THE MILITARY BALANCE

2008

published by

Routledge
Taylor & Francis Group

for

The International Institute for Strategic Studies

ARUNDEL HOUSE | 13–15 ARUNDEL STREET | TEMPLE PLACE | LONDON | WC2R 3DX | UK

THE MILITARY BALANCE 2008

The International Institute for Strategic Studies
ARUNDEL HOUSE | 13–15 ARUNDEL STREET | TEMPLE PLACE | LONDON | WC2R 3DX | UK

DIRECTOR-GENERAL AND CHIEF EXECUTIVE **Dr John Chipman**
EDITOR **James Hackett**

DEFENCE ANALYSTS
GROUND FORCES **Nigel Adderley**
AEROSPACE **Wg Cdr Andrew Brookes**
MARITIME **Jason Alderwick**
DEFENCE ECONOMIST **Mark Stoker**
CONFLICT **Christopher Langton, Hanna Ucko, Kay Floyd and Daniel Slate**

EDITORIAL **Dr Ayse Abdullah, Jessica Delaney, Katharine Fletcher,**
Dr Jeffrey Mazo, Carolyn West
DESIGN AND PRODUCTION **John Buck**
CARTOGRAPHER **Steven Bernard**
ADMINISTRATOR **Clara Catherall**
RESEARCH ASSISTANTS **Chan Le, Bruno Mucciolo, Virginia Comolli,**
Raphaelle Camilleri, Antoine Levesques

This publication has been prepared by the Director-General and Chief Executive of the Institute and his Staff, who accept full responsibility for its contents. The views expressed herein do not, and indeed cannot, represent a consensus of views among the worldwide membership of the Institute as a whole.

FIRST PUBLISHED February 2008

ISBN 978-1-857-43461-3
ISSN 0459-7222

The *Military Balance* (ISSN 0459-7222) is published annually by Routledge Journals, an imprint of Taylor & Francis, 4 Park Square, Milton Park, Abingdon, Oxfordshire OX14 4RN, UK. The 2008 annual subscription rate is: UK£110 (individual rate), UK£222 (institution rate) UK£211 (online only); overseas US$184 (individual rate), US$399 (institution rate), US$379 (online only).

A subscription to the institution print edition, ISSN 0459-7222, includes free access for any number of concurrent users across a local area network to the online edition, ISSN 1479-9022.

Dollar rates apply to subscribers in all countries except the UK and the Republic of Ireland where the pound sterling price applies. All subscriptions are payable in advance and all rates include postage. Journals are sent by air to the USA, Canada, Mexico, India, Japan and Australasia. Subscriptions are entered on an annual basis, i.e. January to December. Payment may be made by sterling cheque, dollar cheque, international money order, National Giro, or credit card (Amex, Visa, Mastercard).

Please send subscription orders to: USA/Canada: Taylor & Francis Inc., Journals Department, 325 Chestnut Street, 8th Floor, Philadelphia, PA 19106, USA. UK/Europe/Rest of World: Routledge Journals, T&F Customer Services, T&F Informa UK Ltd., Sheepen Place, Colchester, Essex, CO3 3LP, UK.

The print edition of this journal is printed on ANSI conforming acid-free paper by Bell & Bain, Glasgow, UK.

CONTENTS

Index of **TABLES**

Index of **MAPS**

The Military Balance 2008
Editor's Foreword

This 2008 edition of *The Military Balance*, the 50th edition of the book, is published in the 50th year of The International Institute for Strategic Studies (IISS). When first published, *The Military Balance* comprised an 11-page pamphlet entitled 'The Soviet Union and the NATO Powers: The Military Balance'. Over the following years, the volume expanded its coverage into more regions, detailing the capabilities of more countries and including information on non-traditional threats, while also giving the reader increasingly detailed information on defence economics.

The Military Balance 2008 is a comprehensive and independent assessment of the military capabilities of 170 nations, and a reference work on developments in global military affairs. In common with recent editions, there is much focus in this edition on operations conducted by the US and its coalition allies in Iraq and by NATO and allied forces in Afghanistan. In both missions, multinational forces continue to grapple with the complexities of creating and maintaining security in order to allow reconstruction efforts to gain ground. In Iraq, while the 'surge' of US troops announced by President George W. Bush in January 2007 contributed to a reduction in violence in Baghdad and some other areas, criminality, intra-communal militia violence and sectarian strife remained commonplace and continued to undermine political and economic initiatives. While Western governments looked for a path to eventual drawdown of their military commitments within the country, this remained contingent on the capability of Iraq's security forces: as Bush said in 2005, 'as the Iraqis stand up, we will stand down'. However, progress so far has been mixed, with advances made in developing the Iraqi army, but less so in the Iraqi police.

The NATO-led International Security Assistance Force (ISAF) and coalition allies have continued to conduct counter-insurgency operations in Afghanistan to address the Taliban-led insurgency. While the military task remains wedded to an international strategy to boost the authority of the Kabul government, its authority is still lacking in many parts of the country. However, there has been an increased effort to train units of the Afghan National Army and police – again, more successful with the former than the latter. While joint Afghan–ISAF operations have brought increased security to some areas, a shortage of military resources hinders operations across the theatre, while the application of national 'caveats' on the use of forces continues to be of concern to commanders.

In East Asia, the Chinese test of an anti-satellite missile in January 2007 focused attention on China's military modernisation efforts, in this case particularly on developments in missile guidance, command and control. Meanwhile,

Beijing's defence White Paper, published in December 2006, gave more information than in previous documents, with particular attention given to the developing aspirations of the service arms of the People's Liberation Army (PLA). However, there continued to be concern, especially in the United States, about a lack of transparency and the consequent difficulty in assessing PLA developments.

Conflict continues to loom large in international perceptions of Africa, and dominates the defence and security debate in that continent. While a new UN–African Union Hybrid Mission in the Darfur region of Sudan had by late 2007 started to deploy initial elements, initially augmenting the AMIS deployment, concerns were still raised over the level of cooperation of Sudan's government as well as the logistical and equipment difficulties that the force would likely encounter. Further east, Ethiopian forces remained in Somalia in support of the transitional government, while an AU presence lacked much of its authorised force-strength. In the Democratic Republic of the Congo, fighting in Kinshasa in early 2007 and continued instability and conflict in the east absorbed the attention of the international community and the UN force, MONUC. Meanwhile, a new international mission is being established by the European Union, designed to support the existing UN presence in Chad and the Central African Republic.

The Military Balance also contains analysis of defence and security developments in Europe, Russia, the Caribbean and Latin America as well as North America. Essays this year focus on unmanned aerial vehicles and the European and US defence industries and it is hoped that *The Military Balance* will feature further analysis of global defence industries in future editions.

As noted in the Foreword to the last edition, the IISS constantly reviews the way in which it analyses military capabilities. Since the end of the Cold War, the Institute has been steadily augmenting its highly regarded quantitative military capability data with more qualitative elements. We will continue to do so. For example, it is important to consider factors that influence a nation's ability or willingness to participate in international military and security operations. The Institute intends to produce, in 2008, a Strategic Dossier examining European military capabilities and considering new metrics that affect a country's ability and willingness to act. Lessons from this work will be carefully studied at the IISS with the objective, where practicable, of integrating these into the Institute's overall capability-assessment process.

James Hackett
Editor, *The Military Balance*

The Military Balance 2008
Preface

The Military Balance is updated each year to provide an accurate assessment of the military forces and defence expenditures of 170 countries. Each edition contributes to the provision of a unique compilation of data and information enabling the reader to discern trends through the examination of editions back as far as 1959. The data in the current edition are according to IISS assessments as at November 2007. Inclusion of a country or state in *The Military Balance* does not imply legal recognition or indicate support for any government.

GENERAL ARRANGEMENT AND CONTENTS

The Editor's Foreword contains a summary of the book and comment on capability analysis.

Part I of *The Military Balance* comprises the regional trends, military capabilities and defence economics data for countries grouped by region. Thus North America includes the US and Canada. Regional groupings are preceded by a short introduction describing the military issues facing the region. There are essays on unmanned aerial vehicles and the US and European defence industries. In this edition the introductory text to the North America section examines the current debate surrounding the evolution of US defence thinking. There are tables depicting aspects of defence activity including selected major training exercises, non-UN and UN multinational deployments, total US aircraft holdings, international defence expenditure, and the international arms trade.

Part II contains information on selected non-state groups with a table showing a synopsis of non-state activity.

Part III comprises reference material.

There are maps showing deployments in Iraq, NATO deployments in Afghanistan, the Russian air defence radar system and developments in Darfur.

The loose Chart of Conflict is updated for 2007 to show data on recent and current armed conflicts, including fatalities and costs

USING THE MILITARY BALANCE

The country entries in *The Military Balance* are an assessment of the personnel strengths and equipment holdings of the world's armed forces. Qualitative assessment is enabled by relating data, both quantitative and economic, to textual comment. The strengths of forces and the numbers of weapons held are based on the most accurate data available or, failing that, on the best estimate that can be made. In estimating a country's total capabilities, old equipments may be counted where it is considered that they may still be deployable.

The data presented each year reflect judgements based on information available to the IISS at the time the book is compiled. Where information differs from previous editions, this is mainly because of changes in national forces, but it is sometimes because the IISS has reassessed the evidence supporting past entries. An attempt is made to distinguish between these reasons for change in the text that introduces each regional section, but care must be taken in constructing time-series comparisons from information given in successive editions.

In order to interpret the data in the country entries correctly, it is essential to read the explanatory notes beginning on page 7.

The large quantity of data in *The Military Balance* has been compressed into a portable volume by extensive employment of abbreviations. An essential tool is therefore the alphabetical index of abbreviations for data sections, which appears at the back of the book.

ATTRIBUTION AND ACKNOWLEDGEMENTS

The International Institute for Strategic Studies owes no allegiance to any government, group of governments, or any political or other organisation. Its assessments are its own, based on the material available to it from a wide variety of sources. The cooperation of governments of all listed countries has been sought and, in many cases, received. However, some data in *The Military Balance* are estimates.

Care is taken to ensure that these data are as accurate and free from bias as possible. The Institute owes a considerable debt to a number of its own members, consultants and all those who help compile and check material. The Director-General and staff of the Institute assume full responsibility for the data and judgements in this book. Comments and suggestions on the data and textual material are welcomed. Suggestions on the style and method of presentation are also much appreciated.

Readers may use data from *The Military Balance* without applying for permission from the Institute on condition that the IISS and *The Military Balance* are cited as the source in any published work. However, applications to reproduce portions of text, complete country entries or complete tables from *The Military Balance* must be referred to the publishers. Prior to publication, applications should be addressed to: Taylor and Francis, 4 Park Square, Milton Park, Abingdon, Oxon, OX14 4RN, with a copy to the Editor of *The Military Balance*.

The Military Balance 2008
Explanatory Notes

ABBREVIATIONS AND DEFINITIONS

Abbreviations are used throughout to save space and to avoid repetition. The abbreviations may have both singular or plural meanings; for example, 'elm' = 'element' or 'elements'. The qualification 'some' means up to, while 'about' means the total could be higher than given. In financial data, '$' refers to US dollars unless otherwise stated; billion (bn) signifies 1,000 million (m). Footnotes particular to a country entry or table are indicated by letters, while those that apply throughout the book are marked by symbols (* for training aircraft counted by the IISS as combat-capable, and † where serviceability of equipment is in doubt). A list of abbreviations for the data sections appears in the reference section (page 491).

COUNTRY ENTRIES

Information on each country is shown in a standard format, although the differing availability of information and differences in nomenclature result in some variations. Country entries include economic, demographic and military data. Military data include manpower, length of conscript service, outline organisation, number of formations and units and an inventory of the major equipment of each service. This is followed, where applicable, by a description of the deployment of each service. Details of national forces stationed abroad and of foreign-stationed forces are also given.

ARMS ORDERS AND DELIVERIES

Tables in the regional texts show selected arms orders and deliveries (contracts) listed by country buyer, together with country supplier and delivery dates, if known. Every effort has been made to ensure accuracy, but some transactions may not be fulfilled or may differ from those reported. Original delivery dates are indicated.

GENERAL MILITARY DATA

Manpower

The 'Active' total comprises all servicemen and women on full-time duty (including conscripts and long-term assignments from the Reserves). Under the heading 'Terms of Service', only the length of conscript service is shown; where service is voluntary there is no entry. 'Reserve' describes formations and units not fully manned or operational in peacetime, but which can be mobilised by recalling reservists in an emergency. Unless otherwise indicated, the 'Reserves' entry includes all reservists committed to rejoining the armed forces in an emergency, except when national reserve service obligations following conscription last almost a lifetime. *The Military Balance* bases its estimates of effective reservist strengths on the numbers available within five years of completing full-time service, unless there is good evidence that obligations are enforced for longer. Some countries have more than one category of 'Reserves', often kept at varying degrees of readiness. Where possible, these differences are denoted using the national descriptive title, but always under the heading of 'Reserves' to distinguish them from full-time active forces.

Other forces

Many countries maintain paramilitary forces whose training, organisation, equipment and control suggest they may be used to support or replace regular military forces. These are listed, and their roles described, after the military forces of each country. Their manpower is not normally included in the Armed Forces totals at the start of each entry. Home Guard units are counted as paramilitary. Where paramilitary groups are not on full-time active duty, '(R)' is added after the title to indicate that they have reserve status. A list of non-state opposition groups which pose a significant threat to a state's security is provided in Part II.

Equipment

Quantities are shown by function and type, and represent what are believed to be total holdings, including active and reserve operational and training units and 'in store' stocks. Inventory totals for missile systems – such as surface-to-surface missiles (SSM), surface-to-air missiles (SAM) and anti-tank guided weapons (ATGW) – relate to launchers and not to missiles. Stocks of equipment held in reserve and not assigned to either active or reserve units are listed as 'in store'. However, aircraft in excess of unit establishment holdings, held to allow for repair and modification or immediate replacement, are not shown 'in store'.

Units and formation strength

Company	100–200
Battalion	500–800
Brigade (regiment)	3,000–5,000
Division	15,000–20,000
Corps (Army)	60,000–80,000

This accounts for apparent disparities between unit strengths and aircraft inventory strengths.

Deployments

The Military Balance mainly lists permanent bases and does not normally list short-term operational deployments. An exception is made in the case of peace-keeping operations. Developments are also described in the text for each regional section. In this edition, the US listing includes general country postings, reflected at times in individual foreign forces listings.

GROUND FORCES

The national designation is normally used for army formations. The term 'regiment' can be misleading. It can mean essentially a brigade of all arms; a grouping of battalions of a single arm; or a battalion group. The sense intended is indicated in each case. Where there is no standard organisation, the intermediate levels of command are shown as headquarters (HQ), followed by the total numbers of units that could be allocated to them. Where a unit's title overstates its real capability, the title is given in inverted commas, with an estimate given in parentheses of the comparable unit size typical of countries with substantial armed forces. For guidelines for unit and formation strengths, see left.

Military formations

The manpower strength, equipment holdings and organisation of formations such as brigades and divisions differ widely from country to country. Where possible, the normal composition of formations is given in parentheses. It should be noted that where both divisions and brigades are listed, only independent or separate brigades are counted and not those included in divisions.

NAVAL FORCES

Categorisation is based on operational role, weapon fit and displacement. Ship classes are identified by the name of the first ship of that class, except where a class is recognised by another name (such as *Udaloy*, *Petya*). Where the class is based on a foreign design or has been acquired from another country, the original class name is added in parentheses. Each class is given an acronym. All such designators are included in the list

Principal Ground Equipment Definitions

The Military Balance uses the following definitions of equipment:

Main Battle Tank (MBT). An armoured, tracked combat vehicle, weighing at least 16.5 metric tonnes unladen, that may be armed with a turret-mounted gun of at least 75mm calibre. Any new-wheeled combat vehicles that meet the latter two criteria will be considered MBTs.

Armoured Combat Vehicle (ACV). A self-propelled vehicle with armoured protection and cross-country capability. ACVs include:

Armoured Infantry Fighting Vehicle (AIFV). An armoured combat vehicle designed and equipped to transport an infantry squad, armed with an integral/organic cannon of at least 20mm calibre. Variants of AIFVs are also included and indicated as such.

Armoured Personnel Carrier (APC). A lightly armoured combat vehicle, designed and equipped to transport an infantry squad and armed with integral/organic weapons of less than 20mm calibre. Variants of APCs converted for other uses (such as weapons platforms, command posts and communications vehicles) are included and indicated as such.

Artillery. A weapon with a calibre of 100mm and above, capable of engaging ground targets by delivering primarily indirect fire. The definition covers guns, howitzers, gun/howitzers, multiple-rocket launchers and mortars.

Principal Naval Equipment Definitions

To aid comparison between fleets, the following definitions, which do not necessarily conform to national definitions, are used:

Submarines. All vessels equipped for military operations and designed to operate primarily below the surface. Those vessels with submarine-launched ballistic missiles are also listed separately under 'Strategic Nuclear Forces'.

Principal Surface Combatant. This term includes all surface ships with both 1,000 tonnes full load displacement and a weapons system for other than self-protection. All such ships are assumed to have an anti-surface ship capability. They comprise: aircraft carriers (defined below); cruisers (over 8,000 tonnes) and destroyers (less than 8,000 tonnes), both of which normally have an anti-air role and may also have an anti-submarine capability; and frigates (less than 8,000 tonnes) which normally have an anti-submarine role. Only ships with a flight deck that extends beyond two-thirds of the vessel's length are classified as aircraft carriers. Ships with shorter flight decks are shown as helicopter carriers.

Patrol and Coastal Combatants. These are ships and craft whose primary role is protecting a state's sea approaches and coastline. Included are corvettes (500–1,500 tonnes with an attack capability), missile craft (with permanently fitted missile-launcher ramps and control equipment) and torpedo craft (with anti-surface-ship torpedoes). Ships and craft that fall outside these definitions are classified as 'patrol' and divided into 'offshore' (over 500 tonnes), 'coastal' (75–500 tonnes), 'inshore' (less than 75 tonnes) and 'riverine'. The prefix 'fast' indicates that the ship's speed can be greater than 30 knots.

Mine Warfare. This term covers surface vessels configured primarily for mine laying or mine counter-measures (such as mine-hunters, minesweepers or dual-capable vessels). They are further classi-fied into 'offshore', 'coastal', 'inshore' and 'riverine' with the same tonnage definitions as for 'patrol' vessels shown above.

Amphibious. This term includes ships specifically procured and employed to disembark troops and their equipment onto unprepared beachheads by means such as landing craft, helicopters or hovercraft, or directly supporting amphibious operations. The term 'Landing Ship' (as opposed to 'Landing Craft') refers to vessels capable of an ocean passage that can deliver their troops and equipment in a fit state to fight. Vessels with an amphibious capability but not assigned to amphibious duties are not included. Amphibious craft are listed at the end of each entry.

Support and Miscellaneous. This term covers auxiliary military ships. It covers four broad categories: 'underway support' (e.g., tankers and stores ships), 'maintenance and logistic' (e.g., sealift ships), 'special purposes' (e.g., intelligence collection ships) and 'survey and research' ships.

Merchant Fleet. This category is included in a state's inventory when it can make a significant contribu-tion to the state's military sealift capability.

Weapons Systems. Weapons are listed in the following order: land-attack missiles, anti-surface ship missiles, surface-to-air missiles, guns, torpedo tubes, other anti-submarine weapons, and helicopters. Missiles with a range of less than 5km, and guns with a calibre of less than 76mm, are not included. Exceptions may be made in the case of some minor combatants with a primary gun armament of a lesser calibre.

Aircraft. All armed aircraft, including anti-submarine warfare and maritime-reconnaissance aircraft, are included as combat aircraft in naval inventories.

Organisations. Naval groupings such as fleets and squadrons frequently change and are often temporary; organisations are shown only where it is meaningful.

Principal Aviation Equipment Definitions

Different countries often use the same basic aircraft in different roles; the key to determining these roles lies mainly in aircrew training. In The Military Balance the following definitions are used as a guide:

Fixed Wing Aircraft

Fighter. This term is used to describe aircraft with the weapons, avionics and performance capacity for aerial combat. Multi-role aircraft are shown as fighter ground attack (FGA), fighter, reconnaissance and so on, according to the role in which they are deployed.

Bomber. These aircraft are categorised according to their designed range and payload as follows:

Long-range. Capable of delivering a weapons payload of more than 10,000kg over an unrefuelled radius of action of over 5,000km;

Medium-range. Capable of delivering weapons of more than 10,000kg over an unrefuelled radius of action of between 1,000km and 5,000km;

Short-range. Capable of delivering a weapons payload of more than 10,000kg over an unrefuelled radius of action of less than 1,000km.

A few bombers with the radius of action described above, but designed to deliver a payload of less than 10,000kg, and which do not fall into the category of FGA, are described as light bombers.

Helicopters

Armed Helicopters. This term is used to cover helicopters equipped to deliver ordnance, including for anti-submarine warfare.

Attack. Helicopters with an integrated fire control and aiming system, designed to deliver anti-armour, air-to-ground or air-to-air weapons;

Combat Support. Helicopters equipped with area suppression or self-defence weapons, but without an integrated fire control and aiming system;

Assault. Armed helicopters designed to deliver troops to the battlefield.

Transport Helicopters. The term describes helicopters designed to transport personnel or cargo in support of military operations.

of abbreviations. The term 'ship' refers to vessels with over 1,000 tonnes full-load displacement that are more than 60 metres (m) in overall length; vessels of lesser displacement, but of 16m or more overall length, are termed 'craft'. Vessels of less than 16m overall length are not included. The term 'commissioning' of a ship is used to mean the ship has completed fitting out and initial sea trials, and has a naval crew; operational training may not have been completed, but otherwise the ship is available for service. 'Decommissioning' means that a ship has been removed from operational duty and the bulk of its naval crew transferred. Removing equipment and stores and dismantling weapons, however, may not have started. Where known, ships in long-term refit are shown as such.

AIR FORCES

The term 'combat aircraft' refers to aircraft normally equipped to deliver air-to-air or air-to-surface ordnance. The 'combat' totals include aircraft in operational conversion units whose main role is weapons training, and training aircraft of the same type as those in front-line squadrons that are assumed to be available for operations at short notice. Training aircraft considered to be combat capable are marked with an asterisk (*). Armed maritime aircraft are included in combat aircraft totals. Operational groupings of air forces are shown where known. Squadron aircraft strengths vary with aircraft types and from country to country.

DEFENCE ECONOMICS

Country entries in Part I include defence expenditures, selected economic performance indicators and demographic aggregates. There are also international comparisons of defence expenditure and military manpower, giving expenditure figures for the past three years in per capita terms and as a % of GDP. The aim is to provide an accurate measure of military expenditure and of the allocation of economic resources to defence. All country entries are subject to revision each year, as new information, particularly that regarding defence expenditure, becomes available. The information is necessarily selective.

Individual country entries show economic performance over the past two years, and current demographic data. Where these data are unavailable, information from the last available year is provided. Where possible, official defence budgets for the current year and previous two years are shown, as well as an estimate of actual defence expenditures for those countries where true defence expenditure is thought to be considerably higher than official budget figures suggest. Estimates of actual defence expenditure, however, are only made for those countries where there are sufficient data to justify such a measurement. Therefore, there will be several countries listed in *The Military Balance* for which only an official defence budget figure is provided but where, in reality, true defence-related expenditure is almost certainly higher.

All financial data in the country entries are shown both in national currency and US dollars at current year, not constant, prices. US dollar conversions are generally, but not invariably, calculated from the exchange rates listed in the entry. In a few cases, notably Russia, a US-dollar purchasing power parity (PPP) rate is used in preference to official or market-exchange rates.

Definitions of terms

Despite efforts by NATO and the UN to develop a standardised definition of military expenditure, many countries prefer to use their own definitions (which are often not made public). In order to present a comprehensive picture, *The Military Balance* lists three different measures of military-related spending data.

- For most countries, an official defence budget figure is provided.
- For those countries where other military-related outlays, over and above the defence budget, are known, or can be reasonably estimated, an additional measurement referred to as defence expenditure is also provided. Defence expenditure figures will naturally be higher than official budget figures, depending on the range of additional factors included.
- For NATO countries, an official defence budget figure as well as a measure of defence expenditure (calculated using NATO's definition) is quoted.

NATO's definition of military expenditure, the most comprehensive, is defined as the cash outlays of central or federal government to meet the costs of national armed forces. The term 'armed forces' includes strategic, land, naval, air, command, administration and support forces. It also includes paramilitary forces such as *gendarmerie*, the customs service and the border guard if these forces are trained in military tactics, equipped as a military force and operate under military authority in the event of war. Defence expenditures are reported in four categories: Operating Costs, Procurement and Construction, Research and Development (R&D) and Other Expenditure. Operating Costs include: salaries and pensions for military and civilian personnel; the cost of maintaining and training units, service organisations, headquarters and support elements; and the cost of servicing and repairing military equipment and infrastructure. Procurement and Construction expenditure covers national equipment and infrastructure spending, as well as common infrastructure programmes. It also includes financial contributions to multinational military organisations, host-nation support in cash and in kind, and payments made to other countries under bilateral agreements. R&D is defence expenditure up to the point at which new equipment can be put in service, regardless of whether new equipment is actually procured. Foreign Military Aid (FMA) contributions of more than US$1 million are also noted.

For many non-NATO countries the issue of transparency in reporting military budgets is fundamental. Not every UN member state reports defence budget (even fewer real defence expenditures) data to their electorates, the UN, the IMF or other multinational organisations. In the case of governments with a proven record of transparency, official figures generally conform to the standardised definition of defence budgeting, as adopted by the UN, and consistency problems are not usually a major issue. The IISS cites official defence budgets as reported by either national governments, the UN, the OSCE or the IMF.

For those countries where the official defence budget figure is considered to be an incomplete measure of total military related spending, and appropriate additional data are available, the IISS will use data from a variety of sources to arrive at a more accurate estimate of true defence expenditure. The most frequent instances of budgetary manipulation or falsification typically involve equipment procurement, R&D, defence industrial investment, covert weapons programmes, pensions for retired military and civilian personnel, paramilitary forces and non-budgetary sources of revenue for the military arising from ownership of industrial, property and land assets.

The principal sources for national economic statistics cited in the country entries are the IMF, the Organisation for Economic Cooperation and Development (OECD), the World Bank and three regional banks (the Inter-American, Asian and African Development Banks). For some countries basic economic data are difficult to obtain. This is the case in a few former command economies in transition and countries currently or recently involved in armed conflict. The Gross Domestic Product (GDP) figures are nominal (current) values at market prices. GDP growth is real not nominal growth, and inflation is the year-on-year change in consumer prices. Two different measures of debt are used to distinguish between OECD and non-OECD countries: for OECD countries, debt is gross public debt (or, more exactly, general government gross financial liabilities) expressed as a proportion of GDP. For all other countries, debt is normally gross foreign debt denominated in current US dollars (not available at time of this publication). Dollar exchange rates relate to the last two years plus the current year. Values for the past two years are annual averages, while current values are the latest monthly value.

Calculating exchange rates

Typically, but not invariably, the exchange rates shown in the country entries are also used to calculate GDP and defence budget and expenditure dollar conversions. Where they are not used, it is because the use of exchange rate dollar conversions can misrepresent both GDP and defence expenditure. For former communist countries, PPP rather than market exchange rates are sometimes used for dollar conversions of both GDP and defence expenditures. Where PPP is used, it is annotated accordingly.

The arguments for using PPP are strongest for Russia and China. Both the UN and IMF have issued caveats concerning the reliability of official economic statistics on transitional economies, particularly those of Russia, some Eastern European and Central Asian countries. Non-reporting, lags in the publication of current statistics and frequent revisions of recent data (not always accompanied by timely revision of previously published figures in the same series) pose transparency and consistency problems. Another problem arises with certain transitional economies whose productive capabilities are similar to those of developed economies, but where cost and price structures are often much lower than world levels.

PPP dollar values are used in preference to market exchange rates in cases where using such exchange rates may result in excessively low dollar-conversion values for GDP and defence expenditure data.

Demographic data

Population aggregates are based on the most recent official census data or, in their absence, demographic statistics taken from US Census Bureau. Data on ethnic and religious minorities are also provided under country entries where a related security issue exists.

Arms trade

The source for the data for the global and regional arms trade is the US Congressional Research Service (CRS). It is accepted that this data may vary in some cases from national declarations of defence exports which is due in part to differences in the publication times of the various sets of data and national definitions of military-related equipment.

Chapter One
North America

THE UNITED STATES

The US Department of Defense is attempting to balance requirements associated with ongoing conflicts, regional security commitments, challenges to the non-proliferation regime and global counter-terrorism efforts. The US Army and US Marine Corps, in particular, are struggling to meet the demands of protracted conflicts in Afghanistan and Iraq. Many veterans are on their third or fourth combat tour; tours that, for army units, are now up to fifteen months long. The army and the marine corps are expanding, but it is unclear whether they will expand sufficiently in time to begin to close the gap between available supply and the high levels of demand for ground forces. All services are attempting to satisfy demand for modernised equipment while at the same time recapitalising existing aircraft, vehicles and weapon systems employed at a high operational tempo across six years of sustained conflict. Although the efforts to stabilise Iraq and Afghanistan remain the immediate priorities for the Department of Defense, a debate is developing over the relevance of these ongoing conflicts to long-term US security requirements. The outcome of that debate and the perceived lessons of the conflicts in Afghanistan and Iraq are likely to have a significant influence on future US defence priorities and force development.

The 'surge' in Iraq and competing security requirements

In January 2007, despite considerable opposition, President George W. Bush decided to reinforce the security effort in Iraq with approximately 30,000 troops. Additional forces were deployed primarily to Baghdad and the 'belts' surrounding the city. The increase brought the number of Brigade Combat Teams (BCTs) or Regimental Combat Teams in Iraq to 20. The objectives of the so-called 'surge' were to improve population security, break the cycle of sectarian violence and defeat 'irreconcilables' to allow progress in moving Iraq's communities toward a political accommodation that would, in turn, lead to sustainable stability. Coalition–Iraqi operations largely succeeded in improving security and reducing violence. It remains unclear, however, whether political and economic initiatives combined with efforts to build institutional capacity, grow Iraqi security forces and reform the security sector will be sufficient to sustain security improvements as US forces are reduced (see p. 225).

Despite improvements in the security situation, support for the sustained commitment of large numbers of US combat forces in Iraq continues to wane in the US Congress, among the public, and even among some senior military officers. Congressional and public pressure is mounting for a reduction in forces in 2008 to a level well below the pre-surge strength of 15 brigades, after which the mission of US forces would shift more rapidly towards providing advice and support to Iraqi army and police units. Although the deterioration in the security situation in 2006 highlighted the danger of transitioning prematurely to Iraqi forces, military leaders such as US Central Command Commander Admiral William Fallon and Chairman of the Joint Chiefs of Staff Admiral Michael Mullen are placing much focus on military preparedness for potential conflicts beyond Iraq. As Admiral Mullen said in October, 'the demands of current operations, however great, should not dominate our training exercises, education curricula, and readiness programs … The conflicts in Iraq and Afghanistan will one day end. We must be ready for who and what comes after.' Some senior defence officials are concerned that continued large-scale commitments in Afghanistan and Iraq are diverting resources from other pressing security requirements and could push the army and the marine corps to breaking point. General George Casey, US Army Chief of Staff, remarked that the 'current demand on our forces exceeds the sustainable supply … we are consuming our readiness as fast as we are building it'.

Expansion of the US Army, US Marine Corps and Special Forces

In January 2007, Secretary of Defense Robert Gates approved an increase of 27,000 in the marine corps by 2012 and the addition of 65,000 soldiers to the army by 2010 (including a previously approved temporary increase of 30,000). Previously, the Department of Defense had deflected periodic calls from members of Congress and others to expand ground forces by describing the wartime demand for troops as a temporary 'spike'. In particular, a larger army did not fit into the vision of former Secretary of Defense Donald Rumsfeld and others of a future joint force that was small, light, fast and capable of waging war quickly and efficiently through the integration of surveillance, communications, information and precision-strike technologies.

The army is executing its plan to transform from a division-based force to one centred around modular BCTs, and now plans to field a total of 76 BCTs, of which 48 will be active, and 28 Army National Guard (ARNG). By the end of 2007, 35 active BCTs are due to have completed the conversion, with three more in the process of converting. The ARNG and Reserves are also in the process of converting forces to the BCT model, with seven BCTs expected to be operational in 2008. While the conversion to BCTs continues, the army is also adjusting the mix of active and reserve forces and increasing the number of units with critical and high-demand skills.

The army and the marine corps both met recruiting targets in 2007. Concerns are growing, however, over the quality of the force, as more army recruits are accepted without high school diplomas and an increasing number require waivers for past criminal behaviour. The services are working to retain qualified leaders for the expanding force; the army expects to pay out approximately US$200 million in retention bonuses in 2008 to keep skilled officers and soldiers in its ranks. Conscription has been discussed in the US media, but is unlikely to be considered seriously.

Special Forces and Special Operations Forces are also expanding. US Army Special Forces will retain their focus on unconventional warfare and continue the process of adding a battalion to each Special Forces group; one new battalion will be added each year between 2008 and 2012. Additionally, the army has formed an active-component brigade-sized civil affairs and psychological operations unit that contains four regionally oriented battalions. Joint Special Operations Command is also increasing its capabilities, including the addition of an additional rifle company per Ranger battalion in the 75th Ranger Regiment and the expansion of the regiment's reconnaissance, fire support and logistical units.

Introduction of new equipment

The services are fielding a wide range of equipment to improve military effectiveness in Afghanistan and Iraq. Protection from improvised explosive devices (IEDs) remains a priority. The US Army and US Air Force continue to improve unmanned aerial vehicle (UAV) capabilities and increase the quantities of surveillance and armed versions of these aircraft (see p. 455). Ground-based surveillance equipment is also proliferating. In 2007, the Pentagon ordered 6,500 Mine Resistant Ambush Protected (MRAP) vehicles and plans to acquire around 15,000 more in time. Meanwhile, the Department of Defense's Joint IED Defeat Organization continues to evaluate and field additional counter-measures to IEDs. Recent developments include sensors that use chemical signatures, electromagnetic waves and spectroscopy to detect concealed IEDs. Other developments aim to neutralise IEDs with electronic jamming or detect and dispose of them using robotic technologies. Many of these technologies have proven successful – for example, Small Unmanned Ground Vehicles had defused over 11,000 IEDs as of November 2007.

In addition to IED-related developments, other systems, such as biometric sensors and databases, have proven particularly valuable in a counter-insurgency environment. The first of three scheduled technological 'spin-outs' from the army's Future Combat System (FCS) programme, the Unattended Ground Sensor, is due to be fielded in 2008. Other spin-out technologies include Non-Line-of-Sight Launch Systems and updated battle command software intended to 'enhance situational awareness and increase soldiers' area of influence and control'.

Trends in doctrinal development

At the end of 2006, the army and marine corps published a joint manual on counter-insurgency, the first major overhaul of US counter-insurgency (COIN) doctrine in two decades. While individual commanders and units were already adapting to the demands of counter-insurgency operations in Iraq and Afghanistan, the manual signalled an institutional shift away from a conventional, enemy-centric approach to armed conflict and towards a population-centric approach that places the use of force more firmly in the context of political goals and considers the influence of social and cultural factors on military operations. General David Petraeus, who, along with US Marine Corps Lieutenant General James Mattis drove the development of the COIN manual, stressed the need to implement the principles contained in it as he assumed command of Coalition forces in Iraq. He emphasised the importance of population security, as well as the need to closely integrate political, economic and military efforts.

In comparison to US joint concepts such as the 'Rapid Decisive Operations' concept under which the initial operations in Afghanistan and Iraq were undertaken, the new counter-insurgency doctrine appears to represent a dramatic shift towards a more sophisticated and historically grounded conception of military operations. With the promotion of General Mattis and his assignment as commander of Joint Forces Command, the command charged with the development of Joint Doctrinal Concepts, it is likely that doctrinal development will in future be less driven by the idea of revolutionary technological change and will take greater account of the political, social, cultural and human dimensions of conflict.

Towards a more comprehensive approach

Recognising the need for a comprehensive approach to counter-insurgency and stability operations, the US government is endeavouring to lay a conceptual foundation for these operations as it commits additional people and resources to the efforts in Afghanistan and Iraq. The new COIN manual states that 'military efforts are necessary and important to counter-insurgency efforts, but they are only effective when integrated into a comprehensive strategy employing all instruments of national power'. A programme known as The Interagency Counterinsurgency Initiative 'seeks to inform and help shape relevant [US government] policy and programs by incorporating the theory and history of counters to organized movements that use subversion or violence rather than established political processes to undermine or overthrow governments, with the goal of focusing appropriate elements of diplomacy, defence, and development on the alleviation of such threats'. The military surge in Iraq was accompanied by the creation of fifteen provincial reconstruction teams (PRTs), the provision of $1.2 billion in new US aid, and coordination with the Iraqi government and security forces to ensure that reconstruction and economic development quickly followed improvements in security. The PRT concept was first introduced in Afghanistan, where PRTs continue to provide access and structure for a multinational development effort at the local level.

Despite these efforts, organisations still lack the capacity to deploy expertise in the areas of recon-

struction, economic development, institutional capacity-building, security-sector reform and the rule of law. Of the additional 300 posts for diplomats and contractors required to staff 15 new Iraq PRTs in 2007, about half have had to be filled, at least temporarily, by military personnel. At the end of October 2007, to address these and other personnel shortfalls, the US Department of State announced plans to order as many as 50 personnel to Iraq if qualified volunteers did not fulfil requirements. If implemented, this would be the first large-scale forced assignment by the State Department since the Vietnam War. The lack of capacity in the State Department and other government agencies may remain a significant problem until Congress provides funding to increase the numbers of qualified civil servants able to deploy to conflict zones.

The future of outsourcing

Shortages of government personnel, both civilian and military, mean that the US employs more than 180,000 contractors in Iraq in a wide range of jobs including logistical support, reconstruction, advisory positions, personal security detachments, facilities security and protection for non-military convoys. US reliance on private security contractors received renewed attention in September 2007 when security contractors hired to protect US diplomats were involved in an incident that left 17 Iraqi civilians dead. This high-profile incident and other events prompted a reconsideration of the role of private security companies and calls for increased oversight and accountability. Defence Secretary Robert Gates described the contractors' objective of protecting their clients at any cost as incompatible with the larger US objective of earning the trust of the Iraqi people. It seems clear that the use of contractors on a large scale has outpaced the development of the legal and administrative frameworks needed to define the scope of contractor responsibilities and lines of authority.

The impact of Afghanistan and Iraq on future US defence policy and force development

Speaking to the Association of the United States Army in October, Gates expressed his belief that 'asymmetric warfare will remain the mainstay of the contemporary battlefield for some time'. US commitments and experiences in Afghanistan and Iraq have driven decisions to increase the size of the Army and US Marine Corps, inspired the development and integration of new technologies, and impelled significant changes in doctrine, training and education. Despite these adaptations, however, it remains to be seen how the US experience in Iraq and Afghanistan will influence US defence policy and force development in the long term. While many leaders agree with Gates's emphasis on asymmetric threats, others are arguing that the true lesson of Afghanistan and Iraq is that the US should in future avoid the protracted commitment of its forces in favour of military operations that promise rapid, decisive results.

While force development efforts will aim to maintain US 'asymmetrical advantages' in the areas of surveillance and precision-strike capabilities, as well as the ability to achieve air supremacy and dominance at sea, it is unclear what effect Afghanistan and Iraq will have on ground forces development. Many defence programmes conceived prior to 2001 are moving forward as planned despite experience that brings into question the premises on which they were based. The army's Future Combat System (FCS) intends to use advanced technology to develop a high degree of situational awareness to allow ground forces to target adversaries from a distance. The technology is also intended to make ground forces significantly more efficient and permit reductions in manpower. It remains uncertain, however, whether FCS-based organisations would improve, or instead detract from, military capabilities in conflicts such as those in Afghanistan and Iraq.

Additionally, there have been few substantive organisational changes within the army based on experiences in Afghanistan and Iraq. For example, the Light and Heavy BCTs, which were designed primarily for conflicts very different from those in which US forces have been engaged since 2001, have undergone no significant organisational revision, despite deficiencies in reconnaissance, combat engineering, logistics and overall formation strength. Critics argue that army organisation and the FCS programme are still driven mainly by 'transformational' theories of the late 1990s, rather than by the reality of recent combat experience.

Introducing AFRICOM

In October 2007, the US established a new Africa Command (AFRICOM) to bring 'consolidated focus' to US engagement in a region formerly divided among three separate combatant commands. Initially operating as a sub-unified command under the US European Command, AFRICOM is expected to be fully operational by October 2008. While some African leaders have expressed concerns about the new command, US officials have emphasised its 'preventative and non-kinetic' nature, and the intention to focus on missions such as humanitarian relief, disaster response and training. They have stressed that the command is intended to have a 'light footprint', without substantial military basing. The new

MAP 1 NEW US UNIFIED COMMAND STRUCTURE

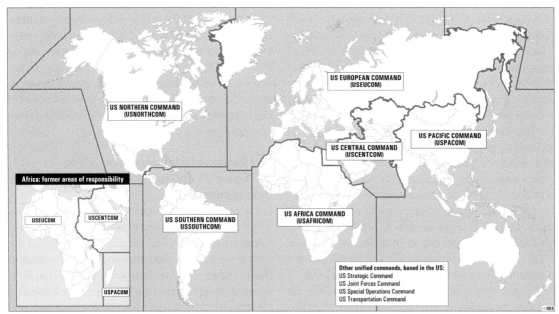

command appears to have the potential to enhance regional security cooperation and assist in state-building, security-sector reform and peace support efforts. The ambition that the command will integrate the efforts of different US government agencies is reflected in its design, with an ambassador-level State Department official serving as deputy to inaugural commander General William Ward.

Other force developments

In October 2007, at a time when much attention was focused on the activities of US ground and air forces, and naval activities in support of ground operations (even while the navy itself has around 6,000 personnel on the ground in Iraq), the US Navy, US Marine Corps and US Coast Guard published a new strategic concept paper entitled 'A Cooperative Strategy for 21st Century Seapower'. Noting that conflict prevention is seen as vital as winning naval battles, as well as placing importance on multinational collaboration, the document observes that 'the expeditionary character and versatility of maritime forces provide the US the asymmetric advantage of enlarging or contracting its military footprint in areas where access is denied or limited'. It envisages the navy achieving six 'strategic imperatives': 'Limit regional conflict with forward deployed, decisive maritime power'; 'Deter major power war'; 'Win our nation's wars'; 'Contribute to homeland defense in depth'; 'Foster and sustain cooperative relationships with more international partners'; and 'Prevent or contain local disruptions before they impact the global system'.

The concept builds upon other initiatives of recent years, such as the 2006 Naval Operations Concept, which articulated the idea of the '1,000-ship navy'. Although the navy desires freedom of action and the ability to project decisive military power, there is also a view that the wide array of maritime-related security threats can best be met with the involvement of partner nations' forces. In September 2007, the pilot mission for the US Global Fleet Station was completed. The six-month deployment of HSV-2 *Swift* was designed to act as an enabler for the 1,000-ship navy concept by transporting teams to conduct maritime training with civil and maritime bodies in seven countries in order to improve capacity in, and interoperability with, the host nations' naval forces.

The navy's Littoral Combat Ship (LCS) programme has run into major difficulties. The LCS is based on a two-hull design programme, with two vessels each scheduled for construction by Lockheed Martin and

General Dynamics. While *USS Freedom*, LCS-1, built by Lockheed Martin, was launched in 2006, the subsequent Lockheed Martin build, LCS-3, was terminated in April 2007, after a stop-work order was given earlier in January. Meanwhile, of the General Dynamics-built vessels, LCS-2 is facing rising costs and LCS-4 was cancelled in November, after General Dynamics and the navy could not agree on a modified contract in the wake of LCS-2's problems. However, the navy still seems committed to the vessels: it is still planning for LCS-1 (which suffered fire damage in 2007) and LCS-2 to enter an operational evaluation phase, and there are plans to transition to a single-hull configuration in fiscal year 2010.

The US Navy also continued its missile defence developments during the year. In November, USS *Lake Erie* launched *Standard* Missile-3 interceptors against two unitary non-separating targets, achieving hit-to-kill intercepts. In an interesting development pointing to interoperability and cooperative activities, a Japanese vessel, the destroyer *Kongo,* also took part, performing long-range surveillance and tracking activities. According to the US Navy, this marked the fourth time an allied military unit had participated in a US *Aegis* BMD test.

Meanwhile, a squadron of US Marine Corps MV-22 *Osprey* tilt-rotor aircraft deployed to Iraq in late 2007. The MV-22 is scheduled to replace the *Sea Knight* helicopter.

The US Air Force is busy developing its UAV capabilities: in November, the MQ-9 *Reaper* dropped its first precision-guided bomb during an operation in Afghanistan. The MQ-9 is substantially larger than the earlier MQ-1 *Predator*, and can carry four 500lb bombs or *Hellfire* air-to-ground missiles (or a mix of the two), in contrast to the MQ-1, which could only carry *Hellfire* (see p. 455). As well as *Predators* and *Reapers*, the air force plans to increase its fleet of *Global Hawks* in coming years.

Meanwhile, air force officials have reportedly expressed interest in boosting F-22 *Raptor* numbers beyond the current order for 183: air force officials had been reported as saying that there was a need for more F-22s until the F-35 Joint Strike Fighter was in production. The late 2007 appropriations bill gave funding for the procurement of 20 further aircraft, also suggesting that the F-22 production line remain open for longer (see p. 24). While 2012 is the year scheduled for F-35 full-rate production, the development schedule for this latter aircraft has caused some concern.

The air force sees as its number one priority the acquisition of a new tanker fleet to replace its KC-135s. It expects to select an aircraft by the end of 2007, and the first order will be for 179 units. The two contenders are Boeing's KC-767 and the Northrop-Grumman–EADS KC-30. More broadly, as the Secretary of the Air Force said before the House Armed Services Committee in October, the force's five procurement priorities are: the new air tanker (KC-X); a replacement rescue helicopter (CSAR-X); new space systems for early warning, communications, weather, and position, navigation and timing; the F-35 Joint Strike Fighter; and the next-generation bomber, due to be fielded by 2018.

UNITED STATES – DEFENCE ECONOMICS

Despite a background of rising interest rates, high oil prices and a slowdown in the domestic property market, the US economy, supported by strong employment growth, had shown significant resilience, whilst buoyant tax revenues had enabled the government to achieve its target of halving the fiscal deficit three years ahead of the scheduled date of financial year (FY) 2009. However, the credit-driven financial turmoil that struck in mid 2007 prompted the International Monetary Fund (IMF) to lower its growth forecast for 2008 by 0.9 percentage points to a rate of 1.9%. Ongoing difficulties in the mortgage market (the trigger for the financial market crisis) are now expected to extend the decline in residential investment, while house-price falls are likely to encourage households to raise their savings rates, thereby dampening consumer spending, and whilst

the weaker dollar may lead to a pick-up in exports, the risks remain biased on the downside. There are a number of reasons for this. Firstly, it is unclear to what extent the cost and availability of credit across the broader economy will be affected by the recent crisis, secondly, the housing market continues to pose significant downside risks and, thirdly, there is a danger that the slowdown in productivity growth may feed through into expectations of future incomes, further depressing consumption and investment spending.

As noted, fiscal developments have remained unexpectedly favourable, with the federal deficit for 2007 forecast to be around 1.2% of GDP, down from 3.6% in FY2004 and less than half the figure budgeted, and the administration has suggested it will balance the budget by FY2012. Official projections, however, do not fully account for the alternative minimum tax relief or war costs in future years and in view of this, the IMF suggests that the deficit will remain above 1% of GDP through to FY2012. Furthermore, the looming fiscal challenges associated with the retirement of the baby-boomer generation, which will begin collecting social security and Medicare benefits in increasing numbers from 2008, is likely to have some restraining influence on discretionary outlays, limiting growth in defence and security accounts over the medium term.

FY2008 DEFENCE BUDGET REQUEST

In February 2007, President Bush submitted his FY2008 defence budget request to Congress. The president asked for a total of US$647.2 billion in national defence funding, of which the Department of Defense

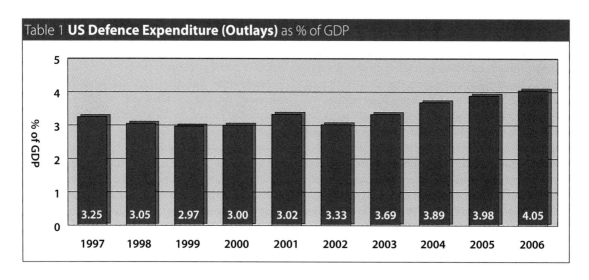

Table 1 **US Defence Expenditure (Outlays)** as % of GDP

Year	% of GDP
1997	3.25
1998	3.05
1999	2.97
2000	3.00
2001	3.02
2002	3.33
2003	3.69
2004	3.89
2005	3.98
2006	4.05

Table 2 **National Defense Budget Authority, FY2006–2012**							
($million)	2006	2007	2008	2009	2010	2011	2012
		Estimate	Request[d]	Plan	Plan	Plan	Plan
Military Personnel	128,485	130,885	135,990	126,955	130,419	135,502	140,488
Operations & Maintenance	213,534	240,693	244,313	174,393	180,565	184,595	189,705
Procurement	105,371	130,547	141,634	110,557	114,770	117,704	123,782
R,D,T & E	72,855	77,131	77,975	77,195	77,071	72,621	70,679
Military Construction	9,530	9,333	19,128	18,435	16,292	14,003	11,367
Family housing	4,426	3,796	2,943	3,165	2,465	2,040	2,038
Other	59,579	7,852	2,655	2,351	1,912	3,078	370
Total Department of Defense	**593,780**	**600,236**	**624,638**	**513,051**	**523,494**	**529,543**	**538,429**
Additional GWOT Supplemental			est. 47,600				
Department of Energy (defence-related)	17,440	17,030	17,369	16,851	16,713	16,985	17,071
Other (defence-related)	5,935	5,180	5,159	4,878	4,950	5,106	5,164
Total National Defense (inlc. GWOT funding)	**617,156**[a]	**622,445**[b]	**695,077**[c]	**534,656**	**544,981**	**551,511**	**560,710**

[a] including US$121.5bn in GWOT supplemental
[b] including US$173bn in GWOT supplementals
[c] including US$189.3bn in GWOT supplemental requests
[d] Budget request only, final appropriations data not available at time of writing

(DoD) would receive US$483.2bn, US$17.4 would be allocated to the defence-related nuclear programmes of the Department of Energy and US$5.2bn was earmarked for the defence-related activities of other agencies. The amount requested also included US$141.7bn for the funding of operations associated with the 'global war on terror', a sum later increased by two separate additional amounts of US$5.3bn and US$43.2bn. Interestingly, the Future Years Defense Plan issued at the same time as the budget request indicated that planned non-war national defence spending would, in real terms, actually fall from US$521bn in FY2009 to US$508bn in FY2012, raising significant questions about the affordability of the DoD's current equipment programme and adding to the concern that the current reliance on supposedly war-related supplemental funding may be distorting the true financial position of the US military (see below). The US$483.2bn requested for the DoD's base budget – that is, for regular operations, excluding the cost of ongoing combat activity – was US$46.8bn higher than the equivalent base budget for FY2007, a real-terms increase of around 8%.

At the time of writing, Congress had agreed to an FY2008 appropriations bill of US$459.6bn. This sum excludes any costs associated with military construction or 'global war on terror' operations, which are subject to separate legislation. Whilst full details were not available, the bill is known to include significant alterations to both the Littoral Combat Ship (LCS)

programme and the army's Future Combat Systems (FCS) family of vehicles (see below).

Whatever the final total for FY2008 defence funding, it seems probable that military spending in the US is nearing something of a plateau, which in turn suggests that important decisions regarding future programmes, ignored in recent years, cannot be indefinitely delayed. Although defence spending is expected to remain high, as the costs of operations in Iraq and Afghanistan continue to increase each year, it is difficult to imagine that Congress will allow the military budget to continue the massive upward trend that has seen it jump from US$335bn in 2001 to a potential total of around US$695bn in 2008. If the budget does peak at around this level, then this is likely to fuel increased competition between the services for their share of the total. Whilst the army has been adding thousands of new troops to its payroll and receiving the lion's share of supplemental spending, the navy and air force have both been reducing personnel in an effort to boost their purchasing power.

It remains to be seen whether, in the future fiscal environment, the Pentagon will be in a position to reset the armed forces to their pre-war condition, whilst also improving its ability to fight asymmetric wars and continuing with the raft of programmes designed to counter a strong conventional threat, without making some significant and difficult decisions regarding its future strategy and equipment programmes.

THE COST OF IRAQ, AFGHANISTAN AND OTHER 'GLOBAL WAR ON TERROR' OPERATIONS SINCE 11 SEPTEMBER 2001

With the FY2007 supplemental enacted in May 2007, Congress has so far approved a total of around US$610bn (excluding any FY2008 funding) for military operations, base security, reconstruction, foreign aid, embassy costs and veterans' health care for the three operations initiated since the 11 September attacks: *Operation Enduring Freedom* (Afghanistan and other counter-terrorist operations); *Operation Noble Eagle* (enhanced security at military bases); and *Operation Iraqi Freedom*. This figure breaks down as follows:

Iraq	US$bn
DoD military operations and other activities	404
Indigenous security forces	19
Diplomatic operations and foreign assistance	25
Veterans' benefits	3
Subtotal	450
Afghanistan	
DoD military operations and other activities	106
Indigenous security forces	11
Diplomatic operations and foreign assistance	10
Veterans' benefits	1
Subtotal	127
Homeland security and other	
DoD military operations and other activities	28
Diplomatic operations and foreign assistance	4
Subtotal	32
TOTAL to end FY2007	**US$610bn**

During 2007, the president made three new war-related supplemental requests for FY2008, which, if enacted, would increase total 'global war on terror' expenditure by a further US$189.3bn. The first request, for US$141.7bn, was, as mentioned above, submitted in February 2007 as part of the defence budget itself, and it included US$71.4bn for operations and maintenance costs and US$32.8bn in procurement accounts. This was followed in July by a request for US$5.3bn to cover the acquisition of additional Mine Resistant Ambush Protected Vehicles (MRAP), and a third request, for US$42.3bn, was submitted in October for 'funding necessary to continue ongoing operations; maintain, repair or replace equipment lost, worn out or stressed by use; enhance force protection; and sustain [the] special pays, benefits and medical services of our all-volunteer force'.

Significant debate continues about the use of supplemental funds, amid criticism that they are in part being used for non-war expenditures and are thus distorting the true financial position of the US armed forces. For the past ten years, DoD financial regulations have defined the cost of 'contingencies' so as to include only incremental costs directly related to operations. Until October 2006, this guidance was used by the services to prepare their estimates for Iraq and the 'global war on terror', with an emphasis on costs 'that would not have been incurred had the contingency operation not been supported', likewise, investment costs were to be calculated 'only if expenditures were necessary to support a contingency operation'. But despite this delimitation, the FY2005–07 supplemental requests have all included requests for the army and Marine Corps modularity and restructuring plan. The DoD has argued that the plan is war-related, because modular units make it easier to rotate units to the war zone; extending the time between deployments and hence improving readiness. Studies by the Congressional Budget Office (CBO), however, have suggested that modularity would only marginally improve rotation schedules, and that Congress's decision to award the funds as supplementals has effectively given the army more room in its regular budget over the past three years than official figures show.

Following new guidance in October 2006 from Deputy Secretary of Defense Gordon England, the status of supplemental funding has become even less clear. In his revised guidance, England instructed the services to submit new requests for FY2007 that would reflect the 'longer war on terror', rather than strictly the requirements of war operations in Iraq and Afghanistan and other counter-terrorist operations. The Congressional Research Service has observed that this new definition appears to open the way for including a far broader range of requirements, given that the needs of the 'longer war' (which, according to national strategy, is now one of the DoD's key missions) are relatively undefined. Indeed, following the new guidance, the FY2007 supplemental request included a navy request of US$450 million for six EA-18G aircraft, and the air force request included US$389m for the procurement of two Joint Strike Fighter aircraft (subsequently denied by Congress). The FY2008 supplemental request includes US$2.6bn for research and development (R&D) for equipment that may not be available for years, US$630m to

Table 3 FY2007 & 08 Global War on Terror Supplementals

US$ in millions

	FY2007	Request Feb 07	MRAP Amendment	Request Oct 07	FY2008 Total
		FY2008			
Military Personnel	17,746	17,070	0	700	17,770
Operations and Maintenance	72,257	71,415	748	8,729	80,892
Procurement	42,025	32,880	4,562	26,598	64,040
R&D	635	1,957	30	603	2,590
Military Construction	1,670	907	0	955	1,863
IED Defeat	4,759	4,108	0	369	4,477
Defense Health Program	2,091	1,023	0	0	1,023
Iraq, and Afghan National					
Security Forces	12,948	4,700	0	1,000	5,700
Working Capital Fund	1,120	1,681	0		1,681
Subtotal	**155,254**	**135,744**	**5,340**	**38,956**	**180,040**
Non-DoD Classified & Additional Emergency Requests	14,244	5,920	0	3,355	9,275
Total	**169,499**	**141,664**	**5,340**	**42,311**	**189,316**

develop 'wide area service architecture networks' to improve communications for the National Security Agency and funds to develop a massive ordnance penetrator bomb (to be dropped from B-2 aircraft) that some members of Congress suggest is not needed in Iraq or Afghanistan, but which may be relevant in relation to Iran's nuclear facilities.

In July 2007, the CBO released estimates of the costs of military operations in Iraq and Afghanistan and other 'global war on terror' operations for the period FY2008–17 in two alternative scenarios. In the first scenario, the US would withdraw most or all of its troops from Iraq by 2010 and keep only a small number of troops (30,000) in Iraq and/or Afghanistan thereafter. The CBO estimated that this arrangement might cost an additional US$406bn–603bn over the period. In the second scenario, the US would draw down its forces from Iraq and Afghanistan much more slowly, to around 75,000 by 2013, and a force this size would be maintained through to 2017. The CBO estimated that covering the costs of these operations would require an additional US$924bn–1,000bn, and suggested that by 2017, the cost of 'global war on terror'-related operations could range from US$1,016bn to US$1,610bn. Reporting to the House Budget Committee in October, the CBO added that since the 'global war on terror' has essentially been financed with borrowed money, a more accurate analysis would also include interest costs, which could add a further US$700bn to the total.

ARMY

Following a public stand-off in August 2006 when the then Army Chief of Staff General Peter Schoomaker refused to submit a new budget plan for FY2008 and beyond unless the army's share of overall spending was increased, the FY2008 budget request included a two-year proposal for the army's base budget to be increased by around US$30bn by FY2009. In addition, as the army continues to bear the brunt of operations in Iraq and Afghanistan, it is receiving increased funding via the annual 'global war on terror' supplemental process. While Congress has approved procurement appropriations of US$22.7bn in the base budget, which is significantly less than was approved for the navy or air force and US$1.5bn less than originally requested by President Bush, in FY2008, the army will also receive a significant proportion of the US$30.5bn requested in the FY2008 supplemental for force protection (including at least US$5.3bn for 1,520 new MRAP vehicles), as well as the US$46.6bn requested for 'reconstitution' or reset costs, i.e., the cost of repairing and replacing equipment.

As noted in *The Military Balance 2007*, the impact of combat operations on the army's readiness levels hit a crisis in 2006 when reset costs for FY2007 rose from an estimated US$7bn to over US$17bn (US$23.7bn including the Marine Corps). At the time the army suggested that whilst fighting continued, and for at least two years after it had ended, US$12.5bn would be needed each year to 'bring a unit back to full readi-

Table 4 US National Defense Budget Function and Other Selected Budgets 1992, 1998–2008

(US$bn)	National Defence Budget Function		Department of Defense		Atomic Energy Defense Activities	Department of Homeland Security	Veterans Adminis tration	Total Federal Government Outlays	Total Federal Budget Surplus/Deficit
FY	BA	Outlay	BA	Outlay	BA	BA (Gross)	BA		
1992	295.1	298.3	282.1	286.9	10.6	n.a.	33.9	1,381	-290
1998	271.3	268.5	258.5	256.1	11.3	11.2	42.7	1,652	69
1999	292.1	274.9	278.4	261.3	12.4	13.0	44.1	1,702	125
2000	304.1	294.5	290.5	281.2	12.2	13.8	45.5	1,789	236
2001	335.5	305.5	319.4	290.9	13.0	16.4	47.4	1,863	128
2002	362.1	348.5	344.9	331.9	14.9	30.5	51.9	2,011	-157
2003	456.2	404.9	437.9	387.3	16.4	30.8	58.9	2,160	-377
2004	490.6	455.9	471.0	436.5	16.8	31.6	60.2	2,293	-412
2005	505.7	495.3	483.9	474.1	17.9	31.9	69.0	2,472	-318
2006	617.1	521.8	593.8	499.3	17.4	32.3	71.0	2,655	-248
2007	622.4	571.8	600.2	548.8	17.0	37.5	74.5	2,784	-244
2008 est	695.1	606.5	624.6	583.3	17.4	34.6	84.4	2,901	-239

Notes

FY = Fiscal Year (1 October–September)
[1] The National Defense Budget Function subsumes funding for the DoD, the DoE Atomic Energy Defense Activities and some smaller support agencies (including Federal Emergency Management and Selective Service System). It does not include funding for International Security Assistance (under International Affairs), the Veterans Administration, the US Coast Guard (Department of Transport), nor for the National Aeronautics and Space Administration (NASA). Funding for civil projects administered by the DoD is excluded from the figures cited here.
[2] Early in each calendar year, the US government presents its defence budget to Congress for the next fiscal year which begins on 1 October. It also presents its Future Years' Defense Program (FYDP), which covers the next fiscal year plus the following five. Until approved by Congress, the Budget is called the Budget Request; after approval, it becomes the Budget Authority.
[3] Definitions of US budget terms: Authorisation establishes or maintains a government programme or agency by defining its scope. Authorising legislation is normally a prerequisite for appropriations and may set specific limits on the amount that may be appropriated. An authorisation, however, does not make money available. Budget Authority is the legal authority for an agency to enter into obligations for the provision of goods or services. It may be available for one or more years.

Appropriation is one form of Budget Authority provided by Congress for funding an agency, department or programme for a given length of time and for specific purposes. Funds will not necessarily all be spent in the year in which they are initially provided. Obligation is an order placed, contract awarded, service agreement undertaken or other commitment made by federal agencies during a given period which will require outlays during the same or some future period. Outlays are money spent by a federal agency from funds provided by Congress. Outlays in a given fiscal year are a result of obligations that in turn follow the provision of Budget Authority.
* The US Coast Guard is funded by the Department of Homeland Security.

ness once it has been rotated out of combat operation' by repairing and replacing equipment and resting and retraining troops.

Again the issue of transparency as regards the use of supplemental funding arises. The DoD's definition of reset now includes not only the replacement of battle losses and equipment repair, but also recapitalisation that typically upgrades current equipment and the repair or replacement of pre-positioned equipment stored overseas that has been earmarked to meet war needs. Given that the army has been planning to recapitalise equipment and modernise pre-positioned equipment in line with its new modular initiative, it is difficult to ascertain whether these expenses should in fact be counted as direct incremental war-related requirements. Likewise, much of the equipment currently being repaired following damage sustained in overseas operations was originally scheduled for repair or replacement at a later date in any case, suggesting that the baseline budget should be reduced to offset the war funding already provided.

The army's FCS family of vehicles once again received less R&D funding than had been originally requested. In FY2007, US$300m was cut from the administration's original FCS request, and for FY2008, Congress approved a budget of US$3.35bn, some US$200m less than had been sought. In making the appropriation, conferees recommended that the army should focus on 'technology spin-outs' from the programme, starting with communications and other software and equipment designed to improve situational awareness, and apply these to *Abrams* tanks, *Bradley* fighting vehicles and high-mobility multipurpose wheeled vehicles.

NAVY

The FY2008 appropriations bill allocated US$37.8bn in procurement funds to the navy, around US$900m less than the administration requested, and conferees expressed their extreme concern over the state of the LCS programme, referring to it as a 'classic example of the way things can go wrong when construction is started prior to the design being complete'. Since the programme's inception, Congress has appropriated funding intended for the construction of six ships, however, due to cost growth and technical problems, only two ships will now be constructed, with the funding already having been provided. However, rather than eliminating LCS funding entirely (as the Senate had suggested), conferees reduced the amount allocated to the programme in FY2008 from US$990m to US$339m and instructed the navy to adopt a new acquisition strategy that would lead to the development of a ship that 'meets future naval requirements and can be affordably procured'. The instruction included a timetable according to which one of the two competing LCS designs currently under construction was to be selected no later than the end of FY2009, to be followed by a full and open competition for future ships that would be opened up to shipyards not currently involved in the programme.

Differences between the House and Senate also emerged over the future of the LPD-17 programme. The original budget request had called for US$1.3bn in FY2008 for the procurement of a ninth vessel. In its version of the appropriations bill, the House increased this sum by a further US$1.7bn to cover the procurement of a tenth ship, but this increase was rejected by the Senate, and the final version of the appropriations bill included a notional US$50m in lead LPD funding for a tenth ship to keep the programme going.

In the FY2007 appropriations bill, conferees had reiterated their support for a 48-ship attack submarine force, but warned that on projected construction schedules, the fleet would fall below this level by 2020. In light of this warning, the FY2008 bill included an additional US$588m for the procurement of a second *Virginia*-class submarine. The final bill also included US$300m for three additional T-AKE combat-supply and dry cargo ships, and an extra US$124m for the advanced procurement of the carrier replacement programme.

In response to the difficulties with the LCS programme and cost overruns in other programmes that together ultimately led to the resignation of the navy's senior acquisitions officer Delores Etter in October 2007, conferees included some robust language regarding the procurement of future naval vessels. In particular they directed that in future the

Table 5 Major US Research & Development, FY2006–FY2008

Classification	Designation	FY2006 Value ($m)	Estimate FY2007 Value ($m)	Request FY2008 [a] Value ($m)
Joint				
UAV	*Global Hawk*	257	247	298
tpt	C-130	243	271	262
Army				
hel	AH-64 *Apache*	104	122	193
hel	Armed Recon Helicopter	88	131	82
FCS	Future Combat System	3,219	3,389	3,563
Navy				
AEA	F/A-18G *Growler*	379	372	272
FGA	F-35 JSF	2,187	2,163	1,707
hel	V-22	192	267	118
hel	VH-71 Executive Aircraft	897	630	271
CVN	Carrier Replacement	300	307	232
DDG	DDG 1000	1,052	808	503
LCS	Littoral Combat Ship	584	329	217
SSN	*Virginia*	168	201	224
AEW	EC-2	619	505	831
sat	MUOS	449	662	611
SAM	Standard	148	176	231
EFV	Amphibious vehicles	243	347	288
JTRS	Joint Tactical Radio	371	796	853
Air Force				
bbr	B-2	281	241	244
tpt	C-17	160	173	181
tpt	C-5	225	150	203
tkr	KC-X	24	69	314
FGA	F-22	413	472	743
FGA	F-15	135	137	101
FGA	F-16	124	152	90
FGA	F-35 JSF	2,264	2,132	1,780
hel	CSAR-X		200	290
sat	AEHF	639	630	603
sat	NAVSTAR GPS	264	490	708
sat	SBIRS	706	664	587
sat	TSAT	416	729	963
sat	Space Based Radar	98	185	

[a] data refer to budget request rather than final appropriations

Table 6 **US Agency for International Development: International Affairs Budget**			
Budget Authority in US$m	FY2006 Actual	FY2007 Estimate	FY2008 Request
Assistance to the New Independent states of the FSU	508	435	351
Assistance for Eastern Europe and the Baltics	357	269	289
Economic Support Fund	2,616	2,603	3,319
International Military Education and Training	85	85	89
Foreign Military Financing	4,464	4,454	4,536
Global HIV/Aids Initiative	1,975	1,852	4,150
Non proliferation, Anti-Terrorism, Demining	405	392	464
International Narcotics Control and Law Enforcement	472	703	634
Andean Counterdrug Initiative	727	569	442
International Disaster and Famine Assistance	361	348	297
Migration and Refugee Assistance	783	750	773
Total International Affairs (excluding supplementals)	**31,389**	**29,916**	**36,186**

secretary of the navy must certify to the Congressional Defence Committees that the 'required research and development and detailed design are mature enough to allow for the initiation of construction with minimal risk of follow-on changes caused by the premature start of construction'. In addition, the Government Accountability Office (GAO) will conduct a review by April 2008 of shipbuilding best practice, examining key decision points in navy and commercial shipbuilding programmes and comparing benchmarks in the two sectors in an effort to improve the cost performance of future navy programmes.

AIR FORCE

While the US$33.2bn the air force will receive in procurement funding in FY2008 is marginally less than the US$33.8bn requested by the Bush administration, Congress confirmed its support for the services' two flagship programmes: the F-35 Joint Strike Fighter and the F-22 *Raptor*, both of which had their budget request met in full. Of the total figure, US$12.0bn is allocated to aircraft procurement, US$4.9bn to missiles and US$12.3bn is set aside for classified programmes.

Spending plans include US$1.4bn for the procurement of six F-35 aircraft, plus a further US$2.0bn in R&D funding, an increase of US$200m which appropriators said would be used for 'production enhancements that will help drive procurement costs down'. There was also US$480m to keep the alternative engine programme running. As well as furnishing US$3.2bn for the procurement of a further 20 F-22 aircraft, the appropriations bill also suggested that the air force should consider extending the F-22 production line beyond its expected closing date in 2009, when the current order for 183 units is due to be complete. Conferees noted that the US$526m that is earmarked for FY2009 to shut the line down should instead be redirected towards the advance procurement items such as speciality metals to support the proposed additional 20 aircraft.

Space programmes for 'space control' and 'counterspace' technologies fared well, with conferees adding funds to a variety of different projects, citing China's successful anti-satellite weapon demonstration in January 2007 as a significant motivation. In total an additional US$100m was made available for a series of programmes, including the Rapid Attack Identification Detection and Reporting System, which aims to identify radio-frequency interference with US satellites, space situational awareness research and the Maui Space Surveillance System. The Space-Based Infrared Radar High, which is chronically behind schedule and over budget, was allocated the administration's full request of US$587m.

The much-needed Combat Search-and-Research (CSAR-X) helicopter programme fared less well, receiving US$295m, some US$185m less than the president had requested. Due to bid protests upheld by the GAO, the contract award for the CSAR-X's system development and demonstration has been delayed until summer 2008. As a result, legislators transferred US$99m of the difference between the requested and allocated sums to the modification of the existing HH-60 helicopter fleet, which, due to the delays in the CSAR-X programme, will perform combat search and rescue operations for several years longer than planned.

CANADA

During a year in which Canada and Russia articulated their positions on Arctic sovereignty (and in which other nations asserted Antarctic sovereignty), Ottawa announced substantive military developments: in early July, Prime Minister Stephen Harper declared the intention to construct up to eight *Polar*-class 5 Arctic

Patrol Vessels at a cost of approximately C$3.1bn, as well as the establishment of a docking and refuelling facility at the deep-water port of Nanisivik inside the eastern entrance to the Northwest Passage. In another naval development, the government announced in June a $3.1bn modernisation programme for Canada's *Halifax*-class frigates, to begin in 2010, with the final ship to be completed in 2017.

In August, Ottawa announced plans for a Canadian Forces Arctic Training Centre, to be initially housed in refurbished facilities in Resolute Bay. As well as cold-weather training activities, the base is due to provide a 'location for pre-positioning training equipment and various types of vehicles in the High Arctic'. The Canadian Rangers, a part-time reserve force 'who provide a military presence in remote, isolated and coastal communities' are also due to be expanded from 4,100 personnel to 5,000.

Also in August, the first of four Canadian C-17s arrived, with the second arriving at Trenton airbase in October and the rest due for delivery by April 2008. The government reactivated 429 Squadron a month earlier, in order to conduct C-17 operations and fleet maintenance. Earlier, in July, a new Expeditionary Air Wing was formed at Bagotville airbase, home to Canada's F-18s, to be composed of a 'Command Element, an Operations Support Flight, and a Mission Support Flight. It will train together and deploy as a team, with aircraft and personnel tailored to the specific requirements of an operation.'

Canadian forces are heavily committed to International Security Assistance Force operations in Afghanistan: Canada has some 2,500 personnel in Afghanistan, centred on a battlegroup in Kandahar and in the Kandahar PRT.

Canada Ca

Canadian Dollar $		2006	2007	2008
GDP	CS$	1.44tr	1.52tr	
	US$	1,273bn	1,568b	
per capita	US$	38,474	46,961	
Growth	%	2.8	2.5	
Inflation	%	2.0	2.0	
Def exp	CS$	16.9bn		
	US$	14.95bn		
Def bdgt	CS$	15.9bn	17.8bn	
	US$	14.1bn	18.4bn	
US$1= CS$		1.13	0.97	

Population   33,390,141,

Age	0 – 14	15 – 19	20 – 24	25 – 29	30 – 64	65 plus
Male	9%	3%	3%	3%	24%	6%
Female	9%	3%	3%	3%	24%	7%

Capabilities

ACTIVE 64,000 (Army 33,300 Navy 11,100 Air 19,600)

CIVILIAN 9,350 (Coast Guard 9,350)

RESERVE 65,773 (Army 28,880 Navy 4,200 Air 2,300 Supplementary Ready Reserve 27,693 Primary Reserve List 2,700)

Canadian Forces operations are organised with four joint operational commands. Canada Command (CANADACOM), is responsible for all domestic and continental operations through six regional sub-commands, Canadian Expeditionary Force Command (CEFCOM) is responsible for all international operations. Canadian Special Operations Forces Command (CANSOFCOM) is responsible for generating all Special Forces operations and has forces permanently assigned to it. Canadian Operational Support Command (CANOSCOM) has responsibility for generation and employment of the operational-level support to CANADACOM and CEFCOM (and if required CANSOFCOM) for logistics, movements, general engineering, health services, communications, human resource management and military police support either through its permanently assigned forces or through augmented force generation. CANADACOM and CEFCOM normally have no permanently assigned forces allocated for operations but receive them from force generation commands, Maritime Command (MARCOM), Land Forces Command (LFC) and Air Command (AIRCOM) each have forces normally assigned to them for force generation by the Chief of Defence Staff (CDS) who has full command. Canadian Forces are expanding and the expected strength will be increasing to 75,000 (approx 39,000 Army, 13,000 Navy and 23,000 Air by uniform)

ORGANISATIONS BY SERVICE

Army (Land Forces) 33,300

FORCES BY ROLE
1 Task Force HQ
Command 3 Bde Gp HQs to form national or cadre of a multi-national TF HQ or a Land Component Command (LCC) of a joint op.

Mech Inf	1 Canadian Mechanised Brigade Group (1 CMBG) with 1 armd regt, (two *Leopard* 1C2 sqns and 1 recce sqn), 2 mech inf bn, 1 lt inf bn, 1 arty regt, 1 AD bty, 1 cbt engr regt); 2 bde gp (2 CMBG and 5 CMBG) with 1 armd recce regt , 2 mech inf bn, 1 lt inf bn, 1 arty regt, 1 AD bty, 1 cbt engr regt
AD	1 indep regt
Spt/Engr	1 indep regt
Cbt spt	3 MP pl, 3 int coys
Logistic	3 Svc bn
Med	3 Fd Amb

EQUIPMENT BY TYPE
MBT 86: 20 *Leopard* 2 A6M on lease; 66 *Leopard* 1C2
RECCE 203 LAV-25 *Coyote*
APC 1,321
  APC (T) 428: 78 Bv-206; ε 289 M-113; 61 M-577
  APC (W) 893: 651 LAV-III *Kodiak* (incl variants); 167 MILLAV *Bison* (incl 25 EW, 32 amb, 32 repair, 32 recovery and 10 C2); 75 RG-31 *Nyala*
ARTY 455
  SP 155mm 76: 18 M-109A4; 58 in store
  TOWED 225 105mm 213: 89 C2 (M-101); 96 C3 (M-101); 28 LG1 MK II; **155mm** 12 M-777
  MOR 81mm 130
    SP 81mm 24 *Bison*
AT
  MSL 554
    SP 17 LAV-TOW
    MANPATS 537: 425 *Eryx;* 112 TOW-2A/TOW-2B (incl 32 TUA M-113 SP; 80 TOW Ground Mount)
  RCL 84mm 987 *Carl Gustav;* M2/M3
  RL 66mm M-72 *LAW*
UAV • TACTICAL 19 *Sperwer; Skylark*
AD
  SAM • SP 34 ADATS
  MANPAD *Starburst*

Reserve Organisations

Canadian Rangers 4,180 Reservists
The Canadian Rangers are a Reserve sub-component of the Canadian Forces, which provide a limited military presence in Canada's sparsely-settled northern, coastal and isolated areas. It is a volunteer, part-time force
Ranger   5 (patrol) gp (163 patrols)

Militia 24,700 reservists
Army	10 (bde gp) HQ
Armd	8 regt
Armd Cav	2 regt
Armd Recce	6 regt
Inf	43 regt
Fd Arty	14 regt, 2 indep bty
ADA	2 regt

Engr	3 regt, 8 sqn
Cbt engr	1 regt
MP	5 coy
Log	19 bn
Medical	11 coy

Navy (Maritime Command) 11,100

EQUIPMENT BY TYPE

SUBMARINES SSK 4:

4 *Victoria* (ex-UK *Upholder*) each with 6 single 533mm TT each with Mk48 *Sea Arrow* HWT, (2 hulls currently operational)

PRINCIPAL SURFACE COMBATANTS 15

DESTROYERS • DDG 3 mod *Iroquois* each with 1 Mk 41 VLS with 29+ SM-2 MR SAM, 2 triple ASTT (6 eff.) each with Mk 46 LWT, 1 76mm gun, 2 CH-124A (SH-3A) *Sea King* ASW hel

FRIGATES • FFG 12 *Halifax* with 2 quad (8 eff.) with 8 RGM-84 *Harpoon* tactical SSM, 2 octuple (16 eff.) Mk 48 *Sea Sparrow* with 16 RIM-7P *Sea Sparrow* SAM, 2 Mk 46 LWT, 2 Twin 324mm ASTT (4 eff.) with 24 Mk 46 LWT, (capacity either 1 CH-124A (SH-3A) *Sea King* ASW hel or 1 CH-124B *Sea King* CH-124 (SH-3) ASW)

PATROL AND COASTAL COMBATANTS 12

MCDV 12 *Kingston*

FACILITIES

Bases Located at Esquimalt (Pacific), Halifax (Atlantic), Ottawa (National HQ), Quebec City (Naval Reserve HQ). Commanders for MARPAC and MARLANT directly or through their respective at-sea fleet commander, act as the MCC for the operational commands of CANADACOM and/or CEFCOM.)

Logistic Support

LOGISTICS AND SUPPORT 16

AOR 2 *Protecteur* each with 3 CH-124A (SH-3A)*Sea King* ASW Hel

YDT 8 : 2 MCM support; 6 diving tender/spt less than 100 tonnes

TRG 6 *Orca* (2 additional vessels expected by 2010)

Reserves 4,200 reservists

HQ	1 HQ located at Quebec
Navy	24 div (tasks: crew 10 of the 12 MCDV; harbour defence; naval control of shipping)

Air Force (Air Command) 19,600 (plus 2,300 reservists integrated within total RCAF structure)

Flying hours   210 hrs/year

FORCES BY ROLE

1 Cdn Air Division (1 Cdn Air Div), HQ Winnipeg, resp for all CF air op readiness, combat air-spt, air tpt, SAR, MR and trg. This HQ is the ACC. HQ for CANADACOM and CEFCOM. 1 Cdn Air Div wgs directly support land forces (tac hel and UAV), maritime forces (maritime hel and long range MP), and Special Forces (hel) with OPCON status. Other wgs undertake directly related air roles (AD, AT, SAR, trg) while remaining under direct 1 Cdn Air Div control.

13 Wgs: 1 Wg (Kingston); 3 Wg (Bagotville); 4 Wg (Cold Lake); 5 Wg (Goose Bay); 8 Wg (Trenton); 9 Wg (Gander); 12 Wg (Shearwater); 14 Wg (Greenwood); 15 Wg (Moose Jaw); 16 Wg (Borden); 17 Wg (Winnipeg); 19 Wg (Comox); 22 Wg (North Bay). An Air Expeditionary Wg (AEW) at Bagotville (up to 550 personnel) will train and deploy together, and will comprise a cmnd element, an ops support Flt and a mission support Flt. The AEW is for use by the op cmds most likely through CANOSCOM when not used in an air component task.

FORCES BY ROLE

Strategic Surveillance	1 (NORAD Regional) HQ located at North Bay with 11 North Warning System Long Range; 36 North Warning System Short Range; 4 Coastal; 2 Transportable (total of 53 Radar stn)
Ftr/FGA	4 sqn with 79 CF-18AM/CF-18BM *Hornet* (1 sqn with 30 at Bagotville of which 29 op; 3 sqn with 30 at Cold Lake of which 29 op, 17 with Op Trg unit, 2 with Test & Eval Unit)
MP	3 sqn (2 in Greenwood, 1 in Comox) with 18 CP-140 *Aurora**)
SAR/Tkr/Tpt	5 sqn (3 in Winnipeg, 1 in Trenton, 1 in Greenwood) with 4 C-17 (by Apr 2008), 29 CC-130 *Hercules* (5 KC-130H, 8 CC-130H, 16 CC-130E; 1 SAR/tpt sqn with 6 CC-115 *Buffalo* (Comox); 1 SAR/tpt sqn with 4 CC-138 *Twin Otter*; 1 sqn with 3 CC-150 *Polaris* A-310 (2 A-310MRTT, 2 Combi Pax/Cargo, 1 VIP/Pax (Trenton); 1 sqn with 6 CC-144 *Challenger* (4 VIP, 2 Medevac) (Trenton)
Hel	9 sqn with 85 CH-146 *Griffon* incl 10 spec ops (6 in Kingston (tac), 1 in Bagotville (cbt spt), 1 in Cold Lake (cbt spt),1 in Goose Bay with (cbt spt)); 3 sqn with 14 CH-149 *Cormorant*; 3 sqn with 28 CH-124 *Sea King* (Shearwater)
Trg	1 school in Moose Jaw with CT-155 *Hawk*, CT-156 *Harvard II*; 1 school in Winnipeg with *Dash-8*; 3 schools in Borden with CH-146 *Griffon*; 1 SAR trg school in Comox with 9 CH-139 *Jet Ranger* utl hel (flying)

EQUIPMENT BY TYPE

AIRCRAFT 107 combat capable

FGA: 89: 61 CF-18AM *Hornet*, 18 CF-18BM *Hornet* (plus 10 CF-18A/B flying until 2009)

MP 18 CP-140 *Aurora*

TPT/TKR 7: 2 A-310MRTT; 5 KC-130H

TPT 43: 4 C-17 by Apr 2008; 24 C-130E/H (16 –E, 8–H, of which 3 grounded though could be fitted with new wings); 6 CC-115 *Buffalo*; 4 CC-138 (DHC-6) *Twin Otter*; 6 CC-144B *Challenger*; 3 CC-150 *Polaris*

TRG 50: 20 CT-155 *Hawk* Mk-115; 26 CT-156 *Harvard* II (T-6A-1 *Texan* II); 4 CT-142 *Dash 8 Nav Trainer*

HELICOPTERS

SAR 14 CH-149 *Cormorant*

ASW 28 CH-124 (SH-3) *Sea King*

UTL 94: 9 CH-139 *Jet Ranger*; 85 CH-146 *Griffon* (incl 10 spec ops)

UAV *Silver Fox*

RADAR 53

AD RADAR • NORTH WARNING SYSTEM 47: 11 Long Range; 36 Short Range

STRATEGIC 6: 4 Coastal; 2 Transportable
MSL
   AAM AIM-7M *Sparrow*; AIM-9L *Sidewinder*; AIM-120C AMRAAM
   ASM AGM-65 *Maverick*
BOMBS
   Conventional: Mk 82; Mk 83; Mk 84
   Laser-Guided: GBU-10/ GBU-12/ GBU-16 *Paveway II*; GBU-24 *Paveway III*

NATO Flight Training Canada

AIRCRAFT
   TRG 47: 26 CT-156 *Harvard II*/T-6A *Texan II*; 21 *Hawk* MK115 (advanced wpns/tactics trg)

Canadian Special Operations Forces Command 1,500

FORCES BY ROLE

Comd	1 HQ
SF	1 regt (3rd Bn Royal Canadian Regt; expanding from 1 to 4 Coy with comd and spt elms) located at CFB Petawawa
Counter-Terrorist	1 (JTF-II) bn (Domestic or specialist foreign ops) located at Dwyer Hill
Special Ops	1 sqn located at CFB Trenton, with 10 CH-146 *Griffon*
NBC	1 coy located at CFB Trenton eqpt. with 4 MILLAV *Bison*

EQUIPMENT BY TYPE
RECCE 4 LAV *Bison* (NBC)
HEL • UTL 10 CH-146 *Griffon*

Canadian Operational Support Command 2,000

Comd	1 HQ
Engr	1 (1 engr support unit) coy
Sigs	(Cdn Forces Joint Sig Regt) regt (strategic and operational signals and information management)
MP	1 (close protection) coy
NBC	3 (3 Cdn support and 4 Cdn movement units) coy (1 supply, 1 postal, 1 movement)
Medical	1 (1 Cdn Forces Field Hospital) bn

Canadian Coast Guard 9,350 (civilian)

Incl. Department of Fisheries and Oceans; all platforms are designated as non-combatant.
PATROL AND COASTAL COMBATANTS 60
   PSO 4 Type-600
   PCO 6: 1 *Tanu*; 2 *Louisbourg*; 1 *Quebecois*; 1 *Arrrow Post*; 1 *Gordon Reid*;
   PCI 9: 4 Type-400; 3 *Post Class*; 1 *Cumella Class*; 1 Type 200
   PB 41: 10 Type 300-A; 31 Type-300B(SAR Lifeboats)
LOGISTICS AND SUPPORT 54
   ACV 4
   AGB 6
     POLAR ICEBREAKER 2: 1 *Gulf* class Type 1300; 1 *Terry Fox* class Type 1200
     RIVER ICEBREAKER 4: 1 Modified R class+ Type 1200; 3 R class Type 1200
   AGOR 10 (fishery)
   AGOS 7
   Navaids 24
   Trg 3
HELICOPTERS
   UTL 27: 16 Bö-105; 6 Bell 206L *Longranger*; 5 Bell 212

DEPLOYMENT

AFGHANISTAN
NATO • ISAF • *Operation Athena* 2,500; 20 *Leopard 2* MBT *Operation Enduring Freedom* • 30 OEF (*Op Archer*)
Bilateral • *Operation Argus* 15
OEF HOA • *Altair* 237
Sperwer UAVs

BOSNIA-HERZEGOVINA
NATO • NATO HQ Sarajevo *Operation Bronze* 8

CYPRUS
UN • UNFICYP • *Operation Snowgoose* 1

DEMOCRATIC REPUBLIC OF CONGO
UN • MONUC • *Operation Crocodile* 10 obs

EGYPT
MFO • *Operation Calumet* 28

EUROPE
NATO (ACE) 292 (Incl AWACS at Geilenkirchen)
SNMG1 *Operation Sextant* 1 FFG (235 pers)

HAITI
UN • MINUSTAH • *Operation Hamlet* 4

IRAQ
UN • UNAMI • *Operation Iolaus* 1 obs

ISRAEL
USSC *OperationProteus* 3

MIDDLE EAST
UN • UNTSO • *Operation Jade* 8 obs
Operation Enduring Freedom (*Op Altair*) 1 FFG

SIERRA LEONE
IMATT *Operation Sculpture* 11

SUDAN
AU • AUMIS • *Operation Augural* 11 obs , 100 APC(W) *Grizzly* and *Husky* recovery veh on loan to AU
UN • UNMIS • *Operation Safari* 8; 22 obs

SYRIA/ISRAEL
UN • UNDOF • *Operation Gladius* 2

UNITED STATES
US CENTCOM *Operation Foundation* 8
US NORTHCOM / NORAD / NATO (ACT) 375 (includes AWACS at Tinker AFB

FOREIGN FORCES

United Kingdom Army 240; Navy 10; Air Force 20
United States Army 8; Navy 40; USAF 86; USMC 9

United States US

United States Dollar $		2006	2007	2008
GDP	US$	13.2tr	13.7tr	
per capita	US$	44,384	45,723	
Growth	%	2.9	1.9	
Inflation	%	3.2	2.6	
National Def Budget				
BA	US$	617bn	622bn	
Outlay	US$	521bn	571bn	
Request				
BA	US$			695bn

Population   301,139,947

Age	0 – 14	15 – 19	20 – 24	25 – 29	30 – 64	65 plus
Male	11%	4%	4%	3%	23%	5%
Female	10%	3%	3%	3%	23%	7%

Capabilities

ACTIVE 1,498,157 (Army 593,327 Navy 341,588 Air 336,081 US Marine Corps 186,661 US Coast Guard 40,500)

CIVILIAN 10,126 (US Special Operations Command 3,376 US Coast Guard 6,750)

RESERVE 1,082,718 (Army 675,450 Navy 128,293 Air 178,875 Marine Corps Reserve 92,000 US Coast Guard 8,100)

ORGANISATIONS BY SERVICE

US Strategic Command

Combined Service 1 HQ located at Offutt AFB (NE)
Five missions   US nuclear deterrent; missile defence; global strike; info ops; ISR

US Navy

SUBMARINES • STRATEGIC • SSBN 14 *Ohio* (mod) SSBN 730 each with up to 24 UGM-133A *Trident D-5* strategic SLBM

US Air Force • Air Combat Command

Bbr 5 sqn (incl. 1 AFR) at 2 AFB with 85 B-52H *Stratofortress* each with up to 20 AGM-86B nuclear ALCM and/or AGM-129A nuclear ACM; 2 sqn at 1 AFB with 20 B-2A *Spirit* each with up to 16 free-fall bombs (or up to 80 when fitted with Small Diameter Bombs); 4 B-52 test hvy bbr; 1 B-2 test hvy bbr

Air Force Space Command

Msl 10 sqn at 3 AFB with 500 LGM-30G *Minuteman III* (capacity 1-3 MIRV Mk12/Mk12A per missile)

Strategic Recce/Intelligence Collection (Satellites)

SPACE BASED SYSTEMS 58+
  SATELLITES 34+
    IMAGERY 3+: *Improved Crystal* (visible and infra-red imagery, resolution 6 inches); some *Lacrosse* (formerly *Indigo*, radar imaging satellite resolution 1–2m)
    ELINT/SIGINT 7: 2 *Orion* (formerly *Magnum*); 2 *Trumpet* (successor to *Jumpseat*); 3 unknown (launched Aug 1994, May 1995, Apr 1996)
    ELECTRONIC OCEAN RECCE SATELLITE: EORSAT (detection of shipping by use of infra-red and radar)
    NAVIGATIONAL SATELLITE TIMING AND RANGING 24 NAVSTAR Block 2R (components of Global Positioning System (GPS) accuracy 1m)
    SENSORS • NUCLEAR DETONATION DETECTION 24: (detects and evaluates nuclear detonations. Sensors deployed in NAVSTAR satellites)

Strategic Defenses – Early Warning

North American Aerospace Defense Command (NORAD), a combined US–Ca org.
SPACE BASED SYSTEMS • SATELLITES 4 Defense Support Programme *DSP* (Infra-red surveillance and warning system. Detects missile launches, nuclear detonations, ac in afterburn, spacecraft and terrestrial infra-red events. Approved constellation: 3 operational satellites; 1 operational on-orbit spare.)
    NORTH WARNING SYSTEM 15 North Warning System Long Range (range 200nm); 40 North Warning System Short Range (range 110–150km)
    OVER-THE-HORIZON-BACKSCATTER RADAR (OTH-B) 2: 1 AN/FPS-118 *OTH-B* (500–3000nm) located at Mountain Home AFB (ID); 1 non-operational located at Maine (ME)
    STRATEGIC 2 Ballistic Missile Early Warning System *BMEWS* located at Thule, GL and Fylingdales Moor, UK; 1 (primary mission to track ICBM and SLBM; also used to track satellites) located at Clear (AK)
    SPACETRACK SYSTEM 11: 8 Spacetrack Radar located at Incirlik (Tu), Eglin (FL), Cavalier AFS (ND), Clear (AK), Thule (GL), Fylingdales Moor (UK), Beale AFB (CA), Cape Cod (MA); 3 Spacetrack Optical Trackers located at Socorro (NM), Maui (HI), Diego Garcia
    USN SPACE SURVEILLANCE SYSTEM *NAVSPASUR* 3 strategic transmitting stations; 6 strategic receiving sites in southeast USA
    PERIMETER ACQUISITION RADAR ATTACK CHARACTERISATION SYSTEM *PARCS* 1 at Cavalier AFS, (ND)
    PAVE PAWS 3 at Beale AFB (CA), Cape Cod AFS (MA), Clear AFS (AK); 1 (phased array radar 5,500km range) located at Otis AFB (MA)
    DETECTION AND TRACKING RADARS Kwajalein Atoll, Ascension Island, Antigua, Kaena Point (HI), MIT Lincoln Laboratory (MA)
    GROUND BASED ELECTRO OPTICAL DEEP SPACE SURVEILLANCE SYSTEM *GEODSS* Socorro (NM), Maui (HI), Diego Garcia

STRATEGIC DEFENCES – MISSILE DEFENCES

SEA-BASED: *Aegis* engagement cruisers and destroyers in Pacific Fleet
LAND-BASED: 21 ground-based Interceptors at Fort Greeley, AK; 3 ground-based interceptors at Vandenburg, CA.

US Army 522,388; 70,939 active reservists (total 593,327)

FORCES BY ROLE

The US Army continues its accelerated transition programme. Last Fiscal Year (2007), the army's operating force have activated or converted approximately 75 percent of its Brigade Combat Teams, operational headquarters and support brigades. The aim at present is to to have an Active Component of 19 HBCT (including 3 ACR), 18 IBCT and 6 SBCT. The Reserve is planned to comprise 10 HBCT, 23 IBCT and 1 SBCT. Main differences are: The SBCT has 3 manoeuvre bn instead of 2, as in the HBCT and IBCT. The HBCT has 2 combined arms bn, an armed recce sqn, an armd fires bn, a Brigade Support Bn (BSB) and a Bde Special Troops Bn (BSTB). The IBCT has two infantry bn, a Reconnaissance, Surveillance and Target Acquisition (RSTA) squadron, a fires bn, a BSB bn and a BSTB bn. The SBCT has three *Stryker* infantry bn, a RSTA squadron, a fires bn, a BSB bn, and engineer, signal, MI and anti-armour coys. The Army currently projects 18 division headquarters in the total force (10 Active and 8 National Guard) All are programmed to convert to modular design by FY09, fully standardizing the division headquarters across the force. The Army is developing plans to grow to include 76 BCTs (48 AC BCTs and 28 RC BCTs) and approximately 225 support brigades.

Comd	6 army HQ; 3 corps HQ (modular by 2009) 10 div HQ
Armd	18 HBCT (*each:* 2 (combined arms) armd / inf bn, 1 armd recce sqn, 1 SP arty bn, 1 BSTB bn, 1 BSB bn)
Armd Cav	1 regt (11th ACR) – OPFOR; 1 heavy regt (3rd ACR) with 3 cav sqn (*each:* 3 cav tps, 1 tk coy, 1 arty bty), 1 air cav sqn with (3 atk tps, 1 lift coy), 1 chemical coy, 1 engr coy, 1 MI coy
Mech Inf	17 IBCT (*each:* 2 (combined arms) armd / inf bn, 1 recce sqn, 1 fd arty bn, 1 BSB, 1 BSTB)
Stryker	6 *Stryker* BCT (*each:* 1 HQ coy, 3 *Stryker* bn, 1 Fd Arty bn, 1 recce sqn, 1 AT coy, 1 engr coy, 1 sigs coy , 1 MI coy ,1 BSB)
Air Aslt	4 BCT (*each:* 2 Air aslt bn, 1 RSTA bn, 1 arty bn, 1 spt bn, 1 bde spec tps bn (1 MI coy, 1 engr coy, 1 sigs coy))
AB	4 BCT (*each:* 2 para bn, 1 recce bn, 1 arty bn, 1 spt bn, 1 spec tps bn (1 MI coy, 1 engr coy, 1 sigs coy)); 1 cbt avn bde (medium) with (2 atk hel bn, 1 aslt hel bn, 1 gen spt avn bn, 1 avn spt bn); 1 AD bn; 1 indep bde (173rd AB) (2 inf bn, 1 recce coy, 1 fd arty bn, 1 spt bn)
Arty	6 (Fires) bde (*each:* HQ coy, 1 MLRS bn, 1 atk UAV coy , 1 TA coy, 1 BSB bn)
AD	4 bn with MIM-104 *Patriot*
Cbt Avn	11 CAB (6 heavy, 3 medium, 2 light) (*each:* 1 aslt hel bn, 2 atk hel bn, 1 avn spt bn, 1 gen spt avn bn); 1 (theatre avn) bde
Spt	13 (Sustainment) bde (*each:* 1 BSTB, 2 Cbt Spt bn, 1 Sigs coy)
Cbt Spt	3 (Manoeuvre enhancement) bde (*each:* 1 spt bn, 1 sigs coy)
BfSB	3 BfSB (*each:* 1 BTB bn, 1 MI bn) forming
WMD / NBC / EOD	1 (CBRNE) comd (1 Chemical bde (2 chemical bn), 1 asymmetric warfare regt (initially under direct FORSCOM C2), 2 EOD gp (*each:* 2 EOD bn))
SF	*See US Special Operations Command*

EQUIPMENT BY TYPE

MBT 7,620+ M1-A1/M1-A2 *Abrams*
RECCE 96 Tpz-1 *Fuchs*
AIFV 6,719 M-2 *Bradley*/M-3 *Bradley* each with 2 TOW msl, 1 30mm cannon
APC 19,931
  APC (T) 14,300 M-113A2/M-113A3
  APC (W) 5,631: 4,131 *Stryker*; MRAP 1,500 (end of 2007) (delivery up to 1,000 per month)
ARTY 6,530
  SP 155mm 2,087 M-109A1/M-109A2/M-109A6
  TOWED 1,547: **105mm** 434 M-102; 416 M-119; **155mm** 697 M-198
  MRL 227mm 830 MLRS (all ATACMS-capable)
  MOR 2,066: **81mm** 990 M-252; **120mm** 1,076 M-120/M-121
AT
  MSL 21,955
    SP 2,005: 1,379 HMMWV; 626 M-901
      MANPATS 19,950: 950 *Javelin* (fire and forget); 19,000 M47 *Dragon*
  RL 84mm M136 (AT-4)
AMPHIBIOUS 124+
  LCU 45: 11 LCU-1600 (capacity either 2 M1-A1 *Abrams* MBT or 350 troops); 34 LCU-2000
  LC 79+: 6 Frank Besson (capacity 32 *Abrams* MBT); 73+ LCM-8 (capacity either 1 MBT or 200 troops)
AIRCRAFT
  RECCE 60: 2 O-2 *Skymaster*
    ARL 9: 3 *Dash-7* ARL-M (COMINT/ELINT); 3 *Dash-7* ARL-1 (IMINT); 3 *Dash-7* ARL-C (COMINT)
    RC-12 49: 37 RC-12D *Guardrail*/RC-12H *Guardrail*/RC-12K *Guardrail*; 12 RC-12P *Guardrail*/RC-12Q *Guardrail*
  EW• ELINT 9 RC-7 *Dash 7*
  TPT 208: 46 C-12C *Huron*/C-12R *Huron*; 90 C-12D *Huron*/C-12F *Huron*/C-12J *Huron*; 3 C-20 *Gulfstream*; 47 C-23A *Sherpa*/C-23B *Sherpa*; 11 C-26 *Metro*; 2 C-31 *Friendship*; 2 C-37; 2 Cessna 182 *Skylane*; 1 U-21 *Ute*; 4 UV-18A *Twin Otter*
  UTL 27: 26 UC-35 *Citation*; 1 UV-20A *Chiricahua*
  TRG 3 T-34 *Turbo Mentor*
HELICOPTERS
  OBS 463 OH-58A *Kiowa*/OH-58C *Kiowa*
  SAR 7 HH-60L *Black Hawk*
  ATK 1,009: 634 AH-64A *Apache*/AH-64D *Apache*; 375 OH-58D *Kiowa Warrior*

ASLT 36 AH-6/MH-6 *Little Bird*
SPEC OP 83: 23 MH-47E *Chinook*; 60 MH-60K *Black Hawk*/MH-60L *Pave Hawk* spec op hel
SPT 399 CH-47 *Chinook*
SAR 7 HH-60 L *Black Hawk*
UTL 1,935; 1,484 UH-60A *Black Hawk*/UH-60L *Black Hawk*/UH-60M *Black Hawk*; 4 UH-60Q *Black Hawk*; 447 UH-1H *Iroquois* utl/UH-1V *Iroquois* spt
TRG 154 TH-67 *Creek*
UAV • TACTICAL 524: 20 *Buster*; 54 RQ-5A *Hunter*; 212 RQ-7A *Shadow*; 4 *I-Gnat*; 126 *Desert Hawk*; 100 BQM-147 *Exdrone*; 17 *Sky Warrior*; 8 MQ-8 *Fire Scout* on order
AD• SAM 1,281+
  SP 798: 703 FIM-92A *Avenger* (veh-mounted *Stinger*); 95 M-6 *Linebacker* (4 *Stinger* plus 25mm gun)
  TOWED 483 MIM-104 *Patriot*
  MANPAD FIM-92A *Stinger*
RADAR • LAND 251: 98 AN/TPQ-36 *Firefinder* (arty); 56 AN/TPQ-37 *Firefinder* (arty); 60 AN/TRQ-32 *Teammate* (COMINT); 32 AN/TSQ-138 *Trailblazer* (COMINT); 5 AN/TSQ-138A *Trailblazer*

Reserve Organisations

Army National Guard 351,350 reservists

Currently capable of manning 8 divs after mobilisation. Under the army's transfomation process, the ARNG will assume an end-state structure consisting of 33 BCT (22 lt and 10 hy), 1 *Stryker* BCT and 1 Scout Gp.

FORCES BY ROLE

Armd	6 armd BCT (transforming)
Stryker	1 *Stryker* BCT (transforming)
Scout	1 gp
Mech	4 div; 5 indep bde
Inf	21 BCT (transforming)
Air Cav	1 sqn (3 air cav tps, 1 aslt tps)
SF	2 gp opcon USSOCOM (*total:* 3 SF bn)
Arty	42 indep bn (likely to become 7 Fires Bde)
Fd Arty	17 bde HQ (mostly non-operational)
Engr	8 bde (40bn)
Avn	2 (heavy) cbt avn bde; 6 (air expeditionary) cbt avn bde (*each:* 1 aslt hel bn, 1 atk hel bn, 1 gen spt avn bn, 1 avn spt bn, 1 spt/sy hel bn (each: 3 spt/sy coy – to become 4)); 5 theatre avn bde (transforming)
WMD	32 WMD-CST (Weapons of Mass Destruction Civil Support Teams)
AD	4 indep bn with MIM-104 *Patriot*; FIM-92A *Avenger*
Spt	9 spt bde, 17 regional spt gps
Cbt Spt	14 (Manoeuvre enhancement) bde (transforming)
Sigs	2 bde

Army Reserve 324,100 reservists

Inf	5 div (exercise); 7 div (trg)
Avn	1 theatre avn bde with (air aslt hel, atk hel and gen spt avn bns),
Engr	4 bde

Sig	1 bde
Spt	8 spt bde, 2 cbt spt bde
Civil Affairs	36 (coys) bn opcon USSOCOM; 12 (4 comd, 8 bde) HQ opcon USSOCOM
Psyops	2 gp opcon USSOCOM
Regional Spt	13 comd gps

Army Stand-by-Reserve 700 reservists
Trained individuals for mobilisation

US Navy 335,702; 5,886 active reservists (total 341,588)

Comprises 2 Fleet Areas, Atlantic and Pacific. All combatants divided into 5 Fleets: 2nd – Atlantic, 3rd – Pacific, 5th – Indian Ocean, Persian Gulf, Red Sea, 6th – Mediterranean, 7th – W. Pacific; plus Military Sealift Command (MSC); Naval Reserve Force (NRF); for Naval Special Warfare Command, see US Special Operations Command element.

EQUIPMENT BY TYPE
SUBMARINES 71
  STRATEGIC • SSBN 14 *Ohio* (Mod) SSBN 730 opcon US STRATCOM each with up to 24 UGM-133A *Trident* D-5 strategic SLBM
  TACTICAL 57
    SSGN 4 *Ohio*, mod eq. with total of 154 *Tomahawk* LAM (3 operational, 1 in refit expected ISD mid 2008)
    SSN 53:
      24 *Los Angeles* each with 4 single 533mm TT each with Mk48 *Sea Arrow* HWT/UGM-84 *Harpoon* USGW
      23 *Los Angeles* imp, each with up to 12 *Tomahawk* LAM, 4 single 533mm TT each with Mk48 *Sea Arrow* HWT/UGM- 84 *Harpoon* USGW
      3 *Seawolf*, each with 8 x 1 660mm TT each with up to 45 *Tomahawk* LAM/UGM-84C *Harpoon* USGW, Mk48 *Sea Arrow* HWT
      3 *Virginia* with SLCM *Tomahawk*, 4 single 533mm TT each with Mk48 ADCAP mod 6 HWT, 1 12 cell vertical launch system (12 eff.)
PRINCIPAL SURFACE COMBATANTS 106
  AIRCRAFT CARRIERS 11
    CVN 10:
      1 *Enterprise* (typical capacity 55 F/A-18 *Hornet* FGA ac; 4 EA-6B *Prowler* ELINT EW ac; 4 E-2C *Hawkeye* AEW ac; 6 S-3B *Viking* ASW ac; 4 SH-60F *Seahawk* ASW hel; 2 HH-60H *Seahawk* SAR hel) with 3 Mk 29 *Sea Sparrow* octuple each with RIM-7M/RIM-7P, 2 Mk 49 RAM (may be fitted) with 21 RIM-116 RAM SAM
      9 *Nimitz* (typical capacity 55 F/A-18 *Hornet* FGA ac; 4 EA-6B *Prowler* ELINT EW ac; 4 E-2C *Hawkeye* AEW ac; 6 S-3B *Viking* ASW ac; 4 SH-60F *Seahawk* ASW hel; 2 HH-60H *Seahawk* SAR hel) each with 2–3 Mk 29 *Sea Sparrow* octuple each with RIM-7M/RIM-7P, 2 Mk 49 RAM with 42 RIM-116 RAM SAM
    CV 1 *Kitty Hawk* (typical capacity 50 F/A-18 *Hornet* FGA ac; 4 EA-6B *Prowler* ELINT EW ac; 4 E-2C *Hawkeye* AEW ac; 6 S-3B *Viking* ASW ac; 4 SH-60F *Seahawk* ASW hel; 2 HH-60H *Seahawk* SAR hel) each with 3 Mk 29 *Sea Sparrow* octuple each with RIM-7M/RIM-7P, 2 Mk 49 RAM with 42 RIM-116 RAM SAM

CRUISERS • CG • *TICONDEROGA* 22 *Aegis* Baseline 2/3/4 (CG-52-CG-74) each with, 1 comd and control, 2 quad (8 eff.) each with RGM-84 *Harpoon* SSM, 2 61 cell Mk 41 VLS (122 eff.) each with SM-2 ER SAM/*Tomahawk* LAM, 2 127mm gun 2 SH-60B *Seahawk* ASW hel, (Extensive upgrade programme scheduled from 2006-2020, to include sensors and fire control systems, major weapons upgrade to include Evolved Sea Sparrow (ESSM), SM-3 / SM-2 capability and 2 MK 45 Mod 2 127mm gun)

DESTROYERS • DDG 52

28 *Arleigh Burke* Flight I/II each with *Aegis* comd and control, 1 32 cell Mk 41 VLS (32 eff.) with ASROC tactical/ASSM SSM/SM-2 ER SAM/*Tomahawk* TLAM, 1 64 cell Mk 41 VLS (64 eff.) with ASROC/ASSM SSM/SM-2 ER SAM/*Tomahawk* TLAM, 2 quad (8 eff.) each with RGM-84 *Harpoon* SSM, 2 Mk 49 RAM with 42 RIM-116 RAM SAM, 2 triple ASTT (6 eff.) each with Mk 46 LWT, 1 127mm gun, 1 hel landing platform

24 *Arleigh Burke* Flight IIA each eq. with *Aegis* comd and control, 1 32 cell Mk 41 VLS (32 eff.) with ASROC tactical/ASSM SSM/SM-2 ER SAM/*Tomahawk* TLAM, 1 64 cell Mk 41 VLS (64 eff.) with ASROC/ASSM SSM tactical/SM-2 ER SAM/*Tomahawk* TLAM, 2 quad (8 eff.) each with RGM-84 *Harpoon* SSM, 2 triple ASTT (6 eff.) each with Mk 46 LWT, 1 127mm gun, 2 SH-60B *Seahawk* ASW hel, (Ongoing programme for 10 additional ships)

FRIGATES 21

FFG 21 *Oliver Hazard Perry* each with 2 triple 324mm ASTT (6 eff.) with 24 Mk 46 LWT, 1 76mm gun, (capacity 2 SH-60B *Seahawk* ASW hel)

LCS 1:

1 *Freedom* with RIM-116 RAM, MK-15 *Phalanx* CIWS, 1 57mm gun, (standard capacity either 2 MH-60 *Seahawk* hel or 1 MH-60 with 3 *Firescout* UAV) (delivery expected '08)

PATROL AND COASTAL COMBATANTS 16:

PFC 8 *Cyclone*

PCI 8

MINE WARFARE • MINE COUNTERMEASURES 9

MCM 9 *Avenger* (MCM-1) each with 1 SLQ-48 MCM system, 1 SQQ-32(V)3 Sonar (mine hunting)

ML (none dedicated)

COMMAND SHIPS • LCC 2:

2 *Blue Ridge* (capacity 3 LCPL; 2 LCVP; 700 troops; 1 SH-3H *Sea King* utl hel)

AMPHIBIOUS

PRINCIPAL AMPHIBIOUS SHIPS 32

LHD 7:

7 *Wasp* (capacity 5 AV-8B *Harrier II* FGA; 42 CH-46E *Sea Knight* spt hel; 6 SH-60B *Seahawk* ASW hel; 3 LCAC(L) ACV; 60 tanks; 1,890 troops) each with 2 Mk 29 *Sea Sparrow* octuple with 32 RIM-7M/RIM-7P, 2 Mk 49 RAM with 42 RIM-116 RAM SAM, (Additional platform in build)

LHA 3:

3 *Tarawa* (capacity 6 AV-8B *Harrier II* FGA ac; 12 CH-46E *Sea Knight* spt hel; 9 CH-53 *Sea Stallion* spt hel; 4 LCU; 100 tanks; 1,900 troops) each with 2 Mk 49 RAM with 42 RIM-116 RAM SAM

LPD 10:

7 *Austin* (capacity 6 CH-46E *Sea Knight* spt hel; 2 LCAC(L) ACV/LCU; 40 tanks; 788 troops)

3 *San Antonio* (capacity 1 UA-53E *Sea Stallion* hel or 2 CH-46 *Sea Knight* or 1 MV-22 *Osprey*; 2 LCAC(L); 14 AAAV; 720 troops) (additional 3 hulls in build; current programme totals 9 units)

LSD 12:

4 *Harpers Ferry* (capacity 2 LCAC(L) ACV; 40 tanks; 500 troops) each with 1–2 Mk 49 RAM with 21–42 RIM-116 RAM SAM, 1 hel landing platform (for 2 Ch-35)

8 *Whidbey Island* (capacity 4 LCAC(L) ACV; 40 tanks; 500 troops) each with 2 Mk 49 RAM with 42 RIM-116 RAM SAM, 1 hel landing platform (for 2 CH-53)

AMPHIBIOUS CRAFT 334

LCU 35

LCVP 8

LCPL 145

LCM 72

ACV 74 LCAC(L) (capacity either 1 MBT or 60 troops)

SF EQUIPMENT 6 DDS opcon USSOCOM

FACILITIES

Bases	1 opcon EUCOM located at Naples, It, 1 opcon EUCOM located at Soudha Bay, Gr, 1 opcon EUCOM located at La Maddalena, It, 1 opcon US Pacific Fleet located at Yokosuka, J, 1 opcon EUCOM located at Rota, Sp, 1 opcon US Pacific Fleet located at Sasebo, J
Naval airbases	1 opcon US Pacific Fleet (plus naval comms facility) located at Andersen AFB, 1 opcon US Pacific Fleet located at Diego Garcia, BIOT
SEWS	1 opcon US Pacific Fleet located at Pine Gap, Aus
Comms facility	1 opcon US Pacific Fleet located at NW Cape, Aus
SIGINT stn	1 opcon US Pacific Fleet located at Pine Gap, Aus
Support facility	1 opcon EUCOM located at Ankara, Tu, 1 opcon EUCOM located at Izmir, Tu, 1 opcon US Pacific Fleet located at Diego Garcia, BIOT, 1 opcon US Pacific Fleet located at Singapore, Sgp

Combat Logistics Force

LOGISTICS AND SUPPORT

AOE 5: 4 *Sacramento* (capacity 2 CH-46E *Sea Knight* spt hel); 1 *Supply* (capacity 3 CH-46E *Sea Knight* spt hel)

Navy Reserve Surface Forces

PRINCIPAL SURFACE COMBATANTS

FFG 8 *Oliver Hazard Perry* in reserve each with 2 triple 324mm ASTT (6 eff.) with 24 Mk 46 LWT, 36 SM-1 MR SAM, 1 76mm gun, (capacity 2 SH-60B *Seahawk* ASW hel)

MINE WARFARE • MINE COUNTERMEASURES 14:

MCM 4 *Avenger* in reserve each with 1 SLQ-48 MCM system, 1 SQQ-32(V)3 Sonar (mine hunting)

MHC 10 *Osprey* in reserve each with 1 SLQ-48 MCM system, 1 SQQ-32(V)2 Sonar (mine hunting)
INSHORE UNDERSEA WARFARE 45 HDS/IBU/MIUW

Navy Stand-by-Reserve 2,500 reservists

Naval Reserve Force 128,293

Naval Inactive Fleet
Under 60–90 days notice for reactivation
PRINCIPAL SURFACE COMBATANTS 20
  AIRCRAFT CARRIERS 5 CV
  BATTLESHIP 1 BB
  CRUISERS 3 CG
  DESTROYERS 12: 4 DD; 8 DDG
AMPHIBIOUS
  LS 5 LKA
  CRAFT 5 LCT
  LOGISTICS AND SUPPORT 7: 5 AG; AO 2

Military Sealift Command (MSC)
Naval Fleet Auxiliary Force
LOGISTICS AND SUPPORT 40:
  AFH 5: 3 *Mars*; 2 *Sirius*
  AEH 5: 5 *Kilauea*
  ARS 2: 2 *Safeguard*
  AH 2:
    2 *Mercy* eqpt. with 1 hel landing platform
  ATF 4: 4 *Powhatan*
  HSV 1
  T-AO 15: 15 *Henry J. Kaiser*
  T-AOE RAS 4: 4 *Supply* class
  T-AKEH 5: 5 *Lewis* and *Clark*
Maritime Prepositioning Program
LOGISTICS AND SUPPORT 32:
  T-AK 6
  T-AKR 24:
    LMSR T-AKR 11: 3; 8 Watson
    T-AKRH 13
  T-AVB 2
Strategic Sealift Force
(At a minimum of 4 Days readiness)
LOGISTICS AND SUPPORT 25:
  T-AOT 4: 4 *Champion*
  T-AK 2
  T-AKR 19
    FSS T-AKR 8: 8 *Algol*
    LMSR T-AKR 11: 7 *Bob Hope*; 2 *Gordon*; 2 *Shughart*
Special Mission Ships
LOGISTICS AND SUPPORT 17:
  HSV 1
  T-AG 1 *Hayes*
  T-AGM 3; T-ARC 1
  T-AGOS 4: 1 *Impeccable*; 3 *Victorious*
  T-AGS 7: 1 *John McDonnell*; 6 *Pathfinder*

US Maritime Administration Support • National Defense Reserve Fleet
LOGISTICS AND SUPPORT 49
  T-AK 42: 39 T-AK (breakbulk); 3 T-AK (heavy lift)
  T-AO 7

Ready Reserve Force
Ships at readiness up to a maximum of 30 days
LOGISTICS AND SUPPORT 56
  T-ACS 10 *Keystone State*
  T-AK 9: 3 T-AK (breakbulk); 6 T-AK (heavy lift)
  T-AKR 31
  T-AOT 6

Augmentation Force • Active
Cargo handling   1 bn

Reserve
Cargo handling   12 bn

Naval Aviation 98,588
Operates from 11 carriers, 11 air wings (10 active 1 reserve). Average air wing comprises 8 sqns: 4 each with 12 F/A-18 (2 with F/A-18C, 1 with F/A18-E, 1 with F/A18-F) 1 with 8 S-3B, 1 with 6 SH-60, 1 with 4 EA-6B, 1 with 4 E-2C.
FORCES BY ROLE

Air wing	11 wg
COMD	2 sqn with E-6B *Mercury*
FGA	8 sqn with F/A-18E *Super Hornet*; 9 sqn with F/A-18F *Super Hornet*; 18sqn with F/A-18C *Hornet*;
ASW	3 sqn with S-3B *Viking*; 10 sqn with SH-60B *Seahawk*; 10 sqn with HH-60H *Seahawk*; SH-60F *Seahawk*
ELINT	2 sqn with EP-3 *Orion*
ELINT/ECM	13 sqn with EA-6B *Prowler*; 2 sqn EA-6B *Prowler*
MP	12 (land-based) sqn with P-3C *Orion**
AEW	10 sqn with total of E-2C *Hawkeye*
MCM	2 sqn with MH-53E *Sea Dragon*
Spt	1 sqn with MH-53E *Sea Dragon*; 7 sqn with MH-60S *Knight Hawk*
Tpt	2 sqn with total of 37 C-2A *Greyhound*
Trg	1 (aggressor) sqn with F/A-18C *Hornet*/ F/A-18D *Hornet* / F/A-18E *Super Hornet*/ F/A-18F *Super Hornet*; 14 sqn with T-2C *Buckeye*/T-34C *Turbo Mentor*/T-44 *Pegasus* /T-44A *Pegasus*; 2 sqn with TH-57B *Sea Ranger*/TH-57C *Sea Ranger*; 1 (aggressor) sqn with F/A-18B *Hornet*/F/A-18 C *Hornet* / F/A-18D *Hornet*; 1 sqn with F/A-18E/F *Super Hornet*

EQUIPMENT BY TYPE
AIRCRAFT 1,171 combat capable
  FGA 939: 116 F/A-18A *Hornet*; 28 F/A-18B *Hornet*; 388 F/A-18C *Hornet*; 137 F/A-18D *Hornet*; 109 F/A-18E *Super Hornet*; 161 F/A-18F *Super Hornet*
  ASW 58 S-3B *Viking**
  ELINT 13 EP-3 *Orion*
  ELINT/ECM 113 EA-6B *Prowler*
  MP 174 P-3C *Orion**
  AEW 68 E-2C *Hawkeye*
  COMD 16 E-6B *Mercury*
  TKR 5 KC-130F *Hercules*

TPT 65: 4 C-12C *Huron*; 37 C-2A *Greyhound*; 1 C-20A *Gulfstream* III; 2 C-20D *Gulfstream* III; 4 C-20G *Gulfstream* IV; 7 C-26D *Metro* III; 1 C-37; 1 CT-39G *Sabreliner*; 2 LC-130F *Hercules*; 1 LC-130R *Hercules*; 5 VP-3A *Orion*

UTL 37: 2 RC-12F *Huron*; 2 RC-12M *Huron*; 2 U-6A *Beaver*; 26 UC-12B *Huron*; 1 UC-35D *Citation Encore*; 4 UP-3A *Orion*

TRG 689: 104 T-2C *Buckeye*; 308 T-34C *Turbo Mentor*; 9 T-38 *Talon*; 1 T-39D *Sabreliner*; 8 T-39G *Sabreliner*; 15 T-39N *Sabreliner*; 55 T-44A *Pegasus*; 74 T-45A *Goshawk*; 75 T-45C *Goshawk*; 17 TA-4J *Skyhawk*; 21 TC-12B *Huron*; 2 TE-2C *Hawkeye*

TRIALS AND TEST 47: 1 EA-18G; 1 NF/A-18A *Hornet*; 2 NF/A-18C *Hornet*; 3 NF/A-18D *Hornet*; 1 NP-3C *Orion*; 11 NP-3D *Orion*; 1 NT-34C *Mentor* test; 1 NU-1B *Otter* test; 2 QF-4N *Phantom* II; 16 QF-4S *Phantom* II; 2 X-26A test; 1 X-31A test; 1 YF-4J *Phantom* II (prototype, FGA); 1 YSH-60 *Seahawk* (prototype); 1 YSH-60 prototype; 1 YSH-60B *Seahawk*; 1 YSH-60F *Seahawk*

HELICOPTERS
MCM 28 MH-53E *Sea Dragon*
OBS 3 OH-58A *Kiowa*
SAR 68: 23 HH-1N *Iroquois*; 4 HH-46D *Sea Knight*; 38 HH-60H *Seahawk*; 3 UH-3H *Sea King*
ATK 4 AH-1Z *Super Cobra*
ASW 220: 148 SH-60B *Seahawk*; 72 SH-60F *Seahawk*
SPEC OP 93: 8 MH-60R *Strike Hawk*; 85 MH-60S *Knight Hawk*
SPT 18: 9 CH-53D *Sea Stallion*; 9 CH-53E *Sea Stallion*
UTL 19: 1 UH-1N *Iroquois*; 4 UH-1Y *Iroquois*; 9 UH-46D *Sea Knight*; 3 UH-60L *Black Hawk*; 2 VH-3A *Sea King* (2 VIP, 1 trials); 5 MV-22 *Osprey*
TRG 132: 44 TH-57B *Sea Ranger*; 82 TH-57C *Sea Ranger*; 6 TH-6B in testing
TEST 3 N-SH-60B *Seahawk*

UAV
RECCE 2: 2 RQ-4A *Global Hawk* (Under evaluation and trials)
TAC 40+: 5 MQ-8B *Fire Scout* (Under evaluation and trials); 35 RQ-2B *Pioneer*

MSL
ASM AGM-65A *Maverick*; AGM-84D *Harpoon*; AGM-84E SLAM/SLAM-ER;
AGM-114B/K/M *Hellfire*; AGM-119A *Penguin* 3; AGM-88A HARM; AGM-154A JSOW
AAM AIM-7 *Sparrow*; AIM-9 *Sidewinder*; AIM-120 AMRAAM; RIM-116 RAM

BOMBS
Conventional: BLU-109 (2,000lb); BLU-117/Mk 84 (2,000-pound); BLU-110/Mk 83 (1,000-pound); BLU-111/Mk 82 (500-pound); Mk 46; Mk 50; Mk 54
Laser-Guided: *Paveway* II; *Paveway* III (fits on Mk 82, Mk 83 or Mk 84)
INS/GPS guided: JDAM (GBU-31/32/38); Enhanced *Paveway* II

Naval Aviation Reserve

FORCES BY ROLE
FGA   2 sqn with F/A-18A *Hornet*; 1 sqn with F/A-18A *Hornet* / F/A-18B *Hornet*

ASW   1 sqn with HH-60F / SH-60F *Seahawk*;
MR   3 sqn with P-3C *Orion*
AEW   1 sqn with E-2C *Hawkeye*
MSC   1 sqn with HH-60H *Seahawk*; 1 sqn with MH-60S
ECM   1 sqn with EA-6B *Prowler*
Log spt   1 wg (3 log spt sqn with C-40A *Clipper*, 3 log spt sqn with C-20 *Gulfstream*, 5 tactical tpt sqn with C-130T *Hercules*, 4 log spt sqn with C-9B *Nightingale*; DC-9)
Trg   1 (aggressor) sqn with F-5E *Tiger* II/F-5F *Tiger* II; 1 (aggressor) sqn with F/A-18 *Hornet*

EQUIPMENT BY TYPE
AIRCRAFT 114 combat capable
FGA 67: 64 F/A-18A *Hornet*; 3 F/A-18B *Hornet*
MP 47 P-3C *Orion**
EW/ELINT 4 EA-6B *Prowler*
AEW 9 E-2C *Hawkeye*
TPT 52: 20 C-130T *Hercules*; 9 C-40A *Clipper*; 15 C-9B *Nightingale*; 8 DC-9
UTL 22: 6 UC-12B *Huron*; 6 UC-12F *Huron*; 10 UC-12M *Huron*
HELICOPTERS 11 attack helicopters
MCM 8 MH-53E *Sea Dragon*
SAR 24: 16 HH-60H *Rescue Hawk*; 8 UH-3H *Sea King*
ASW 11: 5 SH-60B *Seahawk*; 6 SH-60F *Seahawk*

US Marine Corps 175,350; 11,311 active reservists (total 186,661)

3 Marine Expeditionary Force (MEF), 2 Marine Expeditionary Brigade (MEB) drawn from 3 div. The 4th Military Expeditionary Brigade (Anti-Terrorism) was officially deactivated February 2006, and its major subordinate units were reassigned to other commands. The Marine Security Force Battalion (MSFBn), Chemical Biological Incident Response Force (CBIRF) and Anti-Terrorism Battalion (ATBN) are now assigned to the 11 Marine Expeditionary Force. The Marine Security Guard Battalion (MSGBn) is now assigned to Marine Corps Combat Development Command.

FORCES BY ROLE
MARDIV   1st MARDIV (1 cbt engr bn, 1 recce bn, 1 arty regt (4 arty bn), 1 amph aslt bn, 1 armd bn, 2 (LAV-25) lt armd recce bn, 3 inf regt (*each*: 3 inf bn)); 2nd MARDIV (1 cbt engr bn, 1 amph aslt bn, 1 recce bn, 1 arty regt (4 arty bn), 1 lt armd recce bn, 1 armd bn, 3 inf regt (*each*: 3 inf bn)); 3rd MARDIV (1 recce bn, 1 arty regt (2 arty bn), 1 cbt engr bn, 1 cbt sp bn (1 lt armd recce coy, 1 amph aslt coy), 2 inf regt (*each*: 3 inf bn))
Spec Ops   1 force (3 recce bn, 3 MEF recce coy)
Force Service Sp Gp 3 gp; 1 sqn

EQUIPMENT BY TYPE
MBT 403 M1-A1 *Abrams*
RECCE 252 LAV-25 *Coyote* (25mm gun, plus 189 variants excluding 50 mor, 95 ATGW see below)

AAV 1,311 AAV-7A1 (all roles)
ARTY 1,511
   TOWED 926: **105mm:** 331 M-101A1; **155mm** 595 M-198
   MOR 81mm 585: 50 LAV-M; 535 M-252
AT
   MSL 2,299
    SP 95 LAV-TOW
    MANPATS 2,204: 1,121 *Predator* ; 1,083 TOW
   RL 2,764: **83mm** 1,650 SMAW; **84mm** 1,114 AT-4
AD • SAM • MANPAD FIM-92A *Stinger*
UAV 1072: 972 3D Max *Dragon Eye*; 100 BQM-147 *Exdrone*
RADAR • LAND 23 AN/TPQ-36 *Firefinder* (arty)

Marine Corps Aviation 34,700

3 active Marine Aircraft Wings (MAW) and 1 MCR MAW

Flying hours   365 hrs/year on tpt Ac; 248 hrs/year on
              Ac; 277 hrs/year on hel

FORCES BY ROLE

Ftr	2 sqn eqpt. with 12 F/A-18A *Hornet* / F/A-18A+ *Hornet*; 6 sqn eqpt. with 12 F/A-18C *Hornet*; 5 sqn (All Weather) eqpt. with 12 F/A-18D *Hornet*
FGA	7 sqn eqpt. with 14 AV-8B *Harrier II*
ECM	4 sqn eqpt. with total of 20 EA-6B *Prowler*
Tkr	3 sqn eqpt. with total of 36 KC-130F *Hercules* / KC-130J *Hercules* / KC-130R *Hercules*
Atk hel	6 sqn eqpt. with 18 AH-1W *Cobra*; 9 UH-1N *Iroquois*
Spt hel	3 sqn eqpt. with 12 MV-22B *Osprey*; 11 sqn eqpt. with 12 CH-46E *Sea Knight*; 2 sqn eqpt. with 10 CH-53D *Sea Stallion*; 6 sqn eqpt. with 16 CH-53E *Sea Stallion*
Test	1 sqn eqpt. with 4 V-22 *Osprey*; 1 sqn eqpt. with 6 CH-46E *Sea Knight*; 6 CH-53E *Sea Stallion*; 8 VH-60N *Presidential Hawk*; 11 VH-3D *Sea King*
AD	5 bty eqpt. with FIM-92A *Avenger*; FIM-92A *Stinger*
UAV	2 sqn eqpt. with RQ-2B *Pioneer*

EQUIPMENT BY TYPE

AC 362 combat capable
  FGA 362
   F/A-18 231: 38 F/A-18A *Hornet*; 4 F/A-18B *Hornet*; 95 F/A-18C *Hornet*; 94 F/A-18D *Hornet*; 131 AV-8B *Harrier II*
  EW 24 EA-6B *Prowler*
  TKR 38: 6 KC-130F *Hercules*; 25 KC-130J *Hercules*; 7 KC-130R *Hercules*
  TPT 3
   1 C-20G *Gulfstream IV*; C-9; 2 C-9B *Nightingale*
  UTL 22
   UC-12: 11 UC-12B *Huron* utl ac / UC-12F *Huron* utl ac
   UC-35: 11 UC-35C *Citation Ultra* utl ac / UC-35D *Citation Encore* utl ac
  TRG 20
   T-34: 3 T-34C *Turbo Mentor*
   TAV-8: 17 TAV-8B *Harrier*
  ATK 140 AH-1W *Cobra*
  SAR 14
   HH-1: 11 HH-1N *Iroquois*
   HH-46: 3 HH-46D *Sea Knight*

  SPT 368
   CH-46: 181 CH-46E *Sea Knight*
   CH-53: 179: 34 CH-53D *Sea Stallion*; 145 CH-53E *Sea Stallion*
   VH-60N *Presidential Hawk* 8 (VIP tpt)
  UTL 81
   UH-1 70: 69 UH-1N *Iroquois*; 1 UH-1Y *Iroquois*
   VH-3 11: 11 VH-3D *Sea King* (VIP tpt)
  TILTROTOR 60
   MV-22 56: ε56 MV-22B *Osprey* (360 on order, deliveries continuing.)
   V-22 *Osprey* 4
UAV • TACTICAL • RQ-2: some RQ-2B *Pioneer*
MSL
  ASM AGM-65F IR *Maverick* / AGM-65E *Maverick*; AGM-84 *Harpoon*; AGM-114 *Hellfire*
  AAM AIM-9M *Sidewinder*; AGM-88A HARM; *AIM-7 Sparrow*; AIM-120 AMRAAM
BOMBS
  Conventional: CBU-59; CBU-99; MK-82 (500lb), MK-83 (1000lb)
  Laser-Guided: GBU 10/12/16 *Paveway* II (fits on Mk82, Mk 83 or Mk 84)
  INS/GPS Guided: JDAM

Reserve Organisations

Marine Corps Reserve 92,000 reservists

Marine	1 div (1 Amph aslt bn, 1 Recce bn, 1 Cbt Engr bn, 1 Arty bde (5 Arty bn), 1 (LAV-25) Lt Armd Recce bn, 3 Inf regt (*each:* 3 Inf bn))
Spec Ops	1 force (1 MEF recce coy, 1 recce bn)
Force Service Sp Gp	1 gp

Marine Corps Aviation Reserve 11,592 reservists
FORCES BY ROLE

Ftr	2 sqn eqpt. with total of 12+ F/A-18A *Hornet* / F/A-18A *Hornet*
Tkr	2 sqn eqpt. with 12 KC-130T *Hercules*
Atk hel	2 sqn eqpt. with 18 AH-1W *Cobra*; 9 UH-1N *Iroquois*
Spt hel	2 sqn eqpt. with total of 24 CH-46E *Sea Knight*; 2 sqn eqpt. with 8 CH-53E *Sea Stallion*
Trg	1 sqn eqpt. with 13 F-5E *Tiger II* / F-5F *Tiger II* / F-5N *Tiger II*
AD	1 bn (2 bty) eqpt. with FIM-92A *Avenger*

EQUIPMENT BY TYPE

AC 37 combat capable
  FTR • F-5 13
   F-5E 1: 1 F-5E *Tiger II* Ftr Ac / F-5F *Tiger II* Ftr Ac
   F-5N *Tiger II* 12
  FGA • F/A-18 24: 24 F/A-18A *Hornet*
  TKR • KC-130 24: 24 KC-130T *Hercules*
HEL 36 attack helicopters
  ATK • AH-1 36: 36 AH-1W *Cobra*
  SPT 40
   CH-46 24: 24 CH-46E *Sea Knight*
   CH-53 16: 16 CH-53E *Sea Stallion*
  UTL • UH-1 18: 18 UH-1N *Iroquois*

Marine Stand-by Reserve 700 reservists
Trained individuals available for mobilisation

US Coast Guard 40,500 (Military); 6,750 (civilian)

PATROL AND COASTAL COMBATANTS 141
  PSOH 40: 1 *Alex Haley*; 13 *Famous*; 12 *Hamilton*; 14 *Reliance*
  PSO 2
  PFC 5 *Cyclone*
  PBC 94: 45 *Marine Protector*; 49 *Island*
LOGISTICS AND SUPPORT 92
  ABU 16 *Juniper*
  AGB 4: 2; 2 *Polar Icebreaker*
  Trg 2
  WLI 5
  WLIC 13
  WLM 14 *Keeper*
  WLR 18
  WTGB 9
  YTM 11

US Coast Guard Aviation 7,960

AIRCRAFT
  MP 23: 7 HU-25A *Guardian*; 1 HU-25B; 9 HU-25C; 6 HU-25D
  SAR 23 MC-130H *Hercules*
  TPT 10: 6 C-130J *Hercules*; 1 C-37; 2 CN-235-200; 1 C-143A *Challenger*
HELICOPTERS
  SAR 137: 42 HH-60J *Jayhawk*; 95 HH-65C (AS-366G1) *Dauphin II*
  UTL 8 MH-68A (A-109E) *Power*
UAV 1 (trials)

US Air Force (USAF) 336,081 (69,242 officers and 266,839 enlisted personnel)

Flying hours ftr 189, bbr 260, tkr 308, airlift 343

Air Combat Command (ACC)

Comprises 4 numbered air forces and one AFR numbered air force, 23 ac wings. Almost the entire USAF (plus active force ANG and AFR) is divided into 10 Aerospace Expeditionary Forces (AEF). Each AEF is on call for 120 days every 20 months, and at least 2 of the 10 AEFs are on call at any one time. Each AEF with 10,000–15,000 personnel comprises 90 multi-role ftr and bbr ac, 31 intra-theatre refuelling aircraft and 13 aircraft for intelligence, surveillance, reconnaissance and EW missions.

FORCES BY ROLE

HQ (AF)	1 HQ located at Langley AFB (VA)
Bbr	4 (non-STRATCOM mission capable) sqn with 67 B-1B *Lancer*; 4 sqn opcon US STRATCOM with B-52 *Stratofortress*; 2 sqn opcon US STRATCOM with B-2A *Spirit* (16 combat ready)
Ftr	3 sqn with F/A-22A *Raptor*; 15 sqn with F-16C *Fighting Falcon*/F-16D *Fighting Falcon*; 2 sqn with F-117 *Nighthawk*; 8 sqn with F-15E *Strike Eagle*; 8 sqn with F-15C/D *Eagle*
Attack/ FAC	10 sqn with A-10 *Thunderbolt II*/OA-10A *Thunderbolt II*
Recce	3 sqn with RC-135/U-2S; 2 sqn with E-8 J-STARS; OC-135B *Open Skies*
EW	2 sqn with EC-130H *Compass Call Solo*
AEW	1 wg (6 AEW sqn with E-3B *Sentry*/E-3C *Sentry*); E-4B)
SAR	6 sqn with HC-130N *Hercules*/HC-130P *Hercules*/HH-60G *Pave Hawk*
Trg	3 (aggressor) sqn with F-16C/D *Fighting Falcon*; F-15C *Eagle*
UAV	1 wg (6 sqn) with MQ-1 *Predator* , MQ-9 *Predator* and RQ-4A *Global Hawk*

Air Mobility Command (AMC)

Provides strategic, tactical, special op airlift, aero medical evacuation, SAR and weather recce.

FORCES BY ROLE

HQ (AF)	1 HQ located at Scott AFB (IL)
Air	2 Air Forces (*total*: 12 active air wg)
Strategic tpt	2 sqn with C-5 *Galaxy*; 12 sqn with C-17 *Globemaster* III
Tactical tpt	8 sqn with C-130 *Hercules*
Op spt tpt	8 sqn with C-20 *Gulfstream*; C-21 *Learjet*; C-32; C-37; C-40 *Clipper*; VC-25 *Air Force One*; UH-1N *Huey*
Tkr	15 sqn with KC-135 *Stratotanker*; 4 sqn with KC-10A *Extender DC-10*
Weather recce	1 sqn with WC-135

Air Education and Training Command

FORCES BY ROLE

Air	7 sqn (AFR personnel) trained to use ac; 2 air forces (*total*: 11 air wg)
Flying trg	8 wg with T-1 *Jayhawk*; T-37 *Tweet*; T-38 *Talon*; T-43; T-6 *Texan II*
Mission trg	25 sqn with F/A-22A *Raptor*; F-16 *Fighting Falcon*; F-15 *Eagle*; A-10 *Thunderbolt II*; OA-10 *Thunderbolt II*; TU-2S; MC-130 *Hercules*; HC-130 *Hercules*; KC-135 *Stratotanker*; C-130 *Hercules*; C-135 *Stratolifter*; C-17 *Globemaster*; C-21 *Learjet*; C-5 *Galaxy*; HH-60 *Seahawk*; UH-1N *Huey*
Trials and testing	Units with 2 B-1 *Lancer*; B-2 *Spirit*; B-52 *Stratofortress*; F-22 *Raptor*; F-117 *Nighthawk*; F-16 *Fighting Falcon*; F-15A *Eagle*/F-15B *Eagle*/F-15C *Eagle*/F-15D *Eagle*; A-10 *Thunderbolt II*; U-2; EC-130E *Commando Solo*; E-3B *Sentry*; AC-130 *Spectre*; KC-135 *Stratotanker*; C-135 *Stratolifter*; C-17 *Globemaster*; T-38C *Talon*; NC-130 *Hercules*; HH-60 *Seahawk*; UH-1N *Huey*

Reserve Organisations

Air National Guard 106,680 reservists
FORCES BY ROLE

Ftr	3 sqn with F-15 *Eagle*; 1 sqn with F-16 *Fighting Falcon*

FGA	6 sqn with A-10 *Thunderbolt II*/OA-10 *Thunderbolt II*; 3 sqn with F-15A *Eagle*/F-15B *Eagle*; 23 sqn with F-16 *Fighting Falcon*
Special Ops	1 sqn opcon USSOCOM with 6 EC-130J *Commando Solo*; 1 sqn MC-130P *Combat Shadow Hercules*
SAR	6 sqn with HC-130 *Hercules*/MC-130 *Hercules*; HH-60 *Seahawk*
Strategic tpt	3 sqn with C-5A; 1 sqn with C-17 *Globemaster* (+2 sqn personnel only); 20 sqn with C-130E *Hercules*/C-130H *Hercules*/C-130J *Hercules*; 2 sqn with C-21 *Learjet*; C-40
Tac tpt	20 sqn with C-130E *Hercules*/C-130H *Hercules*/C-130J *Hercules*; 1 sqn with C-38 *Astra*; 2 sqn with C-21 *Learjet*;
Tkr	3 sqn with KC-135E *Stratotanker*; 19 sqn with KC-135R *Stratotanker* (+2 sqn personnel only)
Mission trg	7 sqn with F-16 *Fighting Falcon*; F-15 *Eagle*; C-130 *Hercules*
UAV	3 sqn with MQ-1*Predator*

Air Force Reserve Command 72,195 reservists
FORCES BY ROLE

Bbr	1 sqn opcon US STRATCOM with 9 B-52H *Stratofortress*
FGA	4 sqn with A-10 *Thunderbolt* II/OA-10 *Thunderbolt* II (+2 personnel only); 3 sqn with F-16C/D *Fighting Falcon*(+1 sqn personnel only)
Special Ops	1 sqn MC-130P *Combat Shadow Hercules* spec ops ac; 1 sqn opcon USSOCOM with 14 MC-130E *Combat Talon*
SAR	3 sqn with HH-60 *Seahawk*; 2 sqn with HC-130 *Hercules*
Strategic tpt	2 sqn with C-5A *Galaxy* (+2 sqn personnel only); 1 sqn C-17 *Globemaster* (+1 sqn personnel only)
Tac tpt	10 sqn with C-130E *Hercules*/C-130H *Hercules*/C-130J *Hercules*
Tkr	8 sqn with KC-135E/R *Stratotanker* (+2 sqn personnel only); 4 sqn KC-10A *Extender* (personnel only);
Weather recce	1 sqn with WC-130H *Hercules*/WC-130J *Hercules*
Mission trg	3 sqn with F-16 *Fighting Falcon*; A-10 *Thunderbolt II*; C-130 *Hercules*

Civil Reserve Air Fleet
Commercial ac numbers fluctuate
AIRCRAFT • TPT 1,122: 758 long range international cargo and passenger; 218 short range international cargo and passenger; 36 national; 83 aeromedical evacuation

Air Force Stand-by-Reserve 16,858 reservists
Trained individuals for mobilisation
US AIR FORCE INVENTORY
AIRCRAFT 2,658 combat capable, (total aircraft 6,318)

LRSA 179 (170 Active Force; 9 Reserve; 0 Air National Guard): 65 B-1B *Lancer*; 20 B-2A *Spirit*; 85 B-52H *Stratofortress* (9 reserve)
TAC 2,624 (1,778 Active Force; 139 Reserve; 707 Air National Guard): 91 F/A-22A *Raptor*; 40 F-117A *Nighthawk*; 396 F-15A/B/C/D *Eagle* (plus 126 Air National Guard); 217 F-15E *Strike Eagle*; 738 F-16C/D *Fighting Falcon* (plus 69 Reserve; 473 Air National Guard); 143 A-10A *Thunderbolt* II (plus 46 Reserve; 84 Air National Guard); 70 OA-10A *Thunderbolt* II* (plus 6 Reserve; 18 Air National Guard); 21 AC130H/U *Spectre* (soc); 14 EC130H *Compass Call*; 6 EC130J *Commando Solo* (soc) (Air National Guard); 24 MC-130E/H *Combat Talon I/II* (soc) (plus 14 Reserve); 24 MC-130P *Combat Shadow* (plus 4 Reserve)
RECCE 80 (70 Active Force; 10 Reserve; 0 Air National Guard): 5 TU-2S; 28 U-2S; 17 E-8C J-STARS; 10 WC-130J *Hercules* (Reserve); 3 OC-135B *Open Skies*; 14 RC-135V/W *Rivet Joint*; 2 RC-135U *Combat Sent*; 1 WC-135 *Constant Phoenix*
TRIALS & TEST 7 (Active Force: 7; Reserve: 0; Air National Guard: 0): 1 B-2 *Spirit*; 2 B-1B *Lancer*; 4 B-52 *Stratofortress*
COMD/AEW 37 (37 Active Force; 0 Reserve; 0 Air National Guard): 33 E-3B/C *Sentry*; 4 E-4B
TPT 928 (525 Active Force; 156 Reserve; 247 Air National Guard): 32 C-5A *Galaxy* (plus 32 Reserve); 60 C-5B *Galaxy*; 2 C-5C *Galaxy*; 134 C-17A *Globemaster III* (plus 8 Reserve; 8 Air National Guard); 186 C-130E/H/J *Hercules* (plus 106 Reserve; 222 Air National Guard); 5 C-20B *Gulfstream* III; 2 C-20H *Gulfstream* III; 74 C-21A *Learjet* (plus 2 Reserve); 4 C-32A; 9 C-37A; 2 C-40 B/C (plus 2 Reserve); 2 VC-25A (Air Force One); 13 HC- 130P/N *Hercules* (plus 10 Reserve, 13 Air National Guard)
TKR 589 (254 Active Force; 84 Reserve; 251 Air National Guard): 59 KC-10A *Extender* DC-10 (tkr/tpt); 195 KC-135 A/E/R/T *Stratotanker* (plus 84 Reserve, 251 Air National Guard)
TRG 1,572 (1,572 Active Force; 0 Reserve; 0 Air National Guard): 179 T-1A *Jayhawk*; 454 T-6A *Texan* II1; 419 T-37B *Tweet*; 509 T-38A *Talon*; 11 T-43A
TILT-ROTOR 6: 2 CV-22 *Osprey* (testing); 4 CV-22A *Osprey* (soc)
HELICOPTERS 189 (148 Active Force; 23 Reserve; 18 Air National Guard): 64 HH-60G *Pave Hawk* (plus 23 Reserve; 18 Air National Guard); 62 UH-1N *Huey* (TPT); 12 MH-53J *Pave Low* III (soc); MH-53M *Pave Low* IV (soc)
UAV 107 (107 Active Force; 0 Reserve; 0 Air National Guard): 8 MQ-9 *Reaper*; 88 MQ-1 *Predator* (incl 28 SOC) ; 11 RQ-4A *Global Hawk*
MSL 41,422+
ASM 26,422+: 1,142 AGM-86B ALCM; 460 AGM-129A Advanced Cruise Missile; 400+ AGM-130A; 150+ AGM-142 *Popeye*; 17,000+ AGM-65A *Maverick*/AGM-65B *Maverick*/AGM-65D *Maverick*/AGM-65G *Maverick*; 70+ AGM-84B *Harpoon*; 700+ AGM-86C CALCM; 6,500+ AGM-88A HARM/AGM-88B HARM
AAM 15,000+: 5,000+ AIM-120A AMRAAM/AIM-120B AMRAAM/AIM-120C AMRAAM; 3,000+ AIM-7M *Sparrow*; 7,000+ AIM-9M *Sidewinder*

BOMBS

Conventional: BLU-109/Mk 84 (2,000lb); BLU-110/Mk 83 (1,000lb; BLU-111/Mk 82 (500lb)
Laser-guided: *Paveway* II, *Paveway* III (fits on Mk82, Mk83 or Mk84)
INS/GPS guided: JDAM (GBU 31/32/38); GBU-15 (with BLU-109 penetrating warhead or Mk 84); GBU-39B Small Diameter Bomb (250lb); *Enhanced Paveway* III

US Special Operations Command 31,496; 3,376 (civilian); 11,247 reservists (SOF) (total 42,743 plus 3,376 civilians)

Commands all active, reserve, and National Guard Special Operations Forces (SOF) of all services based in CONUS

FORCES BY ROLE

Combined Service   1 HQ located at MacDill AFB (FL)

US Army

SF	5 gp (*each:* 3 SF bn)
Ranger	1 regt (3-4 Ranger bn (QDR increased each bn by one coy))
Sigs	1 bn
Avn	1 regt (160 SOAR) (4 Avn bn)
Psyops	1 gp (5 Psyops bn)
Civil Affairs	1 bn (5 Civil Affairs coy)

EQUIPMENT BY TYPE

UAV 57: 15 *Tern*; 14 *Mako*; 28 *Snowgoose*

Reserve Organisations

Army National Guard

SF 2 gp (*total:* 3 SF bn)

Army Reserve

Psyops   2 gp
Civil Affairs   12 (4 comd, 8 bde) HQ; 36 (coys) bn

US Navy 5,400

The Naval Special Warfare Command (NSWC) is organised around eight SEAL Teams and two SEAL Delivery Vehicle (SDV) Teams. These components deploy SEAL Teams, SEAL Delivery Vehicle Teams, and Special Boat Teams worldwide to meet the training, exercise, contingency and wartime requirements of theater commanders. Operationally up to two of the eight SEAL Teams are deployed at any given time.

FORCES BY ROLE

NSWC	1 comd; 8 SEAL team (48 pl); 2 SDV team

EQUIPMENT BY TYPE

SF 6 DDS

Naval Reserve Force

Delivery veh	1 det
Naval Special Warfare	6 (Gp) det; 3 det; 1 det
Special Boat	2 unit; 2 sqn
HQ	1 (CINCSOC) det

SEAL	8 det

FACILITIES

Navy Special Warfare Command (NSWC), Coronado CA

US Air Force

FORCES BY ROLE

Air Force Special Operations Command (AFSOC) includes about 13,000 active and reserve personnel. AFSOC HQ is at Hurlburt Field, FL, along with the 720th Special Tactics Group, the 18th Flight Test Squadron, and the USAF Special Operations School. The 16th Special Operations Wing (SOW), is at Cannon AFB NM. AFSOC plans to activate the 1st SOW at Hurlburt Field using elements of the 16th SOW. The 352nd Special Operations Group is at RAF Mildenhall, England, and the 353rd Special Operations Group, is at Kadena Air Base, Japan. Reserve AFSOC components include the 193rd Special Operations Wing, ANG, stationed at Harrisburg, PA, the 280th Combat Communications Squadron, ANG, stationed at Dothan, AL, and the 919th Special Operations Wing, AFR, stationed at Duke Field, FL. AFSOC's three active-duty flying units have over 100 fixed and rotary-wing aircraft.

2 wgs and 16 sqn with CV-22A; AC-130H *Spectre*/ AC-130U *Spectre**; MC-130E/H *Combat Talon II*; MC-130W/MC-130P *Combat Shadow*; C-130E *Hercules*; MH-53J *Pave Low III*/MH-53M *Pave Low IV*; U-28A; MQ-1 *Predator* UAV

The first CV-22 tilt rotor squadron is expected to be combat ready in 2009. USSOCOM plans to replace its entire fleet of HH-53 *Pave Low* helicopters over the next two years with CV-22s, but not on a one-for-one basis as USSOCOM presently plans to procure only 50 CV-22s by 2017. USSOCOM would like to increase its MC-130 fleet to 61 aircraft to accommodate the growth of army and marine corps special operations forces.

Reserve Organisations

Air National Guard

Special Ops 1 sqn with 7 EC-130E *Commando Solo*/EC-130H *Compass Call*

Air Force Reserve

Special Ops 1 sqn with 14 MC-130E *Combat Talon*

DEPLOYMENT (incl. detachment postings)

AFGHANISTAN

NATO • ISAF 15,108
United States Central Command
9,650 (*Op Enduring Freedom*)

Army

Cav	1BCT (4th)
Mech inf	1 BCT (3rd)
Inf	1 BCT (27th)
AB	1 div (82nd), 1 div HQ (101st)
Mtn	1 div (10th Mtn)

EQUIPMENT BY TYPE

Atk: AH-64 *Apache*

Utl: UH-60 *Black Hawk*
Spt: CH-47 *Chinook*

Navy
EW: EA-6B *Prowler*
FORCES BY ROLE
1 ARG gp (Part of CTF 150, Fifth Fleet)

Air Force
EQUIPMENT BY TYPE
AIRCRAFT
FGA: F-15E *Strike Eagle;* A-10 *Thunderbolt II*
EW: EC-130 *Compass Call*
Tpt: C-130 *Hercules,*
HELICOPTER
SAR: HH-60 *Pave Hawk,*
UAV: MQ-1 *Predator* , MQ-9 *Reaper,*

ALBANIA
Army 1; Navy 1; USAF 1; USMC 6

ALGERIA
Army 1; USAF 2; USMC 7

ANGOLA
USMC 6

ANTIGUA AND BARBUDA
USAF 2
US Strategic Command
Strategic Defences - Early Warning
RADAR • STRATEGIC 1 DETECTION AND TRACKING RADAR located at Antigua, AB

ARABIAN GULF AND INDIAN OCEAN
United States Central Command
US Navy HQ 5th fleet
5th Fleet's operating forces are rotationally deployed to the region from either the Pacific Fleet or Atlantic Fleet.
Operation Enduring Freedom • Horn of Africa 1,462
FORCES BY ROLE
1 CVSG CVGP; 1 ARG gp

EQUIPMENT BY TYPE
PRINCIPAL SURFACE COMBATANTS 7
AIRCRAFT CARRIERS • CVN 1 CV/CVN
CRUISERS 1 CG
DESTROYERS 4 DDG
FRIGATES 1 FFG
AMPHIBIOUS • PRINCIPAL AMPHIBIOUS SHIPS 6: 1 LPD; 1 LSD;
LHD 4 LHA/LHD

ARGENTINA
Army 4; Navy 3; USAF 14; USMC 8

ARMENIA
Army 1; USMC 6

ASCENSION ISLAND
US Strategic Command
Strategic Defences - Early Warning
RADAR • STRATEGIC 1 DETECTION AND TRACKING RADAR located at USAF Ascension

ATLANTIC OCEAN
United States Northern Command • US Navy HQ 2nd Fleet
FORCES BY ROLE
4–5 CVBG CVGP (2nd Fleet estimated composition)

EQUIPMENT BY TYPE
SUBMARINES 35
STRATEGIC 10 SSBN
TACTICAL 25 SSN
PRINCIPAL SURFACE COMBATANTS 54
AIRCRAFT CARRIERS • CVN 5 CV/CVN
CRUISERS 13 CG
DESTROYERS 18 DDG
FRIGATES 18 FFG
COMMAND SHIPS • LCC 1 *Blue Ridge* (capacity 3 LCPL; 2 LCVP; 700 troops; 1 SH-3H *Sea King* ASW hel)
AMPHIBIOUS
PRINCIPAL AMPHIBIOUS SHIPS 15: 2 LHA; 4 LPD; 4 LPH; 5 LSD
LS 7: 6 LST; 1 LKA

AUSTRALIA
United States Pacific Command
US Navy 26
USMC 603
USAF 61
US Army 21
FACILITIES

SEWS	1 located at Pine Gap, Aus
Comms facility	1 located at NW Cape, Aus
SIGINT stn	1 located at Pine Gap, Aus

AUSTRIA
Army 5; USAF 3; USMC 14

AZERBAIJAN
Army 1; USMC 6

BAHAMAS
Navy 29; USMC 6

BAHRAIN
United States Command
US Army Central Command 29
US Navy Central Command 1,187
US Air Force Central Command 25
US Marines Central Command 148

BARBADOS
USMC 6

BANGLADESH
Army 2; USMC 6

BELARUS
Army 2

BELIZE
Army 1; Navy 1

BELGIUM
United States European Command
HQ Stuttgart–Vaihingen. Commander is SACEUR. (V Corps) Army prepositioned stocks (APS) for 2 armd/mech bdes,

approximately 57% stored in Ge, remainder in Be (22%) Lux (21%) and NL.

US Army Europe 765
Commander is also CINCAFSOUTH
US Navy 92
US Air Force 481
USMC 29

BERMUDA
Navy 4

BOLIVIA
Army 7; Navy 1; USAF 3; USMC 6

BOSNIA-HERZEGOVINA
EU • EUFOR • *Op. Althea* 207

BOTSWANA
Army 4; USMC 6

BRAZIL
Army 9; Navy 4; USAF 6; USMC 22

BRITISH INDIAN OCEAN TERRITORY
US Strategic Command
  Strategic Defences - Early Warning
  RADAR • STRATEGIC 2:
    SPACETRACK SYSTEM 1 Spacetrack Optical Tracker located at Diego Garcia, BIOT
    1 ground based electro optical deep space surveillance system (*GEODSS*) located at Diego Garcia, BIOT
United States Pacific Command
  USAF 643 located at Diego Garcia, BIOT
  US Navy 258 located at Diego Garcia, BIOT
  FORCES BY ROLE
    1 MPS sqn (MPS-2 with equipment for one MEB) located at Diego Garcia, BIOT with 5 logistics and support ships
  FACILITIES
    Naval airbase   1 located at Diego Garcia, BIOT
    Support facility 1 located at Diego Garcia, BIOT

BULGARIA
Army 4; Navy 1; USAF 3; USMC 8

CAMEROON
Army 2; USAF 1; USMC 5

CAMBODIA
Army 3; USMC 7

CANADA
Army 8; Navy 40; USAF 86; USMC 9

CHAD
Army 4; USMC 7

CHILE
Army 7; Navy 5; USAF 11; USMC 15

CHINA
Army 10; Navy 7; USAF 12; USMC 34

COLOMBIA
United States Southern Command
  US Army South 72

Commander Naval Forces South • Navy 3
USAF 7
USMC 42

CONGO, DEMOCRATIC REPUBLIC OF
Army 2; USMC 8

COSTA RICA
Army 1; USMC 7

COTE D'IVOIRE
Army 3; USMC 14

CROATIA
Army 3

CUBA
US Army 311
US Marine Corps 136 located at Guantánamo Bay
US Navy 456 located at Guantánamo Bay

CYPRUS
Army 3; USAF 8; USMC 11

CZECH REPUBLIC
Army 3; USAF 2; USMC 5

DENMARK
Army 2; Navy 5; USAF 6; USMC 6

DJIBOUTI
United States Central Command
  Army 560
  Navy 765
  USAF 340
  USMC 373

DIEGO GARCIA
Navy 203; USAF 37

DOMINICAN REPUBLIC
Army 2; USAF 2; USMC 8

ECUADOR
United States Southern Command
  US Army South 14
  US Navy 2
  US Air Force 19
  Marine Forces South • USMC 6

EGYPT
United States Central Command
  US Air Force 39
  US Army 225
  US Navy 4
  USMC 20
    MFO 1 inf bn; 1 spt bn; 288

EL SALVADOR
Army 7; Navy 1; USMC 13

ESTONIA
Army 1; Navy 1; USMC 7

ERITREA
Army 2

ETHIOPIA
Army 2; USMC 8

ETHIOPIA/ERITREA
UN • UNMEE 5 obs

FINLAND
Army 2; Navy 2; USAF 3; USMC 11

FRANCE
Army 17; Navy 11; USAF 18; USMC 23

GABON
Army 1

GEORGIA
Army 6; USMC 7
UN • UNOMIG 2 obs

GERMANY
United States European Command
1 Combined Service HQ (EUCOM) located at Stuttgart–Vaihingen, Ge

US Army Europe
1 HQ (HQ US Army Europe (USAREUR)) located at Heidelberg, Ge

US Army 43,247,
FORCES BY ROLE
1 armd corps HQ located at Heidelberg, Ge (1 armd div (less 1 bde at Ft Riley), 1 engr bde, 1 avn bde, 1 mech inf div, 1 arty bde, 1 AD bde)

EQUIPMENT BY TYPE
MBT 568 M-1 *Abrams*
AIFV 1,266 M-2 *Bradley* each with 2 TOW msl, 1 cannon
ARTY 312 mor/MRL/SP
HELICOPTERS: 115 atk
US Navy Europe 297
US Air Force Europe 15,067
1 airfield construction HQ (HQ US Airforce Europe (USAFE) located at Ramstein AB, Ge

HQ 3rd Air Force – responsible for all USAF units in Europe
1 ftr wg located at Spangdahlem AB, Ge

US Air Force Air Combat Command (ACC)
1 airlift wg located at Ramstein AB, Ge eqpt. with 16 C-130E *Hercules;* 2 C-20 *Gulfstream;* 9 C-21 *Learjet;* 1 CT-43 Boeing 737

USMC 283

GHANA
Army 4; Navy 1; USMC 10

GIBRALTAR
Navy 2

GUATEMALA
Army 7; USAF 1; USMC 5

GUINEA
Army 2; Navy 1; USMC 6

GUYANA
Army 2

GREECE
European Command
  US Army 9
  US Navy 288 (Base facilities)

Base 1 located at Makri, Gr, 1 located at Soudha Bay, Gr
US Air Force 44
US Air Force Europe • 16th Air Force
Air base 1 located at Iraklion, Gr

USMC 11

GREENLAND (DK)
US Strategic Command
  Strategic Defences
  RADAR • STRATEGIC 2: 1 ballistic missile early warning system (BMEWS) located at Thule, GL
    SPACETRACK SYSTEM 1 Spacetrack Radar located at Thule, GL
United States Northern Command
  US Air Force 138

GUAM
United States Pacific Command
  USMC 5
  USAF 1,706
  US Army 43
  US Navy 1,074
    FORCES BY ROLE
    1 MPS sqn (MPS-3 with equipment for one MEB) eq. with 4 Logistics and Support

    FACILITIES
    Naval airbase   1 located at Andersen AFB (plus naval comms facility)

GUATEMALA
Army 7; USAF 1; USMC 5

GUYANA
United States Southern Command
  US Army 2

HAITI
Army 5; USMC 7
UN • MINUSTAH 3

HONDURAS
United States Southern Command
  US Army 194
  US Navy • Commander Naval Forces South 2
  USAF 208
  USMC 8

HUNGARY
Army 6; USAF 6; USMC 7

ICELAND
Navy 25

INDIA
Army 7; Navy 6; USAF 5; USMC 8

INDONESIA AND TIMOR-LESTE
Army 11; Navy 2; USAF 4; USMC 13

IRAQ
United States Central Command
Operation Iraqi Freedom 168,000: Expected troop levels in Jan 2008 is 160,000 this may decrease to 132,000 by Dec 2008. The combat element comprises 20 BCTs reducing to 19 in Jan 08.

Army

Armd   6 HBCT

Stryker   3 SBCT

Inf   9 IBCT

Army National Guard

Inf 1 bde; 3 BCT

Navy

FORCES BY ROLE

1 CVSG and 1 ARG gp (Both part of CTFs 152 and 158, Fifth Fleet)

USMC

MEF   2 RCT

Air Force

EQUIPMENT BY TYPE

AIRCRAFT

FGA: F-16; A-10

Tpt: C-130 *Hercules*; C-17 *Globemaster* III

HELICOPTER

SAR: HH-60 *Pave Hawk*

UAV: MQ-1 *Predator*

ISRAEL

Army 8; Navy 4; USAF 11; USMC 27

ITALY

European Command

US Army 3,241

1 SETAF HQ Task Force located at Vicenza, It; 2 SETAF para bn located at Vicenza, It; 1 SETAF log unit (in store) (holds eqpt for Theater Reserve Unit (TRU)/Army Readiness Package South (ARPS)) with 116 M-1 *Abrams* MBT; 127 AIFV; 4 APC (T); 1 HQ located at Gaeta, It

US Navy 2,659

1 HQ (HQ US Navy Europe (USNAVEUR)) located at Naples, Italy

Base 1 located at La Maddalena, It

USAF 4,261

1 ftr wg (2 ftr sqn with 21 F-16C *Fighting Falcon*/F-16D *Fighting Falcon* located at Aviano, It)

1 MR sqn located at Sigonella, It, eqpt. with 9 P-3C *Orion*

USMC 55

JAMAICA

Army 2; Navy 3; USMC 7

JAPAN

United States Pacific Command

US Army 2,417

1 HQ (9th Theater Army Area Command) located at Zama, J 1 HQ – HQ USARPAC

US Navy 3,716

Base 1 located at Sasebo, 1 located at Yokosuka

US Pacific Fleet • HQ 7th Fleet

FORCES BY ROLE

1 HQ (7th Fleet) located at Yokosuka, J; 1 MCM sqn located at Sasebo

EQUIPMENT BY TYPE

PRINCIPAL SURFACE COMBATANTS 10:

AIRCRAFT CARRIERS • 1 CVN (Typical composition includes 2 sqn F/A-18C; 1 sqn F/A-18E; 1 sqn F/A-18F); 4 EA-6B *Prowler* EW ac; 4 E-2C *Hawkeye* AEW ac; 4 SH-60F *Seahawk* ASW hel; 2 HH-60H *Seahawk* SAR hel) located at Yokosuka

PRINCIPAL SURFACE COMBATANTS 10: 9 located at Yokosuka.

COMMAND SHIPS • LCC 1 *Blue Ridge* (capacity 3 LCPL; 2 LCVP; 700 troops; 1 SH-3H *Sea King* ASW hel) located at Yokosuka

AMPHIBIOUS 4 at Sasebo

USMC 13,771

1 elems MEF div

USAF 13,164

USAF • 5th Air Force

1 Special Ops gp located at Okinawa – Kadena AB

USAF • AIR COMBAT COMMAND (ACC)

1 ftr wg located at Okinawa – Kadena AB (2 ftr sqn with total of 18 F-16 *Fighting Falcon)* located at Misawa AB); 1 ftr wg located at Okinawa – Kadena AB (1 AEW sqn with 2 E-3B *Sentry*,1 SAR sqn with 8 HH-60G *Pave Hawk,* 2 ftr sqn with total of 24 F-15C *Eagle*/F-15D *Eagle*)

USAF • AIR MOBILITY COMMAND (AMC)

1 airlift wg located at Yokota AB with 10 C-130H *Hercules*; 2 C-12J

JORDAN

Army 1; USAF 10; USMC 8

KAZAKHSTAN

Army 4; USAF 1; USMC 6

KENYA

Army 12; Navy 4; USAF 5; USMC 10

KOREA, REPUBLIC OF

United States Pacific Command • Eighth US Army • US Army

US Army 18,366

FORCES BY ROLE

1 (UN comd) HQ Eighth Army located at Seoul; 1 elems HQ 2ID located at Tongduchon, (1 avn bde (1 aslt hel bn, 1 atk hel bn), 1 armd bde (1 armd inf bn, 2 tk bn), 1 air cav bde (2 atk hel bn), 2 fd arty bn with MLRS, 2 SP arty bn); 1 SAM bn located at Uijongbu, ROK with MIM-104 *Patriot*

EQUIPMENT BY TYPE

MBT 116 M-1 *Abrams*

AIFV 126 M-2 *Bradley* each with 2 TOW msl, 1 cannon

APC 111 APC (T)

ARTY 45 MOR/MRL/SP

USAF 8,369

USAF • 7th Air Force

1 HQ 7th Air Force HQ (AF) HQ (HQ 7th Air Force) located at Osan AB; 1 ftr wg located at Osan AB, ROK (1 ftr sqn with 20 F-16C *Fighting Falcon*/F-16D *Fighting Falcon*, 1 ftr sqn with 24 A-10 *Thunderbolt* II/OA-10 *Thunderbolt* II (12 of each type) located at Osan AB); 1 ftr wg located at Kusan AB (2 ftr sqn with total of 20 F-16C *Fighting Falcon*/ F-16D *Fighting Falcon*); 1 Special Ops sqn

US Navy 244

USMC 135

North America

KUWAIT
Troops deployed as part of *Op Iraqi Freedom*

KYRGYZSTAN
NATO • ISAF 14

LAOS
Army 2; USAF 2

LATVIA
USMC 7

LEBANON
Army 3

LIBERIA
Army 3; USAF 1;USMC 10
UN • UNMIL 5; 7 obs

LITHUANIA
Army 1; Navy 2; USMC 6

LUXEMBOURG
USMC 8

MACEDONIA AND BOSNIA
European Command • USAF 6

MACEDONIA, FORMER YUGOSLAV REPUBLIC
European Command
  US Army 3
  USAF 8
  USMC 16
NATO • KFOR • *Joint Enterprise* 27

MADAGASCAR
Navy 3

MALAYSIA
Army 3; Navy 3; USAF 3; USMC 6

MALI
Army 2; USMC 6

MALTA
Army 1; Navy 2; USMC 6

MAURITANIA
USMC 5

MEDITERRANEAN SEA
European Command
  US Navy 11,800
  USMC 2,200
    HQ 6th Fleet
  US Navy
    FORCES BY ROLE
    1 CVBG gp eqpt. with circa 1 CV

    PRINCIPLE SURFACE COMBATANTS DPG 6; circa 1 spt (fast); 1 MPS gp (MPS-1) eqpt. with 4 Logistics and Support (1 MEF fwd)
    EQUIPMENT BY TYPE
    MBT 116 M-1 *Abrams*
    AIFV 126 M-2 *Bradley* each with 2 TOW Msl, 1 cannon
    APC 111 APC (T)
  SUBMARINES • TACTICAL 3: circa 3 **SSN**

AMPHIBIOUS • PRINCIPAL AMPHIBIOUS SHIPS •
LPD circa 2 **LHD/LPD**
  LOGISTICS AND SUPPORT 6: circa 1 **AE**; circa 1 **AF**; circa 2 **AO**; circa 1 **AOE**; circa 1 **ATF**
USMC 1 MEU gp

MEXICO
Army 7; Navy 2; USAF 5; USMC 22

MIDDLE EAST
UN • UNTSO 3 obs

MOLDOVA
Army 1

MONGOLIA
Army 3; USMC 2

MOROCCO
Army 2; Navy 3; USAF 3; USMC 5

MOZAMBIQUE
USMC 6

MYANMAR
Army 21; Navy 26; USAF 61; USMC 603

NEPAL
Army 4; USMC 6

NETHERLANDS
European Command
  USAF 252
  US Army 273
  US Navy 23
  USMC 14

NEW ZEALAND
Army 2; Navy 2; USMC 1

NICARAGUA
Army 7; USMC 9

NORWAY
European Command
  USAF 38
  US Army 23
    ARTY • SP 155mm 36: 18 M-109 (Army Prepositioned Stocks (APS)); 18 M-198 (APS)
  US Navy 7
  USMC 12

NIGER
Army 1; USMC 6

NIGERIA
Army 3; USAF 4; USMC 16

OMAN
United States Central Command
  USAF 24
  US Army 3
  USMC 10

PACIFIC OCEAN
United States Pacific Command
  USMC 2,027 (at sea)
  US Navy 11,617 (at sea)
    Naval Aviation 1,400 Ac

3rd Fleet
SUBMARINES • TACTICAL 27 SSN
PRINCIPAL SURFACE COMBATANTS 58
  AIRCRAFT CARRIERS • CVN 6 CVN/CV
  CRUISERS 13 CG
  DESTROYERS 24 DDG
  FRIGATES 15 FFG
MINE WARFARE • MINE COUNTERMEASURES 2 MCM
COMMAND SHIPS 2 LCC
LOGISTICS AND SUPPORT 8 AG

PANAMA
Army 7; Navy 2; USAF 1; USMC 9

PAKISTAN
United States Central Command
  US Army 4
  US Navy 2
  USAF 12
  USMC 25

PARAGUAY
Army 4; USAF 1; USMC 5

PERU
Army 15; Navy 14; USAF 4; USMC 15

PHILIPPINES
Army 13; Navy 5; USAF 7; USMC 86

POLAND
Army 10; Navy 1; USAF 6; USMC 12

PORTUGAL
European Command
  USAF 800
  US Army 27
  US Navy 29
  USMC 9
US European Command
Support facility   1 located at Lajes, Por

PUERTO RICO
United States Southern Command • Commander Naval Forces South • US Navy 36
US Special Operations South; 1 HQ (SOCSOUTH) located at Roosevelt Roads
Army 55; USAF 26; USMC 27

QATAR
United States Central Command
  US Army Central Command • US Army 188
  US Navy Central Command • US Navy 4
  USAF 198
  USMC 122

MARSHALL ISLANDS
US Strategic Command 20
  Strategic Defences
  RADAR • STRATEGIC 1 DETECTION AND TRACKING RADAR located at US Army Kwajalein Atoll

ROMANIA
Army 4; Navy 1; USAF 5; USMC 12

RUSSIA
Army 14; Navy 3; USAF 9; USMC 50

RWANDA
USMC 6

SAUDI ARABIA
United States Central Command
  US Army Central Command • US Army 153
  US Navy 23
  USAF 68
  USMC 30

SENEGAL
Army 2; Navy 1; USMC 8

SERBIA
NATO • KFOR • *Joint Enterprise* 1,640

SIERRA LEONE
USMC 1

SINGAPORE
United States Pacific Command
  USMC 12
  USAF 16
  1 log spt sqn located at Singapore, Sgp
  US Navy 80
  US Army 8
  USPACOM
  Support facility   1 located at Singapore, Sgp

SLOVAKIA
USAF 3; USMC 8

SLOVENIA
USAF 6; USMC 2

SOMALIA
Navy 27

SOUTH AFRICA
Army 5; USAF 4; USMC 24

SPAIN
European Command
Base 1 located at Moron, Sp
  USAF 312
  US Army 102
  US Navy 740
  USMC 154

SRI LANKA
Army 2; USMC 8

SUDAN
Army 1; USAF 1
AU • AUMIS 2 obs

SURINAME
Army 1

SWEDEN
  Army 1
  Navy 1
  USAF 5
  USMC 6

SWITZERLAND
Army 1
Navy 1
USAF 4
USMC 13

SYRIA
Army 3
USMC 5

TAJIKISTAN
Army 1

TANZANIA
Army 2
Navy 1
USMC 8

THAILAND
United States Pacific Command
US Army 39
USAF 29
USMC 39
US Navy 7

TOGO
USMC 7

TRINIDAD AND TOBAGO
USMC 6

TUNISIA
Army 4
Navy 3
USAF 1
USMC 7

TURKEY
US Strategic Command 1,573
Strategic Defences
RADAR • STRATEGIC • SPACETRACK SYSTEM 1 Spacetrack Radar located at Incirlik, Tu
European Command
Support facility   1 located at Ankara, Tu, 1 located at Izmir, Tu

US Army 68
US Navy 9
1 air wg (ac on detachment only) located at Incirlik, Tu with F-16 *Fighting Falcon*; F-15E *Strike Eagle*; EA-6B *Prowler*; E-3B *Sentry*/E-3C *Sentry*; HC-130 *Hercules*; KC-135 *Stratotanker*; C-12 *Huron*; HH-60 *Seahawk*

European Command
Air base 1 located at Incirlik, Tu
USMC 18

TURKMENISTAN
USMC 4

UGANDA
Army 2
USMC 9

UKRAINE
Army 6
Navy 1
USAF 3

UNITED ARAB EMIRATES
United States Central Command
USAF 58
US Army 3
US Navy 7
USMC 19

UNITED KINGDOM
US Strategic Command
Strategic Defences
RADAR • STRATEGIC 2: 1 ballistic missile early warning system *BMEWS* located at Fylingdales Moor
SPACETRACK SYSTEM 1: 1 Spacetrack Radar located at Fylingdales Moor
USAF
1 Special Ops gp located at Mildenhall with 5 MC-130H *Combat Talon II*; 5 MC-130P *Combat Shadow*; 1 C-130E *Hercules*; 8 MH-53J *Pave Low III*

European Command
US Army 371
US Navy 475
USAF 9,231
1 ftr wg located at Mildenhall (1 ftr sqn with 24 F-15C *Eagle*/F-15D *Eagle*, 2 ftr sqn with 24 F-15E *Strike Eagle*); 1 tkr wg located at Mildenhall, UK with 15 KC-135 *Stratotanker*

USMC 75

URUGUAY
Army 4
Navy 2
USAF 1
USMC 7

UZBEKISTAN
Army 1
USMC 7

VENEZUELA
Army 3
Navy 1
USAF 6
USMC 7

VIETNAM
Army 4
USAF 1
USMC 8

YEMEN
Army 5
USMC 7

ZAMBIA
Army 1
USMC 7

ZIMBABWE
Army 3
USMC 7

FOREIGN FORCES

Canada 8 USCENTCOM; 375 NORTHCOM (NORAD)

Germany Air Force: 23 *Tornado* IDS Strike/FGA ac located at Holloman AFB (NM); 35 T-37B *Tweet* located at Sheppard AFB (TX); 40 T-38A *Talon* located at Sheppard AFB (TX); Missile trg located at Fort Bliss (TX); School located at Fort Bliss (TX) (GAF Air Defence); some (primary) trg sqn located at Goodyear (AZ) with Beech F-33 *Bonanza;* some (joint jet pilot) trg sqn located at Sheppard AFB (TX); 812 (flying trg) located at Goodyear AFB (AZ); Sheppard AFB (TX); Holloman AFB (NM); FAS Pensacola (FL); Fort Rucker (AL); Army: 1 (battle) Army gp (trg) (army trg area) with 35 *Leopard* 2; 26 *Marder* 1; 12 M-109A3G

Italy Air Force: 38

Korea, Republic of 5 US CENTCOM

Mexico Navy: base located at Mayport (FL)

United Kingdom Army 120; Navy 120; Air Force 160

North America

Table 7 **US Air Capability 2008**

AIRCRAFT (fixed wing & rotary)	AIR FORCE				ARMY	MARITIME						Total
	Active Force	Air Force Reserve	Air National Guard	Total (Air Force)	US Army	Naval Aviation	Naval Aviation Reserve	Marine Corps Aviation	Marine Corps Aviation Reserve	Coast Guard		Total
LRSA	**170**	**9**	**0**	**179**	**0**	**0**	**0**	**0**	**0**	**0**		**179**
B-1B *Lancer*	65			65								65
B-2A *Spirit*	20			20								20
B-52 *Stratofortress*	85	9		94								94
TAC	**1778**	**139**	**707**	**2624**	**9**	**1365**	**127**	**386**	**37**	**23**		**4571**
A-10 *Thunderbolt* II	143	46	84	273								273
AC-130H/U *Spectre* (SOC)	21			21								21
AV-8B *Harrier* II				0				131				131
E-2C *Hawkeye* (AEW)				0		68	9					77
EA-6B *Prowler* (EW)				0		113	4	24				141
EC-130H *Compass Call*	14			14								14
EC-130J *Commando Solo* (spec. op.)			6	6								6
EP-3 *Orion* (EW)				0		13						13
F/A-18A *Hornet*				0		116	64	38	24			242
F/A-18B *Hornet*				0		28	3	4				35
F/A-18C *Hornet*				0		388		95				483
F/A-18D *Hornet*				0		137		94				231
F/A-18E *Super Hornet*				0		109						109
F/A-18F *Super Hornet*				0		161						161
F-117A *Nighthawk*	40			40								40
F-15A/B/C/D *Eagle*	396		126	522								522
F-15E Strike *Eagle*	217			217								217
F-16C/D *Fighting Falcon*	738	69	473	1280								1280
F-22A *Raptor*	91			91								91
F-5E *Tiger* II				0					1			1
F-5N *Tiger* II				0					12			12
HU-25A *Guardian*				0						7		7
HU-25B *Guardian*				0						1		1
HU-25C *Guardian*				0						9		9
HU-25D *Guardian*				0						6		6
MC-130H *Combat Talon* I/II (SOC)	24	14		38								38
MC-130P *Combat Shadow*	24	4		28								28
OA-10 *Thunderbolt* II	70	6	18	94								94
P-3C *Orion*				0		174	47					221
RC-7 *Dash 7* (EW)				0	9							9
S-3B *Viking* (ASW)				0		58						58
RECCE	**70**	**10**	**0**	**80**	**60**	**4**	**0**	**0**	**0**	**0**		**144**
Dash-7 ARL-C				0	3							3
Dash-7 ARL-I				0	3							3
Dash-7 ARL-M				0	3							3
E-8C *Joint Stars*	17			17								17
O-2 *Skymaster*				0	2							2
OC-135B *Open Skies*	3			3								3
RC-12D/H/K *Guardrail*				0	37							37
RC-12F *Huron*				0		2						2

Table 7 US Air Capability 2008

AIRCRAFT (fixed wing & rotary)	AIR FORCE				ARMY	MARITIME						Total
	Active Force	Air Force Reserve	Air National Guard	Total (Air Force)	US Army	Naval Aviation	Naval Aviation Reserve	Marine Corps Aviation	Marine Corps Aviation Reserve	Coast Guard	Total
RC-12M *Huron*				0		2					2
RC-12P/Q *Guardrail*				0	12						12
RC-135U *Combat Sent*	2			2							2
RC-135V/W *Rivet Joint*	14			14							14
U-2S	28			28							28
TU-2S	5			5							5
WC-130 *Hercules*		10		10							10
WC-135 *Constant Phoenix*	1			1							1
COMD / AEW	**37**	**0**	**0**	**37**	**0**	**16**	**0**	**0**	**0**	**0**	**53**
E-3B/C *Sentry* (AWACS)	33			33							33
E-4B	4			4							4
E-6B *Mercury*				0		16					16
TPT	**525**	**156**	**247**	**928**	**235**	**98**	**74**	**25**	**0**	**33**	**1393**
C-12C *Huron*				0	46	4					50
C-12D/F/J *Huron*				0	90						90
C-130 *Hercules*	186	106	222	514			20				534
C-130J *Hercules*				0						6	6
C-143A *Challenger*				0						1	1
C-17 *Globemaster* III	134	8	8	150							150
C-20A *Gulfstream* III				0		1					1
C-20B *Gulfstream* III	5			5	3						8
C-20D *Gulfstream* III				0		2					2
C-20G *Gulfstream* IV				0		4		1			5
C-20H *Gulfstream* III	2			2							2
C-21A *Learjet*	74		2	76							76
C-23A/B *Sherpa*				0	47						47
C-26 *Metro*				0	11						11
C-26D *Metro* III				0		7					7
C-2A *Greyhound*				0		37					37
C-31 *Friendship*				0	2						2
C-32A (Air Force Two)	4			4							4
C-37A	9			9	2	1				1	13
C-40A *Clipper*				0			9				9
C-40B/C	2		2	4							4
C-5A/B/C *Galaxy*	94	32		126							126
C-9B *Nightingale*				0			15	2			17
CN-235-200				0						2	2
Cessna 182 *Skylane*				0	2						2
CT-39G *Sabreliner*				0		1					1
DC-9				0			8				8
MC-130H *Hercules* (SAR)				0						23	23
HC-130P/N	13	10	13	36							36
LC-130F *Hercules*				0		2					2
LC-130R *Hercules*				0		1					1
U-21 *Ute*				0	1						1
U-6A *Beaver*				0		2					2

North America

Table 7 US Air Capability 2008

AIRCRAFT (fixed wing & rotary)	AIR FORCE				ARMY	MARITIME					Total
	Active Force	Air Force Reserve	Air National Guard	Total (Air Force)	US Army	Naval Aviation	Naval Aviation Reserve	Marine Corps Aviation	Marine Corps Aviation Reserve	Coast Guard	
UC-12B *Huron* (UTL)				0		26	6	11			43
UC-12F *Huron* (UTL)				0			6				6
UC-12M *Huron* (UTL)				0			10				10
UC-35 *Citation* (UTL)				0	26						26
UC-35D *Citation Encore*				0		1					1
UC-35C *Citation Ultra*				0				11			11
UP-3A *Orion*				0		4					4
UV-18A *Twin Otter*				0	4						4
UV-20A *Chiricahua* (UTL)				0	1						1
VC-25A (Air Force One)	2			2							2
VP-3A *Orion*				0		5					5
TKR	**254**	**84**	**251**	**589**	**0**	**5**	**0**	**38**	**24**	**0**	**656**
KC-10 A *Extender* (tkr/tpt)	59			59							59
KC-130F *Hercules*				0		5		6			11
KC-130J *Hercules*				0				25			25
KC-130R *Hercules*				0				7			7
KC-130T *Hercules*				0					24		24
KC-135 A/E/R/T *Stratotanker*	195	84	251	530							530
TRG	**1572**	**0**	**0**	**1572**	**3**	**689**	**0**	**20**	**0**	**0**	**2284**
T-1A *Jayhawk*	179			179							179
T-2C *Buckeye*				0		104					104
T-34C *Turbo Mentor*				0	3	308		3			314
T-37B *Tweet*	419			419							419
T-38A *Talon*	509			509		9					518
T-39D *Sabreliner*				0		1					1
T-39G *Sabreliner*				0		8					8
T-39N *Sabreliner*				0		15					15
T-43A	11			11							11
T-44A *Pegasus*				0		55					55
T-45A *Goshawk*				0		74					74
T-45C *Goshawk*				0		75					75
T-6A *Texan* II	454			454							454
TA-4J *Skyhawk*				0		17					17
TAV-8B *Harrier*				0				17			17
TC-12B *Huron*				0		21					21
TE-2C *Hawkeye*				0		2					2
TILT-ROTOR	**6**	**0**	**0**	**6**	**0**	**5**	**0**	**60**	**0**	**0**	**71**
CV-22 *Osprey* (being tested)	2			2							2
CV-22A *Osprey* (SOC)	4			4							4
MV-22A *Osprey*						5					5
MV-22B *Osprey*				0				56			56
V-22 *Osprey*				0				4			4
HELICOPTERS	**148**	**23**	**18**	**189**	**4086**	**588**	**43**	**603**	**94**	**145**	**5748**
AH-1W *Cobra*				0				140	36		176
AH-1Z *Super Cobra*				0		4					4
AH-6/MH-6 *Little Bird**				0	36						36

Table 7 US Air Capability 2008

AIRCRAFT (fixed wing & rotary)	AIR FORCE				ARMY	MARITIME						Total
	Active Force	Air Force Reserve	Air National Guard	Total (Air Force)	US Army	Naval Aviation	Naval Aviation Reserve	Marine Corps Aviation	Marine Corps Aviation Reserve	Coast Guard	Total
AH-64A/D Apache*				0	634							634
CH-46E Sea Knight				0				181	24			205
CH-47D Chinook				0	399							399
CH-53D Sea Stallion				0		9		34				43
CH-53E Sea Stallion				0		9		145	16			170
HH-1N Iroquois				0		23		11				34
HH-46D Sea Knight				0		4		3				7
HH-60G Pave Hawk	64	23	18	105								105
HH-60H Seahawk				0		38	16					54
HH-60J Jayhawk (SAR)				0						42		42
HH-60L Black Hawk (SAR)				0	7							7
HH-65C (AS-366G1) Dauphin II (SAR)				0						95		95
MH-47E Chinook				0	23							23
MH-53E Sea Dragon				0		28	8					36
MH-53J Pave Low III (SOC)	2			2								2
MH-53M Pave Low IV (SOC)	20			20								20
MH-60K/L Black Hawk				0	60							60
MH-60R Strike Hawk						8						8
MH-60S Knight Hawk				0	85							85
MH-68A (A-109E) Power (UTL)				0						8		8
N-SH-60B (TEST)				0		3						3
OH-58A Kiowa				0		3						3
OH-58A/C Kiowa*				0	463							463
OH-58D Kiowa Warrior				0	375							375
SH-60B Seahawk				0		148	5					153
SH-60F Seahawk				0		72	6					78
TH-57B Sea Ranger				0		44						44
TH-57C Sea Ranger				0		82						82
TH-67 Creek (TRG)				0	154							154
TH-6B				0		6						6
UH-1H/V Iroquois				0	447							447
UH-1N Huey (tpt)	62			62								62
UH-1N Iroquois				0		1		69	18			88
UH-1Y Iroquois				0		4		1				5
UH-3H Sea King				0		3	8					11
UH-46D Sea Knight				0		9						9
UH-60A/A/M Black Hawk				0	1484	3						1487
UH-60Q Black Hawk				0	4							4
VH-3A Sea King				0		2						2
VH-3D Sea King (VIP tpt)				0				11				11
VH-60N Presidential Hawk (VIP tpt)				0				8				8
UAV	107	0	0	107	516	42	0	1072	0	0	1737
3D Max Dragon Eye (mini-UAV)				0				972				972
BQM-147 Exdrone				0	100			100				200

Table 7 US Air Capability 2008

AIRCRAFT (fixed wing & rotary)	AIR FORCE				ARMY	MARITIME						Total
	Active Force	Air Force Reserve	Air National Guard	Total (Air Force)	US Army	Naval Aviation	Naval Aviation Reserve	Marine Corps Aviation	Marine Corps Aviation Reserve	Coast Guard		Total
Buster				0	20							20
Desert Hawk				0	126							126
I-Gnat				0	4							4
MQ-1 Predator	88			88								88
MQ-8B Fire Scout (trials)				0		5						5
MQ-9 Reaper	8			8								8
RQ-2B Pioneer				0		35		(some)				35
RQ-4A Global Hawk	11			11		2						13
RQ-5A Hunter				0	54							54
RQ-7A Shadow				0	212							212
TRIALS/TEST	7	0	0	7	0	47	0	0	0	0		54
B-52 Stratofortress	4			4								4
B-1B Lancer	2			2								2
B-2 Spirit	1			1								1
EA-18G				0		1						1
NF/A-18A Hornet				0		1						1
NF/A-18C Hornet				0		2						2
NF/A-18D Hornet				0		3						3
NP-3C Orion				0		1						1
NP-3D Orion				0		11						11
NT-34C Mentor				0		1						1
NU-1B Otter				0		1						1
QF-4N Phantom II				0		2						2
QF-4S Phantom II				0		16						16
X-26A				0		2						2
X-31A				0		1						1
YF-4J Phantom II (prototype, FGA)				0		1						1
YSH-60				0		2						2
YSH-60B Seahawk (prototype)				0		1						1
YSH-60F Seahawk (prototype)				0		1						1
			TOTAL AIRCRAFT (Air Force):	6,318							TOTAL AIRCRAFT (all services):	15,351
			TOTAL Combat Capable (Air Force):	2,658							TOTAL Combat Capable (all services):	4,947

Table 8 **Selected Arms Orders and Deliveries, Canada**

Country Supplier	Classification	Designation	Quantity	Order date	Original Delivery date	Comment
Canada (Ca) US	Tpt	C-17 *Globemaster* III	4	2007	2007	USD660m-670m. 1st ac delivered Aug 2007
US	FGA	CF-18 *Hornet*	36	2007	2007	Upgrade. Supply of 'Sniper' Advanced Targeting Pod (ATP). Deliveries to begin in April 2007. Contract includes spares and integrated logistics support until 2020
US	Hel	CH-148	28	2007	–	Upgrade. USD59.4m to provide Canadian Warning Receiver (RWR)/ Electronic Support Measure (ESM) systems in support of the Canadian Maritime Helicopter Project (MHP)
US	Tpt	C-130J	17	2007	2010	CDN4.9bn (USD4.29bn). To replace C-130 *Hercules* fleet
US	APC	*Buffalo / Cougar*	10	2007	2008	USD8.8m. 5 *Buffalo* mine-clearance vehicles and 5 *Cougar* mine-resistant medium patrol vehicles
dom	FFG	*Halifax*-class	12	2007	–	Halifax-class Modernisation/Frigate Life Extension (HCM/FELEX) project. CAD3.1bn (USD2.9bn). 1st FFG to enter refit in 2010. All to be completed by 2017
US	LAV	LAV-III	33	2007	–	Weapon system upgrade. CAD49m (USD46m)
US	AAM	Evolved *SeaSparrow* Missile (ESSM)	–	2007	–	Part of a USD223m contract issued by the NATO *SeaSparrow* Consortium covering the collective purchase of 294 ESSM
Nl	MBT	*Leopard* 2	100	2007	–	Former Dutch MBT.

Table 9 **Selected arms orders and deliveries, US**

Classification	Designation	FY 2006 Units	FY 2006 Value ($m)	Estimate FY2007 Units	Estimate FY2007 Value ($m)	Request FY2008 [a] Units	Request FY2008 [a] Value ($m)
JOINT							
Trg	JPATS	54	328	48	304	39	245
UAV	Global Hawk	5	359	5	448	5	577
UAV	Medium Size	30	325	26	302	40	550
UAV	Small size	364	324	60	46	300	60
AAM	AMRAAM	132	176	215	203	285	312
ASM	JASSM	75	157	163	207	210	213
ASM	JSOW	420	144	390	124	421	131
PGM	JDAM	11,605	306	10,661	259	4,962	146
SAM	Patriot PAC-3	112	549	112	572	108	550
AIR FORCE							
Tpt	C-17	15	3,697	22	4,597		471
Tpt	C-130J	11	1,144	9	966	9	1,070
Tpt	C-5		111		227		398
Bbr	B-2		61		192		316
FGA	F-16 Upgrades		418		366		329
FGA	F-22	23	3,688	20	3,531	20	3,861
FGA	F-35 JSF		117	2	571	6	1,421
Tilt-rotar	V-22	2	229	2	242	5	495
Sat	NAVSTAR GPS	3	349		96		221
Launcher	EELV	1	603	3	852	5	1,166
Sat	AEHF	1	521				
Sat	Wideband GS		71	1	412	1	325
ARMY							
Hel	AH-64D		1,035		1,414		711
Hel	CH-47	26	646	38	1,130	29	770
Hel	UH-60	49	672	59	1,080	42	705
Hel	Light Utility Helicopter	16	88	26	166	44	230
hel	Armed Recon Helicopter			12	101	37	468
MRL	HIMARS	1,155	190	1,006	237	1,666	250
MBT	M1 Abrams Upgrade	60	893	180	1,632	9	641
AFV	Stryker	494	1,318	100	902	127	1,039
Veh	FHTV	486	369	1,600	1,011	980	483
Veh	FMTV	3,276	674	5,788	1,484	2,862	828
Veh	HMMWV	7,096	1,281	9,253	1,659	3,268	596
Comms	Joint Network Node		678		226		312
Comms	SINCGARS Radio		784		188		137
NAVY and MARINES							
Hel	MH-60S	26	534	18	546	18	503
Hel	MH-60R	12	557	25	913	27	997
Tilt-rotar	V-22	12	1256	14	1,553	21	1,959
Hel	H-1 Upgrade	7	314	11	443	20	518
Recce	E-2C Hawkeye	2	272	2	211		68
FGA	F/A-18 E/F	38	3,211	34	2,974	24	2,545
FGA	F-35 JSF				124	6	1,232
AEA	F/A- 18G Growler	4	351	8	645	18	1,318
Trg	T-45	6	278	12	410		90

Table 9 Selected arms orders and deliveries, US

Classification	Designation	FY 2006 Units	FY 2006 Value ($m)	Estimate FY2007 Units	Estimate FY2007 Value ($m)	Request FY2008 [a] Units	Request FY2008 [a] Value ($m)
tpt	C-130J	7	557	3	243	4	256
SAM	Standard	75	143	75	139	75	159
TCM	Tactical Tomahawk	408	373	355	353	394	383
SLBM	Trident II		905		915	12	1,087
CVN	Carrier Replacement		762		1,107	1	2,848
DDG	DDG 1000		706	2	2,557		2,953
FFG	Littoral Combat Ship	2	470	2	597	3	990
SSN	Virginia	1	2,549	1	2,552	1	2,498
LPD	LPD-17	1	1,514		379	1	1,398
LHA	Amphibious Ship		148	1	1,131		1,377
RCOH	CVN Refueling	1	1,320		1,067		297
auxiliary dry cargo ship	T-AKE	1	386	1	453	1	456

[a] Data refers to budget request rather than final appropriations

Chapter Two

Caribbean and Latin America

FORCE TRANSFORMATION AND MILITARY COOPERATION

The varied security challenges in the Caribbean and Latin America region pose particular problems for militaries operating in an environment of competing demands for limited budgets. While terrorism, drug trafficking, people trafficking, organised crime, money laundering and corruption were identified as major threats to regional security by the Managua Declaration (that emerged from the Seventh Conference of Ministers of Defense of the Americas in October 2006 – see *The Military Balance 2007*, p. 51), military forces are also at times employed on public security tasks as well as humanitarian relief operations while the requirement for national, bilateral and multilateral exercises remains. (The Managua conference also expressed concern over the proliferation of small arms and light weapons, including man-portable air defence systems, and registered a commitment to confidence building and participation in UN peacekeeping operations.)

It is with these above concerns in mind, as well as the broader internal and national security agendas of each nation, that one can view the ongoing examination by some regional governments of the future roles, structures and equipment needs of their military forces. While the ability to conduct conventional operations to counter traditional threats still concerns regional militaries, as does the need to be able to conduct operations such as for disaster relief, several countries have also embarked on modernisation or reorganisation processes designed to better align their armed forces with non-traditional threats. Implementation strategies vary: some nations see a need for structural reform, some for acquisition programmes or mid-life updates; others see benefit in combining these strategies.

Country developments

After assuming the presidency in the wake of a closely fought contest with Andres Manuel López Obrador, **Mexico's** President Felipe Calderón launched, among other policy initiatives, a campaign against organised crime. With drug-related crime reportedly claiming the lives of over 2,000 in 2006, in early December of that year Calderón dispatched over 10,000 army and federal police troops to affected regions.

Mexico's armed forces are employed on missions that include public security tasks, including anti-narcotic operations, and the possible development of intermediate forces within the army is currently the subject of debate. A presidential decree, still to be approved by Congress, talks of establishing a 10,000-strong Cuerpo de Fuerzas Federales de Apoyo (Federal Support Forces) to provide support to civil authorities. The increase in anti-narcotic operations has led to discussion on moves to enhance cooperation between Mexico and the US on common security issues. Illegal immigration and drug smuggling are major concerns for Washington, while arms smuggling from the US to Mexico is of concern to Mexico City. On 22 October, US President George W. Bush asked Congress for an initial US$500 million (out of a total US$1.4 billion) to fund a security cooperation programme with Mexico; the president also requested US$50m relating to the countries of Central America. This programme is envisaged as a multi-year package primarily designed to combat narcotics trafficking and organised crime. Though it was termed 'Plan Mexico' on one occasion by US Secretary of Defense Robert Gates, other officials have been keen to avoid using the term, and it is now referred to as the 'Merida Initiative'. The deployment of US troops or military advisers has been ruled out – although US aid to the Mexican armed forces in the areas of training, intelligence and air mobility is considered to be at the planning stage.

The Mexican navy continues to build indigenous offshore patrol vessels (OPVs) and coastal patrol craft in an effort to increase its patrol capabilities, while the army and air force are preparing for a modernisation process. On 12 October, Mexico's Congress approved funding for three EADS-CASA C-295M aircraft, two UH-60L *Black Hawk* helicopters, tactical radios and 1,000 HMMWVs for 2008. New specialised units, including maritime patrol, search-and-rescue and drug-interdiction units, are also due to be established. The air force recently put its SIVA (Integrated Air Surveillance System) into operation, considerably enhancing Mexico's surveillance capabilities. Developed by a number of companies, including Embraer of Brazil and Raytheon, SIVA is intended to provide air-defence surveillance, tracking and control for the southeast of the country. Meanwhile, in late 2007, Mexico's armed forces were employed in humanitarian operations in the south, particularly the states of Tabasco and Chiapas, after severe flooding.

In late 2006, **Argentina's** army published its Plan Ejército Argentino 2025 (Argentine Army Plan 2025, or PEA 2025), a product of several years' study into how Argentina's forces might be re-equipped and reorganised. The plan envisages the army's 1960s-era corps-level structure transforming to a number of regional divisional commands – northeast, west and south – to address contingencies including possible conflict over resources. Though as yet there have been no structural changes, in late 2006 2 corps was transferred from Santa Fe to a new HQ in Curuzu Cuatia, in a move designed to consolidate forces. Programmes also mentioned in the PEA 2025 documentation include the production of the *Patagon* tank (a hybrid AMX-13/SK-105A2) which is destined to replace the retired AMX-13s; an upgrade of the ageing fleet of M113 armoured personnel carriers (APCs); production of the joint Argentine-Brazilian *Gaucho* 4x4 air-portable light vehicle and upgrade of the UH-1H helicopter fleet to *Huey* II.

In its 'Modernisation of the Defence Sector' document, the Argentine defence ministry stated that in 2007 'a phased action plan was launched to recover in a 5-year period 100% of the aviation capabilities of all three services, in the following priority order: 1) transport aircraft, 2) liaison and training aircraft and helicopters, and 3) fighter-bombers' (see p. 61). Although a number of upgrades have been carried out by local industry, for instance by Lockheed Martin Argentina (formerly Fábrica Militar de Aviones, FMA), Argentina's air force still relies on the *Mirage*/A-4 *Skyhawk* mix that has served it for over 35 years. Replacements in the form of *Mirage* 2000s and F-16s have not yet become available, and the latest addition to the air fleet is the AT-63, a modernised, light-attack derivative of the indigenous IA-63 *Pampa* aircraft, production of which has stalled at a dozen or so units.

Chile's armed forces benefit from a law under which 10% of the value of national copper exports is set aside for defence procurement (see p. 61), and they continue to enjoy a period of recapitalisation. F-16 deliveries have now led to the formation of squadrons and replacement of older *Mirage* aircraft. Meanwhile, the capability of the air force is to be further enhanced with the acquisition of new multi-role A310 tankers, adding to the current converted Boeing 707. The army plans to have an all-professional force, with this desire articulated in the 'Planta de Tropa Profesional' professionalisation plan, which was signed by President Michelle Bachelet and Defence Minister José Goñi and sent to Congress for approval on 22 October. The force has also selected the *Leopard* II as its next-generation main battle tank (MBT). Meanwhile, Chile's navy, which in recent years taken delivery of substantial equipment additions, including second-hand frigates from the UK and the Netherlands, hosted the biennial multinational exercise *Teamwork South 2007*. The two-phase exercise involved assets from Argentina, France, the UK and US as well as 11 vessels from Chile, and concluded in early June.

With a large portion of its forces deployed on UN international peacekeeping missions, **Uruguay's** armed forces are gaining from global experience. Uruguayan troops are currently deployed to the Democratic Republic of the Congo and Haiti, with minor detachments in Egypt, Ethiopia–Eritrea and Western Sahara, among other locations. Procurement funding has recently shifted from the army, which has seen new armour and artillery holdings in recent years, including *Vodnik* and OT-64 APCs and RM-70 multiple rocket launchers, to the navy, which is taking receipt of two *João Belo*-class frigates from Portugal, as well as a number of Bö-105 helicopters.

In July, **Brazil's** President Luiz Inácio 'Lula' da Silva appointed Nelson Jobim, formerly president of the Supreme Court, as defence minister in place of Waldir Pires. The change was made in the wake of the crash of a civilian airliner at São Paulo's Congonhas airport (civilian air traffic control is mainly operated by the military in Brazil), but a number of other aviation incidents had also preceded the changeover. Following Jobim's appointment, it was reported that a process had been initiated that could lead to the production of a new defence doctrine. It is thought that this could increase cooperative activity across the services. There are also plans to increase the military service intake in 2008 to around 100,000.

The army has embarked on a major procurement drive, aiming to acquire some 240 *Leopard* 1A5 MBTs, which are believed to be intended to replace the M-60 and M-41 fleets, and selecting *Urutu* IIIs to replace its EE-9 and EE-11 family of infantry fighting vehicles and APCs. Meanwhile, the navy has a refit, upgrade and acquisition programme aimed at modernising many of its principal surface vessels and its submarine force. It also plans to procure a Type 214 submarine for 2010, and plans for an indigenous nuclear submarine – first proposed some years ago – appear closer to being realised, as the debate over funding looks as if it may be resolved in favour of development. Delayed plans to replace the *Mirage* III and F-5 fleet have seen the arrival of second-hand *Mirage* 2000s and upgrades to the F-5 and AMX fleets, although late in 2007 it was reported that a new procurement programme may lead to the replacement of the F-5/*Mirage* mix (see p. 62). Meanwhile, there have been continued deliveries of the EMB-314 *Super Tucano* light-attack platform, the acquisition of C-295M medium transports as well as the selection of the P-3 *Orion* as Brazil's next-generation maritime patrol aircraft. However, it remains to be seen how several of the proposed projects will be funded, given the proportion of the defence budget assigned to investment (see p. 62).

Peru's armed forces are addressing their operational and maintenance capability requirements through the Núcleo Básico Eficaz (Core Basic Capability) project. The project is centred on a US$650m programme to upgrade aviation assets including *Mirage* 2000s, MiG-29s and Su-25s, as well as the fleet of T-55, AMX-13, M113 and Fiat 6616 armoured vehicles. (For details of the funding that will enable this recapitalisation, see p. 61.) Work has also begun on the development of the Amazon Integrated Air Surveillance System of Peru (Sistema Integral de Vigilancia Amazonica del Peru). The system reportedly has a similar objective to that of Brazil's SIVAM, and is intended to cover Peru's eastern and Amazon regions.

For a number of years, **Colombia's** armed forces have been active in combating guerrillas from the Fuerzas Armadas Revolucionarias de Colombia (FARC) and other groups (see past editions of *The Military Balance* and the IISS *Armed Conflict Database*). In late February 2007, President Alvaro Uribe announced a four-year military upgrade and expansion programme, with total defence spending over the period set to reach around US$28bn. Overall manpower will be increased by over 30,000, with the National Police believed to be the greatest beneficiary with around 20,000 extra personnel. In equipment terms, the only major procurements in recent years have been locally assembled BTR-80 APCs and

Spanish-built 155mm howitzers; most investment has gone into the continued expansion of counter-insurgency and anti-narcotic capabilities. Major air force acquisition programmes have been limited to CAS-oriented UH-60 *Black Hawk* helicopters and EMB-314 *Super Tucano* aircraft.

The role of **Ecuador's** armed forces has been redefined to incorporate the defence of the country's natural resources. However, efforts to transform the armed forces have been affected by the death of Defence Minister Guadalupe Larriva in a January 2007 helicopter crash and resignation of her successor, Lorena Escudero, in August. As noted in the *IISS Strategic Survey* 2007, Ecuador has been building up air and ground forces on its borders, and has been critical of border crossings by Colombian troops claiming to be in 'hot pursuit' of FARC guerrillas. This security issue has increased diplomatic tensions between Ecuador and Colombia, particularly following the December 2006 resumption of aerial eradication along the border. In April 2007, President Rafael Correa launched 'Plan Ecuador' as a 'response of peace, justice, and development' to insecurity in the border region. At an estimated cost of US$135m, the initiative is designed to promote border security by enabling social and economic development in Ecuador's northern border region. According to an August 2007 estimate by the Office of the UN High Commissioner for Refugees, 250,000 Colombians have moved to Ecuador as a result of armed conflict, 'making Ecuador the Latin American country with the highest number of people in need of international protection'.

Meanwhile, there have been reports that Ecuador has been considering the future of the US presence at the Manta airbase on the country's west coast, which is used to support counter-narcotic operations. If agreement is not reached on an extension of the arrangement that has seen the base host US personnel since 1999, the forward operating location could close in 2009.

In August 2007, **Venezuela's** President Hugo Chávez put forward proposals for constitutional reform, which included removal of the limit on presidential terms. The 'new geometry of power' to which the proposals referred would allow the creation of 'special military regions' within the country to be formed in case of a national emergency. Another proposal was for the amendment of Article 328 of the constitution. This article states that the 'national armed forces constitute an essentially professional institution, with no political orientation'. Under the president's proposal, the forces' name would change from 'National' to 'Bolivarian' Armed Forces, and they would be designated an 'essentially patriotic' grouping which, Chávez continued, would be 'popular and anti-imperialist'. Chávez's proposals also included giving the National Guard 'different functions, while the national reserve [would] form the National Bolivarian Militia'. However, on 2 December, the proposals were defeated by a slim majority in a national referendum. Meanwhile, Venezuela is continuing its arms acquisition process. The new Mi-17 and Mi-26 helicopter fleet gives the country an airlift capability that has proved its value in humanitarian relief operations, while the Su-30MKV has served to enhance Venezuelan air capability. Current programmes include the possible acquisition of a new MBT; some 600 infantry fighting vehicles; an air defence network, including *Tor*-M1 batteries; and a number of submarines, including *Kilo*-class boats.

His party's success in the April 2006 parliamentary elections in **Haiti** enabled President René Préval (elected in February 2006) to form his second government. However, the Brazilian-led UN Stabilisation Mission in Haiti (MINUSTAH) is far from being in a position where it is able to withdraw. In February 2007, MINUSTAH launched an offensive against pro-Aristide gangs operating in the Cité Soleil area of Port-au-Prince. The offensive led to the arrest of over 400 gang members, but as noted in the *IISS Strategic Survey* 2007, the poverty and political instability that breed criminality have yet to be addressed. In October 2007, the UN renewed MINUSTAH's mandate for one more year. Meanwhile, the defence force of **Trinidad and Tobago** is pursuing a programme that includes a US$300m order for three 1,500-ton OPVs, to be built by VT Group in the UK. After the contract was signed in April 2007, VT stated that 'design work was to start immediately' and that the 90-metre-long vessels were to be operated by the Trinidad and Tobago Coast Guard, and handed over in 2009.

Caribbean and Latin America

CARIBBEAN AND LATIN AMERICA – DEFENCE ECONOMICS

Economic developments in Latin America continue to be driven by the buoyancy of commodity markets and the ongoing strength of the US economy. In 2004–06, the region as a whole experienced its strongest three-year period of growth since the late 1970s, although growth still lagged behind that of other regions with emerging markets and developing countries. Across the region, growth is forecast to fall modestly to 4.9% in 2007 from 5.5% in 2006, although Chile, Brazil and Argentina are likely to be exceptions. In its 2007 review of the region, the IMF pointed out that recent macroeconomic improvements in Latin America – lower inflation, strengthening fiscal positions and reductions in debt – should make the region more resilient to adverse developments than it was in the past. Defence spending across the region, when measured in US\$, has risen from US\$24.7 bn in 2003 to US\$38.4bn in 2007. This is a result both of a weaker dollar and increased spending on the part of certain countries that have hitherto lacked the financial resources to modernise their armed forces and are facing increasingly obsolete weapons inventories. Not surprisingly, weapons-exporting countries – Russia in particular – have indicated that with buoyant economies and ageing weapons systems, Latin American markets offer good opportunities for the sale of new military equipment.

With its economy continuing to benefit from high oil prices, **Venezuela** once again increased its defence budget. In 2005, the original budget had been set at Bs3.35 trillion, but this rose to Bs5.12tr over the course of the year, likewise in 2006 the original budget of Bs4.47tr was exceeded, with the revised year-end figure reaching Bs5.55tr. The original 2007 budget was set at Bs5.51tr (US\$ 2.56bn), but again this is almost certain to be adjusted upwards by the end of the fiscal year. In addition to the official defence budget, the Venezuelan military has for many years also been the recipient of additional funding under a government financing arrangement known as the Ley Paraguas, or 'Umbrella Law'. This allows the government to borrow overseas in order to finance the acquisition of equipment not covered by the official national defence budget. However, the finance ministry has indicated that this arrangement will be phased out and that future military procurements should be wholly financed by the regular budget and allocations from the National Development Fund (see *The Military Balance 2007*, p. 54). Implementation of this change seems to be underway. In 2005 the Ley Paraguas amounted to US\$640 million; this fell to US\$279m in 2006 and is forecast to reach just US\$100m in 2007.

The growing relationship between Venezuela and Russia was further consolidated during a visit to Moscow by Hugo Chávez in June 2007, after which the Venezuelan president stressed that bilateral cooperation between the two countries should not be restricted to military and technical matters, but embrace wider business and political affairs. In recent years Venezuela has ordered a significant amount of military hardware from Russia, including 100,000 Kalashnikov rifles, over 50 Mi-17V transport and Mi-35M fire support helicopters, and 24 Sukhoi Su-30MKV multi-role fighters, together with an extensive

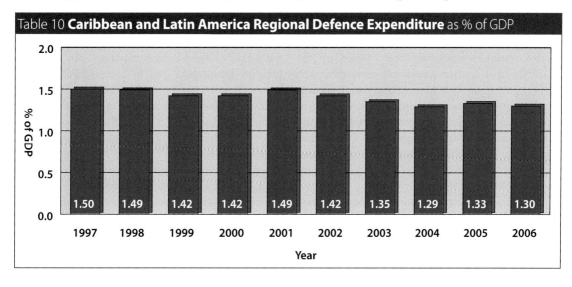

Table 10 **Caribbean and Latin America Regional Defence Expenditure** as % of GDP

Year	1997	1998	1999	2000	2001	2002	2003	2004	2005	2006
% of GDP	1.50	1.49	1.42	1.42	1.49	1.42	1.35	1.29	1.33	1.30

armaments package comprising beyond-visual-range air-to-air missiles, precision-guided air-to-surface weapons, spare parts and crew training programmes. During 2007, two new major deals were signed with Russia whereby Venezuela will purchase five *Kilo*-class diesel-electric submarines, together with torpedoes and possibly long-range *Club*-S anti-ship and land-attack missiles.

Meanwhile, the navy's existing Type 209 submarines are to be refitted. Venezuela's defence minister also announced that the country will take delivery of a number of *Tor* M-1 surface-to-air missile systems that will be used in combination with Chinese-manufactured radars and the air force's new Su-30 aircraft. It also appears probable that these acquisitions will be followed by the purchase of around 600 armoured vehicles to equip the army's cavalry units operating in the border area of Apure state, as well as new units to be deployed in the east.

The sensitivity of conducting weapons business with Venezuela has been well illustrated in recent years. Brazil, France and Spain have all had to cancel proposed deals with Venezuela after pressure from the US. Brazil's aerospace company, Embraer, had intended to sell a number of AMX-T trainer jets and *Super Tucano* light-attack turboprop aircraft to the Venezuelan air force. However, because the aircraft contain US-manufactured parts, the sale required endorsement from the US State Department; this was not forthcoming. Likewise, Spain had to cancel plans to sell 10 C-296 transport aircraft and two CN-235 maritime patrol aircraft for the same reason, whilst the French government vetoed the potential sale of three *Scorpene* submarines in response to US concerns that the acquisition would create a significant imbalance among the navies of the region.

The failure of the armed forces to acquire much-needed transport capabilities has opened up the possibility that another significant arms deal with Russia could occur. It is thought that the air force is studying several plans to acquire a variety of different aircraft. Top of the list is the procurement of at least 10 Il-76 aircraft in both tanker and AWACS configurations, while Venezuela has reportedly also expressed an interest in acquiring 30 An-74 and 10 An-140 transport aircraft from Ukraine.

With its neighbours continuing to modernise their armed forces, **Colombia** increased its defence budget by 11% in 2007, following a 10% rise the previous year. This maintained its position as the country spending the highest proportion of its national

income on defence in the Latin American region. However, as is the case elsewhere in Latin America, the military in Colombia is known to benefit from additional funding derived from departmental or municipal governments, as well as from revenues from the armed forces' own security-related business activities. On top of this, the military and national police in Colombia have also benefited from the 'wealth tax' that raised over US$800m between 2004 and 2006, as well as from annual aid from the US in the form of 'foreign military financing' and financial assistance for counter-narcotics initiatives. In 2007, the Colombian government announced that a new 'wealth tax' would be introduced. The expectation is that it will generate up to US$3.6bn between 2007 and 2010. In addition, for the financial year 2008, President Bush has requested US$79.5m for military training and equipment purchases and US$366m under the Andean Counterdrug Initiative.

In recent years, the Ministry of Defence has become increasingly concerned by the advanced age of much of its conventional force structure – for instance, its frigates are over 20 years old and some of the artillery systems are approaching 50 years. To address this, the government has proposed a 'major overhaul' of its armed forces, outlining a plan to spend around US$28bn, including funds from the new wealth tax, on upgrading and enhancing Colombia's military capabilities. It is thought that this four-year plan will increase the number of police and soldiers by around 36,000, while the navy's four submarines will receive new engines and the air force's *Mirage* and *Kfir* fighter aircraft will receive major upgrades. It is also expected that new combat aircraft and helicopters will be acquired, as well as surveillance aircraft, patrol boats and armoured vehicles.

Chile once again benefited from its position as the world's largest copper exporter with economic growth approaching 6% in 2007, whilst buoyant revenues and government expenditure moderated in line with the structural fiscal surplus rule led to a budget surplus of over 7% of GDP. Following several years of restrained growth in defence spending the budget was boosted by 23% in 2007. However, as noted in previous editions of *The Military Balance*, total spending on national defence-related activities in Chile includes several other elements in addition to the official budget of the Ministry of Defence. These include the proportion of the social security budget that funds military pensions, revenue generated by the military's own business interests and money derived from Chile's copper exports via the Copper Law, under which 10% of the value of copper exports is directed to the armed forces. In general, the official Ministry of Defence budget is used to finance recurring operational expenses, whilst cash from CODELCO (the state mining company) via the Copper Law is primarily allocated to the purchase of foreign military equipment. Taking these additional sources of funding into account, the total national defence-related expenditure in 2007 could be as high as US$5bn, depending on the extent of the funds allocated from the Copper Law. For many years, this law furnished the armed forces with an average of around US$200m a year for the purchase of military equipment. However, since the dramatic increase in copper prices – mainly a result of huge demand from China – this has increased to more than US$1bn. As the funds allocated to the military have increased, so has concern over this arcane funding arrangement, and the government has indicated that it may abolish or modify the law in favour of increasing disbursements from the regular budget. Although no official announcement to this effect has been made, it may help to explain the relatively large 23% increase in the budget between 2006 and 2007.

As a result of the copper-related windfalls of recent years, the military has been active in progressing various procurement programmes. Having taken delivery of F-16 aircraft, *Scorpene* submarines and second-hand frigates from the UK and Netherlands, attention has switched to helicopters and surveillance assets. Although there had been an ambitious plan to procure a single standard rotary-wing aircraft for the army, navy and Carabineros (national police), it seems that there will instead be a series of independent acquisitions. The army is looking to replace its ageing *Puma* battlefield transporters, and has selected a number of second-hand German Eurocopter *Super Puma* EC 225/AS 332s in the first instance. It is also thought to be investigating the possibility of acquiring a number of specialised attack craft for anti-armour and close-support roles. The navy would like to replace its remaining fleet of five ship-borne *Exocet*-armed AS-532 *Cougar* helicopters and their ageing training and utility platforms with ten new units equipped with maritime attack mission systems, whilst the air force has chosen the Bell 412 as its new utility aircraft.

In terms of surveillance capabilities, the navy is currently looking at new platforms to replace its P-3A *Orion* maritime patrol aircraft, whilst the air force is thought to be examining options for replacing the

single – expensive and of limited capability – *Phalcon* airborne early warning (AEW) aircraft that it acquired from Israel over a decade ago. Swedish company Ericsson has made presentations of its advanced *Erieye* AEW radar.

In early 2007, the president of **Peru** confirmed that he was concerned about the state of the country's armed forces and was making a total of US$1.3bn available for military modernisation. This funding will be generated from a combination of a special 'defence fund' set up a few years ago to divert funds from Peru's hydrocarbon revenue to the army, spending austerities elsewhere, and the sale of surplus military property. For the current presidential term, which runs from 2007–11, the military will receive $445m from the defence fund. As hydrocarbon revenues rise with the introduction of new production facilities, funding between 2012 and 2017 will increase to $845m. While all the services are in need of modernisation, the air force is of particular concern, with a maximum of 30% of its aircraft in serviceable condition. Top priority will be the overhaul of 12 *Mirage* 2000 fighters and a number of MiG-29s, armed helicopters and An-32 transports. Other improvements are believed to include overhauling the missile inventory, purchasing air control radars, an air defence weapons system and command and control aircraft.

Mindful of developments elsewhere on the continent, together with the slow deterioration of its armed forces resulting from a lack of funding after the financial crisis, **Argentina** has indicated that, economic conditions permitting, it is poised to embark on a force modernisation programme. Only a fraction of the military's transport fleet – some UH-1 helicopters and C-130 aircraft – is thought to be operational. In the past year, both the defence minister and the foreign minister have made a number of visits abroad in which military and defence cooperation have been high on the agenda. As well as France, with whom it has an historic relationship, Argentina is also thought to be considering the purchase of military equipment from Russia, not least because there is the possibility that any deals between the two countries could be settled through barter arrangements, for instance the exchange of Argentine foodstuffs for Russian equipment. Further evidence that Russia is successfully manoeuvring to become a prime supplier came when the Argentine government fast-tracked a technical–military accord between the two countries that would pave the way for military trade to take place.

The air force's most urgent requirement is for the modernisation of its rotary-wing fleet and its priority is likely to be the acquisition of a number of Mi-17 medium transport helicopters, whilst the army is in need of new APCs. Ukraine has also expressed interest in Argentina, and has held talks with it about the possibility of providing An-70/72 tactical transports to replace the current fleet of C-130 aircraft.

As Argentina's traditional supplier of advanced military equipment, France is expected to benefit from the forthcoming upgrade programme. One likely transaction will involve the replacement of a fleet of Argentine *Mirage* interceptor fighters that are due to retire in 2009. The air force has already requested a first batch of 14 second-hand *Mirage* 2000C/Ds offered by France. Other acquisitions from France may include air-to-air and anti-ship missiles, including the *Mica* and *Exocet* MM40, as well as *Mica* vertical launch short-range air-defence missiles to modernise the navy's surface fleet. The procurement of underwater-launched AM-39 *Exocet* anti-ship missiles with added land-attack capabilities is also being considered as part of a study to upgrade the navy's German-built submarines.

With one eye on developments in Venezuela, **Brazil** appears to be following other Latin American countries with plans to upgrade and modernise parts of its ageing military inventory. However, despite an increase in the defence budget of around 15% in real terms since 2004, in 2007 only 4% of the budget (US$800m) is available for investment, with 80% allocated to personnel and pensions expenditure. As a result, it is difficult to imagine how the reported plan to invest nearly US$8bn in a re-equipment programme will be fulfilled without a significant injection of new resources. The challenges created by the unbalanced budget structure were illustrated in late 2006 when the government was forced to postpone indefinitely the already long-delayed indigenous nuclear submarine construction programme in favour of directing scarce resources to the modernisation of the navy's existing four Type 209 vessels and the construction of a single new Type 214.

The air force appears to have performed yet another U-turn with regard to its long-running fighter replacement programme. Originally known as the F-X project, the plan to acquire 12 next-generation fighter aircraft was cancelled in 2005 due to lack of funds, and instead a dozen second-hand *Mirage* 2000s were purchased, along with a number of second-hand F-5s from Saudi Arabia. However, the Ministry of Defence has been outlining a new procurement programme, under which 24–36 new aircraft will be purchased to equip two squadrons in central and northern Brazil. It is reported that the selection of a platform, most likely the Dassault *Rafale* or Sukhoi Su-35, will be made without a formal bidding process, which would suggest that the issue is being viewed with some urgency. More definite are a $400m contract with Rosoboronexport for Mi-35 assault and Mi-171 multi-role medium helicopters and a $100m contract for the purchase of four Mi-26 heavy-lift helicopters.

The navy has also outlined an ambitious revitalisation plan which calls for the purchase of at least 33 ships by 2025. The procurement of such a large number of vessels was prompted by the retirement of 21 vessels between 1998 and 2006, together with the increase in patrol area due to the expansion of the nation's continental shelf boundaries. The plan includes the acquisition of a further five submarines, doubling the patrol fleet to 30 vessels, and increasing the escort fleet by four and the amphibious fleet to six.

Antigua and Barbuda AB

East Caribbean Dollar EC$		2006	2007	2008
GDP	EC$	2.5bn	2.7bn	
	US$	1.0bn	1.0bn	
per capita	US$	13,934	14,392	
Growth	%	12.2	3.8	
Inflation	%	1.8	3.2	
Def bdgt	EC$	ε13m	ε14m	
	US$	ε4.8m	ε5.2m	
US$1=EC$		2.7	2.7	

Population   69,481

Age	0–14	15–19	20–24	25–29	30–64	65 plus
Male	14%	4%	4%	4%	23%	2%
Female	14%	4%	4%	4%	23%	3%

Capabilities

ACTIVE 170 (Army 125 Navy 45)
(all services form combined Antigua and Barbuda Defence Force)
RESERVE 75 (Joint 75)

ORGANISATIONS BY SERVICE

Army 125

Navy 45
EQUIPMENT BY TYPE
PATROL AND COASTAL COMBATANTS • PCI 3:
1 *Dauntless*; 1 Point; 1 *Swift*; (All vessels less than 100 tonnes)
FACILITIES
Base 1 located at St Johns

FOREIGN FORCES

United States USAF 2; US STRATCOM: 1 DETECTION AND TRACKING RADARS Strategic located at Antigua

Argentina Arg

Argentine Peso P		2006	2007	2008
GDP	P	654bn	759bn	
	US$	214bn	241bn	
per capita	US$	5,371	5,979	
Growth	%	8.5	7.5	
Inflation	%	10.9	9.5	
Def bdgt	P	5.71bn	6.46bn	
	US$	1.87bn	2.05bn	
US$1=P		3.05	3.15	

Population   40,301,927

Age	0–14	15–19	20–24	25–29	30–64	65 plus
Male	13%	4%	4%	4%	19%	4%
Female	12%	4%	4%	4%	19%	6%

Capabilities

ACTIVE 76,000 (Army 41,400 Navy 20,000 Air 14,600) Paramilitary 31,240

RESERVE none formally established or trained

ORGANISATIONS BY SERVICE

Army 41,400
A strategic reserve is made up of Armd, AB and Mech bdes normally subordinate to corps level.

FORCES BY ROLE
Comd   3 corps HQ (mob def)
Mobile   1 Northeast force (1 Jungle bde, 1 Armd bde,
Defence 1 Trg bde); 1 Northern force (1 AB bde (1 Cdo coy), 1 Mech Inf bde, 1 Mtn Inf bde); 1 Patagonia and Southern Atlantic force (1 Mtn Inf bde, 1 Armd bde, 3 Mech Inf bde)
Rapid   1 (Rapid Deployment) force (includes AB bde
Reaction from corps level) (1 Cdo coy)
Mot cav 1 regt (Presidential Escort)
Mot inf 1 bn (army HQ Escort Regt)
Arty   1 gp (bn)
ADA   2 gp
Engr   1 bn
Avn   1 gp

EQUIPMENT BY TYPE
MBT 213: 207 TAM, 6 TAM S21
LT TK 128: 112 SK-105A1 *Kuerassier*; 6 SK105A2 *Kuerassier*; 10 *Patagón*
RECCE 81: 47 AML-90; 34 M1114 *HMMWV*
AIFV 123 VCTP (incl variants)
APC (T) 413: 70 M-113 A1-ACAV; 315 M-113A2 (114 with 20mm cannon); 28 AMX VCI
ARTY 1,103
  SP 155mm 37: 20 Mk F3; 17 VCA 155 *Palmaria*
  TOWED 179: **105mm** 70 M-56 (Oto Melara); **155mm** 109: 25 M-77 *CITEFA*/M-81 *CITEFA*; 84 SOFMA l-33

MRL 105mm 4 SLAM *Pampero*
MOR 883: **81mm** 492; **120mm** 353 *Brandt*
   SP 38: 25 M-106A2; 13 TAM-VCTM
AT
   MSL • SP 3 HMMWV eqpt. with total of 18 TOW-2A
   MANPATS msl
   RCL 150 M-1968
   RL 385+ **66mm** 385 M-72 *LAW*; **78mm** MARA
AIRCRAFT
   TPT 15: 1 *Beech 80 Queen Air*; 1 CASA 212-200 *Aviocar*;
   1 *Cessna 500 Citation I*; 2 DHC-6 *twin Otter*; 3 G-222; 1
   Gaviao 75A; 3 SA-226 *Merlin IIIA*; 3 SA-226AT *Merlin
   IV/IVA*
   UTL 3 *Cessna 207 Stationair*
   TRG 5 T-41 *Mescalero*
HELICOPTERS
   ARMED 6 UH-1H
   SAR 5 SA-315B
   SPT 3 AS-332B *Super Puma*
   UTL 31: 5 A-109; 1 Bell 212; 23 UH-1H *Iroquois*; 2 UH-
   1H-II *Huey II*
   TRG 8 UH-12E
AD
   SAM • STATIC/SHELTER 3 *Roland I*
   GUNS • TOWED 411: **20mm** 230 GAI-B01; **30mm**
   21 HS L81; **35mm** 12 GDF *Oerlikon* (skyguard fire
   control); **40mm** 148: 24 L/60 training, 40 in store; 76
   L/60; 8 L/70
   RADAR • AD RADAR 11: 5 Cardion AN/TPS-44; 6
   Skyguard
      LAND 18+: M-113 A1GE *Green Archer* (mor); 18
      RATRAS (veh, arty*)*

Navy 20,000

Commands: Surface Fleet, Submarines, Naval Avn,
Marines

FORCES BY ROLE

Navy Located at Mar del Plata (SS and HQ Atlantic),
   Ushuaio (HQ South), Puerto Belgrano (HQ
   Centre)

EQUIPMENT BY TYPE
SUBMARINES • TACTICAL • SSK 3:
   1 *Salta* (Ge T-209/1200) with 8 single 533mm TT with 14
   Mk 37/SST-4
   2 *Santa Cruz* (Ge TR-1700) each with 6 single 533mm TT
   with 22 SST-4 HWT
PRINCIPAL SURFACE COMBATANTS 14
   DESTROYERS • DDG 5:
      4 *Almirante Brown* (Ge MEKO 360) each with 2 quad
      (8 eff.) each with MM-40 *Exocet* tactical SSM, 2 B515
      ILAS-3 triple 324mm with 24 A244 LWT, 1 127mm
      gun, (capacity 1 AS-555 *Fennec* or Alouette III utl hels)
      1 *Hercules* (UK Type 42 - utilised as a fast troop
      transport ship), eq with 2 B515 ILAS-3 triple 324mm
      each with A244 LWT, 1 114mm gun, (capacity 1 SH-
      3H *Sea King* utl hels)
   FRIGATES • FFG 9:
      3 *Drummond* (Fr A-69) each with 2 twin (4 eff.) each
      with MM-38 *Exocet* tactical SSM, 2 Mk32 triple 324mm
      each with A244 LWT, 1 100mm gun

6 *Espora* (Ge MEKO 140) 2 twin (4 eff.) each with MM-
38 *Exocet* tactical SSM, 2 B515 ILAS-3 triple 324mm
each with A244 LWT, 1 76mm gun,(capacity either 1
SA-319 *Alouette III* utl hel or 1 AS-555 *Fennec* utl hels)
PATROL AND COASTAL COMBATANTS 15
   PFT 2:
      1 *Interpida* (Ge Lurssen 45m) with 2 single 533mm TT
      each with SST-4 HWT
      1 *Interpida* (Ge Lurssen 45m) with 2 single each with
      1 MM-38 *Exocet* tactical SSM, 2 single 533mm TT each
      with SST-4 HWT
   PCO 7:
      3 *Irigoyen* (US *Cherokee* AT)
      2 *Murature* (US *King*) (trg/river patrol) each with 3
      105mm gun
      1 *Sobral* (US *Sotoyomo* AT)
      1 *Teniente Olivieri* (ex-US oilfield tug)
   PCI 6: 4 *Baradero* less than 100 tonnes (Dabur); 2 Point
   less than 100 tonnes
AMPHIBIOUS 20: 4 **LCM**; 16 **LCVP**
LOGISTICS AND SUPPORT 12
   AORH 1 *Patagonia* (US *Durance*) with 1 SA-316 *Alouette
   III* utl hels
   AORL 1 *Ingeniero Julio Krause*
   AK 3 *Costa Sur*
   AGOR 1 *Commodoro Rivadavia*
   AGHS 1 *Puerto Deseado* (ice breaking capability, use for
   polar research)
   AGB 1 *Almirante Irizar*
   ABU 3 *Red*
   TRG 1 *Libertad*

FACILITIES

Bases	Located at Ushuaio (HQ Centre), Mar del Plata (SS and HQ Atlantic), Buenos Aires, Puerto Belgrano (HQ Centre), Zarate (river craft)
Naval airbases	Located at Trelew, Punta Indio
Construction and Repair Yard	Located at Rio Santiago

Naval Aviation 2,000

AIRCRAFT 28 combat capable
   STRIKE/FGA 3 *Super Etendard* (8 in store)
   ASW 5 S-2T *Tracker**
   MP 6 P-3B *Orion**
   TPT 4: 2 *Beech 200F Super King Air*; 2 F-28 *Fellowship*
   UTL 6: 5 BE-200F/BE-200M; 1 AU-23 *Turbo-Porter*
   TRG 13: 3 EMB-326 *Xavante**; 10 T-34C *Turbo Mentor**
HELICOPTERS
   ASW/ASUW 4 ASH-3H *Sea King*
   UTL 15: 3 AS-555 *Fennec*; 6 SA-316B *Alouette III**;
   6 UH-1H *Iroquois*
MSL
   ASM 21 AM-39 *Exocet*; AS-12 *Kegler*;AS-11 *Kilter*; AS-
   25K CITEFA *Martin Pescador*
   AAM R-550 *Magic*

Marines 2,500
FORCES BY ROLE

Spt/Amph	1 force (1 marine inf bn)

Marine   1 (Fleet) force (1 arty bn, 1 AAV bn, 1 cdo gp, 1 ADA bn, 1 marine inf bn); 1 (Fleet) force (2 marine inf bn, 2 Navy det)

EQUIPMENT BY TYPE

RECCE 12+ ERC-90F *Sagaie*; M1114 *HMMWV*
APC (W) 42: 6 *Grenadier*; 36 M-3 *Panhard*
AAV 25: 15 LARC-5; 10 LVTP-7
ARTY 100
  TOWED 105mm 18: 6 M-101; 12 Model 56 pack howitzer
  MOR 82: 70 **81mm**; 12 **120mm**
AT
  MSL • MANPATS 50 *Cobra*/RB-53 *Bantam*
  RCL 105mm 30 M-1974 FMK-1
  RL 89mm 60 M-20
AD
  SAM 6 RBS-70
  GUNS 30mm 10 HS-816; **35mm** GDF-001

Air Force 14,600 (1,700 conscripts)

4 Major Comds – Air Operations, Personnel, Air regions, Logistics, 8 air bde

Air Operations Command

FORCES BY ROLE

Airspace Defence	1 sqn with 12 *Mirage* EA/DA (*Mirage* III/E)
FGA/Ftr	5 (strategic air) sqn; 2 sqn with 34 A-4AR/OA-4AR *Skyhawk*; 2 sqn with 14 IAI *Dagger Nesher* A/B; 1 sqn with 7 *Mirage* 5 *Mara*; 2 (tac air) sqn with 34 IA-58 *Pucara*
Tac Air	2 sqn with 34 IA-58 *Pucara*
RECCE/Survey	1 sqn with ; 5 *Learjet* 35A
SAR/Utl	3 sqn with 6 Bell 212; 15 *Hughes* 369*; 4 MD-500*; 3 SA-315B *Lama*; 7 UH-1H *Iroquois*; 2 UH-1N
Tpt/Tkr	1 sqn with 5 B-707; 1 sqn with 4 F-27 *Friendship*; 1 sqn with 8 DHC-6 *twin Otter*; 2 sqn with 2 KC-130H *Hercules*; 3 C-130B *Hercules*; 5 C-130H *Hercules*; 1 L-100-30; 1 (Pres) flt with 1 B-757-23ER; 1 S-70 *Black Hawk*; 1 sqn with 6 F-28 *Fellowship*
Trg	Aviation school with 29 B-45 Mentor (basic); 19 EMB-312 Tucano (primary); 7 SU-29AR; 3 MD-500

EQUIPMENT BY TYPE

AIRCRAFT 119 combat capable
  FTR 12 *Mirage* EA/DA (*Mirage* IIIE)
  FGA 89: 34 A-4AR/OA-4AR *Skyhawk*; 7 Mirage 5PA (Mara); 11 IAI *Dagger* A, 3 *Dagger* B; 34 IA-58 *Pucara*
  LEAD-IN FTR TRG: 18 AT-63*
  TKR 2 KC-130H *Hercules*
  TPT 39: 5 B-707; 1 B-757-23ER; 3 C-130B *Hercules*; 5 C-130H *Hercules*; 8 DHC-6 *twin Otter*; 4 F-27 *Friendship*; 6 F-28 *Fellowship*; 1 L-100-30; 5 *Learjet* 35A; 1 *Learjet* LJ60

  TRG 55: 29 B-45 *Mentor*; 19 EMB-312 *Tucano*; 7 SU-29AR (aerobatic team)
HELICOPTERS
  VIP 2: 1 S-70 *Black Hawk*, 1 S-76
  UTL 35: 6 Bell 212; 15 *Hughes* 369*; 4 MD-500D*; 3 SA-315B *Lama*; 7 UH-1H *Iroquois*
  TRG 3 MD-500
MSL
  ASM *Martin Pescador* (ASM-2 Type-93)
  AAM 6 AIM-9L Sidewinder; 30+ R-550 *Magic*; 150+ *Shafrir IV*
AD
  SAM 3 *Roland*; 50 SA-7 (170 msl)
  GUNS 88: **20mm**: 86 Oerlikon/Rh-202 with 9 Elta EL/M-2106 radar; **35mm**: 2 Oerlikon GDF-001 with Skyguard radar
RADAR 6: 5 AN/TPS-43; 1 BPS-1000

Paramilitary 31,240

Gendarmerie 18,000

Ministry of Interior

FORCES BY ROLE

Region   5 comd
Paramilitary   16 bn

EQUIPMENT BY TYPE

RECCE S52 *Shorland*
APC (W) 87: 47 *Grenadier*; 40 UR-416
ARTY • MOR 81mm
AIRCRAFT
  TPT 6: 3 PA-28-236 *Dakota*/PA-31P *Pressurized Navajo*; 3 PC-6 *Turbo-Porter*
  UTL 1 *Cessna* 206
HELICOPTERS
  SPT 3 AS-350 *Ecureuil*
  UTL 3 MD-500C/MD-500D

Prefectura Naval (Coast Guard) 13,240

PATROL AND COASTAL COMBATANTS 32:
  PCO 6: 1 *Mandubi*; 5 *Mantilla*
  PCI 25: 4; 21 PCI all less than 100 tonnes
  PCR 1 Delfin
AIRCRAFT
  TPT 5 CASA 212 *Aviocar*
HELICOPTERS
  SAR 1 AS-565MA
  SPT 1 AS-330L (SA-330L) *Puma*
  UTL 2 AS-365 *Dauphin 2*
  TRG 2 Schweizer 300C

DEPLOYMENT

CYPRUS
UN • UNFICYP 1 inf bn; 294; 2 Bell 212

HAITI
UN • MINUSTAH 562

MIDDLE EAST
UN • **UNTSO** 5 obs

SERBIA
NATO • **KFOR** • *Joint Enterprise* 36
UN • **UNMIK** 1 obs

WESTERN SAHARA
UN • **MINURSO** 1 obs

Bahamas Bs

Bahamian Dollar B$		2006	2007	2008
GDP	B$	6.1bn	6.4bn	
	US$	6.1bn	6.4bn	
per capita	US$	20,081	20,939	
Growth	%	3.4	3.1	
Inflation	%	1.8	2.4	
Def bdgt	B$	40m	45m	
	US$	40m	45m	
US$1=B$		1.0	1.0	

Population   305,655

Age	0–14	15–19	20–24	25–29	30–64	65 plus
Male	14%	5%	4%	4%	19%	3%
Female	14%	5%	4%	4%	21%	4%

Capabilities

ACTIVE 860 (Royal Bahamian Defence Force 860)

ORGANISATIONS BY SERVICE

Royal Bahamian Defence Force 860

EQUIPMENT BY TYPE
PATROL AND COASTAL COMBATANTS 14
  PCO 2 *Bahamas*
  PFC 3 *Protector*
  PCI 2: 1 *Challenger* less than 100 tonnes; 1 *Keith Nelson*
  less than 100 tonnes
  PBF 4 *Boston Whaler* less than 100 tonnes
  PBI 3: 2 *Dauntless* less than 100 tonnes; 1 *Fort Montague*
  less than 100 tonnes
AIRCRAFT
  TPT 4: 1 *Cessna 404 Titan*; 2 PA-31; 1 *Beech* A-350 *Super
  King Air*
FACILITIES
Bases   Located at Coral Harbour, New Providence
      Island

FOREIGN FORCES

Guyana Navy: Base located at New Providence Island

Barbados Bds

Barbados Dollar B$		2006	2007	2008
GDP	B$	6.8bn	7.2bn	
	US$	3.4bn	3.6bn	
per capita	US$	12,147	12,814	
Growth	%	3.9	4.2	
Inflation	%	7.3	5.5	
Def bdgt	B$	ε50m	ε55m	
	US$	ε25m	ε22.5m	
US$1=B$		2.0	2.0	

Population   280,946

Age	0–14	15–19	20–24	25–29	30–64	65 plus
Male	10%	4%	4%	4%	23%	3%
Female	10%	4%	4%	4%	25%	5%

Capabilities

ACTIVE 610 (Army 500 Navy 110)

RESERVE 430 (Joint 430)

ORGANISATIONS BY SERVICE

Army 500
Inf   1 bn (cadre)

Navy 110
FORCES BY ROLE
Navy 1 HQ located at St Ann's Fort
EQUIPMENT BY TYPE
PATROL AND COASTAL COMBATANTS 9
  PCC 1 *Kebir*
  PCI 5: 2 *Dauntless* less than 100 tonnes; 3 *Guardian* less
  than 100 tonnes
  PC 3 *Damen Stan Patrol 4207*
FACILITIES
Bases Located at St Ann's Fort, Bridgetown

Belize Bze

Belize Dollar BZ$		2006	2007	2008
GDP	BZ$	2.4bn	2.6bn	
	US$	1.2bn	1.3bn	
per capita	US$	4,171	4,416	
Growth	%	5.8	4.1	
Inflation	%	4.3	3.3	
Def bdgt	BZ$	ε36m	ε36m	
	US$	ε18m	ε18m	
US$1=BZ$		2.0	2.0	

Population   294,385

Age	0–14	15–19	20–24	25–29	30–64	65 plus
Male	20%	6%	5%	4%	14%	2%
Female	20%	6%	5%	4%	14%	2%

Capabilities

ACTIVE ε1,050 (Army ε1,050)

RESERVE 700 (Joint 700)

ORGANISATIONS BY SERVICE

Army ε1,050

FORCES BY ROLE

Army 3 (Reserve) coy

Inf   3 bn (each: 3 inf coy)

Spt   1 gp

EQUIPMENT BY TYPE

MOR 81mm 6

RCL 84mm 8 Carl Gustav

Maritime Wing

PATROL AND COASTAL COMBATANTS • MISC BOATS/CRAFT ε14 less than 100 tonnes

Air Wing

FORCES BY ROLE

MR/Tpt   some sqn with 1 BN-2A Defender; 1 BN-2B Defender

Trg   unit with 1 Cessna 182 Skylane; 1 T67-200 Firefly

EQUIPMENT BY TYPE

AIRCRAFT

    TPT 2: 1 BN-2A Defender; 1 BN-2B Defender

    TRG 2: 1 Cessna 182 Skylane; 1 T67-200 Firefly

FOREIGN FORCES

United Kingdom Army 70

United States Army 1; Navy 1

Bolivia Bol

Bolivian Boliviano B		2006	2007	2008
GDP	B	89bn	100bn	
	US$	11.1bn	13.1	
per capita	US$	1,238	1,433	
Growth	%	4.6	4.0	
Inflation	%	4.3	8.5	
Def bdgt	B	1.24bn	1.27bn	
	US$	155m	166m	
US$1=B		8.0	7.7	

Population   9,119,152

Age	0–14	15–19	20–24	25–29	30–64	65 plus
Male	18%	6%	5%	4%	14%	2%
Female	18%	6%	5%	4%	16%	3%

Capabilities

ACTIVE 46,100 (Army 34,800 Navy 4,800 Air 6,500) Paramilitary 37,100

ORGANISATIONS BY SERVICE

Army 9,800; 25,000 conscript (total 34,800)

FORCES BY ROLE

HQ: 6 Military Regions

Army   10 div (org, composition varies) (total: 1 (aslt) cav gp, 1 (mot) cav gp, 2 AB regt (bn), 2 mech inf regt, 21 inf bn, 3 mot inf regt, 5 (horsed) cav gp, 6 arty regt (bn), 6 engr bn)

Armd   1 bn

Mech Cav   1 regt

Inf/Presidential Guard 1 regt

SF   3 regt

ADA   1 regt

Avn   2 coy

EQUIPMENT BY TYPE

LT TK 54: 36 SK-105A1 Kuerassier; 18 SK-105A2 Kuerassier

RECCE 24 EE-9 Cascavel

APC 115+

    APC (T) 54+: 4 4K-4FA-SB20 Greif; 50+ M-113

    APC (W) 61: 24 EE-11 Urutu; 22 MOWAG Roland; 15 V-100 Commando

LT VEH 10 Koyak

ARTY 345+

    TOWED 95: **75mm** 34: 24 M-116 pack; 10 M-1935; **105mm** 25 M-101A1; **122mm** 36 (M-30) M-1938

    MOR 250+: **60mm** M-224: **81mm** 250 M-29; Type-W87; **107mm** M-30; **120mm** M-120

AT • MSL• MANPATS 50+ HJ-8 (2 SP on Koyak)

    RCL 106mm M-40A1; **90mm** M-67

    RL 200+: **66mm** M-72 LAW; **73mm** RPG-7V Knout; **89mm** 200+ M-20

AIRCRAFT

    TPT 1 PA-34 Seneca

    UTL 1 Cessna 210 Centurion

AD • GUNS • TOWED 37mm 18 Type-65

Navy 4,800

FORCES BY ROLE

Organised into 6 naval districts with Naval HQ located at Puerto Guayaramerín

EQUIPMENT BY TYPE

PATROL AND COASTAL COMBATANTS 54:

  PCR 1 Santa Cruz
  PBR 53

LOGISTICS AND SUPPORT 19:

  AH 2
  TPT 11 (river tranports)
  SPT 6

FACILITIES

Bases Located at Riberalta, Tiquina, Puerto Busch, Puerto Guayaramerín, Puerto Villarroel, Trinidad, Puerto Suárez, Coral Harbour, Santa Cruz, Bermejo, Cochabamba, Puerto Villeroel

Marines 1,700 (incl 1,000 Naval Military Police)

Marine   6 inf bn (1 in each Naval District)
Mech inf 1 bn
MP   4 (naval MP) bn

Air Force 6,500 (incl conscripts)

FORCES BY ROLE

FGA	2 sqn with 15 AT-33AN *Shooting Star*
Trg/COIN	1 sqn with 18 PC-7 *Turbo Trainer*
SAR/ COMMS	1 sqn with 2 HB-315B *Lama*, 2 AS-532AC *Cougar*
Tpt	1 sqn with 3 *Beech* 90 *King Air*; 2 sqn with 1 RC-130A/ 5 C-130B/1 C-130H *Hercules*; 1 sqn with 3 F-27-400 *Friendship*; 4 IAI-201 *Arava*; 1 CV-440; 1 CV-580; 1 *Aerocommander* 690; 1 *Beech*-1900; 1 BAe-146-100
Liaison	3 sqn with 1 *Cessna* 152; 1 PA-32 *Saratoga*; 3 PA-34 *Seneca*; 14 *Cessna* 206; 1 *Cessna* 210; 1 *Beech* F-33 *Bonanza*
Survey	1 sqn with 1 *Cessna* 402; 2 *Learjet* 25B/25D (secondary VIP role); 5 *Cessna* 206
Trg	3 sqn with 9 *Cessna* 152; 2 *Cessna* 172; 6 T-25; 10 T-34B *Beech Turbo Mentor*; 28 A-122
Hel	1 (anti-drug) sqn with 15 UH-1H *Huey*
AD	1 regt† with *Oerlikon*; 18 Type-65

EQUIPMENT BY TYPE

AIRCRAFT 33 combat capable

  FGA 15 AT-33AN *Shooting Star*
  Trg/COIN 18 PC-7 *Turbo Trainer**
  TPT 30: 3 *Beech* 90 *King Air*; 7 RC-130A/C-130B/C-130H *Hercules*; 1 *Cessna* 152; 1 Cessna 210; 1 CV-440; 1 CV-580; 3 F-27-400 *Friendship*; 1 Aero-Commander 690; 4 IAI-201 *Arava*; 2 *Learjet* 25B/ 25D (secondary VIP role); 1 PA-32 *Saratoga*; 3 PA-34 *Seneca*; 1 *Beech*-1900; 1 BAe-146-100
  UTL 21: 19 *Cessna* 206; 1 *Cessna* 212; 1 *Cessna* 402
  TRG 56: 1 *Beech* F-33 *Bonanza*; 9 *Cessna* 152; 2 *Cessna* 172; 28 A-122; 6 T-25; 10 T-34B *Beech Turbo Mentor*

HELICOPTERS

  ARMED HEL 15 UH-1H *Huey*
  UTL 4: 2 AS-532AC *Cougar*; 2 HB-315B *Lama*
  AD•GUNS 18+: **20mm** *Oerlikon*; **37mm** 18 Type-65

Paramilitary 37,100+

National Police 31,100+

Frontier	27 unit
Paramilitary	9 bde; 2 (rapid action) regt

Narcotics Police 6,000+

  FOE (700) - Special Operations Forces

DEPLOYMENT

AFGHANISTAN

UN • UNAMA 1 obs

CÔTE D'IVOIRE

UN • UNOCI 3 obs

DEMOCRATIC REPUBLIC OF CONGO

UN • MONUC 200; 10 obs

ETHIOPIA/ERITREA

UN • UNMEE 5 obs

GEORGIA

UN • UNOMIG 1 obs

HAITI

UN • MINUSTAH 217

LIBERIA

UN • UNMIL 1; 3 obs

SERBIA

UN • UNMIK 1 obs

SUDAN

UN • UNMIS 1; 16 obs

Brazil Br

Brazilian Real R		2006	2007	2008
GDP	R	2.32tr	2.51tr	
	US$	1,070bn	1,398bn	
per capita	US$	5,689	7,356	
Growth	%	3.7	4.4	
Inflation	%	4.2	3.6	
Def bdgt	R	35.2bn	39.0bn	
	US$	16.2bn	21.6bn	
US$1=R		2.17	1.80	

Population	190,010,647

Age	0–14	15–19	20–24	25–29	30–64	65 plus
Male	13%	5%	5%	5%	20%	2%
Female	13%	5%	5%	5%	20%	4%

Capabilities

ACTIVE 367,901 (Army 238,200 Navy 62,261 Air 67,440)

RESERVE 1,340,000 Paramilitary 385,600

Terms of service 12 months (can be extended to 18)

ORGANISATIONS BY SERVICE

Army 149,200; 89,000 conscript (total 238,200)

FORCES BY ROLE

HQ: 7 Military Command, 12 Military Regions; 8 div (3 with Regional HQ)

Army	1 (frontier) bde (6 army bn)
Armd cav	1 bde (1 arty bn, 1 armd bn, 2 armd cav bn)
Mech cav	4 bde (*each:* 1 armd cav bn, 1 arty bn, 2 Mech cav bn)
Armd Inf	3 bde (*each:* 1 armd cav bn, 1 arty bn, 2 armd inf bn)
SF	1 bde (1 SF bn, 1 Cdo bn) with Training Centre (SF)
Mot Inf	8 bde (*total:* 26 mot inf bn)
Lt inf	1 bde (3 Lt inf bn);6 (jungle) bde
AB	1 bde (1 arty bn, 3 AB bn)
Arty	6 (med) gp
SP Arty	4 gp
ADA	1 (AA and coastal) bde
Engr	2 (railway) bn; 2 gp (*total:* 9 engr bn)
Hel	1 bde (2 hel bn (*each:* 2 hel sqn))

EQUIPMENT BY TYPE

MBT 224: 133 *Leopard* 1 A1BE; 91 M-60A3/TTS

LT TK 112 M-41B/M-41C

RECCE 417: 409 EE-9 *Cascavel*; 8 AV-VBL

APC 803

   APC (T) 583 M-113

   APC (W) 219 EE-11 *Urutu*

ARTY 1,658+

   SP 109: **105mm** 72 M-108/M-7; **155mm** 37 M-109A3

   TOWED 448

      105mm 356: 312 M-101/M-102; 36 L-118 *Light gun*; 8 Model 56 pack howitzer; **155mm** 92 M-114

   MRL 20+: **70mm** SBAT-70; 20 ASTROS II

   MOR 1,080: **60mm** M949 AGR; **81mm** 922 *Commando V*; 20+ Royal Ordinance L-16; **120mm** 77 K6A3; 61 M2

AT

   MSL • MANPATS 30: 18 *Eryx*; 12 *Milan*

   RCL 290: **106mm** 163 M-40A1; **84mm** 127 *Carl Gustav*

   RL 84mm 540 AT-4; ALAC

HELICOPTERS

   SPT 63: 19 AS-550U2 *Fennec* (armed); 8 AS-532 *Cougar*; 4 S-70A *Black Hawk*; 32 AS-365 *Dauphin*

   TRG 16 AS-350 LI *Ecureuil*

AD

   MANPAD 112 SA-18 *Grouse (Igla)* (grouped in pairs)

   GUNS 146: **35mm** 134 GDF-001 towed (some with *Super Fledermaus* radar); **40mm** 12 L/70 (some with BOFI)

Navy 62,261 (incl 11,000+ conscript)

FORCES BY ROLE

Organised into 6 districts with HQ I Rio de Janeiro, HQ II Salvador, HQ III Recife, HQ IV Belém, HQ V Floriancholis, HQ VI Sao Paolo

EQUIPMENT BY TYPE

SUBMARINES • TACTICAL • SSK 5:

4 *Tupi* (Ge T-209/1400) each with 8 single 533mm TT each with MK 24 *Tigerfish* HWT

1 *Tikuna* with 8 single 533mm TT with MK 24 *Tigerfish* HWT (undergoing sea trials)

PRINCIPAL SURFACE COMBATANTS 15

   AIRCRAFT CARRIERS • CV 1:

   1 *Sao Paolo* (ex-Fr *Clemenceau*) (capacity 15-18 A-4 *Skyhawk* FGA ac; 4-6 SH-3D *Sea King* ASW hels/SH-3A *Sea King* ASW hels; 3 AS-355F *Ecureuil II* spt hels/AS-350BA *Ecureuil* spt hels; 2 AS-532 *Cougar* utl hels)

   FRIGATES 10

      FFG 9:

         3 *Greenhaigh* (ex-UK *Broadsword*, 1 low readiness) 4 single each with 1 MM-38 *Exocet* tactical SSM, 2+ sextuple (12 eff.) with 32 *Sea Wolf* SAM, 6 single 324mm ASTT each with Mk 46 LWT, 1 *Lynx* MK21A (*Super Lynx*) utl hel

         6 *Niteroi* each with 4 MM-40 *Exocet* tactical SSM, 1 *Albatros* Octuple with 24 *Aspide* SAM, 2 triple 324mm ASTT (6 eff.) each with Mk 46 LWT, 1 2 tube *Bofors* 375mm (2 eff.), 1 115mm gun, 1 *Lynx* MK21A (*Super Lynx*) utl hel

      FF 1:

         1 *Para* (ex-US *Garcia*) each with 1 Mk16 Mk 112 Octuple with tactical ASROC, 2 triple ASTT (6 eff.) each with Mk 46 LWT, 2 127mm gun, 1 *Lynx* MK21A (*Super Lynx*) utl hel (low readiness, op. capability doubtful)

   CORVETTES • FSG 4:

      4 *Inhauma* each with 1 single with 4 MM-40 *Exocet* tactical SSM, 2 triple ASTT (6 eff.) each with Mk 46 LWT, 1 114mm gun, 1 *Lynx* MK21A (*Super Lynx*) utl hel

PATROL AND COASTAL COMBATANTS 33:

   PCO 14:

      12 *Grajau*; 2 *Imperial Marinheiro* with 1 76mm gun

   PCC 10: 4 *Bracui* (ex-UK *River*); 6 *Piratini* (US PGM)

   PCI 4 *Tracker* (Marine Police)

   PCR 5: 2 *Pedro Teixeira*; 3 *Roraima*

MINE WARFARE • MINE COUNTERMEASURES • MSC 6 *Aratu* (Ge *Schutze*)

AMPHIBIOUS

   PRINCIPAL AMPHIBIOUS SHIPS • LSD 2:

      2 *Ceara* (capacity either 21 LCM or 6 LCU; 345 troops) (US *Thomaston*)

   LS • LST 1:

      1 *Mattoso Maia* (US *Newport*) (capacity 3 LCVP; 1 LCPL; 400 troops)

   LSLH 1 *Garcia D'Avila* (ex UK *Sir Galahad*) (capacity 1 hel; 16 MBT; 340 troops)

   CRAFT 46: 3 LCU; 35 LCVP; 8 LCM

LOGISTICS AND SUPPORT 31:

   AOR 2

   ASR 1

AG 2: 1 (troop carrier); 1 (river tender)
AH 3
AK 5
AGOR 1 *Ary Royal* (Ice-strengthened hull, used for polar research)
AGHS 1 *Sirius*
AGS 4: 1 *Antares*; 3 *Amorim Do Valle* (ex-UK Rover)
ABU 6: 1 (lighthouse tender); 5
ATF 4
TPT 2 (river transport)
TRG 4: 1 *Mod Niteroi*
    AXL 3 *Nascimento*
    AXS 1

Naval Aviation 1,300

FORCES BY ROLE

FGA   1 sqn with 15 A-4 *Skyhawk*/A-4MB *Skyhawk*/TA-4 *Skyhawk*; 3 TA-4MB *Skyhawk*

ASW   1 sqn with 6 SH-3G *Sea King*/SH-3H *Sea King*; 7 SH-3D *Sea King*

Utl   2 sqn with 5 AS-332 *Super Puma*; 4 sqn with 12 AS-350 *Ecureuil* (armed); 8 AS-355 *Ecureuil* (armed)

Atk Hel 1 sqn with 12 Mk21A *Lynx*

Trg   1 sqn with 15 TH-57 *Sea Ranger*

EQUIPMENT BY TYPE

AIRCRAFT 18 combat capable
    FGA 15 A-4 *Skyhawk* FGA/A-4MB *Skyhawk* FGA/TA-4 *Skyhawk* Trg*
    TRG 3 TA-4MB *Skyhawk**
HELICOPTERS
    ASW 25: 12 Mk21A *Lynx*; 6 SH-3G/SH-3H *Sea King*; 7 SH-3D *Sea King*
    SPT 29: 5 AS-332 *Super Puma*; 16 AS-350 *Ecureuil* (armed); 8 AS-355 *Ecureuil* (armed)
    TRG 15 TH-57 *Sea Ranger*
MSL • **ASM**: *Sea Skua*

Marines 14,500

FORCES BY ROLE

Amph 1 (Fleet Force) div (1 comd bn, 1 arty gp, 3 inf bn)

SF   1 bn

Marine 8+ (Regional) gp; 3 bn

Engr   1 bn

EQUIPMENT BY TYPE

LT TK 17 SK-105 *Kuerassier*
RECCE 6 EE-9 *Cascavel*
APC 50
    APC (T) 40 M-113
    APC (W) 10: 5 EE-11 *Urutu*; 5 *Piranha IIIC*
AAV 25: 13 AAV-7A1; 12 LVTP-7
ARTY 49+
    TOWED 41: **105mm** 33: 18 L-118 Light gun; 15 M-101; **155mm** 8 M-114
    MOR 8: **81mm**; **120mm** 8 K6A3
AT
    MSL • **MANPATS** RB-56 *Bill*

RCL 106mm 8 M-40A1
RL 89mm M-20
AD • **GUNS 40mm** 6 L/70 (with BOFI)

Air Force 67,440

COMDABRA (aerospace defence), plus three general cmds – COMGAR (operations), COMGAP (logistics), COMGEP (personnel).

Brazilian air space is divided into 7 air regions, each of which is responsible for its designated air bases.

Air assets are divided among five designated air forces for operations (one temporarily deactivated).

I Air Force operates 3 avn gps (1º/5th, 2º/5th and 1º/11th GAV) and a Tactical Training Group (GITE) providing Air Combat Training for A-29A/B *Super Tucano* and A-27 *Tucano* aircraft. The I Air Force also operates AT-26 *Xavante*, C-95 *Bandeirante* and UH-50 *Esquilo* helicopters.

II Air Force (HQ Rio de Janeiro) has some 240 aircraft organised into 3 Aviation Groups (7th, 8th and 10th GAVs). 7th GAV, responsible for Coastal Patrol, operates P-95A/B Banderhuilas armed for ASV and ASW from 4 air bases. 8th and 10th GAVs, with H-1H, *Super Puma* and *Esquilo* helicopters, are dedicated to SAR/utility, tpt ops and spec ops.

III Air Force (HQ Brasilia) 1st Air Defence Group is equipped with F-5EM/F-5BR *Tiger II*, AT-27 *Tucano* armed trainers and *Mirage* 2000B/C. The main light attack/armed recce force, with anti-narcotic and anti-terrorist roles, comprises 5 air groups with A-29 *Super Tucano*, AT-26 *Xavante* and AMX. 6th GAV, with 5 EMB-145 AEW, 3 EMB-145RS and 5 R-95 electronic recce aircraft, is responsible for electronic surveillance, AEW and reconnaissance.

V Air Force (HQ Rio de Janeiro) operates some 160 air transport and flight refuelling aircraft from 5 air bases. Two tpt gps operate C-295M, ERJ-145 tactical transports, C/KC-130E/H *Hercules* tkr/tpts and KC-137 tankers.

FORCES BY ROLE

AD Ftr 1 gp with F-2000B/C, F-5EM, RC-95, R-99 and R-99A; 3 sqn with F-5EM/AT-27

FGA   2 sqn with A-1A/B; 4 sqn with A-29A/B; 1 sqn with AT-26; 3 sqn with A-27

Recce 1 sqn with A-1A/B; 1 sqn with RT-26

AWACS 1 sqn with R-99A/B

MP   4 sqn with P-95A/ P-95B

Tnk   1 sqn with KC-130, 1 sqn with KC-137

Tpt   1 sqn with VC-96, VC-1A, VC-99A/B, VU-35; 1 sqn with VC-97, VU-9; 2 sqn with C-97; CH/VH-55, 9 sqn with C-95A/B/C and R-95; 1 sqn with R-35A; 1 sqn with C-99, 3 sqn with C-130H/E, 2 sqn with C-98; 1 sqn with C-115 and C-105A

Hel   4 sqn with H-1H; 1 sqn with H-34 (VIP); 2 sqn with H-50/H-55; 1 sqn with H-60L

Trg   1 sqn with T-25, 3 sqn with T-27 (incl. 1 air show. sqn)

EQUIPMENT BY TYPE

AIRCRAFT 309 combat aircraft
    FTR 67 : 12 F-2000 (*Mirage* 2000B/C) ; 49 F-5EM/FM; 6 F-5E

FGA 204: 40 A-1 (AMX); 50 A-29A *Super Tucano*; 50 A-29B *Super Tucano* (75 in service by by mid 2008) ; 10 AT-26A (*Impala* Mk.2); 2 AT-26B (*Impala* Mk.1); 28 AT-26 *Xavante*, 24 AT-27 *Tucano*

RECCE: 12: 4 RA-1 (AMX)*; 4 RT-26 *Xavante*; 4 RC-95

MP: 19: 10 P-95A *Bandeirulha* (EMB-111)*; 9 P-95B (EMB-111)*; 9 P-3AM *Orion* (delivery pending)

ELINT 22: 4 EU-93A (Hawker 800XP); 3 R-99B (EMB-145S); 3 R-35A (Learjet 36); 2 EU-93 (HS-125), 1 EC-93 (HS-125), 9 EC-95 (EMB-110B *Bandeirante*)

AEW 5 R-99A (EMB-145RSA)

SAR 5: 4 SC-95B, 1 SC-130E

TKR 5: 2 KC-130H, 3 KC-137 (1 stored)

TPT 142 : 1 VC-1A (Airbus ACJ); 2 VC-96 (B-737-200); 8 C-115 (DHC-5 *Buffalo*); 12 C-105 *Amazonas* (C-295M); 13 C-130H; 7 C-130E; 10 C-99A (ERJ-145); 59 C-95A/B/C; 4 VC-97 *Brasilia*; 7 C-97 *Brasilia*; 8 VU-9 *Xingu*; 11 VU-93 (BAe125)

UTL 58: 14 C-98 (Cessna 208) *Caravan* I; 3 U-19 *Ipanema*; 13 U-7 (PA-34) *Séneca*; 6 L-42, 22 U-42 *Regente*

TRG 116: 11 A-1B (AMX-T)*; 22 T-25A/C; 42 T-26 *Xavante*; 41 T-27 *Tucano*

HELICOPTERS

UTL 87: 32 H-50 (AS-350B); 8 H-55 (AS-355); 8 H-34; 1 H-34 (AS-332M *Super Puma*); 32 H-1H; 6 H-60L *Blackhawk*

MSL • AAM MAA-1 *Piranha*, *Python* III, Super 530F, *Magic* 2

Paramilitary 385,600+ reservists opcon Army

Public Security Forces 385,600+

In state mil pol org (state militias) under army control and considered army reserve

---

DEPLOYMENT

CÔTE D'IVOIRE
UN • UNOCI 3; 4 obs

ETHIOPIA/ERITREA
UN • UNMEE 7 obs

TIMOR LESTE
UN • UNMIT 3 obs

HAITI
UN • MINUSTAH 1,212

LIBERIA
UN • UNMIL 3

NEPAL
UN • UNMIN 7 obs

SUDAN
UN • UNMIS 24obs

Chile Chl

Chilean Peso pCh		2006	2007	2008
GDP	pCh	77.3tr	85.8tr	
	US$	146bn	173bn	
per capita	US$	9,044	10,630	
Growth	%	4.0	5.9	
Inflation	%	3.4	3.9	
Def exp[a]	pCh	2.48tr		
	US$	4.67bn		
Def bdgt	pCh	1.06tr	1.30tr	
	US$	2.00bn	2.63bn	
US$1=pCh		530	496	

[a] Including estimates for military pensions, paramilitary and Copper Fund

Population   16,284,741

Age	0–14	15–19	20–24	25–29	30–64	65 plus
Male	13%	4%	4%	4%	21%	3%
Female	12%	4%	4%	4%	21%	5%

Capabilities

ACTIVE 64,966 (Army 36,016 Navy 20,450 Air 8,500)
Paramilitary 38,000
Terms of service Army 1 year Navy and Air Force 22 months. Voluntary since 2005

RESERVE 50,000 (Army 50,000)

ORGANISATIONS BY SERVICE

Army 20,016; 16,000 conscript (total 36,016)

FORCES BY ROLE
6 Military administrative regions. Currently being reorganised into 4 armoured, 2 motorised, 2 mountain and 1 special forces brigade.

Army	6 div (org, composition varies)
Composite	15 (reinforced) regt
Armd	4 bde (being created)
Armd Cav	3 regt
Inf	10 regt
Spec Ops	1 bde (4 SF bn)
Arty	2 regt
Sigs	2 regt
Engr	1 regt
Avn	1 bde

EQUIPMENT BY TYPE
MBT 375: 93 *Leopard* 2 A4, 25 (in store) all yet to be delivered; 31AMX-30; 226 *Leopard* 1 (24 in store)
AIFV 139 YPR-765
APC 648
 APC (T) 511: 100 M-113A1; 396 M-113A2; 15 M-113C/M-113R
 APC (W) 137: 106 *Piranha* (6x6); 31 (*Piranha* 8x8 D)

ARTY 687

SP 155mm 71: 24 M-109A3; 47 (AMX) Mk F3

TOWED 188: **105mm** 128: 74 M-101; 54 Model 56 pack howitzer; **155mm** 60: 36 M-68; 24 M-71

MRL 160mm 8 LAR-160

MOR 470+: **SP** 50 (on *Piranha* 6x6); **81mm** 300 M-29; **120mm** 120 FAMAE; M-65

AT

MSL• MANPATS *Milan*; *Spike*

RCL 106mm M-40A1; **57mm** M-18; **66mm** LAW; **84mm** *Carl Gustav*

RL 89mm M-20 (3.5in); M-65

AIRCRAFT

TPT 13: 1 Beech 90 *King Air*; 1 Beech 58 *Baron*; 6 CASA 212 *Aviocar*; 3 CN-235; 2 CE-550 *Citation II*

UTL 3 Cessna 208 *Caravan I* (8 planned)

TRG 6 Cessna R172K *Hawk XP*

HELICOPTERS

SPT 24: 2 AS-332 *Super Puma*; 6 AS-350B3 *Ecureuil*; 1 AS-355F *Ecureuil II*; 10 SA-330 *Puma*; 5 SA-330H/L *Puma*

UTL 20 MD-530F *Lifter* (armed)

TRG 12 Enstrom 280FX

AD

SAM • MANPAD 12+: 12 *Mistral*; *Javelin* some non-operational

GUNS 194: 40 HA-202; **20mm** 94: **SP** 24 *Piranha*/TCM-20; **TOWED** 70: 34 M-167; 36 TCM-20; **25mm SP** 60 M113 *Kuka*

Navy 19,200; 1,250 conscript (total 20,450)

FORCES BY ROLE

Main Command: Fleet includes FF and SS flotilla.

Navy 4 Naval Zones; 1st Naval Zone and main HQ located at Valparaiso (26S-36S); 2nd Naval Zone: at Talcahuano (36S-46S); 3rd Naval Zone at Punta Arenas (46S to Antarctica); 4th Naval Zone at Iquique (18S-26S)

EQUIPMENT BY TYPE

SUBMARINES • TACTICAL • SSK 4:

2 *O'Higgins* (*Scorpene*) each with 6 single 533mm TT with 18 A-184 *Black Shark* HWT & SUT

2 *Thompson* (Ge T-209/1300) each with 8 single 533mm TT with 14 SUT HWT

PRINCIPAL SURFACE COMBATANTS 8

FRIGATES • FFG 8:

1 *Condell* (mod UK *Leander*) with 4 single each with 1 MM-40 *Exocet* tactical SSM, 2 triple ASTT (6 eff.) each with Mk 46 LWT, 2 x 114mm gun, with 1 AS-332F *Super Puma* spt hel

1 *Williams* (ex-UK T22) with 2x12(24eff.) each with *Sea Wolf* naval SAM

2 *Lattore* (ex *NL Jacob Van Heemskerck* class)

2 *Almirante Riveros* (ex *NL Karel Doorman class*)

2 Type 23 (ex-UK *Duke Class* – third of class expected mid 2008)

PATROL AND COASTAL COMBATANTS 38

PFM 7:

3 *Casma* (Il *Sa'ar* 4) each with 8 GI *Gabriel I* tactical SSM, 2 76mm gun

4 *Tiger* (Ge Type 148) each with 4 single each with 1 MM-40 *Exocet* tactical SSM, 1 76mm gun

PCO 6 *Ortiz* (Taitao class)

PCC 17: 1 *Yagan*; 16 *Iquique* (Protector class)

PCI 8 *Grumete Diaz* less than 100 tonnes (Il Dabur)

AMPHIBIOUS • LS 5

LSM 2 *Elicura*

LST 3: 2 *Maipo* (capacity 7 tanks; 140 troops) (Fr *Batral*); 1 *Valdivia* (capacity 400 troops) (ex-US *Newport*)

LOGISTICS AND SUPPORT 10:

AOR 1 *Araucano*

AS 1 (also used as general spt ship)

AKSL 1

AGOR 1 *Vidal Gormez*

AGS 1 *Type 1200* (ice strengthened hull, ex-Ca)

ATF 3: 2 *Veritas*; 1 *Smit Lloyd*

TPT 1

TRG • AXS 1

MSL

SSM: 4 MM-38 *Exocet* tactical SSM

FACILITIES

Bases Located at Valparaiso, Talcahuano, Puerto Montt, Puerto Williams, Iquique, Punta Arenas

Naval Aviation 600

AIRCRAFT 18 combat capable

MP 3 P-3A *Orion*

TPT 15: 3 CASA 212A *Aviocar*; 8 Cessna O-2A *Skymaster**; 4 EMB-111 *Bandeirante*

TRG 7 PC-7 *Turbo Trainer**

HELICOPTERS

ASW 3 Bell 206 AS; 5 NAS-332C *Cougar**

SAR 8: 3 HH-65 *Dauphin*, 5 BO-105S

UTL 6: 4 Bell 206 *JetRange*; 2 Bell 412

MSL •ASM AM-39 *Exocet*

Marines 2,750

FORCES BY ROLE

Amph 1 bn

Marine 4 gp (*total*: 1 SSM bty (Excalibur Central Defence System), 2 Trg bn, 4 inf bn, 4 ADA bty, 4 fd arty bty), 7 security det (one per naval zone).

EQUIPMENT BY TYPE

LT TK 8 *Scorpion*

APC (W) 25 MOWAG *Roland*

ARTY 82

TOWED 32: **105mm** 8 KH-178; **155mm** 24 G-5

MOR 50 **81mm**

RCL 106mm ε30 M-40A1

AD • SAM • MANPAD *Blowpipe*

Coast Guard

Integral part of the Navy

PATROL AND COASTAL COMBATANTS 52

PCC 20: 18 *Alacalufe*; 2 *ONA*

PCI 29: 18 *Rodman*; 11 (LMP, LSR class)

MISC BOATS/CRAFT 3 Defender class

Air Force 7,900; 600 conscript (total 8,500)

Flying hours   100 hrs/year

FORCES BY ROLE

Ftr /FGA	1 sqn with 12 F-5E *Tigre III*; 2 F-5F *Tigre III*; 1 sqn with 6 Block 50 F-16C, 4 F-16D *Puma*; 1 sqn with 11 F-16AM, 7 F-16BM;
	1 (photo) unit with 1 Beech A-100 *King Air*; 3 DHC-6-300 *Twin Otter*; 2 Learjet 35A
AEW ELINT	1 B-707 *Phalcon* with Tpt gp. 6 Beech 99 *Petrel Alfa/Beta*
CCT TKR	2 gps with 14 A-37B *Dragonfly*; 12 A-36CC Halcon; 8 T-36BB ; 2 A-310 MRTT; 1 B-707 *Tanquero*
Tpt Liaison	3 gps with 1 B-737-500 (VIP); 1 B-737 300; 1 C-130B *Hercules*; 2 C-130H *Hercules*; 4 CASA 212 *Aviocar*; 5 DHC-6-100 *Twin Otter*; 8 DHC-6-300; 1 Gulfstream IV; 2 Learjet 35A; 31 PA-28-140 *Cherokee*; 3 Beech 99A7; 6 Cessna O-2A
Trg	1 gp with 38 T-35A/B *Pillan*; 5 CJ-1 *Citation*; 1 Mirage *IIIBE*, 23 T-36 *Halcon*, 2 Bell 206A
Hel	3 gps with 10 UH-1H; 1 BO-105CBS-4; 8 Bell 412; 1 S-70A-39 *Black Hawk*; 3 Bell 206B (trg)
AD	1 regt (5 AD gp) with *Mygale*; *Mistral*; M-163 *Vulcan*/M-167 *Vulcan*; GDF-005; Oerlikon; Crotale

EQUIPMENT BY TYPE
AIRCRAFT 74 combat capable
  FTR 14: 12 F-5E *Tigre III*+; 2 F-5F *Tigre III*+;
  FGA 60: 28 F-16 (6 Block 50 F-16C/4 F-16D; 11 F-16AM; 7 F-16BM); 12 A-37B *Dragonfly*; 12 A-36CC Halcon; 8 T-36BB
  RECCE 6: 1 Beech King Air; 2 Learjet 35A; 3 DHC-6-300
  AEW 1 B-707 (IAI *Phalcon*)
  ELINT 3 Beech 99 Petrel Alfa; 2 Beech 99 Petrel Beta
  TKR 3: 2 A-310 MRTT; 1 B-707 *TanqueroSP*
  TPT 65: 1 B-737-300; 1 B-737-500; 1 C-130B *Hercules*; 2 C-130H *Hercules*; 4 CASA 212 *Aviocar*; 5 DHC-6-100 *Twin Otter*; 8 DHC-6-300 *Twin Otter*; 1 Gulfstream IV; 31 PA-28-140 *Cherokee*; 3 Beech 99A; 6 Cessna 0-2A; 2 Learjet 35A
  TRG 44: 1 Mirage *IIIBE*; 38 T-35A/T-35B *Pillan*; 5 Cessna 525 *Citation CJ-1*
HELICOPTERS
  UTL 23: 1 BO-105CBS-4; 8 Bell 412 *Twin Huey* (delivery in progress) ; 10 UH-1H *Iroquois*; 1 S-70A-39 *Black Hawk*; 3 Bell 206B (trg)
AD
  SYSTEMS: *Mygale*
  SAM *Mistral*
  SP 5 *Crotale*
  GUNS • TOWED 20mm M-163 *Vulcan* SP/M-167 *Vulcan*; **35mm** GDF-005 *Oerlikon*
MSL • AAM AIM-9B *Sidewinder*/AIM-9J *Sidewinder*; *Python* III; *Shafrir*; BVR *Derby*

Paramilitary 38,000

Carabineros 38,000
Ministry of Defence

FORCES BY ROLE
13 Zones
Paramilitary   39 district; 174 comisaria

EQUIPMENT BY TYPE
APC (W) 20 MOWAG *Roland*
MOR 60mm; 81mm
AIRCRAFT
  TPT 10: 4 Cessna 182 *Skylane;* 1 Cessna 550 *Citation V*; 5 PA-31T *Navajo/Cheyenne II*
  UTL 5: 2 Cessna 206; 1 Cessna 208; 2 Cessna 210 *Centurion*
HELICOPTERS • UTL 16: 2 BK-117; 10 BO-105; 2 Bell 206 *JetRanger*; 2 EC-135

NON-STATE ARMED GROUPS

see Part II

DEPLOYMENT

BOSNIA-HERZEGOVINA
EU • EUFOR • *Operation Althea* 21

HAITI
UN • MINUSTAH 503

INDIA/PAKISTAN
UN • UNMOGIP 2 obs

MIDDLE EAST
UN • UNTSO 3 obs

SERBIA
UN • UNMIK 1 obs

Colombia Co

Colombian Peso pC		2006	2007	2008
GDP	pC	320tr	356tr	
	US$	136bn	180bn	
per capita	US$	3,116	4,067	
Growth	%	6.8	6.6	
Inflation	%	4.3	5.5	
Def exp [a]	pC	12.69tr	14.14tr	
	US$	5.37bn	7.14bn	
Def bdgt	pC	9.1tr	10.1tr	16.1tr
	US$	3.83bn	5.10bn	
FMA	US$	89.1	90.0	78.0
US$1=pC		2,361	1,979	

[a] including paramilitaries

Population   44,227,550

Age	0–14	15–19	20–24	25–29	30–64	65 plus
Male	16%	5%	4%	4%	19%	2%
Female	15%	5%	4%	4%	20%	3%

Capabilities

ACTIVE 254,259 (Army 216,921 Navy 27,605 Air 9,733) Paramilitary 144,097

RESERVE 61,900 (Army 54,700 Navy 4,800 Air 1,200 Joint 1,200)

ORGANISATIONS BY SERVICE

Army 43,921; 173,000 conscript (total 216,921)

FORCES BY ROLE

Mech	1 (1st) Div with (1 bde (2nd) (2 Mech Inf bn, 1 COIN bn, 1 mtn inf bn, 1 engr bn, 1 MP bn, 1 Cbt Spt bn, 2 Gaula Anti-Kidnap units); 1 bde (10th) (1 Mech Inf bn, 1 (med)Tk bn, 1 Mech Cav bn, 1 mtn inf bn, 2 Fd Arty bn, 2 engr bn, 1 Cbt Spt bn, 2 Gaula Anti-Kidnap coy); 1 EOD gp
COIN	1 div (2nd) with (1 bde (5th) (3 lt inf bn, 1 Fd arty bn, 1 AD bn, 2 engr bn, 1 Cbt spt bn, 1 Gaula anti-kidnap gp coy); 1 bde (18th) (1 airmob cav bn, 4 lt inf bn, 2 engr bn, 1 cbt spt bn); 1 bde (30th) (1 cav recce bn, 2 lt inf bn, 1 COIN bn, 1 engr bn, 1 cbt spt bn);
Rapid Reaction	3 COIN mobile bde (*each:* 4 COIN bn, 1 cbt spt bn) 1 div (4th) with (1 airmob bde (2 airmob inf bn, 1 lt inf bn, 1 COIN bn, 1 SF (anti-terrorist) bn, 1 airmob engr bn, 1 cbt spt bn, 1 Gaula anti-kidnap gp coy); 1 bde (16th) (1 Mech cav recce bn, 1 lt inf bn, 3 COIN bn, 1 cbt spt bn, 1 Gaula anti-kidnap gp coy); 1 (28th Jungle) bde (2 inf, 3 COIN, 2 marine (riverine) bn, 1 cbt spt bn)
Lt Inf	1 div (3rd) with (1 bde (3rd) (1 cav recce bn, 3 lt inf bn, 1 mtn inf bn, 1 COIN bn, 1 Fd arty bn, 1 engr bn, 1 cbt spt bn, 1 MP bn, 1 Gaula anti-kidnap gp coy); 1 bde (8th) (2 lt inf bn, 1 COIN bn, 1 Fd arty bn, 1 engr bn, 1 Gaula anti-kidnap gp coy); 1 bde (29th) (1 mtn inf bn); 1 (5th)div with 1 (1st) bde (1 cav recce bn, 2 lt inf bn, 1 COIN bn, 1 Fd arty bn, 2 engr bn, 1 cbt spt bn, 1 Gaula anti-kidnap gp coy); 1 bde (6th) (2 lt inf bn,1 mtn inf bn, 1 COIN bn, 1 cbt spt bn, 1 Gaula anti-kidnap gp coy); 1 bde (13th) (2 cav recce bn, 1 airmob inf bn, 2 lt inf bn, 1 mtn inf bn, 1 COIN bn, 1 Fd arty bn, 1 engr bn, 1 cbt spt bn, 2 MP bn); 1 (6th) div with

	1 bde (12th) (2 lt inf bn, 1 mtn inf bn, 1 COIN bn, 1 engr bn, 1 cbt spt bn, 1 Gaula anti-kidnap gp coy); 1 (26th) jungle bde (1 lt jungle inf bn, 1 COIN bn, 1 cbt spt bn, 1 coast guard det); 1 (27th) bde (2 lt inf bn, 1 COIN bn, 2 engr bn, 1 cbt spt bn); 1 div (7th) with 1 (4th) bde (1 cav recce bn, 3 lt inf bn, 1 COIN bn, fd 1 arty bn, 2 engr bn, 1 cbt spt bn, 2 Gaula anti-kidnap gp coy, 1 SF (anti-terrorist) coy); 1 (11th) bde (1 airmob inf bn, 1 lt inf bn, 2 COIN bn, 1 engr bn, 1 cbt spt bn); 1 (14th) bde (3 lt inf bn, 2 COIN bn, 1 engr bn, 1 cbt spt bn); 1 (17th) bde (2 lt inf bn, 1 COIN bn, 1 engr bn, 1 cbt spt bn)
EOD	6 EOD gp (bn)
SF	2 SF gp (bn); 1 SF anti-terrorist bn
Spt/Logistic	1 bde (1 Spt bn, 1 Maint bn, 1 Supply bn, 1 Tpt bn, 1 Medical bn, 1 Logistic bn)
Avn	1 bde (1 Hel bn (2 Cbt hel sqn), 1 Avn bn)
Border Guard	1 bde (Forming - to be 4 bn with 43 AMX-30 (to be delivered)) (1 SF gp)
Counter-Narcotics	1 indep bde (1 Spt bn, 3 Counter-narcotics bn)

EQUIPMENT BY TYPE

RECCE 140: 126 EE-9 *Cascavel*; 6 M-8 (anti-riot vehicle); 8 M-8 eqpt. with 1 single eqpt. with 1 TOW msl

APC 228+

  APC (T) 88: 62 TPM-113 (M-113A1); 26 TPM-113 (M-113A3)

  APC (W) 140+: 80 BTR-80; 56 EE-11 *Urutu*; M-3 *Panhard*; 4 RG-31 *Nyala*

ARTY 654

  TOWED 171: **75mm** 70 M-116 pack; **105mm** 86 M-101; **155mm** 15 155/52 APU SBT-1 (9 delivered in 2006, rest in 2007)

    MOR 483: **81mm** 125 M-1; **107mm** 148 M-2; **120mm** 210 *Brandt*

AT

  MSL• MANPATS 18 TOW (incl 8 SP)

  RCL 106mm 63 M-40A1

  RL 15+: **66mm** M-72 *LAW*; **89mm** 15 M-20; **90mm** C-90C; **106mm** SR-106

AIRCRAFT

  EW • ELINT 2 B-200 Super King Air

  TPT 9: 1 B-727; 1 CASA 212 *Aviocar* (Medevac); 1 CV-580; 1 PA-31 *Navajo* (Medevac); 3 PA-34 *Seneca*; 2 Rockwell *Turbo Commander*

  UTL 3: 1 Cessna 208 *Caravan I*; 2 Cessna 208B *Grand Caravan*

  TRG 5 *Utva-75*

HELICOPTERS

  SPT 18: 14 Mi-17-1V *Hip*; 4 M-17-V5 *Hip*

  UTL 89: 25 Bell 212; 24 UH-1H-II *Huey II*; 32 UH-1N *Twin Huey*; 33 UH-60L *Black Hawk*

TRG 7 Bell 206B
AD
  SAM • TOWED 3 *Skyguard/Sparrow*
  GUNS 39+
    SP 12.7mm 18 M-8/M-55
    TOWED 21+: **35mm** GDF Oerlikon; **40mm** 21 M-1A1
    (radar from 7 eagle eye systems)

Navy 27,605 (incl 7,000 conscript)
FORCES BY ROLE
Navy 1 HQ (Tri-Service Unified Eastern Command HQ)
    located at Puerto Carreño

EQUIPMENT BY TYPE
SUBMARINES • TACTICAL 4
  SSK 2:
    2 *Pijao* (Ge T-209/1200) each with 8 single 533mm TT
    with 14 SUT HWT
  SSI 2 *Intrepido* (It SX-506, SF delivery)
PRINCIPAL SURFACE COMBATANTS • CORVETTES
FSG 4 *Almirante Padilla* each with 2 quad (8 eff.) each with
1 MM-40 *Exocet* tactical SSM, 2 B515 *ILAS-3* triple 324mm
each with A244 LWT, 1 76mm gun, 1 BO-105 / AS-555SN
Fennec utl hel
PATROL AND COASTAL COMBATANTS 93
  PSOH 1 *Reliance*
  PFO 1 *Espartana* (Sp *Cormoran*)
  PCO 4:
    2 *Lazaga*
    2 *Pedro de Heredia* (ex-US tugs) each with 1 76mm
    gun
  PFC 1 *Quita sueno* (US Asheville) with 1 76mm gun
  PCC 2 *Toledo*
  PCI 10: 2 *Jaime Gomez*; 2 *Jose Maria Palas(Swiftships 105)*;
  2 *Castillo Y Rada (Swiftships 110)*; 4 *Point*
  PCR 74: 5 *Nodriza* (PAF-II) with B212 or B412 hel;
  (Additional 2 in build and three ordered); 3 *Arauca*; 20
  Delfin; 4 *Diligente*; 11 *Rio Magdalena*; 9 *Tenerife*; 2 *Rotork*;
  11 *Andromeda* (ex-*Pirahna)*; 9 LPR-40 (Further vessels on
  order)
AMPHIBIOUS 8:
  LCM 1 LCM-8
  LCU 7 *Morrosquillo* (LCU – 1466)
LOGISTICS AND SUPPORT 6:
  AG 2 *Luneburg* (ex-Ge, acts as depot ship for patrol
  vessels)
  AGOR 2 *Providencia*
  AGS 1
  ABU 1
FACILITIES
Bases Located at Puerto Leguízamo, Buenaventura,
    (Pacific) Málaga, (Main HQ) Catagena,
    Barrancabermeja, Puerto Carreño, Leticia, Puerto
    Orocue, Puerto Inirida

Naval Aviation 150
AIRCRAFT
  TPT 9: 3 PA-28-140 *Cherokee*; 2 PA-31 *Navajo*; 2
  Rockwell *Commander* 500; 2 CN-235-200* (MP)
  UTL 2 Cessna 206

HELICOPTERS
  ASW 2 AS-555SN *Fennec*
  UTL 6: 2 BO-105; 4 Bell 412

Marines 14,000
FORCES BY ROLE
SF   1 bn; 1 (River) gp
Marine   2 bde (*each*: 3 Marine bn); 1 (River) bde
Trg   1 bde

EQUIPMENT BY TYPE
no hy equipment
APC (W) 20 BTR-80A

Air Force 9,373
6 Combat Air Commands (CACOM) plus. CACOM 7
(former Oriental Air Group) responsible for air ops in
specific geographic area. Flts can be deployed or 'loaned'
to a different CACOM
CACOM 1. (Capitán Germán Olano Air Base) operates 6
sqn (1 sqn with 9 Kfir C-7; 1 sqn with 11 Mirage- 5COAM
(maybe only 6 op), 2 Mirage- 5CODM (used as command
post); 1 sqn with 8 AC-47T, Hughes 369; 1 sqn with 2 PA-31,
1 PA-42, UH-1H; 1 sqn with 6 T-37C) and is dedicated to air
defence and combat training.
CACOM 2. (CT. Luis F. Gómez Niño Air Base) operates 4
sqn (1 sqn with 7 OV-10; 1 sqn with 12 EMB-312 Tucano*;
1 sqn with 25 EMB-314 Super Tucano*; 1 sqn with MD500,
UH-1H) and is dedicated to anti-insurgency and offensive
operations.
CACOM 3. (Mayor General Alberto Pauwels Rodríguez
Air Base) operates 2 sqn (1 sqn with 9 A-37B/OA-37B; 1
sqn with 8 Bell 212, 2 C-95, 2 Queen Air, 4 T-41D*) and is
dedicated to SAR and MP operations along the Caribbean
Coast.
CACOM 4. (Teniente Coronel Luis Francisco Pinto Parra Air
Base) operates 5 hel sqn (1 sqn with Hughes 369; 1 sqn with
UH-1H, Hughes 369; 1 sqn with Bell 206, Hughes 369; 2
trg sqn with Bell 206, 10 Enstrom F-28F, 6 UH-1F) and is
dedicated to tactical support operations and training.
CACOM 5. (Brigadier General Arturo Lema Posada Air
Base) operates 1 gp with 10 AH-60L Arpia III*, 4 S-70A
Arpia I* and 2 UH-60 (CSAR); and is dedicated to SAR, tpt,
and heavy hel support operations.
CACOM 6. (Capitán Ernesto Esguerra Cubides Air Base)
operates 2 sqn with 5 Schweizer SA-2-337, 5 Cessna IV, 4
Fairchild C-26B, 1 Ce-208 and 1 B-300 Super King Air; and
is dedicated to anti-insurgency opearations.

FORCES BY ROLE

Ftr/FGA/ Recce	1 sqn with *Kfir* C-7; 1 sqn with *Mirage-5COAM*, *Mirage- 5CODM* (used as command post); 1 sqn with AC-47T, *Hughes* 369; 1 sqn with OV-10; 1 sqn with EMB-312 *Tucano**; 1 sqn with EMB-314 *Super Tucano*
Elint/EW	2 sqn with *Schweizer* SA-2-337, Cessna IV, Fairchild C-26B, Ce-208, B-300 *Super King Air*
SAR/ MP	1 sqn with A-37B/OA-37B; 1 sqn with Bell 212, C-95, *Queen Air*, T-41D*

Tpt	1 sqn with C-130B, C-130H; 1 sqn with CN-235M, Arava, C-212, King Air C90, Do 328; 1 (Presidential) sqn with B-727, B-707 (tkr/tpt), B-737-700 (BBJ), F-28, Bell 412
Hel	1 gp with AH-60L *Arpia* III*, S-70A *Arpia* I*, UH-60 (CSAR); 1 sqn with MD500, UH-1H; 1 sqn with Hughes 369; 1 sqn with UH-1H, Hughes 369; 1 sqn with Bell 206, Hughes 369; 2 trg sqn with Bell 206, Enstrom F-28F, UH-1F
Trg	1 (primary trg) sqn with PA-31, PA-42, UH-1H; 1 sqn with T-37C; 1 (primary trg) sqn with T-41D*; 1 sqn with T-27*; 1 sqn basic trg with T-34; 1 sqn multi-engine trg with Cessna 310R

EQUIPMENT BY TYPE

AIRCRAFT 115 combat capable

FGA 22: 9 *Kfir* C-7; 11 *Mirage*-5COAM (maybe only 6 op)); 2 *Mirage*-5CODM

CCT/TRG 67: 8 AC-47T; 9 A-37B/OA-37B *Dragonfly* (to be replaced by 25 A-29 during 2008*); 6 T-37C; 12 EMB-312 *Tucano*; 16 EMB-314 *Super Tucano*; 7 OV-10

RECCE 9: 5 Schweizer SA-2-37, 1 B-300 *Super King Air*; 3 *Aero Commander*

SURVEILLANCE 9: 5 Ce-650 *Citation* IV, 4 C-26B, **ELINT:** 1 C-208

TPT 29: 1 B-737 (BBJ); 1 B-727; 1 B-707 tkr/tpt; 4 C-130B *Hercules* (plus 3 in store); 3 C-130H *Hercules*; 1 King Air C90; 2 *Queen Air* B65; 4 C-212; 3 CN-235M; 1 Ce-208; 1 Ce-550; 2 C-95 (EMB-110P1); 1 F-28T; 1 Arava; 3 Do-328

TRG 37: 13 T-27*; 9 T-34; 13 T-41*; 2 Ce-310R (multi-engine trg)

LIAISON 23: 3 B-300 *Super King Air* (incl 2 Medevac); 1 Ce-185 Floatplane; 2 Ce-210; 2 Ce-337G/H; 1 Ce-401; 3 Ce-404; 2 PA-31 *Navajo*; 1 PA-31T *Navajo*; 1 PA-42 *Cherokee*; 4 PA-34 *Seneca*; 1 PA-44 *Seminole*; 2 *Turbo Commander* 1000

HELICOPTERS

ATK 31: 6 MD-500MD *Defender**; 4 MD530MG *Escorpion**; 7 H369HM*; 10 Sikorksy/Elbit AH-60L *Arpia* III*; 4 S-70A-41 *Arpia* II being upgraded to *Arpia* III

UTL 45: 8 Bell 212 *Rapaz*; 19 UH-1H *Iroquois*; 8 H500C; 2 H500M; 2 UH-60Q; 6 UH-1H

TPT 23: 8 UH-1P *Huey* II; 5 Bell 212 *Twin Huey*; 2 Bell 412HP/SP; 8 UH-60A *Blackhawk*; (15 UH-60L ordered)

TRG 45: 19 UH-1H *Iroquois*, 10 F.28 *Falcon* (on offer for sale), 12 Bell 206B; 2 H500C; 1 H500ME; 1 Bell 212

MSL • AAM *Python* III; R530

Paramilitary 144,097

National Police Force 136,097

AIRCRAFT

2 *King* 300; 2 *Caravan* 208; 1 *Caravan* 208B; 3 Cessna C-152; 5 Cessna 206; 2 *Twin Otter*; 1 C-99; 1 DC-3; 2 C-26SA227-AC; 1 *Turbo Truck*

HELICOPTERS

UTL 62: 10 Bell 206L *LongRanger*; 7 Bell 212; 1 Bell 412; 2 MD 500D/ MD-530F; . 12 UH-1H-II *Huey II*;

Rural Militia 8,000

NON-STATE ARMED GROUPS

see Part II

DEPLOYMENT

EGYPT

MFO 1 Inf bn; 357

FOREIGN FORCES

United States Army 72; Navy 3; USAF 7; USMC:42

Costa Rica CR

Costa **Rican** Colon C		2006	2007	2008
GDP	C	11.3tr	12.9tr	
	US$	20.1bn	22.2bn	
per capita	US$	5,437	6,048	
Growth	%	8.2	6.0	
Inflation	%	11.5	9.1	
Sy Bdgt[a]	C	50.7bn	68.7bn	
	US$	99m	132m	
US$1=C		511	518	

[a] No armed forces. Paramilitary budget

Population	4,133,884

Age	0–14	15–19	20–24	25–29	30–64	65 plus
Male	15%	5%	5%	4%	19%	3%
Female	14%	5%	5%	4%	19%	3%

Capabilities

Paramilitary 9,800

ORGANISATIONS BY SERVICE

Paramilitary 9,800

Civil Guard 4,500

Police	1 (tac) *comisaria*
Provincial	6 *comisaria*
Spec Ops	1 unit
Paramilitary	7 (Urban) *comisaria* (reinforced coy)

Border Police 2,500

Sy 2 (Border) comd (8 *comisaria*)

Coast Guard Unit 400

EQUIPMENT BY TYPE

PATROL AND COASTAL COMBATANTS 20+

PFC 1 *Isla del Coco* (US *Swift* 32m)

PCC 1 *Astronauta* (US Cape)

PCI 8: 5 less than 100 tonnes; 3 Point less than 100 tonnes

MISC BOATS/CRAFT 10: (various)

FACILITIES

Bases Located at Golfito, Punta Arenas, Cuajiniquil, Quepos, Limbe, Moin

Air Surveillance Unit 400

AIRCRAFT
TPT 10: 1 DHC-7 *Caribou*; 2 PA-31 *Navajo*; 2 Cessna T210 *Centurion*; 1 PA-34 *Seneca* ; 4 Cessna U-206G *Stationair*
HELICOPTERS
UTL 2 MD-369E

Rural Guard 2,000

Ministry of Government and Police. Small arms only
Paramilitary 8 comd

Cuba C

Cuban Convertible Peso P		2006	2007	2008
GDP	P	45.2bn		
	US$[a]	41.5bn		
per capita	US$[a]	3,646		
Growth	%	11.1		
Inflation	%	6.2		
Def exp [a]	US$	1.66bn		
US$1=P		21	21	

[a] PPP estimate

Population   11,416,987

Age	0–14	15–19	20–24	25–29	30–64	65 plus
Male	10%	4%	3%	3%	25%	5%
Female	10%	4%	3%	3%	25%	6%

Capabilities

**ACTIVE 49,000 (Army 38,000 Navy 3,000 Air 8,000)
Paramilitary 26,500**
Terms of service 2 years

RESERVE 39,000 (Army 39,000) Paramilitary 1,120,000
Ready Reserves (serve 45 days per year) to fill out Active and Resrve units; see also Paramilitary.

ORGANISATIONS BY SERVICE

Army ε38,000

FORCES BY ROLE

3 Regional comd HQ, 3 army comd HQ

Army   1 (frontier) bde; 14 (reserve) bde
Armd   up to 5 bde
Mech Inf 9 bde (*each:* 1 armd regt, 1 arty regt, 1 ADA regt, 3 Mech inf regt)
AB   1 bde

ADA   1 regt
SAM   1 bde

EQUIPMENT BY TYPE†
MBT ε900 T-34/T-54/T-55/T-62
LT TK PT-76
RECCE BRDM-1/BRDM-2
AIFV ε 50 BMP-1
APC • APC (W) ε500 BTR-152/BTR-40/BTR-50/BTR-60
ARTY 2,030+
  SP 40 2S1 *Carnation* **122mm**/2S3 **152mm**
  TOWED 500 **152mm** D-1 /**122mm** D-30 /**152mm** M-1937/ **122mm** M-30 /**130mm** M-46/ **76mm** ZIS-3 *M-1942*
  MRL SP 175 **140mm** BM-14/**122mm** BM-21
  MOR 1,000 **120mm** M-38 /**82mm** M-41/**120mm** M-43/**82mm** M-43
  STATIC 315: **122mm** 15 JS-2M (hy tk); **85mm** 300 T-34
AT
  MSL • MANPATS AT-1 *Snapper*; AT-3 9K11 *Sagger*
  GUNS 700+: **100mm** 100 SU-100 SP; **85mm** D-44; **57mm** 600 M-1943
AD
  SAM 200 SA-13 *Gopher* SP/SA-14 *Gremlin*; SA-16 *Gimlet* MANPAD/SA-6 *Gainful* SP/SA-7 *Grail* MANPAD/SA-8 *Gecko* SP/SA-9 *Gaskin* SP (300–1800 eff.)
  GUNS 400
    SP 57mm ZSU-57-2 SP/ **23mm** ZSU-23-4 SP/ **30mm** BTR-60P SP
    TOWED 100mm KS-19/M-1939 /**85mm** KS-12/**57mm** S-60 /**37mm** M-1939/**30mm** M-53/**23mm** ZU-23

Navy ε3,000

FORCES BY ROLE

Navy 1 (HQ Western Comd) located at Cabanas; 1 (HQ Eastern Comd) located at Holquin

EQUIPMENT BY TYPE
PATROL AND COASTAL COMBATANTS 7
  PFM 6 *Osa* II† (FSU) each with 4 single each with SS-N-2B *Styx* tactical SSM (missiles removed to coastal defence units)
  PFC 1 *Pauk* II† (FSU) with 1 x4 Manual with SA-N-5 *Grail* SAM, 4 single ASTT, 2 RBU 1200 (10 eff.), 1 76mm gun
MINE WARFARE AND MINE COUNTERMEASURES 5
  MSC 2 *Sonya*† (FSU)
  MHC 3 *Yevgenya*† (FSU)
LOGISTICS AND SUPPORT 1 **ABU**; 1 **TRG**
FACILITIES

Bases Located at Cabanas, Havana, Cienfuegos, Holquin, Nicaro, Punta Movida, Mariel

Coastal Defence

ARTY • TOWED 122mm M-1931/37; **130mm** M-46; **152mm** M-1937
MSL• SSM 2+: Bandera IV (reported); 2 SS-C-3 *Styx*

Naval Infantry 550+

Amph aslt 2 bn

Anti-aircraft Defence and Revolutionary Air Force ε8,000 (incl conscripts)

Air assets divided between Western Air Zone and Eastern Air Zone

Flying hours   50 hrs/year

FORCES BY ROLE

Ftr/ FGA 3 sqn with 2 MiG-29A *Fulcrum*, 1 MiG-29UB, 16 MiG-23ML *Flogger*/ 4 MiG-23MF,/4 MiG-23UM, 4 MiG-21ML

Tpt   1 Exec Tpt sqn with 3 Yak-40 (VIP), 3 An-24, 2 Mi-8P

Hel   2 cbt hel sqn with 8 Mi-17, 4 Mi-35

Trg   2 tact trg sqns with 5 Zlin Z-142 (primary), 7 L-39C (basic), 7+ MiG-21UM*r*

EQUIPMENT BY TYPE

AIRCRAFT 31 combat capable (179 stored)
 FTR/FGA 31: 2 MiG-29 *Fulcrum*; 1 MiG-29UB; 16 MiG-23 ML *Flogger*; 4 MiG-23MF; 4 MiG-23UM; 4 MiG-21ML; (in store: 2 MiG-29; 20 MiG-23BN; 4 MiG-23MF; 6 MiG-23ML; 2 MiG-23UM; 70 MiG-21bis; 28 MiG-21PFM; 30 MiG-21F; 7 MiG-21UM; 4+ MiG-17; 6 MiG-15UTI)
 TPT 12: 3 Yak-40; 3 An-24; 2 Il-76; 2 An-32; 1 An-30; 1 An-2; (in store: 18 An-26 *Curl*; 8 An-2 *Colt*)
HELICOPTERS
 ATK 4 Mi-35 *Hind*
 SPT 10: 2 Mi-8P *Hip*; 8 Mi-17;(in store: 8 Mi-35; 12 Mi-17; 5 Mi-14)
 TRG 59: 25 L-39 *Albatros*; 8 MiG-21U *Mongol A**; 4 MiG-23U *Flogger**; 2 MiG-29UB *Fulcrum**; 20 Z-326 *Trener Master*
AD • SAM SA-3 *Goa*; SA-2 *Guideline* towed
MSL
 ASM AS-7 *Kerry*
 AAM AA-10 *Alamo*; AA-11 *Archer*; AA-2 *Atoll*; AA-7 *Apex*; AA-8 *Aphid*

FACILITIES

Surface To Air   13 with SA-3 *Goa* SAM; SA-2 *Guideline*
Missile Site   Towed SAM (active)

Paramilitary 26,500 active

State Security 20,000
Ministry of Interior

Border Guards 6,500
Ministry of Interior
PATROL AND COASTAL COMBATANTS 20
 PFI 20: 2 *Stenka* less than 100 tonnes (FSU); 18 *Zhuk*

Youth Labour Army 70,000 reservists

Civil Defence Force 50,000 reservists

Territorial Militia ε1,000,000 reservists

FOREIGN FORCES

United States Army: 311; USMC: 136 (located at Guantanamo); USN 456 (located at Guantanamo)

Dominican Republic DR

Dominican Peso pRD		2006	2007	2008
GDP	pRD	1.24tr	1.43tr	
	US$	37.1bn	42.8bn	
per capita	US$	4,019	4,567	
Growth	%	10.7	8.0	
Inflation	%	11.5	9.1	
Def bdgt	pRD	8.6bn	ε9.0bn	
	US$	256m	**268m**	
US$1=pRD		33.6	33.5	
Population	9,365,818			

Age	0–14	15–19	20–24	25–29	30–64	65 plus
Male	17%	5%	5%	4%	18%	3%
Female	16%	5%	4%	4%	17%	3%

Capabilities

ACTIVE 49,910 (Army 40,410 Navy 4,000 Air 5,500)
Paramilitary 15,000

ORGANISATIONS BY SERVICE

Army 15,000
FORCES BY ROLE
5 Defence Zones

Armd   1 bde

Air Cav   1 bde (1 cdo bn, 1 (6th) mtn regt, 1 sqn with 9 OH-58 *Kiowa*; 12 UH-1H *Iroquois*; 4 R-22; 2 R-44 *Raven II*)

Inf   6 bde: 1st and 3rd (*each*: 3 inf bn); 2nd (4 inf bn, 1 Mtn inf bn); 4th and 5th (*each*: 2 bn); 6th (1 inf bn) (*total*: 16 inf bn)

SF   3 bn

Arty   2 bn

Engr   1 bn

Presidential Guard   1 regt

EQUIPMENT BY TYPE
LT TK 9 M-41B (76mm)
APC (W) 8 LAV-150 *Commando*
ARTY 104
 TOWED 105mm 16: 4 M-101; 12 Reinosa 105/26
 MOR 88: **81mm** 60 M-1; **107mm** 4 M-30; **120mm** 24 Expal Model L
AT
 RCL 106mm 20 M-40A1
 GUNS 37mm 20 M3
HEL
 OBS 9: 5 OH-58A *Kiowa*; 5 OH-58C *Kiowa*
 UTL 6: 4 R-22; 2 R-44

Navy 4,000
FORCES BY ROLE
Marine Sy   1 unit

Navy 1 HQ located at Santo Domingo
SEAL 1 unit

EQUIPMENT BY TYPE
PATROL AND COASTAL COMBATANTS 16
PCO 4:
  2 *Balsam*
  2 *Tortuguero* (Ex US ABU)
  PCI 8: 2 *Canopus*; 2 *Swift* (35mm); 4 *Bellatrix* (US Seawart Seacraft) All less than 100 tonnes
  PBR 4 *Damen Stan 1505*
AMPHIBIOUS 1 *Neyba* (Ex US LCU 1675)
LOGISTICS AND SUPPORT 5:
  AG 2 *Draga Contencion*
  AT 3

FACILITIES
Bases Located at Santo Domingo, Las Calderas

Naval Aviation Unit
HELICOPTERS
  SAR / UTL 2 Bell 206A-1 (CH 136)

Air Force 5,500

Flying hours 60 hrs/year

FORCES BY ROLE

SAR/Medivac/ Hel/Liaison	1 sqn with 2 Bell 430 (VIP); 8 Huey II; 12 UH-1H; 3 Schweizer 333; 9 CH-136 Kiowa
Tpt	1 sqn with 3 CASA 212-400 *Aviocar*; 1 Ce-206; 1 PA-31 *Navajo*
Trg	1 sqn with 6 T-35B *Pillan*
AD	1 bn with 4 20mm

EQUIPMENT BY TYPE
AIRCRAFT
TPT/MP 5: 3 CASA 212-400 *Aviocar*; 1 PA-31 *Navajo*; 1 Ce-206
TRG 6 T-35B *Pillan*
HELICOPTERS
UTL 34: 2 Bell 430 (VIP); 9 CH-136 *Kiowa*; 3 Schweizer 333; 8 Huey II; 12 UH-1H
AD • GUNS 20mm 4

Paramilitary 15,000

National Police 15,000

DEPLOYMENT

CÔTE D'IVOIRE
UN • UNOCI 4 obs

Ecuador Ec

Ecuadorian Sucre ES		2006	2007	2008
GDP	ES	882tr	1,075tr	
	US$	35.3bn	43.0bn	
per capita	US$	2,604	3,126	
Growth	%	3.9	2.7	
Inflation	%	3.3	2.1	
Def bdgt	ES	16.3tr	22.9tr	
	US$	653m	918m	
US$1=ES		25,000	25,000	

Population 13,755,680

Age	0–14	15–19	20–24	25–29	30–64	65 plus
Male	17%	5%	5%	4%	16%	2%
Female	16%	5%	5%	4%	17%	3%

Capabilities

ACTIVE 57,100 (Army 47,000 Navy 6,100 Air 4,000)
Paramilitary 400
Terms of Service conscription 1 year, selective

RESERVE 118,000 (Joint 118,000)
Ages 18–55

ORGANISATIONS BY SERVICE

Army 47,000
FORCES BY ROLE

Army	4 div (org, composition varies) (total: 1 Armd bde, 1 SF bde, 1 Arty bde, 1 Engr bde, 1 Avn bde, 3 Jungle bde, 5 Inf bde); 3 (hy mor) coy
Armd cav	1 bde
Armd Recce	3 sqn
Mech Inf	2 bn
Inf	13 bn; 10 (jungle) bn
AB/SF	6 bn
Arty	1 bde
SP Arty	1 gp
MRL	1 gp
ADA	1 gp
Engr	3 bn
Avn	5 bn

EQUIPMENT BY TYPE
LT TK 24 AMX-13
RECCE 67: 25 AML-90; 10 EE-3 *Jararaca*; 32 EE-9 *Cascavel*;
APC 123
  APC (T) 95: 80 AMX-VCI; 15 M-113
  APC (W) 28: 18 EE-11 *Urutu*; 10 UR-416
ARTY 517+
  SP 155mm 5 (AMX) Mk F3
  TOWED 100: **105mm** 78: 30 M-101; 24 M-2A2; 24 Model 56 pack howitzer; **155mm** 22: 12 M-114; 10 M-198
  MOR 412+: **81mm** 400 M-29; **107mm** M-30 (4.2in); **160mm** 12 M-66 *Soltam*

AT
RCL 404: **106mm** 24 M-40A1; **90mm** 380 M-67
AIRCRAFT
TPT 13: 1 Beech 100 *King Air*; 1 Beech 200 *Super King Air*;
2 CASA 212; 2 CN-235; 1 Cessna 500 *Citation I*; 1 DHC-5D
Buffalo; 4 IAI-201 *Arava*; 1 PC-6 *Turbo-Porter*
TRG 5: 3 MX-7-235 *Star Rocket*; 2 CJ-6
HELICOPTERS
ATK 18 SA-342 *Gazelle* (13 w/ HOT)
SPT 13: 2 AS-332B *Super Puma*; 3 AS-350 *Ecureuil*; 5 Mi-17-1V *Hip*; 3 SA-330 *Puma* (in store)
UTL 2 SA-315B *Lama*
AD
SAM • MANPAD 203+: 75 *Blowpipe*; 18 *Chaparral*; 20+
SA-7 *Grail*; 90 SA18 *Grouse (Igla)*
GUNS 240
  SP 44 M-163 *Vulcan*
  TOWED 196: **14.5mm** 128 ZPU-1/-2; **20mm** 38: 28 M-1935, 10 M-167 *Vulcan*; **40mm** 30 L/70/M1A1

Navy 6,100 (including Naval Aviation and Marines)

EQUIPMENT BY TYPE
SUBMARINES • TACTICAL • SSK 2:
2 *Shyri*† (Ge T-209/1300) each with 8 single 533mm TT with 14 SUT HWT
PRINCIPAL SURFACE COMBATANTS 8
FRIGATES • FFG 2:
2 *Presidente Eloy Alfaro*† (ex-UK *Leander* batch II) each with 4 single each with MM-40 *Exocet* tactical SSM, 3 twin (6 eff.) each with Mistral SAM, with 1 Bell 206B *JetRanger II* utl hel
CORVETTES • FSG 6:
6 *Esmeraldas* (4†) each with 2 triple (6 eff.) each with MM-40 *Exocet* tactical SSM, 1 quad (4 eff.) with Aspide SAM, 2 B515 *ILAS-3* triple 324mm each with A244 LWT, 1 76mm gun, 1 hel Landing Platform (upgrade programme ongoing)
PATROL AND COASTAL COMBATANTS 13
PFM 3 *Quito* (Ge Lurssen TNC-45 45m) each with 4 single each with 1 MM-38 *Exocet* tactical SSM, 1 76mm gun (upgrade programme ongoing)
PCC 2 *Espada*
PBR 8 under 100 tonnes
AMPHIBIOUS • LS • LST 1:
1 *Hualcopo* (capacity 150 troops) (US LST-512-1152)
LOGISTICS AND SUPPORT 7:
AOL 1
AG 1
AWT 2
AGOS 1 *Orion*
ATF 1
TRG •AXS 1
FACILITIES
Bases   Located at Guayaquil (main base),
               Galápagos Islands
Naval airbase Jaramijo

Naval Aviation 375

AIRCRAFT
MP 4: 2 CN-235MP (ISD 2007); 2 Beech 200T *Maritime Patrol*

TPT 2: 1 Beech 200 *Super King Air*; 1 Beech 300 *Super King Air*;
TRG 6: 4 T-35C; 2 T-34C *Turbo Mentor*
HELICOPTERS
UTL 6 Bell 206

Marines 1,500

Cdo   1 bn (no hy wpn/veh)
Marine 2 bn (on garrison duties)

Air Force 4,000

Operational Command

FORCES BY ROLE
Air	2 wg
Ftr	1 sqn with 12 *Mirage* F-1JE (F-1E); 1 *Mirage* F-1JB (F-1B)
FGA	3 sqn (1 with 20+ A-37B *Dragonfly*; 1 sqn with 7 Kfir CE; 3 Kfir C-2; 2 *Kfir* TC-2; 1 sqn with 4 BAC-167 *Strikemaster*)
CCT	1 sqn with 5 A-37B; 2 BAC-167 *Strikemaster*

Military Air Transport Group

FORCES BY ROLE
SAR/Liaison	1 sqn with 8 Bell 206B *JetRanger II*; 4 SA-316B/SA-319 *Alouette III*
Tpt	4 sqn with 3 B-727; 4 C-130B *Hercules*, 1 C-130H *Hercules*; 3 DHC-6 *Twin Otter*; 1 F-28 *Fellowship*; 2 Sabreliner 40/60
Liaison	1 Beech E90 *King Air*; 1 *Gaviao* 60; 6 HS-748
TAME	1 mil controlled airline with 2 Airbus A-320; 2 EMB-170; 1 EMB-190
Trg	units with 16 Cessna 150; 15 T-34C *Turbo Mentor*; 5 T-41 *Mescalero*; 1 MXP-650

EQUIPMENT BY TYPE
AIRCRAFT 57+ combat capable
FTR 13: 12 *Mirage* F-1JE; 1 F-1BJ
FGA 44+: 25+ A-37B *Dragonfly*; 7 *Kfir* CE, 4 C.2, 2 TC.2;
6 BAC-167 *Strikemaster*;
TPT 26: 2 A320; 6 HS-748; 3 B-727; 1 Beech E-90 *King Air*; 4 C-130B; 1 C-130H; 2 EMB-170; 1 EMB-190; 3 DHC-6 *Twin Otter*; 1 F-28 *Fellowship*; 2 *Sabreliner* 40/60
TRG 37: 16 Ce-150; 15 T-34C; 1 MXP-650; 5 T-41
HEL 13: 4 SA-316B *Alouette III* / SA-319 *Alouette III* Utl Hel;
8 Bell 206B *JetRanger II*; 1 HB-315B *Gaviao*
MSL •AAM 60 *Python* III; 50 *Python* IV; R-550 *Magic*;
Super 530; *Shafrir*
AD
SAM 7 M-48 *Chaparral*
  SP 6 SA-8 *Gecko*
  MANPAD 185+: 75 *Blowpipe*; SA-7; 20 *Igla*-1 (SA-16) *Gimlet*; 90 SA-18 *Grouse*
GUNS
  SP 28 M-35 with **20mm**
  TOWED 82: **23mm** 34: 34 ZU-23; **35mm** 30: 30 GDF-002 (twin); **37mm** 18: 18 Ch

Paramilitary

Police Air Service
2 B206B *Jet Ranger*, 1 R-22; 1 AS-350B *Ecureuil*

Coast Guard 400
PATROL AND COASTAL COMBATANTS 17+
PCC 9: 2 *Manta* (Ge Lurssen 36m), 3 *Vigilante*
(Protector), 4 *10 de Agosto*
PCI 8: 1 PGM-71; 1 Point; 6 Rio Puyango,
PBR 2 Río Esmeraldas; 4 Piraña
MISC BOATS/CRAFT 8

DEPLOYMENT

CÔTE D'IVOIRE
UN • UNOCI 2 obs

HAITI
UN • MINUSTAH 67

LIBERIA
UN • UNMIL 1; 3 obs

UNMIN
UN • UNMIN 1 obs

SUDAN
UN • UNMIS 20obs

FOREIGN FORCES

United States Army 14; Navy 2; USAF 19; USMC 6

El Salvador EIS

El Salvador Colon C		2006	2007	2008
GDP	C	162bn	175bn	
	US$	18bn	20bn	
per capita	US$	2,714	2,882	
Growth	%	4.2	4.2	
Inflation	%	4.6	4.4	
Def bdgt	C	931m	974m	
	US$	106m	111m	
FMA	US$	9.9m	5.5m	4.8m
US$1=C		8.75	8.75	

Population	6,939,688

Age	0–14	15–19	20–24	25–29	30–64	65 plus
Male	19%	5%	5%	4%	14%	2%
Female	18%	5%	5%	4%	16%	3%

Capabilities

ACTIVE 15,660 (Army 13,850 Navy 860 Air 950)
Paramilitary 12,000
Terms of Service conscription 18 months voluntary

RESERVE 9,900 (Joint 9,900; Registered)

ORGANISATIONS BY SERVICE

Army 9,850; 4,000 conscript (total 13,850)
FORCES BY ROLE
6 Military Zones

Army	1 (special sy) bde (2 Border Guard bn, 2 MP bn)
Armd cav	1 regt (2 armd cav bn)
Inf	5 bde (*each:* 3 inf bn)
Spec Ops	1 gp (1 SF coy, 1 Para bn, 1 (naval inf) army coy)
Arty	1 bde (1 AD bn, 2 fd arty bn)
Engr	1 comd (2 engr bn)

EQUIPMENT BY TYPE
RECCE 9 AML-90; 2 in store
APC (W) 43: 30-35 M-37B1 *Cashuat* (mod); 8 UR-416
ARTY 523+
    TOWED 105mm 54: 36 M-102; 18 M-56
    MOR 469+: **60mm** 306 M-19; **81mm** 151 M-29; **120mm**
    12+: M-74 in store; 12 UBM 52
AT
    RCL 399: **106mm** 20 M-40A1 (incl 16 SP); **90mm** 379 M-67
    RL 94mm 791 LAW
AD
    GUNS 22: **20mm** 18 M-55; 4 TCM-20

Navy 860 (incl some 160 Naval Inf and SF)
EQUIPMENT BY TYPE
PATROL AND COASTAL COMBATANTS 39
    PCC 3 *Camcraft* (30m)
    PCI 3 less than 100 tonnes
    MISC BOATS/CRAFT 33 *River Boats*
AMPHIBIOUS
    LCM 3

FACILITIES
Bases	Located at La Unión
Minor Bases	Located at La Libertad, Acajutla, El Triunfo, Guija Lake

Naval Infantry 160
Sy 1 coy

Naval SF(Commandos) 90
SF 1 coy

Air Force ε750; ε200 conscript (total 950)
Flying hours   90 hrs/year on A-37 *Dragonfly* FGA ac

FORCES BY ROLE
incl AD

FGA/ RECCE	sqn with 9 A-37B *Dragonfly*; 5-6 O-2A *Skymaster* 1 CM-170 *Magister*
Tpt	1 sqn with 1 Bell 407; 4 Bell 412 *Twin Huey*; 7 MD-500; 12 UH-1H *Iroquois* (incl 4 SAR); 1+ sqn with 3 Basler Turbo-67; ; 1 SA-226T *Merlin IIIB*; 2 Cessna 210 *Centurion*
Trg	sqn with 5 *Rallye* 235GT; 5 T-35 *Pillan*; 1 T-41D *Mescalero*; 6 TH-300
Hel	Armed sqn with 3 UH-1M *Iroquois*

EQUIPMENT BY TYPE
AIRCRAFT 14-15 combat capable
  FGA 9 A-37B *Dragonfly*
  RECCE 5-6: **5-6** O-2A *Skymaster**
  TPT 4 : 3 Basler Turbo-67; 1 SA-226T *Merlin IIIB*
  UTL 2 Cessna 210 *Centurion*
  TRG 12: 5 *Rallye* 235GT; 5 T-35 *Pillan*; 1 T-41D *Mescalero*;
  1 CM-170 *Magister* in store
HELICOPTERS
  UTL 27 : 1 Bell 407; 4 Bell 412 *Twin Huey*; 7 MD-500; 12
  UH-1H *Iroquois* (incl 4 SAR); 3 UH-1M *Iroquois* *
  TRG 6 TH-300
MSL • AAM *Shafrir*

Paramilitary 12,000

National Civilian Police 12,000+
Ministry of Public Security
PATROL AND COASTAL COMBATANTS •PBR 10
River Boats
AIRCRAFT • RECCE 1: 1 O-2A *Skymaster*
HELICOPTERS • UTL 3: 1 MD-500D; 1 MD-520N; 1
UH-1H *Iroquois*

DEPLOYMENT

CÔTE D'IVOIRE
UN • UNOCI 3 obs

IRAQ
MNF • *Operation Iraqi Freedom* 380

LIBERIA
UN • UNMIL 3 obs

SUDAN
UN • UNMIS 5 obs

WESTERN SAHARA
UN • MINURSO 6 obs

FOREIGN FORCES

United States: Army 7; Navy 1; USMC 13; 3 P-3C Orion at
Comalapa FOL

Guatemala Gua

Guatemalan Quetzal q		2006	2007	2008
GDP	q	276bn	320bn	
	US$	36.4bn	41.3bn	
per capita	US$	2,920	3.248	
Growth	%	4.9	4.8	
Inflation	%	6.6	6.2	
Def bdgt	q	1.1bn	1.2bn	
	US$	146m	164m	
US$1=q		7.59	7.74	

Population	12,728,111

Age	0–14	15–19	20–24	25–29	30–64	65 plus
Male	21%	6%	5%	4%	13%	2%
Female	20%	6%	5%	4%	14%	2%

Capabilities

ACTIVE 15,500 (Army 13,444 Navy 986 Air 1,070)
Paramilitary 19,000

RESERVE 63,863 (Navy 650 Air 900 Armed Forces
62,313)

(National Armed Forces are combined; the army provides
log spt for navy and air force)

ORGANISATIONS BY SERVICE

Army 13,444
The cavalry regts have a strength of 118, 7 AFV. The arty gp
is 3 bty of 4 guns.

FORCES BY ROLE
15 Military Zones

Armd	6 sqn
Cav	2 regt
Inf	1 (strategic) bde (2 Inf bn, 1 SF pl, 1 recce sqn, 1 (lt) armd bn, 1 arty gp); 5 (regional) bde (*each:* 3 Inf bn, 1 cav regt, 1 arty gp,); 1 (frontier) det
SF	1 bde (1 trg coy, 1 SF coy)
AB	2 bn
Engr	1 bn
MP	1 bde (3 bn)
Trg	1 bn

EQUIPMENT BY TYPE
RECCE 16: 7 M-8 in store; 9 RBY-1 *RAMTA*
APC 52
  APC (T) 15: 10 M-113; 5 in store
  APC (W) 37: 30 *Armadillo*; 7 V-100 *Commando*
ARTY 161
  TOWED 105mm 76: 12 M-101; 8 M-102; 56 M-56
  MOR 85: 81mm 55 M-1; **107mm** 12 M-30 in store;
  120mm 18 ECIA
AT
  RCL 120+: 105mm 64 M-1974 FMK-1 (Arg); **106mm** 56
  M-40A1; **75mm** M-20
  RL 89mm M-20 in store (3.5in)
AD• GUNS • TOWED 32: **20mm** 16 GAI-D01; 16 M-55

Reserves
Inf ε19 bn

Navy 986
EQUIPMENT BY TYPE
PATROL AND COASTAL COMBATANTS 36:
  PCI 10: 6 *Cutlass* less than 100 tonnes; 1 *Kukulkan* less
  than 100 tonnes (US *Broadsword* 32m); 2 *Sewart* less than
  100 tonnes; 1 *Dauntless* less than 100 tonnes
  PCR 20
  PBI 6 *Vigilante*
FACILITIES
Bases Located at Santo Tomás de Castilla, Puerto Quetzal

Marines 650 reservists

Marine 2 bn under strength

Air Force 1,070)

3 air bases – Guatemala City, Santa Elena Petén, Retalhuleu

FORCES BY ROLE

Serviceability of ac is less than 50%

FGA/Trg	1 sqn with 4 A-37B *Dragonfly*; 1 sqn with 6 PC-7 *Turbo Trainer*
Tpt	1 sqn with 4 Basler Turbo-67; 1 Beech 100 *King Air*; 1 Beech 90 *King Air*; 2 F-27 *Friendship*; 4 IAI-201 *Arava*; 1 PA-31 *Navajo*
Liaison	1 sqn with 1 Cessna 310; 2 Cessna 206
Trg	some sqn with 5 Cessna R172K *Hawk XP*; 4 T-35B *Pillan*
Hel	1 sqn with 9 Bell 206 *JetRanger*; 7 Bell 212 (armed); 1 Bell 412 *Twin Huey* (armed); 3 UH-1H *Iroquois*

EQUIPMENT BY TYPE

AIRCRAFT 10 combat capable

FGA 4 A-37B *Dragonfly*

TPT 14: 4 Basler Turbo-67; 1 Beech 100 *King Air*; 1 Beech 90 *King Air*; 1 Cessna 310; 2 F-27 *Friendship*; 4 IAI-201 *Arava*; 1 PA-31 *Navajo*

UTL 2 Cessna 206

TRG 15: 5 Cessna R172K *Hawk XP*; 6 PC-7 *Turbo Trainer**; 4 T-35B *Pillan*

HELICOPTERS

UTL 20: 9 Bell 206 *JetRanger*; 7 Bell 212 (armed); 1 Bell 412 *Twin Huey* (armed); 3 UH-1H *Iroquois*

Tactical Security Group

Air Military Police

Armd	1 sqn
CCT	3 coy
AD	1 bty (army units for air-base sy)

Paramilitary 19,000 active (incl. Treasury Police)

National Police 19,000

Army	1 (integrated task force) unit (incl mil and treasury police)
SF	1 bn
Paramilitary	21 (departments) region

Treasury Police 2,500

DEPLOYMENT

CÔTE D'IVOIRE

UN • UNOCI 5 obs

DEMOCRATIC REPUBLIC OF CONGO

UN • MONUC 105; 6 obs

ETHIOPIA/ERITREA

UN • UNMEE 4 obs

HAITI

UN • MINUSTAH 119

LEBANON

UN • UNIFIL 2

NEPAL

UN • UNMIN 2 obs

SUDAN

UN • UNMIS 1; 8 obs

Guyana Guy

Guyanese Dollar G$		2006	2007	2008
GDP	G$	180bn	192bn	
	US$	0.9bn	0.9bn	
per capita	US$	1,173	1,160	
Growth	%	5.1	5.6	
Inflation	%	6.7	9.6	
US$1=G$		200	204	

Population	769,095

Age	0–14	15–19	20–24	25–29	30–64	65 plus
Male	13%	5%	5%	5%	19%	2%
Female	13%	5%	5%	5%	20%	3%

Capabilities

ACTIVE 1,100 (Army 900 Navy 100 Air 100)
Paramilitary 1,500
Active numbers combined Guyana Defence Force

RESERVE 670 (Army 500 Navy 170)

ORGANISATIONS BY SERVICE

Army 900

FORCES BY ROLE

Inf	1 bn
SF	1 coy
Engr	1 coy
Spt	1 (spt wpn) coy
Presidential Guard	1 bn

EQUIPMENT BY TYPE

RECCE 9: 6 EE-9 *Cascavel* (reported); 3 S52 *Shorland*
ARTY 54
    TOWED 130mm 6 M-46†
    MOR 48: **81mm** 12 L16A1; **82mm** 18 M-43; **120mm** 18 M-43

Navy 100

EQUIPMENT BY TYPE

PATROL AND COASTAL COMBATANTS 5

PCC 1 *Orwell* (ex-UK)
MISC BOATS/CRAFT 4 boats

FACILITIES

Bases   Located at Georgetown, New Providence Island

Air Force 100

FORCES BY ROLE

Tpt   unit with ; 1 Y-12 1 Bell 412 *Twin Huey* ; 1 Rotorway 162F

EQUIPMENT BY TYPE
AIRCRAFT
  TPT 1 Y-12
HELICOPTERS
  UTL 2: 1 Bell 412 *Twin Huey;* 1 Rotorway 162F

Paramilitary 1,500+

Guyana People's Militia 1,500+

DEPLOYMENT

Navy Base located at New Providence Island, Bs

Haiti RH

Haitian Gourde G		2006	2007	2008
GDP	G	200bn	226bn	
	US$	5.1bn	6.4bn	
per capita	US$	583	733	
Growth	%	2.2	3.2	
Inflation	%	14.2	9.0	
US$1=G		40.4	35.4	

Population   8,706,497

Age	0–14	15–19	20–24	25–29	30–64	65 plus
Male	21%	6%	5%	4%	11%	2%
Female	21%	6%	5%	4%	12%	2%

Capabilities

No active armed forces. On June 1st 2004 following a period of armed conflict the United Nations established a multi national stabilisation mission in Haiti (MINUSTAH). The mission has an authorised strength of up to 6,700 military personnel and 1,622 civilian police. A National Police Force of some 2,000 pers remains operational.

FOREIGN FORCES

Argentina 562
Bolivia 217
Brazil 1,212
Canada 4 *(Operation Hamlet)*
Chile 503

Croatia 3
Ecuador 67
France 2
Guatemala 119
Jordan 755
Morocco 1
Nepal 1,109
Pakistan 1
Paraguay 31
Peru 210
Philippines 157
Sri Lanka 960
United States 3; non-UN: Army 5; USMC 7
Uruguay 1,146

Honduras Hr

Honduran Lempira L		2006	2007	2008
GDP	L	175bn	195bn	
	US$	9.3bn	10.4bn	
per capita	US$	1,271	1,191	
Growth	%	6.0	5.4	
Inflation	%	5.6.	6.9	
Def bdgt	L	1.0bn	1.4bn	
	US$	55m	76m	
US$1=L		18.8	18.8	

Population   8,706,497

Age	0–14	15–19	20–24	25–29	30–64	65 plus
Male	21%	6%	5%	4%	13%	2%
Female	20%	6%	5%	4%	14%	2%

Capabilities

ACTIVE 12,000 (Army 8,300 Navy 1,400 Air 2,300)
Paramilitary 8,000

RESERVE 60,000 (Joint 60,000; Ex-servicemen registered)

ORGANISATIONS BY SERVICE

Army 8,300
FORCES BY ROLE
6 Military Zones
Armd cav   1 regt (1 Lt tk sqn, 1 ADA bty, 1 arty bty, 1 Recce sqn, 2 Mech bn)
Inf   1 bde (3 inf bn); 3 bde (*each:* 1 arty bn, 3 inf bn)
Spec Ops   1 (special tac) gp (1 SF bn, 1 Inf/AB bn)
Engr   1 bn
Presidential Guard   1 coy

EQUIPMENT BY TYPE
LT TK 12 *Scorpion*
RECCE 57: 13 RBY-1 *RAMTA*; 40 *Saladin*; 3 *Scimitar*; 1 *Sultan*

ARTY 118+
　TOWED 28: **105mm:** 24 M-102; **155mm:** 4 M-198
MOR 90+: **60mm**; **81mm**; **120mm** 60 FMK-2; **160mm** 30
M-66 *Soltam*
AT • RCL 170: **106mm** 50 M-40A1; **84mm** 120 *Carl Gustav*
AD • GUNS 48: **20mm** 24 M-55A2; 24 TCM-20

Reserves
Inf 1 bde

Navy 1,400
EQUIPMENT BY TYPE
PATROL AND COASTAL COMBATANTS 31
　PFC 3 *Guaymuras* (*Swift* 31m)
　PFI 1 *Copan* less than 100 tonnes (US *Guardian* 32m)
　PC 7: 6 *Swift* 21m; 1 *Swift* 26m
　PBR 5 less than 100 tonnes
　MISC BOATS/CRAFT 15 river boats
AMPHIBIOUS • LCU 1 *Punta Caxinas*
FACILITIES
Bases Located at Puerto Cortés, Puerto Castilla, Amapala

Marines 830
Marine 3 indep coy

Air Force 2,300
FORCES BY ROLE

FGA	1 sqn with 8 A-37B *Dragonfly*; 1 sqn with 8 F-5E *Tiger II*
Tpt	sqn with 1 C-130A *Hercules*; 2 C-47 *Skytrain*
Trg/COIN	some sqn with 2 Cessna 182 *Skylane*; 5 T-41B/D; 9 EMB-312
Liaison	some sqn with 4 Cessna 185; 1 Cessna 401; 1 PA-31 *Navajo*; 1 PA-32T *Saratoga*
Hel	2 sqn with 5 Bell 412SP *Twin Huey*; 2 Hughes 500; 2 UH-1H *Iroquois*

EQUIPMENT BY TYPE
AIRCRAFT 16 combat capable
　FTR 8 F-5E *Tiger II*
　FGA 8 A-37B *Dragonfly*
　TPT 12: 1 C-130A *Hercules*; 2 C-47 *Skytrain*; 2 Cessna 182 *Skylane*; 4 Cessna 185; 1 Cessna 401; 1 PA-31 *Navajo*; 1 PA-32T *Saratoga*
　TRG 14: 5 T-41B/D; 9 EMB-312
HELICOPTERS
　UTL 9: 5 Bell 412SP *Twin Huey*; 2 Hughes 500; 2 UH-1H *Iroquois*
MSL • AAM *Shafrir*

Paramilitary 8,000

Public Security Forces 8,000
Ministry of Public Security and Defence
Region　11 comd

DEPLOYMENT

WESTERN SAHARA
UN • MINURSO 12 obs

FOREIGN FORCES
United States Army: 194; Navy: 2; USAF: 208; USMC: 8

Jamaica Ja

Jamaican Dollar J$		2006	2007	2008
GDP	J$	673bn	737bn	
	US$	10.2bn	10.4bn	
per capita	US$	3,714	3,734	
Growth	%	2.5	1.4	
Inflation	%	8.6	6.6	
Def bdgt	J$	3.7bn	7.5bn	
	US$	57m	105m	
US$1=J$		65.7	71.0	

Population　2,780,132

Age	0–14	15–19	20–24	25–29	30–64	65 plus
Male	17%	5%	5%	4%	15%	3%
Female	17%	5%	5%	4%	15%	4%

Capabilities

ACTIVE 2,830 (Army 2,500 Coast Guard 190 Air 140)
(combined Jamaican Defence Force)

RESERVE 953 (Army 877 Navy 60 Air 16)

ORGANISATIONS BY SERVICE

Army 2,500
FORCES BY ROLE
Inf　2 bn
Engr 1 regt (4 engr sqn)
Spt　1 bn

EQUIPMENT BY TYPE
APC (W) 4 LAV-150 *Commando*
MOR 81mm 12 L16A1

Reserves
Inf 1 bn

Coast Guard 190
EQUIPMENT BY TYPE
PATROL AND COASTAL COMBATANTS 14
　PFC 1 *Fort Charles* (US 34m)
　PFI 1 *Paul Bogle* less than 100 tonnes (US-31m)
　PCI 6: 4 *Dauntless*; 2 *Point* less than 100 tonnes
　PBF 3
　PB 3 *Cornwall* (Damen Stan 4207)
FACILITIES
Bases　　Located at Port Royal, Pedro Cays
Minor Base Located at Discovery Bay

Air Wing 140;
Plus National Reserve

FORCES BY ROLE

Tpt/MP   1 flt with 1 BN-2A *Defender* ; 1 Cessna 210M *Centurio*; 2 DA-40-180FP *Diamond Star* (trg)

SAR/Tpt   2 flt with 4 AS-355N *Ecureuil*; 3 Bell 407; 3 Bell 412EP

EQUIPMENT BY TYPE

AIRCRAFT
TPT 1 BN-2A *Defender*
UTL 1 Cessna 210M *Centurion*
TRG 2 DA-40-180FP *Diamond Star*
HELICOPTERS
SPT 4 AS-355N *Ecureuil*
UTL 6: 3 Bell 407; 3 Bell 412EP

Mexico Mex

Mexican Peso NP		2006	2007	2008
GDP	NP	9.15tr	9.60tr	
	US$	840bn	882bn	
per capita	US$	7,817	8,110	
Growth	%	4.8	2.9	
Inflation	%	3.6	3.9	
Def bdgt[a]	NP	35.2bn	43.4bn	
	US$	3.22bn	3.98bn	
US$1=NP		10.9	10.9	

[a] Excluding paramilitaries

Population	108,700,891

Age	0–14	15–19	20–24	25–29	30–64	65 plus
Male	16%	5%	4%	4%	17%	2%
Female	15%	5%	5%	4%	19%	3%

Capabilities

ACTIVE 248,700 (Army 178,000 Navy 46,400 Air 11,700 Marines 12,600) **Paramilitary 30,700**

RESERVE 39,899 (Armed Forces 39,899)

ORGANISATIONS BY SERVICE

Army 178,000

FORCES BY ROLE
12 regions (total: 45 Army zones (total: 24 Mot Cav regt, 8 Arty regt, 101 Inf bn, 25 indep Inf coy,))

Strategic Reserve	1 corps (1 Cbt Engr bde, 1 Armd bde, 3 Rapid Reaction bde)

Inf   1 corps (Presidential Guard) (1 SF gp, some Spt units, 1 Mech Inf bde, 1 Cbt Engr bn, 1 Logistic bde, 1 MP bde)

SF   1 corps (2 Para bde, 1 Logistic bde, 1 Amph bde)

Para   1 bde

EQUIPMENT BY TYPE

RECCE 271: 150 ERC-90F1 *Lynx* (4 trg); 40 M-8; 41 MAC-1; 40 VBL (8 with *Milan*)
APC 746
  APC (T) 487: 398 AMX-VCI; 52 HWK-11; 34 M-2A1 half-track; 3 M-32 *Recovery Sherman*
  APC (W) 259: 95 BDX; 69: 25 DN-3 *Sedena 1000*; 25 DN-4 *Caballo*; 19 DN-5 *Toro*; 26 LAV-150 ST; 25 MOWAG *Roland*; 44 VCR (3 amb; 5 cmd post)
LT VEH 3,638 M-1038 *HMMVW* (several versions)
ARTY 2075
  SP 75mm 6 DN-5 *Bufalo*
  TOWED 114: **75mm** 18 M-116 pack; **105mm** 96: 40 M-101; 40 M-56; 16 M-2A1/ M-3
  MOR 60mm/81mm/100mm 1,788;
  120mm 167: 75 *Brandt*; 60 M-65; 32 RT61
AT
  MSL • SP 8 *Milan* (VBL)
  RL 1,187+ **64mm** RPG-18 *Fly*/ **82mm** B-300/ **73mm** RPG-16
  GUNS 37mm 30 M3
AD
  GUNS 80
    TOWED 12.7mm 40 M-55; **20mm** 40 GAI-B01

Navy 46,400

Two Fleet Commands: Gulf (6 zones), Pacific (11 zones)

FORCES BY ROLE
Navy 1 HQ located at Acapulco; 1 HQ (exercise) located at Vera Cruz

EQUIPMENT BY TYPE
PRINCIPAL SURFACE COMBATANTS 7
  DESTROYERS • DD 1:
  1 *Netzahualcoyotl* (ex *Quetzacoatl*, ex US *Gearing*) eq with 2 twin 127mm gun (4 eff.), with 1 BO-105 utl hels
  FRIGATES • FF 6:
  2 *Bravo* (ex US *Bronstein*) each with 1 Mk 112 Octuple (8 eff.) with tactical ASROC, 2 triple ASTT (6 eff.) each with Mk 46 LWT, 1 hel Landing Platform
  4 *Allende* (ex US *Knox*) each with 1 Mk 112 Octuple with ASROC/RGM-84C *Harpoon* SSM, 1 Mk 29 GMLS with Sea Sparrow SAM, 2 twin TT (4 eff.) each with Mk 46 LWT, 1 127mm gun, with 1 MD-902 utl hels,
PATROL AND COASTAL COMBATANTS 168
  PSOH 6: 4 *Sierra* (capacity 1 MD-902 *Explorer*); 2 *Oaxaca* each with 1 AS-565 MB *Panther* utl hels (4 addittional hulls in build)
  PFM 2 *Huracan* (ex Il *Aliya*) eq with *Phalanx* CIWS and 4 *Gabriel* SSM
  PCO 24:
  4 *Durango* with 1 57mm gun, each with 1 BO-105 utl hels
  4 *Holzinger* (capacity 1 MD-902 *Explorer*)
  10 *Leandro Valle* (US *Auk* MSF) (being withdrawn from service from 2009 to be replaced with 4 additional *Oaxaca* class)
  6 *Uribe* (Sp 'Halcon') each with 1 BO-105 utl hels
  PCC 25: 20 *Azteca*; 3 *Cabo* (US *Cape Higgon*); 1 *Democrata*; 1 *Caribe*
  PCI 6: 4 *Isla* less than 100 tonnes (US ex *Halter*); 2 *Punta* less than 100 tonnes (US *Point*)
  PCR 48 (Modified *Stridsbat 90*) less than 100 tonnes

PBF 57 all less than 100 tonnes; 48 *Polaris* (Swe CB90); *1 Polaris II* (Swe IC 16M); 6 *Acuario*; 2 *Acuario B*
AMPHIBIOUS • LS • LST 3: 2 *Papaloapan* (ex US *Newport*); 1 *Panuco* (ex US LST -1152)
LOGISTICS AND SUPPORT 19:
  AG 1 *Manzanillo* (troop transport ship, also deployed as SAR and disaster relief ship)
  AK 3
  AGOR 3: 2 *Robert D. Conrad*; 1 *Humboldt*
  AGS 4
  ATF 4
  TRG 4: 1 *Manuel Azuela*; 2 *Huasteco* (also serve as troop transport, supply and hospital ships); **AXS** 1

FACILITIES

Bases   Located at Vera Cruz, Tampico, Chetumal, Ciudad del Carmen, Yukalpetén, Lerna, Frontera, Coatzacoalcos, Isla Mujéres, Acapulco, Ensenada, La Paz, Guaymas, Mayport (FL), US, Salina Cruz, Puerto Madero, Lazaro Cádenas, Puerto Vallarta,

Naval Aviation 1,250

FORCES BY ROLE

AEW   1 sqn with 3 E-2C; 2 Rockwell Sabreliner 60

MR   1 sqn with 8 CASA 212PM *Aviocar**; 1 sqn with 7 L-90 *Redigo*; 5 sqn with 4 *Beech* F-33C *Bonanza*; 1 Cessna 404 *Titan*; 12 MX-7 *Star Rocket*; 7 Lancair IV-P; 4 Beech 55 *Baron*

Tpt   1 sqn with 6 AN-32B *Cline*; 1 VIP sqn with 1 DHC-8 *Dash 8*; 2 Beech 90 *King Air*; 5 Rockwell Turbo Commander 1000; 3 *Learjet* 24

Hel   5 sqn with 21 Mi-17 (Mi-8MT) *Hip H*/Mi-8 *Hip* (8 armed); 2 sqn with 2 PZL MI-2 *Hoplite*; 2 AS-555 *Fennec*; 2 AS-565MB; 6 MD 902 *Explorer*; 2 sqn with 11 BO-105CBS-5

EQUIPMENT BY TYPE
AIRCRAFT 8 combat capable*
  RECCE 15: 8 CASA 212PM *Aviocar** 7 L-90TP *Redigo*
  AEW 3: 3 E-2C *Hawkeye*;
  TPT 24: 6 AN-32B *Cline*; 1 DHC-8 *Dash 8*; 2 Rockwell *Sabreliner 60*; 3 *Learjet* 24; 5 Rockwell *Turbo Commander* 1000; 2 Beech 90 *King Air*; 1 Cessna 404 *Titan*; 4 Beech 55 *Baron*; 7 Lancair IV-P
  TRG 31: 4 Beech F-33C *Bonanza*; 8 Z-242L; 7 L-90 *Redigo*; 12 MX-7 *Star Rocket*
HELICOPTERS
  RECCE 8: 6 MD-902 *Explorer*; 2 AS-565MB *Panther*
  SPT 23: 2 PZL MI-2 *Hoplite*; 21 Mi-17 (Mi-8MT) *Hip H*/Mi-8 *Hip* spt hels
  UTL 14: 2AS-555 *Fennec*; 11 BO-CBS-5; 4 MD-500E; 2 R-22 *Mariner*; 1 R-44

FACILITIES
  Trg School   1 with 8 Z-242L; 1 R-44; 4 MD-500E; 4 *Schweizer* 300C

Marines 12,600

FORCES BY ROLE

Inf   2 bn
Amphibious Reaction Force 2 bde

AB   1 bn
SF   2 coy
Presidential Guard   1 bn

EQUIPMENT BY TYPE
APC (W) 29: 3 BTR-60 (APC-60); 26 BTR-70 (APC-70)
ARTY 122
  TOWED 105mm 16 M-56
  MRL 122mm 6 Firos-25
  MOR 60mm/81mm 100
  RCL 106mm M-40A1
  AD • SAM • MANPAD 5+ SA-18 *Grouse (Igla)*

Air Force 11,700

FORCES BY ROLE

Ftr/CCT   1 sqn with 8 F-5E *Tiger II*; 2 F-5F *Tiger II*; 4 sqn with 43 PC-7, 2 PC-9M

Surv/Recce 1 sqn with 1 EMB-145 *Erieye* (AEW), 2 EMB-145RS (Remote Sensing), 2 SA-2-37B, 4 C-26B

Anti-narc   sqn with 8 Cessna T206H; 50 Bell 206
Spraying

Tpt   1 sqn with 2 C-130A; 2 C-130E; 4 C-130K; 1 L-100-20; 4 B-727; 1 sqn with 2 An-32B, 4 PC-6B, 11 IAI-201 *Arava*; 1 Presidential gp with 1 B-757, 2 B-737; 2 Gulfstream III; 2 Learjet 35; 1 *Turbo Commander*; 4 *Super Puma*; 1 VIP tpt gp with 1 S-70; 1 Cessna 500 *Citation*; 1 Beech-200, 1 C-140

Liaison   6 sqn with 57 Ce-182S; 1 sqn with 3 Ce-206

Hel   1 sqn with 20 MD-530F; 1 sqn with 5 S-70A-24 *Black Hawk*, 4 S-65 *Yas'ur* 2000, 4 B-412, 2 SA-330S; 1 sqn with 10 Mi-8T; 20 Mi-17; 1 Mi-26T; 3 sqn with 24 Bell 212, 6 Bell 206B; 1 sqn with 1 Bell 205A; 8 Bell 206B; 7 Bell 206L

Trg   5 sqn with 11 PT-17; 26 SF-260EU; 28 *Beech* F-33C *Bonanza*; 23 PC-7;

EQUIPMENT BY TYPE
AIRCRAFT 78 combat capable
  FTR 10: 8 F-5E *Tiger II*; 2 F-5F *Tiger II*
  COIN/TRG 68: 66 PC-7, 2 PC-9M*
  RECCE 8: 2 EMB-145RS; 2 SA-2-37A; 4 C-26B
  ANTI-NARC SPRAYING 58: 8 Cessna T206H; 50 Bell 206
  AEW 1 EMB-145AEW *Erieye*
  TPT 41: 4 B-727; 2 B-737; 1 B-757; 1 *Beech* 200; 2 C-130A *Hercules*; 2 C-130 E; 4 C-130K; 1 L-100-20; 1 C-140; 1 *Cessna* 500 *Citation*; 11 IAI-201 *Arava*; ; 2 An-32B; 4 PC-6B; 1 Rockwell *Turbo Commander* 680; 2 Gulfstream III; 2 Learjet 35
  UTL 68: 3 Cessna 206; 57 Cessna 182; 8 Cessna T206H (anti-narc spraying);
  TRG 65: 28 Beech F-33C *Bonanza*; 26 SF-260EU; 11 PT-17;
HELICOPTERS
  CBT 20 MD-530MF
  SPT 147 : 20 Mi-17; 10 Mi-8T; 1 MI-26T; 4 S-65C *Yas'ur* 2000; 6 S-70A-24 *Black Hawk*; 2 SA-330S; 4 AS332L; 1 Bell 205A; 14 Bell 206B *JetRanger II*; 7 Bell 206L; 24 Bell 212; 4 Bell 412 ; 50 Bell 206 (anti-narc spraying)
  MSL • AAM AIM-9J *Sidewinder*

Paramilitary 30,700

Federal Preventive Police 12,700

Public Security Secretariat

AIRCRAFT

TPT 17: 2 An-32B *Cline*; 1 CN-235M; 5 Cessna 182 *Skylane*; 1 Cessna 404 *Titan*; 1 Gulfstream II; 1 Learjet 24; 1 Rockwell *Sabreliner* 60; 5 Rockwell *Turbo Commander* 5

UTL 1 Cessna 210 *Centurion*

HELICOPTERS

SPT 8: 2 AS-350B *Ecureuil*; 4 Mi-17 *Hip*; 1 SA-330C *Puma*; 1 SA-330F *Puma*

UTL 23: 1 AS-555 *Fennec*; 14 Bell 206 *JetRanger*; 1 Bell 212; 5 EC-120; 2 MD-530F *Lifter*

TRG 7 Bell 206B

Rural Defense Militia 18,000

| Inf | 13 units |
| Horsed Cav | 13 units |

DEPLOYMENT

UNITED STATES

Navy

Base   Located at Mayport (FL), US

Nicaragua Nic

Nicaraguan Gold Cordoba Co		2006	2007	2008
GDP	Co	93.0bn	105.0bn	
	US$	5.3bn	5.6bn	
per capita	US$	954	989	
Growth	%	3.7	4.2	
Inflation	%	9.1	8.2	
Def bdgt	Co	613m	675m	
	US$	35m	36m	
US$1=Co		17.5	18.7	

Population	5,675,356

Age	0–14	15–19	20–24	25–29	30–64	65 plus
Male	19%	6%	5%	4%	14%	1%
Female	18%	6%	5%	4%	15%	2%

Capabilities

ACTIVE 14,000 (Army 12,000 Navy 800 Air 1,200)

Terms of service voluntary, 18-36 months

ORGANISATIONS BY SERVICE

Army ε12,000

FORCES BY ROLE

Region 6 comd (*total:* 1 tk coy, 11 inf coy)

Comd   1 regt (1 inf bn, 1 (sy) army bn)

Mil   2 det (*total:* 2 inf bn)

Mech   1 (lt) bde (1 tk bn, 1 mech inf bn, 1 Recce bn, 1 AT gp, 1 fd arty gp (2 fd arty bn))

SF   1 bde (3 SF bn)

Engr   1 bn

Tpt   1 regt (1 (APC) army bn)

EQUIPMENT BY TYPE

MBT 127: 62 T-55; 65 in store

LT TK 10 PT-76 in store

RECCE 20 BRDM-2 (12 with AT-3 9K11 *Sagger*)

APC (W) 166: 102 BTR-152 in store; 64 BTR-60

ARTY 800

TOWED 42: **122mm** 12 D-30; **152mm** 30 D-20 in store

MRL 151: **107mm** 33 Type-63; **122mm** 118: 18 BM-21; 100 GRAD 1P (BM-21P) (single-tube rocket launcher, man portable)

MOR 607: 579 **82mm**: **120mm** 24 M-43: **160mm** 4 M-160 in store

AT

MSL • MANPATS AT-3 9K11 *Sagger* (12 SP on BRDM-2)

RCL 82mm B-10

RL 73mm RPG-16/RPG-7 *Knout*

GUNS 461: **100mm** 24 M-1944; **57mm** 264 ZIS-2 *M-1943*; 90 in store; **76mm** 83 ZIS-3

AD • SAM • MANPAD 200+ SA-14 *Gremlin*/SA-16 *Gimlet*/SA-7 *Grail*

Navy ε800

EQUIPMENT BY TYPE

PATROL AND COASTAL COMBATANTS 24

PFI 5: 3 *Dabur* less than 100 tonnes; 2 *Zhuk†* less than 100 tonnes (FSU)

PBR 19 Assault Craft

FACILITIES

Bases Located at Corinto, Puerto Cabezzas, El Bluff

Air Force 1,200

FORCES BY ROLE

Tpt   sqn with 1 An-2 *Colt*; 4 An-26 *Curl*; 1 Cessna 404 *Titan* (VIP)

Trg/Utl   some sqn with 1 T-41D *Mescalero*

ADA   1 gp with 18 ZU-23; 18 C3-Morigla M1

Hel   some sqn with 1 Mi-17 (Mi-8MT) *Hip H* (VIP); 3 (tpt/armed); 12† (tpt/armed)

EQUIPMENT BY TYPE

AIRCRAFT

TPT 6: 1 An-2 *Colt*; 4 An-26 *Curl*; 1 Cessna 404 *Titan* (VIP)

TRG 1 T-41D *Mescalero*

HELICOPTERS

SPT 16: 1 Mi-17 (Mi-8MT) *Hip H* (VIP); 3 (tpt/armed); 12† (tpt/armed)

AD • GUNS 36: 18 ZU-23; 18 C3-*Morigla* M1

MSL • ASM AT-2 *Swatter*

Panama Pan

Panamanian Balboa B		2006	2007	2008
GDP	B	17.9bn	19.9bn	
	US$	17.9bn	19.9bn	
per capita	US$	5,609	6,138	
Growth	%	8.1	8.5	
Inflation	%	2.5	3.8	
Def bdgt	B	171m	ε200m	
	US$	171m	ε200m	
US$1=B		1.0	1.0	

Population   3,242,173

Age	0–14	15–19	20–24	25–29	30–64	65 plus
Male	16%	5%	4%	4%	19%	3%
Female	15%	5%	4%	4%	18%	3%

Capabilities

ACTIVE 0 Paramilitary 12,000

ORGANISATIONS BY SERVICE

Paramilitary 12,000

National Police Force 11,000
No hy mil eqpt, small arms only

Police	18 coy
SF	1 unit (reported)
Paramilitary	8 coy
Presidential Guard	1 bn under strength
MP	1 bn

National Maritime Service ε600
FORCES BY ROLE
Air Wing 1 HQ located at Amador
EQUIPMENT BY TYPE
PATROL AND COASTAL COMBATANTS 41
  PCO 1 *Independencia* (ex-US *Balsam class*)
  PCC 5: 3; 2 *Panquiaco* (UK *Vosper* 31.5m)
  PCI 10: 3 *Chiriqui* less than 100 tonnes (ex-US); 1 *Negrita* less than 100 tonnes; 5 *Tres De Noviembre* less than 100 tonnes (ex-US *Point*); 1 US MSB Class (MSB 5)
  PBR 25
FACILITIES
Bases Located at Amador, Balboa, Colón

National Air Service 400
FORCES BY ROLE
Tpt   sqn with 1 BN-2B Islander; 5 CASA 212M *Aviocar*; 2 PA-34 *Seneca*; Presidential flt with 1 Gulfstream II; 2 S-76C
Trg   unit with 6 T-35D *Pillan*
Hel   Sqn with 2 Bell 205; 6 Bell 212; 13 UH-1H *Iroquois*

EQUIPMENT BY TYPE
AIRCRAFT
  TPT 9: 1 BN-2B *Islander*; 5 CASA 212M *Aviocar*; 1 Gulfstream II; 2 PA-34 *Seneca*
  TRG 6 T-35D *Pillan*
HELICOPTERS
  TPT 2 S-76C
  UTL 21: 2 Bell 205; 6 Bell 212; 13 UH-1H *Iroquois*

Paraguay Py

Paraguayan Guarani Pg		2006	2007	2008
GDP	Pg	52tr	58tr	
	US$	9.2bn	11.9bn	
per capita	US$	1,419	1,790	
Growth	%	4.3	5.0	
Inflation	%	9.6	7.6	
Def bdgt	Pg	380bn	500bn	
	US$	67m	101m	
US$1=Pg		5,635	4,925	

Population   6,667,147

Age	0–14	15–19	20–24	25–29	30–64	65 plus
Male	19%	5%	4%	4%	16%	2%
Female	19%	5%	4%	4%	15%	3%

Capabilities

ACTIVE 10,650 (Army 7,600 Navy 1,950 Air 1,100)
Paramilitary 14,800
Terms of service 12 months Navy 2 years

RESERVE 164,500 (Joint 164,500)

ORGANISATIONS BY SERVICE

Army 6,100; 1,500 conscript (total 7,600)
The infantry Regiments, each of which forms the major peace-time element of the six Infantry "Divisions" have a strength of a little more than 500. The three Cavalry "Divisions" each have two Regiments with a strength of approximately 750.
FORCES BY ROLE
3 corps HQ

Army	3 corps (*each:* 2 inf div, 1 cav div, 1 arty gp); 6 inf div in total; 20 (frontier) det
Armd Cav	3 regt
Cav	3 div (*each:* 2 (horse) regt)
Inf	6 regt (bn)
Arty	2 gp (bn); 1 gp divided between 2 of the corps
ADA	1 gp
Engr	6 bn
Presidential Guard	1 unit (1 inf bn, 1 SF bn, 1 arty bty, 1 MP bn, 1 (lt) armd sqn)

EQUIPMENT BY TYPE
MBT 5 M4A3 *Sherman*
LT TK 12 M-3A1 *Stuart*
RECCE 30 EE-9 *Cascavel*
APC (W) 10 EE-11 *Urutu*
ARTY 121
   TOWED 105mm 15 M-101
   MOR 81mm 80
   RCL 75mm M-20
   RL 66mm M-72 *LAW*
AD • GUNS 13: **20mm** 3 on M-9; **40mm** 10 M-1A1

Reserves

Cav 4 regt
Inf   14 regt

Navy 1,100; 850 conscript (total 1,950)

EQUIPMENT BY TYPE
PATROL AND COASTAL COMBATANTS 28
   PCR 8: 2 (ROC); 1 *Capitan Cabral*; 2 *Capitan Ortiz* less
than 100 tonnes (ROC *Hai Ou*); 1 *Itapu*; 2 *Nanawa*†
   MISC BOATS/CRAFT 20 craft
AMPHIBIOUS 2 LCT
LOGISTICS AND SUPPORT 3: 2 **AKSL** (also serve as
river transport); 1 **TRG**

FACILITIES

Bases   Located at Asunción (Puerto Sajonia), Bahía Negra,
      Cuidad Del Este

Naval Aviation 100

FORCES BY ROLE

Utl   1 sqn with 2 HB-350 *Esquilo*; 1 OH-13 *Sioux*
Liaison 1 sqn with 2 Cessna 310; 1 Cessna 210 *Centurion*;
      2 Cessna 150; 1 Cessna 410

EQUIPMENT BY TYPE
AIRCRAFT
   UTL 4: 2 Cessna 310; 1 Cessna 210 *Centurion*; 1 *Cessna*
410
   TRG 2 Cessna 150
HELICOPTERS
   SPT 2 HB-350 *Esquilo*
   UTL 1 OH-13 *Sioux*

Marines 700; 200 conscript (total 900)

Marine 3 bn under strength

Air Force 900; 200 conscript (total 1,100)

FORCES BY ROLE

Tac   some sqn with 2 AT-33A *Shooting Star*;
         3 EMB-312 *Tucano*; 5 EMB-326 *Xavante*
SAR/Liaison some sqn with 2 Cessna 402B; 1 PA-32R
         Saratoga; 3 Cessna U-206 *Stationair*; 2 PZL-
         104 *Wilga 80*; I Beech 33 *Debonair*; 2 Beech
         A36 *Bonanza*; 1 Cessna 210 *Centurion*; 1
         EMB-720D *Minuano*; 1 EMB-721C *Sertanejo*;
         1 EMB-810C *Seneca*

Tpt   some sqn with 1 C-47 *Skytrain*; 5 CASA 212
       Aviocar; some (Presidential) flt with 1 B-
       707; 1 DHC-6 *Twin Otter*
Trg   some sqn with 3 T-35A *Pillan*; 4 T-35B
       Pillan; 6 Neiva T-25 *Universal*
Hel   some sqn with 3 HB-350 *Esquilo*; 7 UH-1H
       Iroquois

EQUIPMENT BY TYPE
AIRCRAFT 10 combat capable
   FGA 4: 2 AT-33A *Shooting Star*; 2 in store
   TPT 20: 1 B-707; 1 Beech 55 *Baron* (Army Co-op); 1 C-
   47 *Skytrain*; 5 CASA 212 *Aviocar*; 1 Cessna 310 (Army
   Co-op); 2 Cessna 402B; 1 DHC-6 *Twin Otter*; 1 PA-32R
   Saratoga; 1 Beech 33 *Debonair*; 2 Beech A36 *Bonanza*; 1
   Cessna 210 *Centurion*; 1 EMB-720D *Minuano*; 1 EMB-
   721C *Sertanejo*; 1 EMB-810C *Seneca*;
   UTL 6: 1 Cessna 206 (Army Co-op); 3 Cessna U-206
   Stationair 2 PZL-104 *Wilga 80*
   TRG 21: 3 EMB-312 *Tucano**; 5 EMB-326 *Xavante**; 3 T-
   35A *Pillan*; 4 T-35B *Pillan* ; 6 Neiva T-25 *Universal*
HELICOPTERS
   SPT 3 HB-350 *Esquilo*
   UTL 7 UH-1H *Iroquois*

Paramilitary 14,800

Special Police Service 10,800; 4,000 conscript (total 14,800)

DEPLOYMENT

AFGHANISTAN
UN • UNAMA 1 obs

CÔTE D'IVOIRE
UN • UNOCI 2; 8 obs

DEMOCRATIC REPUBLIC OF CONGO
UN • MONUC 17 obs

ETHIOPIA/ERITREA
UN • UNMEE 4 obs

HAITI
UN • MINUSTAH 31

LIBERIA
UN • UNMIL 1; 3 obs

NEPAL
UN • UNMIN 5 obs

SUDAN
UN • UNMIS 10 obs

Peru Pe

Peruvian Nuevo Sol NS		2006	2007	2008
GDP	NS	305bn	334bn	
	US$	93bn	111bn	
per capita	US$	3,296	3,870	
Growth	%	7.6	7.0	
Inflation	%	2.0	1.5	
Def bdgt	NS	3.6bn	3.8bn	
	US$	1.10bn	1.27bn	
US$1=NS		3.27	3.01	

Population   28,674,757

Age	0–14	15–19	20–24	25–29	30–64	65 plus
Male	16%	5%	4%	4%	18%	2%
Female	15%	5%	4%	4%	18%	3%

Capabilities

ACTIVE 114,000 (Army 74,000 Navy 23,000 Air 17,000) **Paramilitary 84,000**

RESERVE 188,000 (Army 188,000) **Paramilitary 7,000**

ORGANISATIONS BY SERVICE

Army 74,000
FORCES BY ROLE
4 Military Regions
North Region
Cav   1 bde (1st) (4 Mech bn, 1 Arty gp)
Inf   1 bde (1st Reinforced) (1 Tk bn, 3 Inf bn, 1 Arty gp); 2 bde (7th & 32nd) (*each:* 3 Inf bn, 1 Arty gp)
Jungle Inf   1 bde (6th) (4 Jungle bn, 1 Arty gp, 1 Engr bn)

Central Region
Inf   1 bde (1st) (4 Mech bn, 1 Arty gp); 2 bde (2nd & 31st) (*each:* 3 Mot Inf bn, 1 Arty gp); 1 bde (8th) (3 Mot Inf bn, 1 Arty gp, 1 AD bn)
SF   1 bde (1st) (4 SF bn, 1 Airmob Arty gp); 1 bde (3rd) (3 Cdo bn, 1 Airmob Arty gp, 1 AD gp)
Arty   1 gp (Regional Troops)
Avn   1 bde (1 Atk Hel / Recce Hel bn, 1 Avn bn, 2 Aslt Hel / Tpt Hel bn)
Trg   1 armd bde (18th) (1 Armd bn, 2 Tk bn, 1 Armd inf bn, 1 Engr bn, 1 SP Fd Arty gp)

South Region
Armd   1 bde (3rd) (3 Mech Inf bn, 1 Mot Inf bn, 1 Arty gp, 1 AD gp, 1 Engr bn); 1 bde (3rd) (2 Tk bn, 1 Armd inf bn, 1 Arty gp, 1 AD gp, 1 Engr bn)
SF   1 gp (Regional Troops)
Mtn Inf 1 bde (4th) (1 Armd regt, 3 Mot Inf bn, 1 Arty gp); 1 bde (5th) (1 Armd regt, 2 Mot Inf bn, 3 Jungle coy, 1 Arty gp)

Arty   1 gp (Regional Troops)
AD   1 gp (Regional Troops)
Engr   1 bn (Regional Troops)

Eastern Region
Jungle   1 bde (5th) (1 SF gp, 3 Jungle bn, 3 Jungle coy, 1
Inf   Jungle arty gp, 1 AD gp, 1 Jungle Engr bn)

EQUIPMENT BY TYPE
MBT 240: 165 T-55; 75 in store
LT TK 96 AMX-13
RECCE 145: 30 BRDM-2; 15 Fiat 6616; 50 M-3A1; 50 M-9A1
APC 299
  APC (T) 120 M-113A1
  APC (W) 179: 150 UR-416; 25 Fiat 6614; 4 *Repontec*
ARTY 968
  SP • 155mm 12 M-109A2
  TOWED 260
    105mm 152: 44 M-101; 24 M-2A1; 60 M-56; 24 Model 56 pack howitzer; **122mm;** 108 36 D-30; **130mm** 36 M-46; **155mm** 36 M-114
  MRL • 122mm 22 BM-21
  MOR 674+: **81mm/107mm** 350; **120mm** 300+ *Brandt/Expal Model L*
    SP 107mm 24 M-106A1
AT • MSL • MANPATS 350 AT-3 9K11 *Sagger* / HJ-73C
  RCL 106mm M-40A1
AIRCRAFT
  TPT 9: 2 An-28 *Cash*; 3 AN-32B *Cline*; 1 *Beech* 350 *Super King Air*; 2 PA-31T *Navajo/Cheyenne II*; 1 PA-34 *Seneca*
  UTL 8: 3 Cessna U-206 *Stationair;* 1 Cessna 208 *Caravan I*; 4 IL-103
HELICOPTERS
  SPT 36: 15 Mi-17 (Mi-8MT) *Hip H*; 8 in store; PZL MI-2 *Hoplite* 10; MI-26 1; 2 in store
  UTL 2 A-109K?;
  TRG 6 Enstrom F-28F
AD
  SAM • MANPAD 298+: 70 SA-14 *Gremlin*; 128 SA-16 *Gimlet*; 100+ SA-7 *Grail*
  GUNS 165
    SP 23mm 35 ZSU-23-4
    TOWED 23mm 130: 80 ZU-23-2; 50 ZU-23;

Navy 23,000 (incl 1,000 Coast Guard)
Commands: Pacific, Lake Titicaca, Amazon *River*
EQUIPMENT BY TYPE
SUBMARINES • TACTICAL • SSK 6:
  4 *Angamos* (Ge T-209/1200) each with 6 single 533mm TT each with A-185 HWT
  2 *Angamos* in refit/reserve (Ge T-209/1200) each with 6 single 533mm TT each with A-185 HWT
PRINCIPAL SURFACE COMBATANTS 9
  CRUISERS • CG 1 *Almirante Grau* (Nl *De Ruyter*) with 8 single each with 1 Mk 2 Otomat SSM, 4 twin 152mm gun (8 eff.)
  FRIGATES • FFG 8 *Carvajal* (mod It *Lupo*) each with 8 single each with 1 Mk 2 Otomat SSM, 1+ *Albatros* octuple with *Aspide* SAM, 2 triple ASTT (6 eff.) each with A244

LWT, 1 127mm gun, with 1 AB-212 (Bell 212) Utl/SH-3D *Sea King* ASW

PATROL AND COASTAL COMBATANTS 14

PFM 6 *Velarde* (Fr PR-72 64m) each with 4 single each with 1 MM-38 *Exocet* tactical SSM, 1 76mm gun

PCR 5:

2 *Amazonas* each with 1 76mm gun

2 *Maranon* each with 2 76mm gun

1 *Huallaga* with 40 mmgun, (Additional vessel in build)

MISC BOATS/CRAFT 3 craft (for lake patrol)

AMPHIBIOUS • LS • LST 4 *Paita* (capacity 395 troops) (US *Terrebonne Parish*)

LOGISTICS AND SUPPORT 12:

AOR 1 *Mollendo*

AOT 3

ARS 1 *Guardian Rios*

AH 1

AGS 4: 1 *Carrasco*; 2 (coastal survey vessels); 1 (river survey vessel for the Upper Amazon)

TRG • AXS 1

TRV 1

FACILITIES

Bases   Located at Callao (Ocean), Puerto Maldonaldo (*River*), Iquitos (*River*), Talara (Ocean), Puno (Lake), Paita (Ocean), San Lorenzo Island (Ocean)

Naval Aviation ε800

FORCES BY ROLE

MR	2 sqn with 5 Beech 200T *Maritime Patrol*; 3 SH-3D *Sea King*; 3 AB-212 (Bell 212); 1 F-27 *Friendship*
Tpt	1 flt with 2 AN-32B *Cline*
Liaison	1 sqn with 4 Mi-8 *Hip*; 5 Bell 206B *JetRanger II*
Trg	1 sqn with 5 T-34C *Turbo Mentor*

EQUIPMENT BY TYPE

AIRCRAFT

MP 5 Beech 200T *Maritime Patrol*

TPT 2 AN-32B *Cline*

ELINT 1 F-27 *Friendship*

TRG 5 T-34C *Turbo Mentor*

HELICOPTERS

ASW 3 SH-3D *Sea King*

SPT 4 Mi-8 *Hip*

UTL 8: 3 AB-212 (Bell 212); 5 Bell 206B *JetRanger II*

MSL • ASM AM-39 *Exocet*

Marines 4,000

FORCES BY ROLE

Inf	1 (jungle) bn; 2 (indep) bn; 1 gp
Cdo	1 gp
Marine	1 bde (1 arty gp, 1 Spec Ops gp, 1 Recce bn, 1 (Amph veh) Amph bn, 2 inf bn)

EQUIPMENT BY TYPE

APC (W) 35+: 20 BMR-600; V-100 *Commando*; 15 V-200 *Chaimite*

ARTY 18+

TOWED 122mm D-30

MOR 18+: **81mm**; **120mm** ε18

RCL 84mm Carl Gustav; **106mm** M-40A1

AD • GUNS 20mm SP (twin)

Air Force 17,000

FORCES BY ROLE

Air Force divided into five regions – North, Lima, South, Central and Amazon.

Ftr	1 sqn with 15 MiG-29C *Fulcrum*; 3 MiG-29SE *Fulcrum*; 2 MiG-29UB *Fulcrum*
FGA	1 sqn with 10 M-2000P (M-2000E) *Mirage*; 2 M-2000DP (M-2000ED) *Mirage*; 1 sqn with 12 A-37B *Dragonfly*; 3 sqn with 10 SU-25A *Frogfoot A*†; 8 SU-25UB *Frogfoot B*†*
RECCE	1 (photo-survey) unit with 2 *Learjet* 36A; 4 C-26B
Tpt	3 gp; 7 sqn with 7 AN-32 *Cline*; 1 B-737; 2 DC-8-62F; 5 DHC-6 *Twin Otter*; 1 FH-227; 5 L-100-20; 9 PC-6 *Turbo-Porter*; 2 Y-12(II); 1 (Presidential) flt with 1 F-28 *Fellowship*, 1 Falcon 20F
Tkr	1 KC-707-323C
Liaison	sqn with 1 PA-31T *Navajo/Cheyenne II*; 8 UH-1D *Iroquois*
Atk Hel/ Aslt Hel	1 sqn with 6 Mi-24 *Hind*/Mi-25 *Hind D* (plus 10 in store); 8 Mi-17TM *Hip H*;
Spt Hel	3 sqn with 15 Mi-17 *Hip H*; 10 BO-105C; 8 Bell 206 *JetRanger*; 14 AB-212 (Bell 212); 1 Bell 412 *Twin Huey*; ; 6 Schweizer 300C
Trg	drug interdiction sqn with 18 EMB-312 *Tucano*; 10 MB-339A; 6 T-41A/T-41D *Mescalero*; 15 Z-242
AD	6 bn with SA-3 *Goa*

EQUIPMENT BY TYPE

AIRCRAFT 70 combat capable

FTR 18: 15 MiG-29C *Fulcrum*; 3 MiG-29SE *Fulcrum*

FGA 32: 10 A-37B *Dragonfly*; 2 M-2000DP (M-2000ED) *Mirage*; 10 M-2000P (M-2000E) *Mirage*; 10 SU-25A *Frogfoot A*†

RECCE 6: 2 *Learjet* 36A; 4 C-26B

TKR 1 KC-707-323C

TPT 36: 6 An-32 *Cline*; ; 1 B-737; 2 DC-8-62F; 5 DHC-6 *Twin Otter*; 1 *Falcon* 20F; 5 L-100-20; 1 PA-31T *Navajo/Cheyenne II*; 9 PC-6 *Turbo-Porter*; 2 Y-12(II) (incl 4 in stiore)

TRG 59: 18 EMB-312 *Tucano*; 10 MB-339A; 2 MiG-29UB *Fulcrum**; 6 T-41A *Mescalero*/T-41D *Mescalero*; 15 Z-242; 8 SU-25UB *Frogfoot B*†*

HELICOPTERS

ATK 16 Mi-24 *Hind*/Mi-25 *Hind D* (plus 10 in store)

SPT 28: 8 Mi-17TM *Hip H*; 5 MI-8; 15 Mi-17 (Mi-8MT) *Hip H*

UTL 33 : 14 AB-212 (Bell 212); 10 BO-105C; 8 Bell 206 *JetRanger*; 1 Bell 412 *Twin Huey*;

TRG 6 Schweizer 300C

AD

SAM 100+: SA-3 *Goa*; 100+ *Javelin*

MSL
ASM AS-30
AAM AA-2 *Atoll*; AA-8 *Aphid*; AA-10 *Alamo*; AA-12 *Adder*; R-550 *Magic*

Paramilitary • National Police 77,000
(100,000 reported)
APC (W) 100 MOWAG *Roland*

General Police 43,000

Security Police 21,000

Technical Police 13,000

Coast Guard 1,000
Personnel included as part of Navy
PATROL AND COASTAL COMBATANTS 21
  PCC 5 *Rio Nepena*
  PCI 16: 3 *Dauntless* less than 100 tonnes; 13 various
AIRCRAFT
  TPT 2 F-27 *Friendship*

Rondas Campesinas ε7,000 gp
Peasant self-defence force. Perhaps 7,000 rondas 'gp', up to pl strength, some with small arms. Deployed mainly in emergency zone.

NON-STATE ARMED GROUPS
see Part II

DEPLOYMENT

CÔTE D'IVOIRE
UN • UNOCI 3 obs

DEMOCRATIC REPUBLIC OF CONGO
UN • MONUC 7 obs

ETHIOPIA/ERITREA
UN • UNMEE 4 obs

HAITI
UN • MINUSTAH 210

LIBERIA
UN • UNMIL 2; 3 obs

SUDAN
UN • UNMIS 17 obs

Suriname Sme

Suriname Dollar gld		2006	2007	2008
GDP	gld	4.2tr	4.6tr	
	US$	1.54bn	1.69bn	
per capita	US$	3,318	3,588	
Growth	%	5.8	5.3	
Inflation	%	11.3	4.6	
Def bdgt	gld	56bn	ε60bn	
	US$	20m	22m	
US$1=gld		2,740	2,740	

Population   470,784

Age	0–14	15–19	20–24	25–29	30–64	65 plus
Male	15%	5%	5%	4%	19%	3%
Female	14%	5%	4%	4%	19%	3%

Capabilities

ACTIVE 1,840 (Army 1,400 Navy 240 Air 200)
(All services form part of the army)

ORGANISATIONS BY SERVICE

Army 1,400
FORCES BY ROLE
Mech Cav   1 sqn
Inf   1 bn (4 inf coy)
MP   1 bn (coy)

EQUIPMENT BY TYPE
RECCE 6 EE-9 *Cascavel*
APC (W) 15 EE-11 *Urutu*
MOR 81mm 6
RCL 106mm: M-40A1

Navy ε240
EQUIPMENT BY TYPE
PATROL AND COASTAL COMBATANTS 8
  PCI 3 *Rodman†* less than 100 tonnes (100)
  PBR 5
FACILITIES
Base   Located at Paramaribo

Air Force ε200
FORCES BY ROLE
MP   2 CASA 212-400 *Aviocar**
Trg/Tpt   1 sqn with 1 BN-2 *Defender**; 1 PC-7 *Turbo Trainer**
Liaison   1 Cessna U-206 *Stationair*; 1 Cessna 182

EQUIPMENT BY TYPE
AIRCRAFT 4 combat capable
  MP 2 CASA 212-400 *Aviocar**
  TPT 1 BN-2 *Defender**
  UTL 1 Cessna U-206 *Stationair*; 1 Cessna 182
  TRG 1 PC-7 *Turbo Trainer**

Trinidad and Tobago TT

Trinidad and Tobago Dollar TT$		2006	2007	2008
GDP	TT$	114bn	134bn	
	US$	18bn	21bn	
per capita	US$	16,951	20,162	
Growth	%	12.0	6.0	
Inflation	%	8.3	8.5	
Def bdgt	TT$ 326m		ε350m	
	US$ 52m		56m	
US$1=TT$		6.31	6.29	

Population	1,056,608

Age	0–14	15–19	20–24	25–29	30–64	65 plus
Male	11%	5%	6%	4%	22%	4%
Female	10%	5%	5%	4%	20%	5%

Capabilities

ACTIVE 2,700 (Army 2,000 Coast Guard 700)
(All services form the Trinidad and Tobago Defence Force)

ORGANISATIONS BY SERVICE

Army ε2,000

FORCES BY ROLE
Inf 2 bn

SF 1 unit
Spt 1 bn

EQUIPMENT BY TYPE
MOR 46: 60mm ε40; 81mm 6 L16A1
AT
  RCL 84mm ε24 Carl Gustav
  RL 82mm 13 B-300

Coast Guard ε700

FORCES BY ROLE
Marine 1 HQ located at Staubles Bay

EQUIPMENT BY TYPE
PATROL AND COASTAL COMBATANTS 25
  PCO 1 Nelson (ex-UK Island)
  PFC 2 Barracuda (ex-Sw Karlskrona 40m) non-operational
  PCI 10: 4 Plymouth less than 100 tonnes; 4 Point less than 100 tonnes; 2 Wasp less than 100 tonnes
  MISC BOATS/CRAFT 12: 2 Aux Vessels; 10 boats

FACILITIES
Bases Located at Staubles Bay, Hart's Cut, Point Fortin, Tobago, Galeota

Air Wing 50

AIRCRAFT
  TPT 5: 2 C-26 Metro; 1 Cessna 310; 2 PA-31 Navajo

ANTI-CRIME UNIT 4: 1 Sikorski S-76 Sprit; 1 AS-355F Ecureuil 2; 1 Aeros-40B SkyDragon; 1 Westinghouse Skyship 600

Uruguay Ury

Uruguayan Peso pU		2006	2007	2008
GDP	pU	464bn	519bn	
	US$	19.3bn	23.5bn	
per capita	US$	5,633	6,812	
Growth	%	7.0	5.2	
Inflation	%	6.4	8.0	
Def bdgt	pU	5.4bn	5.8bn	
	US$	227	262m	
US$1=pU		24.0	22.1	

Population	3,447,496

Age	0–14	15–19	20–24	25–29	30–64	65 plus
Male	12%	4%	4%	4%	20%	5%
Female	11%	4%	4%	4%	21%	8%

Capabilities

ACTIVE 25,400 (Army 16,800 Navy 5,600 Air 3,000)
Paramilitary 920

ORGANISATIONS BY SERVICE

Army 17,000

Uruguayan units are sub-standard size, mostly around 30%. Div are at most Bde size, while Bn are re-enforced Coy strength. Regts are also Coy size, some Bn size, with the largest formation being the Armd Cav Regt '2 Regimento Tnte. Gral Pablo Ganarza de Caballeria Blindado' with 20 M-41A1UR and 14 M-113 A1. Each tank regt (Sqn size) has only 7 T-55s, while 5 of the 6 Mech Cav Regts have only 6 M-64/-93 on strength.

FORCES BY ROLE
4 Military Regions/div HQ

Cav	1 Armd Cav regt; 6 Mech Cav regt; 2 Tank regt; 1 (Ceremonial) Horse regt
Inf	5 Inf bn; 1 Armd Inf bn; 1 Para bn; 8 Mech Inf bn
Arty	1 Strategic Reserve regt; 5 Field Arty gp
Engr	1 bde (3 engr bn)
Cbt engr	4 bn
AD	1 gp

EQUIPMENT BY TYPE
MBT 15 T-55
LT TK 37: 17 M-24 Chaffee; 20 M-41A1UR
RECCE 114: 4 EE-3 Jararaca (being retired); 15 EE-9 Cascavel; 48 GAZ-39371Vodnik; 47 OT-64 M-93
AIFV 18 BMP-1
APC 104:

APC (T) 17: 14 M-113A1UR; 3 M-93 (MT-LB)
APC (W) 87: 44 *Condor*; 43 OT-64 SKOT
ARTY 196+
SP 122mm 6 2S1 *Carnation*
TOWED 37: **105mm** 32: 24 M-101A1; 8 M-102; **155mm** 5
M-114A1
MRL 122mm 4 RM-70
MOR 149+: **60mm** (ECIA); **81mm** 97; **107mm** 8 M-30;
120mm 44
AT
  MSL • MANPATS 5 *Milan*
  RCL 48: **106mm** 30 M-40A1; **57mm** 18 M-18
UAV • TACTICAL 1 *Charrua*
AD • GUNS • TOWED 19: **20mm** 15: 6 M-167 *Vulcan*; 9
TCM-20 (w/ Elta M-2016 radar); **40mm** 4 L/60

Navy 5,000 (incl 1,600 Prefectura Naval (Coast Guard))

FORCES BY ROLE
Navy HQ located at Montevideo

EQUIPMENT BY TYPE
PRINCIPAL SURFACE COMBATANTS • FRIGATES
FFG 2:
  1 *Montevideo* (ex Fr *Cdt Riviere*) with 2 triple 550mm
  ASTT (6 eff.) each with L3 HWT, 2 single, 2 100mm gun
  1 *Artigas* (ex Ger *Freiburg*) with HB-355 med hel
PATROL AND COASTAL COMBATANTS 10
  PCC 3 (Fr *Vigilante* 42m)
  PCI 3: 2 *Colonia* less than 100 tonnes (US *Cape*); 1
  Paysandu less than 100 tonnes
  PBR 4 *UPF-Class*
MINE WARFARE • MINE COUNTERMEASURES
MSC 3 *Temerario* (Ge *Kondor* II)
AMPHIBIOUS 4: 2 **LCVP**; 2 **LCM**
LOGISTICS AND SUPPORT 7:
  ARS 1 *Vanguardia*
  AG 1 *Luneburg* (ex-Ge, general spt ship)
  AGHS 1 *Hegoland* (ex-Ge)
  ABU 3
  TRG • AXS 1
FACILITIES
Bases   Located at Montevideo, Paysando (river)
Naval airbases Located at La Paloma, Laguna del Sauce

Naval Aviation 280

FORCES BY ROLE
ASW   flt with 1 *Beech* 200T *Maritime Patrol**
Utl / SAR   1 sqn with 2 *Wessex* MK60/HC2; 1 HB-355;
                 4 BÖ-105 M
Trg/Liaison   1 sqn with 2 T-34C *Turbo Mentor*

EQUIPMENT BY TYPE
AIRCRAFT 1combat capable
  ASW / MP 1 Beech 200T *Maritime Patrol**
  TRG 2 T-34C *Turbo Mentor*
HELICOPTERS
  UTL 3: 2 *Wessex* HC2/MK60; 1 HB-355

Naval Infantry 450

Marine 1 bn (under strength)

Coast Guard 1,600

Prefectura Naval (PNN) is part of the Navy
PATROL AND COASTAL COMBATANTS 12
  PCC 3
  MISC BOATS/CRAFT 9 Type-44

Air Force 3,000

Flying hours   120 hrs/year

FORCES BY ROLE
FGA   1 sqn with 9 A-37B *Dragonfly*; 1 sqn with
         4 IA-58B *Pucara*
Tpt   1 sqn with 2 C-130B *Hercules*; 2 EMB-110C
         Bandeirante; 2 Bo105M (VIP); 1 EMB-120RT
         Brasilia; 1 Cessna 172C
Liaison some sqn with 10 Cessna 206H; 5 T-41D; 5 Cessna
         U-17A *Skywagon*
Survey   1 flt with 1 EMB-110B1 *Bandeirante*
Trg   some sqn with 6 PC-7U *Turbo Trainer**; 12SF-
         260EU (SF-260E); 2 B58 *Baron*
Hel   1 sqn with 1 AS-365 *Dauphin* 2; 4 Bell 212; 6 UH-
         1H *Iroquois*; 5 *Wessex* HC2

EQUIPMENT BY TYPE
AIRCRAFT 19 combat capable
  FGA 13: 9A-37B *Dragonfly*; 4 IA-58B *Pucara*
  TPT 19 : 2 C-130B *Hercules*; 2 CASA 212 *Aviocar* (tpt/SAR);
  2 EMB-110C *Bandeirante*; 10 Cessna 206H; 1 EMB-120ER
  Brasilia (VIP); 1 EMB-120RT *Brasilia*; 1 Cessna 172C
  SURVEY: 1 EMB-110BJ *Bandeirante*
  LIAISON 10: 5 T-41D *Mescalero*; 5 Cessna U-17A *Skywagon*
  TRG 20: 6 PC-7U *Turbo Trainer**; 12 SF-260EU (SF-260E);
  2 UB-58 (Beech 58) *Baron*
HELICOPTERS • UTL 16: 1 AS-365N *Dauphin*; 4 Bell 212;
6 UH-1H *Iroquois*; 5 *Wessex* HC2

Paramilitary 920

Guardia de Coraceros 470

Guardia de Granaderos 450

DEPLOYMENT

AFGHANISTAN
UN • UNAMA 1 obs

CÔTE D'IVOIRE
UN • UNOCI 2 obs

DEMOCRATIC REPUBLIC OF CONGO
UN • MONUC 1,324; 45 obs

EGYPT
MFO 87

ETHIOPIA/ERITREA
UN • UNMEE 37; 4 obs; Hel: 2 Bell 212

Caribbean and Latin America

GEORGIA
UN • UNOMIG 4 obs

HAITI
UN • MINUSTAH 1,146

INDIA/PAKISTAN
UN • UNMOGIP 2 obs

NEPAL
UN • UNMIN 3 obs

WESTERN SAHARA
UN • MINURSO 8 obs

Venezuela Ve

Venezuelan Bolivar Bs		2006	2007	2008
GDP	Bs	390tr	473tr	
	US$	182bn	220bn	
per capita	US$	7,060	8,446	
Growth	%	10.3	8.0	
Inflation	%	13.7	18.0	
Def exp	Bs	5.55tr		
	US$	2.58bn		
Def bdgt	Bs	4.47tr	5.51tr	
	US$	2.08bn	2.56bn	
US$1=Bs		2,147	2,147	

Population	26,084,662					

Age	0–14	15–19	20–24	25–29	30–64	65 plus
Male	15%	5%	5%	5%	18%	2%
Female	14%	5%	5%	4%	19%	3%

Capabilities

ACTIVE 115,000 (Army 63,000 Navy 17,500 Air 11,500 National Guard 23,000)
Terms of service 30 months selective, varies by region for all services

RESERVE 8,000 (Army 8,000)

ORGANISATIONS BY SERVICE

Army ε63,000
FORCES BY ROLE

Armd	1 div (4th) (1 armd bde, 1 Lt armd bde, 1 mot cav bde)
Mot Cav	1 div (9th) (1 mot cav bde, 1 ranger bde, 1 sec and spt bde)
Inf	1 div (1st) (1 armd unit; 1 SF unit; 2 inf bde; 1 arty unit; 1 spt unit); 1 div (2nd) (2 inf bde, 2 ranger bde (*each*: 2 ranger bn), 1 special dev and security bde); 1 div (3rd) (1 inf bde, 1 ranger bde(2 ranger bn), 1 comms regt, 1 MP bde)
lt Inf	1 div (5th) (2 Jungle inf bde)
AB	1 para bde

Cbt Engr 1 corps (3 regt)
Avn   1 comd (1 ac bn, 1 armd hel bn, 1 reccce bn)
Logistics 1 Log Comd (2 regt)

EQUIPMENT BY TYPE
MBT 81 AMX-30V
LT TK 109: 31AMX-13; 78 Scorpion 90
RECCE 431: 42 *Dragoon* 300 LFV2; 79 V-100/-150; 310 UR-53AR50 *Tiuna*
APC 71
    APC (T) 25 AMX-VCI
    APC (W) 36 *Dragoon* 300; 10 TPz-1 *Fuchs*
ARTY 370
    SP 155mm 12 (AMX) Mk F3
    TOWED 92: **105mm** 80: 40 M-101; 40 Model 56 pack howitzer; **155mm** 12 M-114
    MRL 160mm 20 LAR SP (LAR-160)
    MOR 246+: **81mm** 165; **120mm** 60 *Brandt*
        SP 21+: **81mm** 21 *Dragoon* 300PM; AMX-VTT
AT
    MSL • MANPATS 24 IMI MAPATS
    RCL 106mm 175 M-40A1
    RL 84mm AT-4
    GUNS 76mm 75 M-18 *Hellcat*
AD
    SAM RBS-70, *Mistral*
    GUNS
        SP 40mm 6+ AMX-13 *Rafaga*
        TOWED 40mm M-1; L/70
AIRCRAFT
    TPT 17: 4 IAI-102/201/202 *Arava*; 1 Beech C90 *King Air*; 12 M28 *Skytruck*
    UTL 8: 2 Cessna 206; 2 Cessna 207 *Stationair*; 1 Cessna 172; 3 Cessna 182 *Skylane*
    TRG 1 C-90 King Air
HELICOPTERS
    ATK 13: 10 Mi-35M2; 3 A-109 (non op)
    SPT 24: 5 Mi-17-1V, 2 AS-61D, 10 Bell 412EP, 2 Bell 412SP, 4 UH-1H, 1 Bell 205A-1
    TPT 1 Mi-26T2
    UTL 8: 4 Bell 206B *Jet Ranger*, 1 Bell 206L-3 *Longranger II*; 3 A-109*
RADAR • LAND RASIT (veh, arty)
MSL • ASM AS-11 *Kilter*

Reserve Organisations

Reserves 8,000 reservists

Armd	1 bn
Inf	4 bn
Ranger	1 bn
Arty	1 bn
Engr	2 regt

Navy ε14,300; ε3,200 conscript (total 17,500)
Naval Commands: Fleet, Marines, Naval Aviation, Coast Guard, Fluvial (River Forces)

FORCES BY ROLE

Navy 1 HQ (HQ *Arauca River*) located at El Amparo;
1 HQ (HQ Fluvial Forces) located at Ciudad
Bolivar; 1 HQ located at Caracas

EQUIPMENT BY TYPE

SUBMARINES • TACTICAL • SSK 2:
2 *Sabalo* (Ge T-209/1300) each with 8 single 533mm TT
each with 14 SST-4 HWT

PRINCIPAL SURFACE COMBATANTS • FRIGATES
FFG 6: *Mariscal Sucre* (It mod *Lupo*) each with 8 single
each with Mk 2 Otomat SSM, 1 Albatros Octuple with 8
Aspide SAM, 2 triple ASTT (6 eff.) each with A244 LWT, 1
127mm gun, 1 AB-212 (Bell 212) utl hels,

PATROL AND COASTAL COMBATANTS 6:
PFM 3 *Federación* (UK Vosper 57m) each with 2 single
each with 1 Mk 2 Otomat SSM
PCO 3 *Constitucion* (UK Vosper 37m) each with 1 76mm
gun

AMPHIBIOUS
LST 4 *Capana* (capacity 12 tanks; 200 troops) (FSU *Alligator*)
CRAFT 4: 1 LCM-8; 2 *Margarita* **LCU** (river comd); 1 **LCVP**

LOGISTICS AND SUPPORT 4
AORH 1
AGOR 1 *Punta Brava*
AGHS 2
ATF 1
TRG • AXS 1

FACILITIES

Bases	Located at Puerto Caballo (SS, FF, amph and service sqn), Caracas, Punto Fijo (patrol sqn)
Minor Bases	Located at Maracaibo (Coast Guard), Ciudad Bolivar, El Amparo, La Guaira (Coast Guard)
Naval airbases	Located at Turiamo, Puerto Hierro, La Orchila

Naval Aviation 500

FORCES BY ROLE

ASW 1 sqn with 7 AB-212 (Bell 212)
MP flt with 3 CASA 212-200 MPA
Spt flt with 4 Bell 412EP *Twin Huey*
Tpt 1 sqn with 1 Beech 200 *Super King Air*;
5 CASA 212 *Aviocar*; 1 Rockwell *Turbo Commander*
980C
Trg 1 sqn with 2 Cessna 310Q; 2 Cessna 402;
1 Cessna 210 *Centurion*

EQUIPMENT BY TYPE

AIRCRAFT 10 combat capable
ASW 7 AB-212 ASW (Bell 212)*
MP 3 CASA 212-200 MPA*
TPT 12: 1 Beech 200 *Super King Air*; 1 Beech C90 *King Air*; 5 CASA 212 *Aviocar*; 2 Cessna 310Q; 2 Cessna 402; 1 Rockwell *Turbo Commander* 980C
UTL 1 Cessna 210 *Centurion*
HELICOPTERS
UTL 5: 1 Bell 206B *JetRanger II* (trg); 4 Bell 412EP *Twin Huey*

Marines ε7,000

FORCES BY ROLE

HQ	1 div HQ
Amph	1 (amph veh) bn
Inf	2 (river) bn; 6 bn
Arty	1 bn (1 AD bn, 3 fd arty bty)
Marine	1 (river) bde; 2 (landing) bde
Engr	1 BCT; 4 bn

EQUIPMENT BY TYPE

APC (W) 32 EE-11 *Urutu*
AAV 11 LVTP-7 (to be mod to -7A1)
ARTY • TOWED 105mm 18 M-56
MOR 120mm 12 *Brandt*
AD • GUNS • SP 40mm 6 M-42

Coast Guard 1,000

EQUIPMENT BY TYPE

PRINCIPAL SURFACE COMBATANTS •
CORVETTES • FS 2:
2 *Almirante Clemente* each with 2 triple ASTT (6 eff.), 2
76mm gun
PATROL AND COASTAL COMBATANTS 45
PCI 20: 12 *Gavion* less than 100 tonnes; 4 *Petrel* (USCG
Point class); 2 Manaure; 2 Guaicapuro
PCR 23: 3 Terepaima (Cougar); 7 Polaris I; 2 Protector;
6 Courage; 5 Interceptor
LOGISTICS AND SUPPORT 2 Los Tanques (salvage
ship)

FACILITIES

Minor Base	1 (operates under Naval Comd and Control, but organisationally separate) located at La Guaira

Air Force 11,500

Flying hours 155 hrs/year

FORCES BY ROLE

Ftr/FGA	1 gp with 14 *Mirage* 50V/DV; 1 gp with 10 CF-5; 2 gp with `17 F-16A/B *Fighting Falcon*; 1 gp with 24 Su-30MKV
COIN	1 gp with 8 OV-10A/E *Bronco**; 3 AT-27*
ECM	1 sqn with 2 *Falcon* 20DC, 2 C-26B
Tpt	3 gp and Presidential flt with A-319CJ, B-737; Gulfstream III/Gulfstream IV; *Learjet* 24D; B-707; C-130H *Hercules*; G-222; HS-748
Liaison	Beech 200 *Super King Air*; Beech 65 *Queen Air*; Beech 80 *Queen Air*; Ce-182/206/208; Shorts 360; Cessna 500 *Citation I*; CE-550 *Citation II*; Cessna 182 *Skylane*
Hel	sqns with AS-332B *Super Puma*; AS-532 *Cougar*, UH-1B/H/N: Bell 212/ 412
Trg	1 gp with 15 EMB-312 *Tucano**; 12 SF-260EV;

EQUIPMENT BY TYPE

AIRCRAFT 94 combat capable
FTR/FGA 68: 24 Su-30MKV; 7 VF-5, 3 NF-5B; 17 F-16A
Fighting Falcon; 4 F-16B *Fighting Falcon*; 10 *Mirage* 50V; 3
Mirage 50DV

COIN 11: 8 OV-10A/E *Bronco**, 3 AT-27*
EW 4: 2 *Falcon* 20DC, 2 C-26B,
TPT 53: 1 A-319CJ; 2 B-707; 1 B-737; 5 Beech 200 *Super King Air*; 2 Beech 65 *Queen Air*; 5 Beech 80 *Queen Air*; 6 C-130H *Hercules*; 10 Ce-182N *Skylane*; 6 Ce-206 *Stationair*; 4 Ce-208B *Caravan*; 1 Ce-500 *Citation I*; 3 CE-550 *Citation II*; 1 *Cessna 551*; 1 G-222; 1 *Learjet* 24D; 2 Shorts 360 *Sherpa*; 1 SD-330 ; 1 Falcon 50 (VIP)
TRG 27: 15 EMB-312 *Tucano**; 12 SF-260E
HELICOPTERS
  CSAR 2 AS-532 *Cougar*
  TPT 16: 6 AS-332B *Super Puma*; 10 AS-532 *Cougar* (incl 2 VIP)
  UTL 10: 3 UH-1B, 5 UH-1H, 2 Bell 412SP
AD
  SAM 10+ *Barak*
    MANPAD: RBS-70
  GUNS
    TOWED 228+: **20mm**: 114 TCM-20; **35mm**; **40mm** 114 L/70
RADARS • LAND *Flycatcher*
MSL ASM AM-39 *Exocet*

AAM AIM-9L *Sidewinder*; AIM-9P *Sidewinder* R530

National Guard (Fuerzas Armadas de Cooperacion) 23,000

(Internal sy, customs) 8 regional comd
APC (W) 44: 24 Fiat 6614; 20 UR-416
MOR 150: 100 **60mm**; 50 **81mm**
PATROL AND COASTAL COMBATANTS • MISC BOATS/CRAFT 52 boats/craft
AIRCRAFT
  TPT 13: 1 Beech 200C *Super King Air*; 1 Beech 55 *Baron*; 2 Beech 80 *Queen Air*; 1 Beech 90 *King Air*; 2 Cessna 185; 4 IAI-201 *Arava* ; 2 Cessna 402C
  UTL/TRG 21: 5 Cessna U-206 *Stationair*; 11 M-28 *Skytruck* ; 3 Cessna 152 *Aerobat*; 1 PZL 106 *Kruk*; 1 PLZ M-26 *Isquierka*
HELICOPTERS • UTL 44+: 4 A-109; 1 AB-212 (Bell 212); 12 Bell 206B/L *JetRanger*; 6 Mi-17; 10 Bell 412; AS-350B; 9 AS-355F *Ecureui*l; 1 Ensrtom F-28C/1 F-280C

Table 11 Selected Arms Orders and Deliveries, Caribbean and Latin America

Country Supplier	Classification	Designation	Quantity	Order date	Original Delivery date	Comment
Argentina (Arg) Fr	LSD	Ouragan	2	2005	2007	First vessel was delivered in 2005. 2nd vessel delayed
US	Hel	SH-3 Sea King	6	2007	2008	USD27m. 2 hel to be used for spares. To enter navy service in 2008
Nl	Tpt	Fokker F28 Fellowship 1000 VIP	1	2007		
Brazil (Br) Fr	FGA	M-2000C Mirage	12	2005	2006	EUR60m (USD72m) Transfer
Sp	Tpt	CASA C-295	12	2005	2006	USD298m. One ac in service. Deliveries continuing
Sp	MP	P-3A Orion	12	2005	2008	Upgrade. USD401m. Upgrade of 8 ac to P-3AM configuration incl Link 11 FLIR, ESM and new radar by EADS-CASA. Option on a 9th upgrade is held, with the remaining 3 to be used as spares source
Sau	Ftr	F-5 Tiger E/F	9	2005	2005	Deliveries continuing
Il	AAM	Derby active radar beyond visual range air-to-air missile	–	2006	2006	–
Fr / dom	PCO	NAPA 500-class	2	2006	2009	Both to be commissioned in 2009
CH	APC	Mowag Piranha IIIC	5	2006	–	To be delivered to the Marines. 4 Piranha in APC configuration, 1 in maintenance role
RF	Hel	Mil Mi-35 / Mi-171	30	2006	–	USD400m
Ge	MBT	Leopard 1A5	270	2006	2008	EUR8m. The contract includes 250 tanks (30 of which to be used for spares) and 20 trg. To replace M-41C and M-60A3 tanks
It	APC	Urutu III	2	2007	–	1 6x6 Puma APC and 1 8x8 Centauro IFV to replace the EE-9 Cascavel and the EE-11 Urutu
RSA	AAM	A-Darter	–	2007	–	–
Chile (Chl) UK	FFG	Type 23 (Project Puente III)	3	2005	2006	GBP134m (USD253.5m) Ex UK RN HMS Norfolk (renamed Almirante Cochrane), Marlborough (to be renamed Almirante Condel) and Grafton (to be renamed Almirante Lynch). Last delivery 2008. First of three - ex HMS Norfolk - transferred October 2006
US	FGA	F-16C	6	2002	2005	4 ac yet to be delivered
US	FGA	F-16D	4	2002	2005	2 ac yet to be delivered
Nl	FGA	F-16AM Block 15	11	2006	2007	Ex RNLAF
Nl	FGA	F-16BM Block 15	7	2006	2007	Ex RNLAF
Ge	MBT	Leopard 2A3	100	2006	–	From German surplus stocks
Fr / Ge	Sat	Satellite	1	2006	2008	USD50m. Negotiations at an advanced stage
Nl / Be	AIFV	YPR-765	160	2006	–	–
US	APC	HMMWV	100	2006	–	–
US	ASSM	Tactical Harpoon Block II AURS	10	2006	2007	Includes 10 Mk 631
Int'l	Tpt	A310	2	2007	2007	EUR76m (USD104m). Secondhand ac. 1 to be used as the new presidential ac.
Sp	MPA	CASA CN-295	3	2007	–	Option for a further 5 ac
Ecuador (Ec) Sp	PCO	Vigilante (aka 6 de Deciembre)-class	3	2004	–	–

Table 11 Selected Arms Orders and Deliveries, Caribbean and Latin America

Country	Supplier	Classification	Designation	Quantity	Order date	Original Delivery date	Comment
Mexico (Mex)	Sp	Hel	AS-565 *Panther*	2	2003	2005	Option for a further 8
Trinidad and Tobago (TT)	UK	PSOH	–	3	2007	2009	GBP150m. (USD296m). For the Coast Guard
Uruguay (Ury)	Sp	Radar	3-D *Lanza* radar	2	2007	–	USD25m. 3-year contract
Venezuela (Ve)	Sp	Tpt	CASA C-295	10	2005	–	Yet to be delivered
	Sp	PCO	PCO	4	2005	–	–
	Sp	ECC	ECC	4	2005	–	–
	Sp	MPA	CASA CN-235	2	2005	–	Yet to be delivered
	PRC	Radar	JYL-1	3	2005	–	USD150m. Contract also includes a fully equipped command-and-control centre, spare parts, training, technical support and the lease of a satellite communication system
	RF	Hel	Mi-35M	3	2005	2006	Combined cost with order for 6 Mi-17V-5 and 1 Mi-26T is USD120m
	RF	Hel	Mi-26T	1	2005	2006	Combined cost with order for 6 Mi-17V-5 and 3 Mi-35M is USD120m
	RF	Hel	Mi-17V-5	5	2005	2006	USD81m. Follow on contract
	RF	Hel	Mi-17V-5 & Mi-35M	38	2006	–	USD384m. 3 Mi-17V-5 delivered in March 2006
	NI	Radar	*Tacticos* Combat Management System	8	2006	2008	Final delivery 2012. Thales NI to install combat management systems on warships built in Spain
	Be / dom	APC	*Iguana* FV4-270 4X4	100	–	–	Lack of a local manufacturer so far
	Sp	PB	Patrol Boat	31	2005	2006	USD199m. Boats will be 30, 20 and 17 metres long

Chapter Three
Europe

The defence debate in Europe in 2007 has at times been dominated by discussion of the proposals, by the United States, to install parts of its ballistic missile defence system in Eastern Europe. The US has been negotiating with the Polish and the Czech governments over the proposed deployment of missile defence facilities and systems, in particular the establishment of a 10-silo long-range interceptor field in Poland and the installation of an X-band radar (like the one currently at Kwajalein Atoll in the Marshall Islands) in the Czech Republic. According to the US Missile Defense Agency, the proposed system is designed to defend the US and its European allies from an evolving ballistic missile threat from the Middle East.

Russia has stressed its opposition to the proposals (see Russia, p. 205). President Vladimir Putin floated the possibility of the Russian-leased radar station at Gaballa in Azerbaijan being used in lieu of new systems in Eastern Europe at the June 2007 G8 summit in Heiligendamm, Germany, but US Secretary of Defense Robert Gates said after a NATO ministerial meeting in Brussels in the same month that he saw the radar in Azerbaijan 'as an additional capability', and that the US 'intended to proceed with … the X-band radar in the Czech Republic'. On a visit to Prague in late October, Gates remarked, in connection with Russia's concerns, that the US could increase transparency in two ways: one could be by allowing Russian observers into the Czech Republic following Czech approval (a proposition that was reported to have received short shrift from Prague); and the other could be to 'tie its activation in to "definitive proof of the threat", including Iranian missile tests'. This latter approach would still entail, according to Gates, the completion of negotiations and construction of sites. At time of writing, despite further talks, Moscow was still opposed to Washington's plans; Foreign Minister Sergei Lavrov said in early October that 'We perceive no threat which would emanate from Iranian territory for Europe or the US … the focus of these facilities clearly affects the security interests of the Russian Federation'.

The June 2007 meeting of NATO defence ministers in Brussels scheduled an assessment of the implications of the US plans for February 2008 and remarked that the 'NATO roadmap on missile defence was clear'. NATO will continue its ongoing project to develop a theatre missile defence (TMD) capability, will 'assess the full implications of the US system for the Alliance, and continue existing cooperation with Russia on [TMD] as well as consultations on related issues'. As noted in *The Military Balance 2006* (p. 48), NATO wishes to establish an Active Layered Theatre Ballistic Missile Defence (ALTBMD) with initial operational capability by 2010. In November 2006, NATO signed a contract for the 'development of an architecture for the protection of deployed NATO forces from ballistic missile threats, and the design of an ALTBMD Integration Test Bed' with a consortium led by SAIC International. ALTBMD will comprise a command-and-control network that is designed to integrate various TMD systems into a single network with the ability to give layered protection against ballistic missiles.

US ballistic missile defence plans for Europe and US moves to set up training bases in Bulgaria and Romania have proved an irritant to Russia. Moscow views any decision to establish a permanent military base in Central Europe as a violation of assurances given to Russia under the 1997 NATO–Russia Founding Act, and at the time of NATO enlargement in 1999, that no new military bases would be placed in new member states. In April, during an address to the Duma, President Putin proposed that Russia suspend its obligations under the 1999 adapted **Conventional Forces in Europe (CFE) Treaty** unless it was ratified by the US and European states.

Originally agreed in 1990, the CFE Treaty set limits on the quantities of particular conventional weapons that could be deployed between the Atlantic and the Urals. After meeting in Oslo in 1992, signatories agreed that individual state holdings would replace blocs as the basis of verification. The 1996 CFE Review Conference addressed concerns about the original 'flank' regime, after the division of former Soviet holdings left Russia with limited equipment, particularly in the North Caucasus (see *The Military Balance 2000–2001*, pp. 35–6.) Consensus that the treaty required adaptation led signatories to meet in

Istanbul in 1999, where an adapted CFE Treaty was negotiated. This established national and territorial ceilings for weaponry, among other points.

Russia's concerns included the failure of NATO states to sign the Adapted Treaty and the failure of new East European and Baltic NATO member states to become states parties to the Treaty. Moscow continues to press for further revision of the treaty on the grounds that the military equipment left to the Baltic states was 'treaty-limited equipment' when it was under Russian control, but is no longer subject to treaty-based restrictions, as the Baltic states are not signatories to the CFE Treaty. Other sticking points in the CFE area concern the limited Russian presence at the Gudauta base in Abkhazia, Georgia, an ongoing point of contention between Russia and Georgia, with the latter continuing to press for closure of the base. Gudauta is viewed by Russia as the support base for the CIS-mandated peacekeeping forces in Abkhazia. There are also tensions between European Organisation for Security and Cooperation in Europe (OSCE) member states and Russia over the continuing presence of Russian troops in Transdniestr.

In July, Putin signed a decree proposing a moratorium on Russia's participation in the CFE Treaty; on 7 November the Duma voted in favour of Putin's proposed moratorium. The moratorium is due to take effect on 12 December 2007, just after the late-November OSCE Ministerial Council meeting.

Meanwhile, in October, Putin remarked – prior to meeting US Secretary of Defense Robert Gates and Secretary of State Condoleezza Rice – that thought should be given to turning bilateral agreements such as the **Intermediate-Range Nuclear Forces Treaty** into global agreements. He continued, 'If we fail to reach this objective I think it will become difficult for us to remain bound by the terms of such agreements when other countries are actively developing these kinds of weapons systems, including countries close to our borders'.

NATO

NATO's ongoing operations in **Afghanistan** constitute the priority area for the Alliance. As noted in the 2007 edition of *The Military Balance*, NATO's International Security Assistance Force (ISAF) took over operational control of the entire country after completing its 'Stage 4' expansion on 5 October 2006. By the end of October 2007, ISAF had 41,144 troops under the command of US General Dan McNeill

(see map, p. 328). As well as combat and the provision of security, NATO forces are also engaged in training the Afghan National Army, often through its Operational Mentoring and Liaison Teams. NATO commanders in theatre repeatedly call for more troops and resources, with a particular demand for more helicopters. The Alliance's planners and commanders on the ground have continued to be vexed by the issue of national 'caveats' that limit the activities a country's forces may undertake. After the Riga Summit in November 2006, some countries relaxed their caveats; for example in April 2007, German *Tornado* aircraft were deployed on a reconnaissance mission in support of NATO ground forces in the south. However, the proposed deployment of an Afghan battalion from Regional Command-North (RC-N) to support operations in the southern Helmand province was cancelled because the embedded training team was German, and Berlin refused to allow it to deploy outside RC-N. Troop-contributing countries have complained about those who do not contribute, or who send only minimal forces. At NATO's Noordwijk meeting in October 2007, Secretary-General Jaap de Hoop Scheffer remarked that he had heard offers from various countries of more resources, including for the south of Afghanistan, but while NATO may have 90% of the forces it needs, shortages still exist.

NATO expansion remains on the agenda. At the Riga Summit in 2006, NATO declared its intention to invite those countries who met NATO standards at the time of the April 2008 Bucharest Summit to join the Alliance. Albania, Croatia and FYROM, the countries currently in the NATO Membership Action Plan (MAP), hope to receive such an invitation. While NATO occasionally signalled that these nations will have to continue to work hard to meet their MAP obligations, and that further enlargement is by no means a foregone conclusion, all three may be invited to join. Furthermore, several Allies, the US in particular, would like to extend MAP status to Georgia (which currently has 'intensified dialogue' status), which would put it on a firmer path to membership in the near to medium term (see discussion of Georgia, p. 106). Ukraine, another potential member, remains politically divided on the question of NATO membership, and it is unlikely that the Alliance will take the initiative on this matter beyond the already ongoing dialogue. Other priorities for discussion at the Bucharest Summit are likely to include Afghanistan, missile defence and a complex agenda for cooperation with other international organisations and partner countries.

An underlying theme for NATO in 2008 will be the question of what role the Alliance should play regarding security issues such as energy infrastructure and cyber warfare. The latter issue gained prominence in May 2007 when numerous government and private websites in Estonia crashed after being hit by denial-of-service attacks in the midst of a row between Russia and Estonia about the removal of a Soviet war memorial in Tallinn. NATO did deploy a small team of experts to monitor the situation, but currently cyber attacks are not treated as falling within the provisions of the Alliance's treaty and thus do not trigger obligations concerning common defence. For the time being, NATO sees ensuring cyber-security as a defensive task connected to infrastructure protection.

The **NATO Response Force** (NRF) was declared to have reached full operational capability on 29 November 2006 during the Riga Summit. General James Jones, then supreme allied commander, Europe, stated that additional resource pledges from Bulgaria, Canada, France, Germany, Italy, Norway, Romania, Spain, Turkey, the UK and the US had helped to fill gaps. Specifically, additional troops, helicopters, transport aircraft, combat support and combat service support have been provided. However, it quickly transpired that the NRF, intended to be key to the transformation of Alliance forces, faced serious difficulties with troop and equipment shortages re-emerging almost immediately after full operational capability was declared. With actual uses for the force remaining unclear, Alliance members have found providing forces for the NRF costly, especially given the simultaneous task of attempting to meet the demands of ongoing military crisis-management missions. As a result, the NRF's future is in doubt. NATO planners are reportedly assessing whether the NRF should be reduced in size, whether its spectrum of operations should be more limited, or whether an amendment to the scheduled six-month rotation might salvage the force.

NATO is making progress with two complementary initiatives in the field of strategic airlift; the Strategic Airlift Interim Solution (SALIS) and the Strategic Airlift Capability (SAC). SALIS entered into force in early 2006 and provides a 16-nation consortium, led by Germany, with access to chartered Antonov An-124-100 transport aircraft. More recently, 15 NATO members plus Finland and Sweden have been in negotiation with Boeing for the purchase of three to four C-17 aircraft to be based in Europe and operated jointly. The first deliveries had been expected in 2007, but initial operational capability has now been pushed back to mid 2008, with full operational capability expected in 2009. In June, the NATO Airlift Management Organisation was created, which will acquire, maintain and support assets on behalf of SAC-participating countries. Participating countries are: Bulgaria, the Czech Republic, Denmark, Estonia, Hungary, Italy, Latvia, Lithuania, the Netherlands, Norway, Poland, Romania, Slovakia, Slovenia and the US (and non-NATO members Finland and Sweden).

EUROPEAN UNION

As of January 2007, the EU's Battlegroups were said to have reached full operational capability, such that from that date there would always be two battlegroups available for near-simultaneous deployment. At the core of these force packages is an infantry battalion, plus designated but mission-tailored combat support and combat service support units. The groups are intended to be able to sustain themselves for 30 days in initial operations, extendable to 120 days if re-supplied. In the second half of 2007, the two battlegroup slots were filled by Italian–Hungarian–Slovenian and Greek–Cypriot–Romanian–Bulgarian battlegroups. In early 2008, the Nordic battlegroup, led by Sweden and with contributions from Finland, Estonia, Ireland and non-EU member Norway, and a Spanish-led group with contributions from Germany, France and Portugal, will be on call. In the second half of 2008, Germany will lead a battlegroup with contributions from France, Belgium, Luxembourg and Spain, with the second battlegroup provided by the UK.

In parallel to progress in the battlegroup initiative, discussions on a possible maritime rapid response concept and a rapid response air initiative have also taken place. Together these would form the EU Military Rapid Response Concept. The goal would be that these land, air and sea elements would be available for use either as stand-alone forces or in joint operations. Signs of movement on these issues were visible when the EU Maritime Task Group was activated for the first time on 7 March. It consisted of vessels from Germany, Belgium, France and the Netherlands. Ultimately, the EU-MTG is intended to mirror the capabilities of the EU Battlegroups in relation to their ability to deploy in various crisis scenarios.

The **EU Operations Centre** (OpsCen) became operational on 1 January 2007, providing the EU with a third option for the command of European Security and Defence Policy (ESDP) missions aside from using NATO assets and capabilities under the Berlin Plus agreement or relying on one of the five national operations headquarters (OHQ) assigned to the EU. (National OHQ have been designated by France, Germany, Greece, Italy and the UK). OpsCen is part of the EU Civil/Military Cell which in turn is located within the EU Military Staff. It has a permanent staff of eight (five officers plus three NCOs), and exists in essence to generate an OHQ for operations involving up to 2,000 troops, in response to a Council decision to deploy. The permanent staff ensures the readiness of facilities and infrastructure, prepares operating procedures and identifies and trains the personnel that would reinforce the OpsCen in case of activation. Once the OpsCen is activated, it should reach initial operating capability within five days, meaning that within this timeframe it should have the ability to plan an autonomous operation. If it is activated for more than 20 days, it should graduate to full operational capability, when it should be able to run autonomous ESDP operations, and is scheduled to have a staff of 89, including 13 civilian experts. The OpsCen was activated for the first time during *MILEX 07/CPX*, the EU military exercise conducted in June.

Following a joint action by the Council of the European Union in April 2006, an EU Planning Team (EUPT) of around 110, including local staff, deployed to **Kosovo** to plan a future ESDP mission which would deal with various issues related to the rule of law, including the judiciary, police, customs and correctional services. The mandate for the EUPT, after several extensions, is expected to run until the end of March 2008 at the earliest. It is envisaged that the eventual mission will comprise some 1,800 civilian personnel, making it by far the biggest effort undertaken by the EU in the field of civilian crisis management. To be mandated for an initial period of two years, the Kosovo mission will be 'integrated', with personnel in the justice, police and customs sectors all working under one single head of mission.

On 15 October, the European Council adopted a joint action on a military operation in **Chad** and the **Central African Republic (CAR)**. To be conducted with the approval of the Chadian and CAR governments, the EUFOR TCHAD/RCA deployment is intended to be for a period of 12 months from the declaration of initial operating capability. The force-generation process for the operation began at the end of October, and lead elements were due to deploy in November. At the time of writing, the force was planned to be up to 4,300 strong, with some 20 contributor countries. France was expected to provide about half of the force. EUFOR TCHAD/RCA is designed to support the UN presence in the east of Chad and the northeast of the CAR. Its objectives are to contribute to the protection of refugees and displaced persons, to facilitate aid delivery by improving the overall security situation, and to help protect UN personnel and facilities. The EU has appointed Irish Lt-Gen. Patrick Nash as the operation commander, and a French brigadier, Jean-Philippe Ganascia, as force commander. The EU OHQ will be located in France. After six months, an assessment will be made over the need for a UN follow-on mission. **France's** President Nicolas Sarkozy, elected in May, has initiated a debate on French defence policy which will lead to the publication of a new White Paper on defence, scheduled for March 2008. The first such document since 1994, this will coincide with the next multi-year military programme law (the current one runs from 2003 to 2008), which has in the past guided, among other things, French defence-reform efforts and equipment programmes. The president appears to see an opportunity for a fundamental review of France's defence priorities. The commission tasked with drawing up the White Paper was instructed to develop a framework for the next 15 years covering defence and security policy, on the assumption that defence spending would be stabilised at 2% of GDP (see p. 108). Sarkozy has repeatedly stated that French defence policy should focus on priority capability needs, and that opportunities for joint programmes and defence-industrial consolidation need to be explored (see p. 451). The French government has openly considered rejoining NATO's integrated military structure. Given that such a move would be highly symbolic and is a sensitive issue domestically, ministerial-level statements have emphasised that a careful weighting of arguments for and against such a move is needed, and that a decision is unlikely before 2009. Initial reactions from within NATO were positive. If the decision to proceed were taken, France's likely demands for senior command posts in NATO and allied support for a strengthened ESDP would have to be balanced with its partners' reluctance on both accounts. President Sarkozy has also indicated that he intends to use France's EU presidency in the second half of 2008 to rewrite the EU's security strategy, which dates from 2003.

A long-awaited White Paper on **German** security policy and the future of the Bundeswehr, published in October 2006, acknowledged that international crisis management missions were the most likely tasks for Germany's military, and would therefore have over-riding influence on the structure and capabilities of the German armed forces. The White Paper high-lighted force protection, reconnaissance, command and control, missile defence, precision stand-off strike and strategic deployability as central to the new capabilities profile. It confirmed previous plans to make up to 15,000 troops available for the NRF, of which up to 5,000 would be on standby. A pool of up to 18,000 German troops is also available to meet EU Headline Goal requirements. A further 1,000 troops are provided within the UN Standby Arrangement System, and 1,000 are available for unilateral rescue and evacuation tasks. The paper also confirmed the differentiation between the three force categories of the Bundeswehr. The response forces, 35,000 strong, are a joint rapid-reaction force with network-centric warfare (NCW) capability for high-intensity missions, including combat. It is from this pool that Germany draws its NRF and EU battlegroup contingents, as well as troops for other demanding missions. Next are the 70,000-strong stabilisation forces, whose purpose is to serve in medium- and low-intensity peace support operations. Up to 14,000 of them are to be deployable at any given time and sustainable for long-term missions. The stabilisation forces will have partial NCW capability. Finally, the 147,500-strong support forces provide combat support for the response and stabilisation forces, such as logistics, transport, medical and command and control. Only some elements of the support forces will have NCW capability. The rationale was to ensure an interven-tion capability within budget limits, since it was not feasible to modernise the entire force.

Defence developments in **Sweden** are also the subject of much debate. The budget squeeze (see p. 110) is a significant problem and threatens to under-mine the reform effort currently being undertaken. For example, the air force was forced to delay the deployment of stand-off precision cruise missiles from 2006–07 to 2012 because of budget cuts. The political context remains volatile, with the minister of defence resigning in early September in part over ongoing budget constraints. As leader of the Nordic Battlegroup, scheduled to be operational by January 2008, Sweden is expected to provide more than 2,000 of over 2,600 personnel, and the country's armed forces are widely thought to have used its leadership of the group as a justification for moves towards an overall transformation of the armed forces. But the uncertain financial situation undermines efforts to conduct medium- and long-term defence planning; it is thus questionable whether recent advances in defence reform can be sustained and developed.

In March 2007, members of the **United Kingdom** Parliament voted to approve the government's plans to take necessary steps 'to maintain the UK's nuclear deterrent beyond the life of the current system', i.e the *Vanguard* SSBNs and *Trident* D5 missiles. Then Prime Minister Tony Blair had made the case for this deci-sion in a parliamentary statement in December 2006, saying that the second *Vanguard* boat would end its extended service life in 2024. This would leave only two SSBNs, which could not guarantee contin-uous patrols. (The UK maintains a continuous at-sea deterrent, with one boat on patrol, one normally in extended refit and the other two operationally available.) As it would take 17 years to design, build and deploy a replacement, he continued, a decision needed to be made in 2007. Blair estimated that the overall cost of the project would be between £15bn and £20bn, taking up on average 3% of the defence budget, although precise costings remain unclear. The govern-ment also committed to an upgrade to the *Trident* D5 submarine-launched ballistic missiles. These decisions did not occur in isolation; there was substantive debate over the future of the UK nuclear deterrent in which the government argued that these investments would not come 'at the expense of the conventional capabili-ties our armed forces need'. In June, the UK defence secretary said in response to a Parliamentary question that 'work has started mobilising MOD and industry to undertake the detailed concept phase for the new class of submarines and on taking forward the UK's participation in the programme to extend the life of the *Trident* D5 missile'. (see Jeremy Stocker, *The United Kingdom and Nuclear Deterrence*, IISS Adelphi Paper no. 386; 'The Future of the UK's Nuclear Deterrent: Decisions Ahead', IISS *Strategic Comments*, vol. 12 no. 2, February 2006.) The other key procurement decision taken during the year was the decision announced in late July, after the Comprehensive Spending Review, of Main Gate approval for the acquisition of two aircraft carriers (see p. 107 and p. 452). At 65,000 tonnes, these will be the largest vessels to have entered Royal Navy service, and are scheduled to have the capability to embark a tailored air group of up to 40 aircraft, including F-35 Joint Strike Fighters.

Meanwhile, *Operation Banner*, UK forces' operations in support of the civil power in Northern Ireland, ended on 31 July after 38 years. 651 service personnel had been killed during the operation, and 6,307 wounded. A remaining permanent garrison of 5,000 will be available for operations worldwide. The task of assisting the police in Northern Ireland 'in the event of extreme public disorder', however, remains, under the name *Operation Helvetic*. Earlier, in March, major UK forces withdrew from Bosnia-Herzegovina after 15 years, following the decision by the EU to reduce its military presence in the country from around 6,000 personnel to around 2,500. Meanwhile, much debate in the UK has centred on operations in Afghanistan and Iraq, and their impact on the military institutionally (including overstretch on the armed forces), and on personnel individually. According to General Sir Richard Dannatt, chief of the UK General Staff, when he spoke in a September address to the IISS, 'the Army that crossed the Line of Departure [into Iraq] on that morning in March 2003 has gone. We have adapted and reformed at an incredible pace in only four years', but he was 'increasingly concerned about the growing gulf between the Army and the Nation'. In Afghanistan, troop deployments rose significantly through the year, with UK forces engaged in high-intensity combat operations against insurgents, primarily in the south (see p. 327). UK troop levels in Afghanistan were scheduled to increase to 7,700 by the end of the year, with numbers in Iraq falling to around 4,500 after Iraqi security forces assumed control of Basra province. Prime Minister Gordon Brown has said that he plans to reduce UK forces in Iraq to 2,500 by spring 2008. According to General Dannatt, the future direction of the UK's armed forces 'is already being shaped by our experiences in Iraq and Afghanistan'.

As noted above, **Georgia** is favoured by some for a deeper relationship with NATO. However, as observed in *The Military Balance 2007*, Moscow views Georgia's ambitions as 'confrontation within its traditional sphere of influence' (p. 96). But despite Russian opposition and the scepticism of some Western European countries, the Georgian bid for NATO membership has been strongly supported by some newer NATO members and by the US Senate, which on 22 March approved a bill expressing support and authorising funding for Georgian and Ukrainian membership. Were Georgia to accede to NATO, the Alliance would be admitting a country with two internal unresolved conflicts: Abkhazia and South Ossetia. Tensions between Georgia and Russia centering on these unresolved conflicts, and US/NATO involvement, have persisted throughout the year. Tbilisi alleged a number of incidents of Russian aircraft violating its airspace, including a claim that on 6 August Russian aircraft entered Georgian airspace several times, on one occasion launching an anti-radiation missile against a radar site near the town of Gori. Moscow has denied the claims. Meanwhile, Georgia continues to contribute to Coalition force levels in Iraq, with an increase to over 2,000 personnel in 2007; Georgian forces are also deployed with NATO's KFOR force in Kosovo.

In October, there were concerns about a possible intervention by **Turkey** in northern Iraq. Turkish forces had been active in operations against the Kurdistan Workers' Party (PKK) following a number of clashes with the organisation. In early October, one incident led to the death of a number of Turkish troops and the capture of eight others. Concurrently, Ankara increased its forces on the border and, on 17 October, Turkey's parliament approved cross-border operations into northern Iraq. Diplomatic activity following this rise in tension resulted in a number of initiatives, including an announcement by the Iraqi government in late October that it would close PKK offices and halt the group's operations in Iraq. In early November, US Secretary of State Rice visited Ankara, saying that the US 'considers the PKK a terrorist organisation and indeed that we have a common enemy, that we must find ways to take effective action so that Turkey will not suffer from terrorist attacks'. Two days later, it was reported that the eight Turkish soldiers held by the PKK had been released, although tensions remained high.

EUROPE – DEFENCE ECONOMICS

The euro-currency area experienced a period of strong economic growth from mid 2006 until the credit-driven financial market turbulence of mid 2007, driven by a broad-based acceleration in investment spending (especially in Germany), a pickup in construction and robust exports. However, data released in the second half of 2007 gave mixed signals about the likely economic performance of Western European countries over coming quarters, and, in the light of uncertain financial markets and probable weaker growth in the US, the risk is that growth will slow. Deteriorating conditions in credit markets are likely to depress consumption, and in those countries where house prices still seem elevated, growth will depend to a large extent on the pace of adjustment of the housing sector to tightening credit conditions. On the fiscal front, several countries in the euro area took advantage of buoyant government revenues in 2006 to improve deficit positions, with the result that the region's fiscal deficit declined from 2.6% of GDP in 2006 to 1.6% of GDP in 2006 and is forecast to fall to 0.9% of GDP in 2007.

Despite the improved fiscal environment, European members of NATO (including Canada) continued the recent trend of allocating a declining proportion of national output to defence. In 2000, the non-US members of NATO committed 2.0% of GDP to defence, but by 2006 this had fallen to 1.75% of GDP and only five European countries (Bulgaria, France, Greece, Turkey and the UK) managed to achieve the NATO guideline level of 2% of national output.

The economy of the **United Kingdom** has remained one of the strongest among the major European countries, with GDP forecast to grow by 3.1% in 2007, while the government's budget deficit is set to narrow to 2.5% of GDP. In October 2007, the government revealed its new three-year Comprehensive Spending Review (CSR) to cover the period 2008–10, which included a pledge to continue increasing the defence budget by a modest annual rate of 1.5% above inflation. However, given that inflation within the defence sector in terms of both operational and investment expenditure is generally accepted to be higher than inflation within the economy at large (the benchmark used to calculate the budget increase), Ministry of Defence (MoD) finances are set to remain under pressure for the foreseeable future. In addition to extra funds from central government, the CSR documents also contained details of 'value for money' reforms that produced savings of £2.8 billion over the previous three years and which are forecast to increase to £2.7bn per year by 2010. Initiatives in the coming three years will include a 5% year-on-year reduction in the MoD's administrative overheads (including a 25% saving in the MoD's head office), the merger of Land Command and the Adjutant General's Command, and the merger of the Defence Logistics Organisation and the Defence Procurement Agency to form Defence Equipment and Support. Asset disposals are also set to continue. Since the 2002 CSR, the MoD has disposed of over £1.5bn in surplus assets and will continue to contribute its share to the government's overall target of disposal of £30bn in surplus assets. During the forthcoming CSR period,

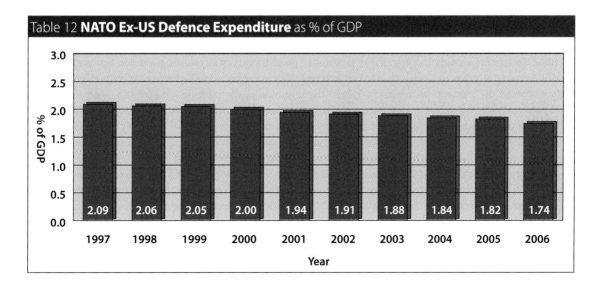

Table 12 **NATO Ex-US Defence Expenditure** as % of GDP

% of GDP

Year	% of GDP
1997	2.09
1998	2.06
1999	2.05
2000	2.00
2001	1.94
2002	1.91
2003	1.88
2004	1.84
2005	1.82
2006	1.74

the MoD will dispose of a further £3bn in surplus assets, of which over 80% will be sold on for housing development.

Notwithstanding the increase in the planned defence budget, questions about the impact of the UK's involvement in Iraq and Afghanistan both on readiness levels and defence finances led the House of Commons Defence Committee to declare that UK armed forces 'are operating in challenging conditions in insufficient numbers and without all the equipment they need'. Between 2001 and March 2007, the government provided an additional £6.6bn on top of the core defence budget to fund international activities; however, it is difficult to isolate the exact cost of such operations, and suspicions remain that the high operational tempo of the UK armed forces is impacting on the core budget. In March 2007, the Defence Select Committee published a report on the Defence Science and Technology Laboratory in which it claimed that UK operations in Iraq and Afghanistan were having a negative impact on research and development (R&D), suggesting that it was inevitable that some long-term R&D funds were being re-directed to provide support for international operations. In late 2006, the National Audit Office claimed that the MoD had failed to tailor its personnel requirements to reflect the current heavy level of operational commitments, concluding that the armed forces were being forced to operate with around 5,000 fewer personnel than they needed. This was followed by a report from the Public Accounts Committee in July 2007 which suggested that the armed forces were closer to 6,000 under strength, leading the MoD to counter that total armed forces manning requirements had in fact decreased due to restructuring across the services designed to 'improve capability and flexibility'.

In December 2006, the government announced its plans to sustain a credible UK nuclear deterrent capability into the 2020s and beyond, and Parliament duly endorsed the plans in March 2007. Whilst the final programme is yet to be decided, the most likely outcome of this decision will include procurement of a new class of nuclear-powered submarines to replace the current *Vanguard* class, together with a programme to extend the life of the *Trident* D5 missile. Although the plan is, so far, effectively uncosted, the CSR makes the optimistic assessment that the renewal of the UK's nuclear deterrent 'will not come at the expense of the conventional capability that our armed forces need'.

In terms of conventional procurement, the biggest decision in the past year was Main Gate approval for the acquisition of two new aircraft carriers. First outlined in the 1998 Strategic Defence Review, the future carrier programme has been delayed for several years, due to in part to the consolidation of the UK maritime industrial sector following the publication of the 2005 Defence Industrial Strategy. At a cost of £2bn each, the new ships will displace 65,000 tonnes and accommodate an air wing of 40 aircraft, including Joint Strike Fighter aircraft. Construction work is to be undertaken by a new Aircraft Carrier Alliance group comprising BAE Systems, Babcock, KBR, Thales and VT Group.

Despite warnings from the prime minister that the country is 'bankrupt' and concern from the EU that **France** is not doing enough to reduce its fiscal deficit, new President Nicolas Sarkozy unveiled a budget for 2008 that does little to help towards the goal of achieving a balanced budget. The target date for achieving this goal has already been moved from 2010 to 2012, and given that the 2008 budget is based on ambitious growth targets of 2.0% to 2.5%, even the revised date looks optimistic. The implications for defence spending have not yet been revealed: a new multi-year allocation plan is due to be revealed in spring 2008, but since the 2008 budget includes a real-terms freeze on public spending – in order to help fund a series of tax cuts aimed at boosting support for contentious welfare and labour reforms – the medium-term outlook for defence looks challenging. Whilst the 2008 defence budget does include €15.9bn for capital investment (only €250m less than programmed), meaning that the 2003–08 defence plan will have been effectively fully funded (the first time any multi-year plan will have been fully funded since their introduction in the early 1960s), Defence Minister Hervé Morin has warned that the next spending blueprint, for 2009–14, will almost certainly lead to cuts in some programmes. Speaking in July, Morin explained to Defence Committee deputies that annual equipment funding would need to increase by 42% over the coming six-year period in order to pay for the programmes currently planned, and that as such an outcome was 'impossible … priorities will have to be defined and choices made'. In addition to the probable cuts in equipment programmes, the MoD will reduce its payroll by 6,000 in 2008. Of particular interest is the fate of the proposed second aircraft carrier to partner the nuclear-powered *Charles de Gaulle*. After some initial hesitation, Sarkozy declared himself in favour of proceeding with the programme, a favourite project of his predecessor

Jacques Chirac. However, before he took up his post, Morin was expressing doubt that there would be sufficient funding to proceed with the acquisition.

Economic growth in **Germany** reached 2.9% in 2006, the highest level for eight years, resulting in a further increase in government revenues. After recording a fiscal deficit of 4% of GDP in 2003 (and thus breaching the rules of the single European currency, which originally set a ceiling of 3% of GDP), the government implemented a series of measures that successfully reduced the deficit to 1.6% of GDP in 2006, and it is forecast to fall again in 2007. Many areas of public spending, including defence, have been frozen during the past few years as the government has attempted to balance its books, but the 2008 federal budget did include a modest increase in defence spending and a pledge to make additional small annual increases until 2011. The 2008 defence budget is €29.3bn, up from €28.4bn the previous year, and it is forecast to grow to €30.3bn in 2011. It should, however, be noted that, of the increase between 2007 and 2008, around €300 million is accounted for by changes in VAT legislation. Of course with parliamentary elections in 2009, there is a real chance that this spending schedule will be amended by a new parliament. Furthermore, behind the headline figures, there is a less positive picture regarding procurement funding.

As illustrated in Table 13, the Bundeswehr Plan 2008 includes a reduction of €2.69bn over four years in the allocation of funds for equipment procurement, compared to the schedule laid out the previous year. It therefore seems fairly certain that without any change to this planned funding, certain equipment programmes will continue to be reduced in size and suffer delays to their projected in-service dates. Not only is the Bundeswehr procurement budget under pressure, but it has emerged that the air force is facing significant financial challenges in keeping its *Tornado* aircraft up to minimum NATO standards for both capability and training. For example, German air crews are often only managing around 100 hours of in-flight training compared to the NATO minimum standard of 180 hours, while some aircraft deployed to Afghanistan are running short of spare parts. One possible solution that has been discussed by the parliamentary defence committee would see the

Table 13 Germany: Equipment Expenditure

Year	Plan 2007	Plan 2008	Difference
2008	€4.69bn	€4.06bn	– €630m
2009	€5.10bn	€4.36bn	– €740m
2010	€5.53bn	€4.74bn	– €790m
2011	€6.06bn	€5.53bn	– €530m
Total	€21.38bn	€18.69bn	– €2.69bn

separation of the financing of out-of-area operations, such as in Afghanistan or off the Lebanese coast, from the defence budget itself.

Despite the challenging budget picture, the MoD was able to proceed with two major equipment programmes during the past year. Probably the most urgent acquisition is of new infantry fighting vehicles for the army, and the 2008 budget included initial funding for the procurement of up to 410 *Puma* vehicles. The original demonstrator vehicle was delivered in December 2005, and an operational evaluation stage began in May 2007, with first deliveries due by the end of 2007. The second major development saw the German Federal Office of Defence Technology and Procurement award the ARGE F125 consortium a contract to build four new multi-purpose frigates for the German navy. The programme, valued at around €2.3bn, will deliver four 6,800-tonne frigates specifically designed to support multinational crisis reaction and stabilisation operations, such as those currently being performed by German frigates in the eastern Mediterranean. The vessels are intended to be delivered at a rate of one a year from 2014. Other naval projects in the pipeline include a third task-force supply vessel and the much delayed naval MH90 helicopter, needed to replace the current fleet of *Sea Kings*.

Unlike other major economies in Europe, **Italy** has made little progress in addressing its sizeable budget deficit. In 2006 the fiscal deficit measured 4.4% of GDP, the highest since the introduction of the single currency, and the fifth year out of six that the government has exceeded the 3% of GDP guideline. Not surprisingly, the government's fiscal challenges have had an impact on defence expenditure, which has remained broadly unchanged, averaging €26bn (including Carabinieri and military pensions) since 2001. Defence spending measured just 1.66% of GDP in 2006, down from 2.0% of GDP in 2001.

Europe

NON-NATO EUROPE – DEFENCE ECONOMICS

In recent years, **Sweden,** like many other European countries, has had to address the fiscal challenges associated with an ageing population. As a result, the government introduced a new stipulation that it must achieve a budget surplus in the region of 2% of GDP and, although this target was reached in 2005, subsequent tax cuts and spending on social programmes, particularly job-creation measures, have pushed the surplus back below the target level.

With public finances under pressure from demographic trends, defence spending has remained virtually unchanged for the past decade, averaging around SEK44bn (including civil defence), meaning that since 2000, defence expenditure has actually fallen from 2.0% of GDP to 1.5% of GDP. In September 2007, the Swedish defence minister resigned when it was revealed that the budget would stay fixed at approximately current levels until at least 2010 and that this would result in a need for significant cuts in investment spending in order to maintain current operational levels. It is proposed that defence equipment spending will be reduced by SEK350m, SEK620m and SEK920m in FY2008, FY2009 and FY2010 respectively, and that these savings, together with efficiency measures, will increase the ability of the Swedish armed forces to participate in international peace-support operations. The scale of the problem currently faced as regards deploying the armed forces was illustrated in November 2007, when the country's supreme commander made a formal request to the Ministry of Defence to reallocate at least SEK550m from the investment budget to enable the effective operation of rapid-response units. In his letter, General Håkan Syrén warned that without the additional money the Nordic Battlegroup, units requiring 10 days' readiness and units requiring 30 days' readiness would not be able to deploy. The general also warned that the real-terms decline in the defence budget was leading to such a low level of defence production that the confidence of the armed forces could be put at risk, and joint operational training was likely to be adversely affected.

As a result of the proposed reduction in investment spending, a number of military programmes are already likely to be terminated. One casualty may well be Kockums' development of a new-generation surface combatant to succeed the current *Visby* class, whilst the navy may pull out of the international programme to develop the Multi-Role Combat Missile, the research for which has so far been conducted by Saab Bofors Dynamics. Programmes already terminated include the *Bamse* air defence missile system and Saab's modular TMS underwater platform.

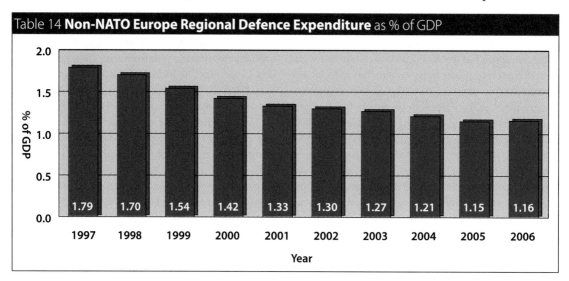

Table 14 **Non-NATO Europe Regional Defence Expenditure** as % of GDP

Year	1997	1998	1999	2000	2001	2002	2003	2004	2005	2006
% of GDP	1.79	1.70	1.54	1.42	1.33	1.30	1.27	1.21	1.15	1.16

Belgium Be

Euro €		2006	2007	2008
GDP	€	314bn	325bn	
	US$	393bn	464bn	
per capita	US$	37,817	44,676	
Growth	%	3.0	2.6	
Inflation	%	2.3	1.1	
Def exp[a]	€	3.54bn		
	US$	4.42bn		
Def bdgt	€	2.69bn	2.75bn	
	US$	3.36bn	3.93bn	
US$1=€		0.80	0.70	

[a] including military pensions

Population   10,392,226

Age	0–14	15–19	20–24	25–29	30–64	65 plus
Male	9%	3%	3%	3%	24%	7%
Female	8%	3%	3%	3%	24%	9%

Capabilities

ACTIVE 39,690 (Army 12,571 Navy 1,605 Air 7,470 Medical Service 1,808 Joint Service 16,236)

RESERVE 2,040

ORGANISATIONS BY SERVICE

Land Component 12,571

FORCES BY ROLE

1 Joint Service Territorial Comd, 1 Comd HQ (COMOPSLAND)

Comd	2 bde HQ
Rapid Reaction	1bde (1 Cdo bn, 2 Para bn, 1 Recce bn, 1 Fd Arty bty, 1 ADA bty, 1 Engr coy, 1 Logistic coy, 1 Medical coy)
Mech	1 bde (1st) (1 Fd Arty regt, 2 Inf regt, 1 Armd regt, 1 Recce regt); 1 bde (7th) (1 SP Fd Arty regt, 1 Recce regt, 1 Logistic bn, 2 Inf regt, 1 Armd regt)
Recce/Psyops	1 unit (CIMIC)
SF	1 gp
ADA	1regt (2 ADA bty with *Mistral*)
Engr	2 bn
MP	1 gp
Logistic	6 bn
EOD	1 unit

FACILITIES

Base   4

Trg Centre   1 (para); 1 (cdo)

EQUIPMENT BY TYPE

MBT 40 *Leopard* 1A5

AIFV 95: 32 YPR-765(25mm); 48 YPR-765 (*Milan*); 15 YPR-765 (PC)

APC 224
 APC (T) 164 M-113
 APC (W) 60 *Pandur*
ARTY 102
 SP 155mm 24 M-109
 TOWED 105mm 12 LG1 MK II
 MOR 66: **81mm** 18; **120mm** 48
AT • MSL • MANPATS 122 *Milan*
SAM 36 *Mistral*
RADARS 9 Land (battlefield surveillance)

Reserves 2,040

Territorial Support Units

Army 11 unit

Navy Component 1,605

EQUIPMENT BY TYPE
PRINCIPAL SURFACE COMBATANTS 2
FRIGATES
FFG 2 *Karel Doorman* each with 2 quad (8eff.) *Harpoon* SSM, 1 Mk 48 *Sea Sparrow* with 16 RIM-7P *Sea Sparrow* SAM, 4 single 324mm MK 32 MOD 9 ASTT with 4 MK 46 MOD 5 HWT, 1 76mm gun, (capacity 1 med hel) (2nd of class to enter service mid 2008 to replace former *Wielingen* class)
PATROL AND COASTAL COMBATANTS
 PCR 1
MINE WARFARE 6
MINE COUNTERMEASURES
MHC 6 *Aster* (Tripartite)
LOGISTICS AND SUPPORT 8: 1 **AG**; 1 **AGOR**; 4 **AT**; 1 **Spt** (log spt/comd, with hel platform); **TRG** 1 **YDT**
FACILITIES
Bases Located at Zeebrugge, Ostend

Naval Aviation
HELICOPTERS
UTL 3 SA-316B *Alouette III*

Air Component 7,470

Flying hours   165 hrs/year on cbt ac. 500 hrs/yr on tpt ac. 200 hrs/yr for trg purposes

FACILITIES

Air bases   Located at Coxijde, Kleine-Brogel, Florennes, Bierset, Beauvechain, Melsbroek

FORCES BY ROLE

AD/FGA/ Recce	2 (Tac) wg with 71 F-16 MLU *Fighting Falcon* (*total*: 1 AD/FGA/Recce sqn, 1 AD/FGA/trg unit, 2 AD/FGA sqn)
SAR	1 unit 4 *Sea King* MK48
Tpt	1 wg with 2 DA-20 *Falcon*; 2 A-310-222; 10 C-130H *Hercules*; 2 ERJ-135 LR; 2 ERJ-145 LR; 2 *Falcon* 20 (VIP); 1 *Falcon* 900B
Trg	1 wg (1 trg sqn with 32 SF-260D/SF-260M, 1 Fr/Be trg unit with 29 *Alpha Jet*)
Hel	1 wg with 32 A-109 (obs); 8 SA-318 *Alouette II*
UAV	1 sqn with 18 B-*Hunter*

Europe (NATO)

EQUIPMENT BY TYPE

AIRCRAFT 71 combat capable
  FGA 71 F-16 MLU *Fighting Falcon* (Mid-Life Update*)*
  EW • ELINT 2 DA-20 *Falcon*
  TPT 19: 2 A-310-222; 10 C-130H *Hercules*; 2 ERJ-135 LR; 2 ERJ-145 LR; 2 *Falcon* 20 (VIP); 1 *Falcon* 900B
  TRG 61: 29 *Alpha Jet*; 32 SF-260D/M
HELICOPTERS
  SAR 4 *Sea King* MK48
  UTL 40: 32 A-109 (obs); 8 SA-318 *Alouette II*
UAV 18 B-*Hunter* systems
SAM 24 *Mistral*
MSL
  AAM AIM-120B AMRAAM; AIM-9M/N *Sidewinder*
  ASM AGM-65G *Maverick*
BOMBS
  Conventional: Mk 84
  Infra-red: 6 LANTIRN
  Laser-Guided: GBU-10/ GBU-12 *Paveway* II; GBU-24 *Paveway* III
  INS/GPS guided: GBU-31 JDAM

DEPLOYMENT

AFGHANISTAN
NATO • ISAF 368 1 F-16

BOSNIA/CROATIA
EU • EUFOR *Operation Althea* 51

CHAD/CENTRAL AFRICAN REPUBLIC
EU • EUFOR Tchad/RCA 100

DEMOCRATIC REPUBLIC OF CONGO
EU • EUPOL KINSHASA 2
UN • MONUC 8 obs

FRANCE
NATO • Air Force
  AIRCRAFT • TRG 29 *Alpha Jet* located at Cazaux/Tours, Fr

LEBANON
UN • UNIFIL II 323
1 inf coy
AIFV Piranha IIIC; 13
APC 17
  APC (T) 14 M-113
  APC (W) 3 Pandur (Ambulance); 8 Dingo II

MIDDLE EAST
UN • UNTSO 2 obs

SERBIA
NATO • KFOR • *Joint Enterprise* 420

SUDAN
UN • UNMIS 5 obs

FOREIGN FORCES

NATO HQ, Brussels; HQ SHAPE, Mons
United Kingdom Army 180; Navy 80; Air Force 140
United States Army 765; Navy 92; USAF 481; USMC 29

Bulgaria Bg

Bulgarian Lev L		2006	2007	2008
GDP	L	49.1bn	53.3bn	
	US$	31.1bn	38.6bn	
per capita	US$	4,208	5,274	
Growth	%	6.1	6.0	
Inflation	%	7.2	8.2	
Def exp	L	1.11bn		
	US$	703m		
Def bdgt	L	1.08bn	1.19bn	
	US$	687m	864m	
FMA (US)	US$	9.9m	10.0m	13.2m
US$1=L		1.58	1.38	

Population 7,322,858

Ethnic groups: Turkish 9%; Macedonian 3%; Romany 3%

Age	0–14	15–19	20–24	25–29	30–64	65 plus
Male	7%	3%	4%	4%	23%	8%
Female	7%	3%	3%	4%	25%	10%

Capabilities

ACTIVE 40,747 (Army 18,773 Navy 4,100 Air 9,344 Central Staff 8,530) **Paramilitary 34,000**
Terms of service 9 months

RESERVE 303,000 (Army 250,500 Navy 7,500 Air 45,000)

ORGANISATIONS BY SERVICE

Army 18,773

Forces are being reduced in numbers the required target by the end of 2008 set out below.

FORCES BY ROLE

Mil District	1 corps HQ
Armd	1 bde
Armd recce	1 regt
Mech Inf	2 bde
Lt inf	1 bde
SF	1 bde
Arty	1 arty bde
MRL	1 bde
Engr	1 regt
NBC	1 regt

EQUIPMENT BY TYPE
MBT 1,474: 400 T-72, 32 in reserve in store; 165 T-55, 877 in reserve in store
RECCE 18 BRDM-1/BRDM-2 (non-op)
AIFV 214: 81 BMP-1; 19 in store; 114 BMP-2 / BMP-3
APC 2,409
  APC (T) 2,169: 626 MT-LB; 1,144 look-a-likes; 399 in reserve in store

APC (W) 240: 120 BTR-60; 120 in reserve in store
ARTY 1,666
  SP • 122mm 692: 358 2S1 *Carnation*; 334 in reserve in store
  TOWED 393: **100mm** 16 M-1944 in store (BS-3); **122mm** 112: 87 (M-30) M-1938 in store; 25 M-1931/37 in store (A-19); **130mm** 60 M-46 in store; **152mm** 205+: 150 D-20; 55 in store; M-1937 (ML-20)
MRL 122mm 222: 216 BM-21; 6 in store
MOR 120mm 359: 210 2S11 SP *Tundzha*; 149 in store
AT
  MSL • MANPATS 436: 200 AT-3 9K11 *Sagger* in store; 236 AT-4 9K111 *Spigot* / AT-5 9K113 *Spandrel*
  GUNS 276: **100mm** 126 MT-12; **85mm** 150 D-44 in store
AD
  SAM • SP 24 SA-8 *Gecko*
  MANPAD SA-7 *Grail*
  GUNS 400 **100mm** KS-19 towed/ **57mm** S-60 towed/ **23mm** ZSU-23-4 SP/ZU-23 towed
  RADARS • LAND GS-13 *Long Eye* (veh); SNAR-1 *Long Trough* (arty); SNAR-10 *Big Fred* (veh, arty); SNAR-2/-6 *Pork Trough* (arty); *Small Fred* / *Small Yawn* (veh, arty)

Army Reserve 250,500 reservists

Army   4 bde

Navy 4,100

EQUIPMENT BY TYPE
SUBMARINES
TACTICAL
  SSK 1 *Slava*† (FSU *Romeo*) with 8 single 533mm TT with 14 SAET-60 HWT
PRINCIPAL SURFACE COMBATANTS 4
  FRIGATES 2
    FFG 1 *Drazki* (*Weilingen*) eq. with 2 twin (4 eff.) each eq. with MM-38 *Exocet* SSM, 1 MK29 *Sea Sparrow* octuple eq. with RIM-7P *Sea Sparrow* SAM, 2 ASTT eq. with total of 2 L5 HWT, 1 mle 54 *Creusot-Loire* 375mm (6 eff.), 1 100mm gun
    FF 1 *Smeli* (FSU *Koni*) with 1 twin (2 eff.) with 2 SA-N-4 *Gecko* SAM, 2 RBU 6000 *Smerch 2* (24 eff.), 2 twin 76mm gun (4 eff.)
    FS 2 *Pauk* each with 1 SA-N-5 *Grail* SAM, 4 single 406mm TT, 2 RBU 1200 (10 eff.)
PATROL AND COASTAL COMBATANTS 19
  PFM 7:
    1 *Tarantul* II with 2 twin (4 eff.) with 4 SS-N-2C *Styx* tactical SSM, 2 quad (8 eff.) with 8 SA-N-5 *Grail* SAM, 1 76mm gun
    6 *Osa* I/II † each with 4 SS-N-2A *Styx*/SS-N-2B *Styx*
  PFI 9 *Zhuk* less than 100 tonnes
  PBI 3 *Nesebar* (ex Belgium *Neustadt*)
MINE COUNTERMEASURES 15
  MSC 7: 4 *Sonya*; 3 *Vanya*
  MSI 8: 6 *Olya*, less than 100 tonnes; 2 *Yevgenya*, less than 100 tonnes
AMPHIBIOUS 8
  LSM 2 *Polnochny* A (FSU) (capacity 6 MBT; 180 troops)
  CRAFT • LCU 6 *Vydra*
LOGISTICS AND SUPPORT 14: 1 **AORL**; 1 **AOL**; 1 **ARS**; 5 **ATS**; 3 **AGS**; 1 **YDG**; 2 **YDT**

FACILITIES
Bases Located at Atya, Balchik, Vidin, Sozopol, Burgas, Varna

Naval Aviation
HELICOPTERS
  ASW 6 Mi-14 *Haze* (3 operational) to be replaced by 6 AS-565MB Panthers 2010–2011

Coastal Arty
FORCES BY ROLE
Arty 2 regt; 20 bty

EQUIPMENT BY TYPE
MSL • TACTICAL • SSM: SS-C-1B *Sepal*; SS-C-3 *Styx*
GUN • 130mm 4 SM-4-1

Naval Guard
Gd 3 coy

Air Force 9,344

Flying hours   30 to 40 hrs/year

FORCES BY ROLE
1 AD Cmd,1 Tactical Aviation Cmd
Ftr/Recce 3rd Fighter Air Base (Graf Ignatievo). 1 sqn with 20 MiG-29A/UB *Fulcrum*; 1 sqn with 26 MiG-21bis/UM *Fishbed*
FGA 22nd Attack Air Base (Bezmer). 2 sqn with 34 Su-25K/UBK *Frogfoot* (5 upgraded to NATO compatibility)
Tpt 16th Tpt Air Base (Sofia) with 2 CJ-27; 1 An-2 *Colt*; 3 An-26 *Curl*; 7 L-410 UVP; 1 TU-134B *Crusty*; 1 PC-12M
Trg Air Trg Base (Dolna Milropolia) with 14 L-39ZA *Albatros* (advanced); 6 PC-9M (basic)
Hel 24th Hel Air Base (Krumovo) with 18 Mi-24D/V *Hind D**; 5 AS 532AL *Cougar*; 17 Mi-17 *Hip*; 6 Bell 206 *JetRanger*

EQUIPMENT BY TYPE
AIRCRAFT 80 combat capable
FTR 46: 20 MiG-29 *Fulcrum A*/UB; 26 MiG-21bis/UM *Fishbed*
FGA 34 Su-25K/UBK *Frogfoot*
TPT 15: 1 An-2 *Colt*; 3 An-26 *Curl*; 2 CJ-27, (3 more to be delivered); 1 AN-30 *Clank*; 7 L-410UVP/L-410UVP-E; 1 TU-134B *Crusty*; 1 PC-12M
TRG 20: 14 L-39ZA *Albatros*; 6 PC-9M (basic)
HELICOPTERS
ATK 18 Mi-24D/V *Hind D** (12 being upgraded to NATO standard)
SPT 23: 5 AS 532AL *Cougar* (7 more to be delivered for tpt/CSAR at rate of 3/yr); 17 Mi-17 *Hip* (6 to be upgraded to NATO standard)
UTL: 6 Bell 206 *JetRanger*
UAV Yastreb-2S
AD
  SAM SA-10 *Grumble* (quad) SP/SA-2 *Guideline* Towed/SA-3 *Goa*/SA-5 *Gammon* static (20 sites, 110 launchers)

MSL
AAM AA-11 *Archer*; AA-2 *Atoll*; AA-7 *Apex*; AA-10 *Alamo*
ASM AS-14 *Kedge*; AS-7 *Kerry*; AS-10 *Karen*
FACILITIES
Air base   1 (ttr/recce), 1 (FGA)
Hel base   1 (hel)
School   2 with L-39ZA *Albatros* trg ac (advanced); PC-9M (basic trg)

Paramilitary 34,000

Border Guards 12,000
Ministry of Interior
FORCES BY ROLE
Paramilitary   12 regt
EQUIPMENT BY TYPE
PATROL AND COASTAL COMBATANTS ε50
   MISC BOATS/CRAFT: ε38 various craft all under 100 tonnes
   PCI ε12 **PB** 2 (FSU, under 100 tonnes)

Railway and Construction Troops 18,000

Security Police 4,000

DEPLOYMENT

AFGHANISTAN
NATO • ISAF 401

BOSNIA-HERZEGOVINA
EU • EUFOR • *Operation Althea* 115

ETHIOPIA/ERITREA
UN • UNMEE 4 obs

IRAQ
MNF • *Operation Iraqi Freedom* 150

LIBERIA
UN • UNMIL 2 obs

SERBIA
NATO • KFOR • *Joint Enterprise* 46
UN • UNMIK 1 obs

Czech Republic Cz

Czech Koruna Kc		2006	2007	2008
GDP	Kc	3.23tr	3.49tr	
	US$	143bn	180bn	
per capita	US$	14,002	17,602	
Growth	%	6.4	5.6	
Inflation	%	2.6	2.5	
Def exp	Kc	55.6bn		
	US$	2.46bn		
Def bdgt	Kc	55.7bn	53.9bn	
	US$	2.46bn	2.78bn	
FMA (US)	US$	3.9m	3.5m	3.0m
US$1=Kc		22.6	19.4	

Population   10,228,744

Ethnic groups: Slovak 3%; Polish 0.6%; German 0.5%

Age	0–14	15–19	20–24	25–29	30–64	65 plus
Male	8%	3%	3%	4%	25%	6%
Female	7%	3%	3%	4%	25%	8%

Capabilities

ACTIVE 23,092 (Joint 23,092) **Paramilitary 3,100**

CIVILIAN 15,992 (MOD Staff 15,992)
Professional armed forces since 2005. Armed Forces being reorganised. Full operational capabilities are planned to be achieved in 2010–12. The Military Forces are Joint Forces composed of Army, Air Force and Joint Forces Support Units

ORGANISATIONS BY SERVICE

Army 16,962
FORCES BY ROLE
Rapid Reaction	1 bde (4th) (2 Mech bn, 1 AB bn)
Mech	1 bde (7th)(1 Armd bn, 2 Mech Inf bn)
SF	1 gp
Arty	1 bde (13th) (2 arty bn)
Recce	1 bn
Presidential Guard	1 bde (Subordinate to Ministry of Interior) (2 Gd bn (*each*: 3 Gd coy), 1 Presidential Sy coy)

EQUIPMENT BY TYPE
MBT 181: 181 T-72CZ
AIFV 508: 257 BMP-1; 175 BMP-2; 76 BPzV
   APC (T) 29 OT-90
   APC (W) 43 OT-64
ARTY 326
   SP 152mm168: 52 M-77 *Dana*; 6 training; 110 in store
   MRL 122mm 60: 16 RM-70; 3 training; 41 in store
   MOR 120mm 138: 85 M-1982; 8 SPM-85; 5 trg; 40 in store
AT• MSL 671
   SP 496: 3 9P133 BRDM-2 *Sagger*; 21 9P148 BRDM-2 *Spandrel*; 472 9S428

MANPATS 175 9P135 (AT-4 9K111) *Spigot*
RADARS • LAND 3 ARTHUR

Active Reserve

FORCES BY ROLE

Territorial Def   14 comd
Inf   14 coy (1 per Territorial comd) (*each:* 1
                          Logistic pl, 3 Inf pl, 1 Cbt Spt pl)

Air Force 6,130 (incl Air Defence Forces)

The principal task is to secure the integrity of the Czech Republic's airspace. This mission is fulfilled within NATO Integrated Extended Air Defence System (NATINEADS) and, if necessary, by means of the national reinforced air defence system of the CR. In addition, the Air Force provides close air support for the Land Forces, and performs tasks associated with the transportation of troops and material.

Flying hours   100hrs/year combat ac 150 for tpt ac
5 Air bases

FORCES BY ROLE

Integrated with Jt Forces
Ftr/FGAe   1 sqn 12 JAS 39C/
                   2 JAS 39D *Gripen*
FGA   1 sqn with 24 L-159; 1 sqn 12 L-39ZA
                   ALCA(Lead-in Ftr Trg)
Tpt   2 sqn with 2 Airbus A-319CJ; 2 Tu-154M
                   Careless; 5 An-26 *Curl*; 1 CL-601 *Challenger*; 8
                   L-410 *Turbolet*; 2 Yak-40 *Codling*
Trg   1 Aviation Trg Centre with 8 L-39C; 8 Z-142C;
                   L-410T; 1 EW-97 *Eurostar*
Hel   2 attack sqn with 38 Mi-24 (Mi-35) *Hind**; 2 aslt/
                   tpt sqn with 31 Mi-17S; 8 PZL W-3RA SOKOL; 1
                   Mi-8 *Hip*
AD   1 (missile) bde

EQUIPMENT BY TYPE

AIRCRAFT 50 combat capable
  FTR/FGA 14: 12 JAS 39C; 2 JAS 39D *Gripen*
  FGA: 24 L-159 ALCA
  TPT 20: 2 Airbus A-319CJ (to replpace 2 TU-154M
  Careless); 2 Tu-154M *Careless*; 5 An-26 *Curl*; 1 CL-601
  Challenger; 8 L-410 *Turbolet*; 2 Yak-40 *Codling*
  TRG 31: 12 L-39ZA*, 8 L-39C *Albatros*; 8 Z-142C; 2 L-410
  Turbolet; 1 EW-97 *Eurostar*
HELICOPTERS
  ATK 38 Mi-24 (Mi-35) *Hind**
  SPT 40: 31 Mi-171S; 1 MI-8; 8 PZL W3A (SOKOL)
  UAV 2 *Sojka* 3
AD • SAM SA-13 *Gopher*; SA-6 *Gainful*; SA-8 *Gecko*; SA-7
Grail
MSL • AAM AIM-9M *Sidewinder*; AIM-120 AMRAAM
BOMBS
  Conventional: GPU Mk 82; Mk 84
  Laser-guided: GBU *Paveway*

Joint Forces Support Units

NBC   1 bn with 1 CW Warning Centre
Engr rescue   1 bde (1 engr bn, 7 engr rescue bn)
CIMIC/Psyops   1 centre

Logistics   1 bde (1 spt bn; 1 supply bn)
EW   1 Centre

Paramilitary 3,100

Border Guards 3,000

Internal Security Forces 100

DEPLOYMENT

AFGHANISTAN
NATO • ISAF 435; 95 field hospital and chemical detachment
Operation Enduring Freedom 35

BOSNIA-HERZEGOVINA
EU • EUFOR *Operation Althea* 5

DEMOCRATIC REPUBLIC OF CONGO
UN • MONUC 3 obs

ETHIOPIA/ERITREA
UN • UNMEE 2 obs

GEORGIA
UN • UNOMIG 5 obs

IRAQ
MNF • *Operation Iraqi Freedom* 99

LIBERIA
UN • UNMIL 3 obs

SERBIA
NATO • KFOR • *Joint Enterprise* 500
UN • UNMIK 2 obs

FOREIGN FORCES

United Kingdom Army 20
United States Army 3; USAF 2; USMC 5

Denmark Da

Danish Krone kr		2006	2007	2008
GDP	kr	1.64tr	1.72tr	
	US$	276bn	328bn	
per capita	US$	50,715	59,914	
Growth	%	3.5	1.9	
Inflation	%	1.9	1.8	
Def exp [a]	kr	23.02bn		
	US$	3.87bn		
Def bdgt	kr	19.8bn	22.7bn	22.2bn
	US$	3.34bn	4.32bn	
US$1=kr		5.94	5.25	
[a] including military pensions				

Population   5,468, 120

Age	0–14	15–19	20–24	25–29	30–64	65 plus
Male	10%	3%	3%	3%	25%	6%
Female	9%	3%	3%	3%	24%	8%

Capabilities

ACTIVE 29,960 (Army 14,240 Navy 3,650 Air 3,830
Joint 8,240 (incl civilians)
Terms of service 4–10 months

Home Guard 53,700 (Army) 40,800 (Navy) 4,500
(Air Force) 5,500 (Service Corps) 2,900

ORGANISATIONS BY SERVICE

Army 8,240; 6,000 conscript (total 14,240)

FORCES BY ROLE

Army	1 (op) comd
Mech inf	1 div (2 Mech Inf bde *each* (1 Tk bn, 2 Mech Inf bn, 1 SP Arty bn, 1 MP coy) - 1 Bde is of Lower Readiness
Recce	1 bn
SF	1 unit
Engr	1 bn
AD	1 bn
Peacekeeping	1 SHIRBRIG bde (UN Stand By High Readiness Brigade)

EQUIPMENT BY TYPE
MBT 231: 51 *Leopard* 2 A4/2A5
RECCE 122: 32 *Eagle1* (MOWAG); 90 *Eagle IV*
APC 395
   APC (T) 282: 242 M-113 (incl variants); 40 IKK (CV)
   APC (W) 113 *Piranha* III (incl variants)
ARTY 859
   SP 155mm 24 M-109
   TOWED 157: **105mm** 60 M-101; **155mm** 97 M-114/M-139
   MRL 227mm 12 MLRS
   MOR 615:
      SP 81mm 53 M-125A2
      TOWED 562: **81mm** 402; **120mm** 160 Brandt
AT
   MSL • SP 56 TOW on M109 (ETS)
   MANPATS 20 TOW
   RCL 84mm 349 *Carl Gustav*
   RL 84mm 4,200 AT-4
HELICOPTERS
   ATK 12 AS-550C2 *Fennec**(with TOW)
   MD-500M OH-6 *Cayuse* 13
UAV 12 *Sperwer* (5 non-operational/all sold to Canada)
AD • SAM • MANPAD FIM-92A *Stinger*
RADAR • LAND ARTHUR

Navy 3,000; 300 civilian; 350 conscript (total 3,650)

EQUIPMENT BY TYPE
PRINCIPAL SURFACE COMBATANTS • CORVETTES
FSG 3 *Niels Juel* each with 2 Mk 141 *Harpoon* quad (8 eff.)
eqpt with RGM-84C *Harpoon* tactical SSM, 2 6 cell Mk 48
VLS (12 eff.) with 12 *Sea Sparrow* SAM, 1 76mm gun
PATROL AND COASTAL COMBATANTS 49
   PSOH 4 *Thetis* each with 2 twin (4 eff.) with *Stingers*, 1
76mm gun, 1 *Super Lynx* MK 90B

PFM 4 *Flyvefisken* (capacity 60 mines) each with 2 Mk 141
Harpoon quad (8 eff.) eqpt with RGM-84C *Harpoon*/RGM-
84L *Harpoon* tactical SSM, 1 6 cell Mk 48 VLS eqpt with 6
Sea Sparrow SAM, 2 single 533mm TT, 1 76mm gun
PFT 2 *Flyvefisken* (Patrol fit) each with 1 Mk 48 *Sea
Sparrow* VLS eqpt with *Sea Sparrow* SAM, 2 single 533mm
TT, 1 76mm gun
PCC 9: 3 *Agdlek*; 6 *Barsoe*
PCI 30 in reserve (Home Guard)
MINE WARFARE 14
   MINE COUNTERMEASURES • MHC 4 *Flyvefisken*
   MCMV 4 *MSF MK-I*
   MHD 6 *Sav*
LOGISTICS AND SUPPORT 17:
   MRV 2 *Holm-class* (Multi Role – MCM, Survey and general
training) (Less than 200 tonnes; six of class expected)
   AE 1 *Sleipner*
   AG 2 *Absalon* (flexible-support-ships) each with 2 octuple
VLS eqpt. with 16 RGM-84 Block 2 *Harpoon* 2 SSM tactical,
4 twin (4 eff.) with *Stingers* SAM, 3 12 cell Mk 56 VLS eqpt.
with 36 RIM-162B Sea Sparrow naval SAM, 1 127mm gun
(capacity 2 LCP, 7 MBT or 40 vehicles; 130 troops)
   AGB 3; **ABU** 2 (primarily use for MARPOL duties); **AK**
4 *Ro/Ro*; **Tpt** 2; **RY** 1

FACILITIES

Bases	Located at Korsøer and Frederikshavn
Naval airbases	Located at Karup, Jutland

Naval Aviation
HELICOPTERS • ASW 8 *Super Lynx* MK90B

Air Force 3,300 (plus 90 civilian, 440 conscript (total 3,830)

Three air bases

Flying hours   165 hrs/year

Tactical Air Comd

FORCES BY ROLE

Ftr/FGA	2 sqn with 48 F-16A/F-16B *Fighting Falcon*
SAR /Spt	1 sqn with 7 S-61A *Sea King*; 8 EH-101 *Merlin*; 1 sqn with 12 AS-550 Fennec (obs)
Tpt	1 sqn with 4 C-130J-30 *Hercules* ; 3 CL-604 *Challenger* (MR/VIP)
Trg	1 flying school with 28 SAAB T-17

EQUIPMENT BY TYPE
AIRCRAFT 48 combat capable
   FTR: 48 F-16A/F-16B *Fighting Falcon*
   TPT 7: 4 C-130J-30 *Hercules* ; 3 CL-604 *Challenger*
   TRG 28 SAAB T-17
HELICOPTERS
   ASW 15: 7 S-61A *Sea King* (being phased out 2008); 8
EH-101 *Merlin* (6 more on order)
   UTL 12 AS-550 *Fennec* (obs)
MSL
   ASM AGM-65 *Maverick*
   AAM AIM-120A AMRAAM; AIM-9L/X *Sidewinder*
BOMBS
   INS/GPS-guided: JDAM (GBU-31/EGBU-12/GBU-24)

Control and Air Defence Group

1 Control and Reporting Centre, 1 Mobile Control and Reporting Centre
4 radar sites
SAM 2 bn; 6 bty with FIM-92A *Stinger*; 36 *I HAWK*

Reserves

Home Guard (Army) 40,800 reservists (To age 50)

Army 5 (local def) region (*each:* up to 2 mot inf bn);
    2 regt cbt gp (*each:* 1 arty bn, 3 mot inf bn)

Home Guard (Navy) 4,500 reservists (to age 50) organised into 30 Home Guard units

PATROL AND COASTAL COMBATANTS 32
PC 32: 18 *MHV800*; 6 *MHV900*; 6 *MHV90*; 2 *MHV70*

Home Guard (Air Force) 5,500 reservists (to age 50)

Home Guard (Service Corps) 2,900 reservists

DEPLOYMENT

AFGHANISTAN
NATO • ISAF 454
UN • UNAMA 1 obs

BOSNIA-HERZEGOVINA
EU • EUFOR • *Operation Althea* 3

DEMOCRATIC REPUBLIC OF CONGO
UN • MONUC 2 obs

ETHIOPIA/ERITREA
UN • UNMEE 3 obs

GEORGIA
UN • UNOMIG 5 obs

INDIA/PAKISTAN
UN • UNMOGIP 5 obs

IRAQ
MNF • *Operation Iraqi Freedom*
1 (bn) inf gp (1 inf/spt hel coy, 1 Scout sqn); 442
NATO • NTM-I 21
UN • UNAMI 3 obs

KYRGYZSTAN
Army 75 (incl C-130 contingent. *Operation Enduring Freedom*)

LIBERIA
UN • UNMIL 2 obs

MIDDLE EAST
UN • UNTSO 11 obs

NEPAL
UN • UNMIN 2 obs

SERBIA
NATO • KFOR • *Joint Enterprise* 1 inf gp (1 scout sqn, 1 inf coy); 363
UN • UNMIK 1 obs

SUDAN
UN • UNMIS 6; 10 obs

FOREIGN FORCES

NATO HQ Joint Command North-East
UN HQ Standby High Readiness Brigade (SHIRBRIG)

Estonia Ea

Estonian Kroon kn		2006	2007	2008
GDP	kn	205bn	228bn	
	US$	16.5bn	20.7bn	
per capita	US$	12,483	15,751	
Growth	%	11.2	8.0	
Inflation	%	4.4	6.0	
Def exp	kn	2.94bn		
	US$	238m		
Def bdgt	kn	2.95bn	4.25bn	4.63bn
	US$	237m	386m	
FMA (US)	US$	4.4m	4.0m	3.0m
US$1=kn		12.4	11.0	

Population 1,315,912

Ethnic groups: Russian 28%; Ukrainian 3%; Belarussian 2%

Age	0–14	15–19	20–24	25–29	30–64	65 plus
Male	8%	4%	4%	3%	21%	6%
Female	8%	4%	4%	3%	24%	11%

Capabilities

ACTIVE 4,100 (Army 3,600 Navy 300 Air 200)
Paramilitary 2,600

RESERVE 16,000 (Joint 16,000)

Terms of service 8 months, officers and some specialists 11 months.

ORGANISATIONS BY SERVICE

Army 2,400; 1,200 conscript (total 3,600)

FORCES BY ROLE
4 Def region; 14 districts

Inf	3 bn
Recce	1 bn
Arty	1 bn
Gd	1 bn
Peacekeeping	1 bn under strength

Reserves

Militia 10,000 reservists
Army 15 (Defence League) Kaitseliit unit

EQUIPMENT BY TYPE
APC 50:
APC (W) 7 Mamba; 43 XA-180 *Sisu*
ARTY 293
  TOWED 62
    105mm 38 M 61-37; 155mm 24 FH-70
  MOR 231
    81mm 51: 41 B455; 10 NM95; 120mm 180: 14 2B11; 166
    41D
  RCL 160
    106mm M-40 30 M-40A1; 90mm 130 PV-1110
FACILITIES
Centre 1 (peace ops)

Navy 300 (inclusive of a platoon size conscript unit)

Lat, Ea and L have set up a joint Naval unit BALTRON
with bases at Liepaja, Riga, Ventspils (Lat), Tallinn (Ea),
Klaipeda (L).
EQUIPMENT BY TYPE
PRINCIPAL SURFACE COMBATANTS • CORVETTES
• FS 1 *Admiral Pitka* with 1 76mm gun
MINE WARFARE • MINE COUNTERMEASURES 6
  MHC 2 *Lindau*; 1 *Admiral Cowan* (ex-UK *Sandown*) (2
  additional units expected mid '08 and early '09)
  MSI 2 *Frauenlob* (*Kalev*)
  ML 1 *Lindormen*
FACILITIES
Bases Located at Tallinn, Miinisadam

Air Force 200

Flying hours   120 hrs/year
FORCES BY ROLE
FACILITIES
Air base   1 air base, 1 surv wg
EQUIPMENT BY TYPE
AIRCRAFT
  TPT 2 An-2 *Colt*
HELICOPTERS • UTL 4 R-44

Paramilitary 2,600

Border Guard 2,430; 170 conscript (total 2,600)

Ministry of Internal Affairs
FORCES BY ROLE
The maritime element of the Border Guard also fulfils the
task of Coast Guard
Paramilitary   1 regt; 3 (rescue) coy
EQUIPMENT BY TYPE
PATROL AND COASTAL COMBATANTS 31
  PCO 2: 1 *Ko*; 1 *Valvas*
  PCC 7: 1 *Vapper*; 1 *Maru*; 3 KBV-100; 1 *Pikker*; 1 *Torm*
  PCI 22: 11 less than 100 tonnes
AIRCRAFT • TPT 2 L-410UVP *Turbolet*
HELICOPTERS • SPT 2 Mi-8 *Hip* (in war, subordinated
to Air Force staff)

DEPLOYMENT

AFGHANISTAN
NATO • ISAF 128; 1 inf coy; 1 EOD team; 1 officer (ISAF
HQ); 120 APC (W) • 9 XA-180 *Sisu*

BOSNIA-HERZEGOVINA
EU • EUFOR • *Operation Althea* 3

IRAQ
MNF • *Operation Iraqi Freedom* 38 (1 inf pl)
NATO • NTM-I 2

MIDDLE EAST
UN • UNTSO 2 obs

SERBIA
NATO • KFOR • *Joint Enterprise* 28

France Fr

Euro €		2006	2007	2008
GDP	€	1.79tr	1.86tr	
	US$	2.24tr	2.66tr	
per capita	US$	36,796	43,664	
Growth	%	2.0	1.9	
Inflation	%	1.9	1.3	
Def exp[a]	€	43.2bn		
	US$	54.0bn		
Def bdgt	€	35.4bn	36.2bn	36.7bn
	US$	44.25bn	51.71bn	
US$1=€		0.80	0.70	

[a] including military pensions

Population   61,083,916

Age	0–14	15–19	20–24	25–29	30–64	65 plus
Male	9%	3%	3%	3%	23%	7%
Female	9%	3%	3%	3%	23%	9%

Capabilities

ACTIVE 254,895 (Army 133,500 Navy 43,995 Air
63,600 Central Staff 5,200 Service de Santé 8,600)
Paramilitary 199,148

CIVILIAN 44,465 (Army 28,500 Navy 10,265 Air
5,700) Paramilitary 1,953

RESERVE 25,350 (Army 11,350 Navy 6,000 Air
8,000) Paramilitary 40,000

ORGANISATIONS BY SERVICE

Strategic Nuclear Forces

Navy 2,200

SUBMARINES • STRATEGIC • SSBN 4
  1 *L'Inflexible* M4 S 615 with 16 M-45 strategic SLBM
  each with 6 TN-75 nuclear warheads, 4 single 533mm

TT each with up to 18 F-17 HWT/L5 HWT/SM-39 *Exocet* tactical USGW

3 *Le Triomphant* S 616 each with 16 M-45 strategic SLBM each with 6 TN-75 nuclear warheads, 4 single 533mm TT each with up to 18 F17 Mod 2 HWT/SM-39 *Exocet* tactical USGW

AIRCRAFT • STRIKE/FGA 24 *Super Etendard*

Air Force 1,800

Air Strategic Forces Command

FGA/Strike	3 sqn with 60 M-2000N *Mirage* each with 2 tactical ASMP, R-550 *Magic* 2 tactical AAM
Tkr	1 sqn with 11 C-135FR; 3 KC-135 *Stratotanker*
Trg	1 unit with 2 *Mystère* 20 (*Falcon* 20)

EQUIPMENT BY TYPE

AIRCRAFT 60 combat capable

  FGA 60 M-2000N *Mirage*

  TKR 14: 11 C-135FR; 3 KC-135 *Stratotanker*

  TRG 2 *Mystère* 20 (*Falcon* 20)

MSL

  ASMP *Storm Shadow*

  AAM R-550 *Magic*

Paramilitary • Gendarmerie 41

Army 133,500; 28,500 (civilian)

FORCES BY ROLE

regt normally bn size

Army	4 (task force) HQ; 1 (land) comd HQ; 5 region HQ
Armd	1 elems bde (Fr/Ge bde 2500 personnel) (1 mech inf regt, 1 armd cav regt); 1 bde (1 armd regt, 2 armd inf regt, 1 SP arty regt, 1 engr rescue regt); 1 bde (1 SP arty regt, 1 engr regt, 2 armd inf regt, 2 armd regt)
Lt armd	2 bde (*each*: 1 arty regt, 1 engr regt, 2 armd cav regt, 2 (APC inf) mech inf regt)
Mech inf	2 bde (*each*: 1 SP arty regt, 1 armd inf regt, 1 armd regt, 1 engr regt, 1 (APC inf) mech inf regt)
Air mob	1 bde (4 cbt hel regt)
Mtn inf	1 bde (1 arty regt, 1 engr regt, 1 armd cav regt, 3 mech inf regt)
AB	1 bde (1 armd cav regt, 1 arty regt, 1 engr regt, 1 spt regt, 4 para regt)
Arty	1 bde (1 SAM regt with *I-HAWK MIM-23B*, 2 MLRS regt, 3 SAM regt with *Roland*)
Engr	1 bde
Sigs	1 bde
EW/Int	1 bde (1 Cav regt, 2 UAV regt, 1 EW regt, 1 Int bn)

Foreign Legion 7,700

Armd	1 regt
Inf	6 regt
Para	1 regt
Engr	2 regt (incl in units listed above)

Marines 14,700

Marine 14 regt (France); 4 regt (Africa); 10 regt (French overseas possessions)

Special Operation Forces ε2,700

FORCES BY ROLE

HQ	1 comd
Para	1 regt
Cbt hel	1 sqn

FACILITIES

Training Centre 3

Reserves 11,350 reservists

Territorial defence forces

Army	1 coy
Spt/engr	14 coy

EQUIPMENT BY TYPE

MBT 968: 354 *Leclerc*; 614 AMX-30

RECCE 1,809: 337 AMX-10RC; 192 ERC-90F4 *Sagaie*; 1,280 VBL M-11

AIFV 601 AMX-10P/PC

APC (W) 4,413: 3,906 VAB; 61 VAB BOA; 172 VAB *Eryx*; 134 VAB HOT; 113 VAB *Milan*; 27 VAB NBC

ARTY 787

  SP 155mm 266: 261 AU-F-1; 5 CAESAR

  TOWED 155mm 105 TR-F-1

  MRL 227mm 55 MLRS

  MOR 120mm 361 RT-F1

AT • MSL • MANPATS 1,195 *Milan*

  RL 84mm AT-4

AIRCRAFT

  TPT 13: 5 PC-6 *Turbo-Porter*; 8 TBM-700

  UTL 2 F406 *Caravan II*

HELICOPTERS

  ATK 2 AS-665 *Tiger**

  RECCE 4 AS-532 *Horizon*

  ASLT 276 SA-342M *Gazelle* (all variants)*

  SPT 106 SA-330 *Puma*

  UTL 5 EC120 (*Colibri*)

UAV 102: 54 CL-289 (AN/USD-502); 18 *Sperwer*; 12 *Eagle I*

  RECCE • TAC 18 SDTI

AD • SAM 455+

  SP 98 *Roland* II/*Roland* I

  TOWED 26+ MIM-23B; *I-HAWK* MIM-23B

  MANPAD 331 *Mistral*

RADAR • LAND 84: 10 *Cobra*; 28 RASIT; 46 RATAC

Navy 43,995; 10,265 (civilian); 2,200 opcon Strategic Nuclear Forces (total 46,195 plus 10,265 civilians)

FORCES BY ROLE

Navy 1 HQ opcon HRF (N) located at Toulon; 1 HQ opcon ALFOST located at Brest

EQUIPMENT BY TYPE
SUBMARINES 10
  STRATEGIC • SSBN 4:
    1 *L'Inflexible* M4 S 615 opcon Strategic Nuclear Forces with 16 M-45 SLBM each with 6 TN-75 nuclear warheads, 4 single 533mm TT each with up to 18 F-17 HWT/L5 HWT/SM-39 *Exocet* tactical USGW
    3 *Le Triomphant* S 616 opcon Strategic Nuclear Forces each with 16 M-45 SLBM each with 6 TN-75 nuclear warheads, 4 single 533mm TT each with up to 18 F17 Mod 2 HWT/SM-39 *Exocet* tactical USGW
  TACTICAL • SSN 6:
    6 *Rubis* each with 4 single 533mm TT with F-17 HWT/SM-39 *Exocet* tactical USGW
PRINCIPAL SURFACE COMBATANTS 35
  AIRCRAFT CARRIERS 2
  CVN 1 *Charles de Gaulle* with 4 octuple VLS each with *Aster* 15 SAM, 2 *Sadral* sextuple each with *Mistral* SAM (capacity 20 *Super Etendard* FTR/FGA ac; 12 *Rafale* M ftr; 3 E-2C *Hawkeye* AEW ac; 2 SA-360 *Dauphin* SAR hel; 3 SA-321 *Super Frelon* SAR hel)
  CVH 1:
    1 *Jeanne d Arc* with 2 triple (6 eff.) each with MM-38 *Exocet* tactical SSM, (capacity 8 SA-319B *Alouette III* ASW hel), 2 100mm gun
  DESTROYERS • DDG 13:
    2 *Cassard* each,with 2 quad (8 eff.) with 8 MM-40 *Exocet* tactical SSM, 1 Mk 13 GMLS with 40 SM-1 MR SAM, 2 single ASTT each with L5 HWT, 1 100mm gun, each eq with 1 AS-565SA *Panther* ASW hel
    7 *Georges Leygues* each with 1 Mk 46 LWT, 8 MM-40 *Exocet* tactical SSM, 1 octuple (8 eff.) with 26 *Crotale* SAM, 2 single ASTT each with L5 HWT, 1 100mm gun, each eq with 2 *Lynx* utl hel
    1 *Forbin* (Undergoing acceptance trials, expected ISD late '08) 1 48-cell VLS eq with *Aster* 15 SAM /*Aster* 30 SAM, 2 *Sadral* sextuple each eq with *Mistral* SAM, 2 twin TT (4 eff.) each eq with MU-90, 2 76mm, eq with 1 NH90 TTH utl hel, (2nd of class in build)
    1 *Suffren* (*Duquesne*) with 4 single with 4 MM-38 *Exocet* tactical SSM, 4 single ASTT each with 1+ L5 HWT, 1 twin (2 eff.) with 48 *Masurca* SAM, 2 100mm gun
    2 *Tourville* each with 6 single with MM-38 *Exocet* tactical SSM, 2 single ASTT with Mk 46 LWT/MU-90, 2 100mm gun, each eq with 2 *Lynx* Mk4 (*Lynx* MK3) ASW hel
  FRIGATES 20
  FFH 11:
    6 *Floreal* each with, 2 single with 2 MM-38 *Exocet* tactical SSM, 1 100mm gun, each eq with 1 AS-565SA *Panther* ASW hel
    5 *La Fayette* (Space for fitting 2 x 8 cell VLS launchers for Aster 15/30), 2 quad (8 eff.) with 8 MM-40 *Exocet* tactical SSM, 1 octuple (8 eff.) with *Crotale* SAM, 1 100mm gun, (capacity either 1 AS-565SA *Panther* ASW hel or 1 SA-321 *Super Frelon* SAR hel)
  FF 9:
    9 *D'Estienne d'Orves* each with 4 MM-40 *Exocet* tactical SSM, 4 single ASTT, 1 100mm gun

PATROL AND COASTAL COMBATANTS 20
  PCO 20: 1 *Arago*; 1 *Grebe*; 10 *L'Audacieuse*; 8 *Leopard* (Instruction)
MINE WARFARE • MINE COUNTERMEASURES 21
  MCCS 1 *Loire*
  MCM SPT 7: 3 *Antares*; 4 *Vulcain*
  MHC 13 *Eridan*
AMPHIBIOUS
PRINCIPAL AMPHIBIOUS SHIPS 8
  LHD 2 *Mistral* (capacity mixed air group of up to 16 NH-90 or SA-330 *Puma* utl hel or AS-532 *Cougar* utl hel or AS-665 *Tigre* atk hel; 2 LCAC or 4 LCM; 60 AVs; 450 troops)
  LPD 2:
    2 *Foudre* (capacity 4 AS-532 *Cougar*; either 2 Edic LCT or 10 LCM; 22 tanks; 470 troops;)
  LS • LST 4 *Batral* (capacity 12 trucks; 140 troops) (additional 1 in reserve)
  CRAFT 19: 4 LCT; 15 LCM
LOGISTICS AND SUPPORT 43:
  AORH 4 *Durance* (capacity either 1 SA-319 *Alouette III* utl hel or 1 AS-365 *Dauphi*; 2 utl hel or 1 *Lynx* utl hel)
  AF 3
  AR 1 *Jules Verne* (capacity 1 SA-319 *Alouette III* utl hel)
  AG 1
  AGOR 2
  AGI 1 *Dupuy de Lome*
  AGM 1
  AGS 3
  YDT 2
  YTM 25
FACILITIES

Bases	1 (HQ) located at Toulon, 1 (HQ) located at Brest, 1 with 2 Frigates; 2 PCI (P 400); 1 *Champlain* LSM (capacity 12 trucks; 140 troops); 3 *Gardian* MP ac (HQ) located at Papeete, PF, 1 located at Dzaoudzi (Mayotte), 1 (HQ) located at Port-des-Galets, 1 located at Fort de France, 1 with 1 *Floreal* FFH; *Albatros* OPV; 2 *Gardian* MP ac located at Nouméa, NC, 1 with 2 PCI; 2 (P 400) located at Cayenne, Gf, 1 located at Lorient, 1 located at Cherbourg
Naval air bases	Located at Nimes-Garons, Landivisiau, Lann-Bihoue, Hyères

Naval Aviation 6,443

Flying hours	180 to 220 hrs/year on *Super Etendard* strike/FGA ac

FORCES BY ROLE

Nuclear Strike	51 *Super Etendard* (incls Strategic Nuclear Forces)
Ftr	1 sqn with 10 *Rafale* M F2; 1 sqn *Rafale* M F2
ASW	2 regt with 31 *Lynx* Mk4 (*Lynx* MK3); 1 sqn with 16 AS-565SA *Panther*
MR	1 sqn with 16 N-262 *Fregate*
MP	2 sqn with 28 *Atlantique* 2*

AEW	1 sqn with 3 E-2C *Hawkeye*
SAR	2 sqn with 9 AS-365F *Dauphin* 2; 8 SA-321 *Super Frelon*
Trg	1 sqn with 21 SA-319B *Alouette III*; 2 unit with N-262 *Fregate*; 8 CAP 10; 9 *Rallye MS-880**

EQUIPMENT BY TYPE
AIRCRAFT 60 combat capable
FTR 10 *Rafale M F1* ; 16 *Rafale M F2* (last 7 to be delivered '08)
STRIKE/FGA 51*Super Etendard* (incl Strategic Nuclear Forces)
MP 37: 28 *Atlantique* 2*; 4 *Falcon* 50M; 5 *Gardian*
AEW 3 E-2C *Hawkeye*
TPT 25: 11 EMB-121 *Xingu*; 14 N-262 *Fregate*
TRG 23: 8 CAP 10; 6 *Falcon* 10 MER; 9 *Rallye MS-880**
HELICOPTERS
SAR 8 SA-321 *Super Frelon*
ASW 77: 16 AS-565SA *Panther*; 31 *Lynx* Mk4 (*Lynx* MK3); 27 SA-319B *Alouette III*
UTL 9 AS-365 *Dauphin* 2
MSL
ASM AM-39 *Exocet*; ASMP
AAM AS 30 *Laser*; MICA; R-550 *Magic 2*

Marines 2,050

Commando Units

Recce	1 gp
Aslt	2 gp
Atk Swimmer	1 gp
Raiding	1 gp

Fusiliers-Marin 1,550

Protection	14 (Naval Base) gp

Public Service Force
Naval personnel performing general coast guard, fishery protection, SAR, anti-pollution and traffic surveillance duties. Command exercised through Maritime Prefectures (Premar): Manche (Cherbourg), Atlantique (Brest), Mediterranee (Toulon)
Ships incl in naval patrol and coastal totals
PATROL AND COASTAL COMBATANTS 5
PSO 1 *Albatros*
PCC 4: 3 *Flamant*; 1 *Sterne*
AIRCRAFT • TPT 4 N-262 *Fregate*
HELICOPTERS • UTL 4 AS-365 *Dauphin* 2

Reserves 6,000 reservists

Territorial Command • Atlantic
CECLANT
Navy 1 HQ located at Brest

Indian Ocean
ALINDIEN
Navy 1 (afloat) HQ located at Toulon

Mediterranean
CECMED
Navy 1 HQ located at Toulon

North Sea/Channel
COMAR CHERBOURG
Navy 1 HQ located at Cherbourg

Pacific Ocean
ALPACI
Navy 1 HQ located at Papeete, PF

Air Force 63,600; 5,700 (civilian); 8,000 reservists;
Flying hours 180 hrs/year

Air Surveillance, Communications and Information Command
FORCES BY ROLE

Air	1 Surveillance & Control sqn with 4 E-3F *Sentry*
Space	1 Helios 1A satellite obs sqn (Creil); 1 picture reception sqn (Colmar)
AD	10 sqn with *Crotale* 3000, *Crotale* upgraded & *Crotale* NG; 20mm 76T2; *Mistral*; ASPIC

Radar Stn 5 (Control)

EQUIPMENT BY TYPE
AIRCRAFT • AEW 4 E-3F *Sentry*
AD
SYSTEMS STRIDA (Control)
SAM *Crotale*; SATCP
GUNS 20mm
LAUNCHER ASPIC
SPACE BASED SYSTEMS • SATELLITES
2 IMAGERY 1: 1 Helios-2a (Creil); SATELLITES 2: 1 (picture reception sqn Colmar)

Air Combat Command
5,000 personnel. Nine airbases incl Djibouti
FORCES BY ROLE

Multi-role	2 AD sqn (St Dizier) plus test and evaluation with 35 *Rafale* F2 (27 F2-B, 8 F2-C)
AD/Test	2 AD sqn (St Dizier) plus test and evaluation sqn (Mont-de-Marsan) with 35 *Rafale* F2 (27 F2-B, 8 F2-C)
FGA	4 sqn with 67 M-2000D *Mirage* (Nancy), 42 F-1CT *Mirage* (Colmar); 1 composite sqn with 10 *Mirage* 2000-C/*Mirage* 2000-D (Djibouti)
Recce	2 sqn with 43 F-1CR *Mirage* (Reims)
EW	1 flt with 2 C-160G *Gabriel* (ESM) (Metz)
OCU	1 sqn eqipped with 17 *Mirage* 2000B; 1 sqn with 10 *Mirage* F1-B (Colmar)

EQUIPMENT BY TYPE
AIRCRAFT 256 combat capable
Multi-role 35: 27 *Rafale* F2-B (twin seat); 8 *Rafale* F2-C (single seat). Incl test and evaluation at Mont-de-Marsan First F3 by mid-2008

FTR 97: 32 M-2000-5 *Mirage*; 65 M-2000C *Mirage*
FGA 109: 67 M-2000D *Mirage*; 42 F-1CT *Mirage*
RECCE: 43 F-1CR *Mirage*
EW • ELINT 2 C-160G *Gabriel* (ESM)
TRG 50: 10 F-1B *Mirage**; 40 M-2000B *Mirage** (incl. 17 for OCU)
MSL
  AAM MICA; R-550 *Magic* 2; Super 530D; R-530F1;
  ASM AS-30L HOT; SCALP; *Apache*
  ASMP *Storm Shadow*
BOMBS
  Conventional: BAP 100, BAT 120; BEATS 120; EU2 SFA
  Laser-guided: GBU-12 *Paveway* II (to be acquired)

Air Mobility Command

4,290 personnel

FORCES BY ROLE

Tpt	1 heavy sqn with 3 A-310-300; 2 A-319; 2 A-340-200 (on lease)
Tkr/tactical tpt	6 sqn with 5 C-130H *Hercules*; 42 C-160 *Transall*; 15 Transall C-160NG
SAR/trg/tpt/utl	7 light sqn with 20 CN-235M; 5 DHC-6 *Twin Otter*; 1 *Mystère* 20 (*Falcon* 20); 4 *Falcon* 50 (VIP); 2 *Falcon* 900 (VIP); 17 TBM-700; 6 EC 725 *Cougar MKII*; AS-555 *Fennec*
OCU	1 sqn with 3 SA-330 *Puma*; 9 AS-555 *Fennec*; 1 unit with C-160 *Transall*
Hel	5 sqn with 7 AS-332 *Super Puma*; 6 AS-355 *Ecureuil*; 26 SA-330 *Puma*; 3 AS-532 *Cougar* (tpt/VIP); 33 AS-555 *Fennec*

EQUIPMENT BY TYPE
AIRCRAFT
  TPT 112: 3 A-310-300; 2 A-319 (VIP); 2 A-340-200 on lease; 5 C-130H; 9 C-130H-30; 42 C-160 *Transall*; 20 CN-235M; 5 DHC-6 *Twin Otter*; 4 *Falcon* 50 (VIP); 2 *Falcon* 900 (VIP); 1 *Mystère* 20 (*Falcon* 20); 17 TBM-700
  TPT/TKR 15 Transall C-160NG
HELICOPTERS
  CSAR 6 EC 725 *Cougar MKII*
  SPT 42: 7 AS-332 *Super Puma*; 6 AS-355 *Ecureuil*; 29 SA-330 *Puma*
  UTL 69: 24 AS-532 *Cougar*; 3 (tpt/VIP); 42 AS-555 *Fennec*

Air Training Command

Over 6,000 personnel

FORCES BY ROLE

Trg some sqns with 31 EMB-121 *Xingu*; 113 *Alpha Jet*; 5 CAP 10; 47 EMB-312 *Tucano*; 138 TB-30 *Epsilon*; 18 *Grob* G120A-F

EQUIPMENT BY TYPE
AIRCRAFT
  TPT 31 EMB-121 *Xingu*
  TRG 321: 113 *Alpha Jet*; 47 EMB-312 *Tucano*; 138 TB-30 *Epsilon* (incl many in storage); 18 *Grob* G120A-F; 5 CAP 10

Force Protection and Security Command

34 protection units
33 fire fighting and rescue sections
3 intervention paratroop commandos

Reserves 4,300 reservists

Paramilitary 99,148

Gendarmerie 3,884 (Administration); 2,078 (Maritime Air (personnel drawn from other departments)); 16,859 (Mobile); 4,741 (Republican Guard, Air Tpt, Arsenals); 5,049 (Schools); 66,537 (Territorial); 1,953 (civilian); 40,000 reservists; 41 opcon Strategic Nuclear Forces (total 139,148 plus 1,953 civilians)

EQUIPMENT BY TYPE
LT TK 28 VBC-90
APC (W) 153 VBRG-170
ARTY MOR 157+ 60mm; 81mm
PATROL AND COASTAL COMBATANTS 41
  PCO 1 *Fulmar*
  PCC 1 *Patra*
  PCR 1 *Stellis*
  PCI 38 (all less than 100 tonnes)
HELICOPTERS
  SPT 32 AS-350B *Ecureuil*
  UTL 17: 8 EC-135; 9 SA-316 *Alouette III*/SA-319 *Alouette III*

NON-STATE ARMED GROUPS

see Part II

DEPLOYMENT

AFGHANISTAN

NATO • ISAF 1,155 (*Operation Pamir*): 6 *Mirage* 2000D/*Mirage* F1; 2 EC-725 CSAR hel; 1 C-130 tpt
Operation Enduring Freedom 821 (*Operation Heracles*)
Operation Enduring Freedom 39 (*Operation Epidote*)

BOSNIA-HERZEGOVINA

EU • EUFOR • Air Force • Air Mobility Command
  AIRCRAFT • TPT 1 TBM-700
EU • EUFOR • *Operation Althea* 73 (*Operation Astrée*)

CENTRAL AFRICAN REPUBLIC

Operation Boali 300
UN • MINURCAT 1 obs

CHAD/CENTRAL AFRICAN REPUBLIC

EU • EUFOR Tchad/RCA 1,500

CHAD

Operation Epervier Army 1,050
FORCES BY ROLE
1 recce sqn with ERC-90F1 *Lynx*; 2 inf coy
Navy 400
Air Force • Air Combat Command
  Ftr: 6 F-1CR *Mirage* recce/F-1CT *Mirage* strike/FGA

TPT/TKR 4: 1 C-135 tkr; 3 C-160 *Transall*
HEL • SPT 3 SA-330 *Puma*

CÔTE D'IVOIRE

Army 3,800
HEL • UTL 1 AS-555 *Fennec*
UN • UNOCI 183; 2 obs

DEMOCRATIC REPUBLIC OF CONGO

EU • EUPOL KINSHASA 12
UN • MONUC 6 obs

DJIBOUTI

Army 2,850
2 (combined) army regt (*each:* 1 engr coy, 1 arty bty, 2 recce sqn, 2 inf coy)
Air Force
1 Air unit with 10 M-2000C/D *Mirage*; 1 C-160 *Transall*; 3 SA-342 *Gazelle*; 7 SA-330 *Puma*; 1 AS-555 *Fennec*; 1 SA-319 *Alouette III*

EGYPT

MFO • Air Force
TPT 1 DHC-6 *Twin Otter*
MFO 15

ETHIOPIA/ERITREA

UN • UNMEE 1

FRENCH GUIANA

Army 1,300 2 army regt; 1 SMA regt
Navy 170
PCI 3 (P 400)
Naval Aviation
MP 1 *Atlantique*
Air Force 1 tpt unit
HEL
SPT 4 SA-330 *Puma*
UTL 3 AS-555 *Fennec*
Gendarmerie
3 coy
HEL • SPT 1 AS-350 *Ecureuil*

FRENCH POLYNESIA

Army 800 (incl Centre d'Expérimentation du Pacifique)
1 marine inf bn; 3 SMA coy

Navy 710
EQUIPMENT BY TYPE
1 FFH with 1 AS-565SA *Panther* ASW hel
PATROL AND COASTAL COMBATANTS 2 PC
AMPHIBIOUS • LS 1 LSM
LOGISTICS AND SUPPORT • AO 1 AOT

FACILITIES
Bases 1 with 2 FF; 2 PCI (P 400); 1 *Champlain* LSM (capacity 12 trucks; 140 troops); 3 *Gardian* MP ac (HQ) located at Papeete
Naval Aviation
AC • MP 2 CASA 235 MPA
Territorial Command • Pacific Ocean
1 Navy HQ located at Papeete, PF
Air Force • Air Mobility Command
1 tpt unit
HEL • SPT 2 AS-332 *Super Puma*

FRENCH WEST INDIES

Army 800
2 marine inf regt; 2 SMA regt
Navy 450
1 FFH
2 PCI
1 LSM
Naval Aviation
AC • MP 3 CASA 235 MPA
HEL • ASW 1 AS-555SN *Fennec*
Air Force • Air Mobility Command
1 tpt unit
HEL • SPT 2 SA-330 *Puma*
Gendarmerie
6 Paramilitary coy
HEL • SPT 2 AS-350 *Ecureuil*

GABON

Army 700
1 recce pl with ERC-90F1 *Lynx*; 1 marine inf bn
HEL • RECCE 4 AS-532 *Horizon*
Navy 1,560
Air Force • Air Mobility Command
AC • TPT 2 C-160 *Transall*
HEL • UTL 1 AS-555 *Fennec*

GEORGIA

UN • UNOMIG 3 obs

GERMANY

Army 2,800 (incl elm Eurocorps and Fr/Ge bde (2,500))
1 (Fr/Ge) army bde (1 army HQ, 1 recce regt, 1 inf regt)

HAITI

UN • MINUSTAH 2

INDIAN OCEAN

Army 1,000 (incl La Reunion and TAAF)
1 marine inf regt; 1 SMA regt
Navy 2 FFH with 2 AS-555 *Fennec* utl hel
1 PC; 2 PCI
LS 1 LSM
Air Force • Air Mobility Command
1 tpt unit
AC • TPT 2 C-160 *Transall*
HEL: 1 spt
UTL 2 AS-555 *Fennec*
Gendarmerie
5 Paramilitary coy
HEL • UTL 1 SA-319 *Alouette III*

KYRGYZSTAN

ISAF 1 C-135 tkr

LA RÉUNION

Navy
FFH 1 *Floreal* (capacity 1 AS-565MA *Panther* SAR hel/AS-332F *Super Puma* ASW/ASUW hel);
2 PCI (P 400)
LS 1 LSM

FACILITIES
Bases 1 located at Dzaoudzi (Mayotte), 1 (HQ) located at Port-des-Galets

LEBANON

UN • UNIFIL II • Army
2 Mech inf coy; 1 Tk sqn; 1,587
MBT 13 *Leclerc*
AIFV 30 AMX-10 P
ARTY • SP • 155mm 4 Grande Cadence de Tir
AD • SAM • MANPAD Mistral
RADARS • LAND 2 Cobra

LIBERIA

UN • UNMIL 1

MARTINIQUE

Navy
Base   Located at Fort de France
Naval   Located at Hyères, Nimes-Garons, Lann-
airbases   Bihoue, Landivisiau

MIDDLE EAST

UN • UNTSO 2 obs

NEW CALEDONIA

Army 1,030
1 marine inf regt; 2 SMA coy
RECCE 6 ERC-90F1 *Lynx*
Navy 510
Bases   1 with 1 *Floreal* FFH; *Albatros* OPV; 2 *Gardian* MP
        aircraft located at Nouméa
Naval Aviation
  AIRCRAFT • MP 3 CASA 235 MPA
Air Force • Air Mobility Command
some air det; 1 tpt unit
  HEL•SPT 5 SA-330 *Puma*
    UTL 2 AS-555 *Fennec*
Gendarmerie
4 Paramilitary coy
  HEL.• SPT 2 AS-350 *Ecureuil*

SENEGAL

Army 610
1 marine inf bn (1 recce sqn with ERC-90F1 *Lynx*)
Navy 230
  Naval Aviation
  AIRCRAFT • MP 1 *Atlantique*
Air Force • Air Mobility Command
  AIRCRAFT • TPT 1 C-160 *Transall*
  HEL • UTL 1 AS-555 *Fennec*

SERBIA

NATO • KFOR • *Joint Enterprise* 1,830

SUDAN

UN • UNMIS 1

TAJIKISTAN

ISAF Air Force • Period deployments from Dushanbe
Armed Forces 150

WESTERN SAHARA

UN • MINURSO 13 obs

FOREIGN FORCES

Belgium Air Force: 29 *Alpha Jet* trg ac located at Cazaux/
Tours
Germany Army: 209 (Ge elm Eurocorps)
Singapore Air Force: 200 Air; some trg sqn with 6 A-4SU
Super Skyhawk; 10 TA-4SU *Super Skyhawk*; 200
United Kingdom Army 10; Navy 10; Air Force 10
United States Army 17; Navy 11; USAF 18; USAMC 23

Germany Ge

Euro €		2006	2007	2008
GDP	€	2.31tr	2.41tr	
	US$	2.88tr	3.44tr	
per capita	US$	35.018	41,782	
Growth	%	2.9	2.4	
Inflation	%	1.8	1.8	
Def exp [a]	€	30.2bn		
	US$	37.77bn		
Def bdgt	€	27.9bn	28.4bn	29.3bn
	US$	34.83bn	4.32bn	
US$1=€		0.80	0.70	

[a] including military pensions

Population	82,400,996

Age	0–14	15–19	20–24	25–29	30–64	65 plus
Male	7%	3%	3%	3%	25%	8%
Female	7%	3%	3%	3%	24%	10%

Capabilities

ACTIVE 245,702 (Army 160,794 Navy 24,328 Air 60,580)
Terms of service 9 months; 10–23 months voluntary. *Reserves:* men to age 45 NCOs and officers to 60.

RESERVE 161,812 (Army 144,548 Navy 3,304 Air 13,960)

ORGANISATIONS BY SERVICE

Army 118,228; 42,566 conscript (total 160,794)

I GE/NL Corps HQ, II GE/US Corps HQ

FORCES BY ROLE
Bde differ in their basic org, peacetime str, eqpt and mob capability; 4 (2 armd, 1 inf and Ge/Fr bde are allocated to the CRF, the remainder to Main Defence Forces (MDF). 1 armd inf div is earmarked for EUROCORPS, 1 armd div (incl 1 Pl bde) to Allied Rapid Reaction Corps (ARRC) and 1 armd inf div to the Multi-National Corps North East

Armd/   5 div (3 armd, 2 armd inf); 12 bde (and the GE
Armd inf elm of the GE/Fr bde)
Mech   4 bde
Air Mob   1 div (1 Avn bde (5 regt), 1 Air mech bde (4 regt))
Inf   1 bde

Mtn Inf	1 bde
Air mob	1 div (1 Avn bde (5 regt), 1 Air mech bde (4 regt))
Spec Ops	1 div (1 SF comd (1 Cdo / SF bde), 2 AB bde (1 Crisis Reaction Force (CRF))
Arty	7 regt
AD	7 regt
Trg	1 bg (trg) with (35 *Leopard* 2; 26 *Marder* 1; 12 M-109A3G)
Engr	7 bde
EW	1 (SIGINT/ELINT) bde
Spt	1 regt
Log	2 bde
Spt arms	1 comd (forming)

EQUIPMENT BY TYPE

MBT 2,035: 1,472 *Leopard* 2 (350 to be upgraded to A6); 563 *Leopard* 1A1/1A3/1A4/1A5 (in store)

RECCE 496: 202 *Fennek*; 210 SPz-2 *Luchs*; 84 Tpz-1 *Fuchs* (NBC)

AIFV 2,218: 2,085 1 A2 *Marder*/1 A3 *Marder*; 133 *Wiesel* (with 20mm gun)

APC 2,300

APC (T) 2,067: 1287 M-113 (incl 317 arty obs and other variants)

APC (W) 1,013: 147 APCV-2 *Dingo*; 909 TPz-1 *Fuchs* (incl variants)

ARTY 1,364

SP 155mm 679; M-109 497: 499 M-109A3G; 180 PzH 2000

TOWED 165: **105mm** 10 M-101; **155mm** 155 FH-70

MRL 227mm 129 MLRS

MOR 120mm 391 *Tampella*

AT • MSL 1,277

SP 194 *Wiesel* (TOW)

MANPATS 1,083 *Milan*

AMPHIBIOUS 13 LCM (river engineers)

HELICOPTERS

ATK 192 BÖ-105, BÖ 105 M (PAH-1) (with HOT)

RECCE 2 BÖ-105M

SPT 93 CH-53G *Stallion*

UTL 136+: 14 EC-135; 12 SA 313 *Alouette II*; 118 UH-1; 118 UH-1D *Iroquois*

UAV 368: 160 AOLOS-289/CL-289 (AN/USD-502); 115 Aladin; 28 LUNA X-2000; 60 KZO; 5 EuroHawk on order

AD

SAM 148+

SP 120 *Roland*

TOWED 28 PAC-3 *Patriot*

MANPAD FIM-92A *Stinger* (incl some *Ozelot* SP)

GUNS 1,288

TOWED 20mm 1,155 Rh 202

SP 35mm 135 *Gepard*

RADAR • LAND 137+: *Cobra*; 18 M-113 A1GE *Green Archer* (mor); 85 RASIT (veh, arty); 34 RATAC (veh, arty)

Navy 20,540; 3,788 conscript (total 24,328)

Undergone extensive reorganisation previous Type Comds have been merged into two Flotillas; Flotilla I combining SS, MCM, PBF and SF whilst Flotilla II comprises 2 FF and Aux squadrons.

EQUIPMENT BY TYPE

SUBMARINES • TACTICAL 12

SSK 12:

8 Type 206A each with 8 x1 533mm ASTT each with DM2 HWT

4 Type 212A (2 further vessels on order) each eq with 6 single 533mm TT with 12 A4 *Seehecht* DM2 HWT

PRINCIPAL SURFACE COMBATANTS 17

FRIGATES 15

FFGHM 3:

3 *Sachsen* each with 2 Mk 141 *Harpoon* quad (8 eff.) each with RGM-84F tactical SSM, 1 32 cell Mk 41 VLS (32 eff.) with 24 SM-2 MR SAM, 32 RIM-162B *Sea Sparrow* SAM, 2 Mk 49 RAM each with 21 RIM-116 *RAM* SAM (capacity either 2 NH-90 utl hel or 2 *Lynx* utl hel)

FFG 12:

4 *Brandenburg* each with 2 twin (4 eff.) each with MM-38 *Exocet* tactical SSM, 2 Mk 49 RAM with 21 RIM-116 *RAM* SAM, 1 Mk 41 VLS with 16 RIM-7M/RIM-7P, 4 x1 324mm ASTT each with Mk 46 LWT, 1 76mm gun, (capacity either 2 MK88 *Sea Lynx* ASW hel or 2 *Sea Lynx* MK88A ASW)

8 *Bremen* each with 2 Mk 141 *Harpoon* quad (8 eff.) each with RGM-84A *Harpoon*/RGM-84C *Harpoon* tactical SSM, 1 Mk 29 *Sea Sparrow* octuple with 16 RIM-7M/RIM-7P, 2 Mk 49 RAM with 21 RIM-116 *RAM* SAM, 2 twin 324mm ASTT (4 eff.) each with Mk 46 LWT,, 1 76mm gun, (capacity either 2 MK88 *Sea Lynx* ASW hel or 2 *Sea Lynx* MK88A ASWs)

CORVETTES 2

FS 2 *Braunschweig* (K130) (further three of class expected 2008–2009)

PATROL AND COASTAL COMBATANTS • PFM 10

10 *Gepard* each with 2 twin (4 eff.) with MM-38 *Exocet* tactical SSM, 1 Mk 49 RAM with 21 RIM-116 *RAM* SAM, 1 76mm gun

MINE WARFARE • MINE COUNTERMEASURES 38:

MHC 15: 10 *Frankenthal*; 5 *Kulmbach*

MSC 5 *Ensdorf*

MSD 18 *Seehund*

AMPHIBIOUS • LC 3

LCM 1

LCU 2 Type 521

LOGISTICS AND SUPPORT 31

AO 2 *Walchensee Type 703*

AOT 2 *Spessart Type 704*

AFH 2 *Berlin Type 702* (capacity either 2 NH-90 utl hel or 2 *Sea King* MK41 SAR hel; 2 RAMs)

AE (AMMO) 1 *Westerwald Type 760*

AG 6: 3 *Schwedeneck Type 748*; 3 *Stollergrund Type 745*

AGOR 1 *Planet Type 751*

AGI 3 *Oste Type 423*

AT 5

Trg 1

SPT 6 *Elbe Type 404* (2 specified for PFM support; 1 specified for SSK support; 3 specified for MHC/MSC support)

Trial Ship 2

FACILITIES

Bases Located at Olpenitz, Wilhelmshaven, Glücksburg
(Maritime HQ), Warnemünde, Eckernförde, Kiel

Naval Aviation 2,260

AIRCRAFT
  MP 10: 2(*Atlantic*), 8 AP-3C *Orion*
  TPT 2 Do-228 (2 pollution control)
HELICOPTERS
  SAR 21 *Sea King* MK41 (SAR)
  ASW 22 *Sea Lynx* MK88A (ASW/ASUW)
MSL • TACTICAL • ASM *Sea Skua*

Air Force 50,310; 10,270 conscript (total 60,580)

Flying hours   150 hrs/year
Missile trg   Located at Fort Bliss (TX), US

Air Force Command

FORCES BY ROLE

Air   3 div
Ftr   4 wg (4 sqn with 76 F-4F *Phantom II*; 2 wg
        with 33 EF-2000 Eurofighter)
FGA   2 wg (4 FGA sqn with 97 Tornado IDS); 1 wg
        (2 FGA sqn with 33 *Tornado* ECR* plus 17 IDS)
Recce   1 wg (2 recce sqn with 42 Tornado IDS (recce))
Radar   3 (tac air control) gp
SAM   3 eg (each 2 SAM gp) with MIM-104 *Patriot*
Trg   sqns with 35 T-37B *Tweet*; 40 T-38A *Talon*

EQUIPMENT BY TYPE

AIRCRAFT 298 combat capable
  FTR 109: 33 EF-2000 *Eurofighter*; 76 F-4F *Phantom II*
  STRIKE/FGA : 156 *Tornado* IDS (incl 42 recce); another
  64 in store
  SEAD 33 *Tornado* ECR*
  TRG 75: 35 T-37B *Tweet*; 40 T-38A *Talon*
AD • SAM • TOWED MIM-104 *Patriot*
MSL
  ASM KEPD 350; AGM-65B/D/G *Maverick*
  ASSM *Kormoran* 2
  ARM AGM-88B HARM
  AAM AIM-9L/Li *Sidewinder*; *Iris*-T; LFK *Iris*-T (being
  introduced); AIM 120A/B AMRAAM
BOMBS
  LGB: GBU-24 *Paveway* III

Transport Command

FORCES BY ROLE

Tkr/tpt 1 (special air mission) wg with 7 A-310
         (4 MRTT, 3 MRT); 6 CL-601 *Challenger*;
         3 AS-532U2 *Cougar II* (VIP)
Tpt   3 wg (*total:* 4 tpt sqn with 80 UH-1D (76 SAR,
         tpt, liaison, 4 VIP)(1 OCU); 3 tpt sqn with 83
         C-160 *Transall* (1 OCU))

EQUIPMENT BY TYPE

AIRCRAFT • TPT 96: 7 A-310 (incl tpt/tkr); 83 C-160
Transall; 6 CL-601 *Challenger* (VIP)

HELICOPTERS • UTL 83: 3 AS-532U2 *Cougar II* (VIP);
80 UH-1D *Iroquois* (76 SAR, tpt, liaison, 4 VIP)

Training

OCU	1 with 23 *Tornado* IDS
NATO joint pilot trg	Sheppard AFB (TX) with 35 T-37B, 40 T-38A

DEPLOYMENT

AFGHANISTAN

EU • EUPOL AFGHANISTAN 60
NATO • ISAF 3,155
  APC(W) 100 *Dingo* II
  SEAD 6 *Tornado* ECR
Tpt C-160
  HEL
    SPT CH-53
UN • UNAMA 1 obs

BOSNIA-HERZEGOVINA

EU • EUFOR • *Operation Althea* 235
  RECCE 28 SPz-2 *Luchs*
  APC (W) TPz-1 *Fuchs*
  HEL
    SPT 3 CH-53 *Sea Stallion*
    UTL • UH-1 4 UH-1D *Iroquois*

DJIBOUTI

Armed Forces
HEl
    SAR 2 *Sea King* MK41
    Utl 2UH-1D *Iroquois*
    Tpt C-160
    Spt CH-53
Operation Enduring Freedom 257

ETHIOPIA/ERITREA

UN • UNMEE 2 obs

FRANCE

Army 209 (Ge elm Eurocorps)

GEORGIA

UN • UNOMIG 12 obs

ITALY

Navy • Naval Aviation
AC 3 Maritime Patrol (in ELMAS/Sardinia)
EU • EUFOR • EUFOR (Air) 200 Air Forces

LEBANON

UN •UNIFIL II • *Maritime Task Force* • Navy 905
  FFG 1
  PB 2
  AE 2

POLAND

Army 67 (Ge elm Corps HQ (multinational))

SERBIA

NATO • KFOR • *Joint Enterprise*
Armed Forces 2,279

MBT 26 *Leopard* C2
RECCE 17 SPz-2 *Luchs*
AIFV 25 *Marder* 1
APC 75
    APC (T) 21; APC (W) 54 TPz-1 *Fuchs*
ARTY SP 155mm 10 M-109A3G
AT • MSL 6 *Wiesel* (TOW)
HEL
    SPT 3 CH-53 *Sea Stallion*
    UTL 9 UH-1D *Iroquois*

SUDAN
AU/UN • UNAMID 250 proposed deployment
UN • UNMIS 5; 31 obs

UNITED STATES
Army
1 (battle) army gp (trg) (army trg area) with 35 *Leopard* 2;
26 *Marder* 1; 12 M-109A3G

Air Force
812 (flying trg) located at Goodyear AFB (AZ), Sheppard
AFB (TX), Holloman AFB (NM), NAS Pensacola (FL), Fort
Rucker (AL)
    STRIKE/FGA 23 *Tornado* IDS located at Holloman AFB
    (NM)
    TRG 75: 35 T-37 *Tweet* located at Sheppard AFB (TX); 40
    T-38 *Talon* located at Sheppard AFB (TX)
NATO • Air Force • Missile trg Located at Fort Bliss (TX), US
Primary trg sqn located at Goodyear AFB (AZ), Joint jet
pilot trg sqn located at Sheppard AFB (TX)
    AIRCRAFT • Trg some Beech F-33 *Bonanza*

UZBEKISTAN
NATO • ISAF 163
    Tpt 6 C-160 *Transall*

FOREIGN FORCES

Canada SNMG 1; 1 FFG; NATO 292
France Army: 1 (Fr/Ge) army bde (1 army HQ, 1 recce regt,
1 inf regt); 2,800 (incl elm Eurocorps and Fr/Ge bde (2,500))
Italy Air Force: 91 (NAEW Force)
Netherlands Air Force: 300 army: 1 mech inf bde (plus spt
elms) (1 armd bn, 1 tk bn); 2,300
United Kingdom Army: 1 army corps HQ (multinational);
1 army corps; 1 armd div; 22,000
United States Army: 1 armd corps HQ located at
Heidelberg (1 armd div ((less 1 bde at Ft Riley)), 1 engr
bde, 1 avn bde, 1 mech inf div, 1 arty bde, 1 AD bde); 43,247
EUCOM: 568 M-1 *Abrams* MBT; 1,266 M-2 *Bradley* AIFV;
312 mor/MRL/SP; 115 atk hel; 1 Combined Service HQ
(EUCOM) located at Stuttgart-Vaihingen; 1 HQ (AF) HQ
(US Airforce Europe (USAFE)) located at Ramstein AB; 1
HQ (US Army Europe (USAREUR)) located at Heidelberg;
1 ftr wg located at Spangdahlem AB (1 ftr sqn with 12 A-10
Thunderbolt II; 6 OA-10 *Thunderbolt II*, 2 ftr sqn each with
21 F-16C *Fighting Falcon*); 1 airlift wg located at Ramstein
AB eqpt with 16 C-130E *Hercules*; 2 C-20 *Gulfstream*; 9 C-
21 *Learjet*; 1 CT-43 *Boeing 737*; 1 Airfield construction HQ
(HQ US Airforce Europe (USAFE)) located at Ramstein AB
Navy: 297; USAF: 15,067; USMC: 283

Greece Gr

Euro €		2006	2007	2008
GDP	€	246bn	263bn	
	US$	308bn	376bn	
per capita	US$	28,770	35,093	
Growth	%	4.3	3.9	
Inflation	%	3.3	2.8	
Def exp[a]	€	5.82bn		
	US$	7.28bn		
Def bdgt	€	3.71bn	3.87bn	
	US$	4.64bn	5.54bn	
US$1=€		0.80	0.70	

[a] including military pensions and procurement

Population   10,706,290
Ethnic groups: Muslim 1%

Age	0–14	15–19	20–24	25–29	30–64	65 plus
Male	7%	3%	3%	4%	24%	8%
Female	7%	3%	3%	4%	24%	10%

Capabilities

**ACTIVE 156,600 (Army 93,500 Navy 20,000 Air
31,500 Joint 11,600) Paramilitary 4,000**

Terms of service All services up to 12 months

**RESERVE 251,000 (Army 198,000 Navy 23,000 Air
30,000)**

ORGANISATIONS BY SERVICE

Army 93,500; ε38% conscript
FORCES BY ROLE
Field army to re-org. Units are manned at 3 different levels
– Cat A 85% fully ready, Cat B 60% ready in 24 hours, Cat C
20% ready in 48 hours

MR	3 regions
Army	1 HQ; 5 corps HQ (incl 1 RRF)
Armd	1 div HQ; 4 bde (*each:* 1 mech inf bn, 1 SP arty bn, 2 armd bn)
Recce	5 bn
Mech inf	3 div HQ; 8 bde (*each:* 1 armd bn, 1 SP arty bn, 2 mech bn)
Inf	1 div HQ ; 3 bde (*each:* 1 armd bn, 1 arty regt, 3 inf regt)
SF	1 comd (1 (cdo) amph bde; 1 cdo parachute bde)
Marine	1 bde
Fd arty	3 bn (incl 2 bn MLRS)
Air Mob	1 bde
ADA	3 bn (incl 2 I-*HAWK* / *TOR* M1)
Avn	1 bde (1 avn regt (2 atk hel bn), 1 Spt hel bn, 3 avn bn)

EQUIPMENT BY TYPE

MBT 1,514: 155 *Leopard* 2; 509 *Leopard* 1; 339 M-60A1/M-60A3; 511 M-48A5

RECCE 242 VBL

AIFV 377 BMP-1

APC (T) 2,105: 432 *Leonidas* Mk1/*Leonidas* Mk2; 1,673 M-113A1/M-113A2

ARTY 3,163

   SP 348: **155mm** 221: 197 M-109A1B/M-109A2/M-109A3GEA1/M-109A5; 24 PzH 2000; **203mm** 127 M-110A2

   TOWED 412: **105mm** 283: 265 M-101; 18 M-56; **155mm** 129 M-114

   MRL 151: **122mm** 115 RM-70 *Dana*; **227mm** 36 MLRS (incl ATACMS)

   MOR 2,252: **81mm** 1,632; **107mm** 620 M-30 (incl 231 SP)

AT

   MSL 1,108

      SP 362: 320 M-901; 42 *Milan* HMMWV

      MANPATS 746: 196 9P163 *Kornet-E*; 262 9K111 AT-4 *Spigot*; 248 *Milan*; 40 TOW

   RCL 4,290:

      SP 106mm 946 M-40A1

      MANPAT 3,344: **84mm** 2,000 *Carl Gustav*; **90mm** 1,344 EM-67

AIRCRAFT

   TPT 3; 1 C-12C *Huron*; 2 C-12R/AP *Huron*

   UTL 38 U-17A

HELICOPTERS

   ATK 32: 20 AH-64A *Apache*; 12 AH-64D *Apache*

   SPT 15 CH-47D *Chinook*

   UTL 114: 14 AB-206 (Bell 206) *JetRanger*; 100 UH-1H *Iroquois*

UAV 12-18 *Sperwer*

AD

   SAM 1,722

      SP 113: 21 SA-15 *Gauntlet*; 38 SA-8B *Gecko*; 54 ASRAD HMMWV

      TOWED 42 I-HAWK *MIM-23B*

      MANPAD 1,567 FIM-92A *Stinger*

   GUNS

      TOWED 683: **20mm** 160 Rh 202; **23mm** 523 ZU-23-2

RADAR • LAND 73: 5 AN/TPQ-36 *Firefinder* (arty, mor); 8 AN/TPQ-37(V)3; 40 BOR-A; 20 MARGOT

National Guard 34,500 reservists

Internal security role

Inf	1 Div
Para	1 regt
Fd Arty	8 bn
ADA	4 bn
Avn	1 bn

Navy 16,000; 4,000 conscript; (total 20,000)

EQUIPMENT BY TYPE

SUBMARINES • TACTICAL • SSK 9:

   8 *Glavkos* (Ge T-209/1100) each with 8 single 533mm TT each with UGM-84C *Harpoon* tactical USGW, SUT HWT

   1 *Papanikolis* (*Poseidon* class) (Ge T-214) (Three more in build; 2nd to be commissioned mid 2008.) eq with 8 single 533mm TT each eq with UGM-84C *Harpoon* USGW, SUT HWT

PRINCIPAL SURFACE COMBATANTS 17

   FRIGATES • FFG 14:

      4 Standard Class Batch I (*Elli class*) (ex-NL *Kortenaer* Batch 2) each with 2 Mk 141 *Harpoon* quad (8 eff.) each with RGM-84A *Harpoon*/RGM-84C *Harpoon* tactical SSM, 1 Mk 29 *Sea Sparrow* octuple with 16 RIM-7M/RIM-7P *Sea Sparrow* SAM, 2 twin ASTT (4 eff.) each with Mk 46 LWT, 1 76mm gun, (capacity 2 AB-212 (Bell 212) utl hel)

      2 Standard Class Batch II (*Elli class*) (ex-NL *Kortenaer* Batch 2) each with 2 Mk 141 *Harpoon* quad (8 eff.) each with RGM-84A *Harpoon*/RGM-84C *Harpoon* tactical SSM, 1 Mk 29 *Sea Sparrow* octuple with 16 RIM-7M/RIM-7P *Sea Sparrow* SAM, 2 twin ASTT (4 eff.) each with Mk 46 LWT, 2 76mm guns, (capacity 2 AB-212 (Bell 212) utl hel)

      4 Standard Class Batch III (*Elli class*) (ex-NL *Kortenaer* Batch 2) each with 2 Mk 141 *Harpoon* quad (8 eff.) each with RGM-84A *Harpoon*/RGM-84C *Harpoon* tactical SSM, 1 Mk 29 *Sea Sparrow* octuple with 16 RIM-7M/RIM-7P *Sea Sparrow* SAM, 2 twin ASTT (4 eff.) each with Mk 46 LWT, 1 76mm gun, (capacity 2 AB-212 (Bell 212) utl hel)

      4 *Hydra* (Ge MEKO 200) each with 2 quad (8 eff.) each with RGM-84G *Harpoon* tactical SSM, 1 16 cell Mk 48 VLS with 16 RIM-7M *Sea Sparrow* SAM, 2 triple ASTT (6 eff.) each with Mk 46 LWT, 1 127mm gun, (capacity 1 S-70B *Seahawk* ASW hel)

   CORVETTES • FS 3:

      3 *Niki* (ex-Ge *Thetis*) each with 2 triple 324mm ASTT (6 eff.) each with Mk 46 LWT, 2 twin 40mm gun (4 eff.)

PATROL AND COASTAL COMBATANTS 40

   PFM 20:

      5 *Kavaloudis* (Fr *La Combattante* II, III, IIIB) each with 6 RB 12 *Penguin* tactical SSM, 2 single 533mm TT each with SST-4 HWT, 2 76mm gun

      4 *Laskos* (Fr *La Combattante* II, III, IIIB) each with 4 MM-38 *Exocet* tactical SSM, 2 single 533mm TT each with SST-4 HWT, 2 76mm gun

      2 *Votsis* (Fr *La Combattante*) each with 2 Mk-141 *Harpoon* twin each with RGM-84C *Harpoon* tactical SSM, 1 76mm gun

      4 *Votsis* (Fr *La Combattante* IIA) each with 4 MM-38 *Exocet* tactical SSM, 1 76mm gun

      5 *Roussen* (*Super Vita*) with 8 MM-40 *Exocet* tactical ASSM

   PFT 4 *Andromeda* (ex No *Nasty*) each with 4 single 533mm TT each with SST-4 HWT

   PC 2 *Stamou* with 4 single SS 12M tactical SSM

   PCO 8: 2 *Armatolos* (ex Dk *Osprey*); 2 *Pirpolitis*; 4 *Machitis*

   PCC 2 *Tolmi*

   PCI 4

MINE COUNTERMEASURES 8

   MHC 2 *Evropi* (ex UK *Hunt*)

   MSC 6 *Alkyon* (ex US MSC-294)

AMPHIBIOUS

   LS • LST 5:

      5 *Chios* (capacity 4 LCVP; 300 troops) each with 1 hel landing platform (for med hel)

   CRAFT 59: 2 LCT; 4 LCU; 31 LCVP; 11 LCM; 7 LCA

   ACV 4 *Kefallinia* (*Zubr*) (capacity either 3 MBT or 10 APC (T)s; 230 troops;)

LOGISTICS AND SUPPORT 21:
AOT 6: 2; 4 (small)
AE 3: 2 AE (ex-Ge *Luneburg*); 1 AE *Etna*
AWT 6
AGHS 3
TPT 2
TRG 1

FACILITIES

Bases Located at Salamis, Patras, Soudha Bay

Naval Aviation

FORCES BY ROLE

ASW   1 Division eq with 11 S-70B *Seahawk*; 8 AB-212 (Bell 212); 2 SA-319 *Alouette III*

MP   2 sqn eq with 6 P-3B *Orion*; 2 CL-415GR (CL-415)

SAR   Flight eq with 2 AB-212 (Bell 212)

EQUIPMENT BY TYPE
AIRCRAFT
  MARITIME PATROL 6 P-3B *Orion*
  SPT 2 CL-415GR (CL-415)
HELICOPTERS 11 attack helicopters
  ASW 11 S-70B *Seahawk*
  UTL 10: 8 AB-212 (Bell 212); 2 SA-319 *Alouette III*
MSL
  ASM AGM-119 *Penguin*
  ASSM MM-40 *Exocet*

Air Force 31,500 (incl 11,000 conscripts)

Tactical Air Force

FORCES BY ROLE

AD/FGA   4 sqn with 71 F-16CG/DG Blk 30,50 *Fighting Falcon*; 3 sqn with 59 F-16CG/DG Block 52+ *Fighting Falcon;* 1 sqn with 15 M-2000-5 Mk 2 *Mirage)*; 2 sqn with 31 M-2000E/BGM *Mirage*; 2 sqn with 35 F-4E *Phantom II*; 2 sqn with 78 A/TA-7E/H *Corsair II*

n with   1 sqn with 19 RF-4E *Phantom II*

AEW   1 sqn with 4 EMB-145H *Erieye*

EQUIPMENT BY TYPE
AIRCRAFT 357 combat capable
  FTR 15 M-2000-5 Mk 2 *Mirage* (10 -5EG, 5 -5BG)
  FGA 323: 31 M-2000EG/BG *Mirage*; (10 being upgraded to 2000-5 standard); 70 F-16C/D *Fighting Falcon* Blk 30, 50 *Fighting Falcon*; 59 F-16 C/D Bl0ck 52+ *Fighting Falcon*; 35 F-4E *Phantom II* ; 78 A/TA-7E/H *Corsair II*
  RECCE 19 RF-4E *Phantom II**
  AEW 6: 4 EMB-145H *Erieye*
MSL
  AAM AIM 120B/C AMRAAM; AIM-7E/F *Sparrow*; AIM-9L/AIM-9P *Sidewinder*; MICA; R-550 *Magic 2*; Super 530; IRIS-T
  ASM AGM-65A/B/G *Maverick*; SCALP EG
  ASSM AM 39 *Exocet*
  ARM AGM-88 HARM
BOMBS
  Conventional: GBU-8B HOBOS
  Laser-guided: GBU-12/ GBU-16 *Paveway* II; GBU-24 *Paveway* III

Air Defence

FORCES BY ROLE

SAM 6 sqn/bty PAC-3 *Patriot* with 36 launchers [MIM-104 (A/B SOJC/D GEM)]; 2 sqn/bty with S-300 PMU-1 with 12 launchers; 12 bty *Skyguard* with SPARROW RIM-7/ GUNS; 9 *Crotale* NG/GR; 4 SA-15 *Gauntlet* (TOR-M1)

EQUIPMENT BY TYPE
AD
  SAM TOWED 61+: 36 PAC-3 *Patriot;* 12 S-300 PMU-1; 9 *Crotale* NG/GR; 4 SA-15 *Gauntlet* (*TOR*-M1); some *Skyguard*/SPARROW
  GUNS 35+ 35mm

Air Support Command

FORCES BY ROLE

CSAR 1 sqn with 6 AS-332 *Super Puma*

Tpt   3 sqn with 5 C-130B *Hercules*; 10 C-130H *Hercules*; 1 YS-11-200; 2 C-47 *Skytrain*; 6 Do-28; 1 sqn with 12 C-27J *Spartan* (8 AT and 4 AAR); 1 sqn with 2 EMB-135; 1 *Gulfstream* V

hel   1 sqn with 4 AS-332 *Super Puma* (SAR); 13 AB-205A (Bell 205A) (SAR); 4 AB-212 (Bell 212) (VIP, tpt); 7 Bell 47G (liaison)

EQUIPMENT BY TYPE
  AIRCRAFT • TPT 39: 5 C-130B *Hercules*; 10 C-130H *Hercules*; 12 C-27J *Spartan* (8 AT and 4 AAR) – being delivered; 2 C-47 *Skytrain*; 6 Do-28; 2 EMB-135; 1 *Gulfstream* V; 1 YS-11-200
HELICOPTERS
  SPT 10 AS-332 *Super Puma*
  UTL 17: 4 AB-212 (Bell 212) (VIP, tpt); 13 AB-205A (Bell 205A) (SAR),
  TRG 7 Bell 47G (liaison)

Air Training Command

FORCES BY ROLE

Trg   5 sqn with T-2C/E *Buckeye*; T-41 D; T-6A/B *Texan II*

EQUIPMENT BY TYPE
  AIRCRAFT • TRG 104: 40 T-2C/E *Buckeye*; 19 T-41D; 20 T-6A *Texan II*; 25 T-6B *Texan II*

Paramilitary • Coast Guard and Customs 4,000

PATROL AND COASTAL COMBATANTS 90: 4 **PCO**; 1 **PFC**; 7 **PCC**; 39 **PBC**; 39 **PBI**
AIRCRAFT • UTL 4
2 Cessna 172RG *Cutlass*
2 TB-20 *Trinidad*

NON-STATE ARMED GROUPS

see Part II

DEPLOYMENT

AFGHANISTAN
NATO • ISAF 137;
  AC • **TPT** 3-4 C-130 *Hercules* per year

BOSNIA-HERZEGOVINA
EU • EUFOR • *Operation Althea* 45

Europe (NATO)

CYPRUS

Army 950 (ELDYK army); ε200 (officers/NCO seconded to Greek-Cypriot National Guard) (total 1,150)
1 armd bn; 1 (incl 950 (ELDYK) army) mech bde; 2 mech inf bn; 1 arty bn
MBT 61 M-48A5 MOLF
APC (T) 80 *Leonidas*
ARTY 24
   TOWED • 155mm 12 M-114
   SP 12: **175mm** 6 M-107; **203mm** 6 M-110A2

ETHIOPIA/ERITREA

UN • UNMEE 2 obs

GEORGIA

UN • UNOMIG 4 obs

LEBANON

UN • UNIFIL II • *Maritime Task Force* • Navy 228
FFG: 1 *Elli* (1 Helo and SEAL team)
PB: 1

SERBIA

NATO • KFOR • *Joint Enterprise* 742

SUDAN

UN • UNMIS 2; 4 obs

WESTERN SAHARA

UN • MINURSO 1 obs

FOREIGN FORCES

United States Army: 9 EUCOM Navy: 288 (Bases located at Makri and Soudha Bay) Air Force: 46 (Base located at Iraklion) USMC: 11

Hungary Hu

Hungarian Forint f		2006	2007	2008
GDP	f	23.56tr	25.79tr	
	US$	112bn	147bn	
per capita	US$	11,241	14,720	
Growth	%	3.9	2.1	
Inflation	%	3.9	7.2	
Def exp	f	277bn		
	US$	1.32bn		
Def bdgt	f	321bn	319bn	
	US$	1.53bn	1.81bn	
FMA (US)	US$	2.4m	2.5m	
US$1=f		210	176	

Population   9,956,108

Ethnic groups: Romany 4%; German 3%; Serb 2%; Romanian 1%; Slovak 1%

Age	0–14	15–19	20–24	25–29	30–64	65 plus
Male	8%	3%	3%	4%	23%	6%
Female	8%	3%	3%	4%	25%	9%

Capabilities

ACTIVE 32,300 (Army 23,950 Air 7,500 Joint 850)
Paramilitary 12,000

RESERVE 44,000 (Army 35,200 Air 8,800)
Terms of service 6 months. Reservists to age 50.

ORGANISATIONS BY SERVICE

Army ε23,950

FORCES BY ROLE
being re-org

Army	1 (Land Forces) force HQ; 1 (garrison) comd; 1 (NBC) bn
Armd	1 bn
Recce	2 bn
Lt inf	2 bde (*total:* 7 Lt inf bn)
Maritime	1 wg
Engr	1 bde
Log	1 regt
MP	1 regt

Reserves 35,200 reservists

Mech inf   4 bde

EQUIPMENT BY TYPE
MBT 238 T-72
AIFV 178 BTR-80A
APC (W) 458 BTR-80
ARTY 573+
   SP 122mm 153+ 2S1 *Carnation* in store
   TOWED 152mm 308 D-20
   MRL 122mm 62+ BM-21 in store
   MOR 82mm 50
AT • MSL • MANPATS 110: 30 AT-4 9K111 *Spigot*; 80 AT-5 9K113 *Spandrel*
AD • SAM 105
   MANPAD 60 SA-14 *Gremlin*
   NAVAL 45 *Mistral*
RADAR • LAND 15: 5 PSZNR-5B; 10 SNAR-10 *Big Fred* (SZNAR-10)

FACILITIES
Training Centre   2

Army Maritime Wing 60

EQUIPMENT BY TYPE
PATROL AND COASTAL COMBATANTS
MINE WARFARE • MINE COUNTERMEASURES
MSR 3 *Nestin*

FACILITIES
Base   Located at Budapest

Air Force Command 7,500

Flying hours   50 hrs/year

FORCES BY ROLE

FGA   1 (tac ftr) wg with 14 JAS-39 *Gripen*; 12 MiG-29B
      Fulcrum; 2 MiG-29UB *Fulcrum*

Tpt   1 (mixed) wg with 5 An-26 *Curl*; 12 Mi-8 *Hip*;
      5 Mi-17 (Mi-8MT) *Hip H*

Atk hel   1 (cbt) sqn with 12 Mi-24 *Hind*

Trg   sqn with 6 L-39ZO *Albatros*; 9 Yak-52

AD   1 (msl) bde; 1 (cmd and radar) regt

SAM   2 (mixed) regt with 45 *Mistral*; 20 SA-6 *Gainful*
      (60 eff.)

EQUIPMENT BY TYPE

AIRCRAFT 28 combat capable

  FTR 12 MiG-29B *Fulcrum**

  FGA 14 JAS-39 *Gripen*(12 C, 2-D)

  TPT 5 An-26 *Curl*

  TRG 17: 6 L-39ZO *Albatros*; 2 MiG-29UB *Fulcrum**; 9 Yak-52

HELICOPTERS

  ATK 12 Mi-24 *Hind*

  SPT 17: 12 Mi-8; 5 Mi-17 (Mi-8MT) *Hip H*

AD

  SAM 65: 45 *Mistral*

    SP 20 SA-6 *Gainful*

MSL

  AAM AIM 120C AMRAAM on order; AA-2C/D *Atoll*;
  AA-8 *Aphid*; 84 AA-10 *Alamo*; 210 AA-11 *Archer*

  ASM AS-12 *Kegler*; AS-7 *Kerry*; AS-10 *Karen*; 97 AT-2
  Swatter; 500 AT-6 *Spiral*

Paramilitary 12,000

Border Guards 12,000 (to reduce)

Ministry of Interior

FORCES BY ROLE

Paramilitary   1 (Budapest) district (7 Rapid Reaction
               coy); 11 (regts/districts) regt

EQUIPMENT BY TYPE

APC (W) 68 BTR-80

DEPLOYMENT

AFGHANISTAN

NATO • ISAF 225

BOSNIA-HERZEGOVINA

EU • EUFOR • *Operation Althea* 158 MP

CYPRUS

UN • UNFICYP 84

EGYPT

MFO 41 MP

GEORGIA

UN • UNOMIG 7 obs

LEBANON

UN • UNIFIL 4

SERBIA

NATO • KFOR • *Joint Enterprise* 484

UN • UNMIK 1 obs

WESTERN SAHARA

UN • MINURSO 6 obs

Iceland Icl

Icelandic Krona K		2006	2007	2008
GDP	K	1.14tr	1.26tr	
	US$	16.3bn	21.1bn	
per capita	US$	54,454	70,049	
Growth	%	2.5	2.1	
Inflation	%	6.7	3.3	
Sy Bdgt [a]	K	e3.2bn		
	US$	45.7m	59.5m	
US$1=K		70	60	

[a] Iceland has no armed forces. Budget is mainly for coast guard.

Population   301,931

Age	0–14	15–19	20–24	25–29	30–64	65 plus
Male	11%	4%	4%	4%	22%	5%
Female	11%	4%	4%	4%	22%	6%

Capabilities

ACTIVE NIL Paramilitary 130

ORGANISATIONS BY SERVICE

Paramilitary

Iceland Coast Guard 130

EQUIPMENT BY TYPE

PATROL AND COASTAL COMBATANTS • PCO 3: 2
Aegir (with hel); 1 *Odinn* (with hel deck)

LOGISTICS AND SUPPORT • RESEARCH CRAFT
1 *Baldur*

AIRCRAFT • TPT 1 F-27-200 *Friendship*

HELICOPTERS

  SPT 1 AS-322L1 *Super Puma*

  UTL 1 AS-365N *Dauphin 2*

FACILITIES

Base   Located at Reykjavik

DEPLOYMENT

AFGHANISTAN

NATO • ISAF • 11 (civilian)

Italy It

Euro €		2006	2007	2008
GDP	€	1.47tr	1.55tr	
	US$	1.84tr	2.22tr	
per capita	US$	31,716	38,203	
Growth	%	1.9	1.7	
Inflation	%	2.2	2.0	
Def exp a	€	24.50bn		
	US$	30.63bn		
Def bdgt	€	12.12bn	12.44bn	
	US$	15.15bn	17.77bn	
US$1=€		0.80	0.70	

a including military pensions and carabinieri

Population   58,147,733

Age	0–14	15–19	20–24	25–29	30–64	65 plus
Male	7%	2%	3%	3%	25%	8%
Female	7%	2%	3%	3%	25%	10%

Capabilities

ACTIVE 186,049 (Army 108,000 Navy 34,000 Air 44,049) Paramilitary 254,300

Terms of service all services 10 months (to be all professional from 2005) Army Reserves have commitment to age 45; Navy Reservists to 39 or in case of officers variable to age 73; Air Force reservists to the age of 25 or 45 for specialists

RESERVE 41,867 (Army 38,633 Navy 3,234)

ORGANISATIONS BY SERVICE

Army 108,000

FORCES BY ROLE

Op	1 comd HQ (COMFOTER)
Raid	1 Div (1st FOD) with (1 Armd bde with (3 tk ,
Reaction	2 Mech inf, 1 arty, 1 engr regt);
	1 Cav bde with (3 cav, 1 amph, 1 arty regt);
	1 AB bde with (1 SF, SF RSTA, 3 para, 1 cbt engr regt);
	1 Air Mob bde with (1Cav, 1 airmob, 2 aviation regt))
Mech	1 Div (2 FOD) with (1 bde with (1 tk, 1 regt, 2 inf, 1 arty, 1 cbt engr regt);
	1 bde with (1 cav, 2 inf, 1 arty regt);
	1 bde with (2 inf, 1cbt engr regt);
	1 bde with (1tk, 2 mech inf, 1 arty, 1 cbt engr regt);
	1 bde (1 cav, 1 mech inf, 1 arty, 1 cbt engr regt))
Mtn Inf	1 div with (2 bdes each with (3 mtn inf , 1 cav,, 1 arty 1 mtn cbt engr regt))
EW	1 (CIS/EW) comd (1 EW/RISTA bde with (1 RISTA , 1 EW, 1 HIMINT bn, 2 sigs bde)
Spt	1 comd
Arty	1 arty bde (1 hy arty regt, 1 NBC regt, 2 arty regt, 1 psyops regt)

AD	1 AD bde (2 (HAWK) SAM regt, 2 SHORAD regt)
Engr	1 engr bde (3 engr, 1 CIMIC regt)
Avn	1 avn bde (1 avn bn, 3 avn regt)
Log	1 log div (8 log regt)

EQUIPMENT BY TYPE
MBT 320: 200 C1 *Ariete*; 120 *Leopard* 1A5
RECCE 300 B-1 *Centauro*
AIFV 200 VCC-80 *Dardo*
APC • APC (T) 1,692: 181 Bv-206; 384 M-113 (incl variants); 1,127 VCC-1 *Camillino*/VCC-2
AAV 14 LVTP-7
ARTY 1,562
  SP 155mm 260 M-109L; 6 PzH 2000
  TOWED 155mm 164 FH-70
  MRL 227mm 22 MLRS
  MOR 1084: **81mm** 256; **120mm** 828: 683, 145 RT-F1
AT
  MSL • MANPATS 1,443: 1,000 *Milan;* 443 I-TOW
  RCL 80mm 482 *Folgore*
  RL 110mm 2000 Pzf 3 *Panzerfaust 3*
AIRCRAFT
  TPT 6: 3 ACTL-1 (Do-228); 3 P-180
HELICOPTERS
  ATK 60 A-129EA *Mangusta*/A-129ESS *Mangusta*
  SPT 23 CH-47C *Chinook*
  UTL 144: 61 AB-205; 43 AB-206 *JetRanger*; 18 AB-212 ; 22 AB-412 (Bell 412) *Twin Huey*
AD
  SAM 132
    TOWED 68: 36 MIM-23 *HAWK*; 32 *Skyguard/Aspide*
    MANPAD 64 FIM-92A *Stinger*
  GUNS • SP 25mm 64 SIDAM

Navy 34,000

FORCES BY ROLE

Fleet	1 Fleet Commander CINCNAV
Navy	Ionian and Strait of Otranto comd; Adriatic comd; Rome comd; Sicily comd; Sardinia comd; Upper Tyrrhenian comd
Maritime	1 High Readiness Forces HQ

EQUIPMENT BY TYPE
SUBMARINES • TACTICAL • SSK 7:
  4 *Pelosi* (imp *Sauro*, 3rd and 4th series) each with 6 single 533mm TT each with 12 Type A-184 HWT / DM2A4 HWT
  1 *Sauro* (2nd series) with 6 single 533mm TT each with 12 Type A-184 HWT
  2 *Salvatore Todaro* (Type 212A) with 6 single 533mm TT each with 12 Type A-184 HWT / DM2A4 HWT
PRINCIPAL SURFACE COMBATANTS 25
AIRCRAFT CARRIERS • CVS 2:
  1 *G. Garibaldi* with 2 single 533mm ASTT with Mk 46 LWT, 2 *Albatros* octuple with (16 eff.) *Aspide* SAM, 4 twin (8 eff.) with up to 4 Mk 2 *Otomat* SSM, (capacity mixed air group of either 15 AV-8B *Harrier II;* 17 SH-3D *Sea King* or EH101 *Merlin)*
  1 *Cavour* with 1 32-cell VLS eq. with Aster 15 Naval SAM; 2 76mm gun; (capacity 8 AV-8B *Harrier II;* 12 EH101 *Merlin)* expected ISD late 2008

DESTROYERS • DDG 3:

1 *Andrea Doria* with 1 48-cell VLS eq. with *Aster* 15 SAM /*Aster* 30 SAM, 2 twin TT (4 eff.) each with MU-90, 3 76mm, (capacity either 1 EH101 spt hel or 1 NH90 TTH utl hel) (Undergoing acceptance trials, ISD expected late'08 – 2nd vessel expected 2009)

2 *Luigi Durand de la Penne* (ex-*Animoso*) each with 2 quad (8 eff.) each with 8 *Milas* AS/Mk 2 *Otomat* SSM, 1 Mk 13 GMLS with 40 SM-1 MR SAM, 2 triple 324mm ASTT (6 eff.) each with Mk 46 LWT, 1 *Albatros* octuple with 16 *Aspide* SAM, 1 127mm gun, (capacity 1 AB-212 (Bell 212) utl hel)

FRIGATES • FFG 12:

4 *Artigliere* each with 8 single each with 1 Mk 2 *Otomat* SSM, 1 *Albatros* octuple with 8 *Aspide* SAM, 1 127mm gun, (capacity 1 AB-212 (Bell 212) utl hel)

8 *Maestrale* each with 4 single with 4 Mk 2 *Otomat* SSM, 1 *Albatros* octuple with 16 *Aspide* SAM, 2 triple 324mm ASTT (6 eff.) each with Mk 46 LWT, 2 single 533mm ASTT each with A-184 *Black Shark* HWT, 1 127mm gun, (capacity 2 AB-212 (Bell 212) utl hel)

CORVETTES • FS 8 *Minerva* each with 1 *Albatros* octuple (8eff.) with *Aspide* SAM, 1 76mm gun

PATROL AND COASTAL COMBATANTS 14

PSOH 10:

4 *Cassiopea* each with 1 76mm gun, eq with 1 AB-212 (Bell 212) utl hel

6 *Comandante Cigala Fuligosi* each with 1 76mm gun, eq with 1 AB-212 (Bell 212) utl hel

PCO 4 *Esploratore*

MINE WARFARE • MINE COUNTERMEASURES 12

MHC 12: 8 *Gaeta*; 4 *Lerici*

AMPHIBIOUS

PRINCIPAL AMPHIBIOUS SHIPS • LPD 3 *San Giorgio* with 1 76mm gun (capacity 4 EH101 *Merlin* ASW hel; 1 CH-47 *Chinook* spt hel; 3 LCM 2 LCVP; 30 trucks; 36 APC (T)s; 350 troops)

CRAFT 26: 17 **LCVP**; 9 **LCM**

LOGISTICS AND SUPPORT 96

AORH 3: 1 *Etna*; 2 *Stromboli*

AOT 7

ARS 1

AKSL 6

AWT 7

AGOR 3

AGHS 1

AGS 2

ABU 5

ATS 7

AT 9 (coastal)

TRG 9: 7 AXS; 2

Trial Ship 1

TRV 1

YDT 2

YTM 32

FACILITIES

Bases Located at La Spezia (HQ), Taranto (HQ), Brindisi, Augusta

Naval Aviation 2,200

FORCES BY ROLE

FGA	Fixed wing strike unit with AV-8B *Harrier II*
ASW	5 sqn eq with AB-212AS (Bell 212 ASW/ASUW); EH-101; SH-3D *Sea King*; EH-101
Aslt hel	some sqn eq with SH-3D *Sea King*; AB-212 (Bell 212)
Trg	Flight with 2 TAV-8B *Harrier*

EQUIPMENT BY TYPE

AIRCRAFT 17 combat capable

  FGA 15 AV-8B *Harrier II*

  TRG 2 TAV-8B *Harrier*

HELICOPTERS 41 attack helicopters

  ASW 41: 27 AB212 ASW ASuW; 8 EH-101 ASW; 6 SH-3D ASW ASuW *Sea King*

  SPT 18: 8 EH-101 ASH; 6 SH-3D ASH *Sea King*; 4 EH-101 EW

  UTL 6 AB-212ASH (Bell 212)

MSL

  ASM AGM-65 *Maverick*; some *Marte* Mk 2

  AAM AIM-120 *AMRAAM*; AIM-9L *Sidewinder*

Marines 2,000

FORCES BY ROLE

Op	1 San Marco regt (1,300 Marine)
Log	1 regt
LC	1 gp

EQUIPMENT BY TYPE

APC (T) 40 VCC-2

AAV 18 AAV-7

ARTY • MOR 12: **81mm** 8 *Brandt*; **120mm** 4 *Brandt*

AT • MSL • MANPATS 6 *Milan*

AD • SAM • MANPAD FIM-92A *Stinger*

Special Forces Command

FORCES BY ROLE

Diving	1 op
Navy SF	1 op
SF	1 comd

FACILITIES

Centre	1 (Research)
School	1

Air Force 44,049

4 Commands – Air Sqn Cmd (air defence, attack, recce, mobility, support, force protection, EW ops); Training; Logistics; Operations (national and international exercises)

FORCES BY ROLE

Ftr	2 sqn with F-2000A *Typhoon*; 3 sqn with F-16A/ F-16B *Fighting Falcon* on lease; 1 sqn with MB-339CD* (slow mover interceptor)
FGA	3 sqn with *Tornado* IDS; 3 (50% of 1 sqn devoted to recce) sqn with AMX *Ghibli*;
ECR/SEAD	1 sqn with *Tornado* ECR*
MR	1 sqn opcon Navy with BR 1150 *Atlantic**
EW	1 sqn with G-222VS

CSAR	1 sqn with HH-3F *Pelican**
SAR	3 det with HH-3F; 4 det with AB-212 (Bell 212)
Tkr/CAL/ tpt	1 sqn with B-707-320C (being replaced by B-767/MRTT); MB-339A RM; 1 sqn with G-222TM
Tpt	2 sqn with C-130J *Hercules*; 1 sqn with C-27J; 1 sqn with P-180, P-166-DL3
Liaison	2 sqn (VIP tpt) with A-319CJ; *Falcon* 50; *Falcon* 900EX; SH-3D *Sea King*.
Trg	1 sqn with F-2000 *Typhoon*; 1 (aerobatic team) sqn with MB-339A; 1 sqn with NH-500D; 4 sqn with AMX-T *Ghibli*; MB-339A; MB-339CD*; SF-260M
AD	3 bty with MIM-14 *Nike Hercules* static SAM; 7 bty with *Spada* towed SAM
UAV	1 sqn with 4 RQ-1B *Predator*

EQUIPMENT BY TYPE

AIRCRAFT 250 combat capable

FTR 54: 27 F-2000A Tranche 1 *Typhoon* (8 -T, 19 -S); first of 52 F-2000 Tranche 2 being delivered; 27 F-16A/4 F-16B *Fighting Falcon* on lease to 2010

STRIKE/FGA 137: 69 *Tornado* IDS; 68 AMX *Ghibli*

ECR/SEAD 16 *Tornado* ECR*

MP 13 BR 1150 *Atlantic**

TPT 90: 4 A-319CJ; 3 B-707-320C (being replaced by 4 B-767/MRTT); 22 C-130J *Hercules*; 2 C-27J; 9 G-222; 4 *Falcon* 50 (VIP); 3 *Falcon* 900EX (VIP); 2 *Falcon* 900 *Easy*; 6 P-166-DL3; 15 P-180 ; 20 SIAI-208 20 (liaison)

TRG 135: 23 AMX-T *Ghibli*; 57 MB-339A (incl 17 aero team, 4 RM, 36 trg); 30 MB-339CD*; 25 SF-260M

HELICOPTERS

SAR 28 HH-3F *Pelican* (of which 6*)

UTL 37: 35 AB-212 (Bell 212) (of which 32 SAR); 2 SH-3D *Sea King* (liaison/VIP)

TRG 50 NH-500D

UAV • RECCE 4 RQ-1B *Predator*. Some *Sky-X* under test.

AD • SAM

TOWED *Spada*

STATIC *Aspide*; MIM-14 *Nike Hercules*

MSL

AAM AIM 120B/C AMRAAM; AIM-7E *Sparrow*; AIM-9L *Sidewinder*; *Sky Flash*; *Aspide* 1A

ARM AGM-88 HARM

ASM AGM-65 *Maverick*; SCALP EG *Storm Shadow*; AS-34 *Kormoran*

BOMBS

Laser-guided/GPS: Enhanced *Paveway* II; Enhanced *Paveway* III

Paramilitary 254,300

Carabinieri 111,367

Police Force with a military status and an all-encompassing jurisdiction, in permanent duty of public security and law enforcement for:

Ministry of Defence; Ministry of Interior; other ministries (Public Health, Environment, Labour, Foreign Affairs, Cultural Activities and Arts)

RECCE 18 Fiat 6616

APC 32

APC (T) 26: 10 VCC-1 *Camillino*; 16 VCC-2

APC (W) 6 *Puma*

AC 1 P180 *Avant*

HELICOPTERS 95+: 95 A-109; AB-206 (Bell 206) *JetRanger*; AB-412 (Bell 412) *Twin Huey*

Mobile and Specialised Branch

Mob/specialised unit	1 corps comd
Specialised unit	1 div (1 Ministry of Foreign Affairs Carabinieri Paramilitary HQ, 8 Paramilitary HQ (*each:* some Paramilitary tps), 1 hel gp)
Spec Ops	1 gp (ROS)
Hel	1 gp
Mobile div	1 div (1 (Special Intervention) GIS Paramilitary gp, 1 AB regt, 2 Mob bde, 1 (mounted) Cav regt, 11 Mob bn, 2 Mob regt)

Territorial

Inter-regional	5 comd
Region	19 comd
Provincial	102 comd

17 Territorial Depts; 1 Group Comd; 536 Company Comd; 37 Lieutenancy Comd; 4,637 Station Comd

Training

FORCES BY ROLE

Trg	1 HQ

FACILITIES

School 5

Customs

(Servizo Navale Guardia Di Finanza)

PATROL AND COASTAL COMBATANTS 83:

PCO 3 *Antonio Zara*

PFC 24 *Corrubia*

PCC 32: 7 *Mazzei*; 25 *Bigliani*

PCI 24 *Meatini*

LOGISTICS AND SUPPORT • TRG 1

Coast Guard

(Guardia Costiera – Capitanerie Di Porto)

PATROL AND COASTAL COMBATANTS 83:

PSO 6 *Saettia*

PCO 1

PFC 4

PCC 9

PCI 76 less than 100 tonnes

LOGISTICS AND SUPPORT • TRG 1 (ex-US *Bannock*)

AIRCRAFT

MP 2 ATR-42 MP *Surveyor*

TPT 14 P-166-DL3

HELICOPTERS • UTL 12 AB-412SP *Griffin*

NON-STATE ARMED GROUPS

see Part II

DEPLOYMENT

AFGHANISTAN
EU • EUPOL AFGHANISTAN 25
NATO • ISAF 2,160
AIFV *Dardo*
AC
Tpt C-130
HEL
ATK 4 A-129 *Mangusta*
Tpt 3 CH-47
UAV 2 *Predator*

ALBANIA
NATO 155 (HQ Tirana)
Delegazione Italiana Esperti (DIA) 25

BOSNIA-HERZEGOVINA
EU • EUFOR • *Operation Althea* 363

CANADA
Air Force 12 (flying trg)

DEMOCRATIC REPUBLIC OF CONGO
EU • EUPOL KINSHASA 4
EU • EUSEC DR Congo 1

EGYPT
MFO 80

GERMANY
Air Force 91 (NAEW Force)

INDIA/PAKISTAN
UN • UNMOGIP 7 obs

IRAQ
NATO • Training Mission 79

LEBANON
UN • UNIFIL II 2,379

MACEDONIA, FORMER YUGOSLAV REPUBLIC
EU • EUPM 3 (HQ SKOPJE + EUPOL *Op Proxima*)
(including logistic support for KFOR)

MALTA
Air Force 16
HEL • UTL 2 AB-212 (Bell 212)
Armed Forces
49 MIATM cbt Sp (Missione Italiana d'Assistenza Tecnico
Militare)

MEDITERRANEAN SEA
NATO • *Active Endeavour* 105
NATO • SNMCMG-2 44

MIDDLE EAST
UN • UNTSO 6 obs

PALESTINIAN AUTONOMOUS AREAS OF GAZA AND JERICHO
TIPH 17

SERBIA
NATO • KFOR • *Joint Enterprise* 2,280
UTL AB205

SOMALIA
AU • AMISOM 2 to be deployed

SUDAN
EU (support to AUMIS) 6
UN • UNMIS 1

UNITED STATES
Air Force 38 (flying trg)

WESTERN SAHARA
UN • MINURSO 5 obs

FOREIGN FORCES
Germany 3 MP ac (in ELMAS/Sardinia); 200
United Kingdom Army 70; Navy 110; Air Force 170
United States EUCOM: 1 HQ located at Gaeta; 31st Ftr Wg HQ, Aviano; 2 SETAF Para bn located at Vicenza; 1 SETAF log unit (in store) (Holds eqpt forTheater Reserve Unit (TRU) /Army Readiness Package South (ARPS)) with 116 M-1 *Abrams*; 127 AIFV; 4 APC (T); Army: 3,241; Navy: 2,659; USAF: 4,261; USMC: 55. Base located at JFC HQ Naples; Base located at La Maddalena

Latvia Lat

Latvian Lat L		2006	2007	2008
GDP	L	11.2bn	12.6bn	
	US$	20.0bn	25.7bn	
per capita	US$	8,792	11,379	
Growth	%	11.9	10.5	
Inflation	%	6.4	9.0	
Def exp	L	156m		
	US$	279m		
Def bdgt	L	176m	231m	289m
	US$	314m	471m	
FMA (US)	US$	5.9m	4.0m	3.0m
US$1=L		0.56	0.49	

Population 2,259,810

Age	0–14	15–19	20–24	25–29	30–64	65 plus
Male	7%	4%	4%	3%	22%	6%
Female	7%	4%	4%	3%	25%	11%

Capabilities

ACTIVE 5,696(Army 1,526 Navy 603 Air 480 Central Support 712 Administration and Command 1,080 Other Forces (TRADOC) 807 SF/MP 488) **Paramilitary 11,034 (National Guard 11,034)**

RESERVE 11,204 (Army 11,204)
Professional from 2007

ORGANISATIONS BY SERVICE

Army 1,526

FORCES BY ROLE

Inf   1 bde (2 inf bn)
SF   1 unit

National Guard 10,483 part-time soldiers

Inf   14 bn
Fd Arty 1 bn
AD   1 bn
Engr   1 bn
NBC   1 bn

EQUIPMENT BY TYPE

MBT 3 T-55 (trg)
RECCE 2 BRDM-2
ARTY 121
  TOWED 100mm 26 K-53
  MOR 95: **71mm**40; **82mm** 5; **120mm** 50
  RL 73mm RPG-7 *Knout*; **84mm** AT-4; **90mm**
  GUNS 143: **76mm** 3; **90mm** 140
AD
  SAM • MANPAD 5 *Strela* 2M (SA-7) *Grail*
  GUNS • TOWED 52: **14.5mm** 2 ZPU-4; **20mm** 10 FK-20;
  23mm 16 GSH-23; **30mm** 2: 1; 1 AK-230; **40mm** 22 L/70

Navy 603

Latvian maritime forces organised with 1 Naval HQ commanding a Naval Forces Flotilla separated into two squadrons, an MCM squadron and a Partrol Boat squadron.

Lat, Ea and L have set up a joint Naval unit* BALTRON with bases at Liepaja, Riga, Ventspils (Lat), Tallinn (Ea), Klaipeda (L).*Each nation contributes 1–2 MCMVs

EQUIPMENT BY TYPE

PATROL AND COASTAL COMBATANTS
  PFB 4 *Storm* with 1 L-70 40mm gun, 1 TAK-76 76mm gun
MINE WARFARE • MINE COUNTERMEASURES 3:
  MHC 1 *Lindau*; 1 *Imanta (ex-Dutch Alkmaa*; a total of 4 further vessels to transfer by '08)
  MSC 2 *Kondor*
LOGISTICS AND SUPPORT 3
  AG 1 *Vidar*
  SPT 1 *Varonis* (C3 and support ship, ex- *Buyskes*)
  YDT 1

FACILITIES

Bases Located at Liepaja, Daugavgriva (Riga)

Air Force 480

AIRCRAFT
  TPT 3: 2 An-2 *Colt*; 1 L-410 *Turbolet*
HELICOPTERS • SPT 6: 4 Mi-17; 2 PZL Mi-2

Administration and Command 759; 296 conscript (total 1,055)

Central Support 590; 192 conscript (total 782)

(LSC)

Other Forces (TRADOC) 457; 187 conscript (total 644)

Paramilitary 11,034

National Guard 551 (full time); 10,483 (part-time) (total 11,034)

DEPLOYMENT

AFGHANISTAN
NATO • ISAF 97

BOSNIA-HERZEGOVINA
EU • EUFOR • *Operation Althea* 1
EUFOR HQ 1

GEORGIA
OSCE 1

IRAQ
MNF • *Operation Iraqi Freedom* 2

SERBIA
NATO • KFOR • *Joint Enterprise* 18

Lithuania L

Lithuanian Litas L		2006	2007	2008
GDP	L	82.0bn	89.9bn	
	US$	29.8bn	37.0bn	
per capita	US$	8,315	10,437	
Growth	%	7.5	8.0	
Inflation	%	3.8	5.2	
Def exp	L	961m		
	US$	349m		
Def bdgt	L	972m	1.14bn	
	US$	353m	470m	
FMA (US)	US$	4.4m	4.0m	3.0m
US$1=L		2.75	2.43	

Population   3,575,439

Ethnic groups: Russian 8%; Polish 7%; Belarussian 2%

Age	0–14	15–19	20–24	25–29	30–64	65 plus
Male	8%	4%	4%	4%	22%	5%
Female	8%	4%	4%	3%	24%	9%

Capabilities

ACTIVE 13,850 (Army 12,500 Navy 450 Air 900)
Paramilitary 14,600
Terms of service 12 months.

RESERVE 6,700 (Army 6,700)

ORGANISATIONS BY SERVICE

Army 5,900; 1,900 conscript (total 7,800)

FORCES BY ROLE

1 mil region

Reaction 1 bde (Iron Wolf) (2 mech inf bn, 2 mot inf bn, 1
Force   arty bn)

SF   1 gp (1 CT unit; 1 Jaeger bn)

Engr   1 bn

Log   1 spt bn (forward); 1 spt bn (main)

Trg   1 regt

EQUIPMENT BY TYPE

RECCE 10 BRDM-2

APC 190+

  APC (T) 187 M-113A1

  APC (W) 3+: M1097A2 HMMWV; 3 M1035A2 HMMWV
  (amb)

ARTY 133

  TOWED 105mm 72 M-101

  MOR 120mm 61 M-43

AT • MSL 28

  SP 10 M1025A2 HMMWV eqpt with *Javelin*

  MANPATS 18 *Javelin*

RCL 84mm 273 *Carl Gustav*

Reserves

National Defence Voluntary Forces 4,700 active
reservists

Territorial Def 5 regt; 36 bn (total: 150 Def coy)

Avn   1 sqn

Navy 300; 150 conscript (total 450)

Lat, Ea and L established a joint Naval unit BALTRON with
bases at Liepaja, Riga, Ventpils (Lat), Tallinn (Ea), Klaipeda
(L), HQ at Tallinn

EQUIPMENT BY TYPE

PRINCIPAL SURFACE COMBATANTS • FRIGATES
•**FFL** 2 *Grisha* III each with 2 twin 533mm ASTT (4 eff.), 1
twin (2 eff.), 2 RBU 6000 *Smerch* 2 (24 eff.)

PATROL AND COASTAL COMBATANTS • PFB 3 *Storm*

MINE WARFARE • MINE COUNTERMEASURES

MHC 2 *Suduvis*

LOGISTICS AND SUPPORT • AG 1 *Vidar*

FACILITIES

Base Located at Klaipeda

Air Force 800; 100 conscript (total 900)

Flying hours 120 hrs/year

FORCES BY ROLE

Tpt   1 base with 1 C-27J *Spartan*; 2 An-2 *Colt*; 3 An-26
       Curl; 2 L-410 *Turbolet*

Trg   1 with 2 L-39ZA *Albatros*

Hel   1 base with 9 Mi-8 *Hip* (tpt/SAR)

AD   1 bn with 18 RBS-70 plus M-48 AD system

EQUIPMENT BY TYPE

AIRCRAFT

  TPT 8: 1 C-27J *Spartan* (2 more to be delivered by 2009); 2
  An-2 *Colt*; 3 An-26 *Curl*; 2 L-410 *Turbolet*

  TRG 2 L-39ZA *Albatros*

HELICOPTERS • SPT: 9 Mi-8 *Hip* (tpt/SAR)

AD • SHORT RANGE MISSILE • 18 RBS-70 plus M-48
AD system

FACILITIES

Air Surveillance and Control Centre

Air base

Radar Stn

Paramilitary 14,600

Riflemen Union 9,600

State Border Guard Service 5,000

Ministry of Internal Affairs

Coast Guard 540

PATROL AND COASTAL COMBATANTS • PCC 3
AMPHIBIOUS • LC • ACV 1: 1 UCAC

DEPLOYMENT

AFGHANISTAN

NATO • ISAF 195

UN • UNAMA 1 obs

BOSNIA-HERZEGOVINA

EU • EUFOR • *Operation Althea* 1 officer

GEORGIA

UN • UNOMIG 2 obs

IRAQ

MNF • *Operation Iraqi Freedom* 5

NATO • NTM-I 4

SERBIA

NATO • KFOR • *Joint Enterprise* 30

Luxembourg Lu

Euro €		2006	2007	2008
GDP	€	33.1bn	36.2bn	
	US$	41.4bn	51.7bn	
per capita	US$	87,213	107,688	
Growth	%	6.2	5.4	
Inflation	%	3.0	2.0	
Def exp	€	203m		
	US$	253m		
Def bdgt	€	203m	263m	
	US$	253m	375m	
US$1=€		0.80	0.70	

Population 480,222

Foreign citizens: ε124,000

Age	0–14	15–19	20–24	25–29	30–64	65 plus
Male	10%	3%	3%	3%	24%	6%
Female	9%	3%	3%	3%	24%	8%

Capabilities

ACTIVE 900 (Army 900) **Paramilitary 612**

ORGANISATIONS BY SERVICE

Army 900

FORCES BY ROLE

Recce 2 coy (1 to Eurocorps/BE div, 1 to NATO pool of deployable forces)

Lt inf 1 bn

EQUIPMENT BY TYPE
ARTY • MOR 81mm 6
AT • MSL• MANPATS 6 TOW
 RL 66mm M-72 *LAW*

Air Force

FORCES BY ROLE
None, but for legal purposes NATO's E-3A AEW ac have Lu registration

Air   1 sqn with 17 E-3A *Sentry* (NATO standard); 3 B-707 (trg)

EQUIPMENT BY TYPE
AIRCRAFT
 AEW 17 E-3A *Sentry* (NATO standard)
 TPT 3 B-707 (trg)

Paramilitary 612

Gendarmerie 612

DEPLOYMENT

AFGHANISTAN
NATO • ISAF 9

BOSNIA-HERZEGOVINA
EU • EUFOR • *Operation Althea* 1

LEBANON
UN • UNIFIL II 2

SERBIA
NATO • KFOR • *Joint Enterprise* 23

FOREIGN FORCES

United States EUCOM: 8

Netherlands Nl

Euro €		2006	2007	2008
GDP	€	527bn	566bn	
	US$	659bn	809bn	
per capita	US$	39,945	48,796	
Growth	%	3.0	2.6	
Inflation	%	1.7	1.4	
Def exp	€	7.92bn		
	US$	9.90bn		
Def bdgt	€	7.91bn	8.13bn	7.93bn
	US$	9.88bn	11.61bn	
US$1=€		0.80	0.70	

Population   16,570,613

Age	0–14	15–19	20–24	25–29	30–64	65 plus
Male	9%	3%	3%	3%	25%	6%
Female	9%	3%	3%	3%	25%	7%

Capabilities

ACTIVE 45,608 (Army 18,266 Navy 10,401 Air 10,141 Paramilitary 6,800)

RESERVE 32,200 (Army 22,200 Navy 5,000 Air 5,000)
Men to age 35, NCOs to 40, officers to 45

ORGANISATIONS BY SERVICE

Army 18,266

FORCES BY ROLE
1 Corps HQ (GE/NL)

Armd recce 1 bn

Mech   2 bde (*each:* 2 Armd inf bn, 1 Tk bn, 1 Armd Recce sqn, 1 Fd Arty bn (2 bty), 1 Engr bn, 1 Maint coy, 1 Medical coy)

Air Mob   1 bde (3 Inf bn, 1 Mor coy, 1 AD bty, 1 Engr coy, 1 Medical coy, 1 Supply coy, 1 Maint coy)

Cdo   1 gp (1 Counter-Terrorist unit, 1 Mtn unit, 1 Amph unit, 1 Para unit)

Fd arty   1 gp (6 arty bn)

Engr   1 gp (3 Engr bn)

AD   1 bn (3 Bty)

Logistic Sp 1 bde (3 Maint coy, 2 Tpt / Supply bn, 1 Medical bn)

EQUIPMENT BY TYPE
MBT 170: 90 *Leopard* 2A6; 80 *Leopard* 2A4 (in store for sale to Canada)
RECCE 202 *Fennek* (incl 48 for arty and 6 for FAC)
AIFV 569: 224 YPR-765 (Used as APC); 345 more (opcon ISAF)
APC • APC (W) 93: 22 TPz-1 *Fuchs*; 71 XA-188 *Sisu*
LFV 25 *Bushmaster* IMV
ARTY 442
 SP 155mm 177: 120 M-109A3; 26 PzH 2000 (to replace M-109); 31 in store
 TOWED 155mm 113: 13 FH-70 (trg); 20 M-114; 80 M-114/M-139

MOR 152: **81mm**: 40; **120mm** 112 *Brandt*
AT
  MSL 883+
    SP 222: 130 *Fennek Spike*; 92 YPR 765 PRAT
    MANPATS 661+: 427 M47 *Dragon; Spike*; 234 TOW
    RCL 84mm *Carl Gustav*
    RL 84mm AT-4
PATROL AND COASTAL COMBATANTS 6: 3 **PBR**; 3 **PCC**
LOGISTICS AND SUPPORT 1 tpt (tk)
UAV • TACTICAL 45: 32 *Sperwer*; 5 *Aladin*; 8 MALE
AD
  SAM
    SP 18 *Fennek* with S*tinger*
    MANPAD 312 FIM-92A *Stinger*
  GUNS• SP35mm 60 *Gepard* (in store for sale)
RADAR • LAND AN/TPQ-36 *Firefinder* (arty, mor); *Squire*

Reserves 22,200 reservists

National Command
Cadre bde and corps tps completed by call-up of reservists (incl Territorial Comd)
Inf 5 bn (Could be mob for territorial defence)

Navy 10,401 (incl 3,100 Marines)
EQUIPMENT BY TYPE
SUBMARINES • TACTICAL • SSK 4:
4 *Walrus* each with 4 single 533mm TT with Mk48 *Sea Arrow* HWT/UGM-84C *Harpoon* tactical USGW (Equipped for *Harpoon* but not embarked)
PRINCIPAL SURFACE COMBATANTS 8
  DESTROYERS • DDG 4:
    4 *Zeven Provinciën* each with 2 Mk 141 *Harpoon* quad (8 eff.) each with 8 RGM-84F *Harpoon* tactical SSM, 1 40 cell Mk 41 VLS (40 eff.) with 32 SM-2 MR SAM, 32 enhanced *Sea Sparrow* SAM (quad pack), 2 twin ASTT (4 eff.) each with Mk 46 LWT, 1 Otobreda 127mm gun, (capacity 1 *Lynx* MK86 ASW hel)
  FRIGATES • FFG 4:
    4 *Karel Doorman* each with, 2 Mk 141 *Harpoon* quad (8 eff.) each with RGM-84A *Harpoon*/RGM-84C *Harpoon*, 1 Mk 48 VLS with 16 RIM-7P *Sea Sparrow* SAM, 2 twin 324mm ASTT (4 eff.) each with Mk 46 LWT 1 76mm gun, (capacity 1 *Lynx* ASW hel)
MINE WARFARE • MINE COUNTERMEASURES • MHC 10 *Alkmaar* (tripartite)
AMPHIBIOUS
  PRINCIPAL AMPHIBIOUS SHIPS • LPD 2:
    1 *Rotterdam* (capacity either 6 *Lynx* utl hel or 4 NH-90 utl hel; either 6 LCVP or 4 LCU or 4 LCM; either 170 APC (T)s or 33 MBT; 600 troops)
    1 *Johan de Witt* (capacity 6 NH-90 utl hel or 4 EH101 *Merlin*; either 6 LCVP or 4 LCU or 4 LCM; either 170 APC (T)s or 33 MBT; 610 troops)
  CRAFT 17: 5 **LCU**; 12 **LCVP**
LOGISTICS AND SUPPORT 15
  AORH 1 *Amsterdam* with capacity for 4 *Lynx* or 2 NH-90
  AOL 1 *Zuiderkruis* with capacity for 2 *Lynx* or NH-90
  AORL 1 *Patria*
  TRG 2
  SPT 1 *Pelikaan*
  TRV 1 *Mercuur*

YDT 4
YFS 4
FACILITIES
Bases   Located at Den Helder, Willemstad (Dutch Antilles)
Naval airbase   Located at De Kooy (hel)

Naval Aviation (part of NL Defence Helicopter Command)
HELICOPTERS 34:
ASW 17 SH-14D *Lynx** (ASW/SAR); some NH-90 NFH (a total of 6 naval variant hels on order 1st delivery expected early 2008)
UTL 17 SH-14D *Lynx** to be replaced by NH-90 NFH (acquisition of 8 NH-90 MTTH in progress)

Marines 3,100
FORCES BY ROLE

Marine	2 Infantry bn (1 cadre); 1 bn (integrated with UK 3 Cdo Bde to form UK/NL Amph Landing Force)
CS	1 Amphibious support bn (1 recce coy, 2 mor coy, 1 AD plt, SF, 2 Ampib. Beach Untis)
CSS	1 bn (2 CSS units, 1 Role 2 medical facility)

EQUIPMENT BY TYPE
ATV 74 BVS-10 *Viking*
APC (W) 17 XA-188 *Sisu*
ARTY • MOR 32: **81mm** 18; **120mm** 14 Brandt
AT • MSL • MANPATS M47 *Dragon*
  RCL 84mm *Carl Gustav*
  RL 84mm AT-4
AD • SAM • MANPAD FIM-92A *Stinger*

Air Force 10,141
Flying hours   180 hrs/year
FORCES BY ROLE

Comd	1 logistics HQ; 1 Tac Air HQ; 1 Education HQ
Ftr/FGA/ Recce	5 (swing role) sqn reducing to 72 F-16 MLU AM/15 F-16 MLU BM *Fighting Falcon* in 2008
SAR	1 sqn with 3 AB-412SP *Griffin*
Tpt	1 sqn with 2 KDC-10 (plus 1 entering service 2008); 2 C-130H/2 C-130H-30 *Hercules*; 2 Fokker 50; 4 Fokker 60; 1 *Gulfstream* IV
Trg	1 sqn with 13 PC-7 *Turbo Trainer*
Hel	1 sqn with 11 CH-47D *Chinook*; 1 sqn with 17 AS-532U2 *Cougar II*; 4 SA-316 *Alouette III*; 1 sqn with 29 AH-64D *Apache*;
AD	4 sqn (*total*: 7 AD Team each with 4 FIM-92A *Stinger*, 4 AD bty with MIM-104 *Patriot* (TMD capable))
NATO, EU	Strategic Airlift Interim Solution (SALIS) 2 An-124 hvy flt transport in full-time lease. Coord Centre in Eindhoven, based in Leipzig, Germany

EQUIPMENT BY TYPE
AIRCRAFT 105 combat capable
FGA 105: 105 reducing to 87 F-16 MLU AM/F-16 MLU BM *Fighting Falcon*
TKR 2 KDC-10 (plus 1 entering service 2008)

TPT 11: 2 C-130H; 2 C-130H-30 *Hercules*; 2 Fokker 50; 4 Fokker 60; 1 *Gulfstream* IV
TRG 13 PC-7 *Turbo Trainer*
HELICOPTERS
ATK 24 AH-64D *Apache*
SPT 11 CH-47D *Chinook*
UTL 24: 3 AB-412SP *Griffin;* 17 AS-532U2 *Cougar II;* 4 SA-316 *Alouette III*
AD • SAM
TOWED 32 MIM-104 *Patriot* (TMD capable with 136 PAC-3 msl, of which 32 delivered)
MANPAD 284 FIM-92A *Stinger*
MSL
AAM AIM-120B AMRAAM; AIM-9L/M/N *Sidewinder*
ASM AGM-114K *Hellfire;* AGM-65D/G *Maverick*
BOMBS
Conventional Mk 82; Mk 84
Laser-guided GBU-10/ GBU-12 *Paveway* II; GBU-24 *Paveway* III (all supported by LANTIRN)
FACILITIES
2 air F-16 air bases

Paramilitary 6,800

Royal Military Constabulary 6,800
FORCES BY ROLE
Paramilitary 6 district (*total:* 60 Paramilitary 'bde')

EQUIPMENT BY TYPE
AIFV 24 YPR-765

DEPLOYMENT

AFGHANISTAN
NATO • ISAF Army: 1,516;
LFV 23 *Bushmaster* IMV;
AIFV YPR-675; 3 Pzh SP
RECCE 12 Fennek
Air Force 8F-16, 6 AH-64D *Apache*; 5 AS-532U2, C-130 tpt; *Sperwer* UAV
Operation Enduring Freedom 6

BOSNIA-HERZEGOVINA
EU • EUFOR • *Operation Althea* 67

BURUNDI
UN • BINUB 1 obs

CHAD/CAR
EU • EUFOR Chad/CAR 100

CURACAO
Navy Base located at Willemstad

DEMOCRATIC REPUBLIC OF CONGO
EU • EUPOL KINSHASA 2; EUSEC 3

GERMANY
Air Force 300

IRAQ
NATO • NTM-I 15

LEBANON
UN • UNIFIL II • *Maritime Task Force*
Navy 149

FFG 1 *Karel Doorman*

MIDDLE EAST
UN •UNTSO 11 obs

NETHERLANDS ANTILLES
Navy 20 NL, Aruba and the Netherlands Antilles operate a Coast Guard Force to combat org crime and drug smuggling. Comd by Netherlands Commander Caribbean. HQ Curaçao, bases Aruba and St. Maarten.
FFG 1
Marines: 1 (cbt) amph det; 1 (2 coy) marine bn (rotation will now be with Army commencing 2008); 1 coy at Aruba Base Located at Willemstad

Air Force
AIRCRAFT • TPT 2 Fokker 60

SERBIA
NATO • KFOR • *Joint Enterprise* 1

SUDAN
AU/UN • UNAMID proposed deployment
UN • UNMIS 5; 7 obs

FOREIGN FORCES
United Kingdom Army 100; Navy 40; Air Force 120
United States EUCOM: Army: 237; Navy: 23; USAF: 252; USMC: 14

Norway No

Norwegian Kroner kr		2006	2007	2008
GDP	kr	2.15tr	2.28tr	
	US$	336bn	422bn	
per capita	US$	72,779	91,265	
Growth	%	2.8	3.5	
Inflation	%	2.2	1.1	
Def exp	kr	32.14bn		
	US$	5.01bn		
Def bdgt	kr	30.6bn	31.2bn	31.5bn
	US$	4.77bn	5.76bn	
US$1=kr		6.41	5.41	

Population   4,627,926

Age	0–14	15–19	20–24	25–29	30–64	65 plus
Male	10%	3%	3%	3%	24%	6%
Female	10%	3%	3%	3%	23%	7%

Capabilities

ACTIVE 15,800 (Army 6,700 Navy 4,100 Air 5,000)
Terms of service 12 months with 4-5 refresher trg periods.

RESERVE 180,300 (Army 83,000 Navy 22,000 Air 25,000 Home Guard 50,300)
Reserves: on 24–72hr readiness; obligation to age of 44, (conscripts remain with fd army units to age of 35, officers to 55, regulars to 60)

ORGANISATIONS BY SERVICE

Army 3,200; 3,500 conscript (total 6,700)

Norway has two brgades one of which is a mobilised bde. Other elements are training and doctrine (TRADOK) and the special forces. The Land Home Guard is separate. For international operations HQ 6 Div has been reorganised to provide a deployable headquaters with joint service capabilities.

FORCES BY ROLE

Army	1 HQ
Mech inf	1 bde (1 Armd bn , 2 mech inf, 1 arty, engr bn);
	1 bde (armd cadre units)
SF	1 bn
ISTAR	1 bn (EW, MI, LR recce, UAV(2009))
Inf	1 (Royal Guard) bn
Border Guard	1mtn inf bn(HQ and garrison coy, patrol coy, trg coy)

EQUIPMENT BY TYPE

MBT 165: 52 *Leopard* 2A4; 2 *Leopard* 1A1NO; 111 *Leopard* 1A5NO

AIFV 157: 104 CV9030N; 53 NM-135 (M-113/20mm)

APC 189

  APC (T) 109 M-113 (incl variants)

  APC (W) ε80 XA-186 *Sisu*/XA-200 *Sisu*

ARTY 434

  SP 155mm 126 M-109A3GN

  MRL 227mm 12 MLRS

  MOR 296:

  SP 36: 81mm 24 M-106A1; 12 M-125A2

  TOWED 81mm 260 L-16

AT

  MSL • SP 97 NM-142 (twin TOW ALT turret)

  MANPATS 744: 424 *Eryx*; 320 TOW /TOW-2

  RCL 84mm 2,517 *Carl Gustav*

  RL 66mm M-72 *LAW*

AD

  SAM • MANPAD 300: 180 RBS-70; 120 in store

  GUNS • TOWED • 20mm 252: 60 Rh 202; 192 in store

RADAR • LAND 12+ *Arthur*

Land Home Guard 46,000 reservists on mobilisation

13 Home Guard Districts, each with Rapid Reaction Forces (4,500 troops in total) as well as Reinforcements and Follow-on Forces (42,000 troops in total). The reinforcements and follow-on forces are 'Home Guard Areas' (company size) comprising a total of 240 units (Coys).

Navy 2,100; 2,000 conscripts (total 4,100)

Joint Command - Norwegian National Joint Headquarters

EQUIPMENT BY TYPE

SUBMARINES • TACTICAL • SSK 6 *Ula* each with 8 single 533mm TT each with A3 *Seal* DM2 HWT

PRINCIPAL SURFACE COMBATANTS • FRIGATES 5

  FFGHM 5 *Fridtjof Nansen* eq. with 2 quad (8 eff.) eq. with total of 8 NSM ASSM, 1 MK41 VLS eq. with 32 enhanced *Sea Sparrow* SAM, 2 twin (4 eff.) eq. with total of 4 *Sting Ray* LWT, 1 76mm; (2 vessels under construction)

PATROL AND COASTAL COMBATANTS • PFM 7:

  3 *Hauk* each with 6 single each with 1 RB 12 *Penguin* tactical SSM, 1 SIMBAD twin (2 eff.) manual with 2 *Mistral* SAM, 1 twin 533mm ASTT (2 eff.) with 2 T-61 HWT (*Hauk Class will be decommissioned in 2008*)

  3 mod *Hauk* each with 6 single each with 1 RB 12 *Penguin* tactical SSM, 1 SIMBAD (2 eff.) manual with 2 *Mistral* SAM, 1 twin 533mm ASTT (2 eff.) with 2 T-61 HWT (*Hauk Class will be decommissioned in 2008*)

  1 *Skjold* each with 8 NSM ASSM; 1 twin (2 eff.) with Mistral Naval SAM; 1 76mm gun (additional 5 units trials/construction)

MINE WARFARE 6

  MINE COUNTERMEASURES • MSC 3 *Alta* **MHC** 3 *Oskoy*

AMPHIBIOUS • CRAFT 20

  LCP 20 S90N

LOGISTICS AND SUPPORT 18

  AS 1 *Horten*

  ATS 1 *Valkyrien*

  AGI 1 *Marajata*

  AGS 5

  RY 1

  TRG 2 *Hessa*

  YDT 7

FACILITIES

Bases Located at Bergen, Ramsund

Coast Guard 321 + 400 conscripts (total 721)

PATROL AND COASTAL COMBATANTS 16

  PSOH 9: 1 *Svalbard*; 3 *Nordkapp* each with 6 single (fitted for but not embarked) with RB 12 *Penguin* tactical SSM, eq with 1 *Lynx* utl hel (SAR/recce); 5 Nornen Class

  PCO 7 (leased from commercial contractors)

  MISC BOATS/CRAFT 6 cutters (for fishery dept)

HELICOPTERS • ASW 6 *Lynx* MK86 (Air Force-manned)

Naval Home Guard 1,800 reservists on mobilization

Consisting of 4 Rapid Reaction Forces (Coy size), with a total of 450 troops each, and 17 'Naval Home Guard Areas' with a total of 1300 troops each. From 2009, the Naval Home Guard will be equipped with 2 vessels of the *Nornen*-class and 12 smaller vessels, deployed along the Norwegian coastline. In addition, a number of civilian vessels can be requisitioned as required.

Air Force 1,800; 3,200 conscript (total 5,000)

Joint Command – Norwegian National HQ

Flying hours   180 hrs/year

FORCES BY ROLE

FGA	3 sqn with 57 F-16A/F-16B *Fighting Falcon*
MR	1 sqn with 4 P-3C *Orion** (MR)); 2 P-3N *Orion* (pilot trg)
SAR	1 sqn with 12 *Sea King* MK43B
EW/CAL	1 sqn with 3 *Falcon* 20C (2 EW, 1 Flight Inspection Service)

Tpt   1 sqn with 6 C-130E *Hercules*
Trg   1 sqn with 15 MFI-15 *Safari*
Hel   2 sqn with 18 Bell 412SP *Twin Huey;* 14 NH90 TTH
SAM   12 bty with NASAMS II

EQUIPMENT BY TYPE
AIRCRAFT 52 combat capable
  FTR 48 F-16A/F-16B *Fighting Falcon* (plus 9 held in reserve)
  MP 6: 4 P-3C *Orion**; 2 P-3N *Orion* (pilot trg)
  TPT 9: 6 C-130H *Hercules* (to be replaced by 4 C-130J from 2008-2010); 3 *Falcon* 20C)
  TRG 15 MFI-15 *Safari*
HELICOPTERS
  SAR 12 *Sea King* MK43B (SAR)
  UTL 18 Bell 412SP *Twin Huey* (12 tpt, 6 SF); 14 NH90 TTH
AD
  SAM
    TOWED NASAMS
  MSL
    AAM AIM-120B AMRAAM; AIM-9L *Sidewinder*
BOMBS
  Laser-guided: EGBU-12 *Paveway* II
  INS/GPS guided: JDAM

AA Home Guard 2,500 reservists on mobilisation

FORCES BY ROLE
Army 2 bn (*total:* 9 army bty)

EQUIPMENT BY TYPE
AD • GUNS 20mm • **TOWED** NM-45

DEPLOYMENT

AFGHANISTAN
NATO • ISAF 508
UN • UNAMA 1 obs

BOSNIA-HERZEGOVINA
EU • EUFOR • *Operation Althea* 8

EGYPT
MFO 9

ETHIOPIA/ERITREA
UN • UNMEE 3 obs

IRAQ
MNF • *Operation Iraqi Freedom* 12

MIDDLE EAST
UN • UNTSO 12obs

NEPAL
UN • UNMIN 3

SERBIA
NATO • KFOR • *Joint Enterprise* 86
UN • UNMIK 1

SUDAN
UN • UNMIS 9; 16 obs

FOREIGN FORCES

United Kingdom Army 10; Navy 20; Air Force 20
United States Army 23; Navy 7; USAF 38; USMC 12

Poland Pl

Polish Zloty z		2006	2007	2008
GDP	z	1.05tr	1.13tr	
	US$	341bn	434bn	
per capita	US$	8,856	11,267	
Growth	%	6.1	6.6	
Inflation	%	1.3	1.8	
Def exp	z	19.32bn		
	US$	6.23bn		
Def bdgt	z	18.0bn	20.15bn	
	US$	5.80bn	7.69bn	
FMA (US)	US$	29.7m	30.0m	27.2m
US$1=z		3.10	2.62	

Population   38,518,241

Ethnic groups: German 1.3%; Ukrainian 0.6%; Belarussian 0.5%

Age	0–14	15–19	20–24	25–29	30–64	65 plus
Male	8%	4%	4%	4%	23%	5%
Female	8%	4%	4%	4%	23%	8%

Capabilities

ACTIVE 127,266 (Army 79,000 Navy 11,600 Air 28,466 Joint 8,200) Paramilitary 21,400
Terms of service 12 months (to be 9 months from 2005)

RESERVE 234,000 (Army 188,000 Navy 12,000 Air 19,000 Joint 15,000)

ORGANISATIONS BY SERVICE

Army 40,000; 39,000 conscript (total 79,000)
Reorganised into Land Forces Command; 2 Mil Districts (Pomeranian and Silesian). Land Forces Command directly controls airmobile bdes and their avn and SF. Transition to lighter forces is continuing but is hampered by lack of funds. The Military Districts have defence forces consisting of 5 territorial bdes. The military police are directly under the Minister of National Defence and are transforming with 15% (2000 personnel) forming special units of bn size to enable their support to counter-terrorism, VIP protection and NATO operations.

FORCES BY ROLE

Comd	1 Mech Corps HQ; element of Ge/Pl/Da Corps HQ
Armd	1 armd cav div (11TH) (3 armd cav, 1 mech bde, 1 recce bn, 1 arty,1 AD regt 1 engr bn)
Mech	1 div (1st) (1 armd ,1 mech, 1 mtn, bde, 1 recce bn, 1 arty, 1 AD regt, 1 engr bn); 1 div (12th) (1 armd cav, 3 mech, 1 coastal bde, 1 arty, 1 AD regt , 1 engr bn); 1 div (16th) 1 Armd, 3 mech bde bde, 1 recce bn, 1 arty, 1 AD regt, , 1 engr bn)
Airmob	1aslt bde (6th) (2 asslt , 1 para bn), 1 air cav bde (25th) (5 spt hel bn)

Recce	2 regt
Arty	2 bde
Engr	2 bde
Avn	1 Air div (32th) (4 Aslt sqn (2 sqn eqpt with Mi-8, 2 sqn eqpt with Mi-17)); combat regt (49th) with (3 attack Sqns eqpt with Mi-24), 1 recce sqn eqpt with (Mi-2)) ; 1 combat regt (56th) (4 sqn (1 atk sqn with Mi-24V, 2 recce sqn eqpt with Mi-2, 1 spt sqn eqpt with Mi-2))

EQUIPMENT BY TYPE

MBT 946: 128 *Leopard* 2 2A4; 232 PT-91 *Tward*; 586 T-72 MBT/T-72M1D/T-72M1

RECCE 490 BRDM-2

AIFV 1402:

AIFV (T) 1,298 BMP-1

AIFV (W) *Patria* AMV 104 *Rosomak*

APC 693 Type Variants

LT VEH 222 M-1038 *HMMVW*

ARTY 956+

  SP 531+: **122mm** 420 2S1 *Carnation*; **152mm** 111 M-77 *Dana*; **203mm**

  MRL 122mm 225: 195 BM-21; 30 RM-70 *Dana*

  MOR 200: **120mm** 125 M-120; **98mm** 75 M-98

AT • MSL • MANPATS 318: 129 AT-3 9K11 *Sagger*; 106 AT-4 9K111 *Spigot*; 18 AT-5 9K113 *Spandrel*; 7 AT-7 9K115 *Saxhorn*; 58 *Spike* LR

HELICOPTERS

  ATK 54: 32 Mi-24D *Hind D*; 22 PZL MI-2URP *Hoplite*

  SPT 97: 36 PZL W-3A *Sokol*/PZL W-3W *Sokol*; 24 Mi-8T *Hip* spt/Mi-8U *Hip* trg; 24 PZL MI-2 *Hoplight* ; 13 Mi-17T *Hip* spt/Mi-17U *Hip H* trg

UAV• TACTICAL 2 MALE on order

AD

  SAM 444

    SP 144: 80 GROM *Poprad*; 64 OSA-AK

    MANPAD 300 *Strzla* 2

  GUNS 450

    SP 23mm 36 ZSU-23-4

    TOWED 23mm 414 ZU-23-2

RADAR • LAND SNAR-10 *Big Fred* (veh, arty)

MSL • TACTICAL • SSM 4 SS-21 *Scarab (Tochka)*

Navy 11,000 conscript 600 (total 11,600)

EQUIPMENT BY TYPE

SUBMARINES • TACTICAL 5

SSK 5:

  4 *Sokol* (ex-*Kilo*) with 8 single 533mm TT

  1 *Orzel* with 6 single 533mm TT with 12 T-53/T-65 HWT

PRINCIPAL SURFACE COMBATANTS 8

  FRIGATES 3

    FFG 2 *Pulawski* (ex US *Oliver Hazard Perry* class) each with 1 Mk 13 GMLS with 36 SM-1 MR SAM, 4 RGM-84D/T *Harpoon* tactical SSM, 2 triple 3x 24mm ASTT (6 eff.) each with 24 A244 LWT, 1 76mm gun, capacity 2 SH-2G *Super Seasprite* ASW hel

    FF 1 *Kaszub* with 2 twin 533mm ASTT (4 eff.) each with SET-53 HWT, 1 quad (4 eff.) with SA-N-5 *Grail* SAM, 2 RBU 6000 *Smerch* 2 (24 eff.), 1 76mm gun

  CORVETTES • FSG 5:

    2 *Gornik* each with 2 twin (4 eff.) each with 4 SS-N-2C *Styx* tactical SSM, 1x4 manual with SA-N-5 *Grail* SAM, 1 76mm gun

3 *Orkan* (ex-GDR *Sassnitz*. Refit programme in progress final vessel due for completion early 2007) each with 2 quad (8 eff.) each with 1 RBS-15M tactical SSM, 1 x4 Manual with SA-N-5 *Grail* SAM, 1 76mm gun

MINE WARFARE • MINE COUNTERMEASURES 20

  MSC 13 *Goplo*

  MHC 7: 3 *Krogulec*; 4 *Mamry*

AMPHIBIOUS 8

  LS • LSM 5 *Lublin* (capacity 9 tanks; 135 troops)

  CRAFT • LCU 3 *Deba* (capacity 50 troops)

LOGISTICS AND SUPPORT 31

  AORL 1

  AOL 2

  MRV 1 Project 890

  ARS 4

  AGI 2 *Moma*

  AGS 4

  ATF 3

  TRG 6: 1 AXS

  YDG 2

  YTM 6

FACILITIES

Bases Located at Kolobrzeg, Gdynia (HQ), Swinoujscie, Hel Peninsula (Spt), Gdynia-Babie Doly

Naval Aviation 1,900

FORCES BY ROLE

ASW / SAR	1 sqn with 10 MI-14PL *Haze A*; 3 MI-14PS *Haze C*; 2 PZL W-3RM *Anakonda*; 1 PZL MI-2
Tpt /Utl	1 sqn with 8 An-28B1R; 2 An-28E
	1 sqn with 1 An-28; 2 An-28TD; 2 PZL W-3T; 5 PZL W-3RM; 2 Mi-17; 1 PZL MI-2, 4 SH-2G

EQUIPMENT BY TYPE

AIRCRAFT

  TPT 3: 1 An-28; 2 An-28TD

  UTL 10: 8 An-28B1R; 2 An-28E

HELICOPTERS

  ASW 14: 10 MI-14PL; 4 SH-2G *Super Seasprite*

  SAR 10: 3 Mi-14PS *Haze C*; 7 PZL W-3RM *Anakonda*

  SPT 6: 2 PZL W-3T *Sokol*; 2 Mi-17 (Mi-8MT) *Hip H*; 2 PZL MI-2

Air Force 28,000 conscript 466 (total 28,466))

2 AD Corps- North and South

Flying hours   160 to 200 hrs/year

FORCES BY ROLE

Multi-role	2 sqn with 23 F-16C/D Block 52+ (11 F-16C, 12 F-16D
Ftr	2 sqn with 32 MiG-29 *Fulcrum* (24 MiG-29A, 8 MiG-29UB)
FGA/Recce	3 sqn with 48 Su-22M-4 *Fitter*
Tpt	1 bde with 8 C-295M; 5 An-26; 10 PZL M-28 *Bryza*. 1 regt with 2 Tu-154M; 8 Yak-40; 2 An-26
Trg	trg units with 28 PZL-130; 76 TS-11; 2 An-28
Hel	5 sqn with 23 PZL W-3 *Sokol*; 16 Mi-2; 12 Mi-8MT; 1 Bell 412 *Twin Huey*; 2 PZL SW-4 (trg)
SAM	3 bde – SA-3 *Goa*; 1 indep regt with SA-3; SA-4 *Ganef*; SA-5 *Gammon*

EQUIPMENT BY TYPE

AIRCRAFT 103 combat capable

Multi Role 23 F-16C/D (first of 36 F-16C & 12 F-16D being delivered).

    FTR 24 MiG-29A

    FGA 48 Su-22M-4

    TPT 31: 5 An-26 *Curl*; 2 An-28 *Cash*; 8 CASA C-295M; 10 M-28 *Bryza TD*; 2 Tu-154 *Careless*; 4 Yak-40 *Codling*. (5 C-130E to be delivered 2007–2009)

    TRG 112: 76 PZL TS-11; 28 PZL-130; 8 MiG-29UB *Fulcrum**

HELICOPTERS

    SPT 51: 23 PZL W-3 *Sokol*; 12 Mi-8MT *Hip*; 16 PZL Mi-2

    UTL 1 Bell 412 *Twin Huey*

    TRG 2 PZL SW-4

AD • SAM 625: 500 SA-3 *Goa*

    SP 75 SA-4 *Ganef*

    STATIC 50 SA-5 *Gammon*

MSL

    AAM AA-8 *Aphid*; AA-3 *Anab*; AA-11 *Archer*. (AIM 120C AMRAAM on order)

    ASM AS-7 *Kerry*

Paramilitary 21,400

Border Guards 14,100

Ministry of Interior and Administration

Maritime Border Guard

PATROL AND COASTAL COMBATANTS 19: 1 PSO; 2 PCO; 1 PCC; 2 PCI; 7 PBF; 6 PB

Prevention Units of Police 6,300; 1,000 conscript (total 7,300)

OPP–Ministry of Interior

DEPLOYMENT

AFGHANISTAN

NATO • ISAF 937

    AGL 40: 20 Mk19 Mod3; 20 Mk19 Mod4

    IFV 25 Rosomack 8x8

BOSNIA-HERZEGOVINA

EU • EUFOR • *Operation Althea* 2 inf coy; 203

CHAD/CENTRAL AFRICAN REPUBLIC

EU • EUFOR Tchad/RCA 350

CÔTE D'IVOIRE

UN • UNOCI 2 obs

DEMOCRATIC REPUBLIC OF CONGO

UN • MONUC 2 obs

ETHIOPIA/ERITREA

UN • UNMEE 3 obs

GEORGIA

UN • UNOMIG 5 obs

IRAQ

MNF • *Operation Iraqi Freedom* 900

Army

FORCES BY ROLE

HEL

    ATK 4: 4 Mi-24V *Hind* E

    SPT 9: 2 Mi-8 *Hip*; 7 PZL W-3 *Sokol*

LEBANON

UN • UNIFIL II 482

LIBERIA

UN • UNMIL 2 obs

SERBIA

NATO • KFOR • *Joint Enterprise* 1 inf bn; 312

UN • UNMIK 1 obs

SUDAN

UN • UNMIS 2 obs

SYRIA/ISRAEL

UN • UNDOF 1 inf bn; 353

WESTERN SAHARA

UN • MINURSO 1 obs

FOREIGN FORCES

Germany Army: 67 (Ge elm Corps HQ (multinational))

Portugal Por

Euro €		2006	2007	2008
GDP	€	155bn	161bn	
	US$	194bn	230bn	
per capita	US$	18,268	21,611	
Growth	%	1.3	1.8	
Inflation	%	3.0	2.0	
Def exp[a]	€	2.46bn		
	US$	3.08bn		
Def bdgt	€	1.91bn	1.88bn	
	US$	2.38bn	2.69bn	
US$1=€		0.80	0.70	

[a] including military pensions

Population 10,642,836

Age	0–14	15–19	20–24	25–29	30–64	65 plus
Male	9%	3%	4%	4%	22%	7%
Female	8%	3%	3%	4%	24%	10%

Capabilities

ACTIVE 42,910 (Army 26,700 Navy 9,110 Air 7,100) **Paramilitary 47,700**

RESERVE 210,900 (Army 210,000 Navy 900)

Reservist obligation to age of 35

ORGANISATIONS BY SERVICE

Army 17,960; 8,740 conscript (total 26,700)

5 Territorial Comd (2 mil region, 1 mil district, 2 mil zone)

FORCES BY ROLE

Army	2 (Task Forces – Azores and Madeira) unit (*total:* 2 AD bty, 3 inf bn)
Mech inf	1 bde (1 SP arty bty, 1 tk gp, 1 engr coy, 1 AD bty, 1 recce sqn, 2 mech inf bn)
Lt inf	1 bde (1 fd arty bn, 2 inf bn)
Spec Ops	1 unit
Cdo	1 bn
AB	1 bde (1 AT coy, 1 engr coy, 1 AD bty, 1 fd arty bn, 1 recce sqn, 2 Para bn)
MP	1 regt

Reserves 210,000 reservists

Territorial Def   3 bde (on mob)

EQUIPMENT BY TYPE

MBT 224: 37 *Leopard* 2A6; 86 M-60A3; 8 M-60A4, 7 M-60; 86 M-48A5
RECCE 40: 15 V-150 *Chaimite;* 25 ULTRAV M-11
APC 353
  APC (T) 280: 240 M-113; 40 M-557
  APC (W) 73 V-200 *Chaimite*
ARTY 350+
  SP 155mm 20: 6 M-109A2; 14 M-109A5
  TOWED 135: **105mm** 97: 21 L-119; 52 M-101; 24 M-56; **155mm** 38 M-114A1
  COASTAL 21: **150mm** 9; **152mm** 6; **234mm** 6 (inactive)
  MOR 174+: **81mm** (incl 21 SP); **107mm** 76 M-30 (incl 14 SP); **120mm** 98 *Tampella*
  AT
  MSL • MANPATS 118: 68 Milan (incl 6 ULTRAV-11); 50 TOW (incl 18 M-113, 4 M-901)
  RCL 402: **106mm** 128 M-40; **84mm** 162 *Carl Gustav;* **90mm** 112
  AD
  SAM • MANPAD 52: 37 *Chaparral;* 15 FIM-92A *Stinger*
  GUNS • TOWED 93: **20mm** 31 Rh 202; **40mm** 62 L/60

Navy 8,775; 335 active reservists (recalled) (total 9.110)

EQUIPMENT BY TYPE

SUBMARINES • TACTICAL • SSK 1 *Albacora* with 12 single 550mm TT (8 bow, 4 stern) each with 12 E14/E15 HWT
PRINCIPAL SURFACE COMBATANTS • FRIGATES 12
  FFG 3:
    3 *Vasco Da Gama* each with 2 Mk 141 *Harpoon* quad (8 eff.) each with RGM-84C *Harpoon* tactical SSM, 2 Mk 36 triple 324mm ASTT each with Mk 46 LWT, 1 Mk 29 *Sea Sparrow* octuple with RIM-7M *Sea Sparrow* SAM, 1 100mm gun, (capacity 2 *Lynx* MK95 (*Super Lynx*) utl hel)
    2 *Karel Dorman class* (*ex-Netherlands* transfer agreed 2006 expected ISD '08 and '09 respectively)
  FF 2 *Commandante Joao Belo* each with 2 Mk32 triple 324mm ASTT each with Mk 46 LWT, 2 100mm gun, 1 hel landing platform
CORVETTES • FSH 7:
    3 *Baptista de Andrade* each with 1 100mm gun, 1 hel landing platform
    4 *Joao Coutinho* each with 2 76mm gun, 1 hel landing platform

PATROL AND COASTAL COMBATANTS 17
  PSOH 1 *Viana do Castelo* (expected ISD early '08)
  PCO 4 *Cacine*
  PCI 9: 5 *Argos;* 4 *Centauro*
  PCR 3: 2 *Albatroz;* 1 *Rio Minho*
AMPHIBIOUS • CRAFT 1 LCU
LOGISTICS AND SUPPORT 10:
  AORLH 1 *Bérrio* (ex UK *Rover*) with 1 hel landing platform (for medium hel)
  AGS 4
  ABU 2
  TRG 3 **AXS**

FACILITIES

Base	Located at Lisbon
Naval airbase	Located at Montijo
Support bases	Leca da Palmeira (North), Portimao (South), Funchal (Madiera), Ponta Delgada (Azores)

Marines 1,725

FORCES BY ROLE

Police	1 det
Lt inf	2 bn
Spec Ops	1 det
Fire spt	1 coy

EQUIPMENT BY TYPE

ARTY •MOR 15 120mm

Naval Aviation

HELICOPTERS • UTL 5 *Lynx* MK95 (*Super Lynx*)

Air Force 7,100

Flying hours   180 hrs/year on F-16 *Fighting Falcon*

FORCES BY ROLE

Air	1 (op) COFA comd; 5 (op) gp
FGA	1 sqn with 19 F-16A/B *Fighting Falcon;* 1 sqn with 21 F-16 MLU *Fighting Falcon*
Surv	1 sqn with 2 CASA 212 *Aviocar*
MR	1 sqn with 6 P-3P/C *Orion**
CSAR/SAR/ Fishery Protection	1 sqn with with 12 EH-101 *Merlin*
Tpt	1 sqn with 24 CASA 212 *Aviocar;* 1 sqn with 3 *Falcon* 50; 1 sqn with C-130H *Hercules*
Liaison/utl	1 sqn with FTB337 *Skymaster(Cessna 337)*
Trg	1 sqn with 16 TB-30 *Epsilon;* 1 sqn with 18 SA-316 *Alouette III;* 1 sqn with 25 *Alpha Jet*

EQUIPMENT BY TYPE

AIRCRAFT 25 combat capable
  FTR 19: 16 F-16A/3 F-16B *Fighting Falcon;* (21 F-16 MLU by 2010)
  MP 6 P-3P *Orion**
  RECCE 2 CASA 212B *Aviocar* (survey)
  TPT 45: 6 C-130H *Hercules* (tpt/SAR); 24 CASA 212A *Aviocar* (tpt/SAR, Nav/ECM trg, fisheries protection). To be replaced by 12 C-295 by end 2007; 12 FTB337 *Skymaster (Cessna 337)* 12 (being phased out); 3 *Falcon* 50 (tpt/VIP)
  TRG 41: 25 *Alpha Jet* (FGA/trg); 16 TB-30 *Epsilon*

HELICOPTERS
SPT 12 EH-101 *Merlin* (6 SAR, 4 CSAR, 2 fishery protection)
UTL 18 SA-316 *Alouette III* (trg, utl)
UAV 34 Armor X7
MSL
AAM AIM-120 AMRAAM; AIM-9J/ AIM-9L/ AIM-9P *Sidewinder*; AIM-7M *Sparrow*
ASM AGM-65A *Maverick;* AGM-84A *Harpoon*
BOMBS
Laser-guided: *Paveway* II

Paramilitary 47,700

National Republican Guard 26,100
APC (W): some *Commando* Mk III (*Bravia*)
HELICOPTERS • UTL 7 SA-315 *Lama*

Public Security Police 21,600

DEPLOYMENT

AFGHANISTAN
NATO • ISAF 162

ANGOLA
Navy 11 (Technical military cooperation)

BOSNIA-HERZEGOVINA
EU • EUFOR • *Operation Althea* 14

CAPE VERDE
Navy 2

CHAD/CAR
EU • EUFOR Chad/CAR 2 hel

DEMOCRATIC REPUBLIC OF CONGO
Navy 33
EU • EUSEC 2

TIMOR LESTE
UN • UNMIT 4 obs

GUINEA BISSAU
Navy 1

IRAQ
NATO • NTM-I 9

LEBANON
UN • UNFIL II 146

MOZAMBIQUE
Navy 7

SAO TOME AND PRINCIPE
Navy 1
Air Force 5
AIRCRAFT • TPT 1: 1 CASA 212 *Aviocar*

SERBIA
NATO • KFOR • *Joint Enterprise* 296
UN • UNMIK 2 obs

SUDAN
AU • AUMIS HQ 1

FOREIGN FORCES
United Kingdom Army 10; Navy 20; Air Force 20
United States EUCOM: Army: 27; Navy: 29; USMC: 9; USAF: 800; USNORTHCOM: Support facility located at Lajes

Romania R

Lei		2006	2007	2008
GDP	lei	342bn	388bn	
	US$	122bn	165bn	
per capita	US$	5,476	7,412	
Growth	%	7.7	6.3	
Inflation	%	6.6	4.2	
Def exp	lei	6.50bn		
	US$	2.32bn		
Def bdgt	lei	6.64bn	7.63bn	9.77bn
	US$	2.37bn	3.24bn	
FMA (US)	US$	12.8m	15.0m	18.4m
US$1=lei		2.80	2.35	

Population 22,276,056
Ethnic groups: Hungarian 9%

Age	0–14	15–19	20–24	25–29	30–64	65 plus
Male	8%	4%	4%	4%	22%	6%
Female	8%	4%	4%	4%	23%	9%

Capabilities

ACTIVE 74,267 (Army 42,200 Navy 8,067 Air 10,500 Joint 13,500) **Paramilitary 79,900**

RESERVE 45,000 (Joint 45,000)

ORGANISATIONS BY SERVICE

Army 42,200
FORCES BY ROLE
1 Joint Ops Comd (corps), 1 Land Forces HQ. Readiness is reported as 70–90% for NATO designated forces and 40–70% for generation and regeneration
HQ	2 corps
Army	8 (generation and regeneration) bde
Mech	1 (NATO Designated) bde
Inf	1 (NATO Designated) bde
Mtn Inf	1 (NATO Designated) bde
Arty	2 bde
Engr	1 bde
Log	2 bde

EQUIPMENT BY TYPE
MBT 366: 5 T-72; 165 T-55; 42 TR-77; 154 TR-85 M1
AIFV 95 MLI-84
APC 1,081
   APC (T) 75 MLVM
   APC (W 1,505: 70 B33 TAB *Zimbru*; 393 TAB-71; 162 TAB-77; 381 TABC-79;

TYPE VARIANTS 499 APC
ARTY 833
   SP 122mm 24: 6 2S1 *Carnation;* 18 Model 89
   TOWED 385: **122mm** 41 (M-30) M-1938 (A-19); **152mm**
   344: 241 M-1981 Model 81; 103 gun/howitzer 85
   MRL 122mm 150 APR-40
   MOR 120mm 274 M-1982
AT
   MSL • MANPATS 138: 12 9P122 *BRDM-2 Sagger;* 78
   9P133 BRDM-2 *Sagger;* 48 9P148 BRDM-2 *Spandrel*
   GUNS 100mm 259: 212 M1977 Gun 77; 47 SU-100 SP
AD • GUNS 60
   SP 35mm 18 *Gepard*
   TOWED 42: **35mm** 24 GDF-203; **37mm** 18
RADARS • LAND 8 SNAR-10 *Big Fred* (veh, arty)

Navy 8,067

Navy HQ with 1 Naval Operational Command (Fleet level),
1 Riverine Flotilla (Danube based)

EQUIPMENT BY TYPE
PRINCIPAL SURFACE COMBATANTS 7
   FRIGATES • FFG 3:
      2 *Regele Ferdinand* (ex UK Type-22), each with 1 76mm
      gun (capacity 1 IAR-330 (SA-330) *Puma*)
      1 *Marasesti* with 4 twin (8 eff.) with 8 SS-N-2C *Styx*
      tactical SSM, each with SA-N-5 *Grail* SAM, 2 triple
      533mm ASTT (6 eff.) each with Russian 53–65 ASW, 2
      RBU 6000 *Smerch 2* (24 eff.), 2 x2 76mm gun (4 eff.),
      (capacity 2 IAR-316 (SA-316) *Alouette III* utl hel)
   CORVETTES • FS 4:
      2 *Tetal* I each with 2 twin 533mm ASTT (4 eff.) each
      with Russian 53-65 ASW, 2 RBU 2500 *Smerch 1* (32 eff.),
      2 twin 76mm gun (4 eff.)
      2 *Tetal* II each with 2 twin 533mm ASTT (4 eff.), 2 RBU
      6000 *Smerch 2* (24 eff.), 1 76mm gun, (capacity 1 IAR-
      316 (SA-316) *Alouette III* utl hel)
PATROL AND COASTAL COMBATANTS 23
   PSO 3 *Zborul* each with 2 twin (4 eff.) each with 4 SS-N-
   2C *Styx* tactical SSM, 1 76mm gun
   PCR 20:
      5 *Brutar* each with 1 BM-21 MRL RL, 1 100mm gun
      3 *Kogalniceanu* each with 2 100mm gun
      12 VD 141 (ex MSI now used for river patrol)
MINE WARFARE 5
   MINE COUNTERMEASURES 4
      MSO 4 *Musca*
   MINELAYERS • ML 1 *Cosar* with up to 100 mines
LOGISTICS AND SUPPORT 13: 1 **AOT**; 3 **AOL**; 2 **AE**; 1
AGOR; 1 **AGS**; 2 **ATF**; 2 **YDG**
   TRG 1 **AXS**

FACILITIES
Base Located at Tulcea, Braila (Danube), Mangalia,
   Constanta (coast)

Naval Infantry

FORCES BY ROLE
Naval inf 1 bn

EQUIPMENT BY TYPE
APC (W) 13: 10 TAB-71M; 3 TABC-79

Air Force 10,500

Flying hours 120 hrs/year

FACILITIES
Air bases   3 combat air bases with Lancer and Puma.
             1 Tpt air base and 1 Trg air base

FORCES BY ROLE
HQ (AF)   1 AF HQ: 1 (op) Air comd)
Ftr   2 sqn with 20 MiG-21 *Lancer* C/*Lancer* B
FGA   4 sqn with 54 MiG-21 *Lancer* A/*Lancer* B
Tpt/survey/   1 tpt ac sqn with 1 An-24 *Coke*, 4 An-26 *Curl*,
spt hel   1 An-30 *Clank*; 5 C-130 B/H *Hercules*; 2 multi-
                role hel sqns with 24 IAR-330 *Puma* SOCAT;
                1 tpt hel with 6 IAR-330 (SA-330) *Puma*
Trg   1 sqn with 17 IAR-99 *Soim*; 1 sqn with 12
                IAK-52; 1 sqn with 12 An-2; 1 sqn with 3 L-39
                Albatros; 1 sqn with 7 IAR-316B (*Alouette III*)
AD   1 bde; 2 regt

EQUIPMENT BY TYPE
AIRCRAFT 74 combat capable
   FTR 20 MiG-21 *Lancer* C/B; (18 MiG-29 in store)
   FGA 54 MiG-21 *Lancer* A/B
   TPT 11: 1 C-130H/4 C-130B *Hercules*; 1 An-24 *Coke*; 4 An-
   26 *Curl*; 1 An-30 *Clank*
   TRG 44: 17 IAR-99 *Soim*; 3 L-39 *Albatros*; 12 IAK-52; 12
   An-2
HELICOPTERS
   SPT 62: 24 IAR-330 *Puma* SOCAT; 38 IAR-330 (SA-330)
   Puma
   UTL 7 IAR-316B (SA-316B) *Alouette III*
UAV 65 *Shadow* 600
AD • SAM 14 SA-2 *Guideline*
MSL
   AAM R-550 *Magic 2*; *Python 3*; AA-8 *Aphid*; AA-11
   Archer; AA-7 *Apex*
   ASM AS-7 (A-921) *Kerry*; AT-3 *Sagger*; SPIKE-ER

Paramilitary 79,900

Border Guards 22,900 (incl conscripts)
Ministry of Interior

Gendarmerie ε57,000
Ministry of Interior

DEPLOYMENT

AFGHANISTAN
NATO • ISAF 536; **APC** *Piranha* IIIC
Operation Enduring Freedom 94
UN • UNAMA 1 obs

BOSNIA-HERZEGOVINA
EU • EUFOR • *Operation Althea* 49

CHAD/CAR
EU • EUFOR Chad/CAR 120

CÔTE D'IVOIRE
UN • UNOCI 7 obs

Europe (NATO)

DEMOCRATIC REPUBLIC OF CONGO
UN • MONUC 22 obs

ETHIOPIA/ERITREA
UN • UNMEE 4 obs

GEORGIA
UN • UNOMIG 2 obs

IRAQ
MNF • *Operation Iraqi Freedom* 489
  APC *Piranha* IIIC
NATO • NTM-I 3

LIBERIA
UN • UNMIL 3 obs

NEPAL
UN • UNMIN 5 obs

SERBIA
NATO • KFOR • *Joint Enterprise* 153
UN • UNMIK 3 obs

SUDAN
UN • UNMIS 12 obs

Slovakia Slvk

Slovak Koruna Ks		2006	2007	2008
GDP	Ks	1.66tr	1.84tr	
	US$	56.5bn	77.9bn	
per capita	US$	10,382	14,298	
Growth	%	8.3	8.8	
Inflation	%	4.4	2.4	
Def exp	Ks	28.2bn		
	US$	957m		
Def bdgt	Ks	28.5bn	28.5bn	
	US$	966m	1.20bn	
FMA (US)	US$	3.9m	4.0m	3.0m
US$1=Ks		29.5	23.7	

Population   5,447,502

Ethnic groups: Hungarian 11%; Romany ε5%; Czech 1%

Age	0–14	15–19	20–24	25–29	30–64	65 plus
Male	9%	4%	4%	4%	23%	5%
Female	8%	4%	4%	4%	24%	7%

Capabilities

ACTIVE 17,129 (Army 7,324 Air 4,280 Cental Staff 2,621 Support and Training 2,904)
Terms of service 6 months

RESERVE 20,000

ORGANISATIONS BY SERVICE

Army 7,324 (incl some conscripts)
1 Land Forces Comd HQ, 1 tri-national bde HQ

FORCES BY ROLE
Rapid Reaction	1 bn
Mech inf	1 bde (1 tk bn, 2 mech Inf bn, 1 recce coy, 1 arty bn, 1 AT bty, 1 AD bty, 1 engr coy); 1 bde (3 Mech Inf bn, 1 Rocket bn, 1 AT bty, 1 recce coy, 1 engr coy, 1 AD bty)
Recce	1 (Special) regt
Engr	1 bn
NBC	1 bn

Reserves ε20,000 on mobilisation

National Guard Force
1 mob base (to form 2 inf bde on mob)

EQUIPMENT BY TYPE
MBT 245 T-72M
AIFV 387: 294 BMP-1; 93 BMP-2
APC 134:
  APC (T) 110 OT-90
  APC (W) 24: 17 OT-64; 7 *Tatrapan* (6x6)
ARTY 341
  SP 193:**122mm** 1 2S1 *Carnation*; 45 in store; **152mm** 131: 119 M-77 *Dana;* 12 in store; **155mm** 16 M-2000 *Zuzana*
  TOWED 122mm 52 D-30
  MRL 84: **122mm** 59 RM-70; **227mm** 25 RM-70/85 *MORAK*
  MOR 120mm 12: 8 M-1982; 4 SPM-85
MSL • MANPATS 466 AT-3 9K11 *Sagger*/AT-5 9K113 *Spandrel* (incl SP on BMP-1/-2 and BRDM)
AD
  SAM • TOWED SA-2 *Guideline*
  SP 48 SA-13 *Gopher*
  MANPAD SA-16 *Gimlet*; SA-7 *Grail*
  RADAR • LAND SNAR-10 *Big Fred* (veh, arty)

Air Force 4,280
Flying hours   57 hrs/year
3 air bases – Sliac air base equipped with cbt and trg ac; Presov air base with atk and spt hel; Kuchyna air tpt wg

FORCES BY ROLE
Ftr	1 wg with 22 MiG-29 *Fulcrum*/MiG-29UB *Fulcrum* (12 Modernised); 21 MiG-21MF/UB *Fishbed*
FGA/ Recce	1 sqn with 3 Su-22M-4 *Fitter K*
Trg	1 L-29 *Delfin*; 15 L-39 *Albatros*
Hel	1 wg with 16 Mi-24D *Hind* D/Mi-24V *Hind E**; 1 Mi-8 *Hip*; 14 Mi-17 (Mi-8MT) *Hip H*; 6 PZL MI-2 *Hoplite*
AD	1 bde with SA-10B *Grumble* system; SA-6 *Gainful*; SA-7 *Grail*

EQUIPMENT BY TYPE
AIRCRAFT 46 combat capable
  FTR 43: 22 MiG-29 /MiG-29 UB *Fulcrum* (12 modernised); 21 MiG-21 MF/MiG-29UB *Fishbed*
  FGA 3 Su-22M-4 *Fitter K*
TRG 16: 1 L-29 *Delfin*, 15 L-39 *Albatross*
HELICOPTERS
  ATK 16 Mi-24D *Hind* D/Mi-24V *Hind E*

SPT 21: 14 Mi-17; 1 Mi-8 *Hip; 6* PZL MI-2 *Hoplite*
AD • SAM
SP SA-10B *Grumble;* SA-6 *Gainful*
MANPAD SA-7 *Grail*
MSL
AAM AA-8 *Aphid;* AA-11 *Archer;* AA-10 *Alamo*
ASM AT-2 *Swatter;* AT-3 *Sagger;* AT-6 *Spiral*

DEPLOYMENT

AFGHANISTAN
NATO • ISAF 59

BOSNIA-HERZEGOVINA
EU • EUFOR • *Operation Althea* 40
EU • EUMM 2 obs

CYPRUS
UN • UNFICYP 196

IRAQ
NATO • NTM-I 2

MIDDLE EAST
UN • UNTSO 2 obs

SERBIA
NATO • KFOR • *Joint Enterprise* 134

SYRIA/ISRAEL
UN • UNDOF 95

Slovenia Slvn

Slovenian Tolar t		2006	2007	2008
GDP	t	7.12tr	7.58tr	
	US$	37.3bn	45.2bn	
per capita	US$	18,558	22,473	
Growth	%	5.7	5.4	
Inflation	%	2.4		
Debt	US$			
Def exp	t	120bn		
	US$	629m		
Def bdgt	t	108bn	126bn	
	US$	568m	750m	
US$1=t		191	168	

Population   2,009,245
Ethnic groups: Croat 3%; Serb 2%; Muslim 1%

Age	0–14	15–19	20–24	25–29	30–64	65 plus
Male	7%	3%	4%	4%	25%	6%
Female	7%	3%	3%	4%	25%	9%

Capabilities

ACTIVE 5,973 (Army 5,973) **Paramilitary 4,500**

RESERVE 20,000 (Army 20,000) **Paramilitary 5,000**

ORGANISATIONS BY SERVICE

Army 5,973
1 Force Comd
FORCES BY ROLE
Inf 1 bde (1 MP bn, 1 engr bn, 2 mot inf bn)
EQUIPMENT BY TYPE
MBT 70: 40 M-84; 30 T-55S1
RECCE 8 BRDM-2
AIFV 26 M-80
APC (W) 64: 28 BOV-3MD; 2 BTR-50PU; 34 *Valuk (Pandur)*
ARTY 140
TOWED 24: **105mm** 6 M-2A1; **155mm** 18 TN-90
MOR 116: **82mm** 60; **120mm** 56: 8 M-52; 16 M-74; 32 MN-9
MSL • SP 24: 12 BOV-3 AT-3 9K11 *Sagger;* 12 BOV-3 AT-4 9K111 *Spigot*
MANPATS AT-3 9K11 *Sagger;* AT-4 9K111*Spigot*

Reserves
Inf   2 bde (on mob) (*each:* 1 tk bn, 1 arty bn, 1 recce bn, 2 inf bn)

Army Maritime Element 47
FORCES BY ROLE
Maritime 1 bn (part of Sp Comd)
EQUIPMENT BY TYPE
PATROL AND COASTAL COMBATANTS • PB 1 *Super Dvora* MKII
FACILITIES
Base   Located at Koper

Air Element 530
FORCES BY ROLE
Air   1 regt
AD   1 regt
EQUIPMENT BY TYPE
AIRCRAFT
TPT 3: 1 L-410 *Turbolet;* 2 PC-6 *Turbo-Porter*
TRG 12: 3 PC-9; 9 PC-9M (armed trainer)
HELICOPTERS
RECCE 2 AS-532 *Horizon*
UTL 11: 3 AB-206 (Bell 206) *JetRanger;* 8 Bell 412 *Twin Huey**
AD
SAM 138
SP 6 *Roland* II
MANPAD 132: 36 SA-16 *Gimlet;* 96 SA-18 *Grouse (Igla)*
GUNS 24
TOWED **12.7mm** 12 M-55
SP **20mm** 12 BOV-3 SPAAG

Paramilitary 4,500

Police 4,500 (armed); 5,000 reservists (total 9,500)
HELICOPTERS • UTL 5: 1 A-109; 2 AB-206 (Bell 206) *JetRanger;* 1 AB-212 (Bell 212); 1 Bell 412 *Twin Huey*

Europe (NATO)

DEPLOYMENT

AFGHANISTAN
NATO • ISAF 42

BOSNIA-HERZEGOVINA
EU • EUFOR • *Operation Althea* 58

IRAQ
NATO • NTM-I 4

MIDDLE EAST
UN • UNTSO 2 obs

SERBIA
NATO • KFOR • *Joint Enterprise* 92

Spain Sp

Euro €		2006	2007	2008
GDP	€	976bn	1.05tr	
	US$	1.22tr	1.50tr	
per capita	US$	30,200	37,226	
Growth	%	3.9	3.7	
Inflation	%	3.6	2.5	
Def exp[a]	€	11.53bn		
	US$	14.41bn		
Def bdgt	€	7.12bn	7.69bn	
	US$	8.90bn	10.99bn	
US$1=€		0.80	0.70	

[a] including military pensions plus extra budgetary expenditure

Population	40,448,191					

Age	0–14	15–19	20–24	25–29	30–64	65 plus
Male	7%	3%	3%	4%	24%	7%
Female	7%	3%	3%	4%	24%	9%

Capabilities

ACTIVE 149,150 (Army 95,600 Navy 23,200 Air 20,900 Joint 9,450) **Paramilitary 73,360**

RESERVE 319,000 (Army 265,000 Navy 9,000 Air 45,000)

ORGANISATIONS BY SERVICE

Army 95,600
4 Area Defence Forces. The principal deployable elements are 1 mech div consisting of 3 mech bde, and the rapid reaction force (FAR) consisting of 1 legion, 1 AB and 1 airmob bde; with arty, cav and sigs regts in support. Spain provides one of the NATO High Readiness Force (Land) HQ which provides the Land Component Command of the NATO Rapid Response Corps Spain NRDC-SP.

FORCES BY ROLE
HQ   1 NRDC-SP HQ (1 NRDC-SP HQ bn)
Cav   1 bde (1 HQ bde, 2 light Cav regt, 1 armd Cav regt, 1 fd arty regt, 1 HQ bn, 1 log bn, 1 engr unit)

Mech inf   1 div with (3 bde (*each:* 1 HQ bn, 1 armd inf / mech regt, 1 mech inf bn, 1 recce bn, 1 fd arty bn, 1 engr bn, 1 log bn, 1 sigs coy))
Lt inf   1 bde (La Legión) with (1HQ bn, 2 inf regt, 1 recce bn, 1 fd arty bn, 1 engr bn, 1 log bn, 1 sigs coy); 2 bde (*each:* 1 HQ bn, 1 inf regt, 1 inf regt/bn, 1 recce/armd bn, 1 fd arty bn, 1 engr bn, 1 log bn, 1 sigs coy); 1 inf bde (Canary Islands Comd) with (1HQ bn, 3 lt inf regt, 1 fd arty regt, 1 AAA regt, 1 engr bn, 1 log bn, 1 spt hel unit, 1 sigs coy)
Inf   1 div (Located in Ceuta) with (1 HQ bn, 1 inf regt, 1 inf bn, 1 cav regt, 1 arty regt, 1 engr bn, 1 log bn, 1 sigs coy); 2 div (Balearic Islands and Melilla comd) (*each:* 1 HQ bn, 1 inf regt, 1 fd arty regt, 1 engr bn, 1 log bn)
Mtn inf   1 bde (2 mtn inf regt, 1 HQ bn, 1 fd arty bn, 1 engr unit, 1 log bn)
AB   1 bde (1 HQ bn, 1 para inf bn, 1 air aslt bn, 1 airmob bn, 1 fd arty bn, 1 engr bn, 1 log bn, 1sigs coy)
SF   1 spec ops comd (1 HQ bde, 1 HQ bn, 3 SF bn, 1 sigs coy)
Arty   1 fd arty comd (1 HQ bde, 3 fd arty regts); 1 coast arty (Ceuta) comd (1 HQ bde, 1 coast arty regt, 1 sigs unit)
AD   1 bde (1HQ, 5 AAA regts, 1 sigs unit)
Engr   1 bde (1 HQ bde, 1 engr regt, 1 engr bridging regt, 1 railway regt, 1 NBC regt)
Sigs/EW   1 bde (1 HQ bde, 2 sigs regt, 2 EW regt)
Avn   1 comd (FAMET) (1HQ bde, 5 hel bn (1 atk,5 spt, , 1log bn, 1sigs bn)
Log   2 div each with (1HQ , 3 log regts)
Med   1 bde with (1HQ, 3 medical regts, 1log unit, 1field hospital)

EQUIPMENT BY TYPE
MBT 323: 108 *Leopard* 2A4; 18 *Leopard* 2A5E; 184 M-60A3TTS; 13 M-48A5E
RECCE 270: 42 B-1 *Centauro*; 228 VEC-3562 *BMR-VEC*
AIFV 144 *Pizarro* (incl variants)
APC 2,022
  APC (T) 1,337 M-113 (incl variants)
  APC (W) 685: 130 BMR-600 (incl variants); 555 BMR-600M1
ARTY 2,013
  SP 170: **105mm** 34 M-108; **155mm** 96 M-109A5 **203mm** 40 M-110A2
  TOWED 290
    105mm 226: 56 L-118 light gun; 170 Model 56 pack howitzer
    155mm 64: 52 M-114; 12 SBT-1
  COASTAL 50:
    155mm 8 SBT 52; **305mm** 3; **381mm** 3; **6in** 36
  MRL 140mm 14 *Teruel*
  MOR 1,489:
    SP 556: **81mm** 446; **120mm** 110 SP
    81mm 594; **120mm** 339
AT
  MSL
    SP 174: 106 *Milan*; 68 *TOW*

MANPATS 458: 28 *HOT*; 298 *Milan*; 132 *TOW*
RCL 106mm 507
AD
  SAM 249
    SP 20: 18 *Roland*; 2 *Spada*
    TOWED 49: 36 I *HAWK* Phase III MIM-23B; 13 *Skyguard/Aspide*
    MANPAD 180 *Mistral*
  GUNS • TOWED 267: **20mm** 175 GAI-B01; **35mm** 92 GDF-002
  RADAR
    AIRBORNE *Sentinel* RMK1
    LAND 2 AN/TPQ-36 *Firefinder* (arty, mor)

Army Aviation (FAMET)

FORCES BY ROLE

Hel   6 bn (4 atk hel bn, 1 spt hel bn, 1 tpt hel bn)
Logistic   1 log bn (1 spt coy, 1 supply coy); 1 sigs bn

EQUIPMENT BY TYPE
HELICOPTERS
ATK AS-665 *Tiger**
OBS 9 OH-58 *Kiowa*
SPT 17+: 17 HT-17D (CH-47D) *Chinook;* HU.21(AS-332) *Super Puma*
UTL 96: 28 BO-105; 6 HU-18 (Bell 212); 15 AS-532UC *Cougar;* 16 AS-532UL *Cougar;* 31 HU-10B (UH-1H) *Iroquois*

Reserves 265,000 reservists

cadre units
Railway   1 regt
Armd Cav   1 bde
Inf   3 bde

Navy 23,200 (incl Naval Aviation and Marines)

FORCES BY ROLE

Navy 1 comd HQ located at Madrid
      1 Strike Group
      2 Frigate Squadrons
      1 Submarine Flotilla
      1 MCM Flotilla

EQUIPMENT BY TYPE
SUBMARINES • TACTICAL • SSK 4:
  4 *Galerna* each with 4 single 533mm TT each with 20 F17 Mod 2/L5
PRINCIPAL SURFACE COMBATANTS 12
  AIRCRAFT CARRIERS • CVS 1 *Principe de Asturias* (capacity 10 AV-8B *Harrier II* FGA ac/AV-8B *Harrier II Plus* FGA ac; 8 SH-3 *Sea King* ASW hel; 2 HU-18 (Bell 212) utl hel
  FRIGATES • FFG 11:
    4 *Alvaro de Bazan* each with 2 twin 324mm ASTT (4 eff.) with 24 Mk 46 LWT, 2 Mk 141 *Harpoon* quad (8 eff.) each with RGM-84F tactical SSM, 1 48 cell Mk 41 VLS (LAM capable) with 32 SM-2 MR SAM, 64 RIM-162B *Sea Sparrow* SAM (quad packs), 1 127mm gun; Baseline 5 Aegis C2, (capacity 1 SH-60B *Seahawk* ASW hel)
    1 *Baleares* (limited operational role only; planned for decommissioning 2009) with 2 Mk 141 *Harpoon* quad (8 eff.) each with RGM-84C *Harpoon* tactical SSM, 1

Mk 112 octuple (8 eff.) with 16 tactical ASROC, 1 Mk 22 GMLS with 16 SM-1 MR SAM, 2 twin ASTT (4 eff.) each with Mk 46 LWT, 1 127mm gun
    6 *Santa Maria* each with 2 Mk32 triple 324mm each with 6 Mk 46 LWT, 1 Mk 13 GMLS with 32 SM-1 MR SAM, 8 RGM-84C *Harpoon* tactical SSM, 1 76mm gun (capacity 2 SH-60B *Seahawk* ASW hel)
MINE WARFARE • MINE COUNTERMEASURES 7
  MCCS 1 *Diana*
  MHO 6 *Segura*
AMPHIBIOUS
  PRINCIPAL AMPHIBIOUS SHIPS • LPD 2 *Galicia* (capacity 6 AB-212 or 4 SH-3D *Sea King;* 4 LCM or 6 LCVP; 130 APC or 33 MBT; 450 troops)
  LS • LST 1 *Pizarro* (2nd ship of class in reserve)
  CRAFT 20 **LCM**
LOGISTICS AND SUPPORT 2:
  AORH 1 *Patino*
  AO 1
FACILITIES
Bases   Located at El Ferrol, Rota (Fleet HQ), Cartagena (ALMART HQ, Maritime Action), Las Palmas (Canary Islands)
Naval Air   Located at Mahón (Menorca), Porto Pi
Stations   (Mallorca)

Navy – Maritime Action Force

FORCES BY ROLE

Navy Canary Islands Maritme Command
      Cadiz Maritime Action Command
      Ferrol Maritime Action Command
      Balear Islands Maritime Area

PATROL AND COASTAL COMBATANTS 31
  PSOH 12: 5 *Descubierta;* 4 *Serviola;* 3 *Alboran*
  PSO 11: 1 *Chilreu;* 9 *Anaga,* 1 *Buquesde Accion Maritime (BAM)* (1st of 4 vessels on order)
  PFC 5 *Barcelo*
  PCC 6: 4 *Conejera* 2 *Toralla*
  PBR 2
LOGISTICS AND SUPPORT 27:
  AWT 2
  AGOR 2 (with ice strengthened hull, for polar research duties in Antarctica)
  AGHS 2
  AGS 2
  ATF 2
  AT 2
  AK 3
  YDT 1
  TRG 11: 1 **AX**; 5 **AXL**; 5 **AXS**

Naval Aviation 814

Flying hours 150 hrs/year on AV-8B *Harrier II* FGA ac; 200 hrs/year on hel

FORCES BY ROLE

COMD/tpt   1 sqn with HU-18 (Bell 212)
FGA   1 sqn with AV-8B *Harrier II Plus;* AV-8B *Harrier II*

ASW	1 sqn with SH-3D *Sea King*; 1 sqn with SH-60B *Seahawk*
EW	1 flt withSH-3D *Sea King* (AEW)
Liaison	1 flt with CE-550 *Citation II*
Trg	1 flight with 1 TAV-8B *Harrier* on lease (USMC)

EQUIPMENT BY TYPE
AIRCRAFT 16 combat capable
  FGA 16: 12 AV-8B *Harrier II Plus*; 4 AV-8B *Harrier II*
  TPT 3 CE-550 *Citation II*
  TRG 1 TAV-8B *Harrier* on lease (USMC)
  MPA 7 P-3 *Orion*
HELICOPTERS
  ASW 24: 3 SH-3D *Sea King* (AEW); 9 more SH-3; 12 SH-60B *Seahawk*
  UTL 18: 8 HU-18 (Bell 212); 10 Hughes 500MD
MSL
  ASM AGM-119 *Penguin*, AGM-65G *Maverick*
  AAM AIM-120 *AMRAAM*, AIM-9L *Sidewinder*

Marines 5,300
FORCES BY ROLE

Marine	1 bde (2500) (1 mech inf bn, 2 inf bn, 1 arty bn, 1 log bn, 1 spec ops unit)
Marine Garrison	5 gp

EQUIPMENT BY TYPE
MBT 16 M-60A3TTS
APC (W) 18 *Piranha*
AAV 19: 16 AAV-7A1/AAVP-7A1; 2 AAVC-7A1; 1 AAVR-7A1
ARTY 18
  SP 155mm 6 M-109A2
  TOWED 105mm 12 M-56 (pack)
AT • MSL • MANPATS 24 TOW-2
  RL 90mm C-90C
AD • SAM • MANPAD 12 *Mistral*

Air Force 20,900
Flying hours 120 hrs/year on hel/tpt ac; 180 hrs/year on FGA/ftr

FORCES BY ROLE

Ftr/OCU	1 sqn with 18 EF *Typhoon*; 2 sqn with 45 F-1CE (F-1C) *Mirage*/F-1EDA/*Mirage* F-1EE (F-1E)
FGA	5 sqn with 90 EF-18A (F/A-18A)/EF-18B (F/A-18B) *Hornet*; 1 EF-18 MLU (First of 67 MLU EF-F18 to be delivered)
MP	1 sqn with 2 P-3A *Orion**; 5 P-3B *Orion** (MR)
EW	1 sqn with 1 B-707; CASA 212 *Aviocar*; 2 *Falcon* 20 (EW)
SAR	1 sqn with 3 F-27 *Friendship* (SAR),3 HU-21 (AS-332) *Super Puma*; 1 sqn with CASA 212 *Aviocar*, 3 HU-21 (AS-332) *Super Puma*; 1 sqn with CASA 212 *Aviocar*, 5 AS-330 (SA-330) *Puma*
Spt	1 sqn with CASA 212 *Aviocar*; 2 Cessna 550 *Citation V* (recce); 15 Canadair CL-215
Tkr/tpt	1 sqn with 5 KC-130H *Hercules*; 1 sqn with 2 Boeing 707

Tpt	1 sqn with 20 CN-235 (18 tpt, 2 VIP); 1 sqn with 7 C-130H/C-130H-30 *Hercules*; 1 sqn with CASA 212 *Aviocar*; 1 sqn with 2 A-310, 2 *Falcon* 900; 1 sqn with 1 Beechcraft C90 *King Air* (VIP), 6 HU-21 (AS-332) *Super Puma*; 1 sqn with 3 Boeing 707, 3 *Falcon* 20
Tkr	1 sqn with 2 A-310; 2 B-707
OCU	1 sqn with EF-18A (F/A-18A) *Hornet*/EF-18B (F/A-18B) *Hornet*
Lead-in trg	2 sqn with 20 F-5B *Freedom Fighter*
Trg	2 (lead-in trg) sqn 2 sqn with 20 F-5B *Freedom Fighter*; 2 sqn with 46 CASA C-101 *Aviojet*; 1 sqn with CASA 212 *Aviocar*; 1 sqn with 22 Beech F-33C *Bonanza* (trg); 2 sqn with 15 EC-120 *Colibri*; 8 S-76C; 1 sqn with 37 E-26 (T-35) *Pillan*

EQUIPMENT BY TYPE
AIRCRAFT 181 combat capable
  FTR 83: 18 *Typhoon* Tranche 1 (87 *Typhoon* on order); 45 F-1CE (F-1C) *Mirage*/F-1EDA *Mirage* F-1EE (F-1E)/*Mirage* F-1EE (F-1E); 20 F-5B *Freedom Fighter* (lead-in ftr trg)
  FGA 91: 90 EF-18A (F/A-18A)/EF-18B (F/A-18B) *Hornet*; 1 EF-18 MLU (first of 67 MLU EF-F18 to be delivered)
  MP 7: 2 P-3A *Orion**; 5 P-3B *Orion** (MR)
  TKR 7: 5 KC-130H *Hercules*, 2 Boeing 707
  TPT 112: 2 A-310; 6 B-707 (incl EW & tkr); 7 C-130H /C-130H-30 *Hercules*; 57 CASA 212 *Aviocar*; 7 CASA C-295 (9 on order to replace some CASA 212); 20 CN-235 (18 tpt, 2 VIP); 2 Cessna 550 *Citation V* (recce); 3 F-27 *Friendship* (SAR); 5 *Falcon*; 20 (3 VIP, 2 EW); 2 *Falcon* 900 (VIP); 1 Beechcraft C90 *King Air*
  SPT/Firefighting 16: 15 Canadair CL-215; 1 CL-415
  TRG 126: 46 CASA C-101 *Aviojet*; 21 DO-27 (liaison/trg); 22 Beech F-33C *Bonanza* (trg); 37 E-26 (T-35) *Pillan*
HELICOPTERS
  SPT 17: 5 AS-330 (SA-330) *Puma*; 12 HU-21 (AS-332) *Super Puma*
  UTL 25: 15 EC-120 *Colibri*; 2 AS-532 (VIP); 8 S-76C
AD
  SAM *Mistral*; R-530
  TOWED *Skyguard*/*Aspide*
MSL
  AAM AIM-120B/C AMRAAM; AIM-9L/ AIM-9M/ AIM-9N/ AIM-9P *Sidewinder*; AIM-7F/M *Sparrow*, R-530
  ARM AGM-88A HARM;
  ASM AGM-65A/G *Maverck*; AGM-84C/D *Harpoon*; Taurus KEPD 350
BOMBS
  Conventional: Mk 82; Mk 83; Mk 84; BLU-109; BPG-2000; BR-250; BR-500; BME-330B/AP; CBU-100 (anti-tank)
  Laser-guided: GBU-10/16 *Paveway* II; GBU-24 *Paveway* III

Central Air Command (Torrejon)
4 Wg

Ftr	2 sqn with EF-18 (F/A-18) *Hornet*

Spt   1 sqn with CASA 212 *Aviocar*; Cessna 550 *Citation V*; 1 sqn with Canadair CL-215/CL-415; 1 sqn with B-707; CASA 212 *Aviocar* (EW); *Falcon* 20; 1 sqn with CASA 212 *Aviocar*; HU-21 (AS-332) *Super Puma* (SAR)

Tpt   1 sqn with A-310; B-707 (tkr/tpt); 1 sqn with HU-21 (AS-332) *Super Puma* (tpt); 2 sqn with CN-235; 1 sqn with CASA C-295; 1 sqn with *Falcon 20/ Falcon* 900; 1 Beechcraft C90 *King Air*

Trg   1 sqn with CASA C-101 *Aviojet*; 1 sqn with E-24 (Beech F-33) *Bonanza*; 1 sqn with CASA 212 *Aviocar*

Eastern Air Command (Zaragosa)

2 Wg

Ftr   2 sqn with EF-18 (F/A-18) *Hornet*

Spt   1 sqn with CASA 212 *Aviocar*; AS-330 (SA-330) *Puma*

Tpt   1 sqn with CASA 212 *Aviocar*; 1 sqn with KC-130H *Hercules* (tkr/tpt); C-130H *Hercules*

OCU 1 sqn with EF-18 (F/A-18) *Hornet*

Strait Air Command (Seville)

4 Wg

Ftr   1 sqn with EF-18 (F/A-18) *Hornet*; 1 sqn with *Typhoon*; 2 sqn with F-1CE (F-1C) *Mirage/Mirage* F-1BE (F-1B)

MP   1 sqn with P-3A *Orion*/P-3B *Orion*

Lead-in trg 2 sqn with F-5B *Freedom Fighter*

Trg   2 sqn with EC-120B *Colibri*; S-76C; 1 sqn with E-26 (T-35) *Pillan*; 1 sqn with CASA C-101 *Aviojet*; 1 sqn with CASA 212 *Aviocar*

Canary Island Air Command (Gando)

1 Wg

FGA 1 sqn with EF-18 (F/A-18) *Hornet*

SAR 1 sqn with F-27 *Friendship*; HU-21 (AS-332) *Super Puma*

Tpt   1 detachment with 2 CN-235

Logistic Support Air Command

Trials and   1 sqn with F-5A *Freedom Fighter* test; F-1
Testing   *Mirage* test; EF-18 (F/A-18) *Hornet* test; CASA 212 *Aviocar* test; CASA C-101 *Aviojet* test

Paramilitary 73,360

Guardia Civil 72,600

9 regions

FORCES BY ROLE

Inf   19 (Tercios) regt (*total*: 56 Rural bn)

Spec Op 6 (rural) gp

Sy   6 (traffic) gp; 1 (Special) bn

EQUIPMENT BY TYPE

APC (W) 18 BLR

HELICOPTERS

   ARMED 26 BO-105ATH

   UTL 12: 8 BK-117; 4 EC135P2

Guardia Civil Del Mar 760

PATROL AND COASTAL COMBATANTS 53

   PCC 15

PCI 1
PBF 22
PB 15

NON-STATE ARMED GROUPS

see Part II

DEPLOYMENT

AFGHANISTAN
NATO • ISAF 742

BOSNIA-HERZEGOVINA
EU • EUFOR • *Operation Althea*; 1 Cav sqn; 2 inf coy 284

DEMOCRATIC REPUBLIC OF CONGO
UN • MONUC 2 obs

ETHIOPIA/ERITREA
UN • UNMEE 3 obs

LEBANON
UN • UNIFIL II 1,100

SERBIA
NATO • KFOR • *Joint Enterprise* 627
UN • UNMIK 2 obs

SUDAN
EU (support to AUMIS) 2

FOREIGN FORCES

United Kingdom Army 10; Air Force 20
United States Army: 102; EUCOM: Base located at Rota; 319 Navy: 740; USAF: 312; USMC: 154

Turkey Tu

New Turkish Lira L		2006	2007	2008
GDP	L	576bn	653bn	
	US$	406bn	549bn	
per capita	US$	5,761	7,711	
Growth	%	6.0	5.0	
Inflation	%	9.6	9.6	
Def exp [a]	L	16.51bn		
	US$	11.63bn		
Def bdgt	L	11.8bn	12.9bn	
	US$	8.30bn	10.88bn	
FMA (US)	US$	14.8m	15.0m	11.8m
US$1=L		1.42	1.19	

[a] including coast guard and gendarmerie

Population   71,158,647

Ethnic groups: Kurds ε20%

Age	0–14	15–19	20–24	25–29	30–64	65 plus
Male	13%	5%	5%	5%	20%	3%
Female	13%	5%	5%	5%	19%	4%

Capabilities

ACTIVE 510,600 (Army 402,000 Navy 48,600 Air 60,000) **Paramilitary 102,200**

Terms of service 15 months. Reserve service to age of 41 for all services. Active figure reducing

RESERVE 378,700 (Army 258,700 Navy 55,000 Air 65,000) **Paramilitary 50,000**

ORGANISATIONS BY SERVICE

Army ε77,000; ε325,000 conscript; 258,700 reservists (total 660,700)

2 armd bde, 1 mech inf bde, 1 inf bde to be disbanded

FORCES BY ROLE

4 Army HQ; 10 corps HQ

Armd	17 bde
Mech inf	15 bde
Inf	2 div
Trg/inf	4 bde
Inf	11 bde
SF	1 comd HQ
Cdo	5 bde
Cbt hel	1 bn
Avn	4 regt; 3 bn (*total*: 1 tpt bn, 2 trg bn)
Trg/arty	4 bde

EQUIPMENT BY TYPE

MBT 4,205: 2,876 M-48A5 T1/M-48A5 T2 (1300 to be stored); 170 *Leopard* 1A1; 227 *Leopard* 1A3; 274 M-60A1; 658 M-60A3

RECCE 250+: ε250 *Akrep*; ARSV *Cobra*

AIFV 650

APC (T) 3,643: 830 AAPC; 2,813 M-113/M-113 A1/M-113A2

ARTY 7,450+

　SP 868+: **105mm** 391: 26 M-108T; 365 M-52T; **155mm** 222 M-44T1; TU SpH *Storm* (K-9) *Thunder*; **175mm** 36 M-107; **203mm** 219 M-110A2

　TOWED 685+: **105mm** M-101A1; **155mm** 523: 517 M-114A1/M-114A2; 6 *Panter*; **203mm** 162 M-115

　MRL 84+: **70mm** 24; **107mm** 48; **122mm** T-122; **227mm** 12 MLRS (incl ATACMS)

　MOR 5,813+

　　SP 1,443+: **81mm**; **107mm** 1,264 M-30; **120mm** 179

　　TOWED 4,370: **81mm** 3,792; **120mm** 578

AT

　MSL 1,283

　　SP 365 *TOW*

　　MANPATS 918: 186 *Cobra*; ε340 *Eryx*; 392 *Milan*

　RCL 3,869: **106mm** 2,329 M-40A1; **57mm** 923 M-18; **75mm** 617

　RL 66mm M-72 *LAW*

AIRCRAFT

　TPT 7: 4 Beech 200 *Super King Air*; 3 Cessna 421

　UTL 98 U-17B

　TRG 63: 34 7GCBC *Citabria*; 25 T-41D *Mescalero*; 4 T-42A *Cochise*

HELICOPTERS

　ATK 37 AH-1P *Cobra*/AH-1W *Cobra*

　OBS 3 OH-58B *Kiowa*

　SPT 50 S-70B *Black Hawk*

　UTL 162: 2 AB-212 (Bell 212); 10 AS-532UL *Cougar*; 12 AB-204B (Bell 204B); 64 AB-205A (Bell 205A); 20 Bell 206 *JetRanger*; ε45 UH-1H *Iroquois*; 9 Bell 412 *Twin Huey*

　TRG 28 Hughes 300C

UAV 215+: AN/USD-501 *Midge*; *Falcon* 600/*Firebee*; CL-89; 19 *Bayraktar* by mid-2007

　RECCE • TAC 196 *Gnat* 750 *Harpy*

AD

　SAM • MANPAD 935: 789 FIM-43 *Redeye* (being withdrawn); 146 FIM-92A *Stinger*

　GUNS 1,664

　　SP 40mm 262 M-42A1

　　TOWED 1,402: **20mm** 439 GAI-D01; **35mm** 120 GDF-001/GDF-003; **40mm** 843: 803 L/60/L/70; 40 T-1

RADAR • LAND AN/TPQ-36 *Firefinder* (arty, mor)

Navy 14,100; 34,500 conscript (total 48,600 inclusive Coast Guard 2,200 and Marines 3,100)

FORCES BY ROLE

HQ 1 (Ankara) Naval Forces Command HQ (1 (Altinovayalova) Training HQ, 1 (Gölcük) Fleet HQ HQ, 1 (Istanbul) Northern Sea Area HQ, 1 (Izmir) Southern Sea Area HQ)

EQUIPMENT BY TYPE

SUBMARINES • TACTICAL 13

SSK 13:

　6 *Atilay* (Ge Type 209/1200) each with 8 single 533mm ASTT each with 14 SST-4 HWT

　7 *Preveze/Gur* (Ge Type 209/1400) each with 8 single 533mm ASTT each with UGM-84 *Harpoon* tactical USGW, *Tigerfish* HWT

PRINCIPAL SURFACE COMBATANTS • FRIGATES 24

FFG 24:

　2 *Barbaros* (MOD Ge MEKO 200 F244, F245) each with 2 Mk 141 *Harpoon* quad (8 eff.) each with RGM-84C *Harpoon* tactical SSM, 1 Mk 29 *Sea Sparrow* octuple with 24 *Aspide* SAM, 2 Mk32 triple 324mm TT each with Mk 46 LWT, 1 127mm gun, 1 AB-212 utl hel

　2 *Barbaros* (MOD Ge MEKO 200 F246, F247) each with 2 Mk 141 *Harpoon* quad (8 eff.) each with RGM-84C *Harpoon* tactical SSM, 1 8 cell Mk 41 VLS with 24 *Aspide* SAM, 2 Mk32 triple 324mm ASTT each with Mk 46 LWT, 1 127mm gun, 1 AB-212 utl hel

　6 *Burak* (Fr *d'Estienne d'Orves*) each with 2 single each with 4 MM-38 *Exocet* tactical SSM, 1 twin Manual with SIMBAD twin, 4 single ASTT each with 4 L5 HWT, 1 100mm gun

　8 *Gaziantep* (ex-US *Oliver Hazard Perry*-class) each with 1 Mk 13 GMLS with 36 SM-1 MR SAM, 4+ RGM-84C *Harpoon* tactical SSM, 2 Mk32 triple 324mm each with 24 Mk 46 LWT, 1 76mm gun, (capacity 1 S-70B *Seahawk* ASW hel)

　2 *Muavenet* (ex-US *Knox*-class) each with 1 Mk16 Mk 112 octuple with ASROC/RGM-84C *Harpoon* SSM (from ASROC launcher), 2 twin 324mm ASTT (4 eff.)

each with 22+ Mk 46 LWT, 1 127mm gun, (capacity 1 AB-212 (Bell 212) utl hel)

4 *Yavuz* (Ge MEKO 200 F244, F245) each with 2 Mk 141 *Harpoon* quad (8 eff.) each with 1 RGM-84C *Harpoon* tactical SSM, 1 Mk 29 *Sea Sparrow* octuple with 24 *Aspide* SAM, 2 Mk32 triple 324mm each with Mk 46 LWT, 1 127mm gun, 1 AB-212 (Bell 212) utl hel

PATROL AND COASTAL COMBATANTS 42

PSO 8: 1 *Trabzon*; 6 *Karamursel* (Ge *Vegesack*); 1 *Hisar*

PFM 24:

8 *Dogan* (Ge *Lurssen-*57) each with 1 76mm gun, 2 quad (8 eff.) each with RGM-84A *Harpoon*/RGM-84C *Harpoon*

8 *Kartal* (Ge *Jaguar*) each with 4 single each with RB 12 *Penguin* tactical SSM, 2 single 533mm TT

6 *Kilic* each with 2 Mk 141 *Harpoon* quad (8 eff.) each with 1 RGM-84C *Harpoon* tactical SSM, 1 76mm gun (Additional vessel due '08)

2 *Yildiz* each with 1 76mm gun, 2 quad (8 eff.) each with RGM-84A *Harpoon*/RGM-84C *Harpoon*

PCO 6 *Turk*

PCC 4 PGM-71

MINE WARFARE 22

MINE COUNTERMEASURES 22:

MCM 6 spt (tenders)

MHC 7: 5 *Edineik* (Fr *Circe*); 2 *Aydin*

MSC 5: 5 *Silifke* (ex-US *Adjutant*)

MSI 4 *Foca* (US *Cape*)

AMPHIBIOUS

LS 5

LST 5:

2 *Ertugrul* (capacity 18 tanks; 400 troops) (US *Terrebonne Parish*)

1 *Osman Gazi* (capacity 4 LCVP; 17 tanks; 980 troops;)

2 *Sarucabey* (capacity 11 tanks; 600 troops)

CRAFT 41: 24 LCT; 17 **LCM**

LOGISTICS AND SUPPORT 49:

AORH 2

AORL 1

AOT 2

AOL 1

AF 2

ASR 1

ARS 1

AWT 13: 11; 2 (harbour)

ABU 2

ATF 3

TPT 1

TRV 3

YTM 17

FACILITIES

Bases Located at Gölcük, Erdek, Canakkale, Eregli, Bartin, Izmir, Istanbul, Foka, Aksaz, Antalya, Mersin, Iskenderun

Marines 3,100

Arty   1 bn (18 guns)

Marine 1 HQ; 1 regt; 3 bn

Naval Aviation

FORCES BY ROLE

ASW   some sqn with 3 AB-204AS (Bell 204AS); 11 AB-212 (Bell 212); 7 S-70B *Seahawk*

Trg   1 sqn with 6 CN-235

EQUIPMENT BY TYPE

AIRCRAFT • TPT 6 CN-235 (MP and ASW)

HELICOPTERS

    ASW 10: 3 AB-204AS (Bell 204AS); 7 S-70B *Seahawk*

    UTL 11 AB-212 (Bell 212)*

Naval Forces Command

HQ Located at Ankara

Fleet

HQ Located at Gölcük

Northern Sea Area

HQ Located at Istanbul

Southern Sea Area

HQ Located at Izmir

Training

HQ Located at Altinovayalova

Air Force 60,000

2 tac air forces (divided between east and west)

Flying hours   180 hrs/year

FORCES BY ROLE

Ftr   3 sqn with F-16C *Fighting Falcon*/F-16D *Fighting Falcon*; 2 sqn with F-4E *Phantom II*; 2 sqn with F-5A *Freedom Fighter*/F-5B *Freedom Fighter*

FGA   5 sqn with F-16C *Fighting Falcon*/F-16D *Fighting Falcon*; 3 sqn with F-4E *Phantom II*

Recce   1 sqn with RF-4E *Phantom II*

AEW   Sqn forming with B-737 AEW&C

SAR   sqn with 20 AS-532 *Cougar* (14 SAR/6 CSAR)

Tpt   1 (VIP) sqn with C-20 *Gulfstream*; CN-235; UC-35 *Citation*; 2 sqn with CN-235; 1 sqn with C-160 *Transall*; 1 sqn with 13 C-130B *Hercules*/C-130E *Hercules*

Tkr   sqn with 7 KC-135R *Stratotanker*

Liaison 10 base flt with CN-235 (sometimes); UH-1H *Iroquois*

OCU   1 sqn with F-4E *Phantom II*; 1 sqn with F-16C *Fighting Falcon*/F-16D *Fighting Falcon*; 1 sqn with F-5A *Freedom Fighter*/F-5B *Freedom Fighter*

Trg   1 sqn with T-37B *Tweet*/T-37C *Tweet*; T-38A *Talon*; 1 sqn with 40 SF-260D; 1 sqn with 28 T-41 *Mescalero*

SAM   4 sqn with 92 MIM-14 *Nike Hercules*; 2 sqn with 86 *Rapier*; 8 (firing) unit with MIM-23 *HAWK*

EQUIPMENT BY TYPE

AIRCRAFT 435 combat capable

    FTR 87 F-5A/F-5B *Freedom Fighter*; (48 being upgraded as lead-in trainers)

FGA 348: 213 F-16C/D *Fighting Falcon* (all being upgraded to Block 50 standard)- further 30 F-16 Bl;ock 52+ on order; 135 F-4E *Phantom II* (88 FGA, 47 ftr (52 upgraded to *Phantom* 2020))

RECCE 35 RF-4E *Phantom II* (recce)

AEW 1 B-737 AEW&C (first of 4)

TKR 7 KC-135R *Stratotanker*

TPT 77: 13 C-130B *Hercules*/C-130E *Hercules*; 16 *Transall* C-160D; some C-20 *Gulfstream*; 46 CN-235 (tpt/EW); 2 UC-35 *Citation* (VIP)

TRG 198: 40 SF-260D (trg); 60 T-37B *Tweet*/T-37C *Tweet*; 70 T-38A *Talon*; 28 T-41 *Mescalero*

HELICOPTERS
UTL 20 UH-1H *Iroquois* (tpt, liaison, base flt, trg schools); 20 AS-532 (14 SAR/6 CSAR)

UAV 18 *Gnat* 750; 10 *Heron*

AD
SAM 178+: 86 *Rapier*
    TOWED: MIM-23 *HAWK*
    STATIC 92 MIM-14 *Nike Hercules*

MSL
AAM AIM-120A/B AMRAAM; AIM-9S *Sidewinder*; AIM-7E *Sparrow*, *Shafrir* 2

ARM AGM-88A HARM

ASM AGM-65A/G *Maverick*; *Popeye* I

BOMBS
Conventional BLU-107; GBU-8B HOBOS (GBU-15)

Infra-Red 40 AN/AAQ 14 LANTIRN; 40 AN/AAQ 13 LANTIRN

Laser-guided *Paveway* I; *Paveway* II

Paramilitary

Gendarmerie/National Guard 100,000; 50,000 reservists (total 150,000)
Ministry of Interior, Ministry of Defence in war

FORCES BY ROLE
Army   1 (Border) div; 2 bde
Cdo   1 bde

EQUIPMENT BY TYPE
RECCE *Akrep*

APC (W) 560: 535 BTR-60/BTR-80; 25 *Condor*

AIRCRAFT
    RECCE • OBS Cessna O-1E *Bird Dog*
    TPT 2 Do-28D

HELICOPTERS
    SPT 33: 14 S-70A *Black Hawk*; 19 Mi-17 (Mi-8MT) *Hip H*
    UTL 23: 1 AB-212 (Bell 212); 8 AB-204B (Bell 204B); 6 AB-205A (Bell 205A); 8 AB-206A (Bell 206A) *JetRanger*

Coast Guard 800 (Coast Guard Regular element); 1,050 (from Navy); 1,400 conscript (total 3,250)
PATROL AND COASTAL COMBATANTS 88:
    PSO 30
    PFC 17
    PCC 8
    PBF 19
    PBI 14

AIRCRAFT
    TPT 3 CN-235 (MP)

HELICOPTERS
    UTL 8 AB-412EP (SAR)

NON-STATE ARMED GROUPS
see Part II

DEPLOYMENT

AFGHANISTAN
NATO • ISAF 1,220

BOSNIA-HERZEGOVINA
EU • EUFOR • *Operation Althea* 1 inf gp; 253

CYPRUS (NORTHERN)
Army ε36,000

1 army corps HQ; some air det; 1 armd bde; 1 indep mech inf bde; 2 inf div; 1 cdo regt; 1 arty bde; 1 avn comd

MBT 449: 8 M-48A2 training; 441: 441 M-48A5T1/M-48A5T2

APC (T) 627: 361 AAPC (incl variants); 266 M-113 (incl variants)

ARTY 648
    TOWED 102: **105mm** 72 M-101A1; **155mm** 18 M-114A2; **203mm** 12 M-115
    SP 155mm 90 M-44T
    MRL 122mm 6 T-122
    MOR 450: **81mm** 175; **107mm** 148 M-30; **120mm** 127 HY-12

AT
    MSL 114: 66 *Milan*; 48 TOW
    RCL106mm 192 M-40A1
       90mm M-67
    RL 66mm M-72 *LAW*

AD GUNS 64+
    TOWED 20mm Rh 202; **35mm** GDF 16 GDF-003; **40mm** 48 M-1

AIRCRAFT • UTL 3 U-17

HELICOPTERS • UTL 4: 1 AS-532UL *Cougar*; 3 UH-1H *Iroquois*

PATROL AND COASTAL COMBATANTS 1 PCI less than 100 tonnes

DEMOCRATIC REPUBLIC OF CONGO
EU • EUPOL Kinshasa 1

GEORGIA
UN • UNOMIG 5 obs

LEBANON
UN • UNIFIL II 746
    1 Engr Bridging coy;
    Maritime Task Force
    Navy Task Force
    FFG 1 *Gaziantep*
    PB 2

PALESTINIAN AUTONOMOUS AREAS OF GAZA AND JERICHO
TIPH 3

SERBIA
NATO • KFOR • *Joint Enterprise* 940

SUDAN

UN • UNMIS 4

FOREIGN FORCES

Israel Air Force: up to 1 ftr det (occasional) located at Akinci with F-16 *Fighting Falcon*

United Kingdom Army 10; Air Force 30

United States US STRATCOM: 1 Spacetrack Radar SPACETRACK SYSTEM Strategic located at Incirlik; EUCOM: Support facility located at Izmir; Support facility located at Ankara; Army: 68; Navy: 9; USAF: 1,573 Air base located at Incirlik; 1 air wg (ac on detachment only) located at Incirlik with F-16 *Fighting Falcon*; F-15E *Strike Eagle*; EA-6B *Prowler*; E-3B *Sentry*/E-3C *Sentry*; HC-130 *Hercules*; KC-135 *Stratotanker*; C-12 *Huron*; HH-60 *Seahawk*; USMC: 18

United Kingdom

British Pound £		2006	2007	2008
GDP	£	1.30tr	1.37tr	
	US$	2.40tr	2.81tr	
per capita	US$	39,720	46,239	
Growth	%	2.8	3.1	
Inflation	%	2.2	2.4	
Def exp	£	29.94bn		
	US$	55.44bn		
Def bdgt[a]	£	28.65bn	29.96bn	34.05bn
	US$	53.1bn	61.1bn	
US$1=£		0.54	0.49	

[a] = Defence Budget data from 2008 expressed in Resource Accounting and Budgeting terms. No cash equivalent available

Population	60,776,238

Ethnic groups: Northern Ireland 1,600,000; Protestant 56%; Roman Catholic 41%

Age	0–14	15–19	20–24	25–29	30–64	65 plus
Male	9%	3%	3%	3%	24%	7%
Female	9%	3%	3%	3%	23%	8%

Capabilities

ACTIVE 180,527 (Army 99,707 Navy 38,900 Air 41,920)

RESERVE 199,280 (Army 134,180 Navy 22,200 Air 42,900)

Includes both trained and those currently under training within the Regular Forces.

ORGANISATIONS BY SERVICE

Strategic Forces 1,000

Armed Forces

RADAR • STRATEGIC 1 Ballistic Missile Early Warning System *BMEWS* located at Fylingdales Moor

Royal Navy

SUBMARINES • STRATEGIC • SSBN 4:

4 *Vanguard* each eq with 4 533mm TT each eq with *Spearfish* HWT, up to 16 UGM-133A *Trident D-5* SLBM (Each boat will not deploy with more than 48 warheads, but each missile could carry up to 12 MIRV, some *Trident* D-5 capable of being configured for sub strategic role)

MSL • STRATEGIC 48 SLBM (Fewer than 160 operational warheads)

Army 95,270; 3,340 (Gurkhas); 1,097 active reservists (total 99,707)

Regt normally bn size

FORCES BY ROLE

1 Land Comd HQ, 1 Corps HQ, 2 deployable div HQ, 8 deployable bde HQ and 1 tri-service Joint Hel Comd. The UK Field Army has a capability to form 36 battlegroups drawing on 5 armd regts, 5 armd recce regts, 6 SP arty regts, 9 armd inf bn, 3 mech inf bn and 20 lt inf bn. Within Joint Hel Comd is 16 Air Aslt Bde with 2 para bn and 2 air aslt bn. The third para bn is not included in the infantry orbat as it is roled as the SF spt gp. Additional spt is provided from theatre troops. For army units within 3 Cdo Bde see the Naval section.

Comd	1 (ARRC) HQ
Armd	1 div (1st) with
	(1 bde (4th) (1 armd regt, 1 Armd Mech Inf regt, 1 Mech regt, 1 Lt inf bn);
	1 Bde (7th) (1 armd regt, 2 Armd Mech Inf regt, 1 Lt inf bn);
	1 bde (20th) (1 armd regt, 2 Armd Mech regt, 1 Lt inf bn) (June 08);
	1 Armd recce regt; 3 SP arty regt; 1 AD regt; 3 cbt engr; 1 engr regt)
Mech	1 div (3rd) with
	(2 Mech bde ((1st and 12th) (*each:* 1 armd regt, 1 Armd Mech Inf regt, 1 Mech inf regt, 1 Lt inf bn);
	1 Mech bde (19th) (1 Mech inf regt, 2 Lt inf bn);
	1 Mech bde (52nd) (5 Lt inf bn);
	3 Recce regt; 2 SP arty regt; 1 arty regt; 1 AD regt; 2 cbt engr regt; 2 engr regt)
Air Aslt	1 bde (16th) (2 para bn, 2 air aslt bn, 1 arty bn, 2 atk hel regt, 1 engr regt)
Arty	1 bde HQ; 1 regt (trg); 1 MLRS regt, 1 STA regt, 1 UAV regt
SF	1 (SAS) regt, 1 SF Spt gp
SF/Recce and Surv	1 regt (600 strong)
Gurkha	2 light bn (1 in 52nd bde above)
Engr	1 Bde (2 EOD regt, 1 Air Spt)
Hel	2 atk regt (incl 1 trg); 3 LUH regt; 4 indep flt
Avn	1 sqn eqpt. with 3 BN-2T-4S *Defender*
NBC	1 (joint) regt (army/RAF)
Log	2 bde
AD	1 bde HQ; (OPCOM Air), 1 regt (*Rapier*)

Home Service Forces • Gibraltar 200 reservists; 150 active reservists (total 350)

Reserves

Territorial Army 37,260 reservists

The Territorial Army has been reorganised to enable the regular army to receive relevant manpower support from their associated territorial unit.

Armd	2 regt
Armd Recce	1 regt, 1 NBC regt
Inf	13bn
SF	2 regt (SAS)
AB	1 bn
Obs	1 regt
Arty	3 lt regt, 1 UAV regt
MLRS	1 regt
Engr	5 regt, 1 EOD regt, 1 sqn, 1 geo sqn , 1 cdo sqn
Avn	2 regt
AD	1 regt

EQUIPMENT BY TYPE

MBT 386 CR2 *Challenger 2*

RECCE 475: 137 *Sabre*; 327 *Scimitar*; 11 Tpz-1 *Fuchs*

AIFV 575 MCV-80 *Warrior*

APC 2,718

  APC (T) 1,883: 380 *Bulldog* Mk 3 (106 up-armoured for Iraq); 771 AFV 432; 597 FV 103 *Spartan*; 135 FV4333 *Stormer*

  APC (W) 835: 649 AT105 *Saxon* (*being phased out, except for Northern Ireland*); 186 *Mastiff* (All by Dec 08)

TYPE VARIANTS 1,675 AIFV/APC

ARTY 877

  SP 155mm 178 AS-90 *Braveheart*

  TOWED 105mm 166 L-118 Light gun/L-119

  MRL 227mm 63 MLRS; GMLRS

  MOR 470: **81mm SP** 110; **81mm** 360

AT • MSL 800+

  SP 60 *Swingfire* (FV 102 *Striker*)

  MANPATS 740 *Milan*; TOW

  RL 94mm LAW-80

AC • RECCE 3 BN-2T-4S *Defender* (4th on order); 1 Beechcraft *King Air* 350ER (3 more on order)

HELICOPTERS

  ATK 67 AH-64D *Apache*

  OBS 133 SA-341 *Gazelle*

  ASLT 99: 77 *Lynx* AH MK7*; 22 *Lynx* AH MK9

UAV • TACTICAL 192+: 192 *Phoenix*; *Hermes* 450; *Desert Hawk*; *Buster*; *Watchkeeper* (from 2010)

AD • SAM 339+

  SP 135 HVM

  TOWED 57+ *Rapier* FSC

  MANPAD 147 *Starstreak* (LML)

RADAR • LAND 157: 4-7 *Cobra*; 150 MSTAR

PATROL AND COASTAL COMBATANTS • MISC BOATS/CRAFT 4 workboats

AMPHIBIOUS 4 LCVP

LOGISTICS AND SUPPORT 6 RCL

Royal Navy 38,600; 300 active reservists (Full Time Reserve Service) (total 38,900)

The Royal Navy has undergone major changes to its organisational structure. Starting in 2002 with Fleet First and ending in 2006 with the single Top Level Budget (TLB) merger.

Operationally, Full Command is held by Commander in Chief FLEET with operational command and operational control delegated for all Units not involved in operations to Commander Operations a 2 star based at Northwood, London. The 2002 review created permanent Battle Staffs allowing for operations to be commanded by either one of two 2 star Commanders or two subordinate 1 star Commanders, depending on the scale of the operation. RN and RM units are also frequently assigned to UK Joint Rapid Reaction Force (JRRF), under the operational command of the Permanent Joint Headquarters (PJHQ). In addition the RN may declare units to various national, NATO or UN commands and groups not listed here.

Administratively, a single top level budget (TLB) merger has brought the Fleet and Personnel/Training Headquarters under a unified structure based at Whale Island, Portsmouth. The new Fleet Headquarters has three main roles: Force Generation – the generation of forces at the appropriate level of readiness to meet the required outputs. Force Deployment – Commander Operations manages maritime operations from the Fleet operations Division located at Northwood. Resource Management – financial management of the Fleet HQ, programming, planning, corporate communications, civilian management, corporate governance and performance management. Below the Fleet HQ, RN surface and sub-surface units are structured administratively into three Flotillas based in Portsmouth, Devonport and Faslane. Aircraft are split between two Typed Air Stations at Culdrose and Yeovilton with a SAR detachment at Prestwick Airport, Scotland. Royal Marines remain under 3 Cdo Bde with a 1 star RM commander, RM Units are located at Arbroath, Plymouth, Taunton and Chivenor.

EQUIPMENT BY TYPE

SUBMARINES 13

  STRATEGIC • SSBN 4:

    4 *Vanguard*, opcon Strategic Forces, each eq with 4 533mm TT each eq with *Spearfish* HWT, up to 16 UGM-133A *Trident D-5* SLBM (Each boat will not deploy with more than 48 warheads, but each missile could carry up to 12 MIRV, some *Trident D-5* capable of being configured for sub strategic role)

  TACTICAL • SSN 9:

    2 *Swiftsure* each with 5 single 533mm TT each with *Spearfish* HWT/ 5 UGM – 84 *Harpoon* tactical USGW

    7 *Trafalgar* each with 5 single 533mm TT each with *Spearfish* HWT/12 *Tomahawk* tactical LAM/5 UGM 84 *Harpoon* tactical USGW

PRINCIPAL SURFACE COMBATANTS 28

  AIRCRAFT CARRIERS • CV 3:

    3 *Invincible* (1 in reserve) with 3 single MK 15 *Phalanx* CIWS, (capacity 'tailored air group' 8–12 *Harrier* GR9A; 4 *Merlin* HM MK1 ASW hel; 4 *Sea King* AEW MK2 AEW hel)

DESTROYERS • DDGH 9:

4 Type-42 Batch 2 each with 1 twin (2 eff.) with 22 *Sea Dart* SAM, 2 single MK 15 *Phalanx* CIWS, 1 114mm gun, (capacity 1 *Lynx* utl hel)

4 Type-42 Batch 3 each with 1 twin (2 eff.) with 22 *Sea Dart* SAM, 2 single MK 15 *Phalanx* CIWS, 1 114mm gun, (capacity 1 *Lynx* utl hel)

1 *Daring* (Type-45) (capacity either 1 *Lynx* MKS ASW hel or 1 *Merlin* HM MK1 ASW hel) (undergoing sea trials, ISD expected '09)

FRIGATES • FFG 17:

4 *Cornwall* (Type-22 Batch 3) each with 2 Mk 141 *Harpoon* quad (8 eff.) each with RGM-84C *Harpoon* tactical SSM, 2 sextuple (12 eff.) each with 1 *Sea Wolf* SAM, 1 *Goalkeeper* CIWS, 1 114mm gun, (capacity 2 *Lynx* utl hel)

13 *Norfolk* (Type-23) each with 2 twin 324mm ASTT (4 eff.) each with *Sting Ray* LWT, 2 Mk 141 *Harpoon* quad (8 eff.) each with 1 RGM-84C *Harpoon* tactical SSM, 1 32 canister *Sea Wolf* VLS with *Sea Wolf* SAM, 1 114mm gun, (capacity either 2 *Lynx* utl hel or 1 *Merlin* HM MK1 ASW hel)

PATROL AND COASTAL COMBATANTS 24:

PSOH 2: 1 *Castle*; 1 mod *River*

PSO 3 *River*

PCI 16 *Archer* (trg)

PBF 2 *Scimitar*

ICE PATROL 1 *Endurance* (RN Manned)

MINE WARFARE • MINE COUNTERMEASURES 16

MCC 8 *Hunt* (incl 4 mod *Hunt* MCC/PCC)

MHO 8 *Sandown*

AMPHIBIOUS

PRINCIPAL AMPHIBIOUS SHIPS 8

LPD 2 *Albion* (capacity 2 med hel; 4 LCVP; 6 MBT; 300 troops)

LPH 1 *Ocean* (capacity 18 hel; 4 LCU or 2 LCAC; 4 LCVP; 800 troops)

LSD 4 *Bay* (capacity 4 LCU; 2 LCVP; 1 LCU; 24 CR2 *Challenger* 2 MBT; 350 troops) (RFA manned)

LS • LSLH 1 *Sir Bedivere* (capacity 1 hel; 16 tanks; 340 troops) (RFA manned)

CRAFT 47: 13 **LCU**; 34 **LCVP**

LOGISTICS AND SUPPORT 5

AGHS 4: 1 *Scott*;2 *Echo*;1 *Gleaner*

AGS 1 *Roebuck*

MSL • STRATEGIC 48 SLBM opcon strategic forces (Fewer than 160 operational warheads)

FORCES BY ROLE

Navy/Marine   1 party located at Diego Garcia, BIOT

FACILITIES

Bases	Located at Portsmouth (Fleet HQ), Faslane, Devonport, Gibraltar
Naval airbases	Located at Prestwick, Culdrose, Yeovilton

Royal Fleet Auxiliary

Support and Miscellaneous vessels are mostly manned and maintained by the Royal Fleet Auxiliary (RFA), a civilian fleet owned by the UK MoD, which has approximately 2,500 personnel with type cmd under CINCFLEET.

LOGISTICS AND SUPPORT 19

AORH 4: 2 *Wave Knight*; 2 *Fort Victoria*

AOR 3 *Leaf*

AORLH 2 *Rover*

AFH 2 *Fort Grange*

AR 1 *Diligence*

AG 1 *Argus* (Aviation trg ship with secondary role as Primarily Casualty Receiving Ship)

RoRo 6

Naval Aviation (Fleet Air Arm) 6,200

FORCES BY ROLE

FGA	1 sqn with 13 *Harrier* GR9A; 1 T10 *Harrier*
ASW/ASUW	5 sqn with *Merlin* HM MK1
ASW/Atk hel	1 sqn eqpt. with Lynx MK3 / Lynx MK8; Lynx MK3 (in indept flt)
AEW	1 sqn with *Sea King* AEW MK7
SAR	1 sqn and detached flt with *Sea King* HAS MK5 utl
Spt	3 sqn with *Sea King* HC MK4; some (Fleet) sqn with 1 Beech 55 *Baron* (civil registration); 1 Cessna 441 *Conquest* (civil registration); 19 *Falcon* 20 (civil registration); 5 *Grob* 115 (op under contract); 1 sqn with 6 *Lynx* AH MK7 (incl in Royal Marines entry)
Trg	1 (operational evaluation) sqn eqpt. with Merlin HM MK1*; Sea King HC MK4; 1 sqn with 10 *Jetstream* T MK2/TMK3; 1 sqn with *Lynx* MK3

EQUIPMENT BY TYPE

AIRCRAFT 13 combat capable

FGA 13 *Harrier* GR8/9A

TPT 21: 1 Beech 55 *Baron* (civil registration); 1 Cessna 441 *Conquest* (civil registration); 19 *Falcon* 20 (civil registration)

TRG 29: 5 Grob 115 (op under contract); 2 *Harrier* T10; 12 *Hawk* T MK1 (spt); 10 *Jetstream* T MK2/T MK3

HELICOPTERS 109 atk hel

ATK 6 *Lynx* AH MK7 (incl in Royal Marines entry)

ASW 103: 64 *Lynx* MK3/*Lynx* MK8; 39 *Merlin* HM MK1

UTL/SAR 16 *Sea King* HAS MK5 Utility

AEW 13 *Sea King* AEW MK7

SPT 37 *Sea King* HC MK4 (for RM)

MSL

ASM *Sea Skua*

AAM AIM-9 *Sidewinder,* AIM-120C *AMRAAM*

Royal Marines Command 7,500 (incl RN and Army elements)

FORCES BY ROLE

LCA	3 sqn opcon Royal Navy; 1 sqn (539 Aslt Sqn RM)
Sy	1 Fleet Protection Group, opcon Royal Navy
Navy	Naval Parties. Various Royal Marines det opcon to RN

Europe (NATO)

SF	4 sqn
Cdo	1 (declared to NATO) bde (1 cdo arty regt (army), 3 cdo regt)
Cdo AD arty	1 bty (army)
Cdo engr	2 sqn (1 army, 1 TA)
Cdo lt hel	2 sqn opcon Royal Navy

EQUIPMENT BY TYPE
APC (T) 150 BvS-10 *Viking*
MOR 81mm
AMPHIBIOUS 28
  ACV 4 *Griffon* 2000 TDX (M)
  LC 24 RRC
HELICOPTERS
  ATK/SPT 43: 6 *Lynx* AH MK7; 37 *Sea King* HC MK4
AD • SAM • SP HVM
RADAR • LAND 4 MAMBA (*Arthur*)

Air Force 41,920

Responsibility for RAF capability rests with Air Command (formed from the merger of Strike Command and Personnel and Training Command on 1 Apr 07). Air Cmd operates from a single, fully integrated HQ at High Wycombe. Its role is to provide a fully operational and flexible combat air force. Air Cmd comprises more than 500 aircraft, 42 stations or units, and it supports operations in the Gulf region and Afghanistan as well as maintaining a RAF presence in Cyprus, Gibraltar, Ascension Island and the Falkland Islands.

Air Cmd operations are delegated to two operational groups. No 1 Group, the Air Combat Group, controls the RAF's combat fast jet aircraft (*Typhoon*, *Tornado* and *Harrier*), and has eight airfields in the UK plus RAF Unit Goose Bay in Canada. No 2 Group, the Combat Support Group, controls Air Transport and Air-to-Air Refuelling (AT/AAR); Intelligence Surveillance, Targeting and Reconnaissance (ISTAR); and Force Protection (FP) assets. No 22 (Training) Gp recruits RAF personnel and provides trained specialist personnel to the RAF and other two Services.

RAF Expeditionary Air Wings, designed to generate a readily identifiable structure that is better able to deploy discrete units of agile, scaleable, interoperable and capable air power, operate from RAF Main Operating Bases as follows:

RAF Waddington – No 34 EAW (ISTAR); RAF Lyneham – No 38 EAW (Air Transport); RAF Coningsby – No 121 EAW (Multi Role); RAF Cottesmore – No 122 EAW (Fighter / Ground Attack); RAF Leuchars – No 125 EAW (Fighter); RAF Leeming – No 135 EAW (Fighter); RAF Marham – No 138 EAW (Fighter/Ground Attack); RAF Lossiemouth – No 140 EAW (Fighter/Ground Attack); RAF Kinloss – No 325 EAW (Maritime Patrol & Surveillance). The deployable elements of each station form the core of each EAW, reinforced by assigned Capability-based Module Readiness System (CMRS) personnel and elements of the Air Combat Support Units (ACSUs). EAWs enable the RAF to train as cohesive Air Power units which are capable of transitioning quickly from peacetime postures and deploying swiftly on operations.

Flying hours   218 hrs/year on *Harrier* GR7 ; 188 hrs/year on *Tornado* GR4; 208 hrs/year on *Tornado* F-3

FORCES BY ROLE

FGA/bbr	5 sqn with *Tornado* GR4
Ftr	4 sqn (incl 1 Op Eval Unit) with *Typhoon*; 3 sqn with *Tornado* F-3
FGA	2 sqn with *Harrier* GR7/ GR7A/GR9/ T10/T12;
ELINT	1 sqn with *Nimrod* R1
Recce	1 sqn with *Sentinel* RMK1; 2 sqn with *Tornado* GR4A
MR	2 sqn with *Nimrod* MR2*
AEW	2 sqn with E-3D *Sentry*
SAR	2 sqn with *Sea King* HAR-3A/*Sea King* HAR-3
Tkr/tpt	1 sqn with *Tristar* C2; *Tristar* K1; *Tristar* KC1; 1 sqn with VC-10C1K; VC-10K3/VC-10K4
Tpt	4 sqn with C-130K/C-130J *Hercules*; 1 (comms) sqn with BAe-125; BAe-146; AS-355 *Squirrel*; 2 BN-2A *Islander* CC2; 3; 1 sqn with 4 C-17 *Globemaster*
OCU	5 sqn with *Typhoon*, *Tornado* F-3; *Tornado* GR4; *Harrier* GR7/T10; *Nimrod* MR2
CAL	1 sqn with *Hawk* T MK1A/*Hawk* T MK1W/ *Hawk* T MK1
Trg	Units (including postgraduate training on 203(R) sqn) with *Sea King* HAR-3; Beech 200 *Super King Air*; *Dominie* T1; Grob 115E *Tutor*; *Hawk* T MK1A/*Hawk* T MK1W/*Hawk* T MK1; *Tucano* T MK1 (Shorts 312); T67M/M260 *Firefly*; *Sea King* HAR-3A
Hel	4 sqn with CH-47 *Chinook*; 3sqn with *Sea King* HAR-3; 2 sqn with *Merlin* HC MK3; 2 sqn with SA-330 *Puma*; 1 sqn *Griffin*
UAV	1 Sqn with *Predator* A/B

EQUIPMENT BY TYPE
AIRCRAFT 341 combat capable
  FTR 117: 49 *Typhoon*; 68 *Tornado* F-3
  STRIKE/FGA 185: 113 *Tornado* GR4; 72 *Harrier* GR7/ GR7A/GR9/T10/T12
  RECCE 29: 24 *Tornado* GR4A*; 5 *Sentinel* RMK1
  MP 15 *Nimrod* MR2*
  ELINT 3 *Nimrod* R1
  AEW 7 E-3D *Sentry*
  TPT 73: 4 C-17A *Globemaster* (5th in service May 08, 6th due delivery 08); 19 C1/C3 (C-130K/C-130K-30 *Hercules*); 24 C4/C5 (15 C-130J-30; 9 C-130J *Hercules*); 6 BAe-125 CC-3 5; 2 BAe-146 MKII; 7 Beech 200 *Super King Air* on lease; 2 BN-2A *Islander* CC2/3
  TPT/TKR 25: 3 *Tristar* C2 (pax); 2 *Tristar* K1 (tkr/pax); 4 *Tristar* KC1 (tkr/pax/cgo); 10 VC-10C1K (tkr/cgo); 4 VC-10K3; 2 VC-10K4
  TRG 359: 38 *Firefly* M260 T67M; 9 *Dominie* T1; 99 Grob 115E *Tutor*; 112 *Hawk* T MK1/1A; 95 *Tucano* T1; 6 *Harrier* T10/T12
HELICOPTERS
  SPT 134: 40 CH-47 HC2/2A *Chinook*; 28 HC MK3 *Merlin*; 37 SA-330 *Puma* HC1; 25 *Sea King* HAR-3A; 4 Bell 412EP *Griffin* HAR-2
  TRG 43: 31 AS-355 *Squirrel*; 12 Bell 412EP *Griffin* HT1
UAV • RECCE/ATK 5: 2 MQ-1 *Predator* A; 3 MQ-9 *Predator* B

MSL
  AAM AIM-120B/AIM-120 C5 AMRAAM; AIM-132 ASRAAM; *Skyflash*; AIM-9L / AIM-9L/I *Sidewinder*
  ARM ALARM
  ASM *Brimstone*; *Storm Shadow*; AGM-65G2 *Maverick*
  ASSM AGM-84D *Harpoon*; *Stingray*
BOMBS
  Conventional Mk 82; CRV-7; BL/IBL/RBL755 (to be withdrawal from service by the end of 2009);
  Laser-Guided/GPS: *Paveway* II; GBU-10 *Paveway* III; *Enhanced Paveway* II/III; GBU-24 *Paveway* IV

Royal Air Force Regiment

FORCES BY ROLE

Air   3 (tactical Survival To Operate (STO)) + HQ; 6 (fd) sqn

Trg   1 (joint) unit (with army) with *Rapier* C

EQUIPMENT BY TYPE

Tri-Service Defence Hel School
HELICOPTERS : 28 AS-350 *Ecureuil*; 7 Griffon HT1

Volunteer Reserve Air Forces
(Royal Auxiliary Air Force/RAF Reserve)

Air   1 (air movements) sqn; 2 (intelligence) sqn; 5 (field) sqn; 1 (HQ augmentation) sqn; 1 (C-130 Reserve Aircrew) flt

Medical 1 sqn

NON-STATE ARMED GROUPS

see Part II

DEPLOYMENT

AFGHANISTAN
NATO • ISAF 7,398 (HQ 100)
Army 5,459
  52 bde HQ, 2 armd recce sqn; 3 inf bn; 1 arty regt; 1 atk hel sqn; elem of (GMRLS; STA , UAV, 2 AD, EOD engr regt) 2 spt regt; 1 medical bn;
  RECCE 32 *Scimitar*
  AIFV 34 *Warrior*
  APC (T) 8 FV 103 *Spartan* 3 *Sultan*; 55 *Viking*
  APC (W) 132 *Mastiff*
  ARTY • TOWED 105mm 18 L-118 Light Gun
  GMRLS 4 M270
  HEL • ATK 12
    8 AH-64D *Apache*; 4 *Lynx* AH MK1; *Lynx* AH MK7
  UAV *Hermes*; *Predator B*
Navy 1,008
  1 naval air sqn
  1 naval strike wg
  1 cdo regt
  AC
    6 *Harrier*
    10 *Sea King*
Air Force 931
  1 tpt hel sqn

  AC
    FGA 12 Harrier GR10
    TPT 5 C-130 *Hercules*
  HEL
    SPT 6 CH-47 *Chinook*
    UTL 2
UN• UNAMA 1

ASCENSION ISLAND
Air Force 23

AUSTRALIA
Army 30
Navy 20

BELGIUM
Army 180
Navy 80
Air Force 140

BELIZE
Army 70

BOSNIA-HERZEGOVINA
EU • EUFOR • *Operation Althea* 21

BRITISH INDIAN OCEAN TERRITORY
  Royal Navy 40
  1 Navy/Marine party located at Diego Garcia, BIOT

BRUNEI
Army 90
Navy 10
Air Force 10

CANADA
Army 240
2 trg units
Navy 10
Air Force 20

CROATIA
EU • EUFOR • *Operation Althea* spt tps; spt/log tps

CYPRUS
Army 1,860
1 inf bn; 1 (spt) engr sqn; 1 hel flt
Navy 40
Air Force 1,060
1 SAR sqn with Bell 412 *Twin Huey*; 1 hel sqn with 4 Bell 412 *Twin Huey*
  AIRCRAFT some (on det)
    HELICOPTERS • UTL 4 Bell 412 *Twin Huey*
    RADAR 1 land (on det)
UN • UNFICYP 1 coy gp 276

CZECH REPUBLIC
Army 20

DEMOCRATIC REPUBLIC OF CONGO
UN • MONUC 6 obs

FALKLAND ISLANDS
Army 200
1 AD Bty *Rapier* FSC

Navy 60
Air Force 20
1 Ftr flt with F-3 *Tornado*; 1 SAR sqn with *Sea King* HAR-3A/*Sea King* HAR-3; 1 tkr/tpt flt with C-130 *Hercules*; VC-10 K3/4
   AD • SAM • TOWED *Rapier* FSC

FRANCE
Army 10
Navy 10
Air Force 10

GEORGIA
UN • UNOMIG 5 obs

GERMANY
Army 21,360; 1 Army corps; 1 army corps HQ, 1 armd div
Navy 30
Air Force 320

GIBRALTAR
Army 40
Royal Navy HQ 20
Air Force 70 some (periodic) AEW det

IRAQ
MNF • *Operation Iraqi Freedom* 6,371
Army 4,151
1 (composite) Army HQ; 1 armd bde; some spt unit
EQUIPMENT BY TYPE
RECCE 30 *Scimitar*
AIFV 29 *Warrior*
APC (T) 117 *Bulldog*
APC (W) 54 *Mastiff*
AC 3 *Defender* AL1
HEL • UTL SH-14D *Lynx*
Royal Navy 982
HEL • SPT 1 sqn *Sea King* HC MK4 (located at Basra)
Air Force 1,238
Air Force 2 *Nimrod* MR2; 4 C-130J; 6 EH101 *Merlin*; 9 *Sea King*; RAF regt detachment
UN • UNAMI 1 obs

ITALY
Army 70
Navy 110
Air Force 70

KENYA
Army 20
BPST (EA) 12

KOSOVO
290

KUWAIT
Army 136
Air Force 10

LIBERIA
UN • UNMIL 3

NEPAL
Army 20
UN• UNMIN 4 obs

NETHERLANDS
Army 100
Navy 40
Air Force 120

NORTHERN IRELAND
Operation Helvetic (resident troops) up to 5,000

NORWAY
Army 10
Navy 20
Air Force 20

OMAN
Army 40
Navy 20
Air Force 20

PORTUGAL
Army 10
Navy 20
Air Force 20

SAUDI ARABIA
Army 20
Navy 10
Air Force 60

SERBIA
NATO • KFOR • *Joint Enterprise* 150
   HEL • SPT 2 SA-341 *Gazelle*
UN • UNMIK 1 obs

SIERRA LEONE
IMATT 115 (incl trg team, tri-service HQ and spt)
UN • UNIOSIL 1 obs

SLOVAKIA
8

SPAIN
Army 10
Air Force 10

SUDAN
UN • UNMIS 4

TURKEY
Army 10
Air Force 30

UNITED STATES
Army 120
Navy 120
Air Force 160

UK STANDING NAVAL DEPLOYMENTS
South Atlantic (APT (S))
Atlantic Patrol Task (South) – South Atlantic and West Africa area • 1 FF/DD; 1 RFA AO

Falkland Islands Patrol Ship • 1 OPV; 1 Ice Patrol Ship (rotational 6 months)

North Atlantic (APT (N))

Atlantic Patrol Task (North) – Caribbean and North Atlantic area • 1 FF/DD; 1 RFA AO

NATO commitments

UK contributes to Standing NATO Maritime Group (SNMG) 1 or 2 • SNMG (2): 1 FF/DD

Standing NATO Mine Countermeasures Group (SNMCMG) 1 or 2 • SNMCMG1: 1 MCM / MCMV

Gulf Patrol Ship (formerly *Armilla*) 1 FF/DD; 1 AO; Additional Personnel contribution:

Naval Transition Team • 35 RN/RM – support training for Iraqi Riverine Patrol Service (IRPS)

FOREIGN FORCES

United States US STRATCOM: 1 BALLISTIC MISSILE EARLY WARNING SYSTEM *BMEWS* Strategic located at Fylingdales Moor; 1 Spacetrack Radar SPACETRACK SYSTEM Strategic located at Fylingdales Moor; USAF: 1 Special Ops gp located at Mildenhall with 5 MC-130H *Combat Talon II*; 5 MC-130P *Combat Shadow*; 1 C-130E *Hercules*; 8 MH-53J *Pave Low III*; EUCOM: Army: 371; Navy: 475; USAF: 9,231; 1 HQ (AF) HQ (3rd US Air Force) located at Mildenhall; 1 ftr wg located at Mildenhall (1 Ftr sqn with 24 F-15C *Eagle*/F-15D *Eagle*, 2 Ftr sqn with 24 F-15E *Strike Eagle*); 1 tkr wg located at Mildenhall with 15 KC-135 *Stratotanker*; USMC: 75

Europe (NATO)

Albania Alb

Albanian Lek		2006	2007	2008
GDP	lek	937bn	1,023bn	
	US$	9.6bn	11.9bn	
per capita	US$	2,667	3,308	
Growth	%	5.0	6.0	
Inflation	%	2.5	2.5	
Def bdgt	lek	13.8bn	17.9bn	21.3bn
	US$	141m	208m	
FMA (US)	US$	3.4m	3.2m	2.6m
US$1=lek		98.1	85.9	

Population	3,600,523

Age	0 – 14	15 – 19	20 – 24	25 – 29	30 – 64	65 plus
Male	14%	5%	4%	4%	20%	4%
Female	13%	5%	4%	4%	19%	4%

Capabilities

ACTIVE 11,020 (Army 6,200 Navy 1,100 Air 1,370
Logistic Support Command (LSC) 1,800 Training and
Doctrine Command (TRADOC) 550) **Paramilitary 500**
Terms of service conscription 12 months

ORGANISATIONS BY SERVICE

Land Forces (Army) Command 6,200

The Alb armed forces are being re-constituted. Restructuring
is now planned to be completed by 2010

FORCES BY ROLE
The army is to consist of:
Rapid Reaction 1 bde
Tk   1 bn
Cdo   1 regt
Arty   1 bn
Engr   1 bn

EQUIPMENT BY TYPE
MBT 40 Type-59
APC (T) 123+: 37 M-113; 86+ Type-531 (Type-63)
ARTY 1,197
   TOWED 270: **122mm** 198 (to be 18 122mm); **130mm** 18;
   152mm 54
   MRL 130mm 18
   MOR 909: **82mm** 259; **120mm** 550 M-120; **160mm** 100
   M-43
AT • MSL 30 HJ-73
AD • GUNS • TOWED 125: **37mm** M-1939 / **57mm** S-60

Navy Forces Command 1,100

FORCES BY ROLE
The Albanian naval element is organised into two naval
flotillas with additional hydrographic, logistics, auxiliary
and training support services.

EQUIPMENT BY TYPE
PATROL AND COASTAL COMBATANTS 31
   PHT 5 *Huchuan*† (PRC) each with 2 single 533mm TT
   PFC 1 *Shanghai* II† (PRC)
   PFI 2 Po-2† (FSU)
   PB 11: 3 Mk3 *Sea Spectre* 8 V-4000; (for Coast Guard
   use)
   PBR 12: 7 *Type2010*; 1 *Type303*; 4 *Type227*; (for Coast
   Guard use)
MINE WARFARE • MINE COUNTERMEASURES 3
   MSC 2 T-301† (FSU)
   MSO 1 T-43
LOGISTICS AND SUPPORT 1 LCT
FACILITIES
Base 1 located at Durrës, 1 located at Vlorë

Air Forces Command 1,370 (incl 500 conscripts)

1 active air base (Rinas), 1 hel base (Farka) and 2 reserve air
bases (Gjader & Kucova)
Flying hours 10 to 15 hrs/year

FORCES BY ROLE
Hel 1 multi-purpose regt (1 recce sqn with 7 AB-206C; 1
   tpt sqn with 3 AB-205A; 2 BO-105; 1 A-109)

EQUIPMENT BY TYPE
HELICOPTERS 13
   RECCE 7 AB-206C
   TPT 6: 3 AB-205A; 2 BO-105; 1 A-109
AD 2 SA-2 bn (12 launchers); one V-SHORAD unit with 18
HN-5A MANPAD systems; 34 AAA guns of 57 & 37mm
calibre

Logistic Support Command (LSC) 1,200; 600 conscript (total 1,800)

The LSC includes a logistics troop school, the central
laboratory, the Central University Military Hospital,
the MoD/GS Motor-pool, the Geographical Institute,
the Design Institute and a depot level maintenance
facility for ground equipment. The authorised strength
is 4,300.

Tpt   1 bde
EOD   1 gp
Maint   1 bn
Supply   1 bde (4 Logistic bn)

Training and Doctrine Command (TRADOC) 490; 60 conscript (total 550)

TRADOC includes the Defence and NCO Academy, the
Basic Training Centre, and five different centres focusing
on all aspects of training and doctrine.
Paramilitary • Border Police ε 500
Ministry of Public Order
Special Police
Internal Security Force
MP 1 (Tirana) bn (plus pl sized units in major towns)

Regional Support Commands

These units were previously the reserve. They are now cadre units (strength 100 each) that are being transformed into the 6 Regional Commands to provide support to the local authorities in case of disaster or other humanitarian crises.

Inf   5 bde
Tk   1 bn

Paramilitary

Border Police ε500
Ministry of Public Order

Special Police
Internal Security Force
MP 1 (Tirana) bn (plus pl sized units in major towns)

DEPLOYMENT

AFGHANISTAN
NATO • ISAF 138

BOSNIA-HERZEGOVINA
EU • EUFOR • *Operation Althea* 70

GEORGIA
UN • UNOMIG 3 obs

IRAQ
MNF • *Operation Iraqi Freedom* 127

FOREIGN FORCES

Ireland 1 OSCE
Italy 155 (NATO HQ Tirana); 25 DIA

Armenia Arm

Armenian Dram d		2006	2007	2008
GDP	d	2.66tr	3.03tr	
	US$	6.4bn	9.2bn	
per capita	US$	2,152	3,080	
Growth	%	13.3	11.1	
Inflation	%	2.9	3.7	
Def bdgt	d	76.4bn	97.9bn	107.2bn
	US$	183m	295m	
FMA (US)	US$	3.9m	3.5m	3.0m
US$1=d		416	331	

a = ppp estimate

Population   2,971,650

Age	0 – 14	15 – 19	20 – 24	25 – 29	30 – 64	65 plus
Male	12%	5%	5%	4%	17%	4%
Female	11%	5%	5%	4%	22%	6%

Capabilities

ACTIVE 42,080 (Army 38,945 Air/AD Joint Command 915 Air and Defence Aviation Forces 2,220) Paramilitary 4,748
Terms of service conscription 24 months. Reserves some mob reported, possibly 210,000 with military service within 15 years.

ORGANISATIONS BY SERVICE

Army 13,840; 25,105 conscripts (total 38,945)
5 Army Corps HQ

FORCES BY ROLE
Army   1 (1st) corps HQ (1 indep Tk bn, 1 Maint bn, 1 indep Recce bn, 2 indep MR regt);
1 (2nd) corps HQ (1 indep Arty bn, 1 indep Tk bn, 1 indep Recce bn, 1 indep Rifle regt, 2 indep MR regt);
1 (3rd) corps HQ (1 indep Sigs bn, 1 indep Rifle regt, 1 indep Arty bn, 1 indep Tk bn, 1 indep Recce bn, 1 indep Rocket bn, 1 Maint bn, 4 indep MR regt);
1 (4th) corps HQ (1 indep Sigs bn, 1 indep SP Arty bn, 4 indep MR regt);
1(5th) corps HQ (with 2 fortified areas) (1 indep MR regt, 1 indep Rifle regt);
MR   1 bde (trg)
SF   1 regt
Arty   1 bde
SP arty   1 regt
AT   1 regt
Engr   1 regt with Demining centre

EQUIPMENT BY TYPE
MBT 110: 102 T-72; 8 T-54
AIFV 104: 80 BMP-1; 7 BMP-1K; 5 BMP-2; 12 BRM-1K
APC (W) 136: 11 BTR-60; 100 look-a-like; 21 BTR-70; 4 BTR-80
ARTY 229
  SP 38: **122mm** 10 2S1 *Carnation*; **152mm** 28 2S3
  TOWED 121: **122mm** 59 D-30; **152mm** 62: 26 2A36; 2 D-1; 34 D-20
  MRL 51: **122mm** 47 BM-21; **273mm** 4 WM-80
  MOR 120mm 19 M-120
AT • MSL 22
  SP 13 9P149 MT-LB *Spiral*
  MANPATS 9 AT-5 9K113 *Spandrel*

Air and AD Joint Command 915
FORCES BY ROLE
AD / Air 1 (Joint) comd
SAM   1 bde; 2 regt; 1 (Radiotech) regt

EQUIPMENT BY TYPE
AD • SAM
  SP SA-4 *Ganef*; SA-6 *Gainful*
  TOWED SA-2 *Guideline*; SA-3 *Goa*

GUNS
SP ZSU-23-4
TOWED 23mm ZU-23-2
RADAR • LAND 4 SNAR-10 *Big Fred*

Air and Defence Aviation Forces 2,220

FORCES BY ROLE

FGA   1 sqn with 1 MiG-25 *Foxbat*; 15 Su-25 *Frogfoot*

Tpt   1 sqn with ; 2 Il-76 *Candid*

Trg   trg unit with 4 L-39 *Albatros*

Hel   1 sqn with 8 Mi-24P *Hind** (attack); 2 Mi-24K *Hind* (recce); 2 Mi-24R *Hind* (cbt spt); 2 Mi-9 *Hip G* (cbt spt); 10 Mi-8MT *Hip H* (cbt spt); 9 PZL MI-2 *Hoplite* (tpt/utl)

EQUIPMENT BY TYPE
AIRCRAFT 16 combat capable
  FTR 1 MiG-25 *Foxbat*
  FGA 15 Su-25 *Frogfoot*
  TPT 2 Il-76 *Candid*
  TRG 4 L-39 *Albatros*
HELICOPTERS
  ATK 8 Mi-24P *Hind**
  RECCE 2 Mi-24K *Hind*
  CBT SPT 23: 2 Mi-24R *Hind*; 10 Mi-8MT *Hip H*; 2 Mi-9 *Hip G*; 9 PZL MI-2 *Hoplite* (tpt/utl)

FACILITIES
Air bases   2

Paramilitary 4,748

Ministry of Internal Affairs
FORCES BY ROLE
Paramilitary   4 bn

EQUIPMENT BY TYPE
AIFV 55: 5 BMD-1; 44 BMP-1; 1 BMP-1K; 5 BRM-1K
APC (W) 24 BTR-152/BTR-60/BTR-70

Border Troops
Ministry of National Security
AIFV 43: 5 BMD-1; 35 BMP-1; 3 BRM-1K
APC (W) 23: 5 BTR-60; 18 BTR-70

DEPLOYMENT

IRAQ
MNF • *Operation Iraqi Freedom* 46

SERBIA
NATO • KFOR • *Joint Enterprise* 34

FOREIGN FORCES
Russia 3,170: Army: 1 mil base at Gumri 74 MBT; 330 ACV; 14 APC (T) / APC (W); 70 Arty/Mor; Military Air Forces: 1 ftr sqn with 18 MiG-29 *Fulcrum*; 1 SAM bty with SA-6 *Gainful*; 2 SAM bty with SA-12A *Gladiator*

Austria A

Euro €		2006	2007	2008
GDP	€	257bn	270bn	
	US$	321bn	386bn	
per capita	US$	39,211	47,040	
Growth	%	3.3	3.3	
Inflation	%	1.7	1.6	
Def bdgt	€	1.81bn	2.25bn	2.03bn
	US$	2.26bn	3.21bn	
US$1=€		0.80	0.70	

Population   8,199,783

Age	0 – 14	15 – 19	20 – 24	25 – 29	30 – 64	65 plus
Male	8%	3%	3%	3%	25%	6%
Female	8%	3%	3%	3%	25%	10%

Capabilities

ACTIVE 39,600 (Army 32,900 Air 6,700)

CIVILIAN 9,500 (Joint 9,500)

RESERVE 66,000 (Joint 66,000)
Air Service forms part of the army. Some 66,000 reservists a year undergo refresher trg, a proportion at a time
Terms of service 6 months recruit trg, 30 days reservist refresher trg for volunteers; 90–120 days additional for officers, NCOs and specialists.

ORGANISATIONS BY SERVICE

Army 15,700; ε17,200 conscript (total 32,900)
FORCES BY ROLE

Army   1 (Land Forces) comd

Mech Inf   1 bde (1 tk bn, 1 mech inf bn, 1 inf bn, 1 SP arty/ recce bn, 1 engr bn, 1 spt bn);
1 bde (1 tk bn, 1 mech inf bn, 1 inf bn 1 SP arty/ recce bn, 1 spt bn

Inf   1 bde (3 inf bn, 1 engr bn, 1 spt bn);
1 bde (3 inf bn, 1 recce/arty bn, 1 engr bn, 1 spt bn)

Provincial Mil   9 comd (*total:* 10 Inf bn, 9 Engr coy)

EQUIPMENT BY TYPE
MBT 114 *Leopard* 2 A4
LT TK 119: 48 SK-105 *Kuerassier*; 71 in store
AIFV 112 *Ulan* (being delivered)
APC 458
  APC (T) 367: 261 4K4E *Saurer*/4K4F *Saurer* (incl look-a-likes); 106 in store
  APC (W) 91: 71 *Pandur*; 20 APCV-2 *Dingo II*
ARTY 684
  SP 155mm 189 M-109A2/M-109A3/M-109A5ÖE
  TOWED 105: **105mm** 85 IFH (deactivated); **155mm** 20 M-1A2 (deactivated)

MRL 128mm 16 M-51 (deactivated)
MOR 374: **107mm** 133; **120mm** 241: 158 M-43; 83 in store
AT • MSL 461
  SP 89 RJPz-(HOT) *Jaguar 1* in store
  MANPATS 372: 307 RB-56 *Bill*; 65 in store
  RCL 1,420: **106mm** 374 M-40A1 in store; **84mm** 1,046 Carl Gustav
AD • GUNS 469: **20mm** 56; 413 in store

Air Force 3,300, 3,400 conscript (total 6,700)

Flying hours   180 hrs/year on hel/tpt ac; 130 hrs/year on FGA/ftr

AF Comd

HQ (AF) is part of Joint Force Cmd.
             2 bde – 1 airspace surveillance, 1 air support

FORCES BY ROLE

Ftr/FGA	1 sqn with 13 F-5E *Tiger II* on lease to be replaced by 15 EF *Typhoon* Tranche 1 between 2007-2009
Recce/ Liaison	1 sqn with 13 PC-6B *Turbo Porter*
Tpt	1 sqn with 3 C-130K *Hercules,* 2 SC.7 3M *Skyvan* (till end 2007)
Hel	1 sqn with 9 S-70A *Black Hawk*; 2 sqn with 23 AB-212 (Bell 212)
SAR/Utl	2 wg with 24 SA-319 *Alouette* III
Recce/ Liaison	3 units with 11 OH-58B *Kiowa*
Trg	Trg units with 16 PC-7 *Turbo Trainer*, 28 Saab 105Öe*, 11 AB-206A (Bell 206A) *JetRanger*
AD	2 bn
Air surv	1 radar bn, some local radar stns

EQUIPMENT BY TYPE
AIRCRAFT 41 combat capable
  FTR 13 F-5E *Tiger II* on lease (First of 15 Typhoon Tranche 1 delivered)
  TPT 18: 3 C-130K *Hercules*; 13 PC-6B *Turbo Porter*; 2 SC.7 3M *Skyvan* (until end 07)
  TRG 44: 16 PC-7 *Turbo Trainer*; 28 Saab 105Öe*
HELICOPTERS
  OBS 11 OH-58B *Kiowa*
  SPT 9 S-70A *Black Hawk*
  UTL 58: 23 AB-212 (Bell 212); 11 AB-206A (Bell 206A) *JetRanger*; 24 SA-319 *Alouette III*
AD
  SAM 76 *Mistral* each with RAC 3D land
  GUNS 146: **20mm** 72; **35mm** 74 each with 30 *Skyguard*
  RADAR 1 *Goldhaube* (1 3DLRR in delivery) with MRCS-403 *Selenia* land, RAC 3D land
MSL • AAM AIM-9P3 *Sidewinder*

DEPLOYMENT

AFGHANISTAN
NATO • **ISAF** 3
UN 1 obs

BOSNIA-HERZEGOVINA
EU • **EUFOR** • *Operation Althea* 178
EU • **EUMM** 5

CHAD/CENTRAL AFRICAN REPUBLIC
EU • **EUFOR** Chad/CAR 160

CYPRUS
UN • **UNFICYP** 5

ETHIOPIA
AU • **AUMIS** 1

ETHIOPIA/ERITREA
UN • **UNMEE** 2 obs

GEORGIA
UN • **UNOMIG** 2 obs

MIDDLE EAST
UN • **UNTSO** 6 obs

NEPAL
UN • **UNMIN** 2 obs

SERBIA
NATO • **KFOR** • *Joint Enterprise* 529
EU • **EUMM** 6 officers

SYRIA/ISRAEL
UN • **UNDOF** 372

WESTERN SAHARA
UN • **MINURSO** 2 obs

Azerbaijan Az

Azerbaijani Manat m		2006	2007	2008
GDP	m	17.7bn	22.0bn	
	US$	20bn	26bn	
per capita	US$	1,212	3,187	
Growth	%	31.0	29.3	
Inflation	%	8.6	16.6	
Def bdgt	m	586m	796m	
	US$	658m	936m	
FMA (US)	US$	3.9m	4.5m	4.3m
US$1=m		0.89	0.85	

Population   8,120,247

Age	0 – 14	15 – 19	20 – 24	25 – 29	30 – 64	65 plus
Male	14%	5%	5%	4%	18%	3%
Female	13%	5%	4%	4%	20%	5%

Capabilities

ACTIVE 66,740 (Army 56,840 Navy 2,000 Air 7,900)
Paramilitary 15,000

Terms of service 17 months, but can be extended for ground forces.

RESERVE 300,000

Reserves some mobilisation, 300,000 with military service within 15 years

ORGANISATIONS BY SERVICE

Army 56,840

5 Army Corps HQ

FORCES BY ROLE

MR   23 bde

Arty 1 bde

MRL   1 bde

AT   1 regt

EQUIPMENT BY TYPE

MBT 220: 120 T-72; 100 T-55

AIFV 127: 20 BMD-1; 44 BMP-1; 41 BMP-2; 1 BMP-3; 21 BRM-1

APC 468

  APC (T) 404: 11 BTR-D; 393 MT-LB

  APC (W) 64: 25 BTR-60; 28 BTR-70; 11 BTR-80

ARTY 270

  SP 122mm 12 2S1 *Carnation*

  TOWED 132: **122mm** 80 D-30; **152mm** 52: 22 2A36; 30 D-20

  GUN/MOR 120mm 26 2S9 *NONA*

  MRL 122mm 53 BM-21

  MOR 120mm 47 PM-38

AT • MSL • MANPATS ε250 AT-3 9K11 *Sagger*/AT-4 9K111 *Spigot*/AT-5 9K113 *Spandrel*/AT-7 9K115 *Saxhorn*

AD • SAM • SP ε40 SA-13 *Gopher*/SA-4 *Ganef*/SA-8 *Gecko* (80–240 eff.)

RADAR • LAND SNAR-1 *Long Trough*/SNAR-2/-6 *Pork Trough* (arty); *Small Fred*/*Small Yawn*/SNAR-10 *Big Fred* (veh, arty); GS-13 *Long Eye* (veh)

Navy 2,000

EQUIPMENT BY TYPE

PATROL AND COASTAL COMBATANTS 5

  PSO 1 *Woodnik 2 Class* (additional trg role)

  PCO 2 *Petrushka*

  PCC 1 *Turk*; 1 *Point*

  PCI 1 *Zhuk*

MINE WARFARE • MINE COUNTERMEASURES 2

  MSI 2 *Yevgenya*

AMPHIBIOUS

  LSM 3: 2 *Polnochny A* (capacity 6 MBT; 180 troops); 1 *Polynochny B* (capacity 6 MBT; 180 troops)

  LCU 2 *Vydra*† (capacity either 3 AMX-30 MBT or 100 troops)

LOGISTICS AND SUPPORT • ARS 1

FACILITIES

Base   Located at Baku

Air Force and Air Defence 7,900

FORCES BY ROLE

Ftr   1 sqn with 23 MiG-25 PD *Foxbat*; 3 MiG-25PU *Foxbat*

FGA   1 regt with 4 MiG-21 *Fishbed*; 6 Su-25 *Frogfoot*; 5 Su-24 *Fencer*; 4 Su-17 *Fitter*; 2 Su-25UB *Frogfoot B*

Tpt   1 sqn with 1 An-12 *Cub*; 3 Yak-40 *Codling*

Trg   28 L-29 *Delfin*; 12 L-39 *Albatros*; 1 Su-17U *Fitter*

Hel   1 regt with 15 Mi-24 *Hind**; 13 Mi-8 *Hip*; 7 PZL MI-2 *Hoplite*

EQUIPMENT BY TYPE

AIRCRAFT 47 combat capable

  FTR 37: 23 MiG-25PD *Foxbat* (+9 in store); 4 MiG-21 *Fishbed* (+1 in store)

  FGA 15: 6 Su-25 *Frogfoot*; 5 Su-24 *Fencer*; 4 Su-17 *Fitter*

  TPT 4: 1 An-12 *Cub*; 3 Yak-40 *Codling*

  TRG 46: 28 L-29 *Delfin*; 12 L-39 *Albatros*; 3 MiG-25PU *Foxbat**; 1 Su-17U *Fitter*; 2 Su-25UB *Frogfoot B**

HELICOPTERS

  ATK 15 Mi-24 *Hind**

  SPT 20: 13 Mi-8 *Hip*; 7 PZL MI-2 *Hoplite*

AD • SAM 100 SA-2 *Guideline* towed/SA-3 *Goa*/SA-5 *Gammon* static

Paramilitary ε15,000

Border Guard ε5,000

Ministry of Internal Affairs

AIFV 168: 168 BMP-1/BMP-2

APC (W) 19 BTR-60/BTR-70/BTR-80

PATROL AND COASTAL COMBATANTS 4

  PFI 2 *Stenka*

  PCI 2 (ex-US)

Militia 10,000+

Ministry of Internal Affairs

APC (W) 7 BTR-60/BTR-70/BTR-80

DEPLOYMENT

AFGHANISTAN

NATO • ISAF 22

IRAQ

MNF • *Operation Iraqi Freedom* 150

SERBIA

NATO • KFOR • *Joint Enterprise* 35

NON-STATE ARMED GROUPS

see Part II

Belarus Bel

Belarusian Ruble r		2006	2007	2008
GDP	r	79.2tr	94.5tr	
	US$	37bn	44bn	
per capita	US$	3,784	4,520	
Growth	%	9.9	7.8	
Inflation	%	7.0	8.1	
Def exp	US$			
Def bdgt	r	599bn	1.13tr	
	US$	279m	525m	
US$1=r		2,144	2.150	

Population 9,724,723

Age	0 – 14	15 – 19	20 – 24	25 – 29	30 – 64	65 plus
Male	8%	4%	4%	4%	22%	5%
Female	8%	4%	4%	4%	24%	10%

Capabilities

ACTIVE 72,940 (Army 29,600 Air 18,170 Joint 25,170) **Paramilitary 110,000**
Terms of service 9–12 months

RESERVE 289,500 (Joint 289,500 with mil service within last 5 years)

ORGANISATIONS BY SERVICE

Joint 25,170 (Centrally controlled units and MOD staff)

Army 29,600
FORCES BY ROLE

MoD Comd Tps
SF   1 bde
SSM   2 bde
Sigs   2 bde

Ground Forces
Arty	1 gp (5 bde) (5 arty bde)
Cbt engr	1 bde
Engr bridging	1 bde
NBC	1 regt
Mob	2 bde

North Western Op Comd
Mech	1 indep bde
Arty	2 regt
MRL	1 regt
SAM	1 bde

Western Op Comd
Mech	2 indep bde
Arty	2 regt

MRL	1 regt
Engr	1 regt
SAM	1 bde

EQUIPMENT BY TYPE
MBT 1,586: 92 T-80; 1,465 T-72; 29 T-55
AIFV 1,588: 154 BMD-1; 109 BMP-1; 1,164 BMP-2; 161 BRM
APC 916
    APC (T) 88: 22 BTR-D; 66 MT-LB
    APC (W) 828: 188 BTR-60; 446 BTR-70; 194 BTR-80
ARTY 1,499
    SP 578: **122mm** 246 2S1 *Carnation*; **152mm** 296: 13 2S19 *Farm*; 163 2S3; 120 2S5; **203mm** 36 2S7
    TOWED 452: **122mm** 202 D-30; **152mm** 250: 50 2A36; 136 2A65; 58 D-20; 6 M-1943
    GUN/MOR 120mm 54 2S9 *NONA*
    MRL 338: **122mm** 213: 5 9P138; 208 BM-21; **132mm** 1 BM-13; **220mm** 84 9P140 *Uragan*; **300mm** 40 9A52 *Smerch*
    MOR 120mm 77 2S12
AT • MSL • MANPATS 480 AT-4 9K11 *Spigot*/AT-5 9K111 *Spandrel*/AT-6 9K114 *Spiral*/AT-7 9K115 *Saxhorn* (some SP)
AD • SAM • SP 350 SA-11 *Gadfly*/SA-12A *Gladiator*/SA-12B *Giant (Twin)*/SA-13 *Gopher*/SA-8 *Gecko* (700–2,100 eff.)
RADAR • LAND GS-13 *Long Eye*/SNAR-1 *Long Trough*/SNAR-2/-6 *Pork Trough* (arty); some *Small Fred*/*Small Yawn*/SNAR-10 *Big Fred* (veh, arty)
MSL • TACTICAL • SSM 96: 36 FROG/SS-21 *Scarab* (*Tochka*); 60 *Scud*

Air Force and Air Defence Forces 18,170
Flying hours   15 hrs/year

FORCES BY ROLE
Ftr	2 bases with 23 Su-27P *Flanker-B*/Su-27UB *Flanker C*; 41 MiG-29S *Fulcrum C*/MiG-29UB *Fulcrum*
FGA/recce	4 sqn with 35 Su-24MK *Fencer D*/Su-24MR *Fencer-E*; 76 Su-25 *Frogfoot*/Su-25UB *Frogfoot B*
Tpt	1 base with 3 An-12 *Cub*; 1 An-24 *Coke*; 6 An-26 *Curl*; 4 IL-76 *Candid*; 1 Tu-134 *Crusty*
Trg	sqns with L-39 *Albatros*
Atk hel	sqns with 50 Mi-24 *Hind*
Spt hel	some (combat) sqn with 8 Mi-24K *Hind G2*; 29 Mi-6 *Hook*; 8 Mi-24R *Hind G1*; 125 Mi-8 *Hip*; 14 Mi-26 *Halo*

EQUIPMENT BY TYPE
AIRCRAFT 175 combat capable
    FTR/FGA 175: 23 Su-27P *Flanker-B* FTR/Su-27UB *Flanker C*; 35 Su-24MK *Fencer D* FGA/Su-24MR *Fencer-E* recce; 41 MiG-29S *Fulcrum C* MiG-29 FTR/MiG-29UB *Fulcrum* MiG-29U; 76 Su-25 *Frogfoot* FGA/Su-25UB *Frogfoot B*
    TPT 27: 3 An-12 *Cub*; 1 An-24 *Coke*; 6 An-26 *Curl*; 4 Il-76 *Candid*; (+12 Il-76 civil available for mil use); 1 Tu-134 *Crusty*
    TRG L-39 *Albatros*
HELICOPTERS
    ATK 50 Mi-24 *Hind*
    RECCE 8 Mi-24K *Hind G2*

Europe
(Non-NATO)

SPT 176: 14 Mi-26 *Halo*; 29 Mi-6 *Hook*; 8 Mi-24R *Hind G1*; 125 Mi-8 *Hip*; 4 Mi-24R *Hind G1*

MSL

ASM AS-10 *Karen*; AS-11 *Kilter*; AS-14 *Kedge*
ARM: AS-11 *Kilter*
AAM AA-10 *Alamo*; AA-11 *Archer*; AA-7 *Apex*; AA-8 *Aphid*

Air Defence

AD data from Uzal Baranovichi EW radar
1 AD bde (2 bn) with SAM/AAA units, ECM/ECCM units
AD • SAM 175 SA-10 *Grumble* (quad) SP/SA-3 *Goa*/SA-5 *Gammon* static (175–700 eff.). First S-300PS delivered to replace SA-3

Paramilitary 110,000

Border Guards 12,000
Ministry of Interior

Militia 87,000
Ministry of Interior

Ministry of Interior Troops 11,000

FOREIGN FORCES

Russia: Military Air Forces: 4 SAM units eqpt with SA-10 *Grumble* (quad)

Bosnia–Herzegovina BiH

Converted Mark		2006	2007	2008
GDP	mark	17.7bn	22.0bn	
	US$	11.4bn	14.3bn	
per capita	US$	2,538	3.136	
Growth	%	6.0	5.8	
Inflation	%	7.5	2.5	
Def bdgt	mark	220m		
	US$	142m		
FMA (US	US$	8.9m	9.0m	
US$1=mark		1.55	1.38	

Population	4,552,198

Age	0 – 14	15 – 19	20 – 24	25 – 29	30 – 64	65 plus
Male	10%	4%	4%	4%	25%	5%
Female	9%	4%	4%	4%	24%	6%

Capabilities

ACTIVE 9,047 (State Joint Operational Command 21 State Joint Staff 19 AFBiH 9007)

The 1995 Dayton Peace Accords had allowed BiH's two entities (The [Muslim-Croat] 'Federation of Bosnia and Herzegovina' and the [Serbian] 'Republika Srpska') to keep the armed forces they had established throughout the armed conflict in 1992 - 1995, with no State armed forces or State control over the Entities' forces. A defence reform process initiated in 2003 resulted in the merger of these separate armies into a single State army by January 2006. By that date, the Entities' defence competencies were completely abolished, as were conscription and the former large reserve forces. The State Forces now consist of three mixed brigades and an air force /air defence regiment and a minor reserve component (about 50% of the standing forces) consisting of former professional soldiers.

ORGANISATIONS BY SERVICE

State Joint Staff 19

State Joint Operational Command 21

AFBiH 9,007

FORCES BY ROLE

Op   1 comd
Mech   3 Mech bde
Spt   1 comd, 1 bde (1 Trg comd, 1 Log unit)

EQUIPMENT BY TYPE

Due to the restructuring process, inconsistencies may exist. The increase from 2006/2007 results from the ongoing transfer of equipment from the Entities to the State armed forces. Numbers now also include stored armaments.

MBT 325: 71 M-84; 50 AMX-30; 45 M-60A3; 142 T-55; 12 T-54, 5 T-34
ACV 1 PT-76
AIFV 132: 25 AMX-10P; 107 M-80
APC 193
  APC (T) 80 M-113A2
  APC (W) 113: 59 BOV, 15 variants; 3 BTR-70; 29 OT-60, 7 variants
ARTY 754+
  SP 122mm 24 2S1 *Carnation*
  TOWED 730: **105mm** 161: 36 L-118 *Light Gun*; 24 M-2A1; 101 M-56; **122mm** 268 D-30; **130mm** 74: 61 M-46; 13 M-82; **152mm** 30: 13 D-20; 17 M-84 **155mm** 197: 119 M-114A2; 78 M-1
  MRL 147: **107mm** 28 Type-63; **122mm** 42: 1 BM-21; 5 GRAD; 36 APR 40; **128mm** 76: 21 M-63; 20 M-77; 35 M-91; **262mm** 1 SVLR
  MOR 568: **82mm** 57; **120mm** 511: 24 M-74; 425 M-75; 23 UK-2; 12 UB M-52; 11 HADID; 16 KROM
AT • MSL
  SP 156: 98 AT-3 9K11 *Sagger* on BMP M-80; 10 *Lovac Tenkova* M-92; 8 POLO 9P122; 9 POLO 9P133; 31 POLO M-83
  MANPATS 260: 157 AT-3 9K11 *Sagger* / *Milan*; 52 AT-4 *Spigot*; 51 HJ-8
  GUNS 100mm 147 MT-12/T-12
AD • SAM
  TOWED SA-2 *Guideline*
  MANPAD SA-14 *Gremlin*; SA-16 *Gimlet*
  GUNS 19+
  SP 20mm BOV-3 SPAAG
  TOWED 19+: **20mm** M-55; **23mm** 19 ZU-23; **30mm** M-53; **57mm** S-60
MSL • SSM 8 FROG-7

Air Wing

FORCES BY ROLE

Avn   1 Avn regt

EQUIPMENT BY TYPE

AC 17 combat capable
  FGA 13: 6 J-21 (J-1) *Jastreb*; 7 J-22 *Orao 1*
  RECCE 2 IJ-21 (RJ-1) *Jastreb*
  TRG 7: 1 G-4 *Super Galeb**; 3 NJ-21 (TJ-1) *Jastreb**; 3 UTVA-75
HEL
  SPT 5: 4 Mi-8; 1 Mi-17 (Mi-8MT) *Hip H*
  UTL 16: 1 Mi-34 *Hermit*; 15 UH-1H *Iroquois*

DEPLOYMENT

DEMOCRATIC REPUBLIC OF CONGO

UN • MONUC 5 obs

ETHIOPIA/ERITREA

UN • UNMEE 5 obs

IRAQ

MNF • *Operation Iraqi Freedom* 49

FOREIGN FORCES

All countries part of EUFOR element, *Operation Althea*
Albania 70
Austria 178; 5 EUMM
Bulgaria 115
Canada 8 NATO HQ (*Op Bronze*)
Chile 21
Czech Republic 5
Estonia 3
Finland 64
France 73 (*Operation Astree*)
Germany 235; 28 SPz-2 *Luchs* RECCE; TPz-1 *Fuchs* APC (W); 3 CH-53 *Sea Stallion* Spt Hel; 4 UH-1D *Iroquois* Utl Hel
Greece 45; 1 C-130 *Hercules* Tpt Ac
Hungary 158
Ireland 25; 1 OSCE
Italy 363
Latvia 1
Lithuania 1
Luxembourg 1; 5 E3-A *Sentry* AEW Ac
Netherlands 67
New Zealand 3 EUFOR Liaison Team
Norway 2
Poland 203; 2 Inf coy
Portugal 14
Romania 49
Slovakia 42;
Slovenia 58
Spain 284
Sweden 24
Switzerland Air Force: 2 AS-532 Utl Hel; 26
Turkey 253
United Kingdom 21
United States Army: 207 (of which Army 175; Navy 15; USAF 10;USMC 7)

Croatia Cr

Croatian Kuna k		2006	2007	2008
GDP	k	251bn	268bn	
	US$	43.1bn	51.9bn	
per capita	US$	9,579	11,559	
Growth	%	4.8	5.6	
Inflation	%	3.2	2.3	
Def bdgt	k	4.04bn	4.51bn	
	US$	693m	875m	
US$1=k		5.83	5.16	

Population   4,493,312

Age	0 – 14	15 – 19	20 – 24	25 – 29	30 – 64	65 plus
Male	9%	3%	4%	3%	23%	6%
Female	8%	3%	3%	3%	24%	10%

Capabilities

ACTIVE 17,660 (Army 12,300 Navy 1,700 Air 1,800 Joint 1,860) **Paramilitary 3,000**

The armed forces of Croatia are subject to arms limitations established under the Dayton Peace Accord. An agreement signed by BiH, its two entities, Cr and FRY on 14 June 1996, established ceilings for holdings of the armed forces of the parties.

Terms of service 6 months. The active total is reported to be up to 31,500.

RESERVE 105,550 (Army 95,000 Navy 8,300 Air 2,250)

ORGANISATIONS BY SERVICE

Joint 1,860 (General Staff)

Army 11,000; 1,300 conscript (total 12,300)

FORCES BY ROLE

Army	2 corps
Armd	2 bde; 1 regt
SF	1 bn
MRL	1 regt
AT	1 regt
ADA	1 regt
Engr	1 regt
Gd	3 regt (org varies)
MP	1 regt

EQUIPMENT BY TYPE

MBT 297: 72 M-84; 3 T-72M; 192 T55; 30 decomissioning
RECCE 1 BRDM-2
AIFV 104: 103 M80; 1 decomissioning
APC 33
  APC (T) 8 M-60PB
  APC (W) 25: 9 BOV-VP; 15 BTR-50; 1 decomissioning

ARTY 1,452

  SP 122mm 8 2S1 *Carnation*

  TOWED 411: **105mm** 146: 61 M-2A1; 29 decomissioning; 56 M-56H1 decomissioning; **122mm** 71: 42 D-30; 29 *M-1938* decomissioning; **130mm** 79: 49 M-46H1; 30 decomissioning; **152mm** 42: 21 D-20; 18 M-84; 3 M 84H1; **155mm** 37: 30 M-1H1; 7 decomissioning; **203mm** 22 M-2 decomissioning

  MRL 222

    SP 42: **122mm** 40: 36 SVLR M96 *Typhoon*; 4 decomissioning; **262mm** 2 M-87 *Orkan*

    TOWED 128mm 180: 68 VLR 128 M91A3; 112 decomissioning

  MOR 804: **82mm** 475: 339 LMB M96; 136 decomissioning; **120mm** 329: 208 M-75; 115 decomissioning; 6 UBM 52

AT • MSL 567

  SP 45 POLO BOV 83

  MANPATS 522+: 418 AT-3 9K11 *Sagger*; 81 AT-4 9K111 *Spigot*; 23 AT-7 9K115 *Saxhorn*; *Milan* (reported)

  RL 73mm RPG-22 *Net*/RPG-7 *Knout*; **90mm** M-79

  GUNS 100mm 132 T-12

AD • GUNS 463

  SP 62: **20mm** 45: 44 BOV-3 SP; 1 decomissioning; **30mm** 17 BOV-3

  TOWED 401: **20mm** 390: 177; 213 decomissioning; **40mm** 11

Navy 1,450; 250 conscript (total 1,700)

Navy Central Command located at Split, with two naval districts; NAVSOUTH and NAVNORTH

FORCES BY ROLE

Navy 1 HQ located at Split

EQUIPMENT BY TYPE

SUBMARINES • TACTICAL 2 SDV

PRINCIPAL SURFACE COMBATANTS • CORVETTES

 • **FSG** 2 *Kralj Petar* each with 2–4 twin (8 eff.) each with RBS-15B tactical SSM

PATROL AND COASTAL COMBATANTS 5

  PFM 1 *Rade Koncar* with 2 twin (4 eff.) each with RBS-15B tactical SSM

  PCC 4 *Mirna*

MINE WARFARE • MINE COUNTERMEASURES 1

MHI 1 *Korcula*

AMPHIBIOUS

  LCT 2

  LCVP 4

LOGISTICS AND SUPPORT 3:

  AGS 1 *Moma* (FSU, trg); **ASR** 1; **AKL** 1;

FACILITIES

Bases   Located at Split, Pula, Sibenik, Dubrovnik, Ploce

Minor Bases Located at Lastovo, Vis

Coastal Defence

FORCES BY ROLE

SSM 3 bty with RBS-15K

Arty 21+ bty

EQUIPMENT BY TYPE

MSL • TACTICAL • SSM RBS-15K

Marines

Inf 2 indep coy

Air Force and Air Defence 1,600; 200 conscript (total 1,800)

Flying hours 50 hrs/year

FORCES BY ROLE

Two air bases

Ftr/FGA	1 sqn with 8 MiG-21bis; 1 trg sqn with 4 MiG-21 UMD *Fishbed*
Tpt	1 tpt ac sqn, 2 tpt hel sqn
Firefighting	1 sqn
Trg	1 trg ac sqn, 1 trg hel sqn

EQUIPMENT BY TYPE

AIRCRAFT 12 combat capable

  FTR 12: 8 MiG-21bis; 4 MiG-21UMD *Fishbed*

  TPT 2 An-32 *Cline*

  Firefighting 5: 1 AT-802F *Air Tractor*; 4 Canadair CL-415

  UTL/TRG 24: 20 PC-9M; 4 UTVA-75 being replaced by 5 Zlin Z242L (basic trg)

HELICOPTERS

  SPT 14: 11 Mi-8MTV, 3 Mi-8T

  UTL 8 Bell 206B *JetRanger II*

AD • RADAR 8: 5 FPS-117; 3 S-600

AD • SAM

  SP SA-10 *Grumble* (quad); SA-9 *Gaskin*

  MANPAD SA-14 *Gremlin*; SA-16 *Gimlet*

MSL • AAM AA-2 *Atoll*; AA-8 *Aphid*

Paramilitary 3,000

Police 3,000 armed

DEPLOYMENT

AFGHANISTAN

NATO • ISAF 199

BURUNDI

UN •BINUB 1 obs

CYPRUS

UN • UNFICYP 4

CÔTE D'IVOIRE

UN • UNOCI 2 obs

ETHIOPIA/ERITREA

UN • UNMEE 4 obs

GEORGIA

UN • UNOMIG 3 obs

HAITI

UN • MINUSTAH 3

INDIA/PAKISTAN
UN • UNMOGIP 8 obs

LEBANON
UN • UNIFIL 1

LIBERIA
UN • UNMIL 5

NEPAL
UN • UNMIN 2 obs

SIERRA LEONE
UN • UNIOSIL 1 obs

SUDAN
UN • UNMIS 5

WESTERN SAHARA
UN • MINURSO 7 obs

FOREIGN FORCES

United Kingdom spt tps; spt/log tps

Cyprus Cy

Cypriot Pound C£		2006	2007	2008
GDP	C£	8.3bn	8.8bn	
	US$	18.4bn	21.5bn	
per capita	US$	23,517	27,222	
Growth	%	3.8	3.8	
Inflation	%	2.5	2.1	
Def bdgt	C£	139m	142m	
	US$	308m	346m	
US$1=C£		0.45	0.41	

Population   788,457

Age	0 – 14	15 – 19	20 – 24	25 – 29	30 – 64	65 plus
Male	11%	4%	4%	3%	22%	5%
Female	10%	4%	4%	3%	22%	6%

Capabilities

ACTIVE 10,000 (National Guard 10,000)
Paramilitary 750
Terms of service conscription, 25 months, then reserve to age 50 (officers 65)

RESERVE 60,000 (National Guard 60,000)

ORGANISATIONS BY SERVICE

National Guard 1,300; 8,700 conscript (total 10,000)

FORCES BY ROLE

Home Guard	1 comd HQ
Army	1 corps HQ
Navy	1 comd HQ
Air	1 comd HQ
Armd	1 bde (3 armd bn)
SF	1 comd (regt) (3 SF bn)
Lt inf	2 div HQ; 2 bde HQ
Arty	1 comd (regt)
Spt	1 (svc) bde

EQUIPMENT BY TYPE
MBT 154: 41 T-80U; 61 AMX-30; 52 AMX-30 B2
RECCE 139: 15 EE-3 *Jararaca*; 124 EE-9 *Cascavel*
AIFV 43 BMP-3
APC 310
   APC (T) 184: 16 AMX-VCI; 168 *Leonidas*
   APC (W) 126 VAB (incl variants)
ARTY 562+
   SP 155mm 24: 12 Mk F3; 12 *Zuzana*
   TOWED 140: **88mm** 36 25-PDR in store; **100mm** 20 M-1944; **105mm** 72 M-56; **155mm** 12 TR-F-1
   MRL 22: **122mm** 4 BM-21; **128mm** 18 M-63 *Plamen*
   MOR 376+: **81mm** 240+: 70+ M-1/M-29 in store; 170 E-44; **107mm** 20 M-2/M-30; **120mm** 116 RT61
AT • MSL • MANPATS 67: 22 HOT; 45 *Milan*
   RCL 184: **106mm** 144 M-40A1; **90mm** 40 EM-67
   RL 1,850+: **66mm** M-72 *LAW*; **73mm** 850 RPG-7 *Knout*; **112mm** 1,000 APILAS
AD • SAM 90
   SP 6 SA-15 *Gauntlet*; *Mistral*
   STATIC 24 *Aspide*
   MANPAD 60 *Mistral*
   GUNS • TOWED 80: **20mm** 36 M-55; **35mm** 24 GDF-003 (with *Skyguard*); **40mm** 20 M-1 in store

Maritime Wing

FORCES BY ROLE
SSM 1 (coastal defence) bty with 3 MM-40 *Exocet*

EQUIPMENT BY TYPE
PATROL AND COASTAL COMBATANTS 6
   PCC 6: 1 *Kyrenia* (Gr *Dilos*); 2 *Rodman 55*; 1 *Salamis*; 2 *Cantieri Vittoria*
MSL • TACTICAL • SSM 3 MM-40 *Exocet*

Air Wing

AIRCRAFT
   TPT 1 BN-2 *Islander*
   TRG 2 PC-9
HELICOPTERS
   ATK 16: 12 Mi-35P *Hind*; 4 SA-342 *Gazelle* (with HOT)
   SPT 2 PZL MI-2 *Hoplite* in store
   UTL 4: 2 Bell 206C *JetRanger III*; 2 UH-1H *Iroquois*

Paramilitary 750+

Armed Police 500+

FORCES BY ROLE
Mech 1 (rapid-reaction) unit

EQUIPMENT BY TYPE
APC (W) 2 VAB VTT
AIRCRAFT • TPT 1 BN-2A *Defender*
HELICOPTERS • UTL 2 Bell 412 *Twin Huey*

Maritime Police 250
PATROL AND COASTAL COMBATANTS 10
   PCC 7: 5 *SAB-12*; 2 *Cantieri Vittoria*
   PFI 3: 2 *Evagoras*; 1 *Shaldag*

FOREIGN FORCES

Argentina 1 inf bn; 294 UNFICYP
Austria 5 UNFICYP
Canada 1 UNFICYP *(Op Snowgoose)*
Croatia 4 UNFICYP
Greece Army: 1 armd bn; 1 (incl 950 (ELDYK) army) mech bde; 2 mech inf bn; 1 arty bn; 61 M-48A5 MOLF MBT; 80 *Leonidas* APC (T); 12 M-114 155mm towed; 6 M-107 175mm SP; 6 M-110A2 203mm SP; 950 (ELDYK army); ε200 (officers/NCO seconded to Greek-Cypriot National Guard)
Hungary 84 UNFICYP
Slovakia 196 UNFICYP
United Kingdom Air Force: 1 SAR sqn with Bell 412 *Twin Huey*; 1 Hel sqn with 4 Bell 412 *Twin Huey*; 1 Inf bn UNFICYP; 1 (spt) engr sqn UNFICYP; 269 UNFICYP; Army: 2,110; 2 inf bn; 1 (spt) engr sqn; 1 hel flt; Air Force: 1,140; ac (on det); 1 land (on det); Royal Navy: 25, 276 UNFICYP
United States Army 3; USAF 8; USMC 11

AREAS WHERE THE GOVERNMENT DOES NOT EXERCISE EFFECTIVE CONTROL

Data presented here represent the de facto situation on the island. This does not imply international recognition as a sovereign state.

Capabilities

ACTIVE 5,000 (Army 5,000) **Paramilitary 150**
Terms of service conscription, 24 months, then reserve to age 50.

RESERVE 26,000 (first line 11,000 second line 10,000 third line 5,000)

ORGANISATIONS BY SERVICE

Army ε5,000
FORCES BY ROLE
Inf 7 bn

EQUIPMENT BY TYPE
ARTY
   MOR 73 **120mm**
AT
   MSL • MANPATS 6 *Milan*
   RCL 36 **106mm**

Paramilitary

Armed Police ε150
SF 1 (Police) unit

Coast Guard
PATROL AND COASTAL COMBATANTS 6
   PCC 5: 2 SG45/SG46; 1 *Rauf Denktash*; 2 US Mk 5
   PCI 1

FOREIGN FORCES

TURKEY
ARMY ε36,000
   1 army corps HQ, some air det, 1 armd bde, 1 indep mech inf bde, 2 inf div, 1 cdo regt, 1 arty bde, 1 avn comd
EQUIPMENT BY TYPE
   MBT 8 M-48A2 MBT
   TRG 441 M-48A5T1/M-48A5T2
   APC (T) 627: 361 AAPC (T) (incl variants); 266 M-113 (T) (incl variants)
   ARTY
      SP 155mm 90 M-44T
      TOWED 102; **105mm** 72 M-101A1; **155mm** 18 M-114A2; **203mm** 12 M-115
      MRL 122mm 6 T-122
      MOR 450: **81mm** 175; **107mm** 148 M-30; **120mm** 127 HY-12
   AT
      MSL • MANPATS 114: 66 *Milan*; 48 TOW
      RCL 106mm 192 M-40A1; **90mm** M-67
      RL 66mm M-72 *LAW*
   AD • GUNS
      TOWED 20mm Rh 202; **35mm** 16 GDF-003; **40mm** 48 M-1
   AC 3 U-17 Utl
      HEL 4: 1 AS-532UL *Cougar* utl; 3 UH-1H *Iroquois* utl
PATROL AND COASTAL COMBATANTS 1 PCI less than 100 tonnes

Finland SF

Euro €		2006	2007	2008
GDP	€	168bn	177bn	
	US$	210bn	253bn	
per capita	US$	40,142	48,269	
Growth	%	5.0	4.3	
Inflation	%	1.3	1.4	
Def exp	€	2.20bn		
	US$	2.75bn		
Def bdgt	€	2.27bn	2.22bn	2.37bn
	US$	2.84bn	3.17bn	
US$1=€		0.80	0.70	

Population   5,238,460

Age	0 – 14	15 – 19	20 – 24	25 – 29	30 – 64	65 plus
Male	9%	3%	3%	3%	24%	6%
Female	9%	3%	3%	3%	24%	10%

Capabilities

ACTIVE 29,300 (Army 20,500 Navy 4,100 Air 4,700)
Paramilitary 3,100
Terms of Service 6-9-12 months (12 months for officers NCOs and soldiers with special duties. 35,000 reservists a year do refresher training: total obligation 40 days (75 for NCOs 100 for officers) between conscript service and age 50 (NCOs and officers to age 60). Reserve total reducing to 340,000.

RESERVE 237,000 (Army 202,000 Air 35,000)
Paramilitary 18,900

ORGANISATIONS BY SERVICE

Army 4,900; 15,600 conscript (total 20,500)
FORCES BY ROLE
Has no peacetime structure. All brigades are reserve based, re-organisation underway, to be complete by 2008. This involves the replacement of the present commands with seven Military Provinces.

Comd	1 (Western) comd (6 Provincial mil districts); 1 (Northern) comd (2 Provincial mil districts); 1 (Eastern) comd (4 Provincial mil districts)
Armd	1 bde with (3 armd bn, 1 AT coy, 1 Fd arty regt, 1 (armd) sigs bn, 1 AD bn, 1 Log bn, 1 engr bn, 1 Armd Recce coy)
Jaeger	1 bde with (4 Jaeger bn, 1 AT coy, 1 HQ coy, 1 sigs coy, 1 AD bn, 1 engr bn, 1 Fd arty regt, 1 Log coy, 1 Recce coy)

EQUIPMENT BY TYPE
MBT 163: 100 *Leopard* 2 A4; 63 T-72
AIFV 182: 60 BMP-1PS; 15 BMP-1TJ; 50 BMP-2; 57 CV90
APC 538
   APC (T) 120: 16 MT-LBU; 98 MT-LBV; 6 BTR-50P
   APC (W) 418: 110 BTR-60; 260 XA-180 *Sisu*/XA-185 *Sisu*; 48 XA-203 *Sisu*
ARTY 1,389
   SP 90 **122mm** PsH 74 (2S1) *Carnation*/**152mm** Telak 91 (2S5)
   TOWED 684: **122mm** 414 H 63 (D-30); **130mm** 36 K 54; **152mm** 180 H 88-38/H 88–40; **155mm** 54 K 83/K 98
   MOR 120mm 615 KRH 92
HEL • SPT 7 Mi-8 *Hip*
UAV • TACTICAL 6 *Ranger*
AD • SAM
   SP ITO 90 (*Crotale* NG); ITO 96 (SA-11) *Gadfly*
   MANPAD ITO 86 (SA-16) *Gimlet*; ITO 86M (SA-18) *Grouse (Igla)*
GUNS 23mm; 30mm; 35mm; 57mm

Reserve Organisations

Reserves 100,000 reservists on mobilisation; 75,000 reservists on mobilisation (local forces); 27,000 reservists on mobilisation (territorial) (total 202,000)
Army 230+ bn (and coys)
Armd 2 bde

Jaeger	9 bde
Inf	11 bde
Engr	16 bn
AD	3 regt

Navy 2,100; 2,000 conscript (total 4,100)
EQUIPMENT BY TYPE
PATROL AND COASTAL COMBATANTS 12
PFM 10:
   4 *Hamina* each with 2 twin (4 eff.) with 4 15SF (RBS-15M) RBS-15 SSM, 1 *Sadral* sextuple with *Mistral* SAM
   2 *Helsinki* each with 4 twin (8 eff.) with 8 15SF (RBS-15M) RBS-15 SSM, 2 *Sadral* sextuple each with *Mistral* SAM
   4 *Rauma* each with 2 single with 2 15SF (RBS-15M) RBS-15 SSM, 2 twin (4 eff.) with 4 15SF (RBS-15M) RBS-15 SSM, 1 *Sadral* sextuple with *Mistral* SAM
PCC 2 *Kiisla*
MINE WARFARE 19
   MINE COUNTERMEASURES • MSI 13: 7 *Kiiski*; 6 *Kuha*
   MINELAYERS • ML 6:
      2 *Hameenmaa* each with 1 *Sadral* sextuple with *Mistral* SAM, 2 RBU 1200 (10 eff.), up to 150–200 mine (undergoing upgrade programme)
      3 *Pansio* each with 50 mine
      1 *Pohjanmaa* with up to 100–150 mine
AMPHIBIOUS
   LCU 7: 2 *Kala*; 3 *Kampela*; 2 *Lohi*
   LCP 66: 36 *Jurmo*; 30 *Meriuisko*
LOGISTICS AND SUPPORT 30:
   AGF 1 *Kustaanmiekka*
   AKSL 15: 6 *Hauki*; 4 *Hila*; 5 *Valas*
   AGB 9: 2 *Karhuj*; 2 *Urho*; 2 *Tarmo*; 2 *Fennica*; 1 *Botnica*
   TRG 4: 2 *Lokki*; 2
   TRIAL 1
FACILITIES

Base	Located at Upinniemi (Helsinki)
Naval airbase	Located at Turku

Coastal Defence
ARTY •COASTAL 158: **130mm** 102: 30 K-53 tk (static); 72 K-54 RT; **100mm** 56 (TK) tank turrets
MSL • TACTICAL • SSM 4 RBS-15K

Air Force 3,100; 1,600 conscript (total 4,700)
Wartime strength – 35,000
3 Air Comds: Satakunta (West), Karelia (East), Lapland (North). Each Air Comd assigned to one of the 3 AD areas into which SF is divided. 3 ftr wings, one in each AD area.

Flying hours   120 hrs/year

FORCES BY ROLE

FGA	3 wg with 54 F/A-18C *Hornet*; 7 F/A-18D *Hornet*
Advanced AD/ Attack trg/recce	3 sqn with 49 *Hawk* MK50/*Hawk* MK51A;1 F-27 *Maritime Enforcer* (ESM/ Elint)

Tpt	1 sqn with 2 C-295M; 1 F-27 *Friendship*; 3 *Learjet* 35A
Liaison	4 sqn with 6 PA-31-350 *Piper Chieftain*; 9 L-90 *Redigo*
Survey	1 sqn with 3 *Learjet* 35A (survey, ECM trg, target-towing)
Trg	Trg unit with 28 L-70 *Vinka*

EQUIPMENT BY TYPE
AIRCRAFT 61 combat capable
  FGA 61: 54 F/A-18C *Hornet*; 7 F/A-18D *Hornet*
  ASW 1 F-27 *Maritime Enforcer* (ESM/Elint)
  TPT 15: 2 C-295M; 1 F-27 *Friendship*; 3 *Learjet* 35A; 3 (survey; ECM trg; tgt-tow); 6 PA-31-350 *Piper Chieftain*
  TRG 86: 49 *Hawk* MK50/*Hawk* MK51A; 28 L-70 *Vinka*; 9 L-90 *Redigo*
MSL • AAM AIM-120 *AMRAAM*; AIM-9 *Sidewinder*

Reservists 35,000 reservists

Paramilitary

Frontier Guard 3,100
Ministry of Interior. 4 Frontier and 2 Coast Guard Districts

FORCES BY ROLE

| Coast Guard | 6 (offshore patrol) sqn eqpt. with 7 ACV; 60 PB |
| Air | 1 (patrol) sqn eqpt. with 2 Do-228 (maritime surv); 3 AS-332 *Super Puma*; 3 AB-206L (Bell 206L) *LongRanger*; 4 AB-412 (Bell 412) *Twin Huey*; 1 AB-412EP (Bell 412EP) *Twin Huey* |

EQUIPMENT BY TYPE
ACV 7
PATROL AND COASTAL COMBATANTS 60 PB
AIRCRAFT • TPT 2 Do-228 (MP)
HELICOPTERS
  SPT 3 AS-332 *Super Puma*
  UTL 8: 4 AB-412 (Bell 412) *Twin Huey*; 1 AB-412EP (Bell 412EP) *Twin Huey*; 3 AB-206L (Bell 206L)

Reserve 18,900 reservists on mobilisation

DEPLOYMENT

AFGHANISTAN
NATO • ISAF 85

BOSNIA-HERZEGOVINA
EU • EUFOR • *Operation Althea* 64

CHAD/CENTRAL AFRICAN REPUBLIC
EU • EUFOR Chad/CAR 60

ETHIOPIA/ERITREA
UN • UNMEE 5 obs

INDIA/PAKISTAN
UN • UNMOGIP 6 obs

LEBANON
UN • UNIFIL II 205

LIBERIA
UN • UNMIL 1

MIDDLE EAST
UN • UNTSO 15 obs

NEPAL
UN • UNMIN 1 obs

SERBIA
NATO • KFOR • *Joint Enterprise* 450
UN • UNMIK 2 obs

SUDAN
UN • UNMIS 1

Georgia Ga

Georgian Lari		2006	2007	2008
GDP	lari	13.8bn	16.1bn	
	US$	7.8bn	9.8bn	
per capita	US$	1,663	2,113	
Growth	%	9.4	11.0	
Inflation	%	9.2	8.5	
Def bdgt	lari	604m	957m	
	US$	339m	583m	
FMA (US)	US$	11.9m	10.0m	10.0m
US$1=lari		1.78	1.64	

Population	4,646,003					

Age	0 – 14	15 – 19	20 – 24	25 – 29	30 – 64	65 plus
Male	10%	4%	4%	3%	21%	6%
Female	9%	4%	4%	3%	23%	9%

Capabilities

ACTIVE 21,150 (Army 17,767 Navy 495 Air 1,310 National Guard 1,578) **Paramilitary 11,700**
Terms of service conscription, 18 months

ORGANISATIONS BY SERVICE

Army 14,000; 3,767 conscript (total 17,767)
FORCES BY ROLE
1 land forces HQ

Recce	1 bn
MRR	2 bde
SF	1 bn
Marine inf	2 bn (1 cadre)
Arty	1 regt
Peacekeeping	1 bn

EQUIPMENT BY TYPE
MBT 128: 102 T-72; 23 T-55; 3 T-54
AIFV 91: 33 BMP-1; 57 BMP-2; 1 BRM-1K
APC 44

APC (T) 10 MT-LB
APC (W) 34: 1 BTR-60; 1 BTR-70; 32 BTR-80
ARTY 109
  SP 39: **152mm** 13 2S3; 24 DANA; 1 2S19 **203mm** 1 2S7
  TOWED 111: **122mm** 94 D-30; **3 M-30 152mm** 14: 3
  2A36; 11 2A65
  MRL 21: **122mm** 15 BM-21; 6 RM70
  MOR 65: **120mm** 26 M-120; 14 2B11;25 M75
AT ε50
  MSL ε10
  GUNS ε40
AD • SAM • SP SA-13 *Gopher*

Navy 495

FORCES BY ROLE

Navy 1 HQ located at Tbilisi

EQUIPMENT BY TYPE

PATROL AND COASTAL COMBATANTS 6
  PFM 1 *Anninos* (ex *La Combattante II*)
  PHM 1 *Matka*
  PCC 4: 2 *Dilos*; 1 *Turk*; 1 *Akhneta*
AMPHIBIOUS 2 LCU

FACILITIES

Bases Located at Tbilisi, Poti

Air Force 1,310 (incl 290 conscript)

1 avn base, 1 hel air base
AIRCRAFT 9 combat capable
  FGA 8: 3 Su-25 *Frogfoot*; 5 Su-25K *Frogfoot A*
  TPT 9: 6 An-2 *Colt*; 1 Tu-134A *Crusty* (VIP); 2 Yak-40
  Codling
  TRG 10: 9 L-29 *Delfin*; 1 Su-25UB *Frogfoot* B*
HELICOPTERS
  ATK 9 Mi-24 *Hind*
  SPT 19: 17 Mi-8T *Hip*; 2 Mi-14
  UTL 7 UH-1H *Iroquois*
AD • SAM 75 SA-2 *Guideline* towed/SA-3 *Goa*/SA-4
Ganef SP/SA-5 *Gammon* static/SA-7 *Grail* MANPAD
(75–150 eff.)

National Guard 1,578 active reservists opcon Army

MRR 1 bde (plus trg centre)

Paramilitary 11,700

Border Guard 5,400

Coast Guard
PATROL AND COASTAL COMBATANTS 14
PFC 1 *Stenka*
PCC 1 *Lindau*
PCI 12: 8 *Zhuk*; 2 *Point*; 2 *Dauntless* (all less than 100
tonnes)

Ministry of Interior Troops 6,300

DEPLOYMENT

IRAQ
MNF • *Operation Iraqi Freedom* 2,000

SERBIA
NATO • KFOR • *Joint Enterprise* 1 inf coy; 184

NON-STATE ARMED GROUPS

see Part II

FOREIGN FORCES

All UNOMIG unless otherwise specified
Albania 3 obs
Austria 2 obs
Bangladesh 8 obs
Bolivia 1 obs
Croatia 3 obs
Czech Republic 5 obs
Denmark 5 obs
Egypt 6 obs
France 3 obs;
Germany 12 obs
Greece 4 obs
Hungary 7 obs
Indonesia 4 obs
Ireland 1 OSCE
Jordan 7 obs
Korea, Republic of 7 obs
Lithuania 2 obs
Moldova 1 obs
Mongolia 1 obs
Nepal 1 obs
Nigeria 1 obs
Pakistan 10 obs
Poland 5 obs
Romania 2 obs
Russia 4 obs; ε1,500 (Abkhazia 15 Independent Pk Bde);
ε3,000 Trans Caucasus MD to be withdrawn from Batumi
Sweden 3 obs
Switzerland 4 obs
Turkey 5 obs
Ukraine 5 obs; 3 OSCE
United Kingdom 5 obs
United States 2 obs
Uruguay 4 obs
Yemen 1 obs

Europe (Non-NATO)

Ireland Irl

Euro €		2006	2007	2008
GDP	€	175bn	187bn	
	US$	219bn	267bn	
per capita	US$	53,850	65,013	
Growth	%	5.7	4.6	
Inflation	%	2.7	2.4	
Def bdgt	€	890m	970m	
	US$	1.11bn	1.38bn	
US$1=€		0.80	0.70	

Population   4,109,086

Age	0 – 14	15 – 19	20 – 24	25 – 29	30 – 64	65 plus
Male	11%	4%	4%	4%	22%	5%
Female	10%	4%	4%	4%	22%	6%

Capabilities

ACTIVE 10,460 (Army 8,500 Navy 1,110 Air 850)

RESERVE 14,875 (Army 14,500 Navy 300 Air 75)

ORGANISATIONS BY SERVICE

Army ε8,500

FORCES BY ROLE

Armd Recce   1 sqn

Inf   3 bde (each: 3 inf bn, 1 cav recce sqn, 1 fd arty regt (2 fd arty bty), 1 fd engr coy, 1 log bn)

Ranger   1 coy

AD   1 regt (1 AD bty)

Constr Engr   1 coy

EQUIPMENT BY TYPE

LT TK 14 Scorpion

RECCE 37: 18 AML-20; 19 AML-90

APC (W) 82: 80 Piranha III (incl variants); 2 XA-180 Sisu

ARTY 537

TOWED 66: **88mm** 42 25-PDR; **105mm** 24 L-118 Light Gun

MOR 471: **81mm** 400; **120mm** 71

AT

MSL • MANPATS 57: 36 Javelin; 21 Milan

RCL 84mm 444 Carl Gustav

RL 84mm AT-4

AD

SAM • MANPAD 7 RBS-70

GUNS • TOWED 40mm 32 L/70 each with 8 Flycatcher

Reserves 14,500 reservists

The Reserve consists of two levels. Of these the "Integrated" Reserve would provide nine rifle companies (one per regular infantry battalion, three cavalry troops (one per regular squadron) and three field batteries (one per regular field artillery regiment) on mobilization. The three reserve brigades form the 'Non-Integrated' Reserve and unlike the regular infantry battalions their component battalions have a variable number of rifle companies, five having four companies each, three having three and one having only two.

Inf   3 bde (Non Integrated)(each: 1 Fd arty regt (2 fd arty bty), 1 Fd engr coy, 1 cav recce sqn,1 log bn)

Inf   9 Coy (integrated); 9 inf bn (non integrated 31 coy)

Cav   3 Tps (integrated)

Arty   3 bty (integrated)

Log   1 bn

AD   3 bty

Navy 1,110

EQUIPMENT BY TYPE

PATROL AND COASTAL COMBATANTS 8

PSOH 1 Eithne with 1 hel landing platform (for Dauphin)

PSO 7: 3 Emer; 2 Orla (UK Peacock) each with 1 76mm gun; 2 Roisin each with 1 76mm gun

FACILITIES

Bases Located at Cork, Haulbowline

Air Corps 850

FORCES BY ROLE

Air   2 ops wg; 2 spt wg; 1 comms and info sqn; 1 air corps college

EQUIPMENT BY TYPE

AIRCRAFT

MP 2 CASA 235 MPA

Police Support 1 Bn Defender 4000

TPT 3: 1 Beech 200 Super King Air; 1 Gulfstream GIV; 1 Learjet 45 (VIP)

UTL 5 Cessna FR-172H

TRG 8 PC-9M

HELICOPTERS:

UTL 11: 2 EC-135 P2 (incl trg/medevac); 3 SA-316B Alouette III; 4 AW139 (2 more for delivery in 2008); 1 EC135 T2 and 1 AS 355N (police support);

DEPLOYMENT

AFGHANISTAN

NATO • ISAF 7

ALBANIA

OSCE 1

BELGIUM

11

BOSNIA-HERZEGOVINA

EU • EUFOR 25

OSCE 1

CHAD/CENTRAL AFRICAN REPUBLIC

EU • EUFOR Chad/CAR 400

CÔTE D'IVOIRE
UN • UNOCI 2 obs

DEMOCRATIC REPUBLIC OF CONGO
UN • MONUC 3 obs

GEORGIA
OSCE 1

LEBANON
UN • UNIFIL 166

LIBERIA
UN • UNMIL 2

MIDDLE EAST
UN • UNTSO 14 obs

MONTENEGRO
OSCE 1

SERBIA
NATO • KFOR • *Joint Enterprise* 220
OSCE 2
UN • UNMIK 4 obs

WESTERN SAHARA
UN • MINURSO 3 obs

Macedonia, Former Yugoslav Republic FYROM

Macedonian Denar d		2006	2007	2008
GDP	d	295bn	314bn	
	US$	6.0bn	7.2bn	
per capita	US$	2,948	3,519	
Growth	%	3.0	5.0	
Inflation	%	3.2	2.0	
Def bdgt	d	6.52bn	7.02bn	
	US$	133m	161m	
FMA (US)	US$	3.9m	3.6m	4.5m
US$1=d		48.8	43.4	

Population	2,055,915

Age	0 – 14	15 – 19	20 – 24	25 – 29	30 – 64	65 plus
Male	11%	4%	4%	4%	22%	5%
Female	10%	4%	4%	4%	22%	6%

Capabilities

ACTIVE 10,890 (Army 9,760 Air Force 1,130)
Paramilitary 7,600
Terms of service 6 months

RESERVE 21,000 (Joint 21,000)

ORGANISATIONS BY SERVICE

Army 9,760

FORCES BY ROLE
2 Corps HQ (cadre)
Tk	1 bn
Inf	2 bde
SF	1 (Special Purpose) unit (1 SF bn, 1 Ranger bn)
Arty	1 (mixed) regt
Engr	1 regt
Border	1 bde

EQUIPMENT BY TYPE
MBT 61: 31 T-72A; 30 T-55A
RECCE 51: 10 BRDM-2; 41 M-1114 HMMWV
AIFV 11: 10 BMP-2; 1 BMP-2K
APC 207
  APC (T) 48: 8 *Leonidas*; 30 M-113A; 10 MT-LB
  APC (W) 159: 58 BTR-70; 12 BTR-80; 89 TM-170 *Hermelin*
ARTY 944
  TOWED 209; **76mm** 65: 55 M-48 *M-1948*; 10 ZIS-3 *M-1942*; **105mm** 36: 18 M-2A1; 18 M-56; **122mm** 108 M-30 *M-1938*
  MRL 18: **122mm** 6 BM-21; **128mm** 12
  MOR 717: **60mm** 234; **82mm** 340; **120mm** 143
AT • MSL • MANPATS 12+: 12 *Milan*; AT-3 *Sagger*
  RCL 57mm; **82mm** M60A

Reserves
Inf	8 bde
Arty	1 regt
AT	1 regt
AD	1 regt

Marine Wing
PATROL AND COASTAL COMBATANTS
  PCR 4

Air Force 1,130
FORCES BY ROLE
FGA	1 sqn with 3 Su-25K *Frogfoot A* (in store); 1 Su-25UB *Frogfoot B* (in store)
Atk hel	1 sqn with 10 Mi-24V *Hind E*; 2 Mi-24K *Hind G2*
Trg	trg unit with 1 Z-143L; 3 Z-242
Trg hel	sqn with 2 UH-1H *Iroquois*
Tpt hel	1 sqn with 3 Mi-17 (Mi-8MT) *Hip H*; 4 Mi-8MTV *Hip H*
Surv	1 sqn with 1 Cessna 337 *Skymaster* on lease

EQUIPMENT BY TYPE
AIRCRAFT 4 combat capable (in store)
  FGA 3 Su-25K *Frogfoot A*; 1 Su-25UB *Frogfoot B* (in store)
  TPT 1 Cessna 337 *Skymaster* on lease (surv)
  TRG 4: 1 Z-143L; 3 Z-242
HELICOPTERS
  ATK 10 Mi-24V *Hind E*
  RECCE 2 Mi-24K *Hind G2*
  SPT 7: 3 Mi-17 (Mi-8MT) *Hip H*; 4 Mi-8MTV *Hip H*
  TRG 2 UH-1H *Iroquois*
  AD • SAM 67
    SP 8 SA-13 *Gopher*
    MANPAD 59: 5 SA-16 *Gimlet*; 54 SA-7 *Grail*

Paramilitary

Police 7,600 (some 5,000 armed)

incl 2 SF units

APC BTR APC (W)/M-113A APC (T)

HELICOPTERS • UTL 3: 1 AB-212 (Bell 212); 1 AB-206B (Bell 206B) *JetRanger II*; 1 Bell 412EP *Twin Huey*

DEPLOYMENT

AFGHANISTAN

NATO • ISAF 129

BOSNIA-HERZEGOVINA

EU • EUFOR • *Operation Althea* 29

IRAQ

MNF • *Operation Iraqi Freedom* 40

NON-STATE ARMED GROUPS

see Part II

Malta M

Maltese Lira ML		2006	2007	2008
GDP	ML	2.2bn	2.3bn	
	US$	6.7bn	7.7bn	
per capita	US$	16,658	19,077	
Growth	%	3.3	3.2	
Inflation	%	2.6	0.6	
Def bdgt	ML	15.1m	13.6m	
	US$	46m	45m	
US$1=ML		0.33	0.30	

Population 401,880

Age	0 – 14	15 – 19	20 – 24	25 – 29	30 – 64	65 plus
Male	9%	4%	4%	4%	23%	6%
Female	9%	3%	4%	4%	23%	8%

Capabilities

ACTIVE 1,609 (Armed Forces of Malta 1,609)

RESERVE 90 (Emergency Volunteer Reserve Force 40 Individual Reserve 50)

ORGANISATIONS BY SERVICE

Armed Forces of Malta 1,609

Comd HQ

Spt tps

No 1 (Infantry) Regt

Inf 1 bn (1 spt coy, 3 rifle coy, 1 HQ coy)

Maritime Squadron

The AFM maritime element is organised into 5 Divisions: Offshore Patrol; Inshore Patrol; Rapid deployment and Training; Marine Engineering and Logistics.

EQUIPMENT BY TYPE

PATROL AND COASTAL COMBATANTS 9

OPV 1 *Diciotti*

PCI 4: 2 *Bremse*; 2 *Swift*

PBC 2 *Marine Protector*

PB 2 *Cantieri Vittoria*

Air Wing

Wing HQ, 1 Base Party. 1 Flt Ops Div; 1 Maint Div; 1 Integrated Logs Div; 1 Rescue Section

EQUIPMENT BY TYPE

AIRCRAFT 4 combat capable (in store)

TPT/MP 2 BN-2B *Islander*

TRG 5 Bulldog T MK1

HELICOPTERS

SAR/UTL 7: 5 *Alouette* III SA-316B; 2 Nardi-Hughes 500M

TRG 2 Bell 47G2

AD • GUNS • TOWED 14.5mm 50 ZPU-4; **40mm** 40 L/70

No 3 (Support) Regt

Airport	1 coy
Ordnance	1 coy
Workshop	1 coy
HQ	1 coy
Engr	1 sqn

Reserves 90

Emergency Volunteer Reserve Force 40

Individual Reserves 50

FOREIGN FORCES

Italy 49 cbt Spt MIATM (Missione Italiana d'Assistenza Tecnico Militare); Air Force: 16; 2 Bell 212 Utl Helicopters

United States Army: 1; Navy 2; USMC: 6

Moldova Mol

Moldovan Leu L		2006	2007	2008
GDP	L	44.1bn	51.1bn	
	US$	3.4bn	4.5bn	
per capita	US$	778	1,047	
Growth	%	4.0	5.0	
Inflation	%	12.7	11.2	
Def bdgt	L	126m	194m	
	US$	9.6m	17.2m	
US$1=L		13.1	11.3	

Population 4,320,490

Age	0 – 14	15 – 19	20 – 24	25 – 29	30 – 64	65 plus
Male	10%	5%	4%	4%	20%	4%
Female	10%	5%	4%	4%	23%	6%

Capabilities

ACTIVE 6,750 (Army 5,150 Air 850) **Paramilitary 3,279**

Terms of service 12 months

RESERVE 66,000 (Joint 66,000)

ORGANISATIONS BY SERVICE

Army 1,671; 3,479 conscript (total 5,150)

FORCES BY ROLE

MoT Inf	3 bde (1st, 2nd and 3rd)
SF	1 bn
Arty	1 bde
Engr	1 bn
Gd	1 (MOD) indep unit
Peacekeeping	1 bn (22nd)

EQUIPMENT BY TYPE

AIFV 44 BMD-1
APC 315
  APC (T) 64: 9 BTR-D; 55 MT-LB
  APC (W) 251: 11 BTR-80; 91 TAB-71; 149 look-a-like
ARTY 148
  TOWED 69: **122mm** 17 (M-30) *M-1938*; **152mm** 52: 21 2A36; 31 D-20
  GUN/MOR • **SP 120mm** 9 2S9 *Anona*
  MRL 220mm 11 9P140 *Uragan*
  MOR 59: **82mm** 52; **120mm** 7 M-120
AT
  MSL • **MANPATS** 117: 71 AT-4 9K111 *Spigot*; 19 AT-5 9K113 *Spandrel*; 27 AT-6 9K114 *Spiral*
  RCL 73mm 138+ SPG-9
  GUNS 100mm 36 MT-12
AD • **GUNS** • **TOWED** 37: **23mm** 26 ZU-23; **57mm** 11 S-60
RADAR • **LAND** 1+: 1 L219/200 *PARK-1* (arty); GS-13 *Long Eye*/SNAR-1 *Long Trough* (arty); *Small Fred/Small Yawn*/SNAR-10 *Big Fred*/SNAR-2/-6 *Pork Trough* (veh, arty)

Air Force 850

(incl air defence)

FORCES BY ROLE

Trg/Tpt	2 sqn with 2 An-2 *Colt*; 1 An-26 *Curl*; 2 An-72 *Coaler*; 8 Mi-8 *Hip*
SAM	1 bde with 12 SA-3 *Goa*

EQUIPMENT BY TYPE

AIRCRAFT • **TPT** 5: 2 An-2 *Colt*; 1 An-26 *Curl*; 2 An-72 *Coaler*
HELICOPTERS • **SPT** 8 Mi-8 *Hip*
AD • **SAM** 12 SA-3 *Goa*

Paramilitary 2,379

Ministry of Interior

OPON 900 (riot police)

Ministry of Interior

DEPLOYMENT

CÔTE D'IVOIRE
UN • UNOCI 4 obs

GEORGIA
OSCE 1
UN • UNOMIG 1 obs

IRAQ
MNF • *Operation Iraqi Freedom* 11

LIBERIA
UN • UNMIL 3 obs

SUDAN
UN • UNMIS 2 obs

NON-STATE ARMED GROUPS

see Part II

FOREIGN FORCES

Russia ε 1,199 (including 365 peacekeepers; Army: 1 (op) army gp (subord. to Moscow MD) (1 SAM regt, 1 MRR bde); 125 Arty/MOR/MRL; 214 ACV; 108 MBT; Air: 7 hel
Ukraine 10 obs

Montenegro Mnt

Euro €		2006	2007	2008
GDP	€	1.8bn	1.9bn	
	US$	2.2bn	2.7bn	
per capita	US$	3,330		
Growth	%	5.5		
Inflation	%	2.6		
Def bdgt	€	e257m		
	US$	e321m		
US$1=€		0.80	0.70	

Population   ε684,736

Capabilities

ACTIVE 5,800 (Army 2,500 Navy 3,300) **Paramilitary 10,100**

Army 2,500

It is likely that the land forces of Montenegro plan to have a strength of 2,400 and that the force will be totally professional. The personnel structure of the security forces is aimed to be compatible with standards of developed democratic countries and the practice of Euro Atlantic structures with 400 officers, 900 non commissioned officers, 900 professional soldiers and 200 civilian administrators. In terms of capacity 60 percent is planned to serve national defence purposes and 40 percent international peacekeeping missions. In addition Montenegro will have to recreate the training facilities that it formerly used in Serbia.

The current military organisation structure will be transformed into one in which the command and training structures would account for 7 percent of the 2,400 soldiers, 50 percent of the soldiers would belong to the land forces, 20 percent to the navy, 10 percent to the air force with 13 percent for the logistic elements. The resulting structure will probably be an all arms light mobile infantry battlegroup with aviation support as well as a small SF unit.

At present Montenegro is setting aside 2.4 percent of GDP for the Army, reducing this figure by 1.1 percent by 2007. Later when Montenegro becomes an integral part of the Euro Atlantic structure the percentage of GDP is expected to be 1.54 percent.

Navy 2,400; 900 Marines (total 3,300)

Current organisation and equipment are outlined below. A new armed forces organisational structure is under development.

EQUIPMENT BY TYPE
SUBMARINES • TACTICAL 6
  SSK 1 *Sava* with 6 Single 533mm TT with 10 Test-71ME HWT
  SSW 3: 3 *Una*†
  SDV 2 †
PRINCIPAL SURFACE COMBATANTS • FRIGATES
FFG 2 *Kotor* each with 4 single each with 1 SS-N-2C *Styx* tactical SSM, 1 twin (2 eff.) with SA-N-4 *Gecko* SAM, 2 RBU 6000 *Smerch* 2 (24 eff.)
PATROL AND COASTAL COMBATANTS 6
  PFM 6: 4 *Rade Koncar* each with 2 single each with 1 SS-N-2B *Styx* tactical SSM ; 2 *Mirna*
MINE WARFARE • MINE COUNTERMEASURES 2
  MHC 2 *Sirius*
AMPHIBIOUS 11
  LCT 1 *Silba* (capacity either 6 medium tk or 7 APCs or 4 towed 130mm or 300 troops) with 1 quad (4 eff.) with SA-N-5 *Grail* SAM, up to 94 mine
  LCU 10: 3 (Type 21); 7 (Type 22)
LOGISTICS AND SUPPORT 4
AOTL 1; **TPT** 2 *Lubin* (PO-91); **AXS** 1
FACILITIES
Bases   Located at Kumbor, Novi Sad (river comd), Bar, Tivat

Marines 900
FORCES BY ROLE
Coast Arty   1 bde with 36 M-46 *Catapult*
MP   1 bn
Mot Inf   2 bde (*each:* 2 army regt (*each:* 2 army bn))
Lt inf   1 bde
EQUIPMENT BY TYPE
ARTY • SP • 130mm 36 M-46 *Catapult*

Air Force
Golubovci (Podgorica) air base under army command.
AC 19: 1 mixed sqn with 15 G-4 Super Galebs (of which 8-9 serviceable); 4 UTVA-75 (basic trg).
HEL 20: 1 sqn with separate army support, tpt and utlity flts. 15 SA 341/SA 342L Gazelle (only half airworthy) and 5 Mi-8T (stored awaiting overhaul)

Paramilitary ε10,100

Montenegrin Ministry of Interior Personnel ε6,000

Special Police Units ε4,100

DEPLOYMENT

LIBERIA
UN • UNMIL 2 obs

FOREIGN FORCES
Ireland 1 OSCE

Serbia Ser

Serbian Dinar d		2006	2007	2008
GDP	d	1.92tr	2.15bn	
	US$	32.3bn	39.4bn	
per capita	US$	3,181	3,879	
Growth	%	5.7	6.0	
Inflation	%	12.7	6.4	
Def bdgt	d	48.3bn	57.0bn	
	US$	811m	1.04bn	
US$1=d		59.6	54.6	

Population   10,150,265

Age	0 – 14	15 – 19	20 – 24	25 – 29	30 – 64	65 plus
Male	9%	4%	4%	4%	22%	6%
Female	9%	4%	4%	4%	23%	8%

Capabilities

ACTIVE 24,257 (Army 11,180, Air Force and Air Defence 4,155, Training Command 3,108, MoD 5,814)

RESERVE 54,249
Terms of service 6 months

ORGANISATIONS BY SERVICE

Army 9,456 conscripts 1,724 (11,180 in total)
Reconstruction continues
FORCES BY ROLE
Comd   1 Land Forces HQ
Mech   4 combined arms bde (comprising armd, mech inf, SP arty, recce, AD units)
Gd   1 bde (Ceremonial, 2 MP bn, 1 anti terrorist bn)
SF   1 bde with (1 anti terrorist, 1 cdo, 1 para bn)
Sig   1 bde
Arty   1 (mixed) bde (3 arty bn, 1MRL bn)
Riverine 1 det (under review)
NBC   1 bn

EQUIPMENT BY TYPE

MBT 224: 209 M-84; 15 T-72
AIFV 332 M-80
ARTY 1169
   SP 122mm 79 2S1 *Carnation*
   TOWED 378: **105mm** 162 M-56; **122mm** 78 D-30;
   130mm 24 M-46; **152mm** 42 M-84; **155mm** 72: 66 M-1; 6
   M-65
   MRL 128mm 81: 20 M-63 *Plamen*; 61 M-77 *Organj*
   MOR 631: **82mm** 385 M-69; **120mm** 246: 41 M-74; 205
   M-75
AT • MSL
   SP 103 BOV-1 AT-3 9K11 *Sagger*
   MANPATS 142+: 142 AT-3 9K11 *Sagger*; AT-4 9K111 *Spigot*
   RCL 650: **105mm** 650 M-65;
AD • SAM 168
   SP 60 SA-6 *Gainful*/ 9K31 *Strela*-1 SA-9 *Gaskin*
   MANPAD 108 *Strela*-2M
   GUNS SP 20mm BOV-3 SPAAG; **30mm** BOV-30;
   M-53/59 SP; **57mm** ZSU-57-2
   TOWED 60+ 12.7mm M-55; **20mm** M-75; **30mm** M-53
   40mm: 60 Bofors

Reserve Organisations

Territorial brigades   8.

Air Force and Air Defence 4,155

Current organisation and equipment are outlined below. A
new AF and AD organizational structure was established
in the first half of 2007.

FORCES BY ROLE

Air Force and Air defence Command - **1**

Ftr	1 comp sqn with MiG-29 *Fulcrum*/MiG-21bis
FGA	2 sqn with J-22 *Orao 1*; G-4 *Super Galeb*
Recce	2 sqn with 4 I-22 *Orao 1**; 3 MiG-21R *Fishbed H**
Tpt	1 comp sqn with An-26, Ya-40, Do-28, Mi-8
Trg	1 comp sqn with UTVA 75 (basic trg), G-4 Super Galeb (adv trg/light atk), SA-341/342 *Gazelle*
SAM	SAM bde (4 bn) with S-125M1T (SA-3); SA-6 Kub, SA-7/14/16 MANPAD

EQUIPMENT BY TYPE

FTR 30: 4 MiG-29A *Fulcrum A;* 1 MiG-29U *Fulcrum;* 20
MiG-21bis *Fishbed L & N;* 5 MiG-21UM *Mongol B*
FGA 27: 16 J-22 *Orao 1*; 11 G-4 *Super Galeb*
RECCE 7: 4 J-22R *Orao 1**; 3 MiG-21R *Fishbed H**
TPT 12: 8 An-26 *Curl*; 2 Do-28 *Skyservant*; 2 Yak-40
Codling
TRG 15 UTVA-75
HELICOPTERS
   SPT 53: 15 Mi-8, 15 H-42, 19 H-42M; 2 Mi-24, 2 Mi-17
AD • SAM 2 bn SA-3; 3 bn SA-6
MSL
   AAM R-60K; R-60MK; R-27R; R-73
   ASM *Maverick*

DEPLOYMENT

CÔTE D'IVOIRE
UN • UNOCI 3 obs

DEMOCRATIC REPUBLIC OF CONGO
UN • MONUC 6

LIBERIA
UN • UNMIL 6 obs

NON-STATE ARMED GROUPS
see Part II

FOREIGN FORCES

All under KFOR cmd unless otherwise specified
Argentina 46; 1 obs UNMIK
Armenia 34
Austria 554; 6 EUMM
Azerbaijan 34
Belgium 420
Bolivia 1 obs UNMIK
Bulgaria 46; 1 obs UNMIK
Chile 1 obs
Czech Republic 445-501 KFOR; 1 obs UNMIK
Denmark 1 inf gp (1 scout sqn, 1 inf coy); 320; 1 obs
UNMIK
Estonia 28
Finland 400; 2 obs UNMIK
France 1,830
Georgia 1 inf coy; 150
Germany 2,279; 26 C2 *Leopard* MBT; 17 SPz-2 *Luchs* recce;
25 *Marder* 1 AIFV; 21 APC (T); 54 TPz-1 *Fuchs* APC (W); 10
M-109A3G 155mm SP; 6 *Wiesel* (TOW) msl; 3 CH-53 *Sea
Stallion* spt hel; 9 UH-1D *Iroquois* utl hel
Greece 742
Hungary 484; 1 obs UNMIK
Ireland 211; 4 obs UNMIK; 5 EUMM; 2 OSCE
Italy 2,280; 1 obs UNMIK
Jordan 2 obs UNMIK
Kenya 1 obs UNMIK
Latvia 18
Lithuania 30
Luxembourg 26
Malawi 1 obs UNMIK
Malaysia 1 obs UNMIK
Mongolia 36
Morocco 279 KFOR
Nepal 1 obs UNMIK
Netherlands 4
New Zealand 1 obs UNMIK
Norway 6; 1 obs UNMIK
Pakistan 1 obs UNMIK
Poland 1 inf bn; 312; 1 obs UNMIK
Portugal 296; 2 obs UNMIK
Romania 153; 3 obs UNMIK
Russia 2 obs UNMIK
Slovakia 134
Slovenia 158

Spain 627; 2 obs UNMIK
Sweden 338
Switzerland 220 (military volunteers) KFOR
Turkey 940
Ukraine 248; 2 obs UNMIK
United Kingdom 150 *Joint Enterprise*; 2 SA-341 *Gazelle*
Spt Hel; 1 Armd Bde; 1 Armd inf bn; 1 inf bn; 1 Engr regt
KFOR; 1 obs UNMIK
United States 1,745; USAF 60; USMC 34
Zambia 1 obs UNMIK

Sweden Swe

Swedish Krona Skr		2006	2007	2008
GDP	Skr	2.81tr	2.90tr	
	US$	384bn	453bn	
per capita	US$	42,602	50,173	
Growth	%	4.2	3.6	
Inflation	%	1.4	1.6	
Def bdgt[a]	Skr	42.6bn	46.9bn	
	US$	5.78bn	7.30bn	
US$1=Skr		7.37	6.42	

[a] Including Civil Defence

Population   9,031,088

Age	0 – 14	15 – 19	20 – 24	25 – 29	30 – 64	65 plus
Male	9%	3%	3%	3%	24%	7%
Female	8%	3%	3%	3%	23%	10%

Capabilities

ACTIVE 24,000 (Army 10,200 Navy 7,900 Air 5,900)
Paramilitary 600 Voluntary Auxiliary Organisations 42,000
Terms of service: Army, Navy 7–15 months; Air Force 8–12 months

RESERVE 262,000 (Army 225,000 Navy 20,000 Air 17,000)

ORGANISATIONS BY SERVICE

Army 5,900; 4,300 conscript (total 10,200)
FORCES BY ROLE
1 Joint Forces Comd, 22 Training Detachments whose main task is to provide support to the Home Guard and other voluntary defence organizations, the Military Districts were disbanded in 2005. The army has been transformed to provide brigade sized task forces depending on the operational requirement. The EU Nordic Battlegroup is now operational.

Army	1 Div HQ (on mobilisation)
Armd	3 regt
Mech	8 bn
Cav	1 regt
Arty	2 bn
AD	1 bn
Engr	3 bn
Log	4 bn

EQUIPMENT BY TYPE
MBT 280: 120 Strv-122 *Leopard 2 (S)*; 160 Strv-121 (*Leopard* 2A4)
AIFV 485 Strv 9040 (CV 9040)
APC 799
  APC (T) 616: 232 Pbv 401A (56 Ambulance version 4020); 334 Pbv 302; 50 Bv S 10 *Viking*
  APC (W) 183 XA-180 *Sisu*/XA-203 *Sisu*
ARTY 258
  TOWED 155mm 50 FH-77B
  MOR 120mm 208
AT • MSL • MANPATS RB-55; RB-56 *Bill*
  RCL 84mm *Carl Gustav*
  RL 84mm AT-4
AIRCRAFT
  TPT 1 CASA 212 *Aviocar*
  UAV • TACTICAL 3 *Sperwer*
AD • SAM
  SP 16 RBS-70
  TOWED RBS-90
  MANPAD RBS-70
  GUNS • SP 40mm 30 Strv 90LV
RADAR • LAND ARTHUR (arty); M-113 A1GE *Green Archer* (mor)

Navy 4,280; 1,300 (Coastal Defence); 320 (Naval Avn); 2,000 conscript; (total 7,900)
FORCES BY ROLE
Maritime forces restructured

Navy	2 surface flotillas
Maritime	1 surveillance and info bn
Amphib	1 Amphib bde (1 Amphib bn)
SS	1 submarine flotilla

EQUIPMENT BY TYPE
SUBMARINES • TACTICAL • SSK 5:
  3 *Gotland* (AIP powered) each with 2 x1 400mm TT with 6 Tp 432/Tp 451, 4 single 533mm TT with 12 Tp 613/Tp 62
  2 *Sodermanland* (AIP fitted) each with 6 single 533mm TT with 12 Tp 613/Tp 62, 6 Tp 432/Tp 451
PRINCIPAL SURFACE COMBATANTS • CORVETTES
FSG 5 *Visby* with 8 RBS-15 SSM, 4 single ASTT each with Tp 45 LWT, Saab 601 mortar
  1 Bofors 57mm, 1 hel landing plaform (for med hel) (1st of class assuming full operational role '08)
PATROL AND COASTAL COMBATANTS 18
PFM 6:
  4 *Göteborg* each with 4 twin (8 eff.) each with 8 RBS-15M tactical SSM, 4 Saab 601 mortars
  2 *Stockholm* each with 4 single ASTT (may not be fitted) each with Tp 431 LWT, 4 twin (8 eff.) each with RBS-15M tactical SSM, 4 Saab 601 mortars
PCR 12 *Tapper*
MINE WARFARE 25
  MINE COUNTERMEASURES 18

MCMV 5: 4 *Styrso*; 1 *Uto*
MHC 7: 2 *Landsort* ; 5 *Koster*
MSD 6: 5 *Sam*; 1 *Sokaren*
MINELAYERS 7
  ML 1 *Carlskrona*
  ML(I) 2
  MLC 4: 1 *Furusund*
AMPHIBIOUS
  LCM 17 *Trossbat*
  LCU 23
  LCPL 145 *Combatboat*
LOGISTICS AND SUPPORT 30:
  ARS 1 *Furusund* (former ML)
  AG 6: 2; 1 *Carlskrona* with 1 hel landing platform (former ML); 1 *Trosso* (mostly used as a depot ship for corvettes and patrol vessels but can also be used as HQ ship); 2 *Arkosund* (former ML)
  AK 1 *Visborg*
  AKSL 1
  AGI 1
  AGS 2
  Trg 3: 2 AXS; 1 *Gassten*
  TPT 1
  TRV 2
  YDT 1
  YTM 2
  YTL 9
FACILITIES
Bases   Located at Muskö, Karlskrona
Support base   Located at Göteborg

Coastal Defence 1,300
FORCES BY ROLE
Amph   1 bde; 1 bn
EQUIPMENT BY TYPE
APC (W) 3+ *Piranha*
ARTY • MOR 81mm; 120mm 70
AD • SAM RBS-70
MSL • SSM 96: 6 RBS-15KA; 90 RBS-17 *Hellfire*
GUNS 24+: **40mm** L-70; **75mm; 105mm; 120mm** 24 CD-80 *Karin* (mobile)

Air Force 2,800; 1,500 conscript; 1,600 active reservists (total 5,900)
Flying hours   110 to 140 hrs/year
Units: F 7, Skaraborg Wing in Såtenäs; F 17, Blekinge Wing in Ronneby; F 21, Norrbotten Wing in Luleå; Helicopter Wing in Linköping (also operates in Luleå, Såtenäs and Ronneby; Air Combat School (LSS) in Uppsala
FORCES BY ROLE
COMD   1 HQ (8 (air base) Air bn)
Ftr/FGA/Recce 4 sqn with 54 JAS 39A/ *Gripen*; 11 JAS 39B/ *Gripen*; 52 JAS 39C/ *Gripen*; 13 JAS 39D *Gripen*: 1 (*Gripen*) sqn (declared for Rapid Reaction Force);
ASW/MP   1 sqn with 1 CASA 212-400 *Aviocar*
SIGINT   1 sqn with 2 S-102B (Gulfstream IV SRA-4)
AEW   1 sqn with 6 S-100B *Argus*

Tpt   4 sqn with 3 Tp-101 (Beech 200) *Super King Air*; 8 C-130E *Hercules*/Tp-84 (C-130H) *Hercules* (7 tpt, 1 tkr); 1 Tp-103 (Cessna 550) *Citation V*; 1 Tp-102A (Gulfstream IV); 1 Tp-100A (VIP)
Trg   1 trg school with 90 SK-60
AD   1 (fighter control and air surv) bn
EQUIPMENT BY TYPE
AIRCRAFT 130 combat capable
  MULTIROLE 130: 54 JAS 39A *Gripen**; 11 JAS 39B *Gripen**; (31 JAS 39A/B to be updated to C/D standard) 52 JAS 39C *Gripen**; 13 JAS 39D *Gripen**
  EW • ELINT 2 S-102B (Gulfstream IV SRA-4)
  AEW 6 S-100B *Argus*
  TPT 14: 8 C-130E *Hercules*/Tp-84 (C-130H) *Hercules* (7 tpt, 1 tkr); 1 Tp-100A (VIP); 3 Tp-101 (Beech 200) *Super King Air*; 1 Tp-102A (Gulfstream IV); 1 Tp-103 (Cessna 550) *Citation V*
  TRG 90: 90 SK-60
MSL
  ASM RB-15F; RB-75 (AGM-65) *Maverick*
  AAM RB-99 (AIM-120B) *AMRAAM*; RB-74 (AIM-9L) *Sidewinder*; RB-71 *(Sky Flash)*
BOMB BK-39

Armed Forces Hel Wing 800 (from all three services); 250 conscripts (total 1,050)
FORCES BY ROLE
Hel   1 bn with 2 HKP-14 (NH 90); 8 HKP-10 (AS-332) *Super Puma* (SAR); 14 HKP-4 (Boeing Vertol 107) (ASW/tpt/SAR); 5 HKP-15 (A-109M); 18 HKP-9A (BÖ-105CB) (trg)
EQUIPMENT BY TYPE
HELICOPTERS
  SPT 24: 2 HKP-14 (NH 90); 8 HKP-10 (AS-332) *Super Puma* (SAR); 14 HKP-4 (Boeing Vertol 107) (ASW/tpt/SAR)
  UTL 23: 18 HKP-9A (BÖ-105CB) trg; 5 HKP-15 (A-109M)

Paramilitary 600

Coast Guard 600
PATROL AND COASTAL COMBATANTS 28
  PSOH 2 *KBV-001*(Delivery expected April and November 2008)
  PSO 2 *KBV-181* (fishery protection)
  PCO 2 *KBV-201*
  PCC 2 *KBV-101*
  PCI 20
LOGISTICS AND SUPPORT 12 **AG** (Pollution Control Craft)

Air Arm
  AIRCRAFT • TPT 2 CASA 212 *Aviocar* (maritime recce)

Voluntary Auxiliary Organisations 42,000

DEPLOYMENT

AFGHANISTAN
NATO • ISAF 340
UN • UNAMA 1 obs

BOSNIA-HERZEGOVINA
EU • EUFOR • 24

CENTRAL AFRICAN REPUBLIC
UN • MINURCAT 1 obs

CHAD/CENTRAL AFRICAN REPUBLIC
EU • EUFOR Chad/CAR 200

DEMOCRATIC REPUBLIC OF CONGO
EU • EUPOL Kinshasa 1
UN • MONUC 5 obs

ETHIOPIA/ERITREA
UN • UNMEE 3 obs

GEORGIA
UN • UNOMIG 3 obs

INDIA/PAKISTAN
UN • UNMOGIP 6 obs

KOREA, REPUBLIC OF
NNSC 5 obs

MIDDLE EAST
UN • UNTSO 7 obs

NEPAL
UN • UNMIN 3 obs

SERBIA
NATO • KFOR 380

SUDAN
AU • AMIS 12
UN • UNMIS 4; 3 obs

Switzerland CH

Swiss Franc fr		2006	2007	2008
GDP	fr	474bn	492bn	
	US$	379bn	417bn	
per capita	US$	50.399	55,191	
Growth	%	3.2	2.4	
Inflation	%	1.1	0.2	
Def bdgt	fr	4.43bn	4.46bn	4.52bn
	US$	3.54bn	3.78bn	
US$1=fr		1.25	1.18	

Population   7,554,661

Age	0 – 14	15 – 19	20 – 24	25 – 29	30 – 64	65 plus
Male	9%	3%	3%	3%	25%	6%
Female	8%	3%	3%	3%	25%	9%

Capabilities

ACTIVE 22,600 (Joint 3,900; 18,700 conscript)

RESERVE 218,200 (Army 161,400 Air 31,300 Armed
Forces Logistic Organisation 11,500 Command
Support Organisation 14,000) Paramilitary 105,000

Terms of service 18 weeks compulsory recruit trg at age 19–
20. Followed by 7 refresher trg courses (3 weeks each) over
a 10-year period between ages 20–30.

ORGANISATIONS BY SERVICE

Joint 3,900 active; 18,700 conscript; 224,700 on
mobilisation; (total 22,600 – 243,400)

Armed Forces Logistic Organisation 11,500
on mobilisation

Log 1 bde

Command Support Organisation ε14,000 on
mobilisation

Spt 1 (comd) bde

Land Forces (Army) 161,400

With the exception of military security all units are non-
active – being re-organised

FORCES BY ROLE

4 Territorial Regions

Armd	1 bde (1 Sigs bn, 3 Tk bn, 1 Armd Recce bn, 1 Engr bn, 2 SP Arty bn, 3 Mech Inf bn); 1 bde (1 Armd Recce bn, 1 Sigs bn, 3 Tk bn, 3 Mech Inf bn, 1 SP Arty bn, 1 Engr bn)
Armd/Arty	1 bde (trg)
Inf	1 bde (trg); 1 bde (1 Sigs bn, 1 Armd Recce bn, 1 SP Arty bn, 1 Engr bn, 3 Inf bn, 1 (mt) Rifle bn); 1 bde (4 Inf bn, 1 Sigs bn, 1 Armd Recce bn, 2 SP Arty bn); 1 bde (1 Sigs bn, 1 Engr bn, 4 Inf bn, 2 SP Arty bn, 1 Armd Recce bn); 1 bde (1 Sigs bn, 1 Engr bn, 2 SP Arty bn, 3 Inf bn, 1 Armd Recce bn, 1 (mt) Rifle bn)
Mtn Inf	1 bde (1 SP Arty bn, 3 Mtn Inf bn, 1 Sigs bn, 1 Armd Recce bn); 1 bde (2 Mtn Inf bn, 1 Armd Recce bn, 1 SP Arty bn, 1 Sigs bn); 1 bde (1 Fd Arty bn, 1 (mt) Rifle bn, 1 Armd Recce bn, 1 Sigs bn, 2 Mtn Inf bn)
Engr Rescue	1 bde (trg)
Sigs	1 bde (trg)
Supply	1 bde (trg)
Sy	1 bde

EQUIPMENT BY TYPE
MBT 224 Pz-87 *Leo* (*Leopard 2*) (134 to be modernised)
RECCE 329: 154 *Eagle I*; 175 *Eagle II*
AIFV 186 CV9030
APC 1,123
    APC (T) 583 M-63/73 (M-113) (around 550 to be dismantled)

APC (W) 540: 25 *Buffalo*; 515 *Piranha* (40 to be re-roled as protected ambulances)

ARTY 884

SP 155mm 224 M-109U

MOR 660: **81mm** 528 M-72; **120mm** 132 M-64

AT • MSL 685

SP 120 TOW-2 SP *Mowag Piranha*

MANPATS 565 M47 *Dragon*

RL 67mm 3,335 PZF 44 *Panzerfaust*

AD • SAM • MANPAD FIM-92A *Stinger*

UAV • TACTICAL *Ranger*

Marine

PATROL AND COASTAL COMBATANTS

PBR 11 *Aquarius*

Air Force 31,300 on mobilisation

6 air base Cmds, 1 flt trg unit, 1 GBAD trg unit, 1 Air Force Cmd trg unit

Flying hours   200–250 hrs/year

FORCES BY ROLE

incl AD units, mil airfield guard units

Ftr   3 sqn with 26 F/A-18C *Hornet*; 7 F/A-18D *Hornet*; 3 sqn with 45 F-5E *Tiger II* (12 on lease to Austria); 1 sqn with 12 F-5F *Tiger II/F-5F*

Tpt   1 sqn with 15 PC-6 *Turbo-Porter*; 1 Do-27; 1 *Falcon-50*; 1 Cessna 560 XL *Citation*; 1 DHC-6 *Twin Otter*; 1 Beech 350 *Super King Air*;

Trg   1 sqn with 37 PC-7 *Turbo Trainer*; 1 sqn with 11 PC-9 (tgt towing)

Hel   6 sqn with 15 AS-332 *Super Puma*; 12 AS-532 *Cougar*; 35 SA-316 *Alouette III* (first of replacement EC635 to be delivered Spring 2008); 1 AS365-N1 *Dauphin*

UAV 1 bn with 4 Systems ADS 95 *Ranger*

EQUIPMENT BY TYPE

AIRCRAFT 90 combat capable

FTR 57: 45 F-5E *Tiger II*; 12 F-5F *Tiger II*

FGA 33: 26 F/A-18C *Hornet*; 7 F/A-18D *Hornet*

TPT 19: 15 PC-6 *Turbo-Porter*; 1 *Falcon-50*; 1 Cessna 560 XL *Citation*; 1 DHC-6 *Twin Otter*; 1 Beech 350 *Super King Air*; 1 Do-27

TRG 48: 37 PC-7 *Turbo Trainer*; 11 PC-9 (tgt towing)

HELICOPTERS

SPT 15 AS-332 *Super Puma*

UTL 48: 12 AS-532 *Cougar*; 35 SA-316 *Alouette III* (being replaced by 18 Eurocopter EC635 by end 2009) ; 1 AS365-N1 *Dauphin*

UAV • RECCE 4 Systems ADS 95 *Ranger*

MSL • AAM AIM-120B *AMRAAM*; AIM-9P *Sidewinder*

Air Defence

FORCES BY ROLE

ADA Up to 15 GBAD bn can be formed. with B/L-84 *Rapier*; FIM-92A *Stinger*; 35mm guns and *Skyguard* fire control radar. These GBAD assets can be used to form AD clusters to be deployed indep as task forces within Swiss territory.

EQUIPMENT BY TYPE

AD • SAM • TOWED Rapier

MANPAD FIM-92A *Stinger*

GUNS 35mm

RADARS • AD RADARS *Skyguard*

Paramilitary

Civil Defence 105,000 reservists

(not part of armed forces)

DEPLOYMENT

AFGHANISTAN

NATO • ISAF 2

BOSNIA-HERZEGOVINA

EU • EUFOR • *Operation Althea* 26; Air Force: 2 AS-532 *Cougar* hel

BURUNDI

UN • BINUB 1 obs

DEMOCRATIC REPUBLIC OF CONGO

UN • MONUC 2 obs

ETHIOPIA/ERITREA

UN • UNMEE 3 obs

GEORGIA

UN • UNOMIG 4 obs

KOREA, REPUBLIC OF

NNSC 5 officers

MIDDLE EAST

UN • UNTSO 9 obs

NEPAL

UN • UNMIN 5 obs

SERBIA

NATO • KFOR • *Joint Enterprise* 220 (military volunteers); 2 hel

Ukraine Ukr

Ukrainian Hryvnia h		2006	2007	2008
GDP	h	538bn	624bn	
	US$	107bn	124bn	
per capita	US$	2,285	2,679	
Growth	%	7.1	6.7	
Inflation	%	9.0	11.5	
Def bdgt	h[a]	8.7bn	9.1bn	11.8bn
	US$	1.72bn	1.81bn	
FMA (US)	US$	10.9m		
US$1=h		5.05	5.03	

[a] = excluding military pensions

Population 46,299,862

Ethnic groups: Russian 22%; Polish 4%; Jewish 1%

Age	0 – 14	15 – 19	20 – 24	25 – 29	30 – 64	65 plus
Male	8%	4%	4%	4%	21%	5%
Female	8%	4%	4%	4%	25%	10%

Capabilities

ACTIVE 129,925 (Army 70,753 Navy 13,932 Air 45,240) Paramilitary 84,900

Terms of Service Army, Air Force 18 months, Navy 2 years

RESERVE 1,000,000 (Joint 1,000,000)

mil service within 5 years

ORGANISATIONS BY SERVICE

Ground Forces (Army) 70,753

FORCES BY ROLE

3 op comd (1 to disband); All corps HQ (except one) to disband

Army 1 (MoD) tps (1 engr bde, 1 sy bde); 1 (ground forces) comd (1 corps HQ (1 arty regt, 1 SAM regt, 1 msl bde, 1 air mob bde, 1 MRL regt, 1 SSM div (3 SSM bde (SS-21)), 2 mech bde))

Arty 1 arty regt

Northern Op Comd

To be disbanded

Comd 1 tps (1 trg bde, 1 avn bde, 1 engr bde, 1 mech bde, 1 tk div)

Southern Op Comd

Comd 1 tps (1 SAM regt, 1 engr regt, 1 mech bde, 1 air mob regt, 1 avn bde)

Army 1 corps (1 SAM regt, 1 arty regt, 1 air mob div (1 arty regt, 2 mech bde), 1 engr regt, 1 arty bde, 1 AB bde, 1 tk div, 1 arty div (2 arty bde, 2 MRL regt), 2 mech bde)

Western Op Comd

Comd 1 tps (1 air mob regt, 1 SAM regt, 1 avn regt, 1 avn bde, 1 mech inf regt, 1 SF bde, 1 engr bde, 1 SSM bde)

Army 1 corps (1 SAM regt, 1 mech div (1 SAM regt, 1 arty regt, 1 tk regt, 3 mech regt), 1 arty bde, 1 engr regt, 1 mech div (1 tk regt, 1 SAM regt, 2 mech regt), 1 arty div (1 MRL regt, 1 MRL bde, 2 arty bde), 2 mech bde)

EQUIPMENT BY TYPE

MBT 2,984: 6 T-84; 167 T-80; 1032 T-72; 1,667 T-64; 112 T-55
RECCE 600+ BRDM-2
AIFV 2,818: BMD 138: 60 BMD-1; 78 BMD-2; 994 BMP-1; 1,434 BMP-2; 4 BMP-3; 458 BRM-1K
APC 1,432
  APC (T) 44: 44 BTR-D
  APC (W) 1,388: 136 BTR-60; 857 BTR-70; 395 BTR-80
ARTY 3,705
  SP 1,226: 122mm 600 2S1 *Carnation*; 152mm 527: 40 2S19 *Farm*; 463 2S3; 24 2S5; 203mm 99 2S7
  TOWED 1,065: 122mm 371: 369 D-30; 2 (M-30) *M-1938*; 152mm 694: 287 2A36; 185 2A65; 215 D-20; 7 ML-70
  GUN/MOR 120mm 69:
    SP 67 2S9 *Anona*
    TOWED 2 2B16 *NONA-K*
  MRL 554: 122mm 335: 20 9P138; 315 BM-21; 132mm 2 BM-13; 220mm 137 9P140 *Uragan*; 300mm 80 9A52 *Smerch*
  MOR 120mm 437: 318 2S12; 119 PM-38
AT • MSL • MANPATS AT-4 9K111 *Spigot*/AT-5 9K113 *Spandrel*/AT-6 9K114 *Spiral*
  GUNS 100mm ε500 MT-12/T-12
HELICOPTERS
  ATK 139 Mi-24 *Hind*
  SPT 38: 38 Mi-8 *Hip*
AD • SAM • SP 435: 60 SA-11 *Gadfly*; ε150 SA-13 *Gopher*; 100 SA-4 *Ganef*; 125 SA-8 *Gecko*
  GUNS 470:
    SP 30mm 70 2S6
    TOWED 57mm ε400 S-60
RADAR • LAND *Small Fred*/*Small Yawn*/SNAR-10 *Big Fred* (arty)
  MSL • SSM 212: 50 FROG; 90 SS-21 *Scarab* (*Tochka*); 72 *Scud*-B

Navy 11,932; 2,000 conscript (total 13,932 incl. Naval Aviation and Naval Infantry)

After intergovernmental agreement in 1997, the Russian Federation Fleet currently leases bases in Sevastopol and Karantinnaya Bays and also shares facilities jointly with Ukr warships at Streletskaya Bay. The overall serviceability of the fleet is assessed as low.

EQUIPMENT BY TYPE

SUBMARINES • TACTICAL • SSK 1 *Foxtrot* (T-641)†
PRINCIPAL SURFACE COMBATANTS 5
  FRIGATES 1
    FF 1 *Hetman Sagaidachny* (RF *Krivak* III) with 1 Twin (2 eff.) with 20 SA-N-4 *Gecko* SAM, 2 quad 533mm ASTT (8 eff.) each with T-53 HWT, 1 100mm gun, (capacity 1 Ka-27 *Helix* ASW hel)

CORVETTES • **FS** 4 *Grisha* (II/V) each with 1 twin (2 eff.) with 20 SA-N-4 *Gecko* SAM, up to 2 RBU 6000 *Smerch 2* (24 eff.), 2 twin 533mm ASTT (4 eff.) each with SAET-60 HWT, 1 76mm gun

PATROL AND COASTAL COMBATANTS 5

PFM 1 *Tarantul II*

PHM 2 *Matka* each with 2 single with 2 SS-N-2C *Styx*/SS-N-2D *Styx*, 1 76mm gun

PFT 1 *Pauk* I with 1 quad with 4 SA-N-5 *Grail* SAM, 4 Single 406mm TT, 1 76mm gun

PCI 1 *Zhuk*

MINE WARFARE • MINE COUNTERMEASURES 4

MHC 1 *Yevgenya*

MSC 1 *Sonya*

MSO 2 *Natya*

AMPHIBIOUS

LS 2:

LSM 1 *Polnochny* C (capacity 6 MBT; 180 troops)

LST 1 *Ropucha* with 4 quad (16 eff.) each with SA-N-5 *Grail* SAM, 2 57mm twin gun (4 eff.), 92 mine, (capacity either 10 MBT or 190 troops; either 24 APC (T)s or 170 troops)

CRAFT ACV 2 *Pomornik* (*Zubr*) each with 2 quad (8 eff.) each with SA-N-5 *Grail* SAM, (capacity 230 troops; either 3 MBT or 10 APC (T)s)

LOGISTICS AND SUPPORT 36

AGF 1 *Bambuk*

AR 1 *Amur* (can also act as a command ship or as a support ship for surface ships and submarines)

AWT 1

AGS 2: 1 *Moma* (mod); 1 *Biya*

ABU 1

TRG • 3 **AXL**

YDG 1

YDT 20; 8 *Yelva*; 12

YTM 6

FACILITIES

Bases — Located at Sevastopol, Kerch, Donuzlav, Chernomorskoye, Odessa, Ochakov

Construction and Repair Yards — Located at Nikolaev, Balaklava

Naval Aviation up to 2,500

AIRCRAFT 10 combat capable

ASW 10 Be-12 *Mail**

TPT 16: 5 An-12 *Cub*; 1 An-24 *Coke*; 8 An-26 *Curl*; 1 Il-18 *Coot*; 1 Tu-134 *Crusty*

HELICOPTERS

ASW 72: 28 Ka-25 *Hormone*; 2 Ka-27E *Helix*; 42 Mi-14 *Haze*

SPT 5: 5 Mi-6 *Hook*

Naval Infantry 3,000

Naval inf 1 bde

Air Forces 45,240

Air — 3 air cmds – West, South, Centre plus Task Force 'Crimea'. Flying hours 40-50hrs/yr

FORCES BY ROLE

Ftr — 5 bde with 80 MiG-29 *Fulcrum*; 36 Su-27 *Flanker*

FGA/bbr — 2 bde with 36 Su-24M *Fencer*; 36 Su-25 *Frogfoot*

Recce — 2 sqn with 23 Su-24MR *Fencer**

Tpt — 3 bde with 3 An-24; 21 An-26; 3 An-30; 2 Tu-134 *Crusty*; 20 Il-76 *Candid*

Spt hel — sqns with 31 Mi-8; 4 Mi-9; 3 PZL Mi-2 *Hoplite*

Trg — sqns with 39 L-39 *Albatros*

EQUIPMENT BY TYPE

AIRCRAFT 211 combat capable

FTR 116: 80 MiG-29 *Fulcrum*; 36 Su-27 *Flanker*

FGA 72: 36 Su-25 *Frogfoot*; 36 Su-24 *Fencer*

RECCE 23 Su-24MR*

TPT 49: 3 An-24 *Coke*; 21 An-26 *Curl*; 3 An-30; 2 Tu-134 *Crusty*; 20 Il-76 *Candid*

TRG 39 L-39 *Albatros*

HELICOPTERS • **SPT** 38: 4 Mi-9; 31 Mi-8 *Hip*; 3 PZL MI-2 *Hoplite*

AD • **SAM** 825 SA-10 *Grumble* (quad)/SA-11 *Gadfly*/SA-12A *Gladiator* SA-2 *Guideline* towed/ SA-3 *Goa* towed/SA-5 *Gammon* **static**/SA-6 *Gainful*

MSL

ASM: AS-10 *Karen*; AS-11 *Kilter*; AS-12 *Kegler*; AS-13 *Kingbolt*; AS-14 *Kedge*; AS-15 *Kent*; AS-9 *Kyle*

ARM: AS-11 *Kilter*; AS-12 *Kegler*

AAM: AA-10 *Alamo*; AA-7 *Apex*; AA-8 *Aphid*; AA-9 *Amos*

Paramilitary

MVS ε39,900 active

(Ministry of Internal Affairs)

FORCES BY ROLE

Mil Region — 4 tps

MP — 1 (Internal Security) tps

Border Guard 45,000 active

Maritime Border Guard

The Maritime Border Guard is an independent subdivision of the State Comission for Border Guards and is not part of the navy.

FORCES BY ROLE

Air Wing — 1 (gunship) sqn

Air — 3 sqn

MCM — 1 sqn

Paramilitary — 2 (river) bde; 1 (aux ship) gp; 4 (cutter) bde

Trg — 1 div

EQUIPMENT BY TYPE

PATROL AND COASTAL COMBATANTS 45

PFT 3 *Pauk* I each with 4 SA-N-5 *Grail* SAM, 4 single 406mm TT, 1 76mm gun

PHT 3 *Muravey* each with 2 single 406mm TT, 1 76mm gun

PFC 10 *Stenka* each with 4 single 406mm TT, 4 30mm gun

PCC 1
PCI 16 *Zhuk*
PBR 12
LOGISTICS AND SUPPORT
AGF 1
AIRCRAFT • TPT: An-24 *Coke*; An-26 *Curl*; An-72
Coaler; An-8 *Camp*
HELICOPTERS • ASW: Ka-27 *Helix A*

Civil Defence Troops 9,500+ (civilian)

(Ministry of Emergency Situations) Army
4 indep bde; 4 indep regt

DEPLOYMENT

DEMOCRATIC REPUBLIC OF CONGO
UN • MONUC 6 obs

ETHIOPIA/ERITREA
UN • UNMEE 3 obs

GEORGIA
UN • UNOMIG 5 obs
OSCE 3

IRAQ
NATO • NTM-I 3

LIBERIA
UN • UNMIL 301; 2 obs

MEDITERRANEAN SEA
NATO • *Active Endeavour*
FS 1

MOLDOVA
10 obs

SERBIA
NATO • KFOR • *Joint Enterprise* 101
UN • UNMIK 3 obs

SUDAN
UN • UNMIS 6 obs

FOREIGN FORCES

Russia ε13,000 Navy: 1 Fleet HQ located at Sevastopol;
1 indep naval inf regt; 102 AIFV/APC (T)/APC (W); 24
arty

Table 15 **Selected Arms Orders and Deliveries, NATO Europe**

	Country Supplier	Classification	Designation	Quantity	Order date	Original Delivery date	Comment
Belgium (Be)	Int'l	Tpt	A-400M	7	2003	2010	–
	NL	FFG	*Karel –Doorman*	2	2005	2006	Transfer. First FFG received March 2007. Second FFG scheduled for transfer March 2008
	CH	APC	Mowag *Piranha* IIIC	242	2006	2010	1st Batch (138 vehicles) all due by 2010, 2nd Batch (81), 3rd Batch (23). 2nd and 3rd Batches due 2010-2015. Total Cost EUR700m (USD844m). Option on another 104
	Ger	APC	*Dingo* II	352	2006	–	Option on another 132 units
	A	APC	*Pandur* II	260	–	2006	–
	Int'l	Hel	NH90	10	2007	–	4 hel in the TTH version, 4 in the NFH version and options for 2 additional ac
	US	FC	Advance targeting	8	2007	2007	Operational upgrade. Supply of *Sniper* Advanced Targeting Pod (ATP)
	US	AAM	Evolved *Sea Sparrow* Missile (ESSM)	–	2007	–	NATO *Sea Sparrow* Consortium for 294 ESSM (USD223m)
Bulgaria (Bg)	It	Trg	C-27J *Spartan*	8	2005	2006	USD257.7m. Deliveries continuing
	Int'l	Hel	AS-532 *Cougar*	12	2005	2008	For Army. Final delivery expected 2009
	Int'l	Hel	AS-565 *Panther*	6	2005	2010	For Navy. Part of a AUR360m (USD460m) deal with the above-mentioned AS-532
Czech Republic (Cz)	dom	MBT	T-72CZ M4	30	2002	2006	To be upgraded to T-72CZ M4 standard
	RF	Atk Hel	Mi-24 *Hind*	7	2002	2006	Part of debt payment
	RF	Tpt	An-70	3	2002	2006	Part of debt payment
	A	APC	*Pandur* II	234	2006	2007	Final deliveries 2012. EUR821m (USD1.04bn). To replace OT-64
	Swe	Radar	*Arthur* artillery radar	1	2004	2006	Kc1.5bn (approx USD65.7m). First unit to be delivered in Sept 2006, to be followed by 2 units in 2007. The *Arthur* system has a lifetime of 20 years
Denmark (Da)	US	Tpt	C-130J *Super Hercules*	4	2000	2004	4th ac delivered to the air force in July 2007
	Swe	AIFV	CV9035	45	2005	2007	DKK1.675bn (GBP156.12m; approx USD272.8m). First delivered in Sept 2007. Final delivery expected 2009
	Nl	FFG	Patrol Frigates	3	2006	2012	DKK4.3bn (USD471m)
	Nl	Radar	APART, force control	5	2006	2012	To equip patrol FFG
	Nl	Radar	SMART-L Force control	3	2006	2012	To equip patrol FFG
	Int'l	Hel	EH101- *Merlin*	6	2007	2009	Hel order to replace 6 EH101 sold to the UK
	Swe	RCWS	*Lemur* RCWS	100	2007	2007	SEK330m (USD50m). To be installed on *Piranha* III APC, *Eagle* IV scout / recce vehicles, and high-mobility cross-country trucks. Due to complete by 2008

Table 15 Selected Arms Orders and Deliveries, NATO Europe

	Country Supplier	Classification	Designation	Quantity	Order date	Original Delivery date	Comment
	US	AAM	Evolved *Sea Sparrow Missile* (ESSM)	–	2007	–	NATO *Sea Sparrow* Consortium for 294 ESSM (USD223m)
	NI	AG	*Absalon*	2	2007	2007	Radar upgrade. Installation of SMART-S Mk2 radar on 2 *Absalon* AG. Second radar to be installed by end of 2007
Estonia (Ea)	SF	APC	*Patria* PaSi XA-180 Sisu	60	2005	2007	USD9.6m
	UK	MCMV	*Sandown*	3	2006	2007	EEK800m (USD65m). Transfer ongoing. Purchase of former UK MCMV. HMS *Sandown* (renamed ENS *Admiral Cowan*) was received in April 2007. Inverness to be delivered in March 2008, Bridport in early 2009
	Int'l	VSHRAD	*Mistral* 2	–	2007	2007	EUR45m (USD48m). Final delivery in 2008.
	Cz / Swe	Tpt / MP	L-410 *Turbolet*	1	2007	–	ac with MSS 6000 maritime surveillance system.
France (Fr)	dom	FGA	*Rafale*	120	1984	2006	120 on order of planned 294. Deliveries expected to 2015
	Dom / Ge	Hel	AS-665 *Tiger*	80	1999	2005	1st batch of 60 ordered 1999. First 8 delivered 2005. Deliveries ongoing
	Ge / dom	ASSM	ANNG (supersonic anti-ship missile)	–	1985	2005	Joint programme with Ge. Work suspended in 2001
	It	Hel	NH-90	160	1987	2003	With Ge, It, NI; orders delayed
	Ge	ATGW	*Trigat*	–	1988	2004	With Ge
	UK	SAM	FSAF (Future surface-to-air-family)	–	1990	2006	With It, UK
	UK	ALCM	SCALP	600	1994	2000	2 orders for delivery over 11 years
	dom	SAM	*Mistral*	1130	1996	2008	Deliveries to 2002
	dom	SLBM	M51	–	1996	2008	To replace M-45
	UK	ASM	*Vesta*	–	1997	2005	In development
	UK	AAM	MICA	225	1998	1999	Further 1,537 to be delivered from 2004
	dom / It	DDG	*Horizon*	4	1999	2005	Joint It/Fr project. *Forbin* commissioned in 2006, *Chevalier Paul* expected commission 2008
	dom	MBT	*Leclerc*	38	2000	2002	Upgrade to Mk2 standard continues
	dom	Sat	*Syracuse* 3	3	2000	2003	Communications satellite
	dom	SSBN	*Le Triomphant* (S 616)	1	2000	2010	4th of class. 3 already in service
	dom	APC	VBCI	700	2000	2008	1st Batch (65 vehicles) due 2008-2009. Then approx 100 vehicles per year until 2013
	Il	UAV	*Eagle*	–	2001	2009	–
	dom / It	FFG	FREMM	17	2002	2012	Multi-mission FFG. EUR11.05bn. (USD13.3bn) Construction to start 2007. First-of-class FNS *Aquitaine* is scheduled to commission in 2012
	Int	Tpt	A-400M	50	2003	2010	Project in development

Table 15 Selected Arms Orders and Deliveries, NATO Europe

	Country Supplier	Classification	Designation	Quantity	Order date	Original Delivery date	Comment
	dom	Arty	*CAESAR* 155mm	72	2004	2007	Deliveries will run until 2011. EUR300m (USD362m)
	dom	AIFV	AMX-10P	108	2005	2008	Upgrade. First deliveries 2008/2009. EUR50m (USD60m)
	Int'l	Hel	EC 725	14	–	2005	6 for air force, 8 for Special Ops Detachment of the French Army Air Corps. 6th hel delivered to air force in May 2007
	dom	APC	VB2L (LAV)	91	2006	2007	–
	dom	Hel	EC-145	7	2006	2007	EUR65m (USD83m) to replace the *Alouette* III. Deliveries to start late 2007/ early 2008
	Int'l	ATGW	*Eryx*	MANPAT	2006	2008	EUR66.5m (USD86.2m). Both training and combat msl. Deliveries between the second half of 2008 and the end of 2011
	It	Gun	76/62 *Super Rapid* naval gun mount	8	2006	2009	EUR40m (USD53.3m). Final delivery by end of 2011. To be installed on first batch of *Aquitaine*-class FFG
	Dom	SSN	*Barracuda*	6	2006	2016	EUR8bn (USD10.5bn). One SSN to be delivered every two years until 2027. First SSN to enter service in 2017
	Int'l	Trg	*Grob* 120A	18	2006	2007	Deliveries to be completed by end 2007. The contract covers a timeframe of 5 years with option for yearly extensions up to 10 years. Ac to be located at the Air Force Flight Training School on the Cognac Air Base
	Int'l	Hel	EC135	37	2007	2008	EUR233m (USD301m). 12 firm orders and 25 options. To be used by French Gendarmerie. Final delivery late 2008
	Int'l	NLACM	*Scalp*	250	2007	2013	EUR910m (USD1.2bn). To be deployed on new SSN and FFG
	US	ASM	AGM-114 *Hellfire* II	–	2007	–	For 40 *Tiger* atk hel fleet. To be completed by 2012. Neither the number of msl nor the contract value has been disclosed. Fr has a total requirement for 680 *Hellfire* msl
	dom	CV	*Charles de Gaulle*-class	1	2007	–	Refit programme
Germany (Ge)	dom	Hel	AS-665 *Tiger*	80	1984	2005	USD2.6bn. First helicopter delivered April 2005. Deliveries continuing
	Int'l	FGA	*Typhoon*	180	1985	2004	Tranche 1 ordered 1998 (44 aircraft). Tranche 2 ordered 2004 (68 aircraft). Tranche 3 order 68. First deliveries 2004
	dom	ATGW	*Trigat*	–	1988	2004	
	Fr	Sat	*Horus*	1	1994	2005	Development with Fr
	Int'l	AAM	IRIS-T (LFK)	–	1997	2003	Development with It, Swe, Gr, Ca, No
	Swe	ASM	KEPD 350 *Taurus*	600	1998	2004	Development with Swe (KEPD-350) Deliveries continuing
	dom	FFG	Type F 125-class	4	1999	2014	EUR2.2bn. Contract at approvals stage
	dom	MBT	*Leopard* 2A5	225	2000	2001	Upgrade to 2A6 continues
	dom	APC	*Boxer*	200	2000	–	Joint programme with Nl continuing

Europe

Table 15 Selected Arms Orders and Deliveries, NATO Europe

Country Supplier	Classification	Designation	Quantity	Order date	Original Delivery date	Comment
dom	FS	K130	5	2000	2007	1st of class preparing for sea trials, expected ISD May 2007. 2nd of class to be launched September 2006, expected ISD 2008
dom / Nl	Recce	Fennek	202	2001	2007	Joint dev with Nl. First deliveries in 2003
dom	MRTT	A-310	4	2001	2004	First ac delivered in 2007
dom	FSG	Type K130	5	2001	2007	Deliveries ongoing. 5th vessel launched 2007
Int'l	Tpt	A-400M	60	2003	2010	Project in development
Swe	APC	Bv-206S	75	2004	–	Order continuing
Dom	APC	Mungo	388	2004	2005	Deliveries continuing
Nl	Hel	NH-90	160	2004	2006	16 hel to be delivered by end of 2007
Dom	AFV	APCV-2 Dingo II	52	2004	–	Deliveries continuing
Dom	LAV	Wiesel 2	32	2004	2005	First 11 in 2005, 15 in 2006 and 6 in 2007
Dom	APC	Puma	410	2004	2006	First production batch in 2006. EUR3.05bn (USD3.7bn)
Fr	C2	Communications	–	2005	2008	USD1.2bn. Secure satcom. Awaiting parliamentary approval 2005.
dom	APC	Dingo II	149	2006	2006	EUR109m (USD139.5m). To be delivered in 2006 and 2007. Dec 2006 contract modification: 100 APC instead of 33 to be delivered to Afghanistan in 2007
dom	ATGW	PARS 3 LR Trigat missiles	680	2006	2014	EUR380m (USD486m). Will be the main armament of the 80 Tiger attack helicopters ordered by the German army
dom	Sat	Phase 2 of the SATCOMBw programme	–	2006	2016	EUR938.7m (USD1.1bn). In orbit delivery of two communications satellites and a number of tactical and strategic ground stations and network control systems
dom	APC	Boxer	400	2006		EUR200m, 200 for army. Option for further 72 units configured as field ambulances
dom	LAV	Wiesel 2	13	2006	2007	EUR9m (USD11.7m). Also two Wiesel 2 driver training vehicles and two training models, plus logistic support
dom	Trucks	MAN SX 45	157	2006	2007	Deliveries to be completed by 2012
dom	SSK	Type 212A	2	2006	–	Due to enter in service from 2012
dom	SSK	Type 212A	2	2007	–	Comms system for 2 new SSK entering service in 2012
dom	SSK	Type 212A	2	2007	–	Propulsion system for 2 new SSK that will enter service in 2012. EUR55m (USD72.3m). The contract includes air independent propulsion systems, DV switchgears and platform management systems
dom	Hel	VFW-Sikorsky CH-53G	40	2007	2007	Upgrade. EUR520m (USD684m). Contract to be completed between 2007 and 2010
Int'l	Hel	EC135	16	–	2007	Rescue hel. Deliveries to be completed in 2 years
Nl	Hel	NH-90	80	2007	2007	Part of a EUR6.6bn contract signed in 2000 for the delivery of 298 hel. 50 hel for the army, 30 hel for the air force.

Table 15 Selected Arms Orders and Deliveries, NATO Europe

Country	Supplier	Classification	Designation	Quantity	Order date	Original Delivery date	Comment
	Nl	Hel	NH-90	42	2007	–	30 hel for the Army Air Corps and 12 for the air force
	Int'l	Trg hel	EC120 B	6	–	2007	To replace Federal Police's Alouette II fleet. First delivery in June 2007. Deliveries to be completed in 7 months
	Int'l	UAV	*EuroHawk* strategic UAV	5	2007	2010	EUR430m (USD559m). Deliveries to be completed before 2015
	Int'l	FF	F125	4	2007	2014	EUR2bn
	dom	AAM	IRIS-T SL	–	2007	–	EUR123m (USD166m). Surface-launched variant of the infra-red guided IRIS-T AAM. To enter service from 2012 as secondary msl for army MEADS
	US	AAM	Evolved *Sea Sparrow* Missile (ESSM)	–	2007	–	Part of a USD223m contract issued by the NATO *Sea Sparrow* Consortium for 294 ESSM
	dom	FF	F123	3	2007	–	Upgrade. EUR6.4m. Naval protection systems for FF all to be installed by 2009
	dom	VIP tpt	A319 / Bombardier *Global* 5000	6	2007	2010	USD270m. 2 A319 to be delivered in 2010, 4 *Global* 5000 to be delivered in 2011. To replace Bombardier *Challenger* 601 fleet
Greece (Gr)	Ge	SSK	Type 214	3	1998	2005	Second of class delivery expected July 2008. Last delivery expected 2010
	Fr	FGA	M-2000EG *Mirage*	15	2000	2007	EUR1.6bn (USD2.1bn)
	Fr	AAM	MICA	200	2000	–	Additional 100 ordered in 2004
	Fr	ALCM	SCALP	56	2000	–	Additional 36 ordered in 2004
	RF	SAM	SA-15 *Gauntlet*	29	2000	2001	*Tor*-M1; additional order of 29 following delivery of first 21
	RF	ATGW	AT-14 *Kornet*	278	2001	–	Two phase purchase
	Nl	Hel	NH-90 TTH	20	2002	2005	Option on further 14
	Ge	MBT	*Leopard* 2 A6	190	2002	2006	(170 MBT, 12 ARV, 8 AVLB) EUR 1.7bn (USD2.05bn). Final delivery expected 2009
	dom	PFM	*Super Vita*	2	2003	2006	First delivery in 2006, second 2007; additional vessels expected
	Ge	MBT	*Leopard* 2 A4	197	2003	2006	183 MBTs, 10 ALVBs, 4 ARVs. EUR 270m (USD333m).
	Ge	MBT	*Leopard* 1 A5	150	2003	2006	Free transfer
	Ge	AIFV	*Kentaurus*	150	2003	2005	Option on further 130
	US	Atk Hel	AH-64D	12	2003	2007	First delivery in January 2007
	US	FGA	F-16C Block 52	30	2005	2009	Programme in development
	US		DB-110 recce system	–	2007	–	Upgrade for new F-16C Block 52 incl 2 recce pods
	dom	FGA	M-2000-5 Mk2 *Mirage*	10	–	2007	Upgrade. Modernisation of M-2000Eg to M- 2000-5 Mk2 standard
	US	AAM	Evolved *Sea Sparrow* Missile (ESSM)	–	2007	–	Part of a USD223m contract issued by the NATO *Sea Sparrow* Consortium for collective purchase of 294 ESSM

Table 15 Selected Arms Orders and Deliveries, NATO Europe

Country Supplier		Classification	Designation	Quantity	Order date	Original Delivery date	Comment
Hungary (Hu)	Swe	FGA	*Gripen*	14	2003	2006	Leased for 12 years
	Pl	UAV	*Sofar* systems	2	2006	2007	EUR800,000 (USD 1.05m). Each system consists of three UAVs and portable and vehicle-mounted ground control stations
Iceland (Icl)	Chl	PCO	–	1	2006	2009	EUR30m (USD39.6m). New patrol vessel to replace Odinn PCO
Italy (It)	Int'l	FGA	*Typhoon*	121	1985	2004	Tranche 1 ordered 1998 (29 aircraft). Tranche 2 ordered 2004 (46 ac). Tranche 3 order 46. First deliveries 2004
	NI	Hel	NH-90 TTH	116	1987	2007	Army order of 60, first deliveries 2007. Navy order of 56, with first deliveries expected in Sept 2006
	UK	SAM	FSAF (Future surface-to-air-family)	–	1990	2006	Future surface-to-air-family, with Fr, UK
	Ge	SSK	Type 212A	2	1997	2005	Built under licence in It; options for 2 more
	dom	APC	*Puma*	540	1999	2003	Deliveries continue
	Ge	Arty	PzH 2000	70	1999	2004	Joint production. Final delivery expected 2008
	Fr	FFG	*Horizon*	4	1999	2007	Joint It/Fr project. First of class launched 2006. 2nd of class expected to be commissioned in 2009
	US	UAV	*Predator*	6	2001	2002	Delivery continuing
	dom /Fr	FFG	FREMM	10	2002	2010	EUR6.5bn (USD7.6bn) est. Multi-mission FF. Project development on-going
	dom	Trg	SF-260EA	30	2003	–	Order continuing
	UK	APC	Bv-206	146	2003	2004	2 orders (first for 112; second for 34) Total order value EUR83m (USD100m). Final delivery expected 2009
	Fr / dom	AIFV	*Dardo*	200	2005	_	Additional order (200 already in service)
	US	Tkr	KC-767	4	_	2007	Conversion of commercial ac into tkr for the Italian Air Force
	dom	Trg	MB-339CD	14	2007	2009	Avionics upgrade. Bach 1 ac reconfigured to Batch 2 standards
Latvia (Lat)	NI	MHC	*Alkmaar*	5	2005	2006	EUR57m (USD69m). Final delivery expected 2008
Lithuania (L)	SF	Trucks	*Sisu* E13TP 8x8 off-road	50	2005	2007	EUR30m (USD40.4). Contract includes a EUR10m option for approx 30 additional trucks. First 26 delivered in August 2007. Deliveries to be completed in 2009
Luxembourg (Lu)	Int'l	Trg	A-400M	1	2003	2010	Programme in development
Netherlands (NI)	Int'l	Hel	NH-90	20	1987	2007	With Fr, Ge, It. Delays announced in 2007. According to 2007 production plans the NI will receive the last 4 hel in 2013
	Ge	Arty	PzH 2000	57	2000	2004	Final delivery in 2009
	dom / Ge	APC	*Boxer*	200	2000	–	Joint programme continuing
	Ge	MBT	*Leopard* 2A5	180	2001	–	Upgrade to 2A6 continues
	US	Tpt	KDC-10	2	2004	2004	Yet to be delivered
	UK	C2	*Bowman*	1405	2005	2005	USD21m. Digital communications for Royal Netherlands Marines. Pending Parliamentary approval

Table 15 **Selected Arms Orders and Deliveries, NATO Europe**

Country Supplier	Classification	Designation	Quantity	Order date	Original Delivery date	Comment
Swe	APC	BvS-10 *Viking*	74	2005	2007	USD76.6m for Royal Netherlands Marines, fitted with *Bowman*. Final deliveries in 2007
US	SAM	PAC-3 *Patriot*	32	2005	2006	Part of 136 msl (USD532m lot 6) procured for US Army allocated for Foreign Military Sales
US	Hel	Ch-47D *Chinook*	5	2005	2007	Approx EUR250m. (USD302m)
US	Tpt	C-130 *Hercules*	4	2005	2008	Ex-USN. Will also be upgraded at the cost of EUR54m (USD65m) First delivery in 2006
Ge / dom	APC	*Boxer* 8X8	200	2006	–	EUR595m (USD747m)
Swe	AIFV	CV9035	184	–	2007	Final delivery expected 2010
US	Ftr	F-16AM/BM	20	2006	2007-08	Upgrade. USD34m. Litening Advanced Targeting Pods
US	Hel	Ch-47F *Chinook*	6	2007	2009	Deliveries between July 2007 and January 2010
US	AAM	Evolved *Sea Sparrow* Missile (ESSM)	–	2007	–	Part of a USD223m contract issued by the NATO *Sea Sparrow* Consortium for collective purchase of 294 ESSM
Norway (No) Sp	FFG	*Fridtjof Nansen*	5	2000	2006	*Roald Amundsen* (F-311), second of class commissioned in May 2007. Final FFG due for commissioning in Sept 2009
US	ATGW	*Javelin*	90	2003	2006	526 missiles
US	MPA	P-3 *Orion*	6	2007	2009	Upgrade: service-life extension kits. USD95m. Final kit delivery March 2010
UK	APC	M113	72	2007	2007	Upgrade kits. USD29.7m. Options for 34 additional sets of kits, storage cases and additional spares
US	Trg	C-130J *Super Hercules*	4	2007	–	NOK3.7bn (USD622m)
dom	ASSM	NSM	–	2007	–	NOK2.2746bn (USD466m). Production will continue through 2014. For 5 new *Fridtjof Nansen* FF and 6 *Skjold* fast attack craft
Swe	FGA	JAS 39 *Gripen*	–	2007	–	Sat comms upgrade and broadband technology development. USD25m. To be completed in 2 years
US	AAM	Evolved *Sea Sparrow* Missile (ESSM)	–	2007	–	Part of a USD223m contract issued by the NATO *Sea Sparrow* Consortium for purchase of 294 ESSM
Fr	MCMV	*Oksoy/Alta*	2	2007		Sonar upgrade involving the delivery of 6 TSM2022 MK3 N hull mounted sonars (HMS)
Poland (Pl) Il	ATGW	NT-D *Dandy*	–	1997	–	For W-3 *Huzar* atk hel
UK	Arty	AS-90 *Braveheart*	72	1999	2007	Licence to produce turret system. First six turrets completed for testing in 2004. First full 18 gun battalion ready in 2007. Deliveries to continue
US	FGA	F-16	48	2002	2006	36 F-16C ac and 12 F-16D ac. First 4 ac delivered in November 2006. Remaining deliveries scheduled by 2008

Europe

Table 15 Selected Arms Orders and Deliveries, NATO Europe

Country	Supplier	Classification	Designation	Quantity	Order date	Original Delivery date	Comment
	Fr	ATGW	Spike-LR	264	2003	2004	USD397m. 264 launchers and 2,675 missiles. To be built in Poland under licence. Final delivery expected 2013
	SF	APC	Patria AMV	690	2003	2004	USD 1.7bn. First two delivered June 2004. 89 to be delivered by end of 2005. Deliveries to continue until 2014
	dom	FSG	Project 621-Gawron	2	2004	2008	Earliest possible delivery 2008. Design based on German MEKO A100. Option for further 5
	Swe	Msl	RBS 15 Mk 3	36	2006	2009	PLN560m (USD178m). The contract covers msl delivery, spare parts, in-service support, training and a simulator. Deliveries continuing until 2012
	dom	Hel	PZL SW-4	22	2006	2007	PLN112m (USD37.8). 9 hel to be delivered in both 2007 and 2008, final deliveries in 2009. Trg simulator also in contract
	dom	IFV	Rosomak 8x8	25	2007	–	Armour upgrade. PLN20m (USD7m). LPA armour for IFV deployed in Afghanistan
	It	FSG	Project 621-Gawron	–	2007	2008	Turbine upgrade. EUR10m (USD13.1m)
	Il	UAV	Orbiter	6	2007	2007	PLN10.56m (USD3.82m). Deliveries to be completed by end of Oct 2007
Portugal (Por)	dom	PSOH	Viana do Castelo (NPO2000)	10	2002	2006	All to be delivered by 2015
	A	APC	Pandur II	260	2005	2006	EUR344.3m (USD415m). Army order of 240 in 11 configurations. Marine order of 20 in 4 versions. Final delivery 2009
	dom	PCC	LFC	5	2005	2008	EUR115m (USD139m). Final delivery 2011
	Sp	Tpt	C-295M	12	2006	2008	EUR270m (USD326m)
	Nl	FF	Karel-Doorman	2	2006	2008	EUR240m (USD306.3m). HrMs Van Nes to be handed over on Dec 2008, HrMs Val Galen on Nov 2009
	US	AAM	Evolved Sea Sparrow Missile (ESSM)	–	2007	–	Part of a USD223m contract issued by the NATO Sea Sparrow Consortium for purchase of 294 ESSM
	Ge	MBT	Leopard 2A6	37	2007	2008	EUR80m (USD113m). Former Dutch MBT
Romania (R)	dom	Hel	IAR-330 Puma	3	–	2007	Upgraded to naval configuration. First hel delivered in Jan 2007. Delivery to be completed by the end of 2008
	CH	APC	Piranha IIIC	31	2006	2007	EUR38m (USD49m). To replace TAB vehicles used by the army in Afghanistan and Iraq
	It	Tpt	C-27J	7	2006	2007	EUR220m (USD293m)
	US	Radar	AN/FPS 117	5	2007	–	Life-extension upgrade to be completed by February 2009
Slovakia (Slvk)	RF	FGA	MiG-29 Fulcrum	12	2004	2006	–
Slovenia (Slvn)	SF	APC	Patria 8x8	135	2007	2007	SIT66.61bn (USD365.9m). First APC delivered by end 2007. Final delivery in 2013

Table 15 Selected Arms Orders and Deliveries, NATO Europe

Country Supplier	Classification	Designation	Quantity	Order date	Original Delivery date	Comment
Spain (Sp) Int'l	FGA	Typhoon	87	1994	2004	Tranche 1 ordered 1998 (20 ac). Tranche 2 ordered 2004 (33 ac). Tranche 3 order 34 ac
Ge	MBT	Leopard 2	219	1998	2003	EUR1.94bn (USD2.34bn).Includes 16 ARVs. Final deliveries in 2008
dom	SSK	S-80 Scorpene	4	2003	2011–14	Earliest delivery expected 2011
dom	LHD	Strategic Projection Ship	1	2003	2008	Multipurpose platform
dom	AIFV	Pizarro	212	2003	2005	EUR707m (USD853m). Five variants. Final deliveries 2010
Ge	Hel	AS-665 Tiger	24	2003	2007	First 3 hel delivered in May 2007
Int'l	Tpt	A-400M	27	2003	2010	–
dom	LCM	LCM-1E	12	2004	2007	EUR32m. To replace LCM-8. 8th LCM delivered in July 2007. Final deliveries in 2009
dom	AOR	AOR	1	2005	2008	USD210m. Similar to Patiño class
dom	Arty	SBT (V07)	72	2005	–	Includes upgrade to 12 APU SBT howitzers from V06 to V07 variant
dom	FFG	Alvaro de Bazan F-100	1	2005	–	Part of a major acquisition package with a potential value of EUR2.5bn (USD3.12bn). Option for one more FFG
dom	PCO	BAM offshore maritime intervention vessel	4	2005	–	Refer to above
dom	AORH	BAC combat logistics vessel	1	2005	2007	Refer to above
Int'l	Hel	NH-90	45	2005	–	EUR 1.3bn. Part of a major acquisition package with a potential value of EUR2.5bn (USD3.12bn). To be used by the three main services. Projected acquisition of 100 hel
Swe	Radar	Arthur	–	2006	2007	Artillery radar. EUR59m (USD77.5m). The number of systems is undiscosed. Final delivery by June 2009
dom	UAV	Searcher Mk II	4	2007	–	EUR17m (USD23m)
US	ATGW	Spike-LR	260	2007	2007	USD424.5m. 2600 msl. Contract to be completed by 2014
Int'l	MP	P-3B	5	2006	–	Operational upgrade
Int'l	SAR	CN-235-500	3	2006	–	SAR and pollution control ac
Int'l	Hel	NH-90 TTH	45	2007	2010	
Int'l	Ac	EC-135	4	2007	–	For the Unidad Militar de Emergencias, a new unit of Sp's armed forces
US	VLS	MK 41 Baseline VII	1	2007	–	To be delivered to an Alvaro de Bazan-class F-105 FF. Part of a USD16m contract including 3 VLS for Australia and 1 VLS for Spain
US	FF	F-100	1	2007	2008	Weapon system upgrade
US	Msl	SM-1	–	2007	–	Support contract. USD 29m including missile assembly and testing work for the Spanish and Egyptian navies

Europe

Table 15 Selected Arms Orders and Deliveries, NATO Europe

Country	Supplier	Classification	Designation	Quantity	Order date	Original Delivery date	Comment
	Int'l	Tpt	C-295 CASA	2	2007	–	EUR46.9m (USD64.2m). It also include the retrofit of an already in-service ac
	US	AAM	Evolved *Sea Sparrow* Missile (ESSM)	–	2007	–	Part of a USD223m contract issued by the NATO SeaSparrow Consortium for purchase of 294 ESSM
Turkey (Tu)	Ge	PCM	*Kilic*	9	1993	2007	Final 2 PCM to be commissioned in 2008 and 2009
	UK	SAM	*Rapier* Mk 2	840	1999	2000	Licence; 80 a year for 10 years. Deliveries continuing
	ROK	Arty	SP Howitzer, *Firtina* 155mm	20	2001	2003	Deliveries continuing. Total requirement of 300- funding permitting.
	US	AEW	B-737 AWACS	4	2002	2006	USD1bn.
	Il	MBT	M-60A1	170	2002	2006	Upgraded by Il.
	dom	MBT	*Leopard* 1A1/1A1A4	162	2002	2006	Fire-control systems upgrade. USD160m. Continuing
	Int'l	Tpt	A-400M	10	2003	2012	Programme in development
	US	FGA	F-16	80	2005	–	USD1.1bn. Upgrade of 70 block 50s and 4 Block 40ac. Original deal included purchase of 295 Sidewinder (AIM-9X). Offset commitments are included
	It	MPA	ATR-72	10	2005	–	USD210m. First five deliveries by 2010. Final deliveries by 2012
	Ge	MBT	*Leopard* 2	298	2005	–	Ex-German Army
	Il	UAV	*Heron*	10	2005	–	–
	US	Hel	Sikorsky S-70B *Seahawk*	17	2006	2009	–
	US	FGA	F-16C/D	216	2006		Upgrade. USD635m. Contract includes 216 modernisation kits, flight testing, training. Contract expires in February 2016
	dom	Tpt	C-130 B/E (*Erciyes* programme)	13	2006	–	Avionics upgrade. USD119m
	dom	SAR	Hel-capable patrol vessel	4	2006	2010	USD325m. Modified Italian *Comandante*-class PCO. For Turkish Coast Guard
	Int'l	Hel	*Mangusta* A 129	30	2007	–	USD2.7bn. Option for further 20 hel. The value of the contract is for the purchase of 50 hel
	US	FGA	F-16 Block 50	30	2007	2011	USD1.78bn. Deliveries to be completed by 2104, when current 213 F-16 will be under modification
	dom	PB	56m PB	16	2007	–	EUR402m (USD545m). Deliveries to be completed by 2015
	dom / ROK	Trg	SKT-1 *Woong-Bee*	55	2007	2009	USD500m. To replace T-37 trg ac
	US	AAM	Evolved *Sea Sparrow* Missile (ESSM)	–	2007	–	Part of a USD223m contract issued by the NATO *Sea Sparrow* Consortium for purchase of 294 ESSM
	US	ASM	AGM-84E *Harpoon*	–	2007	–	USD 12.9m. 10 *Peace Onyx* III F-16 AN/AWW-13 pods to be installed by 2011

Table 15 **Selected Arms Orders and Deliveries, NATO Europe**

Country Supplier	Classification	Designation	Quantity	Order date	Original Delivery date	Comment
United Kingdom (UK)	US	EW	*Soothsayer*	–	–	2006	(USD237m) Battlefield electronic warfare system. First increment (USD130m) delayed to 2008
	Int'l	FGA	*Typhoon*	232	1984	2003	Tranche 1 ordered 1998 (55 ac). Tranche 2 ordered 2004 (89 ac). Tranche 3 order (88 ac)
	dom	SSN	*Astute*	4	1994	2008	First vessel launched June 2007. GBP200m (USD303.8m) per vessel. Fourth vessel ordered on May 2007 / or delivered in 2013
	dom	SAM	PAAMS	–	1994	–	Development with Fr/It
	dom	MPA	*Nimrod* MRA4	12	1996	2009	Orders reduced to 12 ac
	Ca	Recce	*Sentinel* RMK1 (ASTOR)	5	1997	2006	–
	dom	Sat	*Skynet* 5	4	1998	2006	GBP2.5bn (USD4.3bn)
	dom	CET/ETS	*Titan*	66	2001	2007	GBP250m (USD432m) 33 *Titan* bridge-laying vehicles and 33 obstacle/mine-clearing vehicles
	dom	DDG	Type 45- *Daring* class	6	2001	2008	First of class ISD expected 2009
	dom	CET	*Terrier*	60	2002	2008	20 vehicles to be delivered by late 2008
	dom	Trg	*Hawk* Mk 128	44	2003	2008	Initial order for 20, with option for additional 24 exercised.
	US	ATGW	*Javelin*	300	2003	2006	Up to 5,000 msl
	US	PGM	*Paveway* IV	2000	2003	2007	–
	Int'l	Tpt	A-400M	25	2003	2010	–
	Ge	Tpt	A-330	16	2004	–	27-year PFI
	US	Tpt	C-17 *Globemaster* III	6	2005	2008	4 ac originally leased for seven years in 2001. Decision to purchase in 2005, for delivery in 2006, along with a fifth and sixth ac in 2008
	dom	Hel	EH101- *Merlin*	30	2005	2012	Upgrade. GBP750m (USD1.3bn)
	dom	APC	FV432	500	2005	2006	Upgrade. Programme completion in 2008
	dom	Hel	*Sea King* AEW MK7	4	2005	2007	USD56m. 2 ac are to be converted from ASW role, 2 being to built to replace war losses
	dom	Atk Hel	WAH-64		2005	2009	Sighting and targeting upgrade. USD354m. Completion planned for 2010
	It / UK	Hel	*Future Lynx*	70	2006	2014	GBP1bn (USD1.8bn). 70 (40 army, 30 navy) hel with option for further 10. Final delivery 2015. Expected to remain in service for 30 years
	UK / US	CIWS	*Phalanx* Block 1B	16	2006	2007	Upgrade kits. GBP30m (USD57m). Final delivery 2013
	US	FGA	*Harrier* GR9	–	2007	2007	Operational upgrade. Supply of ATP. Full capability deployment in June 2007
	US	FGA	*Harrier* GR10	12	2007	2007	Targeting pod upgrade. AN/AAQ-33 *Sniper* targeting pod for ac deployed in Afghanistan.

Table 15 Selected Arms Orders and Deliveries, NATO Europe

Country Supplier	Classification	Designation	Quantity	Order date	Original Delivery date	Comment
dom	FGA	Tornado	–	2006	2007	GBP947m. Support contract known as ATTAC (Availability Transformation: Tornado Aircraft Contract)
dom	Radar	Commander	2	2007	–	GPB30m. 1 new radar and 1 upgraded ac to be delivered by mid-2008
dom	Trg	Hawk TMK1	131	2007	–	GBP74m. Support contract, known as Hawk Integrated Operational Support (HAWK IOS) contract, aimed at ensuring that agreed levels of sorties can be carried out by Hawk until 2011
dom	APC	BvS10 Viking	21	2007	2008	Prototypes to be delivered by end 2007. The deal follows an initial contract worth USD145m and completed in 2005, to provide the Royal Marine Commandos with 108 Viking systems
Int'l	Hel	EH101-Merlin	6	2007	2007	Modification of 6 former Royal Danish Air Force EH101 Merlin hel to become EH101 Merlin HC Mk3A in RAF service
US	Spt hel	Chinook HC.3	8	2007	2009	Modification contract. GBP50m (USD99m). Originally planned for use with special forces, to be modified for use in spt role by the RAF
Int'l	UAV	Hermes 450	–	2007	2010	USD110m. The contract also covers trg for UK MoD staff, logistic support and provision of management services
dom	CV	–	2	2007	2012	GBP3.9bn (USD8bn). HMS Queen Elizabeth (2012) and HMS Prince of Wales (2015). To be based in Portsmouth
dom	CVH	Ocean	1	2007	2008	Upgrade. GBP30m (USD59.6m). Part of the MoD's Surface Ship Support Alliance
dom	Comms	Falcon	–	2007	–	GBP45m (USD92m). 'Increment C' phase
US / dom	UUV	REMUS 600	2	2007	2009	GBP5.5m (USD11m)

Table 16 Selected Arms Orders and Deliveries, Non-NATO Europe

	Country Supplier	Classification	Designation	Quantity	Order date	Original Delivery date	Comment
Austria (A)	Int'l	FGA	*Typhoon*	15	2003	2007	EUR2bn (USD2.7bn). Final delivery in 2009
Belarus (Bel)	Ukr	Trg	L-39C *Albatros*	10	–	2005	First deliveries end of 2005. Deliveries continuing. Option for additional purchase of 10-20 ac
Croatia (Cr)	dom	MBT	M-95 *Degman*	–	1995	–	On hold due to funding difficulties
	dom / SF	APC	*Patria* 8x8 / 6x6 (XC-361 model)	126	2007	–	EUR200m (USD276m). 84 8x8, 42 6x6
Cyprus (Cy)	Int'l	SAR	Hel	3	2006	–	Option on another 1
	RF	Atk	Mi-35P *Hind-F*	11	2007	–	Upgrade. USD26m contract for airframe and engines refurbishment
Finland (SF)	Fr	ATGW	*Spike*	100	2000	2001	Option on further 70. Deliveries continuing
	Nl	Hel	NH-90	20	2001	2004	First 3 hel to be delivered in 2006. Deliveries continuing
	dom	AIFV	CV9030	45	2004	2006	Deliveries continuing
	It / Ge	MCMV	MCMV 2010 Project' vessel	3	2006	2010	EUR244.8 (USD315m). Three mine countermeasures vessels, a mine countermeasures information system, a life-cycle support and maintenance package. Last vessel expected in 2012
	dom	Trg	*Hawk*	45	2006	–	Modernisation and training efficiency upgrade. EUR20m (USD26.3m). Work to be completed by 2010
	Swe	SAM	RBS 70	–	2006	2008	SEK600m (USD85.5m). Final delivery in 2010
	Int'l	Tpt	MANPAD C-295	2	2006	2007	EUR45m (USD57.3m). Option for another 5 ac. To replace Fokker F-27 ac
	US	FGA	F/A-18C/D *Hornet*	–	2007	–	Second phase of F/A-18C/D *Hornet* Mid-life Update project. AN/AAQ-28(V)4 Litening Advanced Targeting system to be mounted on ac
	No	MCMV	MCMV 2010 Project' vessel	3	2007	2010	Upgrade. NOK180m (USD29.5m)
	Swe	UUV	*Double Eagle*	3	2007	2009	EUR8.51m (USD11.4m). For the 'MCMV 2010 Project' vessels. One UUV in 2010 and one in 2011
	CH	Trg	*Hawk* 66	18	2007	–	EUR40m (USD54m). Ac belonged to CH
	US	Trg	*Hawk* Mk 51 / 51A	30	2007	–	Avionics upgrade. A second level upgrade will be given to a further 15 ac (level 1-upgraded and non-upgraded ac)
	dom	Recce	CBRN Veh	–	2007	–	EUR15m (USD20.4m). Prototype. Lightweight 4x4 recce vehicle
Ireland (Irl)	CH	APC	Mowag *Piranha* IIIH	15	2005	2007	EUR30m.(USD36m). Order for two variants.
	It / UK	Hel	AW-139	2	2006	2008	EUR26m (USD34m)
Sweden (Swe)	dom	FGA	JAS 39A / B / C / D *Gripen*	204	1981	1995	Deliveries continuing. As for 2007, 102 JAS 39A, 20 C, 15 B and 2 D are in service. Total number expected to be reduced to 160
	dom	FSGH	*Visby*	5	1995	2005	Final FSGH launched in 2006 due for commissioning 2008
	Ge	AAM	IRIS-T	–	1997	–	Development with Ge continuing
	dom	ASM	KEPD 350 *Taurus*		1997	2005	Developed with Ge. Also KEPD 150. Currently in production
	SF	APC	XA-203 *Sisu*	167	2000	2001	First order for 104 vehicles. Additional option for 63 vehicles exercised in 2002. Final delivery in 2008

Europe

Table 16 Selected Arms Orders and Deliveries, Non-NATO Europe

	Country Supplier	Classification	Designation	Quantity	Order date	Original Delivery date	Comment
	It	Hel	A-109M Hkp 11	22	2001	2002	Order including 8 hel to be flown from FS. 20 hel still to be delivered as of 2007
	Int'l	Hel	NH-90	25	2001	2007	18 firm orders for 13 TTT I SAR hel and 5 ASW variants, plus 7 options. 2 hel delivered
	Nl	PCO	KBV 001	2	2005	2008	Ordered for Coast Guard. Option for 3rd vessel available
	Int'l	Mor	AMOS 120mm	2	2006	2011	SKR30m (approx USD4m). The two prototypes are to be mounted on a Vv90 tracked chassis.
	UK	Arty	*Archer* Artillery System	24	2007	2009	SEK100m (approx USD13.6m). The *Archer* system consists of a fully automated 155 mm/L52 howitzer mounted on a 6x6 chassis, an ammunition resupply vehicle, a support vehicle and the *Excalibur* guided projectile. Deliveries to continue for 2 years
	UK / RSA	MHPV	RG32M	98	2007	2007	EUR21m (approx USD28.2m). Final delivery due Dec 2007
	Ge	Decoy	*Birdie* 118	–	2007	2007	Bi-spectral Infrared Decoy Improved Efficiency (Birdie) for air force hel
	dom	FGA	JAS 39 *Gripen*	–	2007	–	Helmet-mounted display upgrade. USD54m
Switzerland (CH)	US	AD	*Florako*	1	1999	2008	System upgrade continuing
	UK	AIFV	CV9030CH	154	2000	2002	Deliveries continuing
	dom	APC	Mowag *Piranha* IIIC	8	2006	2007	Electronic Warfare Vehicle variants
	dom	APC	Mowag *Piranha* I	40	2006	2007	Conversions from Tank-destroyers to Ambulances
	dom	APC	Mowag *Piranha* I	160	2006	2008	Re-role of *Piranha* I APC to protected command vehicles. Conversion to be completed by 2010
	Int'l	Tpt/trg hel	EC635	16	2006	2008	Deliveries between March/April 2008 and the end of 2009
	Int'l	Hel	EC135	2	2006	2008	Deliveries between March/April 2008 and the end of 2010
	dom	AEV	*Kodiak*	12	2006	2009	CHF100m (USD82.5m). Contract for 12 AEV modules, six mineclearing modules and logistic support. An additional support. Final deliveries in 2011
	dom	MBT	Pz 87	134	2007	–	Upgrade. The upgraded tanks are likely to be retained to at least 2025.
	Sp	C2	C2 information system	–	2007	–	EUR43m (approx USD57.78m). Extension of 2004 contract. It will run until 2010
Ukraine (Ukr)	RF	Tpt	An-70	5	1991	2008	2 ac due in 2008

Chapter Four
Russia

Fifteen years after the end of the Cold War, and following more than a decade of painful military reform, Russia's armed forces are becoming more capable in a number of key areas. Training across a wide spectrum has increased, particularly in joint-force activity focusing on readiness, deployability and interoperability (see Table 36, p. 440). The improving economic climate and declarations that more will be spent on national defence (see p. 209) have played their part in enabling this long-awaited rebirth which is, nonetheless, still in its early stages. The tense relationship that has developed between Russia and the US, as well as between Russia and NATO, is very much part of the process, with President Vladimir Putin strident in his declarations against US plans to extend its missile-defence infrastructure further into Europe, as well as NATO enlargement. His declared moratorium on future Russian involvement in the Conventional Forces in Europe (CFE) Treaty was another sign of his determination to show that Moscow is no longer prepared to allow the perceived shift in the military balance on its Western borders to go unchallenged (see Europe, p. 101). Russia seeks a re-appraisal of the CFE Treaty, which it sees as being unfairly balanced in favour of NATO.

The resumption of strategic bomber sorties beyond Russian airspace (which had been suspended in the mid-1990s) and the developing military activity within the framework of the Shanghai Cooperation Organisation (SCO) (see p. 325), together with Putin's declared intent to increase defence-industrial production, are as much indications of an increasing ability to produce real military capability as they are the subjects of political speeches designed to portray Putin as the builder of Russia's military. The coincidence of the burgeoning Russian economy and the apparently confrontational posture of the US and NATO on Russia's borders has enabled Putin to boost his popularity and retain strength as he moves into the last months of his second presidential term. But, rather than having a confrontational relationship with the West, Putin is aiming to regain a form of strategic parity for Russia, with this aspiration now a realistic proposition.

Even though Putin would like to establish a balanced strategic relationship with Georgia, bilateral relations have in fact deteriorated and become more complex. Tensions have risen around the unresolved separatist conflicts in Abkhazia and South Ossetia (see Europe p. 106), with a number of serious incidents threatening to worsen relations between Moscow and Tbilisi even further. Strong US support for Georgia in its drive for NATO membership is a source of anger for Russia and is a motivating factor behind its support for the regimes in Sukhumi and Tskhinvali. Despite these growing tensions, Russia has continued to meet its CFE obligations with its base-closure programme in Georgia. At the end of June, the Russian 62nd base at Akhalkalaki was handed over to the Georgian Ministry of Defence and withdrawal from the 12th base at Batumi has commenced, with a final closure date in 2008.

Training activity has underpinned this more confident posture and Russia's determination to display strength in defence. Not only has this been achieved through the Collective Security Treaty Organisation (CSTO) and high-level events organised by the SCO, but also at a national level, with large-scale manoeuvres in the Caucasus and air defence exercises involving significant resources.

INTERNATIONAL MILITARY COOPERATION

Despite tension between Russia and the West there is a degree of pragmatism and cooperation in defence relations, with a number of bilateral and multilateral events taking place among Russia, the US and NATO. For example, in June, Russian ships took part in the NATO Partnership for Peace exercise *BALTOPS 2007* in the Baltic Sea, while in August two minesweepers from the Baltic Fleet took part in *Exercise Open Spirit 2007*, which included 17 ships from Lithuania, the UK, Latvia, Poland, France, Sweden, Germany, Belgium and the Netherlands. In the Pacific Ocean in September, ships from the US 7th Fleet and the Russian Pacific Fleet took part in *Exercise Pacific Eagle 2007*, the largest US–Russian naval exercise in the region since 1998. The USS *Lassen*, an *Arleigh Burke*-class guided-missile destroyer and the USS *Patriot*, a minesweeper, carried out joint training in minesweeping and interception operations with the *Admiral Panteleyev*, an *Udaloy*-class destroyer, and a BT-100 minesweeper. Of note, given the poor Russia–US relationship, was the re-instatement of the *Torgau* exercise series. The most recent exercise took place from 14–16 September 2007. Also of note was the joint exercise, *Shared Purpose*, which ended in Moscow on 1 November, and which focussed on cooperative activities and responsibilities. A similar exercise took place one year earlier in Stuttgart.

In addition to Russia's extensive cooperative equipment programme with India, the two countries are also involved in military-to-military training activities. In September *Exercise Indra-2007* took place at the Pskov base of the 76th Airborne Division within an anti-terrorist scenario involving airborne forces. *Exercise Indra-2008* is planned for September 2008.

While pursuing its defence relationship with NATO and traditional defence partners, the CSTO and the SCO have provided the central framework for Russian international military cooperation. Putin's determination to reassert Russian influence in the South Caucasus and Central Asia has been underlined by the increasing commitment to military training through these two organisations, where the main priorities have been the practice of joint procedures in air defence and anti-terrorist operations (see Table 36). Events such as the CSTO air defence exercises and the SCO exercise *Peace Mission 2007* (see p. 325) serve the aims of improving interoperability between national forces, underscoring Russian influence within the alliances and providing a platform for showcasing Russian equipment.

Further to *Peace Mission 2007*, and serving as an indication of growing defence cooperation between Russia and China, joint training in the Moscow region in August saw the participation of interior and police forces from both countries. The scenario within which joint procedures were practised was based on the search for and destruction of illegal armed groups.

Strategic defence

Against the background of a more assertive Russia trying to regain its position as a major military power, the modernisation of the strategic forces is a priority for President Putin and the Ministry of Defence (MoD). With more financial resources available, the past year has seen developments taking place across the entire spectrum of the strategic forces. The resumption in August of strategic bomber flights by long-range aviation aircraft, which had been suspended since the mid

1990s, served as an indication of Russia's improved financial position as much as its strengthening military power. A large-scale training exercise involving Tu-160, Tu-95 and Tu-22 strategic bombers took place over the Arctic, Atlantic and Indian Ocean regions during 18–21 September, with in-flight refuelling being carried out by Il-78 tanker aircraft. Other flights of a similar nature have taken place in the Asia-Pacific region. The capabilities of the Strategic Rocket Forces (SRF) were further developed with a battalion of the Teikovo Missile Division receiving its complement of three mobile *Topol*-M intercontinental ballistic-missile systems in late 2006. A second battalion is to be equipped with the mobile version this year. The deployment of the static silo-based *Topol*-M systems will be completed in the Saratov and Ivanovo regions in 2010. The intention is to include multiple independently targetable re-entry vehicle (MIRV) capability in the next two or three years. The MIRV will consist of 6–10 warheads, and each will reportedly have a yield of 550 kilotonnes. According to SRF Commander Colonel General Nikolai Solovtsov, there were 44 silo-based systems deployed by the end of 2006. A test of a missile with a MIRV warhead took place in May. A second test took place on 19 October with a missile fired from a mobile launcher in the Plesetsk cosmodrome at a target in the Kura test range in Kamchatka.

In June 2007 a successful test flight of a *Bulava* submarine-launched ballistic missile took place. The missile was fired from a Project 941 *Typhoon*-class submarine located in the White Sea at a target in Kamchatka. Reports indicated that the three-stage missile has a new type of solid propellant for improved thrust. Meanwhile, Project 955 *Borey*-class submarines designated to carry *Bulava* missiles remain in development. It is expected that development will be complete by 2010 with the first *Borey*-class, *Yuri Dolgorukiy*, entering service in 2009. The *Yuri Dolgorukiy*, *Alexander Nevskiy* and *Vladimir Monomakh* will be equipped with 12 launchers each.

Strategic air defence enhancements

As well as enhancing strategic strike capability, the Russian MoD continues to upgrade national strategic air defences. The S-400 *Triumf* surface-to-air-missile air defence system has reportedly been upgraded with a new Kh-96 missile capable of withstanding the effects of jamming devices. The system was reportedly deployed around Moscow in July.

Since the collapse of the Soviet Union, Russia has relied on *Don*, *Daryal* and *Volga* strategic air-defence

Russia

radar systems with elements located outside its borders in Azerbaijan, Ukraine, Belarus and Kazakhstan. The development and deployment of a new radar, *Voronezh-M*, with a greater radius of action, allows missile defence forces to operate without being reliant on information from the other states as the new system can detect targets at the optimum range from within Russian borders. The deployment of the new system at Armavir will negate the need to use the Gaballa radar station in Azerbaijan and the two existing systems in Ukraine, while the new radar located at Lekhtusi near St Petersburg will fill the capability gap left by the loss of an old radar system located at Skrund in Latvia. Gaballa, meanwhile, has been offered to the US as a possible radar site instead of the contentious plan to locate an X-band radar in the Czech Republic – an offer which the US has yet to accept.

REFORM

Selected aerospace capability enhancements

Modernisation and the deployment of new equipment is most evident in the Russian Air Force. The aerospace dimension of non-strategic defence has received strong support from Putin, who stated publicly at the MAKS 2007 air show that the aerospace industry is to be a priority. Even though there is still an emphasis on the export market and less on near-term modernisation of the air force, the drive

to modernise is now clear. The continuing intention to develop a fifth-generation fighter has been highlighted by an announcement that tests on the aircraft will commence in 2009. There is a lack of clarity over whether it will be the joint-production Su-34, to be developed with India, or a wholly domestic product such as the proposed Su-50, developed under the Future Air Complex for Front or Tactical Air Forces.

With the financial allocation for the reconnaissance portion of the aerospace budget set to rise annually there are a variety of enhancements being made, and a number of new reconnaissance capabilities are coming into service. These are separate from the ongoing satellite deployment programme. The Tu-300 reconnaissance unmanned aerial vehicle (UAV) is to have enhanced range and an increase in speed to approximately 950 kilometres per hour. It is believed that the intention is still to develop a UAV with an attack capability, which may have been the original vision for the Tu-300. In another novel move to further enhance its short-range, low-level aerial reconnaissance and observation capability, the air force has trained up to ten airship pilots and is testing *Aerostatika* airships.

To meet a capability gap in the transportation of rapid-deployment troops over distance, the MoD is examining the possibility of replacing Tu-134 aircraft with the new Tu-334. The Tu-334 can carry 102 passengers over a distance of 3,150km and may be used for special forces.

MAP 2 MODERNISING RUSSIA'S EARLY WARNING RADAR SYSTEM

Personnel issues

The biggest problem facing the Russian MoD in its attempt to build modern armed forces seems to centre around personnel (see past issues of *The Military Balance*). The issue goes beyond official and media reports of welfare and morale problems. The downward national demographic trend has reduced numbers of personnel available for service. According to the Main Medical Department of the MoD, around a third of approximately two million candidates eligible by age for conscription service were rejected on health grounds. As an indication of the possible seriousness of the problem one report estimated that, on the basis of current planning, by 2011 there could be 712,000 18-year-old males and a need for 400,000 conscripts. But this forecast is at odds with the more optimistic statement of First Deputy Prime Minister Dmitry Medvedev, who has claimed that Russia's birth rate has increased by 8.5% and the death rate has decreased by 9.5%.

Despite these difficulties, reports show that the target of 133,500 new recruits in the spring draft was achieved. 65% of conscripts in this draft were allocated to the MoD and 35% to other ministries with armed forces. For the first time, no conscripts were allocated to the Border Guard Service, which is now under the remit of the Federal Security Service, and which is to be staffed on a fully contractual basis by 2009.

Within the MoD's armed forces, it is hoped that by January 2008 124,000 servicemen will be volunteers. This would mean that 81 units of various types, the majority being strategic forces, special forces, naval personnel onboard vessels or forces designated for operations, would be fully professional by that date.

Basing and redeployment

In anticipation of the expiry of its lease of the Stavropol base from Ukraine in 2017, Russia has begun the construction of a new base at Novorossiysk. This will be ready for use by the Black Sea Fleet by 2012. The base will have capacity for up to 100 vessels, with infrastructure for the fleet's land-based elements such as aviation and logistics to be added later.

The 33rd and 34th independent motorised mountain brigades (see *The Military Balance 2007*, p. 187) will be fully deployed in their new bases at Botlikh, Dagestan and Zelenchukskaya, Karachaevo-Cherkessia by the end of 2007. According to Defence Minister Anatoly Serdyukov, the brigades will be manned entirely by contract officers and soldiers.

North Caucasus and conflict

The North Caucasus region remains unstable, with high levels of violent extremism, as well as crime fuelled by poverty and unemployment. Chechnya may no longer be Moscow's main area of concern. Dagestan, with deep-rooted Salafism and Wahhabism, suffered from a high level of violence in 2007, with some 80 terrorist attacks in the first half of the year; and Ingushetia has also proved increasingly troublesome for the Kremlin. The nationalist sentiment that existed in all North Caucasian republics in the past has given way to tendencies which are more akin to radical Islam in nature. Salafism, with its promise of equality, is increasingly attractive to young disaffected Muslims across the region. At the same time, organised crime of a particularly violent nature plays its part in creating instability. In this volatile environment, the federal authority seeks to exert some level of control but shows no sign of attempting any regional integration, which leaves a collection of semi-autonomous entities on the border with the problematic South Caucasus.

In Chechnya, the general level of violence has reduced under the stringent regime of President Ramzan Kadyrov, who maintains control through his armed police and military forces, the large majority of whom were formerly rebels. However, the south of the republic remains an area subject to insurgent activity. The total number of troops in the republic is reported as being approximately 30,000. Rising violence in neighbouring Ingushetia led to the deployment in July of 2,500 troops from the Interior Ministry, but with little significant impact. The high degree of anti-Russian feeling among the ethnic Ingush population has led to growing concern that the crisis will only deepen. The so-called 'Ingush Jamaat' are at the heart of the anti-government movement and are gathering increasing support from young disaffected Ingush.

Against this complex background, Moscow appears to be attempting to exert control using its military forces as the main instrument of containment. Aside from the deployment of Interior Ministry troops to Ingushetia and the creation of mountain brigades at bases in Dagestan and Karachaevo-Cherkessia, there has been large-scale training activity focused on the security of Russia's southern border. *Exercise Caucasian Border 2007* took place in July and included more than 400 sorties by Il-76, Su-24, Su-25 and Su-27 aircraft, and helicopters. Airborne and air-landing operations were practiced, and aircraft carried out live-firing on the Tsarskoye and Daryal ranges.

RUSSIA – DEFENCE ECONOMICS

The Russian economy continued its impressive performance of recent years, growing by 7% in 2007 compared to 6.7% in 2006 and 6.4% in 2005. In its 2007 Article IV consultation with Russia, the International Monetary Fund (IMF) commended this strong economic performance, noting that it had been due not only to high oil prices and large capital inflows, but also to good macroeconomic management. In particular it noted that the policy of saving a large proportion of the oil revenue windfall had provided a considerable measure of stability. Growth has also been underpinned by a rise in investment and domestic consumption, spurred by real income growth of over 10%.

On the fiscal front, the non-oil budget deficit continues to grow. Having been as low as 2.9% of GDP in 2004, current projections suggest it will have increased to 7.0% of GDP by 2009. International agencies have warned that this planned increase will lead to upward pressure on inflation and the rouble at a time when the economy is already growing at close to potential. In light of this, the IMF has urged the authorities to adopt a more cautious fiscal policy and delay planned spending increases until the economy can absorb the extra money without putting undue pressure on prices.

Nonetheless, with commodity prices likely to remain at elevated levels, and widely held expectations of policy continuity after the presidential elections suggesting a relatively stable environment, the medium-term economic outlook appears favourable.

Furthermore, despite fears in recent years that the slowing momentum of reform and a lack of clarity regarding the government's role in strategic industries might lead to excessive caution among investors, investment growth has in fact risen, suggesting that investor sentiment is relatively robust and that downside risks to the near-term outlook, in particular from lower oil prices, are limited.

THE 2008 DEFENCE BUDGET

In recent years it has become increasingly difficult to collect and analyse meaningful data on Russia's federal budget, and particularly the finances of Russian national defence, owing to a number of presentational changes. In 2005, federal budget classifications were revised and the chapter entitled 'National Defence' was broadened to include certain military-related expenditures that had previously been allocated under different chapter headings. Then in 2006 and 2007, details of the State Defence Order, comprising procurement, research and development (R&D) and maintenance expenditure, which had been available in 2005, were classified. Unfortunately, in 2008 this trend has continued. There have been widespread changes to the presentation of federal and national defence budget data, not least the switch to a new three-year budget framework, which has been interpreted in some quarters as an attempt by the outgoing Putin administration to impose limits on the freedom of action of its successor.

In March 2007, a draft version of the new three-year budget (2008–10) was presented by the Ministry

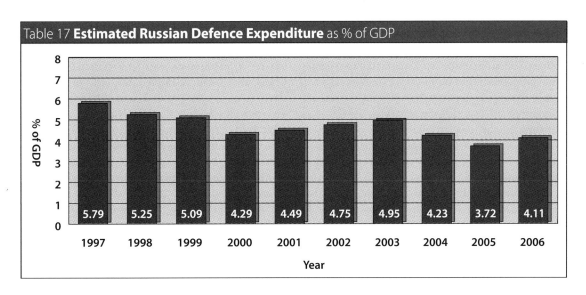

Table 17 **Estimated Russian Defence Expenditure** as % of GDP

Year	1997	1998	1999	2000	2001	2002	2003	2004	2005	2006
% of GDP	5.79	5.25	5.09	4.29	4.49	4.75	4.95	4.23	3.72	4.11

of Finance, which included a summary of spending intentions under the standard functional chapters (National Defence, Education, Social Policy, etc.) and in a format consistent with previous years. However, in April a revised draft was approved by the government, before passing through the Duma and the Council of the Federation, and being signed into law by Putin in July 2007. The later version of the budget had been significantly altered to exclude all classified spending, thereby making it impossible to discern what planned expenditure totals on various chapters were finally approved. Due to the opacity of the second set of data, the figures in Table 18 refer to the original draft budget as presented in March 2007 in which the chapter heading National Defence was allocated R956 billion in 2008, compared to the final outlay of R959.9bn that was eventually signed into law. Of the final outlay some 46.9%, or R450bn, was eventually classified.

Despite the lack of transparency in the budget data it is possible to draw some conclusions. In the past few years, it has been a stated policy that military R&D, alongside improvements in pay and other benefits for service personnel, would be a major budget priority before attention switched to the procurement of new equipment. In 2002, R&D expenditure amounted to R31bn and, in line with medium-term goals, by 2007 this had grown to R120bn. However, the 2008–10 budget indicates that R&D spending will now remain broadly unchanged at around R125bn for the coming three years, suggesting that, as scheduled, more money will now be allocated to the procurement of new weapons systems. In February 2007, then Defence Minister Sergei Ivanov told the State Duma that the 2007–15 State Armament Programme would amount to R5,000bn and that these funds would be used to 'modernise' rather than 'reform' the Russian military. The programme lists a number of new acquisition proposals including 50 *Topol*-M missile systems, 34 new strategic bombers, two multi-purpose nuclear submarines and four diesel submarines, as well as 12 warships. In total the plan envisages the replacement of around 45% of existing military hardware, while a fifth of the total amount is due to be allocated to strategic armaments.

While the trend in Russian national defence spending appears to have shown a rapid increase in recent years, once inflation is factored in the actual rate of growth has broadly matched growth in the economy at large. Since 2000, national defence spending has fluctuated between 2.5–2.8% of GDP

and the new three-year budget appears to maintain this trend, aiming to keep national defence spending at around 2.7% of national output. Indeed, in May 2007 Sergei Ivanov suggested that Russia had no intention of significantly changing the level of defence funding and that the military budget would not become a burden on the economy or social policy.

ARMS TRADE

Russian arms manufacturers enjoyed another successful year in 2006. The US Congressional Research Service (CRS) estimates that actual deliveries of Russian military equipment amounted to US$5.8bn, of which Rosoboronexport (the state arms-export agency) accounted for 80%, while other independent estimates suggest total exports reached as much as US$6.4bn. In terms of new contracts signed, the CRS estimates that Russia achieved sales of US$8.7bn in 2006, 21% of the global market and second only to the US.

Aerospace platforms accounted for 50% of deliveries in 2006, with naval deliveries reaching 27% of the total, while land forces and air defence accounted for 11% and 9% respectively. Major aerospace deliveries included 15 kits to India for the assembly of Su-30MKI aircraft, two Su-30MK2V aircraft to Venezuela (the first of 24), two MiG-29SMT and two MiG-29UBT to Algeria and up to 70 Mi-8/17 helicopters to Venezuela and China. There were two major naval deliveries, both to China: a second Project 956EM destroyer and a Project 636M *Kilo*-class submarine. The most controversial export during the year was the delivery of 29 *Tor*-M1 surface-to-air missile systems to Iran.

While China and India remain Russia's largest trading partners for military equipment, the Kremlin has successfully diversfied the range of customers buying Russian-made weapons systems. In 2006, China and India accounted for 62% of business, down from 74% the previous year, while the share of exports to the Middle East and North Africa grew to 22%, and Latin America jumped from 0.5% to 7.7% of total exports. In all, Russia exported arms to 64 countries in 2006, up from 57 in 2004. Key to the success of the Kremlin's diversification policy has been an innovative approach to alternative financing arrangements. In March 2006, for example, Russia secured a US$7.5bn arrangement with Algeria under which it will supply 40 T-90 main battle tanks, eight S-300 missile systems, 16 Yak-130 advanced jet trainers, 40 MiG-29SMT fighters and 30 Su-30MK interdiction aircraft. Under the terms of the deal, Moscow will write off around US$5bn in debt incurred by Algeria during the Soviet era and Russian energy companies Lukoil and Gazprom will be granted access to Algeria's natural hydrocarbon reserves. More recently, Russia and Indonesia entered into a major arms deal covering aircraft, helicopters and submarines that will be financed by a US$1bn export credit arrangement. Observers also believe that Russia and Libya are close to agreeing a major multi-billion-dollar deal comprising fighter aircraft, submarines and air defence systems that will be financed in part by a debt write-off similar to that agreed with Algeria.

According to the Federal Agency for Military Technical Cooperation, Russia is set to export over US$7bn worth of arms in 2007, with the delivery of at least 50 aircraft to Malaysia, Venezuela, Algeria and India accounting for the bulk of transfers.

Estimating Russian military expenditure

As ever, estimating the real scale of Russian military spending is fraught with difficulty, not least as a result of the recent changes in the presentation of budget data. When taken at face value, the official National Defence chapter heading for 2006 (R666bn) corresponds to 2.50% of GDP, however, as noted above, this figure excludes funds made available to other military-related expenditures such as pensions and paramilitary forces.

Including these additional budget allocations brings overall defence-related expenditure to around R1,052bn, or 3.95% of 2006 GDP. On top of this, there is the revenue from Russian arms exports to consider, approximately US$5.8bn in 2006, a proportion of which is directed to national defence – further inflating the total.

Translated into dollars at the market exchange rate, Russia's official 2006 National Defence chapter heading amounts to US$24.5bn – roughly the equivalent of South Korea's annual defence expenditure. If the additional defence-related items listed in Table 18 are included then this boosts the figure to US$38.8bn, which still appears to be lower than the size of the Russian armed forces and the structure of the military-industrial complex might suggest; thus neither of these figures is particularly useful for comparative analysis.

When assessing macroeconomic data from developing countries where the exchange rate does not fully reflect the purchasing power of the domestic currency,

Table 18 March 2007 Draft Russian National Defence Expenditure 2008–10 (Rbm)

Chapter 2 'National Defence'	2008	2009	2010
Armed Forces of the Russian Federation (including State Defence Order)	698.1	791.8	908.3
Mobilisation of external forces	5.2	5.7	6.2
Mobilisation of the economy	3.5	3.5	3.7
Collective peacekeeping	0.08	0.08	0.12
Military nuclear programmes	17.1	19.8	25.2
International treaty obligations	6.1	6.2	6.2
Applied research and development (R&D)	127.8	124.9	124.9
Other questions of defence	97.9	101.7	109.6
Total Draft National Defence	**955.9**	**1,053.9**	**1,184.5**
Additional defence-related security expenditure			
Internal troops	51.4	57.4	58.2
Security organs	135.3	152.7	162.4
Border troops	65.5	80.0	87.5
Subsidies to closed towns	18.5	19.3	20.4
Ministry of Emergencies	47.0	54.3	55.5
Military pensions	95.0	105.0	118.0
Total Defence-related Expenditure	**1,368.6**	**1,522.6**	**1,686.5**
Total Federal Budget Expenditure	6,500.0	7,177.9	7,598.8
Total Defence-related Expenditure as % of Federal Budget	21.1	21.2	22.2

economists use an alternative methodology know as Purchasing Power Parity (PPP). For example, in 2006 Russian GDP measured US$982bn when converted at market exchange rates, however the World Bank also calculated that in PPP terms, Russia's GDP was equivalent to US$1,704bn. Given that total defence-related expenditure in 2006 amounted to approximately 3.95% of GDP, then this suggests that in PPP terms defence spending measured US$67bn. With the addition of revenue from international arms exports, it is possible that the total may have reached approximately US$70bn.

Note: Although PPP rates may be a useful tool for comparing the macroeconomic data, such as GDP, of countries at different stages of development, as there exists no specific PPP rate to apply to the military sector its use for this purpose should be treated with caution. In addition, there is no definitive guide as to which elements of military spending should be calculated using available PPP rates.

Russia RF

Russian Rouble r		2006	2007	2008
GDP	r	26.6tr	31.3tr	
	US$[a]	1.7tr	2.0tr	
per capita	US$[a]	11,994	14,189	
Growth	%	6.7	7.0	
Inflation	%	9.7	8.1	
Def exp	US$[a]	70.0bn		
Def bdgt	r	666bn	821bn	956bn
	US$	24.57bn	32.99bn	
US$1=r		27.1	24.9	

[a] PPP estimate

Population   141,377,752

Ethnic groups: Tatar 4%; Ukrainian 3%; Chuvash 1%; Bashkir 1%; Belarussian 1%; Moldovan 1%; Other 8%;

Age	0–14	15–19	20–24	25–29	30–64	65 plus
Male	7%	4%	4%	4%	22%	4%
Female	7%	4%	4%	4%	25%	10%

Capabilities

ACTIVE 1,027,000 (Army 360,000 Airborne 35,000 Navy 142,000 Air 160,000 Strategic Deterrent Forces 80,000 Command and Support 250,000) **Paramilitary 418,000**

RESERVE 20,000,000 (all arms)

some 2,000,000 with service within last 5 years; Reserve obligation to age 50

ORGANISATIONS BY SERVICE

Strategic Deterrent Forces ε80,000 (includes personnel assigned from the Navy and Air Force)

Navy
SUBMARINES • STRATEGIC • SSBN 15: 6 *Delta* III† (4 based in Pacific Fleet, 2 based in Northern Fleet) (96 msl) each with 16 RSM-50 (SS-N-18) *Stingray* strategic SLBM; 4 *Delta* IV based in Northern Fleet (80 msl) each with 16 RSM-54 (SS-N-23) *Skiff* strategic SLBM; 2 *Delta* IV in refit in Northern Fleet (16 msl) with 16 RSM-54 (SS-N-23) *Skiff* strategic SLBM; 2 *Typhoon* based in Northern Fleet (40 msl) each with 20 RSM-52 (SS-N-20) *Sturgeon* strategic SLBM; 1 *Typhoon*† in reserve based in Northern Fleet with 20 RSM-52 (SS-N-20) *Sturgeon* strategic SLBM and 1 *Bulava* (SS-N-30) strategic SLBM; 1 *Yury Dolgoruky* (limited OC undergoing sea trials '08; 2 additional units in build)

Strategic Missile Force Troops
3 Rocket Armies operating 284 silo and 258 mobile missile launchers with 508 missiles and 1600 nuclear warheads organised in 12 divs. Launcher gps normally with 10 silos (6 for SS-18) and one control centre

MSL • STRATEGIC 508
ICBM 508: 80 RS-20 (SS-18) *Satan* (at 16 launch gps; mostly mod 4/5, 10 MIRV per msl.); 254 RS12M (SS-25) *Sickle* at 30 op bases (mobile single warhead); 126 RS18 (SS-19) *Stiletto* (at 14 launch gps; mostly mod 3, 6 MIRV per msl.); 48 *Topol*-M (SS-27) silo-based/road mobile single warhead (5 regts) – to be MIRVed during next 2–3 yrs

Long-Range Aviation Command • 37th Air Army

FORCES BY ROLE
Bbr   2 heavy div with 4 regt at 3 air bases operating 79 bbr

EQUIPMENT BY TYPE
AIRCRAFT • LRSA 89: 15 Tu-160 *Blackjack* each with up to 12 KH-55SM/RKV-500B (AS-15B *Kent*) nuclear ALCM; 32 Tu-95MS6 (*Bear* H-6) each with up to 6 Kh-55/RKV-500A (AS-15A *Kent*) nuclear ALCM; 32 Tu-95MS16 (*Bear* H-16) each with up to 16 Kh-55/RKV-500A (AS-15A *Kent*) nuclear ALCM
Test ac 10: 5 Tu-95, 5 Tu-160

Warning Forces
ICBM/SLBM launch-detection capability. Limited number of satellites serviceable
RADAR 1 ABM engagement system located at Pushkino (Moscow). Russia leases ground-based radar stations in Baranovichi (Belarus); Sevastopol and Mukachevo (Ukraine); Balkhash (Kazakhstan); Gaballa (Azerbaijan). It also has radars on its own territory at Lekhtusi, (St. Petersburg); Armavir, (southern Russia); Olenegorsk (northwest Arctic); Pechora (northwest Urals); Mishelevka (east Siberia).
DEFENSIVE ABM 100: 64 9M96 (S-400)/SH-08 *Gazelle*; 36 SH-11 *Gorgon*

Space Forces 40,000
Formations and units withdrawn from Strategic Missile and Air Defence Forces to detect missile attack on the RF and its allies, to implement BMD, and to be responsible for military/dual-use spacecraft launch and control.

Army ε205,000 (incl 35,000 AB); ε190,000 conscript (total 395,000)
FORCES BY ROLE
6 Mil Districts (MD), 1 Special Region; 8 Army HQ, 1 Corps HQ, 7 District trg centre (each = bde – 1 per MD except NC)

Tk	3 div (each: 3 tk regt, 1 MR regt, 1 armd recce bn, 1 arty regt, 1 SAM regt, spt units); 3 reserve div
MR	16 div (each: 3 MR regt, 1 tk regt, 1 recce bn, 1 arty regt, 1 AT bn, 1 SAM regt, 1 tk bn, spt units); 10 indep bde; 4 indep regt; 8 (reserve) div; 6 (reserve) bde
SF	9 (Spetsnaz) bde
Air Aslt	2 bde

AB	4 div (each: 2 para regt, 1 arty regt); 1 bde (trg centre); 3 indep bde (2 under GF control)
Arty	2 div HQ; 16 arty bde ; 3 AT regt
MRL	2 bde; 11 regt
SSM	10 bde each. with 18 SS-21 *Scarab* (*Tochka*) (replacement by *Iskander*-M missile system began during 2005 with 12 per bde)
MGA	5 div (all will be converting to motor rifle)
SAM	12 bde; 1 regt

EQUIPMENT BY TYPE

MBT 23,000: 250–300 T-90 (by end 2008); 4,500 T-80/T-80UD/T-80UM/T-80U; 9,500 T-72L/T-72M; 3,000 T-72; 4,000 T-64A/T-64B; 150 T-62, 350 in store; 1,200 T-55

LT TK 150 PT-76

RECCE 2,000+ BRDM-2

AIFV 15,140+: 1,500+ BMD-1/BMD-2/BMD-3; 8,100 BMP-1; 4,600 BMP-2; 240 BMP-3; 700 BRM-1K; BTR-80A

APC 9,900+

APC (T) 4,000: 700 BTR-D; 3,300 MT-LB

APC (W) 5,900+: 1,000 BTR-50; 4,900 BTR-60/BTR-70/BTR-80; BTR-90

ARTY 26,121+

SP 6,010: **122mm** 2,780: 2,780 2S1 *Carnation*; **152mm** 3,100: 550 2S19 *Farm*; 1,600 2S3; 950 2S5; **203mm** 130: 130 2S7

TOWED 12,765: **122mm** 8,350: 4,600 D-30; 3,750 M-30 *M-1938*; **130mm** 650 M-46; **152mm** 3,725: 1,100 2A36; 750 2A65; 1,075 D-20; 700 M-1943; 100 ML-20 *M-1937*; **203mm** 40 B-4M

GUN/MOR 820+

SP 120mm 820: 30 2S23 *NONA-SVK*; 790 2S9 *NONA-S*

TOWED 120mm 2B16 *NONA-K*

MRL 3,976+: **122mm** 2,970: 2,500 BM-21; 50 BM-16; 420 9P138; **132mm** BM-13; **140mm** BM-14; **220mm** 900 9P140 *Uragan*; **300mm** 106 9A52 *Smerch*

MOR 2,550

SP 240mm 430 2S4

TOWED 2,120: **120mm** 1,820: 920 2S12; 900 PM-38; **160mm** 300 M-160

AT

MSL • MANPATS AT-2 3K11 *Swatter*; AT-3 9K11 *Sagger*; AT-4 9K111 *Spigot*; AT-5 9K113 *Spandrel*; AT-6 9K114 *Spiral*; AT-7 9K115 *Saxhorn*; AT-9 9M114M1 *Ataka*; AT-10 9K116 *Stabber*

RCL 73mm SPG-9; **82mm** B-10

RL 64mm RPG-18 *Fly*; **73mm** RPG-16/RPG-22 *Net*/RPG-26/RPG-7 *Knout*; **105mm** RPG-27/RPG-29

GUNS 526+

SP 57mm ASU-57; **85mm** ASU-85; D-44/SD44

TOWED 526 **100mm**T-12A/M-55; T-12

AD

SAM 2,465+

SP 2,465+: 220 SA-4 A/B *Ganef (twin)* (Army/Front wpn – most in store); 225 SA-6 *Gainful* (div wpn); 550 SA-8 *Gecko* (div wpn); 350 SA-11 *Gadfly* (replacing SA-4/-6); 800 SA-9 *Gaskin*/SA-13 *Gopher* (regt wpn); 200 SA-12A (S-300V) *Gladiator*/SA-12B *Giant (twin)*; 120 SA-15 *Gauntlet* (replacing SA-6/SA-8); SA-19 *Grison* (8 SAM, plus twin 30mm gun); SA-20 (S-400) *Triumph*

MANPAD SA-7 *Grail* (being replaced by -16/-18); SA-14 *Gremlin*; 9K310 (SA-16) *Gimlet*; SA-18 *Grouse (Igla)*

GUNS

SP 23mm ZSU-23-4; **30mm** 2S6; **57mm** ZSU-57-2

TOWED 23mm ZU-23; **57mm** S-60; **85mm** M-1939 KS-12; **100mm** KS-19; **130mm** KS-30

UAV BLA-06; BLA-07; Tu-134 *Reys*; Tu-243 *Reys*/Tu-243 *Reys*-D; Tu-300 *Korshun*; Pchela-1; Pchela-2

MSL • SSM ε200+: 200 SS-21 *Scarab* (*Tochka*); SS-26 *Iskander* (*Stone*); FROG in store; *Scud* in store

FACILITIES

Bases	2 (each = bde+; subord. to North Caucasus MD) located in Georgia, 1 located in Tajikistan, 1 located in Armenia
Training centres	6 (District (each = bde – 1 per MD)), 1 (AB (bde))

Reserves

Cadre formations, on mobilisation form

Tk	2 div; 2 bde
MRR	13 div; 6 bde
Arty	1 div; 4 indep bde
Hy arty	1 bde

Navy 142,000

FORCES BY ROLE

4 major Fleet Organisations and Caspian Sea Flotilla

Northern Fleet

FORCES BY ROLE

1 Navy HQ located at Severomorsk

FACILITIES

Bases	Located at Severodvinsk and Kola Peninsula

EQUIPMENT BY TYPE

SUBMARINES 42

STRATEGIC 11: 8 **SSBN**; 1 in reserve

TACTICAL 23: 13 **SSN**; 3 **SSGN**; 7 **SSK**

SUPPORT 8: 3 **SSAN** (other roles); 5 in reserve (other roles)

PRINCIPAL SURFACE COMBATANTS 10: 1 **CV**; 2 **CGN** (1 in reserve); 1 **CG**; 6 **DDG**

PATROL AND COASTAL COMBATANTS ε14

MINE WARFARE 11 **MCMV**

AMPHIBIOUS 6

LOGISTICS AND SUPPORT 130+

Naval Aviation

EQUIPMENT BY TYPE

AIRCRAFT

BBR 38 Tu-22M *Backfire C*

FTR 20 Su-27 *Flanker*

FGA 10 Su-25 *Frogfoot*

ASW 31: 17 Il-38 *May*; 14 Tu-142 *Bear*

TPT 27: 2 An-12 *Cub* (MR/EW); 25 An-12 *Cub*/An-24 *Coke*/An-26 *Curl*

HELICOPTERS

ASW 42 Ka-27 *Helix A*

ASLT 16 Ka-29 *Helix B*

SPT 15 Mi-8 *Hip* (TPT)

Naval Infantry
Naval inf 1 regt with 74 MBT; 209 ACV; 44 arty

Coastal Defence
Coastal def 1 bde with 360 MT-LB; 134 arty

SAM   1 regt

Pacific Fleet
FORCES BY ROLE
Fleet HQ located at Vladivostok

FACILITIES
Bases located at Kamchatsky, Fokino, Magadan, Petropavlovsk, Gavan, Sovetskya and Vladivostok

EQUIPMENT BY TYPE
  SUBMARINES 23
    STRATEGIC • SSBN 4: 3 and 1 in reserve
    TACTICAL 19: 4 **SSN/SSGN** and 6 in reserve; **SSK** 6 and 3 in reserve
  PRINCIPAL SURFACE COMBATANTS 9: 1 **CG**; 7 **DDG**; 1 **FFG**
  PATROL AND COASTAL COMBATANTS ε25
  MINE WARFARE 8 MCMV
  AMPHIBIOUS 4
  LOGISTICS AND SUPPORT 57

Naval Aviation
EQUIPMENT BY TYPE
  AIRCRAFT
    BBR 14 Tu-22M *Backfire A*
    FTR 30 MiG-31 *Foxhound* A
    ASW 36: 24 Il-38 *May*; 12 Tu-142 *Bear*
    TPT 10 An-12 *Cub* (MR/EW); An-26 *Curl*
  HELICOPTERS
    ASW 31 Ka-28 (Ka-27) *Helix*
    ASLT 6 Ka-29 *Helix*
    SPT 26 Mi-8 *Hip* (TPT)

Naval Infantry
Inf 1 div HQ (Pacific Fleet) (1 arty bn, 1 tk bn, 3 inf bn)

Coastal Defence
Coastal Def 1 div

Black Sea Fleet
The RF Fleet is leasing bases in Sevastopol and Karantinnaya Bays, and is based, jointly with Ukr warships, at Streletskaya Bay. The Fleet's overall serviceability is low.

FORCES BY ROLE
1 Navy HQ located at Sevastopol, Ukr

FACILITIES
Bases located at Sevastopol, Novorossiysk and Temryuk

EQUIPMENT BY TYPE
  SUBMARINES • TACTICAL 1 SSK
  PRINCIPAL SURFACE COMBATANTS 12: 2 **CG**; 3 **DDG**; 7 **FFG/FS**
  PATROL AND COASTAL COMBATANTS ε8
  MINE WARFARE • MINE COUNTERMEASURES MCMV 9

AMPHIBIOUS 2
LOGISTICS AND SUPPORT 90+

Naval Aviation
EQUIPMENT BY TYPE
AIRCRAFT
    FGA 18 Su-24 *Fencers*
    ASW 14 Be-12 *Mail*
    TPT 4 An-12 *Cub* (MR/EW); An-26
HELICOPTERS
    ASW 33 Ka-28 (Ka-27) *Helix*
    SPT 9: 1 Mi-8 *Hip* (TPT); 8 (MR/EW)

Naval Infantry
Naval inf 1 regt with 59 ACV; 14 arty

Baltic Fleet
FORCES BY ROLE
1 Navy HQ located at Kaliningrad

FACILITIES
Bases located at Kronstadt and Baltiysk

EQUIPMENT BY TYPE
  SUBMARINES • TACTICAL 2 SSK
  PRINCIPAL SURFACE COMBATANTS 5: 2 **DDG**; 3 **FFG** some **FS**
  PATROL AND COASTAL COMBATANTS ε18
  MINE WARFARE • MINE COUNTERMEASURES MCMV 15
  AMPHIBIOUS 5
  LOGISTICS AND SUPPORT ε130

Naval Aviation
EQUIPMENT BY TYPE
  AIRCRAFT
    FTR 23 Su-27 *Flanker*
    FGA 26 Su-24 *Fencer*
    TPT 14: 12 An-12 *Cub*/An-24 *Coke*/An-26 *Curl*; 2 An-12 *Cub* (MR/EW)
  HELICOPTERS
    ATK 11 Mi-24 *Hind*
    ASW 19 Ka-28 (Ka-27) *Helix*
    ASLT 8 Ka-29 *Helix*
    SPT 17 Mi-8 *Hip* (TPT)

Naval Infantry
Naval inf 1 regt with 26 MBT; 220 ACV; 52 MRL

Coastal Defence
FORCES BY ROLE
Arty 2 regt with 133 arty
SSM 1 regt with 8 SS-C-1B *Sepal*
AD   1 regt with 28 Su-27 *Flanker* (Baltic Fleet)

EQUIPMENT BY TYPE
AD 50 SAM

Caspian Sea Flotilla
The Caspian Sea Flotilla has been divided between Az (about 25%), RF, Kaz, and Tkm, which are operating a joint flotilla under RF command, currently based at Astrakhan.

FACILITIES
Base located at Astrakhan

EQUIPMENT BY TYPE
PRINCIPAL SURFACE COMBATANTS • FRIGATES
FFG 1
PATROL AND COASTAL COMBATANTS 6
  PFM 3; **PHM** 3
MINE WARFARE • MINE COUNTERMEASURES
5MCMV 5
AMPHIBIOUS 6
LOGISTICS AND SUPPORT ε15

NAVY EQUIPMENT BY TYPE
SUBMARINES 67
  STRATEGIC 15
    SUBMARINES • STRATEGIC • SSBN 15: 6 *Delta* III†
    (4 based in Pacific Fleet, 2 based in Northern Fleet) (96
    msl) each with 16 RSM-50 (SS-N-18) *Stingray* strategic
    SLBM; 4 *Delta* IV based in Northern Fleet (80 msl) each
    with 16 RSM-54 (SS-N-23) *Skiff* strategic SLBM; 2 *Delta*
    IV in refit in Northern Fleet (16 msl) with 16 RSM-
    54 (SS-N-23) *Skiff* strategic SLBM; 2 *Typhoon* based in
    Northern Fleet (40 msl) each with 20 RSM-52 (SS-N-20)
    Sturgeon strategic SLBM; 1 *Typhoon*† in reserve based
    in Northern Fleet with 20 RSM-52 (SS-N-20) *Sturgeon*
    strategic SLBM and 1 *Bulava* (SS-N-30) strategic SLBM;
    1 *Yury Dolgoruky* (limited OC undergoing sea trials '08;
    2 additional units in build)
TACTICAL 52
  SSGN 7:
    5 *Oscar* II each with 2 single 650mm TT each with
    T-65 HWT, 4 single 553mm TT with 24 SS-N-19
    Shipwreck tactical USGW
    2 *Oscar* II (1 in reserve, 1 in refit), with 2 single
    650mm TT each with T-65 HWT, 1 VLS with 24 SS-
    N-19 *Shipwreck* tactical USGW
  SSN 17:
    2 *Akula* II each with 4 single 533mm TT each with
    SS-N-21 *Sampson* tactical SLCM, 4 single 650mm TT
    each with single 650mm TT
    5 *Akula* I each with 4 single 533mm TT each with
    SS-N-21 *Sampson* tactical SLCM, 4 single 650mm TT
    each with T-65 HWT; 3 *Akula* I in reserve
    1 *Sierra* II with 4 single 533mm TT each with, SS-N-
    21 *Sampson* tactical SLCM, 4 single 650mm TT each
    with T-65 HWT/T-53 HWT; 1 *Sierra* II in reserve
    1 *Sierra* I in reserve†
    4 *Victor* III (1 in reserve) each with 4 single 533mm TT
    each with SS-N-21 *Sampson* tactical SLCM, T-65 HWT
  SSK 20:
    15 *Kilo* each with 6 single 533mm TT each with T-53
    HWT; 4 *Kilo* in reserve
    1 *Lada* (Undergoing sea trials)
  SUPPORT • SSAN 8: 1 *Delta Stretch*; 1 *Losharik*; 2 *Paltus*;
  3 *Uniform*; 1 *X-Ray*
PRINCIPAL SURFACE COMBATANTS 62
  AIRCRAFT CARRIERS • CV 1 *Kuznetsov* (capacity 18
  Su-33 *Flanker D* FGA ac; 4 Su-25 *Frogfoot* ac, 15 Ka-27
  Helix ASW hel, 2 Ka-31 *Helix AEW* hel,) with 1 12 cell
  VLS (12 eff.) with 12 SS-N-19 *Shipwreck* tactical SSM, 4
  sextuple VLS (24 eff.) each with 8 SA-N-9 *Gauntlet* SAM

CRUISERS 5
  CGN 1 *Kirov each with* 10 twin VLS (20 eff.) each with
  20 SS-N-19 *Shipwreck* tactical SSM, 2 twin (4 eff.) each
  with 20 SA-N-4 *Gecko* SAM, 12 single VLS each with 8
  SA-N-6 *Grumble* SAM, 10 single 533mm ASTT, 1 single
  ASTT with 1 SS-N-15 *Starfish* ASW, 1 twin 130mm gun
  (2 eff.), (capacity 3 Ka-27 *Helix* ASW hel) (2nd *Kirov*
  undergoing extensive refit currently non operational)
  CG 4:
    1 *Kara*, each with 2 quad (8 eff.) each with SS-N-14
    Silex tactical SSM, 2 twin (4 eff.) each with 36 SA-N-
    3 *Goblet* SAM, 2 (4 eff.) each with 20 SA-N-4 *Gecko*
    SAM, 2 quad (4 eff.) ASTT (10 eff.), (capacity 1 Ka-27
    Helix ASW hel)
    3 *Slava* each with 8 twin (16 eff.) each with SS-N-
    12 *Sandbox* tactical SSM, 8 octuple VLS each with 8
    SA-N-6 *Grumble* SAM, 8 single 533mm ASTT, 1 twin
    130mm gun (2 eff.), (capacity 1 Ka-27 *Helix* ASW
    hel)
DESTROYERS • DDG 16:
    1 *Kashin* (mod) with 2 quad (8 eff.) each with SS-N-25
    Switchblade tactical SSM, 2 twin (4 eff.) each with SA-N-
    1 *Goa* SAM, 5 single 533mm ASTT, 2 76mm gun
    6 *Sovremenny* each with 2 quad (8 eff.) each with SS-
    N-22 *Sunburn* tactical SSM, 2 twin (4 eff.) each with 22
    SA-N-7 SAM, 2 twin 533mm TT (4 eff.), 2 twin 130mm
    gun (4 eff.), (capacity 1 Ka-27 *Helix* ASW hel)
    8 *Udaloy* each with 2 quad (8 eff.) each with SS-N-14
    Silex tactical SSM, 8 octuple VLS each with SA-N-9
    Gauntlet SAM, 2 quad 533mm ASTT (8 eff.), 2 100mm
    gun, (capacity 2 Ka-27 *Helix* ASW hel)
    1 *Udaloy* II with2 quad (8 eff.) each with 1 SS-N-22
    Sunburn tactical SSM, 8 octuple VLS each with SA-
    N-9 *Gauntlet* SAM, 8 SA-N-11 *Grisson* SAM, 10 single
    533mm ASTT, 2 x2 CADS-N-1 CIWS (4 eff.), 2 100mm
    gun, (capacity 2 Ka-27 *Helix* ASW hel)
FRIGATES 14
  FFG 6:
    1 *Gepard* with 2 quad (8 eff.) each with SS-N-25
    Switchblade tactical SSM, 1 twin (2 eff.) with SA-N-4
    Gecko SAM, 2 1 30mm CIWS, 1 76mm gun
    2 *Krivak* I each with 1 quad (4 eff.) with SS-N-14 *Silex*
    tactical SSM, 1 twin (2 eff.) with 20 SA-N-4 *Gecko*
    SAM, 2 quad 533mm ASTT (8 eff.), 2 x12 RL (24 eff.),
    2 100mm gun, 2 x2 76mm gun (4 eff.), (capacity 1 Ka-
    27 *Helix* ASW hel)
    2 *Krivak* II each with 1 quad (4 eff.) with SS-N-14
    Silex tactical SSM, 2 twin (4 eff.) each with 10 SA-N-4
    Gecko SAM, 2 quad 533mm ASTT (8 eff.), 2 x12 RL (24
    eff.), 2 100mm gun
    1 *Neustrashimyy* with 4 octuple (32 eff.) each with 4
    SA-N-9 *Gauntlet* SAM, 6 single 533mm ASTT, 1 RBU
    12000 (10 eff.), 1 100mm gun, (capacity 1 Ka-27 *Helix*
    ASW)
  FF 8 *Parchim* II each with 2 quad (8 eff.) each with 1
  SA-N-5 *Grail* SAM, 2 twin 533mm ASTT (4 eff.), 2 RBU
  6000 *Smerch* 2 (24 eff.), 1 76mm gun
CORVETTES 26:
    3 *Grisha* III with 1 twin (2 eff.) with 20 SA-N-4 *Gecko*
    SAM, 2 twin 533mm ASTT (4 eff.), 2 RBU 6000 *Smerch*
    2 (24 eff.)

22 *Grisha* V each with 1 twin (2 eff.) with 20 SA-N-4 *Gecko* SAM, 2 twin 533mm ASTT (4 eff.), 1 RBU 6000 *Smerch* 2 (12 eff.), 1 76mm gun

1 *Scorpion* with 2 quad (8 eff.) with SS-N-26 *Yakhont* SSM, 1 100mm gun

PATROL AND COASTAL COMBATANTS 74

PFM 41

15 *Nanuchka* III each with 2 triple (6 eff.) each with 1 SS-N-9 *Siren* tactical SSM, 1 twin (2 eff.) eqpt with SA-N-4 *Gecko*, 1 76mm gun

1 *Nanuchka* IV with 2 triple (6 eff.) each with 1 SS-N-9 *Siren* tactical SSM, 1 twin (2 eff.) eqpt with SA-N-4 *Gecko*, 1 76mm gun

4 *Tarantual* II each with 2 twin (4 eff.) each with SS-N-2C *Styx*/SS-N-2D *Styx* tactical SSM

20 *Tarantual* III each with 2 twin (4 eff.) each with SS-N-22 *Sunburn* tactical SSM

1 *Astrakhan* Project 21630 (First of 5–7 on order)

PHM 6:

2 *Dergach* each with 2 quad (8 eff.) each with SS-N-22 *Sunburn* tactical SSM, 1 twin (2 eff.) with 1 SA-N-4 *Gecko* SAM, 1 76mm gun

4 *Matka* each with 2 single each with SS-N-2C *Styx* tactical SSM/SS-N-2D *Styx* tactical SSM

PHT 6:

1 *Mukha* with 2 quad 406mm TT (8 eff.)

5 *Turya* each with 4 single 533mm ASTT

PFC 21:

1 *Pauk* each with 4 single 533mm ASTT, 2 RBU 1200 (10 eff.)

20 ε *Stenka*

MINE WARFARE • MINE COUNTERMEASURES 45

MCO 2 *Gorya*

MSO 12 *Natya*

MSC 26 *Sonya*

MHC 5 *Lida*

AMPHIBIOUS: 45+

PRINCIPAL AMPHIBIOUS SHIPS • LPD

1 *Ivan Rogov* (capacity 4–5 Ka-28 (Ka-27) *Helix* ASW hel; 6 ACV or 6 LCM; 20 tanks; 520 troops)

LS 22

LSM 3:

3 *Polnochny*† B (capacity 6 MBT; 180 troops); (3 in reserve)

LST 19:

4 *Alligator* (capacity 20 tanks; 300 troops)

15 *Ropucha* II and I (capacity either 10 MBT and 190 troops or 24 APC (T) and 170 troops)

CRAFT 23+

LCM 9 *Ondatra*

LCU 3 *Serna* (capacity 100 troops)

ACV 11:

3 *Aist* (capacity 4 lt tk)

3 *Lebed*

2 *Orlan*

3 *Pomornik* (*Zubr*) (capacity 230 troops; either 3 MBT or 10 APC (T))

LOGISTICS AND SUPPORT 370

AOR 5 *Chilikin*

AORL 3: 1 *Kaliningradneft*; 2 *Olekma*

AOL 12: 2 *Dubna*; 5 *Uda*; 5 mod *Altay*

AS 1 *Malina* (Project 2020)

ASR 1 *Elbrus*

ARS 25: 1; 10 *Goryn*; 14 *Okhtensky*

AR 13 *Amur*

ARC 8: 4 *Emba*; 4 *Klasma*

AG 5: 2 *Amga* (msl spt ship); 3 *Bolva* (barracks ship)

ATS 15: 3 *Ingul*; 6 *Katun*; 2 *Neftegaz*; 1 *Prut*; 3 *Sliva*

AH 3 *Ob*

AWT 2 *Manych*

AGOR 4: 2 *Akademik Krylov*; 2 *Vinograd*

AGI 14: 3 *Alpinist*; 2 *Balzam*; 3 *Moma*; 6 *Vishnya*

AGM 1 *Marshal Nedelin*

AGS 61: 8 *Biya*; 19 *Finik*; 6 *Kamenka*; 7 *Moma*; 8 *Onega*; 2 *Sibiriyakov*; 11 *Yug*

AGB 4 *Dobrynya Mikitich*

ABU 12: 8 *Kashtan*; 4 *Sura*

ATF 12 *Sorum*

TRG 12

AXL 10: 10 *Petrushka* (possibly commercially owned)

2 *Smolny*

YDG 27 **YDT** ε130

Naval Aviation ε35,000

4 Fleet Air Forces, each organised in air div; each with 2–3 regt with an HQ elm and 2 sqn of 9–10 ac each; configured recce, ASW, tpt/utl org in indep regt or sqn

Flying hours   ε40 hrs/year

FORCES BY ROLE

Bbr	sqns with 58 Tu-22M *Backfire A*
Ftr/FGA	sqn with 46 Su-27 *Flanker*; 10 Su-25 *Frogfoot*; 58 Su-24 *Fencer*; 30 MiG-31 *Foxhound*
ASW	sqns with 85 Ka-27 *Helix*; 50 Ka-25 *Hormone*; 20 Mi-14 *Haze-A*; sqn with 15 Be-12 *Mail*; 35 Il-38 *May*; 20 Tu-142 *Bear*
MR/EW	sqns with 5 An-12 *Cub*; 2 Il-20 RT *Coot-A*; 8 Mi-8 *Hip*
Tpt	sqns with 37 An-12 *Cub*/An-24 *Coke*/An-26 *Curl*
ATK hel	sqns with 11 Mi-24 *Hind*
Aslt hel	30 Ka-29 *Helix*; 26 Mi-8 *Hip*
Tpt hel	sqns with 22 Ka-25 PS *Hormone* C, Ka-27 PS *Helixe D*; 10 Mi-6 *Hook*; 40 Mi-14 PS *Haze* C

EQUIPMENT BY TYPE

AIRCRAFT 245 combat capable

BBR 58 Tu-22M *Backfire A*

FTR 49 Su-27 *Flanker*; 30 MiG-31 *Foxhound*

FGA 68: 10 Su-25 *Frogfoot*; 58 Su-24 *Fencer*

ASW 20: 20 Tu-142 *Bear**

MP 50: 15 Be-12 *Mail**; 35 Il-38 *May**

EW • ELINT 2 Il-20 RT *Coot-A*

TPT 42: 37 An-12 *Cub*/An-24 *Coke*/An-26 *Curl*; 5 An-12 *Cub*

HELICOPTERS

ATK 11 Mi-24 *Hind*

ASW 155: 85 Ka-27 *Helix*; 50 Ka-25 *Hormone*; 20 Mi-14 *Haze-A*

ASLT 30: 30 Ka-29 *Helix*

SAR 62: 22 Ka-25 PS *Hormone* C/Ka-27 PS *Hormone*-D; 40 Mi-14 PS *Haze* C

SPT 53: 35 Mi-8 *Hip*; 8 more; 10 Mi-6 *Hook*

MSL • TACTICAL

ASM AS-10 *Karen*; AS-11 *Kilter*; AS-12 *Kegler*; AS-4 *Kitchen*; AS-7 *Kerry*; KH-59 (AS-13) *Kingbolt*

Coastal Defence • Naval Infantry (Marines) 9,500

FORCES BY ROLE

Naval inf 3 indep bde (*total:* 1 AT bn, 1 arty bn, 1 MRL bn, 1 tk bn, 4 naval inf bn); 3 indep bn; 3 regt; 1 indep regt;

Inf 1 div HQ (Pacific Fleet) (3 inf bn, 1 tk bn, 1 arty bn)

SF 3 (fleet) bde (1 op, 2 cadre) (*each:* 1 para bn, 1 spt elm, 2–3 underwater bn)

EQUIPMENT BY TYPE

MBT 160 T-55M/T-72/T-80
RECCE 60 BRDM-2 each with AT-3 9K11 *Sagger*
AIFV 150+: ε150 BMP-2; BMP-3; BRM-1K
APC 750+
  APC (T) 250 MT-LB
  APC (W) 500+ BTR-60/BTR-70/BTR-80
ARTY 367
  SP 113: **122mm** 95 2S1 *Carnation*; **152mm** 18 2S3
  TOWED 122mm 45 D-30
  GUN/MOR 113
    SP 120mm 95: 20 2S23 *NONA-SVK*; 75 2S9 SP *NONA-S*
    TOWED 120mm 18 2B16 *NONA-K*
  MRL 122mm 96 9P138
AT • MSL • MANPATS 72 AT-3 9K11 *Sagger*/AT-5 9K113 *Spandrel*
  GUNS 100mm T-12
AD • SAM 320
  SP 70: 20 SA-8 *Gecko*; 50 SA-9 *Gaskin*/SA-13 *Gopher* (200 eff.)
    MANPAD 250 SA-7 *Grail*
  GUNS 23mm 60 ZSU-23-4

Coastal Defence Troops 2,000

FORCES BY ROLE

(All units reserve status)

Coastal Def 1 div; 1 bde
Arty 2 regt
AD 1 regt with 28 Su-27 *Flanker*
SAM 2 regt

EQUIPMENT BY TYPE

MBT 350 T-64
AIFV 450 BMP
APC 320
  APC (T) 40 MT-LB
  APC (W) 280 BTR-60/BTR-70/BTR-80
ARTY 364
  SP 152mm 48 2S5
  TOWED 280: **122mm** 140 D-30; **152mm** 140: 50 2A36; 50 2A65; 40 D-20
  MRL 122mm 36 BM-21
AIRCRAFT • FTR 28 Su-27 *Flanker*
AD • SAM 50

Military Air Forces 160,000 reducing to 148,000 (incl conscripts)

4,000+ ac, 833 in reserve

HQ at Balashikha, near Moscow. The Military Air Forces comprise Long Range Aviation (LRA), Military Transport Aviation Comd (VTA), 5 Tactical/Air Defence Armies comprising 49 air regts. Tactical/Air Defence roles includes air defence, interdiction, recce and tactical air spt. LRA (2 div) and VTA (9 regt) are subordinated to central Air Force comd. A joint CIS Unified Air Defence System covers R, Arm, Bel, Ga, Kaz, Kgz, Tjk, Tkm, Ukr and Uz.

Long-Range Aviation Command • 37th Air Army

Flying hours: 70-80hrs/yr

FORCES BY ROLE

Bbr 2 heavy bbr div; 4 heavy regt (non-strategic); 4 heavy regt (START accountable) with 116 Tu-22M-3/MR *Backfire* C
Tkr 1 base with 20 Il-78 *Midas*/Il-78M *Midas*
Trg 1 hvy bbr trg centre with 30 Tu-134 *Crusty*

EQUIPMENT BY TYPE

AIRCRAFT 124 combat capable
  BBR 124: 8 Tu-22M; 116 Tu-22M-3/Tu-22MR *Backfire C*
  TKR 20 IL-78 *Midas* /Il-78M *Midas*
  TPT 30 Tu-134 *Crusty*

Tactical Aviation

Flying hours 25 to 40 hrs/year

FORCES BY ROLE

Bbr/FGA 7 regt with 241 Su-25A/SM *Frogfoot*; 1 regt forming with 9 Su-34P *Fullback*; 1 bbr div plus 13 FGA regt with 550 Su-24 *Fencer*
Ftr 9 regt with 188 MiG-31 *Foxhound*; 9 regt with 226 MiG-29 *Fulcrum* (24 being upgraded); 6 regt with 281 Su-27 *Flanker* (incl 40 Su-27SM); trg units with 30 MiG-25 *Foxbat*
Recce 4 regt with 40 MiG-25R *Foxbat*; 5 regt with 79 Su-24MR *Fencer*
AEW 1 base with 20 A-50 *Mainstay*/A-50U *Mainstay*
ECM some sqn with 60 Mi-8(ECM) *Hip J*
Trg 2 op conversion centres with 92 trg ac
SAM 35 regt with 1,900+ S-300 (SA-10) *Grumble* (quad) (7,600 eff.). First SA-20/S-400 (*Triumph*) bn op Elektrostal in Moscow region.

EQUIPMENT

AIRCRAFT 1,736 combat capable
  BBR/FGA 800: 241 Su-25A/SM *Frogfoot*; 550 Su-24 *Fencer*; 9 Su-34P *Fullback* (Su-27IB) (6-8 more to be delivered in 2008 - to replace Su-24)
  FTR 725: 188 MiG-31 *Foxhound*; 226 MiG-29 *Fulcrum* (24 being upgraded); 281 Su-27 (18 upgraded to 27SM) incl 40 Su-27SMK *Flanker*; 30 MiG-25 *Foxbat*;
  RECCE 119: 40 MiG-25R *Foxbat**; 79 Su-24MR *Fencer**
  AEW 20 A-50 *Mainstay* AEW/A-50U *Mainstay*

TRG 92: 40 MiG-29 *Fulcrum**; 21 Su-27 Flanker*; 15 Su-25 *Frogfoot;** 16 Su-24 *Fencer** (instructor trg)
HELICOPTERS 60 Mi-8(ECM) *Hip J*
UAV *Pchela*-1T; *Albatross†*; *Expert†*
AD • SAM • SP 1,900+ S-300 (SA-10) *Grumble* (quad) / S-400 (SA-20) *Triumph*
MSL • ARM AS-11 *Kilter;* AS-12 *Kegler;* AS-17 *Krypton*
  ASM AS-14 *Kedge;* AS-15 *Kent;* AS-16 *Kickback;* AS-4 *Kitchen;* AS-7 *Kerry*
  AAM R-27T (AA-10) *Alamo;* R-60T (AA-8) *Aphid;* R-73M1 (AA-11) *Archer*
BOMBS
  Laser-guided KAB-500; KAB-1500L
  TV-guided KH-59 (AS-13 *Kingbolt*); KAB-500KR; KAB-1500KR; KAB-500OD
  INS/GPS/GLONASS guided KH-101; KH-555

Military Transport Aviation Command • 61st Air Army

Flying hours   60 hrs/year

FORCES BY ROLE

Air	9 regt incl. 5 indep regt; 1 div with 12 An-124 *Condor*; 21 An-22 *Cock* (Under MoD control); 210 Il-76 *Candid*
Civilian Fleet	Some sqn (medium and long-range passenger)

EQUIPMENT BY TYPE
AIRCRAFT • TPT 293+: 50 An-12 *Cub;* 12 An-124 *Condor;* 21 An-22 *Cock* (Under MoD control); 210 Il-76M/MD/MF *Candid*

Army Aviation Helicopters
Under VVS control. Units organic to army formations.
Flying hours   55 hrs/year

FORCES BY ROLE

Atk hel	20 regt/sqn with 8 Ka-50 *Hokum;* ε620 Mi-24 *Hind;* 7 Mi-28N *Havoc* (300 by 2010)
Tpt/ECM	mixed regts with 35 Mi-26 *Halo* (hy); 8 Mi-6 *Hook;* ε600 MI-17 (Mi-8MT) *Hip H*/Mi-8 *Hip*

EQUIPMENT BY TYPE
HELICOPTERS 128 atk hel
  ATK 635: 8 Ka-50 *Hokum;* 620 Mi-24 *Hind* D/V/P; 7 Mi-28N *Havoc* (300 by 2010)
  TPT/ECM ε643: 35 Mi-26 *Halo* (hy); 8 Mi-6 *Hook;* ε600 MI-17 (Mi-8MT) *Hip H*/Mi-8 *Hip* Spt

Air Force Aviation Training Schools

EQUIPMENT BY TYPE
AIRCRAFT 980+
  FTR MiG-29 *Fulcrum;* Su-27 *Flanker;* MiG-23 *Flogger*
  FGA Su-25 *Frogfoot*
  TPT Tu-134 *Crusty*
  TRG 336 L-39 *Albatros*

FACILITIES

Aviation Institute	5 sqn regt with MiG-29 *Fulcrum;* Su-27 *Flanker;* MiG-23 *Flogger;* Su-25 *Frogfoot;* Tu-134 *Crusty* tpt; L-39 *Albatros* trg ac

Kaliningrad Special Region 10,500 (Ground and Airborne); 1,100 (Naval Infantry) (total 11,600)
These forces operated under the Ground and Coastal Defence Forces of the Baltic Fleet

Army

FORCES BY ROLE

MR	1 div (2 MR regt, 1 tk regt, 1 SP Arty regt, 1 MRL regt, 1 AT regt, 1 SAM regt, 1 indep tk regt, spt units) (cadre); 1 bde; 1 indep regt (trg)
SSM	1 bde eqpt. with 18 SS-21 *Tochka* (*Scarab*)
Arty	1 MRL regt
Hel	1 indep regt
SAM	1 regt

FACILITIES

Bases	Located at Baltiysk and Kronstadt

EQUIPMENT BY TYPE
MBT 811
ACV 1,239: 865; 374 look-a-like
ARTY 345 ARTY/MOR/MRL

Navy • Baltic Fleet – see main Navy section

Russian Military Districts

Leningrad MD 28,700 (Ground and Airborne); 1,300 (Naval Infantry – subordinate to Northern Fleet) (total 30,000)
Combined Service   1 HQ located at St Petersburg

Army

FORCES BY ROLE

MR	2 indep bde, 1 naval bde
SF	1 (Spetsnaz) bde
AB	1 Air Asslt div (2 air asslt regt, 1 arty regt)
Arty	1 bde, 1 MRL regt, 1 AT regt
SSM	1 bde eq. with 18 SS-21 *Tochka* (*Scarab*)
SAM	2 bde

Reserve

MR	4 Bde

FACILITIES

Training Centre	1 located at Sertolovo (District)

EQUIPMENT BY TYPE
MBT 300
ACV 2,350: 100; 2,250 look-a-like
ARTY 690 MOR/MRL

Navy • Northern Fleet – see main Navy section

Military Air Force
6th Air Force and AD Army

FORCES BY ROLE

PVO	2 corps
Bbr	1 div with 56 Su-24M *Fencer*

Ftr	1 div with 30 MiG-31 *Foxhound*; 55 Su-27 *Flanker*
Recce	1 regt with 20 Su-24MR *Fencer*; 28 MiG-25R/U *Foxbat*; some MiG-31
AEW/AWACS	A-50 *Mainstay*
Tpt	Sqns with An-12, An-24, An-26, Tu-134
Cbt sup	57 Mi-8 *Hip* (incl ECM), some Mi-8PPA, 38 Mi-24, 4 Mi-6

AD • SAM 525 incl S-300V

Moscow MD 86,200 (Ground and Airborne)

Combined Service   1 HQ located at Moscow

Army

FORCES BY ROLE

Army	2 HQ
Tk	1 div (3 tk regt (2 cadre), 1 MR regt, 1 SP arty regt, 1 MRL regt, 1 SAM regt, spt units); 1 div (2 tk regt (cadre), 2 MR regt, (some cadre), arty, MRL SAM,,, spt units cadre)
MR	1 div (3 MR regt, 1 tk regt, 1 SP arty regt, 1 SAM regt, spt units); 1 div (2 MR regt, 2 tk regt, 1 SP Arty regt, 1 SAM regt, spt units); 1 indep bde
SF	1 (Spetsnaz) bde; 1 AB recce regt
AB	2 div (each: 2 para regt, 1 arty regt)
Arty	1 div HQ (3 arty bde), 1 arty bde, 1 MRL bde, 1 MRL regt, 1 AT regt)
SSM	2 bde each eqpt with 18 SS-21 *Scarab* (*Tochka*)
AT	1 regt
Trg	1 HQ (1 AD arty regt, 2 tk regt, 2 MR regt)
SAM	3 bde

Reserve

Tk	1 div
MR	1 bde

EQUIPMENT BY TYPE
MBT 2,500
ACV 3,100: 2,100; 1,000 look-a-like
ARTY 1,300 ARTY/MOR/MRL

Military Air Force

Moscow Air Defence and Air Army has 1 corps. Due to have additional AD regt (2 bn) equipped with S-400 SAM system.

FORCES BY ROLE

352 cbt ac

PVO Air	1 (32 PVO) corps 1 16th Air Army
Ftr	regts with 41 MiG-31 *Foxhound*, 45 MiG-29 *Fulcrum*; 30 Su-27
FGA	regts with 52 Su-25 *Frogfoot*, 80 Su-24 *Fencer*
Recce	regt with 55 Su-24MR
Tpt	regt with An-12, An-24, An-26, An-30, Tu-134
Cbt Spt sup	sqns with 98 Mi-8/ Mi-8PPA/sMV (incl 46 Mi-8(ECM)

Utl	sqns with Mi-8
Trg	30 MiG-29*, 18 Su-27*, 1 Su-25*

UAV Pchela-1T at Combat Training Centre, Egor'evsk, Moscow

EQUIPMENT BY TYPE
AD • SAM 600

Volga-Ural MD 55,000 (Ground and Airborne)

Combined Service   1 HQ located at Yekaterinburg

Army

1 Army HQ

FORCES BY ROLE

Army	1 HQ
MR	1 div (3 MR regt, 1 tk regt, 1 SP arty regt, 1 SAM regt, spt units); 1 div (2 MR regt, 2 tk regt, 1 SP arty regt, 1 SAM regt, spt units); 1 Mil Base (div) (3 MR regt) in Tajikistan; 1 indep PK bde;
SF	2 (Spetsnaz) bde
AB	1 bde, 1 trg centre
Arty	2 bdes, 1 MRL regt
SSM	2 bde each eqpt with 18 SS-21 *Tochka* (*Scarab*)
SAM	2 bde

Reserve

Tk	1 div
MR	1 div

FACILITIES

Training Centre   1 located at Kamshlov (district)

EQUIPMENT BY TYPE
MBT 3,000
ACV 2,300
ARTY 2,700 ARTY/MOR/MRL

Navy • Caspian Sea Flotilla see main Navy section

Military Air Force

5th AF and AD Army has no ac subordinated, incl storage bases

EQUIPMENT BY TYPE
AIRCRAFT •
FTR 34 MiG-31
FGA Su-25 *Frogfoot*
TPT An-12; An-26
COMMS Mi-14
HELICOPTERS •SPT: Mi-6, 25 Mi-8 *Hip* (comms); Mi-24, 24 Mi-26*e*
TRG MiG-25U, MiG-29, Su-25, Su-27; 300 L-39 *Albatros*, Mi-2 *Hoplite*

North Caucasus MD 88,600 (Ground And Airborne); ε1,400 (Naval infantry) (total 90,000)

including Trans-Caucasus Group of Forces (GRVZ)
Combined Service   1 HQ located at Rostov-on-Don

Army

FORCES BY ROLE

Army	1 HQ
MR	1 div (2 MR regt, 1 tk bn, 1 air aslt regt, 1 SP arty regt,1 SAM regt);
	1 div (4 MR regt, 1 tk bn, 1 SP arty regt, 1 SAM regt, spt units);
	1 div (4 MR regt, 1 SP arty regt);
	1 Mil Base (div) 3 MR regt,1 SAM regt, 1 tk bn (Armenia)
	3 indep bde;
SF	2 (Spetsnaz) bde
AB	1 Air Asslt (mtn) div (2 air asslt regt,1 arty regt)
Arty	2 bde,1 MRL bde, 1 MRL regt
SSM	2 bde each eqpt with 18 SS-21 *Tochka* (*Scarab*)
CW	1 (flame thrower) bn
SAM	2 bde; 1 regt

EQUIPMENT BY TYPE
MBT 800
ACV 2,000
ARTY 900 ARTY/MOR/MRL

Navy · Black Sea Fleet – see main Navy section

Military Air Force
6th AF and AD Army

FORCES BY ROLE
360 cbt ac

Bbr	1 div with 62 Su-24 *Fencer* (some 32 likely to be disbanded)
Ftr	1 corps (4 regt with 105 MiG-29 *Fulcrum*; 59 Su-27 *Flanker*)
FGA	1 div with 98 Su-25 *Frogfoot*; 36 L-39
Recce	1 regt with 30 Su-24MR *Fencer*
ECM	1 sqn with 52 Mi-8(ECM) *Hip J*
Tpt	Sqns with An-12, An-24, An-26, Tu-134
Cbt Sup	regts with 58 Mi-8PPA/sMV, 75 Mi-24,
Utl	4 Mi-6, 10 Mi-26
Trg	tac aviation regt

Siberian MD 52,000 (Ground and Airborne)
Combined Service   1 HQ located at Chita

Army

FORCES BY ROLE

Army	2 Army HQ (36th and 41st)
Tk	1 div (3 tk regt, 1 MR regt, 1 armd recce bn, 1 arty regt, 1 SAM regt, spt units)
MR	3 div(85TH,122ND,131ST) (each: 3 MR regt, 1 tk regt, 1 indep tk bn, 1 armd recce bn, 1 arty regt, 1 AT bn, 1 SAM regt, spt units);
	1 indep bde
SF	2 (Spetsnaz) bde
Air aslt	1 bde
Arty	1 div Hq, 3 arty bde,3 MRL regt
SSM	1 bde each eq. with 18 SS-21 *Tochka* (*Scarab*)
SAM	2 bde

FACILITIES
Training Centre   1 located at Peschanka (district)

EQUIPMENT BY TYPE
MBT 4,000
ACV 6,300
ARTY 2,600 MOR/MRL

Military Air Force
14th AF and AD Army (HQ Novosibirsk)
200 cbt ac

FGA/bbr	some sqn with 30 Su-25 *Frogfoot*; 56 Su-24M *Fencer*
Ftr	some sqn with 39 MiG-31 *Foxhound*; 46 MiG-29 *Fulcrum*
Recce	some sqn with 29 Su-24MR *Fencer-E*; MiG-25R/MiG-25U
Tpt	sqns with An-12, An-26
Cbt Sup	sqns with Mi-8PPA/sMV; Mi-24
Utl/Comms	sqns with Mi-8

AD · SAM S-300O

Far Eastern MD 72,500 (Ground and Airborne); 2,500 (Naval infantry) (total 75,000)
Incl Pacific Fleet and Joint Command of Troops and Forces in the Russian Northeast (comd of Pacific Fleet)

Joint Forces Command	1 HQ located at Petropavlovsk
Combined Service	1 HQ located at Khabarovsk

Army

FORCES BY ROLE

Army	2 HQ; 1 corps
MR	5 div (each: 3 MR regt, 1 tk regt, arty regt, 1 SAM regt, spt units);
	1 div (formally MGA) (21st,35A)(1 MR regt, 2 MGA regt, def units, spt units)
MGA	5 div (Converting MR) most (1 tank regt, 2 MR or MGA regt, arty regt, SAM regt)
SF	1 bde
AB	1 bde
Arty	4 arty bde, 3 MRL bde, 1 AT bde)
SSM	2 bde each eq. with 18 SS-21 *Scarab* (*Tochka*)
SAM	3 bde

FACILITIES
Training Centre   1 located at Khaborovsk (district)

EQUIPMENT BY TYPE
MBT 3,000
ACV 6,000
ARTY 4,100 MOR/MRL

Navy · Pacific Fleet see main Navy section

Military Air Force
11th AF and AD Army (HQ Khabarovsk)
361 cbt ac

FGA/bbr	1 regt with 23 Su-27SM; 97 Su-24M *Fencer*

Ftr	sqn with 26 MiG-31 *Foxhound*; ≤100Su-27 *Flanker*;
Recce	sqns with 51 Su-24MR *Fencer*
Tpt	regts with An-12, An-26
Cbt sup	regts with Mi-8PPA/sMV
Comms	sqns with Mi-8; Mi-24, Ka-50
UAV	1 sqn with Pchela-1 (Arseniev, Primorskyy)

AD • SAM S-300P

Paramilitary 419,000

Federal Border Guard Service ε160,000 active

Directly subordinate to the President

FORCES BY ROLE
10 regional directorates
Frontier 7 gp

EQUIPMENT BY TYPE
AIFV/APC (W) 1,000 BMP/BTR
ARTY • SP 90: **122mm** 2S1 *Carnation*; **120mm** 2S12; **120mm** 2S9 *Anona*
PRINCIPAL SURFACE COMBATANTS 14
  FRIGATES 13
    FFG 7:
      7 *Krivak III* (capacity 1 Ka-27 *Helix A* ASW hel; 1 100mm) each with 1 twin (2 eff.) with SA-N-4 *Gecko* naval SAM, 2 quad 533mm TT (8 eff.), 2 RBU 6000 *Smerch 2* (24 eff.), 1 twin 100mm (2 eff.)
    FFL 6: 3 *Grisha* II; 3 *Grisha* III
  CORVETTES • FS 1 *Grisha* V
PATROL AND COASTAL COMBATANTS 180
  PFM 22:
    2 *Pauk II* each with 1 quad (4 eff.) with SA-N-5 *Grail* naval SAM, 2 twin 533mm TT (4 eff.), 2 RBU 1200 (10 eff.), 1 76mm
    20 *Svetlyak* each with 1 quad (4 eff.) with SA-N-5 *Grail* naval SAM, 2 single 406mm TT, 1 76mm
  PFT 17 *Pauk I* each with 1 quad (4 eff.) with SA-N-5 *Grail* naval SAM, 4 single 406mm TT, 1 76mm
  PHT 3: 3 *Muravey*
  PSO 12: 8 *Alpinist*; 4 *Komandor*
  PFC 15: 15 *Stenka*
  PCC 36: 9 *Mirazh*; 27 *Type 1496*
  PCI 12: 12 *Zhuk*
  PCR 32: 3 *Ogonek*; 7 *Piyavka*; 15 *Shmel*; 5 *Vosh*; 2 *Yaz*
  PBF 31: 1 *A-125*; 1 *Mangust*; 1 *Mustang (Project 18623)*; 15 *Saygak*; 12 *Sobol*; 1 *Sokzhoi*
LOGISTICS AND SUPPORT 24: 1 AO
  AK 10: 10 *Neon Antonov*
  AKSL 6: 6 *Kanin*
  AGS 2: 2 *Yug* (primarily used as patrol ships)
  AGB 5: 5 *Ivan Susanin* (primarily used as patrol ships)
  AIRCRAFT • TPT ε86: 70 An-24 *Coke*/An-26 *Curl*/An-72 *Coaler*/Il-76 *Candid*/Tu-134 *Crusty*/Yak-40 *Codling*; 16 SM-92
  HELICOPTERS: ε200 Ka-28 (Ka-27) *Helix* ASW/Mi-24 *Hind* Atk/Mi-26 *Halo* Spt/Mi-8 *Hip* Spt

Interior Troops 170,000 active

FORCES BY ROLE
7 districts
Paramilitary 5 (special purpose) indep div (ODON) (*each:* 2–5 paramilitary regt); 6 div; 65 regt (bn – incl special motorised units); 10 (special designation) indep bde (OBRON) (*each:* 1 mor bn, 3 mech bn); 19 indep bde
Avn gp

EQUIPMENT BY TYPE
MBT 9
AIFV/APC (W) 1,650 BMP-1 /BMP-2/BTR-80
ARTY 35
  TOWED 122mm 20 D-30
  MOR 120mm 15 PM-38
HELICOPTERS • ATK 4 Mi-24 *Hind*

Federal Security Service ε4,000 active (armed)

Cdo unit (incl Alfa, Beta, Zenit units)

Federal Protection Service ε10,000–30,000 active

Org include elm of ground forces (mech inf bde and AB regt)

Mech inf	1 bde
AB	1 regt
Presidential Guard	1 regt

Federal Communications and Information Agency ε55,000 active

MOD • Railway Troops ε50,000

Paramilitary 4 (rly) corps; 28 (rly) bde

Special Construction Troops 50,000

DEPLOYMENT

ARMENIA
Army 3,170

FORCES BY ROLE
1 tk bn; 3 MR regt; 1 avn gp; 1 SAM regt

EQUIPMENT BY TYPE
TK 74 MBT
ACV 330
APC 14 APC (T)/APC (W)
ARTY 70 arty/mor/MRL

FACILITIES
Base 1 located in Armenia

Military Air Forces • Tactical Aviation

FORCES BY ROLE
1 AD sqn with 18 MiG-29 *Fulcrum*; 2 SAM bty with S-300V (SA-12A) *Gladiator*; 1 SAM bty with SA-6 *Gainful*

EQUIPMENT BY TYPE
AIRCRAFT • FTR 18 MiG-29 *Fulcrum*
AD • SAM • SP S-300V (SA-12A) *Gladiator*; SA-6 *Gainful*

Russia

BELARUS

Military Air Forces • Tactical Aviation

FORCES BY ROLE
4 SAM units with S-300 (SA-10) *Grumble (quad)*

EQUIPMENT BY TYPE
AD • SAM • SP some S-300 (SA-10) *Grumble (quad)*

CÔTE D'IVOIRE
UN • UNOCI 9 obs

DEMOCRATIC REPUBLIC OF CONGO
UN • MONUC 28 obs

ETHIOPIA/ERITREA
UN • UNMEE 3 obs

GEORGIA
Army 1,000

FACILITIES
Bases   1 located at Batumi, Ga (subord. to North Caucasus MD) withdrawing 2008

Peacekeeping Forces
3 MR Bn, CIS Abkhazia peacekeeping Force
1 MR bn joint peacekeeping Force South Ossetia
Military Air Forces • Tactical Aviation
HELICOPTERS: 5 atk
UN • UNOMIG 4 obs

KYRGYZSTAN
Military Air Forces ε500
Tactical Aviation
20+ Mi-8 spt hel/ Su-24 *Fencer* FGA ac/ 5 Su-25 *Frogfoot* FGA ac/ Su-27 *Flanker* ftr ac

LIBERIA
UN • UNMIL 4 obs

MEDITERRANEAN SEA
NATO • *Active Endeavour* RFS Ladniy FF

MIDDLE EAST
UN • UNTSO 3 obs

MOLDOVA/TRANSDNESTR
Army 1,199
FORCES BY ROLE
1 (op) army gp (subord. to Moscow MD) 2 MR bn

EQUIPMENT BY TYPE
ACV 214
Military Air Forces • Tactical Aviation
HELICOPTERS 7 Mi-8/Mi-24

NEPAL
UN • UNMIN 8 obs

SERBIA
UN • UNMIK 1 obs

SIERRA LEONE
UN • UNIOSIL 1 obs

SUB-SAHARAN AFRICA
Army 100

SUDAN
UN • UNMIS 122; 14 obs

SYRIA
Army and Navy 150

TAJIKISTAN
Army 5,500
FORCES BY ROLE
1 MR div (subord Volga-Ural MD)
EQUIPMENT BY TYPE
TK 120 MBT
ACV 350
ARTY 190 mor/MRL
Military Air Forces • Tactical Aviation
AIRCRAFT • FGA 5 Su-25 *Frogfoot*; 4 Mi-8

UKRAINE
Navy • Coastal Defence • 13,000 including Naval Infantry (Marines) 1,100

FORCES BY ROLE
1 indep naval inf regt

EQUIPMENT BY TYPE
Arty: 24
AIFV /APC (T) / APC (W): 102
Navy • Black Sea Fleet
1 Fleet HQ located at Sevastopol, Ukr

WESTERN SAHARA
UN • MINURSO 25 obs

Table 19 Selected Arms Orders and Deliveries, Russia

	Country Supplier	Classification	Designation	Quantity	Order date	Original Delivery date	Comment
Russia (RF)	dom	FFG	Project 22350	1	2005	2009	Unit cost estimate USD400m. Navy estimates requirement for up to 20 vessels by 2015.
	dom	LCU	*Dyugon*	1	2005	2007	R200m (approx USD69m)
	UK	ROV	*Panther Plus*	1	2006	2006	Russian Navy. For submarine rescue operations
	dom	FGA	Su-34	24	2006	2006	To be delivered in batches – 2 ac in 2006, 7 ac in 2007, 10 ac in 2008 and 5 ac in 2009-10. First two del in Dec 2006
	dom	SSBN	Project 955 *Borey*	2	1996	2006	Lead boat in class, *Yuri Dolgorukiy* was launched on April 2007. Second boat, *Aleksandr Neveskiy* due to follow in 2007 but now unlikely to be ready before 2009. 3rd SSBN, *Vladimir Monomah*, ordered in 2006 and expected in 2011
	dom	ICBM	SS-27 *Topol*-M	6	2005	2006	–
	dom	MBT	T-90	31	2005	2006	Deliveries continuing
	dom	APC	–	125	2005	2006	–
	dom	Bbr	Tu-160 *Blackjack*	1	2005	2006	Still on order
	dom	Hel	Mi-28N	8	2005	2006	Still on order
	dom	Trg	Yak-130 Advanced Jet Trainer	12	2005	2007	Deliveries due from mid-2006 to end of 2007. The air force has further plans to equip two ftr pilot schools with Yak-130s by 2010, procuring a total of 48 ac to replace L-39s
	dom	MBT	–	139	2005	2006	Repair and modernisation programme
	dom	Arty	–	125	2005	2006	Repair and modernisation programme
	dom	Ac	–	104	2005	2006	Repair and modernisation programme
	dom	Hel	–	52	2005	2006	Repair and modernisation programme
	dom	SRBM	*Iskander*-M (SS-26 *Stone*)	–	–	2007	Five *Iskander*-M bde are due to be operational by 2015
	dom	Bbr	Tu-160	2	2007	2007	Modernisation programme
	dom	IFV	BMP-3	–	2007	–	USD250m

Table 20 Russia: Air Capability 2008

Aircraft (Fixed Wing & Rotary)	Air Force	Army	Maritime	Para-military	Total
LRSA	203	0	58	0	261
Tu-160 *Blackjack*	15				15
Tu-22M	8				8
Tu-22M-3/Tu-22MR *Backfire* C	116		58		174
Tu-95MS6 *Bear*	32				32
Tu-95MS16 *Bear*	32				32
RECCE	119	0	0	0	119
MiG-25R *Foxbat*	40				40
Su-24MR *Fencer*	79				79
COMD/AEW	20	0	37	0	57
Il-38 May (AEW)			35		35
A-50/A-50U *Mainstay*	20				20
Il-20 RT Coot-A			2		2
TAC	1617	0	192	0	1809
Be-12 *Mail*			15		15
Il-20 RT Coot-A			2		2
MiG-25 *Foxbat*	30				30
MiG-29 *Fulcrum*	266				266
MiG-31 *Foxhound*	188		30		218
Su-27 *Flanker* (CDT)*	302		77		379
Su-24 *Fencer*	566		58		624
Su-25 *Frogfoot*	256		10		266
Su-34P (Su-27IB) *Fullback*	9				9
TKR	20	0	0	0	20
Il-78 *Midas*/Il-78M *Midas*	20				20
TPT	323	0	68	86	477
An-12 *Cub*	50		42		92
An-124 *Condor*	12				12
An-22 *Cock*	21				21
An-24 *Coke*			3	some	3
An-26 *Curl*			3	some	3
Il-76M/MD/MF *Candid*	210			some	210
SM-92				16	16
Tu-134 *Crusty*	30			some	30
Tu-142 *Bear* (ASW)			20	some	20

Table 20 Russia: Air Capability 2008

Aircraft (Fixed Wing & Rotary)	Air Force	Army	Maritime	Para-military	Total
TRG(*)	980	0	0	0	980
MiG-29 *Fulcrum*	some				some
Su-27 *Flanker*	some				some
MiG-23 *Flogger*	some				some
Su-25 *Frogfoot*	some				some
Tu-134 *Crusty*	some				some
L-39 *Albatros*	336				336
HEL	60	1278	394	200	1932
Ka-25 *Hormone*			50		50
Ka-25 PS *Hormone* C/D			22		22
Ka-27 *Helix* A			85		85
Ka-28 (Ka-27) *Helix*			83	some	83
Ka-29 *Helix*			30		30
Ka-50 *Hokum*		8			8
Mi-14 *Haze* A			20		20
Mi-14 *Haze* C			40		40
Mi-17 (Mi-8MT) *Hip* H		600			600
Mi-24 *Hind*			11	some	11+
Mi-24 *Hind* D/V/P		620			620
Mi-26 *Halo*		35		some	35+
Mi-28N *Havoc*		7			7
Mi-6 *Hook*		8	10		18
Mi-8 *Hip*			43	some	43+
Mi-8 *Hip* J	60				60
TEST	10	0	0	0	10
Tu-95 *Bear*	5				5
Tu-160 *Blackjack*	5				5
UAV(**)					
Air Force					
Albatross†, Expert†, Pchela-1T,					some
Army					
BLA-06, BLA-07, Pchela-1, Pchela-2, Tu-134 *Reys*, Tu-243 *Reys*/*Reys*-D, Tu-300 *Korshun*					some
Total of Aircraft:					**5665**
Combat Capable(***):					**3169**

Equipment is listed according to type

(CDT)*: Of 77 Su-27 *Flanker* listed under Maritime Forces, 29 are under the command of the Russian Coastal Defence Troops

(*): The total number is 980 aircraft. The exact number of each Russian aircraft belonging to the Air Force Aviation Training Schools is unknown (see Russian capability on page 212)

(**): The current number of Russian UAVs is not known

(***): The Russian combat capable total represents the sum of all LRSA, TAC and TRG ac. Attack helicopters are not counted

Chapter Five
Middle East and North Africa

IRAQ

The Surge

The security situation in Iraq remains highly volatile. According to the United Nations, the mix of criminality, insurgency and sectarian violence in the country led to the deaths of 34,452 Iraqi civilians in 2006, while as of November 2007 US deaths in theatre had totalled 3,845 since March 2003. Although the reinforced security effort in Iraq, the so-called 'surge', has dramatically reduced the violence towards both military and civilians, including in insurgent and terrorist attacks, criminality, intra-communal militia violence and sectarian strife remain commonplace, and still undermine political and economic initiatives. Iraq continues to loom large in global defence-planning debates. The implications of sustained counter-insurgency and stability operations in Iraq – and Afghanistan – are now leading to concern among some US commanders over their relevance to long-term security requirements and force developments (see North America p. 14).

The US response to violence in Iraq can be broadly divided into two phases, corresponding to the commands of General George Casey (from June 2004 until January 2007) and General David Petraeus. Their response has an ongoing impact on other Coalition forces' activities and future dispositions. In 2006, Casey focused on the need to reduce US troop numbers in Iraq. In this plan, as well as handing over authority to Iraqi forces, US bases were to be drawn down from 69 to 11 by the end of 2007. A potential security vacuum would be avoided by enhancing the training of and advisory support given to Iraq's security forces through the Multi-National Security Transition Command-Iraq and the Multi-National Corps-Iraq. As has been detailed in the IISS *Strategic Survey 2007*, the year 2006 bore witness to a series of hasty and unsustainable plans designed to reduce US troop numbers and hand over responsibility to Iraqis as quickly as possible. Lieutenant-General Ray Odierno, Petraeus's deputy commander in Iraq, admitted that 'we've rushed the transition and soon lost many areas that we had before'. Under a new approach, announced by President George W.

Bush in January 2007, the number of US troops was increased and US forces shifted from large bases to patrol bases among the population in areas where sectarian violence had been most severe.

In February, a month after the arrival of Petraeus as commanding general of the Multi-National Force-Iraq, the Baghdad Security Plan (*Operation Fardh al-Qanoon*) – commonly known as 'the surge' – began in earnest. Marking a departure from Casey's approach, it involved increasing force levels by 15%, adding some 30,000 personnel to the 132,000 already in the country. There was particular emphasis on Baghdad, where the number of US soldiers was to rise to 32,500. The plan was designed to deliver order by focusing on population security; soldiers in Baghdad, for example, moved to occupy 28 Joint Security Stations and 28 combat outposts alongside Iraqi army and police forces.

The plan had two phases. The first started in Baghdad on 14 February, and was scheduled to reach its peak by June, when over 160,000 US troops were to be deployed. US combat brigades increased from 15 to 20 between January and June 2007. Tactics were geared towards securing, then clearing and holding areas. Makeshift barriers set up by locals in west Baghdad were cleared and concrete barriers – designed to hinder death squads and suicide bombers – set up in their place. Once areas were cleared, census and identity checks were made, and military commanders used reconstruction funds in an attempt to re-establish basic services and bolster morale among the population in the wake of security operations. Although the surge led to a fall in the rate of sectarian murders and an improvement in economic life, groups such as al-Qaeda in Mesopotamia continued to conduct mass-murder attacks in an attempt to destabilise the security situation and maintain levels of sectarian unrest. Meanwhile, Jaish al-Mahdi (JAM), Shia cleric Moqtada al-Sadr's militia, was relatively restrained, with al-Sadr himself decamping to Iran for the first five months of the surge and JAM largely taking its forces, many of which had been used in the sectarian cleansing of Baghdad neighbourhoods, off the streets.

The second phase of the surge started in June with the final influx of US personnel. Some of these forces were sent to rural areas surrounding Baghdad, which al-Qaeda in Mesopotamia and JAM had both used as safe havens and support bases for operations in the capital. These operations severely disrupted terrorist, insurgent and militia networks, and restricted their freedom of movement. As security improved, communities in Anbar, northern Babil, Diyala and Salahuddin provinces, as well as Baghdad, openly rejected al-Qaeda in Mesopotamia, with many volunteering to help secure their communities.

In late August, an unclassified version of the new US National Intelligence Estimate for Iraq said that there had been 'measurable, but uneven improvements in Iraq's security situation' since the beginning of the surge that had 'checked for now' the rise in violence. On 10 and 11 September 2007, Petraeus and US Ambassador to Iraq Ryan Crocker testified before Congress in a mandated report on the progress of the surge. They argued that violent civilian deaths had declined by 45% in Iraq as a whole and by 70% in Baghdad. The assumption was that if such reductions continued then it would be possible to make limited reductions to US forces by the beginning of 2008.

In early November, Odierno was able to report that US combat deaths in October were at their lowest level since February 2004; attack levels were back to the level before the Samarra mosque bombing in February 2006; detonations of improvised explosive devices were at their lowest level since October 2004; and explosively formed projectile (EFP) explosions had dropped from 99 in July to 78 in August. Further, while there were 52 such attacks in September, in October 30 EFPs exploded, with 23 being found before detonation. In the medium term, the US desires to shift its forces into 'tactical overwatch', whereby control is handed over to Iraqi forces with the US offering support. Odierno said that this was already being practised in some areas, and that there may be a move towards tactical overwatch in Anbar province 'over the next several months', with the same for some neighbourhoods of Baghdad. Such moves would be based on conditions, not time, he continued. However, even if reductions can happen in 2008, it is estimated that President Bush's successor will inherit a situation whereby at least 100,000 troops are still stationed in Iraq.

Iraq's armed forces
One thing has become clear since Petraeus's September testimony and the start of the US presidential election process: the American strategy for victory in Iraq depends upon the capability of Iraq's armed forces. As Bush stated in June 2005, 'as the Iraqis stand up, we will stand down'. Since April 2003, the US has spent $19 billion – matched by $16.6bn from the Iraqi government – in an attempt to train, equip and pay the new Iraqi armed forces, and deliver American ambitions. It is the ability of this force, less than four-and-a-half years old, that will dictate the manner of the US departure from Iraq.

American plans for Iraq's new security forces have gone through several incarnations since the removal of Saddam. In May 2003, in a now much-debated decision, the civilian head of the Coalition Provisional Authority, Paul Bremer, in conjunction with his military adviser Walter Slocombe, disbanded all the existing military organs of the Iraqi state. These included the Ministry of Defence, as well as the Iraqi Army, the Republican Guard, the Special Republican Guard and the Directorate of Military Intelligence. Under this vision of the new post-Ba'athist Iraqi military, a 44,000-strong New Iraqi Corps was to be built from scratch, primarily focused on external defence. The reality of post-Ba'athist Iraq soon put paid to this perhaps idealistic approach, and the ensuing four years were spent building a much larger and more conventional force. By October 2007, the operational arm of this force consisted of around 160,000 police and 163,000 soldiers, and the Iraqi government, with Coalition support, is making significant increases in the size of the army and police forces.

US plans for the 'draw-down' of its own forces from the country envisage a four-stage transfer of power to Iraq's armed forces. To begin with, 'implemented partnerships' are to be established with Iraqi forces, who will then take the leading operational role. This is to be followed by the transition to provincial Iraqi control, finally enabling security self-reliance. Critical to this effort are 6,000 military and civilian advisers, drawn from the US and other Coalition countries. Divided into 500 teams, they are interspersed throughout the Iraqi army and police as advisers and trainers, directing their Iraqi counterparts.

The Ministry of Defence (MoD) and the Iraqi Army
The Iraqi MoD and its minister, the retired Lieutenant-General Abdullah al-Qadir Muhammad Jasim al-Mufraqi, sit at the centre of US transition plans. Amid widespread governmental failure, inefficiency and corruption, the MoD is considered one of the more

MAP 3 **IRAQ**

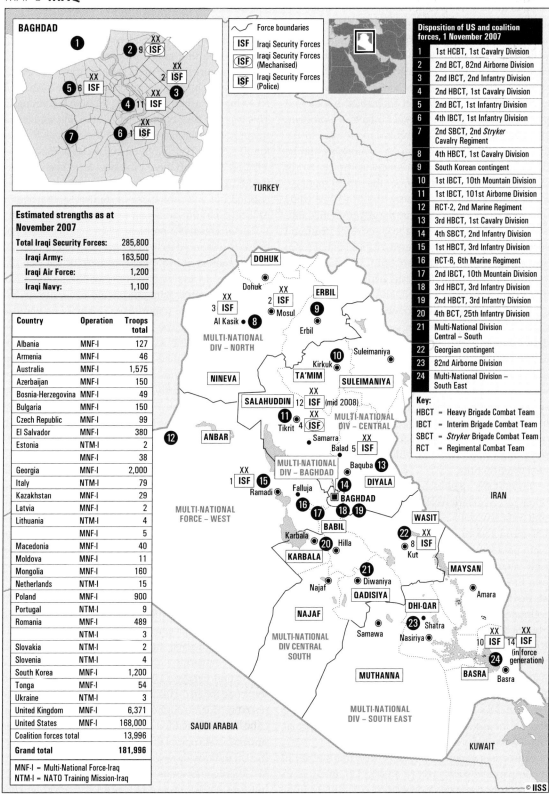

BAGHDAD

Force boundaries

ISF — Iraqi Security Forces
(ISF) — Iraqi Security Forces (Mechanised)
ISF — Iraqi Security Forces (Police)

Disposition of US and coalition forces, 1 November 2007

1	1st HCBT, 1st Cavalry Division
2	2nd BCT, 82nd Airborne Division
3	2nd IBCT, 2nd Infantry Division
4	2nd HBCT, 1st Cavalry Division
5	2nd BCT, 1st Infantry Division
6	4th IBCT, 1st Infantry Division
7	2nd SBCT, 2nd *Stryker* Cavalry Regiment
8	4th HBCT, 1st Cavalry Division
9	South Korean contingent
10	1st IBCT, 10th Mountain Division
11	1st IBCT, 101st Airborne Division
12	RCT-2, 2nd Marine Regiment
13	3rd HBCT, 1st Cavalry Division
14	4th SBCT, 2nd Infantry Division
15	1st HBCT, 3rd Infantry Division
16	RCT-6, 6th Marine Regiment
17	2nd IBCT, 10th Mountain Division
18	3rd HBCT, 3rd Infantry Division
19	2nd HBCT, 3rd Infantry Division
20	4th BCT, 25th Infantry Division
21	Multi-National Division Central – South
22	Georgian contingent
23	82nd Airborne Division
24	Multi-National Division – South East

Key:
HBCT = Heavy Brigade Combat Team
IBCT = Interim Brigade Combat Team
SBCT = *Stryker* Brigade Combat Team
RCT = Regimental Combat Team

Estimated strengths as at November 2007

Total Iraqi Security Forces:	285,800
Iraqi Army:	163,500
Iraqi Air Force:	1,200
Iraqi Navy:	1,100

Country	Operation	Troops total
Albania	MNF-I	127
Armenia	MNF-I	46
Australia	MNF-I	1,575
Azerbaijan	MNF-I	150
Bosnia-Herzegovina	MNF-I	49
Bulgaria	MNF-I	150
Czech Republic	MNF-I	99
El Salvador	MNF-I	380
Estonia	NTM-I	2
	MNF-I	38
Georgia	MNF-I	2,000
Italy	NTM-I	79
Kazakhstan	MNF-I	29
Latvia	MNF-I	2
Lithuania	NTM-I	4
	MNF-I	5
Macedonia	MNF-I	40
Moldova	MNF-I	11
Mongolia	MNF-I	160
Netherlands	NTM-I	15
Poland	MNF-I	900
Portugal	NTM-I	9
Romania	MNF-I	489
	NTM-I	3
Slovakia	NTM-I	2
Slovenia	NTM-I	4
South Korea	MNF-I	1,200
Tonga	MNF-I	54
Ukraine	NTM-I	3
United Kingdom	MNF-I	6,371
United States	MNF-I	168,000
Coalition forces total		13,996
Grand total		**181,996**

MNF-I = Multi-National Force-Iraq
NTM-I = NATO Training Mission-Iraq

TURKEY

DOHUK

Dohuk
Al Kasik
MULTI-NATIONAL DIV – NORTH
NINEVA
Mosul
ERBIL
Erbil
Suleimaniya
Kirkuk
TA'MIM
SULEIMANIYA
SALAHUDDIN
Tikrit
Samarra
Balad
MULTI-NATIONAL DIV – CENTRAL
ANBAR
MULTI-NATIONAL DIV – BAGHDAD
Baquba
DIYALA
Falluja
Ramadi
BAGHDAD
MULTI-NATIONAL FORCE – WEST
BABIL
WASIT
Karbala
Hilla
Kut
MAYSAN
KARBALA
Diwaniya
Najaf
QADISIYA
Amara
NAJAF
DHI-QAR
MULTI-NATIONAL DIV CENTRAL SOUTH
Samawa
Shatra
Nasiriya
BASRA
MUTHANNA
Basra
SAUDI ARABIA
MULTI-NATIONAL DIV – SOUTH EAST
IRAN
KUWAIT

(in force generation)

© IISS

effective ministries in the government. It certainly benefits from being within the protective enclave of the Green Zone. This means that the 50 US civilian advisers working in its central building can operate with a heightened degree of security and access. However, although the MoD had spent 76% of its salary budget by November 2006, it only managed to disburse 1% of its budget for capital goods and projects. This inability to spend budgets is a problem across all Iraqi ministries and is largely due to the insistence of the finance minister, Byan Jabr, that he personally reviews all government contracts worth over US$50,000. In addition to the micro-management of the minister of finance, the MoD has come under aggressive scrutiny from the government's anti-corruption task force, owing to a series of profound corruption scandals it suffered during the interim government of Prime Minister Ayad Allawi in 2004.

In its current form, the Iraqi army consists of ten infantry and one mechanised, one soon-to-be mechanised and one soon-to-be armoured division. Each division has three to five brigades, with two to five light infantry battalions in each (see map). A report to the US Congress in July 2007 asserted that nine army divisions out of 13 and 95 out of 101 battalions were capable of taking the lead role in operations, the second transitional stage. By September, seven provinces out of a countrywide total of 18 were said to be operating under provincial Iraqi control, the third stage, with three more scheduled to transfer over the next three months.

Each of the 163,000 soldiers judged to be operational receives eight weeks' basic training before being sent on active duty, and expects to receive a salary of US$460 a month. Conscripts in the Ba'athist army were paid US$2 a month, which may help to explain why recruiting offices are overrun with volunteers at a time when unemployment is currently running at anything between 25 and 40%. Congressional estimates assess that 75–80% of army solders are Shia, with two of the 13 divisions being at least 50% Kurdish. However, senior ranks of the military are more ethnically and religiously balanced, with three Kurdish divisional commanders, four Shia and four Sunni. (Meanwhile, in late October, the US State Department's Iraq Weekly Status Report estimated that air force and navy personnel numbered approximately 900 and 1,100 respectively.)

There is a general acceptance that Iraq's army is a comparative success story among US attempts to reconstitute the state. However, it still suffers from problems of logistics, shortages of qualified leaders, staff retention, militia infiltration in some units and sectarianism, and is judged to be years away from functioning effectively without sustained Coalition support. The first major problem the army faces is under-manning: many units can only muster between 60–75% of their assigned staff, though they have been receiving replacements to bring them to full strength. This is partly due to the policy of allowing soldiers to travel home each month to give their wages to their families. There is also estimated to be a 15–18% annual attrition rate. Both these problems have been exacerbated by corruption, with muster rolls sometimes padded out with non-existent soldiers so that senior officers can skim money off for personal enrichment.

Sectarianism is a problem in some units, although not as pronounced as in other government ministries. As mentioned above, Shia members of the population make up the vast majority of the junior ranks of the army, while Shia officers are generally underrepresented in the senior staff. This may be because those at the top of the Iraqi Army gained their experience either in the Kurdish militia, the Peshmerga, or in Saddam's armed forces, which had an inherent bias towards a Sunni officer corps. Of much greater concern is the overtly sectarian behaviour of some army divisions. The Fifth Division, based in Diyala province northeast of Baghdad, has repeatedly been accused of perpetrating sectarian violence. It has been charged with facilitating arms shipments to Shia militias and of being dominated by both the JAM and the Badr Brigade, the military wing of the Supreme Council for the Islamic Revolution in Iraq. In July 2007, 30 civilians in Diyala were killed by men wearing army uniforms, and the Fifth Division's Shia commander was replaced at the Coalition's request after repeated complaints that he had been involved in the harassment of Sunni civilians.

In a country deeply enmeshed in violence and long-running sectarian conflict, it is perhaps unsurprising that the army has been tainted by religious and ethnic division. However, the large number of Coalition advisers embedded within its ranks and the close interaction between US and Iraqi forces has limited the scope for an orchestrated campaign of militia colonisation. But throughout 2007 there were worrying signs that an extended campaign of politicisation was underway. As part of the campaign to reduce violence, the US military agreed that Iraqi Prime Minister Nuri al-Maliki could create the Office of the Commander-in-Chief (OCIC). This was designed to bring greater coherence to the Iraqi armed forces with the beginning of the 'surge'. The prime minister has in fact used the OCIC to increase his personal control over the Iraqi Army. There have been numerous reliable reports that key prime ministerial advisers have used his authority to move troops around the battlefield, using mobile telephones to contact officers directly, thus undermining the chain of command. The creation of the OCIC is a development that has undermined the administrative coherence of the MoD and the authority of the defence minister. Analysts judge that this could, if left unchecked, open the Iraqi Army to the sustained politicisation that has done so much to undermine the police force. The possibility would then exist that the Iraqi army could become another sectarian actor, hastening Iraq's further descent into civil war. Under this scenario, US plans for greater Iraqi control over the military would simply deliver it into the hands of the militias and death squads.

The Ministry of the Interior and the Iraqi police force

The Ministry of the Interior and the Iraqi police stand as a stark example of what could happen to the Iraqi army if recent moves to politicise it are not constrained. Unlike the MoD, the Coalition Provisional Authority did not disband the Ministry of Interior or its police force. Instead, in an attempt to get indigenous policing up and running as quickly as possible, it worked through the existing ministry and its personnel. During the Ibrahim al-Jaafari premiership of 2005, the Ministry of Interior was run by Byan Jabr, who had previously been a senior official of the Badr Brigade. He set about integrating its fighters into the ministry and the senior ranks of the police force. Ever since, the ministry and its staff have had a sustained reputation as a bastion of sectarian-motivated violence.

The ministry's main building sits on the opposite side of the Tigris to the Green Zone, while 90 US and Coalition members of the ministry's transition team are lodged at a nearby US army forward-operating base. Meanwhile, the new minister, Jawad al-Bolani, lives and keeps his main office in the Green Zone, which limits his ability to improve the ministry's performance and build capacity. The organisation of policing under the ministry is divided between the general Iraqi Police Service (IPS) and the specialised National Police. The IPS is reported to have 230,000 paid staff assigned. However, owing to militia influence both in Baghdad and across the south of the country, it has developed a reputation for sectarian-motivated action. Command and control of the IPS – in theory at least nationally vested in the Ministry of Interior – has become highly localised, with militia influence undermining formal national and provincial control. The result is that it is difficult to tell the difference between the police and militias in many areas south of Baghdad. The Facilities Protection Service (FPS), over 90,000 strong, is charged with securing fixed locations. Operating under the direct control of the ministries, many FPS units have been infiltrated by militias. A recent decision to bring all of the FPS under the control of the Ministry of Interior aims to re-establish Baghdad's control over these forces.

The National Police was originally created by the Ministry of Interior as a quick-reaction paramilitary force, independent of US advice or oversight. By 2006 it consisted of two divisions, the National Police Commandos and a public order division. The National Police Commandos have been repeatedly accused of acting as a death squad, purging areas of Baghdad of their Sunni residents. By the end of October 2007, the National Police had around 26,300 trained and equipped personnel.

Since taking up his post, al-Bolani has striven to purge the worst offenders from the National Police, removing seven of the nine commanders of the organisation's brigades. He has also dismissed thousands of personnel. However, a recent congressionally mandated report written by retired US General James Jones recommended that in view of the extent to which the National Police had been penetrated by sectarian actors it should be totally disbanded and rebuilt from scratch.

Possible futures

The Iraqi security forces have been clearly identified by the Bush administration as the main vehicle by which the US military commitment to the country can be reduced. It is hoped that troop numbers and associated casualties can eventually be reduced to such a level that Iraq will stop being such a divisive domestic political issue. However, in spite of the billions of dollars spent and the hundreds of thousands of troops and police trained, it still remains to be seen if the Iraqi Army and police will form part of the solution or remain part of the problem.

Through the creation of the Multi-National Security Transition Command-Iraq and the 'surge' of US troops to Baghdad, the Iraqi Army has been built within a clear framework of US and Coalition oversight. In spite of this close attention the army is still very much a 'work in progress'. It is a generation away from being able to act independently of US logistical support. The close attention of US trainers has not stopped the Iraqi Army harbouring, at all levels, sectarian actors bent on using it as a tool in the civil war. The creation by al-Maliki of the OCIC indicates the constant threat to army autonomy from powerful politicians who want it to act for the benefit of one political faction or another. Meanwhile, the case of the Iraqi police, both at a national and local level, serves as a warning of the grave dangers of politicisation that can quickly lead to the sectarian use of forces that the US has armed and trained. If the Iraqi security forces are to act as a central part of any future exit strategy then there needs to be much greater interaction by Coalition personnel with all levels of the security forces over a much greater length of time than current timetables estimate.

OTHER REGIONAL DEVELOPMENTS

Following the summer 2006 fighting in Lebanon and UN Security Council Resolution (UNSCR) 1701 in 2006, the UN Intervention Force in **Lebanon** (UNIFIL II) has acted as a separation force. On 24 August 2007, UNIFIL's mandate was extended by another year, until 31 August 2008, and, as of the end of September 2007, the organisation had over 13,000 military personnel under its command, operating in the area between the border with Israel and the Litani River (see *The Military Balance 2007*, pp. 209–13). On 17 June, the Israeli town of Kiryat Shmona, in the Upper Galilee region, was struck by a number of rockets originating from southern Lebanon. Seven days later, UNIFIL forces were subjected to a bomb attack that killed six Spanish soldiers near the town of Khiyam. Investigators have assessed that the device employed was a remotely controlled car bomb. A second explosion in July, this time near Qasmieyah Bridge, caused no casualties.

Meanwhile, concern has been expressed that weapons may still be finding their way into the hands of Hizbullah forces, notwithstanding the arms embargo noted in UNSCR 1701. In a report in August, the UN Security Council expressed 'grave concern at persistent reports of breaches of the arms embargo along the Lebanon–Syria border'. As well as criticising Israeli violations of Lebanon's air-space, the report also expressed 'concern about the recent statement by Hizbullah that it retains the military

capacity to strike all parts of Israel'. In his report on the implementation of UNSCR 1559, UN Secretary-General Ban Ki-moon said that 'the information I have received also indicates that Hizbullah has compensated for all losses sustained in the course of the war last year and has established a secure network of communications'. During 2007, a number of media reports alleged that Hizbullah forces were now established north of the Litani River; according to the report of a September press conference by the UNIFIL force commander, 'he had recently read an interview by the Minister of Defence of Israel, who said that in his opinion, Hizbullah was operating out of the reach of UNIFIL. It was his opinion as well.' From May to September, Lebanon's military forces were engaged in operations against the Fatah al-Islam group, largely in the Nahr al-Bared refugee camp. It was estimated by the UN Relief and Works Agency that 30,000 inhabitants had fled the camp during fighting, which the organisation classed as the most serious internal fighting in Lebanon since the end of the civil war in 1990.

Israel continued to review the conduct of the military operations in Lebanon in 2006 (see *The Military Balance 2007*). In September 2006, the government mandated the Winograd Commission 'to look into the preparation and conduct of the political and the security levels concerning all the dimensions of the Northern Campaign which started on July 12th 2006'. In April 2007 the committee presented an interim report on the decisions leading up to the conflict. This document said that the Israel Defense Forces (IDF) were not ready for the war and that 'the decision to respond with an immediate, intensive military strike was not based on a detailed, comprehensive and authorized military plan, based on careful study of the complex characteristics of the Lebanon arena'. The IDF, meanwhile, were not creative enough in proposing alternate courses of action and 'did not alert the political decision-makers to the discrepancy between [their] own scenarios and the authorized modes of action, and did not demand – as was necessary under [their] own plans – early mobilization of the reserves so they could be equipped and trained in case a ground operation would be required … Even after these facts became known to the political leaders, they failed to adapt the military way of operation and its goals to the reality on the ground.' In June, former Prime Minister Ehud Barak was elected to the Labor Party leadership in a second-round run-off after Amir Peretz lost a leadership ballot. In mid June, Barak was appointed as the new defence minister in place of Peretz.

The IDF have announced a wide-ranging reform process called 'Tefen 2012' (see p. 234). Presented in September by Chief of Staff Lieutenant-General Gabi Ashkenazi (who replaced Lieutenant-General Dan Halutz after he resigned in January), the process is designed to orient Israel's forces to face a wide range of threats and lays emphasis on bolstering the firepower and mobility of Israel's ground forces. More *Merkava* 4 main battle tanks (MBTs) will be produced, as will more *Namer* armoured personnel carriers, based on the *Merkava* hull. The air force and navy will also receive upgrades, as noted on p. 234. In August, the Israeli Air Force (IAF) base next to Ben Gurion Airport moved to Nevatim in the south. This is part of a plan, according to the IDF, to move various bases southwards. The new base is due to become the IAF's largest, housing the entire cargo aircraft fleet. Meanwhile, it has been reported that the IAF is seeking to expand its cooperation with the army, in the wake of lessons learned in the 2006 fighting in Lebanon. In September, reports surfaced of a possible attack by Israeli forces on a target deep inside Syria. Rumours that an incident had occurred were substantiated by figures in Israel and then by Syria's President Bashar al-Assad in a television interview with the BBC, in which the latter was reported to have said that an 'unused military construction site' was attacked. At the time of writing, details remained vague.

Israel was also, like Saudi Arabia, Egypt and other Gulf states, announced as the prospective recipient of significant packages of US military equipment in mid 2007 (see p. 232).

Israel–Hamas–Palestine. The seizure of power by Hamas forces in June has not led to a reduction in violence in the Gaza Strip. In late October, there were reports of factional fighting among forces from Hamas and Islamic Jihad, as well as a clan supporting Fatah. The seizure of power itself has been termed a military coup. As noted in the IISS *Strategic Survey 2007*, though Fatah's Executive Protection Force 'was competent enough, the majority of Fatah fighters were untrained, poorly organised and seemingly uncommitted to the fight. Hamas personnel, in contrast, were highly disciplined, skilled and fought

effectively under a unified command.' In the wake of the events of June, Palestinian Authority President Mahmoud Abbas sacked a number of his security force personnel. Currently, rocket fire originating from the Gaza Strip is reported to be directed at Israeli territory on a regular basis. As of mid October, according to Israel's foreign affairs ministry, 288 rockets and 454 mortar rounds had landed in Israeli territory since the Hamas takeover. While most of the rockets fired are reported to be of the *Qassam* type, in early October Israeli sources noted that a 122mm *Grad* rocket had also been employed.

While much analysis has been devoted to the unfolding diplomatic situation concerning **Iran's** nuclear programme, the country's military forces have reportedly been upgrading their capabilities. In January, Iran was reported as having completed the receipt of 29 *Tor* M-1 (SA-15 *Guideline*) air-defence systems from Russia, testing the systems in February. It was also reported that Iran received some 10 *Pantsyr* air-defence systems towards mid year, and a new aircraft based on the F-5 airframe, called the *Saeghe*, was reported flying later in the year. In March, naval forces of the Islamic Revolutionary Guards Corps (IRGC) seized 15 UK Royal Navy personnel who were conducting a routine search operation in the Gulf. After a diplomatic stand-off lasting almost two weeks the personnel were freed, with the Royal Navy resuming its boarding operations one month later. Meanwhile, the incident led, in the UK, to naval enquiries and also to protracted debates over the move to permit some of the personnel to sell the story of their captivity to the media. Allegations of Iranian support to insurgents in Iraq and Afghanistan continue, as do concerns over proliferation-related activities. In October, the US designated the IRGC and the Iranian Ministry of Defence and Armed Forces Logistics as 'entities of proliferation concern'. The IRGC-Qods Force was also designated in this way by the US Treasury 'for providing material support to the Taliban and other terrorist organizations'. The IRGC had earlier, in September, seen a new commander appointed when General Mohammad Ali Jafari – who had previously led the IRGC ground forces – replaced General Yahya Rahim Safavi. Jafari was reported as saying that the Basij would come under IRGC command.

MIDDLE EAST AND NORTH AFRICA – DEFENCE ECONOMICS

With oil prices remaining high during 2007, several countries posted healthy budget surpluses and many continued the trend established in recent years of repaying debt and investing in the non-oil sector in an effort to create employment in new industries. Rapid population growth across the region has contributed to some of the highest levels of unemployment in the world and relatively low employment-to-population ratios. In the past, increased public-sector employment has helped to cushion the impact of rising labour supply, but demand for jobs is currently outpacing economy-wide supply by increasing margins. A report by McKinsey & Co. estimated that Saudi Arabia alone would have to create 3.5 million new jobs over the next decade, effectively doubling the current workforce, in order to meet the employment needs of its rising population of working age. The International Monetary Fund has urged oil-producing countries to use the currently favourable economic conditions to implement policies that will address the twin challenges of diversifying oil-dependent economies and providing employment to the rapidly expanding labour force. In this context, the ambitious investment plans of the Gulf Cooperation Council (GCC), totalling some US$700 billion during 2006–10, are expected to make a major contribution. Meanwhile, in the non-oil exporting countries of the Mashreq region, growth remained strong, underpinned by an upturn in foreign direct investment and an overall favourable external environment.

The likelihood of the GCC achieving its medium-term ambition for a single currency by 2010 appears to have receded somewhat, not least given the revelation by Oman that there was only a distant possibility it might join such a scheme, and the decision by Kuwait to revalue its currency and drop the dollar peg. Further pressure comes from sharply rising inflation in both the United Arab Emirates and Kuwait – it is a condition of the GCC's convergence criteria that the inflation rate of individual nations must be kept within 2% of the average inflation figure for all six GCC countries. However, with most countries in the region focusing on economic expansion, domestic inflation is seen as a necessary consequence of government spending and, given demographic challenges, there is little appetite to cut such expenditure.

Despite the windfall revenues generated by high oil prices there had been little evidence over the past few years that this was leading to a noticeable increase in military-related expenditure. However, with tensions over Iran's nuclear ambitions remaining high, there are signs that several countries in the region are now upgrading their military capabilities. As well as allocating higher domestic funding to security forces, Egypt and Israel will receive an increase in external military aid and equipment from the US. In August 2007, the Bush administration unveiled plans for a significant increase in military assistance to Israel (from US$24bn to US$30bn over 10 years) and Egypt (US$13bn over 10 years), as well as significant new weapons exports to Saudi Arabia and other Gulf regional allies, thought to include missile-defence equipment, aircraft and naval assets, and amounting to at least US$20bn. US officials explained that the initiatives were intended to shore up regional security and 'bolster forces of moderation' in the region.

Having refrained from making any major new arms purchases for several years, **Saudi Arabia** has signed a number of high-value deals in the past two years. The largest of its new acquisitions is a contract to purchase 72 Eurofighter *Typhoon* fighter aircraft. Known as 'Project Salam', the deal marks a major evolution in UK–Saudi defence cooperation that will see the UK, as well as other Eurofighter partner nations, supplying the major components for the aircraft while a local supply chain will be built up in the Kingdom. At the heart of the deal is likely to be the establishment of a joint venture company between BAE Systems and the Alsalam Aircraft Company within Saudi Arabia to oversee final assembly work and long-term logistical support. The initial stages of the contract are thought to be worth £4.4bn, although with logistical and training support this could increase to well over £20bn over a 25-year period. From the Saudi perspective the arrangement will create some 15,000 jobs and is, therefore, in line with the government's 'Saudi-isation' policy of boosting employment while building up its own high-tech industrial base through an unprecedented degree of defence-related technology transfers. Under a separate contract, European missile manufacturer MBDA is expecting to confirm a sizeable order for a range of weapons – including *Meteor, Storm Shadow, Brimstone* and advanced short-range air-to-air missiles – to equip both the new *Typhoon* and upgraded *Tornado* aircraft. The first 24 aircraft for the Royal Saudi Air Force (RSAF) will be diverted from the UK's *Typhoon* Tranche 2 order, meaning that the first aircraft is likely to be delivered during 2008, while the remaining 48 aircraft will be delivered from 2011 when the new assembly facility in Saudi Arabia is operational. BAE Systems declared that once it closed the *Typhoon* deal its primary objective in the Kingdom would be to turn its in-country presence into a manufacturing and through-life logistics support operation by developing industrial infrastructure and training Saudi nationals. After the *Typhoon* production facility is established, the focus will move to starting a similar arrangement for the assembly of new *Hawk* trainer aircraft to replace the RSAF's 1980s-vintage platforms. In the longer term it is envisaged that the *Typhoon* logistic support centre will expand to become a regional support centre for *Hawks* in service with Oman, Kuwait and Bahrain.

As noted, MBDA is expecting to conclude negotiations with the RSAF over a comprehensive range of new missiles, some of which are intended for the fleet of *Tornado* IDS aircraft which are currently being upgraded from GR.1 to GR.4 status. So far, around eight Saudi aircraft have been upgraded to *Tornado* Sustainment Programme status, a process which involves two separate stages. The first phase involves the installation of wiring and other hardware to support the integration of precision-guided weapons including new navigation systems, improved radios, new GPS and tabulated cockpit displays, while the second phase will constitute weapons selection and integration.

Other major deals yet to be finalised at the time of writing will likely include a significant helicopter purchase from France. Following a visit to Riyadh in late 2006 by Michèle Alliot-Marie, then France's defence minister, a large Saudi air-force and army delegation visited the Paris Air Show to continue discussions over future equipment requirements. In the first instance it is thought that Saudi Arabia is negotiating the purchase of over 130 helicopters, including 64 NH 90 utility aircraft, 12 *Tiger* attack helicopters, 20 AS 532 *Cougar* combat search and rescue (CSAR) helicopters, 32 AS 650 *Fennec* and four AS 565 *Panther* naval CSAR helicopters. Also linked to the outcome of these talks is the fate of a contract for two Airbus A330 Multi-Role Tanker Transports. As noted in *The Military Balance 2007*, French industry is hopeful that in the longer term, the Saudi armed forces will upgrade their capabilities with the acquisition of FREMM multi-mission frigates, as well as French submarines and main battle tanks.

In August 2006, the US Defence Security Cooperation Agency notified Congress of a range of proposed weapons sales to the Saudi Arabian National Guard amounting to around US$10bn. The largest contract, valued at US$5.8bn, covers the delivery of 724 light-armoured vehicles, while a separate US$2.9bn contract covers the upgrade of 315 M1A2 *Abrams* main battle tanks, plus the delivery of 58 new M1A1 vehicles. Twelve months later it emerged that the US is preparing for additional arms sales to the Kingdom, possibly amounting to at least US$20bn over the coming decade. The package, which has yet to be put to Congress, is likely to include advanced satellite-guided bombs, *Patriot* air-defence systems, aircraft upgrades and new naval assets.

Despite the hostilities with Lebanon during the summer of 2006, **Israel's** economy continues to perform well, leading the IMF to conclude that strong macroeconomic conditions, together with sound domestic policies, have significantly improved Israel's growth performance and prospects. While the extra expenditure attributed to the Lebanese conflict failed to have a dramatic impact on government finances in 2006 – the central government budget deficit actually fell that year – measures adopted in response to the conflict will have a significantly negative impact on the government budget in 2007. As a result, the government has decided to raise the limit on public spending growth to 1.7% (in real terms) from 2007 and has, therefore, adjusted the deficit ceilings upwards for both 2007 and 2008. In 2007, the deficit ceiling will now be 2.9% of GDP and will fall to 2.0% of GDP the following year. According to the Deficit Reduction Law, the central government deficit will not exceed 1% of GDP from 2009 onwards.

Following a drop in defence expenditure over several years, the 2007 defence budget saw this trend reversed with a proposed budget of NS47.8bn, later increased to NS50.9bn to help compensate the IDF for costs incurred during the 2006 conflict in Lebanon. In response to government calls for greater transparency and oversight of defence spending, the Ministry of Defense (MoD) published a 174-page report entitled 'Defence Budget 2007: Unclassified Subjects'. However, beyond the most basic listing of top-line figures, the report covers less than 25% of the country's overall defence budget and provides no guidance as to the proportion of funds allocated to procurement, training, research and development or operational activities.

The increase in the defence budget, originally prompted by the conflict in Lebanon, was underpinned by the publication in June 2007 of a report by the Brodet Committee, which had been commissioned by the prime minister to examine all aspects of Israel's defence budget. The report surprised both the defence and finance ministries – which had expected the committee to conclude that the defence budget should be reduced – by calling for a five-year, rather than annual budget, which should be increased at an annual rate of 1.5%. According to the committee, the IDF should aim to save around NS30bn between 2008 and 2018 by adopting extensive cost-saving and efficiency measures, while the MoD should ring-fence a reserve of NS1bn for unexpected events. The committee believes that savings could be made by: reducing professional army personnel by 2% annually over the next 10 years; setting the retirement age for non-combat personnel at 57; shortening the service of non-combat conscripts from 36 to 32 months; and laying off 500 employees from the MoD over the next four years.

In August 2007, it emerged that Israel had been successful in its negotiations with the US to increase the annual amount of military aid it receives via the Foreign Military Financing (FMF) initiative. Under the new agreement, the US will provide Israel with a US$30bn FMF package between 2009 and 2018, an increase of around 25% over the previous ten-year period. In 2007, US FMF to Israel will amount to US$2.4bn and this will increase by US$150m a year until 2011, when it will be fixed at US$3.1bn. The IDF had been hoping that FMF funding would jump to the new level in one step rather than incrementally over a multi-year period, and as a result it may have to trim certain procurement plans.

Following the publication of the Brodet Report and the conclusion of talks about increased military aid from the US, in September 2007 the IDF published its new five-year plan. Unlike previous plans, Tefen 2012 significantly favours the modernisation of the land forces over other services and specifically aims to improve the manoeuvrability of Israel's ground forces. Focusing on the possibility of continuing conflict with Palestinian groups, a potential conflict with Syria or Hizbullah, the emergence of a nuclear-armed Iran by 2010 and the potential for a 'dramatic change' in the regimes of moderate neighbouring countries, the plan identifies nine core capabilities that need to be maintained or upgraded. It places greatest priority on developing capabilities for the army, which will receive 'hundreds' of new *Namer* infantry fighting vehicles, 'hundreds' of *Stryker* 8x8 medium armoured vehicles, several dozen new *Merkava* 4 MBTs a year and dozens of tactical mini-unmanned aerial vehicles.

With renewed focus on ground forces, the IAF, which has traditionally received highest priority in terms of procurement funding, will be forced to limit its requirements over the next five years. The most high-profile casualty appears to be its hoped-for 100 Joint Strike Fighter aircraft. The request for these has been denied and instead only an initial 25 aircraft will be purchased, with the potential of another 25 in the next five-year plan. The IAF's request for an additional squadron of AH-64D *Apache* attack helicopters has also been limited to just six aircraft. In light of limited new funds there will be no replacement for the ageing KC-707s, which will be upgraded. Likewise, the fleet of 30-year-old F-15 A/Bs will receive a major upgrade, although there are likely to be funds for at least four new C-130 transport aircraft. The navy is probably the service to suffer the most from the new

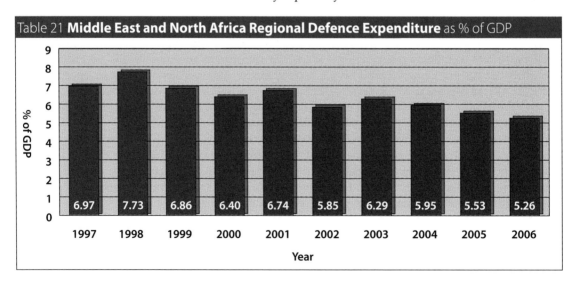

Table 21 **Middle East and North Africa Regional Defence Expenditure** as % of GDP

Year	% of GDP
1997	6.97
1998	7.73
1999	6.86
2000	6.40
2001	6.74
2002	5.85
2003	6.29
2004	5.95
2005	5.53
2006	5.26

plan – procurement funds are currently needed for the acquisition of two additional *Dolphin*-class diesel electric submarines. Although the navy had expected a complete rejection of its request for a new surface combatant, Tefen 2012 does include US$240m for the acquisition of a new multi-mission ship. The most likely vessel is Lockheed Martin's design for the US Navy's Littoral Combat Ship (LCS). Lockheed Martin has been conducting studies for over a year on how the LCS could be best adapted for use by the Israeli navy. A second vessel could then be procured during the next five-year plan.

Tefen 2012 reiterates the conclusions of the Brodet Report, pointing out that even with a modest annual increase of 1.5% in the domestic budget, in addition to increased US military aid, the budget will still not be sufficient to implement all the measures outlined fully and that significant efficiency savings will need to be achieved.

Since the lifting of the EU arms embargo on **Libya** in 2004, Tripoli has indicated its interest in modernising its armed forces, but to date has signed only a few modest contracts. However, observers are predicting that a major new deal will be concluded before long, with France or Russia – both of which have long-standing military relationships with Libya – the most likely counterpart. In the past year, France has agreed to undertake a US$180m upgrade of 12 out of Libya's inventory of 29 *Mirage* F1s – only 12 platforms were deemed suitable to be made airworthy. Under a new French initiative designed to persuade overseas customers to buy new military equipment rather than upgrade older variants, the *Mirage* upgrade will be limited to new-engine installation and verification that the airframe and electronics are still serviceable.

The issue of the five Bulgarian nurses and a Palestinian-born doctor who were accused in Libya of deliberately infecting children in their care with HIV had soured relations between Libya and France, but after their release in August 2007 another two deals were announced. Under one, worth US$200m, EADS will supply Libya with *Milan* anti-tank guided missiles, while the other, a US$160m contract, covers the delivery of *Tetra* communications equipment.

Earlier, in February 2007, France and Libya had signed a framework accord that promised to open the way to significant arms deals between the two countries thought to cover a range of equipment including *Rafale* fighter aircraft, *Tiger* attack helicopters, fast patrol boats, anti-aircraft missiles and a radar system to monitor Libya's airspace and borders. However, as relations between the two countries faltered over the fate of the Bulgarian nurses and the doctor, Russia stepped up its efforts to secure a major arms deal when the head of Libya's military procurement body visited Moscow in May 2007. It is thought that the most likely trade between Russia and Libya would include 12 Su-30MK2 and 12 MiG-29SMT aircraft as well as long- and short-range air-defence systems and one or two *Kilo*-class submarines. If such a deal goes ahead, it is likely to be arranged in a similar way as Russia's 2006 arms-for-debt deal with Algeria. However, the two countries at present appear to be disputing the size of the likely debt, with Russia claiming that it would amount to US$4.4bn, with Tripoli believing the figure is closer to US$1.7bn.

Algeria Ag

Algerian Dinar D		2006	2007	2008
GDP	D	8.2tr	8.9tr	
	US$	113bn	131bn	
per capita	US$	3,430	3,944	
Growth	%	3.6	4.8	
Inflation	%	2.5	4.5	
Def bdgt[a]	D	224bn	ε250bn	
	US$	3.09bn	3.69bn	
US$1=D		72.6	67.7	

[a] Excluding extra-budgetary funding

Population   33,333,216

Age	0–14	15–19	20–24	25–29	30–64	65 plus
Male	15%	6%	6%	5%	17%	2%
Female	14%	6%	6%	5%	17%	2%

Capabilities

ACTIVE 147,000 (Army 127,000 Navy 6,000 Air 14,000) **Paramilitary 187,200**
Terms of service Army 18 months (6 months basic, 12 months civil projects)

RESERVE 150,000 (Army 150,000) to age 50

ORGANISATIONS BY SERVICE

Army 47,000; ε80,000 conscript (total 127,000)
FORCES BY ROLE
6 Mil Regions; re-org into div structure on hold
Armd	2 div (*each*: 3 tk regt, 1 mech regt); 1 indep bde
Mech	3 div (*each*: 1 tk regt, 3 mech regt)
Mech Inf/Mot Inf	5 indep bde
AB /SF	1 div (5 AB regt)
Arty	7 regt
AD	5 bn
Engr	4 indep bn

EQUIPMENT BY TYPE
MBT 895: 325 T-72; 300 T-62; 270 T-54/T-55
RECCE 90: 26 BRDM-2; 64 BRDM-2 each with AT-3 9K11 *Sagger*
AIFV 1,040: 680 BMP-1; 260 BMP-2; 100 BMP-3
APC (W) 750: 300 BTR-60; 150 BTR-80; 150 OT-64; 50 M-3 *Panhard;* 100 TH 390 *Fahd*
ARTY 1,019
  SP 170: **122mm** 140 2S1 *Carnation;* **152mm** 30 2S3
  TOWED 375: **122mm** 160 D-30; 25 D-74; 100 M-1931/37; 60 M-30 *M-1938*; **130mm** 10 M-46; **152mm** 20 ML-20 *M-1937*
  MRL 144: **122mm** 48 BM-21; **140mm** 48 BM-14/16; **240mm** 30 BM-24; **300mm** 18 9A52 *Smerch*
  MOR 330: **82mm** 150 M-37; **120mm** 120 M-1943; **160mm** 60 M-1943

AT
  MSL • MANPATS 200+: 200 Milan; AT-3 9K11 *Sagger;* AT-4 9K111 *Spigot;* AT-5 9K113 *Spandrel*
  RCL 180: **107mm** 60; 60 B-11; **82mm** 120 B-10
  GUNS 300: **57mm** 160 ZIS-2 *M-1943;* **85mm** 80 D-44: **100mm** 50 SU-100 SP (in store); 10 T-12
AD • SAM 288+
  SP 68: ε48 SA-8 *Gecko;* ε20 SA-9 *Gaskin*
  MANPAD 220+: ε220 SA-7A *Grail*/SA-7B *Grail;* SA-14 *Gremlin*/SA-16 *Gimlet;*
  GUNS ε875
  SP ε225 ZSU-23-4
  TOWED ε650: **14.5mm** 100: 60 ZPU-2; 40 ZPU-4; **20mm** 100; **23mm** 100 ZU-23; **37mm** ε100 M-1939; **57mm** 70 S-60; **85mm** 20 M-1939 *KS-12;* **100mm** 150 KS-19; **130mm** 10 KS-30

Navy ε6,000 (incl 500 officers)
EQUIPMENT BY TYPE
SUBMARINES • TACTICAL • SSK 2 *Kilo* (FSU) each with 6 single 533mm TT with 18 Test-71ME HWT (1 in refit)
PRINCIPAL SURFACE COMBATANTS 9
  FRIGATES • FF 3 *Mourad Rais* (FSU *Koni*) each with 1 twin (2 eff.) with 20 SA-N-4 *Gecko* SAM, 2 RBU 6000 *Smerch 2* (24 eff.), 4 76mm gun
  CORVETTES 6
  FSG 3:
    2 *Rais Hamidou* (FSU *Nanuchka* II) each with 4 single each with 1 SS-N-2C *Styx* tactical SSM, 1 twin (2 eff.) with 20 SA-N-4 *Gecko* SAM
    1 *Rais Hamidou* (FSU *Nanuchka* II) with 4 quad (16 eff.) with 16 SS-N-25 *Switchblade* tactical SSM, 1 twin (2 eff.) with 20 SA-N-4 *Gecko* SAM
  FS 3 *Djebel Chenona* each with 2 twin (4 eff.) CSS-N-8 *Saccade* tactical SSM, 1 76mm gun
PATROL AND COASTAL COMBATANTS 20
  PFM 9 *Osa* II each with 4 single each with 1 SS-N-2B *Styx* tactical SSM (3†)
  PFC 11 *Kebir*
AMPHIBIOUS • LS 3
  LSM 1 *Polnochny B* (capacity 6 MBT; 180 troops)
  LST 2 *Kalaat beni Hammad*) (capacity 7 tanks; 240 troops) each with 1 med hel landing platform
LOGISTICS AND SUPPORT 10
  TRG 8: 1 *Daxin;* **AXL** 7 *EL Mouderrib*
  SPT 1
  TRV 1 *Poluchat* (Used for SAR)
FACILITIES
Bases Located at Mers el Kebir, Algiers, Annaba, Jijel

Coast Guard ε500
PATROL AND COASTAL COMBATANTS 15
  PCC 11: 4 *Baglietto;* 7 *Chui- E* (PRC)
  PCI 4 *El Mounkid* less than 100 tonnes
LOGISTICS AND SUPPORT 1 **SPT**

Air Force ε14,000
Flying hours 150 hrs/year

FORCES BY ROLE

Ftr	2 sqn with 12 MiG-25 *Foxbat*; 4 sqn with 25 MiG-29C *Fulcrum*/MiG-29UB *Fulcrum* ; 2 sqn with 18 MiG-23MF/MS/U *Flogger*
FGA	1 sqn with 6 Su-30MKA; 2 sqn each with 17 Su-24M *Fencer*/Su-24MK *Fencer D*; 2 sqn with 38 MiG-23BN *Flogger*
Recce	1 sqn with 4 Su-24E *Fencer*; 1 sqn with 4 MiG-25R *Foxbat*
MR	2 sqn with 6 Beech 200T *Maritime Patrol*
Tpt	2 sqn with 9 C-130H *Hercules*; 8 C-130H-30 *Hercules*; 4 Gulfstream IV-SP; 1 Gulfstream V; 3 Il-76MD *Candid B*; 6 Il-76TD *Candid*; 2 L-100-30; 2 (VIP) sqn with 2 F-27 *Friendship*; 3 *Falcon* 900
Tkr	1 sqn with 6 Il-78 *Midas*
Atk hel	4 sqn with 33 Mi-24 *Hind*
Tpt hel	7 sqn with 8 AS-355 *Ecureuil*; 64 Mi-17/Mi-8 *Hip*; 42 Mi-171
Trg	6 Yak-130 being delivered 2008. 2 sqn with 40 Z-142; 2 sqn with 36 L-39ZA; 7 L-39C *Albatros*; 6 hel sqn with 28 PZL Mi-2 *Hoplite*
AD	3 bde with 725 100mm/130mm/85mm
SAM	3 regt with ε140 SA-2 *Guideline*/SA-3 *Goa*/SA-6 *Gainful*/SA-8 *Gecko* (140-840 eff.)

EQUIPMENT BY TYPE
AIRCRAFT 141 combat capable
  FTR 55: 12 MiG-25 *Foxbat*; 25 MiG-29C *Fulcrum*/MiG-29UB *Fulcrum*; 18 MiG-23MF/MS/U *Flogger*
  FGA 78: 6 Su-30MKA (further 22 to be delivered); 34 Su-24M/Su-24MK *Fencer D*; 38 MiG-23BN *Flogger*
  RECCE 8: 4 MiG-25R *Foxbat**; 4 Su-24E *Fencer**
  MP 6 Beech 200T *Maritime Patrol* (additional units on order)
  TKR 6: 6 Il-78 *Midas*
  TPT 38: 9 C-130H; 8 C-130H-30 *Hercules*; 2 F-27 *Friendship*; 3 *Falcon* 900; 4 Gulfstream IV-SP; 1 Gulfstream V; 3 Il-76MD *Candid B*; 6 Il-76TD *Candid*; 2 L-100-30
  TRG 89: 6 Yak-130; 36 L-39ZA *Albatros*; 7 L-39C; 40 Z-142
HELICOPTERS
  ATK 33 Mi-24 *Hind*
  SPT 114: 8 AS-355 *Ecureuil*; 42 Mi-171; 64 Mi-17 (Mi-8MT) *Hip H*/Mi-8 *Hip*
  TRG 28 PZL Mi-2 *Hoplite*
AD
  SAM ε140 SA-2 *Guideline* Towed/SA-3 *Goa*/SA-6 *Gainful* SP/SA-8 *Gecko* SP (140–840 eff.)
  GUNS 725 **100mm/130mm/85mm**
MSL
  ASM AS-10 *Karen*; AS-12 *Kegler*; AS-14 *Kedge*; AS-17 *Krypton*; AS-7 *Kerry*
  AAM AA-10 *Alamo*; A-11 *Archer*; AA-2 *Atoll*; AA-6 *Acrid*; AA-7 *Apex*; AA-8 *Aphid*

Paramilitary ε187,200

Gendarmerie 20,000
Ministry of Defence

FORCES BY ROLE
Army 6 region

EQUIPMENT BY TYPE
RECCE AML-60/110 M-3 *Panhard* APC (W)
APC (W) 100 TH 390 *Fahd*
HELICOPTERS • SPT PZL Mi-2 *Hoplite*

National Security Forces 16,000
Directorate of National Security. Small arms

Republican Guard 1,200
RECCE AML-60
APC (T) M-3

Legitimate Defence Groups ε150,000
Self-defence militia, communal guards (60,000)

NON-STATE ARMED GROUPS
see Part II

DEPLOYMENT

ETHIOPIA/ERITREA
AU • OLMEE 2 obs
UN • UNMEE 8 obs

SUDAN
AU • AUMIS 13 obs

Bahrain Brn

Bahraini Dinar D		2006	2007	2008
GDP	D	5.9bn	6.8bn	
	US$	15.5bn	17.9bn	
per capita	US$	22,225	25,255	
Growth	%	7.6	6.8	
Inflation	%	2.9	2.9	
Def bdgt[a]	D	182m	205m	210m
	US$	478m	539m	
FMA (US)	US$	15.5m	15.7m	4.3m
US$1=D		0.38	0.38	

[a] Excluding extra-budgetary funding

Population   708,573

Ethnic groups: Nationals 64%; Asian 13%; other Arab 10%; Iranian 8%; European 1%)

Age	0–14	15–19	20–24	25–29	30–64	65 plus
Male	14%	4%	4%	4%	28%	2%
Female	14%	4%	4%	3%	17%	2%

Capabilities

ACTIVE 8,200 (Army 6,000 Navy 700 Air 1,500)
Paramilitary 11,260

ORGANISATIONS BY SERVICE

Army 6,000

FORCES BY ROLE

Armd 1 bde under strength (2 armd bn, 1 recce bn)

Inf 1 bde (2 mech inf bn, 1 mot inf bn)

SF 1 bn

Arty 1 bde (1 lt arty bty, 1 hy arty bty, 1 MRL bty, 2 med arty bty)

Gd 1 (amiri) bn

AD 1 bn (1 ADA bty, 2 SAM bty)

EQUIPMENT BY TYPE

MBT 180 M-60A3

RECCE 46: 22 AML-90; *Ferret* 8 (in store); 8 S52 *Shorland*; 8 *Saladin* (in store)

AIFV 25 YPR-765 (with 25mm)

APC 235+

APC (T) 115 M-113A2

APC (W) 120+: 10+ AT105 *Saxon*; 110 M-3 *Panhard*

ARTY 69

SP **203mm** 13 M-110

TOWED 26: **105mm** 8 L-118 *Light Gun*; **155mm** 18 M-198

MRL **227mm** 9 MLRS (with 30 ATACMS)

MOR 21: **81mm** 12; **120mm** 9

AT • MSL • MANPATS 15 TOW-2A/TOW-2B

RCL 31: **106mm** 25 M-40A1; **120mm** 6 MOBAT

AD • SAM 93

SP 7 *Crotale*

TOWED 8 I-HAWK *MIM-23B*

MANPAD 78: 18 FIM-92A *Stinger*; 60 RBS-70

GUNS 27: **35mm** 15 Oerlikon; **40mm** 12 L/70

Navy 700

EQUIPMENT BY TYPE

PRINCIPAL SURFACE COMBATANTS 3

FRIGATES • FFG 1 *Sabah* (US *Oliver Hazard Perry*) with SM-1 MR SAM, 4+ RGM-84C *Harpoon* tactical SSM, 2 triple ASTT (6 eff.), 1 76mm gun, (capacity either 1 BO-105 utl hel or 2 SH-2G *Super Seasprite* ASW hel)

CORVETTES • FSG 2 *Al Manama* (Ge *Lurssen* 62m with hel deck) each with 2 twin (4 eff.) each with MM-40 *Exocet* tactical SSM, 1 76mm gun, (capacity 1 BO-105 utl hel)

PATROL AND COASTAL COMBATANTS 8

PFM 4 *Ahmed el Fateh* (Ge *Lurssen* 45m) each with 2 twin (4 eff.) each with MM-40 *Exocet* tactical SSM, 1 76mm gun

PFC 2 *Al Riffa* (Ge *Lurssen* 38m)

PCI 2 *Swift* less than 100 tonnes (FPB-20)

AMPHIBIOUS • CRAFT 5

LCU 5: 1 *Loadmaster*; 4 LCU

LOGISTICS AND SUPPORT • SPT 1

FACILITIES

Base Mina Salman

Naval Aviation

EQUIPMENT BY TYPE

HELICOPTERS • SPT 2 BO-105 utl hel

Air Force 1,500

FORCES BY ROLE

Ftr 2 sqn with 17 F-16C *Fighting Falcon*; 4 F-16D *Fighting Falcon*

FGA 1 sqn with 8 F-5E *Tiger II*; 4 F-5F *Tiger II*

Tpt some sqn with 1 B-727; 1 Gulfstream II; 1 Gulfstream III (VIP); 1 RJ-85

VIP 1 unit with 1 S-70A *Black Hawk*; 3 BÖ-105; 1 UH-60L *Black Hawk*

Trg some sqn with 3 T67M *Firefly*, 6 *Hawk* Mk-129

Hel 3 sqn with 24 AH-1E *Cobra*; 6 TAH-1P *Cobra**; 1 sqn with 12 AB-212 (Bell 212)

EQUIPMENT BY TYPE

AIRCRAFT 33 combat capable

FTR 12: 8 F-5E *Tiger II*; 4 F-5F *Tiger II*

FGA 21: 17 F-16C *Fighting Falcon*; 4 F-16D *Fighting Falcon*

TPT 4: 1 B-727; 1 Gulfstream II; 1 Gulfstream III (VIP); 1 RJ-85

TRG 9: 3 T67M *Firefly*; 6 *Hawk* Mk-129

HELICOPTERS

ATK: 24 AH-1E *Cobra*

SPT 1 S-70A *Black Hawk*

UTL 16: 12 AB-212 (Bell 212); 3 BO-105; 1 UH-60L *Black Hawk*

TRG: 6 TAH-1P *Cobra**

MSL

ASM AGM-65D/G *Maverick*

ARM AS-12 *Kegler*

AAM AIM-7 *Sparrow*, AIM-9P *Sidewinder*

MSL some TOW

Paramilitary ε11,260

Police 9,000

Ministry of Interior

HELICOPTERS • UTL 5: 1 BO-105; 2 Bell 412 *Twin Huey*; 2 Hughes 500

National Guard ε2,000

Paramilitary 3 bn

Coast Guard ε260

Ministry of Interior

PATROL AND COASTAL COMBATANTS 22: 7 PCC; 15 PBI (less than 100 tonnes)

LOGISTICS AND SUPPORT 1 SPT

FOREIGN FORCES

United States Army 29; Navy 1,187; USAF 25; USMC 148

Egypt Et

Egyptian Pound E£		2006	2007	2008
GDP	E£	617bn	722bn	
	US$	108bn	130bn	
per capita	US$	1,372	1,624	
Growth	%	6.8	7.1	
Inflation	%	4.2	10.9	
Def exp	E£	24.7bn		
	US$	4.33bn		
Def bdgt	E£	17.3bn	ε19.0bn	
	US$	3.04bn	ε3.42bn	
FMA (US)	US$	1.29bn	1.30bn	1.30bn
US$1=E£		5.70	5.54	

Population   80,264,543

Age	0–14	15–19	20–24	25–29	30–64	65 plus
Male	17%	5%	5%	4%	17%	2%
Female	16%	5%	5%	4%	17%	3%

Capabilities

ACTIVE 468,500 (Army 340,000 Navy 18,500 Air 30,000 Air Defence Command 80,000) **Paramilitary 397,000**

Terms of service 12 months-3 years (followed by refresher training over a period of up to 9 years)

RESERVE 479,000 (Army 375,000 Navy 14,000 Air 20,000 Air Defence 70,000)

ORGANISATIONS BY SERVICE

Army 90,000–120,000; 190,000–220,000 conscript (total 280,000–340,000)

FORCES BY ROLE

Armd	4 div (*each:* 2 armd bde, 1 mech bde, 1 arty bde); 1 (Republican Guard) bde; 4 indep bde
Mech	4 indep bde
Mech Inf	8 div (*each:* 1 arty bde, 1 armd bde, 2 mech inf bde)
Air Mob	2 bde
Inf	1 div, 2 indep bde
SF	1 gp
Cdo	1 gp HQ (5 cdo gp, 1 Counter-Terrorist unit (Unit 777 (Thunderbolt Force (El Saiqa)), str 300.)
Para	1 bde
Arty	15 indep bde
SSM	1 bde with 9 FROG-7; 1 bde with 9 *Scud*-B

EQUIPMENT BY TYPE

MBT 3,505: 755 M1-A1 *Abrams*; 300 M-60A1; 850 M-60A3; 500 T-62 in store; 260 *Ramses II* (mod T-54/55); 840 T-54/T-55 in store
RECCE 412: 300 BRDM-2; 112 *Commando Scout*
AIFV 610: 220 BMP-1 (in store); 390 YPR-765 (with 25mm)

APC 4,160
  APC (T) 2,100 M-113A2 (incl variants);
  APC (W) 2,060: 250 BMP-600P; 500 BTR-50/OT-62 (most in store); 250 BTR-60; 410 Fahd-30/TH 390 *Fahd;* 650 *Walid*
ARTY 4,348
  SP 489: **122mm** 124 SP 122; **155mm** 365: 164 M-109A2; 201 M-109A2/M-109A3
  TOWED 946: **122mm** 526: 190 D-30M; 36 M-1931/37; 300 M-30 *M-1938;* **130mm** 420 M-46
  MRL 498: **122mm** 356: 96 BM-11; 60 BM-21; 50 *Sakr*-10; 50 *Sakr*-18; 100 *Sakr*-36; **130mm** 36 *Kooryong;* **140mm** 32 BM-14; **227mm** 26 MLRS; **240mm** 48 BM-24 in store
  MOR 2,480: **81mm** 50 M-125A2; **82mm** 500; **107mm** 65 M-106; **120mm** 1,835: 35 M-106A2; 1,800 M-1943; **160mm** 30 M-160
AT • MSL 2,362
  SP 262: 52 M-901, 210 YPR 765 PRAT
  MANPATS 2,100: 1,200 AT-3 *Sagger* (incl BRDM-2); 200 *Milan;* 700 TOW-2
  RCL 107mm 520 B-11
UAV R4E-50 *Skyeye*
AD • SAM 2,096+
  SP 96: 50 FIM-92A *Avenger;* 26 M-54 *Chaparral;* 20 SA-9 *Gaskin*
  MANPAD 2,000+: 2,000 *Ayn al-Saqr*/SA-7 *Grail;* FIM-92A *Stinger*
  GUNS 705+
  SP 205: **23mm** 165: 45 *Sinai*-23; 120 ZSU-23-4; **57mm** 40 ZSU-57-2
  TOWED 500+: **14.5mm** 300 ZPU-4; **23mm** 200 ZU-23-2; **57mm** S-60
RADAR • LAND AN/TPQ-36 *Firefinder;* AN/TPQ-37 *Firefinder* (arty/mor)
MSL • TACTICAL • SSM 42+: 9 FROG-7; 24 *Sakr*-80; some (trials); 9 *Scud*-B

Central Zone
Mil Region 1 zone HQ located at Cairo

Eastern Zone
Mil Region	1 zone HQ located at Ismailiya
Armd	1 div
Mech Inf	2 div

Northern Zone
Mil Region	1 zone HQ located at Alexandria
Armd	1 div
Mech Inf	2 div

Southern Zone
Mil Region	1 zone HQ located at Aswan
Armd Cav	1 div
Mech Inf	2 div

Western Zone
Mil Region	1 zone HQ located at Mersa Matruh
Armd	1 div
Mech Inf	2 div

Navy ε8,500 (incl 2,000 Coast Guard); 10,000 conscript (total 18,500)

Two Fleets: Mediterranean and Red Sea. Naval Organisation: 1 Submarine Bde, 1 Destroyer Bde, 1 Patrol Bde, 1 Fast Attack Bde and 1 Special Ops Bde.

FORCES BY ROLE

Navy 1 HQ located at Alexandria; 1 HQ located at Safaqa

EQUIPMENT BY TYPE

SUBMARINES • TACTICAL • SSK 4 *Romeo*† each with 8 single 533mm TT with UGM-84C *Harpoon* tactical USGW

PRINCIPAL SURFACE COMBATANTS 11

DESTROYERS • DD 1 *El Fateh*† training (UK 'Z') with 2 quad 533mm ASTT (8 eff.), 4 114mm gun

FRIGATES • FFG 10:

2 *Abu Qir* (Sp *Descubierta*) each with 2 Mk 141 *Harpoon* quad (8 eff.) each with RGM-84C *Harpoon* tactical SSM, 2 triple ASTT (6 eff.) each with *Sting Ray* LWT, 1 twin tube *Bofors* mortar 375mm (2 eff.), 1 76mm gun

2 *Damyat* (US *Knox*) each with 1 Mk16 Mk 112 octuple with 8 RGM-84C *Harpoon* tactical SSM, tactical ASROC, 2 twin 324mm TT (4 eff.), 1 127mm gun, (capacity 1 SH-2G *Super Seasprite* ASW hel)

4 *Mubarak* (ex-US *Oliver Hazard Perry*) each with 1 Mk 13 GMLS with 4 RGM-84C *Harpoon* tactical SSM, 36 SM-1 MP SAM, 1 76mm gun, (capacity 2 SH-2G *Super Seasprite* ASW hel)

2 *Najim Al Zaffer* (PRC *Jianghu* I) each with 2 twin (4 eff.) each with HY-2 (CSS-N-2) *Silkworm* tactical SSM, 2 RBU 1200 (10 eff.)

PATROL AND COASTAL COMBATANTS 41

PFM 23:

5 *Tiger* class each with 2 single each with Otomat tactical SSM

4 *Hegu* (*Komar* type) (PRC) each with 2 single each with 1 SY-1 tactical SSM

5 *October* (FSU *Komar*) each with 2 single each with 1 SY-1 tactical SSM

3 *Osa* I (FSU) each with 4 single each with 1 SS-N-2A *Styx* tactical SSM

6 *Ramadan* each with 4 single each with 1 Otomat tactical SSM

PFC 18:

5 *Hainan* (PRC) each with 2 triple 324mm TT (6 eff.), 4 x1 RL

3 *Hainan*† in reserve (PRC) each with 2 triple (6 eff.) 324mm TT (6 eff.), 4 single RL

4 *Shanghai* II (PRC)

4 *Shershen* each with 1+ SA-N-5 *Grail* SAM (manual aiming), 1 12 tube BM-24 MPL (12 eff.)

2 *Shershen* (FSU) each with 4 single 533mm TT, 1 8 tube BM-21 MRL (8 eff.)

MINE WARFARE • MINE COUNTERMEASURES 14

MSO 3 *Assiout* (FSU T-43 class)

MSC 4 *Aswan* (FSU *Yurka*)

MHC 5: 2 *Osprey* (US transfer'07); 3 *Dat Assawari*

MHI 2 *Safaga* (*Swiftships*)

AMPHIBIOUS 12

LS • LSM 3:

3 *Polnochny* A (capacity 6 MBT; 180 troops) (FSU)

CRAFT • LCU 9 *Vydra* (capacity either 3 AMX-30 MBT or 100 troops)

LOGISTICS AND SUPPORT 19:

AOT 7 *Toplivo*

AE 1

AR 1

ATF 4

TRG 2: 1 *Tariq* (ex-UK FF); 1 (also used as the Presidential yacht)

TRV 2 *Poluchat*

YDT 2

FACILITIES

Bases Alexandria, Port Said, Mersa Matruh, Port Tewfig, Safaqa, Hurghada, Suez, Al Ghardaqah

Coastal Defence

Army tps, Navy control

MSL • TACTICAL • SSM SSC-2b *Samlet*

LNCHR 3:

3 twin each with 1 Mk 2 Otomat SSM

GUN 100mm; **130mm** SM-4-1; **152mm**

Naval Aviation

All aircraft armed and operated by Air Force

AIRCRAFT • TPT • BEECH 1900: 4 Beech 1900C (Maritime Surveillance)

HELICOPTERS

ATK 5 SA-342 *Gazelle*

ASW 15: 10 SH-2G *Super Seasprite* each with Mk 46 LWT; 5 *Sea King* MK47

UAV 2 *Camcopter* 5.1

Coast Guard 2,000

PATROL AND COASTAL COMBATANTS 75

PCC 45: 5 *Nisr*; 9 *Swiftships*; 21 *Timsah*; 9 *Type83*; 1 *Swift Protector Class* (Additional vessels on order)

PCI 12 *Sea Spectre MKIII*;

PFI 6 *Crestitalia* less than 100 tonnes

PBI 12

Air Force 30,000 (incl 10,000 conscript)

FORCES BY ROLE

Ftr	2 sqn with 53 *Mirage* 5D/E; 2 sqn with 26 F-16A *Fighting Falcon*; 1 sqn with 15 M-2000C *Mirage*; 7 sqn with 113 F-16C *Fighting Falcon*; 6 sqn with 74 MiG-21 *Fishbed*;
FGA	2 sqn with 29 F-4E *Phantom II*; 2 sqn with 44 J-6 (MiG-19S) *Farmer B*; 1 sqn with 12 *Alpha Jet**; 1 sqn with 16 *Mirage* 5E2
ASW/Hel	2 sqn with 10 SH-2G *Super Seasprite**; 5 *Sea King* MK47*; 5 SA-342L *Gazelle** (Navy use)
Tac/Hel/ Tpt	sqns with 3 CH-47C *Chinook*; 16 CH-47D *Chinook* (medium); 25 *Commando* (of which 3 VIP); 12 Mi-6 *Hook*; 2 S-70 *Black Hawk* (VIP, light); 40 Mi-8 *Hip*; 2 AS-61; 2 UH-60A *Black Hawk*; 5 UH-60L *Black Hawk* (VIP); 17 UH-12E
Recce	2 sqn with 14 MiG-21R *Fishbed* H*; 6 *Mirage* 5SDR (*Mirage* 5R)*
MP	1 sqn with 4 Beech 1900C

EW   1 sqn with 1 Beech 1900 (ELINT); 2 C-130H *Hercules* (ELINT); 4 *Commando* 2E (ECM)

AEW   1 sqn with 4 E-2C *Hawkeye*

Tpt   1 regt with 3 B-707-366C; 1 B-737-100; 1 Beech 200 *Super King Air*; 22 C-130H *Hercules*; 5 DHC-5D *Buffalo*; 3 *Falcon* 20; 3 Gulfstream III; 3 Gulfstream IV, first of 6 An-74TK-200A

Atk hel   6 sqn with 36 AH-64A *Apache*; 74 SA-342K *Gazelle* (44 with HOT, 30 with 20mm)

Trg   sqns with 12 F-16B *Fighting Falcon**; 6 F-16D *Fighting Falcon**; 4 DHC-5 *Buffalo*; 24 *Alpha Jet*; 34 EMB-312 *Tucano*; 36 *Gomhouria*; 74 Grob 115EG; 26 L-29 *Delfin*; 10 L-39 *Albatros*; 35 L-59E *Albatros**; 3 M-2000B *Mirage**; 15 MiG-21U *Mongol A**; 6 JJ-6 (MiG-19UTI) *Farmer*; 16 K-8* (80 K-8 being delivered to replace L-29)

UAV   sqn with 20 R4E-50 *Skyeye*; 29 Teledyne-Ryan 324 *Scarab*

EQUIPMENT BY TYPE
AIRCRAFT 489 combat capable
FTR 165: 26 F-16A *Fighting Falcon*; 12 F-16B *Fighting Falcon*; 74 J-7 (MiG-21F) *Fishbed C*; 53 Mirage 5D/E
FGA 235: 15 M-2000C *Mirage*; 113 F-16C *Fighting Falcon*; 6 F-16D *Fighting Falcon*; 16 *Mirage* 5E2; 29 F-4E *Phantom II*; 44 J-6 (MiG-19S) *Farmer B*; 12 *Alpha Jet* 12*
RECCE 20: 14 MiG-21R *Fishbed H**; 6 *Mirage* 5SDR (*Mirage* 5R)*
AEW 4 E-2C *Hawkeye*
TPT 53+: First of 6 An-74TK-200A; 3 B-707-366C; 1 B-737-100; 1 Beech 1900 (ELINT); 4 Beech 1900C; 1 Beech 200 *Super King Air*; 2 C-130H *Hercules* (ELINT); 22 C-130H (tpt); 4 DHC-5; 5 DHC-5D *Buffalo*; 3 Falcon 20; 3 Gulfstream III; 3 Gulfstream IV
TRG 279: 24 *Alpha Jet*; 34 EMB-312 *Tucano*; 36 *Gomhouria*; 74 Grob 115EG; 6 JJ-6 (MiG-19UTI) *Farmer*; 16 K-8* (80 being delivered to replace L-29); 26 L-29 *Delfin*; 10 L-39 *Albatros*; 35 L-59E *Albatros**; 3 M-2000B *Mirage**; 15 MiG-21U *Mongol A**
HELICOPTERS
ELINT 4 *Commando* 2E (ECM)
ATK 115: 36 AH-64A *Apache*; 74 SA-342K *Gazelle* (44 with HOT,30 with 20mm); 5 SA-342L *Gazelle** (Navy use)
ASW 15: 10 SH-2G *Super Seasprite**; 5 *Sea King* MK47*
SPT 98: 3 CH-47C *Chinook*; 16 CH-47D *Chinook* (Medium); 25 *Commando* (of which 3 VIP); 12 Mi-6 *Hook*; 2 S-70 *Black Hawk* (VIP, light); 40 Mi-8 *Hip*
UTL 9: 2 AS-61; 2 UH-60A *Black Hawk*; 5 UH-60L *Black Hawk* (VIP)
TRG 17 UH-12E
UAV 49: 20 R4E-50 *Skyeye*; 29 Teledyne-Ryan 324 *Scarab*
MSL
ASM 245+: 80 AGM-65A *Maverick*; 123 AGM-65D *Maverick*; 12 AGM-65F *Maverick*; 30 AGM-65G *Maverick*; AGM-119 *Hellfire*; AGM-84 *Harpoon*; AM-39 *Exocet*; AS-30L HOT
ARM *Armat*; AS-12 *Kegler*
AAM AA-2 *Atoll*; AIM-7E *Sparrow*/AIM-7F *Sparrow*/ AIM-7M *Sparrow*; AIM-9F *Sidewinder*/AIM-9L *Sidewinder*/AIM-9P *Sidewinder*; R-550 *Magic*; R530

Air Defence Command 30,000; 50,000 conscript; 70,000 reservists (total 150,000)
FORCES BY ROLE
AD 5 div (geographically based) (*total:* 12 SAM bty with M-48 *Chaparral*, 12 radar bn, 12 ADA bde (*total:* 100 ADA bn), 12 SAM bty with I-HAWK MIM-23B, 14 SAM bty with *Crotale*, 18 SAM bn with *Skyguard*, 110 SAM bn with *Pechora* (SA-3A) *Goa*/SA-3 *Goa*; SA-6 *Gainful*; SA-2 *Guideline*)

EQUIPMENT BY TYPE
AD
SYSTEMS: 72+ *Amoun* each with RIM-7F *Sea Sparrow* SAM, 36+ quad SAM (144 eff.), *Skyguard* towed SAM, 36+ twin 35mm guns (72 eff.)
SAM 702+
SP 130+: 24+ *Crotale*; 50+ M-48 *Chaparral*; 56+ SA-6 *Gainful*
TOWED 572+: 78+ I-HAWK *MIM-23B*; SA-2 *Guideline* 282+ *Skyguard*; 212+ *Pechora* (SA-3A) *Goa*/SA-3 *Goa*
GUNS 1,566+
SP • 23mm 266+: 36+ *Sinai*-23 (SPAAG) each with *Ayn al-Saqr* MANPAD SAM, Dassault 6SD-20S land; 230 ZSU-23-4
TOWED 57mm 600 S-60; **85mm** 400 M-1939 *KS-12*; **100mm** 300 KS-19

Paramilitary ε397,000 active

Central Security Forces 325,000
Ministry of Interior; Includes conscripts
APC (W) 100+: 100 *Hussar*; *Walid*

National Guard 60,000
Lt wpns only
FORCES BY ROLE
Paramilitary 8 (cadre status) bde (*each:* 3 paramilitary bn)
EQUIPMENT BY TYPE
APC (W) 250 Walid

Border Guard Forces 12,000
Ministry of Interior; lt wpns only
18 (Border Guard) regt

NON-STATE ARMED GROUPS
see Part II

DEPLOYMENT

DEMOCRATIC REPUBLIC OF CONGO
UN • MONUC 22 obs

GEORGIA
UN • UNOMIG 6 obs

LIBERIA
UN • UNMIL 8 obs

NEPAL
UN • UNMIN 7 obs

Middle East and North Africa

SIERRA LEONE

UN • UNIOSIL 1 obs

SUDAN

AU • AUMIS 34 obs

UN • UNMIS 817 troops; 14 obs

AU/UN • UNAMID 625 proposed deployment

WESTERN SAHARA

UN • MINURSO 20 obs

FOREIGN FORCES

Australia 25 *(Operation Mazurka)*

Canada 28 *(Operation Calumet)*

Colombia 1 inf bn; 357

Fiji 329

Hungary 41 MP

Italy 80

New Zealand 26

Norway 9

United States Army: 225; Navy: 4; USAF: 39; USMC: 20; 288 MFO

Uruguay 87

Iran Ir

Iranian Rial r		2006	2007	2008
GDP	r	2,013tr	2,525tr	
	US$	220bn	271bn	
per capita	US$	3,376	4,143	
Growth	%	6.8	7.1	
Inflation	%	13.6	19.0	
Def bdgt[a]	r	65.6tr	ε78.0tr	
	US$	6.48bn	7.16bn	
US$1=r		9,170	9,320	

[a] Excluding defence industry funding

Population   65,397,521

Ethnic groups: Persian 51%; Azeri 24%; Gilaki/Mazandarani 8%; Kurdish 7%; Arab 3%; Lur 2%; Baloch 2%; Turkman 2%

Age	0–14	15–19	20–24	25–29	30–64	65 plus
Male	14%	6%	7%	5%	17%	2%
Female	13%	6%	6%	5%	16%	2%

Capabilities

ACTIVE 545,000 (Army 350,000 Islamic Revolutionary Guard Corps 125,000 Navy 18,000 Air 52,000) Paramilitary 40,000

Armed Forces General Staff coordinates two parallel organisations: Regular Armed Forces and Revolutionary Guard Corps

RESERVE 350,000 (Army 350,000, ex-service volunteers)

ORGANISATIONS BY SERVICE

Army 130,000; 220,000 conscript (total 350,000)

FORCES BY ROLE

5 Corps–Level Regional HQ

Armd 4 div; some indep bde

Inf 6 div; some indep bde

SF 1 bde

Cdo 2 div; some indep bde

AB 1 bde

Arty 6 gp

Avn some gp

EQUIPMENT BY TYPE

Totals incl those held by Islamic Revolutionary Guard Corps Ground Forces. Some equipment serviceability in doubt

MBT 1,613+: ε100 *Zulfiqar*; 480 T-72; 150 M-60A1; 75+ T-62; 100 *Chieftain* Mk3/Mk5; 540 T-54/T-55/Type-59; 168 M-47/M-48

LT TK 80+: 80 *Scorpion*; *Towsan*

RECCE 35 EE-9 *Cascavel*

AIFV 610: 210 BMP-1; 400 BMP-2

APC 640

  APC (T) 340: 140 *Boragh*; 200 M-113

  APC (W) 300 BTR-50/BTR-60

ARTY 8,196+

  SP 310+ : **122mm** 60+: 60 2S1 *Carnation*; *Thunder* 1; **155mm** 180+: 180 M-109; *Thunder* 2; **170mm** 10 M-1978; **175mm** 30 M-107; **203mm** 30 M-110

  TOWED 2,010+; **105mm** 130 M-101A1; **122mm** 640: 540 D-30; 100 Type-54 (M-30) *M-1938*; **130mm** 985 M-46; **152mm** 30 D-20; **155mm** 205: 120 GHN-45; 70 M-114; 15 Type 88 *WAC-21*; **203mm** 20 M-115

  MRL 876+: **107mm** 700+: 700 Type-63; *Fadjr* 1; HASEB; **122mm** 157: 7 BM-11; 100 BM-21; 50 *Arash/Hadid/Noor*; **240mm** 19: ε10 *Fadjr* 3; 9 M-1985; **333mm** *Fadjr* 5

  MOR 5,000: **60mm**; **81mm**; **82mm**; **107mm** M-30;**120mm** M-65

AT

  MSL • MANPATS 75 AT-3 9K11 *Sagger*/AT-4 9K111 *Spigot*/AT-5 9K113 *Spandrel/Saeqhe* 1/*Saeqhe* 2/*Toophan*/TOW (some AT-3 SP), *Toophan* (TOW)

  RCL 200+: **75mm** M-20; **82mm** B-10; **106mm** ε200 M-40; **107mm** B-11

  RL 73mm RPG-7 *Knout*

AIRCRAFT TPT 17: 10 Cessna 185; 2 F-27 *Friendship*; 1 *Falcon* 20; 4 Rockwell *Turbo Commander* 690

HELICOPTERS

  ATK 50 AH-1J *Cobra*

  SPT 45: 20 CH-47C *Chinook*; 25 Mi-17 (Mi-8MT) *Hip H*/Mi-8 *Hip* spt hel

  UTL 128: 68 AB-205A (Bell 205A); 10 AB-206 (Bell 206) *JetRanger*; 50 Bell 214

UAV • TACTICAL *Mohajer II / Mohajer III / Mohajer IV*

AD • SAM

  SP HQ-7 (reported)

  MANPAD SA-14 *Gremlin*/SA-16 *Gimlet*/SA-7 *Grail*; *Misaq* (QW-1)

GUNS 1,700
   SP 23mm ZSU-23-4; **57mm** ZSU-57-2
   TOWED 14.5mm ZPU-2; ZPU-4; **23mm** ZU-23; **35mm**; **37mm** M-1939; **57mm** S-60
MSL • TACTICAL • SSM 42+: ε30 CSS-8 (175 msl); 12+ *Scud*-B/*Scud*-C (Up to 18. launchers/launch vehicles. 300 msl); *Shaheen*-1 *Hatf*-4/*Shaheen*-2; *Nazeat*; *Oghab*

Islamic Revolutionary Guard Corps 125,000+

Controls Basij (paramilitary) when mob

Islamic Revolutionary Guard Corps Ground Forces 100,000+

Controls Basij (paramilitary) when mob
   Very lightly manned in peacetime. Primary role: internal security; secondary role: external defence, in conjunction with regular armed forces.
Inf some 15 div (Some divs are designated as armd or mech but all are predominantly infantry); some indep bde
AB 1 indep bde

Islamic Revolutionary Guard Corps Naval Forces 20,000+ (incl 5,000 Marines)

FORCES BY ROLE

Navy some (coast-defence) elm (*total:* some SSM bty with HY-2 (CSS-C-3) *Seerseeker*, some arty bty)

EQUIPMENT BY TYPE

PATROL AND COASTAL COMBATANTS 50+
   PFM 10 *Houdong* each with C-802 (CSS-N-8) *Saccade* tactical SSM
   PB 40+ Boghammar Marin (Swe) each with AT (ATGW), RCL, gun (machine guns)
MSL • TACTICAL • SSM HY-2 (CSS-C-3) *Seerseeker*

FACILITIES

Bases Located at Bandar-e Abbas, Khorramshahr, 1 with 40+ Boghammar Marin PB (Swe) each with AT (ATGW), RCL, gun (machine guns) located at Larak, Abu Musa, Al Farsiyah, Halul (oil platform), Sirri

Islamic Revolutionary Guard Corps Marines 5,000+

Marine 1 bde

Islamic Revolutionary Guard Corps Air Force

Controls Iran's strategic missile force.

FORCES BY ROLE

Msl ε1 bde *Shahab*-1/2 with 12–18 lauchers; ε1 bn with ε6 single launchers each with ε4 *Shahab*-3 strategic IRBM

EQUIPMENT BY TYPE

LNCHR 24: 12–18 Satellite Launcher; ε6 single eqpt with ε4 *Shahab*-3 IRBM

Navy 18,000

FORCES BY ROLE

Navy 1 HQ located at Bandar-e Abbas

EQUIPMENT BY TYPE

SUBMARINES • TACTICAL • SSK 3 *Kilo* (RF Type 877) each with 6 single 533mm TT
   SSC 3 *Qadir* (fitted with facility to operate SDV)
PRINCIPAL SURFACE COMBATANTS 5
   FRIGATES • FFG 3 *Alvand* (UK Vosper Mk 5) each with 3 twin (6 eff.) each with CSS-N-4 *Sardine* tactical SSM, 1 single RL, 1 114mm gun
   CORVETTES • FS 2 *Bayandor* (US PF-103) each with 2 76mm gun
PATROL AND COASTAL COMBATANTS 140
   PFM 11 *Kaman* (Fr *Combattante* II) each with 2–4 CSS-N-4 *Sardine* tactical SSM
   PCC 5: 3 *Parvin*; 2 *Kaivan*
   PCI 11 *China Cat* less than 100 tonnes
   PFI 36 less than 100 tonnes
   PBI 40
   PB 37
MINE WARFARE • MINE COUNTERMEASURES 5
   MSC 3: 2 Type-292; 1 *Shahrokh* (in Caspian Sea as trg ship)
   MSI 2 *Riazi* (US *Cape*)
AMPHIBIOUS
   LS 13
      LSM 3 *Iran Hormuz 24* (capacity 9 tanks; 140 troops) (ROK)
      LST 7:
         3 *Hejaz* (mine laying capacity)
         4 *Hengam* each with up to 1 hel (capacity 9 tanks; 225 troops)
      LSL 3 *Fouque*
   CRAFT 8
      UCAC 8: 7 *Wellington*; 1 *Iran*
LOGISTICS AND SUPPORT 26
   AORH 3: 2 *Bandar Abbas*; 1 *Kharg*
   AWT 4 *Kangan*
   SPT 19: 6 *Delvar*; 12 *Hendijan*; 1 *Hamzah*

FACILITIES

Bases Located at Bandar-e Abbas, Bushehr, Kharg Island, Bandar-e Anzelli, Bandar-e Khomeini, Bandar-e Mahshahr, Chah Bahar

Marines 2,600

Marine 2 bde

Naval Aviation 2,600

AIRCRAFT
   MP 3 P-3F *Orion*
   EW • ELINT 3 Da-20 *Falcon*
   TPT 13: 5 Do-228; 4 F-27 *Friendship*; 4 Rockwell *Turbo Commander* 680
HELICOPTERS
   ASW ε10 SH-3D *Sea King*
   MCM 3 RH-53D *Sea Stallion*
   UTL 17: 5 AB-205A (Bell 205A); 2 AB-206 (Bell 206) *JetRanger*; 10 AB-212 (Bell 212)

Air Force ε52,000 (incl 15,000 Air Defence)

FORCES BY ROLE

Some 281 cbt ac (serviceability probably about 60% for US ac types and about 80% for PRC/Russian ac). Includes Islamic Revolutionary Guard Corps Air Force equipment.

Ftr	2 sqn with 25 F-14 *Tomcat*; 1 sqn with 24 F-7M *Airguard*; 2 sqn with 25 MiG-29A *Fulcrum A*/ MiG-29UB *Fulcrum* (incl former Iraq ac)
FGA	1 sqn with 24 F-1E *Mirage* (former Irq ac); 13 Su-25K *Frogfoot A* (former Irq ac); 30 Su-24MK *Fencer D* (including former Iraq ac); 4 sqn with 65 F-4D *Phantom II*/F-4E *Phantom II*; 4 sqn with 60+ F-5E *Tiger II*/F-5F *Tiger II*
Recce	1 (det) sqn with 6+ RF-4E *Phantom II**
MP	1 sqn with 5 P-3MP *Orion**
Tkr/tpt	1 sqn with 3 B-707; 1 B-747
Tpt	5 sqn with 2 Y-7 (An-24) *Coke*; 1 B-727; 4 B-747F; 17 C-130E *Hercules*/C-130H *Hercules*; 10 F-27 *Friendship*; 1 *Falcon* 20; Il-76 *Candid* (former Irq ac); 2 *Jetstar*; 10 PC-6B *Turbo Porter*; 3 Rockwell *Turbo Commander* 680; 9 Y-12; 40 *Iran-140*
Trg	trg units with 20 F-5B *Freedom Fighter**; 4 TB-200 *Tobago*; 8 TB-21 *Trinidad*; 20 Beech F-33A *Bonanza*/Beech F-33C *Bonanza*; 15 EMB-312 *Tucano*; 15 JJ-7 *Mongol A**; 22 MFI-17 *Mushshak*; 40 PC-7 *Turbo Trainer*; 7 T-33 *Shooting Star*
Hel	sqn with 2 CH-47 *Chinook*; *Shabaviz* 2-75 (indigenous versions in production); *Shabaviz* 2061; 2 AB-206A (Bell 206A) *JetRanger*; 30 AB-214C
SAM	16 bn each with ε150 I-HAWK MIM-23B; 5 sqn with FM-80 (*Crotale*); total of 30 *Rapier*; 15 *Tigercat*; 45 SA-2 *Guideline*; 10 SA-5 *Gammon*; FIM-92A *Stinger*; SA-7 *Grail*; 29 TOR-M1 systems (reported delivered early 2007)

EQUIPMENT BY TYPE
AIRCRAFT 319 combat capable
  FTR 118: 25 F-14 *Tomcat*; 25 MiG-29A/UB/U *Fulcrum*; 24 F-1E *Mirage*; 20 F-5B *Freedom Fighter*; 24 F-7M *Airguard*
  FGA 168: 13 Su-25K *Frogfoot A/T/UBK*; 30 Su-24MK *Fencer D*; 65 F-4D *Phantom II*/F-4E *Phantom II*; 60+ F-5E *Tiger II*/F-5F *Tiger II*
  RECCE: 6+ RF-4E *Phantom II**
  MP 5 P-3MP *Orion**
  TPT 104+: 3 B-707; 1 B-727; 4 B-747F; 17 C-130E *Hercules*/ C-130H *Hercules*; 10 F-27 *Friendship*; 1 *Falcon* 20; 1+ Il-76 *Candid*; 40 Iran-140 *Faraz*; 2 *Jetstar*; 10 PC-6B *Turbo Porter*; 3 Rockwell *Turbo Commander* 680; 9 Y-12; 2 Y-7 (An-24) *Coke*; 1 B-747
  UTL 12: 4 TB-200 *Tobago*; 8 TB-21 *Trinidad*
  TRG 119: 20 Beech F-33A *Bonanza*/Beech F-33C *Bonanza*; 15 EMB-312 *Tucano*; 15 JJ-7 *Mongol A*; 22 *MFI-17 *Mushshak*; 40 PC-7 *Turbo Trainer*; 7 T-33 *Shooting Star*
HELICOPTERS
  SPT 2+ CH-47 *Chinook*; *Shabaviz* 2-75 (indigenous versions in production); *Shabaviz* 2061
    UTL 32: 2 AB-206A (Bell 206A) *JetRanger*; 30 AB-214C
  AD • SAM 279+: FM-80 (*Crotale*); 30 *Rapier*; 15 *Tigercat*; ε 150+ I-HAWK MIM-23B; 45 SA-2 *Guideline*; 10 SA-5 *Gammon*; 29 SA-15m *Gauntlet* (TOR-M1) (reported delivered early 2007)
    MANPAD FIM-92A *Stinger*; SA-7 *Grail*
    GUNS • TOWED 23mm ZU-23; **37mm** Oerlikon

MSL
  ASM up to 3,000 AGM-65A *Maverick*/AS-10 *Karen*/AS-11 *Kilter*/AS-14 *Kedge*/C-801K (CSS-N-4) *Sardine* ALCM
  AAM AA-10 *Alamo*; AA-11 *Archer*; AA-8 *Aphid*; AIM-54 *Phoenix*; AIM-7 *Sparrow*; AIM-9 *Sidewinder*; PL-2A; PL-7

Paramilitary 40,000

Law-Enforcement Forces 40,000 (border and security troops); 450,000 on mobilisation (incl conscripts) (total 40,000–490,000)
Part of armed forces in wartime
PATROL AND COASTAL COMBATANTS 130
  MISC BOATS/CRAFT 40 harbour craft
  PCI ε 90
AIRCRAFT • TPT: 2 Iran-140; some Cessna 185/Cessna 310
HELICOPTERS • UTL ε24 AB-205 (Bell 205)/AB-206 (Bell 206) *JetRanger*

Basij Resistance Force up to ε1,000,000 on mobilisation
Paramilitary militia, with claimed membership of 12.6 million, including women and children; perhaps 1 million combat capable; in the process of closer integration with Islamic Revolutionary Guard Corps Ground Forces.
Militia 2,500 bn (claimed); some (full time)

NON-STATE ARMED GROUPS
see Part II

DEPLOYMENT

ETHIOPIA/ERITREA
UN • UNMEE 3 obs

Iraq Irq

Iraqi Dinar D		2006	2007	2008
GDP	US$	42.2bn	55.4bn	
per capita	US$	1,576	2,015	
Growth	%	1.9	2.9	
Inflation	%	53.2	45.0	
US$1=D		1,470	1,232	

Population   27,499,638

Ethnic groups: Arab 75–80% (of which Shi'a Muslim 55%, Sunni Muslim 45%) Kurdish 20–25%

Age	0–14	15–19	20–24	25–29	30–64	65 plus
Male	20%	6%	5%	4%	14%	1%
Female	20%	6%	5%	4%	13%	2%

Capabilities

ACTIVE 494,800 (Army 163,500 Navy 1,100 Air 1,200 Iraqi Police Service 135,000 Ministry of Interior Forces 194,000)

ORGANISATIONS BY SERVICE

Security Forces ε360,100

Figures for Iraqi security forces reflect ongoing changes within the Iraqi security forces.

Army ε163,500 (Includes National Guard)

EQUIPMENT BY TYPE
MBT 77+ T-72; T-55
APC 352+
  APC (T) 236: 100 FV 103 *Spartan*; 100 M-113 A1; 36 BMP-1
  APC (W) 116: 50 BTR-94; 66 BTR-80; (some 600 *DZIK*, being delivered)

Navy 1,100

Iraqi Coastal Defence Force (ICDF)
ICDF crews being trained by UK RN

EQUIPMENT BY TYPE
PATROL AND COASTAL COMBATANTS 12:
  PC 12: 5 (RIB); 5 27m (PRC-built); 2 *Type-200*

FACILITIES
Base Located at Umm Qasr

Department of Border Enforcement

Iraqi Air Force 1,200

Flying around 200 sorties per week.

FORCES BY ROLE

Recce	1 sqn at Basra with 2 SB7 L -360 *Seeker*, 6 CH-2000 SAMA (infrastructure patrols); 1 sqn at Kirkuk with 6 SB7L-360 *Seeker*; 3 Cessna 208B *Grand Caravan* (day-night surveillance, live downlink capability)
Tpt	1 sqn at Baghdad with 3 C-130E *Hercules*
Tpt/utl	4 sqn at Taji with 5 Bell 206-B3 *JetRanger*; 16 UH-1H *Huey* II; 14 Mi-17 2 PZL W-3W
Trg	1 flying trg school Kirkuk with 2 Cessna 172

EQUIPMENT BY TYPE
AIRCRAFT
  RECCE 17: 6 CH-2000 SAMA; 3 Cessna 208B *Grand Caravan* (plus 5 more in 2008) to replace CH-2000 SAMA; 8 SB7L-360 *Seeker*
  TPT 3 C-130E *Hercules*
  TRG 2 Cessna 172
HELICOPTERS
  SPT 16: 14 Mi-17 (14 more to be delivered 2008); 2 PZL W-3WA
  UTL 21: 5 Bell 206-B3 *JetRanger*; 16 UH-1H *Huey* II (20 more to be delivered)

Ministry of Interior Forces ε33,000 (Includes Civil Intervention Force, Emergency Response Unit, Border Enforcement and Dignitary Protection)

Excluding Police

Iraqi Police Service ε135,000 (including Highway Patrol)

National Police ε26,300

FOREIGN FORCES

All under opcon MNF *Operation Iraqi Freedom* unless otherwise specified
Albania 127
Armenia 46
Australia 1,575; C-130 *Hercules*; AP3-C *Orion* MP; FF *Anzac*-class; *Skylark* UAV; 1 obs UNAMI
Azerbaijan 150
Bosnia 49
Bulgaria: 150
Canada 1 obs UNAMI *(Operation Iolaus)*
Czech Republic 99
Denmark 442; 1 (bn) Inf gp (1 Scout sqn, 1 Inf/Spt Hel coy); 21 NTM-I; 3 obs UNAMI
El Salvador 380
Estonia 38; 2 NTM-1
Fiji 223 UNAMI
Georgia 2,000
Italy 79 NTM-1
Kazakhstan 29
Korea, Republic of 1,200
Latvia 2
Lithuania 5; 4 NTM-1
Macedonia, Former Yugoslav Republic of 40
Moldova: 11
Mongolia 160
Netherlands 15 NTM-I
New Zealand 1 obs UNAMI
Poland 900; 4 Mi-24V *Hind* E atk hel; 2 Mi-8 *Hip* spt hel; 7PZL w-3 *Sokol* spt hel
Portugal 9 NTM-I
Romania 489; 3 NTM-1; APC *Piranha* III C
Slovakia 2 NTM-I
Slovenia 4 NTM-I
Ukraine 3 NTM-1

United Kingdom MNF • *Operation Telic* 6,371; Army 4,151; 1 (composite) Army HQ; 1 armd bde; some spt unit; Recce 30 *Scimitar*; AIFV 29 *Warrior*; APC (T) 117 *Bulldog*; APC (W) 54 *Mastiff*; AC 3 *Defender* AL1; SH-14D *Lynx*; Royal Navy 982; 1 sqn *Sea King* HC MK4 (located at Basra); Air Force 1,238; Air Force 2 *Nimrod* MR2; 4 C-130J; 6 EH101 *Merlin*; 9 *Sea King*; RAF regt detachment; UNAMI 1 obs

United States • United States Central Command; *Operation Iraqi Freedom* 168,000: Expected troop levels in Jan 2008 is 160,000 this may decrease to 132,000 by Dec 2008. The combat element comprises 20 BCTs reducing to 19 in Jan 08.

Army	
Armd	6 HBCT
Stryker	3 SBCT
Inf	9 IBCT
Army National Guard	
Inf 1 bde; 3 BCT	

Navy
FORCES BY ROLE
1 CVSG and 1 ARG gp (Both part of CTF 152 and 158, Fifth Fleet)
USMC
MEF   2 RCT

Air Force
EQUIPMENT BY TYPE
AIRCRAFT
  FGA: F-16
  Ftr: A-10
  Tpt: C-130 Hercules; C-17 *Globemaster* III
HELICOPTER
  SAR: HH-60 *Pave Hawk*
  UAV: MQ-1 *Predator*

Israel II

New Israeli Shekel NS		2006	2007	2008
GDP	NS	625bn	665bn	
	US$	140bn	165bn	
per capita	US$	22,111	25,740	
Growth	%	5.2	5.1	
Inflation	%	2.1	**0.4**	
Def exp	NS	49.06bn		
	US$	11.03bn		
Def bdgt	NS	33.5bn	38.0bn	
	US$	7.53bn	9.45bn	
FMA (US)	US$	2.26bn	2.34bn	2.40bn
US$1=NS		4.45	4.02	

Population   6,426,679

Ethnic groups: Jewish 82%; Arab 19% (incl Christian 3%, Druze 2%; Circassian ε3,000)

Age	0–14	15–19	20–24	25–29	30–64	65 plus
Male	14%	4%	4%	4%	20%	4%
Female	13%	4%	4%	4%	20%	6%

Capabilities

ACTIVE 176,500 (Army 133,000 Navy 9,500 Air 34,000) **Paramilitary 8,050**

RESERVE 565,000 (Army 500,000 Navy 10,000 Air 55,000)

Terms of service officers 48 months, other ranks 36 months, women 24 months (Jews and Druze only; Christians, Circassians and Muslims may volunteer). Annual trg as cbt reservists to age 41 (some specialists to age 54) for men, 24 (or marriage) for women

ORGANISATIONS BY SERVICE

Strategic Forces

Israel is widely believed to have a nuclear capability - delivery means include ac, *Jericho* 1 and *Jericho* 2 (IRBM and SRBM)

MSL • STRATEGIC
  IRBM: *Jericho* 2
  SRBM: *Jericho* 1
WARHEADS up to 200 nuclear warheads

Army 26,000; 107,000 conscript; 500,000+ on mobilisation; (total 133,000–633,000)

Organisation and structure of formations may vary according to op situations. Equipment includes that required for reserve forces on mobilisation.

FORCES BY ROLE
3 regional commands each with 2 regular divs; 1-2 regional/ territorial divs; 2 regular bdes
Armd   2 div; 15 bde
Inf   4 div; 12 bde
Para   8 bde
Arty   4 regt
SP arty 8 regt

EQUIPMENT BY TYPE
MBT 3,501: 441 *Merkava* Mk1; 455 *Merkava* MkII; 454 *Merkava* MkIII; 175 *Merkava* MkIV; 111 *Magach-7*; 261 Ti-67 (T-55 mod); 711 M-60/M-60A1/M-60A3; 206 *Centurion*; 126 T-54/T-55/T-62S; 561 M-48A5
RECCE 408: ε400 RBY-1 RAMTA; ε8 Tpz-1 *Fuchs*
APC 10,419+
  APC (T) 10,373+: 276 *Achzarit* (modified T-55 chassis); 6,131 M-113A1/M-113A2; 180 M-2 (some in store); 3,386 M-3 half-track (some in store); ε400 *Nagmachon* (*Centurion* chassis); *Nakpadon*
  APC (W) 46: 34 BTR-152; 6 BTR-40; 6 *Puma* (*Centurion*)
ARTY 5,432
  SP 620: **155mm** 548: 148 L-33; 350 M-109A1; 50 M-50; **175mm** 36 M-107; **203mm** 36 M-110
  TOWED 456: **105mm** 70 M-101A1; **122mm** 5 D-30; **130mm** 100 M-46; **155mm** 281: 50 M-114A1 in reserve; 100 M-46; 50 M-68/M-71; 81 M-839P/M-845P
  MRL 224: **122mm** 58 BM-21; **160mm** 50 LAR-160; **227mm** 60 MLRS; **240mm** 36 BM-24; **290mm** 20 LAR-290
  MOR 4,132: **52mm** 2,000; **81mm** 1,358; **120mm** 652 (towed); **160mm** 122: 104 M-43 in reserve; 18 M-66 *Soltam*
AT
  MSL • MANPATS 1,225+: 900 M47 *Dragon*; AT-3 9K11 *Sagger*; 25 IMI MAPATS; *Gil/Spike*; 300 TOW-2A/TOW-2B (incl *Ramta* (M-113) SP)
  RCL 106mm 250 M-40A1
  RL 82mm B-300
AD • SAM 1,270
  SP 20 Machbet
  MANPAD 1,250: 1,000 FIM-43 *Redeye*; 250 FIM-92A *Stinger*
RADAR • LAND AN/PPS-15 (arty); AN/TPQ-37 *Firefinder* (arty); EL/M-2140 (veh)
MSL 107
  STRATEGIC ε100 *Jericho* 1 SRBM/*Jericho* 2 IRBM
  TACTICAL • SSM 7 *Lance* (in store)

Navy 7,000; 2,500 conscript; 10,000 on mobilisation (total 9,500–19,500)

EQUIPMENT BY TYPE
SUBMARINES • TACTICAL • SSK 3 *Dolphin* (Ge Type-212 variant) each with 6 single 533mm TT each with 5 UGM-84C *Harpoon* tactical USGW, 16 HWT, 4 single 650mm TT
PRINCIPAL SURFACE COMBATANTS • CORVETTES
FSG 3 *Eilat* (*Sa'ar* 5) each with 2 Mk 140 *Harpoon* quad (8 eff.) each with RGM-84C *Harpoon* tactical SSM, 2 32 cell VLS (64 eff.) each with up to 64 *Barak* SAM, 2 triple (6 eff.) TT each with Mk 46 LWT, 1 76mm gun, (capacity either 1 AS-565SA *Panther* ASW hel or 1 AS-366G *Dauphin II* SAR hel)
PATROL AND COASTAL COMBATANTS 52
PFM 10:
  8 *Hetz* (*Sa'ar* 4.5) each with 6 single each with 1 GII *Gabriel II* tactical SSM, 2 Mk 140 twin each with RGM-84C *Harpoon* tactical SSM, 1 32 Cell/Mk 56 (1-32 eff.) with *Barak* SAM, 1 76mm gun
  2 *Reshef* (*Sa'ar* 4) each with 4–6 single each with 1 GII *Gabriel II* tactical SSM, 1 Mk 140 twin with RGM-84C *Harpoon* tactical SSM, 1 76mm gun
PFI 34:
  15 *Dabur* less than 100 tonnes each with 2 single 324mm TT each with Mk 46 LWT
  13 *Super Dvora* MKI and II less than 100 tonnes (SSM, and TT may be fitted) each with 2 single 324mm TT each with Mk 46 LWT
  6 *Super Dvora* MK III; 2 *Shaldag* (Additional vessels in build)
PBF 7: 4 *Tzir'a*; 3 *Stingray*
MISC BOATS/CRAFT • SPECIAL WARFARE SUPPORT
CRAFT: 1 *Katler*
AMPHIBIOUS • CRAFT 2:
LCT 1 *Ashdod*
LCM 1 US type
LOGISTICS AND SUPPORT 3:
AG 2 (ex German Type T45)
Trial 1
FACILITIES
Bases Located at Haifa, Atlit (Naval Commandos), Eilat, Ashdod

Naval Aviation
AC • TPT 2 C-130
HELICOPTERS • ASW 7 AS-565SA *Panther*; 2 SA-366 G *Dauphin*
SAR/UTL 17 Bell 212

Naval Commandos ε300

Air Force 34,000
Responsible for Air and Space Coordination
FORCES BY ROLE
Ftr/FGA   2 sqn with 29 F-15A *Eagle*; 7 F-15B *Eagle*; 17 F-15C *Eagle*; 11 F-15D *Eagle*; 1 sqn with 25 F-15I *Ra'am*; 8 sqn with 90 F-16A *Fighting Falcon*; 16 F-16B *Fighting Falcon*; 52 F-16C *Fighting Falcon*; 49 F-16D *Fighting Falcon*; 2 sqn with 34 F-16I *Sufa*; 3 sqn with some 200+ A-4N *Skyhawk*/F-4 *Phantom II*/*Kfir* C-7 in reserve

ASW	sqn with 5 AS-565SA *Panther* (missions flown by IAF but in non-rated aircrew)
MP	1 sqn with 3 IAI-1124 *Seascan*
EW	6 RC-12D *Guardrail*; 4 Beech 200CT *Super King Air*; 2 EC-130H *Hercules* (ELINT); 15 Do-28; 3 B-707 (ELINT/ECM) being replaced by 3 Gulfstream G-550 *Shavit* (ELINT); 8 IAI-202 *Arava*
AEW	1 sqn with 3 B-707 (with *Phalcon* system)
Tpt	1 sqn with 1 C-47 *Skytrain*
Tpt/tkr	1 sqn with 4 B-707 (transport/tanker)
Tkr	1 sqn with 5 KC-130H *Hercules*
Liaison	1 sqn with 2 BN-2 *Islander*; 8 Beech 80 *Queen Air*; 22 Cessna U-206 *Stationair*
Atk hel	4 sqn with 16 AH-1E *Cobra*; 39 AH-1F *Cobra*; 30 AH-64A *Apache*; *Sarat* (AH-64D) *Apache* (First of 18)
Tpt hel	6 sqn with 41 CH-53D *Sea Stallion*; 24 S-70A *Black Hawk*; 34 Bell 206 *JetRanger*; 55 Bell 212; 10 UH-60A *Black Hawk*; 14 UH-60L *Black Hawk*
Trg	Trg units with 4 Beech 80 *Queen Air*; 43 CM-170 *Magister* (being replaced for lead-in ftr trg by A-4N); 17 Grob 120; 10 TA-4H *Skyhawk**; 16 TA-4J *Skyhawk**
UAV	1 sqn with 22+ *Searcher I/II* (being replaced by MALE (Medium Altitude Long Endurance) *Shoval*; *Delilah*; *Firebee*; *Harpy*; RQ-5A *Hunter*; *Samson*; *Scout*; Silver Arrow *Hermes* 450;
SAM	2 bty each with 9 *Arrow* II; 3 bty each with 16 PAC-2; 17 bty with MIM-23 *HAWK*; 5 bty with MIM-104 *Patriot*; 35 M-163 *Vulcan*

EQUIPMENT BY TYPE
AIRCRAFT 393 combat capable
FTR 193: 90 F-16A *Fighting Falcon*; 16 F-16B *Fighting Falcon*; 27 F-15A *Eagle*; 7 F-15B *Eagle*; 17 F-15C *Eagle*; 11 F-15D *Eagle*; 25 F-15I *Ra'am*
FGA 174: 39 A-4N *Skyhawk*; 52 F-16C *Fighting Falcon*; 49 F-16D *Fighting Falcon*; 34 F-16I *Sufa* (68 more being delivered at rate of 2/month); 200+ A-4N *Skyhawk*/F-4 *Phantom II*/*Kfir* C-7 in reserve
RECCE 6 RC-12D *Guardrail*
ELINT 10: 3 B-707 (ELINT/ECM); 3 Gulfstream G-550; 2 EC-130H *Hercules*AEW; 3 B-707 Phalcon
MP 3 IAI-1124 *Seascan*
TPT/TKR 9: 4 B-707; 5 KC-130H *Hercules*
TPT 45: 5 C-130 Hercules; 2 BN-2 *Islander*; 4 Beech 200CT *Super King Air*; 12 Beech 80 *Queen Air*; 1 C-47 *Skytrain*; 15 Do-28; 6 IAI-202 *Arava*
UTL: 22 Cessna U-206 *Stationair*
TRG 86: 43 CM-170 *Magister* (being replaced for lead-in ftr trg by A-4N); 17 Grob 120; 10 TA-4H *Skyhawk**; 16 TA-4J *Skyhawk**
HELICOPTERS
ATK 94: 16 AH-1E *Cobra*; 39 AH-1F *Cobra*; 30 AH-64A *Apache*; 9 *Sarat* (AH-64D) *Apache* (first of 18)
ASW: 7 AS-565SA *Panther* (missions flown by IAF but with in non-rated aircrew)
SPT 65: 41 CH-53D *Sea Stallion*; 24 S-70A *Black Hawk*
UTL 113: 34 Bell 206 *JetRanger*; 55 Bell 212; 10 UH-60A *Black Hawk*; 14 UH-60L *Black Hawk*

UAV: 44+: 22 *Searcher*; (22+ in store) MK II
RECCE • TAC *Harpy*; RQ-5A *Hunter*, *Samson*, *Scout*; 22
Searcher MK II; 22+ in store; Siver Arrow *Hermes 450*
AD
  SAM • TOWED 48+: 48 PAC-2; MIM-104 *Patriot*; MIM-
  23 HAWK
  GUNS 920
    SP 165 **20mm** 105 M-163 Machbet *Vulcan*; **23mm** 60
    ZSU-23-4
    TOWED 755 **23mm** 150 ZU-23; **20mm/37mm** 455 M-
    167 *Vulcan* towed 20mm/M-1939 towed 37mm/TCM-20
    towed 20mm; **40mm** 150 L/70
  TMD 18 *Arrow* II
MSL
  ASM AGM-114 *Hellfire*; AGM-45 *Shrike*; AGM-62B
  Walleye; AGM-65 *Maverick*; AGM-78D *Standard*; *Popeye* I
  tactical ASM/*Popeye* II
  AAM AIM-120 *AMRAAM*; AIM-7 *Sparrow*; AIM-9
  Sidewinder; *Python* III; *Python* IV; *Shafrir*
BOMB • PGM • JDAM GBU-31

Airfield Defence 3,000 active; 15,000 reservists (total 18,000)

Regional/Territorial Forces

Can be mobilised in 72hrs
Inf 11 (territorial/regional) bde

Reserve Organisations

Reserves ε380,000 reservists
Armd   8 div (*total:* 15 armd bde, 6 arty regt, 4 inf bde,
        6 mech inf bde)
Air Mob 1 div (3 air mob bde, 1 para bde)

Paramilitary ε8,050

Border Police ε8,000
APC • APC (W) *Walid*

Coast Guard ε50
PATROL AND COASTAL COMBATANTS 4:
  PC 3; **PCR** 1 (US)

DEPLOYMENT

TURKEY
Air Force
FORCES BY ROLE
up to 1 ftr det (occasional) located at Akinci, Tu, eqpt. with
F-16 *Fighting Falcon*

EQUIPMENT BY TYPE
AIRCRAFT • FTR: F-16 *Fighting Falcon*

FOREIGN FORCES

Unless specified, figures represent total numbers for
UNTSO mission in Israel, Syria, Lebanon
Argentina 5 obs
Australia 12 obs
Austria 6 obs

Canada 8 obs; 3 (*Operation Proteus*) USSC
Chile 3 obs
China 4 obs
Belgium 2 obs
Denmark 11 obs
Estonia 2 obs
Finland 15 obs
France 2 obs
Ireland 14 obs
Italy 6 obs
Nepal 3 obs
Netherlands 11 obs
New Zealand 8 obs
Norway 12 obs
Russia 3 obs
Slovakia 2 obs
Sweden 7 obs
Switzerland 9 obs
United States 3 obs

Jordan HKJ

Jordanian Dinar D		2006	2007	2008
GDP	D	10.0bn	11.2bn	
	US$	14.1bn	15.8bn	
per capita	US$	2,384	2,606	
Growth	%	6.3	6.0	
Inflation	%	6.3	5.0	
Def bdgt	D	792m	1,132m	
	US$	1.11bn	1.59bn	
FMA (US)	US$	208m	206m	200m
US$1=D		0.71	0.71	

Population   6,053,193
Ethnic groups: Palestinian ε50-60%

Age	0–14	15–19	20–24	25–29	30–64	65 plus
Male	18%	5%	5%	5%	18%	2%
Female	17%	5%	5%	4%	15%	2%

Capabilities

ACTIVE 100,500 (Army 88,000 Navy 500 Air 12,000)
Paramilitary 10,000

RESERVE 65,000 (Army 60,000 Joint 5,000)

ORGANISATIONS BY SERVICE

Army 88,000

Jordan has re-organised from a divisional structure to 4
commands, a strategic reserve and a special operations
command. The strategic reserve still has a divisional structure and the special operations command is responsible
for counter terrorism and unconventional operations. The
Royal Guard also comes under this command.

FORCES BY ROLE

Armd   1 Comd (Southern) (1 armd bde, 1 inf bde); 1 Div (strategic reserve) (3 armd, 1 arty, 1 AD bde)

Mech   1 comd (Northern) (2 mech bde, 1 inf bde, 1 arty bde, 1 AD bde,); 1 comd (Eastern) (2 mech bde ,1 AD bde, 1 arty bde) 1 comd (Central) (1 mech bde, 1 lt inf bde, 1 AD bde, 1 arty bde)

Spec Ops   1 bde (2 ab bn, 1 ab arty bn, 1 psychops unit; 2 SF bn)

EQUIPMENT BY TYPE

MBT 1,100: 390 CR1 *Challenger 1* (*Al Hussein*); 274 FV4030/2 *Khalid*; 88 M-60 *Phoenix*; 180 M-60A1/M-60A3 (being upgraded); 90 *Tariq Centurion* (*Centurion* in store); 78 M-47/M-48A5 (in store)

LT TK 45 *Scorpion* (used as recce)

AIFV 235: 35 BMP-2: ε200 *Ratel-20*

APC • APC (T) 1,345: 1,100 M-113A1; 245 M-113 MK-1 J (indigenous upgrade of M113A1)

ARTY 1,224

  SP 390: **105mm** 35 M-52; **155mm** 273: 253 M-109A1/M-109A2; 20 M-44; **203mm** 82 M-110A2

  TOWED 94: **105mm** 54: 36 M-102; 18 MOBAT; **155mm** 36: 18 M-1/M-59; 18 M-114; **203mm** 4 M-115

  MOR 740:

  SP 81mm 130

  TOWED 610: **81mm** 320; **107mm** 60 M-30; **120mm** 230 Brandt

AT • MSL 670

  SP 20 M-901

  MANPATS 650: 30 Javelin (110 msl); 310 M47 *Dragon*; 310 TOW/TOW-2A

  RL 4,800+: **73mm** RPG-26; **94mm** 2,500 LAW-80; **112mm** 2,300 APILAS

AD • SAM 992+

  SP 152: 92 SA-13 *Gopher*; 60 SA-8 *Gecko*

  MANPAD 840+: 250 FIM-43 *Redeye*; 300 SA-14 *Gremlin*; 240 SA-16 *Gimlet*; 50 SA-7B2 *Grail*; SA-18 *Grouse* (*Igla*)

  GUNS • SP 395: **20mm** 139 M-163 *Vulcan*; **23mm** 40 ZSU-23-4; **40mm** 216 M-42 (not all op)

RADAR • LAND 7 AN/TPQ-36 *Firefinder*/AN/TPQ-37 *Firefinder* (arty, mor)

Navy ε500

EQUIPMENT BY TYPE

PATROL AND COASTAL COMBATANTS 13

  PFI 3 *Al Hussein* less than 100 tonnes (Vosper 30m)

  PB 10: 2 *Al Hashim* (*Rotork*); 4 *Faysal*; 4 *Abduhlla* (*Dauntless*)

FACILITIES

Base   Located at Aqaba

Air Force 12,000

Flying hours   180 hrs/year

FORCES BY ROLE

Ftr   1 sqn with 15 F-1CJ (F-1C) *Mirage/Mirage* F-1BJ (F-1B); 1 sqn with 12 F-16A *Fighting Falcon*; 4 F-16B *Fighting Falcon*

FGA/Recce 1 sqn with 15 *Mirage* F-1EJ (F-1E); 3 sqn with 54 F-5E *Tiger II/F-5F Tiger II*

Surv   sqn with 2 RU-38A *Twin Condor*

Tpt   1 sqn with 4 C-130H *Hercules*; 2 CASA 212A *Aviocar*; 2 CL-604 *Challenger*; 2 CN-235; 2 TB-20 *Trinidad*

VIP   1 (Royal) flt with 1 A-340-211; 2 Gulfstream IV; 1 L-1011 *Tristar*; 3 S-70A *Black Hawk*

Atk hel   2 sqn with 20+ AH-1F *Cobra* with TOW tactical ASM

Tpt hel   2 sqn with 12 AS-332M *Super Puma*; 3 BO-105 (operated on behalf of the police); 13 EC-635 (utl/SAR); 36 UH-1H *Iroquois*; 1 hel sqn dedicated to SF

Trg   3 sqn with 15 *Bulldog* 103 (being replaced by 16 T-67M); 11 CASA C-101 *Aviojet*; 8 Hughes 500D

AD   2 bde (*total*: 14 AD bty with 80 I-HAWK MIM-23B, 3 AD bty with PAC-2 *Patriot*)

EQUIPMENT BY TYPE

AIRCRAFT 100 combat capable

  FTR 100: 54 F-5E *Tiger II/F-5F Tiger II*; 12 F-16A *Fighting Falcon*; 4 F-16B *Fighting Falcon*; 15 Mirage F-1EJ (F-1E); 15 F-1CJ (F-1C) *Mirage* FTR/*Mirage* F-1BJ (F-1B) Trg

  MP 2 RU-38A *Twin Condor*

  TPT 14: 1 A-340-211; 4 C-130H *Hercules*; 2 CASA 212A *Aviocar*; 2 CL-604 *Challenger*; 2 CN-235; 2 Gulfstream IV; 1 L-1011 *Tristar*

  UTL: 2 TB-20 *Trinidad*

  TRG 26: 15 *Bulldog* 103 (being replaced by 16 T-67M *Firefly*); 11 CASA C-101 *Aviojet*

HELICOPTERS

  ATK 20+ AH-1F *Cobra* each with TOW tactical ASM

  SPT 15: 12 AS-332M *Super Puma*; 3 S-70A *Black Hawk*

    UTL 60: 3 BO-105 (operated on behalf of the police); 13 EC-635 (ult/SAR); 8 Hughes 500D; 36 UH-1H *Iroquois*

AD • SAM 80+: PAC-2 *Patriot*; 80 I-HAWK MIM-23B

MSL

  ASM GM-65D *Maverick*

  AAM AIM-7 *Sparrow*; AIM-9 *Sidewinder*; R-550 *Magic*; R530

Paramilitary 10,000 active

Public Security Directorate ε10,000 active

Ministry of Interior

FORCES BY ROLE

Sy 1 (Police Public) bde

EQUIPMENT BY TYPE

LT TK: *Scorpion*

APC (W) 55+: 25+ EE-11 *Urutu*; 30 FV603 *Saracen*

Reserve Organisations 60,000 reservists

Armd   1 (Royal) div (1 arty bde, 1 AD bde, 3 armd bde)

Civil Militia 'People's Army' ε35,000 reservists

Men 16–65, women 16–45

DEPLOYMENT

CÔTE D'IVOIRE
UN • UNOCI 1,062; 7 obs

DEMOCRATIC REPUBLIC OF CONGO
UN • MONUC 66; 25 obs

ETHIOPIA/ERITREA
UN • UNMEE 570; 8 obs

GEORGIA
UN • UNOMIG 7 obs

HAITI
UN • MINUSTAH 755

LIBERIA
UN • UNMIL 123; 7 obs

NEPAL
UN • UNMIN 10 obs

SERBIA
UN • UNMIK 2 obs

SUDAN
AU/UN • UNAMID 360 proposed deployment
UN • UNMIS 10; 7 obs

Kuwait Kwt

Kuwaiti Dinar D		2006	2007	2008
GDP	D	29.6bn	30.7bn	
	US$	102bn	109bn	
per capita	US$	42,205	43,760	
Growth	%	5.0	3.5	
Inflation	%	2.8	2.6	
Def bdgt	D	1.0bn	ε1.1bn	
	US$	3.49bn	ε3.92bn	
US$1=D		0.31	0.31	

Population   2,505,559

Ethnic groups: Nationals 35%; other Arab 35%; South Asian 9%; Iranian 4%; other 17%

Age	0–14	15–19	20–24	25–29	30–64	65 plus
Male	14%	4%	7%	9%	25%	2%
Female	13%	4%	5%	5%	11%	1%

Capabilities

ACTIVE 15,500 (Army 11,000 Navy 2,000 Air 2,500)
Paramilitary 7,100
Terms of service voluntary

RESERVE 23,700 (Joint 23,700)
Terms of service obligation to age 40; 1 month annual trg

ORGANISATIONS BY SERVICE

Army 11,000
FORCES BY ROLE
Army	1 (reserve) bde
Armd	3 bde
Mech/Recce	1 bde
Mech Inf	2 bde
SF	1 unit (forming)
Cdo	1 bn
Arty	1 bde
Engr	1 bde
Gd	1 (Amiri) bde
AD	1 comd (AD bty, 4 (HAWK Phase III), AD bty, 5 (Patriot PAC-2) AD bty, 6 (Amoun (Skyguard/Aspide)) AD bty)

EQUIPMENT BY TYPE
MBT 368: 218 M1-A2 Abrams; 75 M-84; 75 in store
AIFV up to 450: up to 76 BMP-2; up to 120 BMP-3; 254 Desert Warrior (incl variants)
APC 321
    APC (T) 270: 230 M-113A2; 40 M-577
    APC (W) 51: 40 TH 390 Fahd in store; 11 TPz-1 Fuchs
ARTY 218
    SP 155mm 113: 18 AU-F-1 in store; 23 M-109A3; 18 (AMX) Mk F3; 54 PLZ45
    MRL 300mm 27 9A52 Smerch
    MOR 78: 81mm 60; 107mm 6 M-30; 120mm ε12 RT-F1
AT • MSL 118+
    SP 74: 66 HMMWV TOW; 8 M-901
    MANPATS 44+: 44 TOW-2; M47 Dragon
    RCL 84mm ε200 Carl Gustav
AD • SAM 84
    TOWED 24 I HAWK Phase III MIM-23B
    STATIC/SHELTER 12 Aspide
    MANPAD 48 Starburst; Stinger
    GUNS • TOWED 35mm 12+ Oerlikon

Navy ε2,000 (incl 500 Coast Guard)
EQUIPMENT BY TYPE
PATROL AND COASTAL COMBATANTS 10
PFM 10:
    1 Al Sanbouk (Ge Lurssen TNC-45) with 2 twin (4 eff.) each with MM-40 Exocet tactical SSM
    1 Istiqlal (Ge Lurssen FPB-57) with 2 twin (4 eff.) each with MM-40 Exocet tactical SSM
    8 Um Almaradim (Fr P-37 BRL) each with 2 twin (4 eff.) each with Sea Skua tactical SSM, 1 sextuple (6 eff.) (launcher only)
AMPHIBIOUS 2 LCM
LOGISTICS AND SUPPORT • SPT 1 Sawahil
FACILITIES
Base   Located at Ras al Qalaya

Air Force ε2,500

Flying hours 210 hrs/year

FORCES BY ROLE

Ftr/FGA	2 sqn with 31 F/A-18C *Hornet*; 8 F/A-18D *Hornet*
CCT	1 sqn with 11 *Hawk* MK64; 8 *Tucano* T MK52 (Shorts 312); 8†
Tpt	2 sqn with 1 DC-9; 3 L-100-30; 4 AS-332 *Super Puma* (tpt/SAR/atk); 9 SA-330 *Puma*
Trg/atk hel	1 sqn with 16 SA-342 *Gazelle* each with HOT tactical ASM
Atk hel	1 sqn with 16 AH-64D *Apache*

EQUIPMENT BY TYPE

AIRCRAFT 50 combat capable
  FGA 39: 31 F/A-18C *Hornet*; 8 F/A-18D *Hornet*
  TPT 4: 1 DC-9; 3 L-100-30
  TRG 27: 11 *Hawk* MK64*; 8 *Tucano* T MK52 (Shorts 312); 8†
HELICOPTERS
  ATK 16 AH-64D *Apache*
  ASLT 16 SA-342 *Gazelle** each with HOT tactical ASM
  SPT 13: 4 AS-332 *Super Puma* (tpt/SAR/attack); 9 SA-330 *Puma*
MSL
  ASM AGM-65G *Maverick*; AIM-84A *Harpoon*
  AAM AIM-7F *Sparrow*, AIM-9L *Sidewinder*; *Magic* 1

Paramilitary ε7,100 active

National Guard ε6,600 active

FORCES BY ROLE

Armd	1 (armd car) bn
SF	1 bn
Paramilitary	3 (national guard) bn
MP	1 bn

EQUIPMENT BY TYPE

RECCE 20 VBL
APC (W) 92: 70 *Pandur*; 22 S600 (incl variants)

Coast Guard 500

PATROL AND COASTAL COMBATANTS 55
  PCC 7: 3 *Al Shaheed*; 4 *Inttisar* (Aust 31.5m)
  PB 10 *Subahi*
  PBR 38
AMPHIBIOUS • CRAFT 3 LCU

FOREIGN FORCES

Japan Air Self Defense Force 210
Korea, Republic of: some troops part of MNF-I
United Kingdom Army 30; Air Force 10
United States troops deployed as part of *Op Iraqi Freedom*

Lebanon RL

Lebanese Pound LP		2006	2007	2008
GDP	LP	32.0tr	33.1tr	
	US$	21.2bn	21.9bn	
per capita	US$	5,470	5,595	
Growth	%	n.a.	2.0	
Inflation	%	5.6	3.5	
Def bdgt	LP	889bn	953bn	
	US$	588m	631m	
FMA (US)	US$		220m	
US$1=LP		1,510	1,510	

Population 3,921,278

Ethnic groups: Christian 30%; Druze 6%; Armenian 4%, excl ε300,000 Syrian nationals and ε350,000 Palestinian refugees

Age	0–14	15–19	20–24	25–29	30–64	65 plus
Male	14%	4%	5%	6%	17%	3%
Female	13%	4%	5%	5%	20%	4%

Capabilities

ACTIVE 56,000 (Army 53,900 Navy 1,100 Air 1,000)
Paramilitary 20,000
The usual number of Lebanese troops in peacetime is around 56,000. It can increase to 150,000 if there is a recall of conscripts. Conscription ended in Feb 2007.

ORGANISATIONS BY SERVICE

Army 53,900

FORCES BY ROLE

Region	5 comd (Beirut, Bekaa Valley, Mount Lebanon, North, South)
Mech inf	11 bde under strength
Mne cdo	1 regt
SF	5 regt
Cdo	1 regt
Air aslt	1 regt
Arty	2 regt
Presidential Guard	1 bde
MP	1 indep bde
Engr	1 indep regt
Cbt spt	1 indep bde
Logistics	1 indep bde
Medical	1 indep regt

EQUIPMENT BY TYPE

MBT 310: 200 T-54/T-55; 110 M-48A1/M-48A5
RECCE 60 AML
APC 1,257
  APC (T) 1,164 M-113A1/M-113A2
  APC (W) 93: 12 M-3/VTT; 81 VAB VCI
LT VEH 285 M998 HMMVW
ARTY 551

TOWED 157: **105mm** 23: 13 M-101A1; 10 M-102; **122mm** 56: 24 D-30; 32 M-30 *M-1938*; **130mm** 16 M-46; **155mm** 62: 15 M-114A1; 32 M-198; 15 Model-50
MRL 122mm 25 BM-21
MOR 369: **81mm** 158; **82mm** 111; **120mm** 100 Brandt
AT
  MSL • MANPATS 70: 30 ENTAC; 16 *Milan*; 24 TOW
  RCL 106mm 50 M-40A1
  RL 73mm RPG-7 *Knout*; **89mm** M-65
AD • SAM • MANPAD 20 SA-7A *Grail*/SA-7B *Grail*
  GUNS 10+
    SP 40mm 10 M-42A1
    TOWED 20mm; 23mm ZU-23
UAV • TACTICAL 8 *Mohajer IV*

Navy 1,100

EQUIPMENT BY TYPE
PATROL AND COASTAL COMBATANTS 21
  PCI 7: 5 *Attacker*; 2 *Tracker* (ex-UK all units under 100 tonnes)
  PBR 14
AMPHIBIOUS • LS • LST 2 *Sour* (capacity 8 APC; 96 troops) (Fr *Edic*)

FACILITIES

Bases   Located at Jounieh, Beirut

Air Force 1,000

3 air bases

FORCES BY ROLE

Atk hel	1 sqn with SA-342L *Gazelle* at Beirut
Utl hel	2 sqn with UH-1H at Beirut; 1 sqn with UH-1H at Rayak; 1 sqn with UH-1H at Koleyate
Trg hel	1 trg sqn with R-44 *Raven* II at Rayak

EQUIPMENT BY TYPE
AIRCRAFT
  FGA 6 Hawker *Hunter* MK 9, MK6, T66 all grounded (could be refurbished)
  TRG 8: 5 CM-170 *Magister* all grounded (3 could be refurbished)
HELICOPTERS
  ATK 13: 8 SA-342L *Gazelle* (plus 5 grounded – could be refurbished)
  UTL 45 (of which only 20 serviceable): 16 UH-1H *Huey* (+ 7 unserviceable); 4 R-44 *Raven* II (basic trg); 7 Bell 212 unserviceable (5 could be refurbished); 5 *Puma* SA-330 all grounded (3 could be refurbished): 3 SA-330 *Puma* in store; 5 SA-316 *Alouette III* unserviceable (3 could be refurbished); 1 SA-318 *Alouette II* unserviceable (could be refurbished)

Paramilitary ε20,000 active

Internal Security Force ε20,000

Ministry of Interior

FORCES BY ROLE

Police	1 (Judicial) unit
Regional	1 coy
Paramilitary	1 (Beirut Gendarmerie) coy

EQUIPMENT BY TYPE
APC (W) 60 V-200 *Chaimite*

Customs

PATROL AND COASTAL COMBATANTS 7
  PCI 7: 5 *Aztec*; 2 *Tracker* (All vessels less than 100 tonnes)

NON-STATE ARMED GROUPS

see Part II

FOREIGN FORCES

All under UNIFIL comd unless otherwise specified. UNTSO figures represent total numbers for the mission in Israel, Syria, Lebanon, unless otherwise specified.

Argentina 5 obs UNTSO
Australia 12 obs UNTSO
Austria 6 obs UNTSO
Belgium 323, 2 obs UNTSO
Canada 8 obs UNTSO
Chile 3 obs UNTSO
Croatia 1
Cyprus 2
China, People's Republic of 343; 4 obs UNTSO
Denmark 11 obs UNTSO
Estonia 2 obs UNTSO
Finland 205; 15 obs UNTSO
France 1,587; 2 obs UNTSO
Germany 905
Ghana 868
Greece 228
Guatemala 2
Hungary 4
India 884
Indonesia 856
Ireland 166 ; 14 obs UNTSO
Italy 2,379; 6 obs UNTSO
Korea, Republic of 363
Luxemburg 2
Macedonia, Former Yugoslav Republic of 1
Malaysia 362
Nepal 859; 3 obs UNTSO
Netherlands 149; 11 obs UNTSO
New Zealand 8 obs UNTSO
Norway 12 obs UNTSO
Poland 482
Portugal 146
Qatar 203
Russia 3 obs UNTSO
Slovakia 2 obs UNTSO
Spain 1,100
Sweden 7 obs UNTSO
Switzerland 7 obs UNTSO
Tanzania 77
Turkey 746
United States 3 obs UNTSO; 3 non-UN

Libya LAR

Libyan Dinar D		2006	2007	2008
GDP	D	67bn	70bn	
	US$	52.4bn	56.9bn	
per capita	US$	8,884	9,418	
Growth	%	5.6	9.2	
Inflation	%	3.4	16.2	
Def exp	D	759m	807m	
	US$	593m	650m	
US$1=D		1.28	1.24	

Population   6,036,914

Age	0–14	15–19	20–24	25–29	30–64	65 plus
Male	17%	5%	5%	5%	16%	2%
Female	17%	5%	5%	5%	15%	2%

Capabilities

ACTIVE 76,000 (Army 50,000 Navy 8,000 Air 18,000)

Terms of service selective conscription, 1–2 years

RESERVE ε40,000 (People's Militia)

ORGANISATIONS BY SERVICE

Army 25,000; ε25,000 conscript (total 50,000)

FORCES BY ROLE

11 Border Def and 4 Sy Zones

Army	1 (elite) bde (regime sy force)
Tk	10 bn
Mech inf	10 bn
Inf	18 bn
Cdo/para	6 bn
Arty	22 bn
SSM	4 bde
ADA	7 bn

EQUIPMENT BY TYPE

MBT 2,025: 200 T-72; 115 in store; 100 T-62; 70 in store; 500 T-55; 1,040 T-54/T-55 in store

RECCE 120: 50 BRDM-2; 70 EE-9 *Cascavel*;

AIFV 1,000+: 1,000 BMP-1; BMD

APC 945

APC (T) 778: 28 M-113; 750 BTR-50/BTR-60

APC (W) 167: 100 EE-11 *Urutu*; 67 OT-62/OT-64

ARTY 2,421+

SP 444: **122mm** 130 2S1 *Carnation*; **152mm** 140: 60 2S3; 80 M-77 *Dana*; **155mm** 174: 14 M-109; 160 VCA 155 *Palmaria*

TOWED 647+: **105mm** 42+ M-101; **122mm** 250: 190 D-30; 60 D-74; **130mm** 330 M-46; **152mm** 25 M-1937

MRL 830: **107mm** ε300 Type-63; **122mm** 530: ε200 BM-11; ε230 BM-21; ε100 RM-70 *Dana*

MOR 500: **82mm** 428; **120mm** ε48 M-43; **160mm** ε24 M-160

AT • MSL 3,000

SP 40 9P122 BRDM-2 *Sagger*

MANPATS 2,960: 620 AT-3 9K11 *Sagger*; 1,940 AT-3 9K11 *Sagger/* AT-4 9K111 *Spigot* / AT-5 9K113 *Spandrel*; 400 *Milan*

RCL 620: **106mm** 220 M-40A1; **84mm** 400 *Carl Gustav*

RL 73mm 2,300 RPG-7 *Knout*

AD • SAM • SP 424+: 24 *Crotale* (quad); 400 SA-7 *Grail*; SA-13 *Gopher*; SA-9 *Gaskin*

GUNS 490

SP 23mm 250 ZSU-23-4

TOWED 240: **14.5mm** 100 ZPU-2; **30mm** M-53/59; **40mm** 50 L/70; **57mm** 90 S-60

RADAR • LAND RASIT (veh, arty)

MSL • TACTICAL • SSM 45 FROG-7

Navy 8,000 (incl Coast Guard)

EQUIPMENT BY TYPE

SUBMARINES • TACTICAL • SSK 2 *Kyhber*† (FSU *Foxtrot*)

PRINCIPAL SURFACE COMBATANTS 3

FRIGATES • FFG 2 *Al Hani*† (FSU *Koni*) with 2 twin (4 eff.) each with SS-N-2C *Styx* tactical SSM, 2 twin 406mm ASTT (4 eff.) each with USET-95 Type 40 LWT, 1 RBU 6000 *Smerch* 2 (12 eff.)

CORVETTES • FSG 1 *Tariq Ibin Ziyad* (FSU *Nanuchka* II) with 4 single each with 1 SS-N-2C *Styx* tactical SSM

PATROL AND COASTAL COMBATANTS 18

PFM 14:

4 *Al Zuara* (FSU *Osa* II) each with 4 single each with 1 SS-N-2C *Styx* tactical SSM

6 *Sharaba* (Fr *Combattante* II) each with 4 single each with 1 Mk 2 Otomat SSM, 1 76mm gun

PBC 4 *PV-30LS* (constabulary duties, additional units to follow

MINE WARFARE • MINE COUNTERMEASURES •
MSO 4 *Ras al Gelais* (FSU *Natya*)

AMPHIBIOUS 4

LS 1

LST 1 *Ibn Harissa* (capacity 1 SA-316B *Alouette III* utl hel; 11 MBT; 240 troops)

CRAFT 3 LCT

LOGISTICS AND SUPPORT 12:

ARS 1

TPT 10 *El Temsah*

YDT 1

FACILITIES

Bases	Located at Tripoli, Benghazi, Tobruk, Khums

Minor bases Located at Derna, Zuwurah, Misonhah

Coastal Defence

FORCES BY ROLE

Msl 1 bty with SS C-3 *Styx*

EQUIPMENT BY TYPE

MSL • TACTICAL • SSM: some SS-C-3 *Styx*

Naval Aviation

HELICOPTERS • SAR 7 SA-321 *Super Frelon* (air force assets)

Air Force 18,000

Flying hours   85 hrs/year

FORCES BY ROLE

Bbr   1 sqn with 6 Tu-22 *Blinder*

Ftr   9+ sqn with 15 *Mirage* F-1ED (F-1E); 94 MiG-25 *Foxbat*; 75 MiG-23 *Flogger*; 45 MiG-21 *Fishbed*; 3 *Mirage* F-1BD (F-1B); 3 MiG-25U *Foxbat*

FGA   7 sqn with 6 Su-24MK *Fencer D*; 14 *Mirage* F-1AD (F-1A); 40 MiG-23BN *Flogger H*; 53 Su-17M-2 *Fitter D*/Su-20 (Su-17M) *Fitter C*; 15 MiG-23U *Flogger*

Recce   2 sqn with 7 MiG-25R *Foxbat*; 4 *Mirage* 5DP30

Tpt   7 sqn with 2 An-124 *Condor*; 23 An-26 *Curl*; 15 C-130H *Hercules*; G-222; 25 Il-76 *Candid*; 2 L-100-20; 3 L-100-30; 15 L-410 *Turbolet*

Atk hel sqns with 23 Mi-25 *Hind D*; 12 Mi-35 *Hind*

Tpt hel sqns with 4 CH-47C *Chinook* (hy); 35 Mi-17 (Mi-8MT) *Hip H*/Mi-8 *Hip* (med); 5 AB-206 (Bell 206) *JetRanger* (lt); 11 SA-316 *Alouette III*

Trg   sqns with 1 Tu-22 *Blinder*; 90 G-2 *Galeb*; 115 L-39ZO *Albatros*; 20 SF-260WL *Warrior*; 46 PZL Mi-2 *Hoplite*

EQUIPMENT BY TYPE

(many non-operational, many ac in store)

AIRCRAFT 374 combat capable

BBR: 7 Tu-22 *Blinder*

FTR 229: 15 *Mirage* F-1ED (F-1E); 94 MiG-25 *Foxbat*; 75 MiG-23 *Flogger*; 45 MiG-21 *Fishbed*

FGA 113: 6 Su-24MK *Fencer D*; 14 *Mirage* F-1AD (F-1A); 40 MiG-23BN *Flogger H*; 53 Su-17M-2 *Fitter D*/Su-20 (Su-17M) *Fitter C*

RECCE 7 MiG-25R *Foxbat*

TPT 85+: 2 An-124 *Condor*; 23 An-26 *Curl*; 15 C-130H *Hercules*; G-222; 25 Il-76 *Candid*; 2 L-100-20; 3 L-100-30; 15 L-410 *Turbolet*

TRG 250: 90 G-2 *Galeb*; 115 L-39ZO *Albatros*; 15 MiG-23U *Flogger**; 3 MiG-25U *Foxbat**; 4 *Mirage* 5DP30*; 3 *Mirage* F-1BD (F-1B)*; 20 SF-260WL *Warrior*

HELICOPTERS

ATK 35: 23 Mi-25 *Hind D*; 12 Mi-35 *Hind*

SPT 85: 4 CH-47C *Chinook* (hy); 35 Mi-17 (Mi-8MT) *Hip H*/Mi-8 *Hip* spt hel (med); 46 PZL Mi-2 *Hoplite*

UTL 16: 5 AB-206 (Bell 206) *JetRanger* (lt); 11 SA-316 *Alouette III* (lt)

MSL

ASM AS-11 *Kilter*; AS-7 *Kerry*; AS-9 *Kyle*; AT-2 *Swatter*

ARM AS-11 *Kilter*

AAM AA-2 *Atoll*; AA-6 *Acrid*; AA-7 *Apex*; AA-8 *Aphid*; R-550 *Magic*; R530

Air Defence Command

Senezh AD comd and control system

FORCES BY ROLE

AD 5 region (with ε3 AD bde each with 20–24 SA-6 *Gainful*/SA-8 *Gecko* 2–3 AD bde each with 12 SA-3 *Goa*, 5–6 AD bde each with 18 SA-2 *Guideline*); 4 bde with SA-5A *Gammon* (each: 1 radar coy, 2 AD bn with 6 launcher, 4+ ADA bn with guns)

EQUIPMENT BY TYPE

AD

SAM 216+:

SP 72 SA-6 *Gainful*/SA-8 *Gecko* (216–432 eff.)

TOWED 144: 108 SA-2 *Guideline*

STATIC • SA-5: SA-5A *Gammon*; 36 SA-3 *Goa*

GUNS some

NON-STATE ARMED GROUPS

see Part II

DEPLOYMENT

SUDAN

AU • AUMIS 9 obs

Mauritania RIM

Mauritanian Ouguiya OM		2006	2007	2008
GDP	OM	857bn	985bn	
	US$	3.1bn	3.8bn	
per capita	US$	995	1,168	
Growth	%	11.4	0.9	
Inflation	%	6.2	7.6	
Def bdgt	OM	4.8bn	4.8bn	
	US$	17.7m	18.6m	
US$1=OM		271	258	

Population   3,270,065

Age	0–14	15–19	20–24	25–29	30–64	65 plus
Male	23%	5%	4%	4%	12%	1%
Female	23%	5%	4%	4%	13%	1%

Capabilities

ACTIVE 15,870 (Army 15,000 Navy 620 Air 250)

Paramilitary 5,000

Terms of service conscription 24 months authorised

ORGANISATIONS BY SERVICE

Army 15,000

FORCES BY ROLE

6 Mil Regions

Army	2 (camel corps) bn
Armd	1 bn (T-54/55 MBTs)
Armd recce	1 sqn
Inf	8 (garrison) bn
Mot inf	7 bn
Cdo/para	1 bn
Arty	3 bn
ADA	4 bty
Engr	1 coy
Gd	1 bn

EQUIPMENT BY TYPE
MBT 35 T-54/T-55
RECCE 70: 20 AML-60; 40 AML-90; 10 *Saladin*
APC (W) 25: 5 FV603 *Saracen*; ε20 M-3 *Panhard*
ARTY 194
    TOWED 80: **105mm** 36 HM-2/M-101A1; **122mm** 44: 20 D-30; 24 D-74
    MOR 114: **60mm** 24; **81mm** 60; **120mm** 30 *Brandt*
AT • MSL • MANPATS 24 *Milan*
    RCL 114: **75mm** ε24 M-20; **106mm** ε90 M-40A1
    RL 73mm ε48 RPG-7 *Knout*
AD • SAM 104
    SP ε4 SA-9 *Gaskin* (reported)
    MANPAD ε100 SA-7 *Grail*
    GUNS • TOWED 82: **14.5mm** 28: 16 ZPU-2; 12 ZPU-4; **23mm** 20 ZU-23-2; **37mm** 10 M-1939; **57mm** 12 S-60; **100mm** 12 KS-19

Navy ε620

EQUIPMENT BY TYPE
PATROL AND COASTAL COMBATANTS 10
    PSO 1 *Voum-Legleita*;
    PCO 3: 1 *Abourbekr Ben Amer* (Fr OPV 54); 1 *N'Madi* (UK *Jura*, fishery protection); 1 *Arguin*
    PCC 1 *El Nasr* (Fr *Patra*)
    PCI 4 *Mandovi* less than 100 tonnes
    PCR 1 *Huangpu*
FACILITIES
Bases Located at Nouadhibou, Nouakchott

Air Force 250

FORCES BY ROLE
MP   sqn with 2 Cessna 337 *Skymaster*
Tpt   sqn with 2 PA-31T *Navajo/Cheyenne II*; 2 Y-12(II)
COIN sqn with 2 FTB-337 *Milirole*; 5 BN-2 *Defender*; 1 Basler Turbo-67

EQUIPMENT BY TYPE
AIRCRAFT
    RECCE 2 FTB-337 *Milirole*
    TPT 12: 5 BN-2 *Defender*; 1 Basler Turbo-67; 2 Cessna 337 *Skymaster*; 2 PA-31T *Navajo/Cheyenne II*; 2 Y-12(II)
    TRG 4 SF-260E

Paramilitary ε5,000 active

Gendarmerie ε3,000
Ministry of Interior
Regional 6 coy

National Guard 2,000
Ministry of Interior
Aux 1,000

Customs
PATROL AND COASTAL COMBATANTS • PB 1 *Dah Ould Bah* (Fr *Amgram 14*)

DEPLOYMENT

SUDAN
AU • AUMIS 20 obs

Morocco Mor

Moroccan Dirham D		2006	2007	2008
GDP	D	503bn	570bn	
	US$	57.2bn	71.5bn	
per capita	US$	1,721	2,119	
Growth	%	8.0	2.5	
Inflation	%	3.3	2.5	
Def bdgt	D	18.9bn	19.7bn	
	US$	2.16bn	2.47bn	
FMA (US)	US$	12.4m	12.5m	3.6m
US$1=D		8.79	7.97	

Population	33,757,175

Age	0–14	15–19	20–24	25–29	30–64	65 plus
Male	16%	5%	5%	4%	16%	2%
Female	16%	5%	5%	4%	17%	3%

Capabilities

ACTIVE 195,800 (Army 175,000 Navy 7,800 Air 13,000) **Paramilitary 50,000**
Terms of service conscription 18 months authorised; most enlisted personnel are volunteers

RESERVE 150,000 (Army 150,000)
Terms of service obligation to age 50

ORGANISATIONS BY SERVICE

Army ε75,000; 100,000 conscript (total 175,000)

FORCES BY ROLE
2 Comd (Northern Zone, Southern Zone)

Sy	1 light bde
Armd	12 indep bn
Mech/mot inf	8 regt (*each*: 2-3 Mech inf bn)
Mech inf	3 bde
Inf	35 indep bn
Mot inf	3 (camel corps) indep bn
Mtn inf	1 indep bn
Cdo	4 indep unit
Para	2 bde
AB	2 indep bn
Arty	11 indep bn
Engr	7 indep bn
AD	1 indep bn

Royal Guard 1,500

Army	1 bn
Cav	1 sqn

EQUIPMENT BY TYPE

MBT 580: 40 T72, 220 M-60A1; 120 M-60A3; ε200 M-48A5 in store

LT TK 116: 5 AMX-13; 111 SK-105 *Kuerassier*

RECCE 384: 38 AML-60-7; 190 AML-90; 80 AMX-10RC; 40 EBR-75 16 *Eland*; 20 M1114 *HMMWV*

AIFV 70: 10 AMX-10P; 30 MK III-20 *Ratel*-20; 30 MK III-90 *Ratel*-90

APC 765

  APC (T) 400 M-113A1

  APC (W) 365: 45 VAB VCI; 320 VAB VTT

ARTY 2,892

  SP 199: **105mm** 5 Mk 61; **155mm** 134: 44 M-109A1/M-109A1B; 90 (AMX) Mk F3; **203mm** 60 M-110

  TOWED 118: **105mm** 50: 30 L-118 Light Gun; 20 M-101; **130mm** 18 M-46; **155mm** 50: 30 FH-70; 20 M-114

  MRL 35 BM-21

  MOR 1,706

    SP 56: **106mm** 32-36 M-106A2; **120mm** 20 (VAB APC)

    TOWED 1,650: **81mm** 1,100 Expal model LN; **120mm** 550 *Brandt*

AT • MSL 790

  SP 80 M-901

  MANPATS 710: 40 AT-3 9K11 *Sagger*; 440 M47 *Dragon*; 80 Milan; 150 TOW

  RCL 106mm 350 M-40A1

  RL 700: **66mm** 500 M-72 *LAW*; **89mm** 200 M-20

  GUNS 36

    SP 100mm 8 SU-100

    TOWED 90mm 28 M-56

UAV R4E-50 *Skyeye*

AD • SAM 107

  SP 37 M-48 *Chaparral*

  MANPAD 70 SA-7 *Grail*

  GUNS 407

    SP 60 M-163 *Vulcan*

    TOWED 347: **14.5mm** 200: 150-180 ZPU-2; 20 ZPU-4; **20mm** 40 M-167 *Vulcan*; **23mm** 75-90 ZU-23-2; **100mm** 17 KS-19

RADAR • LAND: RASIT (veh, arty)

Navy 7,800 (incl 1,500 Marines)

EQUIPMENT BY TYPE

PRINCIPAL SURFACE COMBATANTS • FRIGATES • FFG 3:

1 *Lt Col Errhamani* (Sp *Descubierto*) with 2 twin (4 eff.) each with MM-38 *Exocet* tactical SSM, 1 *Albatros* octuple with 24 *Aspide* SAM, 2 triple ASTT (6 eff.) each with Mk 46 LWT, (capacity 1 AS-565SA *Panther*), 1 76mm gun

2 *Mohammed V* (Fr *Floreal*) each eq with 2 single each with MM-38 *Exocet* SSM, 1 76mm gun, (capacity 1 AS-565SA *Panther*)

PATROL AND COASTAL COMBATANTS 27

PFM 4 *Cdt El Khattabi* (Sp *Lazaga* 58m) each with 4 single each with MM-40 *Exocet* tactical SSM, 1 76mm gun

PCC 17:

  4 *El Hahiq* (Dk *Osprey* 55, incl 2 with customs)

  6 *LV Rabhi* (Sp 58m B-200D)

2 *Okba* (Fr PR-72) each with 1 76mm gun

5 *Rais Bargach* (under control of fisheries dept)

PFI 6 *El Wacil* (Fr P-32, under 100 tonnes, incl 4 with customs)

AMPHIBIOUS

LS 4:

  LSM 3 *Ben Aicha* (Fr *Champlain* BATRAL) (capacity 7 tanks; 140 troops)

  LST 1 *Sidi Mohammed Ben Abdallah* (US *Newport*) (capacity 3 LCVP; 400 troops)

CRAFT • LCT 1 *Edic* (capacity 8 APCs; 96 troops)

LOGISTICS AND SUPPORT 4:

AK 2; **AGOR** 1 (US lease); 1 **YDT**

FACILITIES

Bases Located at Casablanca, Agadir, Al Hoceima, Dakhla, Tangier

Marines 1,500

Naval inf   2 bn

Naval Aviation

HELICOPTERS • ASW/ASUW 3 AS-565SA *Panther*

Air Force 13,000

Flying hours   100 hrs/year on F-1 *Mirage*/F-5A *Freedom Fighter Tiger*

FORCES BY ROLE

Ftr	1 sqn with 19 F-1CH (F-1C) *Mirage*
FGA	1 sqn with 8 F-5A *Freedom Fighter*; 2 F-5B *Freedom Fighter*; 2 sqn with 20 F-5E *Tiger II*; 3 F-5F *Tiger II*; 2 sqn with 14 *Mirage* F-1EH (F-1E)
Recce	sqn with 4 OV-10 *Bronco**; 2 C-130H *Hercules* (with side-looking radar)
EW	sqn with 2 C-130 *Hercules* (ELINT); 2 *Falcon* 20 (ELINT)
Tpt	sqn with 4 Beech 100 *King Air*; 3 Beech 200 *Super King Air*; 15 C-130H *Hercules*; 6 CN-235; 2 Do-28; 2 *Falcon* 20; 1 *Falcon* 50 (VIP); 2 Gulfstream II (VIP)
Tkr	sqn with 2 KC-130H *Hercules* (tpt/tkr); 1 B-707
Liaison	sqn with 2 Beech 200 *Super King Air*
Atk hel	sqn with 19 SA-342 *Gazelle* (with HOT, 12 with cannon)
Tpt hel	sqn with 8 CH-47D *Chinook* (hy); 24 SA-330 *Puma* (med); 25 AB-205A (Bell 205A); 11 AB-206 (Bell 206) *JetRanger* (lt); 3 AB-212 (Bell 212) (lt); 2 UH-60 *Black Hawk*
Trg	sqn with 7 AS-202 *Bravo*; 19 *Alpha Jet**; 2 CAP 10; 9 T-34C *Turbo Mentor*; 14 T-37B *Tweet* (being replaced by K-8); 4 CAP-231

EQUIPMENT BY TYPE

AIRCRAFT 89 combat capable

FTR 66: 8 F-5A *Freedom Fighter*; 2 F-5B *Freedom Fighter*; 20 F-5E *Tiger II*; 3 F-5F *Tiger II*; 19 F-1CH (F-1C) *Mirage*; 14 *Mirage* F-1EH (F-1E)

FAC 4 OV-10 *Bronco**

TKR 2 KC-130H *Hercules* (tpt/tkr)

TPT 44: 1 B-707; 4 Beech 100 *King Air*; 5 Beech 200 *Super King Air*; 2 C-130 (ELINT); 15 C-130H *Hercules*; 2 C-130H (with side-looking radar); 6 CN-235; 2 Do-28; 2 *Falcon* 20; 2 (ELINT); 1 *Falcon* 50 (VIP); 2 Gulfstream II (VIP)

TRG 51: 7 AS-202 *Bravo*; 19 *Alpha Jet**; 2 CAP 10; 9 T-34C *Turbo Mentor*; 14 T-37B *Tweet* (being replaced by K-8)

TRIALS AND TEST 4 CAP-231

HELICOPTERS

ASLT 19 SA-342 *Gazelle* (7 with HOT, 12 with cannon)

SPT 32: 8 CH-47D *Chinook* (hy); 24 SA-330 *Puma* (med)

UTL 41: 11 AB-206 (Bell 206) *JetRanger* (lt); 3 AB-212 (Bell 212) (lt); 25 AB-205A (Bell 205A); 2 UH-60 *Black Hawk*

MSL

ASM AGM-62B *Walleye* (For F-5E); HOT

AAM AIM-9B/D/J *Sidewinder*; R-550 *Magic*, R530

Paramilitary 50,000 active

Gendarmerie Royale 20,000

FORCES BY ROLE

Coast Guard   1 unit

Para   1 sqn

Paramilitary   1 bde; 4 (mobile) gp

Avn   1 (air) sqn

EQUIPMENT BY TYPE

PATROL AND COASTAL COMBATANTS • MISC BOATS/CRAFT 18 boats

AIRCRAFT • TRG 2 *Rallye* 235 *Guerrier*

HELICOPTERS

SAR 2 SA-360 *Dauphin*

ASLT 6 SA-342K *Gazelle*

SPT 6 SA-330 *Puma*

UTL 8: 3 SA-315B *Lama*; 2 SA-316 *Alouette III* 3 SA-318 *Alouette II*

Force Auxiliaire 30,000 (incl 5,000 Mobile Intervention Corps)

Customs/Coast Guard

PATROL AND COASTAL COMBATANTS 44

PCI 4 *Erraid*

PBF 15

PB 18

MISC BOATS/CRAFT 7 SAR craft

NON-STATE ARMED GROUPS

see Part II

DEPLOYMENT

CÔTE D'IVOIRE

UN • UNOCI 724

DEMOCRATIC REPUBLIC OF CONGO

UN • MONUC 809; 4 obs

SERBIA

NATO • KFOR • *Joint Enterprise* 229

Oman O

Omani Rial R		2006	2007	2008
GDP	R	13.9bn	14.9bn	
	US$	36.6bn	39.2bn	
per capita	US$	11,791	12.235	
Growth	%	5.9	6.0	
Inflation	%	3.2	3.8	
Def bdgt	R	1.24bn	1.23bn	
	US$	3.27bn	3.23bn	
FMA (US)	US$	13.8m	14.0m	10.1m
US$1=R		0.38	0.38	

Population   3,204,897

Expatriates: 27%

Age	0–14	15–19	20–24	25–29	30–64	65 plus
Male	22%	5%	4%	4%	20%	1%
Female	21%	4%	4%	3%	10%	1%

Capabilities

ACTIVE 42,600 (Army 25,000 Navy 4,200 Air 5,000 Foreign Forces 2,000 Royal Household 6,400) Paramilitary 4,400

ORGANISATIONS BY SERVICE

Army 25,000

FORCES BY ROLE

(Regt are bn size)

Armd   1 bde HQ; 2 regt (*each*: 3 tk sqn)

Armd recce   1 regt (3 armd recce sqn)

Inf   2 bde HQ; 8 regt

Rifle   1 indep coy (Musandam Security Force)

AB   1 regt

Inf recce   1 regt (3 recce coy)

Med arty   1 regt (2 Med arty bty)

Fd arty   2 regt

ADA   1 regt (2 ADA bty)

Fd Engr   1 regt (3 fd engr sqn)

EQUIPMENT BY TYPE

MBT 117: 38 CR2 *Challenger 2*; 6 M-60A1; 73 M-60A3

LT TK 37 *Scorpion*

RECCE 145: 13 *Sultan*; 132 VBL (8 with TOW)

APC 216

APC (T) 16: 6 FV 103 *Spartan*; 10 FV4333 *Stormer*

APC (W) 190: 175 *Piranha* (incl variants); 15 AT-105 *Saxon*

ARTY 233

SP 155mm 24 G-6

TOWED 108: **105mm** 42 ROF lt; **122mm** 30 D-30; **130mm** 24: 12 M-46; 12 Type-59-I; **155mm** 12 FH-70

MOR 101: **81mm** 69; **107mm** 20 M-30; **120mm** 12 Brandt

AT • MSL 58
   SP 8 VBL (TOW)
   MANPATS 50: 32 *Milan*; 18 TOW/TOW-2A
   RL 73mm RPG-7 *Knout*; **94mm** LAW-80
AD • SAM 54+
   SP *Mistral* 2
   MANPAD 54: 20 *Javelin*; 34 SA-7 *Grail*
   GUNS 26: **23mm** 4 ZU-23-2; **35mm** 10 GDF-005 (with *Skyguard*); **40mm** 12 L/60 (Towed)

Navy 4,200

EQUIPMENT BY TYPE
PRINCIPAL SURFACE COMBATANTS • CORVETTES
• **FSG** 2 *Qahir Al Amwaj* each with 2 quad (8 eff.) each with MM-40 *Exocet* tactical SSM, 2 triple 324mm TT (6 eff.) (to be fitted) each with MM-40 *Exocet* tactical SSM, 1 octuple (8 eff.) with 16 *Crotale* SAM, 1 76mm gun, with hel landing platform for *Super Lynx* type hel
PATROL AND COASTAL COMBATANTS 11
   PFM 4: 1 *Dhofar* with 2 triple (6 eff.) (not fitted); 3 *Dhofar* each with 2 quad (8 eff.) with MM-40 *Exocet* SSM tactical
   PCC 3 *Al Bushra* (Fr P-400) each with 4 single 406mm TT, 1 76mm gun
   PCI 4 *Seeb* (Vosper 25m, under 100 tonnes)
AMPHIBIOUS
   LS • LST 1 *Nasr el Bahr* (with hel deck) (capacity 7 tanks; 240 troops)
   CRAFT 4: 1 LCU; 3 LCM
LOGISTICS AND SUPPORT 6:
   AK 1 *Al Sultana*
   AGHS 1
   RY 2: 1 *Al Said*; 1 (Royal Dhow)
   TRG 1 *Al Mabrukah* (with hel deck, also used in offshore patrol role)
   SPT 1 (primary role to spt the Royal Yacht on deployment)

FACILITIES
Bases   Located at Muaskar al Murtafaia (Seeb), Alwi, Mainbase HQ located at Widam A'Sahil, Ghanam Island, Musandam, Salalah

Air Force 5,000

FORCES BY ROLE

FGA	1 sqn with 12 Block 50 F-16C *Fighting Falcon*/ F-16D *Fighting Falcon*; 2 sqn with 20 *Jaguar* OS/4 *Jaguar* OB
Ftr/FGA	1 sqn with 4 *Hawk* Mk103; 12 *Hawk* Mk203
Tpt	1 sqn with 3 C-130H *Hercules*; 1 sqn with 10 SC.7 3M *Skyvan* (7 radar-equipped, for MP); 1 sqn with 3 BAC-111
Tpt Hel	2 (med) sqn with 19 AB-205 (Bell 205) *JetRanger*; 3 AB-212 (Bell 212); 16 *Lynx* Mk 300 *Super Lynx* (maritime/SAR)
Trg	1 sqn with 4 AS-202-18 *Bravo*; 8 MFI-17B *Mushshak*; 12 PC-9*; 2 SF-25 *Falke*; 3 AB-206 hel
AD	2 sqn with 40 *Rapier*; 6 *Blindfire*; S713 *Martello*

EQUIPMENT BY TYPE
AIRCRAFT 64 combat capable
   FTR/FGA 52: 12 F-16C/D Block 50 *Fighting Falcon*; 24 *Jaguar* (20 OS (single seat), 4 OB (dual seat)); 4 *Hawk* Mk103; 12 *Hawk* Mk203
   TPT 16: 3 BAC-111; 3 C-130H *Hercules*; 10 SC.7 3M *Skyvan* (7 radar-equipped, for MP)
   TRG 26: 4 AS-202-18 *Bravo*; 8 MFI-17B *Mushshak*; 12 PC-9*; 2 SF-25
HELICOPTERS • UTL 41: 19 AB-205 (Bell 205) to be replaced by 20 NH-90; 3 AB-206 (Bell 206) *JetRanger* (basic rig); 3 AB-212 (Bell 212); 16 *Lynx* Mk 300 *Super Lynx* (maritime/SAR)
AD • SAM 40 *Rapier*
RADAR • LAND 6+: 6 *Blindfire*; S713 *Martello*
MSL
   AAM AIM-9LM *Sidewinder*; AIM-120C AMRAAM
   ASM 20 AGM-84D *Harpoon*; AGM-65 *Maverick*

Royal Household 6,400

(incl HQ staff)
SF 2 regt (1,000 men)

Royal Guard bde 5,000

LT TK 9 VBC-90
APC (W) 73: ε50 Type-92; 14 VAB VCI; 9 VAB VDAA
ARTY • MRL 122mm 6 Type-90A
AT • MSL • MANPATS *Milan*
AD • SAM • MANPAD 14 *Javelin*

Royal Yacht Squadron 150

PATROL AND COASTAL COMBATANTS • MISC BOATS/CRAFT • DHOW 1: 1 *Zinat Al Bihaar*
LOGISTICS AND SUPPORT 2:
   RY 1 (with hel deck)
   TPT 1 *Fulk Al Salamah* (also veh tpt) with up to 2 AS-332C *Super Puma* spt hel

Royal Flight 250

AIRCRAFT • TPT 5: 2 B-747SP; 1 DC-8-73CF; 2 Gulfstream IV
HELICOPTERS • SPT 6: 3 AS-330 (SA-330) *Puma*; 2 AS-332F *Super Puma*; 1 AS-332L *Super Puma*

Paramilitary 4,400 active

Tribal Home Guard 4,000

org in teams of est 100

Police Coast Guard 400

PATROL AND COASTAL COMBATANTS 52
   PCI 5: 3 CG 29 less than 100 tonnes; 1 CG 27 less than 100 tonnes; 1 P-1903 *Type*
   PB 22
   PBF 20
   PBI 5

Police Air Wing

AIRCRAFT • TPT 4: 1 BN-2T Turbine *Islander*; 2 CN-235M; 1 Do-228
HELICOPTERS • UTL 5: 2 Bell 205A; 3 AB-214ST

FOREIGN FORCES

United Kingdom Army 40; Navy 20; Air Force 20
United States Army 3; Air Force 24; Marine Corps 10

Palestinian Autonomous Areas of Gaza and Jericho PA

New Israeli Shekel NS		2006	2007	2008
GDP	US$			
per capita	US$			
Growth	%			
Inflation	%			
US$1=NS				
Population	4,018,332			

Capabilities

ACTIVE 0 Paramilitary 56,000
Personnel strength figures for the various Palestinian groups are not known

ORGANISATIONS BY SERVICE

There is very little data concerning the status of the organisations mentioned below. The Cairo and Washington agreements recognised several organisations under the Palestinian Directorate of Police Force. Some have little or no military significance and it is difficult to estimate the size of the total forces that do. The situation remains uncertain and prone to the many external influences in the region.

Paramilitary

National Forces ε56,000 (reported)
GENERAL SECURITY
Presidential security 3,000
SF 1,200
Police 9000
Preventative Security
Civil Defence 1000
AD • SAM • MANPAD SA-7 *Grail*; *Stinger* reported

NON-STATE ARMED GROUPS

see Part II

FOREIGN FORCES

Italy 17 (TIPH)
Switzerland 5 (TIPH)
Turkey 3 (TIPH)

Qatar Q

Qatari Riyal R		2006	2007	2008
GDP	R	191bn	215bn	
	US$	52bn	59bn	
per capita	US$	59,267	65,106	
Growth	%	10.3	14.2	
Inflation	%	11.8	12.0	
Def bdgt	R	ε8.5bn		
	US$	ε2.33bn		
US$1=R		3.64	3.64	

Population   907,229

Ethnic groups: Nationals 25%; Expatriates 75% of which Indian 18%; Iranian 10%; Pakistani 18%

Age	0–14	15–19	20–24	25–29	30–64	65 plus
Male	12%	4%	4%	5%	37%	3%
Female	12%	4%	3%	3%	12%	1%

Capabilities

ACTIVE 11,800 (Army 8,500 Navy 1,800 Air 1,500)

ORGANISATIONS BY SERVICE

Army 8,500
FORCES BY ROLE
Tk	1 bde (1 tk bn, 1 mech inf bn, 1 mor sqn, 1 AT bn)
Mech inf	3 bn
SF	1 coy
Fd arty	1 bn
Royal Guard	1 bde (3 inf regt)

EQUIPMENT BY TYPE
MBT 30 AMX-30
RECCE 68: 12 AMX-10RC; 20 EE-9 *Cascavel*; 12 *Ferret*; 8 V-150 *Chaimite*; 16 VBL
AIFV 40 AMX-10P
APC 226
 APC (T) 30 AMX-VCI
 APC (W) 196: 36 *Piranha* II; 160 VAB
ARTY 89
 SP 155mm 28 (AMX) Mk F3
 TOWED 155mm 12 G-5
 MRL 4 ASTROS II
 MOR 45: **81mm** 30 L16 (some SP); **120mm** 15 *Brandt*
AT • **MSL** 148
 SP 24 VAB HOT
 MANPATS 124: 24 HOT; 100 *Milan*
 RCL 84mm ε40 *Carl Gustav*

Navy 1,800 (incl Marine Police)
FORCES BY ROLE
Navy 1 HQ located at Doha

EQUIPMENT BY TYPE
PATROL AND COASTAL COMBATANTS 21
PFM 7:
4 *Barzan* (UK *Vita*) each with 2 quad (8 eff.) each with MM-40 *Exocet* tactical SSM, 1 sextuple (6 eff.) with *Mistral* SAM, 1 76mm gun
3 *Damsah* (Fr *Combattante* III) each with 2 quad (8 eff.)
PB 14 (11 operated by Marine Police)
FACILITIES
Bases Located at Doha, Halul Island

Coastal Defence
FORCES BY ROLE
Navy 1 bty with 3 quad (12 eff.) each with MM-40 *Exocet* tactical SSM

EQUIPMENT BY TYPE
LNCHR 3 quad each with MM-40 *Exocet* tactical SSM

Air Force 1,500
FORCES BY ROLE
Ftr/FGA   1 sqn with 6 *Alpha Jet*; 1 sqn with 9 M-2000ED *Mirage*; 3 M-2000D *Mirage*
Tpt   1 sqn with 1 A-340; 2 B-707; 1 B-727; 2 *Falcon* 900
Atk hel   1 sqn with 8 *Commando* MK 3 (*Exocet*); 11 SA-342L *Gazelle* (with HOT)
Tpt hel   sqn with 3 *Commando* MK 2A; 1 *Commando* MK 2C; 2 SA-341 *Gazelle*

EQUIPMENT BY TYPE
AIRCRAFT 18 combat capable
FGA 12: 9 M-2000ED *Mirage*; 3 M-2000D *Mirage*
TPT 6: 1 A-340; 2 B-707; 1 B-727; 2 *Falcon* 900
TRG 6 *Alpha Jet**
HELICOPTERS
ASUW: 8 *Commando* MK 3
ATK 11 SA-342L *Gazelle**
SPT 6: 3 *Commando* MK 2A; 1 *Commando* MK 2C; 2 SA-341 *Gazelle*
AD • SAM 75: 24 *Mistral*
SP 9 *Roland* II
MANPAD 42: 10 *Blowpipe*; 12 FIM-92A *Stinger*; 20 SA-7 *Grail*
MSL
ASM AM-39 *Exocet*; *Apache*; HOT
AAM MICA; R-550 *Magic*

DEPLOYMENT

LEBANON
UN • UNIFIL 203

FOREIGN FORCES
Korea, Republic of: some troops part of MNF-I
United States USCENTCOM: Army 188; Navy 4; Air Force 198; Marine Corps 122

Saudi Arabia Sau

Saudi Riyal R		2006	2007	2008
GDP	R	1.30tr	1.40tr	
	US$	349bn	374bn	
per capita	US$	12,899	13,356	
Growth	%	4.3	4.1	
Inflation	%	2.2	3.0	
Def bdgt[a]	R	110bn	e125bn	
	US$	29.54bn	e33.33bn	
US$1=R		3.75	3.75	

[a] Defence and security budget

Population   27,601,038

Ethnic groups: Nationals 73% of which Bedouin up to 10%, Shi'a 6%, Expatriates 27% of which Asians 20%, Arabs 6%, Africans 1%, Europeans <1%

Age	0–14	15–19	20–24	25–29	30–64	65 plus
Male	19%	5%	6%	6%	17%	1%
Female	19%	5%	4%	4%	12%	1%

Capabilities

ACTIVE 223,500 (Army 75,000 Navy 15,500 Air 20,000 Air Defence 4,000 Industrial Security Force 9,000 National Guard 100,000) Paramilitary 15,500

ORGANISATIONS BY SERVICE

Army 75,000
FORCES BY ROLE
Armd   3 bde (*each*: 3 tk bn ,1 mech bn, 1 fd arty bn, 1 recce bn, 1 AD bn, 1 AT bn)
Mech   5 bde (*each*: 1 tk bn, 3 mech bn, 1 fd arty bn, 1 AD bn, 1 spt bn,)
AB   1 bde (2 AB bn, 3 SF coy)
Arty   1 bde (5 Fd Arty bn, 2 (SP) MRL bn, 1 (SP) Msl bn)
Avn   1 comd (1 Atk Hel bde, 1 Hel bde)
Royal Guard 1 regt (3 lt inf bn)

EQUIPMENT BY TYPE
MBT 910: 115 M1-A2 *Abrams*; 200 in store; 145 AMX-30 in store; 450 M-60A3
RECCE 430: 300 AML-60/AML-90; LAV-AG 130
AIFV 780: 380 AMX-10P; 400 M-2 *Bradley* each with 2 TOW msl, 1 30mm gun
APC 2,240
    APC (T) 1,650 M-113A1/M-113A2/M-113A3 (incl variants)
    APC (W) 590: ε40 AF-40-8-1 *Al-Fahd*; 150 M-3 *Panhard*; 400 *Piranha II*
ARTY 868
    SP 155mm 170: 60 AU-F-1; 110 M-109A1B/M-109A2
    TOWED 238: **105mm** 100 M-101/M-102 in store; **155mm** 130: 40 FH-70 in store; 50 M-114; 40 M-198 in store; **203mm** 8 M-115 in store

MRL 60 ASTROS II
MOR 400:
  SP 220: **81mm** 70; **107mm**150 M-30
  TOWED 180: **81mm/107mm** M-30 70; **120mm** 110 Brandt
AT • MSL 2,040+
  SP 290: 90 AMX-10P HOT; 200 VCC-1 TOW/TOW-2A
  MANPATS 1,750+ : 1,000 M47 *Dragon*; 750 TOW/TOW-2A; HOT
  RCL 450: **84mm** 300 *Carl Gustav*; **106mm** 50 M-40A1; **90mm** 100 M-67
  RL 112mm ε200 APILAS
HELICOPTERS
  ATK 12 AH-64 *Apache*
  SPT 27: 12 S-70A-1 *Desert Hawk*; 15 Bell 406 CS *Combat Scout*
  UTL 28: 6 AS-365N *Dauphin 2* (medevac); 22 UH-60A *Black Hawk* (4 medevac)
AD • SAM 1,000+
  SP *Crotale*
  MANPAD 1,000: 500 FIM-43 *Redeye*; 500 FIM-92A *Stinger*
RADAR • LAND AN/TPQ-36 *Firefinder*/AN/TPQ-37 *Firefinder* (arty, mor)
MSL • TACTICAL • SSM 10+ CSS-2 (40 msl)

Navy 15,500

FORCES BY ROLE

Navy 1 HQ (Eastern Fleet) located at Jubail; 1 HQ (Western Fleet) located at Jeddah; 1 HQ (Naval Forces) located at Riyadh

EQUIPMENT BY TYPE
PRINCIPAL SURFACE COMBATANTS 11
  FRIGATES • FFG 7:
    3 *Al Riyadh* eq with 1 octuple (8 eff.) with MM-40 *Exocet* block II SSM, 2 x 8 cell VLS each eq with *Aster* 15 SAM, 1 x 76mm gun, 4 x 533mm TT each eq with F17P HWT each with 1 hel landing platform (plus hangar for med-sized hel)
    4 *Madina* French F-2000 each with 2 quad (8 eff.) each with Mk 2 Otomat SSM, 1 octuple (8 eff.) with 26 *Crotale* SAM, 4 x1 533mm ASTT each with F17P HWT, 1 100mm gun, (capacity 1 AS-365F *Dauphin 2* utl hel)
  CORVETTES • FSG 4 *Badr* (US *Tacoma*) each with 2 Mk 140 *Harpoon* quad (8 eff.) each with RGM-84C *Harpoon* tactical SSM, 2 triple ASTT (6 eff.) each with Mk 46 LWT, 1 76mm gun
PATROL AND COASTAL COMBATANTS 65
  PFM 9 *Al Siddiq* (US 58m) each with 2 Mk 140 twin each with RGM-84C *Harpoon* tactical SSM, 1 76mm gun
  PCI 17 (US *Halter Marine*, under 100 tonnes)
  PBI 39
MINE WARFARE • MINE COUNTERMEASURES 7
  MCC 4 *Addriyah* (US MSC-322)
  MHO 3 *Al Jawf* (UK *Sandown*)
AMPHIBIOUS 8
  LCU 4 (capacity 120 troops);
  LCM 4 (capacity 80 troops)

LOGISTICS AND SUPPORT 5
  AORH 2 *Boraida* (mod Fr *Durance*) (capacity either 2 AS-365F *Dauphin 2* utl hel or 1 AS-332C *Super Puma* spt hel)
  RY 3
FACILITIES
Bases   HQ (Eastern Fleet) located at Jubail, (HQ Eastern Fleet) Jizan, (HQ Western Fleet) Jeddah, (HQ Naval Forces) Riyadh, Dammam, Al Wajh, Ras al Mishab, Ras al Ghar

Naval Aviation
HELICOPTERS
  ASLT 15 AS-565* each with AS-15TT tactical ASM
  SPT 25: 12 AS-532B *Super Puma*/AS-332F *Super Puma* each with AM-39 *Exocet* tactical ASM; 13 Bell 406 CS *Combat Scout*
  UTL 6 AS-365N *Dauphin 2*

Marines 3,000
FORCES BY ROLE
Inf 1 regt (2 Inf bn)
EQUIPMENT BY TYPE
APC (W) 140 BMP-600P

Air Force 20,000
FORCES BY ROLE

Ftr   1 sqn with 15 *Tornado* ADV; 1 sqn with 27 F-15S *Eagle*; 4 sqn with 66 F-15C; 18 F-15D *Eagle*

FGA   3 sqn with 85 *Tornado* IDS (incl 10 IDS recce); 1 sqn with 22 F-5B *Freedom Fighter*/F-5F *Tiger II*/RF-5E *Tigereye*; 2 sqn with 43 F-15S *Eagle*

AEW   1 sqn with 5 E-3A *Sentry*

Tpt   3 sqn with 7 C-130E *Hercules*; 29 C-130H *Hercules*; 2 C-130H-30 *Hercules*; 4 CN-235; 3 L-100-30HS (hospital ac)

Tkr   sqn with 8 KC-130H *Hercules* (tkr/tpt); 7 KE-3A

OCU   2 sqn with 14 F-5B *Freedom Fighter**

Trg   3 sqn with 25 *Hawk* MK65 (incl aerobatic team); 18 *Hawk* MK65A; 1 sqn with 1 *Jetstream* MK31; sqn with 20 MFI-17 *Mushshak*; 1 sqn with 13 Cessna 172; 2 sqn with 45 PC-9

Hel   2 sqn with 10 AS-532 *Cougar* (CSAR); 22 AB-205 (Bell 205); 13 AB-206A (Bell 206A) *JetRanger*; 17 AB-212 (Bell 212); 16 AB-412 (Bell 412) *Twin Huey* (SAR)

EQUIPMENT BY TYPE
AIRCRAFT 278 combat capable
  FTR 121: 66 F-15C *Eagle*; 18 F-15D *Eagle*; 15 *Tornado* ADV; 22 F-5B/F-5F *Tiger II*/RF-5E *Tigereye**
  STRIKE/FGA 155: 70 F-15S *Eagle*; 85 *Tornado* IDS (incl 10 IDS recce)
  AEW 5 E-3A *Sentry*
  TKR 15: 8 KC-130H *Hercules* (tkr/tpt); 7 KE-3A
  TPT 45: 7 C-130E *Hercules*; 29 C-130H; 2 C-130H-30 *Hercules*; 4 CN-235; 3 L-100-30HS (hospital ac)
  UTL 13 Cessna 172
  TRG 123: 25 *Hawk* MK65 (incl aerobatic team); 18 *Hawk* MK65A; 14 F-5B; 1 *Jetstream* MK31; 20 MFI-17 *Mushshak*; 45 PC-9

HELICOPTERS
UTL 78: 22 AB-205 (Bell 205); 17 AB-212 (Bell 212); 16 AB-412 (Bell 412) *Twin Huey* (SAR); 10 AS-532 *Cougar* (CSAR); 13 AB-206A (Bell 206A) *JetRanger*
MSL
ASM AGM-65 *Maverick*; *Sea Eagle*
ARM ALARM
AAM AIM-7 *Sparrow*; AIM-7M *Sparrow*/AIM-9J *Sidewinder*/AIM-9L *Sidewinder*/AIM-9P *Sidewinder*; *Sky Flash*; AIM-120 AMRAAM

Royal Flt
AIRCRAFT • TPT 16: 1 B-737-200; 2 B-747SP; 4 BAe-125-800; 1 Cessna 310; 2 Gulfstream III, 2 *Learjet* 35; 4 VC-130H
HELICOPTERS
SPT 1 S-70 *Black Hawk*
UTL 3+: AB-212 (Bell 212); 3 AS-61

Air Defence Forces 4,000
FORCES BY ROLE
SAM 16 bty eqpt. with total of 96 PAC-2; 17 bty eqpt. with total of 141 *Shahine*; with 50 AMX-30SA; 16 bty eqpt. with total of 128 MIM-23B *I-HAWK*; 73 units (static defence) eqpt. with total of 68 *Crotale / Shahine*

EQUIPMENT BY TYPE
AD • SAM 1,873
SP 649: 40 *Crotale*; 400 FIM-92A *Avenger*; 141 *Shahine*; 68 *Crotale/Shahine*
TOWED 224: 128 I-HAWK MIM-23B; 96 PAC-2
MANPAD 500 FIM-43 *Redeye*
NAVAL 500 *Mistral*
GUNS 1,220
SP 942: **20mm** 92 M-163 *Vulcan*; **30mm** 850 AMX-30SA;
TOWED 278: **35mm** 128 GDF *Oerlikon*; **40mm** 150 L/70 in store
RADARS • AD RADAR 80: 17 AN/FPS-117; 28 AN/TPS-43; AN/TPS-59; 35 AN/TPS-63; AN/TPS-70

Industrial Security Force 9,000 (to be 32,000)
Newly formed force to protect oil and important installations. Expected to increase by 8,000 per year. The force is part of a new security system that will incorporate surveillance and crisis management. Though the force is trained by Saudi Arabia, Lockheed Martin will contribute considerably with technical support.

National Guard 75,000 active; 25,000 (tribal levies) (total 100,000)
FORCES BY ROLE
Cav   1 (ceremonial) sqn
Mech Inf 3 bde (*each:* 4 army bn (all arms))
Inf   5 bde (*each:* 1 Arty bn, 1 Supply bn, 3 (combined arms) bn)

EQUIPMENT BY TYPE
RECCE 450 LAV-25 *Coyote*
AIFV 1,117 IFV-25

APC • APC (W) 1,820: 720 *Piranha II*; 290 V-150 *Commando*; 810 in store
ARTY • TOWED 77: **105mm** 50 M-102; **155mm** 27 M-198
   MOR 81mm
AT • MSL • MANPATS 116+: 116 TOW-2A (2000 msl); M47 *Dragon*
RCL • 106mm M-40A1
AD • GUNS • TOWED 160: **20mm** 30 M-167 *Vulcan*; **90mm** 130 (M-2)

Paramilitary 15,500+ active

Border Guard 10,500
FORCES BY ROLE
Subordinate to Ministry of Interior. HQ in Riyadh. 9 sub-ordinate regional commands
Mobile Defence some (long-range patrol/spt) units

MP	some units
Border Def	2 (patrol) units
Def	12 (infrastructure) units; 18 (harbour) units
Coastal Def	some units

EQUIPMENT BY TYPE
HEL 6 attack helicopters
ASW/ASUW 6 AS-332F *Super Puma* eqpt. with total of 12 AM-39 *Exocet* ASM tactical
SPT 6 AS-332B *Super Puma*

Coast Guard 4,500
EQUIPMENT BY TYPE
PATROL AND COASTAL COMBATANTS ε 551
PFI 4 *Al Jouf*
PBF 2 *Seaguard*
PBI ε500 less than 100 tonnes; 39 *Simonneau 51Ttype*
PB 6 *StanPatrol2606*
AMPHIBIOUS • CRAFT 13: 8 UCAC; 5 LCAC
LOGISTICS AND SUPPORT 4: 1 Trg; 3 AO (small)
FACILITIES
Base   Located at Azizam

General Civil Defence Administration Units
HELICOPTERS • SPT 10 Boeing Vertol 107

Special Security Force 500
APC (W): UR-416

FOREIGN FORCES
United Kingdom Army 20; Navy 10; Air Force 60
United States USCENTCOM: Army 153; Navy 23; Air Force 68; Marine Corps 30

Syria Syr

Syrian Pound S£		2006	2007	2008
GDP	S£	1.78tr	2.05tr	
	US$	34.3bn	40.2bn	
per capita	US$	1,815	2,081	
Growth	%	4.4	3.9	
Inflation	%	10.0	7.0	
Def bdgt	S£	90.7bn	74.9bn	
	US$	1.73bn	1.46bn	
US$1=S£		52.2	51.1	

ᵃ Excluding extra budgetory funding

Population 19,314,747

Age	0–14	15–19	20–24	25–29	30–64	65 plus
Male	19%	6%	5%	4%	14%	2%
Female	18%	6%	5%	4%	14%	2%

Capabilities

ACTIVE 292,600 (Army 215,000 Navy 7,600 Air 30,000 Air Defence 40,000) **Paramilitary 108,000**

RESERVE 314,000 (Army 280,000 Navy 4,000 Air 10,000 Air Defence 20,000)

Terms of service conscription, 30 months

ORGANISATIONS BY SERVICE

Army 215,000 (incl conscripts)

FORCES BY ROLE
3 Corps HQ

Armd	7 div (*each:* 2 armd; 1 mech; 1 arty bde)
Tk	1 indep regt
Mech	3 div (under strength) (*each:* 1 armd, 2 mech, 1 arty bde)
Inf	4 indep bde
SF	1 div (10 SF gp)
Arty	2 indep bde
AT	2 indep bde
SSM	1 (Coastal Def) bde with SS-C-1B *Sepal* and SS-C-3 *Styx*; 1 bde (3 SSM bn with FROG-7); 1 bde (3 SSM bn with SS-21); 1 bde (3 SSM bn with *Scud*-B/-C)
Border Guard	1 indep bde
Republican Guard	1 div (2 armd, 1 mech, 1 arty bde)

Reserves

Armd	1 div HQ; 4 bde; 2 regt
Inf	31 regt
Arty	3 regt

EQUIPMENT BY TYPE
MBT 4,950: 1,500–1,700 T-72 T-72M; 1,000 T-62K/T-62M; 2,250 T-55/T-55MV (some in store)

RECCE 590 BRDM-2
AIFV up to 2,450 BMP-1/BMP-2/BMP-3
APC (W) 1,500: 500 BTR-152; 1000 BTR-50/BTR-60/BTR-70
ARTY up to 3,440+
  SP 500+: **122mm** 450+: 400 2S1 *Carnation* (*Gvosdik*); 50+ D-30 (mounted on T34/85 chassis); **152mm** 50 2S3 (*Akatsiya*)
  TOWED 2030: **122mm** 1150: 500 D-30; 150 (M-30) M1938; 500 in store (no given designation); **130mm** 700-800 M-46; **152mm** 70 D-20/ML-20 M1937; **180mm** 10 S23
  MRL up to 500: **107mm** up to 200 Type-63; **122mm** up to 300 BM-21 (*Grad*)
  MOR 410+: **82mm**; **120mm** circa 400 M-1943; **160mm** M-160 (hundreds); **240mm** up to 10 M-240
AT • MSL 2,600
  SP 410 9P133 BRDM-2 *Sagger*
  MANPATS 2190+: 150 AT-4 9K111 *Spigot*; 40 AT-5 9K113 *Spandrel*; AT-7 9K115 *Saxhorn*; 800 AT-10 9K116 *Stabber*; 1,000 AT-14 9M133 *Kornet*; 200 *Milan*
  RL 73mm RPG-7 *Knout*; **105mm** RPG-29
AD • SAM 4,184+
  SP 84: 14 SA-8 *Gecko*; 20 SA-9 *Gaskin*; 20 SA-11 *Gadfly*; 30 SA-13 *Gopher*
  MANPAD 4,100+: 4,000+ SA-7 *Grail*/SA-18 *Grouse* (*Igla*); 100 SA-14 *Gremlin*
  GUNS 1,225+
  SP ZSU-23-4
  TOWED 23mm 600 ZU-23; **37mm** M-1939; **57mm** 600 S-60; **100mm** 25 KS-19
MSL • TACTICAL • SSM 94+: 18 *Scud*-B/*Scud*-C/*Scud*-D; 30 look-a-like (North Korea); 18 FROG-7; 18+ SS-21 *Tochka* (*Scarab*); 4 SS-C-1B *Sepal*; 6 SS-C-3 *Styx* (ε850 SSM msl total)

Navy 7,600

EQUIPMENT BY TYPE
PRINCIPAL SURFACE COMBATANTS • FRIGATES • FF
2 *Petya* III each with 1 triple 533mm ASTT (3 eff.) with SAET-60 HWT, 4 RBU 2500 *Smerch* 1 (64 eff.)†, 2 76mm twin gun
PATROL AND COASTAL COMBATANTS 18:
  PFM 10 *Osa* I/II each with 4 single each with 1 SS-N-2C *Styx* tactical SSM
  PFI 8 *Zhuk* less than 100 tonnes
MINE WARFARE • MINE COUNTERMEASURES 5:
  MSC 1 *Natya*
  MSI 3 *Yevgenya*
  MSO 1 T-43 (FSU)
AMPHIBIOUS • LS • LSM 3 *Polnochny* B (capacity 6 MBT; 180 troops)
LOGISTICS AND SUPPORT 3: 2 **AGOR**; 1 **TRG**
FACILITIES
Bases Located at Latakia, Tartus, Minet el-Baida

Naval Aviation

HELICOPTER 13 atk hel
ASW 13: 2 Ka-28 (Ka-27PL) *Helix A* (air force manpower); 11 Mi-14 *Haze*

Air Force 40,000 (incl 10,000 reserves); 60,000 Air Defence (incl 20,000 reserves) (total 100,000)

Flying hours   15 to 25 hrs/year on FGA/ftr; 70 hrs/year;
              50 hrs/year on MBB-223 *Flamingo* trg ac

FORCES BY ROLE

Ftr   4 sqn with 30 MiG-25 *Foxbat*; 4 sqn with 80 MiG-23
         MLD *Flogger*; 3 sqn with 68 MiG-29A *Fulcrum A*

FGA   2 sqn with 60 MiG-23BN *Flogger H*; 1 sqn with
         20 Su-24 *Fencer*; 5 sqn with 50 Su-22 (Su-17M-2)
         Fitter D;7 sqn with 159 MiG-21 *Fishbed*;

Recce   4 sqn with 40 MiG-21H *Fishbed*/MiG-21J *Fishbed**;
         8 MiG-25R *Foxbat**

Tpt   sqn with 1 An-24 *Coke*; 6 An-26 *Curl*;
         2 *Falcon* 20; 1 *Falcon* 900; 4 Il-76 *Candid*; 6 Yak-40
         Codling; 100 Mi-17 (Mi-8MT) *Hip H*/Mi-8 *Hip*;
         20 PZL Mi-2 *Hoplite*

Atk hel sqn with 36 Mi-25 *Hind D*; 35 SA-342L *Gazelle*

Trg   2 PA-31 *Navajo*; 70 L-39 *Albatros*; 35 MBB-223
         Flamingo (basic); 6 MFI-17 *Mushshak*; 20 MiG-21U
         *Mongol A**; 6 MiG-23UM*; 2 MiG-25U *Foxbat**

EQUIPMENT BY TYPE

AIRCRAFT   583 combat capable
   FTR 178: 68 MiG-29A *Fulcrum*; 30 MiG-25 *Foxbat*; 80
   MiG-23MLD *Flogger*
   FGA 289: 20 Su-24 *Fencer*; 60MiG-23BN *Flogger H*; 159
   MiG-21H; 50 Su-22 (Su-17M-2) *Fitter D*
   RECCE 48: 8 MiG-25R *Foxbat**; 40 MiG-21 H/J*
   TPT 22: 1 An-24 *Coke*; 6 An-26 *Curl*; 2 *Falcon* 20; 1 *Falcon*
   900; 4 Il-76 *Candid*; 2 PA-31 *Navajo*; 6 Yak-40 *Codling*
   TRG 139: 70 L-39 *Albatros* (40 armed*); 35 MBB-223
   Flamingo (basic); 6 MFI-17 *Mushshak*; 20 MiG-21U *Mongol
   A**; 6 MiG-23UM*; **2** MiG-25U *Foxbat* *
HELICOPTERS
   ATK 71: 36 Mi-25 *Hind D*; 35 SA-342L *Gazelle*
   SPT 120: 100 Mi-17 (Mi-8MT) *Hip H*/Mi-8 *Hip*; 20 PZL
   Mi-2 *Hoplite*
MSL
   ASM AS-7 *Kerry*; HOT
   AAM AA-10 *Alamo*; AA-2 *Atoll*; AA-6 *Acrid*; AA-7 *Apex*;
   AA-8 *Aphid*

Air Defence Command 60,000

FORCES BY ROLE

AD   2 div (*total*: 25 AD bde (*total*: 150 SAM bty eqpt. with
      total of 148 SA-3 *Goa*; 195 SA-6 *Gainful*; 320 SA-2
      Guideline, some ADA bty eqpt. with total of 4,000
      SA-7A *Grail*/SA-7B *Grail*))

SAM   2 regt (*each*: 2 SAM bn (*each*: 2 SAM bty eqpt.with
      total of 44 SA-5 *Gammon*))

EQUIPMENT BY TYPE

AD • SAM 4,707
   SP 195 SA-6 *Gainful*
   TOWED 468: 320 SA-2 *Guideline*; 148 SA-3 *Goa*
   STATIC/SHELTER 44 SA-5 *Gammon*
   MANPAD 4,000 SA-7A *Grail*/SA-7B *Grail*

Paramilitary ε108,000

Gendarmerie 8,000
Ministry of Interior

Workers' Militia ε100,000
People's Army (Ba'ath Party)

FOREIGN FORCES

All under UNTSO comd unless otherwise specified.
UNTSO overall mission figures for Israel, Syria, Lebanon
unless specified.

Argentina 5 obs
Australia 12 obs
Austria 6 obs; 372 UNDOF
Belgium 2 obs
Canada 8 obs; 2 UNDOF
Chile 3 obs
China, People's Republic of 4 obs
Denmark 11 obs
Estonia 2 obs
Finland 15 obs
France 2 obs
Ireland 14 obs
Italy 6 obs
India 191 UNDOF
Japan 30 UNDOF
Nepal 3 obs
Netherlands 11 obs
New Zealand 8 obs
Norway 12 obs
Poland 353 UNDOF
Russia 3 obs
Slovakia 2 obs; 95 UNDOF
Sweden 7 obs
Switzerland 7 obs
United States 3 obs

Tunisia Tn

Tunisian Dinar D		2006	2007	2008
GDP	D	41.1bn	44.0bn	
	US$	31.1bn	35.2bn	
per capita	US$	3,060	3,425	
Growth	%	4.4	3.9	
Inflation	%	10.0	7.9	
Def bdgt	D	574m	ε625m	
	US$	443m	500m	
FMA (US)	US$	8.4m	8.5m	2.1m
US$1=D		1.32	1.25	

Population   10,276,158

Age	0–14	15–19	20–24	25–29	30–64	65 plus
Male	13%	5%	5%	5%	19%	3%
Female	12%	5%	5%	5%	19%	3%

Capabilities

ACTIVE 35,800 (Army 27,000 Navy 4,800 Air 4,000)
Paramilitary 12,000
Terms of service 12 months selective

ORGANISATIONS BY SERVICE

Army 5,000; 22,000 conscript (total 27,000)

FORCES BY ROLE

Mech 3 bde (*each:* 1 armd regt, 2 mech inf regt, 1 arty regt, 1 AD regt)

SF 1 (Sahara) bde; 1 bde

Engr 1 regt

EQUIPMENT BY TYPE

MBT 84: 30 M-60A1; 54 M-60A3

LT TK 48 SK-105 *Kuerassier*

RECCE 60: 40 AML-90; 20 *Saladin*

APC 268

    APC (T) 140 M-113A1/M-113A2

    APC (W) 128: 18 EE-11 *Urutu*; 110 Fiat 6614

ARTY 276

    TOWED 115: **105mm** 48 M-101A1/M-101A2; **155mm** 67: 12 M-114A1; 55 M-198

    MOR 161: **81mm** 95; **107mm** 48 (some SP); **120mm** 18 Brandt

AT • MSL 590

    SP 35 M-901 ITV TOW

    MANPATS 555: 500 *Milan*; 55 TOW

    RL 89mm 600: 300 LRAC; 300 M-20

AD • SAM 86

    SP 26 M-48 *Chaparral*

    MANPAD 60 RBS-70

    GUNS 127

    SP 40mm 12 M-42

    TOWED 115: **20mm** 100 M-55; **37mm** 15 Type-55 (M-1939)/Type-65

RADAR • LAND RASIT (veh, arty)

Navy ε4,800

EQUIPMENT BY TYPE

PATROL AND COASTAL COMBATANTS 25

    PFM 12:

      3 *Bizerte* (Fr P-48) each with 8 SS 12M tactical SSM

      3 *La Galite* (Fr *Combattante* III) each with 2 Mk 140 *Harpoon* quad (8 eff.) each with MM-40 *Exocet* tactical SSM, 1 76mm gun

      6 *Albatros* (Type 143B) eq with 2 x 76mm gun, 2 twin launcher (4 eff.) for MM-38 *Exocet* SSM, 2 single 533mm TT

    PCC 3 *Utique* (mod PRC *Haizhui* II)

    PCI 10 (less than 100 tonnes)

LOGISTICS AND SUPPORT 6:

    AWT 1

    AGS 1

    ABU 3

    TRG 1 *Salambo* (US *Conrad*, survey)

FACILITIES

Bases Located at Bizerte, Sfax, Kelibia

Air Force 4,000

FORCES BY ROLE

FGA 1 sqn with 12 F-5E *Tiger II*/F-5F *Tiger II*

CCT 1 sqn with 3 MB-326K; 3 MB-326L

Tpt 1 sqn with 8 C-130B *Hercules*; 1 C-130E *Hercules*; 2 C-130H *Hercules*; 1 *Falcon* 20; 5 G-222; 3 L-410 *Turbolet*

Liaison 1 sqn with 2 S-208A

Tpt/utl hel 2 sqn with 6 AS-350B *Ecureuil*; 1 AS-365 *Dauphin* 2; 15 AB-205 (Bell 205); 6 SA-313; 3 SA-316 *Alouette III*; 10 UH-1H *Iroquois*; 2 UH-1N *Iroquois*; 1 sqn with 11 HH-3E

Trg 2 sqn with 12 L-59 *Albatros**; 4 MB-326B; 14 SF-260

EQUIPMENT BY TYPE

AIRCRAFT 27 combat capable

    FTR 12 F-5E *Tiger II*/F-5F *Tiger II*

    FGA 3 MB-326K

    TPT 20: 8 C-130B *Hercules*; 1 C-130E *Hercules*; 2 C-130H *Hercules*; 1 *Falcon* 20; 5G-222; 3 L-410 *Turbolet*

    UTL 2 S-208A

    TRG 33: 12 L-59 *Albatros**; 4 MB-326B; 3 MB-326L; 14 SF-260

HELICOPTERS

    SPT 6 AS-350B *Ecureuil*

    UTL 37: 15 AB-205 (Bell 205); 11 HH-3; 1 AS-365 *Dauphin* 2; 6 SA-313; 3 SA-316 *Alouette III*; 10 UH-1H *Iroquois*; 2 UH-1N *Iroquois*

    MSL • AAM AIM-9J *Sidewinder*

Paramilitary 12,000

National Guard 12,000

Ministry of Interior

PATROL AND COASTAL COMBATANTS 30

    PCC 6 *Kondor* I (ex-GDR)

    PCI 24: 5 *Bremse* (ex-GDR); 4 *Gabes*; 4 *Rodman*; 2 *Socomena*; All units less than 100 tonnes

HELICOPTERS • UTL 8 SA-318 *Alouette II*/SA-319 *Alouette III*

DEPLOYMENT

BURUNDI

UN • BINUB 1

CÔTE D'IVOIRE

UN • UNOCI 2; 5 obs

DEMOCRATIC REPUBLIC OF CONGO

UN • MONUC 462; 30 obs

ETHIOPIA/ERITREA

AU • OLMEE 1 obs

UN • UNMEE 3; 5 obs

United Arab Emirates UAE

Emirati Dirham D		2006	2007	2008
GDP	D	522bn	714bn	
	US$	142bn	195bn	
per capita	US$	54,648	73,622	
Growth	%	9.4	7.7	
Inflation	%	9.3	8.0	
Def bdgtª	D	34.8bn	ε37.0bn	
	US$	9.48bn	ε10.08bn	
US$1=D		3.67	3.67	

ª Excludes possible extra-budgetary procurement funding

Population   2,642,566

Ethnic groups: Nationals 24%; Expatriates 76% of which Indian 30%, Pakistani 20%; other Arab 12%; other Asian 10%; UK 2%; other European 1%

Age	0–14	15–19	20–24	25–29	30–64	65 plus
Male	13%	6%	5%	4%	29%	3%
Female	12%	5%	5%	3%	14%	1%

Capabilities

ACTIVE 51,000 (Army 44,000 Navy 2,500 Air 4,500)

The Union Defence Force and the armed forces of the UAE (Abu Dhabi, Dubai, Ras Al Khaimah, Fujairah, Ajman, Umm al-Qaywayn and Sharjah) were formally merged in 1976 and headquartered in Abu Dhabi. Dubai still maintains independent forces, as do other Emirates to a lesser degree.

ORGANISATIONS BY SERVICE

Army 44,000 (incl Dubai 15,000)

FORCES BY ROLE
GHQ Abu Dhabi

Armd	2 bde
Mech inf	3 bde
Inf	2 bde
Arty	1 bde (3 arty regt)
Royal Guard	1 bde

Dubai Independent Forces
Mech inf 2 bde

EQUIPMENT BY TYPE
MBT 471: 390 Leclerc; 36 OF-40 Mk2 (Lion); 45 AMX-30
LT TK 76 Scorpion
RECCE 113: 49 AML-90; 20 Ferret in store; 20 Saladin in store; 24 VBL
AIFV 430: 15 AMX-10P; 415 BMP-3
APC 880
 APC (T) 136 AAPC (incl 53 engr plus other variants)
 APC (W) 744: 90 BTR-3U Guardian; 120 EE-11 Urutu; 370 M-3 Panhard; 64 TPz-1 Fuchs; 80 VCR (incl variants); 20 VAB
ARV 46

ARTY 501+
 SP 155mm 181: 78 G-6; 85 M-109A3; 18 Mk F3
 TOWED 93: 105mm 73 ROF lt; 130mm 20 Type-59-I
 MRL 72+: 70mm 18 LAU-97; 122mm 48+: 48 Firos-25 (est 24 op); Type-90 (reported); 300mm 6 9A52 Smerch
 MOR 155: 81mm 134: 20 Brandt; 114 L16; 120mm 21 Brandt
AT • MSL 305+
 SP 20 HOT
 MANPATS 285+: 30 HOT; 230 Milan; 25 TOW; Vigilant in store
 RCL 262: 84mm 250 Carl Gustav; 106mm 12 M-40
AD • SAM • MANPAD 40+: 20+ Blowpipe; 20 Mistral
 GUNS 62
 SP 20mm 42 M3 VDAA
 TOWED 30mm 20 GCF-BM2
MSL • TACTICAL • SSM 6 Scud-B (up to 20 msl)

Navy ε2,500

EQUIPMENT BY TYPE
PRINCIPAL SURFACE COMBATANTS 4
 FRIGATES • FFG 2 Abu Dhabi †(NL Kortenaer) each with 2 Mk 141 Harpoon quad (8 eff.) (no weapons embarked) each with RGM-84A Harpoon tactical SSM, 1 Mk 29 Sea Sparrow octuple with 24 RIM-7F/M Sea Sparrow SAM, 2 Twin 324mm TT (4 eff.) each with A244/Mk 46, 1 76mm gun, each with 2 AS-565SA Panthe ASW/ASUW hel
 CORVETTES • FSG 2 Muray Jip (Ge Lurssen 62m) each with 1 SA-316 Alouette III utl hel, 2 quad (8 eff.) each with MM-40 Exocet tactical SSM
PATROL AND COASTAL COMBATANTS 14
 PFM 8:
  6 Ban Yas (Ge Lurssen TNC-45) each with 2 twin (4 eff.) each with MM-40 Exocet tactical SSM, 1 76mm gun
  2 Mubarraz (Ge Lurssen 45m) each with 2 twin (4 eff.) each with MM-40 Exocet tactical SSM, 1 76mm gun
 PCC 6 Ardhana (UK Vosper 33m)
MINE WARFARE • MINE COUNTERMEASURES • MHC 2 Al Murjan (Frankenthal Class Type 332)
AMPHIBIOUS • CRAFT 28
 LCP 16: 12 (capacity 40 troops); 4 (Fast Supply Vessel multi-purpose)
 LCU 5: 3 Al Feyi (capacity 56 troops); 2 (capacity 40 troops and additional vehicles)
 LCT 7
LOGISTICS AND SUPPORT 3: 1 YDT; 2 YTM
FACILITIES
Bases Located at Mina Sakr (Sharjah), Mina Rashid, Khor Fakkan, Mina Zayed (Dubai), Dalma, Abu Dhabi (Main base), Mina Khalid, Mina Jabal (Ras-al-Khaimah)

Naval Aviation
AIRCRAFT • TPT 2 Learjet 35A
HELICOPTERS
 ASW/ASUW 14: 7 AS-332F Super Puma (5 in ASUW role); 7 AS-565 Panther
 UTL 4 SA-316 Alouette III

Air Force 4,500

Incl Police Air Wing
Flying hours   110 hrs/year

FORCES BY ROLE

FGA   3 sqn with 55 F-16E *Falcon* Block 60; 25 F-16F *Falcon* Block 60 (13 to remain in US for trg); 3 sqn with 44 *Mirage* 2000-9DAD/2000-9RAD*e*; 1 sqn with 18 *Mirage* M-2000DAD; 1 sqn with 17 *Hawk* MK63A/*Hawk* MK63C/*Hawk* MK63; 1 sqn with 13 *Hawk* MK102

Recce   1 sqn with 7 M-2000 RAD *Mirage**

SAR   1 sqn with 3 A-109K2; 6 AB-139

Tpt   3 sqn with 1 An-124 *Condor*; 2 Beech 350 *Super King Air*; 4 C-130H *Hercules*; 2 C-130H-30 *Hercules*; 7 CASA 235M-100; 1 DHC-6-300 *Twin Otter*; 4 IL-76 *Candid* on lease; 2 L-100-30

OCU   5 *Hawk* MK61*

Trg   sqn eqpt with 12 Grob 115TA; 30 PC-7 *Turbo Trainer*

Atk hel 2 sqn eqpt with total of 30 AH-64A *Apache*; AS-550C3 *Fennec*; 10 SA-342K *Gazelle* (eqpt with HOT) ASM

Tpt hel 1 sqn eqpt with 15 IAR-330 SOCAT *Puma*/SA-330 *Puma*; 12 CH-47C *Chinook* (SF); 2 AB-139 (VIP); 4 AS-365F *Dauphin 2* (VIP); 9 Bell 206 *JetRanger* trg; 3 Bell 214; 1 Bell 407; 9 Bell 412 *Twin Huey*

EQUIPMENT BY TYPE

AIRCRAFT 184 combat capable

FGA 155: 55 F-16E Block 60 *Desert Eagle*; 25 F-16F Block 60 (13 to remain in US for Trg); 18 *Mirage* 2000-9DAD; 44 *Mirage* 2000-9RAD; 13 *Hawk* MK102

RECCE 7 *Mirage* 2000 RAD*

TPT 23: 1 An-124 *Condor*; 2 Beech 350 *Super King Air*; 4 C-130H; 2 C-130H-30 *Hercules*; 7 CASA 235M-100; 1 DHC-6-300 *Twin Otter*; 4 Il-76 *Candid* on lease; 2 L-100-30

TRG 64: 5 *Hawk* MK61*; 17 *Hawk* MK63 A/*Hawk* MK63C*; 12 Grob 115TA; 30 PC-7 *Turbo Trainer*

HELICOPTERS

ATK 40+: 30 AH-64A *Apache*; AS-550C3 *Fennec*; 10 SA-342K *Gazelle*

SPT 27: 12 CH-47C *Chinook* (SF); 15 IAR-330 SOCAT *Puma* aslt/SA-330 *Puma* spt

UTL 40: 3 A-109K2; 8 AB-139 (incl 2 VIP); 4 AS-365F *Dauphin 2* (VIP); 9 Bell 206 *JetRanger* trg; 3 Bell 214; 1 Bell 407; 9 Bell 412 *Twin Huey*

MSL

ASM AGM-114 *Hellfire*; AS-15 *Kent*; *Black Shaheen*; *Hydra-70*; PGM-1 *Hakeem 1*; PGM-2 *Hakeem 2*; HOT

AAM AIM-9L *Sidewinder*

MICA R-550 *Magic*; AIM-120 AMPAAM

Air Defence

FORCES BY ROLE

AD   2 bde (*each*: 3 bn eqpt. with I-*HAWK* MIM-23B)

SAM   3 short-range bn eqpt with *Crotale*; *Mistral*; *Rapier*; RB-70; *Javelin*; SA-18 *Grouse (Igla)*

EQUIPMENT BY TYPE

AD • SAM

SP *Crotale*; RB-70

TOWED I-*HAWK* MIM-23B; *Rapier*

MANPAD *Javelin*; SA-18 *Grouse (Igla)*

NAVAL *Mistral*

Paramilitary • Coast Guard

Ministry of Interior

PATROL AND COASTAL COMBATANTS 47

PCC 2 *Protector*

PBF 9

PB 21

PBI 15

FOREIGN FORCES

United States USCENTCOM: Army 3; Navy 7; Air Force 58; Marine Corps 19

Yemen, Republic of Ye

Yemeni Rial R		2006	2007	2008
GDP	R	3.89tr	4.23tr	
	US$	19.8bn	21.4bn	
per capita	US$	921	962	
Growth	%	4.0	3.6	
Inflation	%	18.2	12.5	
Def bdgt	R	162bn	179bn	
	US$	823m	908m	
FMA (US)	US$	8.4m	8.5m	4.6m
US$1=R		197	198	

Population   22,211,743

Ethnic groups: Majority Arab, some African and South Asian

Age	0–14	15–19	20–24	25–29	30–64	65 plus
Male	24%	6%	5%	4%	11%	1%
Female	23%	6%	5%	4%	11%	1%

Capabilities

ACTIVE 66,700 (Army 60,000 Navy 1,700 Air Force 3,000, Air Defence 2,000) **Paramilitary 71,200**

Terms of service conscription, 2 years

ORGANISATIONS BY SERVICE

Army 60,000 (incl conscripts)

FORCES BY ROLE

Armd	8 bde
Mech	6 bde
Inf	16 bde
SF	1 bde
Cdo/AB	2 bde
Arty	3 bde
SSM	1 bde
Gd/Central Guard	1 force
AD	2 bn

EQUIPMENT BY TYPE

MBT 790: 50 M-60A1; 60 T-72; 200 T-62; 450 T-54/T-55; 30 T-34

RECCE 145: 80 AML-90; 15 LAV; 50 BRDM-2

AIFV 200: 100 BMP-1; 100 BMP-2

APC 710
  APC (T) 60 M-113A
  APC (W) 650: 60 BTR-40; 100 BTR-60; 20 BTR-152; 470
  BTR-40/BTR-60/BTR-152 in store
ARTY 1,167
  SP 122mm 25 2S1 *Carnation*
  TOWED 310: **105mm** 25 M-101A1; **122mm** 200: 130 D-30;
  30 M-1931/37; 40 M-30 *M-1938*; **130mm** 60 M-46; **152mm**
  10 D-20; **155mm** 15 M-114
  COASTAL 130mm 36 SM-4-1
  MRL 294: **122mm** 280 BM-21 (150 op); **140mm** 14 BM-14
  MOR 502: **81mm** 200; **82mm** 90 M-43; **107mm** 12; **120mm**
  100; **160mm** ε100
AT • MSL • MANPATS 71: 35 AT-3 9K11 *Sagger*; 24 M47
Dragon; 12 TOW
  RCL 75mm M-20; **82mm** B-10; **107mm** B-11
  RL 66mm M-72 *LAW*; **73mm** RPG-7 *Knout*
  GUNS 50+
    SP 100mm 30 SU-100
    TOWED 20+: **85mm** D-44; **100mm** 20 M-1944
AD • SAM ε800
  SP SA-9 *Gaskin*; SA-13 *Gopher*
  MANPAD SA-7 *Grail*; SA-14 *Gremlin*
  GUNS 530
    SP 70: **20mm** 20 M-163 *Vulcan*; **23mm** 50 ZSU-23-4
    TOWED 460: **20mm** 50 M-167 *Vulcan*; **23mm** 100 ZU-
    23-2; **37mm** 150 M-1939; **57mm** 120 S-60; **85mm** 40
    M-1939 KS-12
MSL • TACTICAL • SSM 28: 12 FROG-7; 10 SS-21 *Scarab*
(Tochka); 6 *Scud*-B (ε33 msl)

Navy 1,700

EQUIPMENT BY TYPE
PATROL AND COASTAL COMBATANTS 20
  PFM 4:
    3 *Huangfen*† each with 4 single with 3 YJ-1 (CSS-N-4)
    Sardine tactical SSM
    1 *Tarantul*† with 2 twin (4 eff.) with 4 SS-N-2C *Styx*
    tactical SSM
  PB 10 *Austal*
  PBF 6
MINE WARFARE • MINE COUNTERMEASURES 6
  MHC 5 *Yevgeny* † (FSU)
  MSO 1 *Natya* (FSU)
AMPHIBIOUS
  LS • LSM 1 NS-722 (capacity 5 MBT; 110 troops)
  CRAFT 5:
    LCU 3 *Deba*
    LCM 2 *Ondatra* (FSU)

FACILITIES

Bases   Located at Aden, Hodeida
Minor   These have naval spt eqpt, located at Socotra, Al
Bases   Mukalla, Perim Island

Air Force 3,000

FORCES BY ROLE
Ftr   3 sqn with 10 F-5E *Tiger II*; 16 MiG-29SMT *Fulcrum*;
      2 MiG-29UBT *Fulcrum*; 15 MiG-21 *Fishbed*;

FGA   1 sqn with 30 Su-20 (Su-17M) *Fitter C*/Su-22 (Su-17M-
      2) *Fitter D*
Tpt   1 sqn with 2 An-12 *Cub*; 6 An-26 *Curl*; 3 C-130H
      Hercules; 4 Il-14 *Crate*; 3 Il-76 *Candid*
Trg   1 trg school with 2 F-5B *Freedom Fighter*†*; 12 L-39C;
      4 MiG-21U *Mongol A**; 14 Yak-11 *Moose*; 12 Z-242
Hel   1 sqn with 8 Mi-35 *Hind* (attack); 1 AB-47 (Bell 47);
      9 Mi-8 *Hip*; 2 Bell 212

EQUIPMENT BY TYPE
AIRCRAFT 79 combat capable
  FTR 43: 16 MiG-29SMT *Fulcrum*; 2 -MiG-29UBT; 10 F-5E
  Tiger II; 15 MiG-21 *Fishbed*
  FGA 30 Su-20 (Su-17M) *Fitter C* Su-17 FGA/Su-22 (Su-
  17M-2) *Fitter D*
  TPT 18: 2 An-12 *Cub*; 6 An-26 *Curl*; 3 C-130H *Hercules*; 4
  Il-14 *Crate* 4; 3 Il-76 *Candid*
  TRG 44: 12 L-39C; 4 MiG-21U *Mongol A**; 2 F-5B *Freedom
  Fighter*†*; 14 Yak-11 *Moose*; 12 Z-242
HELICOPTERS
  ATK 8 Mi-35 *Hind*
  SPT 10: 1 AB-47 (Bell 47); 9 Mi-8 *Hip*
  UTL 2 Bell 212

Air Defence 2,000

AD • SAM:
  SP SA-6 *Gainful*; SA-9 *Gaskin*; SA-13 *Gopher*
  TOWED SA-2 *Guideline*; SA-3 *Goa*
  MANPAD SA-7 *Grail*; SA-14 *Gremlin*
MSL • AAM AA-2 *Atoll*; AIM-9 *Sidewinder*

Paramilitary 71,200+

Ministry of the Interior Forces 50,000

Tribal Levies 20,000+

Yemeni Coast Guard Authority ε1,200
PATROL AND COASTAL COMBATANTS 21
  PCI 5 *Interceptor* (French)
  PB 8: 4 *Defender* (US); 4 *Archangel* (US)
  PBI 8

NON-STATE ARMED GROUPS

see Part II

DEPLOYMENT

COTE D'IVOIRE
UN • UNOCI 6 obs

DEMOCRATIC REPUBLIC OF CONGO
UN • MONUC 5 obs

GEORGIA
UN • UNOMIG 1 obs

NEPAL
UN • UNMIN 15 obs

SUDAN
UN • UNMIS 4; 16 obs

WESTERN SAHARA
UN • MINURSO 6 obs

Table 22 **Selected Arms Orders and Deliveries, Middle East and North Africa**

	Country Supplier	Classification	Designation	Quantity	Order date	Original Delivery date	Comment
Algeria (Ag)	RF	FTR	MiG-29 SMT	36	2006	2010	USD3.5bn total cost of order including the order for 28 Su-30 MKA and 16 Yak-130. Option for the purchase of an additional 36 MiG-29 SMT
	RF	FGA	Su-30 MKA	28	2006	2010	USD3.5bn total cost of order including the order for 36 MiG-29 SMT and 16 Yak-130
	RF	Trg	Yak-130	16	2006	2010	USD3.5bn total cost of order including the order for 28 Su-30 MKA and 36 MiG-29 SMT
	RF	AD	S-300PMU-2	8 bn	2006	–	USD1bn
	RF	AD	*Tunguska*-M1 ADGMS	24	2006	–	USD500m. Option of additional 30 systems
	RF	MBT	T-90S	300	2006	–	USD1bn
	RF	ATGW	*Kornet*- E	–	2006	–	USD50m
	RF	ATGW	*Metis*- M1	–	2006	–	USD50m
	RF	MBT	T-72	250	2006	–	Upgrade. USD200m
	RF	IFV	BMP-2	400	2006	–	Upgrade. USD200m
Bahrain (Brn)	Tu	APC	M113A2	–	2007	–	Refit
Egypt (Et)	PRC	Trg	K-8E *Karakorum*	80	1999	2001	78 ac now in service. Deliveries continuing
	RF	SAM	SA-3A *Goa*	50	1999	–	Upgrade to *Pechora*-2 aka SA-3A *Goa* continues
	US	MBT	M1-A1 *Abrams*	125	2004	2005–8	USD277m
	US	ARV	M88A2 *Hercules*	21	2004	–	Deliveries continuing.
	US	SAM	RAM Mk49 GMLS	3	2005	2009	USD24.75m. Upgrade for Fast Missile Craft
	US	ELINT	CS-3000	1	2005	2008	To be delivered in late 2007 / early 2008
	US	MBT	M1-A1 *Abrams*	125	2007		
Iran (Ir)	RF	FGA	Su-24	–	2005	–	Upgrade. Part of USD1.5bn arms deal
	RF	Ftr	MiG-29	–	2005	–	Upgrade. Part of USD1.5bn arms deal
	RF	MBT	T-72	–	2005	–	Upgrade. Part of USD1.5bn arms deal
	RF	AD	96K6 *Pantsyr*-S1E	10	2007	2008	Reportedly obtained via Syria. 10 of 50 *Pantsyr*-S1E ordered by Syr from RF
Iraq (Irq)	PL	Hel	Mi-17V5	10	2005	2008	–
	PL	APC	Dzik3	600	2005	2008	Deliveries to be completed by mid-2008
	PL	APC	BTR-80	115	2005	2006	USD30m
	CH	APC	Spz 63/89	180	2005	2006	Original order was from UAE (blocked by Swiss Parliament) Given by UAE to Iraq
	US	Tpt / ISR	*King Air* 350 ER	6	2007	2007	USD132m. 1 ac for light tpt, 5 for ISR. Final delivery 2008. The deal is part of a potential USD900m contract including 24 *King Air* 350 ER for ISR and 24 *King Air* 350 Er or PZl M-18 *Skytruck* ac for light tpt
Israel (Il)	dom	MBT	*Merkava* Mk IV	200–240	1991	2002	Estimated 50-60 tanks per year over a four year period. First operational unit reported 2004. Continuing
	US	BMD	*Nautilus*	–	1992	–	Joint development with US
	US	ECM	Beech-200CT/T *Super King Air*	4	2000	–	Still on order
	US	FGA	F-16I *Sufa*	102	2001	2006	Deliveries continuing

Table 22 **Selected Arms Orders and Deliveries, Middle East and North Africa**

	Country Supplier	Classification	Designation	Quantity	Order date	Original Delivery date	Comment
	US	Hel	AH-64D	18	2001	2005	Initial contract (USD640m) for 12 AH-64D includes upgrade of 3 Israeli AH-64A to D. Further contract in December 2004 for the purchase of 6 additional units (USD100m). 14 hel now in service. Deliveries continue
	US	AEW	Gulfstream G500	5	2001	–	USD473m. 2 ac being delivered as for June 2007, 2 ac to be transferred to Sgp
	dom	PFI	*Super Dvora* MKIII	4	2005	2006–7	Phase B award after initial order and delivery of first 6 vessels. On order
	dom	PFI	*Shaldag*	3	2005	2006–7	Phase B award after initial order and delivery of first 2 vessels. On order
	US	ASM	JDAM	5000	2004	–	Deliveries continuing
	US	ASM	*Paveway* III	100	2005	–	USD30m. GBU-28B laser guided for F-15I
	dom	C2	Command and Control	–	2005	2008	USD900m. Digital Army Programme (DAP) 2 Divs equiped by 2008
	dom	PFB	*Tzir'a*	4	2005	–	Modified version, still on order
	Ge	SSK	*Dolphine*	2	2006	–	Estimated cost of EUR1bn (USD1.21bn). Completion of first boat planned for 2012
	US	ASM	RGM-84L Block II *Harpoon*	30	2007	–	Part of a USD163m including also 500 AIM-9M *Sidewinder* AAM
	US	AAM	AIM-9M *Sidewinder*	500	2007	–	Part of a USD163m including also 30 RGM-84L Block II *Harpoon* ASM
	dom	AIFV	*Namer*	45	2007	2008	USD67m. Planning to acquire a total of 250 vehicles
	dom	AIFV	*Namer*	45	2007	2008	All-round passive armour upgrade. ILS20m (USD4.8m)
	dom	LGB	*Lizard* 3	–	2007	–	USD15m. Several hundred Lizard 3 kits
Jordan (HKJ)	US	Hel	UH-60L *Black Hawk*	8	2003	2006	3 hel in service. Deliveries continue
	RF	Tpt	IL-76MF *Candid*	2	2005	2007	Option for further 2 ac. Still on order
	US	APC	M113A1	126	2005	2006	USD18.2m. Upgrade to M113A2Mk1
	Tu	Ftr	F-16A / C Block 15	17	2005	2007	Upgrade to Block 40 standard. First ac delivered on schedule
	dom	Recce ac	*Seeker* SB7L	6	2006	2006	–
Kuwait (Kwt)	US	Atk Hel	AH-64D	16	2003	2007	USD212.8m. 6 hel delivered in Feb 2007.
	US	PFB	MK V	12	2006	–	USD175m. Currently in service with the US Navy SEALs. Final delivery expected 2009
	Int'l	AD	*Aspide*	–	2007	–	EUR65m (approx USD87.3m). Upgrade of the standard Aspide msl to the Aspide 2000 configuration. The modernisation is to be performed over three years
Libya (LAR)	Fr	Msl	*Milan* ADT	–	2007	–	EUR296m (USD405m)
Morocco (Mor)	RF	AD	*Tunguska*	–	2005	–	2S6M
	Fr	FF	FREMM	1	2007	2012	EUR470m (USD676m)
	Int'l	Hel	*Puma*	25	2007	–	Refurbishment
	Fr	APC	–	140	2007	–	Upgrade. Unspecified APC
Oman (O)	NI	Hel	NH 90 TTH	20	2003	2008	Maiden flight in May 2007
	US	AAM	AIM-120C AMRAAM	10	2001	2006	On order

Table 22 **Selected Arms Orders and Deliveries, Middle East and North Africa**

Country Supplier	Classification	Designation	Quantity	Order date	Original Delivery date	Comment
US	AAM	AIM-9M *Sidewinder*	100	2001	2006	On order
US	ASM	AGM-84D *Harpoon*	20	2001	2006	On order
Fr	Tpt	A320	2	2007	–	–
UK	PSOH	Project *Khareef*	3	2007	2010	GBP400m (USD785m). Lead ship to be delivered early 2010. Subsequent vessels will follow at 6-month intervals
NI / UK	PSOH	Project *Khareef*	3	2007	2008	Radar and Comms upgrade
Saudi Arabia (Sau) Int'l	FGA	Eurofighter *Typhoon*	72	2005	2008	GBP4.43bn (USD8.9bn). Project Salam
Ge	Recce	Fuchs 2 NBC RS	32	2005	2007	EUR160m (USD205m). 16 NBC recce vehicles, 8 biological warfare detection vehicles, 8 mobile command-post vehicles
Fr	SAM	*Mistral* 2	–	2006	–	*Mistral* is the first of a package of acquisitions of French military equipment, thought to be worth EUR2.5bn
Fr	Tkr	A330-MRTT	2	2007	–	Same package as *Mistral* 2 above
Fr	Hel	NH90	10	2007	–	Same package as Mistral 2 above
Int'l	Utl	*Fennec*	30	2007	–	Same package as Mistral 2 above
US	AEW&C	E-3 *Sentry*	5	2006	–	Comms upgrade. USD16m. Link 16 MIDS
US	Ftr	F-15	–	2007	–	Comms upgrade. USD34.8m. Link 16 MIDS
Tu	APC	M113	300	2007	2008	Upgrade. A follow-on contract could lead to the upgrade of the entire M113 fleet of 3,000 vehicles
US	AEW&C	E-3 *Sentry*	5	2007	–	Comms upgrade. USD49.2m. Link 16, To be completed by 2009
Syria (Syr) RF	Msl	9M133 *Kornet* / 9M131 *Metis* 2	–	2003	–	USD73m. The deal includes several thousand msl
RF	AD	96K6 *Pantsyr-S1E*	50	–	2007	USD730m.
RF	Ftr	MiG-31E *Foxhound*	5	2006	2007	Part of a USD1bn contract covering MiG-31E *Foxhound* and an unspecified number of MiG-29M / M2
RF	Ftr	MiG-29M / M2	–	2006	–	Part of USD1bn contract detailed above
Fr	Hel	AS-350B *Ecureuil*	14	1999	2001	–
US	FGA	F-16E / F *Desert Falcon*	80	2000	2005	55 F-16E and 25 F-16F. With AMRAAM, HARM and *Hakeem* msl. Deliveries continuing
RF	AD	96K6 *Pantsyr-S1E*	50	2000	–	USD734m
US	Atk Hel	AH-64D	30	2002	–	Upgrade from AH-64A to D standard. Programme continuing
dom/Fr	FSG	*Baynunah*	6	2003	2006	First of class being built in France, with delivery due in 2006. All others to be built in UAE. ISD expected 2009
Ge	APC	Tpz-1 *Fuchs* NBC	64	2005	–	USD205m
US / It	Hel	AB-139	8	2005	2005	GBP83m (USD143m) SAR role
Tu	mRL	BPD FIROS 30 122 mm (40-round)	–	–	2005	Upgrade. Deliveries to continue through 2008

Table 22 Selected Arms Orders and Deliveries, Middle East and North Africa

	Country Supplier	Classification	Designation	Quantity	Order date	Original Delivery date	Comment
	dom	LCP	Fast Supply Vessel (FSV)	4	2006	2007	USD20m
	US	AAM	RIM-162 Evolved *Sea Sparrow* Missile (ESSM)	–	2006	2009	For *Baynunah* programme
	US	VLS	Mk 56	–	2006	2009	For RIM-162 ESSM, as part of Baynunah programme
	UK / Sgp / RSA / UEA	Mor	*Agrab (Scorpion)* 120mm MMS	46	2007	2008	AED390m (USD106m)
	Int'l	Tkr/Tpt	Airbus A330 MRTT	3	2007	–	To replace KC-135 tkr
	Int'l	SSM	*Exocet* MM40 Block III	48	2006	–	EUR450m (USD585m). *Exocet* will be placed on *Baynunah*-class FSG. First FSG to be commissioned in 2008. Each vessel is to be equipped with 8 *Exocet*
	US	Hel	AH-64D	30	2007	–	Part of a USD1,149bn contract for the remanufacture of 96 hel for the US Army and 30 hel for the UAE
	US	SAM	RAM Mk 49 Mod 3 GMLS	7	2006	2009	USD80m. 1 GMLS for each of the 6 *Baynunah* FSG and 1 GMLS set for trg
	dom	PB	*Project Al Saber*	12	2007	–	AED127m (USD34.6m). For the Coast Guard
Yemen, Republic of (Ye)	RF	FGA	MiG-29 SMT *Fulcrum*	32	2006	–	USD1.3bn
	RF	FGA	MiG-29	66	2006	2007	Repair old ac in first quarter of 2007. USD1bn

Chapter Six
Sub-Saharan Africa

Defence and security developments in Africa continue to be overshadowed by the problems of conflict and developing political and military capacity. While the United Nations (UN) continues to provide substantial resources in terms of peace-support activities to African nations, it has so far been unable to effect a lasting improvement in the continent's present areas of greatest instability: namely the Darfur region of Sudan and Somalia. Nonetheless, the UN had in October 2007 over 50,000 troops and military observers deployed on seven operations across Africa, and its presence has proved invaluable to the restoration of security and the rule of law in many of these locations, and many African nations are significant participants in these deployments. However, as noted in *The Military Balance 2007* and notwithstanding the earlier African Union (AU) mission in Burundi, optimism that the general operational exposure of AU member states might significantly improve the capacity of African states and regional institutions to better deal with the problems of conflict has been diminished with the continuing failure of the AU Mission in Sudan to prevent violence, in the ongoing absence (at the time of writing) of a fully operational AU/UN Hybrid operation in Darfur (UNAMID).

SUDAN

The January 2005 Comprehensive Peace Agreement (CPA) for southern Sudan came under strain in October 2007 when the Sudan People's Liberation Movement (SPLM) withdrew its ministers from the Government of National Unity, alleging that Khartoum had failed to implement the deal. Among the issues that the SPLM said amounted to a violation of the CPA were Khartoum's 'unwillingness to implement the Abyei Protocol … and intentional delay of North–South border demarcation', and its failure to withdraw its armed forces from the south. (A report by the Abyei Boundaries Commission had recommended that the oil-rich Abyei region should become part of the south.) Talks in late October and early November between Khartoum and the SPLM were inconclusive.

The talks coincided with discussions in the Libyan town of Sirte concerning the violence in Darfur. Two deals concluded in 2006 for Darfur and eastern Sudan had been modelled on the 2005 CPA, and particularly its provisions for sharing power through the allocation of posts and parliamentary seats at the national and state levels. However, as the 2007 edition of the IISS *Strategic Survey* notes (p. 263), the agreements have 'provided no convincing answers to vexed questions relating to land rights, which have been exacerbated by population movements and climate change. Politically, they appear to have had the effect of reinforcing rather than diluting the dominance of President Umar al-Bashir's National Congress Party … [and] it is to be doubted whether they are capable of bringing stability.'

DARFUR, AMIS AND UNAMID

At the talks in Sirte, part of the problem for the UN and AU convenors was the absence of some of Darfur's rebel groups, such as the Justice and Equality Movement and the Sudan Liberation Army-Unity faction, after they were reported to have complained about the invitations to other, smaller groups, as well as the location of the talks (see List of Non-State Groups, p. 474). The UN later reported that it had conducted talks in southern Sudan with some of the groups which did not attend the Sirte discussions.

These difficulties aside, the UN hopes that the talks will form the first part of a three-stage process for Darfur. The second stage is intended to comprise a series of consultations and workshops 'with and among rebel groups, with the hope that they will work out a unified position on the major issues in dispute'. At the time of writing, it was hoped that the third stage – full talks involving all sides – would take place in December, again in Sirte.

In May 2007, the UN was estimating that 200,000 people had died and over two million had been displaced since fighting broke out in 2003 between forces from the Sudanese government, allied Janjaweed militia and rebel groups. Violent clashes continued throughout 2007, as noted in the IISS

MAP 4 **AMIS AND THE PLANNED UNAMID DEPLOYMENT TO DARFUR**

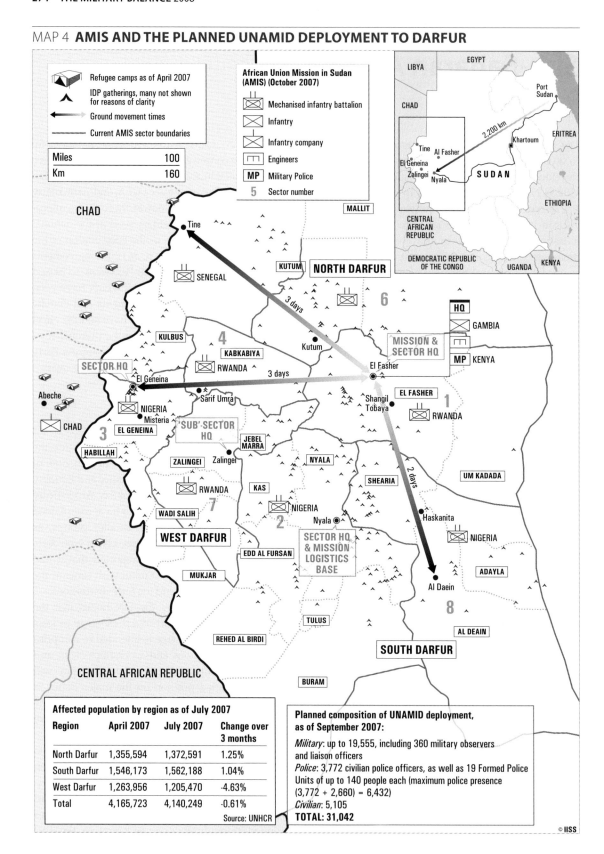

Affected population by region as of July 2007

Region	April 2007	July 2007	Change over 3 months
North Darfur	1,355,594	1,372,591	1.25%
South Darfur	1,546,173	1,562,188	1.04%
West Darfur	1,263,956	1,205,470	-4.63%
Total	4,165,723	4,140,249	-0.61%

Source: UNHCR

Planned composition of UNAMID deployment, as of September 2007:

Military: up to 19,555, including 360 military observers and liaison officers
Police: 3,772 civilian police officers, as well as 19 Formed Police Units of up to 140 people each (maximum police presence (3,772 + 2,660) = 6,432)
Civilian: 5,105
TOTAL: 31,042

© IISS

Armed Conflict Database, even as envoys were shuttling between African cities in an effort to bring an end to hostilities, and at the same time as the UN and the AU were thrashing out the details of the proposed hybrid peacekeeping force due to take over from the African Union Mission in Sudan (AMIS), UNAMID. According to UN Secretary-General Ban Ki-moon's report of 5 November, the month of October alone witnessed heavy fighting in Adilla, in southern Darfur, in Tawilla in the north and in Muhajeriya in the south of the region.

AMIS troops have been present in Darfur since the signing of the N'Djamena Humanitarian Ceasefire Agreement in 2004. In June of that year, 60 military observers, supported by a 300-strong Protection Force, deployed to 16 sites in Darfur to monitor the ceasefire agreement. An AU Peace and Security Commission meeting in October 2004 led to the force expanding to 2,341, including 341 military observers. With these greater numbers AMIS was able to modify its operational parameters, dividing Darfur into eight operational sectors, with eight Sector Headquarters, 29 Group Sites and two Team Sites, and deploying police contingents from African nations. The AMIS military component expanded further in 2005 to 6,171 and, as of late 2007, stands at approximately 7,000.

AMIS forces have not operated without losses in Darfur: in the most serious attack, on 29 September 2007, the AMIS ground site at Haskanita in the south was attacked by militia forces, leaving 10 dead, three missing and 10 wounded. This was one of a string of attacks on AMIS personnel throughout 2007. AMIS forces have been hard pressed, even with the force increases over the years, to operate to best effect in an area as large as Darfur and have been hampered by logistical and equipment deficiencies. The long-proposed UN intervention in Darfur moved a step forward in November 2006, following the decision resulting from high-level consultations in Addis Ababa (between Khartoum, the UN Security Council (UNSC) Permanent 5, the AU and other interested and influential nations, as well as some AMIS troop-contributing countries) to establish a hybrid UN–AU force for Darfur.

Sudan delayed its decision to accept this force until June 2007. UNAMID was formally established under UNSC Resolution 1769 on 31 July and is due to start implementing its mandate no later than 31 December. It has an initial mandate of 12 months' duration, will incorporate the AMIS force, and is scheduled to reach a total of around 20,000 military personnel and 6,000 police officers. (In August 2006 the UN had also expanded the mandate of its existing 10,000-strong UN Mission in Sudan force in southern Sudan.)

Before the UNAMID mission assumes its responsibilities in early 2008, the UN has a three-stage programme of augmenting the existing AMIS and deploying a peacekeeping force, as was agreed at the November 2006 Addis Ababa talks. Firstly, a Light Support Package is scheduled to provide management support to AMIS; it will consist of 105 military personnel, 34 police advisers and 48 civilians, as well as equipment. A total of 36 armoured personnel carriers were also due to be deployed at this stage, with the UN noting that these had been scheduled to arrive with new battalions in late 2007. In late October, the AMIS force commander, Nigerian General Martin Luther Agwai, welcomed newly arrived units, visiting Nigerian battalions 13 and 14 in Nyala and Graida, both in Sector South, and Rwandan battalion 10 in ZamZam, in Sector North. (The Rwandan battalion was airlifted by the US Air Force.) According to the UN, Rwanda was due to complete the deployment of an extra battalion by the end of November.

Secondly, a Heavy Support Package (HSP) was due for deployment starting in mid October 2007, although the Haskanita attack halted movements for a time. Accommodation for the HSP was due to be constructed in El-Fasher, El-Geneina, Zalingeri and El-Obeid. A Chinese engineering contribution, reportedly consisting of over 300 troops, arrived in mid November at Nyala and other contributions were pledged by Egypt, Pakistan, Nigeria and Bangladesh. In total, the HSP should comprise 2,250 military personnel, with 721 police and 1,136 civilians. The UNAMID deployment itself (including contingents formerly with AMIS) will constitute the third stage. Notwithstanding political debate with Khartoum and remaining logistical problems over issues such as the need to secure the necessary real estate, apron space, and day and night flight clearances, as well as the sheer distance heavy equipment has to travel from Port Sudan, the UNAMID deployment is still projected to the earlier noted total of 20,000 in 2008.

In November, Ban Ki-moon noted capability shortfalls in critical areas; even after all the pledges of support, the mission would still require two medium transport companies, three medium helicopter units and a light tactical helicopter unit. Darfur's terrain alone dictates that air transport is necessary for personnel movement, resupply and rapid response in the event of a security emergency. African nations on the whole still possess limited airlift capability; the South African contingent was able to organise its own rotation in the AMIS mission but others were dependent, or were likely to be near-fully dependent, on US, UK, Canadian, French, German or contract aviation assets (Nigeria was able to use its C-130s for some air movements).

Meanwhile, as well as the UNAMID deployment and the ongoing, if shaky, process of political reconciliation, the UN and its partner agencies are as of late 2007 operating the world's largest humanitarian effort in Darfur, as well as in camps in Chad and the Central African Republic (CAR).

CHAD AND THE CENTRAL AFRICAN REPUBLIC

Armed activity in eastern Chad and northern parts of CAR intensified in late 2006 and early 2007, reportedly fuelled by Sudanese support for rebel movements. While the two governments laid the blame primarily on Sudan, rejecting Khartoum's denials, it is clear that these insurgencies have internal, as well as external, origins. Rebel attacks, incursions and counter-insurgency retaliation for the last two years have combined to inflict considerable destruction in frontier areas of Chad and CAR. France, with troops stationed in both countries and fearful of the prospect of a political vacuum, has provided military support to their governments in the form of logistics and intelligence, and, in CAR, more direct participation in the form of Chad-based *Mirage* F-1 fighters and helicopters. Heavy fighting in the east between Chadian forces and a rebel group was followed, at the end of October, by the announcement of a peace deal brokered by Libyan leader Muammar Gadhafi. Under the deal, four rebel groups – the Movement for Resistance and Change, the National Accord of Chad and two factions of the Front for United Forces for Development and Democracy – have reportedly agreed to a ceasefire, with terms including the right for the rebels to form political parties and join Chad's military.

On 15 October 2007, the European Council authorised a military operation in Chad and CAR (EUFOR TCHAD/RCA). This deployment is due to last 12 months from initial operating capability. At the time of writing, France is expected to provide about half of the planned force of 4,300, with Ireland the next-largest contributor and other personnel coming from countries including Poland, Sweden, Austria,

Romania, Belgium, the Netherlands and Finland. With lead elements due to deploy in November 2007, EUFOR TCHAD/RCA is designed to support MINURCAT, the UN presence in the east of Chad and northeast CAR, which was established in September 2007 (see Europe, p. 104).

AFRICOM

In late 2006, the US Department of Defense announced plans to set up a new unified command for Africa, AFRICOM. This replaces the old structure (see US text and map, p. 16) whereby responsibility within the Pentagon for African countries was split between European Command (EUCOM), Pacific Command and Central Command. AFRICOM was deemed to have reached initial operating capability on 1 October 2007, and at that time had approximately 120 core staff members, working out of the EUCOM headquarters in Stuttgart. It will be based there for its first year, during which time it is scheduled to assume control of the programmes and activities currently conducted by the other commands.

According to the Pentagon, AFRICOM will 'enable political and economic growth' by helping to 'build the capability for African partners, and organizations such as the Africa Standby Force, to take the lead in establishing a secure environment'. It is intended that the command should adopt an interagency approach, working with US embassies and diplomatic missions, as well as with personnel from the US Agency for International Development (USAID) and other organisations. However, AFRICOM remains a military command, and 'as directed, U.S. Africa Command conducts military operations to deter aggression and respond to crises'. In July, US Army General William Ward was nominated as the commander of AFRICOM, with Ambassador Mary Carlin Yates (formerly ambassador to Ghana) appointed as deputy to the commander for civil–military activities in October, while Admiral Robert Moeller was appointed as deputy to the commander for military operations.

In mid October, Ward cited the Africa Partnership Station (APS) initiative as a good example of AFRICOM's stress on capacity-building. As part of the APS pilot mission, the USS *Fort McHenry* and HSV *Swift* were sent on a seven-month deployment to West Africa in connection with maritime-security initiatives. US government representatives included individuals from the State Department, Department of Homeland Security, USAID and the US Coast Guard. Personnel from the UK, Spain, Portugal and Germany were also reportedly on board.

Within Africa itself, the reaction to AFRICOM's establishment has been mixed. While Ethiopia and Liberia are among those nations which have greeted the development positively, it was reported that ministers from the Southern Africa Development Community (SADC) decided that its members would not host US forces. The Pentagon, meanwhile, stresses that it does not envisage the need for permanent bases as part of AFRICOM (although the existing presence in Djibouti is planned to be used as an 'enduring forward operating site'), and that only some 20% of the command's personnel will be stationed in Africa. At the time of writing, the location or locations and precise strength of the AFRICOM presence on the continent remained under discussion.

OTHER DEVELOPMENTS

Somalia continues to struggle with the legacy of the 1990s breakdown in central authority and rise of clan-based power struggles. On 6 December 2006, the UNSC approved Resolution 1725, authorising the deployment of an African force in Somalia to protect the Transitional Federal Government (TFG). As detailed in the IISS *Strategic Survey 2007* (p. 256), Somalia's 'Islamic Courts harboured and backed Ethiopian separatist groups and supported Ethiopian Islamists. Christian-dominated Ethiopia, for its part, had strongly supported Abdullahi Yusuf Ahmed's appointment as president of the TFG.' Also in December, Ethiopia sent troops across the border to reinforce the TFG's position in Baidoa, a deployment that was met with an attack by the Islamic Courts reportedly backed by Eritrean troops and foreign jihadists. Ethiopian and TFG forces then pushed their opponents back to Mogadishu, which the Islamic Courts were then forced to vacate after clans withdrew their support. On 7 January, with the consent of the TFG, a US AC-130 aircraft conducted the first of several strikes on suspected terrorist sites in Somalia. Later in January, the AU authorised an 8,000-strong peacekeeping force for Somalia, although by mid year 1,700 Ugandan troops constituted the bulk of the deployed forces, with other nations delaying their contributions. In August, the UNSC voted to extend the mandate of the AU force by another year and instructed the UN secretary-general to prepare for a UN force to replace AU troops, in the wake of

a request from Somalia's prime minister. Meanwhile, at the time of writing, Ethiopian troops remain in Somalia in support of the TFG.

A summit convened by the SADC in Lusaka, Zambia, in mid August saw the launch of the **SADC Brigade (SADCBRIG)** of the **African Standby Force (ASF)** (see *The Military Balance 2004–2005*, p. 219). In 2005, the AU designated five brigades to form the ASF, with one from each African region, setting a target date of 2010 for an operational ASF to be in place. It is planned that contributions to SADCBRIG will remain within each home nation, but 'on call' during prescribed response times – a 'permanent standby arrangement'. The only permanent structure will be the planning elements, located at Gaborone, Botswana, and consisting of military, police and civilian personnel. Botswana will also host the main logistics depot. This is in contrast to the East African Standby Brigade, which has a planning element in Nairobi, as well as the brigade headquarters element and proposed logistical facility in Addis Ababa. Meanwhile, pledges to the **Economic Community of West African States (ECOWAS)** Standby Force (ESF) comprise personnel for a 1,500-strong task force and a brigade of 5,000, with ECOWAS saying that the ESF is scheduled to become operational after certification in 2008. At the June 2007 ECOWAS summit, ministers asked for a further review of the allocated logistics facility at Hastings in Freetown, Sierra Leone, which was handed over to the ESF in 2006.

South Africa's armed forces saw structural change continue in 2007, following the army's 2006 'Vision 2020' document (see p. 280). The army now aims to reinstate a divisional structure in place of the existing system adopted in the late 1990s. It is reported that this change will start in April 2008 with the introduction of staff administrative structures similar to the G1–sections seen in many other armed forces. This is due to be followed by the establishment of land, training and support commands, along with ten brigade headquarters, and one motorised and one mechanised divisional headquarters. South Africa's Special Forces Brigade will continue to operate under the authority of the chief of joint operations and the president. The army plans to recruit some 3,000 new personnel in its January 2008 intake, rising to 7,000 by 2009. In May, the *Project Hoefyster* contract for 264 infantry combat vehicles was awarded. Denel's winning proposal was based on Finland's *Patria* vehicle, and there are scheduled command, mortar, missile, section and fire support variants. The vehicles will eventually replace the army's *Ratels*. In the same month, the new Type 209 submarine SAS *Charlotte Maxeke* arrived in South Africa, while in August the *Valour*-class frigate SAS *Amatola* completed the UK Royal Navy's operational sea-training course at Plymouth; the navy had earlier in the year commissioned the fourth of its *Valour*-class vessels, the SAS *Mendi*.

Nigerian forces have seen continued action against rebels operating in the Niger Delta region. Although the Movement for the Emancipation of the Niger Delta (see List of Non-State Groups, p. 474) declared a ceasefire in the wake of the election of Umaru Yar'Adua as president of Nigeria, this came to an end in October. Since then, rebels have launched attacks in the Delta region and also offshore. On one occasion in late October a clash was reported between Nigerian naval forces and rebels near an offshore oil platform. In the Delta region, raids on oil facilities and pipelines continue. Another attack, by forces as yet unknown, resulted in the deaths of over 20 soldiers from Cameroon in the Bakassi Peninsula. Meanwhile, attacks and instability resulting from gang activity in Port Harcourt led the army to deploy a Joint Task Force in August.

Continuing problems in the **Democratic Republic of the Congo** (see IISS *Strategic Survey* 2007, pp. 271–3) were highlighted by the UN secretary-general's 14 November report to the Security Council. Two sets of events led to renewed conflict: in March, fighting broke out in Kinshasa between government forces and forces loyal to opposition leader Jean-Pierre Bemba (see *The Military Balance 2007*, p. 255). In the east of the country, clashes have taken place between the Armed Forces of the Democratic Republic of the Congo (FARDC) and forces loyal to General Laurent Nkunda. According to the UN, 'the clashes reflect the failure of "mixing", by which pro-Nkunda and Government elements were brought under nominal FARDC command in North Kivu without being fully integrated into the armed forces'. Kinshasa later called for an end to 'mixing' and for the *brassage* of all units, meaning the reintegration and retraining of ex-combatants into the FARDC. Throughout the year

violent incidents and continuing population movements added to instability in the area; in November, a month that saw continuing attacks on government positions by forces loyal to General Nkunda, the chief of staff of the DRC armed forces told a press conference jointly held with the UN force commander that 'peaceful solutions [had] been exhausted'.

In mid to late 2007, **NATO's** Standing Maritime Group 1, one of its four standing maritime groups, conducted a 12,500 nautical mile circumnavigation of Africa. Leaving Rota in Spain on 30 July the group, which comprised six vessels from six NATO nations, conducted 'presence operations' in the Gulf of Guinea and off the Horn of Africa, as well as conducting an exercise with the South African Navy and paying port visits to Cape Town and the Seychelles. In the meantime, CENTCOM's CTF-150 naval task group maintains its focus on maritime-security operations in its area of responsibility, comprising the Gulf of Aden, the Gulf of Oman, the Arabian Sea, Red Sea and the Indian Ocean (see *The Military Balance 2006*, map 4).

The situation in the Temporary Security Zone (TSZ) and adjacent areas between **Ethiopia** and **Eritrea** remains tense. In 2002 the Ethiopia–Eritrea Boundary Commission reported on the delimitation of the common border. In a June 2007 letter to the UN secretary-general, Addis Ababa had reiterated that it was willing to accept the commission's decision, but a September meeting 'failed to resolve the impasse between the two countries [over] demarcation'. In early November, the UN secretary-general said that a military build-up along the border was causing concern and that in the period since his previous report in July 2007 both parties had moved troops and equipment closer to the disputed border. Eritrea was reported to have constructed defences inside the TSZ and to have moved extra troops and equipment into various sectors of the zone. Meanwhile, Ethiopia was reported to have conducted training exercises and reinforced its defences, as well as redeployed troops and equipment (see *The Military Balance 2007*, p. 255, and IISS *Strategic Survey* 2003/4).

SUB-SAHARAN AFRICA – DEFENCE ECONOMICS

In line with the strong trend of recent years, the last seven years have marked the best period of economic growth in Africa since the beginning of the 1970s. Important elements of this growth have included the continuing improvement in cementing macro-economic stability, the beneficial impact of debt relief, increased capital inflows, rising oil production in a number of countries and strong demand for non-oil commodities. However, empirical evidence suggests that while growth episodes occur in sub-Saharan Africa with the same frequency as in other regions, they tend to be shorter in duration and end in painful output collapses.

The International Monetary Fund (IMF) has suggested that with the relative decline in the number of armed conflicts and political instability over the past decade, the main factor determining whether strong growth continues or not will be economic, rather than socio-political, development. In this regard, it will be important to sustain recent improvements in macroeconomic stability, particularly in those oil-exporting countries where increased oil revenue has created strong pressures for increased government spending. At the same time, progress towards more vibrant market-based economies rests on the success of further trade liberalisation. While trade reforms have generally increased the openness of sub-Saharan economies over the past decade, trade regimes in the region remain more restrictive than in the dynamic economies of Asia. However, the issue of improving global market access for regional products – key to progress in this area – has yet to be resolved at the international level.

China continues to establish itself as a major political and economic force in the region. In exchange for securing energy and raw materials to support its spectacular growth, China has built a close relationship with African states and businesses, and has been constructing roads, bridges, railways, dams, power plants, ports, pipelines and telephone lines. Bilateral trade, which is dominated by Chinese oil purchases (accounting for 30% of all Chinese oil imports) has multiplied fivefold since 2000 to US$55.5 billion in 2006. By the end of 2006, the Export–Import Bank of China was financing more than 200 projects in Africa and it expects the total value of these projects to double over the next three years to total some US$20bn, meaning that it could outstrip total infrastructure lending by the World Bank and the African Development Bank. As a result, China now has diplomatic relations with all but five African countries (those five continue to maintain links with Taiwan) – Liberia, Senegal and Chad are the latest to switch.

The increasing influence of China in the region beyond its business and diplomatic interests was illustrated by the visit in November 2006 of a Chinese military delegation to the **Ugandan** Ministry of Defence. During the period 1996 to 2004, it is thought that Chinese arms sales to Uganda probably amounted to little more than US$2–3m. However, central to the latest discussions was an increase in arms supplies, military construction and training, possibly leading to investments worth as

Sub-Saharan Africa

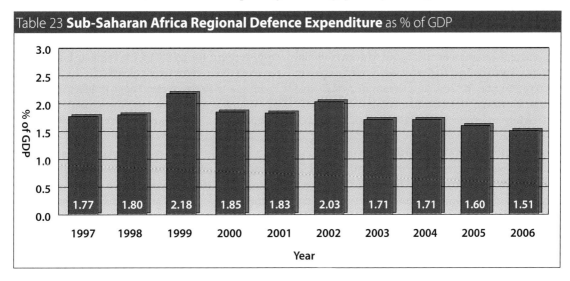

Table 23 **Sub-Saharan Africa Regional Defence Expenditure** as % of GDP

Year	1997	1998	1999	2000	2001	2002	2003	2004	2005	2006
% of GDP	1.77	1.80	2.18	1.85	1.83	2.03	1.71	1.71	1.60	1.51

Table 24 **South Africa's Strategic Armaments Package – Quantities and Costs (Rm)**						
	Cost of 4 frigates per year	Cost of 3 submarines per year	Cost of 30 utility helicopters per year	Cost of 28 fighter aircraft per year	Cost of 24 training aircraft per year	Total cost
2000	1,643	126	154	228	750	2,901
2001	1,846	755	316	446	861	4,223
2002	1,895	1,528	434	1,104	1,381	6,342
2003	2,100	1,461	213	713	1,377	5,864
2004	1,188	1,303	106	1,460	445	4,502
2005	599	1,254	235	3,199	1,045	6,331
2006	378	820	447	2,598	293	4,536
2007	-	753	201	2,794	767	4,515
2008	-	168	286	3,563	257	4,275
2009	-	26	-	1,473	-	1,499
2010	-	-	-	1,346	-	1,346
2011	-	-	-	1,148	-	1,148
Total cost	**9,649**	**8,194**	**2,392**	**20,072**	**7,176**	**47,483**

much as US$1.5bn over the next five years, according to the Ugandan military. Following the donation of 100 military transport vehicles to Uganda in 2006, Chinese companies are currently engaged in building a new army headquarters and upgrading several military barracks. Chinese military experts are also thought to be running the Ugandan armaments factories in Nakasongola, which manufacture ammunition and assemble machine guns and combat vehicles.

The **South African** economy continues to act as an engine for growth throughout Southern Africa with rising employment and booming asset prices, strong public finances and rising international reserves. Indeed, in 2006 strong revenue growth together with restrained public expenditure enabled the government to produce its first budget surplus (0.4% of GDP) for several decades. Against this background of fiscal prudence the South African National Defence Force budget has increased from R13.7bn in 2000 to R25.9bn in 2007, an increase of 25% in real terms. However, the headline figures are slightly misleading as in 2005 the budget was redefined, resulting in responsibility for the management of the armed forces' property portfolio – worth around R1bn – being transferred from the Ministry of Public Works to the Department of Defence (DoD). Even so, the 2007 budget includes an additional R1.2bn over previous forecasts and another R2.3bn in 2008. The additional funds are earmarked for a new defence intelligence project for 'the partial establishment of a strategic imagery and electronic intelligence collec-

tion capability to detect air and maritime movement' and payments towards the eight Airbus A400M military transport aircraft ordered in 2006.

The Special Defence Account used to buy weapons for the armed forces accounts for 34.7% of the total budget in 2007, compared to 39% of the budget in 2005, and by 2009 it will have fallen further, to around 30% of the budget. This trend reflects the gradual reduction in payments towards the 12-year Strategic Armaments Package initiated in the late 1990s, which included the acquisition of four *MEKO*-class A-200 frigates, 3 diesel-electric submarines, 30 utility helicopters, 24 *Hawk* trainer aircraft and 26 *Gripen* fighter aircraft. As illustrated in Table 24, peak expenditure for these acquisitions occurred between 2004 and 2006, and expenditure will slowly be reduced until the scheduled completion of the financing plan in 2011. Personnel-related costs account for 36.5% of the budget, higher than the DoD's long-term target of 30%.

In line with the White Paper published in 2006, procurement funds will now increasingly focus on equipping the army to meet the most likely operational demands placed on it. The army's Vision 2020 plan, which is based on the government's policy of engagement with Africa, will see the army divided into a mechanised division, a motorised division and a special operations brigade. Much of the army's existing inventory is not considered suitable for its new responsibilities and there are four major procurement programmes in progress. In May 2007, the government approved the long-awaited *Project*

Table 25 **South African Defence Budget by Programme, 2003–2009**							
Rand m				Revised	Budget	Budget	Budget
	2003	2004	2005	2006	2007	2008	2009
Administration	1,258	1,436	1,630	1,759	1,934	2,054	2,345
Landward Defence	3,150	3,340	3,431	4,061	4,215	4,507	4,851
Air Defence	2,176	2,242	2,479	2,504	2,651	2,871	3,175
Maritime Defence	1,025	1,097	1,201	1,319	1,388	1,488	1,871
Military Health Support	1,354	1,320	1,556	1,683	1,831	2,000	2,278
Defence Intelligence	133	135	144	143	162	164	181
Joint Support	2,098	2,340	2,373	2,713	3,256	3,612	3,845
Force Employment	1,291	1,242	1,433	1,410	1,471	1,546	1,725
Special Defence Account	8,015	7,045	9,258	8,280	9,011	9,771	8,557
Total	**20,504**	**20,201**	**23,510**	**23,876**	**25,922**	**28,016**	**28,631**

Hoefyster to supply the army with a new generation of infantry combat vehicles. Under the R8.8bn plan, the army will receive 264 vehicles to equip three mechanised infantry battalions. Initially, there will be five variants based on the *Patria* armoured modular vehicle platform equipped with a new modular turret family developed by Denel, which will also serve as the prime contractor. Deliveries are scheduled to run from 2012–22. Three other major army projects are facing delays:

- *Project Guardian*, the R1.2bn very-short-range air-defence element of its wider ground-based air defence system
- *Project Vistula*, the R3.2bn project to acquire more than 1,200 tactical logistical vehicles
- *Project Sepula*, the acquisition of armoured personnel carriers to replace the *Casspir* and *Mamba* models. This project has been referred for further review on an operational level

The air force is also suffering from delays to five major projects including new air-traffic-control radars, new airfield navigation facilities, the upgrade of *Astra* trainers, new fire-fighting vehicles and the upgrade of its national communications network. Despite an annual average increase of 6.5% in its budget between 2003 and 2009, the cost of integrating the new helicopters and jet aircraft is creating pressure on the air force budget and forcing delays to equipment-acquisition and training programmes. In 2007, the Base Support Capability budget, the sub-programme dedicated to airbase infrastructure, will be the largest sub-programme of the entire air force budget, accounting for 31% of total funds. In terms of flying hours, the air force failed to meet its target in 2005 and has warned that over the coming three years it plans to cut back on flying hours for its newest platforms, the *Gripen* fighters and *Hawk* trainers, compared to original targets.

Growth in **Nigeria**, the second-largest economy in sub-Saharan Africa, is forecast to jump from 5.2% in 2006 to 8.2% in 2007, despite ongoing instability in the oil sector. In its third review under the Policy Support Instrument in place with Nigeria, the IMF congratulated the outgoing Olusegun Obasanjo administration on macroeconomic policies which have led to robust growth, lower inflation, a build-up of reserves and a significant reduction in external debt. The rising level of unrest in the Delta region has resulted in a substantial increase in the defence budget from N37bn in 2000 to N122bn in 2007, up 25% from 2006. In addition to the allocation to the Ministry of Defence, the Ministry of Internal Affairs will receive N12bn for the paramilitary units of the Civil Defence Corps. Following the procurement of 15 *Chengdu* F/FT-7NI strike aircraft and trainers from the China National Aero-Technology Import and Export Corporation in 2006, the air force announced that it would be proceeding with the acquisition of two ATR42 maritime patrol aircraft from Finmeccanica and an unknown number of second-hand L-159 fighter aircraft from the Czech Republic. In addition, after a revelation that the air force no longer had the capacity to police the national coastline owing to a lack of capable aircraft, the government approved a US$160m programme to restore out-of-service aircraft and rebuild various facilities, including hangars.

Sub-Saharan Africa

Angola Ang

New Angolan Kwanza AOA		2006	2007	2008
GDP	AOA	2.72tr	3.62tr	
	US$	33.9bn	48.3bn	
per capita	US$	2,831	3,941	
Growth	%	18.6	23.1	
Inflation	%	13.3	11.9	
Def bdgt	AOA	127bn	172bn	
	US$	1.58bn	2.29bn	
USD1=AOA		80.3	75.0	

Population   12,263,596

Ethnic Groups: Ovimbundu 37%; Kimbundu 25%; Bakongo 13%

Age	0–14	15–19	20–24	25–29	30–64	65 plus
Male	22%	5%	4%	4%	14%	1%
Female	22%	5%	4%	4%	13%	2%

Capabilities

ACTIVE 107,000 (Army 100,000 Navy 1,000 Air 6,000)
Paramilitary 10,000

ORGANISATIONS BY SERVICE

Army 100,000

FORCES BY ROLE

Armd/inf   42 regt (dets/gps – strength varies)

Inf   16 indep bde

EQUIPMENT BY TYPE †

MBT 300+: ε200 T-54/T-55; 50 T-62; 50 T-72; T-80/T-84 (reported)

RECCE 600 BRDM-2

AIFV 250+ : 250 BMP-1/BMP-2; BMD-3

APC (W) ε170 BTR-152/BTR-60/BTR-80

ARTY 1,396+

SP 4+: **122mm** 2S1 *Carnation*; **152mm** 4 2S3; **203mm** 2S7

TOWED 552: **122mm** 500 D-30; **130mm** 48 M-46; **152mm** 4 D-20

MRL 90+: **122mm** 90: 50 BM-21; 40 RM-70 *Dana*; **240mm** BM-24

MOR 750: **82mm** 250; **120mm** 500

AT • MSL • MANPATS AT-3 9K11 *Sagger*

RCL 500: 400 **82mm** B-10/**107mm** B-11 †; **106mm** 100†

RL **73mm** RPG-7 *Knout*†

GUNS • SP **100mm** SU-100†

AD • SAM • MANPAD 500 SA-7 *Grail*/SA-14 *Gremlin*/SA-16 *Gimlet*

GUNS • TOWED 450+: **14.5mm** ZPU-4; **23mm** ZU-23-2; **37mm** M-1939; **57mm** S-60

Navy ε1,000

FORCES BY ROLE

Navy 1 HQ located at Luanda

EQUIPMENT BY TYPE

PATROL AND COASTAL COMBATANTS 9

PCI 7: 4 *Mandume*†; 3 *Patrulheiro*†

PBI 2 *Namacurra*

FACILITIES

Base   Located at Luanda

Coastal Defence

MSL • TACTICAL • SSM SS-C-1B *Sepal* (at Luanda base)

Air Force/Air Defence 6,000

FORCES BY ROLE

Ftr	sqn with 20 MiG-21bis /MiG-21MF *Fishbed*; 2 SU-27 *Flanker*
FGA	sqn with 30 MiG-23 *Flogger*; 10 SU-25 *Frogfoot*; 4 SU-24 *Fencer*; 15 SU-22 (SU-17M-2) *Fitter D*
MP	sqn with 1 F-27 MK 200MPA; 7 CASA 212 *Aviocar*
Tpt	sqn with 1 EMB-135BJ Legacy 600 (VIP); 8 AN-12 *Cub*; 4 An-26 *Curl*; 2 AN-32 *Cline*; 2 C-130 *Hercules*; 2 CASA 212 *Aviocar*; 1 IL-62 *Classic*; 1 IL-76TD *Candid*; 4 PC-6B *Turbo Porter*; 9 PC-7 *Turbo Trainer*/PC-9*
Atk hel	sqn with 14 Mi-24 *Hind*/Mi-35 *Hind*; 2 SA-342M *Gazelle* (HOT)
Trg	sqn with 8 EMB-312 *Tucano*; 6 L-29 *Delfin*
Hel	units with Bell 212; 8 AS-565; 25 Mi-17 (Mi-8MT) *Hip H*/Mi-8 *Hip*; 10 IAR-316 (SA-316) *Alouette III* (incl trg)
SAM	5 bn; 10 bty each with 12 SA-3 *Goa*; 10 SA-13 *Gopher*†; 25 SA-6 *Gainful*; 15 SA-8 *Gecko*; 20 SA-9 *Gaskin*; 40 SA-2 *Guideline*

EQUIPMENT BY TYPE

AIRCRAFT 90 combat capable

FTR 22: 2 SU-27 *Flanker*,: 20 MiG-21bis /MiG-21MF *Fishbed*

FGA 59: 10 SU-25 *Frogfoot*; 4 SU-24 *Fencer*; 30 MiG-23 *Flogger*; 15 SU-22 (SU-17M-2) *Fitter D*

MP 8: 1 F-27 MK 200MPA; 7 CASA 212 *Aviocar*

TPT 25: 1 EMB-135BJ Legacy 600 (VIP); 8 AN-12 *Cub*; 4 An-26 *Curl*; 2 AN-32 *Cline*; 2 C-130 *Hercules*; 2 CASA 212 *Aviocar*; 1 IL-62 *Classic*; 1 IL-76TD *Candid*; 4 PC-6B *Turbo Porter*

TRG 23: 9 PC-7 *Turbo Trainer*/PC-9*; 8 EMB-312 *Tucano*; 6 L-29 *Delfin*

HELICOPTERS

ATK 16: 14 Mi-24 *Hind*/Mi-35 *Hind*; 2 SA-342M *Gazelle* (HOT)

SPT 25 Mi-17 (Mi-8MT) *Hip H*/Mi-8 *Hip* spt hel

UTL 18+: Bell 212; 10 IAR-316 (SA-316) *Alouette III* (incl trg); 8 AS-565

AD • SAM 122

SP 70: 10 SA-13 *Gopher*†; 25 SA-6 *Gainful*; 15 SA-8 *Gecko*; 20 SA-9 *Gaskin*

TOWED 52: 40 SA-2 *Guideline*; 12 SA-3 *Goa*

MSL

ASM AS-9 *Kyle*; AT-2 *Swatter*; HOT

AAM AA-2 *Atoll*; AA-6 *Acrid*; AA-7 *Apex*; AA-8 *Aphid*

Paramilitary 10,000

Rapid-Reaction Police 10,000

FOREIGN FORCES
Portugal Navy: 11 (Technical Military Cooperation)
United States USMC 6

NON-STATE ARMED GROUPS
see Part II

Benin Bn

CFA Franc BCEAO fr		2006	2007	2008
GDP	fr	2.45tr	2.62tr	
	US$	4.7bn	5.7bn	
per capita	US$	599	702	
Growth	%	3.8	4.0	
Inflation	%	3.8	3.0	
Def bdgt	fr	24.4bn	e26.2bn	
	US$	47m	e57m	
US$1=fr		522	462	

Population	8,078,314					
Age	0–14	15–19	20–24	25–29	30–64	65 plus
Male	24%	6%	5%	4%	11%	1%
Female	23%	5%	5%	4%	12%	1%

Capabilities

ACTIVE 4,750 (Army 4,300 Navy 100 Air 350)
Paramilitary 2,500
Terms of service conscription (selective), 18 months

ORGANISATIONS BY SERVICE

Army 4,300
FORCES BY ROLE
Armd   1 sqn
Inf   3 bn
Cdo/AB   1 bn
Arty   1 bty
Engr   1 bn

EQUIPMENT BY TYPE
LT TK 18 PT-76 (op status uncertain)
RECCE 31: 14 BRDM-2; 7 M-8; 10 VBL
ARTY 16+
    TOWED 105mm 16: 12 L-118 Light gun; 4 M-101
    MOR 81mm
AT • RL 73mm RPG-7 *Knout*; **89mm** LRAC

Navy ε100
EQUIPMENT BY TYPE
PATROL AND COASTAL COMBATANTS • PB 2 *Matelot Brice Kpomasse* (ex-PRC)

FACILITIES
Naval airbase   Located at Cotonou

Air Force 350
no cbt ac
AIRCRAFT
TPT 13: 2 An-26 *Curl*†; 1 B-707-320† (VIP); 2 C-47 *Skytrain*†; 1 DHC-6 twin *Otter*†; 2 DO-128 *Skyservant*†; 1 F-28 *Fellowship*† (VIP); 3 HS-748†; 1 Rockwell *Commander* 500B†
HELICOPTERS
SPT 2 AS-350B *Ecureuil*†
UTL 6: 5 A-109BA; 1 SE 3130 *Alouette II*†

Paramilitary 2,500

Gendarmerie 2,500
4 (mobile) coy

DEPLOYMENT

CÔTE D'IVOIRE
UN • UNOCI 423; 6 obs

DEMOCRATIC REPUBLIC OF CONGO
UN • MONUC 750; 12 obs

LIBERIA
UN • UNMIL 1; 3 obs

SUDAN
AU • AUMIS 1 obs
UN • UNMIS 7 obs

Botswana Btwa

Botswana Pula P		2006	2007	2008
GDP	P	57.1bn	74.0bn	
	US$	9.8bn	12.3bn	
per capita	US$	5,973	7,524	
Growth	%	2.6	5.0	
Inflation	%	11.0	7.0	
Def bdgt	P	1.68bn	ε1.70bn	
	US$	289m	ε283m	
US$1=P		5.83	6.00	

Population	1,639,131					
Age	0–14	15–19	20–24	25–29	30–64	65 plus
Male	20%	7%	6%	4%	11%	1%
Female	19%	7%	6%	5%	12%	2%

Capabilities

ACTIVE 9,000 (Army 8,500 Air 500) **Paramilitary 1,500**

ORGANISATIONS BY SERVICE

Army 8,500

FORCES BY ROLE

Armd 1 bde (under strength)
Inf 2 bde (*total:* 1 cdo unit, 1 armd recce regt, 1 engr regt, 2 ADA regt, 4 inf bn)
Arty 1 bde
AD 1 bde (under strength)

EQUIPMENT BY TYPE

LT TK 55: ε30 SK-105 *Kuerassier*; 25 *Scorpion*
RECCE 8+: RAM-V-1; ε8 RAM-V-2
APC 156
 APC (T) 6 FV 103 *Spartan*
 APC (W) 150: 50 BTR-60; 50 LAV-150 *Commando* (some with 90mm gun); 50 MOWAG *Piranha* III
ARTY 46
 TOWED 30: **105mm** 18: 12 L-118 *Light* gun; 6 Model 56 pack howitzer; **155mm** 12 Soltam
 MOR 16: **81mm** 10; **120mm** 6 M-43
AT • MSL 6+
 SP V-150 TOW
 MANPATS 6 TOW
 RCL 84mm 30 *Carl Gustav*
 RL 73mm RPG-7 *Knout*
AD • SAM • MANPAD 27: 5 Javelin; 10 SA-16 *Gimlet*; 12 SA-7 *Grail*
 GUNS • TOWED 20mm 7 M-167 *Vulcan*

Air Wing 500

FORCES BY ROLE

Ftr/FGA 1 sqn with 10 F-5A *Freedom Fighter*; 5 F-5D *Tiger II*
Tpt 2 sqn with 10 BN-2 *Defender**; 1 Beech 200 *Super King Air* (VIP); 3 C-130B *Hercules*; 2 CASA 212 *Aviocar*; 2 CN-235; 1 *Gulfstream* IV
Recce 1 sqn with 5 O-2 *Skymaster*
Trg 1 sqn with 6 PC-7 *Turbo Trainer**
Hel 1 sqn with 8 AS-350B *Ecureuil*; 1 Bell 412 *Twin Huey*; 1 Bell 412EP *Twin Huey* (VIP); 5 Bell 412SP *Twin Huey*

EQUIPMENT BY TYPE

AIRCRAFT 31 combat capable
 FTR 15: 10 F-5A *Freedom Fighter*; 5 F-5D *Tiger II*
 RECCE 5 O-2 *Skymaster*
 TPT 19: 10 BN-2 *Defender**; 1 Beech 200 *Super King Air* (VIP); 3 C-130B *Hercules*; 2 CASA 212 *Aviocar* 2; 2 CN-235; 1 *Gulfstream* IV
 TRG 6 PC-7 *Turbo Trainer**
HELICOPTERS
 SPT 8 AS-350B *Ecureuil*
 UTL 7: 1 Bell 412 *Twin Huey*; 1 Bell 412EP *Twin Huey* (VIP); 5 Bell 412SP *Twin Huey*

Paramilitary 1,500

Police Mobile Unit 1,500 (org in territorial coy)

DEPLOYMENT

SUDAN
AU • AUMIS 20 obs
UN • UNMIS 5 obs

Burkina Faso BF

CFA Franc BCEAO fr		2006	2007	2008
GDP	fr	3.16tr	3.32tr	
	US$	6.1bn	7.2bn	
per capita	US$	436	503	
Growth	%	5.9	6.0	
Inflation	%	2.4	0.5	
Def bdgt	fr	44.5bn	e46.6bn	
	US$	85m	e101m	
US$1=fr		522	462	

Population 14,326,203

Age	0–14	15–19	20–24	25–29	30–64	65 plus
Male	24%	6%	5%	4%	11%	1%
Female	23%	5%	5%	4%	12%	1%

Capabilities

ACTIVE 10,800 (Army 6,400 Air 200 Gendarmerie 4,200) **Paramilitary 250**

ORGANISATIONS BY SERVICE

Army 6,400

FORCES BY ROLE

3 Mil Regions
Tk 1 bn (2 tk pl)
Inf 5 regt HQ (*each:* 3 inf bn (*each:* 1 inf coy (5 inf pl)))
AB 1 regt HQ (1 AB bn, 2 AB coy)
Arty 1 bn (2 arty tps)
Engr 1 bn

EQUIPMENT BY TYPE

RECCE 79: 15 AML-60/AML-90; 24 EE-9 *Cascavel*; 30 *Ferret*; 2 M-20; 8 M-8
APC (W) 13 M-3 *Panhard*
ARTY 18+
 TOWED 14: **105mm** 8 M-101; **122mm** 6
 MRL 107mm ε4 Type-63
 MOR 81mm Brandt
AT
 RCL 75mm Type-52 (M-20); **84mm** *Carl Gustav*
 RL 89mm LRAC; M-20
AD • SAM • MANPAD SA-7 *Grail*
 GUNS • TOWED 42: **14.5mm** 30 ZPU; **20mm** 12 TCM-20

Air Force 200

FORCES BY ROLE

Tpt   sqn with 1 B-727 (VIP); 1 Beech 200 *Super King Air*; 1 HS-748; 1 N-262 *Fregate*; 1 Rockwell Commander 500B

Liaison sqn with 2 Cessna 150/Cessna 172; 1 AS-350 *Ecureuil*; 3 Mi-17 (Mi-8MT) *Hip H*/Mi-8 *Hip*; 1 SA-316B *Alouette III*

Trg   sqn with 5 SF-260W *Warrior*/SF-260WL *Warrior**

EQUIPMENT BY TYPE

AIRCRAFT 5 combat capable

  TPT 7: 1 B-727 (VIP); 1 Beech 200 *Super King Air*; 1 HS-748; 1 N-262 *Fregate*; 1 Rockwell Commander 500B, 2 Cessna 150 Trg/Cessna 172 utl

  TRG 5 SF-260W *Warrior* Trg ac/SF-260WL *Warrior**

HELICOPTERS

  ATK 2 Mi-35

  SPT 4: 1 AS-350 *Ecureuil*; 3 Mi-17 (Mi-8MT) *Hip H*/Mi-8 *Hip* spt hel

  UTL 1 SA-316B *Alouette III*

Gendarmerie 4,200

Paramilitary 250

People's Militia (R) 45,000 reservists (trained)

Security Company 250

DEPLOYMENT

DEMOCRATIC REPUBLIC OF CONGO

UN • MONUC 10 obs

SUDAN

AU • AUMIS 4 obs

UN • UNMIS 6 obs

AU / UN • UNAMID Potential deployment

Burundi Bu

Burundi Franc fr		2006	2007	2008
GDP	fr	986bn	1.07tr	
	US$	959m	965m	
per capita	US$	119	115	
Growth	%	5.1	3.5	
Inflation	%	2.7	5.3	
Def bdgt	fr	50.2bn	51.9bn	
	US$	49m	46m	
US$1=fr		1,028	1,127	

Population   8,390,505

Ethnic Groups: Hutu 85%; Tutsi 14%

Age	0–14	15–19	20–24	25–29	30–64	65 plus
Male	23%	6%	5%	4%	10%	1%
Female	23%	6%	5%	3%	11%	2%

Capabilities

ACTIVE 35,000 (Army 35,000) **Paramilitary 31,050**

(Active Forces to be reduced by 14,000). In line with the Pretoria Peace Accord signed in October 2003 rebels from the FDD and government forces are now being integrated into a new National Defence Force.

ORGANISATIONS BY SERVICE

Army 35,000

FORCES BY ROLE

Lt armd 2 bn (sqn)

Inf   7 bn; some indep coy

Arty   1 bn

Engr 1 bn

AD   1 bn

EQUIPMENT BY TYPE

RECCE 55: 6 AML-60; 12 AML-90; 30 BRDM-2; 7 S52 *Shorland*

APC (W) 47: 20 BTR-40; 9 M-3 *Panhard*; 12 RG-31 *Nyala*; 6 *Walid*

ARTY 120

  TOWED 122mm 18 D-30

  MRL 122mm 12 BM-21

  MOR 90: **82mm** 15 M-43; **120mm** ε75

AT

  MSL • MANPATS *Milan* (reported)

  RCL 75mm 60 Type-52 (M-20)

  RL 83mm RL-83 *Blindicide*

AD • SAM • MANPAD ε30 SA-7 *Grail (some SA-7 destroyed in 2006)*

  GUNS • TOWED 150+: **14.5mm** 15 ZPU-4; 135+ **23mm** ZU-23/**37mm** Type-55 (M-1939)

Reserves

Army 10 (reported) bn

Air Wing 200

AIRCRAFT 2 combat capable

  TPT 2 DC-3

  TRG 2 SF-260TP/SF-260W *Warrior**

HELICOPTERS

  ATK 2 Mi-24 *Hind**

  SPT 2 Mi-8 *Hip*

  UTL 3 SA-316B *Alouette III*

Paramilitary 31,050

Marine Police 50

16 territorial districts

PATROL AND COASTAL COMBATANTS 7

  PHT 3 Huchuan†

  Misc Boats/Craft 4

AMPHIBIOUS 1 LCT

LOGISTICS AND SUPPORT 1: 1 spt

General Administration of State Security
ε1,000

Local Defence Militia ε30,000

NON-STATE ARMED GROUPS
see Part II

DEPLOYMENT

SOMALIA
AU • AMISOM 1,700 to be deployed

SUDAN
AU • AUMIS 10 obs

FOREIGN FORCES
All under ONUB comd unless otherwise specified
Algeria 1
Bangladesh 2 obs
Burkina Faso 6 obs
Chad 8 obs
Egypt 2 obs
Ethiopia 2 obs
Ghana 2 obs
Guatemala 1
India 3 obs
Jordan 1; 3 obs
Kenya 192; 1 obs
Korea, Republic of 2 obs
Malawi 2 obs
Mali 7 obs
Namibia 1 obs
Nepal 932; 2 obs
Netherlands 1 obs
Niger 1 obs
Nigeria 1; 5 obs
Pakistan 166; 2 obs
Philippines 2 obs
Portugal 1 obs
Romania 1 obs
Russia 4 obs
Senegal 4; 2 obs
South Africa 862, 3 obs
Thailand 177; 3 obs
Togo 1; 6 obs
Tunisia 1; 8 obs
United States USMC 6
Yemen, Republic of 3 obs

Cameroon Crn

CFA Franc BEAC fr		2006	2007	2008
GDP	fr	9.37tr	9.28tr	
	US$	18.0bn	20.1bn	
per capita	US$	1,107	1,113	
Growth	%	3.8	3.8	
Inflation	%	5.1	2.0	
Def bdgt	fr	134bn	e150bn	
	US$	257m	324m	
US$1=fr		522	462	

Population   18,060,382

Age	0–14	15–19	20–24	25–29	30–64	65 plus
Male	21%	6%	5%	4%	13%	1%
Female	21%	6%	5%	4%	13%	2%

Capabilities

ACTIVE 14,100 (Army 12,500 Navy 1,300 Air 300)
Paramilitary 9,000

ORGANISATIONS BY SERVICE

Army 12,500
FORCES BY ROLE
3 Mil Regions
Armd recce	1 bn
Inf	3 bn (under comd of Mil Regions); 5 bn; 1 bn (trg)
Cdo/AB	1 bn
Arty	1 bn (5 arty bty)
Engr	1 bn
Presidential Guard	1 bn
AD	1 bn (6 AD bty)

EQUIPMENT BY TYPE
RECCE 65: 31 AML-90; 6 AMX-10RC; 15 *Ferret*; 8 M-8; 5 VBL
AIFV 22: 8 LAV-150 *Commando* with 20mm gun; 14 LAV-150 *Commando* with 90mm gun
APC 33
  APC (T) 12 M-3 half-track
  APC (W) 21 LAV-150 *Commando*
ARTY 94+
  TOWED 58: **75mm** 6 M-116 pack; **105mm** 20 M-101; **130mm** 24: 12 Model 1982 gun 82 (reported); 12 Type-59 (M-46); **155mm** 8 I1
  MRL 122mm 20 BM-21
  MOR 16+: **81mm** (some SP); **120mm** 16 Brandt
AT • MSL 49
  SP 24 TOW (on jeeps)
  MANPATS 25 Milan
  RCL 53: **106mm** 40 M-40A2; **75mm** 13 Type-52 (M-20)
  RL 89mm LRAC

AD • GUNS • TOWED 54: **14.5mm** 18 Type-58 (ZPU-2); **35mm** 18 GDF-002; **37mm** 18 Type-63

Navy ε1,300

FORCES BY ROLE

Navy 1 HQ located at Douala

EQUIPMENT BY TYPE

PATROL AND COASTAL COMBATANTS 11
    PCO 2: 1 *Bakassi* (Fr P-48); 1 *L'Audacieux* (Fr P-48)
    PCI 1 *Quartier*
    PCR 2 *Swift*-38
    PB 6: 2 *Rodman* 101; 4 *Rodman* 46
AMPHIBIOUS • LCU 2 (30 ft)

FACILITIES

Bases   Located at Douala, Limbe, Kribi

Air Force 300

FORCES BY ROLE

Air	1 composite sqn; 1 Presidential Fleet
FGA	sqn with 6 MB-326K; 4 *Alpha Jet*†; 5 CM-170 *Magister*
MP	sqn with 2 DO-128D-6 *Turbo SkyServant*
Tpt	sqn with 1 B-707; 3 C-130H-30 *Hercules*; 1 DHC-4 *Caribou*; 4 DHC-5D *Buffalo*; 1 *Gulfstream* III; 1 IAI-201 *Arava*; 2 PA-23 *Aztec*
Atk hel	sqn with 3 Mi-24 *Hind*; 4 SA-342 *Gazelle* (with HOT)
Spt hel	sqn with 1 AS-332 *Super Puma*; 1 AS-365 *Dauphin* 2; 3 Bell 206 *JetRanger*; 1 SA-318 *Alouette II*; 3 SA-319 *Alouette III*; 3 SE 3130 *Alouette II*

EQUIPMENT BY TYPE

AIRCRAFT 15 combat capable
    FGA 15: 6 MB-326K; 4 *Alpha Jet*†; 5 CM-170 *Magister*
    TPT 13: 1 B-707; 3 C-130H-30 *Hercules*; 1 DHC-4 *Caribou*; 4 DHC-5D *Buffalo*; 2 DO-128D-6 *Turbo SkyServant*; 1 *Gulfstream* III; 1 IAI-201 *Arava*
    UTL 2: 2 PA-23 *Aztec*
HELICOPTERS
    ATK 7: 3 Mi-24 *Hind*; 4 SA-342 *Gazelle* (with HOT)
    SPT 1 AS-332 *Super Puma*
    UTL 11: 1 AS-365 *Dauphin* 2; 3 Bell 206 *JetRanger*; 1 SA-318 *Alouette II*; 3 SA-319 *Alouette III*; 3 SE 3130 *Alouette II*

Paramilitary 9,000

Gendarmerie 9,000

Regional Spt 3 gp

DEPLOYMENT

DEMOCRATIC REPUBLIC OF CONGO

UN • **MONUC** 5 obs

SUDAN

AU • **AUMIS** 30 obs

Cape Verde CV

Cape Verde Escudo E		2006	2007	2008
GDP	E	101bn	117bn	
	US$	1.15bn	1.49bn	
per capita	US$	2,729	3,509	
Growth	%	6.5	6.9	
Inflation	%	5.4	2.5	
Def bdgt	E	626m	640m	
	US$	7.1m	8.1m	
US$1=E		87.9	78.8	

Population	423,613

Age	0–14	15–19	20–24	25–29	30–64	65 plus
Male	20%	6%	5%	3%	12%	3%
Female	19%	6%	5%	3%	14%	4%

Capabilities

ACTIVE 1,200 (Army 1,000 Coast Guard 100 Air 100)

Terms of service conscription (selective)

ORGANISATIONS BY SERVICE

Army 1,000

FORCES BY ROLE

Inf 2 bn (gp)

EQUIPMENT BY TYPE

RECCE 10 BRDM-2
ARTY 42
    TOWED 24: **75mm** 12; **76mm** 12
    MOR 18: **82mm** 12; **120mm** 6 M-1943
AT • RL 73mm RPG-7 *Knout*; **89mm** (3.5in)
AD • SAM • MANPAD 50 SA-7 *Grail*
    GUNS • TOWED 30: **14.5mm** 18 ZPU-1; **23mm** 12 ZU-23

Coast Guard ε100

PATROL AND COASTAL COMBATANTS 2
    PCC 1 *Kondor I*
    PCI 1 *Espadarte* less than 100 tonnes

Air Force up to 100

FORCES BY ROLE

MR 1 sqn with 1 Do-228; 1 EMB-110

EQUIPMENT BY TYPE

AIRCRAFT • TPT 2: 1 Do-228; 1 EMB-110

FOREIGN FORCES

Portugal Navy: 2

Central African Republic CAR

CFA Franc BEAC fr		2006	2007	2008
GDP	fr	783bn	832bn	
	US$	1.5bn	1.8bn	
per capita	US$	348	412	
Growth	%	3.8	4.0	
Inflation	%	6.7	3.1	
Def bdgt	fr	ε8.2bn	ε8.5bn	
	US$	ε16m	ε18m	
US$1=fr		522	462	

Population   4,369,038

Age	0–14	15–19	20–24	25–29	30–64	65 plus
Male	21%	6%	5%	4%	12%	2%
Female	21%	6%	5%	4%	13%	2%

Capabilities

ACTIVE 3,150 (Army 2,000 Air 150 Gendarmerie 1,000)

Terms of service conscription (selective), 2 years; reserve obligation thereafter, term n.k.

ORGANISATIONS BY SERVICE

Joint
Combined Service 1 (Intervention and sp) bn

Army ε2,000
FORCES BY ROLE

HQ/Spt	1 regt
Army	1 (combined arms) regt (1 mech bn, 1 inf bn)
Territorial Def	1 regt (bn) (2 Territorial bn (Intervention))

EQUIPMENT BY TYPE
MBT 3 T-55†
RECCE 8 *Ferret*†
APC (W) 39+: 4 BTR-152†; 25+ TPK 4.20 VSC *ACMAT*†; 10+ VAB†
ARTY • MOR 12+: 81mm†; 120mm 12 M-1943†
AT • RCL 106mm 14 M-40†
   RL 73mm RPG-7 *Knout*†; 89mm LRAC†
PATROL AND COASTAL COMBATANTS 9 PCR† less than 100 tonnes

Air Force 150
FORCES BY ROLE
no cbt ac, no armed hel

Tpt	sqn with 1 *Caravelle*; 1 Cessna 337 *Skymaster*; 1 *Mystère* 20 (*Falcon* 20)
Liaison	sqn with 6 AL-60; 6 MH-1521 *M Broussard*
Hel	sqn with 1 AS-350 *Ecureuil*; 1 SE 3130 *Alouette II*

EQUIPMENT BY TYPE
AIRCRAFT • TPT 15: 6 AL-60; 1 *Caravelle*; 1 Cessna 337 *Skymaster*; 6 MH-1521 *M Broussard*; 1 *Mystère* 20 (*Falcon* 20)
HELICOPTERS
   SPT 1 AS-350 *Ecureuil*
   UTL 1 SE 3130 *Alouette II*

Paramilitary

Gendarmerie ε1,000
3 Regional legions, 8 bde

FOREIGN FORCES

Belgium 100 EUFOR Tchad/RCA
Chad 120 CEMAC
Congo 120 CEMA
Gabon 140 CEMAC
France 300 Op *Boali*; 1,500 EUFOR Tchad/RCA; MINURCAT 1 obs
Poland 100 EUFOR Tchad/RCA
South Africa 36 Op Vimbezela
Sweden 200 EUFOR Tchad/RCA

Chad Cha

CFA Franc BEAC fr		2006	2007	2008
GDP	fr	3.41tr	3.46tr	
	US$	6.5bn	7.5bn	
per capita	US$	659	733	
Growth	%	0.5	1.5	
Inflation	%	7,9	3.0	
Def bdgt	fr	30.9bn	33.3bn	
	US$	60m	72m	
US$1=fr		522	462	

Population   10,238,807

Age	0–14	15–19	20–24	25–29	30–64	65 plus
Male	24%	5%	4%	4%	10%	1%
Female	24%	5%	4%	4%	12%	2%

Capabilities

ACTIVE 25,350 (Army 17,000–20,000 Air 350 Republican Guard 5,000) Paramilitary 9,500
Terms of service conscription authorised

ORGANISATIONS BY SERVICE

Army ε17,000–20,000 (being re-organised)
FORCES BY ROLE
7 Mil Regions

Armd	1 bn
Inf	7 bn
Arty	1 bn
Engr	1 bn

EQUIPMENT BY TYPE

MBT 60 T-55
RECCE 174+: 50+ AML-60/AML-90; ε100 BRDM-2; 20 EE-9 *Cascavel*; 4 ERC-90F *Sagaie*
AIFV 9 LAV-150 *Commando* (with 90mm gun)
APC (W) ε20 BTR-60
ARTY 5+
  TOWED 105mm 5 M-2
  MOR 81mm; 120mm AM-50
AT • MSL • MANPATS *Eryx*; Milan
  RCL 106mm M-40A1
  RL 112mm APILAS; **73mm** RPG-7 *Knout*; **89mm** LRAC
AD • GUNS • TOWED 14.5mm ZPU-1/ZPU-2/ZPU-4; **23mm** ZU-23

Air Force 350
FORCES BY ROLE†

COIN   Unit with 2 PC-7 *Turbo Trainer*; 2 SF-260M *Warrior*
Tpt   sqn with 1 An-26 *Curl*; 2 C-130 *Hercules*; 2 Mi-17 (Mi-8MT) *Hip H**
Liaison sqn with 5 FTB-337 *Milirole*; 2 PC-6B *Turbo Porter** (trg)
Atk   sqn with 2 Mi-25V *Hind E*; 2 SA-316 *Alouette III**

EQUIPMENT BY TYPE
AIRCRAFT 4 combat capable
  COIN 4: 2 PC-7 *Turbo Trainer*; 2 SF-260M *Warrior*
  RECCE 5 FTB-337 *Milirole*
  TPT 5: 1 An-26 *Curl*; 2 C-130 *Hercules*; 2 PC-6B *Turbo Porter**
HELICOPTERS
  ATK 2 Mi-25V *Hind E*
  SPT 2 Mi-17 (Mi-8MT) *Hip H**
  UTL 2 SA-316 *Alouette III**

Paramilitary 9,500 active

Republican Guard 5,000

Gendarmerie 4,500

NON-STATE ARMED GROUPS
see Part II

DEPLOYMENT

CENTRAL AFRICAN REPUBLIC
CEMAC 120

CÔTE D'IVOIRE
UN • UNOCI 3 obs

SUDAN
AU • AUMIS 38

FOREIGN FORCES
EUFOR Chad/CAR (HQ Mont Valerien) expects 3,500-4,300 troops by Feb 2008 from:
Austria 160

Belgium 100
Finland 60
France 1,500;
Army 1,050: 1 recce sqn with ERC-90F *Sagaie*; 2 inf coy;
Air Force: 6 F-1CR *Mirage* RECCE/F-1CT *Mirage* Strike/FGA; 1 C-135 *Stratolifter* tpt ac; 3 C-160 *Transall* tpt ac; 3 SA-330 *Puma* spt hel; **Navy:** 400; 100; 300 *Op Boali*
Ireland 400
Netherlands 100
Poland 350
Portugal 2 hel
Romania 120
Sweden 200

Congo RC

CFA Franc BEAC fr		2006	2007	2008
GDP	fr	3.68tr	4.88tr	
	US$	7.1bn	10.6bn	
per capita	US$	1,907	2,779	
Growth	%	6.1	3.7	
Inflation	%	4.8	7.0	
Def bdgt	fr	44bn	e45bn	
	US$	84m	97m	
US$1=fr		522	462	

Population   3,800,610

Capabilities
ACTIVE 10,000 (Army 8,000 Navy 800 Air 1,200)
Paramilitary 2,000

ORGANISATIONS BY SERVICE

Army 8,000
FORCES BY ROLE

Armd   2 bn
Inf   1 bn; 2 bn (gp) (*each:* 1 lt tk tp, 1 (76mm gun) arty bty)
Cdo/AB 1 bn
Arty   1 gp (how, MPL)
Engr   1 bn

EQUIPMENT BY TYPE†
MBT 40+: 25 T-54/T-55; 15 Type-59; T-34 in store
LT TK 13: 3 PT-76; 10 Type-62
RECCE 25 BRDM-1/BRDM-2
APC (W) 68+: 20 BTR-152; 30 BTR-60; 18 *Mamba*; M-3 *Panhard*
ARTY 66+
  SP 122mm 3 2S1 *Carnation*
  TOWED 25+: 76mm ZIS-3 *M-1942*; **100mm** 10 M-1944; **122mm** 10 D-30; **130mm** 5 M-46; **152mm** D-20
  MRL 10+: 122mm 10 BM-21; **122mm** BM-14/**140mm** BM-16
  MOR 28+: 82mm; 120mm 28 M-43

AT • RCL **57mm** M-18
RL **73mm** RPG-7 *Knout*
GUNS **57mm** 5 ZIS-2 *M-1943*
AD • GUNS 28+
SP **23mm** ZSU-23-4
TOWED **14.5mm** ZPU-2/ZPU-4; **37mm** 28 M-1939;
57mm S-60; **100mm** KS-19

Navy ε800

EQUIPMENT BY TYPE
PATROL AND COASTAL COMBATANTS 3+
PFI 3 *Zhuk*†
MISC BOATS/CRAFT: various river boats
FACILITIES
Base   Located at Pointe Noire

Air Force 1,200†

FORCES BY ROLE
FGA   sqn with 12 MiG-21 *Fishbed* (non-op)
Tpt   sqn with 5 An-24 *Coke*; 1 An-26 *Curl*;
1 B-727; 1 N-2501 *Noratlas*
Trg   sqn with 4 L-39 *Albatros*
Hel   sqn with 3 Mi-8 *Hip*; 1 AS-365 *Dauphin 2*;
2 SA-316 *Alouette III*; 2 SA-318 *Alouette II*; 2 Mi-24
Hind

EQUIPMENT BY TYPE†
AIRCRAFT no combat-capable ac
FTR 12 MiG-21 *Fishbed* (non-op)
TPT 8: 5 An-24 *Coke*; 1 An-26 *Curl*; 1 B-727; 1 N-2501
Noratlas
TRG 4 L-39 *Albatros*
HELICOPTERS
ATK 2 Mi-24 *Hind*
SPT 3 Mi-8 *Hip*
UTL 5: 1 AS-365 *Dauphin 2*; 2 SA-316 *Alouette III*; 2 SA-
318 *Alouette II*
MSL AAM AA-2 *Atoll*

Paramilitary 2,000 active

Gendarmerie 2,000
Paramilitary   20 coy

Presidential Guard some
Paramilitary   1 bn

DEPLOYMENT

CENTRAL AFRICAN REPUBLIC
CEMAC 120

SUDAN
AU • AUMIS 14 obs

Côte D'Ivoire CI

CFA Franc BCEAO fr		2006	2007	2008
GDP	fr	9.17tr	9.48tr	
	US$	17.6bn	20.5bn	
per capita	US$	996	1,140	
Growth	%	0.9	1.7	
Inflation	%	2.5	2.5	
Def bdgt	fr	139bn	139bn	
	US$	266m	300m	
US$1=fr			522	462

Population   18,013,409

Age	0–14	15–19	20–24	25–29	30–64	65 plus
Male	20%	6%	5%	4%	14%	1%
Female	21%	6%	5%	4%	13%	1%

Capabilities

ACTIVE 17,050 (Army 6,500 Navy 900 Air 700
Presidential Guard 1,350 Gendarmerie 7,600)
Paramilitary 1,500

RESERVE 10,000 (Joint 10,000)

ORGANISATIONS BY SERVICE

Army 6,500

FORCES BY ROLE
4 Mil Regions
Armd   1 bn
Inf   3 bn
AB   1 gp
Arty   1 bn
ADA   1 coy
Engr   1 coy

EQUIPMENT BY TYPE
MBT 10 T-55
LT TK 5 AMX-13
RECCE 34: 15 AML-60/AML-90; 13 BRDM-2; ERC-90F4
Sagaie
AIFV 10 BMP-1/BMP-2
APC (W) 41: 12 M-3 *Panhard*; 10 *Mamba*; 13 VAB; 6 BTR-80
ARTY 36+
TOWED 4+: **105mm** 4 M-1950; **122mm** (reported)
MRL **122mm** 6 BM-21
MOR 26+: **81mm**; **82mm** 10 M-37; **120mm** 16 AM-50
AT • MSL • MANPATS **AT-14** 9M133 *Kornet* (reported);
AT-5 9K113 *Spandrel* (reported)
RCL **106mm** ε12 M-40A1
RL **73mm** RPG-7 *Knout*; **89mm** LRAC
AD • SAM • MANPAD SA-7 *Grail* (reported)
GUNS 21+
SP **20mm** 6 M3 VDAA
TOWED 15+: **20mm** 10 M3 VDAA; **23mm** ZU-23-2;
40mm 5 L/60

Navy ε900

EQUIPMENT BY TYPE

PATROL AND COASTAL COMBATANTS 3
  PCC 1 *Intrepide* (Fr Patria)
  PBR 2 *Rodman* (fishery protection duties)
AMPHIBIOUS • 2 LCM

FACILITIES

Base   Located at Locodjo (Abidjan)

Air Force 700

Current force structure uncertain; air force neutralised following French attack on 6 Nov 04. Authority given to repair 4 Su-25s and several training ac and helicopters.

EQUIPMENT BY TYPE

AIRCRAFT 6 combat capable†
  FTR 4 Su-25UBK
  TRG 2 BAC-167 *Strikemaster**
HELICOPTERS • **SPT** 8+: 4 Mi-24V; Mi-17; 4 IAR-330L (SA-330L) *Puma*

Paramilitary 10,450

Presidential Guard 1,350

Gendarmerie 7,600

APC (W): some VAB
PATROL AND COASTAL COMBATANTS 4 PB *Patrol boat*

Militia 1,500

Armed Forces 10,000 reservists

NON-STATE ARMED GROUPS

see Part II

FOREIGN FORCES

(All under opcon UNOCI)
Bangladesh 2,728; 10 obs
Benin 423; 6 obs
Bolivia 3 obs
Brazil 3; 4 obs
Chad 3 obs
China, People's Republic of 7 obs
Congo 5 obs
Croatia 2 obs
Dominican Republic 4 obs
Ecuador 2 obs
El Salvador 3 obs
Ethiopia 2 obs
France Army 3,800; UNOCI 183; 2 obs
Ghana 542; 6 obs
Guatemala 5 obs
Guinea 3 obs
India 8 obs
Ireland 2 obs
Jordan 1,062; 7 obs
Kenya 4; 4 obs
Moldova 4 obs
Morocco 724
Namibia 2 obs
Nepal 3 obs
Niger 384; 6 obs
Nigeria 6 obs
Pakistan 1,124; 12 obs
Paraguay 2; 8 obs
Peru 3 obs
Philippines 3; 4 obs
Poland 2 obs
Romania 7 obs
Russia 9 obs
Senegal 328; 9 obs
Serbia 3 obs
Tanzania 2; 1 obs
Tunisia 2; 5 obs
Gambia 3 obs
Tanzania 1; 1 obs
Togo 318; 5 obs
Tunisia 2; 4 obs
Uganda 2; 2 obs
United States Army 3, USMC 14
Uruguay 2 obs
Yemen, Republic of 6 obs
Zambia 2 obs
Zimbabwe 2 obs

Democratic Republic of Congo
DROC

Congolese Franc fr		2006	2007	2008
GDP	fr	4.05tr	5.09tr	
	US$	8.7bn	9.1bn	
per capita	US$	139	141	
Growth	%	5.1	6.5	
Inflation	%	13.2	17.5	
Def bdgt	fr	76.2bn	ε101bn	
	US$	163m	181m	
US$1=fr		467	560	

Population   64,606,759

Capabilities

ACTIVE 134,484 (Army 125,233 Navy 6,703 Air 2,548)

ORGANISATIONS BY SERVICE

Army (Forces Armées de la République Démocratique du Congo (FARDC)) ε111,233

FORCES BY ROLE

Mech inf	1 bde
Inf	14 bde
Cdo	2 regt

EQUIPMENT BY TYPE†

MBT 49: 12-17 Type-59 †; 32 T-55
LT TK 40: 10 PT-76; 30 Type-62† (reportedly being refurbished)
RECCE up to 52: up to 17 AML-60; 14 AML-90; 19 EE-9 *Cascavel*; 2 RAM-V-2
AIFV 20 BMP-1
APC 138:
  APC (T) 3 BTR-50
  APC (W) 135: 30-70 BTR-60PB; 58 M-3 *Panhard†*; 7 TH 390 *Fahd*
ARTY 534+
  TOWED 149: **75mm** 30 M-116 pack; **122mm** 77 (M-30) *M-1938*/D-30/Type-60; **130mm** 42 Type-59 (M-46)/Type-59 I
  MRL 57: **107mm** 12 Type-63; **122mm** 24 BM-21; **128mm** 6 M-51; **130mm** 3 Type-82; **132mm** 12
  MOR 328+: **81mm** 100; **82mm** 200; **107mm** M-30; **120mm** 28: 18; 10 Brandt
AT • RCL 36+: **57mm** M-18; **73mm** 10; **75mm** 10 M-20; **106mm** 16 M-40A1
  GUNS 85mm 10 Type-56 (D-44)
AD • SAM • MANPAD 20 SA-7 *Grail*
  GUNS • TOWED 114: **14.5mm** 12 ZPU-4; **37mm** 52 M-1939; **40mm** ε50 L/60† (probably out of service)

Republican Guard circa 14,000

FORCES BY ROLE

Armd	1 regt
Republican Guard	3 bde

Navy 6,703 (incl. infantry and marines)

EQUIPMENT BY TYPE
PATROL AND COASTAL COMBATANTS 3:
  PFC 1 *Shanghaii* II type 062 fast attack craft (2 additional vessels †)
  PCI 2 *Swiftships†*; 20 various (all under 50ft)
FACILITIES
Bases Located at Kinshasa (*River*), Boma (*River*), Lake Tanganyika, Matadi (Coastal)

Air Force 2,548

AIRCRAFT 5 combat capable
  FTR 2 MiG-23 *Flogger*
  FGA 3 SU-25 *Frogfoot*
HELICOPTERS
  ATK 4 Mi-24/35 *Hind*
  SPT 36: 1 Mi-26 *Halo* (non op); 35 Mi-8 *Hip* (very few serviceable)

Paramilitary • National Police Force
incl Rapid Intervention Police (National and Provincial forces)

People's Defence Force

NON-STATE ARMED GROUPS

see Part II

FOREIGN FORCES

All under opcon MONUC unless otherwise specified
Algeria 5 obs
Bangladesh 1,333; 27 obs
Belgium 2; 9 observers
Benin 750; 20 obs
Bolivia 200; 10 obs
Bosnia and Herzegovina 5 obs
Burkina Faso 12 obs
Cameroon 2 obs
Canada 10 obs (*Operation Crocodile*)
China, Peoples Republic of 218; 1 Inf gp; 14 obs
Czech Republic 3 obs
Denmark 2 obs
Egypt 23 obs
France 12 EUPOL KINSHASA
Germany 1 obs
Ghana 461; 25 obs
Guatemala 105; 9 obs
India 4,376; 49 obs
Indonesia 175; 12 obs
Ireland 3 obs
Italy 4 EUPOL KINSHASA; 1 EUSEC
Jordan 66; 27 obs
Kenya 38 obs
Malawi 110; 28 obs
Malaysia 17 obs
Mali 29 obs
Mongolia 2 obs
Morocco 809; 4 obs
Mozambique 4 obs
Nepal 1,029; 20 obs
Netherlands 2 EUPOL KINSHASA; 3 EUSEC
Niger 20 obs
Nigeria 29 obs
Pakistan 3,560; 46 obs
Paraguay 19 obs
Peru 6 obs
Poland 2 obs
Portugal 22 KINSHASA; 2 EUSEC
Romania 25 obs
Russia 28 obs
Senegal 458; 22 obs
Serbia 6
South Africa 1,186 (*Operation Mistral*); 39 (*Operation Teutonic* – Assist DROC Military); 20 obs; 1 Engr coy; 1 bn gp; air element; air med evacuation team; ac rescue and fire fighting team
Spain 2 obs
Sri Lanka 2 obs
Sweden 5 obs
Switzerland 2 obs

Tunisia 464; 34 obs
Turkey 17
Ukraine 13 obs
United Kingdom 6 obs
United States Army 2; USMC 8
Uruguay 1,324; 46 obs
Yemen, Republic of 2
Zambia 25 obs

Djibouti Dj

Djiboutian Franc fr		2006	2007	2008
GDP	fr	135bn	148bn	
	US$	758m	846m	
per capita	US$	1,559	1,704	
Growth	%	4.8	4.8	
Inflation	%	3.5	3.5	
Def bdgt	fr	3.09bn	2.95bn	
	US$	17.4m	16.9m	
FMA (US)	US$	3.9m	4.0m	3.2m
US$1=fr		178	175	

Population   496,374

Ethnic Groups: Somali 60%; Afar 35%

Age	0–14	15–19	20–24	25–29	30–64	65 plus
Male	22%	5%	5%	4%	14%	2%
Female	22%	5%	5%	4%	12%	2%

Capabilities

ACTIVE 10,950 (Army 8,000 Navy 200 Air 250
National Security Force 2,500) **Paramilitary 1,400**

ORGANISATIONS BY SERVICE

Army ε8,000
FORCES BY ROLE
3 Comd (North, Central and South)
Armd   1 sqn
Inf   1 bn (1 AT pl, 1 mor pl)
Cdo   2 (border) bn
AB   1 coy
Arty   1 bty
Spt   1 bn

EQUIPMENT BY TYPE
RECCE 19: 4 AML-60†; 15 VBL
APC (W) 12 BTR-60†
ARTY 51
    TOWED 122mm 6 D-30
    MOR 45: 81mm 25; 120mm 20 Brandt
AT
    RCL 106mm 16 M-40A1
    RL 73mm RPG-7 *Knout*; 89mm LRAC

AD • GUNS 15+
    SP 20mm 5 M-693 (SP
    TOWED 10: 23mm 5 ZU-23; 40mm 5 L/70

Navy ε200
EQUIPMENT BY TYPE
PATROL AND COASTAL COMBATANTS 7
    PCI 1 *Sawari* less than 100 tonnes
    PB 6: 4 (ex-USCG); 2 *Battalion-17*
FACILITIES
Base   Located at Djibouti

Air Force 250
FORCES BY ROLE
Tpt some sqn with 1 An-28 *Cash*; 2 L-410UVP *Turbolet*;
    1 Cessna U-206G *Stationair*; 1 Cessna 208 *Caravan I*
Hel some sqn with 1 AS-355F *Ecureuil II*; 1 Mi-17 (Mi-
    8MT) *Hip H*

EQUIPMENT BY TYPE
AIRCRAFT
    TPT 4: 1 An-28 *Cash*; 1 Cessna 402 in store; 2 L-410UVP
    Turbolet
    UTL 2: 1 Cessna U-206G *Stationair*; 1 Cessna 208 *Caravan
    I*
HELICOPTERS • SPT 4: 1 AS-355F *Ecureuil II*; 1 in store;
1 Mi-8 in store; 1 Mi-17 (Mi-8MT) *Hip H*

Paramilitary ε2,500 active (3,900 total)

National Security Force ε2,500
Ministry of Interior

Gendarmerie 1,400
Ministry of Defence
FORCES BY ROLE
Paramilitary   1 bn

EQUIPMENT BY TYPE
    PATROL AND COASTAL COMBATANTS 1 PB

DEPLOYMENT

WESTERN SAHARA
UN • MINURSO 2 obs

FOREIGN FORCES

France 2,850 Army: 2 (combined) army regt (*each:* 1
engr coy, 1 arty bty, 2 recce sqn, 2 inf coy) Air Force: 1
Air sqn with 10 M-2000 *Mirage*; 1 C-160 *Transall*; 3 SA-
342 *Gazelle*; 7 SA-330 *Puma*; 1 AS-555 *Fennec*; 1 SA-319
Alouette III
Germany 257; 2 *Sea King* MK41 SAR hel; 2 UH-1D *Iroquois*
utl hel
Korea, Republic of 1
United States Army: 560; Navy: 765; USAF 340; USMC:
373

Equatorial Guinea EG

CFA Franc BEAC fr		2006	2007	2008
GDP	fr	4.24tr	4.99tr	
	US$	8.1bn	10.8bn	
per capita	US$	15,049	19,603	
Growth	%	-5.2	10.1	
Inflation	%	4.5	6.1	
Def bdgt	fr			
	US$			
US$1=fr		522	462	

Population 551,201

Age	0–14	15–19	20–24	25–29	30–64	65 plus
Male	21%	5%	5%	4%	12%	2%
Female	21%	5%	5%	4%	14%	2%

Capabilities

ACTIVE 1,320 (Army 1,100 Navy 120 Air 100)

ORGANISATIONS BY SERVICE

Army 1,100
FORCES BY ROLE
Inf 3 bn

EQUIPMENT BY TYPE
RECCE 6 BRDM-2
APC (W) 10 BTR-152

Navy ε120
EQUIPMENT BY TYPE†
PATROL AND COASTAL COMBATANTS 5
  PC 1 Daphne
  PCI 2 Zhuk
  PBR 2
FACILITIES
Bases Located at Bata, Malabo (Santa Isabel)

Air Force 100
FORCES BY ROLE
Tpt   sqn with 3 CASA 212 Aviocar; 1 Cessna 337
       Skymaster; 1 YAK-40 Codling; 2 SA-316 Alouette III

EQUIPMENT BY TYPE
AIRCRAFT • TPT 5: 3 CASA 212 Aviocar; 1 Cessna 337
Skymaster; 1 YAK-40 Codling
HELICOPTERS • UTL 2 SA-316 Alouette III

Paramilitary

Guardia Civil some
2 coy

Coast Guard
PATROL AND COASTAL COMBATANTS 1 PCI†

Eritrea Er

Eritrean Nakfa ERN		2006	2007	2008
GDP	ERN	18.0bn	21.0bn	
	US$	1.18bn	1.40bn	
per capita	US$	246	285	
Growth	%	2.0	1.3	
Inflation	%	17.3	22.7	
Def bdgt	ERN			
	US$			
USD1=ERN		15.3	15.0	

Population 4,906,585

Ethnic Groups: Tigrinya 50%; Tigre and Kunama 40%; Afar;
Saho 3%

Age	0–14	15–19	20–24	25–29	30–64	65 plus
Male	22%	5%	5%	4%	12%	2%
Female	22%	5%	5%	4%	12%	2%

Capabilities

ACTIVE 201,750 (Army 200,000 Navy 1,400 Air 350)
Terms of service 16 months (4 month mil trg)

RESERVE 120,000 (Army ε120,000)

ORGANISATIONS BY SERVICE

Army ε200,000
FORCES BY ROLE
Army 4 corps
Mech 1 bde
Inf 20 div
Cdo 1 div

EQUIPMENT BY TYPE
MBT 150 T-54/T-55
RECCE 40 BRDM-1/BRDM-2
AIFV/APC 40 BMP-1/BTR-60
ARTY 170+
  SP 25: 122mm 12 2S1 Carnation; 152mm 13 2S5
  TOWED 10+: 122mm D-30; 130mm 10 M-46
  MRL 122mm 35 BM-21
  MOR 120mm/160mm 100+
AT
  MSL • MANPATS 200 AT-3 9K11 Sagger/AT-5 9K113
  Spandrel
  RL 73mm RPG-7 Knout
  GUNS 85mm D-44
AD • SAM • MANPAD SA-7 Grail
  GUNS 70+
    SP 23mm ZSU-23-4
    TOWED 23mm ZU-23

Navy 1,400

FORCES BY ROLE

Navy 1 HQ located at Massawa

EQUIPMENT BY TYPE

PATROL AND COASTAL COMBATANTS 13

PFM 1 Osa II† with 4 Single each with SS-N-2B *Styx* tactical SSM

PFI 4 *Super Dvora* less than 100 tonnes

PCI 3 *Swiftships*

PBF 5

AMPHIBIOUS

LS • LST 2: 1 *Chamo†* (Ministry of Transport); 1 *Ashdod†*

FACILITIES

Bases Located at Massawa, Assab, Dahlak

Air Force ε350

FORCES BY ROLE

Ftr/FGA   sqn with 5 MiG-29 *Fulcrum*; 1 SU-27 *Flanker*; 4 MiG-23 *Flogger†*; 3 MiG-21 *Fishbed†*; 1 MiG-29UB *Fulcrum**

Tpt   sqn with 1 IAI-1125 *Astra*; 3 Y-12(II)

Trg   sqn with 8 L-90 *Redigo*; 4 MB-339CE*

Hel   sqn with 1 Mi-24-4 *Hind*; 4 Mi-17 (Mi-8MT) *Hip H*/Mi-8 *Hip*

EQUIPMENT BY TYPE

AIRCRAFT 18 combat capable

FTR 13: 5 MiG-29 *Fulcrum*; 1 SU-27 *Flanker*; 4 MiG-23 *Flogger†*; 3 MiG-21 *Fishbed†*

TPT 4: 1 IAI-1125 *Astra*; 3 Y-12(II)

TRG 13: 8 L-90 *Redigo*; 4 MB-339CE*; 1 MiG-29UB *Fulcrum**

HELICOPTERS

ATK 1 Mi-24-4 *Hind*

SPT 4 Mi-17 (Mi-8MT) *Hip H*/Mi-8 *Hip*

NON-STATE ARMED GROUPS

see Part II

FOREIGN FORCES

(all UNMEE, unless otherwise indicated; total numbers for forces deployed in Ethiopia and Eritrea)

Algeria 8 obs; 2 obs OLMEE

Austria 2 obs

Bangladesh 5; 8 obs

Bolivia 5 obs

Bosnia-Herzegovina 5 obs

Brazil 7 obs

Bulgaria 4 obs

China 6 obs

Croatia 4 obs

Czech Republic 2 obs

Denmark 3 obs

Finland 5 obs

France 1 obs

Gambia 1, 2 obs

Germany 2 obs

Ghana 3; 10 obs; 3 obs OLMEE

Greece 2 obs

Guatemala 4 obs

India 715, 8 obs

Iran 3 obs

Jordan 570; 8 obs

Kenya 118, 10 obs

Kyrgystan 4 obs

Malaysia 3; 7 obs

Mongolia 4 obs

Namibia 3; 4 obs

Nepal 3 obs

Nigeria 1; 8 obs; 2 obs OLMEE

Norway 3 obs

Pakistan 6 obs

Paraguay 4 obs

Peru 4 obs

Poland 3 obs

Romania 4 obs

Russia 3 obs

South Africa 5 obs; 2 obs OLMEE

Spain 3 obs

Sri Lanka 4 obs

Sweden 3 obs

Switzerland

Tanzania 2, 8 obs

Tunisia 3; 5 obs; 1 obs OLMEE

Ukraine 3 obs

United States 5 obs; Army 2

Uruguay 37; 4 obs

Zambia 3; 10 obs

Ethiopia Eth

Ethiopian Birr EB		2006	2007	2008
GDP	EB	115bn	151bn	
	US$	13.2bn	16.6bn	
per capita	US$	177	217	
Growth	%	9.0	10.5	
Inflation	%	12.3	17.8	
Def bdgt	EB	3.0bn	3.0bn	
	US$	345m	330m	
FMA (US)	US$	2.0m	2.0m	0.8m
US$1=EB		8.7	9.1	

Population	76,511,887

Ethnic Groups: Oromo 40%; Amhara and Tigrean 32%; Sidamo 9%; Shankella 6%; Somali 6%; Afar 4%

Age	0–14	15–19	20–24	25–29	30–64	65 plus
Male	22%	6%	5%	4%	13%	1%
Female	22%	6%	5%	4%	13%	1%

Capabilities

ACTIVE 138,000 (Army 135,000 Air 3,000)

ORGANISATIONS BY SERVICE

Army 135,000 (increased by 15,000 in 2007)

FORCES BY ROLE

4 Mil Regional Commands (Northern, Western, Central, and Eastern) each acting as corps HQ and one functional (Support) Command; strategic reserve of 4 divs and 6 specialist bdes centred on Addis Ababa.

Army 4 corps HQ (*each:* 1 mech div, 4-6 inf div)

EQUIPMENT BY TYPE

MBT 246+ T-54/T-55/T-62
RECCE/AIFV/APC (W) ε450 BRDM/BMP/BTR-60/BTR-152/Type 89
ARTY 460+
  SP 10+: **122mm** 2S1 *Carnation*; **152mm** 10 2S19 *Farm*
  TOWED 400+: **76mm** ZIS-3 *M-1942*; **122mm** ε400 D-30/(M-30) *M-1938*; **130mm** M-46
  MRL 122mm ε50 BM-21
  MOR 81mm M-1/M-29; **82mm** M-1937; **120mm** M-1944
AT • MSL • MANPATS AT-3 9K11 *Sagger*; AT-4 9K111 *Spigot*
  RCL 82mm B-10; **107mm** B-11
  GUNS 85mm εD-44
AD • SAM ε370
  TOWED SA-2 *Guideline*/SA-3 *Goa*
  MANPAD SA-7 *Grail*
  GUNS
    SP 23mm ZSU-23-4
    TOWED 23mm ZU-23; **37mm** M-1939; **57mm** S-60

Air Force 3,000

FORCES BY ROLE

FGA   sqns with 6 SU-27 *Flanker*; 25 MiG-21MF *Fishbed J*; 2 SU-25T *Frogfoot*; 13 MiG-23BN *Flogger H*; 2 SU-25UB *Frogfoot B*
Tpt   sqns with 10 AN-12 *Cub*; 4 C-130B *Hercules*; 6 DHC-6 twin *Otter*; 2 Y-12; 1 YAK-40 *Codling* (VIP)
Atk hel sqn with 25 Mi-24 *Hind*
Spt hel sqn with 12 Mi-17 (Mi-8MT) *Hip H*/Mi-8 *Hip*
Trg   sqn with 12 L-39 *Albatros*; 4 SF-260

EQUIPMENT BY TYPE

AIRCRAFT 48 combat capable
  FTR 31: 6 SU-27 *Flanker*; 25 MiG-21MF *Fishbed J*
  FGA 15: 2 SU-25T *Frogfoot*; 13 MiG-23BN *Flogger H*
  TPT 23: 10 AN-12 *Cub*; 4 C-130B *Hercules*; 6 DHC-6 *Twin Otter*; 2 Y-12; 1 YAK-40 *Codling* (VIP)
  TRG 18: 12 L-39 *Albatros*; 4 SF-260; 2 SU-25UB *Frogfoot B**
HELICOPTERS
  ATK 25 Mi-24 *Hind*
  SPT 12 Mi-17 (Mi-8MT) *Hip H*/Mi-8 *Hip*

NON-STATE ARMED GROUPS

see Part II

DEPLOYMENT

COTE D'IVOIRE
UN • UNOCI 2 obs

LIBERIA
UN • UNMIL 1,804; 19 obs

SUDAN
UN/AU • UNAMID Will deploy up to 2,000 in 2008

FOREIGN FORCES

(all UNMEE, unless otherwise indicated; total numbers for forces deployed in Ethiopia and Eritrea)
Algeria 8 obs; 2 obs OLMEE
Austria 2 obs; 2 AMIS
Bangladesh 5; 8 obs
Bolivia 5 obs
Bosnia-Herzegovina 5 obs
Brazil 7 obs
Bulgaria 4 obs
China 6 obs
Croatia 4 obs
Czech Republic 2 obs
Denmark 3 obs
Finland 5 obs
France 1 obs
Gambia 1, 2 obs
Germany 2 obs
Ghana 3; 10 obs; 3 obs OLMEE
Greece 2 obs
Guatemala 4 obs
India 715, 8 obs
Iran 3 obs
Jordan 570; 8 obs
Kenya 118, 10 obs
Kyrgystan 4 obs
Malaysia 3; 7 obs
Mongolia 4 obs
Namibia 3; 4 obs
Nepal 3 obs
Nigeria 1; 8 obs; 2 obs OLMEE
Norway 3 obs
Pakistan 6 obs
Paraguay 4 obs
Peru 4 obs
Poland 3 obs
Romania 4 obs
Russia 3 obs
South Africa 5 obs; 2 obs OLMEE
Spain 3 obs
Sri Lanka 4 obs
Sweden 3 obs
Switzerland
Tanzania 2, 8 obs
Tunisia 3; 5 obs; 1 obs OLMEE

Ukraine 3 obs
United States 5 obs; Army 2; USMC 8
Uruguay 37; 4 obs
Zambia 3; 10 obs

Gabon Gbn

CFA Franc BEAC fr		2006	2007	2008
GDP	fr	4.72tr	5.15tr	
	US$	9.0bn	11.2bn	
per capita	US$	6,351	7,665	
Growth	%	1.2	4.8	
Inflation	%	4.0	5.5	
Def bdgt	fr			
	US$			
US$1=fr		522	462	

Population   1,454,867

Age	0–14	15–19	20–24	25–29	30–64	65 plus
Male	21%	6%	4%	3%	13%	2%
Female	21%	6%	4%	4%	13%	2%

Capabilities

ACTIVE 4,700 (Army 3,200 Navy 500 Air 1,000)
Paramilitary 2,000

ORGANISATIONS BY SERVICE

Army 3,200
FORCES BY ROLE
Inf   8 coy
Cdo/AB   1 coy
Engr   1 coy
Presidential1 (bn) gp (under direct presidential control)
Guard   (1 ADA bty, 1 arty bty, 1 armd/recce coy, 3 inf coy)

EQUIPMENT BY TYPE
RECCE 70: 24 AML-60/AML-90; 12 EE-3 *Jararaca*; 14 EE-9 *Cascavel*; 6 ERC-90F4 *Sagaie*; 14 VBL
AIFV 12 EE-11 *Urutu* (with 20mm gun)
APC (W) 23+: 9 LAV-150 *Commando*; 12 VXB-170; M-3 *Panhard*
ARTY 51
  TOWED 105mm 4 M-101
  MRL 140mm 8 Teruel
  MOR 39: **81mm** 35; **120mm** 4 Brandt
AT • MSL • MANPATS 4 *Milan*
  RCL 106mm M-40A1
  RL 89mm LRAC
AD • GUNS 41
  SP 20mm 4 ERC-20
  TOWED 37: **23mm** 24 ZU-23-2; **37mm** 10 M-1939; **40mm** 3 L/70

Navy ε500
FORCES BY ROLE
Navy 1 HQ located at Port Gentil

EQUIPMENT BY TYPE
PATROL AND COASTAL COMBATANTS 9
  PFM 1 *Patra*
  PCO 2 *General Ba'Oumar* (Fr P-400)
  PB 6 *Rodman* (all less than 100 tonnes)
AMPHIBIOUS
  LS • LST 1 *President Omar Bongo* (Fr Batral) (capacity 1 LCVP; 7 MBT; 140 troops) with 1 hel landing platform for a medium sized hel
  CRAFT 1 **LCM**

FACILITIES
Base   Located at Port Gentil

Air Force 1,000
FORCES BY ROLE
FGA 1 sqn with 5 *Mirage* 5G/3 *Mirage* 5DG; 4 *Mirage* 5E2; 6 *Mirage* F1-AZ
MP   1 sqn with 1 EMB-111*
CCT 1 (Presidential Guard) sqn with 4 CM-170 *Magister*; 3 T-34 *Turbo Mentor*
Tpt 1 (Presidential Guard) sqn with 1 ATR-42F; 1 EMB-110 *Bandeirante*; 1 *Falcon* 900; 1 AS-332 *Super Puma*; sqn with 1 C-130H *Hercules*; 1 CN-235; 1 EMB-110 *Bandeirante*; 3 L-100-30; 2 YS-11A
Hel 1 sqn with 5 SA-342 *Gazelle**; 3 SA-330C *Puma*/SA-330H *Puma*; 3 SA-316 *Alouette III*/SA-319 *Alouette III*; 2 AB-412 (Bell 412) *Twin Huey*

EQUIPMENT BY TYPE
AIRCRAFT 16+ combat capable
  FGA 15: 5 *Mirage* 5G/DG (*Mirage* 5); 4 *Mirage* 5E2; 6 *Mirage* F1-AZ
  RECCE 1 EMB-111*
  TPT 9: 1 ATR-42F; 1 C-130H *Hercules*; 1 CN-235; 2 EMB-110 *Bandeirante*; 1 *Falcon* 900; 3 L-100-30
  UTL 2 YS-11A
  TRG 7: 4 CM-170 *Magister*; 3 T-34 *Turbo Mentor*
HELICOPTERS
  ATK 5 SA-342 *Gazelle**
  SPT 4: 1 AS-332 *Super Puma*; 3 SA-330C *Puma*/SA-330H *Puma*
  UTL 5: 3 SA-316 *Alouette III*/SA-319 *Alouette III*; 2 AB-412 (Bell 412) *Twin Huey*

Paramilitary 2,000

Gendarmerie 2,000
FORCES BY ROLE
Armd   2 sqn
Paramilitary 3 bde; 11 coy
Avn   1 unit with 2 AS-350 *Ecureuil*; 1 AS-355 *Ecureuil*

EQUIPMENT BY TYPE
HELICOPTERS • SPT 3: 2 AS-350 *Ecureuil*; 1 AS-355 *Ecureuil*

Sub-Saharan Africa

DEPLOYMENT

SUDAN
UN • UNMIS 8 obs
UN/AU • UNAMID proposed deployment

Gambia Gam

Gambian Dalasi D		2006	2007	2008
GDP	D	13.4bn	15.9bn	
	US$	479m	837m	
per capita	US$	292	496	
Growth	%	6.5	7.0	
Inflation	%	1.4	5.0	
Def bdgt	D	ε45m		
	US$	ε1.6		
US$1=D		28	19	

Population	1,688,359

Age	0–14	15–19	20–24	25–29	30–64	65 plus
Male	22%	5%	4%	4%	13%	1%
Female	22%	5%	4%	4%	13%	1%

Capabilities

ACTIVE 800 (Army 800)

ORGANISATIONS BY SERVICE

Gambian National Army 800
Inf   2 bn
Engr   1 sqn
Presidential Guard 1 coy

Marine Unit circa 70
EQUIPMENT BY TYPE
PATROL AND COASTAL COMBATANTS 4: 4 PCI less than 100 tonnes
FACILITIES
Base   Located at Banjul

Air Wing
AIRCRAFT
  FGA 1 Su-25
  TPT 1 Il-62M (VIP)
  UTL 2 AT-802A
FACILITIES
Base   Located at Banjul (Yundum Intl Airport)
FACILITIES
Banjul-Yundum Intl Airport

DEPLOYMENT

CÔTE D'IVOIRE
UN • UNOCI 3 obs

ETHIOPIA/ERITREA
UN • UNMEE 1; 2 obs

LIBERIA
UN • UNMIL 2 obs

NEPAL
UN • UNMIN 4 obs

SUDAN
AU • AUMIS 200
UN • UNMIS 1
UN/AU • UNAMID proposed deployment

Ghana Gha

Ghanaian Cedi C		2006	2007	2008
GDP	C	116tr	140tr	
	US$	12.6bn	14.8bn	
per capita	US$	563	647	
Growth	%	6.2	6.3	
Inflation	%	10.9	9.4	
Def bdgt	C	760bn	980bn	1,228bn
	US$	83m	104m	
US$1=C		9,174	9,436	

Population	22,931,299

Age	0–14	15–19	20–24	25–29	30–64	65 plus
Male	20%	6%	5%	4%	14%	2%
Female	19%	6%	5%	4%	14%	2%

Capabilities

ACTIVE 13,500 (Army 10,000 Navy 2000 Air 1,500)

ORGANISATIONS BY SERVICE

Army 10,000
FORCES BY ROLE
2 Comd HQ
Army   6 inf bn
Recce   1 regt (3 Recce sqn)
AB/SF   2 coy
Arty   1 regt (1 Arty bty, 2 Mor bty)
Fd engr   1 regt (bn)
Trg   1 bn

EQUIPMENT BY TYPE
RECCE 3 EE-9 *Cascavel*
AIFV 19: 6 *Ratel* FSC-90; 13 *Ratel*-20
APC (W) 50 *Piranha*
ARTY 84
  TOWED 122mm 6 D-30
  MOR 78: **81mm** 50; **120mm** 28 *Tampella*
AT • **RCL 84mm** 50 *Carl Gustav*
AD • **SAM** • **MANPAD** SA-7 *Grail*
  GUNS • **TOWED** 8+: **14.5mm** 4+: 4 ZPU-2; ZPU-4; **23mm** 4 ZU-23-2

Navy 2,000

FORCES BY ROLE

Navy 1 (Western) HQ located at Sekondi; 1 (Eastern) HQ located at Tema

EQUIPMENT BY TYPE

PATROL AND COASTAL COMBATANTS 6

PFC 2 *Achimota* (Ge Lurssen 57m)

PCO 4: 2 *Anzole* (US); 2 *Dzata* (Ge Lurssen 45m)

FACILITIES

Bases Located at Sekondi, Tema

Air Force 1,500

Main base Accra. Tpt element at Takoradi

FORCES BY ROLE

Light   2 KA-8 (2 more reported on order).
attack/   7 MB-326K/L-39ZO/MB-339A unserviceable)
Trg

Tpt   1 sqn with 1 *Defender*; 4 F-27 *Friendship*; 3 Cessna 172; 1 F-28 *Fellowship* (VIP)

Trg   flg school with 3 Cessna 172 *

Hel   1 sqn with 3 Mi-171V (one in Accra, 2 on UN duties in S Africa); 2 A-109A; 1 AB-212 (Bell 212); 2 SA-319 *Alouette III*

EQUIPMENT BY TYPE

AIRCRAFT 9 combat capable†

FGA 9: 2 KA-8; 3 MB-326K; 2 L-39ZO; 2 MB-339A

TPT 6: 1 *Defender*; 4 F-27 *Friendship*; 1 F-28 *Fellowship* (VIP)

TRG 3 Cessna 172

HELICOPTERS

SPT 3: 4 Mi-171V

UTL 5: 1 AB-212 (Bell 212) ; 2 A-109A; 2 SA-319 *Alouette* III

DEPLOYMENT

CÔTE D'IVOIRE

UN • UNOCI 542; 6 obs

DEMOCRATIC REPUBLIC OF CONGO

UN • MONUC 461; 24 obs

ETHIOPIA/ERITREA

AU • OLMEE 3 obs

UN • UNMEE 3; 10 obs

LEBANON

UN • UNIFIL 1 inf bn; 868

LIBERIA

UN • UNMIL 859; 12 obs

NEPAL

UN • UNMIN 5 obs

SIERRA LEONE

UN • UNIOSIL 2 obs

SOMALIA

AU • AMISOM proposed deployment

SOUTH AFRICA

2 Mi-171V

SUDAN

AU • AUMIS 23 obs

UN • UNMIS 3

UN/AU • UNAMID proposed deployment

WESTERN SAHARA

UN • MINURSO 8; 8 obs

Guinea Gui

Guinean Franc fr		2006	2007	2008
GDP	fr	17.1tr	20.4tr	
	US$	3.1bn	4.8bn	
per capita	US$	317	486	
Growth	%	2.2	1.5	
Inflation	%	34.7	23.4	
Def bdgt	fr	ε200bn	ε220bn	
	US$	ε36m	ε52m	
US$1=fr		5,550	4,219	

Population   9,947,814

Age	0–14	15–19	20–24	25–29	30–64	65 plus
Male	22%	5%	4%	4%	13%	1%
Female	22%	5%	4%	4%	13%	2%

Capabilities

ACTIVE 12,300 (Army 8,500 Navy 400 Air 800 Gendarmerie 1,000 Republican Guard 1,600) Paramilitary 7,000

Terms of service conscription, 2 years

ORGANISATIONS BY SERVICE

Army 8,500

FORCES BY ROLE

Armd   1 bn

Inf   5 bn

SF   1 bn

Ranger 1 bn

Cdo   1 bn

Arty   1 bn

Engr   1 bn

AD   1 bn

EQUIPMENT BY TYPE†

MBT 38: 8 T-54; 30 T-34

LT TK 15 PT-76

RECCE 27: 2 AML-90; 25 BRDM-1/BRDM-2

APC (W) 40: 16 BTR-40; 10 BTR-50; 8 BTR-60; 6 BTR-152

ARTY 40+

TOWED 20: **76mm** 8 ZIS-3 *M-1942*; **122mm** 12 M-1931/37

MOR 20+: **82mm** M-43; **120mm** 20 M-1943/M-38

AT • MSL • MANPATS AT-3 9K11 *Sagger*
  RCL 82mm B-10
  RL 73mm RPG-7 *Knout*
  GUNS 6+: **57mm** ZIS-2 *M-1943*; **85mm** 6 D-44
AD • SAM • MANPAD SA-7 *Grail*
  GUNS • TOWED 24+: **30mm** M-53 (twin); **37mm** 8 M-1939; **57mm** 12 Type-59 (S-60); **100mm** 4 KS-19

Navy ε400

EQUIPMENT BY TYPE
PATROL AND COASTAL COMBATANTS • PCI 2
Swiftships† less than 100 tonnes
FACILITIES
Bases   Located at Conakry, Kakanda

Air Force 800

FORCES BY ROLE
FGA   sqn with 3 MiG-21 *Fishbed*; 4 MiG-17F *Fresco C*
Tpt   sqn with 1 An-24 *Coke*; 4 AN-14
Trg   sqn with 2 MiG-15UTI *Midget*
Hel   sqn with 1 SA-342K *Gazelle*; 1 SA-330
       Puma; 1† (IAR); 1 Mi-8 *Hip*; 1 SA-316B *Alouette III*

EQUIPMENT BY TYPE†
AIRCRAFT 7 combat capable
  FTR 7: 3 MiG-21 *Fishbed*: 4 MiG-17F *Fresco C*
  TPT 1 An-24 *Coke*
  UTL 4 An-14
  TRG 2 MiG-15UTI *Midget*
HELICOPTERS
  ATK 1 SA-342K *Gazelle*
  SPT 3: 1 SA-330 *Puma†*; 1 (IAR); 1 Mi-8 *Hip*
  UTL 1 SA-316B *Alouette III*
MSL
  AAM: AA-2 *Atoll*

Paramilitary 2,600 active

Gendarmerie 1,000

Republican Guard 1,600

People's Militia 7,000

NON-STATE ARMED GROUPS

see Part II

DEPLOYMENT

CÔTE D'IVOIRE
UN • UNOCI 3 obs

SUDAN
UN • UNMIS 4 obs

WESTERN SAHARA
UN • MINURSO 4 obs

Guinea Bissau GuB

CFA Franc BCEAO fr		2006	2007	2008
GDP	fr	173bn	177bn	
	US$	331m	383m	
per capita	US$	230	260	
Growth	%	2.7	2.5	
Inflation	%	2.0	3.0	
Def exp	fr	ε7.0bn	ε7.4bn	
	US$	ε14m	ε16m	
US$1=fr		522	462	

Population   1,472,041

Age	0–14	15–19	20–24	25–29	30–64	65 plus
Male	21%	5%	5%	4%	13%	1%
Female	21%	5%	5%	4%	13%	2%

Capabilities

ACTIVE 9,250 (Army 6,800 Navy 350 Air 100 Gendarmerie 2,000)
Terms of service conscription (selective).
As a result of the 1998 revolt by dissident army tps, manpower and eqpt totals should be treated with caution.

ORGANISATIONS BY SERVICE

Army 6,800

FORCES BY ROLE
Armd   1 bn (sqn)
Recce 1 coy
Inf   5 bn
Arty   1 bn
Engr   1 coy

EQUIPMENT BY TYPE
MBT 10 T-34
LT TK 15 PT-76
RECCE 10 BRDM-2
APC (W) 55: 35 BTR-40/BTR-60; 20 Type-56 (BTR-152)
ARTY 26+
  TOWED 122mm 18 D-30/*M-1938*
  MOR 8+ : **82mm** M-43; **120mm** 8 M-1943
AT
  RCL 75mm Type-52 (M-20); **82mm** B-10
  RL 89mm M-20
  GUNS 85mm 8 D-44
AD • SAM • MANPAD SA-7 *Grail*
  GUNS • TOWED 34: **23mm** 18 ZU-23; **37mm** 6 M-1939; **57mm** 10 S-60

Navy ε350

EQUIPMENT BY TYPE
PATROL AND COASTAL COMBATANTS 2
  PCI 2 *Alfeite*

FACILITIES
Base Located at Bissau

Air Force 100
FORCES BY ROLE
Ftr/FGA sqn with 3 MiG-17 *Fresco*

Hel sqn with 1 SA-318 *Alouette II*;
2 SA-319 *Alouette III*

EQUIPMENT BY TYPE
AIRCRAFT 3 combat capable
FTR 3 MiG-17 *Fresco*
HELICOPTERS • UTL 3: 1 SA-318 *Alouette II*; 2 SA-319 *Alouette III*

Paramilitary 2,000 active
Gendarmerie 2,000

FOREIGN FORCES
Portugal Navy: 1

Kenya Kya

Kenyan Shilling sh		2006	2007	2008
GDP	sh	1.64tr	1.69tr	
	US$	22.8bn	25.5bn	
per capita	US$	635	689	
Growth	%	6.1	6.4	
Inflation	%	14.5	6.9	
Def bdgt	sh	25.6bn		
	US$	355m		
US$1=sh		72.1	66.6	

Population 36,913,721

Ethnic Groups: Kikuyu ε22–32%

Age	0–14	15–19	20–24	25–29	30–64	65 plus
Male	21%	6%	6%	5%	12%	1%
Female	21%	6%	5%	4%	12%	1%

Capabilities
ACTIVE 24,120 (Army 20,000 Navy 1,620 Air 2,500)
Paramilitary 5,000
(incl HQ staff)

ORGANISATIONS BY SERVICE

Army 20,000
FORCES BY ROLE
Armd 1 bde (3 armd bn)
Air Cav 1 indep bn
Inf 1 bde (2 inf bn); 1 bde (3 inf bn); 1 indep bn
AB 1 bn
Arty 1 bde (2 arty bn)
ADA 1 bn
Engr 1 bde (2 engr bn)

EQUIPMENT BY TYPE
MBT 78 Vickers Mk 3
RECCE 92: 72 AML-60/AML-90; 12 *Ferret*; 8 S52 *Shorland*
APC (W) 62: 10 M-3 *Panhard* in store; 52 UR-416
ARTY 110
  TOWED 105mm 48: 8 Model 56 pack howitzer; 40 lt
  MOR 62: **81mm** 50; **120mm** 12 Brandt
AT • MSL • MANPATS 54: 40 Milan; 14 Swingfire
  RCL 84mm 80 *Carl Gustav*
AD • GUNS • TOWED 94: **20mm** 81: 11 Oerlikon; ε70 TCM-20; **40mm** 13 L/70

Navy 1,620 (incl 120 marines)
EQUIPMENT BY TYPE
PATROL AND COASTAL COMBATANTS 10
  PFM 2 *Nyayo* each with 2 twin (4 eff.) each with 1 Otomat tactical SSM, 1 76mm gun
  PCO 2 *Shujaa* each with 1 76mm gun
  PCI 1 *Mamba*
  PBF 5: 1 *Archangel*; 4 *Defender*
AMPHIBIOUS LCM 2 *Galana*
LOGISTICS AND SUPPORT 1 AT *Tug*
FACILITIES
Base Located at Mombasa

Air Force 2,500
FORCES BY ROLE
FGA sqn with 9 F-5E *Tiger II*/F-5F *Tiger II*†
Tpt sqn with 7 DHC-5D *Buffalo*†; 3 DHC-8 *Dash 8*†; 1 Fokker 70† (VIP); 1 PA-31 *Navajo*†; 12 Y-12(II)†
Atk hel sqn with 11 Hughes 500MD *Scout Defender*† (with TOW); 8 Hughes 500ME†; 15 Hughes 500M†
Spt hel sqn with 12 SA-330 *Puma*†; 5 Mi-17 (Mi-8MT) *Hip H*†
Trg sqn with up to 5 *Bulldog* 103/*Bulldog* 127†; 12 EMB-312 *Tucano*†*; 8 *Hawk* MK52†*; 2 Hughes 500D†

EQUIPMENT BY TYPE†
AIRCRAFT 29 combat capable
  FTR 9 F-5E *Tiger II*/F-5F *Tiger II*†
  TPT 30: 7 DHC-5D *Buffalo*†; 3 DHC-8 *Dash 8*†; 6 Do-28D-2† in store; 1 Fokker 70† (VIP); 1 PA-31 *Navajo*†; 12 Y-12(II)†
  TRG up to 25: up to 5 *Bulldog* 103/*Bulldog* 127†; 12 EMB-312 *Tucano*†*; 8 *Hawk* MK52†*
HELICOPTERS
  ATK 11 Hughes 500MD *Scout Defender*† (with TOW)
  ASLT 8 Hughes 500ME†
  SPT 17: 12 SA-330 *Puma*†; 5 Mi-17 (Mi-8MT) *Hip H*†
  UTL 17: 2 Hughes 500D†; 15 Hughes 500M†
MSL
  ASM AGM-65 *Maverick* (TOW)
  AAM AIM-9 *Sidewinder*

Paramilitary 5,000

Police General Service Unit 5,000
PATROL AND COASTAL COMBATANTS 17
PCI 5 less than 100 tonnes (2 Lake Victoria)
MISC BOATS/CRAFT 12 boats

Air Wing
AIRCRAFT • TPT 7 *Cessna*
HELICOPTERS
  UTL 1 Bell 206L *LongRanger*
  TRG 2 Bell 47G

DEPLOYMENT

CÔTE D'IVOIRE
UN • UNOCI 4; 4 obs

DEMOCRATIC REPUBLIC OF CONGO
UN • MONUC 36 obs

ETHIOPIA/ERITREA
UN • UNMEE 118; 10 obs

LIBERIA
UN • UNMIL 4; 3 obs

SERBIA
UN • UNMIK 2 obs

SIERRA LEONE
UN • UNIOSIL 1 obs

SUDAN
AU • AUMIS 60 obs
UN • UNMIS 831, 7 obs
UN/AU • UNAMID proposed deployment

WESTERN SAHARA
UN • MINURSO 6 obs

FOREIGN FORCES
United Kingdom Army: 12; BPST (EA) 12
United States Army 12; Navy 4; USAF 5; USMC 10

Lesotho Ls

Lesotho Loti M		2006	2007	2008
GDP	M	9.8bn	10.7bn	
	US$	1.45bn	1.59bn	
per capita	US$	716	788	
Growth	%	7.2	4.9	
Inflation	%	6.1	6.6	
Def bdgt	M	ε225m	e230m	
	US$	ε33m	e34m	
US$1=M		6.77	6.75	

Population 2,012,649

Age	0–14	15–19	20–24	25–29	30–64	65 plus
Male	19%	6%	5%	4%	12%	2%
Female	18%	6%	5%	4%	14%	3%

Capabilities

ACTIVE 2,000 (Army 2,000)

ORGANISATIONS BY SERVICE

Army ε2,000
FORCES BY ROLE
Recce 1 coy
Inf 7 coy
Arty 1 bty under strength (with 2x105 guns)
Avn 1 sqn
Spt 1 coy (with 81mm mor)

EQUIPMENT BY TYPE
RECCE 22: 4 AML-90; 10 RBY-1 *RAMTA*; 8 S52 *Shorland*
ARTY 12
  TOWED 105mm 2
  MOR 81mm 10
AT • RCL 106mm 6 M-40

Air Wing 110
AIRCRAFT
  MP 1 CASA 212-400 *Aviocar* (tpt, VIP tpt, casevac)
  TPT 3: 2 CASA 212-300 *Aviocar*; 1 GA-8 *Airvan* 1
HELICOPTERS
  UTL 4: 1 Bö-105LSA-3 (tpt, trg); 2 Bell 412 (SP); 1 Bell 412EP *Twin Huey* (tpt, VIP tpt, SAR)

DEPLOYMENT

SUDAN
AU • AUMIS 10 obs

Liberia Lb

Liberian Dollar L$		2006	2007	2008
GDP	US$	840m	970m	
per capita	US$	276	304	
Growth	%	7.8	9.4	
Inflation	%	7.2	11.2	
Def bdgt	L$			
	US$			
FMA (US)	US$	2.0m	1.6m	1.0m
US$1=L$		58	58	

Population 3,193,942
Ethnic Groups: Americo-Liberians 5%

Age	0–14	15–19	20–24	25–29	30–64	65 plus
Male	21%	6%	5%	4%	13%	1%
Female	21%	6%	5%	4%	13%	1%

Capabilities

ACTIVE 2,400 (Armed Forces 2,400)

ORGANISATIONS BY SERVICE

Armed forces by role 2,400

Armed Forces expected to be created by Dec 2007 and will include General Staff at MOD HQ an Army force, Naval and Air Force wings.

Inf   3 bn (non operational)

Engr   1 sqn (non operational)

Spt   1 sqn (non operational)

NON-STATE ARMED GROUPS

see Part II

FOREIGN FORCES

All under UNMIL cmd unless otherwise specified

Bangladesh 3,195; 17 obs

Benin 1; 3 obs

Bolivia 1; 3 obs

Brazil 1

Bulgaria 2 obs

China, Peoples Republic of 565; 5 obs

Croatia 3

Czech Republic 3 obs

Denmark 2 obs

Ecuador 1; 3 obs

Egypt 8 obs

El Salvador 3 obs

Ethiopia 2,536; 16 obs

Finland 2

France 1

Germany 11

Ghana 857; 12 obs

Indonesia 3 obs

Ireland 422

Jordan 121; 7 obs

Kenya 4; 3 obs

Korea, Republic of 1; 1 obs

Kyrgyzstan 4 obs

Malawi 2

Malaysia 10 obs

Mali 1; 4 obs

Moldova 1; 3 obs

Mongolia 250

Namibia 612; 3 obs

Nepal 42; 3 obs

Niger 3 obs

Nigeria 1,961; 21 obs

Pakistan 2,750; 16 obs

Paraguay 3 obs

Peru 2; 2 obs

Philippines 170; 3 obs

Poland 2 obs

Romania 3 obs

Russia 6 obs

Senegal 601; 3 obs

Serbia 6 obs

Sweden 114

Gambia 4 obs

Togo 1; 2 obs

Ukraine 296; 3 obs

United Kingdom 3

United States 6; 6 obs; Army 3; USAF 1; USMC 10

Zambia 3 obs

Madagascar Mdg

Malagsy Ariary fr		2006	2007	2008
GDP	fr	11.78tr	14.14tr	
	US$	5.5bn	7.8bn	
per capita	US$	291	401	
Growth	%	4.9	6.5	
Inflation	%	10.8	10.1	
Def bdgt	fr	639bn	ε700bn	
	US$	298m	ε385m	
US$1=fr		2,142	1,815	

Population   19,448,815

Age	0–14	15–19	20–24	25–29	30–64	65 plus
Male	22%	5%	4%	4%	12%	1%
Female	22%	5%	4%	4%	13%	2%

Capabilities

ACTIVE 13,500 (Army 12,500 Navy 500 Air 500)
Paramilitary 8,100

Terms of service conscription (incl for civil purposes) 18 months

ORGANISATIONS BY SERVICE

Army 12,500+

FORCES BY ROLE

Army 2 (gp) bn

Engr   1 regt

EQUIPMENT BY TYPE

LT TK 12 PT-76

RECCE 73: ε35 BRDM-2; 10 *Ferret*; ε20 M-3A1; 8 M-8

APC (T) ε30 M-3A1 half-track

ARTY 37+

    TOWED 29: **76mm** 12 ZIS-3; **105mm** 5 M-101; **122mm** 12 D-30

    MOR 8+ : **82mm**M-37; **120mm** 8 M-43

AT • RCL 106mm M-40A1

    RL 89mm LRAC

AD • GUNS • TOWED 70: **14.5mm** 50 ZPU-4; **37mm** 20 Type-55 (M-1939)

Navy 500 (incl some 100 Marines)

EQUIPMENT BY TYPE

PATROL AND COASTAL COMBATANTS 6

PB 6 (ex-USCG)

AMPHIBIOUS 1 LCT† (Fr Edic)

LOGISTICS AND SUPPORT 1 tpt/trg†

FACILITIES

Bases Located at Diégo Suarez, Tamatave, Fort Dauphin, Tuléar, Majunga

Air Force 500

FORCES BY ROLE

Tpt   sqn with 1 An-26 *Curl*; 3†; 1 BN-2 Islander; 2 CASA 212 *Aviocar*; 2 YAK-40 *Codling* (VIP)

Liaison sqn with 1 Cessna 310; 2 Cessna 337 *Skymaster*; 1 PA-23 *Aztec*

Trg   sqn with 4 Cessna 172

Hel   sqn with 6 Mi-8 *Hip*

EQUIPMENT BY TYPE

AIRCRAFT

TPT 14: 1 An-26 *Curl*; 3†; 1 BN-2 *Islander*; 2 CASA 212 *Aviocar*; 1 Cessna 310; 2 Cessna 337 *Skymaster*; 4 YAK-40 *Codling* (VIP)

UTL 5: 4 Cessna 172; 1 PA-23 *Aztec*

HELICOPTERS • SPT 6 Mi-8 *Hip*

Paramilitary 8,100

Gendarmerie 8,100

PATROL AND COASTAL COMBATANTS 5 **PCI** less than 100 tonnes

DEPLOYMENT

SUDAN

AU • AUMIS 9 obs

Malawi Miw

Malawian Kwacha K		2006	2007	2008
GDP	K	294bn	331bn	
	US$	2.2bn	2.4bn	
per capita	US$	163	122	
Growth	%	7.9	5.5	
Inflation	%	9.0	7.0	
Def bdgt	K	2.7bn	ε3.0bn	
	US$	20m	21m	
US$1=K			136	139

Population   13,603,181

Age	0–14	15–19	20–24	25–29	30–64	65 plus
Male	23%	6%	5%	4%	11%	1%
Female	23%	6%	5%	4%	11%	2%

Capabilities

ACTIVE 5,300 (Army 5,300) **Paramilitary 1,500**

ORGANISATIONS BY SERVICE

Army 5,300

FORCES BY ROLE

Inf   3 bn

Para   1 indep bn

Spt   1 (general) bn (1+ marine coy 1 armd recce sqn, 1 engr unit, 2 lt arty bty)

EQUIPMENT BY TYPE

Less than 20% serviceability

RECCE 41: 13 *Eland*; 20 FV721 *Fox*; 8 Ferret

ARTY 17

TOWED 105mm 9 lt

MOR 81mm 8 L16

AD • SAM • MANPAD 15 Blowpipe

GUNS • TOWED 14.5mm 40 ZPU-4

Maritime Wing 220

EQUIPMENT BY TYPE

PATROL AND COASTAL COMBATANTS 14

PCI 2: 1 *Kasungu*† less than 100 tonnes; 1 *Namacurra*† less than 100 tonnes

PBR 12† (various)

AMPHIBIOUS 1 LCU

FACILITIES

Base Located at Monkey Bay (Lake Nyasa)

Air Wing 200

FORCES BY ROLE

Tpt   1 sqn with 2 Basler Turbo-67; 4 Do-228; 1 Hawker 800

Tpt hel   sqn with 1 AS-332 *Super Puma* (VIP); 3 AS-350L *Ecureuil*; 1 SA-330F *Puma*

EQUIPMENT BY TYPE

AIRCRAFT • TPT 7: 2 Basler Turbo-67; 4 Do-228; 1 Hawker 800

HELICOPTERS • SPT 5: 1 AS-332 *Super Puma* (VIP); 3 AS-350L *Ecureuil*; 1 SA-330F *Puma*

Paramilitary 1,500

Mobile Police Force 1,500

RECCE 8 S52 *Shorland*

AIRCRAFT 4

MP 3 BN-2T *Defender* (border patrol)

TPT 1 SC.7 3M *Skyvan*

HELICOPTERS • UTL 2 AS-365 *Dauphin 2*

DEPLOYMENT

DEMOCRATIC REPUBLIC OF CONGO

UN • MONUC 111; 25 obs

SERBIA
UN • UNMIK 1 obs

SOMALIA
AU • AMISOM 1,000 proposed deployment

SUDAN
AU • AUMIS 24 obs
UN • UNMIS 2; 6 obs
UN/AU • UNAMID proposed deployment

Mali RMM

CFA Franc BCEAO fr		2006	2007	2008
GDP	fr	3.1tr	3.3tr	
	US$	5.9bn	7.1bn	
per capita	US$	508		
Growth	%	5.3	5.2	
Inflation	%	1.9	2.5	
Def bdgt	fr	68.9bn	75.0bn	
	US$	132m	162m	
US$1=fr		522	462	

Population   11,995,402

Ethnic Groups: Tuareg 6-10%

Age	0–14	15–19	20–24	25–29	30–64	65 plus
Male	24%	6%	5%	4%	9%	1%
Female	24%	5%	4%	4%	12%	2%

Capabilities

ACTIVE 7,350 (Army 7,350) **Paramilitary 4,800**
Militia 3,000

ORGANISATIONS BY SERVICE

Army circa 7,350
FORCES BY ROLE
Tk   2 bn
Inf   4 bn
SF   1 bn
AB   1 bn
Arty   2 bn
AD   2 bty
Engr   1 bn
SAM   1 bty

EQUIPMENT BY TYPE†
MBT 33: 12 T-54/T-55; 21 T-34
LT TK 18 Type-62
RECCE 20 BRDM-2
APC (W) 50: 30 BTR-40; 10 BTR-60; 10 BTR-152
ARTY 46+
    TOWED 14+: **100mm** 6 M-1944; **122mm** 8 D-30; **130mm**
    M-46 (reported)
    MRL **122mm** 2 BM-21
    MOR 30+: **82mm** M-43; **120mm** 30 M-43

AT • MSL • MANPATS AT-3 9K11 *Sagger*
    RL **73mm** RPG-7 *Knout*
    GUNS **85mm** 6 D-44
AD • SAM 12+
    TOWED 12+ SA-3 *Goa*
    MANPAD SA-7 *Grail*
    GUNS • TOWED 12: **37mm** 6 M-1939; **57mm** 6 S-60

Navy circa 50
EQUIPMENT BY TYPE
PATROL AND COASTAL COMBATANTS 3 PCR† less
than 100 tonnes
FACILITIES
Bases Located at Bamako, Mopti, Segou, Timbuktu

Air Force 400
FORCES BY ROLE
Ftr   1 sqn with 11 MiG-21 *Fishbed*
FGA   sqn with 5 MiG-17F *Fresco C*
Tpt   regt with 2 An-24 *Coke*; 1 An-26 *Curl*
Trg   sqn with 6 L-29 *Delfin*; 1 MiG-15UTI *Midget*; 4 Yak-
    11 *Moose*; 2 Yak-18 *Max*
Hel   sqn with 1 AS-350 *Ecureuil*; 1 Mi-8 *Hip*;
    2 Z-9 (AS-365N) *Dauphin* 2

EQUIPMENT BY TYPE
AIRCRAFT 16 combat capable
    FTR 16: 11 MiG-21 *Fishbed*; 5 MiG-17F *Fresco C*
    TPT 3: 2 An-24 *Coke*; 1 An-26 *Curl*
    TRG 13: 6 L-29 *Delfin*; 1 MiG-15UTI *Midget*; 4 Yak-11
    Moose; 2 Yak-18 *Max*
HELICOPTERS
    SPT 2: 1 AS-350 *Ecureuil*; 1 Mi-8 *Hip*
    UTL 2 Z-9 (AS-365N) *Dauphin* 2

Paramilitary 4,800 active

Gendarmerie 1,800
Paramilitary 8 coy

Republican Guard 2,000

National Police 1,000

Militia 3,000

NON-STATE ARMED GROUPS
see Part II

DEPLOYMENT

DEMOCRATIC REPUBLIC OF CONGO
UN • MONUC 22 obs

LIBERIA
UN • UNMIL 1; 4 obs

SUDAN

AU • **AUMIS** 15 obs
UN • **UNMIS** 10 obs
UN/AU • **UNAMID** proposed deployment

Mauritius Ms

Mauritian Rupee R		2006	2007	2008
GDP	R	205bn	237bn	
	US$	6.5bn	7.9bn	
per capita	US$	5,212	6,295	
Growth	%	3.5	4.7	
Inflation	%	5.5	10.7	
Def bdgt	R	575m	599m	
	US$	18m	20m	
US$1=R		31.7	30.1	

Population   1,250,882

Age	0–14	15–19	20–24	25–29	30–64	65 plus
Male	12%	4%	4%	4%	22%	3%
Female	12%	4%	4%	4%	22%	4%

Capabilities

ACTIVE NIL Paramilitary 2,000

ORGANISATIONS BY SERVICE

Paramilitary 2,000

Special Mobile Force ε1,500

FORCES BY ROLE

Rifle   6 coy
Paramilitary 2 (mob) coy
Engr   1 coy
Spt   1 tps

EQUIPMENT BY TYPE
RECCE BRDM-2; *Ferret*
AIFV 2 VAB with 20mm gun
APC (W) 16: 7 *Tactica*; 9 VAB
ARTY • MOR 81mm 2
AT • RL 89mm 4 LRAC

Coast Guard ε500

PATROL AND COASTAL COMBATANTS 21
  PSOH 1 *Vigilant* (capacity 1 hel) (Ca *Guardian* design)
  PCC 1 SDB-MK5
  PCI 3: 2 *Zhuk*; less than 100 tonnes (FSU); 1 P-2000
  PBI 16
AIRCRAFT • MP 3: 1 BN-2T *Defender*; 2 Do-228-101

Police Air Wing

HELICOPTERS • UTL 2 SA-316 *Alouette III*

Mozambique Moz

Mozambique Metical M		2006	2007	2008
GDP	M	180tr	209tr	
	US$	7.1bn	8.1bn	
per capita	US$	347	388	
Growth	%	8.5	7.0	
Inflation	%	13.2	6.4	
Def bdgt	M	1.45tr	1.48tr	
	US$	57m	57m	
US$1=M		25,400	25,750	

Population   20,905,585

Age	0–14	15–19	20–24	25–29	30–64	65 plus
Male	22%	5%	4%	4%	13%	1%
Female	21%	5%	4%	4%	14%	2%

Capabilities

ACTIVE 11,200 (Army 10,000 Navy 200 Air 1,000)
Terms of service conscription, 2 years

ORGANISATIONS BY SERVICE

Army ε9,000–10,000

FORCES BY ROLE

Inf   7 bn
SF   3 bn
Arty 2-3 bty
Engr 2 bn
Log   1 bn

EQUIPMENT BY TYPE†
Equipment at est 10% or less serviceability
MBT 60+ T-54
RECCE 30 BRDM-1/BRDM-2
AIFV 40 BMP-1
APC (W) 260+: 160 BTR-60; 100 BTR-152; *Casspir*
ARTY 166
  TOWED 102: **76mm** 40 ZIS-3 *M-1942*; **100mm** 20 M-1944; **105mm** 12 M-101; **122mm** 12 D-30; **130mm** 6 M-46; **152mm** 12 D-1
  MRL 122mm 12 BM-21
  MOR 52: **82mm** 40 M-43; **120mm** 12 M-43
AT • MSL • MANPATS 290: 20 AT-3 9K11 *Sagger*; 120 in store; 12 AT-4 9K111 *Spigot*; 138 in store
  RCL 75mm; **82mm** B-10; **107mm** 24 B-12
  GUNS 85mm 18: 6 D-48; 12 Type-56 (D-44)
AD • SAM • MANPAD 250: 20 SA-7 *Grail*; 230 in store
  GUNS 330+
    SP 57mm 20 ZSU-57-2
    TOWED 310+: **20mm** M-55; **23mm** 120 ZU-23-2; **37mm** 100: 90 M-1939; 10 in store; **57mm** 90: 60 S-60; 30 in store

Navy ε200

Bases Located at Pemba - Metangula (Lake Malawi), Nacala, Beira, Maputo

EQUIPMENT BY TYPE

PATROL AND COASTAL COMBATANTS 5
  PBI 2 *Namacurra*
  PBR 3

Air Force 1,000

FORCES BY ROLE

(incl AD units)

FGA   MiG-21bis *Fishbed L & N* non-operational

Tpt   1 sqn with 5 An-26 *Curl*; 2 CASA 212 *Aviocar*;
      4 PA-32 *Cherokee* non-operational

Trg   sqn with 1 Cessna 182 *Skylane*; 7 Z-326 *Trener Master*

Hel   sqn with 4 Mi-24 *Hind*†*; 5 Mi-8 *Hip* non-operational

SAM   bty with 10+ SA-3 *Goa* non-operational;
      SA-2 *Guideline*†

EQUIPMENT BY TYPE

AIRCRAFT
  FTR: some MiG-21bis *Fishbed L & N* non-operational
  TPT 8: 5 An-26 *Curl*; 2 CASA 212 *Aviocar*; 1 Cessna 182
  Skylane
  TRG 11: 4 PA-32 *Cherokee* non-operational; 7 Z-326
  Trener Master
HELICOPTERS
  ATK 4 Mi-24 *Hind*†*
  SPT 5 Mi-8 *Hip* non-operational
AD • SAM 10+ SA-3 *Goa* non-operational
  TOWED: SA-2 *Guideline*†

DEPLOYMENT

SUDAN

AU • **AUMIS** 15 obs
UN • **UNMIS** 3 obs

FOREIGN FORCES

Portugal Navy: 7
United States USMC 6

Namibia Nba

Namibian Dollar N$		2006	2007	2008
GDP	N$	44.5bn	48.6bn	
	US$	6.6bn	7.2bn	
per capita	US$	3,216	3,504	
Growth	%	4.5	4.8	
Inflation	%	5.1	6.3	
Def bdgt	N$	1.33bn	1.68bn	
	US$	197m	248m	
US$1=N$		6.77	6.75	

Population   2,055,080

Age	0–14	15–19	20–24	25–29	30–64	65 plus
Male	20%	6%	5%	4%	13%	2%
Female	19%	6%	5%	4%	14%	2%

Capabilities

**ACTIVE 9,200 (Army 9,000 Navy 200) Paramilitary
6,000**

ORGANISATIONS BY SERVICE

Army 9,000

MOD plans to build new military bases around the county
including at Luiperdsvallei outside Windheek, Osana near
Okahandja, Keetmanshoop, and Karibib

FORCES BY ROLE

Inf	6 bn
AT	1 regt
Cbt Sp	1 bde (1 arty regt)
Presidential Guard	1 bn
AD	1 regt

EQUIPMENT BY TYPE

MBT T-54/T-55†; T-34†
RECCE 12 BRDM-2
APC (W) 60:10 BTR-60; 20 *Casspir*; 30 *Wolf Turbo 2*
ARTY 81
  TOWED 36: **76mm** 12 ZIS-3; **140mm** 24 G2
  MRL 122mm 5 BM-21
  MOR 40: **81mm**; **82mm**
AT • RCL 82mm B-10
  GUNS 12+: **57mm**; **76mm** 12 ZIS-3
AD • SAM • MANPAD 74 SA-7 *Grail*
  GUNS 65
    SP 23mm 15 *Zumlac*
    TOWED 14.5mm 50 ZPU-4

Navy ε200

Fishery protection, part of the Ministry of Fisheries

EQUIPMENT BY TYPE

PATROL AND COASTAL COMBATANTS 6
  PCO 3
  PCC 1 *Oryx*
  PBI 2 Ex *Namacurra*
AIRCRAFT • UTL 1 F406 *Caravan II*
hel 1

FACILITIES

Base   Located at Walvis Bay

Paramilitary 6,000

Police Force • Special Field Force 6,000 (incl Border Guard and Special Reserve Force)

Air Force

FORCES BY ROLE

FGA   sqn with 2 MiG-23 *Flogger* (reported)

Surv   sqn with 5 Cessna 337 *Skymaster*/O-2A *Skymaster*

Tpt   sqn with 2 An-26 *Curl*; 1 *Falcon* 900;
      1 Learjet 36; 2 Y-12

Trg   sqn with 4 K-8

Sub-Saharan
Africa

Hel   sqn with 2 Mi-25 *Hind D*; 2 Mi-17 (Mi-8MT) *Hip H*; 2
       SA-319 *Alouette III*

EQUIPMENT BY TYPE
AIRCRAFT 2 combat capable
   FTR 2 MiG-23 *Flogger* (reported)
   TPT 11: 2 An-26 *Curl*; 1 *Falcon* 900; 1 Learjet 36; 2 Y-12, 5
   Cessna 337 *Skymaster* tpt/O-2A *Skymaster*
   TRG 4 K-8
HELICOPTERS
   ATK 2 Mi-25 *Hind D*
   SPT 2 Mi-17 (Mi-8MT) *Hip H*
   UTL 2 SA-319 *Alouette III*

DEPLOYMENT

CÔTE D'IVOIRE
UN • UNOCI 2 obs

ETHIOPIA/ERITREA
UN • UNMEE 3; 4 obs

LIBERIA
UN • UNMIL 4 ; 2 obs

SUDAN
AU • AUMIS 24 obs
UN • UNMIS 9 obs

Niger Ngr

CFA Franc BCEAO fr		2006	2007	2008
GDP	fr	1.85tr	2.05tr	
	US$	3.5bn	4.4bn	
per capita	US$	283	345	
Growth	%	5.2	5.6	
Inflation	%	0.1		
Def bdgt	fr	ε20bn	ε22bn	
	US$	ε38m	ε47m	
US$1=fr		522	462	

Population   12,894,865
Ethnic Groups: Tuareg 8-10%

Age	0–14	15–19	20–24	25–29	30–64	65 plus
Male	24%	6%	4%	4%	11%	1%
Female	23%	5%	4%	4%	13%	1%

Capabilities

ACTIVE 5,300 (Army 5,200 Air 100) **Paramilitary
5,400**
Terms of service selective conscription (2 year)

ORGANISATIONS BY SERVICE

Army 5,200
FORCES BY ROLE
3 Mil Districts

Armd recce   4 sqn
Inf   7 coy
AB   2 coy
Engr   1 coy
AD   1 coy

EQUIPMENT BY TYPE
RECCE 132: 35 AML-20/AML-60; 90 AML-90; 7 VBL
APC (W) 22 M-3 *Panhard*
ARTY • MOR 40: **81mm** 19 Brandt; **82mm** 17; **120mm** 4
Brandt
AT • RCL 14: **75mm** 6 M-20; **106mm** 8 M-40
   RL 89mm 36 LRAC
AD • GUNS 39
   SP 10 M3 VDAA
   TOWED 20mm 29

Air Force 100
FORCES BY ROLE
Tpt   sqn with 1 An-26 *Curl*; 1 B-737-200 (VIP);
        1 C-130H *Hercules*; 1 Do-28
Liaison sqn with 2 Cessna 337D *Skymaster*

EQUIPMENT BY TYPE
AIRCRAFT • TPT 7: 1 An-26 *Curl*; 1 B-737-200 (VIP); 1
C-130H *Hercules*; 2 Cessna 337D *Skymaster*; 1 Do-28

Paramilitary 5,400
Gendarmerie 1,400
Republican Guard 2,500
National Police 1,500

DEPLOYMENT

BURUNDI
UN • BINUB 1 obs

CÔTE D'IVOIRE
UN • UNOCI 384; 6 obs

DEMOCRATIC REPUBLIC OF CONGO
UN • MONUC 19 obs

LIBERIA
UN • UNMIL 3 obs

SUDAN
UN • UNMIS 1

Nigeria Nga

Nigerian Naira N		2006	2007	2008
GDP	N	15.0tr	16.8tr	
	US$	117bn	136bn	
per capita	US$	892	1,007	
Growth	%	5.6	4.3	
Inflation	%	8.3	5.3	
Def bdgt	N	98bn	122bn	
	US$	768m	988m	
FMA (US)	US$	1.0m	0.8m	1.3m
US$1=N		128	124	

Population   135,031,164

Ethnic Groups: North Hausa and Fulani South-west Yoruba South-east Ibo; these tribes make up ε65% of population

Age	0–14	15–19	20–24	25–29	30–64	65 plus
Male	21%	5%	5%	4%	14%	1%
Female	21%	5%	5%	4%	13%	2%

Capabilities

ACTIVE 80,000 (Army 62,000 Navy 8,000 Air 10,000)
Paramilitary 82,000

Reserves planned, none org

ORGANISATIONS BY SERVICE

Army 62,000

FORCES BY ROLE

Army	1 (comp) div (2 mot inf bde, 1 AB bn, 1 amph bde, 1 engr bde, 1 arty bde, 1 recce bde)
Armd	1 div (1 recce bn, 1 engr bde, 1 arty bde, 2 armd bde)
Mech	2 div (*each:* 1 engr bn, 1 mot inf bde, 1 mech bde, 1 recce bn, 1 arty bde)
Presidential Guard	1 bde (2 Gd bn)
AD	1 regt

EQUIPMENT BY TYPE
MBT 276: 176 Vickers Mk 3; 100 T-55†
LT TK 157 *Scorpion*
RECCE 342: 90 AML-60; 40 AML-90; 70 EE-9 *Cascavel*; 50 FV721 *Fox*; 20 *Saladin* Mk2; 72 VBL (reported)
APC 437+
 APC (T) 317: 250 4K-7FA *Steyr*; 67 MT-LB
 APC (W) 120+: 10 FV603 *Saracen*; 110 *Piranha*; EE-11 *Urutu* (reported)
ARTY 151
 SP 155mm 39 VCA 155 *Palmaria*
 TOWED 112: **105mm** 50 M-56; **122mm** 31 D-30/D-74; **130mm** 7 M-46; **155mm** 24 FH-77B in store
 MRL 122mm 25 APR-21
 MOR 330+: **81mm** 200; **82mm** 100; **120mm** 30+

AT • MSL • MANPATS *Swingfire*
 RCL 84mm *Carl Gustav;* **106mm** M-40A1
AD • SAM 164
 SP 16 *Roland*
 MANPAD 148: 48 *Blowpipe*; ε100 SA-7 *Grail*
 GUNS 90+
 SP 30 ZSU-23-4
 TOWED 60+: **20mm** 60+; **23mm** ZU-23; **40mm** L/70
RADAR • LAND: some RASIT (veh, arty)

Navy 8,000 (incl Coast Guard)
FORCES BY ROLE

Navy   Western Comd HQ located at Apapa; Eastern Comd HQ located at Calabar; Naval Bases at Warri, Port Harcourt, Naval Trg school at Sapele, Delta State.

EQUIPMENT BY TYPE
PRINCIPAL SURFACE COMBATANTS 2
 FRIGATES • FFG 1 *Aradu* (Ge MEKO 360) with 8 single each with 1 Otomat tactical SSM, 1 *Albatros* octuple with 24 *Aspide* SAM, 2 STWS 1B triple 324mm with 18 A244 LWT, 1 127mm gun, (capacity 1 *Lynx* MK 89 SAR hel)
 CORVETTES • FS 1 *Enymiri* (UK Vosper Mk 9) each with 1 x3 *Seacat* Systems (3 eff.) with *Seacat* SAM, 1 2 tube Bofors 375mm (2 eff.), 1 TAK-76 76mm gun
PATROL AND COASTAL COMBATANTS 21
 PFM 1 *Ayam*† (Fr *Combattante*) each with 2 twin (4 eff.) each with 1 MM-38 *Exocet* tactical SSM, 1 76mm gun (Additional 2 vessels†)
 PCO 4 *Balsam* (buoy tenders (ex-US))
 PCC 1 *Ekpe* (Ge *Lurssen* 57m (Additional 2 vessels †)) with 1 76mm gun
 PB 15 *Defender*
MINE WARFARE • MINE COUNTERMEASURES • MCC 2 *Ohue* (mod It *Lerici*)
AMPHIBIOUS • LS • LST 1 *Ambe* (capacity 5 tanks; 220 troops) (Ge)
LOGISTICS AND SUPPORT 5:
 1 **AGHS**; 3 **YTL**; 1 **TRG**

FACILITIES
Bases   Located at Lagos, Apapa, Calabar

Naval Aviation
HELICOPTERS
 SAR 2 *Lynx* MK 89† non-operational
 UTL 2 A-109E *Power*†

Air Force 10,000
FORCES BY ROLE†
Very limited op capability

Ftr/FGA   1 sqn with 12 Jaguar S(N)† non-operational; 3 Jaguar B(N)†; 1 sqn with 6 Alpha Jet; 1 sqn with 12 MiG-21bis/MiG-21FR†; 5 MiG-21MF†; 1 MiG-21U†*

Sub-Saharan Africa

Tpt   2 sqn with 5 C-130H *Hercules*; 3 C-130H-30 *Hercules*; 17 Do-128D-6 *Turbo SkyServant*; 16 Do-228-200 (incl 2 VIP); 5 G-222; 7 AS-332 *Super Puma*; 2 SA-330 *Puma*; 5 Mi-34 *Hermit†*; some (Presidential) flt with 2 *Gulfstream* II/*Gulfstream* IV; 1 B-727; 1 BAe-125-1000; 2 *Falcon* 900

Trg   sqns with 12 MB-339A* (all being upgraded; 24 L-39MS *Albatros†*; 58 *Air Beetle†* (up to 20 awaiting repair); 13 Hughes 300

Hel   sqn with 5 Mi-35 *Hind†*; 5 BO-105D†

EQUIPMENT BY TYPE
AIRCRAFT 75 combat capable
   FTR 17: 5 MiG-21MF *Fishbed J†*; 12 MiG-21bis *Fishbed L & N* MiG-21 FTR/MiG-21FR *Fishbed* Recce†
   FGA 36: 24 L-39MS *Albatros†*; 12 Jaguar N)† non-operational
   TPT 52: 2 *Gulfstream* II/*Gulfstream* IV; 1 B-727; 1 BAe-125-1000; 5 C-130H *Hercules*; 3 C-130H-30 *Hercules*; 17 Do-128D-6 *Turbo SkyServant*; 16 Do-228-200 (incl 2 VIP); 2 *Falcon* 900; 5 G-222†
   TRG 80: 58 *Air Beetle†* (up to 20 awaiting repair); 6 *Alpha Jet* (FGA/trg)*; 3 Jaguar B(N)†*; 12 MB-339AN* (all being upgraded); 1 MiG-21U *Mongol A†*
HELICOPTERS
   ATK 5 Mi-35 *Hind*
   SPT 9: 7 AS-332 *Super Puma*; 2 SA-330 *Puma*
   UTL 10: 5 BO–105D†; 5 Mi-34 *Hermit†*
   TRG 13 Hughes 300
MSL • AAM AA-2 *Atoll*

Paramilitary ε82,000

Coast Guard

Port Security Police ε2,000
PATROL AND COASTAL COMBATANTS • MISC BOATS/CRAFT 60+ boats
AMPHIBIOUS 5+ ACV

Security and Civil Defence Corps • Police 80,000
APC (W) 70+: 70+ AT105 *Saxon†*; UR-416
AIRCRAFT • TPT 4: 1 Cessna 500 *Citation I*; 2 PA-31 *Navajo*; 1 PA-31-350 *Navajo Chieftain*
HELICOPTERS • UTL 4: 2 AB-212 (Bell 212); 2 AB-222 (Bell 222)

NON-STATE ARMED GROUPS
see Part II

DEPLOYMENT

CÔTE D'IVOIRE
UN • UNOCI 6 obs

DEMOCRATIC REPUBLIC OF CONGO
UN • MONUC 26 obs

ETHIOPIA/ERITREA
AU • OLMEE 2 obs
UN • UNMEE 1; 8 obs

GEORGIA
UN • UNOMIG 1 obs

LIBERIA
UN • UNMIL 1,963; 17 obs

NEPAL
UN • UNMIN 8 obs

SIERRA LEONE
UN • UNIOSIL 2 obs

SOMALIA
AU • AMISOM 850 proposed deployment

SUDAN
AU • AUMIS 2,040
UN • UNMIS 10; 12 obs
UN/AU • UNAMID 60 proposed deployment

WESTERN SAHARA
UN • MINURSO 6 obs

Rwanda Rwa

Rwandan Franc fr		2006	2007	2008
GDP	fr	1.63tr	1.82tr	
	US$	3.0bn	3.3bn	
per capita	US$	307	336	
Growth	%	5.3	4.5	
Inflation	%	8.8	8.2	
Def bdgt	fr	39.4bn	33.9bn	
	US$	71m	62m	
US$1=fr		551	546	

Population   9,907,509
Ethnic Groups: Hutu 80%; Tutsi 19%

Age	0–14	15–19	20–24	25–29	30–64	65 plus
Male	21%	6%	5%	4%	12%	1%
Female	21%	6%	5%	4%	13%	2%

Capabilities

ACTIVE 33,000 (Army 32,000 Air 1,000) Paramilitary 2,000

ORGANISATIONS BY SERVICE

Army 32,000
FORCES BY ROLE
Army 4 div (*each*: 3 Army bde)

EQUIPMENT BY TYPE
MBT 24 T-54/T-55
RECCE 106: ε90 AML-60/AML-90/AML-245; 16 VBL
AIFV BMP

APC (W) 16+: 16 RG-31 *Nyala*; BTR; *Buffalo* (M-3 *Panhard*)
ARTY 155+
  TOWED 35+: 105mm 29 Type-54 (D-1); 122mm 6 D-30; 152mm†
  MRL 122mm 5 RM-70 *Dana*
  MOR 115: 81mm; 82mm; 120mm
AD • SAM • MANPAD SA-7 *Grail*
  GUNS ε150: 14.5mm; 23mm; 37mm

Air Force ε1,000

FORCES BY ROLE

Tpt   sqn with An-2 *Colt*; 2-3 AN-8 *Camp*; 1 B-707; 1 BN-2A *Islander*

Trg   sqn with L-39 *Albatros*

Hel   sqn with 5-7 Mi-24V *Hind E*; 8-12 Mi-17MD (Mi-8MTV5) *Hip H*

EQUIPMENT BY TYPE
AIRCRAFT
  TPT 5+: An-2 *Colt*; 2-3 AN-8 *Camp*; 1 B-707; 1 BN-2A *Islander*
  TRG L-39 *Albatros*
HELICOPTERS
  ATK 5–7 Mi-24V *Hind E*
  SPT 8–12 Mi-17MD (Mi-8MTV5) *Hip H*

Paramilitary

Local Defence Forces ε2,000

NON-STATE ARMED GROUPS

see Part II

DEPLOYMENT

SUDAN
AU • AUMIS 3,272
UN • UNMIS 262; 15 obs

Senegal Sen

CFA Franc BCEAO fr		2006	2007	2008
GDP	fr	4.8tr	6.2tr	
	US$	9.2bn	13.5bn	
per capita	US$	755	1,076	
Growth	%	2.1	5.1	
Inflation	%	2.1	5.4	
Def bdgt	fr	77.5bn	e80.0bn	
	US$	148m	e173m	
US$1=fr		522	462	

Population 12,521,851

Ethnic Groups: Wolof 36%; Fulani 17%; Serer 17%; Toucouleur 9%; Man-dingo 9%; Diola 9% (of which 30-60% in Casamance)

Age	0–14	15–19	20–24	25–29	30–64	65 plus
Male	21%	6%	5%	4%	13%	1%
Female	20%	6%	5%	4%	14%	2%

Capabilities

ACTIVE 13,620 (Army 11,900 Navy 950 Air 770)
Paramilitary 5,000
Terms of service conscription, 2 years selective

ORGANISATIONS BY SERVICE

Army 11,900 (incl conscripts)

FORCES BY ROLE
4 Mil Zone HQ

Armd	3 bn
Inf	6 bn
Cdo/AB	1 bn
Arty	1 bn
Engr	1 bn
Presidential Guard	1 bn (horsed)
Construction	3 coy

EQUIPMENT BY TYPE
RECCE 71: 30 AML-60; 27 AML-90; 10 M-8; 4 M-20
APC 28+
  APC (T) 12 M-3 *half-track*
  APC (W) 16+ M-3 *Panhard*
ARTY 34
  TOWED 18: 75mm 6 M-116 pack; 105mm 6 HM-2/M-101; 155mm ε6 Model-50
  MOR 16: 81mm 8 Brandt; 120mm 8 Brandt
AT • MSL • MANPATS 4 *Milan*
  RL 89mm 31 LRAC
AD • GUNS • TOWED 33: 20mm 21 M-693; 40mm 12 L/60

Navy 950

EQUIPMENT BY TYPE
PATROL AND COASTAL COMBATANTS 9
  PCO 4: 1 *Fouta* (Dk *Osprey*); 1 *Njambour* (Fr SFCN 59m); 2 *Saint Louis* (PR-48)
  PFI 3 *Senegal* II
  PCI 2 *Alioune Samb*
AMPHIBIOUS • LCT 2 *Edic* 700
FACILITIES
Bases Located at Dakar and Casamance

Air Force 770

FORCES BY ROLE
MP/SAR   sqn with 1 EMB-111
Tpt   1 sqn with 1 B-727-200 (VIP); 1 DHC-6 twin *Otter*; 6 F-27-400M *Troopship*
Trg   sqn with 4 CM-170 *Magister**; 2 *Rallye* 160; 4 *Rallye* 235 *Guerrier**; 2 *Rallye* 235A
Hel   sqn with 2 SA-330 *Puma*; 1 SA-341H *Gazelle*; 2 SA-318C *Alouette II*

EQUIPMENT BY TYPE
AIRCRAFT 8 combat capable
  RECCE 1 EMB-111
  TPT 8: 1 B-727-200 (VIP); 1 DHC-6 twin *Otter*; 6 F-27-400M *Troopship*

TRG 12: 4 CM-170 *Magister**; 2 *Rallye* 160; 4 *Rallye* 235 *Guerrier**; 2 *Rallye* 235A
HELICOPTERS
  SPT 3: 2 SA-330 *Puma*; 1 SA-341H *Gazelle*
  UTL 2 SA-318C *Alouette II*

Paramilitary 5,000

Gendarmerie 5,000
APC (W) 12 VXB-170

Customs
PATROL AND COASTAL COMBATANTS 2 PCI less than 100 tonnes

NON-STATE ARMED GROUPS

see Part II

DEPLOYMENT

CENTRAL AFRICAN REPUBLIC
UN • MINURCAT 1 obs

CÔTE D'IVOIRE
UN • UNOCI 328; 9 obs

DEMOCRATIC REPUBLIC OF CONGO
UN • MONUC 460; 26 obs

LIBERIA
UN • UNMIL 604; 3 obs

SUDAN
AU • AUMIS 538
UN • UNMIS 5
UN/AU • UNAMID proposed deployment

FOREIGN FORCES

France Army 610: 1 marine inf bn (1 recce sqn with ERC-90F *Lynx*); Navy 230: 1 Atlantic MP ac; Air Force: 1 C-160 *Transall* tpt ac; 1 AS-555 *Fennec* utl hel
United States Army 2; Navy 1; USMC 8

Capabilities

ACTIVE 200 (Army 200) Paramilitary 250

ORGANISATIONS BY SERVICE

Army 200
FORCES BY ROLE
Sy 1 unit
Inf 1 coy

EQUIPMENT BY TYPE†
RECCE 6 BRDM-2†
ARTY• MOR 82mm 6 M-43†
AT • RL 73mm RPG-7 *Knout*†
AD • SAM • MANPAD 10 SA-7 *Grail*†
  GUNS • TOWED 14.5mm ZPU-2†; ZPU-4†; **37mm** M-1939†

Paramilitary

Coast Guard 200 (incl 80 Marines)
EQUIPMENT BY TYPE
PATROL AND COASTAL COMBATANTS 9
  PCC 2: 1 *Andromache* (It *Pichiotti* 42m); 1 *Topaz*
  PCI 7: 1 *Zhuk* less than 100 tonnes; 6 less than 100 tonnes
  AMPHIBIOUS • LCT 1 *Cinq Juin* (govt owned but civilian op)
FACILITIES
Base Located at Port Victoria

National Guard 250

Air Wing 20
AIRCRAFT
  TPT 2: 1 BN-2 *Islander*; 1 Cessna 152
  UTL 1 F406 *Caravan II*

Seychelles Sey

Seychelles Rupee SR		2006	2007	2008
GDP	SR	3.9bn	3.9bn	
	US$	710m	490m	
per capita	US$	8,696	5,938	
Growth	%	5.3	6.1	
Inflation	%	-0.4	4.4	
Def bdgt	SR	77m	ε80m	
	US$	14m	ε10m	
US$1=SR		5.5	8.0	

Population   81,895

Age	0–14	15–19	20–24	25–29	30–64	65 plus
Male	13%	5%	5%	4%	19%	2%
Female	13%	5%	5%	5%	21%	4%

Sierra Leone SL

Sierra Leonean Leone L		2006	2007	2008
GDP	L	4.12tr	4.93tr	
	US$	1.39bn	1.65bn	
per capita	US$	232	269	
Growth	%	7.4	7.4	
Inflation	%	9.5	10.8	
Def bdgt	L	ε70bn	ε75bn	
	US$	ε24m	ε25m	
US$1=L		2,962	2,981	

Population   6,144,562

Age	0–14	15–19	20–24	25–29	30–64	65 plus
Male	22%	5%	4%	4%	12%	2%
Female	23%	5%	4%	4%	13%	2%

Capabilities

ACTIVE 10,500 (Joint 10,500)

ORGANISATIONS BY SERVICE

Total Armed Forces 10,500

The process of disarming the various factions was completed in Jan 2002, with over 45,000 combatants registering. A new, UK-trained, national army has formed, which has an initial target strength of 13-14,000. This initial strength is set to reduce to some 10,000 over a ten year period.

ARTY • MOR 31: **81mm** ε27; **82mm** 2; **120mm** 2
AT • RCL **84mm** *Carl Gustav*
HELICOPTERS • SPT 2 Mi-17 (Mi-8MT) *Hip H*/Mi-8 *Hip*†
AD • GUNS 7: **12.7mm** 4; **14.5mm** 3

Navy ε200

EQUIPMENT BY TYPE
PATROL AND COASTAL COMBATANTS 4
    PCI 1 *Shanghai* III
    PCR 3 (various craft gifted 2006)

FACILITIES
Base   Located at Freetown

NON-STATE ARMED GROUPS

see Part II

DEPLOYMENT

NEPAL
UN • UNMIN 2 obs

TIMOR-LESTE
UN • UNMIT 2 obs

FOREIGN FORCES

(all UNIOSIL)
Bangladesh 1 obs
Canada 11 IMATT
Ghana 1 obs
Kenya 1 obs
Nepal 1 obs
Nigeria 1 obs
Pakistan 1 obs
Russia 1 obs
Sweden 1; 1 obs
United Kingdom 1 obs; Army: ε100 (incl Trg Team, Tri-service HQ and spt); 115 IMATT
United States USMC 1

Somalia SR

Somali Shilling sh		2006*	2007 *	2008
GDP	US$			
per capita	US$			
Debt	US$			

* definitive economic data unavailable

Population   9,118,773

Age	0–14	15–19	20–24	25–29	30–64	65 plus
Male	22%	5%	4%	3%	14%	1%
Female	22%	5%	4%	4%	13%	2%

Capabilities

No national armed forces since 1991. Transitional government attempting to set up armed forces but hampered by defections, money and UN arms embargo. Militia forces of around 1000. Somaliland and Puntland have their own militias. Hy equipment in poor repair or inoperable but Somaliland and Puntland have some artillery available.

NON-STATE ARMED GROUPS

see Part II

FOREIGN FORCES

(all AMISOM, unless otherwise indicated – proposed deployment)
Burundi 1,700
Ethiopia 5,000 (in spt of Somalia's TFG)
Italy 2
Malawi 1,000
Nigeria 850
Uganda 1,500 (in theatre)

South Africa RSA

South African Rand R		2006	2007	2008
GDP	R	1.72tr	1.85tr	
	US$	255bn	277bn	
per capita	US$	5,773	6,249	
Growth	%	5.0	4.7	
Inflation	%	4.5	6.6	
Def exp	R	23.87bn		
	US$	3.52bn		
Def bdgt	R	23.83bn	25.92bn	28.01bn
	US$	3.51bn	3.84bn	
US$1=R		6.77	6.75	

Population   43,997,828

Age	0–14	15–19	20–24	25–29	30–64	65 plus
Male	15%	6%	5%	4%	16%	2%
Female	15%	6%	5%	4%	18%	3%

Capabilities

ACTIVE 62,334 (Army 41,350 Navy 5,801 Air 9,183
South African Military Health Service 6,000)

CIVILIAN 12,382 (Army 6,452 Navy 2,000 Air 2,144
South African Military Health Service 1,786)

RESERVE 41,352 (Army 38,545 Navy 861 Air 831
South African Military Health Service Reserve 1,115)

ORGANISATIONS BY SERVICE

Army 41,350

FORCES BY ROLE

Formations under direct command and control of SANDF
Chief of Joint Operations: 9 Joint Operational Tactical HQs,
tps are provided when necessary by permanent and reserve
force units from all services and SF Bde. 8 type formations.

HQ	2 bde
Tk	1 bn
Armd recce	1 bn
Mech inf	2 bn
SF	1 bde (2 SF bn under strength)
Mot inf	9 bn
AB	1 bn
Arty	1 bn
ADA	1 bn
Engr	2 regt

EQUIPMENT BY TYPE

MBT 167: 34 *Olifant* 1A; 133 *Olifant* 1B in store
RECCE 176: 82 *Rooikat*-76; 94 in store
AIFV 1,200: 534 *Ratel*-20 Mk III-20/ *Ratel*-60 Mk III-60/*Ratel*-
90 Mk III-90 FSV 90; 666 in store
APC (W) 810: 370 *Casspir*; 440 *Mamba*
ARTY 1,467
  SP 155mm 43: 2 G-6; 41 in store
  TOWED 147: **140mm** 75 G2 in store; **155mm** 72: 6 G-5;
  66 in store
  MRL 127mm 51: 26 *Valkiri* Mk I in store (24 tube); 21
  Valkiri Mk II MARS *Bateleur* (40 tube); 4 in store (40
  tube)
  MOR 1,226: **81mm** 1,190 (incl some SP); **120mm** 36
AT • MSL • MANPATS 52: 16 ZT-3 *Swift*; 36 in store
  RCL 106mm 100 M-40A1 (some SP)
  RL 92mm FT-5
AD • GUNS 76
  SP 23mm 36 *Zumlac*
  TOWED 35mm 40 GDF-002
UAV • TACTICAL up to 4 *Vulture*
RADAR • LAND *Cymberline* (mor); M-113 A1GE *Green
Archer* (mor)

Reserve Organisations

Regular Reserve 38,545 reservists

cadre units
Armd 8 regt

Inf	26 bn
AB	1 bn
Arty	7 regt
Engr	4 regt
AD	5 regt

Territorial (all to be disbanded by 2009)

Home Def   128+ ('Cdo') bn

Navy 5,801

FORCES BY ROLE

Navy Fleet HQ and Naval base located at Simon's Town;
    Naval Office located at Pretoria; Naval stations
    Durban and Port Elizabeth

EQUIPMENT BY TYPE

SUBMARINES • TACTICAL • SSK 3 Type 209 with 8
533mm TT
PRINCIPAL SURFACE COMBATANTS • CORVETTES
  FSG 4 *Valour* (MEKO A200) with 2 quad (8 eff.) with MM-
  40 *Exocet* ASSM tactical; 2 octuple VLS with Umkhonto-
  IR naval SAM, (capacity 1 *Lynx* Srs 300 *Super Lynx* ASW/
  ASUW hel)
PATROL AND COASTAL COMBATANTS 22:
  PFM 3 *Warrior* (Il Reshef) each with 6 *Skerpioen* tactical
  SSM (Il Gabriel)
  PCI 19: 16 *Namacurra*; 3 craft less than 100 tonnes
MINE WARFARE • MINE COUNTERMEASURES 4
  MHC 4: 3 *River* (Ge *Navors*) (Limited operational roles;
  training and dive support); 1 in reserve
AMPHIBIOUS 6 LCU
LOGISTICS AND SUPPORT 6:
  AORH 1 *Drakensberg* with 1 spt hel (capacity 4 LCU; 100
  troops)
  AGOS 1 (use for Antarctic survey, operated by private
  co. for Dept of Environment)
  AGHS 1 (UK *Hecla*)
  YTM 3

FACILITIES

Bases Located at Durban Salisbury Island (Naval Station),
    Pretoria, Simon's Town

Air Force 9,183

Air Force office, Pretoria, and 4 op gps
Command & Control: 2 Airspace Control Sectors, 1
Mobile Deployment Wg
1 Air Force Command Post

FORCES BY ROLE

Ftr/FGA	1 supersonic AD sqn with 11 *Cheetah* C; 8 *Cheetah* D
Test/ Evaluation	1 (Lead-in Ftr Trg) sqn with 10 *Hawk* Mk120;1 JAS-39D *Gripen*. (28 Gripen –19 JAS-39C, 9 -39D – on order from 2008)
Tkr/EW/tpt	1 sqn with 3 B-707-320 (only 1/2 op)

Tpt	1 (VIP) sqn with 1 B-737 BBJ; 2 CE-550 *Citation II*; 2 *Falcon* 50; 1 *Falcon* 900; 1 sqn with 11 C-47TP (Basler Turbo-67) (6 maritime, 4 tpt, 1 PR/EW trg); 2 sqns with 2 C-130B;7 C-130BZ *Hercules*; 1 CN-235; 4 CASA 212; 13 Cessna 185; 1 tpt and trg school with 3 Beech 200 *Super King Air*; 1 Beech 300 *Super King Air*; 11 Cessna 208 *Caravan I*; 1 PC-12 *Aviocar*; 9 AF Reserve sqns with ε130 private light tpt ac
Tpt hel	4 mixed sqn with *Oryx* (AS-332B) *Super Puma*; 8 BK-11; 16 A109UH; 1 hel trg school with *Oryx* and A109
Hel	1 (cbt spt) sqn with 11 CSH-1 *Rooivalk**
ASuW/SAR	4 *Super Lynx* 300 deployed on Navy *Valour* class frigates
Trg	1 basic flying trg school with 54 PC-7 MkII *Astra*; 1 air nav school

EQUIPMENT BY TYPE
AIRCRAFT 29 combat capable
FTR 19: 11 *Cheetah* C (plus 2 in store); 8 *Cheetah* D
Lead-In Ftr Trg 10 *Hawk* Mk120 (24 total on order)
Test/Evaluation 1: 1 JAS-39D *Gripen* (28 on order)
TPT 51: 3 B-707-320 (only 1/2 op); 1 B-737 BBJ; 3 Beech 200 *Super King Air*; 1 Beech 300 *Super King Air*; 2 C-130B *Hercules*; 7 C-130BZ *Hercules*; 11 C-47TP (Basler Turbo-67); 4 CASA 212 *Aviocar*; 2 CE-550 *Citation II*; 1 CN-235; 13 Cessna 185; 2 *Falcon* 50; 1 *Falcon* 900
UTL 12: 11 Cessna 208 *Caravan I*; 1 PC-12
TRG 54 PC-7 Mk II *Astra*
HELICOPTERS
ASLT 11 CSH-1 *Rooivalk** (plus 1 that crashed and may be beyond repair)
ASuW/SAR 4 *Super Lynx* 300
SPT 39 *Oryx* (AS-332B) *Super Puma*
UTL 23: 8 BK-117; 16 A109UH (total 30 on order)
UAV *Seeker II*
AD • SAM capability closed down
MSL •AAM V3C *Darter*; V4 *R-Darter*; A-*Darter* being procured for *Gripen*

Ground Defence
FORCES BY ROLE
Air some SAAF regt (*total:* 12 (security) Air sqn)

EQUIPMENT BY TYPE
2 Radar (static) located at Ellisras and Mariepskop; 2 (mobile long-range); 4 (tactical mobile)

FACILITIES
Radar air control sectors   Located at Pretoria, Hoedspruit

South African Military Health Service 6,000; ε1,115 reservists (total 7,115)
A separate service within the SANDF

DEPLOYMENT

BURUNDI
AU • AUSTF • *Operation Curiculum* 736
UN • BINUB 1 obs

CENTRAL AFRICAN REPUBLIC
Operation Vimbazela **(bilateral support)** 36

DEMOCRATIC REPUBLIC OF CONGO
UN • MONUC • *Operation Mistral* 1,186; 15 obs; 1 Engr coy; 1 bn gp; air element; air med evacuation team; ac rescue and fire fighting team
Operation Teutonic (tripartite agreement with Be and DROC) 16

ETHIOPIA/ERITREA
AU • OLMEE • *Operation Espresso* 1
UN • UNMEE 5 obs

NEPAL
UN • UNMIN 5 obs

SUDAN
AU • AUMIS • *Operation Cordite* 620; 1 bn gp; 1 Engr tp (P1); 1 EOD team; 18+ APC
UN • UNMIS 4

UGANDA
AU • *Operation Bongane* 2 obs

Sudan Sdn

Sudanese Dinar d		2006	2007	2008
GDP	d	7.6tr	9.3tr	
	US$	34.8bn	44.8bn	
per capita	US$	844	1,059	
Growth	%	11.8	11.2	
Inflation	%	7.2	8.0	
Def bdgt	d	113bn	ε120bn	
	US$	523m	579m	
US$1=d		217	207	

Population   42,292,929

Ethnic Groups: Muslim 70% mainly in North; Christian10% mainly in South; 52% mainly in South; Arab 39% mainly in North

Age	0–14	15–19	20–24	25–29	30–64	65 plus
Male	22%	6%	5%	4%	13%	1%
Female	21%	5%	5%	4%	13%	1%

Capabilities

ACTIVE 109,300 (Army 105,000 Navy 1,300 Air 3,000) **Paramilitary 17,500**
Terms of service conscription (males 18–30), 2 years

RESERVE NIL Paramilitary 85,000

ORGANISATIONS BY SERVICE

Army 85,000; ε20,000 conscripts (total 105,000)
FORCES BY ROLE
Armd	1 div
Mech inf	1 div; 1 indep bde

Inf	6 div; 7 indep bde
Recce	1 indep bde
SF	5 coy
AB	1 div
Arty	3 indep bde
Engr	1 div
Border Guard	1 bde

EQUIPMENT BY TYPE
MBT 350: 20 M-60A3; 60 Type-59; 270 T-54 / T-55
LT TK 115: 70 Type-62; 45 Type-63
RECCE 238: 6 AML-90; 60 BRDM-1/BRDM-2; 50-80 *Ferret*; 42 M1114 *HMMWV*; 30-50 *Saladin*
AIFV 75 BMP-1/BMP-2
APC 409
  APC (T) 66: 36 M-113; 20-30 BTR-50
  APC (W) 343: 55-80 V-150 *Commando*; 10 BTR 70; 7 BTR-80A; 50-80 BTR-152; 20 OT-62; 50 OT-64; 96 *Walid*
ARTY 1,105+
  SP 40: **122mm** 10 2S1 *Carnation*; **155mm** 30: 20 M-114A1; 10 (AMX) Mk F3
  TOWED 111+ **105mm** 20 M-101; **122mm** 16+: 16 D-30; D-74; M-30; **130mm** 75 M-46/Type-59-I
  MRL 635: **107mm** 477 Type-63; **122mm** 158: 90 BM-21; 50 *Saqr*; 18 Type-81
  MOR 81mm; **82mm**; **120mm** AM-49; M-43
AT • MSL • MANPATS 4+: 4 *Swingfire*; AT-3 9K11 *Sagger*
  RCL 106mm 40 M-40A1
  RL 73mm RPG-7 *Knout*
  GUNS 40+: 40 **76mm** ZIS-3/**100mm** M-1944; **85mm** D-44
AD • SAM • MANPAD 54 SA-7 *Grail*
  GUNS 996+
  SP 20: **20mm** 8 M-163 *Vulcan*; 12 M3 VDAA
  TOWED 976+: 740+ **14.5mm** ZPU-2/**14.5mm** ZPU-4/**37mm** Type-63/**57mm** S-60/**85mm** M-1944; **20mm** 16 M-167 *Vulcan*; **23mm** 50 ZU-23-2; **37mm** 110: 80 M-1939; 30 unserviceable; **40mm** 60
RADAR • LAND RASIT (veh, arty)

Navy 1,300
FORCES BY ROLE
Navy 1 HQ located at Port Sudan
EQUIPMENT BY TYPE
PATROL AND COASTAL COMBATANTS 16
  PBR 8: 4 *Kurmuk*; 4 *Sewart* (all less than 100 tonnes)
  PBI 8: 7 *Ashroora*; 1(armed boat)
AMPHIBIOUS 6
 LCT 2 *Sobat*
LCVP 4
FACILITIES
Bases   Located at Port Sudan, Flamingo Bay (Red Sea), Khartoum (Nile)

Air Force 3,000
The two main air bases are at Khartoum International Airport and Wadi Sayyidna north of Omdurman. The air force also has facilities at civilian airports - El Geneina, Nyala and El Fasher have been used for Darfur ops.

Aircrew trg has been reported at Dezful-Ardestani air base, southern Iran.
FORCES BY ROLE
incl Air Defence
FGA   sqns with 5 A-5 *Fantan*; 5 MiG-29SE; 2 MiG-29UB *Fulcrum*; 10 F-7M (MiG-21); 6 Shenyang J-6
Tpt   sqns with 1 An-26 *Curl* (modified for bombing); 6 An-12, 3 *Falcon 20/Falcon 50*; 4 C-130H *Hercules*; 4 DHC-5D *Buffalo*; 8 Il-76 *Candid*; 2 Y-12
Trg   sqns with 6 K-8 *Karokorum*, 12 PT-6A (CJ-6A)
Hel   sqns with 23 Mi-24V *Hind E**; 20+ Mi-8/Mi-171 (assault); 1 IAR-330 (SA-330) *Puma*
AD   5 bty each with 18 SA-2 *Guideline*
EQUIPMENT BY TYPE
AIRCRAFT 51 combat capable
  FGA 32 5 A-5 *Fantan*; 5 MiG-29SE; 2 MiG-29UB *Fulcrum*; 4 MiG-23BN; 10 F-7 (MiG-21); 6 Shenyang J-6
  TPT 25: 1 An-26 *Curl* (modified for bombing)*; 6 An-12 *Cub*; 4 C-130H *Hercules*; 4 DHC-5D *Buffalo*; 8 Il-76 *Candid*; 2 Y-12
  TRG 18: 12 PT-6A (CJ-6A)*; 6 K-8 *Karokorum**
HELICOPTERS
  ATK 23 Mi-24V *Hind E**
  SPT 21+: 20+ Mi-8/Mi-171 ; 1 IAR-330 (SA-330) *Puma* (10 non operational)
AD • SAM • TOWED: 90 SA-2 *Guideline*

Paramilitary 17,500

Popular Defence Force 17,500 (org in bn 1,000); 85,000 reservists (total 102,500)
mil wing of National Islamic Front

NON-STATE ARMED GROUPS
see Part II

FOREIGN FORCES
(all UNMIS, unless otherwise indicated)
Algeria 13 obs AUMIS
Australia 9; 6 obs
Bangladesh 1,525; 21 obs
Belgium 5 obs
Benin 7 obs; 1 obs AUMIS
Bolivia 11 obs
Botswana 5 obs; 20 obs AUMIS
Brazil 23 obs
Burkino Faso 6 obs; 4 obs AUMIS; UNAMID potential deployment
Burundi 10 obs AUMIS
Cameroon 30 obs AUMIS
Canada 8 (*Operation Safari*), 22 obs; 11 obs AUMIS
Chad 38 AUMIS
China 443, 15 obs; 315 AUMIS
Congo 14 obs AUMIS
Croatia 3
Denmark 6, 10 obs
Ecuador 25 obs

Egypt 815; 1 Air Element; 1 Mech inf det; 1 Tpt pl; 1 Engr det; 1 Minesweeping det; 21 obs; 34 obs AUMIS; UNAMID proposed deployment
El Salvador 5 obs
Fiji 8 obs
Finland 2
France UNMIS 1
Gabon 10 obs; 22 obs AUMIS
Gambia 200 AUMIS, UNAMID proposed deployment
Germany 5; 31 obs; 250 UNAMID proposed deployment
Ghana 23 obs AUMIS; UNAMID proposed deployment
Greece 1; 4 obs
Guatemala 8 obs
Guinea 16 obs
India 2,604; 23 obs
Indonesia 13 obs
Ireland 3 obs
Italy EU 6; UNMIS 1
Jordan 8; 15 obs
Kenya 823; 5 obs; 60 obs AUMIS, UNAMID proposed deployment
Kyrgyzstan 10 obs
Lesotho 10 obs AUMIS
Libya 9 obs AUMIS
Madagascar 9 obs AUMIS
Malawi 2; 6 obs; 24 obs AUMIS; UNAMID proposed deployment
Malaysia 3; 10 obs
Mali 15; 15 obs AUMIS; UNAMID proposed deployment
Mauritania 20 obs AUMIS
Moldova 1 obs
Mongolia 2 obs
Mozambique 3 obs; 15 obs AUMIS
Namibia 10 obs; 24 obs AUMIS
Nepal 197; 8 obs
Netherlands 5; 7 obs
New Zealand 1; 2 obs
Nigeria 13 obs; 2,040 AUMIS. 60 UNAMID proposed deployment
Norway 9; 16 obs
Pakistan 1,559; 23 obs
Paraguay 10 obs
Peru 17 obs
Philippines 20 obs
Poland 2 obs
Portugal AUMIS 1
Romania 12 obs
Russia 122; 15 obs
Rwanda 256; 18 obs; 3,272 AUMIS; 18+ APC
Senegal 538 AUMIS
South Africa 1; 620 AUMIS; 1 bn gp; 1 eng tp (P1); 1 EOD team; 18+ APC
Spain 2 obs
Sri Lanka 6 obs
Sweden 2; 3 obs
Tanzania 20 obs AUMIS

Togo 16 obs AUMIS
Turkey 3
Uganda 9 obs
Ukraine 13 obs
United Kingdom 4
United States 1 obs; Army 1; USAF 1
Yemen, Republic of 20 obs
United States 2 obs AUMIS
Zambia 350; 17 obs; 45 obs AUMIS
Zimbabwe 21 obs

Tanzania Tz

Tanzanian Shilling sh		2006	2007	2008
GDP	sh	15.24tr	17.34tr	
	US$	12.2bn	15.1bn	
per capita	US$	325	395	
Growth	%	6.2	7.1	
Inflation	%	7.3	5.6	
Def bdgt	sh	179bn	ε200bn	
	US$	143m	ε173m	
US$1=sh		1,251	1,152	

Population   38,139,640

Age	0–14	15–19	20–24	25–29	30–64	65 plus
Male	22%	6%	5%	4%	11%	1%
Female	22%	6%	5%	4%	12%	1%

Capabilities

ACTIVE 27,000 (Army 23,000 Navy 1,000 Air 3,000)
Paramilitary 1,400
Terms of service incl civil duties, 2 years

RESERVE 80,000 (Joint 80,000)

ORGANISATIONS BY SERVICE

Army ε23,000
FORCES BY ROLE
Tk   1 bde
Inf   5 bde
Arty 4 bn
Mor   1 bn
AT   2 bn
ADA   2 bn
Engr 1 regt (bn)

EQUIPMENT BY TYPE†
MBT 45: 30 T-54/T-55; 15 Type-59
LT TK 55: 30 *Scorpion*; 25 Type-62
RECCE 10 BRDM-2
APC (W) ε10 BTR-40/BTR-152
ARTY 378
    TOWED 170: **76mm** ε40 ZIS-3; **122mm** 100: 20 D-30; 80 Type-54-1 (M-30) *M-1938*; **130mm** 30 Type-59-I

MRL **122mm** 58 BM-21
MOR 150: **82mm** 100 M-43; **120mm** 50 M-43
AT • RCL **75mm** Type-52 (M-20)
RL **73mm** RPG-7 *Knout*
GUNS **85mm** 75 Type-56 (D-44)

Navy ε1,000

EQUIPMENT BY TYPE
PATROL AND COASTAL COMBATANTS 7
PHT 2 *Huchuan* each with 2 533mm ASTT
PFC 2 *Shanghai II* (PRC)
PCC 3: 2 VT; 1 *Ngunguri*
AMPHIBIOUS • LCU 2 *Yunnan*

FACILITIES
Bases Located at Dar es Salaam, Zanzibar, Mwanza (Lake Victoria)

Air Defence Command ε3,000;

FORCES BY ROLE
Ftr   3 sqn with 6 J-7 (MiG-21F) *Fishbed C*;
          3 J-5 (MiG-17F) *Fresco C*; 10 J-6 (MiG-19S) *Farmer B*
Tpt   1 sqn with 1 Y-5 (An-2) *Colt*; 3 DHC-5D *Buffalo*;
          2 F-28 *Fellowship*; 1 HS-125-700; 3 HS-748; 2 Y-12(II)
Liaison some sqn with 5 Cessna 310; 2 Cessna 404 *Titan*;
          1 Cessna U-206 *Stationair*; 6 Bell 206B *JetRanger II*
Trg   some sqn with 5 PA-28-140 *Cherokee*; 2 MiG-15UTI *Midget*
Hel   some sqn with 4 AB-205 (Bell 205); 4 SA-316

EQUIPMENT BY TYPE
Virtually no air defence assets serviceable.
AIRCRAFT 19 combat capable†
FTR 9: 6 J-7 (MiG-21F) *Fishbed C*; 3 J-5 (MiG-17F) *Fresco C*
FGA 10 J-6 (MiG-19S) *Farmer B*
TPT 24: 5 Cessna 310; 2 Cessna 404 *Titan*; 3 DHC-5D *Buffalo*; 2 F-28 *Fellowship*; 1 HS-125-700; 3 HS-748; 5 PA-28-140 *Cherokee*; 2 Y-12(II); 1 Y-5 (An-2) *Colt*
UTL 1 Cessna U-206 *Stationair*
TRG 2 MiG-15UTI *Midget*
HELICOPTERS
UTL 14: 4 AB-205 (Bell 205); 6 Bell 206B *JetRanger II*; 4 SA-316
AD
SAM 160: 20 SA-3 *Goa*†
   SP 20 SA-6 *Gainful*†
   MANPAD 120 SA-7 *Grail*†
GUNS 200
   TOWED **14.5mm** 40 ZPU-2/ZPU-4†; **23mm** 40 ZU-23; **37mm** 120 M-1939

Paramilitary 1,400 active

Police Field Force 1,400
18 sub-units incl Police Marine Unit

Air Wing
AIRCRAFT • UTL 1 Cessna U-206 *Stationair*

HELICOPTERS
UTL 4: 2 AB-206A (Bell 206A) *JetRanger*; 2 Bell 206L *LongRanger*
TRG 2 AB-47G (Bell 47G) Trg hel/Bell 47G2

Marine Unit 100
PATROL AND COASTAL COMBATANTS • MISC BOATS/CRAFT: some boats

Armed Forces 80,000 reservists

DEPLOYMENT

CÔTE D'IVOIRE
UN • UNOCI 1; 1 obs

ETHIOPIA/ERITREA
UN • UNMEE 2; 8 obs

LEBANON
UN• UNIFIL 77

SUDAN
UN • UNMIS 6; 15 obs

Togo Tg

CFA Franc BCEAO fr		2006	2007	2008
GDP	fr	1.14tr	1.21tr	
	US$	2.2bn	2.6bn	
per capita	US$	394	459	
Growth	%	2.0	2.9	
Inflation	%	2.2	3.2	
Def bdgt	fr	ε18.0bn	ε20.0bn	
	US$	ε34m	ε 43m	
US$1=fr		522	462	

Population   5,701,579

Age	0–14	15–19	20–24	25–29	30–64	65 plus
Male	21%	6%	5%	4%	12%	1%
Female	21%	6%	5%	4%	13%	2%

Capabilities

ACTIVE 8,550 (Army 8,100 Navy 200 Air 250)
Paramilitary 750
Terms of service conscription, 2 years (selective)

ORGANISATIONS BY SERVICE

Army 8,100+
FORCES BY ROLE
Inf   1 regt (some spt unit (trg), 2 armd sqn, 3 inf coy); 1 regt (1 mot inf bn, 1 mech inf bn)
Cdo/Para 1 regt (3 Cdo/Para coy)

Spt   1 regt (1 fd arty bty, 1 engr/log/tpt bn,
             2 ADA bty)
Presidential 1 regt (1 Presidential Guard bn,
Guard   1 Cdo bn, 2 Presidential Guard coy)

EQUIPMENT BY TYPE
MBT 2 T-54/T-55
LT TK 9 *Scorpion*
RECCE 61: 3 AML-60; 7 AML-90; 36 EE-9 *Cascavel*; 3 M-20;
4 M-3A1; 6 M-8; 2 VBL
AIFV 20 BMP-2
APC (W) 30 UR-416
ARTY 30
  SP 122mm 6
  TOWED 105mm 4 HM-2
  MOR 82mm 20 M-43
AT • RCL 22: **75mm** 12 Type-52 (M-20)/Type-56; **82mm** 10
Type-65 (B-10)
  GUNS 57mm 5 ZIS-2
AD • GUNS • TOWED 43 **14.5mm** 38 ZPU-4; **37mm** 5
M-1939

Navy ε200 (incl Marine Infantry unit)
EQUIPMENT BY TYPE
PATROL AND COASTAL COMBATANTS • PFC 2 *Kara*
(Fr *Esterel*)
FACILITIES
Base   Located at Lomé

Air Force 250
FORCES BY ROLE
FGA sqn with 4 EMB-326G; 5 Alpha Jet*
Tpt sqn with 1 B-707 (VIP); 2 Beech 58 *Baron*;
     2 Reims Cessna 337 (Cessna 337) *Skymaster*;
     2 DHC-5D *Buffalo*; 1 F-28-1000 (VIP); 1 DO-27
Trg sqn with 4 CM-170 *Magister**; 3 TB-30 *Epsilon**
Hel sqn with 1 AS-332 *Super Puma*; 1 SA-330 *Puma*; 2 SA-
     315 *Lama*; 1 SA-319 *Alouette III*

EQUIPMENT BY TYPE†
AIRCRAFT 16 combat capable
  FGA 4 EMB-326G
  TPT 8: 1 B-707 (VIP); 2 Beech 58 *Baron*; 2 DHC-5D
  Buffalo; 1 F-28-1000 (VIP); 2 Reims Cessna 337 *Skymaster*
  TRG 13: 5 Alpha Jet*; 4 CM-170 *Magister**; 1 DO-27; 3
  TB-30 *Epsilon**
HELICOPTERS
  SPT 2: 1 AS-332 *Super Puma*; 1 SA-330 *Puma*
  UTL 3: 2 SA-315 *Lama*; 1 SA-319 *Alouette III*

Paramilitary 750

Gendarmerie 750
Ministry of Interior
FORCES BY ROLE
2 reg sections
Paramilitary 1 (mob) sqn

FACILITIES
School 1

DEPLOYMENT

CÔTE D'IVOIRE
UN • UNOCI 318; 5 obs

LIBERIA
UN • UNMIL 1; 4 obs

SUDAN
AU • AUMIS 16 obs

Uganda Uga

Ugandan Shilling Ush		2006	2007	2008
GDP	Ush	18.60tr	20.40tr	
	US$	10.2bn	11.6bn	
per capita	US$	348	384	
Growth	%	5.4	6.2	
Inflation	%	6.5	7.5	
Def exp	Ush	350		
	US$	192		
Def bdgt	Ush	377bn	396bn	406bn
	US$	206m	226m	
US$1=Ush		1,831	1,755	

Population   30,262,610

Age	0–14	15–19	20–24	25–29	30–64	65 plus
Male	25%	6%	5%	4%	10%	1%
Female	25%	6%	5%	4%	10%	1%

Capabilities

ACTIVE 45,000 (Ugandan People's Defence Force
45,000) **Paramilitary 1,800**

ORGANISATIONS BY SERVICE

Ugandan People's Defence Force ε40,000–
45,000
FORCES BY ROLE
Army 5 div (*each:* up to 5 army bde)
Armd 1 bde
Arty 1 bde

EQUIPMENT BY TYPE†
MBT 152 T-54/T-55
LT TK ε20 PT-76
RECCE 46: 40 *Eland*; 6 *Ferret*
APC (W) 79: 15 BTR-60; 20 *Buffel*; 40 *Mamba*; 4 OT-64
ARTY 285+
  TOWED 225+: **76mm** ZIS-3; **122mm** M-30; **130mm** 221;
  155mm 4 G-5
  MRL 107mm (12-tube); **122mm** BM-21
  MOR 60+ : **81mm** L16; **82mm** M-43; **120mm** 60 *Soltam*
AD • SAM • MANPAD 200+: 200 SA-7 *Grail*; SA-16 *Gimlet*
  GUNS • TOWED 20+: **14.5mm** ZPU-1/ZPU-2/ZPU-4;
  37mm 20 M-1939

Air Wing

FORCES BY ROLE

FGA   sqn with 5 MiG-23 *Flogger*; 6 MiG-21 *Fishbed*

Tpt Hel   sqn with 1 Mi-172 (VIP); 3 Mi-17 (Mi-8MT) *Hip H*; 1 non-operational; 3 Bell 206 *JetRanger*; 2 Bell 412 *Twin Huey*

Trg   sqn with 3 L-39 *Albatros*†*; 1 SF-260* non-operational

Hel   sqn with 1 Mi-24 *Hind*; 5 non-operational

EQUIPMENT BY TYPE

AIRCRAFT 14 combat capable
   FTR 11: 5 MiG-23 *Flogger*; 6 MiG-21 *Fishbed*
   TRG 4: 3 L-39 *Albatros*†*; 1 SF-260* (non-operational)
HELICOPTERS
   ATK 6: 1 Mi-24 *Hind*; 5 non-operational
   SPT 5: 1 Mi-172 (VIP); 3 Mi-17 (Mi-8MT) *Hip H*; 1 non-operational
   UTL 5: 3 Bell 206 *JetRanger*; 2 Bell 412 *Twin Huey*

Paramilitary ε1,800 active

Border Defence Unit ε600
Equipped with small arms only

Police Air Wing ε800
HELICOPTERS • UTL 1 Bell 206 *JetRanger*

Marines ε400
PATROL AND COASTAL COMBATANTS 8 PCR less than 100 tonnes

Local Militia Forces • Amuka Group ε3,000; ε7,000 (reported under trg) (total 10,000)

NON-STATE ARMED GROUPS
see Part II

DEPLOYMENT

CÔTE D'IVOIRE
UN • ONUCI 2; 2 obs

SOMALIA
AU • AMISOM 1,500

SUDAN
UN • UNMIS 11 obs

FOREIGN FORCES
South Africa 2 obs *Op Bongane*
United States Army 2; USMC 9

Zambia Z

Zambian Kwacha K		2006	2007	2008
GDP	K	37.4tr	43.4tr	
	US$	10.4bn	11.3bn	
per capita	US$	920	989	
Growth	%	5.9	6.0	
Inflation	%	9.1	11.3	
Def bdgt	K	ε884bn	ε933bn	
	US$	ε245m	ε243m	
US$1=K		3,603	3,825	

Population   11,477,447

Age	0–14	15–19	20–24	25–29	30–64	65 plus
Male	23%	6%	5%	4%	10%	1%
Female	23%	6%	5%	4%	11%	1%

Capabilities

ACTIVE 15,100 (Army 13,500 Air 1,600) **Paramilitary 1,400**

RESERVE 3,000 (Army 3,000)

ORGANISATIONS BY SERVICE

Army 13,500

FORCES BY ROLE

Army   3 bde HQ

Armd   1 regt (1 tk bn, 1 armd recce bn)

Inf   6 bn

Arty   1 regt (1 MRL bn, 2 fd arty bn)

Engr   1 regt

EQUIPMENT BY TYPE

Some equipment†
MBT 30: 20 Type-59; 10 T-55
LT TK 30 PT-76
RECCE 70 BRDM-1/BRDM-2 (ε30 serviceable)
APC (W) 13 BTR-60
ARTY 217
   TOWED 96: 76mm 35 ZIS-3 *M-1942*; 105mm 18 Model 56 pack howitzer; 122mm 25 D-30; 130mm 18 M-46
   MRL 122mm 30 BM-21 (ε12 serviceable)
   MOR 91: 81mm 55; 82mm 24; 120mm 12
AT • MSL • MANPATS AT-3 9K11 *Sagger*
   RCL 12+: 57mm 12 M-18; 75mm M-20; 84mm *Carl Gustav*
   RL 73mm RPG-7 *Knout*
AD • SAM • MANPAD SA-7 *Grail*
   GUNS • TOWED 136: 20mm 50 M-55 (triple); 37mm 40 M-1939; 57mm ε30 S-60; 85mm 16 M-1939 *KS-12*

Reserve 3,000
Inf   3 bn

Air Force 1,600

FORCES BY ROLE

FGA   1 sqn with 8 F-6 (MiG-19); 1 sqn with 12 MiG-21MF *Fishbed J*† (8 undergoing refurbishment)

Tpt   1 sqn with 4 An-26 *Curl*; 4 DHC-5D *Buffalo*; 4 Y-12(II)

VIP   1 Fleet with 1 HS-748; 2 Yak-40 *Codling*

Liaison   sqn with 5 Do-28

Trg   sqns with 2 FT-6*; 8 K-8; 2 MiG-21U *Mongol A**; 5 SF-260MZ (SF-260M)*; 5 SF-260TP; some MFI-17

Hel   1 sqn with 12 Mi-8 *Hip*; some (Liaison) sqn with 10 Bell 47G

AD   3 bty with SA-3 *Goa*; 1 bn

EQUIPMENT BY TYPE
Very low serviceability.
AIRCRAFT 29 combat capable
  FGA 20: 8 F-6 (MiG-19); 12 MiG-21MF *Fishbed J*† (8 undergoing refurbishment)
  TPT 20: 4 An-26 *Curl*; 4 DHC-5D *Buffalo*; 5 Do-28; 1 HS-748; 4 Y-12(II); 2 Yak-40 *Codling*
  TRG 22+: 8 K-8; 2 MiG-21U *Mongol A**; 5 SF-260MZ (SF-260M)*; 5 SF-260TP; 2 FT-6*; some MFI-17
HELICOPTERS
  SPT 12 Mi-8 *Hip*
  TRG 10 Bell 47G
AD • SAM SA-3 *Goa*
MSL • ASM AT-3 *Sagger*

Paramilitary 1,400

Police Mobile Unit 700
Police 1 bn (4 Police coy)

Police Paramilitary Unit 700
Paramilitary 1 bn (3 Paramilitary coy)

DEPLOYMENT

CÔTE D'IVOIRE
UN • UNOCI 2 obs

DEMOCRATIC REPUBLIC OF CONGO
UN • MONUC 24 obs

ETHIOPIA/ERITREA
UN • UNMEE 3; 10 obs

LIBERIA
UN • UNMIL 3 obs

NEPAL
UN • UNMIN 8 obs

SERBIA
UN • UNMIK 1 obs

SIERRA LEONE
UN • UNIOSIL 1 obs

SUDAN
AU • AUMIS 45 obs
UN • UNMIS 353; 14 obs

Zimbabwe Zw

Zimbabwe Dollar Z$		2006	2007	2008
GDP	Z$	909bn	55.1tr	
	US$	5.6bn	3.1bn	
per capita	US$	459	255	
Growth	%	-4.7	-6.2	
Inflation	%	1,016	16,170	
Def bdgt	Z$	25.2bn		
	US$	155m		
US$1=Z$		162*	17,562	

* Redenominated in 2006

Population   12,311,143

Age	0–14	15–19	20–24	25–29	30–64	65 plus
Male	19%	7%	6%	5%	11%	2%
Female	19%	7%	6%	4%	12%	2%

Capabilities

ACTIVE 29,000 (Army 25,000 Air 4,000) Paramilitary 21,800

ORGANISATIONS BY SERVICE

Army ε25,000
FORCES BY ROLE

Armd	1 sqn
Mech	1 bde HQ
Mech inf	1 bn
Inf	5 bde HQ; 15 bn
Cdo	1 bn
Para	1 bn
Arty	1 bde
Fd arty	1 regt
Engr	2 regt
Gd	3 bn
Presidential Guard	1 gp
AD	1 regt

EQUIPMENT BY TYPE
MBT 40: 30 Type-59 mostly non-operational; 10 Type-69 mostly non-operational
AIFV 80 EE-9 *Cascavel* (with 90mm gun)
RECCE 35: 20 *Eland*; 15 *Ferret*†
APC 85
  APC (T) 30: 8 Type-63; 22 VTT-323
  APC (W) 55 TPK 4.20 VSC *ACMAT*
ARTY 242
  TOWED 122mm 20: 4 D-30; 16 Type-60 (D-74)
  MRL 76: **107mm** 16 Type-63; **122mm** 60 RM-70 *Dana*
  MOR 146: **81mm/82mm** ε140; **120mm** 6 M-43
AD • SAM • MANPAD 30 SA-7 *Grail*†
  GUNS • TOWED 116: **14.5mm** 36 ZPU-1/ZPU-2/ZPU-4; **23mm** 45 ZU-23; **37mm** 35 M-1939

Air Force 4,000

Flying hours   100 hrs/year

FORCES BY ROLE

Ftr	1 sqn with 4 F-7N (F-7M) *Airguard*†; 3 F-7II (J-7II) *Fishbed*†; 2 FT-7 (JJ-7) *Mongol A*†
FGA	1 sqn with 3 MiG-23 *Flogger*; 12 Hawker *Hunter*; 1 sqn with 6 K-8 (further 6 on order)
RECCE/Trg/ Liaison	1 sqn with 9 SF-260M; 9 SF-260TP*; 6 SF-260W *Warrior**
RECCE/COIN	1 sqn with 14 Cessna 337 *Skymaster**
Tpt	1 sqn with 1 An-24 *Coke*; 6 BN-2 Islander; 8 CASA 212-200 *Aviocar* (VIP); 1 IL-76 *Candid*
Hel	1 sqn with 4 Mi-35 *Hind**; 2 Mi-35P *Hind* (armed/liaison); 1 SA-319 *Alouette III*; 2 AS-532UL *Cougar* (VIP); 1 trg sqn with 8 Bell 412 *Twin Huey*, 1 SA-319 *Alouette III*
AD	1 sqn with 37mm; 57mm

EQUIPMENT BY TYPE

AIRCRAFT 45 combat capable

FTR 10: 4 F-7N (F-7M) *Airguard*†; 3 MiG-23 *Flogger*; 3 F-7II (J-7II) *Fishbed*†

FGA 18: 6 K-8 (further 6 on order); 12 Hawker *Hunter* FGA* in store

TPT 40: 1 An-24 *Coke*; 6 BN-2 Islander; 10 C-47 *Skytrain* in store; 8 CASA 212-200 *Aviocar* (VIP); 14 Cessna 337 *Skymaster*; 1 IL-76 *Candid*

TRG 32: 2 FT-7 (JJ-7) *Mongol A*†*; 6 K-8; SF-260 24; 9 SF-260M; 9 SF-260TP*; 6 SF-260W *Warrior**

HELICOPTERS

ATK 6: 4 Mi-35 *Hind**; 2 Mi-35P *Hind* (armed/liaison)

UTL 2 AS-532UL *Cougar* (VIP);

TRG 10: 8 Bell 412 *Twin Huey*; 2 SA-319 *Alouette III**;

AD • GUNS 100mm (not deployed); **37mm** (not deployed); **57mm** (not deployed)

FACILITIES

School 1 with 100mm Guns (not deployed); 37mm Guns (not deployed); 57mm Guns (not deployed) (AD)

Paramilitary 21,800

Zimbabwe Republic Police Force 19,500

incl Air Wg

Police Support Unit 2,300

DEPLOYMENT

CÔTE D'IVOIRE

UN • **UNOCI** 2 obs

LIBERIA

UN • **UNMIL** 2 obs

NEPAL

UN • **UNMIN** 2 obs

SUDAN

UN • **UNMIS** 3; 10 obs

Table 26 **Selected Arms Orders and Deliveries, Sub-Saharan Africa**

Country Supplier	Classification	Designation	Quantity	Order date	Original Delivery date	Comment
Cameroon (Crn) Il	Arty	TN-90 155mm	18	–	2006	–
Gabon (Gbn) RSA	Ftr	*Mirage* F1 AZ	–	–	2006	–
Namibia (Nba) Br	PCI	*Tracker* II	4	2004	2009	–
Nigeria (Nga) PRC	Ftr	F-7NI	12	2005	2006	Combined cost with order for 3 FT–7NI is USD251m. Delays occurring
PRC	Trg	FT-7NI	3	2005	2006	Combined cost with order for 12 F–7NI is USD251m. Delays occurring
It	Tpt	G222	6	2005	2005	Upgrade. USD74.5m. Programme to include refurbishment, training and logistical support for Nigeria's fleet of 5 G222s. In addition Nigeria will receive a former Italian Air Force G222
It	Hel	AW 139	4	2006	–	Configured for corporate transport and SAR missions
It	MP / SAR	ATR 42 MP *Surveyor*	2	2007	2009	USD73m
South Africa (RSA) dom	Arty	G-6-52	–	1997	2006	Development complete. Ready for production
Ge	FSG	*Valour* (MEKO A200)	4	1999	2006	EUR924m. First of class delivered 2006. Rest currently undergoing acceptance trials. Expected ISD 2007. 4th FSG, SAS *Mendi,* commissioned March 2007. Letter of intent issued for a 5th vessel in 2006.
Ge	SSK	Type 209/1400	3	1999	2005	Final deliveries 2007. Second Type 209 received April 2007
It	Hel	A-109LUH	30	2000	2005	10 hel delivered. Deliveries continuing
UK	Trg	*Hawk* MK120	24	2000	2005	13 ac delivered. Deliveries continuing
UK	Hel	*Lynx* Srs 300 *Super Lynx*	4	2000	2007	4 hel to go with *Meko* FS
Swe	FGA	JAS 39 *Gripen*	9	2000	2008	Option on further 19
Int'l	Tpt	A-400M	8	2005	2010	USD516m. Long term contract with RSA participation
dom	MBT	*Olifant* Mk1B	13	2005	–	Upgrade. USD27m
dom	UAV	*Vulture*	1	–	2006	Cont. development
Int'l	Msl	Milan ADT	–	2006	2008	EUR18m (USD23m). Milan ADT firing posts, Milan 3 msl and simulators. For inf and SF units
SF / dom	APC	*Patria* 8X8 Armoured Modular Vehicle	264	2007	2012	ZAR8.8bn (USD1.2bn). Deliveries to be completed by 2020
dom	Tpt	A400M	8	2007	–	–
dom	AAM	*A-Darter*	–	2007	–	–
dom	IFV	8x8 IFV	250	2007	–	Based on *Patria* design. 5 variants to be produced: Command, Mor, Msl, Section, and Fire Support vehicles

Table 26 **Selected Arms Orders and Deliveries, Sub-Saharan Africa**

Country Supplier	Classification	Designation	Quantity	Order date	Original Delivery date	Comment
CH	Trg	*Pilatus* PC-7 MKII Astra	35	2007	–	Avionics / life extension upgrade. ZAR400m (USD54m)
Sudan (Sdn) RF	FGA	MiG-29 *Fulcrum*	10	2002	2003	Likely further 12 to be ordered
Uganda (Uga)	Il	Arty	TN-90 155mm	18	–	2006	–
Zimbabwe (Zw) PRC	FGA	FC-1 *Xiaolong*	12	2004	–	Yet to be delivered
PRC	Trg	K-8 *Karakorum*	6	2006	2006	Second batch of K-8. First batch already in service

Chapter Seven
Central and South Asia

CENTRAL ASIA

2007 has proved thus far one of the more stable years in the post-Soviet history of Central Asia. The sudden death of Turkmen President Saparmurat Niyazov in December 2006 led to the succession of a new government led by Gurbanguly Berdymukhammedov. The president of Kazakhstan secured a life-long mandate and effective control over the legislature, while political leaders in Tajikistan and Uzbekistan are expected to remain in power for the foreseeable future, with Uzbek President Islam Karimov indicating that he will stand for another term in the scheduled 23 December 2007 polls. Meanwhile, Kyrgyzstan's President Kurmanbek Bakiev has consolidated power after the 'Tulip Revolution', although effective governance remains an issue and instability cannot be ruled out.

The relative stability of most states has been accompanied by new regional political trends. Firstly, Russia and China continue to strengthen their positions though bilateral ties and multilateral institutions such as the Shanghai Cooperation Organisation (SCO), the CIS Collective Security Treaty Organisation (CSTO) and the Eurasian Economic Community (EurAsEc). In addition, India, Pakistan and Iran have increased their regional engagement through economic and security cooperation. Meanwhile, both the US and the EU continue to signal their interest in Central Asia not only because of its proximity to Afghanistan but also, and increasingly, in the context of their energy-security concerns. In June 2007, the EU Council adopted the EU Strategy towards Central Asia, the first attempt to clearly formulate EU interests and ambitions in the region.

Secondly, there is growing concern in the region about developments in Afghanistan, where NATO has so far been unable to reverse problems such as the volume of narcotics that pass though Central Asia, and the gradual proliferation of insurgency and terrorism into Afghanistan's northern provinces. As a result there is growing concern in Central Asia about possible NATO withdrawal from Afghanistan or the alliance's inability to control growing destabilisation. If this happens, Central Asian states might need to look outside the region for security guarantees, with none possessing the capability to deal with cross-border threats and each feeling vulnerable to the spread of Islamic extremism within its own society.

Such security assurances could come from a combination of three regional mechanisms. The first is the SCO, which remains torn between its identities as a security organisation and as an economic grouping. The second is the CSTO, which has strengthened its role in the region since Uzbekistan re-joined in 2006. Finally, the West remains engaged through NATO and bilateral agreements. Some states seek ties with the West to counter growing dependence on Russia and China.

The Shanghai Cooperation Organisation

The SCO's fifth anniversary was celebrated in China in 2006. Since then the organisation has increased its activities and engagement in Central Asia. 2007 has seen an expansion of economic ties, including discussions on the creation of an SCO 'energy club' (the SCO includes among its members and observers some of the largest oil and gas producers in Eurasia – Russia, Kazakhstan and Iran – and the largest consumers – India and China). Turkmenistan was invited to the 2007 SCO summit in Bishkek as a guest. Should Turkmenistan join the SCO as a full member, or even an observer, the organisation's overall energy 'pool' will become even greater. However, it remains unclear how such a club would function, as its consumers remain in competition and its producers seek to diversify their export routes in order to maximise profits.

In addition to its energy cooperation, the SCO has a security identity. The organisation's largest military exercises were held near Chelyabinsk in Russia in August 2007. *Peace Mission 2007*, called an 'anti-terrorist exercise', preceded the Bishkek summit. But the scale of Russian and Chinese involvement suggests that it was more an exercise in interoperability than an anti-terrorist drill. Over 6,500 personnel and 2,000 pieces of equipment were involved, and this was the first time that Chinese troops were allowed to exercise in Russia in such numbers; it is reported that over 1,600 troops travelled over 10,000km by rail to reach Russia after Kazakhstan refused them passage through its territory. These Chinese troops constituted one ground-force combat group, one air-force combat group and one integrated support group. The exercise scenario saw a group of 'terrorists' capture a town, with SCO forces – acting with close air support and artillery – eliminating opposing forces and freeing the town. After that, Russian forces were tasked with arresting surviving 'terrorists'.

The Russian Air Force contributed six Il-76 *Candid* transport planes (from the High Command's 61st Air Army (military transport aviation)), nine Su-25 *Frogfoot* FGA aircraft (from the 4th Air Force and Air Defence Army, Rostov-on-Don), 14 Mi-24 *Hind* attack helicopters and 18 Mi-8 *Hip* helicopters (from the 5th Air Force and Air Defence Army in Yekaterinburg). Other Russian air contributions included helicopters and aircraft of the Ministry of Internal Affairs, the Federal Security Service (FSB) and other agencies. China provided six Il-76s, eight JH-7-A FGA aircraft, 16 JG-9-W and 16 Mi-17 *Hip* helicopters. Russia and China also contributed 18 122mm and 100mm artillery pieces. The participation of Central Asian militaries was largely symbolic: Uzbekistan did not send troops to the exercise; Kazakhstan deployed 143; Tajikistan 100 and Kyrgyzstan 20. All these depended on Russia for airlift. At $77m, the exercise was significantly more expensive than previous ones.

Both Russia and China, as well as other SCO states, have described the exercise as successful. Moreover, the Russian defence ministry sought to use the exercise to enhance military cooperation within the SCO. Chief of the Russian General Staff General Yuri Baluyevsky proposed conceptual foundations for military cooperation within the SCO and suggested that Russia had already prepared such a document. However, he continued to deny that the SCO is turning into a military grouping, with a similar view expressed by former Defence Minister and now First Deputy Prime Minister Sergei Ivanov in September 2007; Ivanov said that the SCO is an economic organisation. This is the view long advanced by China, which has resisted Russia's efforts to enhance the SCO's security identity at the expense of its economic agenda. However, China's vision of the SCO – that it could be the beginning of a single market – is unlikely to gain support among regional states, which fear Chinese economic expansion. In the meantime, as well as the challenge of defining its identity, the SCO also faces a challenge from potential enlargement. All SCO observer states – Mongolia, India, Pakistan and Iran – have applied to join the organisation as full members, although existing SCO member states have failed so far to reach consensus on which should be admitted and what criteria should be used to guide the enlargement process.

The Collective Security Treaty Organisation

In October 2007, the SCO and CSTO signed a memorandum of cooperation. This is seen as strengthening Russia's influence within the CSTO, since Russia plays a key role in the organisation. Unlike the SCO, the CSTO has many attributes of a declared military alliance, including security guarantees for its members. In 2007, the Russian Duma ratified agreements for Russia to train military personnel from CSTO states, as well as an agreement between Tajikistan and Russia, signed in November 2006, to jointly plan military operations in order to promote both nations' security interests. Russia and Uzbekistan have also agreed on mutual security guarantees, but these agreements have yet to be tested in practice.

For some years the CSTO has been seeking cooperation with NATO, particularly concerning the need to combat drug trafficking from Afghanistan. So far, NATO has been reluctant to enter into such institutional cooperation, preferring to deal with regional states on a bilateral basis, avoiding what they see as a Russian-dominated security structure opposed to a Western security presence in Central Asia. However, regional states are increasingly turning to Russia as a security guarantor, viewing Moscow more positively, in this sense, than NATO and the West.

In October 2007, at the CSTO summit in Dushanbe, leaders agreed to the creation of CSTO peacekeeping forces. It remains unclear where these forces could be deployed. Russian Foreign Minister Sergei Lavrov has ruled out deploying CSTO peacekeepers in conflict zones in Abkhazia or South Ossetia, while CSTO Secretary-General Nikolai Bordyzha suggested that these forces could be deployed for operations, under UN mandate, in various parts of the world.

The CSTO already has joint rapid-response forces tasked to deal with security challenges in Central Asia – the ten-battalion strong Collective Rapid Deployment Force – and is expanding cooperation among its member states' law enforcement and security agencies. In October, moreover, Tajikistan appealed to the CSTO to become more involved in stabilisation efforts in Afghanistan, although no specific steps were agreed.

Afghanistan

NATO and coalition forces remain heavily engaged in counter-insurgency operations to address the Taliban-led insurgency in Afghanistan and to try to enhance the general security environment (see 'Afghanistan Conflict: Military Challenges', IISS *Strategic Comments*, vol. 13, no. 8, October 2007; IISS *Strategic Survey 2007*, pp. 366–7). The positive resolution of this conflict is generally accepted to be of international significance, and one that will require a coordinated long-term, multinational and multi-agency effort. Following the expansion of the International Security Assistance Force (ISAF), under NATO command, to assume responsibility for the country's eastern provinces in October 2006, military actions have seen NATO forces

at times engaged in high-intensity ground combat operations against insurgent forces, where the coalition technical advantage is reduced (see p. 329). Failure in these actions would risk boosting Islamic extremism (not just in Afghanistan), would produce a failed state in an area of strategic importance, and would offer safe haven to terrorist organisations and the narcotics trade. It would also undermine the credibility of NATO in its first major out-of-area combat operation.

The military task remains wedded to an overall international strategy designed to build confidence in

Table 27 Selected Security and Political Developments in Afghanistan, 2007

Month	Event	Month	Event
January	ISAF's Kabul HQ hosts a new joint intelligence-sharing centre set up between ISAF, Afghanistan and Pakistan		ISAF forces are reported to have unintentionally fired rockets into Pakistani territory, killing 10 civilians and injuring 14, following a firefight with Taliban militants on the border
February	Senior Taliban leader Mullah Abdul Gafoor and associates are killed in an ISAF-led airstrike	July	The Taliban is reported to have used heat-seeking surface-to-air missiles for the first time to attack a US C-130 *Hercules* flying over Nimruz province, albeit unsuccessfully
	8 US troops killed, 14 injured, when a CH-47 crashes after an engine failure in Zabul province		
	A further 1,400 UK troops deployed in anticipation of Taliban 'spring offensive'		ISAF announces that it will be using smaller bombs on operations as part of an effort to reduce civilian casualties; another new policy will see Afghan forces conducting house searches instead of foreign forces, in order to improve relations with locals
	Suicide attack at Bagram airbase during visit by US Vice President Cheney		
March	ISAF launches *Operation Achilles*, an operation which ended in May, involved over 5,000 ISAF and Afghan National troops and was focused on operations in northern Helmand	August	ISAF airstrike in Helmand kills two 'Taliban commanders'; local officials claim that at least 19 civilians are killed, while ISAF estimates that the number is three
	Mullah Obaidullah Akhund, former Taliban defence minister, arrested in Quetta, Pakistan		The United Nations Office on Drugs and Crime releases its 2007 Afghanistan Opium Survey, which warns that Afghanistan accounts for 93% of global opium production, with production increasing by 34% since 2006
	Daniele Mastrogiacomo, a reporter for Italy's *La Repubblica*, is released after being held captive by the Taliban for 15 days. He was released after Rome asked Kabul to release five Taliban militants in its custody. *New York Times* reports this was the first time a Western government had openly negotiated with captors to arrange a hostage swap		A total of 21 South Korean hostages are released after having been held by the Taliban since their capture in Ghazni province in July; two were executed early on in their six-week detention. Seoul negotiated directly with the kidnappers, pledging to fulfil its existing plan to withdraw its 200 troops by the end of 2007
	ISAF launches *Operation Now Ruz*, a theatre-wide framework operation designed to maintain freedom of manoeuvre focused on National Highway 1. Afghan National and ISAF forces employed		
April	5 UN workers are killed by a roadside bomb in Kandahar province		Reports claim that the number of insurgent attacks on Afghan and Western troops is at its highest since the 2001 invasion
May	30 civilians are killed in Herat province after a protracted battle between insurgents and US-led forces, leading to protests against the presence of foreign troops in the country and a condemnation of the casualties by President Hamid Karzai	September	The United Nations Security Council extends ISAF's mandate for another year
			A suicide bomber dressed in military uniform targets a bus with Afghan soldiers on board in Kabul, killing at least 30. An almost identical attack in early October kills 12
	Mullah Dadullah, a top-ranking Taliban commander, is killed in Helmand province by US and Afghan troops		
	Taliban announces commencement of its spring offensive	October	ISAF launches *Operation Pamir*, a theatre-wide operation with Afghan forces operation for the period October 2007–March 2008. Designed to maintain pressure on insurgent forces, disrupting their ability to rearm and re-equip
	US airstrikes targeting al-Qaeda operations hit school in Paktika province, killing 7 children		
	ISAF CH-47 *Chinook* crashes in Helmand province killing all (5 US, 1 UK and 1 Canadian soldiers) on board		
	Al-Qaeda announces that its new commander in the country is Mustafa Abu al-Yazid		Associated Press reports there have been over 100 suicide attacks and 5,086 people killed in insurgency-related violence in 2007
	ISAF and Afghan National forces launch *Operation Lastay Kulang* in northern Helmand	November	In the deadliest bomb attack since the 2001 invasion, at least 70 are killed in a suicide attack on a sugar factory in Baghlan province. Among the dead were six members of parliament and many children
June	Karzai survives rocket attacks in Ghazni province close to where he was addressing local villagers		

the Kabul administration of President Hamid Karzai and prevent a reversion to an extremist-dominated Taliban administration. Part of this means giving the lead, in as many areas as possible, to the government in Kabul, and there has been an increase in the international effort to train units of the Afghan National Army and Police. Yet the government still lacks authority in much of the country.

In late October 2007, ISAF had a total of around 41,000 personnel assigned. The force, commanded since February 2007 by US General Dan McNeill, oper-ates in four regional commands, with a fifth based in Kabul (see map). Major contributions included those from the US (over 15,000), the UK (over 7,700), Germany (over 3,000), Italy (over 2,300), Canada (over 1,700), the Netherlands (over 1,500) and Poland (nearly 1,000). Meanwhile, around 9,650 US personnel remain on activities connected with *Operation Enduring Freedom* under the command of Combined Joint Task Force-82. ISAF's role differs according to the stability of the deployed location. Efforts at reconstruction involve 25 Provincial Reconstruction Teams, mostly

MAP 5 **AFGHANISTAN**

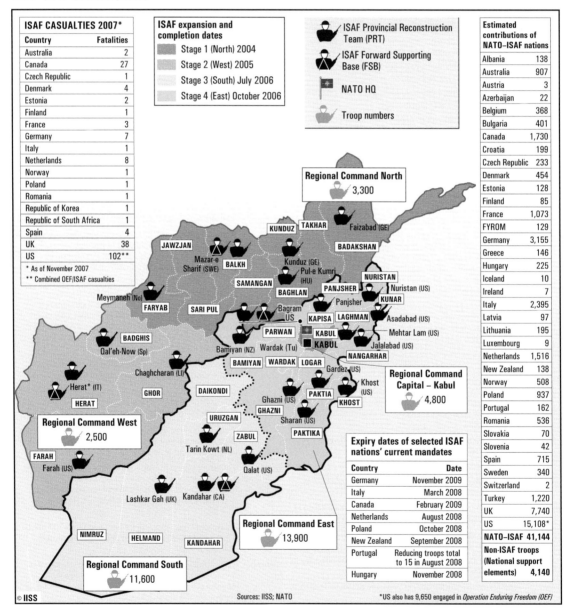

ISAF CASUALTIES 2007*	
Country	Fatalities
Australia	2
Canada	27
Czech Republic	1
Denmark	4
Estonia	2
Finland	1
France	3
Germany	7
Italy	1
Netherlands	8
Norway	1
Poland	1
Romania	1
Republic of Korea	1
Republic of South Africa	1
Spain	4
UK	38
US	102**

* As of November 2007
** Combined OEF/ISAF casualties

ISAF expansion and completion dates
Stage 1 (North) 2004
Stage 2 (West) 2005
Stage 3 (South) July 2006
Stage 4 (East) October 2006

ISAF Provincial Reconstruction Team (PRT)
ISAF Forward Supporting Base (FSB)
NATO HQ
Troop numbers

Estimated contributions of NATO–ISAF nations	
Albania	138
Australia	907
Austria	3
Azerbaijan	22
Belgium	368
Bulgaria	401
Canada	1,730
Croatia	199
Czech Republic	233
Denmark	454
Estonia	128
Finland	85
France	1,073
FYROM	129
Germany	3,155
Greece	146
Hungary	225
Iceland	10
Ireland	7
Italy	2,395
Latvia	97
Lithuania	195
Luxembourg	9
Netherlands	1,516
New Zealand	138
Norway	508
Poland	937
Portugal	162
Romania	536
Slovakia	70
Slovenia	42
Spain	715
Sweden	340
Switzerland	2
Turkey	1,220
UK	7,740
US	15,108*
NATO–ISAF	**41,144**
Non-ISAF troops (National support elements)	**4,140**

Regional Command North 3,300

Regional Command Capital – Kabul 4,800

Regional Command West 2,500

Regional Command East 13,900

Regional Command South 11,600

KUNDUZ TAKHAR Faizabad (GE)
JAWZJAN BADAKHSHAN
Mazar-e Sharif (SWE) BALKH Kunduz (GE) Pul-e Kumri (HU) NURISTAN
SAMANGAN PANJSHER Nuristan (US)
Meymaneh (No) BAGHLAN Panjsher KUNAR
FARYAB SARI PUL Bagram US KAPISA LAGHMAN Asadabad (US)
BADGHIS PARWAN KABUL Mehtar Lam (US)
Qal'eh-Now (Sp) Bamiyan (NZ) Wardak (Tu) KABUL Jalalabad (US)
BAMIYAN WARDAK LOGAR NANGARHAR
Chaghcharan (LI) Gardez (US)
Herat* (IT) DAIKONDI Khost (US)
HERAT GHOR Ghazni (US) PAKTIA KHOST
URUZGAN GHAZNI Sharan (US)
FARAH ZABUL PAKTIKA
Farah (US) Tarin Kowt (NL)
Qalat (US)
Lashkar Gah (UK) Kandahar (CA)
NIMRUZ HELMAND KANDAHAR

Expiry dates of selected ISAF nations' current mandates	
Country	Date
Germany	November 2009
Italy	March 2008
Canada	February 2009
Netherlands	August 2008
Poland	October 2008
New Zealand	September 2008
Portugal	Reducing troops total to 15 in August 2008
Hungary	November 2008

© IISS

Sources: IISS; NATO

*US also has 9,650 engaged in *Operation Enduring Freedom (OEF)*

deployed in the northern and western regions, while combat operations were concentrated in the southern and eastern provinces.

During 2007, insurgents have deployed suicide attacks to a greater extent than previously, indicating not only that the insurgency was spreading geographically but also that tactical lessons and techniques had migrated from the insurgency in Iraq. The attack on Bagram airbase in February 2007, during a visit by US Vice President Dick Cheney, showed that insurgents enjoyed relative freedom of action and possessed accurate information on targets, timings and movements. The level of suicide attacks has increased substantially in the last few years. According to the UN Mission in Afghanistan (UNAMA) in a September 2007 report on suicide bombing in Afghanistan, 'only five attacks occurred between 2001 and 2005, when they escalated unexpectedly to 17 attacks that year. In 2006 there were 123 actual attacks, and in 2007 there were 77 attacks between 1 January and 30 June.'

Although insurgents have shifted towards asymmetric tactics, some conventional engagements occur where, according to the UK Chief of the General Staff, insurgents try to neutralise the technological superiority of the alliance, choosing to fight in areas of limited visibility and where basic soldiering skills are pre-eminent. Combat operations have been intense through mid 2007. However, as a result of joint Afghan–ISAF operations, people and commerce have returned to towns like Sangin, while concerted actions by ISAF and Afghan troops have brought some security to the area around the important Kajaki dam and its associated hydroelectric facility. In March, ISAF's *Operation Achilles* deployed 5,500 troops (4,500 ISAF and 1,000 ANSF) on operations around the Kajaki dam area. However, a project to refurbish the facility has been unable to proceed due to a shortage of troops to hold territory.

A shortage of military resources hinders coalition efforts across the theatre. UK Foreign Secretary David Miliband pointed to this in a November speech, when he said that European nations 'must overcome the blockages to collaboration with NATO' and that while 'EU countries have around 1,200 transport helicopters, yet only about 35 are deployed in Afghanistan'. But it will be difficult for these problems to be remedied to the degree required. Canada and the Netherlands, which both provide substantial combat contributions, face parliamentary debates in late 2007 over the renewal of mandates. ISAF commanders' options are also limited by the operational restrictions placed on nearly a quarter of the force, including troops from Germany, Italy and Spain. About 50 'national caveats' are maintained which, according to some military officers, unduly constrain offensive operations. However, after NATO's Noordwijk meeting in October 2007, Secretary General Jaap de Hoop Scheffer said that he had heard offers from countries, including for the south of Afghanistan.

Nobody, least of all military personnel and commanders, believes there is a military solution to Afghanistan's problems. The longer-term solution to the shortfall in military resources is widely held to be building the capacity of Afghanistan's security forces. But progress has so far been slow: the Afghan National Army comprises fewer than 35,000 men, well below the goal of 70,000 by 2010. However, some problems have been addressed. Retention rates are said to have increased to 45–60% of recruits, though this varies by unit. However, ISAF is falling short on commitments to provide Operational Mentoring and Liaison Teams (OMLTs) – units that the UK CGS called one of the 'key successes' in Afghanistan – to train ANA units on the ground. According to the NATO spokesman in October, 'we have now committed and deployed about half of what we need to meet the current requirement of Afghan battalions, around 20. We have another 10 to 12 in the pipeline. That would still leave us short.' This pressure is increased with the expansion of the Afghan army.

SOUTH ASIA

India

On 28 August 2007, the long-awaited Request for Proposals (RfP) for the $10bn order for 126 Medium Multi-Role Combat Aircraft (MMRCA) for the Indian Air Force (IAF) was released. It invited six aircraft manufacturers, including US manufacturers for the first time, to bid for India's largest defence contract. In addition to Lockheed Martin's F-16 and Boeing's F/A-18 *Super Hornet*, the other contenders are Russia's MiG-35, Sweden's JAS-39 *Gripen,* the French *Rafale*, and the Eurofighter *Typhoon*. While the IAF plans to purchase the first batch of 18 aircraft directly from the manufacturer, the remainder are to be built in India under a transfer of technology agreement. The RfP also has a 50% offset clause, which requires the investment of $5bn in India. The last date for receipt of technical bids is 3 March 2008, with offset proposals due in June 2008.

In addition, negotiations are well advanced for the purchase of six C-130J *Hercules* cargo planes for $1bn from Lockheed Martin. The first four BAE *Hawk* advanced jet trainers arrived in India in November 2007, and the first Airborne Warning and Control Systems (AWACS) aircraft from Israel is expected to arrive by August 2008.

Meanwhile, there were significant differences with Russia over cost escalation of armament systems for contracts already being undertaken. With Russia demanding an increase in the price of contracts, among them for the aircraft carrier *Admiral Gorshkov*, new Sukhoi multi-role fighters and advanced T-90 tanks, delivery was likely to be delayed. After months of denial, the Indian Ministry of Defence finally admitted that the hand over of the *Admiral Gorshkov* would be delayed due to software and cabling problems. Originally planned for August 2008, the aircraft carrier could now be handed over to the Indian navy in mid 2009 or early 2010.

Nonetheless, in view of the delay in releasing the RfP for the MMRCA, the IAF ordered an additional batch of 40 upgraded Sukhoi Su-30 aircraft from Russia in March 2007 for $1.6bn. With a landmark deal in October 2007, India also reiterated its confidence in Russia as its dominant arms supplier and partner in the development of future sophisticated weapon systems. During a visit by the new defence minister, A.K. Antony, to Russia in October 2007, the two countries signed a $10bn agreement for the joint development of the Fifth Generation Fighter Aircraft (FGFA), the Sukhoi T-50 PAK-FA (Future Air Complex for Tactical Air Forces). The two countries are expected to equally share the financial and technological stakes in the project, as is the case for the first major Indo-Russian joint venture project, between India's Defence Research and Development Organisation and Russia's Mashinostroyenia Research and Production Centre, for the development of the 290km-range *BrahMos* supersonic cruise missile.

Following the ongoing deployment of the ship-launched version of the *BrahMos*, it was reported in early September 2007 that a submarine-launched version had been developed, but sea trials were awaiting a suitable platform. The land version of the *BrahMos* was formally adopted by the Indian army on 22 June 2007. The development of an air-launched version of the *BrahMos* is currently in progress, with attempts being made to integrate the missile to the IAF's Su-30 MKI fighters and the Indian navy's IL-38 maritime reconnaissance aircraft. Reportedly,

BrahMos Aerospace is also working on a Mark II version, in an attempt to lead in hypersonic cruise missiles.

On 27 November 2006, India successfully carried out its first missile interception test, when a *Prithvi* surface-to-surface ballistic missile shot down a similar missile off India's east coast, demonstrating a nascent capability to develop an anti-missile shield. This was followed on 2 December 2007 by the first successful test of a new single stage high-speed interceptor missile over the Bay of Bengal. On 12 April 2007, the first successful test of the 3,500km-range nuclear capable *Agni* III missile took place; the first test on 9 July 2006 had failed. While additional tests of the *Agni* III are scheduled, India demonstrated the technical competence for development of a longer-range missile in the near future. The Indian army also held joint exercises with Russia on Russian territory for the first time in late 2007.

India's reach into maritime Asia will be enhanced in the coming years by an ambitious warship-construction programme that projects an expanded carrier-based, multi-dimensional force into the next decade and beyond. In May 2007, the Indian navy published 'Freedom to Use the Seas: India's Maritime Military Strategy'. In his foreword, the chief of the Indian navy, Admiral Sureesh Mehta, said that 'our primary maritime military interest is to ensure national security, provide insulation from external interference, so that the vital tasks of fostering economic growth and undertaking developmental activities can take place in a secure environment. Consequently, India's maritime military strategy is underpinned on "the freedom to use the seas for our national purposes, under all circumstances"'. Elsewhere, the Maritime Strategy reiterates that it bears its title 'because the freedom to use the seas will become crucial if India is to attain her "manifest destiny": and this phrase is used in the most innocuous sense'.

The maritime military strategy focuses on maritime trade and security of energy, maritime domain awareness, strategy for employment in peace, strategy for employment in conflict and strategy for force build-up. On the key issue of nuclear deterrence, it reiterates that 'the most "credible" of all arsenals in a second strike is the nuclear-armed missile submarine'. Mehta also notes that 'the emphasis would be on force multipliers, quality of weapons, sensors and networking of platforms. In other words, the focus would be on critical capabilities than on the number of ships or aircraft.'

India and China have both been expanding their naval forces to secure their growing maritime interests, especially energy security. With India facing unprecedented demand for energy to fuel its economic boom, imports account for over three-quarters of oil usage, with official projections foreseeing oil import dependency increasing to 80% by 2011–12 and to over 90% by 2024–25. China is now dependent on oil imports for 40% of its total demand, of which 80% is sourced from the Persian Gulf and Africa, and passes through the straits of Malacca and Singapore. This has led to a substantial increase in Chinese shipping, with over 6,000 Chinese-flagged ships crossing the Indian Ocean annually.

While the Indian navy now regularly exercises and trains with Southeast Asian navies, the Chinese navy is further building its relations with the Pakistani navy. The tendency for India and Pakistan to be excluded from each other's international engagements has raised concerns over an emerging naval rivalry in the Indian Ocean. In September 2007, for example, the Indian navy participated in the largest-ever multilateral naval exercise in the Bay of Bengal with the US, Australia, Japan and Singapore. This 'quadrilateral' exercise involved three aircraft carriers (two of which were nuclear powered), a nuclear submarine, several frigates and destroyers and over three-dozen fighter aircraft. China was deliberately excluded. The Indian navy also carried out a trilateral joint exercise with the US and Japan along the Pacific coast of East Asia in April 2007. This followed the annual *Malabar* series of exercises with the US Navy, held off Japan for the first time. On August 2007, Indian naval ships also visited Doha, Kuwait, Havana, Al-Jubail, Abu Dhabi, Muscat and Djibouti in the first such deployment of its kind. On 14–16 February 2008, the Indian Navy hosts its first Indian Ocean naval symposium for the Indian Ocean region in New Delhi.

India is suspicious of Chinese activities in Myanmar (where it is helping to develop ports and pipelines), Pakistan (where it is thought to be developing refuelling facilities for Chinese warships at the recently commissioned, Chinese-built Gwadar port on the Makran coast in Baluchistan), and in China's Tibet Autonomous Region (where it is substantially upgrading military-related infrastructure). India perceives these activities as an attempt by China to gain permanent access to the Indian Ocean, and to encircle India strategically. Meanwhile, China has expressed concern over the activities in the Indian Ocean of the 'quadrilateral' group of democratic states – the United States, Japan, Australia and India – and the prospective defence and strategic relationship between India and the US, all seen in Beijing as efforts to contain China.

An increased Chinese naval presence and activities in the Indian Ocean have been countered by bilateral Indian naval exercises with Singapore and Vietnam in the South China Sea. The Indian navy also plans to strengthen its fleet on the eastern front, including the basing of an aircraft carrier in the Bay of Bengal in the next five years, while the Indian air force plans to deploy two squadrons of Sukhoi-30MKI fighters at Tezpur air base in eastern India, neighbouring China.

At the same time, India and China are attempting to develop a bilateral defence relationship. In May 2006, they signed their first MOU on defence cooperation for high-level personnel exchanges, an annual defence dialogue, and joint exercises and training programmes. Following low-scale naval exercises, the first significant army counter-terrorism exercise is scheduled for December 2007 in Kunming, China. But prospects for far-reaching bilateral military exercises are limited.

In April 2004, the Indian Maritime Doctrine perceived 'attempts by China to strategically encircle India' and commented adversely on 'China's vigorous exertions that tend to spill over into our maritime zone'. India's Maritime Strategy three years later was relatively low-key. It simply noted that the Chinese navy was on the path to becoming a blue-water force and that it had an ambitious modernisation programme 'along with attempts to gain a strategic toe-hold in the Indian Ocean Rim'. In the near future, it will be critical to build Sino-Indian naval confidence in the Indian Ocean through maritime cooperation and diplomacy. This could encompass measures such as the establishment of an official bilateral dialogue on maritime security, and attempts to cooperate on issues such as Search & Rescue (SAR) operations, maritime safety and security, and marine environment protection and preservation.

Pakistan

After months of speculation a visibly weakened General Pervez Musharraf stepped down as army chief on 28 November 2007, but was sworn in as president for a second five-year term the following day. Since March 2007, Musharraf faced his gravest domestic challenge since he took power in a military coup on 12 October 1999. His suspension of Chief Justice Iftikhar

Mohammed Chaudhury for alleged abuse of office on 9 March 2007 led to popular street demonstrations demanding the judge's reinstatement and the end of eight years of military rule. On 12 May 2007, violence in Karachi between pro-government forces and local opposition parties and lawyers resulted in 42 deaths. Justice Chaudhury's subsequent reinstatement on 20 July 2007 brought further troubles for Musharraf. With the prospect of the Supreme Court refusing to validate his election, while still in uniform, as president for a second five-year term on 6 October 2007 after opposition boycotts and abstentions, Musharraf imposed a state of emergency on 3 November 2007 citing the worrying increase in violent attacks by jihadi groups and the need to reign in the judiciary.

Chaudhury was placed under house arrest, 2,000 protesters were arrested, and the media was censored. Following former Prime Minister Benazir Bhutto's return to Pakistan after nine years of self-imposed exile and the killing of more than 130 people in two bombings in Karachi on 18 October, her prospective political deal with Musharraf went sour and she vowed to oppose him. This prepared the ground for the return of another former Prime Minister Nawaz Sharif, to Lahore after eight years in exile on 25 November 2007; he had previously been deported from Pakistan on arrival in September 2007. With the suspension of Pakistan from the Commonwealth and pressure from the international community to lift the state of emergency and resign as army chief, Musharraf promised to hold parliamentary elections on 8 January 2008. On 29 November Musharraf announced that emergency rule will be lifted on 16 December.

Notwithstanding growing public opposition to Musharraf's rule, the army and its key group of corps commanders publicly supported him. On 2 October 2007, Musharraf named the director general of the Inter-Services Intelligence (ISI), Lieutenant-General Ashfaq Kayani, as vice chief of the army. Kayani succeeded Musharraf as army chief on 28 November 2007. The Bush administration also reiterated its confidence in Musharraf and his commitment to the campaign against terror, notwithstanding serious concerns over the tribal areas bordering Afghanistan, amidst the siege of the Lal Masjid (Red Mosque) in the centre of Islamabad on 3–11 July 2007, which resulted in over 100 deaths.

Following the failure of its ceasefire agreements with pro-Taliban leaders, the Pakistani army and paramilitary forces continued to clash with local Taliban and al-Qaeda forces in the Federally Administered Tribal Areas bordering Afghanistan, where nearly 80,000 troops have been deployed. The capture of a number of paramilitary personnel has affected morale. On 11 January 2007, outgoing US Director of National Intelligence John Negroponte stated that Pakistan 'remains a major source of Islamic extremism and the home for some top terrorist leaders'. Following the deployment of helicopter gunships and artillery against pro-Taliban militants in November 2007, Pakistani troops began a ground offensive in Swat in the North-West Frontier province. In addition, Pakistani troops are involved in combating a nationalist struggle in Baluchistan province.

With growing US and UK concern over the rise of cross-border infiltration from the tribal areas of Pakistan into Afghanistan, Pakistani security forces have been attempting to beef up their border security checkpoints. But this has had limited impact. With Pakistani and Afghan leaders each alleging the other side is responsible on this issue, the prospect for meaningful bilateral cooperation is limited. At the same time, Pakistan is not permitting US-led military forces in Afghanistan to carry out 'hot pursuit' of the Taliban into Pakistani territory, nor joint military operations with the US against the Taliban on Pakistani territory.

According to the US Congressional Research Service, US arms transfer agreements with Pakistan totalled more than $3.5bn in 2006. Pakistan is currently in the process of acquiring JF-17 joint Pakistan–China fighter aircraft for its air force. It is in negotiations for three German Howaldtswerke-Deutsche Werft GmbH (HDW) U-214 diesel-electric submarines for $1bn. However, the Standing Committee on Defence of the Pakistan Senate has sought an explanation from the Defence Ministry over this prospective contract, alleging that the submarines lack stability in rough seas, have faulty Air Independent Propulsion (AIP) systems, and, critically, are easy to detect.

Pakistan continues to test nuclear-capable ballistic and cruise missiles. On 23 February 2007, it carried out the fifth test of its longest-range ballistic missile, the *Hatf-6* (*Shaheen-2*), with a range of 2,000–2,500km, followed by the third and fourth tests of the new *Hatf-7* (*Babur*) cruise missile with a range of 700km in March 2007 and July 2007. In a significant development, on 28 August 2007 it test-fired its first air-launched cruise missile, the *Hatf-8* (Ra'ad), from a Pakistan Air Force *Mirage* III aircraft. The *Hatf-8* is reported to have a range of 350km, and the capability to carry several kinds of warheads.

SRI LANKA

In a marked deterioration of political stability, the 24-year-old conflict between the Sri Lankan military and the separatist Liberation Tigers of Tamil Eelam (LTTE) shifted from low-intensity warfare to near full-fledged undeclared conventional warfare. Heavy fighting took place between the Sri Lankan military and the LTTE in the east and the north of the country in violation of the five-year-old Norwegian-brokered ceasefire, along with a 'dirty war' carried out by both sides' secretive paramilitary forces. Following the army offensive in the east in December 2006, the military had driven the LTTE from its eastern headquarters in Batticaloa by the end of March 2007. On 11 July, the Sri Lankan military took over the rugged area of Thopigala in the Batticaloa district, the last LTTE stronghold in the eastern province. On 19 July 2007, President Mahinde Rajapakse celebrated the conquest of the eastern province as the 'dawn of the east'.

With the focus of the military now on the north, S.P. Thamilselvan, the head of the LTTE political wing, was killed in a government air raid in Kilinochchi on 2 November 2007. Earlier, on 22 October 2007, the LTTE had mounted a suicide attack on the Sri Lankan air force base at Anuradhapura, 170km northeast of Colombo. The attack destroyed eight aircraft, including five training aircraft, and killed 13 security force personnel, with 21 LTTE cadres killed. On 28 November 2007, two bomb blasts in Colombo killed at least 17 people and injured nearly 40. Although the Sri Lankan armed forces regained territory from the LTTE for the first time in five years in the east, bolstering their confidence, there was little prospect of military victory or talks with the LTTE, which still controlled a vast swathe of land in the north of the island.

A key concern for the Sri Lankan government is the LTTE's new-found light air power. In a daring move on 26 March 2007, two light aircraft of the Air Tigers attacked an air force base near Colombo. The two adapted Czech Morovan ZLIN-143 aircraft, capable of carrying four bombs each, attacked the Katunayake air force base adjacent to the country's sole international airport. Although they failed to destroy any aircraft, three Sri Lankan air force personnel were killed and 16 injured. This was followed on 23 April 2007 with an attack by two LTTE aircraft on the main base complex of the military in the Jaffna peninsula and on April 29 by another against an oil-storage facility near Colombo.

CENTRAL AND SOUTH ASIA – DEFENCE ECONOMICS

India's economy continued to produce unprecedented growth in 2006–07, with real GDP up by 9.2% compared to 9.0% the previous year. However, the composition of the economy continues to change. While the service sector now accounts for over 55% of economic activity, manufacturing continues to grow and India's corporate sector is flourishing as a growing number of Indian companies become multinationals, looking for mergers and acquisitions worldwide. Less impressive is the agricultural sector, the mainstay of the economy employing two-thirds of the workforce, which saw its share of the economy dip below 20%.

The government continues to make slow but steady progress in reducing its high general-budget deficit – down from close to 10% of GDP in 2002 to around 6% of GDP in 2006, with further reductions likely. In 2004, the government introduced a Fiscal Responsibility and Budget Management Act (FRBM) with the aim of gradually reducing the current account deficit by 0.4% of GDP a year and leading to a balanced current budget by 2008. While this target is unlikely to be achieved, the IMF has congratulated Indian authorities on progress so far, which has led to a reduction in general government debt from 86% of GDP in 2002 to 81% in 2006.

Despite the challenging fiscal position, India once again increased its defence budget in 2007. Defence spending (including military pensions) increased to Rs1,126bn (US$27.8bn), from Rs1,015bn in 2006. While this is, on the surface, a 10.9% increase, with inflation running at 7% the real growth in defence

funding is relatively modest. Nonetheless, in real terms the budget has still increased by 30% between 2000 and 2007. In recent years, India's Prime Minister Manmohan Singh has suggested that if the economy continues to grow at the recent rate of 8% a year, he would like to see the core defence budget (excluding military pensions) increase to 3% of GDP. However, despite this oft-stated goal, in 2006 the core budget measured just 2.5% of GDP, down from 2.8% of GDP in 2004, so it appears unlikely that the target will be achieved in the near term. In their May 2007 report to the Finance Ministry, the Indian Parliament Select Committee on Defence supported the call for an increase in defence spending, restating that the target is 3% of GDP.

During a visit to India in January 2007, Russian Defence Minister Sergei Ivanov confirmed that Russia and India were developing their military cooperation to a new level, moving from a buyer–seller relationship to a closer partnership in developing technologies and upgrading weapons, joint R&D and manufacture of military hardware. Over the past five years, Russia has sold arms worth around $10bn to India and further deals amounting to a similar sum are still in the pipeline. During the visit, Russian President Vladimir Putin also initialled wider energy, trade and technology deals, leading Singh to comment that 'Russia remains indispensable to India's foreign policy interests'. However, following ratification of the strategic US–India nuclear agreement in late 2006, the American Industries Association led a trade delegation of 18 major weapons producers, including Boeing, Lockheed Martin, Pratt & Whitney, Raytheon and United Technologies, to New Delhi and Bangalore

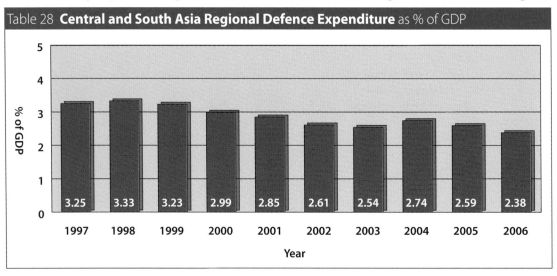

Table 28 **Central and South Asia Regional Defence Expenditure** as % of GDP

Year	1997	1998	1999	2000	2001	2002	2003	2004	2005	2006
% of GDP	3.25	3.33	3.23	2.99	2.85	2.61	2.54	2.74	2.59	2.38

with an eye on India's annual $10bn procurement budget. However, the future of this US–India agreement was, at time of writing, in the balance.

Later in 2007, relations with Russia faltered as Moscow tried to negotiate a price increase in the ongoing Su-30MKI multi-role fighter deal. Under the original terms of the contract, the annual escalation rate was 2.55%, with payments to be made in US dollars. However, with the dollar declining against the rouble, Russian officials proposed to double the escalation rate to 5% or switch to the more stable euro at the prevailing rate. Relations further soured when Moscow asked for additional funds for the modification of the former Russian aircraft carrier, *Admiral Gorshkov*. Details of the original arrangement for the transfer of the ship remain opaque. It is believed that India paid around US$600m for the ship to be refitted to Indian navy standards and that, since then, an additional tranche of US$100m has been requested and paid. Further funds are now sought by Russia to complete additional work stemming from a significant miscalculation in the cost of re-cabling the vessel.

Following years of criticism of the state-run Defence Research and Development Organisation (DRDO), the Ministry of Defence (MoD) made a small but significant allocation of Rs1bn to the private sector in order to fund military R&D. The move confirms the government's intention to reduce dependency on DRDO, which is currently the subject of an investigation by an eight-member government committee looking into the organisation's repeated failure to develop weapon systems on time and within allocated budgets. The committee's report is expected to include reference to several high-profile, over-budget domestic programmes including the Light Combat Aircraft (ten years behind schedule), the advanced nuclear submarine (20 years behind schedule), various missile development programmes (many of which have been abandoned), the *Arjun* Main Battle Tank and the Advanced Light Helicopter. K.P. Singh, the most senior civil servant in charge of defence procurement, indicated that the limited funds are the start of a long-term attempt to dramatically increase private-sector involvement in defence production. In the past, private industry has tended to shun the defence sector due to the high costs associated with military R&D. In terms of production, ten years ago India set a target that it would produce 70% of its own defence equipment, but to date has only reached around 30%.

In another drive to improve India's inefficient procurement procedures, India's comptroller and auditor general (CAG) submitted four separate reports to parliament demanding a 're-engineering' of the entire ministry's complex procurement apparatus. In the reports, the CAG declared that a lack of cooperation among the three services resulted in duplication of purchases, also noting that in nine of 18 army contracts investigated, technical specifications either did not match products available or matched uniquely with a single provider. The watchdog body urged the MoD to pursue greater transparency in procurement and suggested it create a specialised team of acquisition managers.

The 2007 defence budget allocated Rs268.4bn to the air force, including Rs166.5bn (US$3.75bn) in procurement funds. However, with several high-profile acquisitions under way, including 66 BAE *Hawk* jet trainers, three *Phalcon* AEW aircraft and 130 Su-30MKI fighter aircraft, there is little money available for new purchases. During the year, the only significant new order covered the purchase of a further 40 Su-30MKI multi-role fighters from Russia (to supplement the existing order for 140 units). It is believed that this deal will be fast-tracked to try to ensure that India maintains air superiority, with Pakistan in the process of receiving F-16s from the US and J-10s from China, while also developing the advanced JF-17 *Thunder* with China. It is also thought that India's air force has made progress in its long-standing intention to procure 80 Russian medium-lift Mi-17-IV helicopters as a follow-on to 40 acquired five years ago.

Following several delays during which the air force's combat squadron strength has fallen to an all-time modern low of 29 against the sanctioned strength of 45, the MoD finally signed a US$800m deal with Rosoboronexport that will upgrade 78 MiG-29 fighters and extend their life for a further 10–15 years. These upgrades are part of a wider modernisation programme that includes the refurbishment of 125 MiG-21s and 40 MiG-27s with advanced avionics, improved electronic-warfare systems and precision weaponry. The air force is also in the final stage of negotiating a US$1bn deal with Thales for the upgrade of the fleet of *Mirage* 2000I fighters that will extend their life by up to 25 years.

The major procurement decision still facing the air force is their plan to acquire further combat aircraft to replace the ageing fleet of MiG-21 fighters. The initial requirement for the Medium Multi-Role

Table 29 **Indian Defence Budget by Function 2000, 2005–2007**

Current Rsbn	2005 outturn	2006 budget	2006 outturn	2007 budget
Personnel, Operations & Maintenance				
MoD	15.4	19.0	17.2	20.5
Defence Pensions	127.1	132.2	138.0	146.5
Army	306.8	322.9	321.9	340.8
Navy	62.9	67.1	68.1	69.7
Air Force	91.4	98.6	98.7	101.9
Defence Services – R&D	27.9	30.0	30.0	32.0
Defence Ordnance Factories	66.3	69.4	64.1	73.2
Recoveries and Receipts	-69.5	-73.1	-66.7	-77
Sub-total	628.3	666.1	671.3	707.6
Procurement and Construction				
Tri-Service Defence R&D	25.3	24.4	24.4	27.0
Army	96.2	101.9	97.2	114.0
Navy	82.3	90.5	87.0	101.8
Air Force	120.6	148.7	128.9	166.5
Other	5.4	8.6	7.1	9.7
Sub-total	330.0	374.0	344.6	419.0
Total Defence Budget	958.1	1040.2	1015.9	1126.6

Combat Aircraft (MMRCA) was for 126 platforms for the air force, although it now appears that the navy is considering the acquisition of a further 60 aircraft. Contenders for the programme include the F-16, F-18, JAS-39 *Gripen*, MiG-35, Dassault *Rafale* and Eurofighter *Typhoon*. Developing security and military ties with India resulted in the US offering its F-35 *Lightning* II Joint Strike Fighter to India's air force. Other significant future equipment plans for the air force include the procurement of another squadron of Ilyushin Il-78 air-to-air refuellers, an unspecified number of heavy-lift Ilyushin Il-76 transports and two or three Embraer EMB-145 aircraft fitted with a locally developed airborne early warning (AEW) system that will supplement the three *Phalcon* AEW aircraft purchased from Israel, and which became operational in 2007.

The Indian navy was allocated Rs171.5bn, up 10.5% on its 2006 budget, and procurement spending was increased to Rs101.8bn (US$2.56bn), up 17% on the previous year. With the exception of the developments surrounding the acquisition of the *Admiral Gorshkov*, the navy has seen little in the way of new procurement initiatives. Over the next decade, the force plans for a total fleet of 140–145 vessels, of which half will be ocean-going with the remainder assigned to coastal duties. The fleet will be built around two carrier battle groups: one based around the *Gorshkov*; and the other based around the 37,500-tonne Indian-designed air-defence vessel on which construction

began in April 2005. Other procurement initiatives include the acquisition and domestic construction of 6 *Scorpene* submarines to be delivered between 2012 and 2017. The vessels will be constructed at the state-owned Mazagon Dock Ltd, with the French company Amaris transferring necessary technology, as part of the navy's ambitious plans, known as Project 75, to acquire a fleet of 24 diesel-electric submarines. Mazagon Dock is also constructing three Project 15A (*Kolkata*-class) destroyers and three Project 17 (*Talwar*-class) frigates, whilst Goa Shipyard is likely to build eight new mine-countermeasures vessels at a cost of around US$1.3bn.

The Indian army, which accounts for over 80% of the country's active military personnel, received the largest share of the budget, Rs454bn, up 8.3% from the previous year. In recent years the army has suggested that its 'combat ratio' – a measure of their military advantage over Pakistan – has fallen from a level of 1.75:1 in the mid 1970s to as low as 1.2:1. As a result, army chiefs have created a lengthy shopping list of priority acquisitions from new rifles and night-vision equipment to unmanned aerial vehicles and communications and surveillance satellites. The ongoing debacle surrounding the indigenously designed *Arjun* Main Battle Tank (MBT) was re-ignited when parliament suggested the DRDO should seek foreign assistance to overcome ongoing problems with the vehicle. The programme was launched more than 30 years ago, and since then costs have jumped from

Rs155m to at least Rs3bn. An order for an initial 124 units was finally placed a few years ago, but so far only around 15 have been delivered. In order to bridge the capability gap, in 2000 the army signed a contract with Russia for 310 T-90 MBTs which was increased in 2006 by an order for an additional 330 platforms. A key outstanding ground-forces requirement moved further ahead when two 'Request for Proposals' for self-propelled howitzers were issued in mid 2007. The army is seeking to acquire 180 155mm wheeled howitzers under one programme, while an initial 100 tracked guns will be procured under the second. Under the Field Artillery Rationalisation Plan the army intends to acquire a mixture of up to 3,600 155mm towed, wheeled and tracked guns at a cost of over US$5bn.

In separate developments, in early 2007 the Army Aviation Corps (AAC) announced that it had selected Eurocopter's AS 550 *Fennec* light helicopter over the Bell 407 to replace the existing fleet of *Alouette* aircraft. Under the terms of the deal, it was thought that Eurocopter would build 60 units in Europe whilst Hindustan Aeronautics would manufacture the remaining 137 aircraft at its Bangalore facility. However, later in the year the MoD announced that it was investigating the contract, following allegations of 'procedural transgression' over the sale. At the time of writing, the outcome of the investigation is unknown, but the AAC reiterated it was committed to the Vision 2017 programme under which all services' *Alouette* and *Cheetah* helicopters will be replaced.

Pakistan's recent economic performance has been impressive. Growth has accelerated, improvements in public spending and wide-ranging structural reforms have reduced the debt burden and increased efficiency, and government policies have helped lower poverty rates. While the devastating earthquake of October 2005 left a heavy toll in terms of human lives and physical and social infrastructure, it had relatively minor effects on macroeconomic indicators (except for an increase in government spending), owing mainly to the small share that the affected areas contributed to the overall economy. The government allocated Rs275bn for defence in the 2007–08 state budget, an increase of 10% on the previous year. However, as the official budget does not include military pensions and other benefits for retired and serving personnel, military aid from some Gulf states, space programmes or income generated by the armed forces' diverse business interests, true defence expenditure will be considerably higher than the official budget suggests. In addition, due to its special relationship with China, Pakistan is able to purchase Chinese-produced weapons at favourable prices. Pakistan has also been the recipient of substantial US military and economic aid in recent years, which is also unlikely to be reflected in the official budget.

Faced with a US arms embargo imposed after the nuclear tests of the 1990s, Pakistan has successfully diversified its range of military supplier nations, in particular turning to China. At present Pakistan has placed orders with China for four F22-P frigates as well as Z-9C maritime helicopters and JF-17 *Thunder* and J-10 fighter aircraft. In late 2006, during a meeting between the two countries' presidents, China agreed to further military, energy and trade relations, signing a Memorandum of Understanding for the supply of airborne early-warning and control systems (AWACS) which could be used by Pakistan to counter India's acquisition of *Phalcon* AWACS from Israel.

Other foreign suppliers to agree to significant military exports to Pakistan in recent years include the US, which will provide around US$1.5bn in Foreign Military Sales over five years, including new and upgraded F-16 aircraft; Sweden, which is contracted to supply six SAAB 2000 aircraft equipped with the *Erieye* AWACS; Turkey, which has been awarded a contract to build two next-generation fast-attack craft; the Netherlands, with whose authorities negotiations are underway for the supply of second-hand frigates; and Germany and France, from which Pakistan's navy would like to acquire three attack submarines.

Central and South Asia

Afghanistan Afg

New Afghan Afghani Afs		2006	2007	2008
GDP	US$	8.2bn	9.7bn	
per capita	US$	264	304	
Growth	%	7.5	13.0	
Inflation	%	5.1	8.3	
Def exp[a]	US$	ε142m	ε161m	
US$1=Afs		49.1	49.6	

a Domestic budget only

Population   31,888,923

Ethnic groups: Pashtun 38%; Tajik 25%; Hazara 19%; Uzbek 12%; Aimaq 4%; Baluchi 0.5%

Age	0–14	15–19	20–24	25–29	30–64	65 plus
Male	23%	5%	5%	4%	13%	1%
Female	22%	5%	4%	4%	13%	1%

Capabilities

ACTIVE 51,400 (Army 50,000 Air 1,400)

The Afghan Transitional Administration aims to establish control by forming a national army and a national police force encompassing all ethnic and tribal groups. The new Afghan Army (ANA), HQ in Kabul, currently comprises some 35,000 troops. Planned org and national strength of the ANA and national police is outlined below. At present only two (201st and 205) of the five corps are fully manned, 203 has 2 brigades and the remainder one. NATO's ISAF assumed operational control of all regions in Oct 2006. As of Oct 07, ISAF had over 41,000 troops in theatre with over 9,000 US troops remaining on OEF duties.

ORGANISATIONS BY SERVICE

Proposed National Army/Security Services
ε50,000

FORCES BY ROLE

4 regional comd

Army   5 corps (201ˢᵗ Kabul, 203ʳᵈ Gardez, 205ᵗʰ Kandahar, 207ᵗʰ Herat, 209ᵗʰ Mazare Sharif each to be with (3 bde)

Reaction   1 bde (part of 201ˢᵗ corps) with (1 cdo, 1 mech
Force   inf, 1 armd bn)
Lt inf   10 bn

EQUIPMENT BY TYPE

MBT T-62; T-55
RECCE BRDM-1/BRDM-2
AIFV BMP-1/BMP-2
APC (W) BTR-40/BTR-60/BTR-70/BTR-80
ARTY
    TOWED 76mm M-1938; ZIS-3 *M-1942*; 122mm D-30; M-30 *M-1938*; BM 21; 130mm M-46; 140mm BM 14; 152mm D-1; 220 mm BM1 *Oragan*
    MRL 122mm BM-21; 140mm BM-14; 220mm 9P140 *Uragan*

MOR 82mm M-37; 107mm; 120mm M-43
AT • MSL • MANPATS *Milan*; AT4 9K111 *Spigot*
    RCL 73mm SPG9; 82mm B-10
    GUNS 85mm D-48
AD • SAM
    SP SA-13 *Gopher*
    MANPAD SA-7 *Grail*
    GUNS
    SP ZSU-23-4
    TOWED 12.7mm; 14.5mm; 23mm ZU-23; 37mm M-139; 57mm S-60; 85mm M-1939 *KS-12*; 100mm KS-19
MSL • SSM FROG-7; SS-1 *Scud*

Air Force 1,400 (former Mujahideen and Taliban aircrew and logisticians)

3 sqns op out of Kabul

FORCES BY ROLE

TPT   1 sqn (airlift/casevac) with An-26/An-32;
HEL   1 sqn with Mi-17/Mi-35; 1 Presidential VIP sqn with Mi-17

EQUIPMENT BY TYPE

TPT 2 An-26; 2 An-32B
HEL
ATK 6 Mi-35
SPT 7 Mi-17
TRG 2 L-39

NON-STATE ARMED GROUPS

see Part II

FOREIGN FORCES

All under ISAF comd unless otherwise specified. ISAF HQ is likely to become more like a static HQ with contributing NATO countries filling identified posts. The rotation that has been the practice will cease.

Albania 138

Australia 907; 25 *Bushmaster* IMV LFV; 3 C-130J *Hercules*; 2 CH-47 *Chinook*; *Skylark* UAV; 1 obs UNAMA

Austria 3; 1 obs UNAMA

Azerbaijan 22

Bangladesh 2 obs UNAMA

Belgium 368; 1 F-16

Bolivia 1 obs UNAMA

Bulgaria 401

Canada 2,500 ISAF (*Op Athena*); 20 *Leopard* 2 MBT; 12 M-5777 155mm TOWED; *30 Op Enduring Freedom (Op Archer); 15 Op Argus* (bilateral)

Croatia 199

Czech Republic 435; 35 (*Operation Enduring Freedom*)

Denmark 454; 1 obs UNAMA

Estonia 128; 9 XA-180 *Sisu*

Finland 85

France 1,155 (*Operation Pamir*); ISAF: FAF at Oct 07: 150 personnel. 6 *Mirage* 2000D/*Mirage* F1; C-135 tkr, 2 EC 725 CSAR hel, one C-130 tpt.; *821 Op Enduring Freedom (Op Heracles), 39 Op Enduring Freedom (Op Epidote)*

Germany 3,155; 60 EUPOL AFGHANISTAN; 1 obs UNAMA

Greece 1 engr coy; 137; 1 C-130 *Hercules* Tpt Ac

Hungary 1 lt inf coy; 225

Iceland 11 (civilian)

Ireland 7

Italy 2,160; 25 EUPOL AFGHANISTAN

Korea, Republic of 207; 1 obs UNAMA

Latvia 97

Lithuania 195

Luxembourg 9

Macedonia, Former Yugoslav Republic of 129

Mongolia Army: 21 Army (instructors)

Netherlands 1,516; 23 *Bushmaster* IMV LFV; 6 *Op Enduring Freedom*; 8 F-16 at Kandahar, C-130 tpt; 6 AH-64D *Apache* at Tarin Kowt; 5 AS-532U2 *Cougar*

New Zealand 107 *Op Enduring Freedom*; 1 obs UNAMA

Norway 508, 1 obs UNAMA

Paraguay 1 obs UNAMA

Poland 937

Portugal 162

Romania 536; 94 *Op Enduring Freedom*; 1 obs UNAMA

Slovakia 59

Slovenia 42

Spain 715

Sweden 340; 1 obs UNAMA

Switzerland 2 (ISAF HQ + PRT Kunduz)

Turkey 1,220

United Kingdom 7,398 (ISAF)
Army 5,459; 52 bde HQ, 2 armd recce sqn;,3 inf bn; 1 arty regt; 1 atk hel sqn; elem of GMRLS; STA , UAV, 2 AD, EOD engr regt; 2 spt regt; 1 medical bn; 32 *Scimitar*; 29 *Warrior* AIFV; 8 FV 103 *Spartan*, 3 *Sultan*; 55 *Viking* 132 *Mastiff* APC, 18 L-118 Light Gun; GMRLS; 8 AH-64D *Apache*; 4 AH MK1 *Lynx* / AH MK7 *Lynx*; UAV: *Hermes 450*; *Predator B*
Navy 1,008; 1 Naval air sqn; 1 Naval strike wg;1 Cdo regt; 10 *Sea King HC MK 4*
Air Force 931; 1 Tpt Hel sqn; 5 C-130 *Hercules*; 6 CH-47 *Chinook*; 2 utl hel
1 obs UNAMA
RAF/RN: *Harrier* GR7/9 (Joint Force Harrier) rotates with Eurofighter *Typhoon*

United States 15,108 (ISAF); 9,650 (*Operation Enduring Freedom*)
Army: CH-47 Chinook, AH-64 *Apache*, UH-60 *Black Hawk*; HH-60 *Pave Hawk*
Navy: 1 ARG gp (part of CTF150, Fifth Fleet)
USAF: A-10, F-15E. EC-130, EA-6B. C-130 *Hercules*, HH_60, MQ-1 *Predator*, MQ-9 *Reaper*

Uruguay 1 obs UNAMA

Bangladesh Bng

Bangladeshi Taka Tk		2006	2007	2008
GDP	Tk	4.09tr	4.67tr	
	US$	59.4bn	68.0bn	
per capita	US$	403	452	
Growth	%	6.4	5.8	
Inflation	%	6.5	7.2	
Def exp	Tk	64.6bn		
	US$	938m		
Def bdgt	Tk	58.7bn	68.6bn	
	US$	852m	999m	
US$1=Tk		68.9	68.7	

Population   150,448,339

Ethnic groups: Muslim 85%; Hindu 12%

Age	0–14	15–19	20–24	25–29	30–64	65 plus
Male	17%	6%	6%	4%	16%	2%
Female	16%	6%	6%	4%	15%	2%

Capabilities

ACTIVE 150,000 (Army 120,000 Navy 16,000 Air 14,000) Paramilitary 63,910

ORGANISATIONS BY SERVICE

Army 120,000
Some equipment†

FORCES BY ROLE

Armd 1 bde (1 armd regt); 6 regt

Inf   7 div HQ; 17 bde (*total*: 50 inf bn)

Cdo   1 bn

Arty   20 regt

Engr   1 bde

Avn   1 regt (2 sqn)

AD   1 bde

EQUIPMENT BY TYPE
MBT 210 Type-59/Type-69
LT TK 10 Type-62
APC 180+
    APC (T) 50+: ε50 Type-63; MT-LB
    APC (W) 130: 60 BTR-70; 70 BTR-80
ARTY 551+
    TOWED 190+: **105mm** 130: 30 Model 56A1; 100 Model 56/L 10A1 pack howitzer; **122mm** 20 Type-54/54-1 (M-30) *M-1938*; **130mm** 40+ Type-59-1 (M-46)
    MOR 361: **81mm** 11 M-29A1; **82mm** 300 Type-53/87/M31 (M-1937); **120mm** 50 Type-53 (M-1943)
AT • RCL 106mm 200 M-40A1
AIRCRAFT • TPT 6: 5 Cessna 152; 1 Piper *Cheyenne*
AD • SAM • MANPAD 20 HN-5A
    GUNS • TOWED 146: **37mm** 16 Type-55 (M-1939); **57mm** 130: 100 Type 65/74; 30 Type-59 (S-60)

Navy ε16,000

FORCES BY ROLE

Navy 1 HQ located at Dhaka

EQUIPMENT BY TYPE

PRINCIPAL SURFACE COMBATANTS • FRIGATES 4

FFG 1 *Osman* (PRC *Jianghu* I) with 2 twin (4 eff.) each with HY-2 (CSS-N-2) *Silkworm* tactical SSM, 2 RBU 1200 (10 eff.), 4 100mm gun

FF 3:

2 *Abu Bakr*† (UK *Leopard*) each with 2 115mm twin gun (4 eff.)

1 *Umar Farooq*† training (UK *Salisbury*) with 3 *Squid*, 1 115mm twin gun (4 eff.)

PATROL AND COASTAL COMBATANTS 38

PFM 9:

5 *Durbar* less than 100 tonnes (PRC *Hegu*) each with 2 single with 2 SY-1 tactical SSM

4 *Durdarsha* (PRC *Huangfeng*) each with 4 single each with 1 HY-2 (CSS-N-2) *Silkworm* tactical SSM

PHT 4 *Huchuan*† less than 100 tonnes (PRC) each with 2 single 533mm TT each with 2 YU 1 Type 53 HWT

PCO 7:

1 *Nirbhoy* (PRC *Hainan*) with 4 RBU 1200 (20 eff.)

1 *Madhumati*† (*Sea Dragon*) with 1 76mm and 1 40mm gun

5 *Shaheed Ruhul Amin* (ex-UK *Island* class)

PFC 8: 4 *Shaheed Daulat*; 4 *Titas* (RoK *Sea Dolphin*)

PCC 6: 2 *Karnaphuli*; 2 *Meghna* (fishery protection);1 *Ruposhi Bangla*; 1 *Salam*

PCI 4: 2 *Akshay*; 1 *Bakat*; 1 *Bishkali*

MINE WARFARE • MINE COUNTERMEASURES 5

MSI 4 *Shapla* (ex-UK *River*)

MSO 1 *Sagar*

AMPHIBIOUS • CRAFT 11: 2 LCU†; 3 LCVP†; 1 LSL;

LCM: 5 *Yuchin*;

LOGISTICS AND SUPPORT 10

AOR 2 (coastal)

AR 1†

AG 1

ATF 1†

AGHS 1 *Agradoot*

TRG 1 *Shaheed Ruhul Amin*

YTM 3

FACILITIES

Bases Located at Chittagong, Dhaka, Kaptai, Khulna, Mangla

Air Force† 14,000

Three major bases - Bashar AB (consists of Dhaka-Tejgaon and Dhaka-Kurmitola); Matiur Rahman AB (Jessore) and Zahurul Haque AB (Chittagong). Kurmitola is the main fast jet fighter/FGA base. Tejgaon houses two helicopter squadrons. Jessore houses the transport squadrons, the Air Force Academy and the Flying Training Wing. Chittagong has a combat training/light attack squadron plus a helicopter squadron.

Flying hours 17,000+ flying hrs/year

FORCES BY ROLE

FGA	2 sqn with 32 F-7MB, F-7BG (recce capable), FT-7BG, FT-7B *Airguard*; 18 A-5C (Q-5III) *Fantan*; 1 OCU with 8 L-39ZA *Albatros*; 10 FT-6 (MiG-19UTI) *Farmer*
Ftr	1 sqn with 6 MiG-29 *Fulcrum*; 2 MiG-29UB *Fulcrum*
Tpt	1 sqn with 3 An-32 *Club*†, 4 C-130B *Hercules*
Hel	3 sqn with 17 MI-17/MI-171/MI-17MI-IV *Hip*; 2 Bell 206L *LongRanger*; 11 Bell 212
Trg	1 trg school with 10 PT-6 (CJ-6); 8 CM-170 *Magister*†; 12 T-37B *Tweet*

EQUIPMENT BY TYPE†

AIRCRAFT 76+ combat capable

FGA 60+ 32 F-7MB, F-7BG (recce capable), FT-7BG, FT-7B *Airguard*; 18 A-5C (Q-5III) *Fantan*; 10 FT-6 (MiG-19UTI) *Farmer*

FTR 8: 6 MiG-29 *Fulcrum*; 2 MiG-29UB *Fulcrum*

TPT 7: 3 An-32 *Club* †; 4 C-130B *Hercules*

TRG 38: 8 CM-170 *Magister*†; 8 L-39ZA *Albatros**; 10 PT-6 (CJ-6); 12 T-37B *Tweet*

HELICOPTERS

SPT 17 MI-17/MI-171/MI-17MI-IV *Hip*

UTL 13: 2 Bell 206L *LongRanger*; 11 Bell 212

MSL • AAM AA-2 *Atoll*

Paramilitary 63,910

Ansars 20,000+

Security Guards

Armed Police 5,000

Rapid action force (forming)

Bangladesh Rifles 38,000

Border guard

Paramilitary 41 bn

Coast Guard 910

PATROL AND COASTAL COMBATANTS 12

PCI 7 *Bishkali*

PCR 5 *Pabna*

NON-STATE ARMED GROUPS

see Part II

DEPLOYMENT

AFGHANISTAN

UN • UNAMA 2 obs

BURUNDI

UN • BINUB 1 obs

CÔTE D'IVOIRE

UN • UNOCI 2,728; 10 obs

DEMOCRATIC REPUBLIC OF CONGO

UN • MONUC 1,333; 25 obs

EAST TIMOR
UN • UNMIT 4 obs

ETHIOPIA/ERITREA
UN • UNMEE 5; 8 obs

GEORGIA
UN • UNOMIG 8 obs

LIBERIA
UN • UNMIL 3,200; 19 obs

SERBIA
UN • UNMIK 1 obs

SIERRA LEONE
UN • UNIOSIL 1 obs

SUDAN
AU/UN • UNAMID 300 proposed deployment
UN • UNMIS 1,548; 21 obs

TIMOR-LESTE
UN • UNMIT 4 obs

WESTERN SAHARA
UN • MINURSO 8 obs

India Ind

Indian Rupee Rs		2006	2007	2008
GDP	Rs	41.2tr	47.5tr	
	US$	911bn	1,209bn	
per capita	US$	819	1,070	
Growth	%	9.7	8.9	
Inflation	%	6.1	6.2	
Def exp	Rs	1,016bn		
	US$	22.4bn		
Def bdgt	Rs	1,040bn	1,123bn	
	US$	22.9bn	28.5bn	
US$1=Rs		45.3	39.3	

Population   1,129,866,154
Ethnic groups: Hindu 80%; Muslim 14%; Christian 2%; Sikh 2%

Age	0–14	15–19	20–24	25–29	30–64	65 plus
Male	16%	5%	5%	5%	18%	2%
Female	15%	5%	4%	4%	18%	2%

Capabilities

ACTIVE 1,288,000 (Army 1,100,000 Navy 55,000 Air 125,000 Coast Guard 8,000) **Paramilitary 1,300,586**

RESERVE 1,155,000 (Army 960,000 Navy 55,000 Air 140,000) **Paramilitary 987,821**

Army first line reserves (300,000) within 5 years of full time service, further 500,000 have commitment to the age of 50.

ORGANISATIONS BY SERVICE

Strategic Forces Command
In charge of all nuclear assets
FORCES BY ROLE
Msl 2 regt eqpt. with 15 SS-150 *Prithvi*; 1 regt eqpt. with 8-12 *Agni*-1; 1 regt eqpt. with *Agni*-II (both forming); *Agni*-III undergoing trials
EQUIPMENT BY TYPE
MSL • STRATEGIC 42+
    IRBM 12+: 8-12 *Agni*-II; *Agni*-III (under testing)
    SRBM 30 SS-150 *Prithvi* / SS-250 *Prithvi* / SS-350 *Prithvi* (SRBM Strategic)

Army 1,100,000
FORCES BY ROLE
6 Regional Comd HQ (Northern, Western, Central, Southern, Eastern, South Western), 1 Training Comd (ARTRAC), 11 corps HQ (3 strike corps, 8 'holding' corps – incl 1 Desert Corps)

Armd	3 div (*each*: 1 SP arty bde (1 medium regt, 1 SP arty regt), 2–3 armd bde); 8 indep bde; 13 regt each with 55 T-55; 35 regt each with 55 T-72M1; 6 regt each with 55 T-90S; 14 regt each with 55 *Vijayanta*
Mech inf	25 bn
Inf	4 RAPID div (*each*: 1 mech inf bde); 18 div (*each*: 1 arty bde, 2–5 Inf bde); 8 indep bde; 319 bn
Mtn inf	10 div (*each*:3–4 mtn inf bde,1+ arty regt); 2 indep bde
Cdo / AB	1 indep bde
Cdo	6 bn
AB	5 bn
Arty	2 div (*each*: 2 arty bde (*each*: 3 med arty, 1 composite regt (1 SATA/MRL regt))
Med arty	63 regt (bn)
SP med Arty	1 regt (bn)
Fd arty	185 regt
SP fd arty	3 regt (bn)
MRL	4 regt (bn)
SSM	2 (*Prithvi*) regt; 1 (*Agni*) regt; 2 bty (*BrahMos*)
ADA	45 regt
Engr	3 bde
Hel	17 sqn
AD	4 bde; 5 'flak' regt with 320 ZU-23-2 (some SP); 30 'flak' regt with 1,920 L40/70 (*each*: 4 AD bty); 12+ regt
SAM	12 regt; 2 gp (*each*: 2–5 SAM bty)

EQUIPMENT BY TYPE
MBT 4,059 (ε1,133 in reserve): 330 T-90S (to be 1,000+ to replace *Vijayanta* and T-55); ε14 *Arjun*; 1,925 T-72M1 (modification program in progress, incl. thermal sights); 1,008 *Vijayanta* (modified with night-fighting equipment and new fire control systems); 715 T-55 (modifications similar to *Vijayanta*); ε67 in reserve
LT TK 190: 90 AMX-13 in store; ε100 PT-76 (being phased out)

Central and South Asia

RECCE 110 BRDM-2 each with AT-4 *Spigot*/AT-5 *Spandrel*; *Ferret* (used for internal security duties along with some locally built armoured cars)

AIFV 1700+: 700 BMP-1; 1,000+ BMP-2

APC 817+

   APC (W) 317+: ε160 *Casspir*; 157+ OT-62/OT-64 (mainly used for 2nd line duties, such as towing mortars)

   APC (W)/(T) 500+ in reserve in store (Czech and Soviet types)

ARV 166 WZT-3

ARTY up to 11,300+

   SP 100+: **105mm** 80 *Abbot* in store; **130mm** 20 M-46 *Catapult*; **152mm** 2S19 *Farm*

   TOWED up to 4500+: **105mm** up to 1,350+: 600+ IFG Mk1/Mk2/Mk3 (being replaced); up to 700 LFG; 50 M-56; **122mm** 550 D-30; **130mm** 2,200: 1,200 M-46; 500 (in process of upgrading to 155mm); 500 in reserve in store; **155mm** 400 FH-77B

   MRL 180: **122mm** ε150 BM-21/LRAR; **214mm** 30 *Pinaka* (not yet in service)

   MOR 6,520+

      SP 120mm E1

      TOWED 6520+: **81mm** 5,000+ E1; **120mm** ε1,500 AM-50/E1; **160mm** 20 M-58 *Tampella*

AT • MSL

   SP AT-4 9K111 *Spigot*; AT-5 9K113 *Spandrel*

   MANPATS AT-3 9K11 *Sagger* (being phased out); AT-4 9K111 *Spigot*; AT-5 9K113 *Spandrel*; *Milan*

   RCL 84mm *Carl Gustav* (one per inf section); **106mm** 3,000+ M-40A1 (10 per inf bn)

HELICOPTERS

   ASLT 12 *Lancer*

   UTL 150: 50 HAL *Cheetah* (SA-315B) *Lama*; 100 HAL *Chetak* (SA-316B) *Alouette III*

UAV 14+: 14 *Nishant*

   RECCE • TACTICAL *Searcher*

AD • SAM 3,500+

   SP 880+: 180 SA-6 *Gainful*; 50+ SA-8B; 400 SA-9 *Gaskin*; 250 SA-13 *Gopher*;

   MANPAD 2,620+: 620 SA-7 *Grail* (being phased out); 2,000+ SA-16 *Gimlet*

   GUNS 2,339+

      SP 99+: **23mm** 75 ZSU-23-4; ZU-23-2; **30mm** 24 2S6 (60+ more on order)

      TOWED 2,240+: **20mm** Oerlikon (reported); **23mm** 320 ZU-23-2; **40mm** 1,920 L40/70

RADAR • LAND 12+: 12 AN/TPQ-37 *Firefinder*; BSR Mk.2; *Cymbeline*; EL/M-2140; M-113 A1GE *Green Archer* (mor); MUFAR; *Stentor*

AMPHIBIOUS 2 LCVP

MSL • SSM 8-12 PJ-10 *BrahMos*

Reserve Organisations

Reserves 300,000 reservists (1st line reserve within 5 years full time service); 500,000 reservists (commitment until age of 50) (total 800,000)

Territorial Army 160,000 reservists (only 40,000 regular establishment)

Army 3–4 Ecological bn; 29 Departmental unit (raised from government ministries)

Inf   25 bn

AD   20 'flak' regt with 1,280 L40/60

Navy 55,000 (incl 7,000 Naval Avn and 1,200 Marines)

FORCES BY ROLE

Navy Fleet HQ New Delhi; Commands located at Mumbai (Bombay), Vishakhapatnam and Kochi (Cochin)

EQUIPMENT BY TYPE

SUBMARINES • TACTICAL • SSK 16:

   2 *Vela* (FSU *Foxtrot*) each with 10 single 533mm TT (6 forward, 4 aft)

   4 *Shishumar* (Ge T-209/1500) each with 1 single 533mm TT

   4 *Sindhughosh* (FSU *Kilo*) each with 6 single 533mm TT (undergoing phased refit of SS-N-27)

   6 *Sindhughosh* (FSU *Kilo*) with 6 single 533mm TT each with SS-NX-27 *Club-S* tactical SSM

PRINCIPAL SURFACE COMBATANTS 48

   AIRCRAFT CARRIERS • CV 1 *Viraat* (ex-UK *Hermes*) (capacity 30 *Sea Harrier* FRS MK51 (*Sea Harrier* FRS MKI) FGA ac; 7 Ka-27 *Helix* ASW hel/*Sea King* MK42B ASW hel)

   DESTROYERS • DDG 8:

      3 *Delhi* each with 4 quad (16 eff.) each with SS-N-25 *Switchblade* tactical SSM, 2 single with 24 SA-N-7 SAM, 5 x1 533mm ASTT, 1 100mm gun, (capacity either 2 *Sea King* MK42A ASW hel or 2 ALH utl hel)

      5 *Rajput* (ex-FSU *Kashin*) each with 2 twin (4eff.) PJ-10 *BrahMos* ASCM (one ship fitted with phased upgrades in progress for rest of class), 2 Twin (4 eff.) each with SS-N-2C *Styx* tactical SSM, 2 (4 eff.) each with 16 SA-N-1 *Goa* SAM,5 x1 533mm ASTT, 2 RBU 6000 *Smerch* 2 (24 eff.), 2 76mm gun, (capacity either 1 Ka-25 *Hormone*/KA-28 hel)

   FRIGATES 15

      FFG 10:

      3 *Brahmaputra* each with 4 quad (16 eff.) each with SS-N-25 *Switchblade* tactical SSM, 20 SA-N-4 *Gecko* SAM, 2 triple 324mm ASTT (6 eff.), 1 76mm gun, (capacity either 2 HAL *Chetak* (SA-316B) *Alouette III* SA-316 Utl/*Sea King* MK42 ASW hel or 2 *Sea King* MK42 ASW hel) (2 of class awaiting full weapons fit)

      3 *Godavari* each with 2 triple 324mm ASTT (6 eff.), 4 single each with SS-N-2D *Styx* tactical SSM, 1 twin (2 eff.) with 20 SA-N-4 *Gecko* SAM, (capacity either 2 *Sea King* MK42 ASW hel or 2 HAL *Chetak* (SA-316B) *Alouette III* SA-316 Utl/*Sea King* MK42 ASW hel)

      3 *Talwar* each with SS-N-27 *Club* tactical SSM, 6 single with SA-N-7 *Gadfly* SAM, 1 100mm gun, (capacity either 1 KA-31 *Helix B* AEW hel/KA-28 ASW hel or 1 ALH utl hel)

      1 *Shivalik* each with SS-N-27 *Club* tactical SSM, 6 single with SA-N-7 *Gadfly* SAM, 1 76mm gun, (capacity 1 *Sea King* Mk42-B ASW hel). (2 additional vessels expected ISD '08 and '09)

FF 5:

1 *Krishna* (ex-UK *Leander*) trg role

4 *Nilgiri* (ex-UK *Leander*) each with 2 triple 533mm
ASTT (6 eff.), 1 *Limbo* ASW Mor (triple), 2 114mm
gun, eq with 1 ALH/*Chetak* (SA-316B) *Alouette III*
SA-316 Utl

CORVETTES 24

FSG 20:

4 *Khukri* each with 1 76mm gun, 2 twin (4 eff.)
each with SS-N-2C *Styx* tactical SSM, 1 hel landing
platform (For ALH/*Chetak*)

4 *Kora* each with 4 (16 eff.) each with SS-N-25
Switchblade tactical SSM, 1 quad (4 eff.) with SA-N-
5 *Grail* SAM, 1 76mm gun, 1 hel landing platform
(For ALH/*Chetak*)

5 *Veer* (FSU *Tarantul*) each with 4 single each with
SS-N-2D *Styx* tactical SSM, 2 quad (8 eff.) (quad
manual aiming) each with SA-N-5 *Grail* SAM, 1
76mm gun

5 *Vibhuti* (mod *Veer*) each with 4 quad(16 eff.) with
16 SS-N-25 *Switchblade* tactical SSM, 1 quad (4 eff.)
(quad manual aiming) with SA-N-5 *Grail* SAM, 1
76mm gun

2 *Vibhuti* (advanced version) each with 4 quad (16
eff.) each with 16 SS-N-25 *Switchblade* tactical SSM,
1 quad (4 eff.) (manual aiming) with SA-N-5 *Grail*
SAM, 1 76mm gun

FS 4:

4 *Abhay* (FSU *Pauk* II) each with 1 quad (4 eff.)
(quad manual aiming) with SA-N-5 *Grail* SAM, 2 x1
533mm ASTT (twin), 2 RBU 1200 (10 eff.), 1 76mm
gun

PATROL AND COASTAL COMBATANTS 18

PSOH 6 *Sukanya* (capacity 2 HAL *Chetak*)

PCC 7: 5 *Trinkat* SDB MK 5; 2 SDB Mk 3

PFI 5 *Super Dvora* less than 100 tonnes (+2 under
construction)

MINE WARFARE • MINE COUNTERMEASURES 14

MSI 2 *Mahe* less than 100 tonnes (FSU *Yevgenya*)

MSO 12 *Pondicherry* (FSU *Natya*)

AMPHIBIOUS 17

PRINCIPAL AMPHIBIOUS VESSELS • LPD 1

Jalashwa (Ex US *Austin class*) (capacity up to 6 med spt
hel; either 9 LCM or 4 LCM and 2 LCAC; 4 LCVP; 930
troops)

LS 10

LSM 5 *Kumbhir* (FSU *Polnocny* C) (capacity 5 MBT or 5
APC; 160 troops)

LST 5:

2 *Magar* (capacity 15 MBT or 8 APC or 10 trucks;
500 troops)

3 *Magar* mod (capacity 15 MBT or 8 APC or 10
trucks; 500 troops)

CRAFT • LCU 6 *Vasco de Gama* MK2/3 LC (capacity 2
APC; 120 troops)

LOGISTICS AND SUPPORT 32

AORH 3: 1 *Aditya* (mod *Deepak*); 1 *Deepak*; 1 *Jyoti*

AOL 6

ASR 1

AWT 2

AGOR 1 *Sagardhwani*

AGHS 8 *Sandhayak*

AGS 2 *Makar*

ATF 1

TPT 3 *Nicobar*

TRG 3: 1 Tir; 2 **AXS**

TRV 1

FACILITIES

Bases Located at Mumbai (Bombay), Karwar
(under construction), Calcutta,
Vishakhapatnam, Port Blair (Andaman Is),
Kochi (Cochin)

Naval airbase Located at Arakonam, Goa

Naval Aviation 7,000

Flying hours	180 to 240 hrs/year on T-60 trg Aircraft; 180 hrs/year on *Sea Harrier* FRS MK51 (*Sea Harrier* FRS MKI) FGA ac

FORCES BY ROLE

Air	1 HQ located at Arakonam
FGA	1 sqn with 15 *Sea Harrier* FRS MK51 (*Sea Harrier* FRS MKI); 2 T-60*
ASW	6 sqn with 9 Ka-31 *Helix B*; 7 Ka-25 *Hormone*; 18 Ka-28 (Ka-27PL) *Helix A*; 35 *Sea King* MK42A/*Sea King* MK42B; 26 HAL *Chetak* (SA-316B) *Alouette III*
MR	3 sqn with 6 Il-38 *May*; 11 Tu-142M *Bear F*; up to 20 Do-228-201; 15 BN-2 *Defender*
SAR	1 sqn with 6 *Sea King* MK42C; HAL *Chetak* (SA-316B) *Alouette III* (several in SAR role)
Tpt	1 sqn with 10 HAL-784M (HS-748M)
Comms	1 sqn with 10 Do-228
Trg	2 sqn with 6 HJT-16 MKI *Kiran*; 6 HJT-16 MKII *Kiran II*; 8 HPT-32 *Deepak*
UAV	1 sqn with 8 *Searcher* MkII, 4 *Heron*

EQUIPMENT BY TYPE

AIRCRAFT 34 combat capable

FGA 15 *Sea Harrier* FRS MK51 (*Sea Harrier* FRS MKI)

ASW 11 Tu-142M *Bear F**

MP 26: up to 20 Do-228-201; 6 Il-38 *May**

TPT 35: 15 BN-2 *Defender*; 10 Do-228; 10 HAL-784M
(HS-748M)

TRG 22: 6 HJT-16 MKI; 6 HJT-16 MKII *Kiran II*; 8 HPT-
32 *Deepak*; 2 T-60*

HELICOPTERS

ASW 25: 7 Ka-25 *Hormone*; 18 Ka-28 (Ka-27PL) *Helix
A*; 35 *Sea King* MK42A ASW/*Sea King* MK42B ASW/
ASUW*

AEW 9 KA-31 *Helix B*

SAR 6 *Sea King* MK42C

UTL 51+: 4 *Dhruv* ALH 2; 6 HAL *Chetak* (SA-316B)
Alouette III; some (several in SAR role); 25 SA-319
Alouette III

UAV 12: 8 *Searcher* MK II; 4 *Heron*

MSL

ASM *Sea Eagle*; KH-35/*Sea Skua* (*Bear* and *May* a/c now
cleared to fire *Sea Eagle* and Kh-35)

ASCM PJ-10 *BrahMos*

AAM R-550 *Magic* 2/R-550 *Magic* tactical AAM

Marines ε1,200

Amph 1 bde

Cdo   1 (marine) force

Western Command

Navy 1 HQ located at Mumbai (Bombay)

Southern Command

Navy 1 HQ located at Kochi (Cochin)

Eastern Command

Navy 1 HQ located at Vishakhapatnam

Andaman and Nicobar Command (joint command)

Navy 1 HQ located at Port Blair (Andaman Is)

Air Force 125,000

5 regional air comds: Western (New Delhi), South-Western (Gandhinagar), Eastern (Shillong), Central (Allahabad), Southern (Trivandrum)

Maintenance Cmd (Nagpur), Trg Cmd (Bangalore)

Flying hours   180 hrs/year

FORCES BY ROLE

Ftr	3 sqn with 48 MiG-29B *Fulcrum*; 3 sqn with 48 MiG-21FL *Fishbed*
FGA	3 sqn with 48 Su-30 MKI *Flanker*; 3 sqn with 36 M-2000H (M-2000E) *Mirage/* (secondary ECM role); 8 sqn with 120 MiG-21 (3 sqn with 48 MiG-21bis *Fishbed*); 5 sqn with 72 MiG-21M/MF *Fishbed)*; 4 sqn with 64 *Jaguar* S(I) ; 6 sqn with 98 MiG-27ML *Flogger*; 1 sqn with 16 MiG-23BN *Flogger*
Maritime attack	1 sqn with 10 *Jaguar* S(I) with *Sea Eagle* tactical ASM
AEW/ AWACS	1 sqn with 1 IL-76 *Phalcon* (first in IAF service Dec 07, the second Sep 08 and the third in Mar 09)
Recce	1 sqn with Gulfstream IV
Tpt	2 sqn with 24 Il-76 *Candid*; 7 sqn with 112 An-32 *Cline;* some sqns and units with 64 HS-748; 2 sqn with 40 Do-228; 1 flt with 4 B-737; 1 flt with 4 EMB-135BJ
Tkr	1 sqn with 6 Il-78 *Midas*
Atk hel	2 sqn with 20 Mi-24/Mi-35 *Hind*
Hel	9 sqn with 102 Mi-8 *Hip*; 6 sqn with 72 Mi-17 *Hip* H/Mi-17 IV; 1 sqn with 4 Mi-26 *Halo*); 2 sqn with 18 ALH *Dhruv*; 2 sqn with 24 HAL *Cheetah* (SA-315B) *Lam;*: 4 sqn *with* 48 HAL *Chetak* (SA-316B)
Trg	units with 84 HJT-16 *Kiran*; ; 70 HPT *Deepak*; 10 M-2000H*; 13 MiG-21; 8 MiG-21bis; 9 MiG-21M/MF; 6 MiG-21FL; 6 MiG-29UB ; 11 MiG-27ML*;2 MiG-23BN*; 8 *Jaguar* IS/2 –IM; *Hawk* Mk 132 AJT being evaluated
UAV	5 sqn with *Searcher* MkII

SAM   30 sqn with S-123M *Pechora* (SA-3) *Goa*; 8 sqn with OSA-AK (SA-8B *Gecko*); 5 flt with SA-16 *Gimlet*

EQUIPMENT BY TYPE

AIRCRAFT 565 combat capable

FTR 96: 48 MiG-29B *Fulcrum*; 48 MiG-21FL

FGA 392: 48 Su-30 MKI *Flanker*; 36 M-2000H (M-2000E) *Mirage*/M-2000TH (M-2000ED) *Mirage* (secondary ECM role); 98 MiG-27ML *Flogger* J2; 74 *Jaguar* S International (incl 10 maritime attack with *Sea Eagle* tactical ASM); 16 MiG-23BN *Flogger* H/ MiG-23UM; 48 MiG-21bis *Fishbed* L & N; 72 MiG-21M/MF *Fishbed* J (125 MiG-21s being upgraded to MiG-21bis-93)

AEW/AWACS 1 IL-76 *Phalcon* 2 more by Mar 09)

RECCE 3 Gulfstream IV SRA-4;

TKR 6 Il-78 *Midas*

TPT 261: 30 Il-76 *Candid*; 122 An-32 *Cline*; 6 B-707; 6 B-737; 64 BAe-748; 43 Do-228; 4 EMB-135BJ

TRG 237: 6 *Hawk* Mk 132AJT (66 on order) 84 HJT-16 MKII *Kiran* II; 70 HPT-32 *Deepak*; 8 *Jaguar* B(I)*, 40 MiG-21U*; 2 MiG-23BN*; 11 MiG-27UM*, 6 MiG-29UB *Fulcrum**; 10 *Mirage* M-2000H*

HELICOPTERS

ATK 20 Mi-25 *Hind* D/Mi-35 *Hind*

SPT 178: 4 Mi-26 *Halo* (hy tpt); 102 Mi-8; 72 Mi-17 (Mi-8MT) *Hip* H

UTL 80: 8 *Dhruv* ALH (150 on order); 24 HAL *Cheetah* (SA-315B) *Lama* SA-315; 48 HAL *Chetak* (SA-316B) *Alouette III*

UAV: some *Searcher* MK II

AD • SAM S-125 (SA-3B) *Goa*

  SP SA-8B

  MANPAD SA-16 *Gimlet*

MSL • TACTICAL • ASM: AM-39 *Exocet*; AS-11; AS-11B (ATGW); AS-12 *Kegler*; AS-17 *Krypton*; AS-30; AS-7 *Kerry*; *Sea Eagle*

  SSM *Prithvi* MK II

  ARM: AS-11; AS-11B (ATGW); AS-12 *Kegler*; AS-17 *Krypton*

  AAM AA-10 *Alamo*; AA-11 *Archer*; AA-12 *Adder*; AA-7 *Apex*; AA-8 *Aphid*; R-550 *Magic*; Super 530D

Coast Guard ε8,000

Control of the Coast Guard is exercised through the Director General under the Ministry of Defence. The CG is organised into 11 districts with three regional Command Head Quarters at Mumbai, Chennai and Port Blair; in addition there are two air stations at Daman and Chennai and five independent Air Squadrons at Mumbai, Goa, Kochi, Kolkata and Port Blair for maritime surveillance.

EQUIPMENT BY TYPE

PATROL AND COASTAL COMBATANTS 67

  PSOH 14: 5 *Samar* (Additional vessels in build*)*; 9 *Vikram*

  PCO 6 *Sarojini-Naidu*

  PCC 27: 13 *Jija Bai* Mod 1; 8 *Priyadarshini*; 6 *Tara Bai*

  PB 14

  UCAC 6 *Griffon 8000*

AIRCRAFT • TPT 24 Do-228
HELICOPTERS • UTL • SA-316 17 HAL *Chetak* (SA-316B) *Alouette III*

Paramilitary 1,300,586

Assam Rifles 63,883
Ministry of Home Affairs. Security within north-eastern states, mainly army-officered; better trained than BSF
FORCES BY ROLE
Equipped to roughly same standard as an army inf bn
Paramilitary 7 HQ; 40 bn each with 6 81mm mor
EQUIPMENT BY TYPE
ARTY • MOR 81mm 240

Border Security Force 208,422
Ministry of Home Affairs.
FORCES BY ROLE
Paramilitary 157+ bn each with 6 81mm
EQUIPMENT BY TYPE
Small arms, lt arty, some anti-tank weapons
ARTY • MOR 81mm 942+
AIRCRAFT • TPT (air spt)

Central Industrial Security Force 94,347 (lightly armed security guards only)
Ministry of Home Affairs. Guards public-sector locations

Central Reserve Police Force 229,699
Ministry of Home Affairs. Internal security duties, only lightly armed, deployable throughout the country
Paramilitary 2 Mahila (female) bn; 125 bn; 13 rapid action force bn

Defence Security Corps 31,000
Provides security at Defence Ministry sites

Indo–Tibetan Border Police 36,324
Ministry of Home Affairs. Tibetan border security SF/guerrilla warfare and high-altitude warfare specialists
Paramilitary 30 bn

National Security Guards 7,357
Anti-terrorism contingency deployment force, comprising elements of the armed forces, CRPF and Border Security Force

Railway Protection Forces 70,000

Rashtriya Rifles 65,000
Ministry of Defence
Paramilitary 61 bn (in 15 sector HQ. 8 more forming)

Sashastra Seema Bal 31,554
Guards Indo-Nepal/Bhutan borders

Special Frontier Force 10,000
Mainly ethnic Tibetans

Special Protection Group 3,000
Protection of VVIP

State Armed Police 450,000
For duty primarily in home state only, but can be moved to other states. Some bn with GPMG and army standard infantry weapons and equipment
Paramilitary 24 (India Reserve Police (cdo-trained)) bn

Reserve Organisations

Civil Defence 500,000 reservists
Fully train in 225 categorised towns in 32 states. Some units for NBC defence

Home Guard 487,821 reservists (actual str (515,000 authorised str))
In all states except Arunachal Pradesh and Kerala; men on lists, no trg. Not usually armed in peacetime–weapons held in state armouries. Used for civil defence, rescue and fire-fighting teams in wartime.
Paramilitary 6 bn (Special battalions created to protect tea plantations in Assam)

NON-STATE ARMED GROUPS
see Part II

DEPLOYMENT

AFGHANISTAN
400 commandos

BURUNDI
UN • ONUB 3 obs

CÔTE D'IVOIRE
UN • UNOCI 8 obs

DEMOCRATIC REPUBLIC OF CONGO
UN • MONUC 4,380; 53 obs

ETHIOPIA/ERITREA
UN • UNMEE 715; 8 obs

LEBANON
UN • UNIFIL 884

SUDAN
UN • UNMIS 2,606; 20 obs

SYRIA/ISRAEL
UN • UNDOF 191

TAJIKISTAN
IAF Forward Op Base, Farkhar

FOREIGN FORCES
Total numbers for UNMOGIP mission in India and Pakistan
Chile 2 obs
Croatia 8 obs
Denmark 4 obs

Finland 6 obs
Italy 7 obs
Korea Republic of 9 obs
Sweden 6 obs
Uruguay 2 obs

Kazakhstan Kaz

Kazakhstani Tenge t		2006	2007	2008
GDP	t	9.7tr	11.5tr	
	US$	78bn	96bn	
per capita	US$	5,115	6,252	
Growth	%	10.7	8.7	
Inflation	%	8.6	8.6	
Def bdgt	t	81bn	142bn	
	US$	648m	1,183m	
FMA (US)	US$	3.5m	3.5m	2.0m
US$1=t		125	120	

Population   15,284,929

Ethnic groups: Kazak 51%; Russian 32%; Ukrainian 5%; German 2%; Tatar 2%; Uzbek 2%

Age	0–14	15–19	20–24	25–29	30–64	65 plus
Male	12%	6%	5%	4%	19%	3%
Female	12%	5%	5%	4%	21%	6%

Capabilities

ACTIVE 49,000 (Army 30,000 Navy 3,000 Air 12,000 MoD 4,000) **Paramilitary** 31,500

Terms of service 24 months

ORGANISATIONS BY SERVICE

Army 30,000

4 regional comd: Astana, East, West and Southern.

FORCES BY ROLE

Mech Inf	10 bde (1 Bde Astana Region, 4 Bde East Region, 5 bde South Region)
Air Aslt	4 bde
Arty	7 bde
MRL	1 bde
AT	2 bde
SSM	1 bde
Coastal Def	1 (West Region) bde
Cbt Engr	3 bde
SSM	1 bde
Peacekeeping	1 (KAZBRIG) bde

EQUIPMENT BY TYPE

MBT 980 T-72
RECCE 280: 140 BRDM; 140 BRM
AIFV 1,430: 730 BMP-1; 700 BMP-2
APC 370

APC (T) 180 MT-LB
APC (W) 190 BTR-70/BTR-80
ARTY 1,460
  SP 240: **122mm** 120 2S1 *Carnation*; **152mm** 120 2S3
  TOWED 670: **122mm** 400 D-30; **152mm** 270: 180 2A36; 90 2A65
  GUN/MOR 120mm 25 2S9 *Anona*
  MRL 380: **122mm** 200 BM-21; **220mm** 180 9P140 *Uragan*
  MOR 120mm 145 2B11/M-120
AT • MSL • MANPATS AT-4 9K111 *Spigot*; AT-5 9K113 *Spandrel*; AT-6 9K115 *Spiral*
  RL 73mm RPG-7 *Knout*
  GUNS 100mm 68 MT-12/T-12
MSL • SSM 12 SS-21 *Tochka* (*Scarab*)

FACILITIES

Training centre   1

Navy 3,000

PATROL AND COASTAL COMBATANTS

PCI 12: 4 *Almaty*; 1 *Dauntless*; 5 *Guardian*; 2 *Zhuk*

Air Force 12,000 (incl Air Defence)

1 air force div, 164 cbt ac, 14 atk hel

Flying hours   100 hrs/year

FORCES BY ROLE

Comd	regt with 2 Tu-134 *Crusty*; 1 Tu-154 *Careless*
Ftr	1 regt with 40 MiG-29 *Fulcrum*; 1 regt with 42 MiG-31 *Foxhound*; 16 MiG-25 *Foxbat*
FGA	1 regt with 14 Su-24 *Fencer*; 1 regt with 14 Su-25 *Frogfoot*; 1 regt with 25 Su-27 *Flanker*
Recce	1 regt with 12 Su-24 *Fencer**
Atk hel	some regt with 40+ Mi-24V
Trg	some regt with 12 L-39 *Albatros*; 4 Yak-18 *Max*
Hel	some regt with 20 Mi-171V5, 50 Mi-8 *Hip*, 6 UH-1H
SAM	some regt with 100 SA-2 *Guideline*/SA-3 *Goa*; SA-10 *Grumble* (quad); SA-4 *Ganef*/SA-5 *Gammon*; SA-6 *Gainful* (60 eff.)

EQUIPMENT BY TYPE

AIRCRAFT 163 combat capable
  FTR 98: 42 MiG-31 *Foxhound* (20 to be upgraded to MiG-31BM by end 2008); 40 MiG-29 *Fulcrum*; 16 MiG-25 *Foxbat*
  FGA 65: 14 Su-25 *Frogfoot*; 14 Su-24 *Fencer*; 12* Su-24 (recce), 25 Su-27 *Flanker*
  TPT 3: 2 Tu-134 *Crusty*; 1 Tu-154 *Careless*
  TRG 16: 12 L-39 *Albatros*; 4 Yak-18 *Max*
HELICOPTERS
  ATK 40+ Mi-24V (first 9 upgraded)
  SPT 76: 20 Mi-171V5; 50 Mi-8 *Hip*; 6 UH-1H
AD • SAM 147+
  SP 47+: 20 SA-6 *Gainful*; 27+ SA-4 *Ganef* /SA-5 *Gammon* static; SA-10 *Grumble* (quad)
  TOWED 100 SA-2 *Guideline*; SA-3 *Goa*
MSL
  ASM AS-10 *Karen*; AS-11 *Kilter*; AS-7 *Kerry*; AS-9 *Kyle*
  ARM AS-11 *Kilter*

AAM AA-6 *Acrid*; AA-7 *Apex*; AA-8 *Aphid;* AA-12 on MiG-31BM

Paramilitary 31,500

Government Guard 500

Internal Security Troops ε20,000
Ministry of Interior

Presidential Guard 2,000

State Border Protection Forces ε9,000
Ministry of Interior.
HEL • SPT 1 Mi-171

DEPLOYMENT

IRAQ
MNF • *Operation Iraqi Freedom* 29

NEPAL
UN • UNMIN 1 obs

Kyrgyzstan Kgz

Kyrgyzstani Som s		2006	2007	2008
GDP	s	113bn	126bn	
	US$	2.8bn	3.6bn	
per capita	US$	540	681	
Growth	%	2.7	7.6	
Inflation	%	5.6	7.0	
Def bdgt	s	1.44bn	1.46bn	
	US$	36m	41m	
FMA (US)	US$	1.9m	1.5m	1.5m
US$1=s		40.1	35.0	

Population   5,284,149

Ethnic groups: Kyrgyz 56%; Russian 17%; Uzbek 13%; Ukrainian 3%

Age	0–14	15–19	20–24	25–29	30–64	65 plus
Male	16%	6%	5%	4%	15%	3%
Female	15%	6%	5%	4%	17%	4%

Capabilities

ACTIVE 10,900 (Army 8,500 Air 2,400) Paramilitary 9,500
Terms of service 18 months

ORGANISATIONS BY SERVICE

Army 8,500
FORCES BY ROLE
MR   2 bde; 1(mtn) bde
SF   1 bde
Arty   1 bde
AD   1 bde

EQUIPMENT BY TYPE
MBT 150 T-72
RECCE 30 BRDM-2
AIFV 320: 230 BMP-1; 90 BMP-2
APC (W) 35: 25 BTR-70; 10 BTR-80
ARTY 246
  SP 122mm 18 2S1 *Carnation*
  TOWED 141: **100mm** 18 M-1944; **122mm** 107: 72 D-30; 35 M-30 *M-1938*; **152mm** 16 D-1
  GUN/MOR 120mm 12 2S9 *Anona*
  MRL 21: **122mm** 15 BM-21; **220mm** 6 9P140 *Uragan*
  MOR 120mm 54: 6 2S12; 48 M-120
AT • MSL • MANPATS 26+: 26 AT-3 9K11 *Sagger*; AT-4 9K111 *Spigot*; AT-5 9K113 *Spandrel*
  RCL 73mm SPG-9
  RL 73mm RPG-7 *Knout*
  GUNS 100mm 18 MT-12/T-12
AD • SAM • MANPAD SA-7 *Grail*
  GUNS 48
    SP 23mm 24 ZSU-23-4
    TOWED 57mm 24 S-60

Air Force 2,400
FORCES BY ROLE
Tac   1 regt with 4 L-39 *Albatros* ; 1 (comp avn) regt with 48 MiG-21 *Fishbed*; 2 An-12 *Cub*; 2 An-26 *Curl*
Ftr   1 regt with 4 L-39 *Albatros*
Hel   1 regt with 9 Mi-24 *Hind*; 23 Mi-8 *Hip*
SAM some regt with SA-3 *Goa*; SA-4 *Ganef*; SA-2 *Guideline*

EQUIPMENT BY TYPE
AIRCRAFT 52 combat capable
  FTR 72: 48 MiG-21 *Fishbed*; 24 in store
  TPT 4: 2 An-12 *Cub*; 2 An-26 *Curl*
  TRG 28: 4 L-39 *Albatros**; 24 in store
HELICOPTERS
  ATK 9 Mi-24 *Hind*
  SPT 23 Mi-8 *Hip*
AD • SAM
  SP SA-4 *Ganef*
  TOWED SA-2 *Guideline*; SA-3 *Goa*

Paramilitary 9,500

Border Guards 5,000 (Kgz conscripts, RF officers)

Interior Troops 3,500

National Guard 1,000

DEPLOYMENT

ETHIOPIA/ERITREA
UN • UNMEE 4 obs

LIBERIA
UN • UNMIL 4 obs

SUDAN
UN • UNMIS 8 obs

FOREIGN FORCES

Denmark Army: 75 (incl C-130 contingent) *Operation Enduring Freedom*

Russia Military Air Forces: 20+ Mi-8 *Hip* spt hel/Su-24 *Fencer* FGA ac/Su-25 *Frogfoot* FGA ac/Su-27 *Flanker* ftr ac; ε500

United States 14 in support of ISAF

Nepal N

Nepalese Rupee NR		2006	2007	2008
GDP	NR	582bn	643bn	
	US$	8.0bn	10.2bn	
per capita	US$	283	353	
Growth	%	2.8	2.5	
Inflation	%	8.0	6.5	
Def bdgt	NR	11.5bn	10.9bn	
	US$	158m	173m	
US$1=NR		72.7	63.0	

Population   28,901,790

Ethnic groups: Hindu 90%; Buddhist 5%; Muslim 3%

Age	0–14	15–19	20–24	25–29	30–64	65 plus
Male	20%	6%	5%	4%	14%	2%
Female	19%	5%	5%	4%	14%	2%

Capabilities

ACTIVE 69,000 (Army 69,000) **Paramilitary 62,000**

ORGANISATIONS BY SERVICE

Army 69,000

FORCES BY ROLE

Army	3 div HQ; 1 (valley) comd
Inf	7 bde (*total:* 16 Inf bn); 44 indep coy
SF	1 bde (1 AB bn, 1 cav sqn, 2 indep SF coy)
Ranger	1 bn
Arty	1 bde (1 arty regt, 1 AD regt)
Engr	1 bde (4 engr bn)
Royal Guard	1 bde (1 MP bn)

EQUIPMENT BY TYPE

RECCE 40 *Ferret*
APC (W) 40 *Casspir*
ARTY 95+
    TOWED 25: **75mm** 6 pack; **94mm** 5 3.7in (mtn trg); **105mm** 14: 8 L-118 Light Gun; 6 pack howitzer non-operational
    MOR 70+: **81mm; 120mm** 70 M-43 (est 12 op)
AD • GUNS • TOWED 32+: **14.5mm** 30 Type-56 (ZPU-4); **37mm** (PRC); **40mm** 2 L/60

Air Wing 320

AIRCRAFT • TPT 2: 1 BAe-748; 1 SC.7 3M *Skyvan*

HELICOPTERS
    SPT 7: 1 AS-332L; 2 AS-322L1 *Super Puma*; 1 AS-350 *Ecureuil*; 3 MI-17 (Mi-8MT) *Hip H*
    UTL 5: 2 Bell 206L *LongRanger*; 1 HAS-315B (SA-315B) *Lama*; 2 SA-316B *Alouette III*

Paramilitary 62,000

Armed Police Force 15,000
Ministry of Home Affairs

Police Force 47,000

NON-STATE ARMED GROUPS

see Part II

DEPLOYMENT

CÔTE D'IVOIRE
UN • UNOCI 3 obs

DEMOCRATIC REPUBLIC OF CONGO
UN • MONUC 1,030; 20 obs

ETHIOPIA/ERITREA
UN • UNMEE 3 obs

GEORGIA
UN • UNOMIG 1 obs

HAITI
UN • MINUSTAH 1,109

LEBANON
UN • UNIFIL 859

LIBERIA
UN • UNMIL 44; 3 obs

MIDDLE EAST
UN • UNTSO 3 obs

SERBIA
UN • UNMIK 1 obs

SIERRA LEONE
UN • UNIOSIL 1 obs

SUDAN
AU/UN • UNAMID proposed deployment
UN • UNMIS 8; 8 obs

FOREIGN FORCES

United Kingdom Army: 20; UNMIN 4 obs
UN: 60 (projected UN requirements as of 29 Nov 2006)
Austria 2 obs
Brazil 7 obs
Croatia 2 obs
Ecuador 1 obs
Finland 1 obs
Gambia 4 obs

Ghana 5 obs
Guatemala 2 obs
Indonesia 6 obs
Japan 6 obs
Jordan 10 obs
Kazakhstan 1 obs
Malaysia 7 obs
Nigeria 8 obs
Norway 3 obs
Paraguay 5 obs
Republic of Korea 5 obs
Romania 5 obs
Russia 8 obs
South Africa 5 obs
Sweden 3 obs
Switzerland 5 obs
Thailand 7 obs
United States Army 4; USMC 6
Uruguay 3 obs
Yemen 15 obs
Zambia 8 obs
Zimbabwe 2 obs

Pakistan Pak

Pakistani Rupee Rs		2006	2007	2008
GDP	Rs	7.7tr	8.7tr	
	US$	128bn	144bn	
per capita	US$	773	849	
Growth	%	6.9	6.4	
Inflation	%	7.9	7.8	
Def exp	Rs	250bn		
	US$	4.14bn		
Def bdgt	Rs	250bn	275bn	
	US$	4.14bn	4.53bn	
FMA (US)	US$	297m	n.a.	300m
US$1=Rs		60.2	60.6	

Population   169,270,617
Ethnic groups: Hindu less than 3%

Age	0–14	15–19	20–24	25–29	30–64	65 plus
Male	20%	6%	5%	4%	14%	2%
Female	19%	5%	5%	4%	14%	2%

Capabilities

ACTIVE 619,000 (Army 550,000 Navy 24,000 Air 45,000) Paramilitary 304,000

ORGANISATIONS BY SERVICE

Army 550,000

FORCES BY ROLE
Army 9 corps HQ
Armd 2 div; 7 (indep) bde

Mech 1 (indep) bde
Inf 1 (area) comd; 18 div; 6 bde
SF 1 gp (3 SF bn)
Arty 9 (corps) bde; 5 bde
Engr 7 bde
Avn 1 (VIP) sqn; 5 (composite) sqn
Hel 10 sqn
AD 1 comd (3 AD gp (total: 8 AD bde))

EQUIPMENT BY TYPE
MBT 2,461+: 45 MBT 2000 Al-Khalid; 320 T-80UD; 51 T-54/T-55; 1,100 Type-59; 400 Type-69; 275+ Type-85; 270 M-48A5 in store
APC 1,266
　APC (T) 1,100 M-113
　APC (W) 166: 120 BTR-70/BTR-80; 46 UR-416
ARTY 4,291+
　SP 260: 155mm 200 M-109/M-109A2; 203mm 60 M-110A2/M-110
　TOWED 1,629: 105mm 329: 216 M-101; 113 M-56; 122mm 570: 80 D-30 (PRC); 490 Type-54 M-1938; 130mm 410 Type-59-I; 155mm 292: 144 M-114; 148 M-198; 203mm 28 M-115
　MRL 122mm 52 Azar (Type-83)
　MOR 2,350+: 81mm; 120mm AM-50; M-61
AT
　MSL 10,500+
　　SP M-901 TOW
　　MANPATS 10,500 HJ-8/TOW
　RCL 3,700: 75mm Type-52; 106mm M-40A1
　RL 73mm RPG-7 Knout; 89mm M-20
　GUNS 85mm 200 Type-56 (D-44)
AIRCRAFT
　RECCE 30 Cessna O-1E Bird Dog
　TPT 4: 1 Cessna 421; 3 Y-12(II)
　UTL 90 SAAB 91 Safrai (50 obs; 40 liaison)
HELICOPTERS
　ATK 26: 25 AH-1F Cobra (TOW); 1 Mi-24 Hind
　SPT 54: 31 SA-330 Puma; 10 Mi-8; 13 MI-17 (Mi-8MT) Hip H
　UTL 81: 26 Bell-412; 5 AB-205A-1 (Bell 205A-1); 13 Bell 206B JetRanger II; 12 SA-315B Lama; 20 SA-319 Alouette III; 5 UH-1H Iroquois
　TRG 22: 12 Bell 47G; 10 Hughes 300C
UAV Bravo; Jasoos; Vector
AD
　SAM • MANPAD 2,990+: 2,500 Mk1/Mk2; 60 FIM-92A Stinger; HN-5A; 230 Mistral; 200 RBS-70
　GUNS • TOWED 1900: 14.5mm 981; 35mm 215 GDF-002/GDF-005; 37mm 310 Type-55 (M-1939)/Type-65; 40mm 50 L/60; 57mm 144 Type-59 (S-60); 85mm 200 Type-72 (M-1939) KS-12
RADAR • LAND AN/TPQ-36 Firefinder (arty, mor); RASIT (veh, arty)
MSL • TACTICAL • SSM 166: 95 Hatf 1; 50 Hatf 3 (PRC M-11); 15 Hatf 5 Ghauri (up to 20); 6 Shaheen 1 Hatf-4

Navy 24,000 (incl ε1,400 Marines and ε2,000 Maritime Security Agency (see Paramilitary))

EQUIPMENT BY TYPE
SUBMARINES • TACTICAL 8

SSK 5:

2 *Hashmat* (Fr *Agosta 70*) each with 4 x1 533mm ASTT with 20 F17P HWT/UGM- 84 *Harpoon* tactical USGW

3 *Khalid* (Fr *Agosta 90B*) each with 4 x1 533mm ASTT with 20 F17 MOD 2 HWT; 4 SM-39 *Exocet* tactical USGW

SSI 3: 3 MG110 (SF delivery)

PRINCIPAL SURFACE COMBATANTS • FRIGATES 6

FFG 6:

4 *Tariq* (UK *Amazon*) each with 2 Mk-141 *Harpoon* twin each with RGM-84D *Harpoon* tactical SSM, 2 single each with TP 45 LWT, 1 114mm gun, (capacity 1 *Lynx* utl hel)

2 *Tariq* each with 1 sextuple (6 eff.) with LY-60 (Aspide) SAM, 2 triple 324mm ASTT (6 eff.) each with Mk 46 LWT, 1 114mm gun, (capacity 1 *Lynx* utl hel)

PATROL AND COASTAL COMBATANTS 8

PFM 4 *Jalalat* II each with 2 twin (4 eff.) each with C-802 (CSS-N-8) *Saccade* tactical SSM

PCC 2: 1 *Larkan*; 1 *Rajshahi*

PBF 2 *Kaan* 15

MINE WARFARE • MINE COUNTERMEASURES • MHC 3 *Munsif* (Fr *Eridan*)

LOGISTICS AND SUPPORT 10

AORH 2:

1 *Fuqing* with 1 SA-319 *Alouette III* utl hel

1 *Moawin* with 1 *Sea King* MK45 ASW hel

AOT 3: 1 *Attock*; 2 *Gwadar*

AGS 1 *Behr Paima*

YTM 4

FACILITIES
Bases Located at Ormara, Gwadar, Karachi

Marines ε1,400
Cdo 1 gp

Naval Aviation
AIRCRAFT 16 ac combat capable

MP 16: 3 *Atlantic* (also ASW)*; 3 F-27-200 MPA*; 10 P-3C *Orion**

HELICOPTERS

ASW 12: 6 *Lynx* MK3; 6 *Sea King* MK45 ASW hel

UTL 6: 2 SA-319B *Alouette III*; 4 SA-316 *Alouette III*

MSL • ASM AM-39 *Exocet*

Air Force 45,000

FORCES BY ROLE
3 regional comds: Northern (Peshawar) Central (Sargodha) Southern (Masroor). The Composite Air Tpt Wg, Combat Cadres School and PAF Academy are Direct Reporting Units.

Ftr	2 sqn with 50 *Mirage* IIIEP/OD; 1 sqn with 21 F-16A *Fighting Falcon*; 11 F-16B *Fighting Falcon*; 5 sqn with 77 F-7PG *Skybolt*; 2 sqn with 55 F-7PG (F-7MG) *Airguard;* first 2 delivered of 24 F-16 C/D
FGA	1 sqn with 13 *Mirage* IIIEP each with AM-39 *Exocet* tactical ASM; 2 sqn with 41 A-5C (Q-5III) *Fantan;* 2 sqn with 10 *Mirage* 5PA3 (A5uW); 40 5PA2/5PA *Mirage;* 2 FC-1/JF-17 *Thunder* undergoing test and evaluation (150+ on order);
ELINT/ECM	1 sqn with 2 Da-20 *Falcon*
Recce	1 sqn with 15 *Mirage* IIIRP (*Mirage* IIIR)*
SAR	6 sqn with SA-316 *Alouette III*; 1 sqn with 4 Mi-171 (SAR/liaison)
Tpt	sqns with 1 An-26 *Curl*; 3 B-707; 1 Beech 200 *Super King Air;* /11 C-130B /C-130E *Hercules;* 4 CN-235; 2 F-27-200 *Friendship* (1 with navy); 1 *Falcon* 20; 1 L-100 *Hercules;* 1 Y-12; 1 Beech F-33 *Bonanza*
Trg	sqns with 25 FT-5 (MiG-17U); 15 FT-6 (MiG-19UTI); 12 K-8; 20 FT-7 (JJ-7) *Mongol*; 80 MFI-17B *Mushak;* 3 *Mirage* 5DPA/5DPA2; 2 *Mirage* IIIB*; 7 *Mirage* IIIOD*; 20 T-37C *Tweet*
SAM	1 bty with 6 CSA-1 (SA-2) *Guideline;* SA-16 *Gimlet;* 6 bty each with 24 *Crotale*

EQUIPMENT BY TYPE
AIRCRAFT 360 combat capable

FTR 216: 55 F-7PG (F-7MG) *Airguard;* 77 F-7P *Skybolt;* 21 F-16A *Fighting Falcon;* 11 F-16B *Fighting Falcon;* first 2 delivered of 24 F-16C/D on order; 50 *Mirage* III EP

FGA 106: 2 FC-1/JF-17 *Thunder* delivered (150+ on order); 41 A-5C (Q-5III) *Fantan;* 10 *Mirage* 5PA3 (ASuW), 40 *Mirage* 5PA /*Mirage* 5PA2**;** 13 *Mirage* IIIEP each with AM-39 *Exocet* tactical ASM

RECCE 15 *Mirage* IIIRP (*Mirage* IIIR)*

EW • ELINT 2 Da-20 *Falcon*

TPT 25: 1 An-26 *Curl;* 3 B-707; 1 Beech 200 *Super King Air;* 11 C-130B *Hercules*/C-130E *Hercules;* 4 CN-235; 2 F-27-200 *Friendship* (1 with navy); 1 *Falcon* 20; 1 L-100 *Hercules;* 1 Y-12; 1 Beech F-33 *Bonanza*

TRG 184: 25 FT-5 (MiG-17U) *Fresco;* 15 FT-6 (MiG-19UTI) *Farmer;* 12 K-8; 20 FT-7 (JJ-7) *Mongol A Trg*;* 80 MFI-17B *Mushshak;* 3 *Mirage* 5DPA/*Mirage* 5DPA2*****; 2 *Mirage* IIIB* (trg); 7 *Mirage* IIIOD (*Mirage* IIID)*; 20 T-37C *Tweet*

HELICOPTERS 19: 4 Mi-171; 15 SA-316 *Alouette III*

AD • SAM 150+

TOWED 150: 6 CSA-1 (SA-2) *Guideline;* 144 *Crotale*

MANPAD SA-16 *Gimlet*

RADAR • LAND 51+: 6 AR-1 (AD radar low level); some *Condor* (AD radar high level); some FPS-89/100 (AD radar high level)

MPDR 45 MPDR/MPDR 60 MPDR 90 (AD radar low level)

TPS-43G Type 514 some (AD radar high level)

MSL ASM: AGM-65 *Maverick;* AM-39 *Exocet*

AAM AIM-9L *Sidewinder*/AIM-9P *Sidewinder;* R-Darter, Super 530

FACILITIES

Radar air control sectors	4
Radar control and reporting station	7

Paramilitary up to 304,000 active

Coast Guard
PATROL AND COASTAL COMBATANTS 28
PB 1
PBF 4
MISC BOATS/CRAFT 23

Frontier Corps up to 65,000 (reported)
Ministry of Interior

FORCES BY ROLE
Armd recce   1 indep sqn
Paramilitary   11 regt (*total:* 40 paramilitary bn)

EQUIPMENT BY TYPE
APC (W) 45 UR-416

Maritime Security Agency ε2,000
PRINCIPAL SURFACE COMBATANTS •
DESTROYERS • **DD** 1: 1 *Nazim* (US *Gearing*, no ASROC)
PATROL AND COASTAL COMBATANTS 7:
  PCO 4 *Barkat*
  PCC 3: 2 *Subqat* (PRC *Shanghai*); 1 *Sadaqat* (ex-PRC *Huangfen*)

National Guard 185,000
Incl *Janbaz* Force; *Mujahid* Force; National Cadet Corps; Women Guards

Northern Light Infantry ε12,000
Paramilitary   3 bn

Pakistan Rangers up to 40,000
Ministry of Interior

NON-STATE ARMED GROUPS
see Part II

DEPLOYMENT

BURUNDI
UN • BINUB 1 obs

CÔTE D'IVOIRE
UN • UNOCI 1,124; 12 obs

DEMOCRATIC REPUBLIC OF CONGO
UN • MONUC 3,579; 55 obs

ETHIOPIA/ERITREA
UN • UNMEE 6 obs

GEORGIA
UN • UNOMIG 10 obs

HAITI
UN • MINUSTAH 1

LIBERIA
UN • UNMIL 3,403; 15 obs

SERBIA
UN • UNMIK 2 obs

SIERRA LEONE
UN • UNIOSIL 1 obs

SUDAN
AU/UN • UNAMID 445 proposed deployment
UN • UNMIS 1,567; 20 obs

TIMOR LESTE
UN • UNMIT 4 obs

WESTERN SAHARA
UN • MINURSO 8 obs

FOREIGN FORCES
Unless specified, figures represent total numbers for UNMOGIP mission in India and Pakistan
Chile 2 obs
Croatia 8 obs
Denmark 4 obs
Finland 6 obs
Italy 7 obs
Korea Republic of 9 obs
Sweden 6 obs
United Kingdom some (fwd mounting base) air elm located at Karachi
United States USCENTCOM: 35 (*Operation Enduring Freedom*); Army: 4; Navy: 2; USAF: 12; USMC: 25
Uruguay 2 obs

Sri Lanka Ska

Sri Lankan Rupee Rs		2006	2007	2008
GDP	Rs	2.8tr	3.4tr	
	US$	27.5bn	30.3bn	
per capita	US$	1,325	1,446	
Growth	%	7.4	6.5	
Inflation	%	9.5	17.0	
Def bdgt	Rs	70bn	139bn	
	US$	686m	1,230m	
US$1=Rs		102	113	

Population   20,926,315
Ethnic groups: Sinhalese 74%; Tamil 18%; Moor 7%

Age	0–14	15–19	20–24	25–29	30–64	65 plus
Male	13%	4%	5%	4%	20%	3%
Female	12%	4%	5%	4%	22%	4%

Capabilities

ACTIVE 150,900 (Army 117,900 Navy 15,000 Air 18,000) **Paramilitary 62,200**

RESERVE 5,500 (Army 1,100 Navy 2,400 Air Force 2,000) **Paramilitary 30,400**

ORGANISATIONS BY SERVICE

Army 78,000; 39,900 active reservists (recalled) (total 117,900)

FORCES BY ROLE

9 Div HQ

Armd	3 regt
Armd recce	3 regt (bn)
Air mob	1 bde
Inf	33 bde
SF	1 indep bde
Cdo	1 bde
Fd arty	1 light regt; 2 (med) regt
Fd engr	3 regt

EQUIPMENT BY TYPE

MBT 62 T-55AM2/T-55A
RECCE 15 *Saladin*
AIFV 62: 13 BMP-1; 49 BMP-2
APC 217
   APC (T) 35 Type-85
   APC (W) 182: 31 *Buffel*; 21 FV603 *Saracen*; 105 *Unicorn*; 25 BTR-80/BTR-80A
ARTY 963
   TOWED 157: **88mm** 3 25-pdr; **122mm** 74; **130mm** 40 Type-59-I; **152mm** 40 Type-66 (D-20)
   MRL 122mm 22 RM-70 *Dana*
   MOR 784: **81mm** 520; **82mm** 209; **120mm** 55 M-43
AT • RCL 40: **105mm** ε10 M-65; **106mm** ε30 M-40
   GUNS 85mm 8 Type-56 (D-44)
UAV 1 *Seeker*
AD • GUNS • TOWED 27: **40mm** 24 L/40; **94mm** 3 (3.7in)
RADAR • LAND 2 AN/TPQ-36 *Firefinder* (arty)

Navy 15,000 (incl 2,400 recalled reservists)

FORCES BY ROLE

Navy 1 (HQ and Western comd) located at Colombo

EQUIPMENT BY TYPE

PATROL AND COASTAL COMBATANTS 131
   PSOH 2: 1 *Reliance*; 1 *Sayaru* (Ex Indian *Sukanya*)
   PSO 1 *Jayesagara*
   PFM 2 *Nandimithra* (Il *Saar* 4) each with 3 single each with 1 GII *Gabriel II* tactical SSM, 1 76mm gun
   PCC 11: 3 *Abeetha* (PRC mod *Shanghai*); 2 *Prathapa* (PRC mod *Haizhui*); 3 *Ranajaya* (PRC *Haizhui*); 1 *Ranarisi* (PRC *Shanghai* II); 2 *Weeraya* (PRC *Shanghai*)
   PBF 57: 29 *Colombo*; 3 *Dvora*; 3 *Killer* (ROK); 6 *Shaldag*; 5 *Trinity Marine*; 8 *Super Dvora* all vessels less than 100 tonnes; 3 *Simonneau*
   PBR 51
   PB 7
AMPHIBIOUS
   LSM 1 *Yuhai* (capacity 2 tanks; 250 troops)
   CRAFT 8
      LCU 2 *Yunnan*
      LCM 2
      LCP 3 *Hansaya*
      ACV 1 M 10 (capacity 56 troops)

LOGISTICS AND SUPPORT 3: 1 AK; 1 TPT; 1 SPT/TRG

FACILITIES

Bases   Located at Trincomalee (Main base and Eastern Comd), Kankesanthurai (Northern Comd), Galle (Southern Comd), Medawachiya (North Central Comd) and Colombo (HQ and Western Comd)

Air Force 18,000

FORCES BY ROLE

FGA /Ftr	1 sqn with 4 MiG-27M *Flogger J2*; 1 FT-7 (JJ-7) *Mongol A*, 3F-7M; 2 FT-5 (MiG-17U) *Fresco*; 1 MiG-23UB *Flogger C* (conversion trg); 1 sqn with 7 *Kfir* C-2; 2 *Kfir* C-7; 1 *Kfir* TC-2
Tpt	1 sqn with 7 An-32B *Cline*; 2 C-130K *Hercules*; 1 Cessna 421C *Golden Eagle*; 3 Y-12; 5 Cessna 150
Atk hel	1 sqn with 1 Mi-24V *Hind E*; 12 Mi-35P *Hind*; 10 Bell 212
Trg	Trg sqn with 10 PT-6 (CJ-6); 2 K-8; 5 SF-260TP;
Hel	2 sqn with 3 MI-17 (Mi-8MT) *Hip H*; 6 Bell 412 *Twin Huey* (VIP); 5 Bell 206 *JetRanger* (incl basic trg)
Reserves	Air Force Regt, 3 sqn; airfield construction, 1 sqn

EQUIPMENT BY TYPE

AIRCRAFT 22 combat capable
   FTR 3 F-7M
   FGA 13: 7 *Kfir* C-2; 2 *Kfir* C-7; 4 MiG-27M *Flogger J2*
   TPT 13: 7 An-32B *Cline*; 2 C-130K *Hercules*; 1 Cessna 421C *Golden Eagle*; 3 Y-12
   TRG 25: 5 Cessna 150; 2 FT-5 (MiG-17U*) *Fresco*; 1 FT-7* (JJ-7) *Mongol A*; 2 K-8; 2 *Kfir* TC-2*; 1 MiG-23UB *Flogger C* (conversion trg)*; 7 PT-6 (CJ-6); 5 SF-260TP
HELICOPTERS
   ATK 13: 1 Mi-24V *Hind E*; 12 Mi-35P *Hind*
   SPT 6: 3 MI-17 (Mi-8MT) *Hip H*; 3 in store
   UTL 21: 5 Bell 206 *JetRanger*; 10 Bell 212; 6 Bell 412 *Twin Huey* (VIP)
UAV 3
   RECCE 3: 2 *Searcher*; 1 *Scout*

Paramilitary ε88,600

Home Guard 13,000

National Guard ε15,000

Police Force 30,200; 1,000 (women); 30,400 reservists (total 61,600)

Ministry of Defence

Special Task Force 3,000

anti-guerrilla unit

NON-STATE ARMED GROUPS
see Part II

DEPLOYMENT

DEMOCRATIC REPUBLIC OF CONGO
UN • MONUC 4 obs

ETHIOPIA/ERITREA
UN • UNMEE 4 obs

HAITI
UN • MINUSTAH 960

SUDAN
UN • UNMIS 3 obs

WESTERN SAHARA
UN • MINURSO 2 obs

Tajikistan Tjk

Tajikistani Somoni Tr		2006	2007	2008
GDP	Tr	9.0bn	11.0bn	
	US$	2.7bn	3.2bn	
per capita	US$	394	453	
Growth	%	7.0	7.5	
Inflation	%	10.0	9.9	
Def bdgt	Tr	239m	ε300m	
	US$	72m	87m	
US$1=Tr		3.29	3.43	

Population   7,076,598
Ethnic groups: Tajik 67%; Uzbek 25%; Russian 2%; Tatar 2%

Age	0–14	15–19	20–24	25–29	30–64	65 plus
Male	19%	6%	5%	4%	13%	2%
Female	19%	6%	5%	4%	14%	3%

Capabilities

ACTIVE 8,800 (Army 7,300, Air Force/Air Defence 1,500) **Paramilitary 7,500**
Terms of service 24 months

ORGANISATIONS BY SERVICE

Army 7,300
FORCES BY ROLE
MR   3 bde with 1 trg centre
Air Aslt 1 bde
Arty   1 bde
SAM   1 regt
EQUIPMENT BY TYPE
MBT 37: 30 T-72; 7 T-62
AIFV 23: 8 BMP-1; 15 BMP-2
APC (W) 23 BTR-60/BTR-70/BTR-80

ARTY 23
    TOWED 122mm 10 D-30
    MRL 122mm 3 BM-21
    MOR 120mm 10
AD • SAM 20+
    TOWED 20 SA-2 *Guideline*; SA-3 *Goa*
    MANPAD FIM-92A *Stinger* (reported); SA-7 *Grail*

Air Force/Air Defence 1,500
FORCES BY ROLE
Tpt some sqn with 1 Tu-134A *Crusty*
Hel sqn with 4 Mi-24 *Hind*; 12 Mi-17TM *Hip H*/Mi-8 *Hip*
EQUIPMENT BY TYPE
AIRCRAFT • TPT 1 Tu-134A *Crusty*
HELICOPTERS
    ATK 4 Mi-24 *Hind*
    SPT 12 Mi-17TM *Hip H*/Mi-8 *Hip*

Paramilitary 7,500
Interior Troops 3,800
National Guard 1,200
Emergencies Ministry 2,500
Border Guards

FOREIGN FORCES
France Air Force: 2 C-160 *Transall* tpt ac; 150
India Air Force: 1 Fwd Op Base located at Farkhar
Russia Army: 120 MBT; 350 ACV; 190 Arty/mor/MRL; 1 MR div (subord to Volga-Ural MD); 5,500; Military Air Forces: 5 Su-25 *Frogfoot* FGA ac

Turkmenistan Tkm

Turkmen Manat TMM		2006	2007	2008
GDP	TMM	110tr	134tr	
	US$	10.2bn.	12.2bn	
per capita	US$	2,021.	2,369	
Growth	%	9.0	10.0	
Inflation	%	8.2	6.5	
Def bdgt	TMM	ε2.0tr		
	US$	ε183m		
USD1=TMM		10,881	11,015	

Population   5,136,262
Ethnic groups: Turkmen 77%; Uzbek 9%; Russian 7%; Kazak 2%

Age	0–14	15–19	20–24	25–29	30–64	65 plus
Male	18%	6%	5%	4%	15%	2%
Female	17%	6%	5%	4%	16%	3%

Capabilities

ACTIVE 22,000 (Army 18,500 Navy 500 Air 3,000)
Terms of service 24 months

ORGANISATIONS BY SERVICE

Army 18,500

FORCES BY ROLE

5 Mil Districts

MR	3 div; 2 bde; 1 div (trg)
Air aslt	1 indep bn
Arty	1 bde
MRL	1 regt
AT	1 regt
Engr	1 regt
SAM	2 bde
Msl	1 (Scud) bde

EQUIPMENT BY TYPE

MBT 670 T-72

RECCE 170 BRDM/BRDM-2

AIFV 942: 930 BMP-1/BMP-2; 12 BRM

APC (W) 829 BTR-60/BTR-70/BTR-80

ARTY 548

SP 40: **122mm** 2S1 *Carnation;* **152mm** 2S3

TOWED 269: **122mm** 180 D-30; **152mm** 89: 17 D-1; 72 D-20

GUN/MOR 120mm 17 2S9 *Anona*

MRL 125: **122mm** 65: 9 9P138; 56 BM-21; **220mm** 60 9P140 *Uragan*

MOR 97: **82mm** 31; **120mm** 66 PM-38

AT

MSL • MANPATS 100 AT-3 9K11 *Sagger*; AT-4 9K111 *Spigot*; AT-5 9K113 *Spandrel*; AT-6 9K115 *Spiral*

RL 73mm RPG-7 *Knout*

GUNS 100mm 72 MT-12/T-12

AD • SAM 53+

SP 53: 40 SA-8 *Gecko*; 13 SA-13 *Gopher*

MANPAD SA-7 *Grail*

GUNS 70

SP 23mm 48 ZSU-23-4

TOWED 57mm 22 S-60

MSL • SSM 10 SS-1 *Scud*

Navy 500

Intention to form a navy/coast guard and currently has a minor base at Turkmenbashy with 6 boats. A Caspian Sea Flotilla (see Russia) is operating as a joint RF, Kaz, Tkm flotilla under RF comd based at Astrakhan.

EQUIPMENT BY TYPE

PATROL AND COASTAL COMBATANTS 6

PB 1 *Point* class

PBI 5 *Kalkan*

FACILITIES

Minor base   Located at Turkmenbashy

Air Force 3,000

incl Air Defence

FORCES BY ROLE

Ftr / FGA   2 sqn with 22 MiG-29 *Fulcrum*; 65 Su-17 *Fitter*; 2 MiG-29U *Fulcrum*; 2 Su-25MK

Tpt /Utl   1 sqn with 1 An-26 *Curl*; 10 Mi-24 *Hind*; 8 Mi-8 *Hip*

Trg   1 unit with 3 Su-7B; 2 L-39 *Albatros*

SAM   sqns with 50 SA-2 *Guideline*/SA-3 *Goa*/SA-5 *Gammon*

EQUIPMENT BY TYPE

AIRCRAFT 94 combat capable

FTR 22 MiG-29 *Fulcrum*

FGA 67: 65 Su-17 *Fitter*; 2 Su-25MK (+41 more being refurbished)

TPT 1 An-26 *Curl*

TRG 7: 2 L-39 *Albatros*; 2 MiG-29U *Fulcrum**; 3 Su-7B*

HELICOPTERS

ATK 10 Mi-24 *Hind*

SPT 8 Mi-8 *Hip*

AD • SAM 50 SA-2 *Guideline* towed/SA-3 *Goa*/SA-5 *Gammon* static

Uzbekistan Uz

Uzbekistani Som s		2006	2007	2008
GDP	s	20.7tr	25.6tr	
	US$	17.0bn	20.0bn	
per capita	US$	624	722	
Growth	%	7.3	8.8	
Inflation	%	14.2	12.2	
Def bdgt	s	ε103bn		
	US$	ε84m		
US$1=s		1,219	1,277	

Population   27,780,059

Ethnic groups: Uzbek 73%; Russian 6%; Tajik 5%; Kazak 4%; Karakalpak 2%; Tatar 2%; Korean <1%; Ukrainian <1%

Age	0–14	15–19	20–24	25–29	30–64	65 plus
Male	17%	6%	5%	4%	15%	2%
Female	16%	6%	5%	4%	16%	3%

Capabilities

ACTIVE 67,000 (Army 50,000 Air 17,000)

Paramilitary 20,000

Terms of service conscription 12 months

ORGANISATIONS BY SERVICE

Army 50,000

FORCES BY ROLE

4 Mil Districts; 2 op comd; 1 Tashkent Comd

Tk	1 bde
MR	11 bde
Mtn Inf	1 (lt) bde
Air Aslt	3 bde
AB	1 bde
SF	1 bde
Arty	6 bde
MRL	1 bde

EQUIPMENT BY TYPE
MBT 340: 70 T-72; 100 T-64; 170 T-62
RECCE 19: 13 BRDM-2; 6 BRM
AIFV 399: 120 BMD-1; 9 BMD-2; 270 BMP-2
APC 309
 APC (T) 50 BTR-D
 APC (W) 259: 24 BTR-60; 25 BTR-70; 210 BTR-80
ARTY 487+
 SP 83+: **122mm** 18 2S1 *Carnation*; **152mm** 17+: 17 2S3; 2S5 (reported); **203mm** 48 2S7
 TOWED 200: **122mm** 60 D-30; **152mm** 140 2A36
 GUN/MOR 120mm 54 2S9 *Anona*
 MRL 108: **122mm** 60: 24 9P138; 36 BM-21; **220mm** 48 9P140 *Uragan*
 MOR 120mm 42: 5 2B11; 19 2S12; 18 PM-120
AT • MSL • MANPATS AT-3 9K11 *Sagger*; AT-4 9K111 *Spigot*
 GUNS 100mm 36 MT-12/T-12

Air Force 17,000

FORCES BY ROLE
7 fixed wg and hel regts.
FGA/Bbr 1 regt with 23 Su-24 *Fencer*; 11 Su-24MP *Fencer F* (recce); 1 regt with 20 Su-25 *Frogfoot*/Su-25BM *Frogfoot*; 26 Su-17MZ (Su-17M) *Fitter C*/Su-17UMZ (Su-17UM-3) *Fitter G*
Ftr 1 regt with 30 MiG-29 *Fulcrum*/MiG-29UB *Fulcrum*; 25 Su-27 *Flanker*/Su-27UB *Flanker C*
ELINT/Tpt 1 regt with 26 An-12 *Cub*/An-12PP *Cub*; 13 An-26 *Curl*/An-26RKR *Curl*
Tpt sqns with 1 An-24 *Coke*; 1 Tu-134 *Crusty*
Trg sqns with 5 L-39 *Albatros*
Hel 1 regt with 29 Mi-24 *Hind* (attack); 1 Mi-26 *Halo* (tpt); 52 Mi-8 *Hip* (aslt/tpt); 1 regt with 2 Mi-6AYa *Hook* (cmd post); 26 Mi-6 *Hook* (tpt)

EQUIPMENT BY TYPE
AIRCRAFT 135 combat capable

FTR 55: 30 MiG-29 *Fulcrum* FTR/MiG-29UB *Fulcrum*; 25 Su-27 *Flanker* FTR/Su-27UB *Flanker C*
FGA 69: 20 Su-25 *Frogfoot* FGA/Su-25BM *Frogfoot**; 23 Su-24 *Fencer*; 26 Su-17MZ (Su-17M) *Fitter C*/Su-17UMZ (Su-17UM-3)
RECCE/EW 11 Su-24MP *Fencer F**
ELINT/Tpt 39: 26 An-12 *Cub* Tpt/An-12PP *Cub*; 13 An-26 *Curl* Tpt/An-26RKR *Curl* ELINT EW
TPT 2: 1 An-24 *Coke*; 1 Tu-134 *Crusty*
TRG 14: 5 L-39 *Albatros*; 9 in store
HELICOPTERS
 ATK 29 Mi-24 *Hind*
 COMD 2 Mi-6AYa *Hook*
 SPT 79: 1 Mi-26 *Halo* (tpt); 26 Mi-6 *Hook* (tpt); 52 Mi-8 *Hip* (aslt/tpt)
AD • SAM 45
 TOWED SA-2 *Guideline*; SA-3 *Goa*
 STATIC SA-5 *Gammon* static
MSL
 ASM AS-10 *Karen*; AS-11 *Kilter*; AS-12 *Kegler*; AS-7 *Kerry*; AS-9 *Kyle*
 ARM: AS-11 *Kilter*; AS-12 *Kegler*
 AAM AA-10 *Alamo*; AA-11 *Archer*; AA-8 *Aphid*

Paramilitary up to 20,000

Internal Security Troops up to 19,000
Ministry of Interior

National Guard 1,000
Ministry of Defence

NON-STATE ARMED GROUPS
see Part II

FOREIGN FORCES
Germany 6 C-160 *Transall* Tpt Ac; 163

Table 30 Selected Arms Orders and Deliveries, Central and South Asia

Country Supplier	Classification	Designation	Quantity	Order date	Original Delivery date	Comment
Bangladesh PRC (Bng)	FGA	F-7MG	16	2005	2006	Deliveries delayed
RF	APC	BTR-80	60	2005	2006	Purchased for UN deployments
PRC	SAM	QW-2 MANPAD	_	2004	2006	
India (Ind) RF	FGA	Su-30 MKI	238	1996	_	USD8.5bn. In 2000 it was agreed that 140 ac would be completed in India. Licensed Production of 138 ac continuing
Fr	SSK	*Scorpene*	6	2005	2012	EUR2bn (USD2.55bn) First delivery expected in 2012, with one per year thereafter.
dom	SLCM	*Sagrika*	–	1983	–	Under development; estimated 300km range
dom	FGA	LCA - *Tejas*	8	1983	2012	Light Combat Aircraft. Total requirement of 220 ac
dom	FGA	LCA - *Tejas*	20	2006	_	INR24.39bn
dom	Hel	ALH - *Dhruv*	20	2006	_	INR9.55bn. Revised order
dom	DDG	Project 15A	3	2003	2008	Follow on to Project 15 *Delhi*-class. First of class ISD expected 2009
dom	UAV	*Nishant*	12	2005	–	For Indian Army. Deliveries continue
dom	MBT	*Arjun*	124	1999	–	Low-rate production began in 2004
dom	Trg	HJT-36 *Sitara*	16	1999	2007	Not yet in service
RF	CV	*Kiev*-class *Admiral Gorshkov*	1	1999	2008	USD1bn. Contract includes 16 MiG 29 K. CV renamed INS Vikramaditya. Delay announced in 2007
dom	ICBM	*Surya*	–	1999	2008	Still in development. 1st Test-flight 2005
RF	MBT	T-90	310	2000	–	186 tanks delivered. Production of remaining 124 will begin in 2007 and will see the delivery of kit form MBT
RF	SSK	*Sindhughosh*	10	2002	–	Upgrade programme continuing
dom	MBT	T-72 VT	500-600	2002	–	Upgrade programme continuing
Il	AEW	IAI-707 *Phalcon*	3	2004	2007	Still on order
RF	FGA	MiG-29K *Fulcrum* D	24	2004	2007	USD1.5bn incl 4 two seat MiG-29KUB. To equip INS *Vitramaditya* (ex CV *Gorshkov*). First delivery expected in 2007. Final delivery in 2009
UK	Trg	*Hawk* Mk132 AJT (Advanced Jet Trainer)	66	2003	2007	USD1.7bn. Delivery expected to start in September 2007 at the rate of 2 ac per month. Final delivery in 2010
dom	FGA	MiG-27	40	2005	–	Upgrade programme continuing
RF	MLRS	*Smerch*-M BM 9K58	28	2005	2006	USD500m. Deliveries continuing
It	AGHS	Oceanographic survey vessel	1	2005	2008	EUR40m (USD48m)
dom	LCA	*Tejas*	20	2005	2010	INR20bn (USD444.4m)
dom	CV	Air Defence Ship (Project 71)	1	2001	2012	USD730m. Indigenous carrier programme. Vessel laid down 2005
RF	FFG	*Talwar*	3	2006	2012	INR55.14bn (USD1.2bn) Option exercised in 2006. Final delivery expected 2013
RF / dom	ASCM	*BrahMos*	_	2006	_	Estimated USD88m. Built jointly with Russia to arm *Talwar* and *Kolkata*-class FFG

Table 30 Selected Arms Orders and Deliveries, Central and South Asia

	Country Supplier	Classification	Designation	Quantity	Order date	Original Delivery date	Comment
	RF	SLCM	*Novator* 3M14E *Klub*-S	28	2006	–	INR8.44bn (USD182m)
	dom	FGA	*Jaguar* IS	20	2006	–	INR23.4bn
	dom	SRBM	*Prithvi*	54	2006	–	INR12.13bn
	dom	Trg	HJT-36	12	2006	–	INR4.86bn
	RF	Ftr	MiG-29	67	2006	2006	Life extension upgrade. INR40bn (USD888m). To be completed in 2010
	US	SAR	UH-3H	6	2006	–	USD39m. US Navy surplus hel for LPD transfer
	dom	AAM	*Mistral*	–	2006	–	For a new combat version of *Dhruv* hel. Number of msl and value remain undisclosed. The basic fit for the *Dhruv* will be 4 ATAM in 2 launchers. To be deployed in 2009
	dom	Hel	*Dhruv*	20	2006	2008	Turret upgrade. THL-20 Turrets for Dhruv hel
	dom	LCA	*Tejas*	24	2007	–	Engine upgrade. USD100m. F404-GE-In20 afterburning turbofan engines for 20 Tejas LCA
	RF	FGA	Su-30 MKI	40	2007	2008	USD1.6bn. First 4 ac to be delivered in early 2008
Kazakhstan (Kaz)	RF	Ftr	MiG-31	20	2007	2007	Upgrade to MiG-31BM configuration. USD60m. 10 ac to be modernised in 2007, 10 ac in 2008
Pakistan (Pak)	dom	Sat	*Badr* 2	–	1993	–	In development. Range 3,000km. Based on *Taepo-dong* 2
	dom	MRBM	*Hatf* 6	–	1993	–	First test reported in 2004. Current status unknown. Possibly in limited production.
	dom	SSM	*Shaheen* 2	–	1994	–	In production mid-1999. Range 750km. Based on M-9. Aka *Hatf* 4
	US	MP	P-3C *Orion*	8	2004	2007	USD970m
	PRC	FF	*Jiangwei* II (type 053H3)	4	2005	2009	Dubbed F-22P (*Zulfiquar*) by Pak. Final delivery 2013
	US	FTR	F-16	54	2006	2007	Follow on order. Estimated between USD1.6bn and USD1.8bn. 36 F-16 A & B; 18 F-16 C & D
	It	UAV	*Galileo Falco*	4	2006	2006	–
	Swe	AEW	*Erieye*	6	2006	2008	SEK8.3bn (USD1.05bn)
	Ge	UAV	EMT LUNA	3 to 4	2006	–	Still on order
	US	Msl	SM-2 Block II AURS	10	2006	–	With 10Mk 631
	Tu	PFM	RTP 33 (*Kaan* 33) class	2	2006	2007	Delivery of first vessel expected in Oct 2007. Second of class to be delivered in Jan 2008
	dom / PRC	Ftr	JF-17 (FC-1)	150	2006	2007	8 ac to be delivered in 2007. Pak / PRC cooperation
	US	FTR	F-16C/D Block 50/52	36	2006	–	USD3bn
	US	Radar	AN/APG-68(V)9 Fire Control Radar	54	2006	–	USD99.5m. Deliveries to be completed by 2010. 36 radars (plus 7 spares) will accompany the new F-16C/D Block 50/52; 10 (plus 1 spare) will be allocated to the retrofits of older F-16s in service
	PRC	Ftr	F-10 (*Jian*-10)	36	2006	–	–

Table 30 **Selected Arms Orders and Deliveries, Central and South Asia**						
Country Supplier	Classification	Designation	Quantity	Order date	Original Delivery date	Comment
PRC	FF	F-22P	4	2007	–	Each FF to cost approx USD200m. Improved version of Jiangwei II FF. Final delivery 2013
PRC	Hel	Z-9	_	2007	–	For F-22P FF
US	MP	P-3C *Orion*	7	2007	–	Mission system upgrade and sustainment work. USD186.5m
US	FGA	F-16	_	2007	–	EW upgrade. USD78m. Installation of AN/ALQ-173 (V) advanced integrated defence EW system on Pak's F-16. To be completed in Jan 2010
US	FGA	F-16	52	2007	2008	EW upgrade. USD49.75m. Installation of AN/APG-68 (V)9 airborne fire-control radars. To be completed in 2010
US	ATGW	TOW	_	2007	–	USD185m. Tube-launched, optically tracked, wire-guided msl
US	AMRAAM	Advanced AMRAAM	500	2007	2008	USD284m also including 200 Sidewinder AAM. To be completed in 2011
US	AAM	AIM-9M *Sidewinder*	200	2007	–	Part of a USD284m contract including 500 AMPAAM
US	FTR	F-16 Block 52	18	2007	–	Targeting upgrade. USD44.5m. AN/AAQ-33 Sniper Advanced Targeting Pod

Chapter Eight
East Asia and Australasia

NORTHEAST ASIA

China, Taiwan and the Koreas

On 11 January 2007, China successfully tested a direct-ascent anti-satellite missile. This launch was not notified in advance or subsequently made public by China until the US issued a statement of complaint on 18 January. Designated the SC-19 by the US military, the missile has been assessed as a two-stage solid-fuelled medium-range missile fired from a mobile launcher; the target was an ageing Chinese weather satellite in an 850km low earth orbit. The manner of interception, and the guidance and command and control systems that must have been developed, have given pause for thought: 'the attack was executed on a spacecraft that was flying as fast – 7.42km per second – as an intercontinental ballistic missile re-entering the earth's atmosphere. Further, the satellite's destruction involved the employment of a unitary hit-to-kill warhead ... Finally, the satellite intercept occurred along the ascent trajectory of the offensive missile's flight'(Ashley Tellis, 'China's Military Space Policy', *Survival*, vol. 49, no. 3, Autumn 2007, pp. 41–2).

China's belated disclosure of this event, and the sharp and surprised international reaction, led to speculation over the degree of consultation and coordination over the test between its civil and military hierarchies. No conclusive answer has been found. However, as noted in an IISS *Strategic Comment* in January 2007, 'it seems almost unimaginable that a test did not receive explicit concurrence at the highest levels of the Chinese system, including by Hu' – that is, President Hu Jintao, chairman of the Central Military Commission. The test left a persistent legacy in orbit: by July 2007, NASA was calling the event the worst satellite fragmentation of the space age, noting that the US Space Surveillance Network was tracking more than 2,200 objects of at least 5cm in size. Furthermore, it noted that the debris cloud 'extends from 200km to 4,000km in altitude' and that 'the debris orbits are spreading rapidly and will essentially encircle the globe by the end of the year'.

While the ASAT test may have attracted most attention, over the past year Chinese force developments and budget increases have prompted continued calls for greater transparency over its military activities and intentions. When the topic was addressed by Lieutenant-General Zhang Qinsheng, deputy chief of the PLA General Staff, at the Sixth IISS *Shangri-La Dialogue* in June, he said that 'the rise of a country's military power is a dynamic process' which is difficult to evaluate precisely. 'Therefore it takes time to achieve "transparency". Anyhow, it is obvious to all that China is gradually making progress in "military transparency".' Indeed, Beijing announced in September 2007 that it would report its annual defence outlays and arms sales to the UN Military Expenditure Transparency Mechanism and Register of Conventional Arms.

However, the publication, in May 2007, of the US Department of Defense's (DoD) congressionally mandated 'Annual Report to Congress of the Military Power of the People's Republic of China' continued to point to US concern over China's military policy. While the ASAT test and increases in defence spending received prominent and critical attention, many other issues disconcerted the Pentagon. As noted in the IISS *Strategic Survey 2007*, in briefings these developments were couched in terms of 'surprise' – indicating puzzlement at Chinese intentions and hinting at the increasing success and deliberation with which China appeared to be concealing its military programmes. The report said that while the Chinese near-term focus on preparing for contingencies in the Taiwan Strait, including the possibility of US intervention, appeared to be a driver of its modernisation plans, analysis suggested that Beijing was also developing capabilities for other regional contingencies. Meanwhile, China's pursuit of area denial and anti-access strategies was expanding to include space and cyber-space, as well as the land, sea and air dimensions. China was seen as 'laying the foundation for a force able to accomplish broader regional and global objectives'. Military-to-military contacts have continued, though, culminating in an early November visit to Beijing by US Secretary of Defense Robert Gates. An agreement to establish a telephone hotline between the Pentagon and the ministry in Beijing was announced during a meeting between Gates and General Cao Gangchuan, China's Minister of National Defence.

Beijing published a White Paper on 'China's National Defence in 2006' in December of that year. The Pentagon report noted that 'as declaratory policy, the paper reflects a modest improvement in transparency, but it does not adequately address the composition of China's military forces, or the purposes and desired end-states of China's military development'. Observers generally gave China credit for including in its report more detail and data than in previous White Papers. Particularly noted were some of the more forward-leaning aspirations set out for the various service arms of the People's Liberation Army (PLA), while statements on strategic policy and military interoperability included seeing 'joint operations as the basic form'. According to Beijing, the army aims to move from 'regional defense to trans-regional mobility', improving air-ground integrated operations, long-distance manoeuvres, assault and special-operations capabilities. Meanwhile, the navy 'aims at gradual extension of the strategic depth for offshore defensive operations and enhancing its capabilities in integrated maritime operations and nuclear counterattacks' and the air force has as its objective a move away from territorial air defence to offensive and defensive operations, increasing its capabilities 'in the areas of air strike, air and missile defense, early warning and reconnaissance, and strategic projection'. Furthermore, 'The Second Artillery aims to improve its force structure with nuclear and conventional missiles, raising capabilities in strategic deterrence and conventional strike.' Statements on nuclear policy were also included, with more detail than previously seen. China's nuclear strategy was described as self-defensive and deterrent in nature, and there was a stated commitment to a policy of no first use. China's nuclear force, the document continued, was under the direct command of the Central Military Commission.

Force developments

Buoyed by a booming economy and an increasing international presence, China is continuing to modernise its military capabilities. At the Seventeenth Communist Party Congress in October 2007, Hu declared that 'in keeping with the new trends in world military affairs and the new requirements of China's development, we must promote innovation in military theory, technology, organization and development'.

An internal debate among military and defence industry policymakers appears to be nearing a conclusion as to whether to embark on an aircraft-carrier programme. A Chinese admiral was quoted at the annual parliamentary meeting in Beijing in March 2007 as saying that the Chinese shipbuilding industry was currently conducting research and development in aircraft-carrier construction and could be ready to build a vessel by the end of the decade. Other senior defence policymakers have also publicly said that China has the necessary industrial and technological expertise to build a modest-sized carrier or refurbish the ex-Soviet aircraft carrier *Varyag*, currently sitting in port in Dalian. Furthermore, as noted by the DoD report, Lieutenant-General Wang Zhiyuan, vice chairman of the Science and Technology Committee of the PLA's General Armament Department, stated in October 2006 that the 'Chinese army will study how to manufacture aircraft carriers so that we can develop our own ... Aircraft carriers are indispensable if we want to protect our interests in oceans.'

But naval developments can also be seen through the prism of strategic imperatives other than potential power-projection, particularly what the Pentagon terms area-denial and anti-access activities. While the May 2007 US report notes that ballistic missiles could form part of a strategy to increase the risk for surface ship activity, 'advanced mines, submarines, maritime strike aircraft, and modern surface combatants equipped with advanced anti-ship cruise missiles (ASCM) would form a supporting layer of defense for [China's] long-range anti-access systems'. The development of submarine capabilities is at the heart of the navy's immediate goals, even while debates take place over aircraft-carrier capability. The People's Liberation Army Navy (PLAN) is acquiring new types of nuclear and conventional submarines. Two *Shang*-class SSNs and one *Jin*-class SSBN are reported to have entered service in the past 12–24 months, while the diesel-electric *Song*-class SSK has continued to add to the conventional submarine force. The navy is also absorbing eight Type 636 diesel-electric *Kilo*-class SSKs that have been delivered from Russia. According to the Pentagon the newest of these are equipped with the supersonic SS-N-27B *Sizzler* ASCM. The Chinese navy also received two Type 956EM *Sovremenny* II guided-missile destroyers (DDG) from Russia. These are significantly more capable than two earlier model *Sovremennys*, which Russia has offered to upgrade to the latest design. Deliveries of domestically built warships have also been taking place, including two Type 052C *Luyang* II-Class DDGs, two Type 051C *Luzhou* Class DDGs as well as three Type 054A *Jiangkai* frigates.

The PLA Air Force is also undergoing modernisation. As noted, China's 2006 White Paper pointed out that the air force's mission is expanding. The top procurement priority at present is the J-10, which represents a generational advance in Chinese domestic combat fighter capabilities. The J-10s are likely to serve alongside the PLAAF's Su-27 (J-11) and Su-30MKK multi-role fighter aircraft as well as Chinese third-generation J-8II *Finback* fighters; two regiments of J-10s are currently believed to be in service in Anhui and Yunnan provinces. The Chengdu Aircraft Corporation, which produces the J-10, is reported to be working on an upgraded version of the aircraft called the Super-10 that will reportedly be equipped with a more powerful Russian-supplied engine with thrust-vectoring and passive phased-array radar.

Meanwhile, as noted in *The Military Balance 2007*, China is also developing airborne early-warning and control (AEW&C) platforms. This includes the KJ-200 programme, which is based on the *Shaanxi Y-8* transport aircraft and is being configured for the AEW&C role as well as intelligence collection and maritime surveillance, and the KJ-2000 Airborne Warning and Control system that is based on the Russian A-50 AWACS platform.

The pace of ground-force modernisation is slow in comparison to other services. The PLA is believed to have so far only acquired around 160 Type-99 main battle tanks (MBT) since the beginning of the decade. With the clearly stated goal of military chiefs being to pursue a dual-track strategy of engaging in limited modernisation of mechanised capabilities while emphasising the long-term construction of a network-enabled force, the PLA has consequently opted instead to procure larger numbers of the cheaper Type 96 MBTs and rearm its existing fleet of Type 59 and Type 63 light tanks.

The acquisition of ballistic, tactical, cruise and air-launched missiles has been a priority for the PLA over the past decade. Several new models of intercontinental ballistic missiles (ICBM), M-series tactical battlefield missiles, cruise missiles and air-to-air missiles are now entering service. These include the three-stage solid-propellant ICBM *Dongfeng* 31 and improved long-range *Dongfeng* 31A. According to Taiwanese and US intelligence estimates, the PLA currently has more than 900 short-range ballistic missiles deployed in the Nanjing Military Region, consisting of CSS-6 and CSS-7 models.

Meanwhile, China has continued to be active in deploying its forces overseas. As of September 2007, China had substantial bodies of troops with the following UN missions: MONUC in the Democratic Republic of the Congo, UNIFIL in southern Lebanon, UNMIL in Liberia and UNMIS in Sudan. Chinese forces also participated in the *Peace Mission 2007* exercises with Russia and other members of the Shanghai Cooperation Organisation, despatching over 1,500 troops and equipment (see p. 325).

Taiwan's own drive to modernise its armed forces has intensified, although the inability of Taiwan's legislature to agree on a US package of defence enhancements has slowed progress. The political stalemate was finally broken in June 2007 when approval was given for the acquisition, from the US, of 12 P-3C *Orion* ASW aircraft and upgrades to Taiwan's existing arsenal of *Patriot* Advanced Capability II missiles. These major hardware items had already been approved by the Bush Administration in 2001. The Pentagon sought US Congressional approval in September for the sale of the *Orions*, along with a mobile operations command centre and 144 SM-2 Block 3A *Standard* missiles designed to improve Taiwan's air-defence capabilities, in deals worth $2.23 billion.

Another top priority for the outgoing administration of Chen Shui-bian is to receive Washington's approval for 66 F-16C/D fighters (see *The Military Balance 2007*), which are considered crucial to offset Beijing's Su-30s and J-10s. In the event that the F-16 request is denied, the Taiwanese defence industry is believed to be considering an upgrade to its *Ching-Kuo* Indigenous Defence Fighter, with an improved flight-control system and increased weapons-carrying capacity. Meanwhile, the Taiwanese army is also seeking the purchase of 30 AH-6D *Apache Longbow* attack helicopters, worth $2.2bn, to strengthen its ground defences. The package requires parliamentary approval before it can be submitted to the US for consideration.

Taiwan has begun testing its own long-range cruise missile, the *Hsiung-feng* 2E, which according to Taiwanese military chiefs has not yet entered operational service. While this missile was absent from the island's National Day military parade in October, the first for 16 years, equipment displayed included the *Hsiung-feng* 3 surface-to-air and anti-ship missile, the under-development *Tien Kung* 3 anti-tactical ballistic missile, and an unmanned aerial vehicle that could be used for battlefield reconnaissance. As well as this modernisation effort, there is a move by the armed forces to turn itself into a professional volunteer force. The Taiwanese Defence Ministry is continuing to trim the length of compulsory military service for army recruits from 20 months to 12 months beginning in 2008, while candidates contesting the presidential election have made the establishment of an all-volunteer force within the next 4–6 years a major issue.

While **North Korea** may have halted its nuclear programme, Pyongyang continues to work on its ballistic-missile capabilities. A new medium-range ballistic missile, reportedly capable of reaching the US Territory of Guam, was publicly displayed for the first time in April. This was followed a month later by several missile firings, towards the sea, of the KN-02, a new short-range solid-fuel missile. Meanwhile, **South Korea's** defence spending continues to rise. In September 2007, Seoul announced that its 2008 defence budget would be increased by 9% to $27bn following a 9.7% rise in its 2007 military outlay. This significant jump in military expenditure will help to pay for a major overhaul of the military's organisational structure as it prepares to assume greater responsibility from the US military. Seoul has been pursuing a number of major programmes and reforms over the past year, including the launch in May 2007 of the KDX-III, the country's first *Aegis*-equipped warship; and the launch, in July 2007, of the second KSS-2 (Type 214) Air Independent Propulsion submarine. The defence ministry also approved plans to proceed with the indigenous development of a new class of 3,000-tonne submarines, which would be nearly twice the displacement of the KSS-2.

Japan's defence policy continued to demonstrate signs of new activity at the start of 2007, but its momentum subsequently slowed later in the year as a result of domestic political upheavals. Prime Minister Shinzo Abe attempted to push through a number of changes to the national military establishment and capabilities; to maintain the strengthening of the US–Japan alliance, following on from the record of cooperation in the 'war on terror' and the work of his predecessor Junichiro Koizumi; and to seek to establish a range of complementary new security relationships in East Asia and beyond.

Abe's administration oversaw the final elevation of the Japan Defence Agency to full ministerial status as the Japan Ministry of Defence (MOD) in January 2007, thus providing the first official acknowledgement in the post-war period of an equal role for the defence bureaucracy in devising national security policy. Abe's attempts to 'normalise' Japanese defence policy also included plans for the creation of a new Japan National Security Council (JNSC) to provide expert advice to the prime minster and cabinet on defence and security issues. Furthermore, in April the National Diet passed a new law to enable a national referendum on constitutional revision, while in the same month Abe established an Advisory Council to consider the legal foundations of Japanese security policy, including the exercise of the right of collective self-defence in support of the US.

Japanese moves to revise national security policy were matched by the unveiling of and plans for the procurement of new Japan Self Defense Forces (JSDF) capabilities. The first of the Maritime Self Defense Force's (MSDF) new *Hyuga*-class 13,500-tonne helicopter-carrying destroyers (DDHs) was launched in August. These are Japan's largest naval vessels built in the post-war period, resemble helicopter carriers, and will provide a highly flexible new asset for the MSDF. In addition to its primary role of air defence the *Hyuga* will offer a step-change in capability, with its ability to act as a command platform and support wider maritime operations. The Air Self Defense Force (ASDF) rolled out its first PAC-3 Ballistic Missile Defence (BMD) units in March, and rehearsed BMD deployments in central Tokyo in September.

However, Japan's defence plans were dominated in 2007 by consideration of the F-X candidates for the replacement of its ageing F-4 fighters. The preference was for the US F-22 *Raptor*. During his visit to Washington DC in April, Abe requested that the US release data on the F-22, although the US Congress has so far maintained its ban on overseas sales of the F-22. Japan's MOD has considered an upgraded F-18 and Eurofighter *Typhoon* as alternatives, but in its 2008 budget request it indicated the intent for the time being to upgrade its F-15 fighters and to develop its own stealth-technology fighter prototype. In addition, Japan will push ahead with the development and procurement of an indigenously developed P-X replacement for its P-3C, although it has deferred procurement of another indigenously developed C-X long-range transport.

Japan's domestic politics have acted to constrain defence planning. The defeat of Abe's governing Liberal Democratic Party (LDP) in the National Diet Upper House elections in July handed the opposition Democratic Party of Japan (DPJ) a strong veto position on much security legislation, and forced the eventual resignation of Abe at the start of September. Abe was succeeded by Yasuo Fukuda later the same month. As a result, Abe's plans for a JNSC are currently in abeyance, and the issue of constitutional revision has been pushed off the domestic political agenda. Moreover, defence planning has been hampered by the MOD's high leadership turnover, with four different ministers in 2007: Akio Kyuma; Yuriko Koike; Masahiko Komura; and, as of the end of 2007, Shigeru Ishiba, who has served in the post before.

Japan's domestic travails have had an impact on US–Japan alliance cooperation. Abe sought to press ahead with plans for the realignment of US bases in Japan in line with the May 2006 bilateral Defence Policy Review Initiative. Abe's administration passed legislation in April to facilitate the relocation of US Marine Corps (USMC) bases from Okinawa to Guam. However, continued local political opposition in Okinawa means that the key base issue of the relocation of the USMC air station at Futenma remains unresolved. Meanwhile, new negotiations were due to take place in late 2007 over Host Nation Support. The US has requested an increase in Japanese funding for US bases in Japan.

Concurrently, there has been much debate over Japanese support for the 'war on terror'. Abe succeeded in April in passing a two-year extension, until July 2009, of legislation enabling the ASDF transport mission in Kuwait to support the US-led coalition in Iraq, and a six-month extension until the start of November 2007 of legislation enabling the MSDF mission to provide refuelling and logistical support to coalition ships in the Indian Ocean engaged in *Operation Enduring Freedom* (OEF) in Afghanistan. The DPJ, since capturing control of the Upper House in July, had refused to cooperate with the LDP in extending the MSDF mission, on grounds that the despatch is unconstitutional due to the lack of sufficient UN mandates. The DPJ argued that Japan should instead look to participate in the ISAF operation logistically – an operation clearly mandated by the UN. As of the start of November Fukuda had been unsuccessful in his attempt to pass a new law in the Diet to extend the mission and thus on 1 November the vessels, in the absence of a legal mandate, were ordered home.

Abe's administration, at the same time as seeking to bolster the alliance relationship with the US, further sought to complement the alliance by seeking security cooperation with a number of like-minded US partners. The Japan–Australia Joint Declaration on Security Cooperation was concluded in March, specifying cooperation in counter-terrorism, maritime security, peace operations and disaster relief. Abe visited India in September and stressed the

new 'strategic' aspects of the bilateral relationship. Japan–India–US joint exercises were held in April; a Japan–US–Australia security dialogue took place in the same month; Japan, Australia, India and the US all participated in military exercises in the Bay of Bengal in September, and all four from 2007 onwards are engaged in a quadrilateral security dialogue. Further trilateral US–Japan–Australia exercises were held near Japan in October. In addition, Abe visited Europe in January and stressed Japan's desire for closer security relations with individual European states and NATO.

SOUTHEAST ASIA AND AUSTRALASIA

During 2006–07, there was substantial evidence of continuing efforts by several Southeast Asian states to modernise their armed forces, with particular emphasis on improving conventional-warfare capabilities. Driven in part by the availability of increased resources for defence as a result of economic growth that has revived after the recession of the late 1990s, military modernisation programmes in maritime Southeast Asia also reflected continued tensions and rivalry amongst members of the Association of Southeast Asian Nations (ASEAN), despite their intention to establish an ASEAN Security Community by 2020.

Though they rely on conscripts and reservists for the bulk of their manpower, and lack combat experience, the **Singapore** Armed Forces (SAF) are ahead of their Southeast Asian counterparts in terms of their doctrinal and organisational response to new military technologies and new security challenges. The '3G' (Third Generation) SAF concept emphasises the development of network-centric forces with greatly improved firepower as a way of compensating for Singapore's lack of geographical hinterland and relatively small population. There has been particular emphasis on developing Singapore's air force, which is being fundamentally reorganised, with five new functional commands replacing the pre-existing structure in which air bases were the main organisational units. Air Defence and Operations Command – the air force's 'high-readiness core' that will oversee peacetime operational commitments – became operational in January 2007, and UAV Command stood up in May. The reorganisation will be complete by mid 2008.

Singapore's air force continues to benefit from major new equipment procurement. In April 2007,

Singapore ordered four Gulfstream G550 CAEW (conformal airborne early warning aircraft), with third-generation *Phalcon* radars integrated by Israel Aircraft Industries' Elta division, to replace the present E-2Cs, with deliveries scheduled for 2008–10. During May, UAV Command unveiled its new Elbit *Hermes* 450 MALE-UAVs, up to 16 of which are equipping its third squadron. In October, an order was announced for 12 more F-15SG combat aircraft, bringing to 24 the total ordered so far. Though touted as 'fighters', it seems likely that Singapore will operate these aircraft primarily in the strike role. The requirement announced in August for provision of a Fighter Wings Course to replace the present advanced flying training squadron based at Cazaux in France is likely to result in a public–private partnership arrangement.

During the current decade, the changing international and regional security environment has forced Singapore's army to adapt to a wider array of potential challenges, and it has stressed its role alongside the police force (which includes the 1,800-strong paramilitary Singapore Gurkha Contingent) in counter-terrorism and the protection of critical national infrastructure, such as the Jurong Island petrochemical complex and Changi international airport. The addition to its order of battle of an 'active' (in other words, full-time conscript) infantry battalion tasked with POI (protection of installations) has strengthened 2 People's Defence Force Command (essentially a division-strength light infantry formation, hitherto wholly reservist), which now has specific responsibility for 'Island Defence'. New legislation gives troops powers to search and arrest.

However, Singapore's army has simultaneously maintained its drive to become a highly networked force equipped to deter conventional military aggression. Under the Singapore Armed Forces IKC2 (Integrated Knowledge-based Command and Control) doctrine, there is great emphasis on integrating 'sensors and shooters'. Surveillance (particularly through UAVs), battlefield awareness and networked communications are clearly at the core of the army's thinking. The most recent biennial Army Open House (AOH) in late August 2007 provided an opportunity to display new equipment. Though Singapore's army has operated upgraded *Centurions* (known locally as *Tempests*) since the 1970s, these were never shown in public or even acknowledged officially for fear of provoking the city-state's neighbours, neither of which operated MBTs. However, with increased confidence on the regional stage, and following Malaysia's order

for 48 PT-91M MBTs from Poland in 2003, Singapore has been markedly less reserved about publicising its acquisition from Germany of 66 refurbished ex-Bundeswehr *Leopard* 2A4 MBTs plus 30 further examples for spare parts, following an order in December 2006. Though Singapore displayed only a solitary *Leopard* at AOH, this was a significant indication of greater openness. Intriguingly, the Malaysian army showed its own MBTs for the first time the very next day, when six newly delivered PT-91Ms joined the country's 50th Merdeka (Independence) Day parade in central Kuala Lumpur. The *Leopard* aside, the range of current equipment displayed at AOH emphasised the extent to which Singapore's army has benefited from the procurement of locally developed arms and vehicles – such as the *Bionix* MkII IFV, *Pegasus* 155mm lightweight air-portable artillery, *Primus* 155mm SP artillery, and *Skylark* tactical UAVs – tailored to its own specific requirements.

Imminent procurement for Singapore's army includes multiple-launch rocket systems and new wheeled armoured vehicles. In September 2007, the US Defense Security Cooperation Agency announced Singapore's requirement for 18 M142 HIMARS (High Mobility Artillery Rocket System) launchers and associated equipment, likely to cost $330 million. If tailored to local requirements, HIMARS could provide the army with a long-range precision strike capability. An order for sufficient locally developed ST Kinetics AV81 *Terrex* 8×8 armoured fighting vehicles to equip three infantry battalions was expected in late 2007.

The Singapore navy's two main current procurement projects involve frigates and submarines. In May 2007 the navy commissioned the first of six *Formidable*-class frigates (based on the French *La Fayette*-class); the whole class is due to be operational by 2009. The two ex-Swedish navy *Västergötland*-class submarines ordered in November 2005 will supplement (rather than replace) Singapore's four *Challenger*-class boats from 2010. In September 2007, the navy again sent one of its *Endurance*-class LSTs to the Gulf for a three-month deployment in support of multinational operations.

Malaysia's armed forces continue to receive new equipment, though on a more modest scale than Singapore's. The most significant development during 2007 was the arrival of the Su-30MKM combat aircraft ordered in 2003. Six were delivered mid year, and all were expected to be in service at the new air-force base of Gong Kedak in Kelantan state by the year's end. All 10 PC-7 MkII training aircraft ordered in 2006 had been delivered by April. In July, Defence Minister Najib Tun Razak announced plans to replace the air force's 20 remaining S-61A *Nuri* helicopters. Apart from two *Lekiu* II-class frigates, for which BAE Systems received a letter of intent during 2006, and two *Scorpene* submarines due for delivery in 2009 (the first of which was launched in October), other major procurement in prospect for the navy includes two LPD-type 'multi-role support ships'.

Indonesia's armed forces are benefiting from increased budgetary allocations to compensate for the government's efforts to constrain the military's non-budgetary income sources. When President Putin visited Jakarta in September 2007, he and President Susilo Bambang Yudhoyono signed a much-heralded loan agreement under which Moscow agreed to provide credit worth $1bn for the purchase of Russian defence equipment, including 10 Mi-17V-5 and 5 Mi-35PN helicopters, 30 BMP-3 infantry combat vehicles, and two Type 636 *Kilo*-class submarines. It had been anticipated that this agreement with Russia might cover three Su-30MK and three Su-27SM combat aircraft, but instead Jakarta is negotiating with India to purchase as many as 44 Su-30MKIs from the Hindustan Aeronautics-IRKUT-BrahMos consortium which is already producing them for the Indian Air Force. If India is able to provide suitable financing, the Indonesian air force will receive six Su-30MKI MkIIIs in the first instance, with 38 more being delivered by 2014. Indonesia is also negotiating to buy 100 light battlefield-surveillance radars and naval spares from India. In November 2007, Indonesia's navy is expected to commission the first of four large vessels – three LPDs and one fleet command ship – ordered from South Korea in 2005. Two of the LPDs will be built in Indonesia, and all are expected to be in service by 2012.

Driven in part by the need to replace its navy's ageing *Exocet* and *Harpoon* anti-ship missiles in order to maintain a deterrent capability against external intervention, since early 2005 Indonesia has indicated serious interest in acquiring more modern naval cruise missiles or developing and manufacturing such missiles indigenously, though with Chinese technical assistance. In mid 2005, Indonesia purchased three CSS-N-8/YJ-2 *Saccade* missile systems; it has also shown interest in the Indo-Russian PJ-10 *BrahMos* missile system.

In **Thailand**, the armed forces, which usurped Thaksin Shinawatra's elected government in September 2006, awarded themselves substantial funding increments in the 2007 and 2008 budgets, which respectively saw 34% and 28% increases in the allocation to the military. Following constrained budgets in the wake of the 1997–98 financial crisis, this greatly expanded funding has allowed renewed major procurement. In late September, a cabinet meeting approved the acquisition of 96 Ukrainian BTR-3E1 armoured vehicles, large quantities of Israeli-made light machine guns and assault rifles, and new C-801 anti-ship missile rounds for the navy's *Chao Phraya*-class frigates. Though the government claimed that the new army equipment was not intended for use in any particular area, it would clearly be of relevance to the army's counter-insurgency operations in Thailand's troubled southernmost provinces. In October, the cabinet approved $1.1bn in funding for major air force procurement from Sweden, consisting of 12 JAS-39C/D multi-role fighters and two Saab S-1000 *Erieye* AEW aircraft. Funding for the purchase will be spread over the decade from 2008–17.

During 2007 the Thai army, supported by the police, continued intensive operations in the country's three southernmost provinces, where the Malay–Muslim separatist insurgency has revived since January 2004. Bombings, arson and shootings by the 5,000 or so insurgents continued throughout the year. The insurgents continued to demonstrate tactical ingenuity, introducing new means of triggering roadside improvised explosive devices. In late April it was reported that the government planned to deploy a further 15,000 troops to the deep south, particularly to protect lines of communication. These would supplement 20–30,000 troops already there. Simultaneously, though, Bangkok has relied increasingly on 'army rangers', locally recruited militia troops who have earned a reputation in the south for abusing non-combatants. In May, the government allocated an additional 1 billion baht ($30m) to support security operations in the south. In July, the director of the Southern Border Provinces Administrative Centre (a multi-agency organisation revived in November 2006), Pranai Suwanrath, spoke of significantly strengthening village defences by 2009. Equipment ordered during 2007 is intended to enhance the army's counter-insurgent capabilities.

Since 2002, the Armed Forces of the **Philippines** (AFP) have remained largely dependent on US military aid – supplied essentially to bolster Manila's military capability against the Abu Sayyaf Group (ASG) in the country's south – to fund their equipment purchases. However, in September 2007, the

Philippines' blossoming relationship with Beijing brought an offer of military assistance when China's defence minister, Cao Gangchuan, visited Manila. As part of a package of bilateral agreements (reportedly including one covering oil exploration in disputed areas of the South China Sea), Cao promised an initial $6.6m worth of assistance for the AFP as a 'confidence-building measure'. This will be used to fund the supply of non-lethal army equipment, initiate a Chinese-language programme within the AFP, support AFP participation in naval exercises with the PLAN, and provide places for AFP officers on courses in China. Cao reportedly pledged much larger military assistance in the longer-term.

By early 2007, *Oplan Ultimatum*, the largest offensive since 2002–03 by the AFP in the south of the country, had substantially weakened the ASG. The operation had substantial support from the United States' armed forces, notably the 150-strong, forward-deployed Joint Special Operations Task Force–Philippines. Though *Oplan Ultimatum* succeeded in further reducing the ASG's strength, the Muslim insurgent group continued to pose a serious threat to security. In early July, an AFP operation to free a kidnapped Italian priest resulted in a combined force of ASG guerrillas and Moro Islamic Liberation Front (MILF) elements killing 14 AFP personnel. An ensuing investigation assigned some blame to the AFP for allowing its troops to stray without warning into territory controlled by the MILF, violating a ceasefire agreement. The incident stimulated a renewed AFP offensive against the ASG, but also the establishment of a Joint Monitoring and Assistance Team to improve communications between the AFP and MILF.

The latest version of Canberra's Defence Capability Plan 2006–2016, released in June 2006, outlined likely major procurement for **Australia**'s armed forces over the coming decade. Subsequently, a series of announcements has provided more detail. In March 2007, it was announced that 24 F-18E/F *Super Hornet* strike aircraft would be delivered from 2010 to bridge the gap between the retirement of the air force's fleet of F-111s and the likely entry into service of the F-35 Joint Strike Fighter from 2013. It also became clear that Canberra had selected the C-27J to succeed the air force's *Caribou* light transport aircraft, though an order seemed likely only after the federal election in November. In June, the defence department announced that Spanish designs had been selected for two key naval requirements. The *Hobart*-class next-generation Air Warfare Destroyer (AWD) will be based on the Navantia 100. Three *Aegis*-equipped AWDs, costing approximately $7.3m, will enter service from 2014–17. A Navantia design will also provide the basis for two large *Canberra*-class amphibious ships (essentially helicopter carriers) to enter service from 2013. In July, the defence department – concerned to find an eventual replacement for the air force's AP-3C fleet – granted 'first pass approval' for negotiations with the US Navy over Australian participation in the P-8A Multi-mission Maritime Aircraft programme.

EAST ASIA AND AUSTRALASIA – DEFENCE ECONOMICS

With **Australia** having recorded more than 15 years of continuous economic growth, in 2007 the International Monetary Fund (IMF) commended Australian authorities for their exemplary macro-economic management, which 'is now widely recognized as being at the forefront of international best practice'. The Fund noted that sound fiscal, monetary and structural policies, against a background of sizeable terms of trade gains, have created the conditions for continued expansion, supported by high employment levels. The government's healthy budget surplus (1.3% of GDP in 2007) led to a 10% increase in the defence budget, which rose from A\$19.9bn in 2006 to A\$22.0bn in 2007. The budget included details of a further A\$14bn to be spent over the next decade, meaning that in the past 18 months the government has committed to A\$41bn worth of new defence initiatives over the next ten years: A\$16bn in the 2006 budget, A\$14bn in the 2007 budget and A\$11bn in the period between budgets (A\$10bn to expand the army by two light infantry divisions and A\$1bn on a range of recruitment and retention initiatives).

The 2007 budget focuses heavily on two particular issues: new procurement and further measures designed to boost recruitment and retention in the Australian Defence Force (ADF). The major procurement development announced during the year was the decision to acquire 24 Boeing F/A-18F Block II *Super Hornet* multi-role aircraft at a cost of A\$6bn over a 10-year period. While the Australian air force remains fully committed in the medium term to

acquiring the Joint Strike Fighter (JSF), with an initial requirement of three squadrons, the procurement of the *Super Hornets* is designed to insure against any potential slippage in the JSF programme. Australia is expecting to receive its first JSF in 2013 and has indicated that in the long term it will consider operating either a mixed fleet of *Super Hornets* and JSFs or opt for a fourth squadron of JSFs, although it is thought that the preferred solution would be to operate four squadrons of JSF aircraft and 'on-sell' the *Super Hornets*. The 2007 budget provides an initial A\$620m for the procurement of the aircraft.

In addition to the *Super Hornet* funding the 2007 budget includes another A\$8bn in new initiatives for the coming decade:

- A\$2.1bn to boost retention and recruitment
- A\$1.8bn of additional logistics funding
- A\$1.3bn for C-17 personnel and operating costs
- A\$1.3bn for operational supplementation (Iraq, Afghanistan and Timor Leste)
- A\$950m for improved housing
- A\$392m on intelligence initiatives

However, despite the announced total of A\$41bn in new funding for the coming decade, doubts remain over whether the ADF will be able to finance all its planned operational activities and procurement programmes. It seems inevitable that, with rising personnel costs and escalating investment levels, money available for operating activities will be squeezed. There is particular concern that there are insufficient funds planned to cover the additional

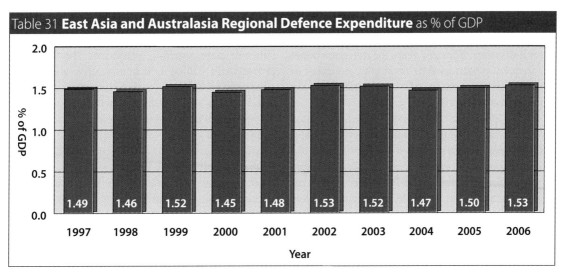

Table 31 **East Asia and Australasia Regional Defence Expenditure** as % of GDP

Year	% of GDP
1997	1.49
1998	1.46
1999	1.52
2000	1.45
2001	1.48
2002	1.53
2003	1.52
2004	1.47
2005	1.50
2006	1.53

East Asia and Australasia

personnel and operating costs associated with the delivery of new equipment such as the *Wedgetail* Airborne Early Warning and Control aircraft, armed reconnaissance helicopters and air-to-air refuelling aircraft, all due for delivery in 2009.

Furthermore, due to delays in the *Wedgetail* and M113 upgrade projects, A$400m of investment was deferred from 2006 into the two subsequent years; this was compounded by the 2007 budget, which deferred a further A$1.8bn to at least 2010 and beyond. Therefore a total of A$2.2bn in new capability will now arrive behind schedule, while the approval of projects from the 2006 Defence Capability Plan has already fallen behind schedule – even though the document is just over 12 months old. The result is that investment in major capital equipment needs to grow from A$4.8 in 2007 to A$6.9bn by 2010.

A strong economic performance, led by sound macroeconomic policies and a favourable external environment, enabled **Indonesia** to complete the early repayment of its remaining obligations to the IMF in October 2006. With a buoyant domestic economy, the official defence budget – which had averaged Rp23 trillion between 2004 and 2006 – jumped to Rp32.6tr in 2007, enabling Jakarta to conclude a number of significant procurement programmes. It should be noted that the official defence budget does not capture the true extent of Indonesian defence expenditure, as it fails to include military pensions and benefits for retired personnel, overseas procurement (often financed through barter arrangements) or the revenue generated by the military's considerable business interests. With the release of the 2007 budget, Defence Minister Juwono Sudarsono revealed that Indonesia would prioritise land, air and sea transport capabilities over the coming decade in order to deal with non-military threats such as natural disasters. In recent years the defence budget has frequently been used to assist with a number of natural disasters, including the 2004 tsunami and the Sidoarjo mudflows.

In late 2006, the Indonesian president visited Moscow, where a number of nuclear, aerospace and defence agreements were signed. Under the terms of a US$1bn export credit arrangement, Russia will supply the armed forces with three Su-27 interceptor/ground attack aircraft, three Su-30MK multi-role fighters (including armaments and spares), two submarines, 10 Mi-17 multi-role helicopters, 5 Mi-35 attack helicopters, 20 BMP-3 armoured infantry fighting vehicles and two packages of anti-ship missiles.

Indonesia is thought to have opted for Russian rather than American equipment for fear of a repeat of the 11-year partial US arms embargo, during which Indonesia encountered difficulty obtaining spare parts for its F-16 aircraft, many of which were grounded as a result.

Having remained virtually static at around THB80bn between 2000 and 2006, **Thailand's** defence budget jumped to THB115bn in 2007 and is forecast to reach THB143bn in 2008. Prior to the military coup in late 2006, then-Prime Minister Thaksin Shinawatra had authorised a substantial 10-year US$6bn defence procurement plan that included a wide range of weapons systems for all three services. However, it now appears that this ambitious initiative has been shelved and will be replaced by a more modest three-year programme, casting doubt on the acquisition of certain major systems. In revealing the new budget, the Thai Ministry of Defence suggested that the increase in funding was primarily to address the security situation in the south of the country rather than to provide for new equipment procurement. It was also revealed that the new government would discontinue the former prime minister's strategy of bartering Thai commodities and agricultural products for military equipment. In 2005, for example, the army purchased armoured vehicles from China in exchange for dried fruit, and there were long-standing plans to acquire new fighter aircraft from Russia in exchange for Thai chickens. Despite scaling down the previous 10-year procurement plan, recent purchases by Malaysia, Vietnam and Indonesia of modern Sukhoi aircraft propelled the Thai government to announce that it would begin the process of replacing the air force's ageing fleet of F-5s. In October 2007, it was confirmed that Thailand will purchase 12 JAS 39 *Gripen* multi-role combat aircraft from Saab as well as two *Erieye* airborne early warning platforms. The US$1.1bn procurement will be split into two five-year phases – between 2008 and 2012, six *Gripen* aircraft and one *Erieye* aircraft will be delivered, whilst the remaining platforms will be delivered between 2013–17.

In June 2007, the army requested a total of THB17.6bn to fund counter-insurgency operations by the Internal Security Operation Command in the south over the coming four years. The money is categorised as a so-called 'secret budget', meaning that it can be spent by officials without having to account to the government. However, critics of the government's strategy in the south have pointed out that the vast majority of these funds will be accounted for

Table 32 China – Estimated Total Military-Related Revenue 2005

	RMB bn	US$bn at market exchange rates	US$bn incl. PPP estimates
Official PLA budget (Including local militia funding)	244	29.8	71.0
Foreign weapons purchase (1998–2005 average)	14.7	1.8	1.8
Subsidies			
Loss-making enterprises	4.8	0.58	0.58
Defence Industry	40.9	5.0	5.0
R&D	36.7	4.48	4.48
New Product Expenditure	42.3	5.16	5.16
Arms Exports (50% of annual average 1998–2005)	2.9	0.35	0.35
People's Armed Police			
Central Funding	28.5	3.47	13.1
Local Funding	4.1	0.5	1.88
Total	418.9	51.1	103.4
% of GDP	2.24		

by salaries and welfare benefits for the 20,000 troops deployed in the region and that the remainder was insufficient to fund military training programmes and deal with emergencies that are likely to arise. The distribution of funds will fall from THB5.2bn in 2008 to just THB500m in 2011, suggesting that although the army expects the insurgency to last for four years it is also expecting to have made huge progress by the end of the period.

Despite continuing pressure from Washington to make progress on the 'special' arms-procurement package offered to **Taiwan** in 2001, to date there has been only modest advancement with the initiative. Originally the US had offered Taipei a comprehensive package including submarines, maritime patrol aircraft and PAC-3 air defence systems; however, persistent delaying tactics by the government's opponents in the Taiwanese legislature have left elements of the programme in some doubt. Indeed, it was only in mid 2007 that the go-ahead for the acquisition of 12 second-hand P-3C *Orion* aircraft was finally agreed, while the procurement of the PAC-3 systems appears to have little chance of success after the Taipei legislature agreed to fund the upgrade of existing PAC-2 units rather than purchase new units. In 2007, out of the total defence budget of NT$311bn, only minimal funds for the US procurement package were made available: NT$6.1bn towards the P-3C *Orion* aircraft, NT$3.5bn to begin upgrading three PAC-2 systems to PAC-3 standard and just NT$200m for a study evaluating the proposed acquisition of eight diesel-electric submarines. Whereas the original total package had a value of some US$17bn, so far only around US$200m

has been made available. In a related development, the government froze one-third of the NT$16bn outlay for the proposed purchase of 66 F-16C/D aircraft, a procurement that Washington says is dependent on the successful conclusion of the 'special' arms package. While Taiwan has repeatedly declared that it intends to boost defence spending to 3% of GDP, the 2007 budget will only amount to 2.2% of preliminary figures for national output.

Once again the **Chinese** economy continued to drive growth in the region as surging investment and exports resulted in GDP growth of 11.5%, the fifth year of double-digit economic growth. And, although growth is likely to slow in light of softer external demand and policy measures designed to achieve a more balanced and inclusive economy – dependent more on private consumption and services and less on exports, investment and industry – the economy is still expected to grow by around 10% in 2008.

In 2006, the National People's Congress endorsed the 11th Five-Year Programme (2006–11), which continued the government's emphasis of recent years on achieving balanced, equitable and sustainable growth. Of the 22 major goals outlined in the programme, just two relate to economic growth, while the remainder focus on population growth, the use of natural resources, the environment and living standards. The new programme is notable for its strong emphasis on rural development and includes a pledge to raise farmers' incomes and to promote public services in the countryside.

Although the five-year plan makes no reference to defence-related spending, it was unsurprising when the official state budget for 2007 included a substantial increase in the defence budget, up 25% to RMB350bn (US$46.7bn when converted at market exchange rates (MER)). However, as illustrated in the essay 'Calculating China's Defence Expenditure' in *The Military Balance 2006,* the official defence budget, while a helpful indicator of the overall trend in military spending, does not reflect the true level of resources devoted to the People's Liberation Army (PLA).

According to the 2006 White Paper, the official defence budget is broadly distributed in equal shares among three categories: personnel, operations and equipment. However, it is widely understood that the official budget takes no account of several other military-related expenditures, including weapons purchased from overseas, revenue generated by China's own arms exports, subsidies to the defence industry, or R&D funding. In addition, attempts to calculate China's true military burden should include funds allocated to the People's Armed Police.

In attempting to arrive at a figure for total Chinese defence expenditure there is also the problem of exchange rates. At the 2005 MER – RMB8.19 to US$1 – China's GDP measured US$2.2tr; however, in the case of developing economies, it is conventional to use a different methodology know as Purchasing Power Parity (PPP). PPP rates are a technique used to make the comparison of a range of goods and services

between different countries more meaningful. For example, the World Bank has calculated that at PPP rates, China's 2005 GDP was the equivalent of US$8.5tr, nearly four times greater than suggested by using the MER. In calculating the figures in Table 32, *The Military Balance* uses a combination of PPP and MER rates which are applied to different parts of military expenditure.

The results of this methodology indicate that total military-related revenue available to the PLA in 2005 amounted to RMB418.9bn, about 1.7 times the official state-budget figure of RMB244bn, which equals 2.24% of GDP. Converted into US dollars at the prevailing market exchange rate this would equal US$51.1bn; if, however, certain elements of the budget are converted at the World Bank PPP rate then the US-dollar equivalent figure jumps to US$103.4bn, illustrating the sensitivity of using different approaches to this difficult subject.

Note: Although the use of PPP rates may be a useful tool when comparing macro economic data, such as GDP, between countries at different stages of development, because there exists no specific PPP rate to apply to the military sector its use for this purpose should be treated with caution. In addition, there is no definitive guide as to which elements of military spending should be calculated using available PPP rates.

Australia Aus

Australian Dollar A$		2006	2007	2008
GDP	A$	965bn	1,069bn	
	US$	731bn	792bn	
per capita	US$	36,077	47,558	
Growth	%	2.7	4.4	
Inflation	%	3.5	2.2	
Def exp[a]	A$	22.7bn		
	US$	17.2bn		
Def bdgt	A$	19.9bn	21.9bn	
	US$	15.1bn	19.9bn	
US$1=A$		1.32	1.10	

a Including military pensions

Population 20,434,176

Ethnic groups: Asian 4%; Aborigines <1%

Age	0–14	15–19	20–24	25–29	30–64	65 plus
Male	10%	4%	3%	3%	24%	6%
Female	10%	3%	3%	3%	23%	7%

Capabilities

ACTIVE 51,293 (Army 25,259 Navy 12,784 Air 13,250)

RESERVE 21,450 (Army 17,200 Navy 1,850 Air 2,400)

The High Readiness Reserve (announced by the Australian Government in May 2006) of 2,800 army and 1,400 air force personnel is intended to strengthen the Australian Defence Force (ADF) with members trained to the same skill levels as the Regular Force. The High Readiness Reserve will be available for deployment within the same timeframes of 28 days or less.

ORGANISATIONS BY SERVICE

Army 25,259

Land Command
FORCES BY ROLE
1 Land HQ, 1 Deployable Joint Force HQ, 1 Logistic Support Force HQ

Mech	1 bde HQ (1st) (1 armd regt, 1 recce regt, 1 mech inf bn ((7th), 1 lt inf bn (5th) (7th RAR, to be at full strength by 2008), 1 med arty regt, 1 cbt engr regt, 1 cbt spt regt, 1 cbt service spt bn)
Surv	3 (regional force) units
EW	1 regt
Mot inf	1 bde HQ (7th) (1 recce regt, 2 mot inf bn, 1 inf bn, (1 lt inf bn (8/9) being raised to be op by 2010), 1 fd arty regt, 1 cbt engr regt, 1 cbt spt regt, 1 cbt service spt bn)
Lt inf	1 bde HQ (3rd) (1 Para bn (converting to light infantry by 2008), 2 inf bn, 1 APC sqn, 1 fd arty regt, 1 cbt engr regt, 1 cbt spt regt, 1 cbt service spt bn)
Para	1 bn (3 RAR) (converting to lt inf remaining with 3 bde)
Avn	1 bde HQ; 1 Avn regt (1 Special Ops sqn, 1 Avn regt (2 recce hel sqn), 1 (FW) surv sqn, 1 Avn regt (2 tpt hel sqn, 1 spt hel sqn))
STA	1 (20th) regt (1 STA bty, 1 UAV bty, 1 combat service support bty)

Force support 3 bn
AD 1 regt
Construction 2 sqn

Special Operations Command
FORCES BY ROLE
1 Special Operations HQ

SF	1 SAS regt
Cdo	2 bn (4th RAR and 1st cdo (reserve))
Sigs	1 coy
Combat Service support	2 coy
Incident Response	1 regt

EQUIPMENT BY TYPE
MBT 172: 101 M1-A1 *Abrams;* 71 *Leopard 1* A3 in store (decommissioned)
AIFV (W) 299 ASLAV-25 (all variants, being delivered)
APC APC (T) 487: 364 M-113 (350 to be upgraded), 119 in store; 4 M-113AS4
LFV 299 *Bushmaster* IMV (being delivered)
ARTY 566
    TOWED 270: **105mm** 234: 109 L-118 Light Gun; 125 L-5/M-2A2; **155mm** 36 M-198
    MOR 81mm 296
AT • MSL • MANPATS *Javelin*
    RCL 651: **84mm** 577 *Carl Gustav;* **106mm** 74 M-40A1
AMPHIBIOUS 21: 6 LCM-2000 (not yet operational);15 LCM-8 (capacity either 1 MBT tank or 200 troops); 6 LCM-2000 (not yet operational)
AIRCRAFT • TPT 3 Beech 350 B300 (on lease)
HELICOPTERS 22 attack helicopters
    ATK 22 AS-665 *Tiger* (delivery from July 2004, ongoing)
    SPT 44: 6 CH-47D *Chinook;* 34 S-70 A-9 (S-70A) *Black Hawk;* 4 NH-90 TTH (of 40 army order)
    UTL 66: 41 Bell 206B-1 *Kiowa* (to be upgraded); 25 UH-1H *Iroquois* in store (decommissioned)
AD • SAM 48
    TOWED 18 *Rapier* B1M in store (decommissioned)
    MANPAD 30 RBS-70
RADAR • LAND 21: 7 AN/TPQ-36 *Firefinder* (arty, mor); 14 RASIT (veh, arty)

Training Command 3,160

Reserve Organisations

Land Command 17,200 reservists

East Asia and Australasia

FORCES BY ROLE

Comms	1 div HQ, 6 bde HQ
Inf	1 bde HQ (8th) (1 APC sqn, 2 inf bn, 1 fd arty regt, 1 cbt engr regt, 1 combat service support bn);
	1 bde HQ (5th) (1 armd recce regt, 2 inf bn, 1 fd arty regt, 1 cbt engr regt, 1 combat service support bn);
	1 bde HQ (13th) (1 armd recce sqn, 2 inf bn, 1 fd arty bty, 1 cbt engr sqn, 1 combat service support bn);
	1 bde HQ (9th) (1 APC sqn, 2 inf bn, 2 fd arty bty, 1 cbt engr sqn, 1 combat service support bn);
	1 bde HQ (4th) (1 armd recce regt, 2 inf bn, 1 med arty regt, 1 cbt engr regt, 1 combat service support bn);
	1 bde HQ (11th) (1 armd recce sqn, 2 inf bn, 1 cbt engr sqn, 1 combat service support bn)
Sigs	1 regt
Engr	2 regt
Construction	

Navy 12,784

EQUIPMENT BY TYPE

SUBMARINES • TACTICAL • SSK 6 *Collins* each with UGM-84C *Harpoon* tactical USGW, 6 single 533mm TT each with 1 Mk48 *Sea Arrow* HWT

PRINCIPAL SURFACE COMBATANTS • FRIGATES 12

FFG 4:

3 *Adelaide* each with 1 Mk 13 GMLS each with RGM-84C *Harpoon* SSM, SM-1 MR naval SAM, 2 Mk32 triple 324mm ASTT each with Mk 46 LWT, 1 76mm, 2 S-70B *Seahawk* ASW hel (SM-2 capability upgrades in progress)

1 *Adelaide* (Mod) eqpt with 1 Mk 13 GMLS eqpt. with RGM-84C *Harpoon* SSM, SM-2 MR naval SAM, 1 8 cell Mk 41 VLS (32 eff.) eqpt. with up to 32 RIM-162 Evolved *Sea Sparrow* naval SAM, 2 Mk32 triple 324mm ASTT eqpt. with Mk MU90 LWT, 1 76mm, 2 S-70B *Seahawk* ASW hel

FF 8 *Anzac* (Ge MEKO 200) each with 1 8 cell Mk 41 VLS (32 eff.) each with up to 32 RIM-162 *Evolved Sea Sparrow* naval SAM, 2 triple 324mm ASTT eqpt. with Mk 46 LWT, 1 127mm, 1 SH-2G *Super Seasprite* ASW hel

PATROL AND COASTAL COMBATANTS • PCO 11 *Armidale* each with 1 25mm gun

MINE WARFARE • MINE COUNTERMEASURES 8

MHC 6 *Huon*

MSC 2 *Bandicoot*

MSD 3

AMPHIBIOUS

PRINCIPAL AMPHIBIOUS SHIPS • LPH 2:

2 *Kanimbla* (capacity either 4 UH-60 *Black Hawk* utl hel or 3 *Sea King* MK-50A utl hel; 2 LCM; 450 troops)

LS • LST 1 *Tobruk* (capacity 2 *Sea King* MK-50A utl hel; 2 LCM; 2 LCVP; 40 APC and 18 *Leopard* 1 A3 MBT; 500 troops)

LANDING CRAFT 20:

LCH 6 *Balikpapan* (capacity 3 MBT or 13 APC)

LCM 14

LOGISTICS AND SUPPORT 23

AORH 2: 1 *Success*; 1 *Sirius*

AOL 4 *Warrigal*

AE 3 *Wattle*

ASR 3

AGHS (SVY) 2 *Leuwin*

AGS 4 *Paluma*

TRG 2: 1 **AXL**; 1 **AXS**

TRV 3

Naval Aviation 990

FORCES BY ROLE

ASW	1 sqn
ASUW	1 sqn
Spt	1 sqn
Trg	1 sqn

EQUIPMENT BY TYPE

HELICOPTERS 46

ASW 27: 16 S-70B-2; 11 SH-2G *Super Seasprite*

MAR SPT 6 *Sea King* MK50A

SPT 13 AS-350BA *Ecureuil*

FACILITIES

Bases Located at Sydney (NSW), Darwin (NT), Cairns (QLD), Stirling (WA), Jervis Bay(NSW), Nowra (NSW), Flinders(SA).

Fleet Command

Navy 1 HQ located at Stirling

Naval Systems Comd

Navy 1 HQ located at Canberra

Air Force 13,250

Flying hours 175 hrs/year on F/A-18 *Hornet* FGA; 200 hrs/year on F-111 *Aardvark* bbr ac

FORCES BY ROLE

Air Cmnd coordinates air force operations. HQ Air Cmnd is responsible for developing and delivering the capability to command and control air operations. The air commander controls the activities of six subordinate Force Element Groups – Air Cbt, Air Lift, Aerospace Ops support, Combat Support, Surveillance and Response, Air Force Training.

Air cbt	1 gp with 135 ac and 2,000 personnel, (1 ftr/tac wg (1 OCU, 3 ftr sqn with 55 F/A-18A *Hornet*; 16 F/A-18B *Hornet*), 1 recce/strike wg (2 FGA/recce sqn with 17 F-111C *Aardvark*; 4 RF-111 *Aardvark* (photo recce); 5 F-111G *Aardvark* (op trg); 2 LIFT sqn with 33 *Hawk* MK127));1 Fwd air cbt dev unit with 4 PC-9/A(F)

Surv/ Response	1 gp (1 sqn, 1 OCU MP component) with 19 AP-3C *Orion*; 1 sqn surv component with 6 Boeing 737-700 '*Wedgetail*' AEW&C on order for intro service 2007; 1 control and reporting wg with 4 tactical AD radars; 1 radar surv unit with *Jindalee* Operational Radar Network correlation centre at Edinburgh (S. Australia), 2 *Jindalee* radar sensors at Laverton (W.Australia) and Longreach (N. Queensland); 1 *Jindalee* facility at Alice Springs; 2 AD Command & Control Centres at Williamtown (NSW) and Tindal (NT)
SAR	S-76 (civil contract) at 4 air bases
Airlift	1 gp (1 tkr/tpt sqn with 4 B-707-338C, 1 tpt sqn with 2 C-17 (2 more on order); 1 special purpose/VIP tpt sqn with 2 B-737 BBJ; 3 CL-604 *Challenger*, 1 light tact tpt sqn with 14 DHC-4 *Caribou*, 2 medium tpt sqn with; 12 C-130H *Hercules*; 12 C-130J *Hercules*)
Trg	Air trg wg manages: ADF Basic Flying Training School (Tamworth) PC-9/A; No 2 Flying Training School (Pearce) PC-9/A; Combat Survival and Training School (Townsville); Central Flying School and Roulettes Aerobatic Team (East Sale); School of Aviation Warfare (East Sale); School of Air Traffic Control (East Sale); and No 32 Squadron with 8 Beech 300 *Super King Air* (navigation trg) (East Sale). Flt trg schl with 58 PC-9/A
Cbt sup gp	2 cbt spt wgs; 1 Expeditionary cbt spt wg; 1 airfield def wg (3 sqn); 1 Health Services Wg
Reserve Training Wing	13 Sqn (Darwin); 21 Sqn (Williams); 22 Sqn (Richmond); 23 Sqn (Amberley); 24 Sqn (Edinburgh); 25 Sqn (Perth); 26 Sqn (Williamtown); 27 Sqn (Townsville); 28 Sqn (Canberra); 29 Sqn (Hobart).

EQUIPMENT BY TYPE
AIRCRAFT 120 combat capable
BBR 22: 17 F-111C *Aardvark*; 5 F-111G *Aardvark* (7 F-111G in store)
FGA 71: 55 F/A-18A *Hornet*; 16 F/A-18B *Hornet*
LIFT 33 *Hawk* Mk127
RECCE 4 RF-111C *Aardvark**
MP 19 AP-3C *Orion**
AWACS 6 B-737 *Wedgetail* being delivered
TPT 51: 2 C-17 *Globemaster* (2 more by 2008); 4 B-707 (tkr/tpt); 2 B-737 BBJ (VIP); 12 C-130H *Hercules*; 12 C-130J *Hercules*; 3 CL-604 *Challenger* (VIP); 14 DHC-4 *Caribou*
TRG 70: 62 PC-9/A(incl 4 PC-9/A(F) for tgt marking); 8 Beech 300 *Super King Air* (navigation trg);
HELICOPTERS • UTL 5–7 S-76 (civil contract)
RADAR • AD RADAR 8
OTH-B *Jindalee* 4
Tactical 4
MSL • TACTICAL •
ASM AGM-84A *Harpoon*; AGM-142E *Raptor*; AGM-158 *JASSM* on order

AAM AIM-120 AMRAAM; AIM-9M *Sidewinder*; AIM-132 ASRAAM: AIM-7M *Sparrow*;
BOMBS
Conventional: Mk 82 500lb GP; Mk 84 2,000lb GP; BLU-109/B 2,000lb penetrator
Laser-guided: *Paveway* II/IV
INS/GPS guided: JDAM on order

Paramilitary

Australian Customs Service
PATROL AND COASTAL COMBATANTS 10:
PSOH 1 *Triton*
PSO 1
PCC 8 *Bay*
AIRCRAFT
MP/Surv 14: 6 BN-2B *Islander*; 5 DHC-8 *Dash 8*; 3 F406 *Caravan II*
SAR 1 AC50 *Shrike*
HELICOPTERS • UTL 1 Bell 206L *LongRanger*; 1 Bell 214

DEPLOYMENT

AFGHANISTAN
NATO • ISAF
907

EQUIPMENT BY TYPE
LFV 25 *Bushmaster* IMV
Tpt 3 C-130J *Hercules*
HEL 2 *Chinook*
UAV *Skylark*
UN • UNAMA 1 obs

EGYPT
MFO 25 (*Operation Mazurka*)

IRAQ
MNF • *Operation Iraqi Freedom*
Air force
AIRCRAFT • MARITIME PATROL 4: 2 P-3C *Orion* ; 2 C-130H
Army 1,575 (*Operation Catalyst*); UAV *Skylark*
Navy FF 1 *Anzac-class*
UN • UNAMI 1 obs

MALAYSIA
Army 115
1 inf coy (on 3-month rotational tours)
Air force 1 AP-3C crew (13)

MIDDLE EAST
UN • UNTSO 12 obs

PAPUA NEW GUINEA
Army 38 1 trg unit

SOLOMON ISLANDS
RAMSI
FORCES BY ROLE
140 police/military (*Operation Anode*)

EQUIPMENT BY TYPE
AIRCRAFT • TPT 2 DHC-4 *Caribou*
HEL: *2 UH-1H*

SUDAN
UN • UNMIS 17; 6 obs

TIMOR LESTE
Joint 850 (*Operation Astute*)
EQUIPMENT BY TYPE
APC (T): some M-113
AC • TPT 3 C-130
HEL • OBS 4 OH-58 *Kiowa*
  UTL 4 UH-60 *Blackhawk*
UN • UNMIT 4 obs

FOREIGN FORCES

New Zealand Army: 9 (air navigation) trg
Singapore Air Force: School located at Pearce with 27 S-211 trg ac (flying trg); Op trg sqn located at Oakey with 12 AS-332 *Super Puma* Spt/AS-532 *Cougar* utl (flying trg); 230
United Kingdom Army 30; Navy 20
United States USPACOM: SEWS located at Pine Gap; comms facility located at NW Cape; SIGINT stn located at Pine Gap; Army: 21; Navy: 26; USAF: 61; USMC: 603

Brunei Bru

Brunei Dollar B$		2006	2007	2008
GDP	B$	18.5bn		
	US$	11.8bn		
per capita	US$	31,054		
Growth	%	2.7	4.4	
Inflation	%	0.2	1.2	
Def bdgt	B$	ε515m	519m	
	US$	328m	355m	
US$1=B$		1.57	1.46	

Population   386,511
Ethnic groups: Muslim 71%; Malay 67%; Chinese 16%; non-Malay indigenous 6%

Age	0–14	15–19	20–24	25–29	30–64	65 plus
Male	15%	5%	4%	5%	22%	1%
Female	14%	4%	4%	4%	19%	2%

Capabilities

ACTIVE 7,000 (Army 4,900 Navy 1,000 Air 1,100)
Paramilitary 2,250

RESERVE 700 (Army 700)

ORGANISATIONS BY SERVICE

Army 4,900

FORCES BY ROLE
Inf   3 bn
Spt   1 bn (1 armd recce sqn, 1 engr sqn)
Reserves   1 bn
EQUIPMENT BY TYPE
LT TK 20 *Scorpion* (16 to be upgraded)
APC (W) 39 VAB
ARTY • MOR 81mm 24
AT • RL 67mm *Armbrust*

Navy 1,000

FORCES BY ROLE
SF 1 sqn
EQUIPMENT BY TYPE
PATROL AND COASTAL COMBATANTS 6+
  PFM 3 *Waspada* each with 2 MM-38 *Exocet* tactical SSM
  PFI 3 *Perwira*
AMPHIBIOUS • CRAFT 4 LCU

Air Force 1,100

FORCES BY ROLE
MP 1 sqn with 1 CN-235M
Trg 1 sqn with 4 PC-7 *Turbo Trainer*; 2 SF-260W *Warrior*; 2 Bell 206B *JetRanger II*
Hel 1 sqn with 5 Bö-105 (armed, 81mm rockets); 1 sqn with 4 S-70A *Black Hawk*; 1 S-70C *Black Hawk* (VIP); 10 Bell 212; 1 Bell 214 (SAR)
AD 2 sqn with 12 *Rapier* each with *Blindfire*; 16 *Mistral*
EQUIPMENT BY TYPE
AIRCRAFT
  MP 1 CN-235M
  TRG 6: 4 PC-7 *Turbo Trainer*; 2 SF-260W *Warrior*
HELICOPTERS
  SPT 5: 4 S-70A *Black Hawk*; 1 S-70C *Black Hawk* (VIP)
  UTL 18: 5 Bö-105 (armed, 81mm rockets); 2 Bell 206B *JetRanger II*; 10 Bell 212; 1 Bell 214 (SAR)
AD • SAM 28: 12 *Rapier* each with *Blindfire*; 16 *Mistral*

Paramilitary ε2,250

Gurkha Reserve Unit 400-500
2 bn

Royal Brunei Police 1,750
PATROL AND COASTAL COMBATANTS
PCI 7 less than 100 tonnes

DEPLOYMENT

PHILIPPINES
IMT 10

FOREIGN FORCES

Singapore Air Force: 500; trg school; 1 hel det with *Super Puma*
United Kingdom Army: 90; Navy: 10; Air Force: 10

Cambodia Cam

Cambodian Riel r		2006	2007	2008
GDP	r	29.8tr	33.9tr	
	US$	7.3bn	8.5bn	
per capita	US$	524	600	
Growth	%	10.8	9.5	
Inflation	%	4.7	6.5	
Def bdgt	r	503bn	557bn	
	US$	123m	139m	
US$1=r		4,103	4,000	

Population   14,131,858

Ethnic groups: Khmer 90%; Vietnamese 5%; Chinese 1%

Age	0–14	15–19	20–24	25–29	30–64	65 plus
Male	18%	7%	6%	3%	14%	1%
Female	18%	6%	5%	3%	16%	2%

Capabilities

ACTIVE 124,300 (Army 75,000 Navy 2,800 Air 1,500 Provincial Forces 45,000) **Paramilitary 67,000**

Terms of service conscription authorised but not implemented since 1993

ORGANISATIONS BY SERVICE

Army ε75,000

FORCES BY ROLE
6 Military Regions (incl 1 special zone for capital)

Armd	3 bn
Recce	some indep bn
Inf	22 div (established str 3,500; actual str <1500); 3 indep bde; 9 indep regt
AB/SF	1 regt
Arty	some bn
Protection	1 bde (4 bn)
Engr construction	1 regt
Fd engr	3 regt
AD	some bn

EQUIPMENT BY TYPE
MBT 150+: 50 Type-59; 100+ T-54/T-55
LT TK 20+: Type-62; 20 Type-63
RECCE BRDM-2
AIFV 70 BMP-1
APC 190+
  APC (T) M-113
  APC (W) 190: 160 BTR-60/BTR-152; 30 OT-64
ARTY 428+
  TOWED 400+ **76mm** ZIS-3 *M-1942*/**122mm** D-30 /**122mm** M-30 *M-1938* /**130mm** Type-59-I
  MRL 28+: **107mm** Type-63; **122mm** 8 BM-21; **132mm** BM-13-16 (BM-13); **140mm** 20 BM-14-16 (BM-14)
  MOR 82mm M-37; **120mm** M-43; **160mm** M-160
AT • RCL 82mm B-10; **107mm** B-11

AD • GUNS • TOWED 14.5mm ZPU-1/ZPU-2/ZPU-4; **37mm** M-1939; **57mm** S-60

Navy ε2,800 (incl. 1,500 Naval Infantry)

EQUIPMENT BY TYPE
PATROL AND COASTAL COMBATANTS 10
  PFC 2 *Stenka*
  PCR 2 *Kaoh Chhlam*
  PB 6

FACILITIES
Bases Located at Phnom Penh (river), Ream (maritime)

Naval Infantry 1,500

Inf	7 bn
Arty	1 bn

Air Force 1,500

FORCES BY ROLE

Ftr	1 sqn with 14 MiG-21bis *Fishbed L & N†*; 5 MiG-21UM *Mongol B†* (up to 9 to be upgraded by IAI: 2 returned but status unclear)
Recce/trg	some sqn with 5 P-92 *Echo* (pilot trg/recce); 5 L-39 *Albatros** (lead-in trg)
Tpt	1 (VIP (reporting to Council of Ministry)) sqn with 2 An-24RV *Coke*; 1 AS-350 *Ecureuil*; 1 AS-365 *Dauphin 2*; 1 sqn with 1 Bn-2 *Islander*; 1 Cessna 421; 2 Y-12
Hel	1 sqn with 1 Mi-8P *Hip K* (VIP); 2 Mi-26 *Halo*; 13 MI-17 (Mi-8MT) *Hip H*/Mi-8 *Hip*

EQUIPMENT BY TYPE
AIRCRAFT 24 combat capable
  FTR 14 MiG-21bis *Fishbed L & N†*
  TPT 6: 2 An-24RV *Coke*; 1 BN-2 *Islander*; 1 Cessna 421; 2 Y-12
  UTL 5 P-92 *Echo* (pilot trg/recce)
  TRG 10: 5 L-39 *Albatros** (lead-in trg); 5 MiG-21UM *Mongol B*†*
HELICOPTERS • SPT 18: 1 AS-350 *Ecureuil*; 2 Mi-26 *Halo*; 13 MI-17 (Mi-8MT) *Hip H*/Mi-8 *Hip*; 1 Mi-8P *Hip* (VIP); 1 AS-365 *Dauphin 2*

Provincial Forces 45,000+

Reports of at least 1 inf regt per province, with varying numbers of inf bn with lt wpn

Paramilitary

Police 67,000 (including gendarmerie)

NON-STATE ARMED GROUPS

see Part II

DEPLOYMENT

SUDAN
UN • UNMIS 136; 10 obs

China, People's Republic of PRC

Chinese Yuan Renminbi Y		2006	2007	2008
GDP	Y	20.9tr	25.2tr	
	US$	2.62tr	3.35tr	
per capita	US$	2,000	2,539	
Growth	%	11.1	11.5	
Inflation	%	1.5	4.5	
Def exp[a]	US$	ε122bn		
Def bdgt[b]	Y	280bn	350bn	
	US$	35.3bn	46.7bn	
US$1=Y		7.97	7.51	

[a] PPP estimate including extra-budgetary military expenditure
[b] Official defence budget at market exchange rates

Population 1,321,851,888

Ethnic groups: Tibetan, Uighur and other non-Han 8%; Xinjiang: Muslim ε60% of which Uighur ε44%. Tibet: Chinese ε60%; Tibetan ε40%

Age	0–14	15–19	20–24	25–29	30–64	65 plus
Male	11%	5%	4%	4%	24%	4%
Female	10%	5%	4%	4%	23%	4%

Capabilities

ACTIVE 2,105,000 (Army 1,600,000 Navy 255,000 Air 250,000) Paramilitary 1,500,000

Terms of service selective conscription; all services 2 years

RESERVE some 800,000

Overall organisation: Army leadership is exercised by the four general headquarters/departments. A military area command exercises direct leadership over the Army units under it. The Army has 18 combined corps, which are mobile combat troops. Each of the Navy, Air Force and Second Artillery Force have a leading body consisting of the headquarters, political department, logistics department and armaments department. These direct the military, political, logistical and equipment work of their respective troops, and take part in the command of joint operations.

ORGANISATIONS BY SERVICE

Strategic Missile Forces (100,000+)

Offensive

The Second Artillery Force organises and commands its own troops to launch nuclear counterattacks with strategic missiles and to conduct operations with conventional missiles. It comprises missile and training bases, and relevant support troops

Org as 20 launch bdes within 6 msl armies; org varies by msl type; one testing and one trg base

MSL • STRATEGIC 806

ICBM 46: circa 6 DF-31 (CSS-9) (1 bde); circa 20 DF-4 (CSS-3) (2 bde); 20 DF-5A (CSS-4 Mod 2) (4 bdes)

IRBM 35: circa 33 DF-21 (CSS-5) (4 bde); circa 2 DF-3A (CSS-2 Mod) (1 bde)

SRBM 725

500 DF-11A/M-11A (CSS-7 Mod 2) (4 bdes); 225 DF-15/M-9 (CSS-6) (2 bdes)

Navy

SUBMARINES • STRATEGIC • SSBN 3:

1 *Xia* equiped with 12 JL-1 (CSS-N-3) strategic SLBM

2 *Jin* equiped with up to 12 JL-2 (CSS-NX-4) strategic SLBM (full operational status unkown; 3rd and 4th vessels in build)

Defensive

RADAR • STRATEGIC: some phased array radar; some detection and tracking radars (covering Central Asia and Shanxi (northern border)) located at Xinjiang

People's Liberation Army ε800,000; ε800,000 conscript (reductions continue) (total 1,600,000)

FORCES BY ROLE

Group army: strength from 30–65,000, org varies, normally with 2–3 mech/mot inf div/bde, 1 armd div/bde, 1 arty div/bde, 1 SAM/AAA or AAA bde, cbt readiness category varies with 10 GA at category A and 8 at category B (reorg to bde structure in progress)

Army	18 (group) armies (*total:* 1 mech inf bde, 1 AT bde, 12 armd bde, 12 ADA bde, 14 arty bde, 15 inf div, 2 amph aslt div, 22 mot inf bde, 24 mot inf div, 3 mech inf div, 4 AT regt, 7 arty div, 9 armd div, 9 (SAM/AAA) AD bde)
Arty/air	(coastal defence) air forces
Mil region	7 comd
Provincial mil	28 district
Inf	5 (border) indep regt
Mot inf	1 indep bde; 1 indep regt
Mtn inf	2 (indep) bde
AB	1 (manned by AF) corps (3 AB div, 35,000 AB)
Arty	1 indep regt
SSM	1 indep bde; 9 (coastal defence) regt
ADA	1 indep regt
Engr	1 indep bde; 50 regt
Sigs	50 regt
Avn	2 (indep) regt (trg); 8 indep regt
Gd	4 (garrison) comd (with 1 mtn inf bde, 12 inf div, 4 inf bde, 87 (bn) inf regt)
AD	8 (coastal defence) regt

North East–Shenyang MR ε250,000

Army 3 gp ((Heilongjiang, Jilin, Liaoning MD): 2 armd, 1 mech, 4 mot, 1 arty div; 2 armd, 5 mot, 3 arty, 1 SAM/ AAA, 3 AAA, 1 ATK bde)

North–Beijing MR ε300,000

Army 3 gp ((Beijing, Tianjin Garrison, Inner Mongolia, Hebei, Shanxi MD): 2 armd, 1 mech, 5 mot, 1 arty div; 3 armd, 7 mot inf, 4 arty, 2 SAM/AAA, 3 AAA bde; 1 ATK regt)

West–Lanzhou MR ε220,000

Army 2 gp ((incl Ningxia, Shaanxi, Gansu, Qing-hai, Xinjiang, South Xinjiang MD): 1 armd, 2 mot inf, 1 arty div; 1 armd, 2 mot inf, 1 arty, 1 AAA bde; 1 ATK regt)

South-West–Chengdu–MR ε180,000

Army 2 gp ((incl Chongqing Garrison, Sichuan, Guizhou, Yunnan, Tibet MD): 4 mot inf, 1 arty div; 2 armd, 1 arty, 2 AAA bde)

South–Guangzhou MR ε180,000

Army 2 gp ((Hubei, Hunan, Guangdong, Guangxi, Hainan MD): 1 mech, 3 mot inf, 1 arty div; 2 armd, 1 arty, 1 SAM/AAA, 1 AAA bde. Hong Kong: ε7,000 with 1 inf bde (3 inf, 1 mech inf, 1 arty regt, 1 engr bn), 1 hel unit)

Centre–Jinan MR ε190,000

Army 3 gp ((Shandong, Henan MD): 2 armd, 1 mech inf, 3 mot inf, 1 arty div; 1 armd, 1 mech inf, 4 mot inf, 2 arty, 2 SAM/AAA, 1 AAA bde, 1 ATK regt)

East–Nanjing MR ε250,000

Army 3 gp ((Shanghai Garrison, Jiangsu, Zhejiang, Fujian, Jiangxi, Anhui MD): 2 armd, 1 mech inf, 3 mot inf, 1 arty div; 1 armd, 4 mot inf, 2 arty, 2 SAM/AAA, 1 AAA bde; 1 ATK regt)

EQUIPMENT BY TYPE

MBT 7,660+: 5,000+ Type-59-II/Type-59-I; 300 Type-79; 1,000 Type-88A/Type-88B; 1,200 Type-96; ε160 Type-98A/99

LT TK 1,000: 400 Type-62-I; 600 Type-63A

AIFV 1,000 Type-86A *WZ-501*

APC 3,500+

APC (T) 2,600: 2,300 Type-63-II/Type-63-I/Type-63A/Type-63C; 300 Type-89-I

APC (W) 900+: 200 Type-77-II; 600+ Type-92; 100 WZ-523

ARTY 17,700+

SP 1,200: **122mm** 700: ε200 Type-70-I; ε500 Type-89; **152mm** ε500 Type-83

TOWED 14,000: 13,850 **100mm** Type-59 (M-1944)/**122mm** Type-54-1 (M-30) *M-1938*/Type-83/Type-60 (D-74)/**130mm** Type-59 (M-46)/Type-59-I/**152mm** Type-54 (D-1)/Type-66 (D-20); **155mm** 150 Type 88 WAC-21

GUN/MOR 120mm 100 2S23 *NONA-SVK*

MRL 2,400+

SP 122mm Type-89/**130mm** Type-70

TOWED 122mm Type-81/**130mm** Type-82 /**273mm** Type-83/**320mm** Type-96 (WS-1)

MOR

SP 82mm Type-82

TOWED 81mm Type-W87; **82mm** Type-53 (M-37)/Type-67 /Type-82; **100mm** Type-71 (reported); **120mm** Type-55 (incl SP); **160mm** Type-56 (M-160)

AT • MSL 7,200

SP 24 HJ-9 *Red Arrow 9*

MANPATS 7,176 HJ-73A/HJ-73B/HJ-73C/HJ-8A/HJ-8C/HJ-8E

RCL 75mm Type-56; **82mm** Type-65 (B-10)/Type-78; **105mm** Type-75

RL 62mm Type-70-1

GUNS 300+: **100mm** Type-73 (T-12)/Type-86; **120mm** 300+ Type-89 SP

HELICOPTERS

SAR 7 SA-321 *Super Frelon*

ATK 31 WZ-9

ASLT 8 SA-342 *Gazelle* (with HOT)

SPT 260: 53 AS-350 *Ecureuil*; 45 Mi-171; 50 Mi-171V5; 3 Mi-6 *Hook*; 19 S-70C2 (S-70C) *Black Hawk*; 40 MI-17 (Mi-8MT) *Hip H*; 50 Mi-8T *Hip*

UTL 69+: 61 AS-365 *Dauphin 2*/Z-9 (AS-365N) *Dauphin 2*; 8 SA-316 *Alouette III*; Z-10

UAV ASN-15 (hand-launched); ASN-104; ASN-105; ASN-206; W-50; WZ-5; D-4 NPU (Xian NPU)

AD • SAM 284+:

SP 284: 200 HQ-7A; 60 SA-15 *Gauntlet* (Tor-M1); 24 HQ-61A *Red Leader*

MANPAD HN-5A/HN-5B *Hong Nu*; FN-6/QW-1/QW-2

GUNS 7,700+

SP 37mm Type-88; **57mm** Type-80

TOWED 23mm Type-80 (ZU-23-2); **25mm** Type-85; **35mm** Type-90 (GDF-002); **37mm** Type-55 (M-1939)/Type-65/Type-74; **57mm** Type-59 (S-60); **85mm** Type-56 (M-1939) *KS-12*; **100mm** Type-59 (KS-19)

RADAR • LAND *Cheetah* (arty); RASIT (veh, arty); Type-378 (veh)

MSL • SSM HY-2 (CSS-C-3) *Seerseeker*; HY-4 (CSS-C-7) *Sadsack*

Reserves

Inf	30 div (*each*: 3 inf regt, 1 arty regt)
Arty	3 div
AD	12 div
Logistic/Spt7 bde	

Navy ε215,000; 40,000 conscript (total 255,000)

The Navy organises and commands maritime operations conducted independently by its troops or in support of maritime operations. There are three fleets under the Navy, namely the Beihai Fleet, Donghai Fleet and Nanhai Fleet. Each fleet has flotillas, aviation divisions, etc. under its command. In major directions and key target areas there are also corps or division level command posts.

SUBMARINES 62

STRATEGIC • SSBN 3:

1 *Xia* equiped with 12 JL-1 (CSS-N-3) strategic SLBM

2 *Jin* equiped with up to 12 JL-2 (CSS-NX-4) strategic SLBM (full operational status unknown; 3rd and 4th vessels in build)

TACTICAL 59

SSN 6:

4 *Han* (Type 091) each with YJ-82 SSM, 6 single 533mm TT

2 *Shang* (Type 093), 6 single 533mm TT (full operational status unknown, 3rd vessel in build)

SSG 1 mod *Romeo* (Type SSG) with 6 YJ-1 (CSS-N-4) *Sardine* SSM, 8 single 533mm TT (test platform)

SSK 51:

12 *Kilo* each with SS-N-27 *Club* ASCM; 6 single 533mm TT with up to 18 *Test-71/96 HWT*

19 *Ming* (imp, type ES5E) each with 8 single 533mm TT

8 *Romeo*† (Type ES3B) each with 8 533mm TT

10 *Song* each with YJ-2 (CSS-N-8) *Saccade* SSM, 6 single 533mm TT

2 *Yuan* each with 6 533mm TT (undergoing sea trials)

SS 1 *Golf* (SLBM trials)

PRINCIPAL SURFACE COMBATANTS 75

DESTROYERS • DDG 29:

2 *Luyang* each with 4 quad (16 eff.) each with YJ-83 SSM, 2 x24 (48 eff.) each with 48 SA-N-7 *Grizzly* SAM, 2 triple 324mm TT (6 eff.) each with Yu-7 LWT, 1 100mm, (capacity 1 Ka-28 *Helix* A ASW hel)

4 *Hangzhou* (RF *Sovremenny*) each with 2 quad (8 eff.) each with SS-N-22 *Sunburn* SSM, 2 SA-N-7 *Grizzly* SAM, 2 twin 533mm ASTT (4 eff.), 2 RBU 1000 *Smerch* 3, 2 twin 130mm (4 eff.), (capacity either 1 Z-9C (AS-565SA) *Panther* ASW/ASUW hel or 1 Ka-28 *Helix* A ASW hel)

2 *Luyang* II each with 2 quad (8 eff.) each with YJ-62 SSM, 8 sextuple VLS (48 eff.) with total of 48 HQ-9 SP SAM, 2 triple 324mm TT (6 eff.) each with Yu-7 LWT, 1 100mm, (capacity 2 Ka-28 *Helix* A ASW hel)

1 *Luda* III with 2 triple (6 eff.) each with HY-2 (CSS-N-2) *Silkworm* SSM / YJ-1 (CSS-N-4) *Sardine* SSM, 4 twin (8 eff.) each with 2 YJ-1 (CSS-N-4) *Sardine* SSM, 2 triple 324mm ASTT (6 eff.), 2 twin 130mm (4 eff.)

11 *Luda* Type-051 each with 2 triple 324mm ASTT (6 eff.), 2 FQF 2500 (24 eff.), 2 twin 130mm (4 eff.)

1 *Luhai* with 4 quad (16 eff.) each with YJ-83 SSM, 1 octuple (8 eff.) with 8 HQ-7 SAM, 2 triple 324mm ASTT (6 eff.) each with Yu-7 LWT, 1 twin 100mm (2 eff.), (capacity either 2 Z-9C (AS-565SA) *Panther* ASW/ASUW hel or 2 Ka-28 *Helix* A ASW hel)

2 *Luhu* (Type 052A) each with 4 quad (16 eff.) each with YJ-83 SSM, 1 octuple (8 eff.) with HQ-7 SAM, 2 triple 324mm ASTT (6 eff.) each with Yu-7 LWT, 2 FQF 2500 (24 eff.), 1 twin 100mm (2 eff.), (capacity 2 Z-9C (AS-565SA) *Panther* ASW/ASUW hel)

2 *Luzhou* eq. with 2 quad (8 eff.) YJ-83 (C-803) SSM; SA-N-6 *Grumble* SAM

1 *Luda* II each with 2 triple 324mm ASTT (6 eff.), 2 triple (6 eff.) each with HY-2 (CSS-N-2) *Silkworm* SSM, 1 twin 130mm (2 eff.), (mine-laying capability), (capacity 2 Z-9C (AS-565SA) *Panther* ASW/ASUW hel)

3 *Luda* mod Type-051DT each with 2 quad (8 eff.) each with YJ-1 (CSS-N-4) *Sardine* SSM, 1 octuple (8 eff.) with HQ-7 *Crotale* SAM, 2 FQF 2500 (24 eff.), 2 twin 130mm (4 eff.), mines (capability)

FRIGATES • FFG 46:

11 *Jianghu* Type I each with 2 triple (6 eff.) each with 1 SY-1 (CSS-N-1) *Scrubbrush* SSM, 4 RBU 1200 (20 eff.), 2 100mm

9 *Jianghu* Type II each with 1 triple (3 eff.) with SY-1 (CSS-N-1) *Scrubbrush* SSM, 2 RBU 1200 (10 eff.), 1 twin 100mm (2 eff.), (capacity 1 Z-9C (AS-565SA) *Panther* ASW/ASUW hel)

3 *Jianghu* Type III each with 8 YJ-1 (CSS-N-4) *Sardine* SSM, 4 RBU 1200 (20 eff.), 2 twin 100mm (4 eff.)

1 *Jianghu* Type IV with 1 triple (3 eff.) with 1 SY-1 (CSS-N-1) *Scrubbrush* SSM, 4 RBU 1200 (20 eff.), 1 100mm, 1 Z-9C (AS-565SA) *Panther* ASW/ASUW hel

6 *Jianghu* Type V each with 1 triple (3 eff.) with SY-1 (CSS-N-1) *Scrubbrush* SSM, 2 RBU 1200 (10 eff.), 1 twin 100mm (2 eff.), (capacity 1 Z-9C (AS-565SA) *Panther* ASW/ASUW hel)

4 *Jiangwei* I each with 2 triple (6 eff.) each with 1 YJ-8 SSM, 1 sextuple (6 eff.) with 1 HQ-61 (CSA-N-2) SAM, 2 RBU 1200 (10 eff.), 1 twin 100mm (2 eff.), (capacity 2 Z-9C (AS-565SA) *Panther* ASW/ASUW hel)

10 *Jiangwei* II each with 2 quad (8 eff.) each with YJ-83 SSM, 1 octuple (8 eff.) with 1 HQ-7 SAM, 2 RBU 1200 (10 eff.), 2 100mm, (capacity 2 Z-9C (AS-565SA) *Panther* ASW/ASUW hel)

2 *Jiangkai* each with 2 quad (8 eff.) each with YJ-83 SSM, 1 octuple (8 eff.) with HQ-7 SAM, 2 triple 324mm TT (6 eff.) each with Yu-7 LWT, 2 RBU 1200 (10 eff.), 1 100mm, (capacity either 1 Ka-28 *Helix* A ASW hel or 1 Z-9C (AS-565SA) *Panther* ASW/ASUW hel)

PATROL AND COASTAL COMBATANTS 233

PFM 63:

16 *Houxin* each with 4 YJ-1 (CSS-N-4) *Sardine* SSM

7 *Houjian* each with 6 YJ-1 (CSS-N-4) *Sardine* SSM

15 *Huangfeng/Hola* (FSU *Osa* I-Type) each with ε 4 SY-1 (CSS-N-1) *Scrubbrush* SSM

25 *Houbei* each with 4 YJ-82 (CSS-N-8) *Saccade* SSM

PFC 93 *Hainan* each with ε4 RBU 1200 (20 eff.)

PCC 27:

2 *Haijui* each with 4 RBU 1200 (20 eff.)

25 *Haiqing* each with 2 type-87 (12 eff.)

PCI 50: 15 *Haizui* less than 100 tonnes; 35 *Shanghai* II less than 100 tonnes

MINE WARFARE 65

MINE COUNTERMEASURES 64

MSO 14 T-43

MSC 4 *Wosao*

MSD • MSD INSHORE 46: 4 *Futi* Class (Type 312); 42 in reserve

MINELAYERS • ML 1 *Wolei*

AMPHIBIOUS

LS 74

LSM 47:

1 *Yudao*

1 *Yudeng* (capacity 6 tanks; 180 troops)

13 *Yuhai* (capacity 2 tanks; 250 troops)

22 *Yuliang* (capacity 5 tanks; 250 troops)

10 *Yunshu* (capacity 6 tanks)

LST 27:

7 *Yukan* (capacity 10 tanks; 200 troops)

10 *Yuting* (capacity 10 tanks; 250 troops; 2 hel)

10 *Yuting* II (capacity 4 LCVP; 10 tanks; 250 troops)

LC 160

LCU 130:

10 *Yubei* (capacity 10 tanks or 150 troops)

120 *Yunnan*

LCM 20 *Yuchin*

ACV 10 UCAC

LOGISTICS AND SUPPORT 204

AORH 5: 2 *Fuqing*; 2 *Fuchi*; 1 *Nanyun*

AOT 50: 7 *Danlin*; 20 *Fulin*; 2 *Shengli*; 3 *Jinyou*; 18 *Fuzhou*

AO L 5 *Guangzhou*

AS 8: 1 *Dazhi*; 5 *Dalang*; 2 *Dazhou*

ASR 1 *Dajiang* with 2 SA-321 *Super Frelon*

ARS 2: 1 *Dadong*; 1 *Dadao*

AG 6: 4 *Qiongsha* (capacity 400 troops); 2 *Qiongsha* (hospital conversion)

AK 23: 2 *Yantai*; 2 *Dayun*; 6 *Danlin*; 7 *Dandao*; 6 *Hongqi*

AWT 18: 10 *Leizhou*; 8 *Fuzhou*

AGOR 5: 1 *Dahua*; 2 *Kan*; 1 *Bin Hai*; 1 *Shuguang*

AGI 1 *Dadie*

AGM 5 (space and missile tracking)

AGS 6: 5 *Yenlai*; 1 *Ganzhu*

AGB 4: 1 *Yanbing*; 3 *Yanha*

ABU 7 *Yannan*

ATF 51: 4 *Tuzhong*; 10 *Hujiu*; 1 *Daozha*; 17 *Gromovoy*; 19 *Roslavl*

TRG 2: 1 *Shichang*; 1 *Daxin*

YDG 5 *Yen Pai*

Naval Aviation 26,000

AIRCRAFT 792 combat capable

BBR 130: 100 H-5,F-5,F-5B (Il-28) *Beagle* (torpedo-carrying lt bbr); 30 H-6D

FTR 346: 50 J-8B *Finback*; 20 J-8D *Finback*; 50 J-8 *Finback/J-8A Finback*; 200 J-8IIA *Finback*; 26 J-7 (MiG-21F) *Fishbed C*

FGA 296: 18 JH-7; 30 Q-5 *Fantan*; 48 Su-30Mk2 *Flanker*; ε200 J-6 (MiG-19S) *Farmer B*

ASW 4 PS-5 (SH-5)

RECCE 7 HZ-5 (Il-28R) *Beagle*

MP 4 Y-8X

TKR 3 HY-6

TPT 66: 4 Y-8 (An-12BP) *Cub A*; 50 Y-5 (An-2) *Colt*; 4 Y-7 (An-24) *Coke*; 6 Y-7H (An-26) *Curl*; 2 Yak-42

TRG 73: 16 JJ-6 (MiG-19UTI) *Farmer**; 4 JJ-7 *Mongol A**; 53 PT-6 (CJ-6)

HELICOPTERS

ASW/ASUW 25 Z-9C (AS-565SA) *Panther*

SAR 35: 15 SA-321; 20 Z-8,Z-8A (SA-321Ja) *Super Frelon*

ASW 10 Ka-28 (Ka-27PL) *Helix A*

SPT 8 Mi-8 *Hip*

MSL • TACTICAL • ASM YJ-61 (CAS-1 (improved)) *Kraken*; YJ-8K (CSS-N-4) *Sardine*; YJ-83 (CSSC-8) *Saccade*

Marines ε10,000

FORCES BY ROLE

Army   3 (also have amph role) div

Marine inf 2 bde (*each*: 1 inf bn, 1 AD bn, 1 (armd) mech inf bn, 2 amph recce bn, 2 arty bn, 2 tk bn)

EQUIPMENT BY TYPE

LT TK 150 Type-63A

APC (T) 60 Type-63

APC (W) Type-92

ARTY • TOWED 122mm Type-83

MRL 107mm Type-63

AT • MSL • MANPATS HJ-73; HJ-8

AD • SAM • MANPAD HN-5 *Hong Nu*/*Red Cherry*

North Sea Fleet

Coastal defence from DPRK border (Yalu River) to south of Lianyungang (approx 35°10′N); equates to Shenyang, Beijing and Jinan MR, and to seaward; 9 coastal defence districts

FORCES BY ROLE

Navy 1 HQ located at Qingdao

FACILITIES

Support bases Located at Lushun

East Sea Fleet

Coastal defence from south of Lianyungang to Dongshan (approx 35°10′N to 23°30′N); equates to Nanjing Military Region, and to seaward; 7 coastal defence districts

FORCES BY ROLE

Navy 1 HQ located at Dongqian Lake (Ninsbo)

FACILITIES

Bases Located at Fujian, Zhousnan, Dongqian Lake (Ninsbo)

South Sea Fleet

Coastal defence from Dongshan (approx 23°30′N) to Vn border; equates to Guangzhou MR, and to seaward (including Paracel and Spratly Islands)

FORCES BY ROLE

Navy 1 comd HQ located at Guangzhou

FACILITIES

Bases Located at Yulin, Guangzhou, Zuanjiang

Air Force 250,000

The Air Force organises and commands air operations conducted independently or with Air Force personnel as the main fighting force, as well as air defence operations in the Beijing area. It has an air command in each of the Shenyang, Beijing, Lanzhou, Jinan, Nanjing, Guangzhou and Chengdu military area commands. Within an air command are aviation divisions, ground-to-air missile divisions (brigades and regiments), anti-aircraft artillery brigades (regiments), radar brigades (regiments) and other support troops.

32 air divs (22 ftr, 3 bbr, 5 attack, 2 tpt). Up to 4 regt, each with 10–15 ac,1 maint unit, some tpt and trg ac, make up an air div; Varying numbers of air divs in the mil regions – many in the south-east.

Flying hours 130 hrs/year on J-8 *Finback*; 180 hrs/year on Su-27 *Flanker*/Su-30 *Flanker*; 80 hrs/year on H-6 (Tu-16) *Badger* bbr; 130 hrs/year on J-7 (MiG-21F) *Fishbed*

FORCES BY ROLE

Bbr   5 regt with up to 50 H-6E/H-6F/H-6H (of which some with YJ-63 cruise missile); 1 (nuclear ready) regt with 20 H-6 (Tu-16) *Badger*

Ftr   3 regt with 28 J-8 IIB *Finback*; 3 regt with 62 J-8D *Finback*; 16 regt with 400 J-7II *Fishbed*/J-7IIA; 1 regt with 11 J-8F *Finback*; 9 regt with 116 J-11 (Su-27SK) *Flanker*; 12 regt with 296 J-7E *Fishbed*; 5 regt with 32 Su-27UBK *Flanker*; 2 regt with 36 J-7C *Fishbed*; 1 regt with 24 J-7G *Fishbed*; 4 regt with 80 J-8 *Finback*; 1 regt with 24 J-8 IID *Finback*; 2 regt with 40 J-8III *Finback*

FGA   4 regt with 73 Su-30MKK *Flanker*; 12 regt with 408 Q-5C *Fantan*/Q-5D *Fantan*; 2 regt each with 31 J-10; 3 regt each with 70 JH-7/7A

ELINT/   2 regt with 45 JZ-6 (MiG-19R); some regt
Recce   with ε126 JZ-7 (MiG-21R) *Fishbed H*; 1 Tu-154M *Careless*; 1 regt with 8+ JZ-8 *Finback*

AEW/   1 regt with A-50 *Mainstay*; 4 Y-8
AWACS

Tpt   1 regt with 16 Tu-154M *Careless*; 3 regt with 18 Il-76MD *Candid B*; 30 IL-76TD to support 15th and 16th Airborne armies; 3 regt with; 170 Y-5 (An-2) *Colt*; 41 Y-7 (An-24) *Coke*/Y-7H (An-26) *Curl*; 15 B-737-200 (VIP); 5 CL-601 *Challenger*; 2 Il-18 *Coot*; 20 Y-11; 8 Y-12

Tkr   1 regt with 10 HY-6. 8 Il-78M on order to extend Su-30MKK ops

ADA   1 bde located in Centre; 1 bde located in East; 1 bde located in North-East

Trg   1 regt with 12 H-6H; some regt with CJ-6/-6A/-6B); Y-7; JL-8 (K-8); JJ-6; JJ-7

Hel   regts with ε30–40 hel; 6 AS-332 *Super Puma* (VIP); 50 Mi-8 *Hip*; 20 Z-9 (AS-365N) *Dauphin 2*; 4 Bell 214

SAM   3 div located in North; 2 bde located in South; 1 bde located in North-East; 2 bde located in East; 1 bde located in South West; 100+ unit with 60+ HQ-7; 24 HQ-9; 144 S-300PMU2 (SA-10C) *Grumble*/SA-10D *Grumble*; 500+ HQ-2 (SA-2) *Guideline*/HQ-2A/HQ-2B(A); 160 (Strategic Air Defence) unit with 850 S-300PMU1 (SA-10B) *Grumble*/S-300PMU2 (SA-10C) *Grumble*

EQUIPMENT BY TYPE

AIRCRAFT 1,762 combat capable
BBR up to 82: up to 20 H-6 (Tu-16) *Badger*; up to 50 H-6E/H-6F/H-6H
FTR 1,179: 400 J-7II/J-7IIA *Fishbed*; 36 J-7C *Fishbed*; 296 J-7E *Fishbed*; 24 J-7G *Fishbed*; 80 J-8; 62 J-8D *Finback*; 11 J-8F *Finback*; 28 J-8 IIB *Finback*; 24 J-8 IID *Finback*; 40 J-8III *Finback*; 62 J-10; 116 Su-27SK (J-11) *Flanker*
FGA 551: 73 Su-30MKK *Flanker*; 70 JH-7/JH-7A; 408 Q-5C *Fantan*/Q-5D *Fantan*
RECCE 179+: 45 JZ-6 (MiG-19R); 126 JZ-7 (MiG-21R) *Fishbed H*; 8+ JZ-8 *Finback*
AEW 4+: A-50 *Mainstay*; 4 Y-8
TKR 18: 10 HY-6; 8 IL-78M on order
TPT 296: 15 B-737-200 (VIP); 5 CL-601 *Challenger*; 2 Il-18 *Coot*; 18 Il-76MD *Candid B* (30 on order); 17 Tu-154M *Careless*; 20 Y-11; 8 Y-12; 170 Y-5 (An-2) *Colt*; 41 Y-7 (An-24) *Coke*/Y-7H (An-26) *Curl*
TRG 522: 400 CJ-6/-6A/-6B; 50 JJ-7; 40 JL-8 (K-8); 32 Su-27UBK *Flanker*

HELICOPTERS

SPT 56: 6 AS-332 *Super Puma* (VIP); 50 Mi-8 *Hip*
UTL 24: 20 Z-9 (AS-365N) *Dauphin 2*; 4 Bell 214
UAV CH-1 *Chang Hong*; *Chang Kong 1*; BQM-34 *Firebee*; *Harpy*

AD

SAM 1,578+
  SP 1,078+: 60+ HQ-7; 24 HQ-9; 850 S-300PMU1 (SA-10B) *Grumble*/S-300PMU2 (SA-10C) *Grumble*; 144 S-300PMU2 (SA-10C) *Grumble*/SA-10D *Grumble*
  TOWED 500+ HQ-2 (SA-2) *Guideline* Towed/HQ-2A/HQ-2B(A)
GUNS 16,000 **100mm/85mm**
MSL • TACTICAL 4,500+
  ASM: AS-14 *Kedge*; AS-17 *Krypton*; AS-18 *Kazoo*; YJ-63
  AAM 4,500+: 100 AA-12 *Adder*; 1,200 P-27 (AA-10) *Alamo*; 3,200 P37 (AA-11) *Archer*; PL-12; PL-2B; PL-5B; PL-8

Paramilitary ε1,500,000 active

People's Armed Police ε1,500,000
Ministry of Public Security
Police 45 div (14 each with 4 regt, remainder no standard organisation; 1–2 div per province)

Border Defence Force 100,000+

Comms 69,000+

Internal Security ε800,000

NON-STATE ARMED GROUPS
see Part II

DEPLOYMENT

CÔTE D'IVOIRE
UN • UNOCI 7 obs

DEMOCRATIC REPUBLIC OF CONGO
UN • MONUC 1 inf gp; 218; 16 obs

ETHIOPIA/ERITREA
UN • UNMEE 6 obs

LEBANON
UN • UNIFIL 343

LIBERIA
UN • UNMIL 565; 5 obs

MIDDLE EAST
UN • UNTSO 4 obs

SIERRA LEONE
UN • UNIOSIL 1obs

SUDAN
AU • **AUMIS** 315
UN • **UNMIS** 446; 14 obs

TIMOR-LESTE
UN • **UNMIT** 3 obs

WESTERN SAHARA
UN • **MINURSO** 1; 13 obs

Fiji Fji

Fijian Dollar F$		2006	2007	2008
GDP	F$	5.1bn		
	US$	2.9bn		
per capita	US$	3,254		
Growth	%	3.6	-3.1	
Inflation	%	2.5	4.5	
Def bdgt	F$	74m	80m	
	US$	43m	51m	
US$1=F$		1.73	1.55	

Population   918,675

Ethnic groups: Fijian 51%; Indian 44%; European/Others 5%

Age	0–14	15–19	20–24	25–29	30–64	65 plus
Male	16%	5%	5%	4%	18%	2%
Female	15%	5%	5%	4%	18%	2%

Capabilities

ACTIVE 3,500 (Army 3,200 Navy 300)

RESERVE ε6,000
(to age 45)

ORGANISATIONS BY SERVICE

Army 3,200 (incl 300 recalled reserves)
FORCES BY ROLE
Inf   7 bn (incl 4 cadre)
Spec Ops 1 coy
Arty   1 bty
Engr   1 bn
EQUIPMENT BY TYPE
ARTY 16
    TOWED 85mm 4 25-pdr (ceremonial)
    MOR 81mm 12
HELICOPTERS
    SPT 1 AS-355 *Ecureuil*
    UTL 1 AS-365 *Dauphin 2*

Navy 300
EQUIPMENT BY TYPE
PATROL AND COASTAL COMBATANTS 7
    PCC 3 *Kula*
    PCI 4: 2 *Levuka*; 2 *Vai*

LOGISTICS AND SUPPORT 2
    AGHS 1 *Tovutu*
    TRG 1 *Cagi Donu* (Presidential Yacht)
FACILITIES
Bases Located at Viti (trg), Walu Bay

DEPLOYMENT

EGYPT
MFO 3 inf coy; 329

IRAQ
UN • **UNAMI** 223

SOLOMON ISLANDS
RAMSI 1 inf coy; 122 *(Helpem Fren)*

SUDAN
UN • **UNMIS** 7 obs

TIMOR LESTE
UN • **UNMIT** 1 obs

Indonesia Indo

Indonesian Rupiah Rp		2006	2007	2008
GDP	Rp	3,338tr	3,846tr	
	US$	364bn	425bn	
per capita	US$	1,572	1,809	
Growth	%	5.5	6.2	
Inflation	%	13.1	6.2	
Def exp[a]	US$	ε10.3		
Def bdgt	Rp	23.6tr	32.6tr	
	US$	2.59bn	3.60bn	
FMA (US)	US$	1.0m	15.7bn	
US$1=Rp		9,159	9,060	

[a] including extra-budgetary funding

Population   234,693,997

Ethnic groups: Javanese 45%; Sundanese 14%; Maduerse 8%; Malay 8%; Chinese 3%; other 22%

Age	0–14	15–19	20–24	25–29	30–64	65 plus
Male	15%	5%	5%	5%	19%	2%
Female	14%	4%	5%	5%	19%	3%

Capabilities

ACTIVE 302,000 (Army 233,000 Navy 45,000 Air 24,000) **Paramilitary 280,000**
Terms of service 2 years selective conscription authorised

RESERVE 400,000
Army cadre units; numercal str n.k., obligation to age 45 for officers

ORGANISATIONS BY SERVICE

Army ε233,000

11 Mil Area Command 150,000

Provincial (KOREM) and District (KODIM) Comd

Cav	8 bn
Inf	2 bde (6 bn); 60 bn
AB	5 bn
Fd arty	10 bn
Engr	7 bn
Avn	1 composite sqn
Hel	1 sqn
AD	7 bn

Special Forces Command (KOPASSUS) ε5,000

SF 3 gp (total: 2 cdo/para unit, 1 counter-terrorist unit (Unit 81), 1 trg unit, 1 (int) SF unit)

Strategic Reserve Command (KOSTRAD) 40,000

Comd	2 div HQ
Armd	2 bn
Inf	3 bde (9 bn); 1 indep (3rd) bde
AB	2 bde
Fd arty	2 regt (6 bn)
AD	1 regt (2 bn)
Engr	2 bn

EQUIPMENT BY TYPE
LT TK 350: 275 AMX-13 (to be upgraded); 15 PT-76; 60 *Scorpion* 90
RECCE 142: 55 *Ferret* (13 upgraded); 69 *Saladin* (16 upgraded); 18 VBL
AIFV 11 BMP-2
APC 356
  APC (T) 115: 75 AMX-VCI; 40 FV4333 *Stormer*
  APC (W) 241: 80 BTR-40; 34 BTR-50PK; 22 *Commando Ranger*; 45 FV603 *Saracen* (14 upgraded); 60 LAV-150 *Commando*
ARTY 1,060
  TOWED 185: **76mm** 50 M-48 *M-1948*; **105mm** 130: 120 M-101; 10 M-56; **155mm** 5 FH-2000
  MOR 875: **81mm** 800; **120mm** 75 Brandt
AT • RCL 135: **106mm** 45 M-40A1; **90mm** 90 M-67
  RL 89mm 700 LRAC
AIRCRAFT • TPT 11: 3 DHC-5 *Buffalo*; 6 NC-212 (CASA 212) *Aviocar*; 2 Rockwell *Turbo Commander* 680
HELICOPTERS
  ATK 2 Mi-35P *Hind*
  SPT 10 Mi-17 *Hip*
  UTL 37: 8 Bell 205A; 12 NB-412 (Bell 412) *Twin Huey*; 17 NBO-105 (Bö-105)
  TRG 12 Hughes 300C
AD • SAM 68: 51 *Rapier*; 17 RBS-70
  GUNS • TOWED 413: **20mm** 121 Rh 202; **40mm** 36 L/70; **57mm** 256 S-60

Navy ε45,000 (including Marines and Aviation)

EQUIPMENT BY TYPE
SUBMARINES • TACTICAL • SSK 2 *Cakra*† each with 8 single 533mm TT with 14 SUT HWT

PRINCIPAL SURFACE COMBATANTS 29
  FRIGATES 11
    FFG 10:
      6 *Ahmad Yani* each with 2 Mk 141 *Harpoon* quad (8 eff.) each with RGM-84A *Harpoon* tactical SSM, 2 SIMBAD twin manual each with *Mistral* SAM, 2 triple 324mm ASTT (6 eff.) each with Mk 46 LWT, 1 76mm gun, (capacity either 1 HAS-1 *Wasp* ASW hel or 1 NBO-105 (Bö-105) utl hel)
      3 *Fatahillah* each with 2 twin (4 eff.) each with MM-38 *Exocet* tactical SSM, 2 B515 *ILAS-3*/triple 324mm ASTT (2-6 eff.) (not on *Nala*) with 12 A244/Mk 46, 1 2 tube *Bofors* 375mm (2 eff.), 1 120mm gun
      1 *Hajar Dewantara* (trg) with 2 twin (4 eff.) each with MM-38 *Exocet* tactical SSM, 2 single 533mm ASTT each with SUT HWT, (capacity 1 NBO-105 (Bö-105) utl hel)
    FF 1 *Samadikun* † each with 2 triple 324mm ASTT (6 eff.) each with Mk 46 LWT, 1 76mm gun
  CORVETTES • FS 18:
    16 *Kapitan Patimura*† each with 4 x1 400mm ASTT, Twin each with SA-N-5 *Grail* SAM, 2 RBU 6000 *Smerch* 2 (24 eff.), 1 57mm gun
    2 *Sigma* each with 2 *Tetral* quad (8eff.) *Mistral* SAM, each with 4 MM-40 *Exocet* Block II tactical SSM, 2 triple 324mm ASTT (6eff.), 1 76mm gun; (2 additional vessels in build)
PATROL AND COASTAL COMBATANTS 41
  PFM 4 *Mandau* each with 4 MM-38 *Exocet* tactical SSM
  PCT 4 *Singa* each with 2 single 533mm TT
  PCO 8: 4 *Kakap*; 4 *Todak*
  PCC 21:
    13 *Kobra* KAL-35 each with 2 20mm gun
    8 *Sibarau*
  PC 4
MINE WARFARE • MINE COUNTERMEASURES 11
  MCC 2 *Pulau Rengat*
  MSC 9 *Palau Rote*†
AMPHIBIOUS
  PRINCIPAL AMPHIBIOUS VESSELS • LPD 1 *Tanjung Dalpele* (capacity 2 LCU); (3 LPD and 1 LPD with command facilities on order. Deliveries expected from mid '08)
  LS • LST 26: 1 *Teluk Amboina* (capacity 16 tanks; 200 troops); 12 *Teluk Gilimanuk*; 7 *Teluk Langsa* (capacity 16 tanks; 200 troops); 6 *Teluk Semangka* (capacity 17 tanks; 200 troops)
  CRAFT 54 LCU
LOGISTICS AND SUPPORT 28
  AGF 1 *Multatuli*
  AORLH 1 *Arun* (ex-UK *Rover*)
  AOT 3: 2 *Khobi*; 1 *Sorong*
  AKSL 6
  AGOR 7: 5 *Baruna Jaya*; 1 *Jalanidhi*; 1 *Burujulasad*
  AGHS 1
  ATF 2
  TRG • AXS 2
  YTM 3
  TPT 2 *Tanjung Nusanive* (troop transport)

Naval Aviation ε1,000

AIRCRAFT

MP 27: 2 CASA 235 MPA; 15 GAF N-22B *Searchmaster B*; 10 GAF N-22SL *Searchmaster L*

TPT 15: 1 CN-235M; 2 DHC-5 *Buffalo*; 4 CASA 212-200 *Aviocar*; 4 PA-34 *Seneca*; 4 Rockwell *Commander* 100; 6 PA-38 *Tomahawk*

HELICOPTERS

ASW 9 HAS-1 *Wasp*

SPT 14: 8 PZL Mi-2 *Hoplite* AS-332; 6 NAS-322L *Super Puma*

UTL 22: 3 EC-120B *Colibri* (+6 on order); 2 NB-412 (Bell 412) *Twin Huey**; 17 NBO-105 (Bö-105)

Marines ε20,000

FORCES BY ROLE

SF   1 bn

Marine   1st marine corps gp (total: 3 marine bn) based Surabaya; 1 indep marine corp gp (total: 3 bn) based Jakarta; 1 marine bde (total: 3 bn) based Teluk, Rata and Sumatra

Cbt spt   1 regt (arty, AD)

EQUIPMENT BY TYPE

LT TK 55 PT-76†

RECCE 21 BRDM

AIFV 34: 24 AMX-10P; 10 AMX-10 PAC 90

APC (W) 100 BTR-50P

ARTY 62+

TOWED 50+: **105mm** 22 LG1 MK II; **122mm** 28 M-38 M-1938

MRL 140mm 12 BM-14

MOR 81mm

AD • GUNS 150: **40mm** 5 L/60 / L/70; **57mm** S-60

Fleet Command

FORCES BY ROLE

Navy   Two fleets: East (Surabaya), West (Jakarta). Planned; 1 HQ (Surabaya): 3 commands: Riau (West); Papua (East); Makassar (Central)

Forward   1 Kupang (West Timor); 1 Tahuna
Operating Bases   (North Sulawesi)

Air Force 24,000

2 operational cmds (East and West) plus trg cmd. Only 45% of ac op

FORCES BY ROLE

Ftr   1 sqn with 8 F-5E *Tiger II*; 4 F-5F *Tiger II*

Ftr/FGA 1 sqn with 2 Su-30 MKI *Flanker* (multi-role); 2 Su-27SK *Flanker* (AD); 1 sqn with 7 F-16A 3 F-16B *Fighting Falcon*; 1 sqn with 11 A-4E *Skyhawk*; 1 TA-4H *Skyhawk*; 2 TA-4J *Skyhawk*; 2 sqn with 7 *Hawk* MK109; 28 *Hawk* MK209

FAC   1 flt with 12 OV-10F *Bronco** mostly non-operational

MR   1 sqn with 3 B-737-200

Tpt/Tkr 5 sqn with 1 B-707; 8 C-130B *Hercules*; 2 KC-130B *Hercules*; 4 C-130H *Hercules*; 6 C-130H-30 *Hercules*; 10 NC-212 (CASA 212) *Aviocar*; 10 CN-235-110; 5 Cessna 401; 2 Cessna 402; 6 F-27-400M *Troopship*; 1 F-28-1000; 2 F-28-3000; 3 L-100-30; 1 SC.7 3M *Skyvan* (survey); 4 Cessna 207 *Stationair*

Trg   3 sqn with 2 Cessna 172; 39 AS-202 *Bravo*; 7 *Hawk* MK53*; 7 KT-1B; 19 SF-260M/SF-260W *Warrior*; 20 T-34C *Turbo Mentor*; 6 T-41D *Mescalero*

Hel   3 sqn with 10 S-58T; 5 NAS-332L (AS-332L) *Super Puma* (VIP/CSAR); 11 NAS-330 (SA-330) *Puma* (1 NAS-330SM VIP); 12 EC-120B *Colibri*

EQUIPMENT BY TYPE

AIRCRAFT 94 combat capable

FTR 24: 2 Su-27SK *Flanker* (AD); 7 F-16A *Fighting Falcon*; 3 F-16B *Fighting Falcon*; 8 F-5E *Tiger II*; 4 F-5F *Tiger II*

FGA 48: 2 Su-30 MKI *Flanker* (multi-role); 11 A-4E *Skyhawk*; 7 *Hawk* MK109; 28 *Hawk* MK209 (FGA/ftr)

FAC 12 OV-10F *Bronco** mostly non-operational

TKR 2 KC-130B *Hercules*

TPT 62: 1 B-707; 3 B-737-200; 8 C-130B *Hercules*; 4 C-130H *Hercules*; 6 C-130H-30 *Hercules*; 10 CN-235-110; 5 Cessna 401; 2 Cessna 402; 6 F-27-400M *Troopship*; 1 F-28-1000; 2 F-28-3000; 3 L-100-30; 10 NC-212 (CASA 212) *Aviocar*; 1 SC.7 3M *Skyvan* (survey)

UTL 6: 2 Cessna 172; 4 Cessna 207 *Stationair*

TRG 101: 39 AS-202 *Bravo*; 7 *Hawk* MK53*; 7 KT-1B; 19 SF-260M/SF-260W *Warrior*; 20 T-34C *Turbo Mentor*; 6 T-41D *Mescalero*; 1 TA-4H *Skyhawk**; 2 TA-4J *Skyhawk**

HELICOPTERS

SAR 10 S-58T

SPT 16: 5 NAS-332L (AS-332L) *Super Puma* (VIP/CSAR); 11 NAS-330 (SA-330) *Puma* (1 NAS-330SM VIP)

UTL 12 EC-120B *Colibri*

MSL • TACTICAL

ASM AGM-65G *Maverick*

AAM AIM-9P *Sidewinder*

Special Forces (Paskhasau)

Special Ops   3 (PASKHASAU) wg (*total*: 6 special ops sqn); 4 indep coy

Paramilitary ε280,000 active

Naval Auxiliary Service

PATROL AND COASTAL COMBATANTS 71

PCC 65 *Kal Kangean*

PCI 6 *Carpentaria*

Customs

PATROL AND COASTAL COMBATANTS • PCI 55

Marine Police

PATROL AND COASTAL COMBATANTS 85

PSOH 2 *Bisma*

PCC 14 *Bango*

PC 37

PBI 32

Police ε280,000 (including 14,000 police 'mobile bde' (BRIMOB) org in 56 coy, incl CT unit (Gegana))

APC (W) 34 *Tactica*
AIRCRAFT • TPT 5: 2 Beech 18; 2 NC-212 (CASA 212) *Aviocar*; 1 Rockwell *Turbo Commander* 680
HELICOPTERS • UTL 22: 3 Bell 206 *JetRanger*; 19 NBO-105 (Bö-105)

KPLP (Coast and Seaward Defence Command)

Responsible to Military Sea Communications Agency
PATROL AND COASTAL COMBATANTS 11
   PSO 2 Arda Dedali
   PCC 9: 4 *Golok* (SAR); 5 *Kujang*
   LOGISTICS AND SUPPORT • ABU 1 *Jadayat*

Reserve Organisations

Kamra People's Security ε40,000 (report for 3 weeks' basic training each year; part time police auxiliary)

NON-STATE ARMED GROUPS

see Part II

DEPLOYMENT

DEMOCRATIC REPUBLIC OF CONGO
UN • MONUC 175; 15 obs

GEORGIA
UN • UNOMIG 4 obs

LEBANON
UN • UNIFIL 856

LIBERIA
UN • UNMIL 3 obs

NEPAL
UN • UNMIN 6 obs

SUDAN
UN • UNMIS 10 obs

Japan J

Japanese Yen ¥		2006	2007	2008
GDP	¥	507tr	512tr	
	US$	4.34tr	4.65tr	
per capita	US$	34,051	36,515	
Growth	%	2.2	2.0	
Inflation	%	0.2	-0.3	
Def bdgt	¥	4.81tr	4.80tr	
	US$	41.14bn	43.65bn	
US$1=¥		117	110	

Population   127,467,972
Ethnic groups: Korean <1%

Age	0–14	15–19	20–24	25–29	30–64	65 plus
Male	7%	3%	3%	3%	24%	8%
Female	7%	3%	3%	3%	24%	10%

Capabilities

ACTIVE 240,400 (Ground Self-Defense Force 148,300 Maritime Self- Defense Force 44,500 Air 45,900 Central Staff 1,700) **Paramilitary 12,250**

RESERVE 41,800 (Navy 1,000 Air 800 General Reserve Army (GSDF) 33,800 Ready Reserve Army (GSDF) 6,200)

ORGANISATIONS BY SERVICE

Ground Self-Defense Force 148,300

FORCES BY ROLE
5 Army HQ (regional comds)

Composite	1 bde
Army	9 div
Armd	1 div
Inf	4 bde
Spec ops	1 unit
AB	1 bde
Arty	1 bde; 2 unit
Engr	5 bde
Hel	1 bde
Trg	3 bde; 1 regt
AD	2 bde; 3 gp

EQUIPMENT BY TYPE
MBT 900: 600 Type-74; 300 Type-90
RECCE 100 Type-87
AIFV 70 Type-89
APC 790
   APC (T) 330 Type-73
   APC (W) 460: 230 Type-82; 230 Type-96
ARTY 1,920
   SP 230: **155mm** 150: 110 Type-75; 40 Type-99; **203mm** 80 M-110A2
   TOWED 155mm 420 FH-70
   MRL 227mm 100 MLRS

MOR 1,150
SP 120mm 20
TOWED 1,130: **81mm** 690; **107mm** 80; **120mm** 360
AT
MSL • MANPATS 650: 20 Type-64; 200 Type-79 *Jyu-MAT*; 430 Type-87 *Chu-MAT*
RCL 2,760: **SP 106mm** 40 Type-60; **84mm** 2,720 *Carl Gustav*
RL 680 **89mm**
AIRCRAFT
TPT 10 LR-2 (Beech 350) *Super King Air*
UTL 10 LR-1 (MU-2)
HELICOPTERS
ATK 85: 5 AH-64D *Apache;* 80 AH-1S *Cobra*
SPT 53: 3 EC-225LP (VIP); 50 CH-47J (CH-47D) *Chinook/CH-47JA Chinook*
UTL 300: 120 OH-60 (MD-500); 150 UH-1J (UH-1H) *Iroquois*; 30 UH-60JA (UH-60L) *Black Hawk*
AD • **SAM** 720
SP 170: 60 Type-81 *Tan-SAM;* 110 Type-93 *Kin-SAM*
TOWED 190 MIM-23B *I-HAWK*
MANPAD 360: 50 FIM-92A *Stinger;* 310 Type-91 *Kin-SAM*
GUNS 60
SP 35mm 50 Type-87 SP
TOWED 35mm 10 (twin)
MSL • SSM • COASTAL 100 Type-88

Maritime Self- Defense Force 44,500

Surface units organised into 4 Escort Flotillas with a mix of 7–8 warships each. Bases Yokosuka, Kure, Sasebo, Maizuru. SSK organised into 2 Flotillas with bases at Kure and Yokosuka. Remaining units assigned to 5 regional districts.

EQUIPMENT BY TYPE
SUBMARINES • TACTICAL • SSK 16:
6 *Harushio* each with 6 single 533mm TT each with T-89 HWT/UGM-84C *Harpoon* tactical USGW
10 *Oyashio* each with 6 single 533mm TT each with UGM-84C *Harpoon* tactical USGW
PRINCIPAL SURFACE COMBATANTS 53
DESTROYERS 44
DDG 40:
6 *Asagiri* each with 2 triple 324mm ASTT (6 eff.) each with Mk 46 LWT, 1 Mk 112 octuple (8 eff.) with tactical ASROC, 2 Mk 141 *Harpoon* quad (8 eff.) each with RGM-84C *Harpoon* tactical SSM, 1 Mk 29 *Sea Sparrow* octuple with 16 RIM-7F/M *Sea Sparrow* SAM, 1 76mm gun, (capacity 1 SH-60J/K *Seahawk* ASW hel)
1 *Atago* (*Aegis* Base Line 7) each with 2 quad SSM launchers (8 eff.) with tactical SSM-1B, 1 MK 41 VLS (64 eff.) with SM-2 MR SAM, tactical ASROC, 1 MK 41 VLS (32 eff.) with SM-2 MR SAM, 2 triple 324mm ASTT (6 eff.) each with MK 46 LWT, 1 127mm gun, (capacity 1 SH-60J *Seahawk* ASW hel)
2 *Hatakaze* each with 2 Mk 141 *Harpoon* quad (8 eff.) each with RGM-84C *Harpoon* tactical SSM, 1 Mk 13 GMLS with 40 SM-1 MR SAM, 2 triple 324mm ASTT (6 eff.), 2 127mm gun, 1 hel landing platform
11 *Hatsuyuki* each with 1 Mk 112 octuple (8 eff.) with

tactical ASROC, 2 Mk 141 *Harpoon* quad (8 eff.) each with RGM-84C *Harpoon* tactical SSM, 1+ Mk 29 *Sea Sparrow* octuple with 16 RIM-7F/M *Sea Sparrow* SAM, 2 triple ASTT (6 eff.) each with Mk 46 LWT, 1 76mm gun, (capacity 1 SH-60J/K *Seahawk* ASW hel)
4 *Kongou* (with hel deck) *Aegis* Baseline 4/5 each with 2 Mk 141 *Harpoon* quad (8 eff.) each with RGM-84C *Harpoon* tactical SSM, 1 29 cell Mk 41 VLS (29 eff.) with SM-2 MR SAM, tactical ASROC, 1 61 cell Mk 41 VLS (61 eff.) with SM-2 MR SAM, tactical ASROC, 2 triple 324mm ASTT (6 eff.), 1 127mm gun
9 *Murasame* each with 2 quad (8 eff.) each with tactical SSM-1B, 1 16 cells Mk 41 VLS with up to 16 tactical ASROC, 1 16 cell Mk 48 VLS with RIM-7M *Sea Sparrow* SAM, 2 triple 324mm TT (6 eff.) each with Mk 46 LWT, 2 76mm gun, (capacity 1 SH-60J/K *Seahawk* ASW hel)
2 *Tachikaze* each with 1 Mk 13 GMLS with 8-16 RGM-84C *Harpoon* tactical SSM, 32 SM-1 MR SAM, 1 Mk 112 octuple (8 eff.) with up to 16 tactical ASROC, 1 2 triple 324mm ASTT (6 eff.) each with Mk 46 LWT, 127mm gun
5 *Takanami* (*Improved Murasame*) each with 2 quad SSM launchers (8 eff.) each with tactical SSM-1B, 1 32 cell Mk 41 VLS (32 eff.) with tactical ASROC/RIM-7M/ESSM *Sea Sparrow* SAM, 2 triple 324mm TT (6 eff.) each with Mk 46 LWT, 1 *Otobreda* 127mm gun, (capacity 1 SH-60J/K *Seahawk* ASW hel)
DD 4:
2 *Haruna* each with 1 Mk 112 octuple (8 eff.) with tactical ASROC, 1 Mk 29 *Sea Sparrow* octuple with RIM-7F/M *Sea Sparrow* SAM, 2 triple ASTT (6 eff.) each with Mk 46 LWT, 2 127mm gun, (capacity 3 SH-60J/K *Seahawk* ASW hel)
2 *Shirane* each with 1 Mk 112 octuple (8 eff.) with tactical ASROC, 1+ Mk 29 *Sea Sparrow* octuple with 24+ RIM-162A *Sea Sparrow* SAM, 2 triple ASTT (6 eff.) each with Mk 46 LWT, 2 127mm gun, (capacity 3 SH-60J/K *Seahawk* ASW hel)
FRIGATES • FFG 9:
6 *Abukuma* each with 2 Mk 141 *Harpoon* quad (8 eff.) each with RGM-84C *Harpoon* tactical SSM, 1 Mk 112 octuple (8 eff.) with tactical ASROC, 2 triple ASTT (6 eff.) each with Mk 46 LWT, 1 76mm gun
1 *Ishikari* with 2 Mk 141 *Harpoon* quad (8 eff.) each with RGM-84C *Harpoon* tactical SSM, 2 triple ASTT (6 eff.) each with Mk 46 LWT, 1 Type 71/ 4 tube Mitsubishi 375mm Bofors (4 eff.), 1 76mm gun
2 *Yubari* each with 2 Mk 141 *Harpoon* quad (8 eff.) each with RGM-84C *Harpoon* tactical SSM, 2 triple ASTT (6 eff.), 1 Type 71/ 4 tube Mitsubishi 375mm Bofors (4 eff.), 1 76mm gun
PATROL AND COASTAL COMBATANTS 9
PFM 6 *Hayabusa* each with 4 tactical SSM-1B, 1 76mm gun
PHM 3 *Ichi-Go* each with 4 tactical SSM-1B
MINE WARFARE • MINE COUNTERMEASURES 31
MCM SPT 4:
2 *Nijma*
2 *Uraga* each with 1 hel landing platform (for MH-53E)

MSO 3 *Yaeyama*
MSC 24: 3 *Hatsushima*; 12 *Sugashima*; 9 *Uwajima*
AMPHIBIOUS
  LS • LST 5:
    3 *Osumi* each with 1 hel landing platform (for 2 x CH-47) (capacity 10 Type-90 MBTs; 2 LCAC(L) ACV; 330 troops)
    2 *Yura* (capacity 70 troops)
  LANDING CRAFT 18
    LCU 2 *Yusotei*
    LCM 10
    ACV • LCAC(L) (capacity either 1 MBT or 60 troops)
LOGISTICS AND SUPPORT 76:
  AOE 5: 2 *Mashuu*; 3 *Towada*
  AS 1 *Chiyoda* (also has submarine rescue facilities)
  ASR 1 *Chihaya*
  ARC 1 *Muroto*
  AG 3: 2 *Kurihama*; 1 *Asuka* (wpn trials)
  AGOS 2 *Hibiki*
  AGS 4: 2 *Futami*; 1 *Suma*; 1 *Nichinan*
  AGB 1 *Shirase*
  ATF 22
  TRG 6: 1 *Kashima*; 1 *Shimayuki*; 2 *Yamagiri* TV35 with 2 triple ASTT (6 eff.) each with Mk 46 LWT, 1 Mk 112 octuple (8 eff.) with tactical ASROC, 1 Type 71/ 4 tube Mitsubshi 375mm Bofors (4 eff.), 4 76mm gun; 1 *Tenryu* (trg spt ship); 1 *Kurobe* (trg spt ship)
  SPT 3 *Hiuchi*
  YDT 6
  YTM 21
FACILITIES
Bases Located at Kure, Sasebo, Yokosuka, Maizuru, Ominato

Naval Aviation ε9,800

FORCES BY ROLE
7 Air Groups
ASW 5 sqn (land based, 1 trg) with SH-60J/K *Seahawk*; 4 sqn (shipboard) with SH-60J *Seahawk*
MR 9 sqn(1 trg) with P-3C *Orion*
EW 1 sqn with EP-3 *Orion*; OP-3C
MCM 1 sqn with MH-53E *Sea Dragon*
SAR 7 sqn with UH-60J *Black Hawk*; 1 sqn with *Shin Meiwa* US-1A
Tpt 1 sqn with YS-11M; LC-90
Trg 1 sqn with OH-6D (MD-500MD); OH-6DA (MD-500ME); 4 sqn with T-5; TC-90; YS-11T

EQUIPMENT BY TYPE
AIRCRAFT 80 combat capable
  MP 80 P-3C *Orion**
  SAR 7: 5 *Shin Meiwa* US-1A; 2 *Shin Meiwa* US-2
  TPT 9: 4 YS-11M; 5 LC-90
  TRG 63: 33 T-5; 24 TC-90; 6 YS-11T
HELICOPTERS 99 combat capable
  ASW 99: 84 SH-60J *Seahawk*; 15 SH-60K
  MCM 9 MH-53E *Sea Dragon*
  SAR 18 UH-60J *Black Hawk*
  SPT 14 EH101 (currently being delivered)

  UTL 4: 3 S-61A *Black Hawk*; 1 USH-60K
  TRG 9: 4 OH-6D (MD-500MD); 5 OH-6DA (MD-500ME)

Air Self-Defense Force up to 45,900

Flying hours 148 hrs/year on aircraft
FORCES BY ROLE
7 cbt wings
Ftr 7 sqn with 130 F-15J *Eagle*; 3 sqn with 70 F-4EJ (F-4E) *Phantom II*; 2 sqn with 40 Mitsubishi F-2
Recce 1 sqn with 20 RF-EJ (RF-4E) *Phantom II**
EW 2 sqn with 1 Kawasaki EC-1; 10 YS-11E
AEW 2 sqn with total of 10 E-2C *Hawkeye*; 4 E-767 (AWACS)
SAR 1 wg with 20 U-125A *Peace Krypton*; LR-1 (MU-2); 30 UH-60J *Black Hawk*; 10 KV-107 (Boeing Vertol 107)
Tkr 1 sqn with 1 KC-767A
Tpt 3 sqn with 20 C-1; 10 C-130H *Hercules*; YS-11; 1 sqn with B-747-400 (VIP); 4 (hy-lift) flt with 10 CH-47 *Chinook*
Liaison some sqn with 10 U-4; 90+ T-4
CAL 1 sqn with U-125-800 *Peace Krypton*; YS-11
Test 1 wg with F-15 *Eagle*; 10 Kawasaki T-4
Trg 5 wg; 12 sqn with 20 F-15 *Eagle**; 20 Mitsubishi F-2B; ; 80 T-4; 30 T-7; 10 T-400

EQUIPMENT BY TYPE
AIRCRAFT 280 combat capable
  FTR 260: 150 F-15 *Eagle*; 40 Mitsubishi F-2; 70 F-4EJ (F-4E) *Phantom II*
  RECCE 20 RF-EJ (RF-4E) *Phantom II**
  EW 1 Kawasaki EC-1
  AEW 14: 10 E-2C *Hawkeye*; 4 E-767 (AWACS)
  SAR 20 U-125A *Peace Krypton*
  TPT 30: 20 C-1; 10 C-130H *Hercules*
  TKR: 1 KC-767A (first of 4)
  UTL 10 U-4
  TRG 250+: 10 T-4; 20 Mitsubishi F-2B; 80 T-4; 90+ more; 30 T-7; 10 T-400; 10 YS-11E,
HELICOPTERS
  SAR 30 UH-60J *Black Hawk*
  SPT 20: 10 CH-47 *Chinook*; 10 KV-107 (Boeing Vertol 107)

Air Defence

FORCES BY ROLE
ac control and warning
AD 4 wg; 28 radar sites; 1 (Air Base Defence) gp with Type-81 *Tan-SAM*; FIM-92A *Stinger*; Type-91 *Kin-SAM*; M-167 *Vulcan*
SAM 6 gp, comprising 24 SAM sqn each with 4 bty of 8 launchers MIM-104 *Patriot*) 16 bty of PAC-3 from 2006; two delivered 2007

EQUIPMENT BY TYPE
AD • SAM 192+
  SP Type-81 *Tan-SAM*
  TOWED 192+ MIM-104 *Patriot*; PAC-3
  MANPAD FIM-92A *Stinger*; Type-91 *Kei-SAM*
  GUNS • TOWED 20mm M-167 *Vulcan*

MSL
ASM ASM-1Type-80; ASM-2 Type-93;
AAM AAM-4 (Type-99); AIM-7 *Sparrow*; AIM-9 *Sidewinder*; Type-90 (AAM-3)

FACILITIES
Radar stn   28 (ac control and warning)

Paramilitary 12,250

Coast Guard
Ministry of Transport, no cbt role
PATROL AND COASTAL COMBATANTS 348
PSOH 24: 1 *Izu*; 1 *Kojima* (trg); 2 *Mizuho*; 1 *Shikishima*; 10 *Soya*; 1 *Miura*; 1 *Nojima*; 7 *Ojika*
PSO 60: 22 *Shiretoko*; 3 *Aso*; 14 *Teshio*; 2 *Takatori*; 15 *Bihoro*; 4 *Amani*;
PCO 3 *Tokara*
PFC 27 *PS-Type*
PCC 60 *PC-Type*
PCI 174: 170 *CL-Type*; 4 *FM-Type*
LOGISTICS AND SUPPORT 74: 4 ABU; 13 AGHS; 54 small tenders; 3 Trg
AIRCRAFT
MP 2 *Falcon 900*
SAR 2 SAAB 340B
TPT 17: 10 LR-2 (Beech 350) *Super King Air*; 5 Beech 200T; 2 *Gulfstream V* (MP)
UTL 6: 1 Cessna U-206G *Stationair*; 5 YS-11A
HELICOPTERS
SPT 4 AS-332 *Super Puma*
UTL 40: 4 Bell 206B *JetRanger II*; 26 Bell 212; 8 Bell 412 *Twin Huey*; 3 S-76C

NON-STATE ARMED GROUPS
see Part II

DEPLOYMENT

KUWAIT
210

MIDDLE EAST
UN • UNDOF 30

NEPAL
UN • UNMIN 6 obs

FOREIGN FORCES
United States Army: 2,417; Navy: 3,716; USAF: 13,164; USMC 13,771; USPACOM: 9 principal surface combatants located at Yokosuka; 1 *Kitty Hawk* aircraft carrier located at Yokosuka; 1 *Blue Ridge* LCC (capacity 3 LCPL; 2 LCVP; 700 troops; 1 SH-3H *Sea King* utl hel) located at Yokosuka; 4 amphibious vessels located at Sasebo; base located at Sasebo; base located at Yokosuka; 1 HQ (7th Fleet) located at Yokosuka; 1 5th Air Force HQ located at Okinawa–Kadena AB; 1 HQ (9th Theater Army Area Command) located at Zama (HQ USARPAC)); Elms MEF div; 1 ftr wg located at Okinawa–Kadena AB (2 ftr sqn with total of 18 F-16 *Fighting Falcon* located at Misawa AB); 1 ftr wg located

at Okinawa–Kadena AB (1 SAR sqn with 8 HH-60G *Pave Hawk*, 1 AEW sqn with 2 E-3B *Sentry*, 2 ftr sqn with total of 24 F-15C *Eagle*/F-15D *Eagle*); 1 MCM sqn located at Sasebo; 1 special ops gp located at Okinawa–Kadena AB; 1 airlift wg located at Yokota AB with 10 C-130E *Hercules*; 4 C-21 *Learjet*; 4 C-9 *Nightingale*

Korea, Democratic Peoples Republic of DPRK

North Korean Won		2006*	2007 *	2008
GDP	US$			
per capita	US$			
Def bdgt	won			
	US$			

US$1=won

* definitive economic data not available

Population   23,301,725

Age	0–14	15–19	20–24	25–29	30–64	65 plus
Male	12%	4%	4%	3%	22%	3%
Female	12%	4%	4%	3%	23%	5%

Capabilities

ACTIVE 1,106,000 (Army 950,000 Navy 46,000 Air 110,000) Paramilitary 189,000
Terms of service Army 5–12 years Navy 5–10 years Air Force 3–4 years, followed by compulsory part-time service to age 40. Thereafter service in the Worker/Peasant Red Guard to age 60.

RESERVE 4,700,000 (Army 600,000, Armed Forces 4,035,000 Navy 65,000), Paramilitary 3,500,000
Reservists are assigned to units (see also Paramilitary)

ORGANISATIONS BY SERVICE

Army ε950,000
FORCES BY ROLE

Army	corps tps: 14 arty bde (incl 122mm, 152mm, SP, MRL); 1 (FROG) SSM regt; 1 *Scud* SSM bde, 6 hy arty bde (incl MRL)
Armd	1 corps; 15 bde
Mech	4 corps
Inf	12 corps; 27 div; 14 bde
Arty	2 corps; 21 bde
MRL	9 bde
Capital Defence	1 corps

Special Purpose Forces Command 88,000

Army	6 sniper bde
Recce	17 bn
Amph	2 sniper bde
SF	8 Bureau of Reconnaissance bn

Lt inf 9 bde

AB 2 sniper bde; 3 bde; 1 bn

Reserves 600,000

Inf 40 div; 18 bde

EQUIPMENT BY TYPE

MBT 3,500+ T-34/T-54/T-55/T-62/Type-59

LT TK 560+: 560 PT-76; M-1985

APC 2,500+

APC (T) Type-531 (Type-63); VTT-323

APC (W) 2,500 BTR-40/BTR-50/BTR-60/ BTR-80A/BTR-152

ARTY 17,900+

SP 4,400: **122mm** M-1977/M-1981/M-1985/M-1991; **130mm** M-1975/M-1981/M-1991; **152mm** M-1974/M-1977; **170mm** M-1978/M-1989

TOWED 3,500: **122mm** D-30/D-74/M-1931/37; **130mm** M-46; **152mm** M-1937/M-1938/M-1943

GUN/MOR 120mm (reported)

MRL 2,500: **107mm** Type-63; **122mm** BM-11/M-1977 (BM-21)/M-1985/M-1992/M-1993; **240mm** M-1985/M-1989/M-1991

MOR 7,500: **82mm** M-37; **120mm** M-43; **160mm** M-43

AT • MSL

SP AT-3 9K11 *Sagger*

MANPATS AT-1 *Snapper*; AT-4 9K111 *Spigot*; AT-5 9K113 *Spandrel*

RCL 82mm 1,700 B-10

AD • SAM • MANPAD ε10,000+ SA-16 *Gimlet*/SA-7 *Grail*

GUNS 11,000

SP 14.5mm M-1984; **23mm** M-1992; **37mm** M-1992; **57mm** M-1985

TOWED 11,000: **14.5mm** ZPU-1/ZPU-2/ZPU-4; **23mm** ZU-23; **37mm** M-1939; **57mm** S-60; **85mm** M-1939 *KS-12*; **100mm** KS-19

MSL • SSM 64+: 24 FROG-3/FROG-5/FROG-7; ε10 *No-dong* (ε90+ msl); 30+ *Scud*-B/*Scud*-C (ε200+ msl)

Navy ε46,000

FORCES BY ROLE

Navy 2 (Fleet) HQ located at Tasa-ri; 1 HQ located at Nampo; 1 HQ located at Toejo Dong

EQUIPMENT BY TYPE

SUBMARINES • TACTICAL 63

SSK 22 PRC Type-031/FSU *Romeo*† each with 8 single 533mm TT with 14 SAET-60 HWT

SSC 21 *Sang-O*† each with 2 single 533mm TT each with Russian 53–65 ASW

SSI 20†

PRINCIPAL SURFACE COMBATANTS 8

FRIGATES • FF 3:

2 *Najin* each with 2 single each with 1 SS-N-2 tactical SSM, 2 RBU 1200 (10 eff.), 2 100mm sun

1 *Soho* with 4 single each with 1 SS-N-2 tactical SSM, 2 RBU 1200 (10 eff.), 1 100mm gun, 1 hel landing platform (for med hel)

CORVETTES • FS 5:

4 *Sariwon* each with 1 85mm gun

1 *Tral* each with 1 85mm gun

PATROL AND COASTAL COMBATANTS 335+

PTG 16:

6 *Sohung*

10 *Soju* each with 4 single each with 1 SS-N-2 tactical SSM

PFM 18:

4 *Huangfen* each with 4 single each with 1 SS-N-2 tactical SSM

6 *Komar* each with 2 single each with 1 SS-N-2 tactical SSM

8 *Osa* II each with 2 single each with 1 SS-N-2 tactical SSM

PHT 100: 60 *Ku Song*; 40 *Sin Hung*

PFC 19:

6 *Hainan* each with 4 RBU 1200 (20 eff.)

13 *Taechong* each with 2 RBU 1200 (10 eff.)

PFI 12 *Shanghai* II

PC 6 *Chong-Ju* each with 2 RBU 1200 (10 eff.), 1 85mm gun

PCI 164 (less than 100 tons); 18 FSU SO-1, 54 *Chong-Jin*, 59 *Chaho*, 33 *Sinpo*

MINE WARFARE • MINE COUNTERMEASURES 24: 19 *Yukto* I; 5 *Yukto* II

AMPHIBIOUS

LSM 10 *Hantae* (capacity 3 tanks; 350 troops)

CRAFT 251:

LCPL 96 *Nampo* (capacity 35 troops)

LCM 25

LCVP 130 (capacity 50 troops)

LOGISTICS AND SUPPORT 23:

AS 8 (converted cargo ships); **ASR** 1 Kowan; **AGI** 14 (converted fishing vessels)

FACILITIES

Bases Located at Tasa-ri, Koampo, Chodo-ri, Sagon-ni, Pipa Got, Nampo (West Coast); Puam-Dong, Toejo Dong, Chaho Nodongjagu, Mayang-do, Mugye-po, Najin, Songjon-pardo, Changjon, Munchon (East Coast)

Coastal Defence

FORCES BY ROLE

SSM 2 regt (*Silkworm* in 6 sites, and probably some mobile launchers)

EQUIPMENT BY TYPE

ARTY • TOWED 122mm M-1931/37; **152mm** M-1937

COASTAL 130mm M-1992; SM-4-1

Air Force 110,000

4 air divs. 1st, 2nd and 3rd Air Divs (cbt) responsible for N, E and S air defence sectors respectively. 8th Air Div (trg) responsible for NE sector. 33 regts (11 ftr/fga, 2 bbr, 7 hel, 7 pt, 6 trg) plus 3 indep air bns (recce/EW, test and evaluation, naval spt). The AF controls the national airline. Approx 70 full time/contingency air bases.

Flying hours 20 hrs/year on ac

FORCES BY ROLE

Bbr 3 (lt) regt with 80 H-5 (Il-28) *Beagle*

Ftr/FGA	1 regt with 20 MiG-29 *Fulcrum*; 1 regt with 18 Su-7 *Fitter*; 6 regt with 107 J-5 (MiG-17F) *Fresco C*; 5 regt with 120 J-7 (MiG-21F) *Fishbed C*; 4 regt with 159 J-6 (MiG-19S) *Farmer B*; 1 regt with 46 MiG-23 *Flogger*; 1 regt with 34 Su-25 *Frogfoot*
Tpt	regts with ε300 Y-5 (An-2) *Colt* (to infiltrate 2 air force sniper brigades deep into ROK rear areas); 6 An-24 *Coke*; 2 Il-18 *Coot*; 4 Il-62M *Classic*; 2 Tu-134 *Crusty*; 4 Tu-154 *Careless*
Aslt hel	regt with 24 Mi-24 *Hind*
Trg	regts with 6 MiG-21 *Fishbed*; 35 FT-2 (MiG-15UTI) *Midget*; 180 CJ-5 (Yak-18)/CJ-6
Hel	some regt with 48 Z-5 (Mi-4) *Hound*; 15 Mi-17 (Mi-8MT) *Hip H*/Mi-8 *Hip*; 139 PZL Mi-2 *Hoplite*; 80 Hughes 500D (Tpt)
SAM	19 bde with a total of 3,400 SAM; 133 SA-3 *Goa*; 179+ SA-2 *Guideline*; 38 SA-5 *Gammon*; + SA-14 *Gremlin*/SA-16 *Gimlet*/SA-7 *Grail* (Possible Western systems, reverse-engineered *Stinger*)

EQUIPMENT BY TYPE

AIRCRAFT 590 combat capable
  BBR 80 H-5 (Il-28) *Beagle*
  FTR 299: 20 MiG-29 *Fulcrum*; 46 MiG-23 *Flogger*; 6 MiG-21; 120 J-7 (MiG-21F) *Fishbed C*; 107 J-5 (MiG-17F) *Fresco C*
  FGA 211: 34 Su-25 *Frogfoot*; 18 Su-7 *Fitter*; 159 J-6 (MiG-19S) *Farmer B*
  TPT 318: 6 An-24 *Coke*; 2 Il-18 *Coot*; 4 Il-62M *Classic*; 2 Tu-134 *Crusty*; 4 Tu-154 *Careless*; ε300 Y-5 (An-2) *Colt* (to infiltrate 2 air force sniper brigades deep into ROK rear areas)
  TRG 215: 180 CJ-5 (Yak-18)/CJ-6; 35 FT-2 (MiG-15UTI) *Midget*

HELICOPTERS
  ATK 24 Mi-24 *Hind*
  SPT 202: 48 Z-5 (Mi-4) *Hound*; 15 MI-17 (Mi-8MT) *Hip H*/Mi-8 *Hip* Spt; 139 PZL MI-2 *Hoplite*
  UTL 80 Hughes 500D (Tpt)
UAV *Shmel*
AD • SAM 3400+
  TOWED 312+: 179+ SA-2 *Guideline*; 133 SA-3 *Goa*
  STATIC/SHELTER 38 SA-5 *Gammon*
  MANPAD 3,050+ SA-7 *Grail*/SA-14 *Gremlin*/SA-16 *Gimlet* (Possible Western systems, reverse-engineered *Stinger*)
MSL • AAM AA-10 *Alamo*; AA-11 *Archer*; AA-2 *Atoll*; AA-7 *Apex*; AA-8 *Aphid*; PL-5; PL-7

Paramilitary 189,000 active

Security Troops 189,000 (incl border guards, public safety personnel)
Ministry of Public Security

Worker/Peasant Red Guard 3,500,000+ reservists
Org on a provincial/town/village basis; comd structure is bde–bn–coy–pl; small arms with some mor and AD guns (but many units unarmed)

DEPLOYMENT

SUB-SAHARAN AFRICA
Army (Advisers in some 12 African countries)

Korea, Republic of ROK

South Korean Won		2006	2007	2008
GDP	won	847tr	891tr	
	US$	888bn	971bn	
per capita	US$	18,176	19,790	
Growth	%	5.0	4.8	
Inflation	%	2.2	2.5	
Def bdgt	won	23.5tr	ε24.7tr	
	US$	24.6bn	ε26.9bn	
US$1=won		954	918	

Population   49,044,790

Age	0–14	15–19	20–24	25–29	30–64	65 plus
Male	10%	3%	4%	4%	25%	4%
Female	9%	3%	4%	4%	25%	5%

Capabilities

ACTIVE 687,000 (Army 560,000 Navy 63,000 Air 64,000) Paramilitary 4,500
Terms of service conscription: Army 26 months; Navy and Air Force 30 months; First Combat Forces (Mobilisation Reserve Forces) or Regional Combat Forces (Homeland Defence Forces) to age 33

RESERVE 4,500,000 Paramilitary 3,500,000
Being re-organised

ORGANISATIONS BY SERVICE

Army 420,000; 140,000 conscript (total 560,000)

FORCES BY ROLE
Commands: 3 fd Army, 1 special warfare, 1 capital defence, 1 army avn

Army	10 corps
Mech inf	5 div (*total*: 1 recce bde, 1 fd arty bde, 1 engr bde, 3 tk bde, 3 mech inf bde)
Inf	17 div (*each*: 1 arty regt (4 arty bn), 1 recce bn, 1 engr bn, 1 tk bn, 3 inf regt); 2 indep bde
SF	7 bde
Air aslt	1 bde
Counter-Infiltration	3 bde
SSM	3 bn
ADA	3 bde
SAM	2 (*Nike Hercules*) bn (10 sites); 3 (I *HAWK*) bn (24 sites)

EQUIPMENT BY TYPE

MBT 2,330: 1,000 Type-88 *K1*; 80 T-80U; 400 M-47; 850 M-48

AIFV 2,040: 40 BMP-3; 2,000 *Doosan*

APC 2,480

  APC (T) 2,260: 1,700 KIFV; 420 M-113; 140 M-577

  APC (W) 220; 20 BTR-80; 200 KM-900/-901 (Fiat 6614)

ARTY 10,774+

  SP 1,089+: **155mm** 1076: ε36 K-9 *Thunder*; 1,040 M-109A2; **175mm** M-107; **203mm** 13 M-110

  TOWED 3,500+: **105mm** 1,700 M-101/KH-178; **155mm** 1,800+ KH-179/M-114/M-115

  MRL 185: **130mm** 156 *Kooryong*; **227mm** 29 MLRS (all ATACMS capable)

  MOR 6,000: **81mm** KM-29 (M-29); **107mm** M-30

AT • MSL • MANPATS AT-7 9K115 *Saxhorn*; TOW-2A

  RCL 57mm; 75mm; 90mm M-67; **106mm** M-40A2

  RL 67mm PZF 44 *Panzerfaust*

  GUNS 58

    SP 90mm 50 M-36

    TOWED 76mm 8 M-18 *Hellcat* (AT gun)

HELICOPTERS

  ATK 60 AH-1F *Cobra*/AH-1J *Cobra*

  SPEC OP 6MH-47E (MH-47E) *Chinook*

  SPT 21: 3 AS-332L *Super Puma*; 18 CH-47D *Chinook*

  UTL 337: 12 Bö-105; 130 Hughes 500D; 45 MD-500; 20 UH-1H *Iroquois*; 130 UH-60P *Black Hawk*

AD • SAM 1,090+

  SP *Chun Ma Pegasus*

  TOWED 110 I-*HAWK* MIM-23B

  STATIC 200 MIM-14 *Nike Hercules*

  MANPAD 780+: 60 FIM-43 *Redeye*; ε200 FIM-92A *Stinger*; 350 *Javelin*; 170 *Mistral*; SA-16 *Gimlet*

  GUNS 330+

    SP 170: **20mm** ε150 KIFV *Vulcan* SPAAG; **30mm** 20 BIHO *Flying Tiger*

    TOWED 160: **20mm** 60 M-167 *Vulcan*; **35mm** 20 GDF-003; **40mm** 80 L/60/L/70; M1

RADAR • LAND AN/TPQ-36 *Firefinder* (arty, mor); AN/TPQ-37 *Firefinder* (arty); RASIT (veh, arty)

MSL • SSM 12 NHK-I/-II *Hyonmu*

Reserves

1 army HQ

Inf 23 div

Navy 44,000; ε19,000 conscript (total 63,000)

EQUIPMENT BY TYPE

SUBMARINES • TACTICAL 12

  SSK 10:

    9 *Chang Bogo* each with 8 single 533mm TT each with SUT HWT

    1 *Son Won-ill* each with 8 single 533mm TT each with SUT HWT (further 2 of class in build)

  SSI 2 KSS-1 *Dolgorae* each with 2 single 406mm TT

PRINCIPAL SURFACE COMBATANTS 44

  DESTROYERS • DDG 7:

    1 *Sejong* KDX-3 each with 2 Mk 41 *Harpoon* quad (8 eff.) each with RGM-84 *Harpoon* tactical SSM, 2 32/64 cell

Mk 41 VLS with *Sea Sparrow* SAM and ESSM, 1 127mm gun, (capacity *Super Lynx* utl hel); (further 2 of class in build)

    3 *Kwanggaeto Daewang* KDX-1 each with 2 Mk 41 *Harpoon* quad (8 eff.) each with RGM-84 *Harpoon* tactical SSM, 1 16 cell Mk 48 VLS with *Sea Sparrow* SAM, 1 127mm gun, (capacity 1 *Super Lynx* utl hel)

    3 *Chungmugong Yi Sun-Jhin* KDX-2 each with 2 Mk 141 *Harpoon* quad (8 eff.) each with 8 RGM-84C *Harpoon* tactical SSM, 2 Mk 41 VLS-32 cells each with SM-2 MR SAM, 1 127mm gun (capacity 1 *Super Lynx* utl hel)

FRIGATES • FFG 9:

  9 *Ulsan* each with 2 Mk 141 *Harpoon* quad (8 eff.) each with 1 RGM-84C *Harpoon* tactical SSM, 2 triple ASTT (6 eff.) each with Mk 46 LWT, 2 76mm gun

CORVETTES • FS 28:

  4 *Dong Hae* each with 2 triple ASTT (6 eff.) each with Mk 46 LWT

  24 *Po Hang* each with 2 MM-38 *Exocet* tactical SSM (fitted on some vessels), 2 triple ASTT (6 eff.) each with Mk 46 LWT

PATROL AND COASTAL COMBATANTS ε75

  PFI 75 *Sea Dolphin*

MINE WARFARE 10

  MINE COUNTERMEASURES 9

    MHC 6 *Kan Kyeong*

    MSC 3 *Yang Yang*

  MINELAYERS • ML 1 *Won San*

AMPHIBIOUS

PRINCIPAL AMPHIBIOUS SHIPS • LPD 1 *Dodko* (capacity 2 LCVP; 10 tanks; 700 troops)

  LS 11

    LST 8: 4 *Alligator* (capacity 20 tanks; 300 troops); 4 *Un Bong* (capacity 16 tanks; 200 troops)

    ACV 3 *Tsaplya* (capacity 1 MBT; 130 troops)

  CRAFT 36: 6 LCT; 20 **LCVP**; 10 **LCM**

LOGISTICS AND SUPPORT 24

  AORH 3 *Chun Jee*

  ARS 1

  AG 1 *Sunjin* (trials spt)

  ATS 2

  AGOR 17 (civil manned, funded by the Min. of Transport)

FACILITIES

Bases Located at Pusan, Mukho, Cheju, Pohang, Mokpo, Chinhae (Fleet HQ and 3rd Fleet), Donghae (1st Fleet), Pyongtaek (2nd Fleet)

Naval Aviation

AIRCRAFT 8 combat capable

  MP ASW 8 P-3C *Orion**

  UTL 5 F406 *Caravan II*

HELICOPTERS

  ASW 24: 11 *Lynx* MK99; 13 *Lynx* MK99-A

  UTL 5 IAR-316 (SA-316) *Alouette III*

Marines 28,000

FORCES BY ROLE

Spt   some unit

Marine 2 div; 1 bde

EQUIPMENT BY TYPE
MBT 60 M-47
AAV 102: 42 AAV-7A1; 60 LVTP-7
ARTY TOWED: 105mm; 155mm
LNCHR: some single (truck mounted) each with RGM-84A *Harpoon* tactical SSM

Air Force 64,000

FORCES BY ROLE
4 Cmds (Ops, Southern Combat Logs, Trg), Tac Airlift Wg and Composite Wg are all responsible to ROK Air Force HQ.

FGA/Ftr	1 wg with 40 F-15K; 2 wg with 104 KF-16C *Fighting Falcon*; 49 KF-16D *Fighting Falcon* 2 wg with 60 F-4D *Phantom II*; 70 F-4E *Phantom II*; 3 wg with 150 F-5E *Tiger II*; 35 F-5F *Tiger II*
FAC	1 wg with 20 Cessna O-1A *Bird Dog*; 20 KO-1
ELINT	(SIGINT) sqn with 4 *Hawker* 800XP
Recce/ TAC	1 gp with 4 *Hawker* 800RA; 18 RF-4C *Phantom II**; 5 RF-5A *Tiger II**; 100 *Harpy*; 3 *Searcher*
SAR	1 sqn with 4 Bell 212; 5 UH-1H *Iroquois*
CCT	1 wg with first of 44 A-50 *Golden Eagle*
Tpt	some wg with 1 B-737-300 (VIP); 2 BAe-748 (VIP); 1 C-118 *Liftmaster*; 10 C-130H *Hercules*; 20 CN-235-220/CN-235M; 3 AS-332 *Super Puma*; 6 CH-47 *Chinook*; 7 KA-32 *Helix C* (SAR); 3 VH-60 *White Knight*
Trg	some sqn with 25 F-5B *Freedom Fighter**; 17 *Hawk* MK67; 85 KT-1; 30 T-38 *Talon*; 15 T-50; 20 Il-103

EQUIPMENT BY TYPE
AIRCRAFT 555 combat capable
FTR/FGA 532: 40 F-15K *Eagle*; 25 F-5B *Freedom Fighter**; 150 F-5E *Tiger II*; 35 F-5F *Tiger II*; 103 KF-16C *Fighting Falcon*; 49 KF-16D *Fighting Falcon*; 60 F-4D *Phantom II*; 70 F-4E *Phantom II*
RECCE 67: 4 Hawker 800RA; 20 Cessna O-1A *Bird Dog*; 20 KO-1 ; 18 RF-4C *Phantom II**; 5 RF-5A *Tiger II**
EW • ELINT 4 Hawker 800XP
TPT 34: 1 B-737-300 (VIP); 2 BAe-748 (VIP); 1 C-118 *Liftmaster*; 10 C-130H *Hercules*; 20 CN-235-220/CN-235M
TRG 167: 17 *Hawk* MK67; 85 KT-1; 30 T-38 *Talon*;   20 Il-103; 15 T-50
HELICOPTERS
SPT 9: 3 AS-332 *Super Puma*; 6 CH-47 *Chinook*
UTL 19: 4 Bell 212; 7 KA-32 *Helix C* (SAR); 5 UH-1H *Iroquois*; 3 VH-60 *White Knight*
UAV 100+: some *Night Intruder*
RECCE • TAC 103: 100 *Harpy*; 3 *Searcher*
MSL • TACTICAL
ASM AGM-130; AGM-142 *Popeye*
AGM AGM-65A *Maverick*; AGM-84 *Harpoon*; AGM-84-H SLAM-ER
ARM AGM-88 *HARM*
AAM AIM-120B *AMRAAM*/AIM-120C5 *AMRAAM*; AIM-7 *Sparrow*; AIM-9 *Sidewinder*

Paramilitary ε4,500 active

Civilian Defence Corps 3,500,000 reservists (to age 50)

Maritime Police ε4,500

PATROL AND COASTAL COMBATANTS 87+:
PSO 6: 1 *Sumjinkang*; 3 *Mazinger*; 1 *Han Kang*; 1 *Sambongho*
PCO 12: 6 *Sea Dragon/Whale*; 6 *430 Ton*
PCC 31: 4 *Bukhansan*; 5 Hyundai Type; 22 *Sea Wolf/Shark*
PCI ε20
PBI 18 *Seagull*
LOGISTICS AND SUPPORT • ARS 10
HELICOPTERS • UTL 9 Hughes 500

DEPLOYMENT

AFGHANISTAN
Operation Enduring Freedom 207 (engr/med)
UN • UNAMA 1 obs

DJIBOUTI
Operation Enduring Freedom • Horn of Africa 1

GEORGIA
UN • UNOMIG 7 obs

INDIA/PAKISTAN
UN • UNMOGIP 9 obs

IRAQ
MNF • *Operation Iraqi Freedom* 1,200

KUWAIT
MNF • *Operation Iraqi Freedom* some

LEBANON
UN • UNIFIL 363

LIBERIA
UN • UNMIL 1; 1 obs

NEPAL
UN • UNMIN 5 obs

QATAR
MNF • *Operation Iraqi Freedom* some

SUDAN
UN • UNMIS 1; 7 obs

FOREIGN FORCES

Sweden NNSC: 5 obs
Switzerland NNSC: 5 officers
United States Army: 18,366; Navy: 244; USAF 8,369; USMC: 135; USPACOM: 116 M-1 *Abrams* MBT; 126 M-2 *Bradley* AIFV each with 2 TOW Msl, 1 cannon; 111 APC (T); 45 mor/MRL/SP; 1 HQ 7th Air Force HQ (AF) HQ (HQ 7th Air Force) located at Osan AB; 1 (UN Comd) HQ Eighth Army HQ located at Seoul; 1 ftr wg located at Kusan AB (2 ftr sqn with 20 F-16C *Fighting Falcon*/F-16D *Fighting Falcon*); 1 ftr wg located at Kusan AB (1 ftr sqn with 20 F-16C *Fighting Falcon*/F-16D *Fighting Falcon*, 1 ftr sqn with 24 A-10 *Thunderbolt II*/OA-10 *Thunderbolt II* (12 of each type) located at Osan AB); 1 elems HQ 2ID armd inf HQ located at Tongduchon (1 avn bde (1 aslt hel bn, 1 atk hel bn), 1 armd bde (1 armd inf bn, 2 tk bn), 1 air cav bde (2 atk hel bn), 2 SP arty bn, 2 fd arty bn with MLRS); 1 special ops sqn; 1 SAM bn located at Uijongbu with MIM-104 *Patriot*

Laos Lao

New Lao Kip		2006	2007	2008
GDP	kip	35.5tr	40.0tr	
	US$	3.5bn	4.2bn	
per capita	US$	547	638	
Growth	%	7.6	7.1	
Inflation	%	6.8	4.0	
Def bdgt	kip	ε135bn		
	US$	13.3m		
US$1=kip		10,159	9.618	

Population   6,521,998

Ethnic groups: lowland Lao Loum 68%; upland Lao Theung 22%; highland Lao Soung incl Hmong and Yao 9%; Chinese and Vietnamese 1%

Age	0–14	15–19	20–24	25–29	30–64	65 plus
Male	21%	6%	5%	4%	13%	1%
Female	21%	5%	5%	4%	14%	2%

Capabilities

ACTIVE 29,100 (Army 25,600 Air 3,500) **Paramilitary 100,000**

Terms of service 18 month minimum conscription

ORGANISATIONS BY SERVICE

Army 25,600

FORCES BY ROLE
4 Mil Regions

Armd	1 bn
Inf	5 div; 7 indep regt; 65 indep coy
Arty	5 bn
ADA	9 bn
Engr	1 regt
Avn	1 (liaison) lt flt
Engr construction	2 regt

EQUIPMENT BY TYPE
MBT 25: 15 T-54/T-55; 10 T-34/85
LT TK 10 PT-76
APC (W) 50: 30 BTR-40/BTR-60; 20 BTR-152
ARTY
   TOWED 82: 75mm 20 M-116 pack; **105mm** 20 M-101; **122mm** 20 D-30/M-30 *M-1938*; **130mm** 10 M-46; **155mm** 12 M-114
   MOR 81mm; 82mm; 107mm M-1938/M-2A1; **120mm** M-43
AT • RCL 57mm M-18/A1; **75mm** M-20; **106mm** M-40; **107mm** B-11
   RL 73mm RPG-7 *Knout*
AD • SAM • MANPAD SA-7 *Grail*
   GUNS
      SP 23mm ZSU-23-4
      TOWED 14.5mm ZPU-1/ZPU-4; **23mm** ZU-23; **37mm** M-1939; **57mm** S-60

Army Marine Section ε600

PATROL AND COASTAL COMBATANTS (Riverine) 52+:
40 **PBR**; 12 **PCR** less than 100 tonnes
AMPHIBIOUS LCM 4

Air Force 3,500

FORCES BY ROLE

FGA	2 sqn with up to 22 MiG-21bis *Fishbed L & N†*; up to 2 MiG-21UM *Mongol B†*
Tpt	1 sqn with 4 An-2 *Colt*; 5 Y-7 (An-24) *Coke*; 3 An-26 *Curl*; 1 An-74 *Coaler*; 1 Y-12; 1 Yak-40 *Codling* (VIP)
Trg	sqn with 8 Yak-18 *Max*
Hel	1 sqn with 3 SA-360 *Dauphin*; 1 KA-32T *Helix C* (5 more on order); 1 Mi-26 *Halo*; 1 Mi-6 *Hook*; 9 Mi-8 *Hip*; 12 Mi-17 (Mi-8MT) *Hip H*

EQUIPMENT BY TYPE
AIRCRAFT 22† combat capable
   FTR up to 22 MiG-21bis *Fishbed L & N†*
   TPT 15: 4 An-2 *Colt*; 3 An-26 *Curl*; 1 An-74 *Coaler*; 1 Y-12; 5 Y-7 (An-24) *Coke*; 1 Yak-40 *Codling* (VIP)
   TRG up to 10: 2 MiG-21UM *Mongol B†*; 8 Yak-18 *Max*
HELICOPTERS
   SAR 3 SA-360 *Dauphin*
   SPT 24: 1 KA-32T *Helix C* (5 more on order); 1 Mi-26 *Halo*; 1 Mi-6 *Hook*; 9 Mi-8; 12 Mi-17 (Mi-8MT) *Hip H*
MSL • AAM AA-2 *Atoll†*

Paramilitary

Militia Self-Defence Forces 100,000+

Village 'home guard' or local defence

Malaysia Mal

Malaysian Ringgit RM		2006	2007	2008
GDP	RM	546bn	647bn	
	US$	149bn	192bn	
per capita	US$	6,117	7,735	
Growth	%	5.9	5.8	
Inflation	%	3.6	2.1	
Def bdgt[a]	RM	11.73bn	13.36bn	
	US$	3.20bn	3.96bn	
US$1=RM		3.66	3.37	

[a] Excluding extra-budgetary funding

Population   24,821,286

Ethnic groups: Malay and other indigenous (Bunipatre) 64%; Chinese 27%; Indian 9%; Sabah and Sarawak non-Muslim; 1m+ Indo and Pi illegal immigrants

Age	0–14	15–19	20–24	25–29	30–64	65 plus
Male	17%	5%	5%	4%	18%	2%
Female	16%	5%	4%	4%	18%	3%

Capabilities

ACTIVE 109,000 (Army 80,000 Navy 14,000 Air 15,000) Paramilitary 24,600

RESERVE 51,600 (Army 50,000, Navy 1,000 Air Force 600) Paramilitary 244,700

ORGANISATIONS BY SERVICE

Army 80,000 (to be 60–70,000)

FORCES BY ROLE

2 mil regions, 1 HQ fd comd, 4 area comd (div)

Armd	5 regt
Mech inf	1 bde (3 mech bn)
Inf	11 bde (28 bn)
SF	1 bde (3 SF bn)
AB	1 bde (10th) (Rapid Deployment Force) (1 lt tk sqn, 1 light arty regt, 3 AB bn)
Med arty	2 regt
Fd arty	7 regt
MRL	1 regt
ADA	3 regt
Engr	5 regt
Hel	1 sqn
Arty loc	1 regt

EQUIPMENT BY TYPE
MBT 6 PT-91M *Twardy* (48 ordered)
LT TK 26 *Scorpion* 90
RECCE 418: 140 AML-60/AML-90; 92 *Ferret* (60 mod); 186 SIBMAS
AIFV 111 *Doosan*
APC 1,020
   APC (T) 347: 211 *Adnan* (incl variants); 25 FV4333 *Stormer*; 111 KIFV (incl variants)
   APC (W) 673: 452 *Condor* (150 upgraded); 37 M-3 *Panhard*; 184 LAV-150 *Commando*
ARTY 414
   TOWED 164: **105mm** 130 Model 56 pack howitzer; **155mm** 34: 12 FH-70; 22 G-5
   MRL 18 *ASTROS II* (equipped with 127mm SS-30)
   MOR 81mm 232
AT • MSL • MANPATS 60: 18 AT-7 9K115 *Saxhorn*; 24 *Eryx*; 18 HJ-8
   RCL 260: **84mm** 236 *Carl Gustav*; **106mm** 24 M-40
   RL 73mm 584 RPG-7 *Knout*
AMPHIBIOUS • LCA 165 *Damen* Assault Craft 540 (capacity 10 troops)
HELICOPTERS • UTL 20: 9 SA-316B *Alouette III*; 11 A109
AD • SAM • MANPAD 48+: 48 *Starburst*; *Anza*; SA-18 *Grouse (Igla)*
   GUNS • TOWED 60: **35mm** 24 GDF-005; **40mm** 36 L40/70

Reserves

Territorial Army
5 highway sy bn

Border Security 2 bde (being created from existing Territorial units)

Inf   16 regt

Navy 14,000
PRINCIPAL SURFACE COMBATANTS 11
   FRIGATES 3:
   FFG 2 *Lekiu* each with 2 B515 *ILAS-3* triple 324mm each with *Sting Ray* LWT, 2 quad (8 eff.) each with MM-40 *Exocet* tactical SSM, 1 *Sea Wolf* VLS with 16 *Sea Wolf* SAM, (capacity 1 *Super Lynx* ASW/ASUW hel)
   FF 1 *Hang Tuah* trg with 3 *Limbo* non-operational, 1 57mm gun, 1 hel landing platform (for *Wasp* or *Super Lynx*)
   CORVETTES 8
   FSG 6:
      4 *Laksamana* each with 1 quad (4 eff.) with 12 *Aspide* SAM, 2 B515 *ILAS-3* triple 324mm each with A244 LWT, 3 twin (6 eff.) each with Mk 2 *Otomat* SSM, 1 76mm gun
      2 *Kedah* (MEKO) each fitted for MM-40 *Exocet* tactical SSM; each fitted for RAM CIWS and 1 76mm gun (Further 4 of class in build)
   FS 2:
      2 *Kasturi* each with 2 twin (4 eff.) each with MM-38 *Exocet* tactical SSM, 1 Mle 54 *Creusot-Loire* 375mm Bofors (6 eff.), 1 100mm gun, 1 hel landing platform (For 1 Westland *Wasp* HAS Mk 1)
PATROL AND COASTAL COMBATANTS 14
   PFM 8:
      4 *Handalan* each with 2 twin (4 eff.) each with MM-38 *Exocet* tactical SSM, 1 57mm gun
      4 *Perdana* each with 2 single each with 1 MM-38 *Exocet* tactical SSM, 1 57mm gun
   PFC 6 *Jerong*
MINE WARFARE • MINE COUNTERMEASURES •
MCO 4 *Mahamiru*
AMPHIBIOUS
   LS • LST 1 *Sri Inderapura* (capacity 10 tanks; 400 troops)
   CRAFT 115 LCM/LCU
LOGISTICS AND SUPPORT 9
   AOR 2; **AOL** 4; **AGS** 2; **TRG •AXS** 1
FACILITIES
Bases   Located at Tanjung Pengelih, Semporna, Langkawi (under construction), Lumut, Labuan, Kuantan

Naval Aviation 160
HELICOPTERS
   ASW 6 *Wasp*†
   ASW/ASUW 6 *Lynx* Srs300 *Super Lynx*
   UTL 6 AS-555 *Fennec*

Special Forces
Mne cdo   1 unit

Air Force 15,000
1 Air Op HQ, 2 Air Div, 1 trg and Log Cmd, 1 Intergrated Area Def Systems HQ

Flying hours   60 hrs/year

FORCES BY ROLE

Ftr 1 sqn with 16 MiG-29N / 2 MiG-29NUB *Fulcrum* (to be withdrawn from service)

FGA 1 sqn with 8 F/A-18D *Hornet*; 1 sqn with 18 Su-30MKM; 2 sqn with 8 *Hawk* MK108; 15 *Hawk* MK208

FGA/Recce 1 sqn with 13 F-5E *Tiger II*/F-5F *Tiger II*; 2 RF-5E *Tigereye*

MR 1 sqn with 4 Beech 200T

SF 1 Air Force Commando unit (air field defence/SAR)

Tpt 2 sqn with 4 KC-130H *Hercules* (tkr); 4 C-130H *Hercules*; 8 C-130H-30 *Hercules*; 9 Cessna 402B (2 modified for aerial survey); 1 (VIP) sqn with 1 B-737-700 BBJ; 1 BD700 *Global Express*; 1 F-28 *Fellowship*; 1 *Falcon* 900; 2 S-61N; 2 S-70A *Black Hawk*; 1 A-109; 1 sqn with 6 CN-235

Trg 1 trg school with 8 MB-339A; 20 MD3-160; 34 PC-7/MK II *Turbo Trainer*; 13 SA-316 *Alouette III*

Hel 4 (tpt/SAR) sqn with 20 S-61A-4 *Nuri*; 2 S-61N; 2 S-70A *Black Hawk*

SAM 1 sqn with *Starburst*

EQUIPMENT BY TYPE

AIRCRAFT 68 combat capable

FTR 29: 13 F-5E *Tiger II*/F-5F *Tiger II*; 16 MiG-29N *Fulcrum* (to be withdrawn from service)

FGA 28: 8 F/A-18D *Hornet*; 18 Su-30MKM; 8 *Hawk* MK108

RECCE 2 RF-5E *Tigereye*

MP 4 Beech 200T

TKR 4 KC-130H *Hercules*

TPT 31: 1 B-737-700 BBJ; 1 BD700 *Global Express*; 4 C-130H *Hercules*; 8 C-130H-30 *Hercules*; 6 CN-235; 9 Cessna 402B (2 modified for aerial survey); 1 F-28 *Fellowship*; 1 *Falcon* 900

TRG 79: 15 *Hawk* MK208*; 8 MB-339AB; 20 MD3-160 ; 2 MiG-29NUB *Fulcrum**; 34 PC-7/9 PC-7 MK II *Turbo Trainer*

HELICOPTERS

ASW 20 S-61A-4 *Nuri*

SPT 8: 4 S-61N; 4 S-70A *Black Hawk*

UTL 14: 1 A-109; 13 SA-316 *Alouette III*

UAV • RECCE • TAC 3 *Eagle* 150; *Aludra*

AD • SAM •MANPAD *Starburst*

MSL

ASM AGM-65 *Maverick*; AGM-84D *Harpoon*

AAM AA-10 *Alamo*; AA-11 *Archer*; AIM-7 *Sparrow*; AIM-9 *Sidewinder*

Paramilitary ε24,600

Police-General Ops Force 18,000

FORCES BY ROLE

Police 5 bde HQ; 2 (Aboriginal) bn; 19 bn; 4 indep coy

Spec Ops 1 bn

EQUIPMENT BY TYPE

RECCE ε100 S52 *Shorland*

APC (W) 170: 140 AT105 *Saxon*; ε30 SB-301

Malaysian Maritime Enforcement Agency ε4,500

EQUIPMENT BY TYPE

PATROL AND COASTAL COMBATANTS 40:

PSO 2 *Musytari* each with 1 100mm gun, 1 hel landing platform

PCC 18: 14 *Kris*; 4 *Sabah*

PC 5

PBF 14

TRG 1

Marine Police 2,100

EQUIPMENT BY TYPE

PATROL AND COASTAL COMBATANTS 150

PFI 30: 9 *Imp* PX; 15 *Lang Hitam*; 6 *Sangitan*

PBI 120

LOGISTICS AND SUPPORT 8: 2 **AT**; 6 **tpt**

FACILITIES

Bases Located at Kuala Kemaman, Penang, Tampoi, Sandakan

Police Air Unit

AIRCRAFT

TPT 7 PC-6 *Turbo-Porter*

UTL 10: 4 Cessna 206; 6 Cessna 208 *Caravan I*

HELICOPTERS

SPT 2 AS-355F *Ecureuil II*

UTL 1 Bell 206L *LongRanger*

Area Security Units (R) 3,500

(Auxillary General Ops Force)

Paramilitary 89 unit

Border Scouts (R) 1,200

in Sabah, Sarawak

People's Volunteer Corps 240,000 reservists (some 17,500 armed)

RELA

Customs Service

PATROL AND COASTAL COMBATANTS 44

PFI 8: 2 *Combatboat* 90H; 6 *Perak*

MISC BOATS/CRAFT 36 craft

NON-STATE ARMED GROUPS

see Part II

DEPLOYMENT

DEMOCRATIC REPUBLIC OF CONGO

UN • MONUC 17 obs

ETHIOPIA/ERITREA

UN • UNMEE 3; 7 obs

LEBANON

UN • UNIFIL 362

LIBERIA

UN • UNMIL 10 obs

NEPAL
UN • UNMIN 7 obs

PHILIPPINES
IMT 60

SERBIA
UN • UNMIK 1 obs

SUDAN
UN • UNMIS 4; 8 obs

TIMOR LESTE
UN • UNMIT 2 obs
Operation Astute 209

WESTERN SAHARA
UN • MINURSO 20; 12 obs

FOREIGN FORCES

Australia Air Force: 12 Army: 1 inf coy (on 3-month rotational tours); 115

Mongolia Mgl

Mongolian Tugrik t		2006	2007	2008
GDP	t	2.7tr	3.7tr	
	US$	2.3bn	3.2bn	
per capita	US$	826	1,113	
Growth	%	8.6	8.5	
Inflation	%	5.1	6.7	
Def bdgt	t	ε22bn	ε24bn	
	US$	19m	20m	
FMA (US)	US$	3.0m	3.0m	1.0m
US$1=t		1,179	1,179	

Population 2,874,127

Ethnic groups: Kazak 4%; Russian 2%; Chinese 2%

Age	0–14	15–19	20–24	25–29	30–64	65 plus
Male	15%	6%	5%	5%	17%	2%
Female	14%	6%	5%	5%	18%	2%

Capabilities

ACTIVE 8,600 (Army 7,500 Air 800 Construction Troops 300) **Paramilitary 7,200**
Terms of service conscription: males 18–25 years, 1 year

RESERVE 137,000 (Army 137,000)

ORGANISATIONS BY SERVICE

Army 4,200; 3,300 conscript (total 7,500)
FORCES BY ROLE
MRR 6 (under strength) regt
Lt inf 1 bn (rapid deployment – 2nd bn to form)

AB 1 bn
Arty 1 regt

EQUIPMENT BY TYPE
MBT 370 T-54/T-55
RECCE 120 BRDM-2
AIFV 310 BMP-1
APC (W) 150 BTR-60
ARTY 570
  TOWED ε300: **122mm** D-30/M-30 *M-1938*; **130mm** M-46; **152mm** ML-20 *M-1937*
  MRL 122mm 130 BM-21
  MOR 140: **120mm**; **160mm**; **82mm**
AT • GUNS 200: **85mm** D-44 /D-48; **100mm** M-1944 /MT-12

Air Forces 800
FORCES BY ROLE
Tpt 1 sqn with 1 A-310-300; 6 An-2 *Colt*; 1 An-26 *Curl*; 1 B-737
Atk hel 1 sqn with 11 Mi-24 *Hind*; 2 Mi-8 *Hip*
AD 2 regt with 150 S-60/ZPU-4/ZU-23

EQUIPMENT BY TYPE
AIRCRAFT • TPT 9: 1 A-310-300; 6 An-2 *Colt*; 1 An-26 *Curl*; 1 B-737
HELICOPTERS
  ATK 11 Mi-24 *Hind*
  SPT 2 Mi-8 *Hip*
AD • GUNS • TOWED 150: **14.5mm** ZPU-4; **23mm** ZU-23; **57mm** S-60

Paramilitary 7,200 active

Border Guard 1,300; 4,700 conscript (total 6,000)

Internal Security Troops 400; 800 conscript (total 1,200)
Gd 4 unit

Construction Troops 300

DEPLOYMENT

AFGHANISTAN
Army 21 (instructors)

DEMOCRATIC REPUBLIC OF CONGO
UN • MONUC 2 obs

ETHIOPIA/ERITREA
UN • UNMEE 1 obs

GEORGIA
UN • UNOMIG 1 obs

IRAQ
MNF • *Operation Iraqi Freedom* 160

LIBERIA
UN • UNMIL 250

SERBIA

NATO • KFOR • *Joint Enterprise* 36

SUDAN

UN • UNMIS 2 obs

WESTERN SAHARA

UN • MINURSO 3 obs

Myanmar My

Myanmar Kyat K		2006	2007	2008
GDP	K	11.9tr		
	US$[a]	37.0bn		
per capita	US$[a]	788		
Growth	%	12.7		
Inflation	%	25.7		
Def bdgt	K	ε40bn		
	US$[b]	ε6.9bn		
US$1=K		5.78	6.42	

[a] PPP estimate

[b] defence budget at official exchange rate

Population   47,373,958

Ethnic groups: Burmese 68%; Shan 9%; Karen 7%; Rakhine 4%; Chinese 3+%; Other Chin, Kachin, Kayan, Lahu, Mon, Palaung, Pao, Wa, 9%

Age	0–14	15–19	20–24	25–29	30–64	65 plus
Male	13%	5%	5%	5%	18%	2%
Female	13%	5%	5%	5%	19%	3%

Capabilities

ACTIVE 406,000 (Army 375,000 Navy 16,000 Air 15,000) Paramilitary 107,250

ORGANISATIONS BY SERVICE

Army ε375,000

FORCES BY ROLE

12 regional comd, 4 regional op comd, 14 military op comd, 34 tactical op comd (TDC)

Armd 10 bn
Inf   100 bn; 337 bn (regional comd)
Lt inf 10 div
Arty   7 bn; 37 indep coy
AD   7 bn

EQUIPMENT BY TYPE

MBT 150: 50 T-72; 100 Type-69-II
LT TK 105 Type-63 (ε60 serviceable)
RECCE 115: 45 *Ferret*; 40 Humber *Pig*; 30 Mazda
APC 325
    APC (T) 305: 250 Type-85; 55 Type-90
    APC (W) 20 *Hino*

ARTY 388+
    TOWED 278+: **76mm** 100 M-48 *M-1948*; **88mm** 50 25-pdr; **105mm** 96 M-101; **122mm**; **130mm** 16 M-46; **140mm**; **155mm** 16 *Soltam*
    MRL 30+: **107mm** 30 Type-63; **122mm** BM-21 (reported)
    MOR 80+: **82mm**Type-53 (M-37); **120mm** 80+: 80 Soltam; Type-53 (M-1943)
AT
    RCL 1,000+: **106mm** M-40A1; **84mm** ε1,000 *Carl Gustav*
    RL 73mm RPG-7 *Knout*
    GUNS 60: **57mm** 6-pdr; **76.2mm** 17-pdr
AD • **SAM** • **MANPAD** HN-5 *Hong Nu/Red Cherry* (reported); SA-16 *Gimlet*
    GUNS 46
        SP 57mm 12 Type-80
        TOWED 34: **37mm** 24 Type-74; **40mm** 10 M-1

Navy ε16,000

EQUIPMENT BY TYPE
PRINCIPAL SURFACE COMBATANTS • CORVETTES
• **FS** 3 *Anawrahta* each with 1 76mm gun
PATROL AND COASTAL COMBATANTS 67:
    PFM 6 *Houxin* each with 2 twin (4 eff.) each with 4 C-801 (CSS-N-4) *Sardine* tactical SSM
    PTG 8 *Myanmar* each with 2 twin (4 eff.) each with 4 C-801 (CSS-N-4) *Sardine* tactical SSM
    PCO 2 *Indaw*
    PCC 10 *Hainan*
    PFI 3 *PB-90*
    PCI 9: 6 PGM 401; 3 *Swift*
    PCR 29: 15 less than 100 tonnes 2 *Nawarat*; 10 Y-301; 2 *Imp* Y-301
AMPHIBIOUS • CRAFT 15: 5 **LCU**; 10 **LCM**
LOGISTICS AND SUPPORT 12
    AOT 1; **AK** 1; **AKSL** 5; **AGS** 3; **ABU** 1; **YDT** 1

FACILITIES
Bases Located at Bassein, Mergui, Moulmein, Seikyi, Rangoon (Monkey Point), Sittwe

Naval Infantry 800

Navy 1 bn

Air Force ε15,000

FORCES BY ROLE

Ftr	3 sqn with 8 MiG-29B *Fulcrum*; 50 F-7 (MiG-21F) *Fishbed C*; 10 FT-7 (JJ-7) *Mongol A**; 2 MiG-29UB *Fulcrum**
FGA	2 sqn with 22 A-5M (Q-5II) *Fantan*
CCT	2 sqn with 12 G-4 *Super Galeb**; 12 PC-7 *Turbo Trainer**; 9 PC-9*
Tpt	1 sqn with 2 An-12 *Cub*; 3 F-27 *Friendship*; 4 FH-227; 5 PC-6A *Turbo Porter*/PC-6B *Turbo Porter*
Trg/liaison	sqn with 1 Ce-550 *Citation II*; 4 Cessna 180 *Skywagon*; 12 K-8

Hel 4 sqn with 10 PZL W-3 *Sokol*; 11 Mi-17 (Mi-8MT) *Hip H**; 18 PZL Mi-2 *Hoplite**; 12 Bell 205; 6 Bell 206 *JetRanger*; 9 SA-316 *Alouette III*

EQUIPMENT BY TYPE
AIRCRAFT 125 combat capable
FTR 58: 8 MiG-29B *Fulcrum*; 50 F-7 (MiG-21F) *Fishbed C*
FGA 22 A-5M (Q-5II) *Fantan*
TPT 15: 2 An-12 *Cub*; 1 Ce-550 *Citation II*; 3 F-27 *Friendship*; 4 FH-227; 5 PC-6A *Turbo Porter/PC-6B Turbo Porter*
UTL 4 Cessna 180 *Skywagon*
TRG 57: 10 FT-7 (JJ-7) *Mongol A**; 12 G-4 *Super Galeb**; 12 K-8; 2 MiG-29UB *Fulcrum**; 12 PC-7 *Turbo Trainer**; 9 PC-9*
HELICOPTERS
SPT 39: 10 PZL W-3 *Sokol*; 11 Mi-17 (Mi-8MT) *Hip H**; 18 PZL MI-2 *Hoplite**
UTL 27: 12 Bell 205; 6 Bell 206 *JetRanger*; 9 SA-316 *Alouette III*

Paramilitary 107,250

People's Police Force 72,000

People's Militia 35,000

People's Pearl and Fishery Ministry ε250
PATROL AND COASTAL COMBATANTS 11
PCC 3 *Indaw*
PCI 8: 5 *Carpentaria*; 3 *Swift*

NON-STATE ARMED GROUPS

see Part II

New Zealand NZ

New Zealand Dollar NZ$		2006	2007	2008
GDP	NZ$	160bn	170bn	
	US$	103bn	135bn	
per capita	US$	25,162	32,772	
Growth	%	1.6	2.8	
Inflation	%	3.5	2.0	
Def bdgt	NZ$	2.40bn	2.17bn	
	US$	1.54bn	1.68bn	
US$1=NZ$		1.56	1.29	

Population 4,115,771

Ethnic groups: Maori 15%; Pacific Islander 6%

Age	0–14	15–19	20–24	25–29	30–64	65 plus
Male	11%	4%	4%	4%	22%	5%
Female	10%	3%	3%	4%	22%	7%

Capabilities

ACTIVE 9,051 (Army 4,580 Navy 2,034 Air 2,437)

RESERVE 2,243 (Army 1,762 Navy 291 Air Force 190)

ORGANISATIONS BY SERVICE

Army 4,580
FORCES BY ROLE
2 Land Force Gp HQ

Recce	1 sqn
Inf	2 bn
SF	1 sqn
Arty	1 regt (2 fd arty bty, 1 AD tp)
Engr	1 regt under strength

EQUIPMENT BY TYPE
APC (W) 105 NZLAV
LFAV 188 *Pinzgauer*
ARTY 74
   TOWED 105mm 24 L-118 Light Gun
   MOR 81mm 50
AT • MSL 24 *Javelin*
   RCL 84mm 42 *Carl Gustav*
AD • SAM • MANPAD 12 *Mistral*

Reserves

Territorial Force 1,762 reservists
Responsible for providing trained individuals for top-up and round-out of deployed forces
Trg 6 (Territorial Force Regional) regt

Navy 2,034
FORCES BY ROLE
Navy 1 (Fleet) HQ and 1 Naval Base located at Auckland
EQUIPMENT BY TYPE
PRINCIPAL SURFACE COMBATANTS • FRIGATES
   FF 2 *Anzac* each with 1 octuple Mk41 *Sea Sparrow* (8 eff.) with RIM-7M *Sea Sparrow* SAM, 2 triple 324mm TT (6 eff.), 1 MK 15 *Phalanx* CIWS guns, 1 127mm gun, with 1 SH-2G (NZ) *Super Seasprite* ASW hel,
PATROL AND COASTAL COMBATANTS 6:
   PSO 2 *Otago* (capacity 1 SH-2G *Super Seasprite*) (2nd of class to commission '08)
   PCO 4 *Rotoiti* (Final 2 vessels of class expected to commission '08)
LOGISTICS AND SUPPORT 5
   MRV 1 *Canterbury* (capacity 4 NH90 tpt hel; 1 SH-2G *Super Seasprite* ASW hel; 2 LCM; 16 NZLAV; 16 trucks; 250 troops)
   AO 1 *Endeavour*
   AGHS (SVY) 1 *Resolution*
   Diving tender/spt 1 *Manawanui*
   Trg 1
FACILITIES
Base Located at Auckland

Air Force 2,437
3 air bases – Auckland, Palmerston North and Blenheim
Flying hours 190

FORCES BY ROLE

MR   1 sqn with 6 P-3K *Orion* (being upgraded)

Tpt   1 sqn with 2 B-757-200 (being upgraded); 5 C-130H *Hercules* (being upgraded);

Hel   1 sqn with 14 UH-1H *Iroquois* (to be replaced by 8 NH90 in 2009),

ASW   1 sqn RNZAF/RNZN sqn with 5 SH-2G(NZ) *Super Seasprite*

Trg   Fg Trg Wg with 13 Airtrainer CT-4E ; 5 Beech 200 *King Air* (leased); 5 Bell 47G trg hel (to be replaced by 6 twin-turbine T/LUH aircraft)

EQUIPMENT BY TYPE

AIRCRAFT 6 combat capable
  MP 6 P-3K *Orion**
  TPT 7: 2 B-757-200; 5 C-130H *Hercules*
  TRG 13 CT-4E (leased); 5 Beech 200 *King Air* (leased)
HELICOPTERS
  UTL 14 UH-1H *Iroquois* (to be replaced by 8 NH90 in 2009)
  ASW 5 SH-2G(NZ)
  TRG 5 Bell 47G
MSL • ASM AGM-65B *Maverick*/AGM-65G *Maverick*

DEPLOYMENT

AFGHANISTAN
NATO • ISAF 107 (PRT Bamiyan)
Operation Enduring Freedom 14
UN • UNAMA 1 obs

ANTARCTICA
Operation Antarctica 26

AUSTRALIA
Army 9 (navigation) trg
Navy HMNZS *Te Kaha*/*Endeavour* E Australia 230

BOSNIA-HERZEGOVINA
EU • EUFOR • *Operation Althea* 3

EGYPT
MFO 26

KOREA
UNCMAC 3

IRAQ
UN • UNAMI 1 obs

LEBANON
10

MIDDLE EAST
UN • UNTSO 8 obs

SERBIA
UN • UNMIK 1 obs

SOLOMON ISLANDS
RAMSI 44 Police

SUDAN
UN • UNMIS 1; 2 obs

TIMOR LESTE
Armed Forces 180 (*Operation Astute*)
UN • UNMIT 1 obs

Papua New Guinea PNG

Papua New Guinea Kina K		2006	2007	2008
GDP	K	14.1bn	14.8bn	
	US$	4.6bn	5.2bn	
per capita	US$	815	896	
Growth	%	2.6	5.2	
Inflation	%	2.3	3.0	
Def bdgt	K	91m	94m	
	US$	30m	33m	
US$1=K		3.05	2.85	

Population   5,795,887

Age	0–14	15–19	20–24	25–29	30–64	65 plus
Male	19%	5%	5%	5%	16%	2%
Female	19%	5%	4%	4%	15%	2%

Capabilities

ACTIVE 3,100 (Army 2,500 Air 200 Maritime Element 400)

ORGANISATIONS BY SERVICE

Army ε2,500

FORCES BY ROLE
Inf   2 bn
Engr   1 bn

EQUIPMENT BY TYPE
ARTY • MOR 3+: 81mm; 120mm 3

Maritime Element ε400

FORCES BY ROLE
Navy   1 HQ located at Port Moresby
Maritime some sqn located at Lombrun (Manus Island) with Patrol and Coastal Combatants

EQUIPMENT BY TYPE
PATROL AND COASTAL COMBATANTS 4:
  PCC 4 *Pacific*
AMPHIBIOUS 2:
  LSM 2 *Salamaua*
  CRAFT 6: 4 (civil manned); 2
FACILITIES
Bases   Located at Alotau (forward), Kieta (forward), Lombrun (Manus Island), Port Moresby

Air Force 200

FORCES BY ROLE
Tpt 1 sqn with 1 CASA 212 *Aviocar*; 2 CN-235; 3 IAI-201 *Arava*

Hel some sqn with 4 UH-1H *Iroquois*†

EQUIPMENT BY TYPE
AIRCRAFT • TPT 6: 1 CASA 212 *Aviocar*; 2 CN-235; 3 IAI-201 *Arava*
HELICOPTERS • UTL 4 UH-1H *Iroquois*†

DEPLOYMENT

SOLOMON ISLANDS
RAMSI some

FOREIGN FORCES

Australia Army: 1 trg unit; 38

Philippines Pi

Philippine Peso P		2005	2006	2007
GDP	P	6.03tr	6.63tr	
	US$	118bn	151bn	
per capita	US$	1,314	1,655	
Growth	%	5.4	6.3	
Inflation	%	6.2	3.0	
Def bdgt	P	46.6bn	49.3bn	
	US$	909m	1,121m	
FMA (US)	US$	29.7m	17.6m	11.1m
US$1=P		51.3	44.0	

Population	91,077,287					
Age	0–14	15–19	20–24	25–29	30–64	65 plus
Male	18%	5%	5%	4%	16%	2%
Female	17%	5%	5%	4%	16%	2%

Capabilities

ACTIVE 106,000 (Army 66,000 Navy 24,000 Air 16,000) Paramilitary 40,500

RESERVE 131,000 (Army 100,000 Navy 15,000 Air 16,000) Paramilitary 40,000 (to age 49)

ORGANISATIONS BY SERVICE

Army 66,000

FORCES BY ROLE
5 Area Unified Comd (joint service), 1 National Capital Region Comd

Lt reaction	3 coy
Spec Ops	1 comd (1 Scout Ranger regt, 1 SF regt, 1 lt armd bde (regt))
Lt inf	8 div (*each:* 1 arty bn, 3 inf bde)
Arty	1 regt HQ
Engr	5 bn
Presidential Guard	1 gp

EQUIPMENT BY TYPE
LT TK 65 *Scorpion*
AIFV 85 YPR-765
APC 370
    APC (T) 100 M-113
    APC (W) 270: 100 LAV-150 *Commando*; 150 *Simba*; 20 V-200 *Chaimite*
ARTY 282+
    TOWED 242: **105mm** 230 M-101/M-102/M-26/M-56; **155mm** 12 M-114/M-68
    MOR 40+: **81mm** M-29; **107mm** 40 M-30
AT • RCL 75mm M-20; **90mm** M-67; **106mm** M-40A1
AIRCRAFT
    TPT 3: 1 Beech 80 *Queen Air*; 1 Cessna 170; 1 P-206A
    UTL 1 Cessna 172
UAV *Blue Horizon*

Navy ε24,000

EQUIPMENT BY TYPE
PRINCIPAL SURFACE COMBATANTS • FRIGATES
    FF 1 *Rajah Humabon* with 3 76mm gun
PATROL AND COASTAL COMBATANTS 62
    PCO 13:
        3 *Emilio Jacinto* each with 1 76mm gun
        8 *Miguel Malvar* each with 1 76mm gun
        2 *Rizal* each with 3 Twin ASTT (6 eff.)†, 2 76mm guns
    PFC 1 *Cyclone*
    PCC 14: 3 *Aguinaldo*; 3 *Kagitingan*; 8 *Thomas Batilo*
    PCI 34: 22 *Jose Andrada*; 10 *Conrado Yap*; 2 *Point*
AMPHIBIOUS
    LS • LST 7:
        2 *Bacolod City* (*Besson*-class) each with 1 hel landing platform (capacity 32 tanks; 150 troops)
        5 *Zamboanga del Sur* (capacity 16 tanks; 200 troops)
    CRAFT 39: 3 **LCU**; 6 **LCVP**; 30 **LCM**
LOGISTICS AND SUPPORT 6: AOL 1; AR 1; AK 1; AWT 2; TPT 1

FACILITIES
Bases Located at Sangley Point/Cavite, Zamboanga, Cebu

Naval Aviation
AIRCRAFT • TPT 6
    4 BN-2A *Defender*
    2 Cessna 177 *Cardinal*
HELICOPTERS • UTL 7 BO-105

Marines 7,500
FORCES BY ROLE
Marine 2 bde (*total:* 6 marine bn)

EQUIPMENT BY TYPE
APC (W) 24 LAV-300
AAV 85: 30 LVTP-5; 55 LVTP-7
ARTY 150+
    TOWED 105mm 150 M-101
    MOR 107mm M-30

Air Force ε16,000

FORCES BY ROLE

PAF HQ, 5 Cmds (AD, tac ops, air ed and trg, air log and spt, air res)

Ftr	1 sqn with 15 Augusta S-211*
RECCE	1 Rockwell *Turbo Commander* 690A
MP	1 sqn with 1 F-27 MK 200MPA; 1 GAF N-22SL *Nomad*
SAR/Comms	4 sqn with 6 AB-412SP *Griffon*; 27 UH-1M *Iroquois*
Tpt	1 sqn with 2 C-130B *Hercules*; 2 C-130H *Hercules*; 4 C-130K *Hercules*; 1 sqn with 2 Cessna 210 *Centurion*; 1 GAF N-22B *Nomad*; 1 sqn with 1 F-27-200 *Friendship*
FAC	1 sqn with 15 OV-10 *Bronco**
Trg	1 sqn with 12 SF-260TP; 1 sqn with 11 T-41D *Mescalero*; 1 sqn with 6 R172 *Hawk* XP
Hel	4 sqn with 40 UH-1H *Iroquois*; 1 (VIP) sqn with 1 S-70 A-5 (S-70A) *Black Hawk*; 1 SA-330L *Puma*; 6 Bell 412EP *Twin Huey*/Bell 412SP *Twin Huey*; 2 sqn with 5 AUH-76; 20 MD-520MG

EQUIPMENT BY TYPE

30 combat capable

AIRCRAFT

FAC 15 OV-10 *Bronco*

MP 1 F-27 MK 200MPA

TPT 15: 2 C-130B *Hercules* (6 in store); 2 C-130H *Hercules*; 4 C-130K *Hercules*; 1 F-27-200 *Friendship*; 1 L-100-20 in store; 1 Rockwell *Turbo Commander* 690A

UTL 4: 2 Cessna 210 *Centurion*; 1 GAF N-22B; 1 GAF N-22SL *Nomad*;

TRG 44: 15 Augusta S-211*; 6 R172 *Hawk* XP; 12 SF-260TP; 11 T-41D *Mescalero*

HELICOPTERS

ASLT 25: 5 AUH-76; 20 MD-520MG

SPT 2: 1 S-70 A-5 (S-70A) *Black Hawk*; 1 SA-330L *Puma*

UTL 79: 6 AB-412SP *Griffon*; 6 Bell 412EP *Twin Huey*/Bell 412SP *Twin Huey*; 40 UH-1H *Iroquois*; 27 UH-1M *Iroquois*

UAV 2 *Blue Horizon* II

MSL • AAM AIM-9B *Sidewinder*

Paramilitary

Philippine National Police 40,500

Deptartment of Interior and Local Government

FORCES BY ROLE

Aux	62,000
Provincial	73 comd
Regional	15 comd

EQUIPMENT BY TYPE

PATROL AND COASTAL COMBATANTS • PCI 14 Rodman

AIRCRAFT

TPT 2 BN-2 *Islander*

TRG 3 Lancair 320

Coast Guard

PATROL AND COASTAL COMBATANTS 61

PCO 5: 4 *San Juan*; 1 *Balsam*

PCC 6: 4 *Ilocosnorte*; 2 *Tirad*

PCI 29: 4 *Agusan*; 3 *De Haviland*; 22 *Swift*

PBR 11

PB 10

HELICOPTERS: 3 SAR

Citizen Armed Force Geographical Units
40,000 reservists

CAFGU

Militia 56 bn (part-time units which can be called up for extended periods)

NON-STATE ARMED GROUPS

see Part II

DEPLOYMENT

CÔTE D'IVOIRE
UN • UNOCI 3; 4 obs

HAITI
UN • MINUSTAH 157

LIBERIA
UN • UNMIL169; 3 obs

SUDAN
UN • UNMIS 12 obs

TIMOR LESTE
UN • UNMIT 3 obs

FOREIGN FORCES

Brunei 10

Libya 5

Malaysia 60

United States Army 13; Navy 5; USAF 7; USMC 86

Singapore Sgp

Singapore Dollar S$		2006	2007	2008
GDP	S$	209bn	227bn	
	US$	131bn	155bn	
per capita	US$	29,261	34,149	
Growth	%	7.9	7.5	
Inflation	%	1.0	1.2	
Def bdgt	S$	10.05bn	10.58bn	
	US$	6.32bn	7.24bn	
US$1=S$		1.59	1.46	

Population 4,553,009

Ethnic groups: Chinese 76%; Malay 15%; Indian 6%

Age	0–14	15–19	20–24	25–29	30–64	65 plus
Male	8%	3%	3%	4%	27%	3%
Female	8%	3%	3%	4%	29%	4%

Capabilities

ACTIVE 72,500 (Army 50,000 Navy 9,000 Air 13,500)
Paramilitary 93,800
Terms of service conscription 24 months

RESERVE 312,500 (Army 300,000 Navy 5,000 Air 7,500) **Paramilitary 44,000**
Annual trg to age of 40 for army other ranks, 50 for officers

ORGANISATIONS BY SERVICE

Army 15,000; 35,000 conscripts (total 50,000)

FORCES BY ROLE

Combined Arms	3 div (mixed active/reserve formations) (*each:* 2 inf bde (*each:* 3 inf bn), 1 armd bde, 1 recce bn, 1 AD bn, 1 engr bn, 2 arty bn)
Rapid Reaction	1 div (mixed active/reserve formations) (1 amph bde (3 amph bn), 1 air mob bde, 1 inf bde)
Recce/lt armd	4 bn
Inf	8 bn
Cdo	1 bn
Arty	4 bn
Engr	4 bn
MI	1 bn

Reserves

9 inf bde incl in mixed active/inactive reserve formations listed above; 1 op reserve div with additional inf bde; People's Defence Force Comd (homeland defence) with inf bn 12

Recce/lt armd	ε8 bn
Inf	ε60 bn
Cdo	ε1 bn
Arty	ε12 bn
Engr	ε8 bn

EQUIPMENT BY TYPE
MBT 196: 96 *Leopard* 2A4 (all expected by 2008); 80–100 *Tempest* (*Centurion*) (being replaced)
LT TK ε350 AMX-13 SM1
RECCE 22 AMX-10 PAC 90
AIFV 272+: 22 AMX-10P; 250 IFV-25; M-113A1/M-113A2 (some with 40mm AGL, some with 25mm gun);
APC 1,280+
  APC (T) 1,000+: 250 IFV-40/50; 750+ M-113A1/M-113A2; ATTC *Bronco*
  APC (W) 280: 250 LAV-150 *Commando*/V-200 *Commando*; 30 V-100 *Commando*
ARTY 265
  SP 155mm 36: ε18 *Pegasus* (replacing 105mm); ε18 SSPH-1 *Primus*
  TOWED 107: **105mm** 37 LG1; **155mm** 70: 18 FH-2000; 52 FH-88;
  MOR 112+
    SP 90+ **81mm**; **120mm** 90: 40 on *Bronco*; 50 on M-113
    TOWED 160mm 12 M-58 *Tampella*

AT • **MSL** • **MANPATS** 30+ *Milan/Spike MR*
  RCL 290: **84mm** ε200 *Carl Gustav*; **106mm** 90 M-40A1
  RL 67mm *Armbrust*; **89mm** M-20
AD • **SAM** 75+
  SP *Mistral*; RBS-70; SA-18 *Grouse* (*Igla*) (on V-200/M-113)
  MANPAD *Mistral*/RBS-70/SA-18 *Grouse* (*Igla*)
  GUNS 30
  SP 20mm GAI-C01
  TOWED 20mm GAI-C01
UAV *Skylark*
RADAR • **LAND** AN/TPQ-36 *Firefinder*; AN/TPQ-37 *Firefinder* (arty, mor)

FACILITIES

Training camp	3 located in Taiwan (Republic of China) incl inf, arty and armd, 1 located in Thailand, 1 located in Brunei

Navy 2,200; 1,800 conscript; ε5,000 active reservists (total 9,000)

EQUIPMENT BY TYPE
SUBMARINES • **TACTICAL** • **SSK** 4 *Challenger* each with 4 single 533mm TT
PRINCIPAL SURFACE COMBATANTS 9:
  FRIGATES • **FFGHM** 3 *Formidable* (3 additional vessels in build) each with 8 RGM-84 *Harpoon* SSM, 4 octuple (32 eff.) VLS with *Aster15* SAM, 1 76mm gun, (capacity for 1 S-70B *Sea Hawk*)
  CORVETTES • **FSG** 6 *Victory* each with 2+ Mk 140 *Harpoon* quad (8 eff.) each with 1 RGM-84C *Harpoon* tactical SSM, 2 octuple (16 eff.) each with 1 *Barak* SAM, 2 triple ASTT (6 eff.), 1 76mm gun
PATROL AND COASTAL COMBATANTS 29:
  PFM 6 *Sea Wolf* each with 2 Mk 140 *Harpoon* quad (8 eff.) each with RGM-84C *Harpoon* tactical SSM, 1 twin (2 eff.) with *Mistral* SAM (manually operated), 4 (8 eff.) each with GI *Gabriel I* tactical SSM, 1 57mm gun
  PCO 11 *Fearless* each with 2 *Sadral* sextuple each with *Mistral* SAM, 1 76mm gun
  PBI 12
MINE WARFARE • **MINE COUNTERMEASURES**
  MHC 4 *Bedok*
AMPHIBIOUS
  LS • **LST** 4 *Endurance* each with 2 twin (4 eff.) each with *Mistral* SAM, 1 76mm gun with hel deck (capacity 2 hel; 4 LCVP; 18 MBTs; 350 troops)
  LANDING CRAFT 34 LCU
LOGISTICS AND SUPPORT 2 :
  AS 1 *Kendrick*
  Trg 1

FACILITIES
Bases Located at Changi, Tuas (Jurong)

Air Force 13,500 (incl 3,000 conscript)

Air Defence and Operations Command; Unmanned Aerial Vehicle (UAV) Command; Participation Command (coordinates airlift, close air support and maritime air surveillance in support of the other services. Will also raise, train and sustain RSAF helicopters, divisional ground-based air-defence systems and tactical support elements). Two Commands are still to be formed - Air Combat Command and Air Power Generation Command – will probably be established in the second half of 2008 to complete the restructuring process.

FORCES BY ROLE

FGA/Recce 3 sqn with 51 F-16C *Fighting Falcon*/F-16D *Fighting Falcon* (some used for recce with pods); 2 sqn with 28 F-5S *Tiger II*; 9 F-5T *Tiger II*

Recce/tkr/tpt 1 sqn with 4 KC-130B *Hercules* (trk/tpt); 1 KC-130H *Hercules*; 5 C-130H *Hercules* (2 Elint); 1 sqn with 9 F-50 (5 *Maritime Enforcer,*4 tpt)

AEW 1 sqn with 4 E-2C *Hawkeye*

Tkr 1 sqn with 4 KC-135R *Stratotanker*

Trg 1 sqn with 9 F-16C/D at Luke AFB, AZ; AH-64D *Apache* located at Marana, (AZ), US; 6+ CH-47D *Chinook* located at Grand Prairie, (TX), US; 1 sqn with 4 A-4SU *Super Skyhawk*; 10 TA-4SU *Super Skyhawk*; 1 sqn with 27 S-211

Hel 1 sqn with 12 AH-64D *Apache*;1 sqn with 10 CH-47SD *Super D Chinook*; 2 sqn with 18 AS-332M *Super Puma* (incl 5 SAR); 12 AS-532UL *Cougar*; Trg: 6 EC-120B *Colibri* (leased)

UAV 2 sqn with *Searcher* MkII; 1 sqn with *Hermes* 450

Staffed by personnel from all three services and the joint staff. Comprised of HQ unit, four squadrons and a training school. 119 and 128 Sqns operate the *Searcher* UAV, while the 116 Sqn is equipped with the *Hermes* 450. The fourth unit provides logistics support. There are two other major structures in UAV Cmd: the operations and systems development group; and the standards office/simulator centre. The former includes a governance branch, ISTAR branch and operations centre.

EQUIPMENT BY TYPE

AIRCRAFT 102 combat capable
  FGA 97: 60 F-16C *Fighting Falcon*/F-16D *Fighting Falcon* (incl reserves); 28 F-5S *Tiger II*; 9 F-5T *Tiger II*
  MP 5 F-50 *Maritime Enforcer**
  AEW 4 E-2C *Hawkeye*
  TKR 9: 4 KC-130B *Hercules* (trk/tpt); 1 KC-130H *Hercules*; 4 KC-135R *Stratotanker*
  TPT 9: 5 C-130H *Hercules* (2 Elint); 4 F-50
  TRG 41: 27 S-211; 10 TA-4SU; 4 A-4SU *Super Skyhawk*
HELICOPTERS
  ATK 12 AH-64D *Apache*
  SPT 40: 18 AS-332M *Super Puma* (incl 5 SAR); 10 CH-47SD *Super D Chinook*; 12 AS-532UL *Cougar*
  TRG 12: EC-120B *Colibri* (leased); 6+ CH-47D *Chinook*
UAV some *Hermes* 450; 40 *Searcher* MK II
MSL • TACTICAL
   ASM: AGM-45 *Shrike*; *Hellfire*; AGM-65B/G *Maverick*; AGM-84 *Harpoon*; AM-39 *Exocet*
   AAM AIM-120C *AMRAAM* in store (US); AIM-7P *Sparrow*; AIM-9N *Sidewinder*/AIM-9P *Sidewinder*

Air Defence Systems Divison

FORCES BY ROLE

4 (field def) sqn

Air Defence Bde

FORCES BY ROLE

Air Some bde (*total:* 1 AD sqn with Oerlikon, 1 AD sqn with 18+ MIM-23 *HAWK*, 1 AD sqn with *Rapier-Blindfire*)

EQUIPMENT BY TYPE
RADAR • AD *Blindfire*

Air Force Systems Bde

Air Some bde (*total:* 1 AD sqn with radar (mobile), 1 AD sqn with LORADS)

Divisional Air Def Arty Bde

Attached to army divs

FORCES BY ROLE

AD some bde (*total:* 1 AD bn with 36 *Mistral*, 1 AD bn with SA-18 *Grouse (Igla)*, 3 AD bn with RBS-70)

EQUIPMENT BY TYPE
AD • SAM 36+
   TOWED *Mistral*; RBS-70
   MANPAD SA-18 *Grouse (Igla)*

Paramilitary 93,800 active

Civil Defence Force 81,800 incl. 1,600 regulars, 3,200 conscripts, 23,000 reservists; 54,000+ volunteers; 1 construction bde (2,500 conscripts)

Singapore Police Force (including Coast Guard) 8,500; 3,500 conscript; 21,000 reservists (total 33,000)

EQUIPMENT BY TYPE
PATROL AND COASTAL COMBATANTS 90
   PCI 12 *Swift*
   PBF 32
   PBC 2 *Manta Ray*
   PB 56: 12 *Shark*

Singapore Gurkha Contingent (under police) 1,800

6 coy

DEPLOYMENT

AUSTRALIA
Air Force 230

EQUIPMENT BY TYPE
AIRCRAFT • TRG 27 S-211
HELICOPTERS: 12 AS-332 *Super Puma* Spt/AS-532 *Cougar* Utl

FACILITIES
School 1 with 12 AS-332 *Super Puma* Spt/AS-532 *Cougar* utl (flying trg) located at Oakey, Aus, 1 with 27 S-211 trg ac (flying trg) located at Pearce, Aus

BRUNEI
Army trg camp
Air Force hel det

FORCES BY ROLE
500; 1 hel det with AS-332 *Super Puma*

FRANCE
Air Force
FORCES BY ROLE
200; 1 trg sqn
EQUIPMENT BY TYPE
AIRCRAFT • FGA 4 A-4SU *Super Skyhawk*
  TRG 10 TA-4SU *Super Skyhawk*

TAIWAN (REPUBLIC OF CHINA)
Army
Training camp   3 (incl inf, arty and armd) located in
               Taiwan (Republic of China)

NEPAL
UN • **UNMIN** 2 obs

TIMOR LESTE
UN • **UNMIT** 2 obs

THAILAND
Army
Training camp   1 located in Thailand (arty, cbt engr)

UNITED STATES
Air Force
AIRCRAFT • FGA 9 F-16C/F-16D *Fighting Falcon* located
at Luke AFB, (AZ)
HELICOPTERS
  ATK AH-64D *Apache* located at Marana, (AZ), US
  SPT 6+ CH-47D *Chinook* located at Grand Prairie, (TX),
  US

FOREIGN FORCES

New Zealand Army: 1 spt unit; 11
United States Army 8; Navy 80; USAF 16; USMC 12;
USPACOM: 1 support facility located at Singapore; 1 log
spt sqn located at Singapore

Taiwan (Republic of China) ROC

New Taiwan Dollar NT$		2006	2007	2008
GDP	NT$	11.50tr	12.31tr	
	US$	351bn	379bn	
per capita	US$	15,225	16,352	
Growth	%	4.7	4.1	
Inflation	%	0.6		
Def bdgt	NT$	254bn	311bn	341bn
	US$	7.73bn	9.58bn	
US$1=NT$		32.8	32.5	

Population   23,174,294

Ethnic groups: Taiwanese 84%; mainland Chinese 14%

Age	0–14	15–19	20–24	25–29	30–64	65 plus
Male	10%	4%	4%	4%	24%	5%
Female	9%	3%	4%	4%	23%	5%

Capabilities

ACTIVE 290,000 (Army 200,000 Navy 45,000 Air
45,000) **Paramilitary 17,000**
Terms of service 20 months

RESERVE 1,657,000 (Army 1,500,000 Navy 67,000
Air Force 90,000)
Army reservists have some obligation to age 30

ORGANISATIONS BY SERVICE

Army ε200,000 (incl MP)
FORCES BY ROLE
Comd	4 defence HQ
Army	3 corps
Armd	5 bde
Armd inf	1 bde
Inf	28 bde
Avn/SF	1 comd (1 spec war bde, 3 avn bde)
Mot inf	3 bde
SSM	1 coastal def bn

Missile Command
AD 1 AD Msl comd (2 AD / SAM gp (*total:* 6 SAM bn
    eqpt. with total of 100 MIM-23 *HAWK*; with up to
    6 PAC-3 *Patriot* (systems); up to 6 Tien Kung I *Sky
    Bow* / Tien Kung II *Sky Bow*))

Reserves
Lt inf 7 div

EQUIPMENT BY TYPE
MBT 926+: 376 M-60A3; 100 M-48A5; 450+ M-48H *Brave
Tiger*
LT TK 905: 230 M-24 *Chaffee* (90mm gun); 675 M-41/Type-64
AIFV 225 CM-25 (M-113 with 20–30mm cannon)
APC 950
  APC (T) 650 M-113
  APC (W) 300 LAV-150 *Commando*
ARTY 1,815+
  SP 405: **105mm** 100 M-108; **155mm** 245: 225 M-109A2/M-
  109A5; 20 T-69 ; **203mm** 60 M-110
  TOWED 1,060+: **105mm** 650 T-64 (M-101); **155mm** 340+:
  90 M-59; 250 T-65 (M-114); M-44; **203mm** 70 M-115
  COASTAL 127mm ε50 US Mk 32 (reported)
  MRL 300+: **117mm** *Kung Feng* VI; **126mm** *Kung Feng* III/
  Kung Feng IV; RT 2000 *Thunder* (KF towed and SP)
  MOR
    SP 81mm M-29
    TOWED 81mm M-29; **107mm**
AT • MSL 1,000
  SP TOW
  MANPATS TOW
  RCL 500+: **90mm** M-67; **106mm** 500+: 500 M-40A1; Type-
  51
HELICOPTERS
  ATK 101: 62 AH-1W *Cobra*; 39 OH-58D *Warrior*
  SPT 9 CH-47SD *Super D Chinook*

East Asia and
Australasia

UTL 80 UH-1H *Iroquois*
TRG 30 TH-67 *Creek*
UAV *Mastiff* III
AD • SAM up to 678+
    SP 76: 74 FIM-92A *Avenger*; 2 M-48 *Chaparral*
    TOWED up to 137: 25 MIM-104 *Patriot*; 100 MIM-23
    HAWK; up to 6 PAC-3 *Patriot* (systems); up to 6 *Tien
    Kung* I *Sky Bow*/Tien Kung II *Sky Bow*
    MANPAD 465+ FIM-92A *Stinger*
    GUNS 400
        SP 40mm M-42
        TOWED 40mm L/70
MSL • SSM *Ching Feng*

Navy 45,000

FORCES BY ROLE

Navy 3 district; 1 (ASW) HQ located at Hualein; 1 Fleet
    HQ located at Tsoying; 1 New East Coast Fleet

EQUIPMENT BY TYPE

SUBMARINES • TACTICAL • SSK 4:
    2 *Hai Lung* each with 6+ single 533mm TT each with 20+
    SUT HWT
    2 *Hai Shih* (trg only) each with 4 Single 533mm TT (aft)
    each with SUT HWT, 6 (fwd) each with SUT HWT
PRINCIPAL SURFACE COMBATANTS 26
    DESTROYERS • DDG 4 *Keelung* (ex US *Kidd*) with 2
    quad with 8 RGM-84L *Harpoon* SSM, 2 Mk 112 octuple
    with 16 ASROC, 2 twin (4 eff) eqpt with SM-2 MR naval
    SAM, 2 127mm guns, (capacity 2 med hel)
    FRIGATES • FFG 22:
    8 *Cheng Kung* each with 2 quad (8 eff.) each with *Hsiung
    Feng* tactical SSM, 1 Mk 13 GMLS with 40+ SM-1 MR
    SAM, 2 triple ASTT (6 eff.) each with Mk 46 LWT, 1
    76mm gun, (capacity 2 S-70C *Defender* ASW hel)
    8 *Chin Yang* each with 1 Mk 112 octuple with ASROC/
    RGM-84C *Harpoon* SSM, 2 Twin 324mm ASTT (4 eff.)
    each with Mk 46 LWT, 1 127mm gun, (capacity 1 MD-
    500 utl hel)
    6 *Kang Ding* each with 2 quad (8 eff.) each with *Hsiung
    Feng* tactical SSM, 1 quad (4 eff.) with *Sea Chaparral* SAM,
    2 triple 324mm ASTT (6 eff.) each with Mk 46 LWT, 1
    76mm gun, (capacity 1 S-70C *Defender* ASW hel)
PATROL AND COASTAL COMBATANTS 70
    PTG 1 *Kwang Hua*
    PFM 61:
    47 *Hai Ou* each with 2 single each with 2 *Hsiung Feng*
    tactical SSM
    12 *Jinn Chiang* each with 1 quad (4 eff.) with 4 *Hsiung
    Feng* tactical SSM
    2 *Lung Chiang* each with 4 single each with 4 *Hsiung
    Feng* tactical SSM
    PFC 8 *Ning Hai*
MINE WARFARE • MINE COUNTERMEASURES 12
    MSC 8: 4 *Yung Chuan*; 4 *Yung Feng*
    MSO 4 *Aggressive* (Ex US)
COMMAND SHIPS • LCC 1 *Kao Hsiung*
AMPHIBIOUS
    PRINCIPAL AMPHIBIOUS SHIPS • LSD 2:
    1 *Shiu Hai* (capacity either 2 LCU or 18 LCM; 360
    troops) with 1 hel landing platform

    1 *Chung Cheng* (capacity 3 LCU or 18 LCM)
    LS 17
        LSM 4 *Mei Lo*
        LST 13: 11 *Chung Hai* (capacity 16 tanks; 200 troops); 2
        Newport (capacity 3 LCVP, 400 troops)
    LANDING CRAFT 290: 20 LCU; 100 **LCVP**; 170 **LCM**
LOGISTICS AND SUPPORT 11:
    AOE 1 *WuYi* with 1 hel landing platform
    ARS 6
    AK 3 *Wu Kang* with 1 hel landing platform (troop tpt
    capacity 1,400 troops)
    AGOR 1 *Ta Kuan*

FACILITIES

Bases Located at Makung (Pescadores), Keelung, Tsoying,
    Hualein, Suo

Marines 15,000

FORCES BY ROLE

Marine 3 bde
Spt some amph elm

EQUIPMENT BY TYPE

AAV 150 LVTP-5A1
ARTY • TOWED 105mm; 155mm
AT • RCL 106mm

Naval Aviation

FORCES BY ROLE

ASW 3 sqn with 20 S-70C *Defender**
MR 2 sqn with 24 S-2E *Tracker*; 8 S-2G *Tracker*

EQUIPMENT BY TYPE

AIRCRAFT 32 combat capable
    ASW 32: 24 S-2E *Tracker**; 8 S-2G *Tracker**
HELICOPTERS • ASW 20 S-70C *Defender**

Air Force 45,000

Flying hours 180 hrs/year

FORCES BY ROLE

Ftr	3 sqn with 47 *Mirage* 2000-5EI (M-2000-5E); 10 *Mirage* 2000-5DI (M-2000-5D)
FGA	6 sqn with 136 F-16A *Fighting Falcon*/F-16B *Fighting Falcon*; 1 sqn with 22 AT-3 *Tzu-Chung*; 6 sqn with 89 F-5E *Tiger II*/F-5F *Tiger II* some in store; 6 sqn with 128 *Ching Kuo*
Recce	1 sqn with 10 F-16A *Fighting Falcon*/F-16B *Fighting Falcon* ; 1 sqn with 8 RF-5E *Tigereye*
EW	1 sqn with 2 C-130HE *Tien Gian*; 2 CC-47 (C-47) *Skytrain*
AEW	1 sqn with 6 E-2T (E-2) *Hawkeye*
SAR	1 sqn with 17 S-70C *Black Hawk*
Tpt	2 sqn with 19 C-130H *Hercules* (1 EW); 1 (VIP) sqn with 4 B-727-100; 1 B-737-800; 10 Beech 1900; 3 Fokker 50
Trg	Trg school with 42 T-34C *Turbo Mentor*; 36 AT-3A/AT-3B *Tzu-chung*
Hel	sqn with 3 CH-47 *Chinook*; 14 S-70 *Black Hawk*; 1 S-62A (VIP)

EQUIPMENT BY TYPE

AIRCRAFT 478 combat capable

FTR 292: 89 F-5E *Tiger II*/F-5F *Tiger II* (some in store); 146 F-16A/F-16B *Fighting Falcon*; 10 *Mirage* 2000-5DI (M-2000-5D); 47 *Mirage* 2000-5EI (M-2000-5E)

FGA 150: 128 *Ching Kuo*; 22 *Tzu-Chung AT-3*

RECCE: 8 RF-5E *Tigereye*

EW 2 C-130HE *Tien Gian*

AEW 6 E-2T (E-2) *Hawkeye*

TPT 39: 4 B-727-100; 1 B-737-800; 10 Beech 1900; 19 C-130H *Hercules* (1 EW); 2 CC-47 (C-47) *Skytrain*; 3 Fokker 50

TRG 78: 36 AT-3A *Tzu-Chung*/AT-3B *Tzu-Chung**; 42 T-34C *Turbo Mentor*

HELICOPTERS

SPT 34: 3 CH-47 *Chinook*; 14 S-70; 17 S-70C *Black Hawk*

UTL 1 S-62A (VIP)

MSL • TACTICAL

ASM AGM-65A *Maverick*; AGM-84 *Harpoon*

ARM *Sky Sword* IIA

AAM AIM-120C *AMRAAM*; AIM-4D *Falcon*; AIM-9J *Sidewinder*/AIM-9P *Sidewinder*; MICA ; R-550 *Magic 2*; *Shafrir*; *Sky Sword* I/II

Paramilitary 17,000

Coast Guard 17,000

New service formed with the merging of agencies from the ministry of finance, customs and marine police.

PATROL AND COASTAL COMBATANTS 48

PSO 14: 2 *Ho Hsing*; 2 *Taipei*; 2 *Mou Hsing*; 1 *Yun Hsing*; 3 *Dao Hsing*; 4 *Shun Hu*

PCO 1 *Shun Hsing*

PCC 20: 4 *Hai Cheng*; 4 *Hai Ying*; 12 var

PBF 13

Thailand Th

Thai Baht b		2006	2007	2008
GDP	b	7.81tr	8.32tr	
	US$	207bn	244bn	
per capita	US$	3,198	3,752	
Growth	%	5.0	4.0	
Inflation	%	4.6	2.0	
Def bdgt	b	ε86.0bn	115bn	
	US$	2.27bn	3.37bn	
FMA (US)	US$	1.5m	1.3m	0.5m
US$1=b		37.8	34.1	

Population   65,068,149

Ethnic groups: Thai 75%; Chinese 14%; Muslim 4%

Age	0–14	15–19	20–24	25–29	30–64	65 plus
Male	11%	4%	4%	5%	22%	4%
Female	11%	4%	4%	4%	23%	4%

Capabilities

ACTIVE 306,600 (Army 190,000 Navy 70,600 Air 46,000) **Paramilitary 113,700**

Terms of service 2 years

RESERVE 200,000 Paramilitary 45,000

ORGANISATIONS BY SERVICE

Army 120,000; ε70,000 conscript (total 190,000)

4 Regional Army HQ, 2 Corps HQ

FORCES BY ROLE

Armd air cav	1 regt (3 air mob coy)
Rapid reaction	1 force (1 bn per region forming)
Cav	2 div; 1 indep regt
Recce	4 coy
Mech inf	2 div
Armd inf	3 div
Inf	8 indep bn
SF	2 div
Lt inf	1 div
Arty	1 div
ADA	1 div (6 ADA bn)
Engr	1 div
Hel	some flt
Economic development	4 div

EQUIPMENT BY TYPE

MBT 333: 53 M-60A1; 125 M-60A3; 50 Type-69 (trg) in store; 105 M-48A5

LT TK 515: 255 M-41; 104 *Scorpion*; 50 in store; 106 *Stingray*

RECCE 32+: 32 S52 Mk 3; M1114 *HMMWV*

APC 950

APC (T) 790: 340 M-113A1/M-113A3; 450 Type-85

APC (W) 160: 18 *Condor*; 142 LAV-150 *Commando*

ARTY 2,473+

SP 155mm 20 M-109A2

TOWED 553: **105mm** 353: 24 LG1 MK II; 285 M-101/-Mod; 12 M-102; 32 M-618A2; **130mm** 15 Type-59-I; **155mm** 185: 42 GHN-45 A1; 50 M-114; 61 M-198; 32 M-71

MRL 130mm Type-85 (reported)

MOR 1,900

SP 33: **81mm** 21 M-125A3; **120mm** 12 M-1064A3

TOWED 1,867: **81mm**; **107mm** M-106A1

AT • MSL 318+

SP 18+ M-901A5 (TOW)

MANPATS 300 M47 *Dragon;*

RCL 180: **75mm** 30 M-20; **106mm** 150 M-40

RL 66mm M-72 *LAW*

AIRCRAFT

RECCE 40 Cessna O-1A *Bird Dog*

TPT 10: 2 Beech 1900C; 2 Beech 200 *Super King Air*; 2 CASA 212 *Aviocar*; 2 *Jetstream* 41; 2 Short 330UTT

UTL 10 U-17B

TRG 33: 18 MX-7-235 *Star Rocket*; 15 T-41B *Mescalero*

HELICOPTERS

ATK 5 AH-1F *Cobra*

SPT 6 CH-47D *Chinook*
UTL 159: 65 AB-212 (Bell 212)/Bell 206 *JetRanger*/Bell 214/ Bell 412 *Twin Huey*; 92 UH-1H *Iroquois*; 2 UH-60L *Black Hawk*
TRG 42 Hughes 300C
UAV • RECCE • TACTICAL *Searcher*
AD • SAM
    STATIC *Aspide*
    MANPAD FIM-43 *Redeye*; HN-5A
    GUNS 202+
        SP 54: **20mm** 24 M-163 *Vulcan*; **40mm** 30 M-1/M-42 SP
        TOWED 148+: **20mm** 24 M-167 *Vulcan*; **37mm** 52 Type-74; **40mm** 48 L/70; **57mm** 24+: ε6 Type-59 (S-60); 18+ non-operational
RADAR • LAND AN/TPQ-36 *Firefinder* (arty, mor); RASIT (veh, arty)

Reserves

Inf 4 div HQ

Navy 44,751 (incl Naval Aviation, Marines, Coastal Defence); 25,849 conscript (total 70,600)

FORCES BY ROLE

Air wing   1 div

Navy   1 (Fleet) HQ located at Sattahip; Mekong River Operating Unit HQ located at Nakhon Phanom

EQUIPMENT BY TYPE

PRINCIPAL SURFACE COMBATANTS 20
    AIRCRAFT CARRIERS • CVH 1:
        1 *Chakri Naruebet* (capacity 9 AV-8A *Harrier†* FGA ac; 6 S-70B *Seahawk* ASW hel)
    FRIGATES 10
        FFG 8:
            2 *Chao Phraya* each with 4 twin (8 eff.) each with CSS-N-4 *Sardine* tactical SSM, 2 (4 eff.) non-operational each with HQ-61 (CSA-N-2) SAM non-operational, 2 RBU 1200 (10 eff.), 2 twin 100mm gun (4 eff.), 2 twin 37mm gun (4 eff.), 1 hel landing platform
            2 *Kraburi* each with 4 (8 eff.) each with CSS-N-4 *Sardine* tactical SSM, 2 twin (4 eff.) with HQ-61 (CSA-N-2) SAM, 2 RBU 1200 (10 eff.), 1 twin 100mm gun (2 eff.), 2 twin 37mm gun (4 eff.), (capacity 1 AB-212 (Bell 212) utl hel)
            2 *Naresuan* each with 2 Mk 141 *Harpoon* quad (8 eff.) each with RGM-84A *Harpoon* tactical SSM, 1 8 cell Mk 41 VLS with RIM-7M *Sea Sparrow* SAM, 2 triple 324mm TT (6 eff.), 1 127mm gun, (1 *Lynx* SRS 300 *Super Lynx* ASW/ASUW hel)
            2 *Phuttha Yotfa Chulalok* (leased from US) each with 1 Mk 112 octuple with RGM-84C *Harpoon* tactical SSM, tactical ASROC, 2 Twin ASTT (4 eff.) with 22 Mk 46 LWT, 1 127mm gun, (capacity 1 AB-212 (Bell 212) utl hel)
        FF 2:
            1 *Makut Rajakumarn* with 2 triple ASTT (6 eff.), 2 114mm gun
            1 *Pin Klao* (trg) with 6 single 324mm ASTT, 3 76mm gun

CORVETTES 9
    FSG 2 *Rattanakosin* each with 2 Mk 140 *Harpoon* quad (8 eff.) each with RGM-84A *Harpoon* tactical SSM, 1 *Albatros* octuple with *Aspide* SAM, 2 triple ASTT (6 eff.), 1 76mm gun
    FS 7:
        3 *Khamronsin* each with 2 triple ASTT (6 eff.), 1 76mm gun
        2 *Tapi* each with 6 single 324mm ASTT each with Mk 46 LWT, 1 76mm gun
        2 *Pattani* each with 1 76mm gun
PATROL AND COASTAL COMBATANTS 87
    PFM 6:
        3 *Prabparapak* each with 2 single each with 1 GI *Gabriel I* tactical SSM, 1 triple (3 eff.) with GI *Gabriel I* tactical SSM, 1 40mm gun, 1 57mm gun
        3 *Ratcharit* each with 2 twin (4 eff.) each with MM-38 *Exocet* tactical SSM, 1 76mm gun
    PSO 3 *Hua Hin* each with 2 20mm gun, 1 76mm gun
    PFC 3 *Chon Buri* each with 2 76mm gun
    PC 6 *Sattahip* each with 1 40mm gun, 1 76mm gun
    PCC 3 each with 1 40mm gun, 1 76mm gun
    PCI 44: 9 *Swift*; 10 T-11; 13 T-213; 3 T-81; 9 T-91
    PCR 6
    PBR 16
MINE WARFARE • MINE COUNTERMEASURES 19
    MCC 2 *Bang Rachan*
    MCM SPT 1 *Thalang*
    MCMV 2 *Lat Ya*
    MS ε12
    MSC 2 *Bangkeo*
AMPHIBIOUS:
    LS 9: 2
        LSM 1 *Kut* (capacity 4 tanks)
        LST 6:
            4 *Chang* each with 6 40mm gun (capacity 16 tanks; 200 troops)
            2 *Sichang* training each with 2 40mm gun, 1 hel landing platform (capacity 14 tanks; 300 troops)
    LANDING CRAFT • LCU 13: 3 *Man Nok*; 6 *Mataphun* (capacity either 3–4 MBT or 250 troops); 4 *Thong Kaeo*
LOGISTICS AND SUPPORT 15:
    AORH 1 *Similan* (1 hel)
    AOR 1 *Chula*
    AOL 5: 4 *Prong*; 1 *Samui*
    AWT 1
    AGOR 1
    AGS 1
    ABU 1
    TRG 1
    YPT 1
    YTM 2

FACILITIES

Bases   Located at Bangkok, Sattahip, Songkhla, Phang Nga, Nakhon Phanom

Naval Aviation 1,940

AIRCRAFT 17 combat capable
    FGA 7 AV-8A *Harrier†*
    RECCE 9 *Sentry* 02-337

MP 10: 5 DO-228-212*; 3 F-27 MK 200MPA*; 2 P-3T (P-3A) *Orion**

TPT 2 F-27-400M *Troopship*

UTL 8: 2 CL-215-III; 5 GAF N-24A *Search Master*; 1 UP-3T (UP-3A) *Orion*

TRG 16: 14 TA-7; 4 TA-7C *Corsair II*; 2 TAV-8A *Harrier*†

HELICOPTERS

8 atk hel

ASW 6 S-70B *Seahawk*

ASW/ASUW 2: 2 *Lynx SRS 300 Super Lynx*

UTL 17: 5 AB-212 (Bell 212); 5 AB-214ST; 5 S-76B; 2 *Super Lynx*

MSL • TACTICAL • ASM: AGM-84 *Harpoon*

Marines 23,000

FORCES BY ROLE

Recce	1 bn
Amph aslt	1 bn
Inf	2 regt
Arty	1 regt (1 ADA bn, 3 fd arty bn)
Marine	1 div HQ

EQUIPMENT BY TYPE

APC (W) 24 LAV-150 *Commando*

AAV 33 LVTP-7

ARTY • TOWED 48: **105mm** 36 (reported); **155mm** 12 GC-45

AT • MSL 24+

  TOWED 24 HMMWV TOW

  MANPATS M47 *Dragon*; TOW

AD • GUNS 12.7mm 14

Air Force ε46,000

4 air divs, one flying trg school

Flying hours   100 hrs/year

FORCES BY ROLE

FTR/ FGA	3 sqn with 41 F-16A *Fighting Falcon*; 9 F-16B *Fighting Falcon*; 2 sqn with 34 L-39ZA/MP *Albatros*; 1 sqn with 3 (1 aggressor) sqn with 35 F-5E *Tiger II*/F-5F *Tiger II* (32 being upgraded), 2 F-5B
Recce/ ELINT	1 sqn with 3 IAI-201 *Arava*, 2 Learjet 35A
Tpt	1 sqn with 9 Basler *Turbo-67*; 15 GAF N-22B *Nomad*; 1 sqn with 4 BAe-748; 3 G-222; 1 sqn with 7 C-130H *Hercules*; 5 C-130H-30 *Hercules*
VIP	1 (Royal Flight) sqn with 1 A-310-324; 1 Airbus A319CJ; 1 B-737-200; 2 BAe-748; 2 B737-400; 2 Beech 200 *Super King Air*; 6 SA-226AT *Merlin IV/IVA*; 3 AS-532A2 *Cougar MKII*; 3 AS-332L *Super Puma*; 2 Bell 412 *Twin Huey*
Utl	1 sqn with 22 AU-23A *Peacemaker**, 1 sqn with 12 L-39EA*, 1 with 10 *Alpha Jet**
Liaison	1 sqn with 2 Beech 65 *Queen Air*; 1 Beech E90 *King Air*; 3 Rockwell *Commander* 500; 3 Cessna 150; 12 T-41D *Mescalero*
Survey	1 sqn with 3 SA-226AT *Merlin IV/IVA*; 3 GAF N-22B *Nomad*
Trg	Trg school with 29 CT-4B/E *Airtrainer*; 23 PC-9; 6 Bell 206B *JetRanger II*
Hel	1 sqn with 20 UH-1H *Iroquois*; 1 sqn with 13 Bell 212

EQUIPMENT BY TYPE

AIRCRAFT 165 combat capable

  FTR/FGA 87: 35 F-5E *Tiger II*/F-5F *Tiger II* (32 being upgraded), 2 F-5B; 41 F-16A *Fighting Falcon*; 9 F-16B *Fighting Falcon*

  TPT 57: 1 A-310-324; 1 A-319CJ; 1 B-737-200; 2 B737-400; 6 BAe-748; 9 Basler Turbo-67; 2 Beech 200 *Super King Air*; 2 Beech 65 *Queen Air*; 1 Beech E90 *King Air*; 7 C-130H *Hercules*; 5 C-130H-30 *Hercules*; 3 G-222; 3 IAI-201 *Arava*; 2 Learjet 35A; 3 Rockwell *Commander* 500; 9 SA-226AT *Merlin IV/IVA*

  UTL 40: 22 AU-23A *Peacemaker**; 18 GAF N-22B *Nomad*

  TRG 123: 10 *Alpha Jet**; 29 CT-4B/E *Airtrainer*; 3 Cessna 150; 46 L-39ZA/MP *Albatros**; 23 PC-9; 12 T-41D *Mescalero*

HELICOPTERS

  SPT 19: 3 AS-332L *Super Puma*; 3 AS-532A2 *Cougar MKII*; 13 Bell 212

  UTL 28: 6 Bell 206B *JetRanger II*; 2 Bell 412 *Twin Huey*; 20 UH-1H *Iroquois*

MSL

  AAM AIM-120 *AMRAAM*; AIM-9B *Sidewinder*/AIM-9J *Sidewinder*; *Python* III

  ASM: AGM-65 *Maverick*

Paramilitary ε113,700 active

Border Patrol Police 41,000

Marine Police 2,200

PATROL AND COASTAL COMBATANTS 124

  PSO 3: 1 *Srinakrin*; 2 *Hameln*

  PCC 3: 2 *Chasanyabadee*; 1 *Yokohama*

  PCI 13: 6 *Ital* Thai Marine; 1 *Burespadoog kit*; 3 *Cutlass*; 3 *Technautic* 810-812 series

  PBR 80

  PB 25

National Security Volunteer Corps 45,000 – Reserves

Police Aviation 500

AIRCRAFT

  TPT 16: 2 CN-235; 1 Fokker 50; 8 PC-6 *Turbo-Porter*; 3 SC.7 3M *Skyvan*; 2 Short 330UTT

  UTL 6 AU-23A *Peacemaker*

HELICOPTERS • UTL 67: 20 AB-212 (Bell 212); 27 Bell 205A; 14 Bell 206 *JetRanger*; 6 Bell 412 *Twin Huey*

Provincial Police 50,000 (incl est. 500 Special Action Force)

Thahan Phran (Hunter Soldiers) ε20,000

Volunteer irregular force

Paramilitary   13 regt (*each*: 107 Paramilitary coy)

NON-STATE ARMED GROUPS
see Part II

DEPLOYMENT

NEPAL
UN • UNMIN 7 obs

SUDAN
UN • UNAMID proposed deployment
UN • UNMIS 2; 12 obs

FOREIGN FORCES
United States Army 39; Navy 7; USAF 29; USMC 39

Timor Leste TL

Timorian Escudo TPE	2006	2007	2008

Population	1,040,880					

Age	0–14	15–19	20–24	25–29	30–64	65 plus
Male	19%	6%	5%	3%	16%	1%
Female	18%	6%	5%	3%	16%	2%

Capabilities
ACTIVE 1,286 (Army 1,250 Naval Element 36)

ORGANISATIONS BY SERVICE

Army 1,250
Training began in Jan 2001 with the aim of deploying 1,500 full-time personnel and 1,500 reservists
Inf 2 bn

Naval Element 36

FOREIGN FORCES
All under UNMIT comd unless otherwise specified
Australia M-113 APC (T); 4 OH-58 *Kiowa* obs hel; UH-60 Blackhawk; 3 C-130; 4 *Blackhawk*; 850 *(Operation Astute)*; 4 obs
Bangladesh 4 obs
Brazil 3 obs
China, People's Republic of 3 obs
Fiji 1 obs
Libya 2 obs
Malaysia 209 *(Operation Astute)*; 2 obs
New Zealand 180 *(Operation Astute)*; 1 obs
Pakistan 4 obs
Philippines 3 obs
Portugal 4 obs
Sierra Leone 1 obs
Singapore 2 obs

Vietnam Vn

Vietnamese Dong d		2006	2007	2008
GDP	d	979tr	1,145tr	
	US$	61.1bn	71.2bn	
per capita	US$	724	835	
Growth	%	8.2	8.3	
Inflation	%	7.5	7.3	
Def bdgt	d	ε55tr	ε60tr	
	US$	3.43bn	3.73bn	
US$1=d		15,994	16,080	

Population 85,262,356
Ethnic groups: Chinese 3%

Age	0–14	15–19	20–24	25–29	30–64	65 plus
Male	14%	6%	5%	5%	17%	2%
Female	13%	5%	5%	4%	19%	3%

Capabilities
ACTIVE 455,000 (Army 412,000 Navy 13,000 Air 30,000) **Paramilitary 40,000**
Terms of service 2 years Army and Air Defence, 3 years Air Force and Navy, specialists 3 years, some ethnic minorities 2 years

RESERVES 5,000,000

ORGANISATIONS BY SERVICE

Army ε412,000
9 Mil Regions (incl capital), 14 Corps HQ
FORCES BY ROLE

Armd	10 bde
Mech inf	3 div
Inf	58 div (div strength varies from 5,000 to 12,500); 15 indep regt
SF	1 bde (1 AB bde, 1 demolition engr regt)
Fd arty	10+ bde
Engr	8 div; 20 indep bde
Economic construction	10–16 div

EQUIPMENT BY TYPE
MBT 1,315: 70 T-62; 350 Type-59; 850 T-54/T-55; 45 T-34
LT TK 620: 300 PT-76; 320 Type-62/Type-63
RECCE 100 BRDM-1/BRDM-2
AIFV 300 BMP-1/BMP-2
APC 1,380
  APC (T) 280: 200 M-113 (to be upgraded); 80 Type-63
  APC (W) 1,100 BTR-40/BTR-50/BTR-60/BTR-152
ARTY 3,040+
  SP 30+: **152mm** 30 2S3; **175mm** M-107
  TOWED 2,300 **76mm**; **85mm**; **100mm** M-1944; **105mm** M-101/M-102; **122mm** D-30/Type-54 (M-30) *M-1938* /Type-60 (D-74); **130mm** M-46; **152mm** D-20; **155mm** M-114

GUN/MOR 120mm 2S9 *Anona* (reported)

MRL 710+: 107mm 360 Type-63; **122mm** 350 BM-21; **140mm** BM-14

MOR 82mm; **120mm** M-43; **160mm** M-43

AT • MSL • MANPATS AT-3 9K11 *Sagger*

RCL 75mm Type-56; **82mm** Type-65 (B-10); **87mm** Type-51

GUNS

SP 100mm Su-100; **122mm** Su-122

TOWED 100mm T-12 (arty)

AD • SAM • MANPAD SA-7 *Grail*/SA-16 *Gimlet*/SA-18 *Grouse* (Igla)

GUNS 12,000

SP 23mm ZSU-23-4

TOWED 14.5mm/30mm/37mm/57mm/85mm/100mm

MSL • SSM *Scud*-B/*Scud*-C (reported)

Navy ε13,000

FORCES BY ROLE

Navy 1 HQ located at Haiphong

EQUIPMENT BY TYPE

SUBMARINES • TACTICAL • SSI 2 DPRK *Yugo*†

PRINCIPAL SURFACE COMBATANTS 11

FRIGATES • FF 5:

3 FSU *Petya* II each with 2 x5 406mm ASTT (10 eff.), 4 RBU 6000 *Smerch* 2 (48 eff.), 4 76mm gun

2 FSU *Petya* III each with 1 triple 533mm ASTT (3 eff.), 4 RBU 2500 *Smerch* 1 (64 eff.), 4 76mm gun

CORVETTES • FSG 6:

4 FSU *Tarantul* each with 2 twin (4 eff.) each with SS-N-2D *Styx* tactical SSM

2 BPS-500 with 2 quad (8 eff.) each with SS-N-25 *Switchblade* tactical SSM non-operational, SA-N-5 *Grail* SAM (manually operated)

PATROL AND COASTAL COMBATANTS 38

PFM 10:

8 *Osa* II each with 4 single each with 1 SS-N-2 tactical SSM

2 *Svetlyak* (Further 2 on order)

PFT 3 FSU *Shershen*† each with 4 single 533mm TT

PHT 5:

2 *Turya*†

3 *Turya*† each with 4 single 533mm TT

PCI 16: 2 FSU *Poluchat*; 4 FSU SO-1; 10 *Zhuk*†

PBR 4 *Stolkraft*

MINE WARFARE • MINE COUNTERMEASURES 14

MCMV 5 K-8

MSC 7: 4 *Sonya*; 1 *Vanya*; 2 *Yurka*

MSI 2 *Yevgenya*

AMPHIBIOUS

LS 6

LSM 3:

1 *Polnochny* A† (capacity 6 MBT; 180 troops)

2 *Polnochny* B† (capacity 6 MBT; 180 troops)

LST 3 US LST-510-511 (capacity 16 tanks; 200 troops)

LANDING CRAFT 23: 5 **LCU**; 18 **LCM**

LOGISTICS AND SUPPORT 20:

AKSL 17; **AWT** 1; **AGS** 1; **AT** 1

NAVAL SHIP ASSET 2 floating dock

Naval Infantry ε27,000

FACILITIES

Bases Located at Hanoi, Ho Chi Minh City, Da Nang, Cam Ranh Bay, Ha Tou, Haiphong, Can Tho

People's Air Force 30,000

3 air divs (each with 3 regts), a tpt bde

FORCES BY ROLE

Ftr	7 regt with 140 MiG-21bis *Fishbed L*
FGA	2 regt with 4 Su-30MKK *Flanker*; 7 Su-27SK/5 Su-27UBK *Flanker*; 53 Su-22M-3 /Su-22M-4 *Fitter* (some recce designated)
ASW SAR	1 regt (The PAF also maintains Vn naval air arm) with 3 Ka-25 *Hormone*; 10 Ka-28 (Ka-27PL) *Helix A*; 2 KA-32 *Helix C*; 4 PZLW-3 *Sokol*
MR	1 regt with 4 Be-12 *Mail*
Tpt	3 regt with 12 An-2 *Colt*; 12 An-26 *Curl*; 4 Yak-40 *Codling* (VIP); 4 Mi-6 *Hook*; 30 MI-17 (Mi-8MT) *Hip H*/Mi-8 *Hip*; 12 UH-1H
Atk hel	1 regt with 26 Mi-24 *Hind*
Trg	Trg regt with 18 L-39 *Albatros*; 10 MiG-21UM *Mongol B**; 10 BT-6 (Yak-18) *Max*
AD/ SAM	4 bde with 100mm; 130mm; 37mm; 57mm; 85mm; some (People's Regional) force (*total*: ε1,000 AD unit, 6 radar bde with 100 radar stn)

EQUIPMENT BY TYPE

AIRCRAFT 219 combat capable

FTR 140 MiG-21bis *Fishbed L & N*

FGA 64: 4 Su-30MKK *Flanker*; 7 Su-27SK *Flanker*; 53 Su-22M-3/M-4 *Fitter* (some recce dedicated)

ASW 4 Be-12 *Mail*

TPT 28: 12 An-2 *Colt*; 12 An-26 *Curl*; 4 Yak-40 *Codling* (VIP)

TRG 43: 10 BT-6 (Yak-18) *Max*; 18 L-39 *Albatros*; 10 MiG-21UM *Mongol B**; 5 Su-27UBK *Flanker**

HELICOPTERS

ATK 26 Mi-24 *Hind*

ASW 13: 3 Ka-25 *Hormone**; 10 Ka-28* (Ka-27PL) *Helix A*

SPT 48: 2 KA-32s *Helix C*; 4 Mi-6 *Hook*; 30 MI-17 (Mi-8MT) *Hip H*/Mi-8 *Hip* Spt; 12 UH-1H *Iroquois*

SAR 4 PZL W-3 *Sokol*

AD • SAM

SP SA-6 *Gainful*

TOWED SA-2 *Guideline*; SA-3 *Goa*

MANPAD SA-7 *Grail*; SA-16 *Gimlet*

GUNS 37mm; 57mm; 85mm; 100mm; 130mm

MSL

ASM AS-14 *Kedge*; AS-17 *Krypton*; AS-18 *Kazoo*; AS-9 *Kyle*

AAM AA-10 *Alamo*; AA-12 *Adder*; AA-2 *Atoll*; AA-8 *Aphid*

FACILITIES

SAM site	66 with SA-16 *Gimlet* MANPAD/SA-2 *Guideline* Towed/SA-3 *Goa*/SA-6 *Gainful* SP/SA-7 *Grail* MANPAD

Paramilitary 40,000 active

Border Defence Corps ε40,000

Local Forces ε5,000,000 reservists

Incl People's Self-Defence Force (urban units), People's Militia (rural units); comprises of static and mobile cbt units, log spt and village protection pl; some arty, mor and AD guns; acts as reserve.

ARTY • MOR
AD • GUNS

Table 33 **Selected Arms Orders and Deliveries, East Asia and Australasia**

	Country Supplier	Classification	Designation	Quantity	Order date	Original Delivery date	Comment
Australia (Aus)	dom	LACV	*Bushmaster*	299	1999	2006	Reduced from 370.
	US	AEW	B-737 *Wedgetail*	6	2000	2006	AUD3.4bn (USD2.4bn). Order increased from 4 to 6 in 2004. Final deliveries by 2008
	Sp	Hel	AS-665 *Tiger*	22	2001	2004	First delivery December 2004. Delivery of remaining 15 hel continuing
	dom	LACV	*Bushmaster*	300	2002	–	266 LACV delivered as of June 2007
	dom	FFG	*Adelaide*	4	2003	2006	Upgrade to enhance self-defence and attack capabilities. HMAS *Sydney* delivered in 2006. HMAS *Melburne*, *Darwin* and *Adelaide* to be delivered by 2008.
	Int'l	Tkr/Tpt	A-330-200	5	2004	2008	AUD1.46bn (USD1.05bn)
	dom	EW	*Soothsayer*	–	2005	–	Revived EWSP (Electronic Warfare Self Protection) fit to C-130H, CH-47 and S-70A-9s with MILDS (Missile Launch and Detection System)
	Il	UAV	I-View 250A	15	2006	2008	AUD145m.(USD104m)
	dom	Hel	NH-90	40	2005	2007	USD1bn. First 12 aircraft expected by 2007. Additional 28 aircraft scheduled for delivery by 2009
	US	Tpt	C-17 *Globemaster* III	4	2005	2006	AUD2bn. (USD1.4bn) First delivered in late 2006. All expected by 2008. Second ac delivered in May 2007
	dom	FFG	*Anzac*	–	2005	2009	USD260m. Upgrade to be complete by 2012.
	US	C2	*Aegis*	3	2006	2013	AUD1bn (USD720m) Purchased as long-lead items for planned RAN AWD, due in service by 2013.
	Int'l / dom	Hel	MRH-90	46	2006	2007	AUD2bn (USD1.47bn) replacement programme. First 4 built in Europe and remaining 42 in Australia
	US	Msl	AGM-158	–	2006	2009	
	–	APC	M113	–	–	2010	AUD590m upgrade contract
	Ca	C2	Digital communications system for deployable land forces	–	2006	2007	AUD26m (USD19.5m). Remaining options could bring the project to up to AUD800m. Final delivery 2016
	Int'l	SSK	*Collins*	6	2006	2007	Comms upgrade AUD400m (USD220.9m). Contract including acquisition of a new heavyweight torpedo
	US	ASM	Tactical *Harpoon* Block II AURS	2	2006	2007	USD44m. Includes 2 warheads sections, 2 Mk 992 exercise/ warhead container and 1 Mk 607 air-launch container
	US / Il	UAV (Tac)	TUAV unit	2	2006	–	AUD145m (USD114m). Each unit consists of 4 air vehicles, 2 ground-control stations and support systems for the new 20th Surveillance and Target Acquisition Regt. To commence ops in 2009
	Ge	APC	M113	–	2006	–	GPS upgrade. AUD11m (USD8.6m). TALIN 500 hybrid GPS/inertial navigation system
	It / dom	SURV	*Dash* 8 / Hel	12	2007	–	Upgrade. EU20m. The contract will run up to 2020. 10 ATOS Surveillance Information Management will be installed on *Dash* 8 ac, 2 on hel

Table 33 Selected Arms Orders and Deliveries, East Asia and Australasia

Country Supplier	Classification	Designation	Quantity	Order date	Original Delivery date	Comment
UK	MP	AP-3C *Orion*	–	2007	2011	Electronic surv upgrade. USD76m. Electronic Surveilance System. The contract is part of a series of up to USD600m upgrades
dom	UAV	*ScanEagle*	–	2007	–	AUD11.5m (USD9.1m) lease contract to provide recce and surv services for the Army until new TUAV with I-View capabilities becomes operational in 2009
dom	DD	*Hobart*	3	2007	–	USD8bn. To enter service in 2013
US	VLS	MK 41 *Baseline* VII	3	2007	–	For 3 *Hobart*-class AWD DD. Part of a USD16m contract including 3 VLS for Aus and 1 VLS for Sp
US	DD	–	3	2007	2008	Weapon system upgrade. *Aegis* Weapon System to be delivered for *Hobart* class. Part of a USD260m contract including 3 *Aegis* for Aus and 1 *Aegis* for Sp
dom	LHD	*Canberra*	2	2007	2012	AUD3bn (USD2.5bn). To replace HMAS *Manoora nad Kanimbla*
Int'l	Hel	AW119 Ke light single / A109 Power / Grand Light twin / AW139 medium twin	8	2007	–	3 of 8 hel are A109
dom / US	AUV	REMUS 600 / REMUS 100 Autonomous Underwater Vehicle	2	2007	2007	AUD1.9m (USD1.6m)
US	FGA	F/A-18F Block II *Super Hornet*	24	2007	2010	AUD6bn (USD4.6bn). Final delivery in 2011
US	FGA	F/A-18F Block II *Super Hornet*	24	2007	2009	Engine upgrade. USD428m contract for the provision of F414-GE-400 turbofan engines
US	FGA	F/A-18F Block II *Super Hornet*	24	2007	2008	Radar upgrade. USD24m contract covering ALR-67 (V) 3 digital radar warning receiver (RWR) systems. Completion in 2011
dom	LACV	*Bushmaster*	143	2007	–	AUD99m (USD82m). Extension to 2002 contract. Inf, ambulance, mor and direct-fire variants. Deliveries to be completed by 30 March 2009
US	AAM	Evolved *SeaSparrow* Missile (ESSM)	–	2007	–	USD223m NATO *SeaSparrow* Consortium for 294 ESSM
dom	FFG	*Anzac*	–	2007	–	Upgrade and maintenance. AUD104m. 9-year alliance agreement with option for extension for 6 years
US	FFG	*Anzac*	4	2007	–	Mk 92 fire control system upgrade to support deployment to SM-2 msl. USD20.6m. To be completed by 2009
dom	LACV	*Bushmaster*	254	2007	–	AUD300m (USD240m)
Sp	DD	F100	3	2007	2014	USD8bn. 2nd to be delivered in 2016, 3rd in 2017
Sp / dom	LCM	–	2	2007	2013	USD3bn. 2nd to be delivered in 2015

Table 33 Selected Arms Orders and Deliveries, East Asia and Australasia

Country Supplier	Classification	Designation	Quantity	Order date	Original Delivery date	Comment
dom	AORH	*Durance*	1	2007	–	Second phase refit of HMAS *Success*. AUS24m (USD19.8m). The first phase was completed in early 2007
China, People's Republic of (PRC) dom	ICBM	CSS-X-10	–	1985	–	DF-41 – range 12,000km. It is believed that the programme was either halted or terminated in 2002. It is possible that it has been restarted with a new performance requirement
dom	IRBM	CSS-9	–	1985	–	DF-31 – range 8,000km. Successfully tested Aug 1999. 6 reported as operationally deployed. Programme continuing
dom	ICBM	CSS-NX-5	–	1985	2009	For development; range 8,000km. Reportedly to equip the new Type 094 SSBN
dom	SSBN	Type 094	4	1985	2008	Construction reportedly began 1999. First of class launched 2004. Currently undergoing sea-trials. Full commissioning status unknown
dom	Hel	EC-120 *Colibri*	–	1990	2005	With Pak (150 units)
dom	FGA	J-10	–	1993	–	100 ac in service as of 2007
dom	IRBM	DF-21X	–	1999	–	Modernised DF-15. Development continuing
RF	AEW	A-50 *Mainstay*	6	2000	2004	Delivered but not fully operational
RF	Tpt	IL-76TD	30	2005	–	Combined cost with order for 8 IL-78M tankers is reported to be EUR850-1.5bn (USD1-1.8bn)
RF	Tkr	IL-78M	8	2005	–	Combined cost with order for 30 IL-76TD Transport aircraft is reported to be EUR850-1.5bn (USD1-1.8bn)
RF	Ac	Be-103	6	2007	–	Amphibian ac
Indonesia (Indo) dom	MP	NC212-200	3	1996	2000	Delays due to financial difficulties. First delivered in late 2006. 2 ac in March 2007
dom	Hel	NAS-332 *Super Puma*	16	1998	–	Deliveries should have been completed in 2004. As for June 2007, only 7 hel have been delivered. Only 5 hel are operational. Contract to be reviewed
RF	Hel	Mi-8 *Hip*	8	2000	2004	Currently four delivered. Deliveries continuing
ROK	LPD	Multi-role vessel	4	2003	2008	–
Nl	FS	*Sigma*	4	2004	2008	USD1.9bn First batch of 2 ordered in 2004. Second batch of 2 ordered 2006. First deliveries due 2008. KRI *Diponegoro* delivered in 2007. Remaining FS to be named *Hasanuddin* (Nov 2007), *Sultan Iskandar Muda* (late 2008) and *Frans Kaisiepo* (early 2009)
PI	PB	NS-935 (Type B-2)	5	2004	2007	USD24.5m. PB will be named KP *Kutilang* (638), KP *Bangau* (639), KP *Balibis* (640), KP *Pelikan* (641), KP *Punai* (642) and handed over to the Sea Police Unit
PI	MP/Tpt	PZL M-28 *Skytruck*	10	2005	2006	USD75m contract for Indonesian Police and naval forces. All were expected by the end of 2006
PI	AD	*Kobra* AD system	–	2005	2007	USD40m. Final delivery in 2008. To replace 51 MBDA *Rapier* Mk 1

Table 33 **Selected Arms Orders and Deliveries, East Asia and Australasia**

Country Supplier	Classification	Designation	Quantity	Order date	Original Delivery date	Comment
Fr	APC	LAV Renault	32	2006	–	To be delivered 3 months after confirmation in Lebanon
Pl	Radar	CNPEP radar *Kobra*	1	2006	2008	USD40m
Sp	Tpt	CASA C-212-400	–	2006	–	–
RF	Ftr	Su-27	3	2006	2008	Part of USD1bn deal
RF	Ftr	Su-27MK	3	2006	2008	Refer to above
RF	Hel	Mi-17	10	2006	–	Refer to above
RF	Hel	Mi-35P	5	2006	–	Refer to above
RF	AIFV	BMP-3F	20	2006	–	Refer to above
RF	ASSM	ASM package	2	2006	–	Refer to above
RF	SSK	*Kilo* or *Lada*	2	2006	–	Refer to above
RF	Ftr	Su-27SKM / Su-27MK2	6	2007	2008	USD330-350m. Final delivery in 2010. 3 Su-27SKM and 3 Su-27MK2
RF	Hel	Mi-17	10	2007	–	For the army
RF	Atk / Aslt	Mi-35	3	2007	–	For the army
Japan (J) dom	AAM	XAAM-5	–	1994	2001	Development continuing
dom	BMD	TMD	–	1997	–	Joint development with US from late 1998. Programme continuing.
dom	Recce	Satellites	4	1998	2002	Deliveries continuing. Programme consists of 2 optical, 2 radar satellite/ first launched in 2003
dom / US	FGA	Mitsubishi F-2A / F-2B	130	1999	2000	Deliveries continuing.
dom	Utl	U-125A Peace *Krypton* (aka *Hawker* U-125A)	27	1995	1995	USD76m. 22 ac in service. Deliveries continuing
dom	Trg	T-X	50	2000	–	Development programme to replace Fuji T-3s. Delayed
dom	Hel	AH-64D *Apache*	55	2001	2006	Five delivered in 2007. Designation AH-64DJP
US	Tkr/Tpt	B-767A	3	2002	2007	Deployment of first tkr in 2007
UK	Hel	EH-101 *Merlin*	14	2003	2006	First helicopter delivered March 2006. Further deliveries continuing
dom	DDGH	Improved *Kongou*	4	2002	2007	Missile upgrade. To be upgraded to *Aegis* BMD Block IV *Standard* and equipped with *Standard* SM-3 Block 1A ABM. First vessel due in 2007. Remaining ships are to follow at one-year intervals
Dom	DDGH	Future Destroyer-class	2	2004	2009	First of class expected commission in 2009
US	AD	PAC-3 *Patriot*	16	2005	2006	Two deployed near Tokyo in 2007
US	SAM	*Raytheon* SM-3	9	2006	–	USD458m
US	AWACS	E-767	4	2006	–	Radar upgrade. USD108m. Radar System Improvement Programme (RSIP)
Ca / dom	MP	*Dash* 8 Q300	3	2006	–	To be delivered to the Coast Guard
US	VLS	Mk 48	3	2007	–	USD7.6m kits to allow VLS mounted on *Murasame*-class DD to use RIM-162C ESSM
US	Recce	F-15	–	2007	–	Radar upgrade. Fleet to be equipped with advanced synthetic aperture radar (SAR) pods

Table 33 **Selected Arms Orders and Deliveries, East Asia and Australasia**

Country Supplier	Classification	Designation	Quantity	Order date	Original Delivery date	Comment
Korea, Republic of (ROK) dom	DDG	KDX-3	3	2002	2008	First of class expected in-service date 2008. Final vessel due 2012
dom	SAM	Type-91 Kin-SAM	–	1998	2003	Development continuing
US	AAV	AAV-7A1	57	1998	2006	Licence. Following delivery of 103 from US
dom	SAM	MSAM	–	1998	2008	Programme continuing
Ge	SSK	KSS-2 (Type 214)	3	2000	2007	Final vessel due 2009. 2nd vessel launched in June 2007
dom	SAM	SM2	–	2000	2008	–
RF	Trg	IL-103	23	2002	2004	15 ac in service. Deliveries in progress
US	FGA	F-15K *Eagle*	40	2002	2005	First phase of F-X fighter programme. Deliveries continuing
US	FGA	F-15K	20	2006	2009	USD2bn. Second phase of the 2002 contract. Subject to presidential approval
dom	Trg	T-50 *Golden Eagle*	25	2003	2005	Deliveries in progress. Additional purchases of 75 approved. First 2 ac delivered Jan 2006
dom	FFGH	*Ulsan* I (aka FFX Programme)	6	2006	2015	KRW1.7bn (USD1.8bn). To replace the *Ulsan*-class FFG
dom / Int'l	FFGH	*Ulsan* I (aka FFX Programme)	6	2006	–	Combat systems upgrade. KRW156.4bn (USD160m). Due for completion 2011
Ge	SAM	*Patriot*	48	2006	–	
US	ASM	AGM-84L *Harpoon* Block II	20 + 42	2006	–	USD37.5m for the last 20
dom	ASCM	*Haeseong (Sea Star)*	30	–	2007	–
US	AEW&C	Boeing 737	4	2006	2009	USD1.7bn. 2 ac in 2011
dom	Trg	T-50 / TA-50	50	2006	–	Approx USD1bn
dom	SSK	KSS-III	3	2006	2015	Construction expected to start in 2010 or 2011. Further 3 or 6 SSK to follow in a second phase. To replace *Chang Bogo*-class (Type 209) KSS-I SSK
dom	ASCM	*Haeseong (Sea Star)*	100	2006	2010	KRW270m (USD294m)
dom / Int'l	FFGH	*Ulsan* I (aka FFX Programme)	6	2007	–	Sonar upgrade. Hull-mounted sonar (HMS). Completion scheduled for 2009
US	FGA	F-15K *Eagle*	20	2007	2012	USD2.4bn. Second phase of F-X fighter programme. Option for further 20 ac
US	Msl	AIM-9X *Sidewinder* / SM-2 Block IIIB / SM-2 Block IIIA	312	2007	–	Up to USD427m. 102 *Sidewinder*, 150 SM-2 IIIB, 60 SM-2 IIIA
US	AAM/SAM	AIM-9M	11	2007	–	Upgrade. Part of a USD300m including the upgrade of 200 AIM-9X for Pak and 57 for Mal
Malaysia (Mal) Ge	FFG	MEKO A100	6	1997	2004	First two of class commissioned. Remaining four expected ISD 2010
It	SAM	*Rapier*	–	2002	2006	–
Sp	SSK	*Scorpene*	2	2002	2007	EUR23.7m (USD29.3m). First delivered March 2007, named *Tunku Abdul Rahman*. Both expected commission in 2009
RF	Hel	Mi-8 Hip	10	2003	2005	Deliveries continuing
PI	MBT	PT-91M *Twardy*	48	2003	2005	MUR1.4bn (USD368m). Deliveries continuing

Table 33 **Selected Arms Orders and Deliveries, East Asia and Australasia**

	Country Supplier	Classification	Designation	Quantity	Order date	Original Delivery date	Comment
	RF	FGA	Su-30MKM *Flanker*	18	2003	2005	USD900m. 6 ac delivered in May 2007. Final delivery by 2008
	Int	Tpt	A-400M	4	2006	2013	MYR907m (USD246m). Final delivery by 2014
	Ge	Radar	TRM-L3D	2	2006	2008	EUR20m (USD23.6m). Surveillance and target acquisition radar system
	dom / Fr	MP	Beech *King Air* 200 TB	2	2006	2007	Upgrade contract, including installation of the Thales Airborne Maritime Situation Control System
	dom / Fr	MHC	*Mahamiru (Lerici)*	2	2006	–	Upgrade. MYR94m (USD24.9m) modernising contract including the replacement of the existing TSM 2022 Mk I sonar with the TSM 2022 Mk III sonar
	US	ASM	Tactical *Harpoon* Block II AURS	2	2006	2007	–
	US	AAM	AIM-9M	57	2007	–	Upgrade. Part of a USD300m including the upgrade of 200 AIM-9X for Pak and 57 for ROK
	dom / US	FFGH	*Lekiu*	2	2007	–	Follow-up contract following a first order issued in the 1990s
	PI	MBT	PT-91M	–	2007	–	Serial production
	dom	UAV	ALUDRA	–	2007	–	MYR5m (USD1.4m). To meet Army and Navy requirements
	Br	MRL	*Astros* II	18	2007	–	–
	Cz	Radar	VERA-E	–	2007	–	–
	Tu	Mor	120 mm	–	2007	–	–
Myanmar (My)	Ind	MP	BN-2 *Defender*	2	2007	2007	Transfer from Ind. To be used on relief and humanitarian missions only. Not yet delivered
	PRC	FF	–	1	–	2007	
New Zealand (NZ)	US	Tpt	C-130H *Hercules*	5	2004	2010	Upgrade. Life-extension programme. All aircraft due for completion by 2010
	US	MP	P-3K *Orion*	6	2005	2010	Upgrade.
	Fr	Hel	NH-90	8	2006	2010	NZD771m (USD477m). Final delivery by 2013
	Il	FF	ANZAC	2	2006	2007	Upgrade. USD3.5m for the fitting of Mini-*Typhoon* remote-controlled weapon stations aboard of HMNZS *Te Mana* (2007) and *Te Kaha* (2008)
	US	Tpt	C-130H *Hercules*	5	2007	2007	Upgrade programme in addition to 2004 life-extension contract. NZS21.2m (USD15.6m) for Electronic Warfare Self-protection systems (EWSPS). All ac due for completion by 2011
Philippines (Pi)	dom	LST	LST	1	–	–	–
	dom	LCU	LCU	4	–	–	–
Singapore (Sgp)	US	AAM	AIM-120 AMRAAM	100	2000	–	Only to be delivered if under military threat
	US	FGA	F-16 *Fighting Falcon*	20	2000	2003	Deliveries continuing

Table 33 Selected Arms Orders and Deliveries, East Asia and Australasia

Country Supplier	Classification	Designation	Quantity	Order date	Original Delivery date	Comment
Fr	FFG	Formidable	6	2000	2005	Modified Lafayette-class. First vessel arrived in Singapore, mid-2005. Expected ISD 2007. All ships expected ISD by 2009. RSS Formidable commissioned in May 2007. Remaining FFG to be named RSS Intrepid, Steadfast, Tenacious, Stalwart and Supreme.
Swe	SSK	Vastergötland	2	2005	2010	Likely to replace two of the Challenger class that entered service in 2000
US	Hel	S-70 B Seahawk	6	2005	2008	Final delivery expected 2010. To operate with Formidable-class FFGs
US	Ftr	F-15SG Eagle	12	2005	2008	–
US	Radar	APG-63 (v)3 AESA system	–	2006	–	–
US	Trg	Pilatus PC-21	19	2006	2008	The contract covers the supply of Pilatus ac, engineering and logistic support, maintenance, and simulators for the RSAF's 130 Sqn for 20 years
Ge	MBT	Leopard 2A4	96	2006	2007	66 refurbished and 30 spare MBT, Final delivery by mid-2008
dom / UK		Submarine support and rescue ship (SSRV)	1	2007	2009	SGD400m (USD261.8m). To replace Mv Kendrick and MV Avatar
US	AEW	Gulfstream 500 (G550)	4	2007	2008	Final delivery in 2010. To replace E-2C Hawkey AEW ac. Option for further 2 ac now a firm contract. 5th and 6th ac where delivered to II
US	Tpt	C-130 Hercules	10	2007	–	Avionics upgrade. To be completed in 7 years
US	Ftr	F-15SG Eagle	12	2007	2010	8 ac were included as an option in the original 2005 contract. As part of the contract 28 GbU-10 and 56 GBU-12, several thousands cartridges and practice bombs will be delivered
Taiwan (Republic of China) (ROC)	dom	PFM	Jinn Chiang	24	1992	2010	12 delivered by 2005. All expected to be delivered by 2010
	Dom	ASM	Hsiung Feng 2E	–	2005	–	Programme continuing
	US	ATGW	Javelin	360	2002	–	USD51m
	US	AAV	AAV-7A1 RAMS/RS	54	2003	2006	USD156m
	US	Ftr	F-16 A/B	146	2006	2008	USD9.3m upgrade contract including the upgrade of AN/ALR-56M radar warning receiver, and of 185 central processing units
	US	ASM	AGM-84L Harpoon Block II	60	2007	–	USD125m
Thailand (Th)	PRC	APC	WMZ 551	97	2005	–	USD51.3m. Delivery date yet to be released
	Uk	Hel	Super Lynx	2	–	2005	–
	NI	HSV	Hydrographic Survey Vessel	1	2005	2008	Under Construction
	RSA	APC	Reva 4×4	100	2007	–	–

Table 33 **Selected Arms Orders and Deliveries, East Asia and Australasia**

Country Supplier	Classification	Designation	Quantity	Order date	Original Delivery date	Comment
Ukr	APC	BTR-3E1 8x8	96	2007	–	THB4bn (USD134m). Amphibious APC. To be completed in 2–3 years.
US	Radar	TSP-77 long-range air surv	1	2007	2009	As part of a multi-phase national air defence system
PRC	ASSM	C-802	50	2007	–	THB1,600m
dom / US	Tpt	C-130H	12	2007	–	Avionics upgrade. THB1bn
Swe	FGA	JAS 39 *Gripen*	12	2007	2008	THB3404bn (USD1.1bn). To replace F-5B/E *Tiger* II ac. First to enter service in 2010. Final delivery in 2017
Swe	AEW	*Erieye*	2	2007	2008	Pat of a USD1.1bn including the purchase of 12 JAS 39 *Gripen* ac. Final delivery by 2017
Fr	FF	Type 25T *Naresuan*	2	2007	–	Landing system upgrade. EUR5m (USD7m)
US	Hel	MH-60S	2	2007	2009	USD58m. For *Naresuan*-class FF
Vietnam (Vn) PL	MPA/tpt	PZL M-28B Bryza-1R	10	2005	2005	Part of Polish support contract. 1 ac in service. Up to 12 ac may ultimately be acquired. Owned by the Coast Guard but appeared by the Army Air Force
PL	MBT	T-72	150	2005	2005	Part of USD150m Polish support contract to supply ac electronics and equipment
RF	PCI	*Svetlyak*	4	2006	–	2 vessels delivered 2002. Further 2 vessels expected 2007. Option for further 8 PCI
dom	FS	FS	3	–	2006	Project ongoing
RF	FFG	*Gepard*	2	2005	–	Components may be supplied for the construction of 2 further ships in Ho Chi Minh City

Chapter Nine
Country comparisons – commitments, force levels and economics

Table 34 UN Deployments 2007–2008

Region/Country	Deployment Location	Operational Organisation	No. of Troops	No. of mil observers	Total Number
North America					
Canada	RH	MINUSTAH	4		4
	DROC	MONUC		10	10
	Irq	UNAMI		1	1
	Syrian Golan Heights	UNDOF	2		2
	Cy	UNFICYP	1		1
	Sdn	UNMIS	8	22	30
	Il, Syr, RL	UNTSO		8	8
United States	RH	MINUSTAH	3		3
	Eth and Er	UNMEE		5	5
	Lb	UNMIL	5	7	12
	Ga	UNOMIG		2	2
	Il, Syr, RL	UNTSO		3	3
NATO Europe					
Belgium	DROC	MONUC		8	8
	RL	UNIFIL	323		323
	Sdn	UNMIS		5	5
	Il, Syr, RL	UNTSO		2	2
Bulgaria	Eth and Er	UNMEE		4	4
	Kosovo	UNMIK		1	1
	Lb	UNMIL		2	2
Czech Republic	DROC	MONUC		3	3
	Eth and Er	UNMEE		2	2
	Kosovo	UNMIK		2	2
	Lb	UNMIL		3	3
	Ga	UNOMIG		5	5
Denmark	DROC	MONUC		2	2
	Afg	UNAMA		1	1
	Irq	UNAMI		3	3
	Eth and Er	UNMEE		3	3
	Kosovo	UNMIK		1	1
	Lb	UNMIL		2	2
	N	UNMIN		2	2
	Sdn	UNMIS	6	10	16
	Ind and Pak	UNMOGIP		5	5
	Ga	UNOMIG		5	5
	Il, Syr, RL	UNTSO		11	11
Estonia	Il, Syr, RL	UNTSO		2	2
France	CAR	MINURCAT		1	1
	Western Sahara	MINURSO		13	13
	RH	MINUSTAH	2		2
	DROC	MONUC		6	6
	RL	UNIFIL	1587		1587
	Eth and Er	UNMEE		1	1
	Lb	UNMIL	1		1
	Sdn	UNMIS	1		1

Table 34 UN Deployments 2007–2008

Region/Country	Deployment Location	Operational Organisation	No. of Troops	No. of mil observers	Total Number
	CI	UNOCI	183	2	185
	Ga	UNOMIG		3	3
	Il, Syr, RL	UNTSO		2	2
Germany	Afg	UNAMA		1	1
	RL	UNIFIL	905		905
	Eth and Er	UNMEE		2	2
	Sdn	UNMIS	5	31	36
	Ga	UNOMIG		12	12
Greece	Western Sahara	MINURSO		1	1
	RL	UNIFIL	228		228
	Eth and Er	UNMEE		2	2
	Sdn	UNMIS	2	4	6
	Ga	UNOMIG		4	4
Hungary	Western Sahara	MINURSO		6	6
	Cy	UNFICYP	84		84
	RL	UNIFIL	4		4
	Kosovo	UNMIK		1	1
	Ga	UNOMIG		7	7
Italy	Western Sahara	MINURSO		5	5
	RL	UNIFIL	2379		2379
	Sdn	UNMIS	1		1
	Ind and Pak	UNMOGIP		7	7
	Il, Syr, RL	UNTSO		6	6
Lithuania	Afg	UNAMA		1	1
	Ga	UNOMIG		2	2
Luxembourg	RL	UNIFIL	2		2
Netherlands	Bu	BINUB		1	1
	RL	UNIFIL	149		149
	Sdn	UNMIS	5	7	12
	Il, Syr, RL	UNTSO		11	11
Norway	Afg	UNAMA		1	1
	Eth and Er	UNMEE		3	3
	Kosovo	UNMIK		1	1
	N	UNMIN		3	3
	Sdn	UNMIS	9	16	25
	Il, Syr, RL	UNTSO		12	12
Poland	Western Sahara	MINURSO		1	1
	DROC	MONUC		2	2
	Syrian Golan Heights	UNDOF	353		353
	RL	UNIFIL	482		482
	Eth and Er	UNMEE		3	3
	Kosovo	UNMIK		1	1
	Lb	UNMIL		2	2
	Sdn	UNMIS		2	2

Table 34 UN Deployments 2007–2008

Region/Country	Deployment Location	Operational Organisation	No. of Troops	No. of mil observers	Total Number
	CI	UNOCI		2	2
	Ga	UNOMIG		5	5
Portugal	RL	UNIFIL	146		146
	Kosovo	UNMIK		2	2
	Timor-Leste	UNMIT		4	4
Romania	DROC	MONUC		22	22
	Afg	UNAMA		1	1
	Eth and Er	UNMEE		4	4
	Kosovo	UNMIK		3	3
	Lb	UNMIL		3	3
	N	UNMIN		5	5
	Sdn	UNMIS		12	12
	CI	UNOCI		7	7
	Ga	UNOMIG		2	2
Slovakia	Syrian Golan Heights	UNDOF	95		95
	Cy	UNFICYP	196		196
	Il, Syr, RL	UNTSO		2	2
Slovenia	Il, Syr, RL	UNTSO		2	2
Spain	DROC	MONUC		2	2
	RL	UNIFIL	1100		1100
	Eth and Er	UNMEE		3	3
	Kosovo	UNMIK		2	2
Turkey	RL	UNIFIL	746		746
	Sdn	UNMIS	4		4
	Ga	UNOMIG		5	5
United Kingdom	DROC	MONUC		6	6
	Afg	UNAMA		1	1
	Irq	UNAMI		1	1
	Cy	UNFICYP	276		276
	SL	UNIOSIL		1	1
	Kosovo	UNMIK		1	1
	Lb	UNMIL	3		3
	N	UNMIN		4	4
	Sdn	UNMIS	4		4
	Ga	UNOMIG		5	5

Non-Nato Europe

Region/Country	Deployment Location	Operational Organisation	No. of Troops	No. of mil observers	Total Number
Albania	Ga	UNOMIG		3	3
Austria	Western Sahara	MINURSO		2	2
	Syrian Golan Heights	UNDOF	372		372
	Cy	UNFICYP	5		5
	Eth and Er	UNMEE		2	2
	N	UNMIN		2	2
	Ga	UNOMIG		2	2
	Il, Syr, RL	UNTSO		6	6

Table 34 UN Deployments 2007–2008

Region/Country	Deployment Location	Operational Organisation	No. of Troops	No. of mil observers	Total Number
Bosnia-Herzegovina	DROC	MONUC		5	5
	Eth and Er	UNMEE		5	5
Croatia	Bu	BINUB		1	1
	Western Sahara	MINURSO		7	7
	RH	MINUSTAH	3		3
	Cy	UNFICYP	4		4
	RL	UNIFIL	1		1
	SL	UNIOSIL		1	1
	Eth and Er	UNMEE		4	4
	Lb	UNMIL	5		5
	N	UNMIN		2	2
	Sdn	UNMIS	5		5
	Ind and Pak	UNMOGIP		8	8
	CI	UNOCI		2	2
	Ga	UNOMIG		3	3
Cyprus	RL	UNIFIL	2		2
Finland	Eth and Er	UNMEE		5	5
	Kosovo	UNMIK		2	2
	Lb	UNMIL	1		1
	N	UNMIN		1	1
	Sdn	UNMIS	1		1
	Ind and Pak	UNMOGIP		6	6
	Il, Syr, RL	UNTSO		15	15
Ireland	Western Sahara	MINURSO		3	3
	DROC	MONUC		3	3
	RL	UNIFIL	166		166
	Kosovo	UNMIK		4	4
	Lb	UNMIL	2		2
	CI	UNOCI		2	2
	Il, Syr, RL	UNTSO		14	14
Macedonia, Former Yugoslav Republic	RL	UNIFIL	1		1
Moldova	Lb	UNMIL		3	3
	Sdn	UNMIS		2	2
	CI	UNOCI		4	4
	Ga	UNOMIG		1	1
Montenegro	Lb	UNMIL		2	2
Serbia	DROC	MONUC	6		6
	Lb	UNMIL		6	6
	CI	UNOCI		3	3
Sweden	CAR	MINURCAT		1	1
	DROC	MONUC		5	5
	Afg	UNAMA		1	1
	SL	UNIOSIL		1	1
	Eth and Er	UNMEE		3	3
	N	UNMIN		3	3

Table 34 UN Deployments 2007–2008

Region/Country	Deployment Location	Operational Organisation	No. of Troops	No. of mil observers	Total Number
	Sdn	UNMIS	4	3	7
	Ind and Pak	UNMOGIP		6	6
	Ga	UNOMIG		3	3
	Il, Syr, RL	UNTSO		7	7
Switzerland	Bu	BINUB		1	1
	DROC	MONUC		2	2
	N	UNMIN		5	5
	Ga	UNOMIG		4	4
	Il, Syr, RL	UNTSO		9	9
Ukraine	DROC	MONUC		6	6
	Eth and Er	UNMEE		3	3
	Kosovo	UNMIK		3	3
	Lb	UNMIL	301	2	303
	Sdn	UNMIS		6	6
	Ga	UNOMIG		5	5
Russia					
Russia	Western Sahara	MINURSO		25	25
	DROC	MONUC		28	28
	Eth and Er	UNMEE		3	3
	Kosovo	UNMIK		1	1
	Lb	UNMIL		4	4
	N	UNMIN		8	8
	Sdn	UNMIS	122	14	136
	CI	UNOCI		9	9
	Ga	UNOMIG		4	4
	Il, Syr, RL	UNTSO		3	3
Middle East and North Africa					
Algeria	Eth and Er	UNMEE		8	8
Egypt	Western Sahara	MINURSO		20	20
	Sierra Leone	UNIOSIL		1	
	DROC	MONUC		22	22
	Lb	UNMIL		8	8
	N	UNMIN		7	7
	Sdn	UNMIS	817	14	831
	Ga	UNOMIG		6	6
Iran	Eth and Er	UNMEE		3	3
Jordan	RH	MINUSTAH	755		755
	DROC	MONUC	66	25	91
	Eth and Er	UNMEE	570	8	578
	Kosovo	UNMIK		2	2
	Lb	UNMIL	123	7	130
	N	UNMIN		10	10
	Sdn	UNMIS	10	7	17
	CI	UNOCI	1062	7	1069
	Ga	UNOMIG		7	7
Morocco	DROC	MONUC	809	4	813

Table 34 UN Deployments 2007–2008

Region/Country	Deployment Location	Operational Organisation	No. of Troops	No. of mil observers	Total Number
	CI	UNOCI	724		724
Qatar	RL	UNIFIL	203		203
Tunisia	Bu	BINUB		1	1
	DROC	MONUC	462	30	492
	Eth and Er	UNMEE	3	5	8
	CI	UNOCI	2	5	7
Yemen	Western Sahara	MINURSO		6	6
	DROC	MONUC		5	5
	N	UNMIN		15	15
	Sdn	UNMIS	4	16	20
	CI	UNOCI		6	6
	Ga	UNOMIG		1	1
Central and South Asia					
Bangladesh	Bu	BINUB		1	1
	Western Sahara	MINURSO		8	8
	DROC	MONUC	1333	25	1358
	Afg	UNAMA		2	2
	SL	UNIOSIL		1	1
	Eth and Er	UNMEE	5	8	13
	Kosovo	UNMIK		1	1
	Lb	UNMIL	3200	19	3219
	Sdn	UNMIS	1548	21	1569
	Timor-Leste	UNMIT		4	4
	CI	UNOCI	2728	10	2738
	Ga	UNOMIG		8	8
India	DROC	MONUC	4380	53	4433
	Syrian Golan Heights	UNDOF	191		191
	RL	UNIFIL	884		884
	Eth and Er	UNMEE	715	8	723
	Sdn	UNMIS	2606	20	2626
	CI	UNOCI		8	8
Kazakhstan	N	UNMIN		1	1
Kyrgyzstan	Eth and Er	UNMEE		4	4
	Lb	UNMIL		4	4
	Sdn	UNMIS		8	8
Nepal	RH	MINUSTAH	1109		1109
	DROC	MONUC	1030	20	1050
	RL	UNIFIL	859		859
	SL	UNIOSIL		1	1
	Eth and Er	UNMEE		3	3
	Kosovo	UNMIK		1	1
	Lb	UNMIL	44	3	47
	Sdn	UNMIS	8	8	16
	CI	UNOCI		3	3
	Ga	UNOMIG		1	1

Table 34 UN Deployments 2007–2008

Region/Country	Deployment Location	Operational Organisation	No. of Troops	No. of mil observers	Total Number
	Il, Syr, RL	UNTSO		3	3
Pakistan	Bu	BINUB		1	1
	Western Sahara	MINURSO		8	8
	RH	MINUSTAH	1		1
	DROC	MONUC	3579	55	3634
	SL	UNIOSIL		1	1
	Eth and Er	UNMEE		6	6
	Kosovo	UNMIK		2	2
	Lb	UNMIL	3403	15	3418
	Sdn	UNMIS	1567	20	1587
	Timor-Leste	UNMIT		4	4
	CI	UNOCI	1124	12	1136
	Ga	UNOMIG		10	10
Sri Lanka	Western Sahara	MINURSO		2	2
	RH	MINUSTAH	960		960
	DROC	MONUC		4	4
	Eth and Er	UNMEE		4	4
	Sdn	UNMIS		3	3
East Asia and Australasia					
Australia	Afg	UNAMA		1	1
	Irq	UNAMI		1	1
	Sdn	UNMIS	17	6	23
	Timor-Leste	UNMIT		4	4
	Il, Syr, RL	UNTSO		12	12
Cambodia	Sdn	UNMIS	136	10	146
China	Western Sahara	MINURSO	1	13	14
	DROC	MONUC	218	16	234
	RL	UNIFIL	343		343
	SL	UNIOSIL		1	1
	Eth and Er	UNMEE		6	6
	Lb	UNMIL	565	5	570
	Sdn	UNMIS	446	14	460
	Timor-Leste	UNMIT		3	3
	CI	UNOCI		7	7
	Il, Syr, RL	UNTSO		4	4
Fiji	Irq	UNAMI	223		223
	Sdn	UNMIS		7	7
	Timor-Leste	UNMIT		1	1
Indonesia	DROC	MONUC	175	15	190
	RL	UNIFIL	856		856
	Lb	UNMIL		3	3
	N	UNMIN		6	6
	Sdn	UNMIS		10	10
	Ga	UNOMIG		4	4

Table 34 UN Deployments 2007–2008

Region/Country	Deployment Location	Operational Organisation	No. of Troops	No. of mil observers	Total Number
Japan	Syrian Golan Heights	UNDOF	30		30
	N	UNMIN		6	6
Korea, Republic of	Afg	UNAMA		1	1
	RL	UNIFIL	363		363
	Lb	UNMIL	1	1	2
	N	UNMIN		5	5
	Sdn	UNMIS	1	7	8
	Ind and Pak	UNMOGIP		9	9
	Ga	UNOMIG		7	7
Malaysia	Western Sahara	MINURSO	20	12	32
	DROC	MONUC		17	17
	RL	UNIFIL	362		362
	Eth and Er	UNMEE	3	7	10
	Kosovo	UNMIK		1	1
	Lb	UNMIL	10		10
	N	UNMIN		7	7
	Sdn	UNMIS	4	8	12
	Timor-Leste	UNMIT		2	2
Mongolia	Western Sahara	MINURSO		3	3
	DROC	MONUC		2	2
	Eth and Er	UNMEE		4	4
	Lb	UNMIL	250		250
	Sdn	UNMIS		2	2
	Ga	UNOMIG		1	1
New Zealand	Afg	UNAMA		1	1
	Irq	UNAMI		1	1
	Kosovo	UNMIK		1	1
	Sdn	UNMIS	1	2	3
	Timor-Leste	UNMIT		1	1
	Il, Syr, RL	UNTSO		8	8
Philippines	RH	MINUSTAH	157		157
	Lb	UNMIL	169	3	172
	Sdn	UNMIS		12	12
	Timor-Leste	UNMIT		3	3
	CI	UNOCI	3	4	7
Singapore	N	UNMIN		2	2
	Timor-Leste	UNMIT		2	2
Thailand	N	UNMIN		7	7
	Sdn	UNMIS	2	12	14
Caribbean and Latin America					
Argentina	Western Sahara	MINURSO		1	1
	RH	MINUSTAH	562		562

Table 34 UN Deployments 2007–2008

Region/Country	Deployment Location	Operational Organisation	No. of Troops	No. of mil observers	Total Number
	Cy	UNFICYP	294		294
	Kosovo	UNMK		1	1
	Il, Syr, RL	UNTSO		5	5
Bolivia	RH	MINUSTAH	217		217
	DROC	MONUC	200	10	210
	Afg	UNAMA		1	1
	Eth and Er	UNMEE		5	5
	Kosovo	UNMIK		1	1
	Lb	UNMIL	1	3	4
	Sdn	UNMIS	1	16	17
	CI	UNOCI		3	3
	Ga	UNOMIG		1	1
Brazil	RH	MINUSTAH	1212		1212
	Eth and Er	UNMEE		7	7
	Lb	UNMIL	3		3
	N	UNMIN		7	7
	Sdn	UNMIS	24		24
	Timor-Leste	UNMIT		3	3
	CI	UNOCI	3	4	7
Chile	RH	MINUSTAH	503		503
	Kosovo	UNMIK		1	1
	Ind and Pak	UNMOGIP		2	2
	Il, Syr, RL	UNTSO		3	3
Dominican Republic	CI	UNOCI		4	4
Ecuador	RH	MINUSTAH	67		67
	Lb	UNMIL	1	3	4
	N	UNMIN		1	1
	Sdn	UNMIS		20	20
	CI	UNOCI		2	2
El Salvador	Western Sahara	MINURSO		6	6
	Lb	UNMIL		3	3
	Sdn	UNMIS		5	5
	CI	UNOCI		3	3
Guatemala	RH	MINUSTAH	119		119
	DROC	MONUC	105	6	111
	RL	UNIFIL	2		2
	Eth and Er	UNMEE		4	4
	N	UNMIN		2	2
	Sdn	UNMIS	1	8	9
	CI	UNOCI		5	5
Honduras	Western Sahara	MINURSO		12	12
Paraguay	RH	MINUSTAH	31		31
	DROC	MONUC		17	17
	Afg	UNAMA		1	1
	Eth and Er	UNMEE		4	4

Table 34 UN Deployments 2007–2008

Region/Country	Deployment Location	Operational Organisation	No. of Troops	No. of mil observers	Total Number
	Lb	UNMIL	1	3	4
	N	UNMIN		5	5
	Sdn	UNMIS		10	10
	CI	UNOCI	2	8	10
Peru	RH	MINUSTAH	210		210
	DROC	MONUC		7	7
	Eth and Er	UNMEE		4	4
	Lb	UNMIL	2	3	5
	Sdn	UNMIS		17	17
	CI	UNOCI		3	3
Uruguay	Western Sahara	MINURSO		8	8
	RH	MINUSTAH	1146		1146
	DROC	MONUC	1324	45	1369
	Afg	UNAMA		1	1
	Eth and Er	UNMEE	37	4	41
	N	UNMIN		3	3
	Ind and Pak	UNMOGIP		2	2
	CI	UNOCI		2	2
	Ga	UNOMIG		4	4
Sub- Saharan Africa					
Benin	DROC	MONUC	750	12	762
	Lb	UNMIL	1	3	4
	Sdn	UNMIS		7	7
	CI	UNOCI	423	6	429
Botswana	Sdn	UNMIS		5	5
Burkino Faso	DROC	MONUC		10	10
	Sdn	UNIMIS		6	6
Cameroon	DROC	MONUC		5	5
Chad	CI	UNOCI		3	3
Djibouti	Western Sahara	MINURSO		2	2
Ethiopia	Lb	UNMIL	1804	19	1823
	CI	UNOCI		2	2
Gabon	Sdn	UNMIS		8	8
The Gambia	Eth and Er	UNMEE	1	2	3
	Lb	UNMIL		2	2
	N	UNMIN		4	4
	Sdn	UNMIS	1		1
	CI	UNOCI		3	3
Ghana	Western Sahara	MINURSO	8	8	16
	DROC	MONUC	461	24	485
	RL	UNIFIL	868		868
	SL	UNIOSIL		2	2
	Eth and Er	UNMEE	3	10	13
	RL	UNMIL	859	12	871
	N	UNMIN		5	5

Table 34 UN Deployments 2007–2008

Region/Country	Deployment Location	Operational Organisation	No. of Troops	No. of mil observers	Total Number
	Sdn	UNMIS	3		3
	CI	UNOCI	542	6	548
Guinea	Western Sahara	MINURSO		4	4
	Sdn	UNMIS		4	4
	CI	UNOCI		3	3
Kenya	Western Sahara	MINURSO		6	6
	DROC	MONUC		36	36
	SL	UNIOSIL		1	1
	Eth and Er	UNMEE	118	10	128
	Kosovo	UNMIK		2	2
	Lb	UNMIL	4	3	7
	Sdn	UNMIS	831	7	838
	CI	UNOCI	4	4	8
Malawi	DROC	MONUC	111	25	136
	Kosovo	UNMIK		1	1
	Sdn	UNMIS	2	6	8
Mali	DROC	MONUC		22	22
	Lb	UNMIL	1	4	5
	Sdn	UNMIS		10	10
Mozambique	Sdn	UNMIS		3	3
Namibia	Eth and Er	UNMEE	3	4	7
	Lb	UNMIL	4	2	6
	Sdn	UNMIS		9	9
	CI	UNOCI		2	2
Niger	Bu	BINUB		1	1
	DROC	MONUC		19	19
	Lb	UNMIL		3	3
	Sdn	UNMIS	1		1
	CI	UNOCI	384	6	390
Nigeria	Western Sahara	MINURSO		6	6
	DROC	MONUC		26	26
	SL	UNIOSIL		2	2
	Eth and Er	UNMEE	1	8	9
	Lb	UNMIL	1963	17	1980
	N	UNMIN		8	8

Table 34 UN Deployments 2007–2008

Region/Country	Deployment Location	Operational Organisation	No. of Troops	No. of mil observers	Total Number
	Sdn	UNMIS	10	12	22
	CI	UNOCI		6	6
	Ga	UNOMIG		1	1
Rwanda	Sdn	UNMIS	262	15	277
Senegal	CAR	MINURCAT		1	1
	DROC	MONUC	460	26	486
	Lb	UNMIL	604	3	607
	Sdn	UNMIS	5		5
	CI	UNOCI	328	9	337
Sierra Leone	N	UNMIN		2	2
	Timor-Leste	UNMIT		1	1
South Africa	Bu	BINUB		1	1
	DROC	MONUC	1186	15	1201
	Eth and Er	UNMEE		5	5
	N	UNMIN		5	5
	Sdn	UNMIS	4		4
Tanzania	RL	UNIFIL	77		77
	Eth and Er	UNMEE	2	8	10
	Sdn	UNMIS	6	15	21
	CI	UNOCI	1	1	2
Togo	Lb	UNMIL	1	4	5
	CI	UNOCI	318	5	323
Uganda	Sdn	UNMIS		11	11
	CI	UNOCI	2	2	4
Zambia	DROC	MONUC		24	24
	SL	UNIOSIL		1	1
	Eth and Er	UNMEE	3	10	13
	Kosovo	UNMIK		1	1
	Lb	UNMIL		3	3
	N	UNMIN		8	8
	Sdn	UNMIS	353	14	367
	CI	UNOCI		2	2
Zimbabwe	Lb	UNMIL		2	2
	N	UNMIN		2	2
	Sdn	UNMIS	3	10	13
	CI	UNOCI		2	2

Table 35 **Non-UN Deployments 2007–2008**

Region/ Country	Deployment Location	International Organisation	Operational Organisation	Operational Name	Task	Total Number
North America						
Canada	Afg	NATO	ISAF	ATHENA	Assisting the Afghan government in providing security	2,500
	Afg	US Coalition	OEF - HOA	ALTAIR	Global military response to 'War on Terror'	237
	Afg		OEF- AFG	ARCHER	Canadian support to the National Training Centre, Combined Joint Task Force 76 (CJTF-76) and Combined Security Transition Command - Afghanistan (CSTC-A)	30
	Afg	bilateral		ARGUS	Canadian Strategic Advisory Team supporting the Afghan Government	15
	BiH	NATO		BRONZE	NATO HQ Sarajevo	8
	Et		MFO	CALUMET	Supervise the implementation of the security provisions of the Egyptian–Israeli Peace Treaty	28
	Jerusalem	USSC		PROTEUS	Assisting the Office of the US Security Coordinator	3
	SL	IMATT		SCULPTURE	Providing Sierra Leonean soldiers with military training and advice	11
	Sdn	AU		AUGURAL	Supporting of the AU Mission in Darfur for the establishment of lasting peace in the Sudan	11
	US, Tampa, FL, and Brn	US CENTCOM		Task Force Tampa or FOUNDATION	Maintaining effective liaison with HQ US CENTCOM with regard to the campaign against terrorism.	8
United States	Afg	NATO	ISAF		Assisting the Afghan government in providing security across Afghan territory	15,108
	Afg	US Coalition		ENDURING FREEDOM	Global military response to 'War on Terror'	9,650
	BiH	EU	EUFOR	ALTHEA	Establishing and maintaining security in Bosnia and Herzegovina with accordance of Dayton/Paris Agreement	207
	Et		MFO		Supervise the implementation of the security provisions of the Egyptian–Israeli Peace Treaty	288
	Horn of Africa - Dj	CJTF-HOA			Detecting, disrupting, and defeating transnational terrorist groups operating in the region. Military training and counterterrorist training	2,038
	Irq	US Coalition	MNF-I	Iraqi Freedom	Fighting terrorism, delivering humanitarian support to the Iraqi people, securing Iraq's oil fields and resources, helping the transition to a representative self-government	168,000
	Kgz	NATO	ISAF		Assisting the Afghan government in providing security across Afghan territory	14
	FYROM	NATO	KFOR	JOINT ENTERPRISE	Establishing and maintaining security in Kosovo	27
	Ser	NATO	KFOR	JOINT ENTERPRISE	Establishing and maintaining security in Kosovo	1,640
	Sdn	AU	AMIS		Military Observers	2
NATO Europe						
Belgium	Afg	NATO	ISAF		Assisting the Afghan government in providing security across Afghan territory	368
	Cha / CAR	EU	EUFOR Tchad/ RCA		Bridging military operation in eastern Cha and north eastern CAR in support to MINURCAT	100
	DROC	EU	EUPOL KINSHASA		Police training and to monitor, mentor, and advise the IPU (Integrated Police Unit)	2
	Ser	NATO	KFOR	JOINT ENTERPRISE	Establishing and maintaining security in Kosovo	420

Table 35 Non-UN Deployments 2007–2008

Region/ Country	Deployment Location	International Organisation	Operational Organisation	Operational Name	Task	Total Number
Bulgaria	Afg	NATO	ISAF		Assisting the Afghan government in providing security	401
	BiH / Cr		EUFOR	ALTHEA	Establishing and maintaining security in Bosnia and Herzegovina with accordance of Dayton/Paris Agreement	115
	Irq	US Coalition	MNF-I	Iraqi Freedom	Fighting terrorism, delivering humanitarian support to the Iraqi people, securing Iraq's oil fields and resources, helping the transition to a representative self-government	150
	Ser and Mnt	NATO	KFOR	JOINT ENTERPRISE	Establishing and maintaining security in Kosovo	46
Czech Republic	Afg	NATO	ISAF		Assisting the Afghan government in providing security	435
	Afg	NATO	ISAF		Field Hospital and Chemical Detachment	95
	Afg	US Coalition		ENDURING FREEDOM	Special forces involved in the global military response to 'War on Terror'	35
	BiH	EU	EUFOR	ALTHEA	Establishing and maintaining security in Bosnia and Herzegovina in accordance with Dayton/Paris Agreement	5
	Irq	US Coalition	MNF-I	Iraqi Freedom		99
	Ser	NATO	KFOR	JOINT ENTERPRISE	Establishing and maintaining security in Kosovo	500
Denmark	Afg	NATO	ISAF		Assisting the Afghan government in providing security	454
	Ser and Mnt	NATO	KFOR	JOINT ENTERPRISE	Establishing and maintaining security in Kosovo	363
Estonia	Afg	NATO	ISAF		Military assistance and training	128
	BiH	EU	EUFOR	ALTHEA	Establishing and maintaining security in Bosnia and Herzegovina in accordance with Dayton/Paris Agreement	3
	Irq	NATO	NTM-I		NATO Training Mission in Iraq; Baghdad	2
	Irq	US Coalition	MNF-I	Iraqi Freedom	Fighting terrorism, delivering humanitarian support to the Iraqi people, securing Iraq's oil fields and resources, helping the transition to a representative self-government	38
	Ser	NATO	KFOR	JOINT ENTERPRISE	Establishing and maintaining security in Kosovo	28
France	Afg	NATO	ISAF	PAMIR	Assisting the Afghan government in providing security	1,155
	Afg	US Coalition		ENDURING FREEDOM or HERACLES	Global military response to 'War on Terror'	821
	Afg	US Coalition		ENDURING FREEDOM or EPIDOTE	Contributing to the formation of Afghan battalions	39
	BiH	EU	EUFOR	ASTRÉE	Establishing and maintaining security in Bosnia and Herzegovina in accordance with Dayton/Paris Agreement	73
	CAR			BOALI	Restructuring local armed forces and supporting FOMUC	300
	Cha			EPERVIER	Maintaining the territorial integrity of Chad under the 1976 bilateral agreement	1,100
	Cha / CAR	EU	EUFOR Tchad/ RCA		Bridging military operation in eastern Cha and north eastern CAR in support of MINURCAT	1,500
	DROC	EU	EUPOL KINSHASA		Police training and to monitor, mentor, and advise the IPU (Integrated Police Unit)	12
	Ser	NATO	KFOR	JOINT ENTERPRISE	Establishing and maintaining security in Kosovo	1,830

Table 35 Non-UN Deployments 2007–2008

Region/ Country	Deployment Location	International Organisation	Operational Organisation	Operational Name	Task	Total Number
Germany	Afg	EU	EUPOL AFGHANISTAN		Contributing to the establishment of sustainable and effective civilian policing arrangements under Afghan ownership and in accordance with international standards	60
	Afg	NATO	ISAF		Assisting the Afghan government in providing security. Unspecified number of troops deployed in Uzbekistan	3,155
	BiH	EU	EUFOR	ALTHEA	Establishing and maintaining security in Bosnia and Herzegovina with accordance of Dayton/Paris Agreement	235
	Horn of Africa	US Coalition		ENDURING FREEDOM	Global military response to 'War on Terror'	257
	Ser	NATO	KFOR	JOINT ENTERPRISE	Establishing and maintaining security in Kosovo	2,279
Greece	Afg	NATO	ISAF		Assisting the Afghan government in providing security	137
	BiH	EU	EUFOR	ALTHEA	Establishing and maintaining security in Bosnia and Herzegovina with accordance of Dayton/Paris Agreement	45
	Ser and Mnt	NATO	KFOR	JOINT ENTERPRISE or ELDYKO	Establishing and maintaining security in Kosovo	742
Hungary	Afg	NATO	ISAF		Assisting the Afghan government in providing security	225
	BiH	EU	EUFOR	ALTHEA	Establishing and maintaining security in Bosnia and Herzegovina with accordance of Dayton/Paris Agreement	158
	Et		MFO		Supervise the implementation of the security provisions of the Egyptian–Israeli Peace Treaty	41
	Ser	NATO	KFOR	JOINT ENTERPRISE	Establishing and maintaining security in Kosovo	484
Iceland	Afg	NATO	ISAF		Civilian assistance and training; Crisis Response Unit under Ministry of Foreign Affairs	11
Italy	Afg	EU	EUPOL AFGHANISTAN		Contributing to the establishment of sustainable and effective civilian policing arrangements under Afghan ownership and in accordance with international standards	25
	Afg	NATO	ISAF		Assisting the Afghan government in providing security	2,395
	Alb	NATO	JFC Naples	NATO HQ Tirana	Facilitate coordination between the Government of Albania, organisations of the international community and NATO	155
	Alb		DIE (Delegazione Italiana Esperti)		Italian delegation of experts, supporting transformation of Alb military	25
	BiH	EU	EUFOR	ALTHEA	Establishing and maintaining security in Bosnia and Herzegovina in accordance with Dayton/Paris Agreement	363
	DROC	EU	EUPOL KINSHASA		Police training and to monitor, mentor, and advise the IPU (Integrated Police Unit)	4
	DROC	EU	EUSEC DR Congo		EU advisory and assistance mission for security reform in the DROC	1
	Et		MFO		Supervise the implementation of the security provisions of the Egyptian–Israeli Peace Treaty	80
	Irq	NATO	NTM-I		Training Iraqi forces	79
	Mediterranean Sea	NATO SNMG2		ACTIVE ENDEAVOUR	Global military response to 'War on Terror'	105

Table 35 Non-UN Deployments 2007–2008

Region/ Country	Deployment Location	International Organisation	Operational Organisation	Operational Name	Task	Total Number
	Palestinian Autonomous Areas of Gaza and Jericho		TIPH 2		Establishing and maintaining security in Hebron and economic development	17
	Ser	NATO	KFOR	JOINT ENTERPRISE	Establishing and maintaining security in Kosovo	2,280
	SR	AU	AMISOM		Security and peacekeeping. To be deployed	2
	Sdn	EU			EU support to UN authorized African Union Mission in Sudan (AMIS)	6
Latvia	Afg	NATO	ISAF		Assisting the Afghan government in providing security	97
	BiH	EU	EUFOR	ALTHEA	Establishing and maintaining security in Bosnia and Herzegovina with accordance of Dayton/Paris Agreement	1
	Ga	OSCE	EDSO/OSCE			1
	Irq	US Coalition	MNF-I	Iraqi Freedom	Fighting terrorism, delivering humanitarian support to the Iraqi people, securing Iraq's oil fields and resources, helping the transition to a representative self-government	2
	Ser and Mnt	NATO	KFOR	JOINT ENTERPRISE	Establishing and maintaining security in Kosovo	18
Lithuania	Afg	NATO	ISAF		Assisting the Afghan government in providing security	195
	BiH	EU	EUFOR	ALTHEA	Establishing and maintaining security in Bosnia and Herzegovina in accordance with Dayton/Paris Agreement	1
	Irq	NATO	NTM-I		NATO Training Mission in Iraq	4
	Irq	US Coalition	MNF-I	Iraqi Freedom	Fighting terrorism, delivering humanitarian support to the Iraqi people, securing Iraq's oil fields and resources, helping the transition to a representative self-government	5
	Ser	NATO	KFOR	JOINT ENTERPRISE	Establishing and maintaining security in Kosovo	30
Luxembourg	Afg	NATO	ISAF		Assisting the Afghan government in providing security	9
	BiH	EU	EUFOR	ALTHEA	Establishing and maintaining security in Bosnia and Herzegovina in accordance with Dayton/Paris Agreement	1
	Ser	NATO	KFOR	JOINT ENTERPRISE	Establishing and maintaining security in Kosovo	23
Netherlands	Afg	NATO	ISAF		Assisting the Afghan government in providing security	1516
	Afg	US Coalition		ENDURING FREEDOM	Global military response to 'War on Terror'	6
	BiH	EU	EUFOR	ALTHEA	Establishing and maintaining security in BiH with accordance of Dayton/Paris Agreement	67
	Cha/CAR	EU	EUFOR Tchad/ RCA		Bridging millitary operation in eastern Chad and north eastern CAR in spt of MINURCAT	100
	DROC	EU	EUSEC and EUSEC FIN		Providing advice and assistance to the Congolese authorities in charge of security	3
	DROC	EU	EUPOL KINSHASA		Police training and to monitor, mentor, and advise the IPU (Integrated Police Unit)	2
	Gaza Strip	EU	EU BAM Rafah		Monitoring the operations of Rafah border crossing point	
	Irq	NATO	NTM-I		NATO Training Mission in Iraq; Baghdad	15
	Ser	NATO	KFOR	JOINT ENTERPRISE	Establishing and maintaining security in Kosovo	1

Table 35 Non-UN Deployments 2007–2008

Region/ Country	Deployment Location	International Organisation	Operational° Organisation	Operational Name	Task	Total Number
	Sdn	AU / UN	UNAMID		Proposed deployment. Support the implementation of the Darfur Peace Agreement, as well as to protect its personnel and civilians	N/A
Norway	Afg	NATO	ISAF		Assisting the Afghan government in providing security across Afghan territory	508
	BiH	EU	EUFOR	ALTHEA	Establishing and maintaining security in Bosnia and Herzegovina in accordance with Dayton/Paris Agreement	8
	Et		MFO		Supervise the implementation of the security provisions of the Egyptian–Israeli Peace Treaty	9
	Ser	NATO	KFOR	JOINT ENTERPRISE	Establishing and maintaining security in Kosovo	86
Poland	Afg	NATO	ISAF		Military assistance and training	937
	BiH	EU	EUFOR	ALTHEA	Establishing and maintaining security in Bosnia and Herzegovina in accordance with Dayton/Paris Agreement	203
	Cha / CAR	EU	EUFOR Tchad/ RCA		Bridging military operation in eastern Cha and north eastern CAR in support to MINURCAT	350
	Irq	US Coalition	MNF-I	Iraqi Freedom	Fighting terrorism, delivering humanitarian support to the Iraqi people, securing Iraq's oil fields and resources, helping the transition to a representative self-government	900
	Ser	NATO	KFOR	JOINT ENTERPRISE	Establishing and maintaining security in Kosovo	312
Portugal	Afg	NATO	ISAF		Assisting the Afghan government in providing security across Afghan territory	162
	BiH	EU	EUFOR	ALTHEA	Establishing and maintaining security in Bosnia and Herzegovina in accordance with Dayton/Paris Agreement	14
	Cha/CAR	EU			Bridging millitary operation in eastern Chad and north eastern CAR in spt of MINURCAT	some
	DROC	EU	EUSEC		Military assistance	2
	Irq	NATO	NTM-I		NATO Training Mission in Iraq; Baghdad	9
	Ser	NATO	KFOR	JOINT ENTERPRISE	Establishing and maintaining security in Kosovo	296
	Sdn	EU	AMIS		HQ	1
Romania	Afg	NATO	ISAF		Military assistance and training	536
	Afg	US Coalition		ENDURING FREEDOM	Global military response to 'War on Terror'	94
	BiH	EU	EUFOR	ALTHEA	Establishing and maintaining security in Bosnia and Herzegovina in accordance with Dayton/Paris Agreement	49
	Cha/CAR	EU			Bridging military operation in eastern Chad and north eastern CAR in spt of MINURCAT	120
	Irq	US Coalition	MNF-I	Iraqi Freedom	Fighting terrorism, delivering humanitarian support to the Iraqi people, securing Iraq's oil fields and resources, helping the transition to a representative self-government	489
	Irq	NATO	NTM-I		Training Iraqi security and defence forces	3
	Mediterranean Sea	NATO		ACTIVE ENDEAVOUR	Global military response to 'War on Terror'	1 FF
	Ser	NATO	KFOR	JOINT ENTERPRISE	Establishing and maintaining security in Kosovo	153
Slovakia	Afg	NATO	ISAF		Assisting the Afghan government in providing security	59

Table 35 Non-UN Deployments 2007–2008

Region/ Country	Deployment Location	International Organisation	Operational Organisation	Operational Name	Task	Total Number
	BiH	EU	EUFOR	ALTHEA	Establishing and maintaining security in Bosnia and Herzegovina in accordance with Dayton/Paris Agreement	40
	BiH	EU	EUMM		Monitor political and security developments, borders, inter-ethnic issues and refugee returns	2
	Irq	NATO	NTM-I		Training Iraqi security and defence forces	2
	Ser	NATO	KFOR	JOINT ENTERPRISE	Establishing and maintaining security in Kosovo	134
Slovenia	Afg	NATO	ISAF		Assisting the Afghan government in providing security	42
	BiH	EU	EUFOR	ALTHEA	Establishing and maintaining security in Bosnia and Herzegovina in accordance with Dayton/Paris Agreement	58
	Irq	NATO	NTM-I		NATO Training Mission in Iraq; Baghdad	4
	Ser	NATO	KFOR	JOINT ENTERPRISE	Establishing and maintaining security in Kosovo	92
Spain	Afg	NATO	ISAF		Military assistance and training	742
	BiH	EU	EUFOR	ALTHEA	Establishing and maintaining security in Bosnia and Herzegovina in accordance with Dayton/Paris Agreement	284
	Ser	NATO	KFOR	JOINT ENTERPRISE	Establishing and maintaining security in Kosovo	627
	Sdn	EU			Logistics and Training in support of AMIS II	2
Turkey	Afg	NATO	ISAF		Assisting the Afghan government in providing security	1220
	BiH	EU	EUFOR	ALTHEA	Establishing and maintaining security in Bosnia and Herzegovina in accordance with Dayton/Paris Agreement	253
	DROC	EU	EUPOL KINSHASA		Police training and to monitor, mentor, and advise the IPU (Integrated Police Unit)	1
	Palestinian Autonomous Areas of Gaza and Jericho		TIPH 2		Establishing and maintaining security in Hebron and economic development	3
	Ser	NATO	KFOR	JOINT ENTERPRISE	Establishing and maintaining security in Kosovo	940
United Kingdom	Afg	NATO	ISAF	HERRICK	Assisting the Afghan government in providing security	7,398
	BiH	EU	EUFOR	ALTHEA	Establishing and maintaining security in Bosnia and Herzegovina in accordance with Dayton/Paris Agreement	21
	Irq	US Coalition	MNF-I	Iraqi Freedom or TELIC	Fighting terrorism, delivering humanitarian support to the Iraqi people, securing Iraq's oil fields and resources, helping the transition to a representative self-government	6,371
	Kya	BPST (EA)			The British Peace Support Team coordinates and delivers peace support training across East Africa	12
	Ser	NATO	KFOR	JOINT ENTERPRISE	Establishing and maintaining security in Kosovo	150
	SL	IMATT			Providing Sierra Leonean soldiers with military training and advice	115
Non-Nato Europe						
Albania	Afg	NATO	ISAF		Assisting the Afghan government in providing security across Afghan territory	138
	BiH	EU	EUFOR	ALTHEA	Establishing and maintaining security in Bosnia and Herzegovina in accordance with Dayton/Paris Agreement	70

Table 35 Non-UN Deployments 2007–2008

Region/ Country	Deployment Location	International Organisation	Operational Organisation	Operational Name	Task	Total Number
	Irq	US Coalition	MNF-I	*Iraqi Freedom*	Fighting terrorism, delivering humanitarian support to the Iraqi people, securing Iraq's oil fields and resources, helping the transition to a representative self-government	127
Armenia	Irq	US Coalition	MNF-I	*Iraqi Freedom*	Fighting terrorism, delivering humanitarian support to the Iraqi people, securing Iraq's oil fields and resources, helping the transition to a representative self-government	46
	Ser	NATO	KFOR	*JOINT ENTERPRISE*	Establishing and maintaining security in Kosovo	34
Austria	Afg	NATO	ISAF		Military assistance and training	3
	BiH	EU	EUFOR	*ALTHEA*	Establishing and maintaining security in Bosnia and Herzegovina in accordance with Dayton/Paris Agreement	178
	BiH	EU	EUMM		Monitor political and security development borders, inter-ethnic and refugee issues	5
	Cha/CAR	EU			Bridging military operation in eastern Chad and north eastern CAR in spt of MINURCAT	160
	Eth	AU	AMIS II			1
	Ser	NATO	KFOR	*JOINT ENTERPRISE*	Establishing and maintaining security in Kosovo	529
Azerbaijan	Afg	NATO	ISAF		Assisting the Afghan government in providing security across Afghan territory	22
	Irq	US Coalition	MNF-I	*Iraqi Freedom*	Fighting terrorism, delivering humanitarian support to the Iraqi people, securing Iraq's oil fields and resources, helping the transition to a representative self-government	150
	Ser	NATO	KFOR	*JOINT ENTERPRISE*	Establishing and maintaining security in Kosovo	35
Bosnia-Herzegovina	Irq	US Coalition	MNF-I	*Iraqi Freedom*	De-mining	49
Croatia	Afg	NATO	ISAF		Assisting the Afghan government in providing security across Afghan territory	199
Finland	Afg	NATO	ISAF		Assisting the Afghan government in providing security across Afghan territory	85
	BiH	EU	EUFOR	*ALTHEA*	Establishing and maintaining security in Bosnia and Herzegovina in accordance with Dayton/Paris Agreement	64
	Cha/CAR	EU			Bridging millitary operation in eastern Chad and north eastern CAR in spt of MINURCAT	60
	Ser	NATO	KFOR	*JOINT ENTERPRISE*	Establishing and maintaining security in Kosovo	450
Georgia	Irq	US Coalition	MNF-I	*Iraqi Freedom*	Fighting terrorism, delivering humanitarian support to the Iraqi people, securing Iraq's oil fields and resources, helping the transition to a representative self-government	2,000
	Ser	NATO	KFOR	*JOINT ENTERPRISE*	Establishing and maintaining security in Kosovo	184
Ireland	Afg	NATO	ISAF		Assisting the Afghan government in providing security across Afghan territory	7
	Alb	OSCE	OSCE Presence in Albania			1
	BiH	EU	EUFOR	*ALTHEA*	Establishing and maintaining security in Bosnia and Herzegovina in accordance with Dayton/Paris Agreement	25
	BiH	OSCE	OSCE Mission to Bosnia-Herzegivina			1
	Be, Brussels		Head of Military Staff			1

Table 35 Non-UN Deployments 2007–2008

Region/ Country	Deployment Location	International Organisation	Operational Organisation	Operational Name	Task	Total Number
	Be, Brussels	EU	EU Military Staff			4
	Be, Brussels	EU	Permanent Representative			3
	Be, Brussels	PfP	Liaison Office of Ireland			2
	Be, Mons	SHAPE	Partnership Coordination Cell/SHAPE		Military Representative	1
	Cha / CAR	EU	EUFOR Tchad/ RCA		Bridging military operation in eastern Cha and north eastern CAR in support of MINURCAT	400
	Ga	OSCE	OSCE Mission in Georgia			1
	Mnt	OSCE	OSCE Mission in Montenegro			1
	US, New York	EU	EU Military Staff			1
	Ser	NATO	KFOR	*JOINT ENTERPRISE*	Establishing and maintaining security in Kosovo	220
	A, Vienna	OSCE	Higher Level Planning Group		Staff Officer	1
	A, Vienna	OSCE	Irish Delegation		Military Adviser	1
	Ser	OSCE	OSCE Mission in FRY			2
Macedonia, Former Yugoslav Republic of	Afg	NATO	ISAF		Assisting the Afghan government in providing security	129
	BiH	EU	EUFOR	*ALTHEA*	Establishing and maintaining security in Bosnia and Herzegovina in accordance with Dayton/Paris Agreement	29
	Irq	US Coalition	MNF-I	*Iraqi Freedom*	Fighting terrorism, delivering humanitarian support to the Iraqi people, securing Iraq's oil fields and resources, helping the transition to a representative self-government	40
Moldova	Ga	OSCE			Military Observer	1
	Irq	US Coalition	MNF-I	*Iraqi Freedom*	Fighting terrorism, delivering humanitarian support to the Iraqi people, securing Iraq's oil fields and resources, helping the transition to a representative self-government	11
Sweden	Afg	NATO	ISAF		Assisting the Afghan government in providing security	340
	BiH	EU	EUFOR	*ALTHEA*	Establishing and maintaining security in Bosnia and Herzegovina in accordance with Dayton/Paris Agreement	24
	Cha / CAR	EU	EUFOR Tchad/ RCA		Bridging military operation in eastern Cha and north eastern CAR in support of MINURCAT	200
	DROC	EU	EUPOL KINSHASA		Police training and to monitor, mentor, and advise the IPU (Integrated Police Unit)	1
	ROK		NNSC		Monitoring cease-fire between North and South Korea	5
	Ser	NATO	KFOR	*JOINT ENTERPRISE*	Establishing and maintaining security in Kosovo	380
	Sdn	AU	AMIS		Performing peacekeeping operations related to the Darfur conflict	12
Switzerland	Afg	NATO	ISAF		Assisting the Afghan government in providing security	2
	BiH	EU	EUFOR	*ALTHEA*	Establishing and maintaining security in Bosnia and Herzegovina with accordance of Dayton/Paris Agreement	26

Table 35 Non-UN Deployments 2007–2008

Region/Country	Deployment Location	International Organisation	Operational Organisation	Operational Name	Task	Total Number
	ROK		NNSC		Monitoring cease-fire between North and South Korea	5
	Ser	NATO	KFOR	*JOINT ENTERPRISE or SWISSCOY*	Establishing and maintaining security in Kosovo	220
Ukraine	Irq	NATO	NTM-I		Training Iraqi forces	3
	Mediterranean Sea	NATO		*ACTIVE ENDEAVOUR*	Global military response to 'War on Terror'	FF
	Mol	Russia, Moldova, Ukraine			Joint Peacekeeping Force in Pridnestrovye (Transdnistria) region of Moldova Republic	10
	Ser	NATO	KFOR	*JOINT ENTERPRISE*	Establishing and maintaining security in Kosovo	101
Russia						
Russia	Mediterranean Sea	NATO		*ACTIVE ENDEAVOUR*	Global military response to 'War on Terror'	FF
	Mol	Russia, Moldova, Ukraine			Joint Peacekeeping Force in Pridnestrovye (Transdnistria) region of Moldova Republic	1,199
Middle East and North Africa						
Algeria	Er and Eth	AU	OLMEE		Military Observers	2
	Sdn	AU	AMIS		Military Observers	13
Egypt	Sdn	AU	AMIS		Military Observers	34
	Sdn	AU / UN	UNAMID		Proposed deployment. Support the implementation of the Darfur Peace Agreement, as well as to protect its personnel and civilians	625
Jordan	Sdn	AU / UN	UNAMID		Proposed deployment. Support the implementation of the Darfur Peace Agreement, as well as to protect its personnel and civilians	360
Libya	Pi		IMT		International Monitoring Team overseeing the implementation of the ceasefire agreement between the Armed Forces of the Philippines and the Moro Islamic Liberation Front (MILF)	5
	Sdn	AU	AMIS		Military Observers	9
Mauritania	Sdn	AU	AMIS		Military Observers	20
Morocco	Ser	NATO	KFOR	*JOINT ENTERPRISE*	Medical and Humanitarian	229
Tunisia	Er and Eth	AU	OLMEE		Military Observers	1
Central and South Asia						
Bangladesh	Sdn	AU / UN	UNAMID		Proposed deployment. Support the implementation of the Darfur Peace Agreement, as well as to protect its personnel and civilians	300
India	Afg				Commandos to guard Indian road-builders working on the Zaranji-Delaram highway that will connect Kandahar with the Iranian border	400
Kazakhstan	Irq	US Coalition	MNF-I	*Iraqi Freedom*	Fighting terrorism, delivering humanitarian support to the Iraqi people, securing Iraq's oil fields and resources, helping the transition to a representative self-government	29
Nepal	Sdn	AU / UN	UNAMID		Proposed deployment. Support the implementation of the Darfur Peace Agreement, as well as to protect its personnel and civilians	N/A

Table 35 Non-UN Deployments 2007–2008

Region/ Country	Deployment Location	International Organisation	Operational Organisation	Operational Name	Task	Total Number
Pakistan	Sdn	AU / UN	UNAMID		Proposed deployment. Support the implementation of the Darfur Peace Agreement, as well as to protect its personnel and civilians	445
East Asia and Australasia						
Australia	Afg	NATO	ISAF		Assisting the Afghan government in providing security	907
	Et		MFO	*MAZURKA*	Supervise the implementation of the security provisions of the Egyptian–Israeli Peace Treaty	25
	Irq	US Coalition	MNF-I	*CATALYST*	Rehabilitation and Reconstruction of Iraq	1575
	Solomon Islands		RAMSI	*ANODE*	Restore law and order, strengthen government institutions, reduce corruption, re-invigorate the economy	140
	Tl	Timor-Leste Coalition Force		*ASTUTE*	To assist the Government of Timor Leste to bring security, peace and confidence to its people	850
Brunei	Pi		IMT		International Monitoring Team overseeing the implementation of the ceasefire agreement between the Armed Forces of the Philippines and the Moro Islamic Liberation Front (MILF)	10
China, People's Republic of	Sdn	AU	AMIS		Performing peacekeeping operations related to the Darfur conflict	315
Fiji	Et		MFO		Supervise the implementation of the security provisions of the Egyptian–Israeli Peace Treaty	329
	Solomon Islands		RAMSI	*HELPEM FREN*	Help the Solomon Islands Government restore law and order, strengthen government institutions, reduce corruption and re-invigorate the economy	122
Japan	Kwt				Humanitarian Reconstruction Support. Air force contribution	210
Malaysia	Pi		IMT		International Monitoring Team overseeing the implementation of the ceasefire agreement between the Armed Forces of the Philippines and the Moro Islamic Liberation Front (MILF)	60
	Tl	Timor-Leste Coalition Force		*ASTUTE*	To assist the Government of Timor Leste to bring security, peace and confidence to its people	209
Mongolia	Irq	US Coalition	MNF-I	*Iraqi Freedom*	Fighting terrorism, delivering humanitarian support to the Iraqi people, securing Iraq's oil fields and resources, helping the transition to a representative self-government	160
	Ser	NATO	KFOR	*JOINT ENTERPRISE*	Establishing and maintaining security in Kosovo	36
New Zealand	Afg	NATO	ISAF		Assisting the Afghan government in providing security	8
	Afg	US Coalition		*ENDURING FREEDOM*	Global military response to 'War on Terror'. Provincial Reconstruction Team	122
	Antarctica			*Operation Antarctica*	Scientific research and management of Scott Base	26
	BiH	EU	EUFOR	*Liaison Team*	Establishing and maintaining security in Bosnia and Herzegovina in accordance with Dayton/Paris Agreement	3
	Et		MFO		Supervise the implementation of the security provisions of the Egyptian–Israeli Peace Treaty	26

Table 35 **Non-UN Deployments 2007–2008**

Region/ Country	Deployment Location	International Organisation	Operational Organisation	Operational Name	Task	Total Number
	Gulf Region	US Coalition		*ENDURING FREEDOM*	Global military response to 'War on Terror'	5
	Solomon Islands		RAMSI		Fostering long-term stability, security and prosperity through support for improved law, justice and security, and for more effective, accountable and democratic government	44
	TI	Timor-Leste Coalition Force		*ASTUTE*	To assist the Government of Timor Leste to bring security, peace and confidence to its people	180
	US (FL)	US Coalition		*ENDURING FREEDOM*	Global military response to 'War on Terror'	4
Korea, Republic of	Afg	NATO	ISAF		Military assistance and training	207
	Horn of Africa - Dj	CJTF-HOA			Detecting, disrupting, and defeating transnational terrorist groups operating in the region. Military training and counterterrorist training	1
	Irq	US Coalition	MNF-I	*Iraqi Freedom*	Fighting terrorism, delivering humanitarian support to the Iraqi people, securing Iraq's oil fields and resources, helping the transition to a representative self-government. Some troops deployed in Kuwait and Qatar	1,200
	US, Tampa, FL, and Brn	US CENTCOM		*Task Force Tampa* or *FOUNDATION*	Maintaining effective liaison with HQ US CENTCOM with regard to the campaign against terrorism.	5
Thailand	Sdn	AU / UN	UNAMID		Proposed deployment. Support the implementation of the Darfur Peace Agreement, as well as to protect its personnel and civilians	N/A

Caribbean and Latin America

Region/ Country	Deployment Location	International Organisation	Operational Organisation	Operational Name	Task	Total Number
Argentina	Ser	NATO	KFOR	*JOINT ENTERPRISE*	Establishing and maintaining security in Kosovo	36
Chile	BiH	EU	EUFOR	*ALTHEA*	Peacekeeping in accordance with Dayton/ Paris Agreement	21
Colombia	Et		MFO		Supervise the implementation of the security provisions of the Egyptian–Israeli Peace Treaty/Military Observers	357
El Salvador	Irq	US Coalition	MNF-I	*Iraqi Freedom*	Fighting terrorism, delivering humanitarian support to the Iraqi people, securing Iraq's oil fields and resources, helping the transition to a representative self-government	380
Uruguay	Et		MFO		Supervise the implementation of the security provisions of the Egyptian–Israeli Peace Treaty	87

Sub-Saharan Africa

Region/ Country	Deployment Location	International Organisation	Operational Organisation	Operational Name	Task	Total Number
Benin	Sdn	AU	AMIS		Military Observers	1
Botswana	Sdn	AU	AMIS		Military Observers	20
Burkina Faso	Sdn	AU	AMIS		Military Observers	4
	Sdn	AU / UN	UNAMID		Proposed deployment. Support the implementation of the Darfur Peace Agreement, as well as to protect its personnel and civilians	N/A
Burundi	SR	AU	AMISOM		Security and peacekeeping. To be deployed	1,700
	Sdn	AU	AMIS		Military Observers	10
Cameroon	Sdn	AU	AMIS		Military Observers	30
Chad	Sdn	AU	AMIS		Performing peacekeeping operations related to the Darfur conflict	38
Congo	Sdn	AU	AMIS		Military Observers	14
Ethiopia	SR	AU	AMISOM		Security and peacekeeping. To be deployed	5,000

Table 35 Non-UN Deployments 2007–2008

Region/ Country	Deployment Location	International Organisation	Operational Organisation	Operational Name	Task	Total Number
	Sdn	AU / UN	UNAMID		Proposed deployment. Support the implementation of the Darfur Peace Agreement, as well as to protect its personnel and civilians	N/A
Gabon	Sdn	AU	AMIS		Military Observers	22
Ghana	Er and Eth	AU	OLMEE		Military Observers	3
	SR	AU	AMISOM		Proposed deployment. Security and peacekeeping	N/A
	Sdn	AU	AMIS		Military Observers	23
	Sdn	AU / UN	UNAMID		Proposed deployment. Support the implementation of the Darfur Peace Agreement, as well as to protect its personnel and civilians	N/A
Kenya	Sdn	AU	AMIS		Military Observers	60
	Sdn	AU / UN	UNAMID		Proposed deployment. Support the implementation of the Darfur Peace Agreement, as well as to protect its personnel and civilians	N/A
Lesotho	Sdn	AU	AMIS		Military Observers	10
Madagascar	Sdn	AU	AMIS		Military Observers	9
Malawi	SR	AU	AMISOM		Proposed deployment. Security and peacekeeping	1,000
	Sdn	AU	AMIS		Military Observers	24
	Sdn	AU / UN	UNAMID		Proposed deployment. Support the implementation of the Darfur Peace Agreement, as well as to protect its personnel and civilians	N/A
Mali	Sdn	AU	AMIS		Military Observers	15
	Sdn	AU / UN	UNAMID		Proposed deployment. Support the implementation of the Darfur Peace Agreement, as well as to protect its personnel and civilians	N/A
Mozambique	Sdn	AU	AMIS		Military Observers	15
Namibia	Sdn	AU	AMIS		Military Observers	24
Nigeria	SR	AU	AMISOM		Proposed deployment. Security and peacekeeping	850
	Sdn	AU	AMIS		Peacekeeping	2,040
	Sdn	AU / UN	UNAMID		Proposed deployment. Support the implementation of the Darfur Peace Agreement, as well as to protect its personnel and civilians	60
	Er and Eth	AU	OLMEE		Military Observers	2
Rwanda	Sdn	AU	AMIS		Peacekeeping and military observers	3,272
Senegal	Sdn	AU	AMIS		Performing peacekeeping operations related to the Darfur conflict	538
	Sdn	AU / UN	UNAMID		Proposed deployment. Support the implementation of the Darfur Peace Agreement, as well as to protect its personnel and civilians	N/A
South Africa	Bu	AU	AUSTF	CURICULUM	Special Task Force	763
	CAR	Bilateral support		VIMBEZELA	Bilateral military support	36
	DROC	Tripartite agreement with Belgium		TEUTONIC 2	Assisting DROC gvt to disarm rebels	16
	Er and Eth	AU	OLMEE	ESPRESSO	Assisting United Nations (UN) in implementing and monitoring peace agreement	1

Table 35 Non-UN Deployments 2007–2008

Region/ Country	Deployment Location	International Organisation	Operational Organisation	Operational Name	Task	Total Number
	Sdn	AU	AMIS	*CORDITE*	Performing peacekeeping operations related to the Darfur conflict	620
	Uga	AU		*BONGANE*	Observer mission to northern Uga and Sdn	2
The Gambia	Sdn	AU	AMIS		Peacekeeping and military observers	200
	Sdn	AU / UN	UNAMID		Proposed deployment. Support the implementation of the Darfur Peace Agreement, as well as to protect its personnel and civilians	N/A
Togo	Sdn	AU	AMIS		Military Observers	16
Uganda	SR	AU	AMISOM		Security and peacekeeping	1,500
Zambia	Sdn	AU	AMIS		Military Observers	45

Table 36 Selected Operations and Training Activity 2007

Date	Title	Location	Aim	Principal Participants/Remarks
North America: US & Canada				
April	RED FLAG ALASKA 07 (-1)	US (Pacific Alaskan Range Complex)	Series of multilateral air cbt trg ex	US; Aus; Fr (Mirage, C-130, C-160, 1 E-3 AWACS). Over 1,300 pers
30 April–17 May	ALASKA SHIELD / ARDENT SENTRY / NORTHERN EDGE 07	US (Rhode Island; Indiana; Alaska)	Inter-agency DISTEX	DHS, FEMA, NORAD, USNORTHCOM. USNORTHCOM's largest and most complex Ex
01–13 May	UNITAS 48-07 ATLANTIC	Arg (coast)	Multilateral naval ex with live fire, interdiction, ASW and ADEX air ops	Arg; Br; Chl; Sp; US (SOUTHCOM). Obs: Bol; Et; Ge; Nba; Por; RSA
31 May–15 June	RED FLAG ALASKA 07 (-2)	see above	see above	US; Sng; Aus. Total: 1,400 pers. Obs: Mal; No
June	COPE NORTH	US (Guam)	Bilateral joint air ex	US; J (first live weapon drops from 8 F-2 FGA ac.)
04–15 June	BALTIC OPERATIONS (BALTOPS) 07	Baltic Sea (Da; Swe; Ge)	Multilateral naval ex, part of NATO's Partnership for Peace Ex series	US; Da; Ge; RF; Nl; L; Lat; Fr; Pl; Swe; UK
18–26 June	UNITAS 48-07 PACIFIC	Offshore western Latin America	Multilateral naval ex focused on EW, AAW, AD, ASW, MSO	Chl; Co; Pe; US (SOUTHCOM). Obs: Mex. Incl in Partnership of the Americas 07 (PoA) initiative
12–27 July	RED FLAG ALASKA 07 (-3)	see above	see above	J (6 F-15); Mgl; Sp; Th; Tu; US; Da; SF; Fr; Ge; UK; Ind; Indo; Ska; Mex
August	NORTHERN VIKING 07	Icl (Keflavik)	Multilateral NATO air ex focused on refuelling issues	No (2 F-16 and 1 P-3C Orion, SF and logistics); Icl (coastguard vessels, 1 hel); Da; Lat; US (3 F-15s, KC-135); NATO (E-3A AWACS)
August	NANOOK	Ca (Iqaluit, Baffin Island Coastal and Hudson Strait areas)	National DISTEX and CN ex; cold weather trg	Ca (600 pers. 1 FF, 1 OPV, 1 SSK, 2 CC138 ac, 2 CH-146 hel, 1 CP-140 MPA, 1 CF-18 FGA)
September	BOLD QUEST	US (Nellis AFB; Fort Irwin, Calif.)	NATO Advanced Concept Technology Demonstration ex, testing combat identification technologies	Aus, Be, Ca, Fr, Ge, Nl, Swe, UK, US, NATO. Over 850 pers. USJFCOM's largest Ex of 2007
Caribbean and Latin America				
May	FUERZAS ALIADAS HUMANITARIAS (FAHUM) 07	Gua	Multilateral DISTEX (information sharing)	AB; Bs; Bds; Bze; DR; DR; Grenada; Guy; Ja; RH; Montserrat; St Kitts and Nevis; St. Lucia; St. Vincent and the Grenadines; Sme; Turks and Caicos; TT; US
May	TRADEWINDS 07	Bze	Multilateral DISTEX	Bze; CARICOM; Ca; US (400 pers); UK (BATSUB)
June	TEAMWORK SOUTH	Chl	Multilateral naval ex aimed at improving task force comms and coordination	Arg; Chl; Fr; UK; US. (18 vessels, 1 sub, ac.)
June	FUERZAS COMMANDO 07	Hr	Multilateral SF ex to improve CT ops	Arg; Bol; Br; Chl; Co; CR; DR; Ec; ElS; Gua; Hr; Ja; Nic; Pan; Py; Pe; US; Ury. Obs: Mex
11–15 July	PRATA	Br	Bilateral air border patrol ex	Br; Arg
29 August– September	FUERZAS ALIDAS / PANAMAX 07	Pan (Canal approaches); Hr (Soto Cano AFB).	Multilateral PoA 07 ex focused on interdiction, C2, stability and humanitarian assistance ops	Arg; Co; Gua; Pan; Br; DR; Hr; Pe; Ca; Ec; Nic; US; Chl; Fr; Nl; Ury. Obs: ElS; Mex; Py; UK. Over 30 ships, 12 ac, 7,500 pers
Europe				
March	ICEX 2007	North Pole	ASW ice ex	UK (1SSN); US (1SSN)
March	n.k.	Ge (Lehnin)	EU Battle Group PKO ex	Ge; Nl; SF. Over 800 pers
05–15 March	COLD RESPONSE 2007	No (Bodo AFB)	Multilateral air ex focused on Expeditionary Air Wing concept for NATO or EU	Be; Da; Nl; No; Por; Cz; Ge; Lat; L; Swe; Ca; SF. Eqpt included: 27 F-16s, 3 C-160 (Ge), 1 E-3A AWACS (NATO), 1 E-3D Sentry (UK).Pers: 4,500 land; 500 naval from 18 nations Largest SF Ex in Europe in 2007
26–27 April	SMART RAVEN	L (Vilnius, Siauliai).	Multilateral air interdiction ex (PSI)	L; US; Pl; Lat; Ea. Obs from 19 nations

Table 36 **Selected Operations and Training Activity 2007**

Date	Title	Location	Aim	Principal Participants/Remarks
May	*NOBLE LIGHT I*	It	Multilat NRF ex focused on NBC ops (NRF-9)	Gr; Cz; Tu; Fr; R; Bg; It; UK; US
14–25 May	*NOBLE MARINER / NOBLE AWARD / NOBLE SWORD*	Southern Baltic Sea and Kattegat.	Multilateral NATO naval ex incl amphibious and expeditionary capabilities; concurrently air ops ex; with naval and air ex focused on C2 trg (NRF context)	17 NATO countries (Be; Ca; Da; Ea; Fr; Ge; Gr; It; Lat; Nl; No; Pl; Por; Sp; Tu; UK; US), SF, Swe. With *NOBLE AWARD* and *NOBLE SWORD* over 80 Maritime Units, 73 ac
27–29 May	*ADRIATIC GATE*	Slvn (Portorož; Koper).	Multilateral NBC interception ex (PSI)	26 nations incl. US, Montenegro, BiH. Obs: 40 nations
June	*COOPERATIVE MAKO*	Mediterranean Sea	Multilateral naval MSO ex	NATO nations
June	*MILEX*	Be (Brussels); Swe (Enkoping).	Multilateral EU CPX and crisis management ex.Brussels ops centre activated	27 nations. Brussels HQ manned by Nordic BG. Obs incl NATO, UN, OSCE, some non-EU NATO, EU accession candidates, Ca, US, RF, Ukr, Med Partners
04–23 June	*STEADFAST JACKPOT 07*	It; Tu; No; Sp	NRF C2 ex based on UN Chapter 7 op scenario	26 NATO nations incl No; Sp; Tu; It. Over 2,000 pers, incl C2 at Naples, It and Stavanger, No. 7th ex since 2000
09–22 July	*SEA BREEZE 07*	Ukr (Mykolayiv region, Odessa and Yuzhny)	Multilateral naval PfP ex focused on PKO support and CT	NATO: Arm; Az; Ca; Ga; Ge; Gr; Lat; FYROM; Mol; R; Tu; Ukr; US. Over 22 ships, 9 ac, 2,500 pers
August	*MEDCEUR 2007*	Mol (Bulboaca)	Multilateral DISTEX	13 NATO nations. PfP: Arm; Alb; Az; Bel; Ga; Kaz; Kgz; FYROM; Ser; Ukr; Cr; Mol; US. Second PfP ex in Mol
September–December	*TORGAU 07*	RF (Nizhny Novgorod); Ge (Grafenwoehr, Hohenfels trg ranges).	Bilateral army PKO CPX, designed to increase div-level interoperability	RF; US. First since 2005
03–14 September	*BOLD AVENGER 07*	No (Orland airbase) and North Sea	Multilateral NATO ex, focused on tac air ops within NRF context	13 NATO members: Be; Ca; Cz; Fr; Ge; Gr; No; Pl; R; Sp; Tu; UK; US. Over 100 ac, incl cbt, tkr, AEW; around 1,450 pers
14–18 September	*AFRICA 07*	RSA	Multilateral naval MSO ex	Standing NATO Maritime Group 1 (US; Nl; Ge; Ca; Por; Da); RSA
17–28 September	*NEPTUNE WARRIOR / SKYLANCE*	UK (Cumbria; Northumberland; Scotland).	Multilateral C2 ex	Fr; Ca; US; NZ; UK - eqpt incl Ftr, FGA, AEW, MP along with NATO ac & naval assets
01–12 October	*NOBLE MIDAS 2007*	Offshore Cr.	Multilateral NATO ex with extensive amphibious assault trg	Cr and NATO: Bg; Fr; Ge; Gr; It; Nl; No; R; US; Sp; Tu; UK. Obs: Ca; Alb; Mnt. Over 9,000 NRF pers, 50 ships, 1 CV, amphibious vehs, FF, cruisers, 6 sub, 60 NATO member ac, 23 hel. First NATO ex in non-member country
30 October	*COOPERATIVE LONGBOW / LANCER*	Alb (Tirana)	Multilateral NATO PfP ex, based on a UN-mandated crisis response scenario	NATO: Ca; Gr; Hu; Pol; Tu; UK; US. Partners Alb; Arm; A; Az; Bel; FYROM; Ga; Kaz; Mol; CH; Ukr; Mnt. Med Dialogue: Il. Obs: UAE; Q; Mor. Also: RF; J
Russia & Collective Security Treaty Organisation				
29–31 May	*ISSYK KUL ANTI-TERROR 07*	Kgz (Issyk Kul).	Multilateral joint pol-mil CT ex focused on mtn ops and hostage rescue	SCO: RF; Kgz; Kaz; Tjk; Uz; PRC. Obs: Pak; Ir; Ind; Mgl
June–September	*COMBAT COMMONWEALTH 07*	RF	Multilateral AD ex	RF; Arm; Bel; Kaz; Uz; Kgz
July	n.k.	RF (Barents Sea)	Naval ex	RF (Over 7,000 pers, 30 vessels and 30 ac incl. Su-27, MiG-29, Su-24, Mi-24, Tu-22M3)
09–17 August	*PEACE MISSION (RUBEZH)*	PRC (Urumchi) to RF (Chebarkul, Chelyabinsk)	Shanghai Cooperation Organisation-led CT, CN ex	Kaz; Kgz; PRC (1,700); RF (2,000); Tjk; Uz. Over 7,500 pers, 1,500 air and land assets incl. 36 RF and 46 PRC ac. Other SCO members: air aslt coy or SF units. Obs: Pak; Ir; Ind; Mgl. First ex involving all SCO states

Table 36 **Selected Operations and Training Activity 2007**

Date	Title	Location	Aim	Principal Participants/Remarks
11–20 September	*INDRA 07*	RF (Pskov).	Air asslt ex based on a CT scenario (UN-mandated)	RF (76 AB Div); Ind (160+ pers, air force assets). 400 SF from RF and Ind
28 October– 03 November	*EAST 07*	RF (Far Eastern district)	CT ex	RF
Middle East & North Africa				
07–08 February	*SAEQA- THUNDERBOLT*	Ir	AD and atk ex	IRGC (naval and air-force). Eqpt incl *Tor*-M1
10–20 March	*JUNIPER COBRA*	Il	NBC MD computer assisted ex focused on multi-tier interoperability	Il, US. Around 500 pers. Eqpt: PAC-2/3; *Arrow; Aegis;* THAAD
April–May	*NEON FALCON 07*	Brn	Naval ex elms ashore and at sea	US (DDG); Brn
20–30 April	*ARABIAN GAUNTLET 07*	Persian Gulf	Multilateral mine exercise and MARSEC ex	Et, US, Irq and 12 others. The world's largest MCM ex
14–30 May	*INFINITE MOONLIGHT 07*	HKJ	Air ex	US (4,000 troops plus hel); HKJ
November	*BRIGHT STAR 07*	Et	Multilateral air and ground ex	Et; Fr; Ge; Gr; It; HKJ; Kwt; Nl; UAE; UK; US
Sub–Saharan Africa				
22 January– 15 February	*XENON MERCURY*	Moz	DISTEX	UK; Moz
June	*NATURAL FIRE / NATIVE FURY*	East Africa.	DISTEX focused on CIMIC, humanitarian ops and and med. assistance	Kya; Tz; Uga; US
10–19 July	*AFRICA ENDEAVOR 07*	RSA (Didholo base).	Multilateral C3I ex, designed to support CT ops and enhance PKO by the African Standby Force ahead of 2010 World Cup	US; Ag; Ang; Be; Bn; Btwa; BF; Bu; Crn; CV; Cha; Gam; Ls; RMM; Mor; Nba; Ngr; Nga; Sen; RSA; Swe; Uga; Z
21 August– 08 September	*FLINTLOCK*	RMM (Bamako).	CPX, with CT and PKO elms. Part of the Trans-Sahara Counter-Terrorism Initiative	Ag; Cha; RIM; Mor; Ngr; Nga; Sen; Tn; RMM; BF; Fr; Nl; UK; US (SOCEUR, USAFRICOM)
November– December	*WEST AFRICAN TRAINING CRUISE 07*	n.k.	Multilateral CT ex	Gha; Sen; Gui; Mor; US
East Asia and Australasia				
29 January – 09 February	*COPE TIGER 07*	Th (Korat and Udon AFBs).	Multilateral ex incl AD, civic assistance and cbt trg	Th; Sgp; US. Largest air cbt ex in Th
February	*TEMPEST EXPRESS 11*	Sgp	DISTEX	20+ Asian countries, US PACOM
19 February– 04 March	*BALIKATAN 07*	Pi	Promote interoperability and enhance Pi CT capabilities, involving civil-mil ops and NGOs	US; Pi
April	*INDRA 07*	Western Pacific Ocean	Naval CT, CN and MARSEC ex incl AD and ASW elms	Ind (3 DDG, 1 FSG, 1 AO); RF (incl 2 DDG, 1 FFG, 1 SSK, MS gp, 1 AO.)
08–18 May	*COBRA GOLD 07*	Th	Improve interoperability through field training ex, CAX and humanitarian/civic action activties	Th (3,090); US (PACOM, 2,000); J (47); Sgp (70); Indo (27). Obs: Aus; Bng; Bru; Ind
June	*TALISMAN SABRE*	Aus	AB and amphib ex. Merges Exs *TANDEM THRUST, KINGFISHER* and *CROCODILE*	US (20,000 pers). Aus (7,500 pers). Incl 1 CVBG; 30 vessels; 2 SSN and 100+ ac
August	*KHAAN QUEST 07*	Mgl (Ulan Bator)	Improve interoperability in UN-sponsored peace enforcement ops	US (200 pers); Mgl (600 pers); ROK; Indo; Bng; Tonga; Bru; Ska; Cam. Obs: PRC; RF; Mal; J
September	*WARRIOR 07*	PRC (Taonan trg base, Shenyang mil area).	Field training ex	PRC; Obs: 35 countries incl SCO members, ASEAN, US, UK, Fr. 1 PRC Mot Div, 10,000 tps
Central and South Asia				
4–10 March	*AMAN (PEACE)*	Pak (Offshore Karachi)	Naval ex focused on CT in Arabian Sea	Pak; US; Aus; PRC; Fr; RF; UK; Brn; Et; Indo; HKJ; Mal; Q; Sau and 9 other countries

Table 36 Selected Operations and Training Activity 2007

Date	Title	Location	Aim	Principal Participants/Remarks
April	*MALABAR 07 (-1)*	Okinawa coast	Naval ex incl surface, air, MP, and ASW trg	US (6,500 pers, 7 ships); Ind
July	*INDRA DHANUSH 07*	UK (Waddington)	Air ex incl IAF Tactics and Cbt Development Establishment and RAF Air Warfare Centre	Ind (FGA); UK (Ftr, FGA, Trg, AEW). Sequel to the 2006 ex in Ind. First UK/Ind ex in UK
04–09 September	*MALABAR 07 (-2)*	Bay of Bengal (Visakhapatnam, Andaman and Nicobar Is.)	Naval Ex incl ASW, MSO, humanitarian and cbt elms	US (2 CVBG, 1 SSN); Ind; J; Aus; Sgp. Over 20,000 pers, 28 ships and 150 ac. First invitation for J, Sng, Aus. The Indian Navy's largest ex
09–21 September	*STEPPE EAGLE 07*	Kaz (Ili district nr Alamaty).	PfP ex focused on Kazakh PKO Bde	Kaz; US; UK; Obs: Tu; PA; NATO pers
14–16 October	*PACIFIC SHIELD 07*	J (Izu–Oshima island, Tokyo).	Naval PSI ex with WMD intercept and MP elms	J; Aus; UK; Fr; NZ; Sgp; US. Obs: 40 countries

Table 37 **International Comparisons of Defence Expenditure and Military Manpower, 2004–2006**

current US$ m	US$ m			Defence Expenditure per capita US$			% of GDP			Number in Armed Forces (000)	Estimated Reservists (000)	Paramilitary (000)
	2004	2005	2006	2004	2005	2006	2004	2005	2006	2008	2008	2008
North America												
Canada	11,501	13,224	14,958	354	403	452	1.2	1.2	1.2	64	66	0
USA	455,908	495,300	535,943	1,556	1,675	1,796	3.9	4.0	4.0	1,498	1,083	0
NATO Europe												
Belgium	4,311	4,231	4,428	417	408	427	1.2	1.1	1.1	40	2	0
Bulgaria	623	669	703	83	90	95	2.6	2.5	2.3	41	303	34
Czech Republic	1,984	2,237	2,464	194	218	241	1.8	1.8	1.7	23	0	3
Denmark	3,579	3,472	3,876	661	639	711	1.5	1.3	1.4	30	54	0
Estonia	182	205	238	136	154	179	1.6	1.5	1.4	4	16	3
France	53,363	53,181	54,003	883	877	887	2.6	2.5	2.4	255	25	99
Germany	38,263	38,250	37,775	464	464	458	1.4	1.4	1.3	246	162	0
Greece	5,940	6,786	7,286	558	636	682	2.2	2.4	2.4	157	251	4
Hungary	1,531	1,601	1,323	153	160	133	1.5	1.4	1.2	32	44	12
Iceland	40	48	46	136	161	153	0.3	0.3	0.3	0	0	0.13
Italy	34,345	33,699	30,635	592	580	527	2.0	1.9	1.7	186	42	254
Latvia	176	204	279	76	89	122	1.3	1.3	1.4	6	11	11
Lithuania	310	305	349	86	85	97	1.4	1.2	1.2	9	7	15
Luxembourg	236	245	254	511	523	535	0.7	0.7	0.6	0.9	0	0.612
Netherlands	9,440	9,616	9,904	578	586	601	1.5	1.5	1.5	46	32	0
Norway	4,888	4,887	5,015	1,069	1,064	1,088	1.9	1.6	1.5	16	180	0
Poland	4,630	5,545	6,235	120	144	162	1.8	1.9	1.8	127	234	21
Portugal	2,866	3,159	3,080	272	299	290	1.6	1.7	1.6	43	211	48
Romania	1,530	1,976	2,324	68	88	104	2.0	2.0	1.9	74	45	80
Slovakia	730	824	957	135	152	176	1.7	1.7	1.7	17	20	0
Slovenia	494	516	629	246	257	313	1.5	1.5	1.7	6	20	5
Spain	12,746	13,121	14,415	316	325	357	1.2	1.2	1.2	149	319	73
Turkey	9,390	10,328	11,630	136	148	165	3.1	2.8	2.9	510	379	102
United Kingdom	50,120	56,335	55,444	832	932	915	2.3	2.5	2.3	181	199	0
Subtotal NATO Ex-US	253,220	264,665	268,247	448	467	472	1.84	1.82	1.74	2,263	2,662	765
Total NATO	709,128	759,965	804,190	827	881	928	2.78	2.82	2.81	3,761	3,705	765
Non-NATO Europe												
Albania	105	116	141	30	33	39	1.4	1.3	1.5	11	0	0.5
Armenia	98	125	184	33	42	62	2.8	2.5	2.9	42	0	5
Austria	2,250	2,263	2,630	275	276	321	0.8	0.7	0.8	40	66	0
Azerbaijan	245	314	658	31	40	82	2.8	2.5	3.3	67	300	15
Belarus	219	248	279	21	24	29	0.9	0.8	0.8	73	290	110

Table 37 International Comparisons of Defence Expenditure and Military Manpower, 2004–2006

current US$ m	US$ m 2004	US$ m 2005	US$ m 2006	Defence Expenditure per capita US$ 2004	2005	2006	% of GDP 2004	2005	2006	Number in Armed Forces (000) 2008	Estimated Reservists (000) 2008	Paramilitary (000) 2008
Bosnia	204	175	142	47	39	32	2.2	1.7	1.2	9	0	0
Croatia	606	600	693	135	133	154	1.7	1.5	1.6	18	106	3
Cyprus	228	274	240	293	352	306	1.4	1.7	1.3	10	60	0.75
Finland	2,515	2,758	2,750	482	528	526	1.4	1.4	1.3	29	237	3
Georgia	84	214	339	18	46	73	1.6	3.4	4.4	21	0	12
Ireland	919	948	1,113	231	236	274	0.5	0.5	0.5	10	15	0
Macedonia	136	128	134	67	63	65	2.5	2.3	2.2	11	21	8
Malta	52	49	46	132	122	114	0.9	0.8	0.7	2	0.09	0
Moldova	9	9	10	2	2	2	0.4	0.3	0.3	6	66	2
Montenegro	n.a.	n.a.	54	n.a.	n.a.	80	0.0	0.0	2.4	6	0	10
Serbia	740	634	812	68	59	80	3.3	2.8	2.5	24	54	0
Sweden	5,837	5,837	5,780	650	648	641	1.7	1.6	1.5	24	262	0.6
Switzerland	3,651	3,606	3,473	490	481	462	1.0	1.0	0.9	23	218	0
Ukraine	1,013	1,080	1,723	21	23	37	2.2	1.3	1.6	130	1,000	85
Total	18,912	19,376	21,200	137	141	155	1.21	1.15	1.16	556	2,695	255
Russia [1]												
Russia	59,600	58,000	70,000	414	404	493	4.23	3.72	4.11	1,027	20,000	419
Middle East and North Africa												
Algeria	2,805	2,877	3,096	87	88	94	3.3	2.8	2.7	147	150	187
Bahrain	474	500	532	699	726	761	4.3	3.8	3.4	8	0	11
Egypt	3,589	3,834	4,337	47	49	55	4.5	4.1	4.0	469	479	397
Iran	5,328	6,481	7,160	83	100	110	3.3	3.5	3.3	545	350	40
Iraq	n.a.	n.a.	n.a.	n.a.	n.a.	n.a.	n.a.	n.a.	n.a.	495	0	0
Israel	10,235	10,767	11,031	1,651	1,715	1,737	8.4	8.3	7.9	177	565	8
Jordan	920	973	1,115	164	169	189	8.1	7.6	7.9	101	65	10
Kuwait	3,284	3,568	3,497	1,455	1,528	1,446	5.8	4.5	3.4	16	24	7
Lebanon	609	564	589	161	147	152	3.0	2.7	2.8	56	0	20
Libya	715	721	593	127	125	100	2.2	1.8	1.1	76	40	0
Mauritania	18	18	18	6	6	6	1.2	1.0	0.6	16	0	5
Morocco	1,990	2,054	2,161	62	63	65	4.0	4.0	3.8	196	150	50
Oman	3,008	3,695	3,276	1,036	1,231	1,056	12.0	11.9	9.0	43	0	4
Palestinian Autonomous Areas of Gaza and Jericho	n.a.	n.a.	n.a.	n.a.	n.a.	n.a.	n.a.	n.a.	n.a.	0	0	56
Qatar	2,060	2,198	2,335	2,452	2,547	2,638	6.6	5.2	4.5	12	0	0
Saudi Arabia	20,910	25,372	29,541	811	960	1,093	8.4	8.0	8.5	224	0	16
Syria	1,524	1,502	1,739	85	81	92	5.9	5.3	5.1	293	314	108

Table 37 International Comparisons of Defence Expenditure and Military Manpower, 2004–2006

current US$ m	Defence Expenditure US$ m			Defence Expenditure per capita US$			% of GDP			Number in Armed Forces (000) 2008	Estimated Reservists (000) 2008	Paramilitary (000) 2008
	2004	2005	2006	2004	2005	2006	2004	2005	2006			
Tunisia	447	471	435	45	47	43	1.6	1.6	1.4	36	0	12
UAE	8,910	8,747	9,482	3,530	3,412	3,643	8.6	6.9	6.7	51	0	0
Yemen	842	584	824	42	28	38	6.3	3.7	4.2	67	0	71
Total	**67,669**	**74,925**	**81,760**	**198**	**216**	**231**	**5.95**	**5.53**	**5.26**	**3,028**	**2,137**	**1,002**
Central and Southern Asia												
Afghanistan	121	119	143	4	4	5	2.0	1.6	1.7	51	0	0
Bangladesh	775	841	938	5	6	6	1.4	1.5	1.6	150	0	64
India	19,821	21,726	22,428	19	20	20	2.9	2.7	2.5	1,288	1,155	1,301
Kazakhstan	426	596	648	28	39	43	1.0	1.1	0.8	49	0	32
Kyrgyzstan	33	34	36	7	7	7	1.5	1.4	1.3	11	0	10
Maldives	39	46	56	114	132	156	5.0	6.1	6.1	n.a.	n.a.	n.a.
Nepal	116	154	158	4	6	6	1.7	2.1	2.0	69	0	62
Pakistan	3,644	4,050	4,156	23	25	25	3.8	3.7	3.2	619	0	304
Sri Lanka	558	616	943	28	31	46	2.8	2.6	3.4	151	6	62
Tajikistan	45	62	73	6	9	10	2.2	2.7	2.7	9	0	8
Turkmenistan	145	154	184	30	31	36	2.1	1.9	1.8	22	0	0
Uzbekistan	62	76	85	2	3	3	0.5	0.5	0.5	67	0	20
Total	**25,784**	**28,475**	**29,848**	**17**	**19**	**19**	**2.74**	**2.59**	**2.38**	**2,486**	**1,161**	**1,831**
East Asia and Australasia												
Australia	13,907	15,550	17,208	698	774	849	2.3	2.3	2.4	51	21	0
Brunei	298	309	328	815	830	864	3.8	3.2	2.8	7	0.7	2
Cambodia	105	111	123	8	8	9	2.0	1.8	1.7	124	0	67
China [2]	87,150	103,400	121,872	20	23	27	1.4	1.3	1.3	2,105	800	1,500
Fiji	56	49	43	64	55	47	2.1	1.6	1.5	4	6	0
Indonesia	2,568	2,869	3,645	11	13	16	1.0	1.0	1.0	302	400	280
Japan	45,152	43,910	41,144	355	345	323	1.0	1.0	0.9	240	42	12
Korea, North	n.a	n.a	n.a	n.a.	n.a.	n.a.	n.a.	n.a.	n.a.	1,106	4,700	189
Korea, South	17,463	21,504	24,645	361	442	505	2.6	2.7	2.8	687	4,500	5
Laos	11	12	13	2	2	2	0.5	0.4	0.4	29	0	100
Malaysia	2,742	3,110	3,206	117	130	131	2.3	2.4	2.1	109	52	25
Mongolia	17	17	19	6	6	7	1.0	0.9	0.8	9	137	7
Myanmar	5,889	6,944	6,920	127	148	147	15.6	18.8	18.7	406	0	107
New Zealand	1,221	1,449	1,544	306	359	379	1.2	1.3	1.5	9	0	0
Papua New Guinea	24	30	30	4	5	5	0.6	0.7	0.6	3	2	0
Philippines	825	1,375	909	10	16	10	0.9	1.4	0.8	106	0	131
Singapore	5,102	5,578	6,321	1,172	1,260	1,407	4.8	4.8	4.8	73	313	94

Table 37 International Comparisons of Defence Expenditure and Military Manpower, 2004–2006

current US$ m	US$ m			Defence Expenditure per capita US$			% of GDP			Number in Armed Forces (000)	Estimated Reservists (000)	Paramilitary (000)
	2004	2005	2006	2004	2005	2006	2004	2005	2006	2008	2008	2008
Taiwan	7,542	7,978	7,738	332	348	336	2.3	2.2	2.2	290	1,657	17
Thailand	1,954	2,021	2,275	31	31	35	1.2	1.1	1.1	306	200	114
Timor Leste	n.a.	n.a.	n.a.	n.a.	n.a.	n.a.	n.a.	n.a.	n.a.	1	0	0
Vietnam	2,781	3,153	3,439	34	38	41	6.1	6.0	5.6	455	5,000	40
Total[3]	194,806	219,368	241,421	64	69	72	1.47	1.50	1.53	6,422	17,962	2,600
Caribbean, Central and Latin America												
Caribbean												
Antigua and Barbuda	4	5	5	65	70	70	0.5	0.5	0.5	0.17	0.075	0
Bahamas, The	34	36	40	113	119	132	0.6	0.6	0.7	0.86	0	0
Barbados	24	25	25	85	90	89	0.8	0.8	0.7	0.61	0.43	0
Cuba	1,276	1,416	1,660	113	125	146	4.0	4.0	4.0	49	39	27
Dominican Republic	153	273	256	17	30	28	0.7	0.8	0.7	50	0	15
Haiti	n.a.	n.a.	n.a.	n.a.	n.a.	n.a.	n.a.	n.a.	n.a.	2.7	n.a	2.7
Jamaica	53	56	57	20	21	21	0.6	0.6	0.6	3	0.953	0
Trinidad and Tobago	70	64	52	65	59	48	0.6	0.4	0.3	3	0	0
Central America												
Belize	16	16	18	58	57	63	1.5	1.5	1.5	1	0.7	0
Costa Rica	98	95	99	25	24	24	0.5	0.5	0.4	0	0	10
El Salvador	106	106	106	16	16	16	0.7	0.6	0.6	16	10	12
Guatemala	98	90	146	8	7	12	0.4	0.3	0.4	16	64	19
Honduras	52	53	55	7	7	8	0.7	0.6	0.6	12	60	8
Mexico	2,876	3,123	3,229	27	29	30	0.4	0.4	0.4	249	40	31
Nicaragua	32	34	35	6	6	6	0.7	0.7	0.7	14	0	0
Panama	140	158	171	45	50	54	1.1	1.0	1.0	0	0	12
South America												
Argentina	1,629	1,780	1,873	42	45	47	1.1	1.0	0.9	76	0	31
Bolivia	148	147	156	17	17	17	1.7	1.6	1.4	46	0	37
Brazil	9,612	13,281	16,206	52	71	86	1.4	1.5	1.5	368	1,340	386
Chile	3,424	4,143	4,677	216	259	290	3.6	3.5	3.2	65	50	38
Colombia	3,971	4,937	5,377	94	115	123	4.0	4.0	4.0	254	62	144
Ecuador	588	593	653	45	44	48	1.9	1.8	1.9	57	118	0.4
Guyana	n.a.	n.a.	n.a.	n.a.	n.a.	n.a.	n.a.	n.a.	n.a.	1	0.67	2
Paraguay	52	58	67	8	9	10	0.7	0.8	0.7	11	164	15
Peru	923	1,097	1,108	34	39	39	1.3	1.4	1.2	114	188	84
Suriname	22	21	20	49	49	44	1.9	1.6	1.3	2	0	0

Table 37 International Comparisons of Defence Expenditure and Military Manpower, 2004–2006

current US$ m	US$ m			Defence Expenditure per capita US$			% of GDP			Number in Armed Forces (000)	Estimated Reservists (000)	Paramilitary (000)
	2004	2005	2006	2004	2005	2006	2004	2005	2006	2008	2008	2008
Uruguay	188	240	227	55	70	66	1.4	1.4	1.2	25	0	0.9
Venezuela	1,680	2,454	2,588	67	97	101	1.5	1.7	1.4	115	8	0
Total	**27,267**	**34,300**	**38,908**	**50**	**62**	**70**	**1.29**	**1.33**	**1.30**	**1,551**	**2,146**	**875**
Sub-saharan Africa												
Horn Of Africa												
Djibouti	16	12	17	34	26	36	2.4	1.8	2.3	11	0	1
Eritrea	72	65	n.a.	16	14	n.a.	7.7	6.3	n.a.	202	120	0
Ethiopia	348	300	345	5	4	5	3.6	2.7	2.6	138	0	0
Somali Republic	n.a.	n.a.	n.a.	n.a.	n.a.	n.a.	n.a.	n.a.	n.a.	n.a	n.a	n.a
Sudan	426	453	524	11	11	13	2.0	1.7	1.5	109	0	18
Central Africa												
Burundi	45	50	49	6	6	6	6.6	6.2	5.1	35	0	31
Cameroon	286	222	257	17	13	15	1.8	1.3	1.4	14	0	9
Cape Verde	7	7	7	16	17	17	0.7	0.7	0.6	1	0	0
Central African Republic	15	15	16	4	4	4	1.2	1.1	1.0	3	0	0
Chad	51	56	59	5	6	6	1.1	1.0	0.9	25	0	10
Congo	76	79	84	22	22	23	1.7	1.4	1.2	10	0	2
Democratic Republic of Congo (Zaire)	196	150	163	3	2	3	3.0	2.1	1.9	134	0	0
Equatorial Guinea	7	7	8	13	14	14	0.2	0.1	0.1	1	0	0
Gabon	17	19	21	13	14	15	0.2	0.2	0.2	5	0	2
Rwanda	45	56	72	5	7	7	2.3	2.3	2.4	33	0	2
East Africa												
Kenya	296	353	355	9	10	10	1.8	1.8	1.6	24	0	5
Madagascar	272	269	298	16	15	16	6.2	5.3	5.4	14	0	8
Mauritius	11	10	18	9	8	15	0.2	0.2	0.3	0	0	2
Seychelles	16	13	14	193	157	172	2.3	1.8	2.0	0.2	0	0.25
Tanzania	122	135	143	3	4	4	1.1	1.1	1.2	27	80	1
Uganda	168	196	192	6	7	7	2.2	2.1	1.9	45	0	2
West Africa												
Benin	n.a.	n.a.	47	n.a	6	6	n.a	n.a	1.0	5	0	3
Burkina Faso	74	76	85	6	6	6	1.4	1.3	1.4	11	0	0
Cote d'Ivoire	252	249	266	15	14	15	1.6	1.5	1.5	17	10	0.25
Gambia, The	2	2	2	1	1	1	0.4	0.4	0.3	1	0	0
Ghana	56	76	83	3	3	4	0.6	0.7	0.7	14	0	0
Guinea	82	55	36	9	6	4	2.1	1.7	1.2	12	0	7

Table 37 International Comparisons of Defence Expenditure and Military Manpower, 2004–2006

current US$ m	Defence Expenditure US$ m			Defence Expenditure per capita US$			% of GDP			Number in Armed Forces (000)	Estimated Reservists (000)	Paramilitary (000)
	2004	2005	2006	2004	2005	2006	2004	2005	2006	2008	2008	2008
Guinea Bissau	10	12	13	8	9	9	3.6	3.9	4.0	9	0	0
Liberia	n.a.	n.a.	n.a.	n.a.	n.a.	n.a.	n.a.	n.a.	n.a.	2	0	0
Mali	103	120	132	9	11	11	2.1	2.3	2.2	7	0	5
Niger	32	33	38	3	3	3	1.1	1.0	1.1	5	0	5
Nigeria	572	854	768	5	7	6	0.9	0.9	0.7	80	0	82
Senegal	108	124	149	9	11	12	1.3	1.4	1.6	14	0	5
Sierra Leone	23	24	24	4	4	4	2.1	2.0	1.7	11	0	0
Togo	32	33	34	6	6	6	1.6	1.6	1.6	9	0	0.75
Southern Africa												
Angola	958	1,189	1,588	83	101	132	4.7	3.6	4.7	100	0	10
Botswana	312	305	289	190	186	176	3.4	3.2	3.0	9	0	2
Lesotho	33	35	33	16	17	16	2.4	2.4	2.3	2	0	0
Malawi	13	13	20	1	1	1	0.7	0.6	0.9	5	0	2
Mozambique	70	58	57	4	3	3	1.2	0.9	0.8	11	0	0
Namibia	169	166	197	84	82	96	2.9	2.7	3.0	9	0	6
South Africa	3,132	3,697	3,527	70	83	80	1.4	1.5	1.4	62	0	41
Zambia	122	163	245	11	15	22	2.3	2.3	2.4	15	3	1
Zimbabwe	251	136	156	19	11	13	5.3	2.3	2.8	29	0	22
Total	8,896	9,885	10,433	13	14	14	1.71	1.60	1.51	1,270	213	287
Summary												
US	455,908	495,300	535,943	1,556	1,675	1,796	3.89	3.98	4.05	1,498	1,083	0
NATO Ex-US	253,220	264,665	268,247	448	467	472	1.84	1.82	1.74	2,263	2,622	765
Total NATO	709,128	759,965	804,190	827	881	928	2.78	2.82	2.81	3,761	3,705	765
Non-NATO Europe	18,912	19,376	21,200	137	141	155	1.21	1.15	1.16	556	2,695	255
Russia [1]	59,600	58,000	70,000	414	404	493	4.23	3.72	4.11	1,027	20,000	419
Middle East and North Africa	67,669	74,925	81,760	198	216	231	5.95	5.53	5.26	3,028	2,137	1,002
Central and South Asia	25,784	28,475	29,848	17	19	19	2.74	2.59	2.38	2,486	1,161	1,863
East Asia and Australasia [3]	194,806	219,368	241,421	64	69	72	1.47	1.50	1.53	6,422	17,962	2,600
Caribbean, Central & Latin America	27,267	34,300	38,908	50	62	70	1.29	1.33	1.30	1,551	2,146	875
Sub-Saharan Africa	8,896	9,885	10,433	13	14	14	1.71	1.60	1.51	1,270	213	287
Global totals [4]	1,112,062	1,204,293	1,297,759	175	188	199	2.63	2.64	2.66	23,862	53,724	8,831

[1] PPP estimate.
[2] Defence expenditure figure includes PPP estimates and extra budgetary expenditure. Per capita and % of GDP figures refer to the official budget only, converted at *official exchange rates*.
[3] Regional defence expenditure total includes PPP estimates and extra budgetary expenditure for China. Per capita and % of GDP totals are calculated using China's official budget only converted at official exchange rates.
[4] Global defence expenditure totals includes PPP estimates. Global per capita totals and % of GDP totals include China's official budget only, converted at *official exchange rates*.

Table 38 Arms Deliveries to Developing Nations
Leading Recipients in 2006
(current US$m)

1	Saudi Arabia	4,100
2	China	2,900
3	Israel	1,500
4	Egypt	1,400
5	Taiwan	1,000
6	India	800
7	Chile	800
8	Venezuela	700
9	South Korea	600
10	Malaysia	500

Table 39 Arms Transfer Agreements to Developing Nations
Leading Recipients in 2006
(current US$m)

1	Pakistan	5,100
2	India	3,500
3	Saudi Arabia	3,200
4	Venezuela	3,100
5	Algeria	2,100
6	Israel	2,100
7	Brazil	1,100
8	Iraq	900
9	Indonesia	600
10	South Korea	500

Table 40 Global Arms Deliveries
Leading Suppliers in 2006
(current US$m)

1	United States	14,008
2	Russia	5,800
3	UK	3,300
4	Germany	1,000
5	China	700
6	Canada	600
7	France	400
8	Netherlands	300
9	Israel	200
10	Spain	200
11	Sweden	200

Table 41 Global Arms Transfer Agreements
Leading Suppliers in 2006
(current US$m)

1	United States	16,905
2	Russia	8,700
3	Ukraine	3,100
4	Germany	1,900
5	Israel	1,700
6	Austria	1,500
7	Sweden	1,100
8	Italy	900
9	China	800
10	Spain	700
11	Netherlands	600

Table 42 Value of Global Arms Deliveries and Market Share by Supplier 1999–2006 (constant 2006US$m – % in italics)

	Total	US		Russia		UK		France		Germany		Italy		All Other European		China		Others	
1999	45,873	20,678	45.1	4,446	9.7	5,805	12.7	5,064	11.0	2,470	5.4	865	1.9	3,952	8.6	618	1.3	1,976	4.3
2000	37,746	15,182	40.2	5,041	13.4	6,481	17.2	3,880	10.3	1,440	3.8	240	0.6	3,481	9.2	1,080	2.9	1,920	5.1
2001	30,758	10,504	34.2	5,471	17.8	4,423	14.4	2,212	7.2	698	2.3	582	1.9	3,608	11.7	1,048	3.4	2,212	7.2
2002	30,446	11,276	37.0	4,083	13.4	5,104	16.8	1,588	5.2	1,361	4.5	567	1.9	3,176	10.4	1,021	3.4	2,269	7.5
2003	33,486	11,733	35.0	4,772	14.3	4,883	14.6	2,664	8.0	2,220	6.6	444	1.3	4,218	12.6	777	2.3	1,776	5.3
2004	33,959	12,336	36.3	5,917	17.4	2,904	8.6	5,701	16.8	1,936	5.7	215	0.6	1,721	5.1	968	2.9	2,259	6.7
2005	26,204	11,955	45.6	3,224	12.3	3,016	11.5	2,288	8.7	624	2.4	312	1.2	2,080	7.9	936	3.6	1,768	6.7
2006	27,008	14,008	51.9	5,800	21.5	3,300	12.2	400	1.5	1,000	3.7	100	0.4	1,200	4.4	700	2.6	500	1.9

Table 43 Value of Global Arms Transfer Agreements and Market Share by Supplier, 1999–2006 (constant 2006US$m – % in italics)

	Total	US		Russia		UK		France		Germany		Italy		All Other European		China		Others	
1999	43,372	14,225	32.8	6,299	14.5	1,853	4.3	1,976	4.6	4,940	11.4	865	2.0	7,040	16.2	3,582	8.3	2,594	6.0
2000	45,587	20,983	46.0	8,041	17.6	720	1.6	5,521	12.1	1,440	3.2	240	0.5	4,921	10.8	720	1.6	3,000	6.6
2001	35,720	31,371	87.8	6,518	18.2	698	2.0	4,889	13.7	1,397	3.9	1,280	3.6	3,143	8.8	1,397	3.9	3,026	8.5
2002	32,063	14,822	46.2	6,466	20.2	794	2.5	567	1.8	1,134	3.5	454	1.4	4,991	15.6	454	1.4	2,382	7.4
2003	31,685	16,147	51.0	4,994	15.8	666	2.1	2,775	8.8	1,665	5.3	666	2.1	2,331	7.4	555	1.8	1,887	6.0
2004	41,710	13,634	32.7	5,809	13.9	6,885	16.5	2,367	5.7	1,829	4.4	645	1.5	6,992	16.8	753	1.8	2,797	6.7
2005	46,322	13,457	29.1	7,488	16.2	2,912	6.3	8,320	18.0	1,768	3.8	1,456	3.1	6,032	13.0	2,600	5.6	2,288	4.9
2006	40,305	16,905	41.9	8,700	21.6	3,100	7.7	500	1.2	1,900	4.7	900	2.2	5,200	12.9	800	2.0	2,300	5.7

US DoD Price Deflator. All data rounded to nearest $100m. Source: Richard F. Grimmett, Conventional Arms Transfers to Developing Nations 1999-2006 (Washington DC: Congressional Research Service)

Table 44 Arms Deliveries to Middle East and North Africa, by Supplier
(current US$m)

1997–2002	US	Russia	China	Major West European*	All other European	Others	Total
Algeria		400	200		400	100	1,100
Bahrain	500						500
Egypt	4,500	200	200	100	100		5,100
Iran		400	100			400	900
Iraq					100	100	200
Israel	3,300			900		100	4,300
Jordan	200			100		100	400
Kuwait	1,300	100	200	600		200	2,400
Lebanon							–
Libya		100			200	100	400
Morocco				100	200		300
Oman					100		100
Qatar				200			200
Saudi Arabia	8,900			15,200	2,900	100	27,100
Syria		200		100	100		400
Tunisia							–
UAE	200	300		2,700	400	100	3,700
Yemen		200	100	100	100	200	700

2003–2006	US	Russia	China	Major West European*	All other European	Others	Total
Algeria		500	100				600
Bahrain	300			100			400
Egypt	5,100	100	300		200	100	5,800
Iran		300	200		100	100	700
Iraq					200	200	400
Israel	5,200	100			100		5,400
Jordan	400				100	100	600
Kuwait	900		200				1,100
Lebanon							–
Libya		100			100		200
Morocco	100	100		100		100	400
Oman	600			300			900
Qatar							–
Saudi Arabia	4,400			13,500	700	100	18,700
Syria		300				200	500
Tunisia							–
UAE	600	200		5,400	200	200	6,600
Yemen		400			100	100	600

* Major West European includes UK, Germany, France, Italy

All data rounded to nearest $100m

Source: Richard F. Grimmett, Conventional Arms Transfers to Developing Nations 1999–2006
(Washington DC: Congressional Research Service)

Chapter Ten

2007 in review: major developments in the European and US defence industries

Europe's largest defence manufacturers have undergone important changes over the past year, while their US counterparts enjoyed another year of booming business and rising profits as a result of substantial Pentagon spending on the acquisition of equipment and services.

Significant alterations were made to the governance and management structure of the **European Aeronautic Defence and Space Company (EADS)**, owner of the aircraft manufacturer Airbus. EADS had been put together in 2000 as a French–German–Spanish political construct in reaction to expansion by the UK's BAE Systems. Its major shareholders are Daimler of Germany with 22.5% and the French state with 15%, with France's Lagardère holding 7.5% and SEPI of Spain 5.5%. Remaining shares are traded on the stock market, from where state-controlled Vneshtorgbank of Russia acquired 5% in 2006. On establishment, EADS was carefully structured to reflect a balance between French and German interests: it had co-chairmen and co-chief executives from each country. While this double-headed system may have been useful, and was perhaps even necessary in the early days, the shared management was widely seen as too cumbersome and an obstacle to the creation of a streamlined, effective, transnational company.

Two factors forced change. First, the company's main operating unit, Airbus, ran into production difficulties with its new A380 passenger aircraft, as well as other problems, resulting in losses that all but wiped out EADS's profits in 2006 and the first half of 2007. The company rushed to make management changes at Airbus and to introduce an efficiency programme that would include the disposal of many factories. Secondly, Nicolas Sarkozy, who had attempted to alter the structure of EADS during a previous tenure as finance minister, was elected president of France in May 2007. Sarkozy immediately broached the subject with German Chancellor Angela Merkel.

Germany continued to block any changes that would tilt the French–German balance in EADS. However, in July the two government leaders met in Toulouse, home to Airbus, and agreed that EADS would have a single chairman (Rüdiger Grube of Germany), and a single chief executive (Louis Gallois of France), and that the other then co-chief executive, Germany's Thomas Enders, would become chief executive of Airbus. These moves, as well as changes to the company's board, were widely welcomed as steps towards more efficient management of EADS and Airbus. However, further challenges loomed, including implementation of the Airbus cost-savings programme, an investigation over alleged insider trading in EADS shares, and a delay to the Airbus A400M military transport aircraft.

INDUSTRY CONSOLIDATION

The French firm **Thales**, Europe's leading defence electronics company, also experienced structural change during the year. The company acquired the space interests of Alcatel-Lucent in a deal approved by the European Commission in April. Alcatel-Lucent received an increased stake in Thales – rising to 21% from 9.5% – in part-payment. At the same time, the French state's holding fell from 31.3% to 27.3%. Thales continued to look for opportunities to expand, and in a separate step to consolidate France's naval industries, it acquired 25% of the shipyard group **DCN** in March 2007, with the remainder still held by the French state. The French government's aim was to trigger a broader consolidation of European naval shipyards, a goal which has long been elusive and may remain so, with national concerns and jobs given precedence.

Similar national consolidation moves were under way between British naval yards, at the behest of the UK Ministry of Defence (MoD). **Babcock International**, which operates the Rosyth and Faslane naval repair and refit yards in Scotland, acquired the Devonport Royal Dockyard in southwest England in June 2007 for some £350m. Devonport's former majority owner, KBR (formerly Kellogg Brown & Root) of the US, was obliged to sell after the MoD objected to the November 2006 spin-off and stock market flotation of KBR by its parent company, Halliburton. Devonport is deemed a 'strategic asset' by the UK, and is important to the MoD as it houses a dry dock in which nuclear submarines are to be refitted and refuelled. Lord Drayson, formerly the UK minister for defence procurement, sought guarantees about the future financial condition of KBR, and asked that the share offering be delayed until such guarantees had been received. However, the company went ahead with its plans and the sale of Devonport, effectively forced due to the ministry's concerns, was the result.

The other major naval base and shipyard, at Portsmouth in the south of England, will form part of a broader restructuring of Britain's naval shipyards, also ordered by the MoD. The Defence Industrial Strategy, a policy document published in December 2005, had said that 'consolidation should occur as a matter of urgency'. Drayson made clear that contracts for the construction of two new aircraft carriers would not be signed until the industry had been rationalised. Accordingly, the two warship builders **BAE Systems** and **VT Group** (formerly Vosper Thornycroft) announced in July 2007 that they would combine their surface shipbuilding activities – BAE owns the Scotstoun and Govan shipyards in Glasgow, Scotland, as well as the submarine construction yard at Barrow in northwest England, and VT has a yard for the construction of smaller warships at Portsmouth. The new joint venture will manage all these yards except Barrow, as well as fleet support at Portsmouth, with the aim of achieving substantial savings for the MoD that will justify the retention of the base. In return, the partners are to have a 15-year partnership agreement with the MoD providing a defined future workload for design, construction and through-life support of surface vessels. In announcing the order for the aircraft carriers in July 2007, the government detailed that sections of the two vessels – which at some 65,000 tonnes' displacement will be the largest-ever Royal Navy vessels – would be built at all the yards, and assembled at Babcock's Rosyth facility. The design is provided by Thales, and discussions continued on France's plans to build a carrier to the same design.

Its future presence in naval shipbuilding thus apparently confirmed, **BAE Systems,** Europe's biggest defence company, meanwhile continued to build its global businesses in the land systems area – and to expand its rapidly growing presence in the United States. It has diversified considerably away from its past concentration on military aircraft construction and now provides equipment, sub-systems and services to all branches of military forces, especially in the US.

Having acquired United Defense, makers of the *Bradley* fighting vehicle, in 2005, BAE Systems bought Armor Holdings for about $4.5 billion in 2007. Armor Holdings, which had previously bought the vehicle maker Stewart & Stevenson, added considerably to the range of products that the group – in competition with General Dynamics and other suppliers – could offer the US Army as it sought to acquire substantial numbers of Mine-Resistant Ambush Protected vehicles. BAE Systems also won sizeable contracts for the refurbishment and upgrade of *Bradleys*.

There were several other significant developments for the UK-based company. In June 2007, BAE Systems announced the appointment of a committee of external experts headed by Lord Woolf, formerly the UK's lord chief justice, to 'review and evaluate the company's policies and processes – and their application – relating to ethics and business conduct'. This followed the controversial decision by the UK Serious Fraud Office, at the government's request, to drop an investigation into company payments to Saudi Arabia, a major customer. Then Prime Minister Tony Blair said that failure to abandon the inquiry would have led to 'the complete wreckage of a vital strategic relationship and the loss of thousands of British jobs'. Nine months after the decision was announced, Saudi Arabia signed in September 2007 a contract to buy 72 Eurofighter *Typhoon* aircraft for £4.4bn – a deal that will bring considerable benefit not only to BAE Systems but also to EADS, **Finmeccanica** of Italy and many other European companies.

In addition to the Saudi order for Eurofighter *Typhoons*, several large international procurements have reached important milestones over the past year. Nine countries signed up to the production, sustainment and follow-on development phase of the $300bn F-35 *Lightning* II Joint Strike Fighter programme: the United States, United Kingdom, Italy, the Netherlands, Turkey, Canada, Australia, Denmark and Norway. The UK committed to this phase after prolonged wrangles over technology transfer appeared to be resolved.

In October 2007, the UK government chose a partnership between Thales and Boeing to be the systems integrator for a planned family of some 3,000 medium-weight armoured vehicles, called the Future Rapid Effects System. It was, meanwhile, evaluating three vehicles for the utility vehicle role: the German–Dutch *Boxer*, the General Dynamics *Piranha*, and the VBCI from Nexter (formerly GIAT Industries) of France. Trials were held in mid year, and a decision on the utility-variant designer was due later in November.

US DEVELOPMENTS

BAE Systems' purchase of Armor Holdings was the largest corporate deal of the year in the US, where the defence mergers and acquisitions market tends to be more active than in Europe. Among other transactions, **ITT Corporation** announced plans to acquire EDO Corporation, a maker of defence electronic systems, for $1.7bn, and **Textron** agreed to acquire AAI Corporation, a maker of unmanned aerial vehicles, for $1.1bn.

Meanwhile, the largest US defence companies concentrated on their healthy business with the US Department of Defense, where acquisition spending continued to be boosted by defence-budget increases and supplementary budget appropriations arising from military operations in Iraq and Afghanistan. **Lockheed Martin**, **Boeing**, **Northrop Grumman**, **Raytheon** and **General Dynamics** all reported higher profits, revenues and profit margins for the first half of 2007, and all continued to receive a steady flow of new contract awards. The bountiful nature of the current US defence budget was illustrated by the fact that some of the funding for the Joint Strike Fighter – which remains years from full production – was included in a 2007 emergency supplemental request (see US defence economics, p. 24). Companies continued to be cautious in their forecasts, in anticipation of a spending slowdown which so far has not yet materialised. Apart from acquisitions of new equipment, the defence industry has been boosted by replacement, repair and improvements to equipment used on operations – especially by ground forces – and by rapid growth in operational support services.

Customers continued to signal, however, that they wanted significant improvements in industrial performance and efficiency. The US Navy cancelled Lockheed Martin's contract to build a second prototype of the Littoral Combat Ship, as the projected cost rose by more than half. Separately, the US Coast Guard reduced the role of a Northrop Grumman–Lockheed Martin joint venture which had been appointed in 2002 to manage its Deepwater modernisation programme. It said it could acquire 12 fast-response cutters – one of a number of purchases within the $24bn programme – more cheaply than could the joint venture.

SIGNS OF TRANSATLANTIC INTEGRATION

Several US procurement decisions indicated that the climate for European companies seeking transatlantic business could be improving after the political difficulties of recent years. Following the selection in 2005 of a US version of Finmeccanica's AgustaWestland EH-101 as the presidential Marine One helicopter, the US Army in 2006 chose the UH-72A, a version of the EC145 produced by the Eurocopter unit of EADS, as its Light Utility Helicopter. Deliveries began immediately, with the potential for up to 322 purchases. The US Coast Guard, as part of its Deepwater programme, ordered five more EADS CASA HC-235A multi-mission aircraft, bringing orders so far to eight. The US Army chose the C-27J, produced by the Alenia Aeronautica division of Finmeccanica, as its new cargo aircraft, with an order for 78. Thales won a large US order for software-defined handheld radios. Meanwhile, the US Air Force's impending decision on in-flight refuelling tankers, delayed following an earlier procurement scandal involving Boeing and Pentagon officials, loomed large as a test for the US defence prospects of EADS, as its Airbus A330 competed with the Boeing 767 for an initial order for 80 aircraft.

These procurements drew attention to the chronically difficult market conditions facing foreign competitors in the US market, where overseas companies must often work through US companies to win orders – for example, Lockheed Martin is prime contractor for the Marine One helicopters and L-3 Communications for the C-27J aircraft. They are also subject to many other restrictions. Although British companies such as BAE Systems and **Rolls-Royce** have been successful in building US portfolios, and can deal directly with their customers, they too have to work within security restrictions.

In June 2007, significant progress was made with the agreement of a Defence Trade Cooperation Treaty between the United Kingdom and United States. Under this, a trusted community of official bodies and commercial contractors would be able to trade goods and information between the two countries without obtaining export licences. The US and Australia signed an equivalent treaty immediately afterwards. Both have still to be ratified, and could face opposition in the US Congress. While details needed clarification, the agreements, if ratified, seemed likely to end a long campaign for a British waiver to the US International Traffic in Arms Regulations (ITAR), since companies within the trusted community would no longer need to seek licences under ITAR, at least for some types of goods. However, the prospects for such arrangements being extended to the other European countries with large defence industries seem limited for the time being.

A EUROPEAN STRATEGY?

European nations have for years pondered how to create a streamlined defence industry that could both compete on the world stage and meet Europe's capability needs as efficiently as possible. Many obstacles have stood in the way: protection of national interests, cultures, industries and technologies; security of supply concerns; failure to harmonise equipment requirements; bureaucratic wrangling and inertia; and the sheer difficulty of merging companies across borders. During 2007, the European Union added its weight to the argument as its European Defence Agency (EDA) began to develop a strategy to strengthen the continent's defence technological and industrial base (DTIB). The chairman of a meeting of the EDA's ministerial steering board, at which a series of steps were agreed in September, said: 'Ministers have recognised that individual member states can no longer sustain their separate DTIBs on a purely national basis, and that we need to specialise and become more dependent on each other at a European level'. Among the areas of future action the EDA identified were: identification of key industrial capabilities; security of supply; increased competition in the defence equipment market; deepening and diversifying the supplier base; and improved armaments cooperation.

While the record of the past suggested that such an initiative was likely to make only slow progress, there were indications of political support – vital for success – in the two biggest defence-spending countries. Britain, which has been trying hard to implement its Defence Industrial Strategy, has been working on an updated version. President Sarkozy of France signalled his intention to propel the debate when he said at the Paris Air Show in June that Europe must have a defence industrial strategy that should be 'neither in thrall to nor opposed to the rules of competition'. He said: 'Europe can no longer afford the luxury, with its combined defence budgets still well below that of the US, of having five surface-to-air missile programmes, three combat aircraft projects, six attack submarine programmes and about 20 armoured vehicle programmes'. He called the *juste retour* work-sharing formula 'a poison which hinders and weakens the implementation of European ... programmes'.

Meanwhile, Europe's defence manufacturers will wait to see whether the future behaviour of their customers, whose fragmented capability hinders genuine industrial rationalisation, will match the political rhetoric. More effective coordination of customers' requirements would facilitate the creation of a more streamlined industry meeting European rather than national needs, and would enable governments to deliver better value for their taxpayers' money.

More from the IISS on defence industries

'Russia's Defence Industry – Phoenix from the Ashes?', IISS *Strategic Comments*, vol. 13, no. 8, October 2007.
'Britain's Defence-Industrial Strategy – Radical Remedies?', IISS *Strategic Comments*, vol. 12, no. 1, February 2006.
'Consolidating Europe's Defence Industries – Big Rewards, Big Obstacles', IISS *Strategic Comments*, vol. 11, no. 4, June 2005.
Kapstein, Ethan B., 'Capturing Fortress Europe: International Collaboration and the Joint Strike Fighter', *Survival*, vol 46. no. 3, Autumn 2004, pp. 137–60.
The Military Balance, all years.
Strategic Survey 2007, Strategic Survey 2006.

Chapter Eleven
Unmanned aerial vehicles: current developments and future utility

While unmanned vehicles have been used for civilian and military purposes on land, sea and air for many years, the recent proliferation in the type, employment and utility of unmanned aerial vehicles (UAVs) has served to heighten attention on these platforms. Traditionally often used in a reconnaissance role, UAVs – directed by operator input or using autonomous control – are showing increasing potential for integration with front-line combat forces, and are viewed as having increasing utility as combat platforms. Globally, it is expected that more than 9,000 UAVs will be purchased over the next ten years, and spending on these technologies in the US alone is scheduled to increase from $4 billion in the 1990s to $14bn between 2001 and 2010. Currently, at least 32 countries are developing more than 250 models of UAV, and 38 countries already operate such systems. However, these emerging technologies are not without their drawbacks: development costs, as well as operating costs, can be substantial; personnel savings may be more imagined than real; and a rise in the numbers and sophistication of platforms means more supporting infrastructure, such as communications bandwidth, is needed.

FROM KOSOVO TO AFGHANISTAN AND IRAQ

In 1999, the US, France, Germany, Italy and the UK employed UAVs to an unprecedented extent during operations over Kosovo. In many cases used in a reconnaissance and target identification role, the aircraft proved increasingly useful for NATO military planners, often providing controllers with real-time information. On 12 June 1999, for example, staff in the Combined Air Operations Centre in Italy saw, via a camera in a UAV, previously hidden Serb MiG-21s taking off from Pristina airfield before the Russians arrived. However, issues such as the time taken for a decision to engage and direct assets on to an identified target (the 'sensor-to-shooter time'), as well as UAV vulnerabilities, provided valuable lessons. NATO lost upwards of 40 UAVs during the 78-day air operation to enemy action and tech-

nical failure. As the majority of UAVs were based in the Former Yugoslav Republic of Macedonia, Serb defenders could plan on them approaching at no more than 100 knots from a limited number of directions. It was therefore relatively easy to position guns and surface-to-air missiles (SAMs) under likely flight paths. Nonetheless, these 40 UAV losses meant around 40 fewer lives were at risk, which meant in turn that fewer resources for rescuing downed aircrew were required and the risk of political difficulties arising from searches for missing pilots, or the display of captured pilots, was reduced.

Coalition forces deployed in Afghanistan in 2001 to dislodge the Taliban regime used UAVs in novel ways, particularly against moving or mobile targets. Former US Air Force (USAF) chief of staff General John Jumper tired of UAV sensors finding a target, only for the quarry to escape because no strike aircraft were nearby. The US defence department decided to test the *Predator* UAV with *Hellfire* missiles during *Operation Enduring Freedom*. On one occasion a *Predator* supplied real-time video pictures of a night-time Taliban convoy stopping at a hotel, enabling nearby F-15s to attack the building. The *Predator* then tracked fleeing Taliban vehicles and destroyed them with its own *Hellfires*. (Video images from *Predator* were relayed to General Tommy Franks, then-commander of US Central Command in Florida, who authorised the *Hellfire* strikes.) However, it is worth remembering that Taliban and al-Qaeda fighters had virtually no air defences, and that the basic *Predators* proved to be slow, vulnerable with no on-board self-protection and prone to icing in winter.

The way in which around 100 US UAVs were employed during the opening stages of *Operation Iraqi Freedom* in 2003 reflected the lessons of operations in the Balkans and Afghanistan. UAVs had been in Iraqi skies before 2003. On 26 December 2002, an Iraqi MiG-25 fired two missiles at a *Predator*, shooting it down. The *Hellfire*-equipped *Predators* were then fitted with *Stinger* air-to-air missiles to confer limited air-defence capability. Older-model *Predators*, stripped of their expensive sensor systems, were deployed in the initial phase of the campaign as bait to attract SAM lock-on for subsequent targeting by coalition suppression of enemy air defence (SEAD) assets. Besides the long-endurance reconnaissance role, UAVs were used in the hunt for mobile missile launchers and high-value individuals: when UAVs observed a building housing a reported Ba'ath Party gathering, strikes were executed using Joint Direct Attack Munitions (JDAMs).

CURRENT DEVELOPMENTS

Some elements of coalition ground forces in Iraq now use a miniature UAV called *Desert Hawk* for aerial surveillance. The small, 3kg remote-controlled aircraft, made essentially from expandable polypropylene, is launched by a bungee cord and controlled through a portable computer system. Security forces in Iraq use *Desert Hawk* as part of a comprehensive programme, in cooperation with foot patrols, aimed at disrupting insurgent and terrorist activity. Between 750 and 800 remotely piloted aircraft are, as of late 2007, operating over Iraq and Afghanistan. One *Global Hawk* (effectively the UAV version of the U2 aircraft) operates in the Persian Gulf region while about two dozen of the USAF's 90-plus *Predators* are flying in the two countries. The 20.1m-wingspan MQ-9 *Reaper* (also known as *Predator* B), the first USAF hunter-killer UAV, or unmanned combat aerial vehicle (UCAV), is designed to pursue time-sensitive targets and destroy or disable them with munitions such as 500lb bombs and *Hellfire* missiles. (In contrast to the *Reaper*, the MQ-1 *Predator* A has a wingspan of 14.8m.) On 9 November 2006 the USAF became the first service to establish an attack squadron equipped with *Reapers*, at Creech Air Force Base, Nevada. At the same time, the UK's Royal Air Force (RAF) is standing up its first UCAV squadron comprising one flight with armed MQ-1L *Predator* As and one with a pair of MQ-9As, although the latter will not initially carry weapons. For the UK, these Platforms will fill the gap between the man-portable *Desert Hawk* on the tactical level and manned Airborne Stand-Off Radar Sentinel Intelligence, Surveillance and Reconnaisance platforms at the strategic level. The RAF deployed MQ-9A to Afghanistan in late 2007, with two air vehicles and one ground station. These are an interim solution until the UK's *Watchkeeper* UAV, with electro-optical/infrared (EO/IR) and Synthetic Aperture Radar (SAR) sensors, enters service from 2010. *Watchkeeper* is based on the Israeli *Hermes* 450; such is the value of UAVs in Iraq that, since 20 June 2007, Elbit *Hermes* 450 UAVs procured under an Urgent Operational Requirement are now delivering imagery support to British personnel in southern Iraq.

In July 2007, Northrop Grumman's X-47B *Pegasus* beat Boeing's X-45C to win the US Navy's UCAS-D development contract. At a cost of over $70 million each, *Pegasus* is designed to survive on long-range strike, surveillance, SEAD and electronic-attack missions over hostile airspace. The X-47B has a single non-afterburning F100 engine and 7,700kg internal fuel capacity, giving it twice the range of the F-35C, the naval variant of the Joint Strike Fighter. With airborne refuelling, *Pegasus* could remain airborne for 50 hours or more. It is due to carry two 2,000lb JDAMs and few of its systems will differ from those of manned aircraft. The first *Pegasus* is scheduled to fly in late 2009. It will begin a series of detailed flight envelope and land-based carrier integration and qualification events beginning in 2010, with the first actual at-sea carrier landings planned for late 2011.

While UCAS-D is clearly an ambitious project, it can be argued that historically the US Navy (USN) has been slow to develop and introduce UAVs, particularly when compared to the air force. The first to enter the arena were tactical systems such as the *Pioneer*, primarily used by the US Marine Corps. However, as doctrine, concepts of operations and development programmes have progressed, UAVs are increasingly seen as a force multiplier in the littoral and maritime environment. Current projects under development include Northrop Grumman's *Firescout* vertical take-off and landing UAV. This project has moved from the systems-development and demonstration phase and has now entered initial low-rate production for the USN. *Firescout* is specifically designed to operate in support of the Littoral Combat Ship; operational tasks include real-time video imagery collection, intelligence gathering, communications-relay, precision targeting and battle damage assessment. Arming studies on *Firescout* are underway, with a number of options under consideration, including a range of laser and electro-optical guided missiles and rocket systems. To meet the need for 'persistent surveillance' the navy's Broad Area Maritime Surveillance programme will deliver a fleet of unmanned long-range maritime intelligence, surveillance and reconnaissance air vehicles. The USN is evaluating both

Global Hawk and marinised versions of *Predator* B to deliver this capability.

Meanwhile, UAVs are proving useful away from formal combat zones. After the December 2004 Indian Ocean tsunami, Indian military UAVs were pressed into service to help search dogs find bodies resting in jungles and among urban rubble. *Global Hawks* will soon be flying homeland-defence and counter-drug missions over the US, while in late 2007 UAVs were operating in support of fire-fighting activities in California. Meanwhile, as noted in the IISS *Strategic Survey 2007* (p. 73), high-altitude UAVs 'are increasingly able to fill some of the roles of satellites, including communications and remote sensing'; geostationary communications relay and reconnaissance UAVs would be significantly cheaper to build and launch than their satellite equivalents. Further uses could include monitoring or carrying out tasks in dangerous environments, such as zones subject to high levels of radiation, or carrying payloads that could be injurious to the health of a pilot, such as directed-energy weapons. But the military utility of UAVs garners the greatest attention. US Air Combat Command tasked a *Global Hawk* to fly on an official mission for the first time in November 2006. The USAF, which is expected to purchase a total of 54 *Global Hawks*, plans to deploy them to combatant commands, including Pacific Command and European Command, by 2010.

TECHNOLOGICAL POTENTIAL

Current technical programmes under way around the world have the potential to revolutionise UAV design and application. The US defence department's Defense Advanced Projects Research Agency has a Morphing Aircraft Structures programme, which has the objective of advancing 'high-performance aircraft concepts designed to change shape substantially during flight to create multi-point optimized, aerodynamically and structurally efficient, state-changing aircraft'. Indeed, presuming progress in these technological programmes, one can conceive that by 2050 UAVs shaped for endurance will monitor national borders, changing shape into swifter-moving attack craft when programmed or ordered to intercept an intruder. They may also be built with self-repairing materials capable of detecting flaws, and sealing holes during flight; work on self-healing technology is also underway in the US. The world's smallest UAV is currently the

Table 45 **UAV Capability**	
Region	**Countries**
North America	Ca, US
Caribbean & Latin America	Ury
NATO Europe	Be, Bg, Cz, Da, Fr, Ge, Gr, It, Nl, Pl, Por, R, Tu, UK
Non-NATO Europe	Swe, CH, SF
Russia	RF
Middle East and north Africa	Et, Ir, Il, RL
Sub-Saharan Africa	Mor, RSA
Central and south Asia	Ind, Pak, Sgp, Ska
East Asia and Australasia	PRC, Mal, DPRK, Pi, ROK, ROC, Th

See individual country entries for further information

15cm-long electrically powered *Black Widow*. It can fly for 30 minutes and download live colour video from its onboard camera to the ground. Future UAVs that depend on stealth and miniaturisation may well dominate the battlespace. Capitalising on advancements in microcircuits and nanotechnology, small UAVs launched by hand could be used as sensors, to mark targets for precision air strikes, and to detect radiological, chemical or biological contamination. Other developments could provide submarines with a UAV-based reconnaissance capability, while UAVs might also act as virtual mobile-phone towers, providing a battlefield or famine-relief effort with temporary communications coverage.

Meanwhile, in 2005, 'The U.S. Air Force Remotely Piloted Aircraft and Unmanned Aerial Vehicle' strategic vision paper noted that 'the Air Force should begin examining the feasibility and practicality of unmanned cargo delivery and air refueling systems'. In August 2006, Boeing demonstrated for the first time the ability of a UAV – in this case a modified Learjet – autonomously to maintain a steady refuelling station behind a KC-135R tanker; some analysts believe that such automated UAV refuelling systems could be operational by 2020.

PERSISTENCE

The ability of UAVs to remain in the air for substantial periods, or 'persistence', is one of the prime benefits of the developing technology. The UK has signed a four-year, £124m deal with a consortium to design the *Taranis* UCAV, a *Hawk* trainer-size jet capable of delivering weapons to a battlefield in another continent with a 'fully integrated autonomous intelligent system'. The aircraft could remain in the air for more than 24 hours, a far higher degree of persistence in hostile airspace than than can be achieved with conventional fast jets. A decision will be taken around 2010 on whether such a large UCAV will form part of the UK's Future Combat Air Capability programme, alongside current and upgraded manned fighters.

The French Air Force is also considering whether to adopt a UCAV from 2020 as a replacement for its last *Mirage* 2000s and to complement the Dassault *Rafale*. It is pushing for a pan-European project known as *Système de Combat Aérien Futur - Europe*. One technology demonstrator for this project, the Dassault-led *Neuron*, continues towards a first flight scheduled for 2011, under a contract signed in February 2006. The *Neuron* demonstrator measures 10m long by 12m wide and weighs 5 tonnes. The aircraft is scheduled to have unmanned autonomous air-to-ground attack capabilities with precision-guided munitions, relying on an advanced stealth airframe that reduces radar and infrared cross-sections to penetrate target airspace undetected at a speed of about Mach 0.8. Other payloads, such as reconnaissance devices, are to be validated at a later stage. Another contemplated feature is the ability to control UCAV 'swarm flight' in automatic mode with an advanced fighter like the *Rafale* or JAS-39 *Gripen* grouping and controlling the *Neurons*. The *Neuron* programme is led by the Délégation Générale pour l'armement (DGA), the French defence procurement agency. DGA acts as the programme executive on behalf of the participating countries, and has entrusted development of the first *Neuron* demonstrator to Dassault Aviation and its European partners. These include SAAB (Sweden) in particular, HAI (Greece), Alenia (Italy), EADS-CASA (Spain), and RUAG Aerospace (Switzerland). According to Dassault Aviation, the French government will provide half of the €400m ($480m) programme budget, while the remaining funds will be supplied by the other participating member nations.

Future UAVs employing stealth and miniaturisation will be able to 'perch and stare' for long periods. QinetiQ's project *Zephyr* is little more than a flying wing, 18m wide and covered in solar cells. The cells power small propellers and charge batteries that will keep the craft flying at night. *Zephyr* is being developed for long missions, three to six months in duration, and to fly at extreme altitudes – around 20km – conducting surveillance tasks currently undertaken by manned U2 aircraft.

In September, *Zephyr* exceeded the official world-record time for the longest-duration unmanned flight, with a 54-hour flight over New Mexico.

RELIABILITY

UAV designers and engineers will have to meet robust performance and reliability targets before politicians and civil aviation authorities will allow them wider freedom to operate. Only 66% of UAV missions over Kosovo were completely fault free. Since 11 September 2001, upwards of 30 *Predators* have been lost in Iraq and Afghanistan to bad weather, pilot error, enemy fire or mechanical failure. The UAV squadron at Balad airbase in Iraq generated over 175 combat sorties and 3,279 flying hours in June 2007 but lost two MQ-1 *Predators* in two days in August. Hostile activity did not appear to be a factor in either case. And once jet-powered UAVs become as reliable as manned aircraft, and are equipped with systems to enhance self-protection in regions where air superiority is not assured, the cost differential between UAVs and manned platforms, often seen as the chief benefit of UAVs, may be narrowed.

COORDINATION

The possibility of 'swarm flight', as with the Dassault *Neuron* discussed above, underlines the importance of command and control developments under the rubric of 'network-centric warfare'. During *Operation Iraqi Freedom* there were helicopter–UAV de-confliction incidents where a UAV strayed above its designated airspace and a helicopter, avoiding ground fire, stayed below. The proliferation of UAVs, and manned fixed- and rotary-wing assets, has led to increasingly crowded airspace: in November 2004 a 2kg US Army *Raven* surveillance UAV collided with a *Kiowa* scout helicopter, causing no injuries or serious damage but raising safety concerns.

A sense-and-avoid capability is required to prevent mid-air collisions. Standards for sense-and-avoid have been suggested by Eurocontrol, the European Organisation for the Safety of Air Control, and are being developed for regulation by the US Federal Aviation Administration, but sense-and-avoid requirements and capabilities for use in NATO-controlled airspace do not exist. NATO is studying the various sense-and-avoid systems in development, as well as prospects for using these systems in civil aviation, with the hope of then setting a NATO standard for air operations. One option might be for Automatic Dependent Surveillance-Broadcast to be used above 5,000m, while the Sense-and-Avoid Display System would be best for high-density low-altitude airspace (where tactical UAVs and helicopters operate), with Laser Obstacle Avoidance Monitoring best employed for beyond-line-of-sight low-density low-altitude airspace.

A solution to the lack of standard communications frequencies, waveforms and sensor suites among UAVs, highlighted by combat experience, may be a standard package for collecting and disseminating information, plus data-link technology that can share information among aircraft, satellites and other networks. BAE Systems has successfully networked ground and surveillance radars with UAVs, fusing the information from dispersed ground and airborne sensors into a single battlespace picture visible across numerous systems in real time. The technology, known as Decentralised Data Fusion, was recently demonstrated during a series of flight trials in Australia. It effectively networked eight separate pieces of equipment: two UAVs which were operating autonomously; a ground surveillance radar; a weapons-locating radar which was detecting live artillery firing at fixed and mobile targets; two soldiers in the field with electronic binoculars and palm-top computers; and two soldiers moving through the battlefield in vehicles.

LIMITATIONS

UAVs have become victims of their own success, with military staffs adding more sensor packages and extending the range of missions. *Global Hawk*, the top-of-the-range unmanned reconnaissance vehicle, has gone from a base cost of $10m in 1994 to its present cost of $28.2m with basic SAR and EO/IR sensors. The projected cost of *Global Hawk* by 2007–11 with upgraded EO/IR and SAR plus a signals intelligence package is $43.1m. The key factors behind this cost escalation are the sensor suites and the continual addition of requirements. When costs for all aircraft, ground stations, support equipment and spares are taken into account, procurement costs have soared to $130.5m for each *Global Hawk*.

Success in future operations will rely on the successful passage of real-time information, yet a single *Global Hawk* consumes five times the bandwidth used by the entire US military contingent deployed in 2001 during *Operation Enduring Freedom* in Afghanistan. The bandwidth available to US forces in *Operation Iraqi Freedom* was 42 times higher than in *Desert Storm* and will likely increase by a similar factor in the not-too-distant future. In part this will result from the fact that UCAVs of the UCAS-D calibre will have to pass much more information to personnel on the ground than the manned F-22 or B-2. If UAVs are to provide a large part of deployed forces' reconnaissance, surveillance and target acquisition, they need a large amount of bandwidth to send sensor data to the reach-back locations for analysis, as well as to the local commanders for their situational awareness. When the analysis is complete, bandwidth is then needed to push the important sensor findings back to the theatre. Bandwidth is a finite resource and needs careful management. In the 2001 *Enduring Freedom* campaign in Afghanistan, the approximately 17,000 US forces in theatre used 700 megabytes (MB) of bandwidth, or about 42 kilobytes (KB) per person. Now NATO is planning for 60MB of bandwidth for about 8,000 NATO personnel, or about 7.7KB/person of capability. This reduction in capability is seemingly at odds with the likely draws on bandwidth needed to enable the reach-back centres to contribute effectively to the activities of forward-deployed forces.

Meanwhile, the manpower savings that UAVs bring are sometimes overestimated. While a *Predator* can orbit for 20 hours, it requires two crew operating for eight hours each – a total of six crew per *Predator* – and that is just the operator budget. The analysts, datalink managers, engineers in the deployed location and the further crews required to launch and recover in-theatre mean that current unmanned aircraft operations are deceptively manpower intensive. A *Predator* squadron requires as many personnel as a fast jet unit. Furthermore, in future those operating UAVs remotely may never have experienced actual combat in a manned platform. Coupled with the difficulty of assessing a fast-moving operational environment through systems and video-screen displays, the simplicity of 'drag and drop' computer-based operations serve to lessen the operator's understanding of the combat environment experienced by those serving on the ground.

The great appeal of UAVs was once political, as well as financial. In 2001, the US Senate Armed Services Committee noted that 'the American people are coming to expect that military operations are casualty-free'. But in the midst of operations in Iraq, Afghanistan and elsewhere, there has perhaps been a revision in this judgement: as of 21 September 2007, the Pentagon had confirmed 3,792 military fatalities in Iraq. Given this possible change in perception, UAVs may well have to justify their place on merit. Although unit costs may presently be below many manned platforms, such cost differences may narrow as systems presently found on manned aircraft are further integrated into UAVs. The rising costs of UAV systems, coupled with their increasing technological sophistication and that of related infrastructure, mean that these aircraft must be complementary to the forces of the proposed purchaser and affordable, with procurement driven by operational and strategic requirements.

PART TWO
Non-State Groups

Table 46 Non-State Activity Reference

Place	Activity	Groups/Trends	Reference
Caribbean, Central and Latin America			
Colombia, Ecuador	Insurgency	FARC, border insecurity	p. 57
Europe			
Turkey	Terrorism, separatism	PKK, cross-border attacks	p. 106
Russia			
Russia, N. Caucasus	Crime, insurgency, separatism	Chechen rebels, violence in Ingushetia	p. 208
Middle East and North Africa			
Iraq	International terrorism	al-Qaeda, insurgency	p. 225
Iraq	Opposition to foreign presence	Mahdi Army, internecine conflict	p. 226
Israel/Lebanon	Terrorism	Hizbullah	p. 230
Israel/Palestine	Domestic terrorism	Hamas	p. 231
Sub-Saharan Africa			
Nigeria	Militias	Niger Delta, oil production	p. 278
Somalia	Anti-transitional govt.	Union of the Islamic Courts (UIC) militias	p. 277
Sudan	Opposition to Government	JEM	p. 273
Sudan	Opposition to Government	SLA-Unity, AMIS and UN	p. 273
Sudan	Opposition to Government	SPLM	p. 273
Central and South Asia			
Afghanistan	Insurgency	Taliban, insecurity spreading beyond the Afghan borders	p. 326
Pakistan	Terrorism	Local Taliban and al-Qaeda forces in FATA	p. 332
Sri Lanka	Separatism, Terrorism	LTTE, renewed violence	p. 333
East Asia and Australasia			
Philippines	Crime, Terrorism	Actions against ASG	p. 365
Philippines	Separatism	MILF-ASG attack in July	p. 366
Thailand	Insurgency, separatism	Attacks in the south continue	p. 365

Table 47 **Selected Non-State Groups and Affiliates**

Definition

In this table, a 'non-state group' is an organised force, which may be armed, has a recognised political or ideological goal, and acts independently from state or government, but may have the support of a state. Groups are only included if they are assessed as having an effective structure. The definition mostly covers groups that might be variously described as guerrilla, militia, or paramilitary. They may be terroristic or engage in criminal violence. Some may be non-violent in their declared aims but may engage in radical propagandist activity likely to lead to violence.

Notes A active, **C** cease-fire, **D** dormant (inactive for the past 12 months)

Origin	Organisation * aka	Estb.	Est. Strength	Status	Operates	Aims and Remarks
North America						
US	18th Street Gang/Mara 18	1960s	n.k	A	EIS, Mex, US	Organised crime, turf wars; predominantly Hispanic org
US	Hizb ut-Tahrir in America	1993	n.k.	A	New York, Orange County, Chicago and Milwaukee	Similar ideology to Hizb ut-Tahrir (see UK)
US	Mara Savatrucha (MS-13)	1980s	8–10,000	A	EIS, Gua, Hr, US, C. America	Criminal; originated from Pico Union in Los Angeles, spread through US and C. America
Caribbean and Latin America						
Chl	Frente Patriotico Manuel Rodriguez – Dissidente (FPMR-D) / Manuel Rodriguez Patriotic Front Dissidents	1983	50-100	D	Chl	Communist party that sought to overthrow the regime of Augusto Pinochet; splinter grp continued violent campaign after 1989
Co	Autodefensas Unidas de Colombia (AUC) / United Self-Defense Forces of Colombia	1997	10,000	A/C	N. and N.W. Co	Protect the Co govt from guerrilla movements; umbrella organization for right-wing paramilitaries; close financial connections to drug cartels
Co	Ejercito de Liberación Nacional (ELN) / National Liberation Army	1964	3,000	A	Bol, N., N.E., and S.W. Co	Anti-US 'Maoist-Marxist-Leninist' grp, equality for the rural poor by instituting popular democracy; peace talks with govt since 1999
Co	Ejercito Popular de Liberación (EPL) / Popular Liberation Army	1967	500	A	Co	Rid Co of 'US imperialism' and indigenous oligarchies, creation of communist state
Co	Ejercito Revolucionario del Pueblo (ERP) / People's Revolutionary Army	1990s	350	A	Co	Previously ELN faction, shares communist beliefs
Co	Ejército Revolucionario Guevarista (ERG) / Guevarist Revolutionary Army	1993	100	A	Antioquia, Choco, Risralda	Socialist revolution; ELN faction
Co	Fuerzas Armadas Revolucionarias de Colombia (FARC)/ Revolutionary Armed Forces of Colombia	1964	12,000+	A	Co	Overthrow current democratic govt and replace with communism; exerts controls over drug protection industry
Ec	Grupos de Combatientes Populares (GCP) / People's Fighters Group	1994	n.k.	A	Ec	Opposes govt's economic policies, oligarchs and 'traitors'; militant branch of Ec's Marxist-Leninist Communist Party
Ec	Izquierda Revolucionaria Armada / Armed Revolutionary Left	2004	n.k.	A	Ec	Anti-govt; commercial and political targets
Ec	Milicias Revolucionarias del Pueblo (MRP) / People's Revolutionary Militias	n.k.	n.k.	A	Ec	Anti-globalisation, insurrection against current Ec govt, anti-US war in Iraq
Mex	Los Zetas	late 1990s	100	A	Mex	Control drug trade through Mex to the US
Mex	Popular Revolutionary Army (ERP)	1996	n.k.	A	Mex	Overthrow Mex govt; has agitated for better conditions for the rural poor and coordinates armed insurgent grps in Mex
Pe	Movimiento Revolucionario Túpac Amaru (MRTA) / Túpac Amaru Revolutionary Movement	1983	100	A	Upper Huallaga river valley	Estb Marxist regime and seeks to rid Pe of 'imperialist elements'; less active since Pe govt's 1999 counter-terrorist ops

Table 47 Selected Non-State Groups and Affiliates

Origin	Organisation * aka	Estb.	Est. Strength	Status	Operates	Aims and Remarks
Pe	Sendero Luminoso (SL)/Shining Path	1960s	500	A	Upper Huallaga and Ene river valleys	Estb peasant revolutionary regime in Pe based on communist ideals, control of coca-producing regions; less active since Pe govt's 2000 counter-terrorist ops
RH	Armée Cannibale/Revolutionary Artibonite Resistance Front (RARF) / National Revolutionary Front for the Liberation of Haiti	2003	n.k.	A	RH	Anti-Aristide, seeks to gain control of RH; informal alliance of Armée Cannibale, anti-govt gangs, and former soldiers of the disbanded RH army
Ve	Las Autodefensas Unidas de Venezuela (AUV) / United Self-Defense Forces of Venezuela	2002	n.k.	A	Tachira	Anti-leftist govt and Communism; Ve version of AUC
Europe						
Alb	Albanian National Army (ANA) / Armaj Kombetare Shiqitare (AKSh)	1999	n.k.	A	Kosovo; FYROM	Insurgent Alb grp for united Alb state, most membership from the disbanded KLA and NLA
Alb	Hakmarrje per Drejtesi / Vengeance for Justice	Early 1990s	n.k.	A	Alb	An organised armed and criminal grp associated with the former communist special services in Alb; aims to revive old communist status quo
Alb/Ser/ Mnt	n.k.	1990s	n.k.	A	Tu; Alb; FYROM, Kosovo; Ser; Mnt; BiH; Cr; and most EU countries	A large number of hierarchical organised criminal grps whose main aim is financial profit
Bg	VIS-1/VIS-2	1991-92	n.k.	D	Bg	An organised criminal grp founded as a private security company (VIS-1) and later transformed into insurance company (VIS-2)
BiH	Convicts' Brigade	1992	n.k.	D	BiH; Cr	Annex Croat-populated parts of BiH to Cr (during the 1990s wars in the Balkans)
BiH	New BiH / Nova BiH	n.k.	n.k.	A	BiH	Unitary BiH state comprising a Muslim majority and Serb and Cr minorities (assumed)
Da	n.k.	n.k.	n.k.	A	Da	On 4 Sept 2007 police arrested 9 men suspected of planning attacks
Fr	Armata Corsa	1999	30+	A	Corsica	Self determination for Corsica, transfer of detained terrorists back to Corsica, end of organised crime in Corsica
Fr	Clandestini Corsi	2004	n.k.	A	Corsica	Rid Corsica of foreigners, stop drug trafficking on Corsica
Fr	Front de Libération Nationale de la Corse (FLNC) / National Liberation Front of Corsica	1976	600	A	Corsica	Leftist grp for Corsican indp, preserve Corsican language and culture
FYROM	Ushtria Cliirimtare e Kosoves (UCK) / Kosovo Liberation Army (KLA)	1992/03	5–12,000+	D	Kosovo	Loose grp desiring autonomy for Kosovars, eventual unifcation with other Albs
FYROM	Ushtria Cliirimtare Kombetare (UCK) / National Liberation Army (NLA)	1999-01	2–3,000+	D	FYROM	Greater Albania, overlapping membership with AKSh, KLA, UCPMB, not to be confused with Kosovo's UCK
Ga	Abkhaz separatist regime	early 1990s	1,500+	C	Abkhazia	Separate, indp Abkhazia, protection of Abkhaz culture from Ga dominance
Ga	South Ossetian separatist regime	early 1990s	n.k.	C	S. Ossetia, Ga	Seeks an indp S. Ossetia
Ga	White Legion and Forest Brothers	1997	2–300+	D	Abkhazia, Ga	Ga grp destabilising Abkhazia

Table 47 Selected Non-State Groups and Affiliates

Origin	Organisation * aka	Estb.	Est. Strength	Status	Operates	Aims and Remarks
Ge	n. k.	n.k.	n.k.	A	Ge	Two failed bomb attacks on trains in Koblenz and Dortmund, seven arrests
Gr	Epanastatiki Pyrines / Revolutionary Nuclei (RN)	1983	100	A	Athens	Remove US influence, anti-govt
Gr	Epanastatikos Aghonas / Revolutionary Struggle	2003	n.k.	A	Athens	Anti-capitalist grp, similar ideology to RN
It	Brigate Rosse/Partito Comunista Combattente (BR/PCC) / New Red Brigades / Communist Combatant Party	1984	50	A	It	Opposed to It's foreign and labour policies, anti-NATO
It	Federazione Anarchia Informale (FAI) / Informal Anarchist Federation	2003	n.k.	A	It	Anarchist grp, opposes current 'European order'
It	Fronte Rivoluzionario per il Comunismo (FRC) / Revolutionary Front for Communism	1996	n.k.	A	It	Marxist-Leninist grp, anti-globalisation
It	Mafia – Ndrangheta clan	1991	10,000	A	S. It; International	End of the Pelle-Vottari clan, conducts international violence and crime. Carried out assassinations in Germany. Accused of trafficking nuclear waste
It	Nuclei di Iniziativa Proletaria Rivoluzionaria (NIPR) / Revolutionary Proletarian Initiative Nuclei	2000	12+	A	It	Opposes It's foreign and labour policies, supports Marxist-Leninist ideology
It	Nuclei Proletari per il Comunismo (NPC)/Proletarian Combatant Groups /Proletarian Nuclei for Communism	2003	n.k.	A	It	Marxist class-struggle, seeks creation of anarchist state, anti-imperialist grp
It	Nuclei Territoriali Anti-imperialisti (NTA) / Anti-Imperialist Territorial Nuclei	1995	20	A	N. It	Opposes US and NATO, condemns It's foreign and labour polices
Kosovo (UN)	Vetevendosje / Self-Determination	after 2000	n.k.	A	Kosovo	Radical ethnic Alb movement; indp Kosovo state free of UN administration; oppose decentralisation
Moldova	Transnistrian separatist regime	1992	7,500	A	Transnistria	Separate state of Transnistria
Ser	Liberation Army of Presevo, Medvedja and Bujanovac (UCPMB)	2000	800	D	Presevo Valley; Ser; W. and N. FYROM	Annex Kosovo for ethnic Albs
Ser/Mnt	The Surcin Group	1990s	n.k.	A	Ser; Mnt; W. Europe	An organised criminal grp based in the Belgrade suburb of Surcin; profit-making
Sp	Euskadi ta Askatasuna (ETA)	1959	300	A	Basque regions	Indp homeland on Marxist principles in Basque autonomous regions; declared permanent cease-fire Mar 2006. Broke ceasefire 2007
Sp	Grupos de Resistencia Antifascista Primero de Octubre/ First of October Antifascist Resistance Group (GRAPO)	1975	20	A	Sp	Replace govt in Sp with Communist regime
Swe	Global Intifada	2002	n.k.	A	Swe	Leftist grp opposed to capitalism, imperialism and current world order
Tu	Front Islamique des Combattants du Grand Orient / Great Eastern Islamic Raiders Front (IBDA-C)	1970s	100	A	Tu	Advocates 'uncorrupted Islamic rule' in Tu and rejects current regime; Sunni Salafist grp
Tu	Partiya Karkaren Kurdistan (PKK)/People's Congress of Kurdistan (Kongra-Gel)	1978	3,000	A	N. Ir; N. Irq; Syr; Tu	Revolution to free Kurdish people and estb indp Kurdish state; Marxist-Leninist, in 1999 'peace initiative' claimed halt to use of force; terminated cease-fire in June 2004

Table 47 Selected Non-State Groups and Affiliates

Origin	Organisation * aka	Estb.	Est. Strength	Status	Operates	Aims and Remarks
Tu	People's Defence Forces/Hêzên Parastina Gel (HPG)	n.k.	3,000+	A	Tu	Militant wing of the People's Congress of Kurdistan
Tu	Revolutionary People's Liberation Party-Front/ Devrimci Halk Kurtuluş Partisi/Cephesi (DHKP-C)	1978	1,000	A	Tu; Asia; Europe	Marxist grp opposed to the US and to NATO; seeks 'revolution'
Tu	Teyrbazen Azadiya Kurdistan (TAK) / Kurdistan Freedom Hawks	2004	n.k.	A	Tu	Opposes Tu's policies on the Kurdish issue, targets businesses and govt installations; separatist grp
Tu	TKP/ML-TIKKO/Turkiye Komunist Partisi/Marksist-Leninist-Turkiye Isci Koylu Kurtulus Ordusu	1972	1,000	A	Tu	Communist, anti-Western grp; TKP/ML changed name to the Maoist Communist Party (MKP) and TIKKO changed name to the People's Liberation Army (HKO) in Jan 2003
Tu	Turkish Hizbullah	1994	200+	A	Tu	Estb indp Islamic state
UK	Al Muhajiroun/The Emigrants	1996	n.k.	n.k.	UK; Irl	Islamist grp emerging after the split of Hizb-ut-Tahrir (Islamic Party of Liberation), notorious for praising 9/11; officially disbanded on 13 Oct 2004; al-Firqat un-Naajiyah/ The Saved Sect (aka The Saviour Sect) and al-Ghurabaa/The Strangers are believed to have emerged from al Muhajiroun
UK	Continuity Irish Republican Army (CIRA)/Continuity Army Council	1994	30	A	UK; Irl	Reunify Irl, opposed Sinn Fein's adoption of the July 1997 cease-fire
UK	Irish National Liberation Army (INLA)/People's Liberation Army (PLA)/People's Republican Army (PRA) /Catholic Reaction Force (CRF)	1975	50	C	UK; Irl	Unified Irl with Marxist-Leninist political and social infrastructures, remove British forces from N. Irl and unite it with Irl; armed wing of Irish Republican Socialist Party
UK	Irish Republican Army (IRA)/Official Irish Republican Army (OIRA)	1922	250	D	UK; Irl	Unite N. Irl with the Republic of Irl; declared end to 'armed struggle' 28 July 2005 including PIRA
UK	Loyalist Volunteer Force (LVF)/Red Hand Defenders	1996	300	C	UK; Irl	No political settlement with nationalists in N. Irl, maintain strong ties with UK; UVF faction
UK	Movement for Islamic Reform in Arabia (MIRA)	1996	n.k.	A	UK	Aims to counter domestic problems associated with the ruling al-Saud family
UK	Orange Volunteers	1970s	25	C	UK; Irl	No political settlement with nationalists in N. Irl; destabilise peace process
UK	Provisional Irish Republican Army (PIRA) / Provos	1969	300+	D	International; UK; Irl	Remove British forces from N. Irl, unite N. Irl with Republic of Irl. Declared end to 'armed struggle' 28 July 2005
UK	Real Irish Republican Army (RIRA)/True IRA	1997	200	A	UK; Irl	Unification of Irl, opposed Sinn Fein's adoption of July 1997 cease-fire; armed wing of 32 County Sovereignty Committee
UK/Mor	Secret Organisation Group of al-Qaeda of Jihad Org in Europe/Abu Hafs al-Masri Brigade	2004-05	n.k.	A	UK; Irl	Ideologically opposed to Western culture; possibly resp for July 2005 London bombings
UK	Ulster Defence Association (UDA)/Ulster Freedom Fighters (UFF)	1971	200+	A	UK; Irl	Protect Loyalist community, backed the 1998 Good Friday Agreement; largest loyalist para-military grp in N. Irl, armed wing of Ulster Democratic Party. Said that it would put its 'arms beyond use' on 11 Nov 07
UK	Ulster Volunteer Force (UVF)/Protestant Action Force/ Protestant Action Group	1966	150+	C	UK; Irl	Safeguard N. Irl's constitutional position within UK, protect Loyalist community; armed wing of Progressive Unionist Party
Russia						
RF	Chechen Rebels	n.k.	2–3,000	A	Chechnya, Dagestan	Indp state (Muslim mercenaries), some demands for an Islamist state

Table 47 Selected Non-State Groups and Affiliates

Origin	Organisation * aka	Estb.	Est. Strength	Status	Operates	Aims and Remarks
RF	Chyornyye Vdovy (Black Widows)	1999	30+	A/D	Chechnya	Female suicide bombers for Chechen indp, avenge death of relatives in the Chechen conflict
RF	Ingush Mujahideen	2007	n.k.	A	Ingushetia, Chechnya	Similar aims to other N. Caucasus grps
RF	Islamic International Peacekeeping Brigade (IIPB)	1998	400	A	Chechnya; Az; Ga; Tu	Withdrawal of RF forces from Chechnya, fully indp Chechen state; members participated in the Oct 2002 Dubrovka theatre attack in Moscow
RF	Islamist Terror Group/Jama'at Yarmuk	2004	n.k.	A	N. Caucasus	Autonomous N. Caucasus region; resp for Nalchik bombing in 2005
RF	Jama'at of Dagestan 'Shariat'/Shariah Jama'at/Dzhenet	2004	n.k.	A	Dagestan	Separatists seeking indp for Dagestan
RF	Mujahideen of Kabardino-Balkaria	2007	n.k.	A	N.Caucasus	Pro-radical Islam
RF	Nogai Jamaat	1997	n.k.	A/D	Stavropol, Shelkovskii district, Nogaiskii district, parts of Karachaevo-Cherkessia, Chechnya	Assist in the 'Caucasus resistance movement'; aid ethnic Chechen grps
RF	Riyadus-Salikhin Reconnaissance and Sabotage Battalion of Chechen Martyrs (RSRSBCM)	2002	50	A	Chechnya	Withdrawal of RF forces from Chechnya
RF	Silence Association / Amanat Jama'at	n.k.	n.k.	A	Chechnya	Wahhabi Chechen separatist grp
RF	Special Purpose Islamic Regiment (SPIR)	1996	100	A	Chechnya; Az; Ga; Tu	Withdrawal of RF forces from Chechnya, indp Chechen state; members participated in the Oct 2002 Dubrovka theatre attack in Moscow
RF	Western Resistance Front	2007	100	A	Ingushetia	Similar aims to other N. Caucasus grps
Middle East and North Africa						
Ag	al-Qaeda in the Maghreb (AQM)	2006–7	n.k.	A	Ag; RIM	Anti-West, suicide tactics, possible ambitions for a pan-Maghreb insurgency
Ag	Armed Islamic Group/Groupe Islamique Armée (GIA)/al-Jama'ah al-Islamiyah al-Musallah	1992	100	D	Ag; RMM	Fundamentalist Islamic state in Ag, refused Jan 2002 peace plan; strength undermined by splinter grps
Ag	Dhamat Houmet Daawa Salafia	n.k.	n.k.	A	Ag	Previously known as Katibat el Ahoual, emerged when leader, Mohammed Benslim, broke away from GIA
Ag	Islamic Salvation Army/Armée Islamique du Salut (AIS)	1992	4,000+	C	Ag	Socialist republic in Ag within framework of Islamic principles; armed wing of Front Islamique du Salut (FIS); cease-fire with govt 1997
Ag	Salafist Group for Preaching and Combat/Groupe Salafiste pour la Prédication et le Combat (GSPC)/aka Group for Call and Combat	1998	500	C	Ag; Cha; Nga; RMM; International	Estb a fundamentalist Islamic state in Ag, attacks Western targets; linked to GIA and AQM
Brn	Islamic Front for the Liberation of Bahrain (IFLB)	1981	n.k.	D	Brn; Ir	Anti-monarchy, restore national parliament; politically active as Islamic Action Party

Table 47 Selected Non-State Groups and Affiliates

Origin	Organisation * aka	Estb.	Est. Strength	Status	Operates	Aims and Remarks
Et	al-Gama'a al-Islamiyya/Islamic Group (IG)	1977	500	A	Afg; Et	Overthrow of the regime of Hosni Mubarak, estb an Islamic state in Et; anti-Western al-Qaeda affiliated members
Et	Al-ikhwān al-muslimūn / Muslim Brotherhood	1928	n.k.	D	International	Promotes Muslim rights and Islam as a way of life; joined Et democratic process; active in armed conflict in Ag, Kashmir and Afg; Sunni
Et	al-Jihad/Egyptian Islamic Jihad/Jihad Group/Islamic Jihad/Vanguards of Conquest	1973	300	A	Cairo, Et; Arg; Pak; RL; Sdn; UK; Ye; International	Islamic state in Et, anti-US and West; merged linked to al-Qaeda in 2001, but retains some indp
Et	Islamic Brigades of Pride	2005	n.k.	A	Et	Anti-US and other 'colonial powers, 'against' oppression of Islamic brothers in Iraq and Palestinian territories'
Et	Takfir Wal Hijra/Excommunication and Exodus	early 1970s	300+	A	Ag; Et; RL; Sdn	Joined with deported Afg/Pak Mujahideen in N. Africa to cleanse society of infidels; offers intellectual inspiration to al-Qaeda and other militant grps; amorphous extremist Wahhabi sect, original grp was Muslim Brotherhood offshoot in Et, resp for death of President Anwar Sadat
Et/Syr	Abdullah Azzam Brigades of al-Qaeda in Syria and Egypt	2004	n.k.	A	Et; HKJ	Claimed responsibility for 2005 USS Ashland and Kearsarge attack at Aqaba HKJ, 2005 Sharm el-Sheikh attacks and 2004 attacks in Taba
HKJ	Jund al-Sham/the Zarqawi Network/Jama'at al-Tawheed wa'Jihad	n.k.	500–1,000	A	HKJ; Irq; Syr; International	Oppose US invasion of Iraq, anti-monarchy in HKJ; Islamist extremist grp
HKJ	Tawhid and Jihad/Jama'at Al-Tawhid Wa'al-Jihad (JTJ)	1990s	n.k.	A	Irq	Overthrow interim govt and expel US Coalition forces, estb Sharia Law
Il	Hilltop Youth/Noar Ha'Gvaot	2000–01	100-	A	Il;PA	Several right-wing dissident youth grps seeking to protect and encourage Jewish settlements, supports 'Avoda Ivrit' (Jewish labour) and wants to exclude Palestinians from the Occupied Territories; suspected of PA school bombing attempts and roads
Il	Kahane Chai/Kach	1990	30+	A	Il; PA	Seeks to restore the biblical land of Il by annexing all disputed territories, forcibly removing Palestinians
Ir	Hizbî Dēmokiratî Kurdistanî Êran / Democratic Party of Iranian Kurdistan (DPKI) / Kurdish Democratic Party of Iran (KDPI)	1995	1,200–1,800	A/D	Ir	Kurdish autonomy in Ir
Ir	Islamic Action in Iraq	n.k.	n.k.	D	Ir; Irq	Previously sought to overthrow the Hussein govt and replace with an Islamic state, reemerged as a legitimate political party in 2003, as the 'Organisation of Islamic Action in Iraq'
Ir	Kurdestan org of the Communist Party of Iran /The Revolutionary org of Working People of Iranian Kurdistan (KOMALA)	1967	200	A	Ir	Communist govt in Ir; formed Communist Party of Ir in 1983
Ir	Movement of Islamic Action of Iraq	1982	n.k.	A/D	Ir; Irq	Shi'ite faction that supported Iran during the Ir-Irq war; possibly still active as Islamic Action in Iraq
Ir	Mujahedin-e Khalq org (MEK or MKO)/ National Council of Resistance (NCR)/National Council of Resistance Iran (NCRI)/People's Mujahedin of Iran (PMOI)	1960	3,000	A	Ir	Advocates secular Muslim regime and NCRI rule

Table 47 Selected Non-State Groups and Affiliates

Origin	Organisation * aka	Estb.	Est. Strength	Status	Operates	Aims and Remarks
Ir	National Liberation Army of Iran (NLA)	1987	6–8,000	A	Ir, Irq	Largest and most active armed Ir dissident grp, armed wing of NCRI or MKO. Forces quarantined in Iraq
Ir	The Arbav Martyrs of Khuzestan	2005	n.k.	A	Ir	Separatist group
Irq	1920 Revolutionary Brigade	2003	n.k.	A/D	W. of Baghdad, Khan Dari, Fallujah, Irq	End of US presence, liberation and Islamic govt for Irq; disbanded into Islamic Conquest and Islamic Jihad/Twentieth Revolution Brigades; Sunni
Irq	Abu Bakr al-Siddiq Fundamentalist Brigades/Abu Bakr al-Siddiq Salafi Brigades	2004	n.k.	A	Irq	Seeks removal of coalition troops from Irq and release of female prisoners from US custody
Irq	Abu Nidal org (ANO)/Fatah Revolutionary Council/ Fatah al-Majlis al-Thawry/Black September /Arab Revolutionary Brigades/Revolutionary org of Socialist Muslims	1974	300	D	International	Destroy Il; ops in LAR and Et shut down by govts in 1999
Irq	Al-Dawa	1968	2,000	A	Irq	Islamic rule in Irq; Shia Muslim fundamentalist grp
Irq	Al-Faruq Brigades/Jihadist Al Faruq Brigades / Media Commission for the Mujahideen in Iraq	2003	n.k.	A	Irq	Nationalist-Islamist grp, militant wing of 'Islamic Movement in Iraq'
Irq	al-Jaish al-Islami fi al-Iraq / Islamic Army in Iraq (IAI) / al-Aqsa Support Division	2005	thousands	A	Irq	Drive coalition forces out of Irq
Irq	Al-Mujahideen Brigades	2004	n.k.	A	Fallujah, Ramadi, Khaldiya, Irq	Oppose US forces in Iraq
Irq	al-Qaeda in Iraq/al-Qaeda Organization in the Land of the Two Rivers/Tanzim Qa'idat al-Jihad fi Bilad al-Rafidayn	2004	n.k.	A	Irq; HKJ	Expel coalition, overthrow Irq govt
Irq	Ansar al-Islam/Jund al-Islam/Army of Supporters of Islam	2001	500	A	Irq	Estb Islamic state in Irq, opposes coalition forces; believed to be broken up by US-led invasion
Irq	Ansar al-Jihad/Supporters of Jihad	2004	n.k.	A	Irq	Seeks release of all prisoners in Irq and termination of armed ops in Fallujah; nationalist-Islamist grp
Irq	Ansar al-Sunnah Army	2002–3	n.k.	A	N. and W. Irq	Opposes US presence in Irq, supports Islamic society in Irq; collection of small Islamist grps including remnants of Ansar al Islam
Irq	Army of the Followers of Sunni Islam/Jaish Ansar al-Sunnah	2004	n.k.	A	Irq	Oppose US-led coalition in Irq
Irq	Badr Org/Badr Corps	1982	10,000	A	S. Irq	Mutual agreement signed with PUK against Irq; armed wing of Supreme Council for Islamic Revolution (SCIRI), Shiite
Irq	Brigades of Imam al-Hassan al-Basri	2005	n.k.	A	Irq	Joined al-Qaeda in Iraq in 2005; Sunni-Islamist grp
Irq	Cells of the People	2006	n.k.	A	al-Anbar, Irq	Against Irq govt and US presence
Irq	Divine Wrath Brigades/Kata'ib al-Ghadab al-Ilahi	2004	n.k.	A/D	Irq	Opposes Irq govt and Western presence; supports Moqtada al-Sadr
Irq	Iraqi Hizbullah	2003	2–300	A	Irq	Opposes US presence in Irq; Shia grp
Irq	Islamic Conquest/Hamas of Iraq	2007	n.k.	A	Irq	Similar aims of parent org: 1920 Revolutionary Brigades

Table 47 **Selected Non-State Groups and Affiliates**

Origin	Organisation * aka	Estb.	Est. Strength	Status	Operates	Aims and Remarks
Irq	Islamic Jihad Brigades of Muhammad's Army/Jaish Muhammed	2003	200+	A	Irq	Coalition of small Islamist grps; opposes US forces, assassinates those it deems as 'collaborators'
Irq	Islamic Jihad/Twentieth Revolution Brigades	2007	n.k.	A	Irq	Jihad, similar aims to 1920 Revolutionary Brigade
Irq	Islamic Resistance Brigades	2004	n.k.	A	Irq	Opposes US presence in Irq
Irq	Islamic State of Iraq (ISI)	2006	n.k.	A	Irq	Islamic state for Irq, anti-West, publishes online instructions of 'how to destabilise a state'. Protect the Sunni Irq people and defend Islam, by the Khalf al-Mutayibeen; alliance of insurgent grps
Irq	Jaish al-Mahdi / Mahdi Army	2003	6–10,000	A	S. and C. Irq	'Defend Shia rights and faith from US invasion', opposes foreign forces
Irq	Jaish al-Taifa al-Mansoura/Army of the Victorious Community	2003	n.k.	A	Irq	Removal of US-led coalition, estb of Sharia law; member of Mujahideen Shura Council
Irq	Mujahideen Shura Council	2006	n.k.	A/D	Irq	'Manage the battle and insurgency against US occupation'; umbrella org for 6+ radical Islamic grps; disbanded 2007, now part of ISI
Irq	Party for Freedom and Life in Kurdistan (PFLK)	n.k.	n.k.	A	N. Irq	Kurdish autonomy in N. Irq, targeted by Ir
Irq	Patriotic National Islamic Front for the Liberation of Iraq	2007	n.k.	A	Irq	End of foreign presence, estb a 'political system with greater equality and freedom'
Irq	Patriotic Union of Kurdestan (PUK)/Yakêti Niştimanî Kurdistan	1975	10,000	A	Irq	'Revitalise resistance and rebuild a democratic Kurdish society;' evolved into a political movement
Irq	Saddam Fedayeen/Saddam's Men of Sacrifice	1995	30,000	A	Irq and N. Irq	Resists US occupation, attacks US interests and people; Ba'athist militia created under Saddam regime
Irq	Saraya al-Shuhuada al-Jihadiyah fi al-Iraq/Jihadist Martyrs Brigades in Iraq	2004	n.k.	A	Irq	Opposes US presence in Irq; Iraqi Islamist grp
Irq	Tha'ar Allah/Revenge of Allah	2003	n.k.	A	Basra, Irq	Opposes US presence in Irq; Shia grp
LAR	al-Jama'at al-Islamiyah al-Muqatilah / Libyan Islamic Fighting Group (LIFG)	1995	300	A	LAR; Middle East	Anti-LAR govt, wage 'international jihad'
Mor	Ansar al-Islam in the Muslim Desert	2007	n.k.	A	Mor	Jihad against govts in the Maghreb, seeks to reacquire historical Muslim lands in Andalucia; anti-Western
Mor	Groupe Islamique Combatant Marocain (GICM) / Moroccan Islamic Combatant Group	1990s	n.k.	A	Afg; Et; Mor; Tu; W. Europe	Estb an Islamic state in Mor, supports al-Qaeda
Mor	Sahrawi People's Liberation Army (SPLA)	1973	3–6,000	C	Mor	Indp Western Sahara; armed wing of the Frente Popular para la Liberacion de Saguia el-Hamra y del Rio de Oro (Polisario Front)
Mor/UK	Salafya Al-Aihadya/Abu Hafs al-Masri Brigade/Assirat Al-Moustakim	n.k.	200–1000	A	Mor; Sp; UK	Jihad against West; loose network of Salafist grps suspected of bombings in Madrid, London and Casablanca
PA	Al-Aqsa Martyrs Brigades	2000	n.k.	A	Il; PA	Create a PA nation state, remove settlers from West Bank, Gaza Strip and Jerusalem; associated with, not officially backed, by former PA leadership
PA	Al-Jabhah al-sha'biyyah li-tahrir filastin / Popular Front for the Liberation of Palestine (PFLP)	1967	1,000	A	Il; PA	Armed struggle against Il; Marxist–Leninist
PA	Al-Quds Brigades/Jerusalem Battalions/Jerusalem Brigades/al-Quds Battalions	late 1970s	n.k.	A	Il; PA; Syr	Militant wing of Palestinian Islamic Jihad

Non-State Groups

Table 47 Selected Non-State Groups and Affiliates

Origin	Organisation * aka	Estb.	Est. Strength	Status	Operates	Aims and Remarks
PA	Al-Saika/Vanguard of the Popular Liberation War	1968	300	A/D	Il; PA	Militant wing of PA faction of Syr Ba'ath Party, nominally part of PLO
PA	Democratic Front for the Liberation of Palestine (DFLP)/Al-Jabha al-Dimuqratiya Li-Tahrir Filastin	1969	100+	A	Il; PA	Achieve PA national goals through revolution; Marxist–Leninist grp which splintered from PFLP
PA	Fatah Tanzim	1995	1,000+	A	Il; PA	Counter-balance to the military wings of Hamas and Palestinian Islamic Jihad
PA	Hamas (Islamic Resistance Movement/Izz al-Din al-Qassam Brigades (IDQ)	1987	500+	A	Il; PA	Estb an Islamic PA state in place of Il
PA	Jabha at-tahrir al-arabiyya / Arab Liberation Front	1969	500	D	Il; PA	Achieve national goals of PA; faction of PLO formed by leadership of Irq Ba'ath party
PA	Palestine Islamic Jihad (PIJ)/Shaqaqi faction/Shalla faction	1970s	500	A	Il; PA	Destroy Il and establish Islamic state in PA
PA	Palestine Liberation Front (PLF)/Jabhat al-Tahrir al-Filistiniyyah	1977	300–400	D	Il; PA	Armed struggle against Il; splintered from PFLP
PA	Palestinian Resistance Committees (PRC)/Salah al-Din Battalions/Salah al-Din Brigades	late 2000	n.k.	A	Il	Claimed responsibility for roadside bombs, suspected in 2003 attack on US embassy employees; composed of members from PIJ, Hamas, Al-Aqsa Martyrs Brigade
PA	Popular Front for the Liberation of Palestine – General Command (PFLP–GC)	1968	500	D	Il; PA; RL; Syr	Armed struggle against Il; Marxist–Leninist, split from PFLP to focus on fighting rather than politics
RL	Ansar Allah/Followers of God	1994	n.k.	A	RL	Ideological ties with Hizbullah, similar aims
RL	Asbat al-Ansar/League of Partisans	1990's	300	A	RL	Advocates Salafism, opposed to any peace with Il, estb Sunni Islamic state in RL
RL	Hizbullah (Party of God)/Islamic Jihad/Revolutionary Justice org/Org of the Oppressed on Earth	1982	2,000	A	Bekaa Valley, Beirut; LAR; Arg; Br; Py; S. RL; S. America	Ir-style Islamic republic in RL, remove all non-Islamic influence; Shi'ite, formed to resist Il occupation of S. RL with political representation in Lebanese Assembly; some cells operate internationally
Sau	Al-Haramain Brigades	2003	n.k.	A	Sau	Anti-monarchy in Sau, implement Sharia, expel the West
Sau	al-Qaeda in the Arabian Penninsula (AQAP)	2004	n.k.	A	Sau	Linked to al-Qaeda
Tn	Tunisian Combatant Group/Groupe Combattant Tunisien/Jama'a Combattante Tunisien	2000	n.k.	A	Afg; W. Europe	Creation of an Islamic state in Tn, anti-US grp
Ye	al-Houthi rebels	2004	n.k.	A	Sa'ada province; Ye	Overthrow Ye govt, anarchy; affiliated with Zaidi Muslims
Ye	Islamic Army of Aden (IAA)/Aden-Abyan Islamic Army (AAIA)/Jaysh Adan-Abiyan al-Islami	1998	30	D	S. Ye	Overthrow of the Ye govt and conduct ops against US and other Western interests in Ye, Salafist
Ye	Yemeni Islamic Jihad	1990's	200+	A	Ye	Establishment of Sharia law in Ye and opposes Western intervention; al-Qaeda affiliated Islamist grp of ex-Afghan Mujahideen
Ye/Afg	al-Qaeda in Yemen	2000	n.k.	A	Ye	More radical than traditional insurgents in Ye; anti-West, estb Sharia law in Ye

Table 47 Selected Non-State Groups and Affiliates

Sub-Saharan Africa

Origin	Organisation * aka	Estb.	Est. Strength	Status	Operates	Aims and Remarks
Ang	Frente de Libertacao do Enclave de Cabinda – Forcas Armadas de Cabinda/ Front for the Liberation of the Enclave of Cabinda – Armed Force of Cabinda (FLEC–FAC)	1980s	300	C	Cabinda, Ang	Indp of Cabinda region; grew from FLEC in the 1980s
Ang	Frente de Libertacao do Enclave de Cabinda – Renovada (FLEC–Renovada)/Front for the Liberation of Cabinda – Renewed	1980s	250	C	Cabinda, Ang	Indp of Cabinda region; grew from FLEC in the 1980s
Ang	União Nacional para a Independencia Total de Angola (UNITA)/National Union for the Total Independence of Angola	1966	5,000	C	Ang; DROC; Nba	Strive for govt proportionally representative of all ethnic grps, clans and classes; peace agreement with govt April 2002
Bu	Forces pour la Défense de la Démocratie (FDD)/Forces for the Defence of Democracy	1994	16–20,000	A	Bu; DROC; W. Tz	Restore constitution and institutions set by 1993 elections and form national army; to be disarmed under Lusaka Peace Accord but continues attacks against Bu govt, believed involved in DROC conflict; armed wing of National Council for the Defence of Democracy
Bu	Parti pour la Libération du Peuple Hutu (Palipehutu)/ Forces for National Liberation	1980	2–3,000	A	Bu; Tz borders	Liberate Hutus and estb ethnic quotas based on 1930s Be census; armed wing of Forces Nationales de Libération
CAR	Armee populaire pour la restauration de la Republique de la democratie - Popular Army for the Reconstruction of the Republic and Democracy (APRD)	2005	700–1000	A	Ouham-Pende, Ouham and Nana-Grebizi provinces, CAR	Call for political dialogue and aim for the improvement of the security situation in CAR N.W.
CAR	Front Democratique du Peuple Centrafricain (FDPC)	2005	n.k.	C	N.W. CAR	Similar aims to APRD
CAR	Mouvement Patriotique pour la Restauration de la Republique Centrafricaine (MPRC)	2005	n.k.	D	Bossangoa, CAR	Overthrow of President Francois Bozize
CAR	Union des forces democratiques pour le rassemblement - Union of Democratic Forces for Unity (UFDR)	2006	150–200	C	Vakaga and Bamingui-Bangoran Provinces, N.E. CAR	Protest against President Bozize's exclusionist policy, and corruption; demands a power-sharing agreement or that Bozize step down
CAR	Union des Forces Republicaines (UFR)	2005	n.k.	A	Paoua, CAR	Protect villages from attacks by the army and Presidential Guards
CAR	Zaraguinas / Coupeurs de route	n.k.	n.k.	A	Cha and Crn border areas; CAR	Armed banditry with no clear political agenda; composed of CAR and Cha nationals
Cha	Mouvement pour la Démocratie et la Justice au Tchad (MDJT) /Movement for Democracy and Justice in Chad	1998	n.k.	C	Tibesti region, N. Cha	Overthrow Cha govt; peace agreement with govt Dec 2003
Cha	The Platform for Change, Unity and Democracy/Socle pour le Changement, l'Unité et la Démocratie (SCUD)	2005	n.k.	A	E. Cha	Anti-govt, seeks to exert control over E. Cha
CI	Forces Nouvelles/New Forces	2003	20–26,000	A	Bouake, Man, Danane, N. CI	Coalition of MPCI, MPIGO and MJP
CI	Front pour la Liberation du Grand Ouest/The Front for the Liberation of the Great West (FLGO)	2002	7,000	A	Guiglo, Toulepleu, W. CI	Pro-Gbagbo militia

Non-State Groups

Table 47 Selected Non-State Groups and Affiliates

Origin	Organisation * aka	Estb.	Est. Strength	Status	Operates	Aims and Remarks
CI	Front pour la securite du Centre-Ouest/Front for the Security of the Centre-West (FSCO)	2002	14,000	A	Gagnoa	Pro-Gbagbo militia
CI	Groupe des patriotes pour la paix/The Group of Patriots for Peace (GPP)/Convention des Patriotes pour la Paix (CPP)/Front de Liberation Nationale (FLN)	2002	6,000	A	S. CI	Umbrella org made up of half a dozen pro-govt militias
CI	Mouvement patriotique de Côte d'Ivoire/Patriotic Movement of Côte d'Ivoire (MPCI)	2002	10,000	C	Bouake, Korhogo, N. and C. CI	Overthrow President Gbagbo; represents disgruntled soldiers and civilians, merged with Forces Nouvelles; cease-fire with govt Oct 2002
CI	Mouvement populaire ivoirien du Grand Ouest/Ivorian Popular Movement for the Great West (MPIGO)	2002	2,000, combined with MJP	C	Binhouye, W. CI	Avenge death of General Guei, defend the rights of the Yacouba ethnic grp; merged with Forces Nouvelles; Linas-Marcoussis peace agreement Jan 2003
CI	Mouvement pour la justice et la paix/Movement for Justice and Peace (MJP)	2002	2,000	C	Town of Man	Similar objectives to MPIGO; combined forces
CI	Union des Patriotes pour la Libération Totale de la Côte d'Ivoire (UPLTCI) / Union of Patriots for the Total Liberation of the Côte d'Ivoire	2003	thousands	A	Abidjan, W. and S.W. CI	Pro-govt militia; armed wing of the Convention of Patriots for Peace (CPP)
CI	Young Patriots (FESCI)/Union pour la Liberation Totale de la Côte d'Ivoire/The Unions for the Total Liberation of Côte d'Ivoire (UPLTCI)/Congres panafricain des jeunes patriotes/Pan-African Congress of Young Patriots (COJEP)	n.k.	150,000	A	Abidjan, S. CI	Pro-govt; student membership consists of networks and political parties
Dj	Front pour la restauration de l'Unité Nationale et de la Démocratie (FRUD)/Front for the Restoration of National Unity and Democracy	1991	hundreds	C	Dj	Represent Afar population of Dj and estb multi-party elections; following 1994 split, one faction signed agreement with govt to become legitimate political party, joined 1995 coalition govt
DROC	Allied Democratic Forces (ADF)	1995	100+	A	N.E. DROC, Uga	Undermine Uga govt
DROC	Congres Nationale de la defense du peuple/ Armée Nationale du Congo (CNDP/ANC)	2006	3,000+	A	N.Kivu, DROC	Protection of Congolese Tutsi population, return of the 45,000-60,000 Congolese Tutsi refugees living in Rwa, disarmament of the FDLR
DROC	Forces Armées du Peuple Congolais (FAPC) / Armed Forces of the Congolese People	n.k.	n.k.	C	DROC	Split from UPC, has incorporated the Popular Front for Democracy in Congo (FPDC), elements from RCD-ML, APC
DROC	Forces de Résistance Patriotique d'Ituri (FRPI) / Patriotic Resistance Forces in Ituri	n.k.	5,000	C	DROC	Armed wing of Nationalist Integrationist Front (FNI), primarily Lendu
DROC	Mai Mai fighters	n.k.	1,700	A	Kongolo, Mitwaba, Katanga, DROC	Indigenous militia
DROC	Mouvement de Libération Congolais (MLC) / Movement for the Liberation of Congo	1998	18,000	C	N. DROC	Transformed into political party; integrated with national army; 'Fight dictatorship in the Democratic Republic of the Congo'; first faction to break from RCD
DROC	National Army for the Liberation of Uganda (NALU)	n.k.	n.k.	A	N.E. DROC	Undermine Uga govt
DROC	Parti pour l'unite et la Sauvegarde de l'Integrite du Congo (PUSIC) / Party for Unity and the Safeguard of the Integrity of Congo	n.k.	2–5,000	C	Ituri province	Hema militia supporting Hema against Lendu in DROC's ethnic conflict

Table 47 Selected Non-State Groups and Affiliates

Origin	Organisation * aka	Estb.	Est. Strength	Status	Operates	Aims and Remarks
DROC	Patriotes Resistants Congolais (Pareco)	2007	n.k.	A	N. Kivu, DROC	Protect the local population from attacks by Gen. Nkunda's forces; alleged coalition of Mai-Mai forces and ethnic self-defence grps
DROC	Rassemblement Congolais pour la Démocratie – Mouvement de Libération (RCD–ML) / Congolese Rally for Democracy – Liberation Movement	1999	2–3,000	D	N. Kivu, DROC	Overthrow DROC govt
DROC	Rassemblement Congolais pour la Démocratie – Goma (RCD–GOMA) / Congolese Rally for Democracy – Goma	1998	20,000	D	Kivu, DROC	Estb democracy in the DROC
DROC	Rasta	n.k.	n.k.	A	S. Kivu, DROC	Breakaway faction of the FDLR(Rwa) - alliance with the Mai-Mai Mudundu 40 grp
DROC	Union des Patriotes Congolais (UPC) / Union of Congolese Patriots	2002	n.k.	C	Ituri province, DROC	Seek to preserve Hema political advantages over the majority Lendu and wants Hema share of resources in Ituri; now part of transitional govt
Er	Alliance of Eritrean National Forces (AENF)	1999	3,000	A	Er	Overthrow Er govt; coalition of Er armed grps
Er	Harakat al Khalas al Islami / Eritrean Islamic Jihad/ Islamic Salvation Movement (EJIM)	1990s	hundreds	A	Er, Eth, Sdn	Overthrow Er govt, estb new govt based on Islamic law; conglomerate of many grps
Eth	Ogaden National Liberation Army (ONLA)	1984	n.k.	A	Eth	'Restore rights of Ogaden population' and obtain right to self-determination; armed wing of ONLF
Gam	Green Boys/22 July Movement	1994	n.k.	A	Banjul, Gam	Pro-govt activists; affiliated with the Alliance for Patriotic Reorientation and Construction
Gub	Military junta/ Mané followers	1998	200	D	Border with Sen	Anti-govt; composed of national armed forces members
Gui	Guinean dissidents/Movement of the Democratic Forces of Guinea/Rassemblement des Forces Démocratiques de Guinée (RFDG)	2000	1,000	A	Gui	Anti-Gui govt; fought with SL and Lb during 2000 border confrontation
Gui	Movement of the Democratic Forces of Guinea/ Rassemblement des Forces Démocratiques de Guinée (RFDG)	late 1990's	1,800	D	S. Gui	Anti-govt; possibly composed of ex-army officers
Gui	Young Volunteers	2000	10,000	A	Gui	Pro-govt; previously countered the 2000-01 attacks by RFDG, SL's RUF and Lb fighters; several have been disarmed and reintegrated
Lb	Former Government of Liberia (GoL) militias and para-militaries	1997	15,000	A	Lb	Defended Charles Taylor govt after the 1997 elections; uses RUF child soldiers
Lb	Liberians United for Reconciliation and Democracy (LURD)	2000	3–8,000	A	Lofa county, N.W. Lb	Against Charles Taylor's govt; dissatisfied with 1997 Abuja Peace Accords process; officially disbanded in Nov 2004, but remains an organised force
Lb	Movement for Democracy in Liberia (MODEL)	2003	1–5,000	C	CI border, E. and S.E. Lb	Overthrow of Charles Taylor's govt; currently disarming but still organised
Lb	Revolutionary United Front (RUF)	1991	n.k.	C	Lb, SL	Overthrow SL govt; cease-fire with govt Nov 2000, disarmament programme completed Jan 2002
Nga	Al Sunna Wal Jamma/Followers of the Prophet	2002	200	A	Nga	Estb an Islamic state in Nga; strong university student membership
Nga	Arewa People's Congress (APC)	1999	n.k.	A	N. Nga	Defend the rights of the Hausa-Fulani tribe, terminate violence from S. Nga

Non-State Groups

Table 47 Selected Non-State Groups and Affiliates

Origin	Organisation * aka	Estb.	Est. Strength	Status	Operates	Aims and Remarks
Nga	Bakassi Boys/Anambra State Vigilante Service (AVS)/Abia State Vigilante Service (AVS)/Imo State Vigilante Service (IVS)/ASMATA Boys	1999	n.k.	D	S.E. Nga	Aimed to terminate violence by 'Maf' (mafia); emerged from several grps in Abia state, formed in response to robberies, violence and intimidation by 'Maf'
Nga	Egbesu Boys of Africa (EBA)	late 1990s	thousands	D	Ijaw regions, Nga	Promote Ijaw interests and assert control over oil company policies and wealth in Niger Delta; suspected armed wing of Ijaw Youth Council
Nga	Federated Niger Delta Ijaw Communities (FNDIC)	1997	3,000	A	S.E. Nga	Protect Ijaw interests and benefits; redistribute oil revenues
Nga	Grand Alliance of the Niger Delta(GAND)	2006/2007	n.k.	A	Niger Delta	Threatens energy companies unless they employ unemployed youth, and demands repeal of land laws of 1978.
Nga	Movement for the Emancipation of the Niger Delta (MEND)	2006	100+	C	Ngr Delta	Intimidate oil companies, seeks local redistribution of revenues
Nga	Hisba/Hisbah Groups	2001	n.k.	A	Nga	Full implementation of Sharia law in states that adopted it, especially in N. Nga
Nga	Movement for the Actualisation of the Sovereign State of Biafra (MASSOB)	1999	thousands	A	S.E. Nga	Secession of Biafra
Nga	Niger Delta People's Volunteer Force (NDPVF)	2003	n.k.	A	Rivers State around Buguma	Seeks increase in oil revenues and employment of local youths
Nga	Niger Delta Vigilante (NDV)	1998/2003	n.k.	A	Rivers State	Similar objectives to other Niger Delta forces
Nga	Niger Delta Volunteer Force (NDVF)	1980s	thousands	A/D	Niger Delta	Seeks distribution of oil profits and employment of local youths
Nga	O'dua People's Congress (OPC)	1994	4,000	A	S.W. Nga	Indep for the Yoruba people of S.W. Nga, protect the interests of the Yoruba ethnic grp
Nga	Zamfara State Vigilante Service (ZSVS)	1999	n.k.	A	Zamfara State	Strict adherence to Sharia law; operates in 6-man teams
Ngr	Arab and Peulh self-defence militias / Comité de vigilance de Tassara (CVT) / Comité d'Autodéfense (CAD)	1992	n.k.	D	Ngr Manga region	To prevent Tuareg and Toubou rebels from stealing cattle and property in order to fund their war effort
Ngr	Iduwini Youths	2004	n.k.	A	S. Ngr	Opposes exploitation of environment; Iduwini advocacy grp, armed wing of Iduwini Naitonal Movement for Peace and Development (INMPD)
Ngr	Le Mouvement des Nigeriens pour la Justice (MNJ)	n.k.	n.k.	A	N. Ngr	Tuareg-led; anti-govt corruption, irresponsible development policies, economic inequality, ethnic inequality; opposes development of Ingall
Ngr	Niger Movement for Justice (MNJ)	1991	n.k.	A	Ngr	Representation for Tuareg people, access to uranium resources
Ngr	Tuareg and Toubou rebel groups/Union des forces de la résistance armée (UFRA)/Union of Armed Resistance Forces/Forces armées révolutionnaires du Sahara (FARS)/Revolutionary Armed Forces of the Sahara/Front Démocra	1992	7,000	D	Ngr	Anti-peace agreements; split into 13 different grps
RC	Ninja Rebels	2002	n.k.	C	RC	Rebel movement led by Pasteur Ntumi; peace agreement with govt in 2003
RMM	Democratic Alliance for Change	2006	n.k.	A/C	N.E. RMM	Composed of former Tuareg rebels who deserted the army out of dissatisfaction with the peace process

Table 47 Selected Non-State Groups and Affiliates

Origin	Organisation * aka	Estb.	Est. Strength	Status	Operates	Aims and Remarks
RMM	Patriotic Movement of Ganda Koy/Mouvement Patriotique Ganda Koy (MPGK)	1994	n.k.	A	RMM	Against displacement of indigenous people in S.; anti MFUA
RMM	United Movement and Fronts of Azawad/United Movement and Fronts of Azawad (MFUA)	1991	3–10,000	A/D	Goa, Kidal, Timbuktu, N.E. RMM	Coalition of the MPA, FIAA, FPLA and ARLA: Arab and Tuareg anti-govt rebels; demand to end economic and political marginalisation of the North
RSA	People Against Gangsterism and Drugs (PAGAD)	1995	50	A	Cape Town area	Combat and eradicate crime, gangsterism and drugs; anti-Western, views RSA govt as threat to Muslim values
RSA	Qibla	1980s	300	A	Cape Town area	Estb an Islamic state in RSA; allied to PAGAD
Rwa	Forces Démocratiques pour la Liberation du Rwanda (FDLR)/Armie pour la liberation du Rwanda (ALIR) / Democratic Forces for the Liberation of Rwanda/Army for the Liberation of Rwanda	2000	3,000+	A	S. Kivu, Katanga, DROC	Reinstate Hutu control of Rwa; ALIR superseded by FDLR in 2001, consists of survivors of genocide in the DROC
Rwa/DROC	Mai-Mai Militia/Alliance pour la Resistance Democratique (ARD)/Popular Self-Defence Forces (FAP)	1997	n.k.	A	DROC, Rwa	Protect the DROC from foreign influence; indigenous militia aligned with the FDLR, unwilling to be part of coalition govt
Sdn	Eastern Front	2005	5,200	C	E. Sdn	Opposes the marginalisation of Beja and Rashaida ethnic grps, demand control over the region's resources; coalition of the Beja Congress and the Free Lions; possible links with JEM
Sdn	Janjaweed Militias	2002–03	20,000	A	W. Sdn	Janjaweed is a generic term for tribal Arab militias displacing the African population of Darfur; Rizigat tribe biggest element
Sdn	Justice and Equality Movement (JEM)	2002–03	thousands	A	Darfur	Defence of Darfur population, protests regional under-development; National Movement for Reform and Development is aligned
Sdn	Justice Front	2007	4,000	A	Al-Duayn, Darfur, Sdn	Tribal Arab militia under Khartoum displacing African population of Darfur
Sdn	New Sudan Brigade	1995	2,000	A	E. Sdn	Eastern branch of SPLA
Sdn	Sudan Alliance Forces	1994	500	A	E. Sdn	Overthrow Sdn govt and 'establish progressive and secular democracy,' played major role in opening new war front in East since 1997
Sdn	Sudan Liberation Movement/Army (SLM/A) / SLM-Classic / SLM-Unity / Group 19 (G19)	2003	thousands	C	Darfur, Sdn	Defence of the African population of Darfur, self determination for Darfur, democracy in Sdn
Sdn	Sudan People's Liberation Army (SPLA)	1983	20,000–30,000	C	S. Sdn	Secular and democratic Sdn; armed wing of Sudan People's Liberation Movement (SPLM); cease-fire with govt July 2002, recreated as police
Sdn	United Revolutionary Force Front (URFF)	2007	n.k.	A	Sdn	Arab group opposed to government; formed from Democratic Popular Front Army; similar aims to JEM
Sdn	The Beja Congress	1993	500	A	E. Sdn	Overthrow Sdn govt and estb autonomous Beja state; controls area of E. Sdn centred around Garoura and Hamshkoraib
Sdn	United Front for Liberation and Development (UFLD)	2007	n.k.	A	Sdn	Similar to aims of Sudan Liberation Army, alliance between several Sdn armed grps
Sen	Mouvement des Forces Démocratiques de Casamance (MFDC)/Movement of the Democratic Forces of Casamance	1982	2–4,000	C	Sen, close to GuB, Gam border	Indp Casamance; involved in peace talks with govt since 2000; military wing factionalised into Front Sud and Front Nord

Non-State Groups

Table 47 **Selected Non-State Groups and Affiliates**

Origin	Organisation * aka	Estb.	Est. Strength	Status	Operates	Aims and Remarks
SL	Armed Forces Revolutionary Council (AFRC)	1997	n.k.	D	Freetown	Disaffected members of the armed forces, estb during coup d'état
SL	Civil Defence Force (CDF)	1990's	37,000+	C	SL	Defence of tribal communities against RUF and govt
SL	Independent RUF (RUF–I)	2002	500	C	Lb border	Against cease-fire signed between other grps and govt in Jan 2002; split from RUF in 2002
SL	Revolutionary United Front (RUF)	1980s	20,000	D	Gui; Lb; SL	Overthrow SL govt; cease-fire with govt Nov 2000, became political party, disarmament programme completed Jan 2002
SL	West Side Boys (WSB)	n.k.	hundreds	D	Rokel Creek area near Occra Hills in Port Loko district	Members included former SL Army members; conducted armed robberies and attacks
SR	Al-Ittihad al-Islami (AIAI)/Islamic Union	1992	2,000	A	Eth; Kya; SR	Estb an Islamic regime in SR and Eth
SR	Alliance for the Liberation of Somalia (ALS) / Alliance for the Re-Liberation of Somalia (ARS)	2007	300+	A	SR	Remove the Eth-backed govt through military struggle or diplomatic efforts
SR/Irq	Islamic Courts Council (ICC) / Somali National Alliance (SNA) / United Somali Congress (USC)	1989	n.k.	A	S. Mogadishu	Militia of the Hawiye clan, led by Aideed family; overthrew Siad Barre, struggles for political power,connected to PRM
SR	Popular Resistance Movement in the Land of the two Migrations (PRM)	2007	n.k.	A	Mogadishu, S. SR	Militant wing of the ICC led by Shabaab militia, against reconciliation, led by Sharif Sheikh Ahmed
SR	Rahanweyn Resistance Army (RRA)	1996	n.k.	A	S. SR	Local autonomy; allied to SDM
SR	Somali Democratic Movement (SDM)	1992	n.k.	A	S. SR	Local autonomy; allied to RRA
SR	Somali National Front (SNF)	1991	2–3,000	A	SR	Marehans fighting for control of S. Gedo region bordering Kya, pro-Siad Barre
SR	Somali National Movement (SNM)	1982	5,000+	A	N. SR	Independence for Somaliland
SR	Somali Patriotic Movement (SPM)	1989	2–3,000	A	SR	Ogaden tribal militia that helped overthrow Barre govt
SR	Somali Salvation Democratic Front (SSDF)	1978	3,000	A	N.E. SR	Independence for Puntland
SR	Union of Islamic Courts (UIC)/Ittihād al-mahākim al-islāmiyya/Joint Islamic Courts or Union of Islamic Courts	1991	n.k.	A	RL, SR	Estb an Islamic regime in SR; supported by Er, linked to Hizbullah
SR	United Somali Congress Ali Mahdi Faction	1990's	10,000	A	N. SR	Anti Aideed, Abgal clan militia
SR/Irq	Islamic Courts Union (ICU)/Ittihād al-mahākim al-islāmiyya/Joint Islamic Courts	n.k.	n.k.	A/D	SR	Similar insurgency tactics to Irq; expel Eth forces; links with Hizbullah
Uga	Allied Democratic Front/Uganda Allied Democratic Army	1996	200	A	W. Uga	Replace Uga govt with regime based on Sharia law
Uga	Lord's Resistance Army (LRA)	1989	1,500+	A	Gulu and Kitgum district, Sdn	'Rule Uganda according to biblical ten commandments and create Great Nile Republic in Northern Uganda,' Christian fundamentalist, extensive use of child soldiers
Uga	West Nile Bank Front (WNBF)	1995	1,000	C/D	DROC; Uga	Anti govt grp dominated by West Nile tribes and former army officers under Idi Amin

Table 47 Selected Non-State Groups and Affiliates

Origin	Organisation *aka	Estb.	Est. Strength	Status	Operates	Aims and Remarks
Central and South Asia						
Afg	al-Qaeda	1988	n.k.	A	International	'Re-estb the Muslim state' worldwide; international network of Osama bin Laden
Afg	al-Qaeda in Afghanistan	n.k.	3,000	A	Afg, tribal areas	Re-estb the Muslim state in Afg; anti-West; communicates through the Global Islamic Media Front (GIMF)
Afg	Hizb-e Islami Gulbuddin (HIG)	1977	n.k.	A	Afg; Pak	Force foreign troops to withdraw from Afg and estb an Islamic fundamentalist state
Afg	Jaish-ul-Muslimin	2004	n.k.	A	Afg	Opposes US govt and Afg govt, demands release of al-Qaeda and Taliban prisoners in Guantanamo Bay, cessation of UN work in Afg
Afg	Saif-ul-Muslimeen/Saif-ul-Muslimeen Lashkar Jihad/Sword of Muslims	2003	n.k.	A/D	E. Afg	Anti-Afg govt and Western presence
Afg	Taliban	mid 1980s	thousands	A	Afg	Deobandi. Remove foreign forces, overthrow government
Afg	United Islamic Front for the Salvation of Afghanistan	mid 1980s	15,000	D	Afg	Anti-Taliban group based on former Northern Alliance
Bng	Harkat ul-Jihad i-Islami, Bangladesh Cell (HUJI-B)/Bangladesh Taleban	1992	3,000+	A	Bng	Recruit Bng and Ind Muslims to fight in Kashmir under HuM; estb by al-Qaeda
Bng	Hizbut Towhid (HT)	1994	n.k.	A	Bng	Anti-traditional govt
Bng	Islami Biplobi Parishad (IBP)	2001	n.k.	A	Bng	Estb Islamic state
Bng	Islami Ch'atra Shibir (ICS)	1941	n.k	A	Bng	Militant org seeking Taliban-style regime in Bng; student wing of Jamaat-e-Islami, Bng's third biggest political party
Bng	Jagrata Muslim Janata Bangladesh (JMJB)/Awakened Muslim Masses of Bangladesh	1998	n.k.	A	Bng	End activities of left-wing extremist grps in N.W., estb of Islamic rule in Bng; Taliban ideology, possibly splinter of JMB
Bng	Jama'at ul Mujahideen Bangladesh (JMB)	1998	10,000	A	Bng	Estb Islamic rule in Bng, opposes democracy
Bng	Purba Bangla Communist Party (PBCP)	1968	1,000+	A	Bng	Armed struggle, 'rid Bangladesh of class exploitation', estb Communist govt
Bng	Shahadat al Hiqma	1996	n.k.	A	N. Bng	Liberation struggle
Bng	Shanti Bahini/Peace Force	1976	3,000	D	Bng	Fights for autonomy of Chittagong Hill Tracts; armed wing of Parbatya Chattagram Jana Sanghati Samity (PCJSS), disbanded 1998 with possible remaining cells
Bng/Ind	Borok National Council of Tripura (BNCT)	2000	n.k.	A	Bng; Ind	Splinter grp of separatist National Liberation Front of Tripura (NLFT)
Bng/Ind	Jama'at ul-Mujahideen (JUM)	1990	n.k.	A	N.E. Ind	Seeks annexation of Jammu and Kashmir to Pak with no negotiations, advocates violence as the only solution; splinter of Ind/Pak HUJI, pro-Pak Islamic grp; different from Jama'at ul-Mujahideen, which is splinter from Hizb ul-Mujahideen
Bng/My	Rohingya Solidarity org (RSO)	1982	100–200+	A	Bng, My	Separate state for Rohingya Muslims in Arakan region of My
Ind	Achik National Volunteers Council (ANVC)	1995	n.k.	A	Meghalaya, Bng; My	Estb Achik homeland in the Garo Hills area
Ind	Adivasi Cobra Force (ACF)/Adivasi Cobra Militant Force (ACMF)	1996	350	C	Ind	Protection of Assam; cease-fire with govt 2001

Non-State Groups

Table 47 Selected Non-State Groups and Affiliates

Origin	Organisation * aka	Estb.	Est. Strength	Status	Operates	Aims and Remarks
Ind	All Muslim United Liberation Front of Assam (AMULFA)	mid 1990s	n.k	A	N.E. Ind	Collection of Islamist grpps that coordinates subversive activities in N.E. Ind
Ind	All Tripura Tiger Force (ATTF)	1990	500–600	A	Bng; Ind	Indp Tripura and expulsion of Bengali-speaking immigrants from Tripura
Ind	Al-Umar Mujahideen (AUM)/Al Madina	1989	700	A	Kashmir	Merger of Jammu and Kashmir with Pak
Ind	Arunachal Dragon Force (ADF)/East India Liberation Front (EILF)	1996	60	A	Arunachel Pradesh, Ind	Resist domination of Adi tribe, estb homeland for tribe of Tai-Khamtis
Ind	Babbar Khalsa International (BKI) / ISYF	1981	hundreds	A/D	Ind	Estb indp Sikh state called Khalistan in N.W. Ind
Ind	Bodo Liberation Tigers (BLT)/Bodo Liberation	1996	2,600	C/D	Assam, Ind; Bhutan	Creation of Bodo state under control and protection of Ind's constitution; peace accord with govt 2003
Ind	Bru National Liberation Front (BNLF)	1997	100+	C	Assam, Mizoram, Tripura	Protect rights of Reangs in Mizoram, possibly will attempt to negotiate a separate Reang homeland
Ind	Daughters of the Faith/Dukhtaran-e-Millat	2005	n.k.	A	Kashmir, Ind	Promotes strict Islamic rule for Kashmir; women's org
Ind	Hmar People's Convention-Democracy (HPC-D)	1986	100–150	A	Mizoram	Indp Hmar state in Hmar areas of Assam Manipur, Mizoram
Ind	Hynniewtrep National Liberation Council (HNLC)	1992	n.k.	A	Meghalaya	Estb Khasi homeland in Meghalaya, expel Garos and others
Ind	Indo-Burmese Revolutionary Front (IBRF)	1989	n.k.	A	N.E. Ind	Grp facilitating cooperation among N.E. Ind insurgents and foreign grps
Ind	International Sikh Youth Federation (ISYF),BKI	1985	n.k	A	Ind, UK; N. America; Europe	Estb indep Sikh state called Khalistan
Ind	Kamtapur Liberation org (KLO)	1995	300	A	Assam	Separate Kamtapur state
Ind	Kanglei Yawol Kanna Lup (KYKL)	1994	n.k	A	Manipur	Rebuild society in Manipur
Ind	Kuki National Army (KNA)	1991	600	A	Ind/My border	Estb indp Kukiland comprising parts of Ind and My
Ind	Manipur People's Liberation Front (MPLF)	1999	n.k.	A	Ind	Estb indp socialist Manipur. A coalition of UNLF, the RPF and the People's Revolutionary Party of Kangleipak
Ind	Maoist Communist Centre (MCC)	1969	1,000+	D	Bihar, Jharkhand	People's govt through 'armed struggle', merged with the People's War Group (PWG) in Sept 2004 to form CPI-M
Ind	Muslim United Liberation Tigers of Assam (MULTA)	1996	n.k	A	N.E. Ind	Islamist state indp of Ind
Ind	National Democratic Front of Bodoland (NDFB)	1988	1,500	A	Assam, Ind; Bhutan; My	Seeks autonomy for Bodoland in areas N. of River Brahmaputra
Ind	National Liberation Front of Tripura (NLFT)	1989	800	A	Bng; Ind	To estb indp for Tripura through armed struggle
Ind	National Socialist Council of Nagaland-Isaac Muivah (NSCN-IM)	1988	4,500	C	Assam, Manipur, Nagaland	Estb a greater socialist Nagaland; cease-fire renewed in July 2005
Ind	People's Liberation Army (PLA)	1978	n.k	A	Manipur	Unite Manipur's ethnic grps to liberate Manipur from Ind; transtribal org
Ind	People's Revolutionary Party of Kangleipak (PREPAK)	1977	200	A	Mizoram, N. Tripura	Expel 'outsiders' from Manipur

Table 47 Selected Non-State Groups and Affiliates

Origin	Organisation * aka	Estb.	Est. Strength	Status	Operates	Aims and Remarks
Ind	Rabha National Security Force (RNSF)	late 1990s	120	A	Assam	Separate homeland for Rabhas
Ind	Ranvir Sena/Ranvir Kisan Maha Sangh/Ranvir Mahila Sangh	1994	400	A	Ind	Eliminate left wing extremist grps in Bihar, especially PWG, MCC; supported by some upper caste land owners
Ind	Sanjukta Mukti Fouj (SMF)	1996	1,500	A	Assam	Estb an autonomous and socialist Assam; affiliated militarily with ULFA
Ind	Students Islamic Movement of India (SIMI)	1977	400	A	Ind	Overthrow current Ind govt, 're-establish the Caliphate,' Sharia based rule, propagate Islam, oppose democracy, secularism, nationalism; wage jihad
Ind	Tamil National Retrieval Troops (TNRT)	late 1980s	30	A	Ind	Estb Tamil homeland in Ind; LTTE sponsored grp
Ind	The Communist Party of India (CPI-Maoists)/Naxalites	1980/2004	6,500+	A	Ind	Estb a 'compact revolutionary zone' of control from N. border to Andhra Pradesh, convert to indp communist state; Maoist grp aiming to seize political power through 'armed struggle', merger between Maoist Communist Centre (MCC) and People's War Group (PWG) in 2004
Ind	Tripura Liberation org Front (TLOF)	1992	n.k.	A	Ind	Secession of Tripura from Ind
Ind	United Kuki Liberation Front (UKLF)	1990s	n.k.	A	Kuki	United Kuki state within Manipur
Ind	United Liberation Front of Assam (ULFA)	1979	3,000	A	Assam	Estb sovereign socialist Assam through 'armed struggle'
Ind	United Liberation Front of Barak Valley (ULFBV)	2002	50+	A	Assam	Separate homeland for tribal people of Karimgnj and Hailakandi
Ind	United National Liberation Front (UNLF)/Manipur Peoples' Army (MPA)	1964	n.k.	A	Assam	Indp and socialist Manipur
Ind	United People's Democratic Solidarity (UPDS)	1999	150	A	Assam	Secession of Karbi 'nation' from N. Assam; union of Karbi National Volunteers (KNV) and Karbi Peoples Front (KPF)
Ind/My	National Socialist Council of Nagaland-Khaplang (NSCN-K)	1988	2,000	C	Ind; My	Estb greater Nagaland in parts of Ind and My; believed to still have armed units; ceasefire with govt 1997
Ind/Pak	Al-Badr Mujahideen	1998	100+	A	Kashmir	'Liberate' Kashmir from Ind forces; split from Hizb-ul Mujahideen
Ind/Pak	Harkat ul-Mujahideen (HUM)/Harkat ul-Ansar (HUA)	1985	300–500	A	Kashmir; Afg; BiH; My; Pi; RF; Tjk	Seeks Kashmir's accession to Pak to solidify pan-Islamic entity, conducts 'armed struggle' against those that oppose Islam; Splinter of Ind/Paki HUJI, pro-Pak Islamic grp, wants to recruit 5,000 fighters
Ind/Pak	Harkat ul-Mujahideen al-Almi	2001–02	n.k.	A	Kashmir	Seek unification of Kashmir with Pak; splinter of HuM, implicated in assassination attempt on President Musharraf
Ind/Pak	Hizb ul-Mujahideen (HM)	1989	1500+	A	Kashmir	Pro-Pak Islamic grp; armed wing of Jama'at-e-Islami
Ind/Pak	Jaish-e-Mohammed (JeM)/The Army of Muhammad/ JeM Eastern Command	2000	100–400	A	Jammu, Kashmir	Seeks to expel Ind from Jammu and Kashmir, integration with Pak; under command Abdalla Banda Akbar
Ind/Pak	Jama'at ul-Mujahideen (JuM)	1990s	n.k.	A	Kashmir	Annexation of Jammu and Kashmir to Pak through violence; splinter grp of HM
Ind/Pak	Lakshar-e-Jabbar (LeJ)/The Army of the Omnipotent Almighty	n.k.	n.k.	A	Kashmir	Introduction of Sharia law
Ind/Pak	Lashkar-e-Toiba (LT)/Jama'at ud Dawa (JUD)	1989	300	A	Jammu, Kashmir	Seeks restoration of Islamic rule in Ind; armed wing of Markaz-ud-Dawa-wal-Irshad (MDI)

Table 47 Selected Non-State Groups and Affiliates

Origin	Organisation * aka	Estb.	Est. Strength	Status	Operates	Aims and Remarks
Ind/Pak	Save Kashmir Movement	2002	50	A	Jammu, Kashmir	Opposes Ind rule in Kashmir
Ind/Pak	Tehrik-e-Jihad	1997	n.k.	A	Kashmir	Self-determination for Kashmir, Kashmir to join Pak
N	Akhil Krantikari/All Nepal National Independent Students' Union (ANNISU-R)	2004	n.k.	n.k.	N	Opposes N monarchy, seeks student action to reinstitute democracy; student wing of CPN-M
N	Communist Party of Nepal (Maoist)/United People's Front	late 1990s	8–14,000; up to 200,000 sympathisers	C	N	Overthrow monarchy and replace with Maoist republic; declared 'People's War' in 1996; headed by 'Prachanda;' armed wing of Samyukta Jana Morcha (UPF); peace agreement and disarmament accord
Pak	al-Qaeda in Pakistan	2007	n.k.	A	N. Waziristan, Pak	Umbrella grp for Jaish-e-Mohammed, Lashkar-e-Jhangvi and Sipah-e-Sahaba; exists to further the three grp's aims
Pak	Baluch Liberation Army (BLA)	2003	n.k.	A	Pak	Fights for the right of the Baluch people; separatist/nationalist grp
Pak	Baluch People's Liberation Front (BPLF)/Popular Front for Armed Resistance/Baluch Students' org	1963–76	3,000+	A	Afg, Pak	Indp land for Baluch Muslims; al-Qaeda connection
Pak	Haqiqi Muttahida Qaumi Movement (MQM-H)	1992	n.k.	A	Pak	Splinter faction from MQM-A, engineered by govt to act as counterweight to MQM-A, which it thought more of a threat
Pak	Jama'at ul-Fuqra (JF)/Community of the Impoverished	1980	1,000–3,000	A	Pak, N. America	'Purify Islam through violence'
Pak	Jund Allah/God's Brigade	2001–02	20+	A	Pak	Islamist grp, implicated in assassination attempt on President Musharraf
Pak	Lashkar-e-Jhangvi (LIJ)	1996	300	A	Pak	Protect Sunni community from Shia extremism and terrorism
Pak	Lashkar-e-Omar (LeO)/al-Qanoon	2001–02	multiple cells 5–15 each	A	Pak	Anti-US attacks in Pak region; conglomeration of HUJI, LeJ, JeM members
Pak	Muttahida Qaumi Movement (MQM)/Muttahida Qaumi Movement-Altaf (MQM-A)	1984	3,000	A	Pak	Mohajir rights in Pak, more political power, improve socio-economic status; disputes over territory with MQM-H
Pak	Sipah-e-Muhammad (SMP)/Army of Muhammad	1993	30,000 followers	A	Punjab	Protect Shia community from Sunni extremism and terrorism; splinter of TJP
Pak	Sipah-e-Sahaba (SSP)/Millat e Islamia Pakistan	1985	3–6,000	A	Pak	Sunni state in Pak, opposes Pak/US alliance; operates also as political party
Pak	Tehreek-e-Nafaz-e-Shariat-e-Mohammadi / Movement for the Enforcement of Islamic Laws (TNSM) / Black Turbans	1989	n.k.	A	Malakand, Pak; Afg	Pak jihadist movement; banned in Jan 2002 by General Musharraf
Pak	Tehrik-e-Jaferia	1992	n.k.	A	Pak	Create Islamic society, protect rights of Shia Muslims
Ska	Liberation Tigers of Tamil Eelam (LTTE)/ World Tamil Association/ World Tamil Movement	1972	8–11,000	A	N. and E. Ska	Indp Tamil state; began armed conflict in 1983, on-going peace negotiations; possible commercial link with al-Qaeda; broke 2002 cease-fire in 2007
Uz	Hizb ut-Tahrir/Islamic Party of Liberation	1952	5–10,000	A	Uz; International	Estb Islamic Caliphate in C. Asia, jihad against US, its allies, and moderate Muslim regimes; seeks to estb an Islamic state or caliphate in Indo
Uz	Islamic Jihad Group	2002	n.k.	A	Uz	Opposes secular rule, seeks Islamic state
Uz	Islamic Movement of Uzbekistan (IMU)/Islamic Movement of Turkestan (IMT)	1997	2,000+	A	Arg; Ir; Kaz; Kgz; Pak; PRC; Tjk; Uz	Seeks creation of fundamentalist Islamic state in Uz and across C. Asia; coalition of Islamic militants from Uz, other C. Asian states and PRC; links to al-Qaeda, Taliban and ETIM

Table 47 Selected Non-State Groups and Affiliates

Origin	Organisation * aka	Estb.	Est. Strength	Status	Operates	Aims and Remarks
East Asia and Australasia						
Aus	n.k.	2004	20+	A	Sydney, Melbourne	Spread radical Islam, target Westerners; led by Abu Bakr, several cells emulating al-Qaeda tactics and ideology
Cam	Party of Democratic Kampuchea (Khmer Rouge)	1960	1–2,000	D	Cam	Destabilise the Cam govt
Indo	Gerakan Aceh Merdeka (GAM)/Free Aceh Movement/ Tentara Nasional Aceh (TNA)	1976	2,000	C	Aceh	Indp Islamic state in Aceh; Tentara Nasional Aceh is the armed wing, underground since 1996; GAM disarmed and TNI left Aceh under peace accords in Dec 2005
Indo	Jemaah Islamiah (JI)/Islamic Group/Community	1993–94	500+	A/D	Indo; Mal; Pi; Th	Estb indp Islamic state encompassing Indo, Mal, S. Pi, S. Th; active faction Thoifah Muqatilah conducted 2005 Bali bombings
Indo	Laskar Jihad/Holy War Warriors	2000	500+	D	Maluku	Remove Christians from Maluku, Islamic state in Indo
Indo	Mujahideen KOMPAK	2001	n.k.	A	Indo	Estb Islamic govt in Indo; JI splinter grp
Indo	Organisasi Papua Merdeka (OPM)/Free Papua Movement	1962	150	A	Indo	Indp for W. Papua
Indo	South Maluku Republic/Republik Maluku Selatan (RMS)	1998	n.k.	A	E. Ind	Maluku indp; Christian separatist grp
J	Aum Supreme Truth/Aum Shinrikyo/Aleph	1987	1,500–2,000	D	J; RF	'Take over Japan and then the world;' released Sarin on Tokyo subway in 1995 and other chemical attacks in J
J	Chukaku-Ha /Kansai Revolutionary Army (KRA)	1957	3,500	D	J	Protests J's imperial system and Western 'imperialism'
J	Japanese Red Army/Anti-Imperialist International Brigade (AIIB)	1970	30–40	D	J; RL	Overthrow the J govt and monarchy, help foment world revolution
Lao	Underground Government of the Free Democratic people of Laos	2000	n.k.	A	Lao	Supports democracy; anti-communist govt
Lao	United Lao National Liberation Front (ULNLF)/Lao National Liberation Movement (LNLM)	1975	2,000	A	N. Lao	Overthrow current govt; pro-royalist right wing
Mal	Malaysian Mujahideen Group/Kumpulan Mujahideen Malaysia (KMM)	1995	90–100	D	Indo; Mal; Pi	Estb Muslim state comprising Indo, Mal and S. Pi; allegedly linked to JI
My	All Burma Students Democratic Front (ABSDF)	1988	2,000	A	My	'Liberate Myanmar from dictatorship, establish democracy and transform into federal union'
My	Chin National Army (CNA)/Chin National Front	1988	800–1,000	A	Chin state, W. My	Overthrow My govt; armed wing of Chin National Front
My	Democratic Karen Buddhist Army (DKBA)	1994	100–500	C	My; Th	Indp for Karen minority, ongoing conflict with KNLA; splinter grp of Karen National Union (KNU), armed wing of Democratic Karen Buddhist org
My	Kachin Independence Army (KIA)	1961	8,000	C	Khmer range, N. My	Promote Buddhism; armed wing of Kachin Independence org
My	Karen National Liberation Army (KNLA)	1948	2–4,000	A	Th border	Estb Karen State with right to self-determination, ongoing conflict with DKBA; armed wing of KNU
My	Karenni National Progressive Party (KNPP)	1948	800–2,000	A	Kayah State, N. My	Indp of Karenni State; armed wing of Karenni National Progressive Party
My	Kayin National Union (KNU)/Karen National Union	1959	5,000	A	My; Th	Independent homeland for the Karen people

Non-State Groups

Table 47 **Selected Non-State Groups and Affiliates**

Origin	Organisation * aka	Estb.	Est. Strength	Status	Operates	Aims and Remarks
My	Mon National Liberation Army (MNLA)	1958	1,000	C	Th border	Represent Mon minority; armed wing of New Mon State Party
My	Mong Thai Army (MTA)	1964	3,000	C	Th border	Protect Shan population
My	Myanmar National Democratic Alliance Army (MNDAA)	1989	1,000	C	E. Shan State, PRC–Lao border	Oppose My mil rule; formerly part of Communist Party of Burma (CPB)
My	Palaung State Liberation Army (PSLA)	1963	700	C	N. of Hsipaw	Greater autonomy for Palaung population
My	Shan State Army (SSA)/Shan State Progress Army (SSPA)	1964	3,000	C	S. Shan State	Freedom and democracy for Shan State
My	United Wa State Army (UWSA)	1989	15,000	C	Wa Hills	Splinter grp of CPB
My	Vigorous Burmese Student Warriors (VBSW)	1999	n.k.	A	My, Th	Opposes military regime in My; anti-govt grp
Pi	Abu Sayyaf Group (ASG)	1991	300	A	S. Pi, Mal	Indp Islamic state in W. Mindanao and Sulu; split from MNLF
Pi	al-Khobar	2007	n.k.	A	S. Cotabato province, Pi	Similar ideology to MILF and JI reported
Pi	Bangsamoro Army	1972–73	15,000	C	S. Pi	Muslim separatist movement; armed wing of the Moro National Liberation Front
Pi	Kabataang Makabayan (KM)/Nationalist/Patriotic Youth	1964	n.k.	A	Pi	Student wing of Communist Party of the Philippines
Pi	Moro Islamic Liberation Front (MILF)	1977	11,000+	C	S. Pi	Indp Islamic state in Bangsa Moro and neighbouring islands; split from MNLF; cease-fire with govt Aug 2001
Pi	Moro Islamic Reformist Group	1978	900	A	S. Pi	Indp Islamic state in S. Pi; split from MNLF
Pi	New People's Army (NPA)	1969	6,000+	A	Pi	Overthrow the Pi govt through guerrilla warfare; armed wing of Communist Party of the Philippines
PRC	East Turkestan Liberation Org (ETLO)/Sharqiy Türkistan Azatliq Tashkilati/ East Turkestan Islamic Movement (ETIM)	1990	600	A	Kgz, N.W. PRC, C. Asia	Estb separate E. Turkestan state for Uighur population; links to al-Qaeda, IMU and IMT
Th	Pattani Islamic Mujahideen Movement/Gerakan Mujahideen Islam Pattani (GMIP)	1995	20+	A	S. Th	Estb a Muslim state in S. Th
Th	Pattani United Liberation org (PULO)	1968	100	A	Th	Fighting for the separation of Th's mainly Muslim South
Th	Runda Kumpulan Kecil (RKK)	2005	3,000	A	S.Th	Indp state of Pattani
Th	United Front for the Independence of Pattani/Bersatu	1989	60+	A	Th	Estb an indp Islamic state in S. Th; umbrella grp including PULO, New PULO, and BRN
Th/Mal	Barisan Revolusi Nasional (BRN)	1960	60-80	A	S.Th	Muslim separatist movement in Th

PART THREE
Reference

Table 48 **Designations of Aircraft**

NOTES

1 [Square brackets] indicate the type from which a variant was derived: 'Q-5 ... [MiG-19]' indicates that the design of the Q-5 was based on that of the MiG-19.

2 (Parentheses) indicate an alternative name by which an aircraft is known, sometimes in another version: 'L-188 ... *Electra* (P-3 Orion)'

shows that in another version the Lockheed Type 188 *Electra* is known as the P-3 *Orion*.

3 Names given in 'quotation marks' are NATO reporting names, e.g., 'Su-27...*"Flanker"*'.

4 For country abbreviations, see 'Index of Country Abbreviations' (p. 495).

Type	Name/designation	Country of origin/Maker
Fixed-wing		
A-1	*AMX*	**Br/It** AMX
A-1	*Ching-Kuo*	**ROC** AIDC
A-3	*Skywarrior*	**US** Douglas
A-4	*Skyhawk*	**US** MD
A-5	*(Q-5)*	**PRC** SAF
A-7	*Corsair* II	**US** LTV
A-10	*Thunderbolt*	**US** Fairchild
A-36	*Halcón* (C-101)	**Sp** CASA
A-37	*Dragonfly*	**US** Cessna
A-50	*'Mainstay'* (Il-76)	**RF** Beriev
A300		**UK/Fr/Ge/Sp** Airbus Int
A310		**UK/Fr/Ge/Sp** Airbus Int
A340		**UK/Fr/Ge/Sp** Airbus Int
AC-47	*(C-47)*	**US** Douglas
AC-130	*(C-130)*	**US** Lockheed
Air Beetle		**Nga** AIEP
Airtourer		**NZ** Victa
AJ-37	*(J-37)*	**Swe** Saab
Alizé	*(Br 1050)*	**Fr** Breguet
Alpha Jet		**Fr/Ge** Dassault–Breguet/Dornier
AMX		**Br/It** Embraer/Alenia/Aermacchi
An-2	*'Colt'*	**Ukr** Antonov
An-12	*'Cub'*	**Ukr** Antonov
An-14	*'Clod'* (Pchyelka)	**Ukr** Antonov
An-22	*'Cock'* (Antei)	**Ukr** Antonov
An-24	*'Coke'*	**Ukr** Antonov
An-26	*'Curl'*	**Ukr** Antonov
An-28/M-28	*'Cash'*	**Ukr** Antonov/**Pl** PZL
An-30	*'Clank'*	**Ukr** Antonov
An-32	*'Cline'*	**Ukr** Antonov
An-72	*'Coaler-C'*	**Ukr** Antonov
An-74	*'Coaler-B'*	**Ukr** Antonov
An-124	*'Condor'* (Ruslan)	**Ukr** Antonov
Andover	[HS-748]	**UK** BAe
Arava		**Il** IAI
AS-202	*Bravo*	**CH** FFA
AT-3	*Tsu Chiang*	**ROC** AIDC
AT-6	*(T-6)*	**US** Beech

Type	Name/designation	Country of origin/Maker
AT-11		**US** Beech
AT-26	*EMB-326*	**Br** Embraer
AT-33	*(T-33)*	**US** Lockheed
Atlantic	*(Atlantique)*	**Fr** Dassault–Breguet
AU-23	*Peacemaker* [PC-6B]	**US** Fairchild
AV-8	*Harrier* II	**US/UK** MD/BAe
Aztec	*PA-23*	**US** Piper
B-1	*Lancer*	**US** Rockwell
B-2	*Spirit*	**US** Northrop Grumman
B-5	*H-5*	**PRC** HAF
B-6	*H-6*	**PRC** XAC
B-52	*Stratofortress*	**US** Boeing
B-65	*Queen Air*	**US** Beech
BAC-167	*Strikemaster*	**UK** BAe
BAe-125		**UK** BAe
BAe-146		**UK** BAe
BAe-748	*(HS-748)*	**UK** BAe
Baron	*(T-42)*	**US** Beech
Basler T-67	*(C-47)*	**US** Basler
Be-6	*'Madge'*	**RF** Beriev
Be-12	*'Mail'* (Tchaika)	**RF** Beriev
Beech 50	*Twin Bonanza*	**US** Beech
Beech 95	*Travel Air*	**US** Beech
BN-2	*Islander, Defender, Trislander*	**UK** Britten-Norman
Boeing 707		**US** Boeing
Boeing 727		**US** Boeing
Boeing 737		**US** Boeing
Boeing 747		**US** Boeing
Boeing 757		**US** Boeing
Boeing 767		**US** Boeing
Bonanza		**US** Beech
Bronco	*(OV-10)*	**US** Rockwell
BT-5	*HJ-5*	**PRC** HAF
Bulldog		**UK** BAe
C-1		**J** Kawasaki
C-2	*Greyhound*	**US** Grumman
C-5	*Galaxy*	**US** Lockheed
C-7	*DHC-7*	**Ca** DHC
C-9	*Nightingale* (DC-9)	**US** MD

Type	Name/designation	Country of origin/Maker
C-12	*Super King Air (Huron)*	US Beech
C-17	*Globemaster* III	**US** McDonnell Douglas
C-18	[Boeing 707]	US Boeing
C-20	(*Gulfstream* III)	US Gulfstream
C-21	(*Learjet*)	US Learjet
C-22	(Boeing 727)	US Boeing
C-23	(*Sherpa*)	UK Shorts
C-26	*Expediter/Merlin*	US Fairchild
C-27	*Spartan*	It Alenia
C-32	[Boeing 757]	US Boeing
C-37A	[Gulfstream V]	US Gulfstream
C-38A	(*Astra*)	Il IAI
C-42	(Neiva *Regente*)	Br Embraer
C-46	*Commando*	US Curtis
C-47	DC-3 (*Dakota*) (C-117 *Skytrain*)	US Douglas
C-54	*Skymaster* (DC-4)	US Douglas
C-91	HS-748	UK BAe
C-93	HS-125	UK BAe
C-95	EMB-110	Br Embraer
C-97	EMB-121	Br Embraer
C-101	*Aviojet*	Sp CASA
C-115	DHC-5	Ca De Havilland
C-117	(C-47)	US Douglas
C-118	*Liftmaster* (DC-6)	US Douglas
C-123	*Provider*	US Fairchild
C-127	(Do-27)	Sp CASA
C-130	*Hercules* (L-100)	US Lockheed
C-131	Convair 440	US Convair
C-135	[Boeing 707]	US Boeing
C-137	[Boeing 707]	US Boeing
C-140	(*Jetstar*)	US Lockheed
C-141	*Starlifter*	US Lockheed
C-160	*Transall*	Fr/Ge EADS
C-212	*Aviocar*	Sp CASA
C-235	*Persuader*	Sp/Indo CASA/Airtech
C-295M		Sp CASA
Canberra		UK BAe
CAP-10		Fr Mudry
CAP-20		Fr Mudry
CAP-230		Fr Mudry
Caravelle	SE-210	Fr Aérospatiale
CC-115	DHC-5	Ca DHC
CC-117	(*Falcon 20*)	Fr Dassault
CC-132	(DHC-7)	Ca DHC
CC-137	(Boeing 707)	US Boeing
CC-138	(DHC-6)	Ca DHC
CC-144	CL-600/-601	Ca Canadair
CF-5a		Ca Canadair
CF-18	F/A-18	US MD
CH-2000	*Sama*	HKJ/JAI
Cheetah	[*Mirage* III]	RSA Atlas
Cherokee	PA-28	US Piper
Cheyenne	PA-31T [*Navajo*]	US Piper
Chieftain	PA-31-350 [*Navajo*]	US Piper

Type	Name/designation	Country of origin/Maker
Ching-Kuo	A-1	ROC AIDC
Citabria		US Champion
Citation	(T-47)	US Cessna
CJ-5	[Yak-18]	PRC NAMC (Hongdu)
CJ-6	[Yak-18]	PRC NAMC (Hongdu)
CL-215		Ca Canadair
CL-415		Ca Canadair
CL-600/604	*Challenger*	Ca Canadair
CM-170	*Magister* [*Tzukit*]	Fr Aérospatiale
CM-175	*Zéphyr*	Fr Aérospatiale
CN-212		Sp/Indo CASA/IPTN
CN-235		Sp/Indo CASA/IPTN
Cochise	T-42	US Beech
Comanche	PA-24	US Piper
Commander	Aero-/TurboCommander	US Rockwell
Commodore	MS-893	Fr Aérospatiale
CP-3	P-3 *Orion*	US Lockheed
CP-140	*Acturas* (P-3 *Orion*)	US Lockheed
CT-4	*Airtrainer*	NZ Victa
CT-114	CL-41 *Tutor*	Ca Canadair
CT-133	*Silver Star* [T-33]	Ca Canadair
CT-134	*Musketeer*	US Beech
CT-156	*Harvard* II	US Beech
Dagger	(*Nesher*)	Il IAI
Dakota		US Piper
Dakota	(C-47)	US Douglas
DC-3	(C-47)	US Douglas
DC-4	(C-54)	US Douglas
DC-6	(C-118)	US Douglas
DC-7		US Douglas
DC-8		US Douglas
DC-9		US MD
Deepak	(HPT-32)	Ind HAL
Defender	BN-2	UK Britten-Norman
DHC-3	*Otter*	Ca DHC
DHC-4	*Caribou*	Ca DHC
DHC-5	*Buffalo*	Ca DHC
DHC-6	*Twin Otter*, CC-138	Ca DHC
DHC-7	*Dash-7* (*Ranger*, CC-132)	Ca DHC
DHC-8		Ca DHC
Dimona	H-36	Ge Hoffman
Do-27	(C-127)	Ge Dornier
Do-28	*Skyservant*	Ge Dornier
Do-128		Ge Dornier
Do-228		Ge Dornier
E-2	*Hawkeye*	US Grumman
E-3	*Sentry*	US Boeing
E-4	[Boeing 747]	US Boeing
E-6	*Mercury* [Boeing 707]	US Boeing
E-26	T-35A (*Tamiz*)	Chl Enear
EA-3	[A-3]	US Douglas
EA-6	*Prowler* [A-6]	US Grumman
EC-130	[C-130]	US Lockheed
EC-135	[Boeing 707]	US Boeing

Type	Name/designation	Country of origin/Maker
EF-111	*Raven* (F-111) .... **US** General Dynamic
Electra	(L-188) .... **US** Lockheed
EMB-110	*Bandeirante* .... **Br** Embraer
EMB-111	*Maritime Bandeirante* .... **Br** Embraer
EMB-120	*Brasilia* .... **Br** Embraer
EMB-121	*Xingu* .... **Br** Embraer
EMB-145	(R-99A/-99B) .... **Br** Embraer
EMB-201	*Ipanema* .... **Br** Embraer
EMB-312	*Tucano* .... **Br** Embraer
EMB-314	*Super Tucano* .... **Br** Embraer
EMB-326	*Xavante* (MB-326) .... **Br** Embraer
EMB-810	[*Seneca*] .... **Br** Embraer
EP-3	(P-3 *Orion*) .... **US** Lockheed
ERJ-145	.... **Br** Embraer
Etendard/Super Etendard .... **Fr** Dassault
EV-1	(OV-1) .... **US** Rockwell
F-1	[T-2] .... **J** Mitsubishi
F-4	*Phantom* .... **US** MD
F-5	-A/-B *Freedom Fighter* -E/-F *Tiger* II ... **US** Northrop
F-6	J-6 .... **PRC** SAF
F-7	J-7 .... **PRC** CAC-GAIC
F-8	J-8 .... **PRC** CACC
F-10	J-10 .... **PRC** SAC
F-11	J-11 .... **PRC** SAC
F-14	*Tomcat* .... **US** Grumman
F-15	*Eagle* .... **US** MD
F-16	*Fighting Falcon* .... **US** GD
F-18	[F/A-18], *Hornet* .... **US** MD
F-21	*Kfir* .... **Il** IAI
F-22	*Raptor* .... **US** Lockheed
F-27	*Friendship* .... **NI** Fokker
F-28	*Fellowship* .... **NI** Fokker
F-35	*Draken* .... **Swe** SAAB
F-50/-60	.... **NI** Fokker
F-104	*Starfighter* .... **US** Lockheed
F-111	EF-111 .... **US** GD
F-117	*Nighthawk* .... **US** Lockheed
F-172	(Cessna 172) .... **Fr/US** Reims-Cessna
F-406	*Caravan* .... **Fr** Reims
F/A-18	*Hornet* .... **US** MD
Falcon	*Mystère-Falcon* .... **Fr** Dassault
FB-111	(F-111) .... **US** GD
FBC-1	*Feibao* [JH-7] .... **PRC** CAC-GAIC
FC-1	(*Sabre* 2, *Super-7*) .... **PRC/RF/Pak** CAC/MAPO/Pak
FH-227	(F-27) .... **US** Fairchild-Hiller
Firefly	(T-67M) .... **UK** Slingsby
Flamingo	MBB-233 .... **Ge** MBB
FT-5	JJ-5 .... **PRC** CAF
FT-6	JJ-6 .... **PRC** SAF
FT-7	JJ-7 .... **PRC** GAIC
FTB-337	[Cessna 337] .... **US** Cessna
G-91	.... **It** Aeritalia
G-115E	*Tutor* .... **Ge** Grob
G-222	.... **It** Alenia

Type	Name/designation	Country of origin/Maker
Galaxy	C-5 .... **US** Lockheed
Galeb	.... **FRY** SOKO
Genet	SF-260W .... **It** SIAI
GU-25	(*Falcon* 20) .... **Fr** Dassault
Guerrier	R-235 .... **Fr** Socata
Gulfstream	.... **US** Gulfstream Aviation
Gumhuria	(*Bücker* 181) .... **Et** Heliopolis
H-5	[Il-28] .... **PRC** HAF
H-6	[Tu-16] .... **PRC** XAC
H-36	*Dimona* .... **Ge** Hoffman
Halcón	[C-101] .... **Sp** CASA
Harrier	(AV-8) .... **UK** BAe
Hawk	.... **UK** BAe
Hawker 800XP	(BAe-125) .... **US** Raytheon
HC-130	(C-130) .... **US** Lockheed
HF-24	*Marut* .... **Ind** HAL
HFB-320	*Hansajet* .... **Ge** Hamburger FB
HJ-5	(H-5) .... **PRC** HAF
HJT-16	*Kiran* .... **Ind** HAL
HPT-32	*Deepak* .... **Ind** HAL
HS-125	(*Dominie*) .... **UK** BAe
HS-748	[*Andover*] .... **UK** BAe
HT-2	.... **Ind** HAL
HU-16	*Albatross* .... **US** Grumman
HU-25	(*Falcon* 20) .... **Fr** Dassault
Hunter	.... **UK** BAe
HZ-5	(H-5) .... **PRC** HAF
IA-50	*Guaraní* .... **Arg** FMA
IA-58	*Pucará* .... **Arg** FMA
IA-63	*Pampa* .... **Arg** FMA
IAI-201/-202	*Arava* .... **Il** IAI
IAI-1124	*Westwind, Seascan* .... **Il** IAI
IAI-1125	*Astra* .... **Il** IAI
Iak-52	(Yak-52) .... **R** Aerostar
IAR-28	.... **R** IAR
IAR-93	*Orao* .... **FRY/R** SOKO/IAR
IAR-99	*Soim* .... **R** IAR
Il-14	'Crate' .... **RF** Ilyushin
Il-18	'Coot' .... **RF** Ilyushin
Il-20	'Coot-A' (Il-18) .... **RF** Ilyushin
Il-22	'Coot-B' (Il-18) .... **RF** Ilyushin
Il-28	'Beagle' .... **RF** Ilyushin
Il-38	'May' .... **RF** Ilyushin
Il-62	'Classic' .... **RF** Ilyushin
Il-76	'Candid' (tpt),'Mainstay' (AEW) .... **RF** Ilyushin
Il-78	'Midas' (tkr) .... **RF** Ilyushin
Il-82	'Candid' .... **RF** Ilyushin
Il-86	'Camber' .... **RF** Ilyushin
Il-87	'Maxdome' .... **RF** Ilyushin
Impala	[MB-326] .... **RSA** Atlas
Islander	BN-2 .... **UK** Britten-Norman
J-5	[MiG-17F] .... **PRC** SAF
J-6	[MiG-19] .... **PRC** SAF
J-7	[MiG-21] .... **PRC** CAC/GAIC

Type	Name/designation	Country of origin/Maker
J-8	Finback	**PRC** SAC
J-10	[IAI *Lavi*]	**PRC** SAC
J-11	[Su-27]	**PRC** SAC
J-32	Lansen	**Swe** SAAB
J-35	Draken	**Swe** SAAB
J-37	Viggen	**Swe** SAAB
JA-37	(J-37)	**Swe** SAAB
Jaguar		**Fr/UK** SEPECAT
JAS-39	Gripen	**Swe** SAAB
Jastreb		**FRY** SOKO
Jetstream		**UK** BAe
JH-7	[FBC-1]	**PRC** XAC
JJ-5	[J-5]	**PRC** CAF
JJ-6	[J-6]	**PRC** SAF
JJ-7	[J-7]	**PRC** GAIC
JZ-6	(J-6)	**PRC** SAF
K-8		**PRC/Pak/Et** Hongdu/E
KA-3	[A-3]	**US** Douglas
KA-6	[A-6]	**US** Grumman
KT-1B		**ROK** KAI
KC-10	*Extender* [DC-10]	**US** MD
KC-130	[C-130]	**US** Lockheed
KC-135	[Boeing 707]	**US** Boeing
KE-3A	[Boeing 707]	**US** Boeing
KF-16	(F-16)	**US** GD
Kfir		**Il** IAI
King Air		**US** Beech
Kiran	HJT-16	**Ind** HAL
Kraguj		**FRY** SOKO
KT-1		**ROK** KAI
L-4	Cub	**US** Piper
L-18	Super Cub	**US** Piper
L-19	O-1	**US** Cessna
L-21	Super Cub	**US** Piper
L-29	Delfin	**Cz** Aero
L-39	Albatros	**Cz** Aero
L-59	Albatros	**Cz** Aero
L-70	Vinka	**SF** Valmet
L-100	C-130 (civil version)	**US** Lockheed
L-188	Electra (P-3 Orion)	**US** Lockheed
L-410	Turbolet	**Cz** LET
L-1011	Tristar	**US** Lockheed
Learjet	(C-21)	**US** Gates
LR-1	(MU-2)	**J** Mitsubishi
M-28	Skytruck/Bryza	**Pl** MIELEC
Magister	CM-170	**Fr** Aérospatiale
Marut	HF-24	**Ind** HAL
Mashshaq	MFI-17	**Pak/Swe** PAC/SAAB
Matador	(AV-8)	**US/UK** MD/Bae
Maule	M-7/MXT-7	**US** Maule
MB-326		**It** Aermacchi
MB-339	(Veltro)	**It** Aermacchi
MBB-233	Flamingo	**Ge** MBB
MC-130	(C-130)	**US** Lockheed

Type	Name/designation	Country of origin/Maker
Mercurius	(HS-125)	**UK** BAe
Merlin		**US** Fairchild
Mescalero	T-41	**US** Cessna
Metro		**US** Fairchild
MFI-17	Supporter (T-17)	**Swe** SAAB
MiG-15	'Midget' trg	**RF** MiG
MiG-17	'Fresco'	**RF** MiG
MiG-19	'Farmer'	**RF** MiG
MiG-21	'Fishbed'	**RF** MiG
MiG-23	'Flogger'	**RF** MiG
MiG-25	'Foxbat'	**RF** MiG
MiG-27	'Flogger D'	**RF** MiG
MiG-29	'Fulcrum'	**RF** MiG
MiG-31	'Foxhound'	**RF** MiG
MiG-35	'Fulcrum'	**RF** MiG
Mirage		**Fr** Dassault
Missionmaster	N-22	**Aus** GAF
Mohawk	OV-1	**US** Lockheed
MS-760	Paris	**Fr** Aérospatiale
MS-893	Commodore	**Fr** Aérospatiale
MU-2	LR-1	**J** Mitsubishi
Musketeer	Beech 24	**US** Beech
Mystère-Falcon		**Fr** Dassault
N-22	Floatmaster, Missionmaster	**Aus** GAF
N-24	Searchmaster B/L	**Aus** GAF
N-262	Frégate	**Fr** Aérospatiale
N-2501	Noratlas	**Fr** Aérospatiale
Navajo	PA-31	**US** Piper
NC-212	C-212	**Sp/Indo** CASA/Nurtanio
NC-235	C-235	**Sp/Indo** CASA/Nurtanio
Nesher	[Mirage III]	**Il** IAI
NF-5	(F-5)	**US** Northrop
Nightingale	(C-9)	**US** MD
Nimrod	[Comet]	**UK** BAe
Nomad		**Aus** GAF
O-1	Bird Dog	**US** Cessna
O-2	(Cessna 337 Skymaster)	**US** Cessna
OA-4	(A-4)	**US** MD
OA-37	Dragonfly	**US** Cessna
Orao	IAR-93	**FRY/R** SOKO/IAR
Ouragan		**Fr** Dassault
OV-1	Mohawk	**US** Rockwell
OV-10	Bronco	**US** Rockwell
P-3	Orion [L-188 Electra]	**US** Lockheed
P-92		**It** Teenam
P-95	EMB-110	**Br** Embraer
P-166		**It** Piaggio
P-180	Avanti	**It** Piaggio
PA-18	Super Cub	**US** Piper
PA-23	Aztec	**US** Piper
PA-28	Cherokee	**US** Piper
PA-31	Navajo	**US** Piper
PA-32	Cherokee Six	**US** Piper
PA-34	Seneca	**US** Piper

Type	Name/designation	Country of origin/Maker
PA-36	*Pawnee Brave*	**US** Piper
PA-38	*Tomahawk*	**US** Piper
PA-42	*Cheyenne III*	**US** Piper
PBY-5	*Catalina*	**US** Consolidated
PC-6	*Porter*	**CH** Pilatus
PC-6A/B	*Turbo Porter*	**CH** Pilatus
PC-7	*Turbo Trainer*	**CH** Pilatus
PC-9		**CH** Pilatus
PC-12		**CH** Pilatus
PD-808		**It** Piaggio
Pillán	T-35	**Chl** Enaer
PL-1	*Chien Shou*	**ROC** AIDC
PLZ M-28	[An-28]	**Pl** PZL
Porter	PC-6	**CH** Pilatus
PS-5	[SH-5]	**PRC** HAMC
PZL M-28	M-28 [An-28]	**Pl** PZL
PZL-104	*Wilga*	**Pl** PZL
PZL-130	*Orlik*	**Pl** PZL
Q-5	A-5 *'Fantan'* [MiG-19]	**PRC** NAMC (Hongdu)
Queen Air	(U-8)	**US** Beech
PD-808		**It** Piaggio
Rafale		**Fr** Dassault
R-160		**Fr** Socata
R-235	*Guerrier*	**Fr** Socata
RC-21	(C-21, *Learjet*)	**US** Learjet
RC-47	(C-47)	**US** Douglas
RC-95	(EMB-110)	**Br** Embraer
RC-135	[Boeing 707]	**US** Boeing
RF-4	(F-4)	**US** MD
RF-5	(F-5)	**US** Northrop
RF-35	(F-35)	**Swe** SAAB
RF-104	(F-104)	**US** Lockheed
RG-8A		**US** Schweizer
RT-26	(EMB-326)	**Br** Embraer
RT-33	(T-33)	**US** Lockheed
RU-21	(*King Air*)	**US** Beech
RV-1	(OV-1)	**US** Rockwell
S-2	*Tracker*	**US** Grumman
S-208		**It** SIAI
S-211		**It** SIAI
SA 2-37A		**US** Schweizer
Saab 340H		**Swe** SAAB
Sabreliner	(CT-39)	**US** Rockwell
Safari	MFI-15	**Swe** SAAB
Safir	SAAB-91 (SK-50)	**Swe** SAAB
SB7L-360	(*Seeker*)	**Aus/HKJ** KADDB/Seabird
SC-7	*Skyvan*	**UK** Short
SE-210	*Caravelle*	**Fr** Aérospatiale
Sea Harrier	(*Harrier*)	**UK** BAe
Seascan	IAI-1124	**Il** IAI
Searchmaster	N-24 B/L	**Aus** GAF
Seneca	PA-34 (EMB-810)	**US** Piper
Sentinel	(Global Express)	**Ca** Bombardier
Sentry	(O-2)	**US** Summit

Type	Name/designation	Country of origin/Maker
SF-37	(J-37)	**Swe** SAAB
SF-260	(SF-260W *Warrior*)	**It** SIAI
SH-5	PS-5	**PRC** HAMC
SH-37	(J-37)	**Swe** SAAB
Sherpa	Short 330, C-23	**UK** Short
Short 330	(*Sherpa*)	**UK** Short
Sierra 200	(*Musketeer*)	**US** Beech
SK-35	(J-35)	**Swe** SAAB
SK-37	(J-37)	**Swe** SAAB
SK-60	(SAAB-105)	**Swe** SAAB
SK-61	(*Bulldog*)	**UK** BAe
Skyvan		**UK** Short
SM-90		**RF** Technoavia
SM-1019		**It** SIAI
SP-2H	*Neptune*	**US** Lockheed
SR-71	*Blackbird*	**US** Lockheed
Su-7	*'Fitter-A'*	**RF** Sukhoi
Su-15	*'Flagon'*	**RF** Sukhoi
Su-17/-20/-22	*'Fitter-B' - '-K'*	**RF** Sukhoi
Su-24	*'Fencer'*	**RF** Sukhoi
Su-25	*'Frogfoot'*	**RF** Sukhoi
Su-27	*'Flanker'*	**RF** Sukhoi
Su-29		**RF** Sukhoi
Su-30	*'Flanker'*	**RF** Sukhoi
Su-33	(Su-27K) *'Flanker-D'*	**RF** Sukhoi
Su-34	(Su-27IB) *'Flanker-C2'*	**RF** Sukhoi
Su-35	(Su-27) *'Flanker'*	**RF** Sukhoi
Su-39	(Su-25T) *'Frogfoot'*	**RF** Sukhoi
Super		**Fr** Dassault
Shrike Aerocommander		**US** Rockwell
Super Galeb		**FRY** SOKO
T-1		**J** Fuji
T-1A	*Jayhawk*	**US** Beech
T-2	*Buckeye*	**US** Rockwell
T-2		**J** Mitsubishi
T-3		**J** Fuji
T-6A	*Texan* II	**US** Beech
T-17	(*Supporter*, MFI-17)	**Swe** SAAB
T-23	*Uirapurú*	**Br** Aerotec
T-25	Neiva *Universal*	**Br** Embraer
T-26	EMB-326	**Br** Embraer
T-27	*Tucano*	**Br** Embraer
T-28	*Trojan*	**US** North American
T-33	*Shooting Star*	**US** Lockheed
T-34	*Mentor*	**US** Beech
T-35	*Pillán* [PA-28]	**Chl** Enaer
T-36	(C-101)	**Sp** CASA
T-37	(A-37)	**US** Cessna
T-38	*Talon*	**US** Northrop
T-39	(*Sabreliner*)	**US** Rockwell
T-41	*Mescalero* (Cessna 172)	**US** Cessna
T-42	*Cochise* (*Baron*)	**US** Beech
T-43	(Boeing 737)	**US** Boeing
T-44	(*King Air*)	**US** Beech

Type	Name/designation	Country of origin/Maker
T-47	(Citation)	**US** Cessna
T-67M	(Firefly)	**UK** Slingsby
T-400	(T-1A)	**US** Beech
TB-20	Trinidad	**Fr** Aérospatiale
TB-21	Trinidad	**Fr** Socata
TB-30	Epsilon	**Fr** Aérospatiale
TB-200	Tobago	**Fr** Socata
TBM-700		**Fr** Socata
TC-45	(C-45, trg)	**US** Beech
TCH-1	Chung Hsing	**ROC** AIDC
TL-1	(KM-2)	**J** Fuji
Tornado		**UK/Ge/It** Panavia
TR-1	[U-2]	**US** Lockheed
Travel Air	Beech 95	**US** Beech
Trident		**UK** BAe
Trislander	BN-2	**UK** Britten-Norman
Tristar	L-1011	**US** Lockheed
TS-8	Bies	**Pl** PZL
TS-11	Iskra	**Pl** PZL
Tu-16	'Badger'	**RF** Tupolev
Tu-22	'Blinder'	**RF** Tupolev
Tu-22M	'Backfire'	**RF** Tupolev
Tu-95	'Bear'	**RF** Tupolev
Tu-126	'Moss'	**RF** Tupolev
Tu-134	'Crusty'	**RF** Tupolev
Tu-142	'Bear F'	**RF** Tupolev
Tu-154	'Careless'	**RF** Tupolev
Tu-160	'Blackjack'	**RF** Tupolev
Tucano	(EMB-312/314)	**Br** Embraer
Turbo Porter	PC-6A/B	**CH** Pilatus
Twin Bonanza	Beech 50	**US** Beech
Twin Otter	DHC-6	**Ca** DHC
Typhoon		**Ge,Sp,Ir,UK** Eurofighter
Tzukit	[CM-170]	**Il** IAI
U-2		**US** Lockheed
U-3	(Cessna 310)	**US** Cessna
U-4	Gulfstream IV	**US** Gulfstream
U-7	(L-18)	**US** Piper
U-8	(Twin Bonanza/Queen Air)	**US** Beech
U-9	(EMB-121)	**Br** Embraer
U-10	Super Courier	**US** Helio
U-17	(Cessna 180, 185)	**US** Cessna
U-21	(King Air)	**US** Beech
U-36	(Learjet)	**US** Learjet
U-42	(C-42)	**Br** Embraer
U-93	(HS-125)	**UK** BAe
U-125	BAe 125-800	**UK** BAe
U-206G	Stationair	**US** Cessna
UC-12	(King Air)	**US** Beech
UP-2J	(P-2J)	**US** Lockheed
US-1		**J** Shin Meiwa
US-2A	(S-2A, tpt)	**US** Grumman
US-3	(S-3, tpt)	**US** Lockheed
UTVA-66		**FRY** UTVA

Type	Name/designation	Country of origin/Maker
UTVA-75		**FRY** UTVA
UV-18	(DHC-6)	**Ca** DHC
V-400	Fantrainer 400	**Ge** VFW
V-600	Fantrainer 600	**Ge** VFW
Vampire	DH-100	**Ca** DHC
VC-4	Gulfstream I	**US** Gulfstream
VC-10		**UK** BAe
VC-11	Gulfstream II	**US** Gulfstream
VC-25	[Boeing 747]	**US** Boeing
VC-91	(HS-748)	**UK** BAe
VC-93	(HS-125)	**UK** BAe
VC-97	(EMB-120)	**Br** Embraer
VC-130	(C-130)	**US** Lockheed
VFW-614		**Ge** VFW
Vinka	L-70	**SF** Valmet
VU-9	(EMB-121)	**Br** Embraer
VU-93	(HS-125)	**UK** BAe
WC-130	[C-130]	**US** Lockheed
WC-135	[Boeing 707]	**US** Boeing
Westwind	IAI-1124	**Il** IAI
Winjeel	CA-25	**Aus** Boeing
Xavante	EMB-326	**Br** Embraer
Xingu	EMB-121	**Br** Embraer
Y-5	[An-2]	**PRC** Hua Bei
Y-7	[An-24/-26]	**PRC** XAC
Y-8	[An-12]	**PRC** STAF
Y-12	Turbo/Twin Panda	**PRC** HAMC
Yak-11	'Moose'	**RF** Yakovlev
Yak-18	'Max'	**RF** Yakovlev
Yak-28	'Firebar' ('Brewer')	**RF** Yakovlev
Yak-38	'Forger'	**RF** Yakovlev
Yak-40	'Codling'	**RF** Yakovlev
Yak-42	'Clobber'	**RF** Yakovlev
Yak-52	(IAK 52)	**R** Aerostar
Yak-55		**RF** Yakovlev
YS-11		**J** Nihon
Z-142/143		**Cz** Zlin
Z-226		**Cz** Zlin
Z-242		**Cz** Zlin
Z-326		**Cz** Zlin
Z-526		**Cz** Zlin
Zéphyr	CM-175	**Fr** Aérospatiale

Tilt-Rotor Wing

V-22	Osprey	**US** Bell/Boeing

Helicopters

A-109	Hirundo	**It** Agusta
A-129	Mangusta	**It** Agusta
AB-...	(Bell 204/205/206/212/214, etc.)	**It/US** Agusta/Bell
AH-1	Cobra/Sea Cobra	**US** Bell
AH-2	Rooivalk	**RSA** Denel
AH-6	(Hughes 500/530)	**US** MD
AH-64	Apache	**US** Hughes

Type	Name/designation	Country of origin/Maker
ALH	*Adv Light Hel* . . . . **Ind** HAL
Alouette **II**	SA-318, SE-3130 . . . .**Fr** Aérospatiale
Alouette **III**	SA-316, SA-319 . . . .**Fr** Aérospatiale
AS-61	(SH-3) . . . .**US/It** Sikorsky/Agusta
AS-313 – AS-365/-366	(ex-SA-313 – SA-365/-366) **Fr** Aérospatiale
AS-332	*Super Puma* . . . .**Fr** Aérospatiale
AS-350	*Ecureuil* . . . .**Fr** Aérospatiale
AS-355	*Ecureuil* II . . . .**Fr** Aérospatiale
AS-365	*Dauphin* . . . .**Fr** Aérospatiale
AS-532	*Cougar* . . . . **Fr** Eurocopter
AS-550/555	*Fennec* . . . .**Fr** Aérospatiale
AS-565	*Panther* . . . . **Fr** Eurocopter
ASH-3	(*Sea King*) . . . .**It/US** Agusta/Sikorsky
AUH-76	(S-76) . . . .**US** Sikorsky
Bell 47	(*Sioux*) . . . .**US** Bell
Bell 205	. . . .**US** Bell
Bell 206	. . . .**US** Bell
Bell 212	. . . .**US** Bell
Bell 214	. . . .**US** Bell
Bell 222	. . . .**US** Bell
Bell 406	*Kiowa* . . . .**US** Bell
Bell 407	. . . .**Ca** Bell
Bell 412	. . . .**US** Bell
Bö-105	(NBö-105) . . . .**Ge** MBB
CH-3	(SH-3) . . . .**US** Sikorsky
CH-34	*Choctaw* . . . . **US** Sikorsky
CH-46	*Sea Knight* . . . .**US** Boeing-Vertol
CH-47	*Chinook* . . . .**US** Boeing-Vertol
CH-53	*Stallion* (*Sea Stallion*) . . . .**US** Sikorsky
CH-54	*Tarhe* . . . . **US** Sikorsky
CH-113	(CH-46) . . . .**US** Boeing-Vertol
CH-124	SH-3 (*Sea King*) . . . . **US** Sikorsky
CH-136	Kiowa . . . .**Ca** Bell
CH-139	Bell 206 . . . .**US** Bell
CH-146	Bell 412 . . . .**Ca** Bell
CH-147	CH-47 . . . .**US** Boeing-Vertol
CH-149	*Cormorant* (Merlin) . . . .**UK/It** Westland/Agusta
Cheetah	[SA-315] . . . . **Ind** HAL
Chetak	[SA-319] . . . . **Ind** HAL
Commando	(SH-3) . . . . **UK/US** Westland/Sikorsky
Dhruv	. . . . **Ind** HAL
EC-120B	*Colibri* . . . . **Fr/Ge** Eurocopter
EH-60	(UH-60) . . . . **US** Sikorsky
EH-101	*Merlin* . . . .**UK/It** Westland/Agusta
F-28F	. . . .**US** Enstrom
FH-1100	(OH-5) . . . .**US** Fairchild-Hiller
Gazela	(SA-342) . . . . **Fr/FRY** Aérospatiale/SOKO
Gazelle	SA-341/-342 . . . .**Fr** Aérospatiale
H-34	(S-58) . . . .**US** Sikorsky
H-76	S-76 . . . .**US** Sikorsky
HA-15	Bö-105 . . . .**Ge** MBB
HB-315	*Gavião* (SA-315) . . . . . .**Br/Fr** Helibras Aérospatiale
HB-350	*Esquilo* (AS-350) . . . . . .**Br/Fr** Helibras Aérospatiale
HD-16	SA-319 . . . .**Fr** Aérospatiale

Type	Name/designation	Country of origin/Maker
HH-3	(SH-3) . . . .**US** Sikorsky
HH-34	(CH-34) . . . .**US** Sikorsky
HH-53	(CH-53) . . . .**US** Sikorsky
HH-65	(AS-365) . . . . **Fr** Eurocopter
Hkp-2	*Alouette* II/SE-3130 . . . . **Fr** Aérospatiale
Hkp-3	AB-204 . . . . **It/US** Agusta/Bell
Hkp-4	KV-107 . . . . **J/US** Kawasaki/Vertol
Hkp-5	Hughes 300 . . . .**US** MD
Hkp-6	AB-206 . . . . **It/US** Agusta/Bell
Hkp-9	BÖ-105 . . . .**Ge** MBB
Hkp-10	AS-332 . . . .**Fr** Aérospatiale
HR-12	OH-58 . . . .**US** Bell
HSS-1	(S-58) . . . .**US** Sikorsky
HSS-2	(SH-3) . . . .**US** Sikorsky
HT-17	CH-47 . . . .**US** Boeing-Vertol
HT-21	AS-332 . . . .**Fr** Aérospatiale
HU-1	(UH-1) . . . . **J/US** Fuji/Bell
HU-8	UH-1B . . . .**US** Bell
HU-10	UH-1H . . . .**US** Bell
HU-18	AB-212 . . . . **It/US** Agusta/Bell
Hughes 300	. . . .**US** MD
Hughes 500/520	*Defender* . . . .**US** MD
IAR-316/-330	(SA-316/-330) . . . .**R/Fr** IAR/Aérospatiale
Ka-25	'Hormone' . . . .**RF** Kamov
Ka-27/-28	'Helix-A' . . . .**RF** Kamov
Ka-29	'Helix-B' . . . .**RF** Kamov
Ka-32	'Helix-C' . . . .**RF** Kamov
Ka-50	*Hokum* . . . .**RF** Kamov
KH-4	(Bell 47) . . . . **J/US** Kawasaki/ Bell
KH-300	(Hughes 269) . . . . **J/US** Kawasaki/MD
KH-500	(Hughes 369) . . . . **J/US** Kawasaki/MD
Kiowa	OH-58 . . . .**US** Bell
KV-107	[CH-46] . . . . **J/US** Kawasaki/Vertol
Lynx	. . . .**UK** Westland
MD-500/530	*Defender* . . . .**US** McDonnell Douglas
Merlin	EH-101 . . . .**UK/It** Westland/Augusta
MH-6	(AH-6) . . . .**US** MD
MH-53	(CH-53) . . . .**US** Sikorsky
Mi-2	'Hoplite' . . . . **RF** Mil
Mi-4	'Hound' . . . . **RF** Mil
Mi-6	'Hook' . . . . **RF** Mil
Mi-8	'Hip' . . . . **RF** Mil
Mi-14	'Haze' . . . . **RF** Mil
Mi-17	'Hip-H' . . . . **RF** Mil
Mi-24, -25, -35	'Hind' . . . . **RF** Mil
Mi-26	'Halo' . . . . **RF** Mil
Mi-28	'Havoc' . . . . **RF** Mil
NAS-330	(SA-330) . . . . **Indo/Fr** Nurtanio/Aérospatiale
NAS-332	AS-332 . . . . **Indo/Fr** Nurtanio/Aérospatiale
NB-412	Bell 412 . . . . **Indo/US** Nurtanio/Bell
NBö-105	Bö-105 . . . . **Indo/Ge** Nurtanio/MBB
NH-300	(Hughes 300) . . . . **It/US** Nardi/MD
OH-6	*Cayuse* (Hughes 369) . . . .**US** MD
OH-13	(Bell 47G) . . . .**US** Bell

OH-23	*Raven* ....**US** Hiller	
OH-58	*Kiowa* (Bell 206) ....**US** Bell	
OH-58D	(Bell 406) ....**US** Bell	
Oryx	(SA-330) ....**Fr** Aérospatiale	
PAH-1	(Bö-105) ....**Ge** MBB	
Partizan	(*Gazela*, armed) .... **Fr/FRY** Aérospatiale/SOKO	
RH-53	(CH-53) ....**US** Sikorsky	
S-58	(*Wessex*) ....**US** Sikorsky	
S-61	SH-3 ....**US** Sikorsky	
S-65	CH-53 ....**US** Sikorsky	
S-70	UH-60 ....**US** Sikorsky	
S-76	....................................**US** Sikorsky	
S-80	CH-53 ....**US** Sikorsky	
SA-313	*Alouette* II ....**Fr** Aérospatiale	
SA-315	*Lama [Alouette* II] ....**Fr** Aérospatiale	
SA-316	*Alouette* III (SA-319) ....**Fr** Aérospatiale	
SA-318	*Alouette* II (SE-3130) ....**Fr** Aérospatiale	
SA-319	*Alouette* III (SA-316) ....**Fr** Aérospatiale	
SA-321	*Super Frelon* ....**Fr** Aérospatiale	
SA-330	*Puma* ....**Fr** Aérospatiale	
SA-341/-342	*Gazelle* ....**Fr** Aérospatiale	
SA-360	*Dauphin* ....**Fr** Aérospatiale	
SA-365/-366	*Dauphin* II (SA-360) ....**Fr** Aérospatiale	
Scout	(*Wasp*) ....**UK** Westland	
SE-316	(SA-316) ....**Fr** Aérospatiale	
SE-3130	(SA-318) ....**Fr** Aérospatiale	
Sea King	[SH-3] ....**UK** Westland	
SH-2	*Sea Sprite* ....**US** Kaman	

SH-3	(*Sea King*) ....**US** Sikorsky
SH-34	(S-58) ....**US** Sikorsky
SH-57	Bell 206 ....**US** Bell
SH-60	*Sea Hawk* (UH-60) ....**US** Sikorsky
Sokol	W3 .... **PI** PZL
TH-50	Esquilo (AS-550) ....**Fr** Aérospatiale
TH-55	Hughes 269 ....**US** MD
TH-57	*Sea Ranger* (Bell 206) ....**US** Bell
TH-67	Creek (Bell 206B-3) ....**Ca** Bell
Tiger	AS-665 ....**Fr** Eurocopter
UH-1	*Iroquois* (Bell 204/205/212) ....**US** Bell
UH-12	(OH-23) ....**US** Hiller
UH-13	(Bell 47J) ....**US** Bell
UH-19	(S-55) ....**Ca** Bell
UH-34T	(S-58T) ....**US** Sikorsky
UH-46	(CH-46) ....**US** Boeing/Vertol
UH-60	*Black Hawk* (SH-60) ....**US** Sikorsky
VH-4	(Bell 206) ....**US** Bell
VH-60	(S-70) ....**US** Sikorsky
W-3	*Sokol* .... **PI** PZL
Wasp	(*Scout*) ....**UK** Westland
Wessex	(S-58) ....**US/UK** Sikorsky/Westland
Z-5	[Mi-4] ....**PRC** HAF
Z-6	[Z-5] ....**PRC** CHAF
Z-8	[AS-321] ....**PRC** CHAF
Z-9	[AS-365] ....**PRC** HAMC
Z-11	[AS-352] ....**PRC** CHAF

Table 49 List of Abbreviations for Data Sections

– part of unit is detached/less than
* combat capable
" unit with overstated title/ship class nickname
+ unit reinforced/more than
< under 100 tonnes
† serviceability in doubt
ε estimated

AAA anti-aircraft artillery
AAM air-to-air missile
AAV amphibious assault vehicle
AB airborne
ABM anti-ballistic missile
ABU sea-going buoy tender
ac aircraft
ACCS Air Command and Control System
ACP airborne command post
ACV air cushion vehicle / armed combat vehicle
AD air defence
ADA air defence artillery
adj adjusted
AE auxiliary, ammunition carrier
AEW airborne early warning
AF Air Force
AFB Air Force Base / Station
AFS logistics ship
AG misc auxillary
AGB icebreaker
AGF command ship
AGHS hydrographic survey vessel
AGI intelligence collection vessel
AGL automatic grenade launcher
AGM air-to-ground missile
AGOR oceanographic research vessel
AGOS oceanographic surveillance vessel
AGS survey ship
AH hospital ship
AIFV armoured infantry fighting vehicle
AK cargo ship
aka also known as
AKR fast sealift ship / cargo ship
AKSL stores ship (light)
ALARM air-launched anti-radiation missile
ALCM air-launched cruise missile
amph amphibious/amphibian
AMRAAM advanced medium-range air-to-air missile
AO tanker with RAS capability
AOE auxillary fuel and ammunition, RAS capability
AORH tanker with hel capacity
AORL replenishment oiler light
AORLH oiler light with hel deck
AOT tanker
AP armour-piercing/anti-personnel

APC armoured personnel carrier
APL anti-personnel land-mine
AR/C repair ship/cable
ARG amphibious ready group
ARL airborne reconnaissance low
ARM anti-radiation missile
armd armoured
ARS salvage ship
ARSV armoured reconnaissance/ surveillance vehicle
arty artillery
ARV armoured recovery vehicle
AS anti-submarine
ASaC airborne surveillance and control
ASCM anti-ship cruise missile
ASM air-to-surface missile
ASR submarine rescue craft
ASROC anti-submarine rocket
ASSM anti-surface-ship missile
ASTROS II artillery saturation rocket System
ASTT anti-submarine torpedo tube
ASW anti-submarine warfare
ASuW anti-surface warfare
AT tug / anti-tank
ATBM anti-tactical ballistic missile
ATF tug, ocean going
ATGW anti-tank guided weapon
ATK anti-tank / attack
ATTACMS army tactical missile system
ATTC all terrain tracked carrier
AV armoured vehicle
AVB aviation logistic ship
avn aviation
AWACAS airborne warning and control system
AWT water tanker
AXL training craft
AXS training craft, sail
BA budget authority (US)
Bbr bomber
BCT brigade combat team
bde brigade
bdgt budget
BfSB Battlefield surveillance brigade
BG battle group
BMD ballistic missile defence
bn battalion/billion
BSB brigade support battalion
BSTB brigade special troops battalion
bty battery
C2 command and control
CAB combat aviation brigade
CALCM conventional air-launched cruise missile
CAS close air support
casevac casualty evacuation

CASM conventionally armed stand-off missile
cav cavalry
cbt combat
CBU cluster bomb unit
CCS command and control systems
cdo commando
CET combat engineer tractor
CFE Conventional Armed Forces in Europe
C/G/GN/L cruiser/guided missile/guided missile, nuclear powered/light
cgo cargo (freight) aircraft
CIMIC civil-military cooperation
CIWS Close in Weapons System
CLOS command to line of sight
COIN counter insurgency
comb combined/combination
Comd command
COMINT Communications Intelligence
Comms communications
CS combat support
CSAR combat search and rescue
CSG Carrier Strike Group
C-RAM counter rocket, artillery and mortar
CT counter terrorism
CTOL conventional take off and landing
CV/H/N/S aircraft carrier/helicopter/ nuclear powered/VSTOL
CVBG carrier battlegroup
CW chemical warfare/weapons
DD/G/GH destroyer/guided missile/with helicopter
DDS dry dock shelter
def defence
demob demobilised
det detachment
div division
dom domestic
DSCS defense satellite communications system
ECM electronic counter measures
ECR electronic combat and reconnaissance
EELV evolved expendable launch vehicle
ELINT electronic intelligence
elms elements
engr engineer
EOD explosive ordnance disposal
eqpt equipment
ESG Expeditionary Strike Group (US)
ESM electronic support measures
est estimate(d)
ETS engineer tank systems
EW electronic warfare
EWSP electronic warfare self protection
excl excludes/excluding
exp expenditure
FAC forward air control

FF/G/H/L frigate/guided missile/ helicopter/light
FGA fighter ground attack
flt flight
FMA Foreign Military Assistance
FMTV family of medium transport vehicles
FROG free rocket over ground
FS/G corvette/guided missile
FSSG Force Service Support Group
FSTA future strategic tanker aircraft
Ftr fighter
FW fixed-wing
FY fiscal year
GBAD ground-based air defences
GBU guided bomb unit
gd guard
GDP gross domestic product
GMLS guided missile launch sytem
GNP gross national product
gp group
GEODSS ground based electro optical deep space surveillance system
GW guided weapon
HARM high-speed anti-radiation missile
hel helicopter
HIMARS high mobility artillery rocket system
HMMWV high-mobility multi-purpose wheeled vehicle
HMTV high mobility tactical vehicle
HOT High-subsonic Optically Teleguided
how howitzer
HQ headquarters
HSV high speed vessel
HVM high-velocity missile
HWT heavyweight torpedo
hy heavy
IBU inshore boat unit
ICBM inter-continental ballistic missile
IFV infantry fighting vehicle
IMET International Military Education and Training
imp improved
incl includes/including
indep independent
inf infantry
IRBM intermediate-range ballistic missile
IRLS infra-red line scan
ISD in service date
ISTAR intelligence, surveillance, target acquisition and reconnaissance
JDAM Joint Direct Attack Munition
JSF Joint Strike Fighter
JSTARS Joint Surveillance Target Attack Radar System
LACV light armoured combat vehicle
LAM land-attack missile
LAMPS light airborne multi-purpose system
LANTIRN low-altitude navigation and targeting infra-red system night

LAV light armoured vehicle
LAW light anti-tank weapon
LCA/D/H/M/PA/PL/T/U/VP landing craft / assault / dock / heavy / medium / personnel aircushion / personnel light / tank / utility / vehicles and personnel
LCC amphibious command ship
LCS littoral combat ship
LFV light forces vehicles
LGB laser-guided bomb
LHA landing ship assault
LHD amphibious assault ship
LIFT lead-in ftr trainer
LKA amphibious cargo ship
log logistic
LORADS long range radar display system
LP/D/H landing platform / dock / helicopter
LPV lifespan patrol vessel
LRAR long range artillery rocket
LRSA long-range strike/attack
LS/D/L/LH/M landing ship / dock / logistic / logistic helicopter / medium
LST landing ship tank
LWT lightweight torpedo
MAMBA mobile artillery monitoring battlefield radar
MANPAD man portable air defence
MANPAT man portable anti-tank
MARDIV marine division
MAW marine aviation wing
MBT main battle tank
MCC mine countermeasure coastal
MCD mine countermeasure diving support
MCDV maritime coastal defence vessel
MCI mine countermeasure inshore
MCLOS manual CLOS
MCM mine countermeasures
MCMV mine countermeasures vessel
MCO mine countermeasures ocean
MCV mine countermeasures vessel
MD military district
MEADS medium extended air defence system
MEB marine expeditionary brigade
mech mechanised
med medium
MEF marine expeditionary force
MEU marine expeditionary unit
MGA machine gun artillery
MH/C/D/I/O mine hunter / coastal / drone / inshore /ocean
mil military
MIRV multiple independently targetable re-entry vehicle
MIUW mobile inshore undersea warfare
mk mark (model number)
ML minelayer
MLRS multiple-launch rocket system
MLU mid-life update

MLV medium launch vehicle
mne marine
mob mobilisation/mobile
mod modified/modification
mor mortar
mot motorised/motor
MP maritime patrol
MPA maritime patrol aircraft
MPS marine prepositioning squadron
MR maritime reconnaissance / motor rifle
MRAP mine resistant ambush protected
MRAAM medium-range air-to-air missile
MRBM medium-range ballistic missile
MRL multiple rocket launcher
MRTT multi-role tanker transport
MS/A/C/D/I/O/R mine sweeper / auxiliary / coastal / drone / inshore / ocean /
msl missile
MSTAR manportable surveillance and target acquisition radar
Mtn mountain
NAEW NATO Airborne Early Warning & Control Force
n.a. not applicable
n.k. not known
NBC nuclear biological chemical
NCO non-commissioned officer
NLACM naval land attack cruise missile
nm nautical mile
NMD national missile defence
NMP net material product
nuc nuclear
O & M operations and maintenance
OBS observation/observer
OCU operational conversion unit
OOV objects of verification
op/ops operational/operations
OPFOR opposition training force
OPV off-shore patrol vessel
org organised/organisation
OSV oceanographic survey vessel
OTH/-B over-the-horizon/backscatter (radar)
OTHR/T over-the-horizon radar/targeting
PAAMS principal anti-air missile system
para paratroop/parachute
pax passenger/passenger transport aircraft
PB/C/I/O/R patrol boat / coastal / inshore / offshore / riverine
PC/C/I/M/O/R/T/F patrol craft / coastal / inshore / with SSM / offshore / riverine / torpedo / fast
PDMS point defence missile system
pdr pounder
pers personnel
PF/C/I/M/O/T fast patrol craft / coastal / inshore / with SSM / offshore / torpedo
PGM precision guided munitions
PHM patrol hydrofoil with SSM
PHT patrol hydrofoil with torpedo

Pk peacekeeping

PPP purchasing-power parity

PR photo-reconnaissance

prepo pre-positioned

PSO/H offshore patrol vessel over 60 metres / with helicopter

PTG guided missile patrol craft

PTRL/SURV patrol / surveillance

PVO anti-aircraft defence (Russia)

qd quadrillion

R&D research and development

RAM rolling airframe missile

RAS replenishment at sea

RCL ramped craft logistic

RCWS remote controlled weapon station

recce reconnaissance

regt regiment

RIB rigid inflatable boat

RL rocket launcher

ro-ro roll-on, roll-off

RPV remotely piloted vehicle

RR/C/F rapid-reaction corps/force

RRC rapid raiding craft

RV re-entry vehicle

RY royal yacht

SACLOS semi-automatic CLOS

SAM surface-to-air missile

SAR search and rescue

sat satellite

SDV swimmer- delivery vehicles

SEAD suppression of enemy air defence

SEWS satellite early warning station

SF special forces

SHORAD short range air defence

SIGINT signal intelligence

SLAM stand-off land-attack missile

SLBM submarine launched ballistic missile

SLCM submarine launched cruise missile

SLEP service life extension programme

SMAW shoulder-launched multi-purpose assault weapon

SOC special operations capable

SP self propelled

SPEC OP special operations

spt support

sqn squadron

SRAM short-range attack missile

SRBM short range ballistic missile

SS diesel submarine

SSAN submersible auxiliary support vessel

SSBN ballistic-missile submarine nuclear-fuelled

SSC diesel submarine coastal

SSG attack submarine diesel, non-ballistic missile launchers

SSGN SSN with dedicated non-ballistic missile launchers

SSI diesel submarine inshore

SSK Ptrl submarine with ASW capability

SSM surface-to-surface missile

SSN attack submarine nuclear powered

START Strategic Arms Reduction Talks/Treaty

STO(V)L short take-off and (vertical) landing

str strength

SUGW surface-to-underwater GW

SURV surveillance

SUT surface and underwater target

sy security

t tonnes

tac tactical

TASM tactical air-to-surface missile

temp temporary

THAAD Theater High Altitude Area Defense (US)

TIPH Temporary International presence in Hebron

tk tank

tkr tanker

TLAM tactical land-attack missile

TLE treaty-limited equipment (CFE)

TMD theatre missile defence

torp torpedo

TOW tube launched optically wire guided

tpt transport

tr trillion

TRG / trg training

TRIAD triple AD

TRV torpedo recovery vehicle

TT torpedo tube

UAV unmanned aerial vehicle

UCAV unmanned combat aerial vehicle

URG under-way replenishment group

USGW underwater to surface guided weapon

utl utility

V(/S)TOL vertical(/short) take-off and landing

veh vehicle

VLS vertical launch system

VSRAD very short range air defence

wg wing

WLIC Inland construction tenders

WMD weapon(s) of mass destruction

WTGB Icebreaker tugs

YDG degaussing

YDT diving tender

YTL light harbour tug

YTM medium harbour tug

Index of Countries and Territories

Index of **Country/Territory Abbreviations**